TWELFTH EDITION

ACCOUNTANTS' HANDBOOK

VOLUME TWO:

SPECIAL INDUSTRIES AND SPECIAL TOPICS

BECOME A SUBSCRIBER!

Did you purchase this product from a bookstore?

If you did, it's important for you to become a subscriber. John Wiley & Sons, Inc. may publish, on a periodic basis, supplements and new editions to reflect the latest changes in the subject matter that you ***need to know*** in order to stay competitive in this ever-changing industry. By contacting the Wiley office nearest you, you'll receive any current update at no additional charge. In addition, you'll receive future updates and revised or related volumes on a 30-day examination review.

If you purchased this product directly from John Wiley & Sons, Inc., we have already recorded your subscription for this update service.

To become a subscriber, please call **1-877-762-2974** or send your name, company name (if applicable), address, and the title of the product to:

mailing address: **Supplement Department**
John Wiley & Sons, Inc.
One Wiley Drive
Somerset, NJ 08875
e-mail: **subscriber@wiley.com**
fax: **1-732-302-2300**

For customers outside the United States, please contact the Wiley office nearest you:

Professional & Reference Division
John Wiley & Sons Canada, Ltd.
22 Worcester Road
Etobicoke, Ontario M9W 1L1
CANADA
Phone: 416-236-4433
Phone: 1-800-567-4797
Fax: 416-236-4447
Email: canada@wiley.com

John Wiley & Sons Australia, Ltd.
33 Park Road
P.O. Box 1226
Milton, Queensland 4064
AUSTRALIA
Phone: 61-7-3859-9755
Fax: 61-7-3859-9715
Email: brisbane@johnwiley.com.au

John Wiley & Sons, Ltd.
The Atrium
Southern Gate, Chichester
West Sussex PO 19 8SQ
ENGLAND
Phone: 44-1243-779777
Fax: 44-1243-775878
Email: customer@wiley.co.uk

John Wiley & Sons (Asia) Pte., Ltd.
2 Clementi Loop #02-01
SINGAPORE 129809
Phone: 65-64632400
Fax: 65-64634604/5/6
Customer Service: 65-64604280
Email: enquiry@wiley.com.sg

Twelfth Edition

ACCOUNTANTS' HANDBOOK

VOLUME TWO:

Special Industries and Special Topics

Lynford Graham
D.R. Carmichael

JOHN WILEY & SONS, INC.

Published by John Wiley & Sons, Inc., Hoboken, New Jersey.

Published simultaneously in Canada.

ISBN: 978-1-118-17181-3 (book); 978-1-118-40709-7 (ebk); 978-1-118-40710-3 (ebk); 978-1-118-40711-0 (ebk)

Printed in the United States of America

10 9 8 7 6 5 4 3 2 1

CONTENTS

Preface

About the Editor

About the Contributors

VOLUME ONE: FINANCIAL ACCOUNTING AND GENERAL TOPICS

1 **Financial Accounting and Auditing Organizations**
LYNFORD GRAHAM, CPA, PHD, CFE
Bentley University

2 **Framework of Financial Accounting Concepts and Standards: A Historical Perspective**
REED K. STOREY, PHD, CPA
Financial Accounting Standards Board

3 **Future Directions in Financial Accounting Standards: The Potential Role of International Accounting Standards**
TOM JONES

4 **Financial Statements: Form and Content**
JAN R. WILLIAMS, PHD, CPA
College of Business Administration, University of Tennessee

5 **Securities and Exchange Commission Reporting Requirements**
WENDY HAMBLETON, CPA
BDO USA, LLP

6 **Management Discussion and Analysis**
SYDNEY K. GARMONG, CPA
Crowe Horwath LLP
BRAD A. DAVIDSON, CPA
Crowe Horwath LLP

7 **Introduction to Internal Control Assessment and Reporting**
LYNFORD GRAHAM, CPA, PHD, CFE
Bentley University

8 **Accounting for Business Combinations**
JAMES MRAZ, CPA, MBA
University of Maryland, University College

9 **Consolidation, Translation, and the Equity Method**
JAMES MRAZ, CPA, MBA
University of Maryland, University College

10 Analyzing Financial Statements
NOAH P. BARSKY, PHD, CPA, CMA
Villanova University
FRANK J. GRIPPO, MBA, CPA, CFE
William Paterson University
B. SCOTT TEETER, MBA, CMA
The Ryland Group, Inc.

11 Cash, Loans, and Investments
MICHAEL A. ANTONETTI, CPA, CMA
Crowe Horwath LLP

12 Revenues and Receivables
ALAN S. GLAZER, PHD, CPA
Franklin & Marshall College
CYNTHIA L. KROM, PHD, CPA
Franklin & Marshall College
HENRY R. JAENICKE, PHD, CPA
Late of Drexel University

13 Inventory
RICHARD R. JONES, CPA
Ernst & Young LLP
ANNA T. SZURGOT, CPA
Ernst & Young LLP

14 Goodwill and Other Intangible Assets
JAMES MRAZ, CPA, MBA
University of Maryland, University College

15 Leases
FRANCIS E. SCHEUERELL, JR., CPA
Navigant Consulting

16 Property, Plant, Equipment, and Depreciation
GEORGE I. VICTOR, CPA
Giambalvo, Stalzer & Company, CPAs, P.C.

17 Accounting for Income Taxes
LYNNE GLENNON, CPA, MST
Financial Accounting Standards Board

18 Liabilities
FREDERICK GILL, CPA
American Institute of Certified Public Accountants, Accounting Standards Team

19 Shareholders' Equity
GEORGE I. VICTOR, CPA
Giambalvo, Stalzer & Company, CPAs, P.C.

20 Partnerships and Joint Ventures
FRANCIS E. SCHEUERELL, JR., CPA
Navigant Consulting

21 Prospective Financial Statements
DON M. PALLAIS, CPA

VOLUME TWO: SPECIAL INDUSTRIES AND SPECIAL TOPICS

22 **Personal Financial Statements**
George I. Victor, CPA
Giambalvo, Stalzer & Company, CPAs, P.C.

23 **Stock-Based Compensation**

24 **Fair Value Measurement**
Mark L. Zyla, CPA/ABV, CFA, ASA
Acuitas, Inc.

25 **Valuation of Assets, Liabilities, and Nonpublic Companies**
Neil J. Beaton, CPA/ABV/CFF, CFA, ASA
Grant Thornton, LLP

26 **Accounting for Derivatives: A Primer**
Ira G. Kawaller
Kawaller & Co.

27 **Pension Plans and Other Postretirement and Postemployment Benefits**
Jason Flynn, FSA, MAAA
Deloitte Consulting LLP
Timothy Geddes, FSA, MAAA
Deloitte Consulting LLP
Daniel Thomas, EA, MAAA
Deloitte Consulting LLP

28 **Not-for-Profit Organizations**
Richard F. Larkin, CPA
BDO USA, LLP

29 **Cost-Volume-Revenue Analysis for Nonprofit Organizations**
JAE K. SHIM, PhD
California State University, Long Beach

30 **Financial Institutions**
Zabihollah Zabi Rezaee, PhD, CPA, CMA, CIA, CGFM, CFE, CSOXP, CGRCP, CGOVP
The University of Memphis

31 **Real Estate and Construction**
Benedetto Bongiorno, CPA, CRE
Natural Decision Systems, Inc

32 **Federal Government Accounting, Budgeting, and Auditing**
David M. Zavada, CPA, MPA
Partner, Kearney & Company

33 **State and Local Government Accounting**
Cynthia Pon, CPA
Macias Gini O'Connell LLP
Richard A. Green, CPA
Macias Gini O'Connell LLP
Caroline H. Walsh, CPA
Macias Gini O'Connell LLP

34 Oil, Gas, and Other Natural Resources
Bill Godshall, CPA
Frazier & Deeter, LLC

35 Health Care Organizations
Martha Garner, CPA
PwC LLP

36 Regulated Utilities
Darin W. Kempke, CPA
KPMG Partner, Power and Utility Audit Sector Leader

37 Producers or Distributors of Films
Francis E. Scheuerell, Jr., CPA
Navigant Consulting

38 Estates and Trusts
Philip M. Herr, JD, CPA, PFS
AXA Equitable Life Insurance Company
Elizabeth Lindsay-Ochoa, JD, LLM (Taxation)
AXA Equitable Life Insurance Company

39 Bankruptcy
Grant W. Newton, PhD, CPA, CIRA
Pepperdine University

40 Detecting Fraud
W. Steve Albrecht
Brigham Young University
Conan C. Albrecht
Brigham Young University

41 Forensic Accounting in Litigation Consulting Services, Investigations, and Compliance Matters
Yogesh Bahl, CPA, MBA
Deloitte Financial Advisory Services LLP
Frank Hydoski, PhD
Deloitte Financial Advisory Services LLP

42 Introduction to E-Discovery
Jack Moorman
PricewaterhouseCoopers LLP
Greg Schaffer
PricewaterhouseCoopers LLP

43 Financial Expert Witness Challenges and Exclusions: Results and Trends in Federal and State Cases Since *Kumho Tire*
Lawrence F. Ranallo, CPA
PricewaterhouseCoopers LLP
Keith R. Ugone, PhD
Analysis Group, Inc.

Index

PREFACE

The twelfth edition of *Accountants' Handbook* continues the tradition established in the first edition nearly 90 years ago of providing a comprehensive single reference source for understanding current financial statement and reporting issues. It is directed to accountants, auditors, executives, bankers, lawyers, and other preparers and users of accounting information. Its presentation and format facilitates the quick comprehension of complex accounting-related subjects updated for today's rapidly changing business environment.

This edition of the *Handbook* continues the presentation of two soft-cover volumes; this edition contains a total of 43 chapters. To provide a resource with the encyclopedic coverage that has been the hallmark of this *Handbook* series, this edition again focuses on financial accounting and related topics, including those auditing standards and audit reports that are the common ground of interest for accounting and business professionals.

A few years make quite a difference in the modern accounting and auditing world. Sarbanes-Oxley is part of the fabric of today's business environment, but we wrestle with a codification of generally accepted accounting principles that has reoriented our approach to citing the accounting literature and day-to-day updates on U.S. and Securities and Exchange Commission progress toward adopting International Financial Reporting Standards in the United States. Auditors of public companies continue to follow the growing Standards of the Public Company Accounting Oversight Board, and such Standards continue to diverge from those set by the Auditing Standards Board of the American Institute of Certified Public Accountants and adopted by the Government Accountability Office in its Yellow Book Standards. In 2011, the AICPA implemented a new codification of its literature, more aligned with the presentation format of the International Federation of Accountant's International Audit and Attest Standards Board format. The "clarity" standards are designed to better highlight the requirements of the standards and significantly align AICPA and IAASB Standards. Chapter 3 in this edition (by Tom Jones) reviews the recent revolution in accounting standards and the contemporary issues in merging U.S and international GAAP. There are also new chapters on fair value (Mark Zyla) and private company valuation issues (Neil Beaton). A new and comprehensive chapter on financial institutions by Zabihollah Rezaee addresses contemporary industry issues including those raised in the Dodd-Frank Financial Reform Act of 2010. We are in the middle of a significant revolution in the health care industry, and there remain a myriad of uncertainties surrounding the future in this industry at the date of publication.

In addition, most chapters have incorporated some international accounting perspectives when possible. Fraud continues to be an important element in our business environment, as we continue to focus on fraud and fraud-related issues. These topics have become more prominent in the business literature and in practice, and management and auditors have, by law and regulation, assumed greater responsibility for preventing and detecting fraud.

References to the professional accounting literature in this edition include references to the new Financial Accounting Standards Board Codification (Accounting Standards Codification, or ASC) in each chapter. Sometimes the original literature is also cited, where it can be helpful in understanding the development of thought and can help orient us to the prior literature. We have retained the chapter by Reed Storey on the development of the conceptual framework and plan to carry it forward because of its unique insight and historical content. In this edition we have also eliminated a number of redundant and overlapping chapters and those that were very specific to historical issues.

This edition of the *Handbook* is divided into two convenient volumes. *Volume One: Financial Accounting and General Topics* includes:

- A comprehensive review of the framework of accounting guidance today and the organizations involved in its development, including the development of international standards
- A compendium of specific guidance on general aspects of financial statement presentation, disclosure, and analysis, including SEC filing regulations
- Coverage of specific financial statement areas from cash through shareholders' equity, including coverage of financial instruments

Volume Two: Special Industries and Special Topics includes:

- Comprehensive coverage of the specialized environmental and accounting considerations for key industries, including a chapter on the film industry
- Coverage of accounting standards applying to pension plans, retirement plans, and employee stock compensation and other capital accumulation plans
- Diverse topics, including reporting by partnerships, estates and trusts, and valuation, bankruptcy, and forensic accounting

The specialized expertise of the individual authors remains a critical element in this edition, as it has been in all prior editions. Although the editor worked with the authors, in the final analysis, each chapter is the work and presents the viewpoint of the individual author or authors.

Content of the chapters in this edition has been prepared and/or reviewed by professionals practicing in accounting firms, financial executives, university professors, and financial analysts and executives. Every major international accounting firm is represented among the authors. These professionals bring to bear their own and their firms' experiences in dealing with accounting practice problems. All of the authors and technical reviewers are recognized authorities in their fields and have made significant contributions to the twelfth edition of the *Handbook*.

Our greatest debt is to the authors and reviewers of this edition. We deeply appreciate the value and importance of their time and efforts. We also acknowledge our debt to the editors of and contributors to 11 earlier editions of the *Handbook*. This edition draws heavily on the accumulated knowledge of those earlier editions.

Finally, we wish to thank John DeRemigis and Brandon Dust at John Wiley & Sons, Inc., for handling the many details of organizing and coordinating this effort.

For convenience, the pronoun "he" is used in this book to refer nonspecifically to the accountant and the businessperson. We intend this pronoun to include women.

L. Graham
D. R. Carmichael

ABOUT THE EDITOR

Lynford Graham, CPA, PhD, CFE, is a Certified Public Accountant with more than 30 years of public accounting experience in audit practice and national policy development groups. He is a visiting professor of accountancy and executive in residence at Bentley University in Waltham, Massachusetts. He was a partner and the director of audit policy for BDO Seidman, LLP, and was a national accounting and SEC consulting partner for Coopers & Lybrand, responsible for the technical issues research function and database, auditing research, audit automation and audit sampling techniques. Prior to joining BDO Seidman LLP, Dr. Graham was an associate professor of accounting and information systems and a graduate faculty fellow at Rutgers University in Newark, NJ, where he taught financial accounting courses. Dr. Graham is a member of the American Institute of Certified Public Accountants and a past member of the AICPA Auditing Standards Board. He is a Certified Fraud Examiner and a member of the Association of Certified Fraud Examiners. Throughout his career he has maintained an active profile in the academic as well as the business community. In 2002 he received the Distinguished Service Award of the Auditing Section of the AAA. His numerous academic and business publications span a variety of topical areas including information systems, internal controls, expert systems, audit risk, audit planning, fraud, sampling, analytical procedures, audit judgment, and international accounting and auditing. Dr. Graham holds an MBA in industrial management and PhD in business and applied economics from the University of Pennsylvania (Wharton School).

ABOUT THE CONTRIBUTORS

Michael A. Antonetti, CPA, CMA, is a partner with Crowe Horwath LLP. Mr. Antonetti has over 20 years of experience providing assurance and business advisory services to clients in many industries including manufacturing, distribution, banking, professional services, transportation and hospitality. Mr. Antonetti's experience also includes assisting clients with merger, acquisition, and divestiture transactions and application of related accounting standards. Mr. Antonetti also serves clients with international operations in Europe, Asia, and North and South America.

Yogesh Bahl, CPA, MBA, has more than 18 years of experience in leading global forensic investigations, delivering dispute consulting services, and helping companies manage enterprise risks. He leads the National Life Sciences Practice and the Northeast Antifraud practice. Yogesh specializes in assisting companies manage issues involving accounting, third parties, strategic alliances, and intellectual property. He has helped companies address and resolve multimillion-dollar issues involving accounting and finance, business partner reporting, unclear contract terms, and supply chain infiltration. In addition, Yogesh's experience includes strengthening the financial and audit-related provisions in various types of agreements including licensing, collaboration, distribution, and co-promotion agreements. By leveraging his advisory experience with corporations, Yogesh is effective when testifying on industry practice, breach of contract, accounting, and intellectual property matters.

Noah P. Barsky, PhD, CPA, CMA, is an associate professor at the Villanova School of Business. He earned his BS and MS in accounting from The Pennsylvania State University and his PhD from the University of Connecticut. His professional experience includes practice in the fields of accounting and finance as an analyst, auditor, and business consultant as well as instructional design and delivery for global professional services firms. He has been recognized with multiple national and international awards and grants for his scholarly writing and curriculum innovation.

Neil Beaton, CPA, ABV, CFAI, ASA, MBA is a managing director with Alvarez & Marsal Valuation Services in Seattle, Washington. He specializes in the valuation of public and privately held businesses and intangible assets for purposes of litigation support (marriage dissolutions, lost profits claims and others), acquisitions, sales, buy-sell agreements, ESOPs, incentive stock options, and estate planning and taxation. He also performs economic analysis for personal injury claims and for wrongful termination and wrongful death actions. His primary areas of concentration are valuations of early-stage, venture-backed company and litigation support across a broad spectrum of financial and economic matters. With more than 23 years of valuation and litigation support experience, Mr. Beaton has been involved in valuing companies in all major industries and has provided expert testimony in a number of domestic and international venues. Prior to joining A&M, Mr. Beaton spent nine years with Grant Thornton, where he most recently served as the Global Lead of Complex Valuation. He is a co-chair of the AICPA's Valuation of Private Equity Securities Task Force and a member of the AICPA's Mergers & Acquisitions Disputes Task Force. He is a member of the Business Valuation Update Editorial Advisory Board and on the Board of Experts, *Financial Valuation and Litigation Expert*.

Benedetto Bongiorno, CPA, CRE, has more than 40 years of public accounting experience providing auditing, accounting, and consulting services to both public and private real estate companies.

He has served as national director of real estate for Deloitte & Touche and BDO and has many years of experience in research and practical application of specially developed substantive analytical audit procedures and technologically based tools. He has made major contributions in public accounting, both in real estate and financial audits and in the field of continuous audit. As a cofounder and head of audit and accounting consulting services at Natural Decision Systems, Inc., he was awarded U.S. patents in both continuous assurance and internal control. Mr. Bongiorno continues to apply his extensive expertise in improving real evaluation techniques, transparency, and cost-effective auditing strategies through consulting for public accounting firms as well as both public and privately held companies.

Brad A. Davidson, CPA, is partner in charge of the Securities and Exchange Commission competency center of the national office of Crowe Horwath LLP. The Assurance Professional Practice group (or national office) has responsibility for technical consultations, quality control, and communications of current SEC and accounting developments. Brad specializes in the financial institutions industry. He serves as Crowe's representative to the Center for Audit Quality's SEC Regulations Committee, which meets quarterly with SEC staff to discuss emerging financial reporting issues. In December 2010, Brad served as steering committee chair of the American Institute of Certified Public Accountants annual national conference on current Securities and Exchange Commission and Public Company Accounting Oversight Board developments. Earlier in his career, he completed a two-year professional fellowship with the AICPA in Washington, DC.

Jason Flynn, FSA, MAAA, is a principal in the Human Capital Total Rewards practice at Deloitte Consulting LLP, where he provides broad technical guidance and advisory consulting with regard to pension and retiree medical benefit plans to a wide spectrum of clients including multinational clients. Jason serves as a national leader for Deloitte Consulting's retirement practice.

Sydney Garmong, CPA, is partner in the audit practice with Crowe Horwath LLP and located in Washington, DC. Her primary responsibility is to address accounting and regulatory issues affecting financial institutions. She is a member of the American Institute of Certified Public Accountants Depository Institutions Expert Panel, which maintains an ongoing liaison with various regulatory and standard-setting agencies that impact financial institutions, including the federal bank regulators, the Securities and Exchange Commission, and the Financial Accounting Standards Board. In addition to addressing technical issues, Sydney is a frequent speaker at industry and regulatory conferences. Prior to joining Crowe Horwath, she was a senior manager at the AICPA in Washington, DC. During her time with the AICPA, she addressed financial institution and financial instrument accounting, auditing, and regulatory matters.

Martha Garner, CPA, is a managing director in PricewaterhouseCoopers' national office specializing in health care, not-for-profit, and governmental accounting and financial reporting matters. She currently chairs the American Institute of Certified Public Accountants' Health Care Expert Panel and has served on numerous Financial Accounting Standards Board, Government Accounting Standards Board, and AICPA task forces and committees. She is a contributing author for *Montgomery's Auditing* (John Wiley & Sons, 1998) and the *Financial and Accounting Guide for Not-for-Profit Organizations* (John Wiley & Sons, 2012), and has authored articles and publications on a variety of accounting topics.

Timothy Geddes, FSA, MAAA, is a senior manager in the Human Capital Total Rewards practice at Deloitte Consulting LLP, where he provides broad technical guidance and advisory consulting with regard to pension and retiree medical benefit plans to a wide spectrum of domestic and multinational clients. Timothy serves on the American Academy of Actuaries Pension Committee and has spoken at numerous national actuarial meetings.

Frederick Gill, CPA, is senior technical manager on the Accounting Standards Team at the American Institute of Certified Public Accountants, where he provides broad technical support to the

Accounting Standards Executive Committee. During his over 20 years with the AICPA, he participated in the development of numerous AICPA Statements of Position, Audit and Accounting Guides, Practice Bulletins, issues papers, journal articles, and practice aids. He was a member of the U.S. delegation to the International Accounting Standards Committee, represented the U.S. accounting profession on the United Nations Intergovernmental Working Group of Experts on International Standards of Accounting and Reporting, and was a member of the National Accounting Curriculum Task Force. Previously he held several accounting faculty positions.

Alan S. Glazer, PhD, CPA (inactive), is the Henry P. and Mary B. Stager Professor of Business at Franklin & Marshall College, Lancaster, Pennsylvania. He was associate director of the Independence Standards Board's conceptual framework project and has been a consultant to several AICPA committees. His articles on auditor independence, not-for-profit organizations, and other issues have been published in the *Journal of Accountancy*, *CPA Journal*, *Issues in Accounting Education*, *Accounting Horizons*, and other academic and professional journals. He is also coauthor of a three-volume series of portfolios on financial statement analysis published by Bloomberg BNA.

Lynne M. Glennon, CPA, MST, is a full-time instructor for DePaul University's Master of Science in Taxation program. She currently teaches accounting for income taxes, transactions in property, and taxation of corporations and shareholders on campus as well as online for a national CPA firm. Prior to teaching full time, she worked in both industry and public accounting for 20 years as a tax director and tax consultant. As director of tax planning for Global Hyatt Corporation, she was primarily responsible for tax planning support on large-scale restructurings and mergers, acquisitions and dispositions, and management and control of the federal audit process, including communications with the Internal Revenue Service. As senior manager in Deloitte & Touche's lead tax services group, she focused on corporate and partnership taxation and served a number of multinational clients in the manufacturing, distribution, and service industries. Ms. Glennon is a Certified Public Accountant in the State of Illinois and a member of the American Institute of Certified Public Accountants. She is a graduate of the University of Notre Dame with a BA in economics; her MST degree is from DePaul University.

Bill Godshall, CPA. Since joining Coopers & Lybrand in 1990, Bill has had extensive experience in the energy and mining sector of assurance practices at two international accounting firms. He has worked on oil and gas audit and attestation engagements; utility audits, controls projects, and attestation engagements; and mining joint venture costs reviews. Bill also assisted his energy and mining clients with special accounting and auditing projects in the areas of derivatives, asset retirement obligations, leasing, and other complex topics. Bill spent two years at the Public Company Accounting Oversight Board, where he authored the inspection guidance for derivative accounting and auditing areas that is still in place today. In addition, Bill led the inspection of the audits of several energy and natural resource Securities and Exchange Commission issuers. Bill joined Frazier & Deeter's assurance practice in 2005 and serves as the lead partner for the assurance group's quality control function.

Richard A. Green, CPA, has over 25 years of auditing, accounting, and consulting experience, including all phases of external and internal auditing. Mr. Green leads the Sacramento public sector assurance practice of Macias Gini & O'Connell LLP. He served on the Governmental Accounting Standards Board Task Force on Pension Accounting Research and was recently appointed to the American Institute of Certified Public Accountants' State and Local Government Expert Panel Pension Comment Letter Task Force. Mr. Green is the engagement partner on the largest pension plan in the nation, the State of California Public Employees' Retirement System.

Frank J. Grippo, MBA, CPA, CFE, is an associate professor of accounting at William Paterson University in Wayne, NJ. He earned his BS in accounting from Seton Hall University and his MBA from Fairleigh Dickinson University. Prior to teaching, he was an auditor with Arthur Andersen & Co. His firm performs financial and accounting consulting for various nonprofit organizations, specializing in internal control structures, auditing, and fraud detection. Clients include well-known health and welfare, religious, and educational organizations.

Wendy Hambleton, CPA, is an audit partner working in the National SEC Department in BDO Seidman LLP's Chicago office. Prior to joining the SEC Department, Ms. Hambleton worked in the firm's Washington, DC, practice office. She works extensively with clients and engagement teams to prepare SEC filings and resolve related accounting and reporting issues. Ms. Hambleton coauthors a number of internal and external publications, including the AICPA's *Guide to SEC Reporting* and Warren Gorham & Lamont's *Controller's Handbook* chapter on public offering requirements.

Philip M. Herr, JD, CPA, PFS, is a senior case design analyst in the advance markets unit of AXA Equitable Life Insurance Company located in New York City. He is a former adjunct professor at Fairleigh Dickinson University, School of Continuing Education, and New Jersey City University. Phil specializes in the areas of: tax; estate and trusts; business succession and planning; personal financial planning; Employee Retirement Income Security Act issues and transactions; retirement, employee benefit, and executive compensation planning; and the use of life insurance, annuities, and insurance products. Phil is admitted to the New York and U.S. Tax Court Bars and is a member of the New York State Bar Association, American Institute of Certified Public Accountants, New York State Society of Certified Public Accountants, and Association for Advanced Life Underwriting. Phil holds life, health, and variable insurance licenses in New Jersey and New York and Financial Industry Regulatory Authority 7, 24, 55, 63 and 65 securities licenses.

Frank Hydoski, PhD, is a director in the New York Forensics & Dispute Services practice of Deloitte Financial Advisory Services LLP. He is responsible for developing new products and approaches in forensic accounting and investigations for clients in both the private and public sector. Mr. Hydoski is internationally recognized for his work in complex investigations, especially those requiring information technologies to facilitate forensic analysis. He was the chief investigator examining the United Nations Oil-for-Food Programme and led a crucial part of the massive forensic effort in the investigation of Holocaust-era accounts held by Swiss banks.

Henry R. Jaenicke, PhD, CPA, was the C. D. Clarkson Professor of Accounting at Drexel University. He is the author of *Survey of Present Practices in Recognizing Revenues, Expenses, Gains, and Losses* (FASB, 1981) and is the coauthor of the twelfth edition of *Montgomery's Auditing* (John Wiley & Sons, 1998). He has served as a consultant to several American Institute of Certified Public Accountants committees, the Independence Standards Board, and the Public Oversight Board.

Richard R. Jones, CPA, is a senior partner in the National Accounting Standards Professional Practice Group of Ernst & Young LLP, where he is responsible for assisting the firm's clients in understanding and implementing today's complex accounting requirements. Mr. Jones's fields of expertise are in the areas of impairments, equity accounting, real estate, leasing, and various financing arrangements.

Tom Jones was the vice chairman of the International Accounting Standards Board from its founding in 2001 until 2009. Prior to this he was a trustee and vice chairman of the Financial Accounting Foundation, which oversees the Financial Accounting Standards Board. He was a member of the ITF and was chairman of the American Bankers Association CFO Committee. He has been elected to the Financial Executives International Accounting Hall of Fame. Mr. Jones's corporate experience includes 20 years with Citibank/Citicorp as executive vice president and principal financial officer. He previously served for 15 years with IT&T in Italy, Belgium, and New York.

Ira G. Kawaller is the founder and principal of Kawaller & Co., a boutique consulting firm that specializes in assisting commercial enterprises with their use of derivative contracts. He is also the managing partner of the Kawaller Fund. He can be reached at Kawaller@kawaller.com; additional biographical information about Dr. Kawaller can be accessed at *www.kawaller.com/Ira_Kawaller_vita.pdf*.

Darin W. Kempke, CPA, is a partner at KPMG LLP in its Philadelphia office. He is the national audit sector leader for KPMG's power and utility practice. He has been working with power and utility clients (regulated and nonregulated) all over the world in his 21-plus years in the industry both with Arthur Andersen LLP and currently with KPMG LLP. He specializes in business and accounting services to regulated and nonregulated energy companies, provides energy thought leadership for publications and the KPMG Global Energy Institute, is a frequent speaker on the power and utility conference and webinar circuit. He spent time in the KPMG LLP Department of Professional Practice working on energy issues including derivatives, leases, emissions, and variable interest entities. He is a Certified Public Accountant licensed in Missouri, Kansas, New York, New Jersey, Pennsylvania, and the District of Columbia. He is a graduate of the University of Kansas with a BS in accounting and a BS in business administration.

Cynthia L. Krom, PhD, CPA, CFE, is assistant professor of accounting and organizations at Franklin & Marshall College, Lancaster, Pennsylvania. She is active in the New York State Society of Certified Public Accountants as well as the American Accounting Association. She has published articles on the Bank Secrecy Act and terrorism financing in professional journals, and her research interests include strategic bankruptcy and accounting history.

Richard F. Larkin, CPA, is technical director of not-for-profit accounting and auditing for BDO USA, LLP, in Bethesda, MD. Previously he was the technical director of the Not-for-Profit Industry Services Group in the national office of PricewaterhouseCoopers. He is a Certified Public Accountant with over 40 years of experience serving not-for-profit organizations as independent accountant, board member, treasurer, and consultant. He teaches, speaks, and writes extensively on not-for-profit industry matters and is active in many professional and industry organizations. He has been a member of the Financial Accounting Standards Board Not-for-Profit Advisory Task Force and the American Institute of Certified Public Accountants Not-for-Profit Organizations Committee and chaired the AICPA Not-for-Profit Audit Guide Task Force. He participated in writing both the third and fourth editions of *Standards of Accounting and Financial Reporting for Voluntary Health and Welfare Organizations*, and the AICPA Practice Aid *Financial Statement Presentation and Disclosure Practices for Not-for-Profit Organizations* (1999). He graduated from Harvard College and has an MBA from Harvard Business School. He is a coauthor of the fourth, fifth, and sixth editions of *Financial and Accounting Guide for Not-for-Profit Organizations* (John Wiley & Sons).

Elizabeth Lindsay-Ochoa, JD, LLM (Taxation), joined AXA Equitable in July 2002. Her primary focus is in estate and charitable planning. She has presented to Certified Public Accountants, attorneys, and financial professionals on charitable and estate-planning topics. Speaking engagements have included the Association of Fundraising Professionals International Conference on Fundraising; the American Bar Association Real Property, Trust and Estate; and the ABA Tax Section and the Association for Advanced Life Underwriting. Liz has written articles for the *Tax News Quarterly*, *Probate and Property*, and *National Underwriter*. She also has submitted comments to Congress, the Federal Deposit Insurance Company, and the Internal Revenue Service as part of her committee work for the ABA. Liz graduated from Michigan State University with a BA in telecommunications. In 2001, she received her JD from Thomas M. Cooley Law School and, in 2005, her LLM (taxation) from the University of Denver. Previously, Liz was a fellow with the Charitable Planning and Organizations Committee with the ABA's RPTE section (2005–2007). She is the chair of the Non-Tax Issues Affecting the Planning and Administration of Estates and Trust and an acquisitions editor for ABA RPTE publications. Liz is admitted to practice law in Michigan, Colorado (inactive), New York, and Connecticut. She is a member of the Colorado and Michigan Bar Associations and the National Committee on Planned Giving. She also holds Financial Industry Regulatory Authority Series 7, 66 and 24 securities registrations.

James Mraz, CPA, MBA, is a professor of accounting and business at the University of Maryland University College. Mr. Mraz has taught accounting and business for over 30 years in several colleges. Mr. Mraz has also conducted accounting accuracy reviews for John Wiley & Sons since 2005 and completed the instructor's manual for Prentice Hall's Accounting Information System's textbook. Mr. Mraz was a government auditor for 33 years while serving in the Marine Corps, Department of Health & Human Services, and the Department of Defense. Mr. Mraz served as chief financial officer for a resale and recreation government organization.

Grant W. Newton, PhD, CPA, CIRA, is a professor of accounting at Pepperdine University. He is the author of the two-volume set *Bankruptcy and Insolvency Accounting: Practice and Procedures: Forms and Exhibits, Sixth Edition* (John Wiley & Sons, 2006) and coauthor of *Bankruptcy and Insolvency Taxation, Second Edition* (John Wiley & Sons, 1994). He is a frequent contributor to professional journals and has lectured widely to professional organizations on bankruptcy-related topics.

Don M. Pallais, CPA, has his own practice in Richmond, VA. He is a former member of the American Institute of Certified Public Accountants Auditing Standards Board and the AICPA Accounting and Review Services Committee. He has written a host of books, articles, and continuing professional education courses on accounting topics.

Cynthia Pon, CPA, has over 20 years of professional experience providing auditing, accounting, and consulting services to the private and public sectors. Ms. Pon leads the San Francisco Bay Area public sector assurance practice of Macias Gini & O'Connell LLP, bringing extensive experience in federal, state, and local financial and compliance auditing. She is experienced in the application of generally accepted accounting principles and has been recognized by the Governmental Accounting Standards Board for her leadership in assisting California governments with early implementation of its standards. Ms. Pon also serves on the Government Finance Officers Association Special Review Committee for Comprehensive Annual Financial Report awards and has instructed numerous governmental clients on a variety of accounting and audit issues and challenges.

Zabihollah Rezaee, PhD, CPA, is the Thompson-Hill Chair of Excellence and Professor of Accountancy at the University of Memphis and has served a two-year term on the Standing Advisory Group of the Public Company Accounting Oversight Board. He received his BS degree from the Iranian Institute of Advanced Accounting, his MBA from Tarleton State University in Texas, and his PhD from the University of Mississippi. Professor Rezaee holds a number of certifications, including Certified Public Accountant, Certified Fraud Examiner, Certified Management Accountant, Certified Internal Auditor, Certified Government Financial Manager, Certified Sarbanes-Oxley Professional, Certified Corporate Governance Professional, and Certified Governance Risk Compliance Professional. He has also been a finalist for the SOX Institute's SOX MVP 2007, 2009, and 2010 Award. Professor Rezaee has published over 180 articles in a variety of accounting and business journals and made more than 200 presentations at national and international conferences. He has also published seven books: *Financial Institutions, Valuations, Mergers, and Acquisitions: The Fair Value Approach* (John Wiley & Sons, 2007); *Financial Statement Fraud: Prevention and Detection* (John Wiley & Sons, 2002); *U.S. Master Auditing Guide, Third Edition* (Commerce Clearing House, 2004); Audit Committee Oversight Effectiveness Post-Sarbanes-Oxley Act; *Corporate Governance Post-Sarbanes-Oxley: Regulations, Requirements, and Integrated Processes (John Wiley & Sons, 2007); Corporate Governance and Business Ethics* (John Wiley & Sons, 2008); and *Financial Services Firms: Governance, Regulations, Valuations, Mergers and Acquisitions* (John Wiley & Sons, 2011).

Francis E. Scheuerell, Jr., CPA, is a managing director at Navigant Consulting and is a Certified Public Accountant and certified management accountant. Frank has almost 30 years of diverse business experience in all areas of financial management and technical accounting, including accounting for business combinations, restatements, corporate restructurings, spin-offs, inventory, leases, revenue recognition, income taxes, equity method investments, segments, and consolidations, including variable interest entities. He has extensive experience addressing accounting and reporting issues for the real estate, construction, health care, hospitality, software, entertainment, retail, and manufacturing industries. Frank has served as an interim executive and/or consultant for numerous billion-dollar companies facing complex and extensive financial reporting issues. He has managed teams restating financial results and rebuilding financial reporting infrastructures while helping to restore regulator and investor confidence in those organizations. Frank has represented and testified on behalf of clients at Securities and Exchange Commission and NASDAQ hearings. Additionally, he has served as an expert witness in a securities litigation case. He has assisted numerous clients with their initial public offering or private place memorandums. He is an accomplished public speaker and author of numerous articles, publications, and continuing professional education seminars. Frank was a Project Manager—Research and Technical Activities for the Financial Accounting Standards Board and is a graduate of Illinois State University.

Jae K. Shim, PhD, is a professor of accounting and finance at California State University, Long Beach, and chief executive officer of Delta Consulting Company, a financial consulting and training firm. Dr. Shim received his MBA and PhD degrees from the University of California at Berkeley (Haas School of Business). He has been a consultant to commercial and nonprofit organizations for over 30 years. Dr. Shim has also published numerous articles in professional and academic journals and has over 50 college and professional books to his credit.

Reed K. Storey, PhD, CPA, had more than 30 years of experience on the framework of financial accounting concepts, standards, and principles, working with both the Accounting Principles Board, as director of Accounting Research of the American Institute of Certified Public Accountants, and the Financial Accounting Standards Board, as senior technical advisor. He was also a member of the accounting faculties of the University of California, Berkeley, the University of Washington, Seattle, and Bernard M. Baruch College, CUNY, and a consultant in the executive offices of Coopers & Lybrand (now PricewaterhouseCoopers LLP) and Haskins & Sells (now Deloitte & Touche, LLP).

B. Scott Teeter, MBA, CMA, is the vice president of land acquisition and development for the Austin/San Antonio, TX, division of Ryland Homes. He earned his BS in finance from The Pennsylvania State University and his MBA from the Wharton School of the University of Pennsylvania.

Daniel Thomas, EA, MAAA, is a specialist leader in the Human Capital Total Rewards practice at Deloitte Consulting LLP, where he serves as an actuarial specialist for the Deloitte audit teams and as a technical resource and reviewer within Deloitte's pension actuarial practice.

George I. Victor, CPA, is a partner in Giambalvo, Stalzer & Company, CPAs, P.C., and is the firm's director of quality control, where he is responsible for formulating the firm's accounting and auditing policy standards, including monitoring, consulting, technical research, staff training, and review of completed engagements. Mr. Victor has extensive experience in providing accounting and advisory services to both privately held and Securities and Exchange Commission–reporting companies. He also provides consulting services in areas of quality control, U.S. generally accepted accounting principles, and International Financial Reporting Standards matters to other certified public accounting firms in the United States and abroad. He is a member of the American Institute of Certified Public Accountants as well as the New York State Society of CPAs, where he serves as a member of its board of directors, chaired various committees, and serves as a member of the Editorial Board of the *CPA Journal*. He is an adjunct professor at the City University of New York. Mr. Victor has been published or quoted in various professional journals and books and frequently lectures on accounting and auditing related topics.

Jan R. Williams, PhD, CPA, is the Ernst & Young Professor and Dean, College of Business Administration, at the University of Tennessee. He is past president of the American Accounting Association and a frequent contributor to academic and professional literature on financial reporting and accounting education. Most recently he has been involved in the redesign of the CPA Examination and is a frequent speaker on this and other topics of professional significance.

Caroline H. Walsh, CPA, has over 33 years of specialized experience in auditing and consulting for local government agencies, nonprofit, and corporate enterprises. Ms. Walsh serves as the Quality Control Partner at Macias Gini & O'Connell LLP and leads the firm's Professional Standards Group. From October 2006 through 2009, Ms. Walsh served on the American Institute of Certified Public Accountants American Institute of Certified Public Accountants State and Local Government Expert Panel, where her role was to provide review and technical support services for the public accounting profession, including drafting and updating the AICPA guides for Audits of State and Local Governments and Government Auditing Standards and Circular A-133 Audits. Since 2009, Ms. Walsh has participated on the Expert Panel Task Force, which reviews and comments on the recent *Governmental Accounting Standards Board* due process documents related to accounting and reporting for pension benefits. In 2009, she was appointed for a three-year term to the GASB Advisory Committee, a standing committee whose members review the GASB staff's annual proposed changes and additions to the GASB's *Comprehensive Implementation Guide*.

David M. Zavada, CPA, MPA, is a partner with Kearney & Company in Alexandria, VA, where he specializes in providing accounting and audit services to the federal government. He is a former chief of the Financial Standards and Grants Branch within the Office of Federal Financial Management at the Office of Management and Budget and deputy to the Controller of the U.S. Government. He was director of the Office of Financial Management at the Department of Transportation, Federal Aviation Administration, and served as the Assistant Inspector General, Office of Audits at the Department of Homeland Security. In all of these positions David played a leadership role in developing and implementing government-wide financial management policies.

Mark L. Zyla, CPA/ABV, CFA, ASA, is managing director of Acuitas, Inc., an Atlanta, GA–based valuation and litigation consultancy firm. As a valuation specialist, Mark has provided consulting for numerous valuations in financial reporting and other types of engagements. He was the 2011 chair of the American Institute of Certified Public Accountants National Business Valuation Conference and presented AICPA's Fair Value Measurement Workshop. He is the author of *Fair Value Measurements, Second Edition: Practical Guidance and Implementation* (John Wiley & Sons).

CHAPTER 22

PERSONAL FINANCIAL STATEMENTS

George I. Victor, CPA

Giambalvo, Stalzer & Company, CPAs, P.C.

22.1 WHAT ARE THEY? AND WHY DO WE NEED THEM? 2

(a) What Is a Personal Financial Statement? 2
(b) Whose Financial Statement Is It? 2
(c) Why Are They Needed? 2
(d) Cash, Accrual, or Something Else? 6
(e) Which Asset/Liability Goes First? 6

22.2 PRACTICAL TIPS 7

(a) Due Diligence in the Accountant–Client Relationship 7
(b) Understanding of the Engagement to All Parties 7
(c) Value of Written Representations 8
(d) Operating Rules Are Otherwise Known as Applicable Professional Standards 8

22.3 RULES AND GUIDANCE IN PRESENTING ASSET VALUES 9

(a) Start by Using the Estimated Current Value 9
(b) What Is Owed from Others? 9
(c) Stock Market and Other Markets 10
(d) Limited Partnership Interests Are Limited 11
(e) Gold, Silver, and Other Precious Metals 11
(f) Options on Assets Other Than Marketable Securities 11
(g) Life Insurance 11
(h) A Real Challenge Is Valuing a Closely Held Business 12
(i) Real Estate 13
(i) Location, Location, Location 13
(j) Personal Property 13
(k) Intangible Assets 13
(l) Future Interests 14

22.4 RULES AND GUIDANCE IN PRESENTING LIABILITIES 14

(a) Start by Using the Estimated Current Amount of the Debt or Liability 14
(b) Fixed Commitments 14
(c) Contingencies, Risks, and Uncertainties 15
(d) Paying the Devil His Due: Income Taxes 15

22.5 PROVISION FOR INCOME TAXES 15

(a) Definition 15
(b) Computing the Provision for Income Taxes 15
(c) Tax Basis 16
(d) Disclaimer 16
(e) Omission of Disclosure 16

22.6 STATEMENT OF CHANGES IN NET WORTH 16

(a) Definition 16
(b) Uses 17
(c) Format 17

22.7 DISCLOSURES 17

22.8 COMPILATION 18

22.9 REVIEW 19

22.10 AUDITS 20

22.11 REPORTS 20

(a) Standard Compilation Report 21
(b) Reporting When Substantially All Disclosures Are Omitted 22
(c) Reporting When the Accountant Is Not Independent 23
(d) Reporting on Prescribed Forms 23

(e) Reporting When There Is a Departure from Generally Accepted Accounting Principles 24
(f) Standard Review Report 24
(g) Standard Audit Report 25

22.12 COMPILED STATEMENTS ONLY FOR CLIENT INTERNAL USE 26

22.13 SOURCES AND SUGGESTED REFERENCES 26

22.1 WHAT ARE THEY? AND WHY DO WE NEED THEM?

(a) WHAT IS A PERSONAL FINANCIAL STATEMENT? A standard definition of a *personal financial statement* is: a listing of everything owned or owed presented in a uniform way so that the user of the statement can understand it.

A personal financial statement presents the personal assets and liabilities of an individual, a couple or a family. It is not a financial statement on a business owned by the person; however, it does contain important information about such business interests.

The essential purpose of a personal financial statement is to measure wealth at a specified date—to take a snapshot of the person's financial condition. It does this by presenting:

- Estimated current values of assets
- Estimated current amounts of liabilities
- A provision for income taxes based on the taxes that would be owed if all the assets were liquidated and all the liabilities paid on the date of the statement
- Net worth

Although both personal and business financial statements are presented for the purpose of informing a reader about the finances of the entity being presented, the statements have many significant differences (see Exhibit 22.1).

The basic personal financial statement containing this information is called a *statement of financial condition,* not a balance sheet. Values and amounts for one or more prior periods may be included for comparison with the current values and amounts, but this is optional. The statement of changes in net worth is also optional (also see Section 22.6). It presents the major sources of increase or decrease in net worth (see Exhibit 22.2).

(b) WHOSE FINANCIAL STATEMENT IS IT? Normally, a personal financial statement is compiled for an individual and his or her spouse or one or the other person individually.

A personal financial statement covering a whole family usually presents the assets and liabilities of the family members in combination, as a single economic unit. However, the members may have different ownership interests in these assets or liabilities. For example, the wife may have a remainder interest in a testamentary trust, whereas the husband may own life insurance with a net cash surrender value. It may be useful, especially when the statement is to be used in a divorce case, to disclose each individual's interests separately. This may be done in separate columns within the statement, in the notes to the statement, or in additional statements for each individual.

Often an individual covered by the statement is one of a group of joint owners of assets, as with community property or property held in joint tenancy. In this case, the statement should include only the individual's interest as a beneficial owner under the laws of the state. If the parties' shares in the assets are not clear, the advice of an attorney may be needed to determine whether the person should regard any interest in the assets as his or her own and, if so, how much. The statement should make full disclosure of the joint ownership of the assets and the grounds for the allocation of shares.

(c) WHY ARE THEY NEEDED? Many individuals or families use personal financial statements for investment, tax, retirement, gift and estate planning, or for obtaining credit. A personal financial

	Personal	Business
Objective	Measurement of wealth	Reporting of earnings; evaluation of performance
Uses	Facilitation of financial planning; Procuring of credit; Provision of disclosures to the public or the court	Procuring of credit; Information for shareholders; Regulatory requirements
Valuation	Current value	Historical cost
Method of accounting	Accrual	Accrual
Classification	None: assets presented in order of liquidity, liabilities in order of maturity	Assets and liabilities classified as current or long-term
Excess of assets over liabilities	Net worth	Equity earnings

Exhibit 22.1 Personal and Business Financial Statements Compared

JAMES AND JANE PERSON
Statements of Financial Condition
December 31, 20X3 and 20X2

	December 31	
	20X3	**20X2**
Assets		
Cash	$ 3,700	$ 15,600
Bonus receivable	20,000	10,000
Investments		
Marketable securities (Note 2)	160,500	140,700
Stock options (Note 3)	28,000	24,000
Kenbruce Associates (Note 4)	48,000	42,000
Davekar Company, Inc. (Note 5)	550,000	475,000
Vested interest in deferred profit-sharing plan	111,400	98,900
Remainder interest in testamentary trust (Note 6)	171,900	128,800
Cash value of life insurance ($43,600 and $42,900), less loans payable to insurance companies ($38,100 and $37,700) (Note 7)	5,500	5,200
Residence (Note 8)	190,000	180,000
Personal effects (excluding jewelry) (Note 9)	55,000	50,000
Jewelry (Note 9)	40,000	36,500
	$1,384,000	$1,206,700
Liabilities		
Income taxes—current year balance	$ 8,800	$400
Demand 10.5% note payable to bank	25,000	26,000
Mortgage payable (Note 10)	98,200	99,000
Contingent liabilities (Note 11)		
	132,000	125,400
Estimated income taxes on the differences between the estimated current values of assets and the estimated current amounts of liabilities and their tax bases (Note 12)	239,000	160,000
Net worth	1,013,000	921,300
	$1,384,000	$1,206,700

The notes are an integral part of these statements.

Exhibit 22.2 Illustrative Financial Statements
Source: SOP No. 82-1(FASB ASC 274-10).

	Year ended December 31	
	20X3	20X2
Realized increases in net worth		
Salary and bonus	$ 95,000	$ 85,000
Dividends and interest income	2,300	1,800
Distribution from limited partnership	5,000	4,000
Gains on sales of marketable securities	1,000	500
	103,300	91,300
Realized decreases in net worth		
Income taxes	26,000	22,000
Interest expense	13,000	14,000
Real estate taxes	4,000	3,000
Personal expenditures	36,700	32,500
	79,700	71,500
Net realized increase in net worth	23,600	19,800
Unrealized increases in net worth		
Marketable securities (net of realized gains on securities sold)	3,000	500
Stock options	4,000	500
Davekar Company, Inc.	75,000	25,000
Kenbruce Associates	6,000	
Deferred profit-sharing plan	12,500	9,500
Remainder interest in testamentary trust	43,100	25,000
Jewelry	3,500	
	147,100	60,500
Unrealized decrease in net worth		
Estimated income taxes on the differences between the estimated current values of assets and the estimated current amounts of liabilities and their tax bases	79,000	22,000
Net unrealized increase in net worth	68,100	38,500
Net increase in net worth	91,700	58,300
Net worth at the beginning of year	921,300	863,000
Net worth at the end of year	$1,013,000	$921,300

The notes are an integral part of these statements.

Exhibit 22.2 ***Continued***

JAMES AND JANE PERSON
Notes to Financial Statements

Note 1 The accompanying financial statements include the assets and liabilities of James and Jane Person. Assets are stated at their estimated current values and liabilities at their estimated current amounts.

Note 2 The estimated current values of marketable securities are either (*a*) their quoted closing prices or (*b*) for securities not traded on the financial statement date, amounts that fall within the range of quoted bid and asked prices.

Marketable securities consist of the following:

	December 31, 20X3		December 31, 20X2	
	Number of Shares or Bonds	**Estimated Current Values**	**Number of Shares or Bonds**	**Estimated Current Values**
Stocks				
Jaiven Jewels, Inc.	1,500	$ 98,813		
McRae Motors, Ltd.	800	11,000	600	$ 4,750
Parker Sisters, Inc.	400	13,875	200	5,200
Rosenfield Rug Co.			1,200	96,000
Rubin Paint Company	300	9,750	100	2,875
Weiss Potato Chips, Inc.	200	20,337	300	25,075
		153,775		133,900
Bonds				
Jackson Van Lines, Ltd. (12% due 7/1/X9)	5	5,225	5	5,100
United Garvey, Inc. (7% due 11/15/X6)	2	1,500	2	1,700
		6,725		6,800
		$160,500		$140,700

Note 3 Jane Person owns options to acquire 4,000 shares of stock of Winner Corp. at an option price of $5 per share. The option expires on June 30, 20X5. The estimated current value is its published selling price.

Note 4 The investment in Kenbruce Associates is an 8% interest in a real estate limited partnership. The estimated current value is determined by the projected annual cash receipts and payments capitalized at a 12% rate.

Note 5 James Person owns 50% of the common stock of Davekar Company, Inc., a retail mail order business. The estimated current value of the investment is determined by the provisions of a shareholders' agreement, which restricts the sale of the stock and, under certain conditions, requires the company to repurchase the stock based on a price equal to the book value of the net assets plus an agreed amount for goodwill. At December 31, 20X3, the agreed amount for goodwill was $112,500, and at December 31, 20X2, it was $100,000.

A condensed balance sheet of Davekar Company, Inc., prepared in conformity with generally accepted accounting principles, is summarized below:

	December 31	
	20X3	**20X2**
Current assets	$3,147,000	$2,975,000
Plant, property, and equipment—net	165,000	145,000
Other assets	120,000	110,000
Total assets	3,432,000	3,230,000
Current liabilities	2,157,000	2,030,000
Long-term liabilities	400,000	450,000
Total liabilities	2,557,000	2,480,000
Equity	$ 875,000	$ 750,000

Exhibit 22.2 ***Continued***

The sales and net income for 20X3 were $10,500,000 and $125,000 and for 20X2 were $9,700,000 and $80,000.

Note 6. Jane Person is the beneficiary of a remainder interest in a testamentary trust under the will of the late Joseph Jones. The amount included in the accompanying statements is her remainder interest in the estimated current value of the trust assets, discounted at 10%.

Note 7. At December 31, 20X3 and 20X2, James Person owned a $300,000 whole life insurance policy.

Note 8. The estimated current value of the residence is its purchase price plus the cost of improvements. The residence was purchased in December 20X1, and improvements were made in 20X2 and 20X3.

Note 9. The estimated current values of personal effects and jewelry are the appraised values of those assets, determined by an independent appraiser for insurance purposes.

Note 10. The mortgage (collateralized by the residence) is payable in monthly installments of $815 a month, including interest at 10% a year through 20Y8.

Note 11. James Person has guaranteed the payment of loans of Davekar Company, Inc., under a $500,000 line of credit. The loan balance was $300,000 at December 31, 20X3, and $400,000 at December 31, 20X2.

Note 12. The estimated current amounts of liabilities at December 31, 20X3, and December 31, 20X2, equaled their tax bases. Estimated income taxes have been provided on the excess of the estimated current values of assets over their tax bases as if the estimated current values of the assets had been realized on the statement date, using applicable tax laws and regulations. The provision will probably differ from the amounts of income taxes that eventually might be paid because those amounts are determined by the timing and the method of disposal or realization and the tax laws and regulations in effect at the time of disposal or realization.

The estimated current values of assets exceeded their tax bases by $850,000 at December 31, 20X3, and by $770,300 at December 31, 20X2. The excess of estimated current values of major assets over their tax bases are—

	December 31	
	20X3	**20X2**
Investment in Davekar Company, Inc.	$430,500	$355,500
Vested interest in deferred profit-sharing plan	111,400	98,900
Investment in marketable securities	104,100	100,000
Remainder interest in testamentary trust	97,000	53,900

Exhibit 22.2 ***Continued***

statement may also be required for disclosure to the court in a divorce case or to the public when the individual is a candidate or an incumbent of public office. Another example of the use of a specialized personal financial statement was where the statement was used in litigation to show the solvency of an individual who had been the holder of a business franchise that was terminated due to an "alleged" insolvency.

(d) CASH, ACCRUAL, OR SOMETHING ELSE? American Institute of Certified Public Accountants (AICPA) Statement of Position (SOP) No. 82–1 (Financial Accounting Standards Board [FASB] ASC 274–10; see Section 22.2(d)) establishes the use of estimated current values and amounts and the accrual basis of accounting as generally accepted accounting principles (GAAP) for personal financial statements. The American Institute of Certified Public Accountants (AICPA) *Personal Financial Statements Guide* (the *Guide*) allows accountants to prepare, compile, review, or audit personal financial statements on other comprehensive bases of accounting, such as historical cost, tax, or cash. In actual practice, there are many variations on a theme, but the methodologies and approaches should be disclosed and should not be misleading to the user of the statement.

(e) WHICH ASSET/LIABILITY GOES FIRST? Cash is king (and the most liquid of the assets). So cash is at the top of the list. Assets are presented in order of liquidity and liabilities in order of maturity. No distinction is made between current and long-term assets and liabilities because there is no operating cycle on which to base that distinction in a person's financial affairs.

Assets and liabilities of a closely held business that is conducted as a separate entity are not combined with similar personal items in a personal financial statement. Instead, the estimated current net value of the person's investment in the entity is shown as one amount. But if the person owns a business activity that is not conducted as a separate entity, such as a real estate investment with a related mortgage, the assets and liabilities of the activity are shown as separate amounts.

22.2 PRACTICAL TIPS

(a) DUE DILIGENCE IN THE ACCOUNTANT–CLIENT RELATIONSHIP. As is the case with any potential business relationship, before accepting an engagement involving personal financial statements, the accountant ordinarily would evaluate certain aspects of the potential client relationship.

The accountant may wish to consider facts that might bear on the integrity of the prospective client. Consideration of the character and reputation of the individual helps to minimize the possibility of association with a client who lacks integrity. The extent of the accountant's inquiries before acceptance might depend on his or her previous knowledge of the client and the nature of the client's financial activities. The accountant may want to consult predecessor accountants or auditors, attorneys, bankers, and others having business relationships with the individual regarding facts that might bear on the integrity of the prospective client. This does not suggest that, in accepting an engagement, the accountant vouches for the integrity or reliability of a client. However, prudence suggests that an accountant be selective in determining his or her professional relationships. It is not unknown for a seemingly high-profile potential client, complete with private jet and an entourage of assistants, to be a fraudster, destined for more humble quarters in a prison.

The accountant may also wish to consider circumstances that present unusual business risk, such as considering whether an individual is in serious financial difficulty and if that fact could have a bearing on the integrity of the information presented to the accountant for the preparation of the financial statements.

In addition, the accountant may want to consider up front the effect of any lack of independence on the type of report he may issue in compliance with professional standards. Statements on Standards for Accounting and Review Services (SSARS) No. 19 permits the accountant to issue a compilation report on personal financial statements of an individual with respect to whom the accountant is not independent. However, the accountant must be independent to issue a review report or an audit opinion. For example, if a prospective client requesting a personal financial statement is the co-owner of a business with the spouse of the accountant, the accountant is not independent and can issue a compilation only.

Before accepting an engagement involving personal financial statements, the accountant may want to ask the potential client about the availability of records and consider whether available records provide a basis sufficient for providing the services requested. Incomplete or inadequate accounting records are likely to give rise to problems in compiling, reviewing, or auditing personal financial statements. Because of the informal nature of most personal financial records, the accountant should evaluate the need to perform other accounting services in conjunction with personal financial records. AICPA Interpretation No. 101–3, *Performance of Nonattest Services,* should be consulted for guidance.

Professional standards require the accountant to attain a certain level of knowledge of the client's financial activities. Before accepting an engagement, the accountant should consider whether he or she can obtain an appropriate understanding of the nature of the prospective client's financial activities and the specialized accounting principles and practices related to any of the client's financial activities.

(b) UNDERSTANDING OF THE ENGAGEMENT TO ALL PARTIES. Once the accountant has decided to accept an engagement involving personal financial statements, SSARS No. 19, *Compilation and Review Engagements,* states: "[T]he accountant should establish an understanding with management regarding the services to be performed for compilation engagements and should document the understanding through a written communication with management."

The individuals requesting personal financial statements may not be familiar with the accountant's service or its limitations and may confuse such engagements with audits. It is important that both parties have an understanding of the engagement, and a written understanding is the best one to prevent misunderstandings. An engagement letter would normally include:

- Type of service being provided (compilation, review, or audit)
- Statements to be produced
- Applicable standards
- Client and accountant/auditor responsibilities
- Differences among compilations, reviews, and audits
- Indication that the engagement cannot be relied on to disclose errors, fraud, or illegal acts
- Fees

(c) VALUE OF WRITTEN REPRESENTATIONS. Talk is cheap and can be easily misconstrued or, in retrospect, be unclear as to facts and circumstances. During an engagement, the client will ordinarily make many representations to the accountant. Documentation of these representations in written form will indicate their continuing appropriateness and reduce the possibility of misunderstanding. The actual content of the letter will depend on the circumstances of the particular engagement.

Generally accepted auditing standards (GAAS) require that an independent auditor performing an audit in accordance with GAAS obtain written representations from management for all financial statements and periods covered by the auditor's reports. The representation should be addressed to the auditor and should be made as of a date no earlier than the date of the auditor's report.

SAARS No. 19 requires that the accountant obtain a representation letter from the client as part of every review engagement as well. Compilation engagements do not contemplate tests of accounting records and of responses to inquiries by obtaining corroborating evidential matter. However, because of the informal nature of most personal financial records, it is advisable to obtain written representation from the client to confirm the oral representations made in all personal financial statement engagements.

(d) OPERATING RULES ARE OTHERWISE KNOWN AS APPLICABLE PROFESSIONAL STANDARDS. The primary authoritative guidance for accountants on the preparation of personal financial statements is SOP No. 82–1, *Accounting and Financial Reporting for Personal Financial Statements,* issued by the AICPA (FASB ASC 274–10).

Accountants are often engaged to compile, review, or audit personal financial statements. These different types of engagements are governed by different standards. Standards for compilation of financial statements prescribed by SSARS No. 19 are applicable to the compilation of personal financial statements in the same manner as they apply to the compilation of other financial statements.

However, AICPA release SSARS No. 6, *Reporting on Personal Financial Statements Included in Written Personal Financial Plans,* provides an exemption from the performance and reporting standards of SSARS No. 19 for personal financial statements included in written personal financial plans as long as both of the next conditions exist:

1. The accountant establishes an understanding with the client, preferably in writing, that the financial statements (a) will be used solely to assist the client and the client's advisors to develop the client's personal financial goals and objectives and (b) will not be used to obtain credit or for any purposes other than developing the financial plan.
2. Nothing comes to the accountant's attention during the engagement that would cause the accountant to believe that the financial statements will be used to obtain credit or for any purposes other than developing the client's financial goals and objectives.

If an accountant prepares a personal financial statement under this exemption, he or she should issue a written report stating the restricted purpose of the statement and noting that it has not been audited, reviewed, or compiled. (See also Sections 22.8 and 22.9.)

Standards for review of financial statements prescribed by SSARS No. 19 apply to the review of personal financial statements in the same manner as to the review of other financial statements (also see Section 22.8), and GAAS apply to the audit of personal statements in the same manner as to the audit of other financial statements.

Accountants may also be asked to report on specified elements, accounts, or items of a personal financial statement. In those circumstances, the guidance provided by Statement on Auditing Standards (SAS) No. 62, *Special Reports,* Statements on Standards for Attestation Engagements (SSAE) No. 10, *Attestation Standards,* as amended, and SSARS No. 19. The authors highly recommend the use of the AICPA *Guide.* The *Guide,* which was prepared by the AICPA Personal Statements Task Force, provides excellent guidance about the application of professional standards to personal statement engagements. The *Guide* was originally published in 1982–1983 but has been updated periodically to include changes resulting from the issuance of authoritative pronouncements since that time.

22.3 RULES AND GUIDANCE IN PRESENTING ASSET VALUES

(a) START BY USING THE ESTIMATED CURRENT VALUE. According to SOP No. 82–1 (FASB ASC 274–10), personal financial statements must present assets at their estimated current values.

The definition of *estimated current value* as shown in SOP No. 82–1 (FASB ASC 274–10) is "the amount at which the item could be exchanged between a buyer and a seller, each of whom is well informed and willing, and neither of whom is compelled to buy or sell." Sales commissions and other costs of disposal should be considered if they are expected to be material to the value.

SOP No. 82–1 (FASB ASC 274–10) recognizes that determining the estimated current value of some assets may be difficult. Judgment should be exercised if the costs of determining the estimated current value of such assets outweigh the benefits. For example, some unique collections may not have a readily determinable value, as there are few benchmark transactions or no discernible market for these items (as there are for some stamp, coin, and car collections) on which to base a valuation. In such cases, the valuation may be a conservative one, despite the enthusiastic valuation of the assets by their owner.

In general, the best way to determine estimated current value is by reference to recent transactions involving market prices of similar assets in similar circumstances, such as published prices for marketable securities.

If recent market prices are not available, other methods may be used. SOP No. 82–1 (FASB ASC 274–10) recommends:

- Capitalization of past or prospective earnings
- Liquidation value
- Appraisals
- Adjustment of historical cost based on changes in a specific price index
- Discounted amounts of projected cash receipts and payments

Whatever method is used, it should be consistently applied from period to period for the same asset unless there is a change in circumstances. Should there be a change in the method or the circumstances surrounding a particular asset, a disclosure regarding such a change should be made in the notes to the statements.

If the client requests a change in the method used to calculate the value of an asset and it is not supported by a significant change surrounding the circumstances surrounding the asset, this is a departure from GAAP, and the accountant's report should be modified.

(b) WHAT IS OWED FROM OTHERS?. Debts or obligations that are owed from others are called *receivables.* When they represent near-term commitments, they often do not carry any provision for interest to be paid, as it would be a nominal amount. The theory, however, is that such notes or promises, when they are far in the future, be presented at the discounted (net of interest) amounts of cash expected to be collected, using the prevailing interest rate at the date of the statement to discount these cash flows.

Even though there is no interest noted in an agreement, the face amount of the note showing the balance owed may not be the amount that should be shown on the statement of condition. Within many families and within certain religious, cultural, or ethnic groups, the concept of interest is not recognized. As a result, the face amount of the amount owed may not appear to specify that there is any interest involved but may, in fact, include an implicit interest amount. Another issue faced in valuation is the determination of the discount when faced with a risk of collectability. For example, a valuation engagement for an estate involved a note receivable from a corporation that was near bankruptcy. After reviewing the statements of the company, the accountant discounted the value of the note by 40 percent, by using a high interest rate to compensate for the risk. In a similar manner, a note from one family member to another may be discounted more heavily based on the poor condition of the debtor.

(c) STOCK MARKET AND OTHER MARKETS. Marketable securities are stocks, bonds, unfulfilled futures contracts, options on traded securities, certificates of deposit, and money market accounts for which market quotations are publicly available. The estimated current value of a marketable security is its closing price on the date of the statement, less any expected sales commission to be paid. Individual retirement accounts (IRAs) and Keogh accounts should be presented net of the penalty charge for early withdrawal.

- If the security was not traded on that date but published bid and ask prices are available, SOP No. 82–1 (FASB ASC 274–10) states that the estimated current value should be within the range of those prices. Using the principle of conservatism, one school of thought suggests that if there is a wide gap between bid and asked amounts, then the selected price should be toward the lower end of the range.
- If bid and asked prices are not available for the date of the statement, the estimated current value is the closing price on the last day that the security was traded, unless the trade occurred so far in the past as to be meaningless by the date of the statement.
- On over-the-counter securities, unfortunately, the market does not speak with a single voice. Different quotations may be given by the financial press, quotation publications, financial reporting services, and various brokers. In such a case, the mean (average) of the bid prices, of the bid and asked prices, or of the prices quoted by a representative sample of brokers may be used as the estimated current value.
- Movement of large blocks of stock may also pose a problem. If a large block of stock was dumped on the market, the market price may be adversely affected. However, a controlling interest might be worth more, share for share, than a minority interest. Market prices may need to be adjusted for these factors to determine estimated current value. Preparers should consult a qualified stockbroker for an opinion on a particular situation such as this. Discounts for blockage as it relates to accounting and fair value are issues of contemporary accounting discussion for large companies as well as smaller ones.
- Restrictions on the transfer of a stock are yet another factor that might call for an adjustment of market prices to determine estimated current value.
- Options values should be reported at published prices. If prices are not available, value should be determined on the basis of the value of the asset subject to option, considering exercise price and the length of the option period.

Because of the importance of valuations to taxing authorities, some valuations may result in challenges, even though they may conform to accounting practice. For example, when valuing the transfer of stock for gift tax purposes, an accountant discounted the value of the stock by 5 percent for blockage. The facts supported the small discount of 5 percent since, although the stock was regularly traded, it was not traded in large quantities. Unfortunately, the Internal Revenue Service did not agree with the valuation, and, in order to avoid a costly appeals process and possible litigation, a lower, compromise discount was proposed and accepted.

(d) LIMITED PARTNERSHIP INTERESTS ARE LIMITED. Since limited partnership interests are limited by the terms of the agreement, they should be discounted to reflect the lack of participation and transferability.

Except for publicly traded limited partnerships, accountants may value the asset by taking the value of the assets less liabilities and discounting the result based on the nature and extent of restrictions contained in the partnership agreement, also giving consideration to the actual operation of the partnership as it relates to distribution of cash flow. In one engagement we found that in a limited partnership that owned and operated a business, the manager/general partner was underpaid for duties and responsibilities. After determining the appropriate compensation and adjusting cash flow downward, we reduced the value of the partnership interests.

If the interests in a limited partnership are actively traded, the estimated current value of such an interest should be based on the prices of recent trades. If interests in the partnership are not actively traded, the value of reasonably comparable securities, or the current value of the partnership's underlying assets may be used to measure the value of the interest (see Section 22.3(h)). When this method is used, the person should consider discounting the value of the interest for lack of marketability and lack of control over the general partner. As with the valuation of private equity securities, discounts should not be based on arbitrary rules of thumb but on the facts and circumstances of the valuation. In practice, discounts they can vary significantly (e.g., 5 to 60 percent) based on the nature and number of the issues.

If it is not feasible to estimate the current value of the partnership's underlying assets (and the interests are not actively traded), and the entity is in an early stage of development, the estimated current value of the interest may be shown as the amount of cash that the person has invested. If the underlying assets of the partnership are considered to be virtually worthless, however, the interest should be valued at zero.

The person's share of the partnership's negative tax basis, if any, should be included in the computation of the provision for income taxes (see Section 22.5).

The statement should disclose the person's share of any recourse debts of the partnership and any commitments for future funding. If the person's interest in the partnership represents a substantial proportion of ownership, it may be useful to disclose summarized financial information about the partnership as an investment in a closely held business (see Section 22.3(h)).

(e) GOLD, SILVER, AND OTHER PRECIOUS METALS. The estimated current value of precious metals, like that of marketable securities, is their closing price on the date of the statement, less the expected sales commission.

(f) OPTIONS ON ASSETS OTHER THAN MARKETABLE SECURITIES. Options to buy assets other than marketable securities should first be valued at the difference between the exercise price and the asset's current value. Then this difference should be discounted at the person's borrowing rate over the option period, if this is material. The borrowing rate should reflect the cost of any loan secured by the asset.

Because we are valuing the option, not the asset, we need to find out if the option is in the money. That is, would it make economic sense to exercise the option because the current value is higher than the exercise price? If it is not higher, then the option has no current value.

(g) LIFE INSURANCE. The estimated current value of a life insurance policy is its cash surrender value, less any loans against it. This information may be obtained from the insurance company.

Disclosure of the face value of the policy is required by SOP No. 82–1 (FASB ASC 274–10). It may also be useful to disclose the death benefits that would accrue to family members covered by the statement.

(h) A REAL CHALLENGE IS VALUING A CLOSELY HELD BUSINESS. Can a business with liabilities in excess of its assets have value? Answer. It all depends on the facts. One business that had a negative net worth sold for approximately $4 million due to the intangibles of a customer list and its established name. The challenge is finding those assets. Another company was worth more than it would appear due to its trained and in-place workforce.

If the person has a material investment in a closely held business that is conducted as a separate entity, the statement should disclose:

- Name of the company
- Person's percentage of ownership
- Nature of the business
- Summarized financial information on the company's assets, liabilities, and results of operations, based on the company's financial statements for the most recent year
- Basis of presentation of the company's statements, such as GAAP, tax, or cash
- Any significant loss contingencies

Determining the estimated current value of an investment in a closely held business, whether a proprietorship, partnership, joint venture, or corporation, is notoriously difficult. The objective is to approximate the amount at which the investment could be exchanged, on the date of the statement, between a well-informed and willing buyer and seller, neither of whom is compelled to buy or sell. This value is presented as a single item in the statement of financial condition, and a condensed balance sheet of the company should be presented in the notes.

SOP No. 82–1 (FASB ASC 274–10) recognizes several methods, or combinations of methods, for determining the estimated current value of a closely held business:

- Appraisals
- Multiple of earnings
- Liquidation value
- Reproduction value
- Discounted amounts of projected cash receipts
- Adjustments of book value
- Cost of the person's share of the equity of the business

SOP No. 82–1 (FASB ASC 274–10) says that if there is an existing buy-sell agreement specifying the amount that the person will receive when he or she withdraws, retires, or sells out, it should be considered, but it does not necessarily determine estimated current value.

While all of the methods listed are valid valuation methods, the difficulty is determining which method or methods are most appropriate for the particular business being valued. It is also important to keep in mind that estimated current value is based on the accrual basis of accounting. If the business being valued keeps it books on the cash or tax basis of accounting, the amounts utilized in determining the estimated current value should be adjusted to the accrual basis.

A question that SOP No. 82–1 (FASB ASC 274–10) does not address is whether an accountant preparing a personal financial statement should try to value a closely held business at all. Competence in valuing businesses requires a considerable degree of specialized knowledge, and often accountants' litigation liability coverage excludes valuations.

In addition, the Professional Ethics Executive Committee (PEEC) of the AICPA has issued Interpretation 101–3, *Performance of Nonattest Services.* This interpretation states that independence would be impaired if a member performs an appraisal or valuation service for an attest client where the results of the service, individually or in the aggregate, would be material to the statements, and the appraisal or valuation involves a significant degree of subjectivity. Since valuations and appraisals generally involve a significant degree of subjectivity, independence would often be impaired if the valuation were performed by the accountant issuing a report on the statement. For these reasons, the certified public accountant (CPA) should refrain from valuing the business interest himself or herself. Qualified independent appraisers are often readily accessible to value the business, which will significantly aid in obtaining an objective valuation.

Various business valuation accrediting organizations exist. Some of the best known are the ABA (Accreditation in Business Valuation, by the AICPA), the ASA (Accredited Senior Appraiser of the American Society of Appraisers), and the CBA (Certified Business Appraiser, of the Institute of Business Appraisers). Such organizations generally set standards for objectivity and report preparation and require qualifying examinations and appraisal experience to receive the credential. Additionally, to be an ABA, the candidate must be a CPA.

(i) REAL ESTATE

(i) Location, Location, Location. Estimated current values may be based on:

- Sales of similar properties in similar circumstances
- Discounted amounts of projected cash flows from the property
- Appraisals based on estimates of selling prices and selling costs obtained from independent real estate agents or brokers familiar with similar properties in similar locations
- Appraisals used to obtain financing
- Assessed value for property taxes, considering the basis of the assessment and its relationship to market values in the area

The estimated current value of a property should be presented net of expected sales commissions and closing costs.

Pitfalls sometimes encountered with real estate include environmental problems, zoning restrictions, floodplains, or other hazardous conditions or encumbrances. For example, a property of significant value would be valued at a much lower value because if it was leased by another entity at below-market value on a long-term lease.

(j) PERSONAL PROPERTY. Personal property includes but is not limited to cars, jewelry, antiques, and art. These items should be valued at appraisal values derived from a specialist's opinion or at the values given in published guides, such as *Kelley's Blue Book* for automobiles. If the costs of an appraisal seem to outweigh the benefits and if the valuation is not significant to the overall recorded amount, then, historical costs are often used. Appraisers can be located through the American Society of Appraisers.

From a practical perspective, personal property that has appreciated in value is generally conservatively valued if the purpose of the statement of condition is collateral for lending purposes. Accordingly, it may often be prudent to simply use the cost basis.

(k) INTANGIBLE ASSETS. Patents, copyrights, and other intangible assets should be presented at the net proceeds of a current sale of the asset or the discounted amount of cash flow arising from its future use. If the amounts and timing of receipts from the asset cannot be reasonably estimated, the asset should be presented at its purchased cost, evaluated for impairment.

The real issue is often to identify such assets. Frequently, they are not visible to the accountant or recognized by the person engaging the accountant. Questioning and experience are used to identify potential intangibles that might have a recognizable value. For example, a patent may be owned and used within a business enterprise without a designated, separate cash flow. Sometimes anomalies arise, such as a line of greeting cards being valued at greater than the value of the aggregate business that had created and owned the line of greeting cards. Such situations can arise when some product lines are not profitable.

(l) FUTURE INTERESTS. These future interests should be shown in a personal financial statement:

- Guaranteed minimum portions of pensions
- Vested interests in pension or profit-sharing plans
- Deferred compensation contracts
- Beneficial interests in trusts
- Remainder interests in property subject to life estates
- Fixed amounts of alimony for a definite future period
- Annuities

Any other future interests should also be shown, so long as they are nonforfeitable rights for fixed or determinable amounts; are not contingent on the holder's life expectancy or the occurrence of a particular event, such as disability or death; and do not require future performance of service by the holder.

The presentation of future interests should be at the discounted amount of estimated future receipts, using an appropriate interest (discount) rate as of the date of the statements.

22.4 RULES AND GUIDANCE IN PRESENTING LIABILITIES

(a) START BY USING THE ESTIMATED CURRENT AMOUNT OF THE DEBT OR LIABILITY. Payables and other liabilities are presented at their estimated current amounts. This is the amount of cash to be paid, discounted by the rate implicit in the transaction in which the debt was incurred. Accounting Principles Board (APB) Opinion No. 21, *Interest on Receivables and Payables* (FASB ASC 835–30), explains how to determine this rate.

Although certain kinds of liabilities are not discounted in business financial statements, all liabilities should be presented at their discounted amounts in personal financial statements. No distinction is made between current and long-term liabilities.

With some home mortgages and other debts, the person may be able to pay off the debt currently at an amount less than the present value of future payments. If this alternative exists, the debt should be presented at the lower amount, as that is the amount the liability could be satisfied if paid today.

Personal liabilities, such as home mortgages, are shown separately from investment liabilities, such as margin accounts. Obligations related to limited partnership investments should be shown if the person is personally liable for them. Debt that was included in the valuation of an investment in a closely held business, however, should not be shown again in this section of the personal statement.

In addition to discounting because of the terms of the obligation, it may be appropriate to reflect the poor condition of the creditor in the valuation. For example, a 30 percent discount rate was applied to value a $100,000 debt that was payable over 10 years. The discounted value reflected the uncertainty of the later payments, and the reduced valuation was used in creditor negotiations.

(b) FIXED COMMITMENTS. Child support, alimony, pledges to charities, and other noncancelable commitments to pay future sums should be presented as liabilities at their discounted amounts if they have all of these characteristics:

- The commitment is for a fixed or determinable amount.
- The commitment is not contingent on someone else's life expectancy or the occurrence of a particular event, such as death or disability.
- The commitment does not require future performance by others, as an operating lease does.

(c) CONTINGENCIES, RISKS, AND UNCERTAINTIES. During life we enter into many open transactions, which often may lead to unexpected consequences. While we are waiting for the son's or daughter's business to succeed, the lease we cosigned for their business location may become an unanticipated and unwelcome liability, particularly if it requires reaching for the checkbook. Items like this must be disclosed.

Among the contingent liabilities that should be considered for disclosure are:

- Personal guarantees on others' loans
- Liabilities for limited partnership obligations
- Lawsuits against the person
- Inadequate medical insurance coverage
- Noncoverage for personal liability

Statement of Accounting Standards (SFAS) No. 5, *Accounting for Contingencies,* as amended (FASB ASC 450–10), provides guidance on whether a contingent liability should be recorded, disclosed in a footnote, or omitted. This pronouncement says, in short, that a liability should be recorded if its related contingent loss or range of loss can be estimated and its occurrence is probable. If the amount of loss cannot be estimated but its occurrence is either probable or possible, the related liability should be disclosed in a footnote. If its occurrence is remote, neither recording nor disclosure is required.

(d) PAYING THE DEVIL HIS DUE: INCOME TAXES. Income taxes currently payable include any unpaid income taxes for past tax years, deferred income taxes arising from timing differences, and the estimated amount of income taxes accrued for the elapsed portion of the current tax year to the date of the statement.

If the statement date coincides with the tax year-end, then there is obviously no difficulty in estimating the amount for the current year. If the dates do not coincide, the estimate should be based on taxable income to date and the tax rate applicable to estimated taxable income for the whole year. The taxes for the current year should be shown net of amounts withheld from pay or paid with estimated tax returns.

Estimated income taxes are shown after the liabilities but before net worth on the statement of condition.

22.5 PROVISION FOR INCOME TAXES

(a) DEFINITION. The personal financial statement should show an estimate for the income taxes that would be owed if all of the person's assets were sold, and all of his or her liabilities paid, on the date of the statement. This estimate, known as a *provision,* should be shown under its full title as given in SOP No. 82–1 (FASB ASC 274–10): "Estimated income taxes on the differences between the estimated current values of assets and the estimated current amounts of liabilities and their tax bases." It is presented in the statement as one amount and is shown between liabilities and net worth. A note discloses the methods and assumptions used to compute it (refer back to Exhibit 22.2).

(b) COMPUTING THE PROVISION FOR INCOME TAXES. Currently applicable income tax laws and regulations—state, local, and federal—should be used in computing the provision for income taxes. Items for consideration include:

- Recapture of depreciation
- Available carryovers of losses, credits, or deductions
- Exclusion for the gain on the sale of a residence
- Deductible state income taxes
- Alternative minimum taxes

Because most of these considerations apply to some assets or liabilities but not to others, the provision for income taxes should be computed separately for each asset and each liability. It is not necessary, however, to disclose all these computations in the note. For example, note 12 in Exhibit 22.2 shows only the excess of estimated current values over the tax bases of major assets.

(c) TAX BASIS. It is often difficult to determine the tax basis of an asset or liability acquired long ago or by inheritance or trade. In such a case, the preparer may use a conservative estimate of the tax basis in computing the provision for income taxes, with a note disclosing how the estimate was determined.

(d) DISCLAIMER. SOP No. 82–1 (FASB ASC 274–10) requires a statement that:

> the provision will probably differ from the amounts of income taxes that might eventually be paid because those amounts are determined by the timing and the method of disposal, realization, or liquidation and the tax laws and regulations in effect at the time of disposal, realization, or liquidation.

This statement should be made in the note (see Exhibit 22.2, note 12).

(e) OMISSION OF DISCLOSURE. In addition to omitting the deferred tax liability, some practitioners also do not estimate the income tax liability for the provision for income taxes. This departure from GAAP must be disclosed in the report. In our experience, many personal statements are prepared in connection with bank requirements for loans. We have found that for most of those loans, the banks are not concerned with the amount of estimated taxes on appreciation in value of assets. What they are concerned with are the unpaid income tax obligations for the current and prior years and other short-term liquidity issues. If not provided by the client, one technique to obtain the federal tax liability is to obtain a transcript of the individuals' current and prior tax-year records. The transcripts are available if a power of attorney, Form 2848, has been filed with the Internal Revenue Service.

22.6 STATEMENT OF CHANGES IN NET WORTH

(a) DEFINITION. A statement of changes in net worth is an *optional* statement that presents the major sources of change in a person's net worth.

Whereas the statement of financial condition may or may not show amounts for prior periods and thus may not show change in net worth, the statement of changes in net worth should present:

- Increases in net worth produced by income
- Increases in the estimated current values of assets
- Decreases in the estimated current amounts of liabilities
- Decreases in the provision for income taxes
- Decreases in net worth produced by expenses
- Decreases in the estimated current values of assets
- Increases in the estimated current amounts of liabilities
- Increases in the provision for income taxes

The statement of changes in net worth does not attempt to measure net income. It combines income and other changes because the financial affairs of an individual are a mixture of business and personal activities.

The accountant is not precluded from undertaking an engagement to issue a compilation report on a statement of financial condition when a statement of changes in net worth has not been prepared.

(b) USES. Accountants have often found that lenders do not require a statement of changes in net worth from persons seeking credit and that credit seekers, for their part, are not eager to reveal so much information about their standard of living. But a statement of changes in net worth can be very useful in financial planning by providing information about how much an individual will have to increase earnings or decrease consumption to achieve a desired level of wealth—or how much he or she may decrease earnings or increase consumption and still achieve the same goal.

(c) FORMAT. The sample statement of changes in net worth shown in Exhibit 22.2 distinguishes realized from unrealized sources of increase or decrease in net worth, thus dividing the sources into four categories: realized increases, realized decreases, unrealized increases, and unrealized decreases.

22.7 DISCLOSURES

SOP No. 82–1 (FASB ASC 274–10) states that personal statements should include sufficient disclosures to make the statements adequately informative. These disclosures can be made in the body of the statements or in the notes. The next list, although not exhaustive, indicates the nature and type of information that should ordinarily be disclosed:

- A clear indication of the individuals covered by the statement
- Assets, presented at their estimated current values, and liabilities, presented at their estimated current amounts
- The methods used to determine estimated current values of assets and estimated current amounts of liabilities, and any change in these methods from one period to the next
- Whether any assets shown in the statement are jointly held, and the nature of the joint ownership
- If the person's investment portfolio is material in relation to his or her other assets and is concentrated in one or a few companies or industries, the names of the companies or industries and the estimated current values of the securities
- If the person has a material investment in a closely held business, these points, at a minimum should be disclosed:
  - The name of the business, the business form (corporation, partnership, etc.) and the person's percentage of ownership
  - The nature of the business
  - Summarized information about assets, liabilities, and results of operations for the most recent year based on the statements of the business, including information about the basis of presentation (e.g., GAAP, income tax basis, or cash basis) and any significant loss contingencies
- Descriptions of intangible assets and their useful lives
- The face amount of life insurance owned by the individuals
- Nonforfeitable rights, such as pensions based on life expectancy that do not have the characteristics discussed earlier in the assets section regarding future interests
- This tax information:
  - The methods and assumptions used to compute the estimated income taxes on the differences between the estimated current values of assets and the estimated current amounts of liabilities and their tax bases and a statement that the provision will probably differ from the amounts of income taxes that might eventually be paid because those amounts are determined by the timing and the method of disposal, realization, or liquidation
  - Unused operating loss and capital loss carryforwards
  - Other unused deductions and credits, with their expiration periods, if applicable

  - The differences between the estimated current values of major assets and the estimated current amounts of major liabilities or categories of assets and liabilities
- Maturities, interest rates, collateral, and other pertinent details relating to receivables and debt
- Related party transactions, such as notes receivable or notes payable to other family members
- Contingencies such as pending lawsuits and loan guarantees
- Noncancelable commitments, such as operating leases that do not have the characteristics required for inclusion
- Subsequent events, such as a decline in value of an asset after the statement date

It is important to reinforce that the disclosures listed are not all-inclusive. GAAP other than those discussed in SOP No. 82–1 may apply to personal statements. Should a situation arise that is covered by an FASB or other pronouncement, the accountant should look to that source for guidance.

22.8 COMPILATION

The standards applicable to compilations of financial statements in SSARS No. 19 are applicable to personal financial statements. SSARS No. 19 states that an accountant should establish an understanding with management regarding the services to be performed for compilation engagements and should document the understanding through a written communication with management. Such an understanding reduces the risks that either the accountant or management may misinterpret the needs or expectations of the other party. The AICPA *Guide* includes sample engagement letters for compilations, reviews, and audits in Appendix A.

The accountant should also have a general understanding of:

- Nature of the individual's financial transactions
- Form of available records
- Qualifications of accounting personnel, if any
- Accounting basis on which the statements are to be presented
- Form and content of the statements

For example, the statements may be on a GAAP, cash, or tax basis.

A compilation requires an understanding of the individual's business and personal records necessary to compile personal financial statements in an appropriate format.

Knowledge required is generally gained through experience with the client's records, such as bank statements, tax returns, broker's statements, property insurance policies, wills, leases, safe deposit box contents, records of closely held business, and through inquiries. The accountant must consider other services that may be necessary to compile an individual's financial statements, such as utilizing a specialist to determine the value of an asset.

Ordinarily an accountant can compile personal statements based on the individual's representation of the estimated current values of assets and the estimated current amounts of liabilities. The accountant should have a clear understanding of the methods used to determine the estimated current values of significant assets and the estimated current amounts of significant liabilities and be satisfied that those methods are appropriate, considering the circumstances of the engagement. The accountant is not an appraiser of assets or an expert in determining present values for items such as pension plans and other assets and liabilities that may appear in personal financial statements. Therefore, it may be appropriate for the accountant to rely on the services of an expert, such as a real estate appraiser or an actuary, in gathering and evaluating client information.

In a compilation, the accountant is not required to make inquiries or perform other procedures to verify, corroborate, or review information supplied by the individual. However, if the accountant has reason to believe that the information supplied by the client is not correct, is incomplete, or is otherwise unsatisfactory to support the compilation of personal financial statements, he or she should attempt to obtain additional or revised information. If the client refuses to provide additional or revised information, or if the accountant cannot otherwise obtain the needed information, he or she should withdraw from the engagement.

Before issuing the report, the accountant should read the compiled personal statements and consider whether they appear to be appropriate in form and free from obvious material errors.

The term *errors* refers to mistakes (intentional or unintentional) in compiling financial statements, including arithmetical or clerical mistakes, and mistakes in applying accounting standards, which includes inadequate disclosure. Examples of errors that might occur in personal financial statements prepared in conformity with SOP No. 82–1 (FASB ASC 274–10) include:

- Failure to record estimated income taxes on the differences between the estimated current values of assets and the estimated current amounts of liabilities and their tax bases
- Not disclosing the method utilized to estimate current values and amounts
- Presenting asset or liability amounts at an obviously inappropriate value or amount

SSARS No. 19 permits an accountant to compile financial statements that omit substantially all disclosures required by GAAP. Also, since GAAP for personal financial statements involve measurement principles different from those for other reporting entities, the accountant should disclose the use of estimated current values and amounts in the report if the disclosure is not provided in the financial statements.

If the accountant believes that the methods used to determine the estimated current values of assets and the estimated current amounts of liabilities are not in accordance with SOP No. 82–1 (FASB ASC 274–10), or if he or she believes that the methods are not appropriate in light of the nature of each asset and liability, the accountant should modify the report because of a departure from GAAP or should withdraw from the engagement.

If uncertainties are encountered in personal financial statements, the accountant is not required to modify the standard report, provided the financial statements appropriately disclose the matter. However, the accountant may wish to draw attention to such uncertainty in an explanatory paragraph of the compilation report. If so, the accountant should follow the guidance in SSARS No. 19.

The *Guide* encourages the use of a representation letters in personal statement compilation engagements.

22.9 REVIEW

Standards for reviews of personal financial statements are established in SSARS No. 19. The next items are applicable to reviews:

- reaching an understanding with the client
- gaining an understanding of the individuals' transactions
- understanding the methods used to determine estimated current values of significant assets and the estimated current amounts of significant liabilities
- becoming satisfied that those methods are appropriate
- utilizing the services of an expert when necessary
- reading the statements to ensure they are appropriate in form and free from material error, whether caused unintentionally or due to fraud.

In addition to those items, the accountant must perform inquiry and analytical procedures sufficient to provide a reasonable basis for expressing limited assurance that there are no material modifications that should be made to the client's personal financial statements for them to be in conformity with GAAP or other comprehensive basis of accounting. Analytical procedures include developing an expectation about the relationships between data and comparing recorded amounts to those expectations. The accountant should also consider making inquiries of management concerning their knowledge of fraud in a review engagement. Procedures performed should be documented to support the conclusions reached by the accountant.

Further, before issuing the review report, the accountant should read the reviewed personal statements and consider whether they appear to be appropriate in form and free from obvious material errors, whether unintentional or caused by fraud. The accountant should also consider making inquiries of managers concerning their knowledge of fraud.

A review does not include obtaining an understanding of internal control or assessing control risk, tests of accounting records and of responses to inquiries by obtaining corroborating evidential matter, and certain other procedures ordinarily performed during an audit. Thus, a review does not provide assurance that the accountant will become aware of all significant matters that would be disclosed in an audit. However, if the accountant becomes aware of information that appears incorrect, incomplete, or otherwise unsatisfactory, he or she should perform the additional SSARS No. 19 procedures considered necessary to achieve limited assurance that there are no material modifications that should be made to the financial statements for them to be in conformity with the basis of reporting.

SSARS No. 19 requires a written representation letter in all review engagements. An example representation letter appropriate for a compilation, review, or audit engagement is reproduced in the *Guide*.

Further, whereas a compilation can be completed without disclosures, a review cannot.

22.10 AUDITS

GAAS apply to audits of personal financial statements, as they do to other audit engagements. As with any financial statement, the audit objective in personal financial statement engagements is to attest to the fairness of the assertions embodied in the statements. Special attention must be given to the establishment of estimated current values and amounts in accordance with SOP No. 82–1 (FASC ASC 274–10).

GAAS requires a study and evaluation of internal accounting control, tests of accounting records and of responses to inquiries, and other evidential procedures considered necessary in the circumstances of the engagement. Because internal control is not usually a consideration, most of the independent auditors' effort in forming an opinion of personal financial statements consists of gathering evidential matter to support the assertions of existence and valuation of assets and the rights and obligations associated with those assets. SAS No. 101, *Auditing Fair Value Measurements and Disclosures,* provides important guidance when auditing a personal financial statement, as does a June 2003 *Journal of Accountancy* article, "The Auditor's Approach to Fair Value."

Often, as a result of the inadequacy of personal financial records, significant restrictions are imposed on the auditor's efforts to obtain needed evidential matter to support an opinion on personal financial statements. In such a situation, it is not possible to express an unqualified opinion. For this reason, most personal financial statement engagements are compilations, with some reviews.

22.11 REPORTS

The *Guide* discusses specific auditor reports relevant to compilation, review, and audit engagements that incorporate the basic reporting standards in the applicable SSARS and SAS.

Because a statement of financial condition is the only personal financial statement required by SOP No. 82–1 (FASB ASC 274–10), often the accountant is engaged to report on that statement only. Occasionally, an individual will need or want the accountant to report on both the statement of financial condition and a statement of changes in net worth. Usually the accountant is asked to report on current-period statements only, although sometimes comparative statements (covering more than one date) are requested.

Reporting standards in the SSARS apply to compilations and reviews of personal financial statements. In a compilation or review engagement, an accountant is required to issue a report whenever the compilation or review is complete; and this requirement is applicable to the personal financial statements of an individual, as specified by SSARS No. 1. However, if an engagement is not completed, a report is unlikely to be issued.

(a) STANDARD COMPILATION REPORT. Personal financial statements compiled by an accountant should be accompanied by a report containing seven areas of information:

1. *Title.* The accountant's compilation report should have a title that clearly indicates that it is the accountant's compilation report. The accountant may indicate that he or she is independent in the title, if applicable. Appropriate titles would be "Accountant's Compilation Report" or "Independent Accountant's Compilation Report."
2. *Addressee.* The accountant's report should be addressed as appropriate in the circumstances of the engagement.
3. *Introductory paragraph.* The introductory paragraph in the accountant's report should
   a. Identify the entity whose financial statements have been compiled
   b. State that the financial statements have been compiled
   c. Identify the financial statements that have been compiled
   d. Specify the date or period covered by the financial statements
   e. Include a statement that the accountant has not audited or reviewed the financial statements and, accordingly, does not express an opinion or provide any assurance about whether the financial statements are in accordance with the applicable financial reporting framework
4. *Management's responsibility for the financial statements and for internal control over financial reporting.* The report should include a statement that the individuals whose financial statements are compiled are responsible for the preparation and fair presentation of the financial statements in accordance with the applicable financial reporting framework and for designing, implementing, and maintaining internal control relevant to the preparation and fair presentation of the financial statements.
5. *Accountant's responsibility.* This statement indicates that the accountant's responsibility is to conduct the compilation in accordance with SSARSs issued by the AICPA. The statement should indicate that the objective of a compilation is to assist management in presenting financial information in the form of financial statements without undertaking to obtain or provide any assurance that there are no material modifications that should be made to the financial statements.
6. *Signature of the accountant.* The accounting firm or the accountant, as appropriate, should sign manually or in print.
7. *Date of the accountant's report.* The date of the compilation report (the date of completion of the compilation should be used as the date of the accountant's report) must be included.

Any other procedures the accountant performs in connection with the engagement should not be mentioned in the report.

The compilation report is addressed to the individual whose financial statement(s) are compiled. The date of the report is the date of the completion of the compilation procedures. Also, each page of the statement of financial condition (and the statement of changes in net worth, if presented) should include a reference "See Accountant's Compilation Report."

An example of a compilation report for a personal financial statement follows.

(INDEPENDENT) ACCOUNTANT'S COMPILATION REPORT

John and Jane Doe

City, State

I (We) have compiled the accompanying statement of financial condition of John and Jane Doe as of December 31, 20XX. I (We) have not audited or reviewed the accompanying financial statement and, accordingly, do not express an opinion or provide any assurance about whether the financial statement is in accordance with accounting principles generally accepted in the United States of America.

The individuals are responsible for the preparation and fair presentation of the financial statement in accordance with accounting principles generally accepted in the United States of America and for designing, implementing, and maintaining internal control relevant to the preparation and fair presentation of the financial statement.

My (Our) responsibility is to conduct the compilation in accordance with Statements on Standards for Accounting and Review Services issued by the American Institute of Certified Public Accountants. The objective of a compilation is to assist the individuals in presenting financial information in the form of financial statements without undertaking to obtain or provide any assurance that there are no material modifications that should be made to the financial statement.

Firm's Signature

Report Date

(b) REPORTING WHEN SUBSTANTIALLY ALL DISCLOSURES ARE OMITTED. An accountant may be asked to compile personal financial statements that omit substantially all disclosures required by SOP No. 82–1 (FASB ASC 274–10), including disclosures that might appear in the body of the statements. Such reporting is appropriate provided the omission of the disclosures is clearly indicated in the accountant's compilation report and the accountant is not aware that the disclosures are being omitted for the purpose of misleading the intended users of the statements. For example, it would not be appropriate to omit from personal financial statements intended for use in obtaining a home mortgage informative disclosures that would be important to the financial institution in making the loan decision. If disclosures are omitted, and certain selected information is presented in the footnotes—for example, information important in obtaining a mortgage loan—such information should be labeled "Selected Information—Substantially All Disclosures Required by GAAP Are Not Included."

If substantially all disclosures are omitted from the personal financial statements and the statements do not disclose that the assets are presented at their estimated current values and that the liabilities are presented at their estimated current amounts, the accountant should include this disclosure in the compilation report. If the statements have been presented on a comprehensive basis of accounting other than GAAP, that basis of accounting, if not disclosed in the statements, must be included in the accountant's report.

An example of a compilation report for a personal financial statement with substantially all disclosures omitted follows.

Compilation—Substantially All Disclosures Omitted

(INDEPENDENT) ACCOUNTANT'S COMPILATION REPORT

John and Jane Doe

City, State

I (We) have compiled the accompanying statement of financial condition of John and Jane Doe as of December 31, 20XX. I (We) have not audited or reviewed the accompanying financial statement and, accordingly, do not express an opinion or provide any assurance about whether the financial statement is in accordance with accounting principles generally accepted in the United States of America.

The individuals are responsible for the preparation and fair presentation of the financial statement in accordance with accounting principles generally accepted in the United States of America and for designing, implementing, and maintaining internal control relevant to the preparation and fair presentation of the financial statement.

My (Our) responsibility is to conduct the compilation in accordance with Statements on Standards for Accounting and Review Services issued by the American Institute of Certified Public Accountants. The objective of a compilation is to assist the individuals in presenting financial information in the form of financial statements without undertaking to obtain or provide any assurance that there are no material modifications that should be made to the financial statement.

John and Jane Doe have elected to omit substantially all of the disclosures required by accounting principles generally accepted in the United States of America. If the omitted disclosures were included in the statement of financial condition, they might influence the user's conclusions about the financial condition of John and Jane Doe. Accordingly, the financial statement is not designed for those who are not informed about such matters.

Firm's Signature

Report Date

(c) REPORTING WHEN THE ACCOUNTANT IS NOT INDEPENDENT. An accountant may issue a compilation report on the personal financial statements of an individual even though he or she is not independent with respect to that individual. In such cases, the accountant must modify the compilation report. by adding an additional paragraph to the compilation report stating:

I am [we are] not independent with respect to [name of individual].

The accountant is not precluded from disclosing a description about the reason(s) that his or her independence is impaired. Three examples of descriptions the accountant may use follow.

I am (We are) not independent with respect to [name of individual] as of and for the year ended December 31, 20XX, because I (a member of the engagement team) had a direct financial interest with [name of individual].

I am (We are) not independent with respect to [name of individual] as of and for the year ended December 31, 20XX, because an individual of my immediate family (an immediate family member of one of the members of the engagement team) was employed by [name of individual].

I am (We are) not independent with respect to [name of individual] as of and for the year ended December 31, 20XX, because I (we) performed certain accounting services (the accountant may include a specific description of those services) that impaired my (our) independence.

If the accountant elects to disclose a description about the reasons his or her independence is impaired, the accountant is required to include all reasons for lack of independence in the description.

(d) REPORTING ON PRESCRIBED FORMS. Sometimes an accountant is requested by an individual to assist in assembling data for the completion of a standard preprinted loan form and sign the form or to sign such a form the client has compiled. SSARS No. 3, *Compilation Reports on Statements Included in Certain Prescribed Forms* (as amended by SSARS Nos. 5, 7, 15, 17 and 19), provides an alternative form of standard compilation report when a prescribed form or related instructions call for a departure from GAAP by specifying a measurement principle not in conformity with GAAP or by failing to request the disclosures required by GAAP.

SSARS No. 3 (as amended by SSARS Nos. 5, 7, 15, 17 and 19) is appropriate for prescribed forms that request information from personal financial statements that have been compiled or reviewed by an accountant.

As stated in SSARS No. 3 (as amended by SSARS Nos. 5, 7, 15, 17 and 19), a prescribed form is any standard preprinted form designed or adopted by the body to which it is to be submitted, for example, forms used by credit agencies. There is a presumption in SSARS No. 3 (as amended by SSARS Nos. 5, 7, 15, 17 and 19) that the information required by a prescribed form is sufficient to meet the needs of the body that designed or adopted the form. Therefore, there is no need for that body to be advised of departures from GAAP SOP No. 82–1 required by the prescribed form or related instructions.

An accountant should not sign a preprinted accountant's report that does not conform to the guidance in SSARS No. 19 regarding the standard compilation report. If the preprinted report form cannot be appropriately revised, the accountant should attach his or her own report following the guidance provided in SSARS No. 3 (as amended by SSARS Nos. 5, 7, 15, 17 and 19) or SSARS No. 19, as appropriate.

(e) REPORTING WHEN THERE IS A DEPARTURE FROM GENERALLY ACCEPTED ACCOUNTING PRINCIPLES. An accountant compiling or reviewing personal statements may become aware of a departure from GAAP involving either measurement principles or disclosure principles, or both. If the accountant determines that explaining the GAAP deficiencies in the personal statements in the report will not adequately communicate the problems to potential statement users, the accountant should withdraw from the engagement and issue no report.

If the accountant believes he or she can appropriately communicate the departure in the compilation or review report, the departure should be described in a separate paragraph of the report. The separate paragraph(s) should explain what GAAP requires, the client's departure, and the effects of the departure on the statements, if such effects have been determined. If the effects have not been determined, this fact should also be disclosed in the separate paragraph(s).

For example, if the client has reported an investment at cost rather than at fair value as required by GAAP for personal financial statements, and the accountant cannot persuade the individual to change the amount, the accountant's report should explain the GAAP departure.

Some departures from GAAP are not as easy to detect. For example, a client going through a divorce may want to change the method utilized from previous financial statements to estimate the fair value of an asset. If the sole purpose of the change is to manipulate the distribution of property in the divorce, the change in method is a departure from GAAP.

(f) STANDARD REVIEW REPORT. An example review report for a personal financial statement is shown next.

> INDEPENDENT ACCOUNTANT'S REVIEW REPORT
>
> John and Jane Doe
>
> City, State
>
> I (We) have reviewed the accompanying statement of financial condition of John and Jane Doe as of December 31, 20XX. A review includes primarily applying analytical procedures to the individuals' financial data and making inquires of the individuals. A review is substantially less in scope than an audit, the objective of which is the expression of an opinion regarding the financial statement as a whole. Accordingly, I (We) do not express such an opinion.
>
> The individuals are responsible for the preparation and fair presentation of the financial statement in accordance with accounting principles generally accepted in the United States of America and for designing, implementing, and maintaining internal control relevant to the preparation and fair presentation of the financial statement.
>
> My (Our) responsibility is to conduct the review in accordance with Statements on Standards for Accounting and Review Services issued by the American Institute of Certified Public Accountants. Those standards require me (us) to perform procedures to obtain limited assurance that there are no material modifications that should be made to the financial statement. I (We) believe that the results of my (our) procedures provide a reasonable basis for our report.
>
> Based on my (our) review, I am (we are) not aware of any material modifications that should be made to the accompanying statement of financial condition in order for it to be in conformity with accounting principles generally accepted in the United States of America.
>
> Firm's Signature
>
> Report Date

Reviews of personal financial statements are not requested as frequently as compilations. Reviews require inquiry and analytical procedures and carry more professional responsibility on the part of the accountant than does a compilation engagement. Further, users of these reports may not understand the concept of limited assurance. As a result, the accountant should take care in determining the type of engagement required and in accepting the engagement. As a matter of simple economics, compilations are the least expensive service. They provide the lowest assurance value to the reader but still may be sufficient for the purpose for which they are prepared.

Audits of personal financial statements are the least common of the three types of engagements primarily because of the general lack of adequate accounting records supporting personal assets and liabilities and the transactions data affecting those balances. Additionally, the required tests and procedures cause this to be a more costly service. Recent requirements regarding the auditor's responsibility to apply procedures relevant to the detection of fraud and other requirements, such as the assessment of the design of the system of internal controls, make little sense in the context of personal statements. Also, the standards requiring presentation of a statement of financial condition with assets at estimated fair values and liabilities at estimated current amounts may create audit difficulties. Fair value estimates involve uncertainty and subjectivity that may not lend themselves to producing evidence that can be efficiently or effectively audited. The auditor may be unable to obtain sufficient competent evidential matter to support an opinion on personal financial statements. Many such engagements that start out as audits end up with a disclaimer of opinion because of scope restrictions on the auditor's ability to obtain necessary evidence.

(g) STANDARD AUDIT REPORT. The auditor's standard report appropriate for personal financial statements is presented next.

> INDEPENDENT AUDITOR'S REPORT
>
> I [We] have audited the accompanying statement of financial condition of [James and Jane Person] as of [date], and the related statement of changes in net worth for the [period] then ended. These financial statements are the responsibility of [James and Jane Person]. My [Our] responsibility is to express an opinion on these financial statements based on my [our] audit.
>
> I [We] conducted my [our] audit in accordance with generally accepted auditing standards in the United States of America. Those standards require that I [we] plan and perform the audit to obtain reasonable assurance about whether the financial statements are free of material misstatement. An audit includes examining, on a test basis, evidence supporting the amounts and disclosures in the financial statements. An audit also includes assessing the accounting principles used and significant estimates made by [James and Jane Person], as well as evaluating the overall financial statement presentation. I [We] believe that my [our] audit provides a reasonable basis for my [our] opinion.
>
> In my [our] opinion, the financial statements referred to above present fairly, in all material respects, the financial condition of [James and Jane Person] as of [date], and the changes in their net worth for the [period] then ended in conformity with accounting principles generally accepted in the United States of America.

Paragraphs 9 and 10 of SAS No. 62, *Special Reports,* paragraphs 9 and 10, provides guidance concerning disclosures in personal financial statements presented on a comprehensive basis of accounting other than GAAP, such as the cash or tax basis of accounting. Similar informative disclosures are appropriate to those required by GAAP for the same or similar issues.

SSARS No. 6 provides an exception for the performance and reporting standards in SSARS No. 19 for personal financial statements included in written personal financial plans. Such statements included in written personal financial plans frequently exclude disclosures required by GAAP and contain other GAAP departures. These exceptions exist because the statements are prepared to facilitate the financial plan and not for credit purposes.

An accountant, according to SSARS No. 6, may submit a written personal financial plan containing unaudited personal financial statements to a client without complying with the compilation and review performance and reporting standards when all these conditions are met:

- An understanding is reached with the client, preferably in writing, that the financial statements will be used solely to assist the client's advisors to develop the client's personal financial goals and objectives.
- The document will not be used to obtain credit or for any purposes other than developing the personal plan.

- Nothing comes to the accountant's attention during the engagement to cause him or her to believe that the statements will be used to obtain credit or for any purposes other than the personal financial plan or its implementation by an insurance agent, broker, attorney, or like agent.

If these objectives are met, the next report, as prescribed in SSARS No. 6, may be used in place of the standard compilation report for personal financial statements included in personal financial plans:

> The accompanying statement of financial condition of [James and Jane Person], as of [date], was prepared solely to help you develop your personal financial plan. Accordingly, it may be incomplete or contain other departures from generally accepted accounting principles and should not be used to obtain credit or for any purposes other than developing your financial plan. We have not audited, reviewed, or compiled the statement.

Each of the personal financial statements should include a reference to the accountant's report.

22.12 COMPILED STATEMENTS ONLY FOR CLIENT INTERNAL USE

In accordance with SSARS No. 19, when an accountant submits unaudited financial statements to a client that are not expected to be used by a third party, he or she should include a reference on each page of the financial statements restricting their use, such as "Restricted for Management's Use Only" or "Solely for the information and use by the management of [*name of entity*] and not intended to be and should not be used by any other party."

If the accountant becomes aware that the financial statements have been distributed to third parties, he or she should discuss the situation with the client and determine the appropriate course of action, including considering requesting that the client have the statements returned. If the accountant requests that the financial statements be returned and the client does not comply with that request within a reasonable period of time, the accountant should notify known third parties that the financial statements are not intended for third-party use, preferably in consultation with his or her attorney.

1. Issue a compilation report in accordance with the reporting requirements discussed in AR Sections 100.11–.19 of the AICPA Code of Professional Standards, vol. 2.
2. Document an understanding with the individual through the use of an engagement letter, preferably signed by the individual, regarding the services to be performed and the limitations on the use of those financial statements. Such an understanding reduces the risk that the accountant or the client may misinterpret the needs or expectations of the other party; if the accountant believes an understanding with the client has not been established, he or she should decline to accept or perform the engagement.
3. Include a reference on each page of the financial statements restricting their use such as "Restricted for Client's Use Only" or "Solely for the information and use by the client [name of individual] and not intended to be and should not be used by any other party."

22.13 SOURCES AND SUGGESTED REFERENCES

Accounting Principles Board. APB Opinion No. 21, *Interest on Receivables and Payables* (FASB ASC 835-30). New York: AICPA, 1971.

American Institute of Certified Public Accountants. Statements on Standards for Accounting and Review Services No. 6, *Reporting on Personal Financial Statements Included in Written Personal Financial Plans*. New York: Author, 1986.

American Institute of Certified Public Accountants, Accounting and Review Services Committee. Statement on Standards for Accounting and Review Services No. 19, *Compilation and Review Engagements*. New York: Author, 2009.

American Institute of Certified Public Accountants, Accounting Standards Division. Statement of Position No. 82–1, *Accounting and Financial Reporting for Personal Financial Statements* (FASB ASC 274–10). New York: Author, 1982.

Auditing Standards Board. Statement on Auditing Standards No.101, *Auditing Fair Value Measurements and Disclosures*. New York: AICPA, 2003.

Bull, I. O. "Personal Financial Statements—Suggestions for Improvement," *CPA Journal* (December 1984): 42.

Financial Accounting Standards Board. Statement of Financial Accounting Standards No. 5, *Accounting for Contingencies* (FASB ASC 450–10). Stamford, CT: Author, 1975.

Kinsman, M. D., and B. Samuelson. "Personal Financial Statements: Valuation Challenges and Solutions," *Journal of Accountancy* (September 1987): 139.

Menelaides, S. L., L. E. Graham, and G. Fishbach. "The Auditor's Approach to Fair Value," *Journal of Accountancy* (June 2003): 73.

Personal Financial Statements Task Force. *Personal Financial Statements Guide, With Conforming Changes as of May 1, 2005*. New York: AICPA, 2005.

CHAPTER 23

STOCK-BASED COMPENSATION

23.1 HISTORY OF ACCOUNTING FOR STOCK-BASED COMPENSATION 1
- (a) Stock Option Backdating Scandal 4

23.2 ACCOUNTING FOR STOCK-BASED COMPENSATION 5
- (a) Stock Option Accounting Using Fair Value 5
- (b) Non-Public Company Option 6
- (c) Restricted Stock Options 7
- (d) Employee Stock Option Plans 7

23.3 ESTIMATING FAIR VALUE 8
- (a) Black-Scholes Option Pricing Models 9
  - (i) Expected Volatility 10
  - (ii) Expected Dividends 11
  - (iii) Expected Option Lives 11
- (b) Lattice/Binomial Option Pricing Models 11
  - (i) Computing the Option Price 13
  - (ii) Changing Methods 13

23.4 SPECIAL TOPICS 13
- (a) Awards to Nonemployees for Goods and Services 13
- (b) Awards Classified as Liabilities 14
- (c) Stock Appreciation Rights as Compensation 15
- (d) Modifications of Awards 15
- (e) Income Taxation of Stock Compensation Plans 15
- (f) Earnings per Share 16
  - (i) Diluted Earnings per Share 16
- (g) Obtaining and Retaining Supporting Data 17

23.5 DISCLOSURE 17
- (a) Notes to the Financial Statements 17
- (b) Disclosure Example 17

23.6 ACCOUNTING STANDARDS CODIFICATION 20

23.7 INTERNATIONAL PERSPECTIVE 20

23.8 SOURCES AND SUGGESTED REFERENCES 20

23.1 HISTORY OF ACCOUNTING FOR STOCK-BASED COMPENSATION

The nature and types of stock-based compensation plans and awards have changed constantly over the years. However, the two most significant problems in determining the appropriate accounting for such awards have remained the same:

1. Measurement of compensation cost (i.e., the determination of total compensation cost to be allocated to expense for financial reporting purposes)
2. Allocation of compensation cost (i.e., the determination of the period(s) over which total compensation cost should be allocated to expense and the method of allocation)

A chapter on this topic in earlier editions of the *Handbook* was written by Peter T. Chingos, CPA of Mercer Human Resources Consulting, Walton T. Conn Jr., CPA, and John R. Deming, CPA, from KPMG Peat Marwick. The chapter has been rewritten for this edition by the editor.

The motivation to issue and to receive stock options is easy to understand.

- By issuing stock options in lieu of cash compensation, the entity incurs no cash payment and may generate a permanent contribution to capital if the recipient purchases the shares.
- The payment serves as motivation to the recipient and supposedly aligns its focus toward future profitability of the entity better than cash payments.
- It can provide tax benefits to the participant.
- Under some historical methods of accounting, but to a lesser extent today, the stock option has less impact on the profitability of the company than a comparable cash payment.

To be sure, employees are compensated by being awarded stock options when they contribute services. However, historically, employers did not incur any cost in compensating employees with stock options, any more than employers do in issuing previously unissued shares of their stock when they receive money from new stockholders. Preexisting stockholders are the ones to incur a cost when employees are awarded stock options:

- A cost of contingent dilution of their ownership interest
- A real cost of actual dilution of their ownership interest

Ironically, after centering its consideration of reporting in connection with the awarding of employee stock options on the concept of compensation cost, the Financial Accounting Standards Board (FASB) initially agreed that employers incur no cost when compensating employees with options, although they do incur a cost in using up the services provided by the employees for which they are awarded options: "[I]ssuances of equity instruments result in the receipt of... services, which give rise to expenses as they are used in an entity's operations."[1] As with all accounting practices that initially have objectives other than the simple measurement of the economic effects of events, accounting for stock options has undergone significant revision over the years. Early accounting guidance saw little value in issuing options when the options were out of the money (the option price exceeded the market price) at the date of issue. However, the options had real economic value to employees since, as the stock price rose (whether due to company growth, general economic trends, or inflation), employees were able to cash in on stock that had a value greater than the market price. In addition, over many years, the general tendency of market prices was to rise. All this resulted in a kind of off-the-books treatment for stock options. Had such plans been for a trivial number of shares, perhaps concern would be less. However, modest share awards morphed into significant awards. Shareholders were seeing the dilution of their ownership due to the awards. The accounting and economic transparency of the whole issue was begging for clarification and disclosure; thus began the march toward disclosure and a rethinking of the nature of the economic events being recorded.

The accounting literature addressed the accounting for stock-based compensation in several pronouncements:

- Accounting Principles Board (APB) Opinion No. 25, *Accounting for Stock Issued to Employees* (1972); also see Interpretation of APB Opinion No. 25, *Accounting for Stock Issued to Employees* (1973).
- FASB Statement of Financial Accounting Standard No. 123, *Accounting for Stock-Based Compensation* (1995).
- FASB Statement No. 148, which provided additional guidance for transitional issues to the preferred fair value method (2002).

These standards and a host of Emerging Issues Task Force discussions and decisions (EITFs) were superseded by Statement No. 123R, *Share Based Payment,* in 2004.

---

[1] FASB, Statement of Standards No. 123, *Accounting for Stock-Based Compensation,* par. 89.

Subsequent to the issuance of APB Opinion No. 25 (1972), the trend toward the adoption by enterprises of more complex plans and awards continued. Of particular significance was the increase in the number of combination plans—plans that provide for the granting of two or more types of awards to individual employees. In many combination plans, the employee, or the enterprise, must make an election from alternative awards as to the award to be exercised, thereby canceling the other awards granted under the plan.

Following the issuance of APB Opinion No. 25, there was also a significant increase in the number of plans that provided for the granting of variable awards to employees. A variable award is one that at the date the grant is awarded, (1) the number of shares of stock (or the amount of cash) an employee is entitled to receive, (2) the amount an employee is required to pay to exercise rights with respect to the award, or (3) both the number of shares an employee is entitled to receive and the amount an employee is required to pay are unknown. One of the most popular variable awards is the stock appreciation right (SAR). SARs are rights granted that entitle an employee to receive, at a specified future date(s), the excess of the market value of a specified number of shares of the granting employer's capital stock over a stated price. The form of payment for amounts earned under an award of SARs may be specified by the award (i.e., stock, cash, or a combination thereof), or the award may permit the employee or employer to elect the form of payment.

Considerable disagreement continued to exist as to the appropriate method of accounting for variable awards. As a result, significant differences arose in the methods used by employers to account for variable awards, which led to numerous requests of the FASB for clarification. In December 1978, the FASB provided this clarification through the issuance of FASB Interpretation No. 28, *Accounting for Stock Appreciation Rights and Other Variable Stock Option or Award Plans.* In paragraph 2 of the Interpretation, the FASB specified that:

> APB Opinion No. 25 applies to plans for which the employer's stock is issued as compensation or the amount of cash paid as compensation is determined by reference to the market price of the stock or to changes in its market price. Plans involving SARs and other variable plan awards are included in those plans dealt with by [APB] Opinion No. 25.

The Interpretation provided specific guidance in the application of APB Opinion No. 25 to variable awards, particularly in those more troublesome areas where the greatest divergence in accounting existed prior to its issuance.

However, APB Opinion No. 25, as interpreted, failed to incorporate criteria that can be consistently applied to all types of plans. As a result, as new types of plans have evolved and changes in the tax laws have occurred, new interpretations and guidance have been required, resulting in a steady stream of pronouncements by the FASB and the EITF since 1978.

The FASB undertook a major project in 1984 to reconsider the accounting for stock-based compensation, whether issued to employees or issued to vendors, suppliers, or other nonemployees. In October 1995, the FASB issued FASB Statement No. 123, *Accounting for Stock-Based Compensation.* This Statement allowed companies to retain the current approach set forth in APB Opinion No. 25, as amended, interpreted, and clarified; however, companies were encouraged to adopt a new accounting method based on the estimated fair value of employee stock options. Companies that do not follow the fair value method are required to provide expanded disclosures in the footnotes.

Thus, the FASB settled on a compromise solution to a complex issue that had become extremely politicized. The vast majority of entities did not elect the fair value method of accounting for stock options. As a result, multiple presentations of the results of operations were common. FASB Statement No. 123 was preceded by an Exposure Draft that proposed a new accounting method that would report compensation expense in connection with virtually all stock options issued to employees. However, those who receive stock options believed a requirement to change to the new method could threaten their stock options: The *Wall Street Journal* reported that "FASB's chairman . . . Dennis Beresford . . . says he scoffed at the doomsday arguments during a heated discussion aboard one corporate jet. The executives he was debating invited him to exit the craft—at

20,000 feet."[2] And Beresford himself reported that "the CEO of one of United States' most successful companies . . . said that if the FASB was allowed to finalize the draft as proposed 'it would end capitalism.'"[3]

To prevent this "disaster," the U.S. Congress prepared a bill entitled the Accounting Standards Reform Act, which, if enacted, would have required the Securities and Exchange Commission (SEC) to pass on all new standards approved by the FASB. The bill stated, in part, that "any new accounting standard or principle, and any modification . . . shall become effective only following an affirmative vote of a majority of a quorum of the member of the [Securities and Exchange] Commission." The bill was proposed simply to pressure the SEC to prevent the FASB from making this particular exposure draft final. Once again, political pressure on the setting of accounting standards was observed, despite the long-term objectives of the profession to resist this mistake.

Needless to say, Statement No. 123 as it was finally issued did not radically alter the landscape, but it did provide an alternative (preferred) accounting treatment based on trying to measure the fair value of the award at the date of grant. By addressing the issuance of stock to their parties for goods and services, these Statements essentially replaced Opinion No. 25 and most of the countless interpretations and EITFs that had arisen over the years.

In Statement No. 123R, the transition became complete for public entities, as they now were required to measure stock compensation at fair value. Statement No. 123R replaced Statement No. 123 and Opinion No. 25 in their entirety. Statement No. 148 provided additional transition guidance for those companies moving to a fair value measurement approach from the intrinsic value method.

Private companies can follow a modified fair value method. The complexity of providing a fair value measure in securities that may have no observable market value or measurable volatility leads to the need for this practical exception. They can also elect an intrinsic value method and revalue the options each period.

Today, some issues remain in debate, but consensus is converging on some sort of fair value measurement for such stock compensation plans and the recognition of compensation expense in conjunction with the share award. International accounting standards are essentially similar to current U.S. generally accepted accounting principles (GAAP), with the usual assortment of minor differences that will provide endless hours of debate in reconciliation. The remainder of the chapter addresses the application of current GAAP.

(a) STOCK OPTION BACKDATING SCANDAL. Around 2005, academic and analyst research uncovered a phenomenon that led to the discovery that corporations were backdating the measurement dates at which executive stock option grants were valued in order to enhance the value of the awards to corporate executives. The research of Eric Lie at the University of Iowa[4] is largely credited with exposing the scandal by demonstrating that share values often rose significantly in the days subsequent to the date that the stock option awards were made. Why was this pattern so strong?

By backdating the options, an option was valued at a lower value of the stock at some previous date. From a financial accounting measurement perspective, the stock would then be valued at market value on that prior date. Consequently the corporation might not recognize the full compensation expense because there might be less or no intrinsic value of the award on the grant date. By valuing the share award at market value of an earlier date, it could also be better argued that the award was "performance based" (Section 162(m) of the 1993 Tax Code) because of its lack of an intrinsic value. Thereby it met the reasonable compensation requirement so that any corporate

[2] J. Helyar and J. S. Lublin, "Corporate Coffers Gush with Currency of an Opulent Age," *Wall Street Journal,* August 10, 1998.

[3] D. R. Beresford, "How to Succeed as a Standard Setter by Trying Really Hard," *Accounting Horizons,* September 1997, p. 83.

[4] See E. Lie, "On the Timing of CEO Stock Option Awards," *Management Science* 51, no. 5 (May 2005): 802 – 812; and E. Lie, with R. A. Heron, "Does Backdating Explain the Stock Price Pattern around Executive Stock Option Grants?" *Journal of Financial Economics* 83, no. 2 (February 2007): 271–295.

compensation deduction for the issued shares would not be denied as "unreasonable compensation." Furthermore, the fact that the award was priced at, and not below, the market price meant that no tax would be due on the award in the year it was granted. Had the true grant date been used to value the award, the immediate economic benefit of the award to the recipient and to the corporation would be lessened.

More than 100 companies were identified as having participated in the practice of backdating options. There is debate as to whether this practice was illegal or unethical. Indeed, it distorted economic measurement and was rigged to achieve certain self-serving objectives. In any case, under provisions of the Sarbanes-Oxley Act of 2002, companies must publicly report awards within two days. If followed, this provision would substantially reduce the time frame in which such practices could be followed.

23.2 ACCOUNTING FOR STOCK-BASED COMPENSATION

(a) STOCK OPTION ACCOUNTING USING FAIR VALUE. In general, share-based plans are considered compensatory unless the benefit to the grantee is the same as available to all shareholders. In making that determination, the purchase price of the shares and the number of shares are considered. Even plans that may be treated as noncompensatory under federal tax laws (such as employee stock option plans [ESOPs]) are accounted for as compensatory plans.

Under GAAP, stock option awards to employees and executives are accounted for by measuring the fair value of the option at the grant date[5] and apportioning that value across the period of service as compensation expense. The period of service is the time in service required to vest[6] in the award.

A person is deemed an employee if the grantor consistently represents the person to be an employee under common law, as illustrated in case law and under U.S. Internal Revenue Service Revenue Ruling 87–14. For such a person to be a common law employee, the grantor must represent the person as an employee for payroll tax purposes. However, simply representing a person as an employee for payroll tax purposes is insufficient to indicate that the person is an employee. Facts and circumstances determine the employee status of any individual.

A nonemployee member of a grantor's board of directors ordinarily does not meet that definition of an employee. However, application of GAAP accounting is required to be applied to stock compensation granted to such a person for services provided as a director if the person (1) was elected by the grantor's shareholders or (2) was appointed to a board position to be filled by shareholder election when the existing term expires. Employee status is not involved for awards granted to people for advisory or consulting services in a nonelected capacity or to nonemployee directors for services outside their role as directors, such as legal or investment banking advice or for loan guarantees. The rules for exchanging stock for goods and services would be applied to this situation.

To illustrate the straightforward fair value accounting for the issue of stock options, suppose Smith is granted 500 options of ASAP Corporation stock on January 1, 2012. The option vests after three years of service and can be exercised for five years. The price of a share at the date of grant is $20, and the option to Smith is to purchase shares at $20. The fair value of the option is determined by reference to an acceptable share-pricing model such as the Black-Scholes method or the lattice (binomial method). These methods are described later in the chapter in Section 23.3.

---

[5] The grant date is when there is a mutual understanding by the employer and employee of the key terms and conditions of an award. Under ASC 718-10-25-5, *Compensation—Stock Compensation,* that understanding exists at the date the award is approved in accordance with the relevant corporate governance requirements if both of these are met: (1) The recipient does not have the ability to negotiate the key terms and conditions of the award with the employer, and (2) it is expected that the key terms and conditions of the award will be communicated to an individual recipient shortly. (See also IRS Ruling 87-41).

[6] Vesting occurs when the recipient's right to receive or retain shares no longer is subject to any restrictive conditions (e.g., service period requirement).

Under past accounting (the intrinsic method), often there was no value at the grant date, since the option price and the share price were often the same. However, the use of fair value would identify a measure of value based on historical stock behavior and other factors. Suppose the award is valued at $3,000. The accounting for the first year (and each succeeding year) of service is:

Compensation expense	1,000	
Additional paid-in capital (APIC)—Options		1,000

Suppose in year 5, Smith exercises all 500 of the options for $30 each. The APIC associated with the options is converted to permanent capital. The subsequent appreciation of the award value to Smith is not reflected in the accounting.

Cash	15,000	
APIC—Options	3,000	
Capital stock at par ($10)		5,000
APIC—Stock		13,000

A potential weakness in even this method is the failure to measure the actual value of the options if there is a change after the valuation at the grant date. However, if the terms of the award are modified during the period, a remeasurement of the compensation is generated that may result in a change in the compensation expense.

If Smith fails to meet the vesting requirements regarding the options—say he is lured away by another opportunity—the options are canceled, the APIC accumulated to date is reversed, and the associated compensation expense to date is treated as a correction of an estimate and taken though income. Suppose that after two years, Smith leaves the company. The entry to record the event would be:

APIC—Options	2,000	
Compensation expense		2,000

However, if the options expire in year 5 because Smith is vested, but he never purchases the shares, then the APIC from the options is converted to permanent APIC. This entry still recognizes that the options had some value at the date of grant.

An additional complexity in the estimation of fair value is that forfeitures of options are to be estimated when determining the compensation expense. Under previous accounting, forfeitures were recognized as they occurred. However, significant changes in these estimates of forfeiture are acceptable as changes in an estimate during the option life.

Sometimes share awards are not based on future service but on current and past service. In such cases, the value of these awards would be recorded as compensation in the period of the award.

(b) NON-PUBLIC COMPANY OPTION. Private companies may elect to value stock options using a modified fair value method as of the date of the grant. One of the difficulties in pricing private equity securities is the lack of an active market for the shares. The FASB has suggested that in lieu of observable stock volatility in the specific security, the entity could use an index of volatility from a relevant industry segment source when specifying the volatility in a valuation formula such as Black-Scholes. Nonvested or vested stock awards should be valued at fair value as of the grant date.

In some circumstances, a second alternative for nonpublic companies when accounting for share-value or liability awards is the use of an intrinsic value method that is updated and revalued each reporting period. Under the intrinsic value method, the difference between the offer price and the market value of the security is the identified compensation expense. Because the fair value method is considered preferable accounting (Accounting Standards Codification [ASC] 250, *Accounting Changes and Error Corrections*), switching to an intrinsic value method is not contemplated.

When fair value methods are used, the accounting entries and measurement procedures are the same as for public companies. If the entity adopts the intrinsic value method, then at the date of grant, there may be no compensation expense if the value of a share ($20) and the option price for a share ($20) are the same. However, if a year later the value of a share increases to $25, then $5 per option (assume 1,000 options) is recognized as compensation for over the service period (e.g., 3 years). Thus, compensation for year 1 is one-third times $5,000, or $1,667. Future changes would be treated as changes in estimates. For example, if the share value fell to $22 in the next year, then a reconsideration of the entire value would result in a $2,000 valuation to be allocated to the three periods. Since two periods have passed, two-thirds of the $2,000 should have been charged to compensation ($1,333). Since more than that was charged in year 1, the compensation account would be reduced (negative compensation expense) by $334 and APIC—Options adjusted for a similar amount. And so on for the last year. One can easily see how the difficulties of valuing private entity shares and the seesaw effects of this accounting method can become an issue for private entities.

The complexities of valuing private equity entities are discussed in Chapter 25 in this *Handbook.*

(c) RESTRICTED STOCK OPTIONS. Today the issuance of restricted shares is a more popular option than issuance of stock options. Issuing restricted stock as a form of compensation is beneficial to the recipient since the share (and not the option to purchase) is assigned to the recipient. Therefore, unless the recipient forfeits the shares during the service period, the award generally has a value whether the stock price goes up and down. Because of the value of these awards, the number of shares involved is generally a fraction of the number of options that it would take to be comparable in a stock option plan. This also has the advantage of less dilution to the existing shareholders. Additionally, since the recipient is a shareholder, it is believed the award better aligns the objectives of the entity with the objectives of the recipient.

At the time of the award, the value is recorded as unearned compensation and is amortized to compensation over the service period. For an award valued at $20,000 at the date of grant the entry is:

Unearned compensation	20,000	
Common stock ($10)		10,000
APIC		10,000

Compensation is recognized over the period of service:

Compensation expense	5,000	
Unearned compensation		5,000

If the recipient forfeits the award because the service requirements are not met, the original stock issuance is reversed and the remaining deferred compensation is canceled. The compensation recorded to date is also reversed through income, as a correction of an estimate.

Common stock	10,000	
APIC	10,000	
Unearned compensation		15,000
Compensation expense		5,000

(d) EMPLOYEE STOCK OPTION PLANS. ESOPs usually do not present accounting problems since often they are stock sales to employees with a modest discount to offset the usual middleman costs of selling shares to the public. Employers offer these plans to encourage employees to better align the individual's long-term financial objectives with the employer's financial success. Supposedly, this "skin in the game" better aligns the objectives of the employee and employer when compared to pure cash compensation plans. If certain conditions are met, the plan may qualify under

Section 423 of the Internal Revenue Code (IRC), which allows employees to defer taxation on the difference between the market price and the discounted purchase price. A plan that qualifies under Section 423 of the IRC as a noncompensatory plan permits discounts of up to 15 percent.

ESOPs are formal plans, specifying the broad opportunity to all or most employees to purchase stock at a discount from the market price. Broad-based ESOPs are generally considered compensatory unless the discount from market price is relatively small. Plans that provide a discount of, say, 5 percent or less often would be considered noncompensatory under GAAP; discounts in excess of this amount generally would be considered from a GAAP perspective as compensatory unless the company can justify a higher discount. A company may justify a discount in excess of 5 percent if the discount from market price does not exceed the greater of (1) the per share discount that would be reasonable in a recurring offer of stock to stockholders or (2) the per share amount of stock issuance costs avoided by not having to raise a significant amount of capital by a public offering. If a company cannot provide adequate support for a discount in excess of 5 percent, the entire amount of the discount (including the 5 percent benchmark amount) should be treated as compensation cost.

For example, if an ESOP provides that employees can purchase the employer's common stock at a price equal to 85 percent of its market price at the date of purchase; compensation cost would be based on the entire discount of 15 percent unless the discount in excess of 5 percent can be otherwise justified.

If an ESOP meets these three criteria, the discount from market price is generally not considered stock-based compensation:

1. The plan incorporates no option features other than these, which may be incorporated:
   a. Employees are permitted a short period of time (not exceeding 31 days) after the purchase price has been fixed in which to enroll in the plan.
   b. The purchase price is based solely on the stock's market price at the date of purchase, and employees are permitted to cancel participation before the purchase date.
2. The discount from the market price is 5 percent or less (or the company is able to justify a higher discount).
3. Substantially all full-time employees meeting limited employment qualifications may participate on an equitable basis.

Awards granted under compensatory plans do not always result in recognition of compensation expense by the employer. An employer recognizes compensation expense with respect to awards granted pursuant to a compensatory plan only if the application of the measurement principle results in the determination of compensation cost.

23.3 ESTIMATING FAIR VALUE

In the Exposure Draft preceding FASB Statement No. 123R, it was proposed that the lattice/binomial method be used for valuing stock options. The final Standard permitted, without preference, either the lattice method or the Black-Scholes-Merton (aka Black-Scholes) method. Initially the Black-Scholes method was selected overwhelmingly because of its simplicity and its similar result to the lattice method under certain stable market conditions. It still is favored in the United States, although lattice methods are more popular elsewhere.

The Black-Scholes model uses fixed assumptions about volatility, dividends, and risk-free interest rates over the life of the option. Stock purchases are assumed to occur at a point in time. While these modeling characteristics are not an issue in stable markets, they become less realistic in unstable markets, such as have been experienced in 2008 through the date of this writing.

An advantage of the lattice model in periods of instability is that it permits modeling of the stock option value with the ability to change assumptions between periods or model alternative scenarios for stock prices and interest rates. For example, a higher volatility might be ascribed to the early years in the model with a diminishing volatility in future years. Dividend yields are also subject to change in such unstable markets.

Under the lattice model, a portion of the options can be assumed to be converted to shares in specific periods. Historical patterns of exercise may be of no use when markets are unstable. Thus, rethinking of the likely exercise under changing price conditions is desirable.

Regardless of the method selected, GAAP requires the development of reasonable and supportable estimates for each model input. A weakness of all these models is that they are based on prognostications regarding future events and economic factors. While they may reflect the best thinking at the time the valuation is taking place, they do not necessarily reflect the true value of the option as measured by actual events to take place going forward.

(a) BLACK-SCHOLES OPTION PRICING MODELS. In first addressing the issue of estimating fair value of equity instruments, the FASB noted that it was not aware of any quoted market prices, such as a futures market, that would be appropriate for valuing employee stock options.[7] Accordingly, GAAP requires that the fair value of a stock option (or its equivalent) be estimated using an option-pricing model, such as the Black-Scholes or a binomial pricing model, that considers these assumptions or variables:

- *Exercise price of the option.*
- *Expected life of the option.* This considers the outcome of service-related conditions (i.e., vesting requirements and forfeitures) and performance-related conditions. Expected life is typically less than the contractual term due to assumed forfeitures.
- *Current price of the underlying stock.* This refers to the stock price at the date of grant.
- *Expected volatility of the underlying stock.* This is an estimate of the future price fluctuation of the underlying stock for a term commensurate with the expected life of the option. Volatility is not required for nonpublic companies.
- *Expected dividend yield on the underlying stock.* This estimate should reflect a reasonable expectation of dividend yield commensurate with the expected life of the option.
- *Risk-free interest rate during the expected term of the option.* This is the rate currently available for zero-coupon U.S. government issues with a remaining term equal to the expected life of the options.

The option pricing model utilized should consider management's expectations relative to the life of the option, future dividends, and stock price volatility. Both the volatility and dividend yield components should reflect reasonable expectations commensurate with the expected life of the option. As there is likely to be a range of reasonable expectations about factors such as expected volatility, dividend yield, and lives of options, a company may use the low end of the range for expected volatility and expected option lives and the high end of the range for dividend yield (assuming that one point within the ranges is no better estimate than another). These estimates introduce significant judgment in determining the value of stock-based compensation awards.

Despite the imprecision of measuring fair value through option pricing models, and particularly in light of the fact that most stock options issued to employees are not transferable and are forfeitable, the FASB believes that it has addressed these issues by valuing at zero those options that are expected to be forfeited and by valuing options that vest based on the length of time they are expected to remain outstanding rather than on the stated term of the options.

During the last 20 years, a number of mathematical models for estimating the fair value of traded options have been developed. The most commonly used methodologies for valuing options include the Black-Scholes model, binomial pricing models, the Monte Carlo simulation models, and the minimum value method. The minimum value of a stock option can be determined by a simple present value calculation that ignores the effect of expected volatility but is no longer GAAP.

---

[7] However, if a futures market is found to exist that closely tracks the terms of the options, it could be argued that this would be a better reference point for fair value than the calculated values from theoretical options pricing models.

Assumptions:

Exercise price—$40 (equals current price of underlying stock)
Expected dividends—0%, 2%, and 4%
Expected risk-free rate of return—7%
Expected volatility—0%, 20%, 30%, and 40%
Expected term—6 years

Fair values calculated using a Black-Scholes option pricing model

Dividend Rate	0%	Volatility 20%	30%	40%
0%	$13.35	$15.14	$17.56	$20.16
2%	8.87	11.42	13.98	16.57
4%	4.96	8.45	11.05	13.58

Exhibit 23.1 Estimated Option Values

The Black-Scholes and binomial pricing models were originally developed for valuing traded options with relatively short lives and are based on complex mathematical formulas. Option values derived under these models are sensitive to both the expected stock volatility and the expected dividend yield. Exhibit 23.1 illustrates the relative effect of changes in expected volatility and dividend rates using a generalized Black-Scholes option pricing model. Software packages that include option pricing models are available from numerous software vendors. Form-based tools are available on the Internet.

As shown in Exhibit 23.1, option values increase as expected volatility increases, and option values decrease as expected dividend yield increases. It is interesting to note that in instances where higher expected volatility is coupled with higher dividend yields, the binomial (lattice) model generally produces higher option values than the Black-Scholes model due primarily to increased sensitivity to compounded dividend yields in the binomial model. Nevertheless, current GAAP permits the use of either model.

(i) Expected Volatility. *Volatility* is the measure of the amount that a stock's price has fluctuated (historical volatility) or is expected to fluctuate (expected volatility) during a specified period. Volatility is expressed as a percentage; a stock with a volatility of 25 percent would be expected to have its annual rate of return fall within a range of plus or minus 25 percentage points of its expected rate about two-thirds of the time. For example, if a stock currently trades at $100 with a volatility of 25 percent and an expected rate of return of 12 percent, after one year the stock price should fall within the range of $87 to $137 approximately two-thirds of the time (using simple interest for illustration). Stocks with high volatility provide option holders with greater economic upside potential and, accordingly, result in higher option values under the Black-Scholes and binomial option pricing models.

Volatility is often computed as the standard deviation of recent historical returns on the stock. Suppose a stock is currently selling at $10 and the standard deviation of prices (e.g., based on daily closing prices over a relevant period) was $2.00; this would result in an estimated volatility of $2.00/$10 = 20 percent.

GAAP suggests that estimating expected future volatility should begin with calculating historical volatility over the most recent period equal to the expected life of the options. Thus, if the weighted-average expected life of the options is six years, historical volatility should be calculated for the six years immediately preceding the option grant, unless that period can be argued to be unrepresentative.

Companies should modify historical stock volatility to the extent that recent experience indicates that the future is reasonably expected to differ from the past. Although historical averages may be the best available indicator of expected future volatility for some mature companies, there are legitimate exceptions, including: (1) a company whose common stock has only recently become publicly traded with little, if any, historical data on its stock price volatility; (2) a company with only a few years of public trading history where recent experience indicates that the stock has generally become less volatile; and (3) a company that sells off a line of business with significantly different volatility than the remaining line of business. In such cases, it is appropriate for companies to adjust historical volatility for current circumstances or use the average volatilities of similar companies until a longer series of historical data is available. Recent aberrations in the stock market make powerful arguments for the unrepresentativeness of recent year volatility.

GAAP does not allow for a company with publicly traded stock to ignore volatility simply because its stock has little or no trading history. For private companies, the use of an industry-specific index is an accepted method to estimate volatility if there is no company specific data from which to estimate this factor. Using an industry index for an appropriate sector and company size, the Black-Scholes estimation can be applied.

(ii) Expected Dividends. The assumption about expected dividends should be based on publicly available information. While standard option pricing models generally call for expected dividend yield, the model may be modified to use an expected dividend amount rather than a yield. If a company uses expected payments, any history of regular increases in dividends should be considered. For example, if a company's policy has been to increase dividends by approximately 3 percent per year, its estimated option value should not assume a fixed dividend amount throughout the expected life of the option.

Some companies with no history of paying dividends might reasonably expect to begin paying small dividends during the expected lives of their employee stock options. These companies may use an average of their past dividend yield (zero) and the mean dividend yield of an appropriately comparable peer group.

Because of the turbulent markets following 2008, the dividend yield estimate may be more appropriately specified by looking at current and future rather than past trends.

(iii) Expected Option Lives. The expected life of an employee stock option award should be estimated based on reasonable facts and assumptions on the grant date. Three factors should be considered: (1) the vesting period of the grant, (2) the average length of time similar grants have remained outstanding, and (3) historical and expected volatility of the underlying stock. The expected life must at least include the vesting period and, in most circumstances, will be less than the contractual life of the option.

Option value increases at a higher rate during the earlier part of an option term. For example, a two-year option is worth less than twice as much as a one-year option if all other assumptions are equal. As a result, calculating estimated option values based on a single weighted-average life that includes widely differing individual lives may overstate the value of the entire award. Companies are encouraged to group option recipients into relatively homogeneous groups and calculate the related option values based on appropriate weighted-average expectations for each group. For example, if top-level executives tend to hold their options longer than middle management, and nonmanagement employees tend to exercise their options sooner than any other groups, it would be appropriate to stratify the employees into these three groups in calculating the weighted-average estimated life of the options. Alternatively, separate models might be applied to each of the groups and aggregated for valuation purposes.

(b) LATTICE/BINOMIAL OPTION PRICING MODELS. It is not unusual for a large proportion of employees to exercise their options upon vesting. They do this so they can lock-in the value of the option and not risk that future values will decline.[8] Other executives or employees may hold their options

---

[8] See J. N. Carpenter, "The Exercise and Valuation of Executive Stock Options," *Journal of Financial Economics* 48 (1998): 127–158.

and exercise based on their assessment of how likely it is the stock price will rise further before the expiration date. Lattice models can better capture the impact of these varying exercise patterns when calculating the value of the option.

A lattice/ binomial[9] model for pricing options is a tree diagram that traces the estimated option prices over the life of the option and hypothetical "actions" at those points in the diagram. The roots of this approach lie in the research of John C. Cox, Stephen A. Ross, and Mark Rubinstein that was published in 1979.[10] The value of the options is derived by backward induction through the tree structure to the present. The discrete periods in the tree can be months, quarters, or annual periods. Probabilities can be assigned to stock price rises or declines at each node. The tree builds from period to period through the option life.

Suppose an initial stock price at the grant date of $10. At the end of the first modeling period, say there is a 50 percent chance the stock price will rise and a 50 percent chance it will fall. The volatility is used to estimate the potential rise and fall. In addition, the risk-free interest rate is used to estimate a likely trend for the stock even apart from volatility, and the dividend yield reduces the value. For example, assume a 2 percent risk-free rate and no expected dividends. The node representing an increase in value would be $10 × 1.02 × volatility (e.g., 15%) = 11.73, assuming no dividends. Similarly, the decrease node is computed using the same variables but assuming a negative price trend ($10 × 1.02 =10.20 – (15% of 10.20 = 1.53) = $8.67. In the next period, the increase and decrease would also be similarly modeled from each first stage nodes.

Following this procedure, a probabilistic tree of expected stock prices can be constructed over the life of the options. Once options become vested, estimates can be made of the number of options that are still in force and when they will be exercised. To estimate the fair value of the options, the outcomes of the estimated future purchases (net of forfeitures) and lapses can be calculated and discounted back to the present period. Probabilities are used to weight the potential outcomes before summarization. For example, suppose a node had a present value of $4.00 but a probability of 10 percent in the completed tree; then a .40 value would be used in the summarization of the values of the nodes in reaching the value of the option.

When senior executives and other employees exhibit different characteristics of purchasing shares (e.g., different rates of turnover of personnel before vesting, different patterns of purchase—later versus earlier), these different characteristics can be factored into a single model or more simply modeled separately for each unique group before summarization.

The inputs for the lattice model are similar to the inputs to the Black-Scholes model. They include:

- Stock price on the grant date
- Exercise price of the option
- Risk-free rate over the life of the option
- Expiration of the option
- Expected life of the option—this may be less than the contractual life due to a stock purchase before the expiration date
- Dividend yield of the option's underlying stock over the life of the option
- Volatility of the underlying stock of the option (ASC 718 requires the use of expected volatility)
- Exercise multiple over the life of the option due to suboptimal exercise behavior—redeeming earlier than the optimal date
- Vesting period of the option grant

---

[9] The binomial aspect of this technique is that the outcomes are based on two potential outcomes (price rise or price decline). Multinomial models are exceedingly complex but may allow for more flexibility in representing alternative scenarios.

[10] J. C. Cox, S. A. Ross, and M. Rubinstein, "Option Pricing: A Simplified Approach," *Journal of Financial Economics* (September 1979) pp. 229-263.

- Blackout period, if any[11]
- Annual turnover rate of executives or employees
- Number of time periods in the option life (month, quarter, year)
- The possible increase in value from period to period and its probability
- The possible decline in value from period to period and its respective probability (1.0, minus the probability of an increase, from prior bullet point.) A strength of the lattice approach is its ability to handle changing estimates through the life of the options. For example, if the current risk-free rate is artificially low, say at 1.5 percent, in future periods, the risk-free rate can be increased in the model to better track expectations. With the increase in flexibility come the risk of bias in determining the factors, and since compensation expense is the result of the combination of the assumptions and estimates.

(i) Computing the Option Price. The options can be valued once the tree of prices is completed over the life of the option. For the most part shares will not be purchased if the option price is greater than the market value (out of the money). The option holder will exercise or not exercise his or her right to purchase shares when permitted under the agreement at the dates allowed. When assessing whether options might be exercised, the price at each node is compared to the option price. If there is an intrinsic value, options might be exercised. If there is no intrinsic value, options are assumed not to be exercised. There are also assumptions factored in regarding employees who may leave the plan along the way and the number of remaining options at various points in time.

Stock may not be purchased, even if allowed, at an early point before expiration since holders may expect further appreciation. At the final point, however, all option holders will either exercise or not exercise the option to purchase. Even if the options are in the money, not all holders may purchase shares for one reason or another.

The payoff at the expiration date is the difference between the share price ($20) and the price at each final node in the lattice chart at that date. Similarly, the payoffs at prior nodes can be calculated. One can make estimates at each of the nodes after the vesting point as to how many shares will be issued and at the various option values at that point. Probabilities are used to weight the outcomes at various times in the analysis. Present values can then be used to determine the value of the options at the grant date.

Once completed, these calculations are generally not updated for changes in the assumptions and estimates, unless a plan change is implemented partway through the option lives.

For complex options or options with embedded uncertainty (e.g., real options or "Asian" options), other models may be more appropriate, such as a Monte Carlo simulation of various option scenarios.

Computer and other Web-based programs are generally required to develop these calculations in a realistic scenario. Both the Black-Scholes and lattice methods can be developed in Excel or a similar spreadsheet program.

(ii) Changing Methods. Changes from the Black-Scholes method to the preferable binomial method are accounted for as a change-in-estimate. Changes from the binomial to the Black-Scholes methods would require significant justification.

23.4 SPECIAL TOPICS

(a) AWARDS TO NONEMPLOYEES FOR GOODS AND SERVICES. For want of better placement, the accounting for exchanges of stock for goods and services has historically been handled by the

---

[11] During a blackout period, employees cannot exercise the options even after they are vested. This blackout period often lowers the option value but may increase it when stock values are expected to rise significantly during the blackout period. The effect depends on two factors: the length of the blackout period and the estimated stock value at the date of exercise. A reason for a blackout period is to suspend options activity around an earnings release date.

various Standards addressing stock options. This issue has been handled rather consistently over the years amid the rather tortured accounting thought and different treatments afforded stock option plans and recognizing compensation expense. Fair market value has long been the concept applied in accounting for such transactions.

When valuing the fair value of the goods and services in an exchange with nonemployees, the fair value of the stock or the exchanged good or service is used, whichever is more reliably measurable (ASC 505-50, *Equity Based Payments to Non-Employees*). In some cases, the fair value of goods or services received from suppliers, consultants, attorneys, or other nonemployees is more reliably measurable and indicates the fair value of the equity instrument issued. This has been long-standing GAAP and was reconfirmed during the EITF's discussion of Issue No. 96-18, *Accounting for Equity Instruments That Are Issued to Other Than Employees for Acquiring, or in Conjunction with Selling, Goods or Services.* Additionally, SEC Staff Accounting Bulletin No. 107 instructs companies to use, by analogy, the guidance in Statement No. 123R as it applies to employees for equity compensation granted to nonemployees (ASC 505).

Some such transactions are more complex: The exchange may span several periods; the issuance of the equity instruments may be contingent on service or delivery of goods that must be completed by the provider of the goods or services in order to vest in the equity instrument; or fully vested, nonforfeitable equity instruments issued to a grantee may contain terms that may vary based on the achievement of a performance condition or certain market conditions. In certain cases, the fair value of the equity instruments to be received may be more reliably measurable than the fair value of the goods or services to be given as consideration.

Critical to determining the valuation of the expense or asset when the value of the stock is used to value the transaction is the "measurement date." When there is no "performance commitment" in the contract, the measurement date is generally the date of the completion of the service or delivery of the good.

When a performance commitment exists, under ASC 505-50, the measurement date is the performance commitment date. Whether a benchmark performance measure, such as penalties or damages if the contract is not fulfilled by a certain date or in a certain way, or some other contingency is involved, requires a careful analysis of the agreement. If disincentives for nonperformance are written into the agreement, it is likely that the agreement will be considered to have a performance commitment as defined by GAAP. Such provisions need to go beyond the mere risk of legal action or risk of forfeiting part of the award for nonperformance.

When a multiperiod project is involved—for example, a construction project that spans several periods—estimated expense is recognized each service or activity period, based on the measured stock valuation. If accounting rules require recognition of the transaction before the settlement date, it may be necessary to adjust the already recognized asset or expense for the facts at the date when the value of the exchanged stock is known.

(b) AWARDS CLASSIFIED AS LIABILITIES. Under certain circumstances, certain share awards might be classified as a liability rather than an equity award, such as when the award calls for potential settlement in cash or other assets. Another example of a liability award is one involving mandatorily redeemable shares. In general, equity awards are not reclassified as liabilities if the company only occasionally settles awards for cash or withholds shares to satisfy tax withholding requirements. However, certain provisions of share-based awards may cause them to be classified as liabilities, such as if an award provides for a puttable or callable repurchase term within six months of the vesting period or stock purchase or if the provision is based on other than fair value. An award indexed to a factor other than performance, service, or market condition may also classify the award as a liability award. ASC 480, *Distinguishing Liabilities from Equity,* identifies criteria that should be used when determining whether an instrument is a liability or equity item. Examples of liability awards include cash-settled SARs and restricted/performance share units.

These liability awards must be revalued each period and not valued only at the inception, as stock awards are valued. Compensation is measured prior to vesting by the portion of the service period passing and also by the change in the value of the award at each measurement period. After vesting, further value changes would also be charged to compensation.

Thus, for these types of awards, the key measurement date shifts from the grant date to the settlement date, when the value of the award is known. This is in contrast with the measurement date for equity awards.

(c) STOCK APPRECIATION RIGHTS AS COMPENSATION. SARs are a common means of structuring employee bonus awards. Essentially, the stock price at the measurement date is the benchmark for determining the award. Increases in the stock value each period until the end date determine the compensation value of the award until the final measurement date when the value is known. Changes in valuations from year to year are treated on a cumulative basis as changes in estimates. These plans may be structured so the recipient receives stock, cash, or some combination of assets in settlement. When the recipient can demand cash payment, GAAP accounting recognizes a liability and compensation expense. The measurement is made each reporting period.

Whether a public company, where fair value is required, or a nonpublic company where fair value, modified fair value, or intrinsic value may be selected, awards must be valued each reporting period.

(d) MODIFICATIONS OF AWARDS. Circumstances such as changing the option price, extending the life of an award, or changing the vesting periods can trigger a modification of an award. If an equity award is modified after the grant date, the value of the option is remeasured. The process for determining the amounts involved in the change require the fair valuation of the original award to the date of the change and a fair valuation of the modified agreement. Cancellations of awards if replaced with a new award would also be accounted for as modifications. Additional compensation expense may be recognized in the period of the change.

Some award modifications may result in liability awards becoming share awards and vice versa. In general, the measurement issue is the same—valuing the new plan under GAAP and then valuing the modified plan at the point of modification, and recognizing a difference in compensation expense. The GAAP for the modified plans will follow the GAAP for those types of plans going forward. For example, if the new plan is treated as a liability, then the plan will be valued and compensation adjusted each period going forward.

(e) INCOME TAXATION OF STOCK COMPENSATION PLANS. Taxation and accounting rules do not share common rules as they relate to stock option plans. The entity deductibility for tax purposes for stock option plans is based on the intrinsic value (e.g., market value − exercise price) of the option at the exercise date (the "true" value of the option) and not on any of the compensation computations that are required under GAAP. Thisdivergence gives rise to the recognition of expense over the service period but a tax benefit available only at a later measurement point. Complexities are also introduced when shares are forfeited since some compensation expenses might have been recognized on unanticipated forfeitures and failures to exercise options, but they will never result in any tax benefit. Thus, some portion of compensation expense may give rise to a temporary difference for deferred tax purposes (ASC 740, *Income Taxes*).

If the intrinsic value at exercise exceeds the compensation expense recognized in the income statement, that excess tax benefit is treated as a contribution to paid-in capital. A reverse situation, where there is a tax accrual deficiency, would be accounted for as additional compensation expense. If the reason for the excess or deficiency is from a change in tax rates, then that change would flow through the tax expense provision and not through equity or compensation expense accounts.

If there is a realized tax benefit from the stock compensation plan, ASC 718 directs that the cash flow effect of the excess benefit be reported as both a *cash inflow from financing activities* and a *cash outflow from operating activities,* regardless of whether the direct or indirect cash flow methods are being followed.

(f) EARNINGS PER SHARE. Stock-based compensation awards impact basic and diluted earnings per share to the extent of compensation expense or credits to compensation expense, net of income tax effects, recognized by the employer for financial reporting purposes. When awards will be settled through issuance of shares of common stock, diluted earnings per share may reflect further dilution because of the incremental number of shares of the employer's common stock deemed to be outstanding. Stock-based compensation arrangements that may be settled in either common stock or cash at the election of either the entity or the employee are presumed to be settled in common stock (absent compelling evidence to the contrary), and the resulting potential common shares are included in the computation of diluted earnings per share if the effect is dilutive.

The impact of stock-based compensation awards on earnings per share applies to the earnings per share computations regardless of the method of accounting for stock-based compensation. Net income available to common stockholders (the numerator) may differ between methods because of the differences in determining compensation cost under different methods. Furthermore, the weighted-average number of common shares outstanding (the denominator) in computations of diluted earnings per share may differ due to the differences in the determination of the assumed number of shares to be purchased. For example, the amount of compensation cost attributed to future services and not yet recognized and the amount of tax benefits that would be credited to stockholders' equity assuming exercise of the options generally would differ depending on whether a company is accounting for stock-based compensation under fair value or the intrinsic methods.

In most cases, performance awards will not be reflected in diluted earnings per share until the performance condition has been satisfied.

(i) Diluted Earnings per Share. The denominator in the diluted earnings per share computation is increased to include the number of additional common shares that would have been outstanding if the dilutive potential common shares had been issued. Accordingly, the dilutive effect of all outstanding options (and their equivalents such as nonvested stock) that are subject only to time-based vesting are reflected in diluted earnings per share. Stock-based compensation awards that are subject to performance-based vesting are treated as contingently issuable shares.

Dilutive options that are issued during a period or that expire or are canceled during a period are included in the denominator of diluted earnings per share for the period they are outstanding. Similarly, dilutive options exercised during the period are included in the denominator for the period prior to actual exercise. The common shares issued upon exercise of the options or warrants are included in the denominator for the period after the exercise date as part of the weighted-average number of common shares outstanding.

Contingently issuable shares are included in the computation of diluted earnings per share as of the beginning of the period in which the conditions are satisfied (or as of the date of the agreement providing for contingently issuable shares, if later). If all necessary conditions have not been satisfied by the end of the period, the number of contingently issuable shares included in diluted earnings per share is based on the number of shares, if any, that would be issuable if the end of the reporting period were the end of the contingency period. Performance-based vesting describes vesting that depends on both (1) an employee rendering service to the employer for a specified period of time and (2) the achievement of a specified performance target.

As with variable awards subject only to time-based vesting, for stock-based compensation awards subject to performance-based vesting, (1) the number of shares issuable pursuant to the award; (2) the option or purchase price, if any; or (3) both the number of shares issuable and the option or purchase price are not known at the date the award is granted.

If all necessary conditions have not been satisfied by the end of the reporting period, the number of contingently issuable shares included in diluted earnings per share is based on the number of shares, if any, that would be issuable if the end of the reporting period were the end of the contingency period and if the result would be dilutive. Those contingently issuable shares are included in the denominator of diluted earnings per share as of the beginning of the reporting period (or as of the date of the agreement providing for contingently issuable shares, if later).

(g) OBTAINING AND RETAINING SUPPORTING DATA. Obtaining and retaining the data and means to apply the methodology approaches required for the computations and disclosures is important to the use of the fair value and intrinsic methods. Because further changes in the current Standards may be forthcoming, or private entities may become public, it behooves an entity to consider what data might be necessary should there be proposed changes. For example, a nonpublic entity about to become public needs to consider the transition to its different status and the different GAAP rules that may apply going forward. A further convergence of U.S. GAAP to International Financial Reporting Standards (IFRS) may also signal data issues for all entities.

23.5 DISCLOSURE

(a) NOTES TO THE FINANCIAL STATEMENTS. The notes to the financial statements of all entities should disclose information to assist users to understand the nature of share-based payment transactions and the effects of those transactions on the financial statements. The footnote requirements have evolved over time. In addition to FASB requirements, the SEC is active in specifying disclosures it believes important to achieving transparency.

Under ASC 718, the required disclosures include:

- A description of and the terms of the share-based payment awards. A nonpublic company should disclose its policy for measuring compensation cost.
- The most recent income statement should provide the number and weighted-average exercise prices of the share options and equity instruments.
- For each income statement, the weighted-average grant-date fair value of equity options and the intrinsic value of options exercised during the year should be presented. For fully vested share options and those expected to vest at the date of the latest statement of financial position, the company should provide the number, weighted-average exercise price, aggregate intrinsic value, and contractual terms of options outstanding and currently exercisable.
- If more than one share-based plan is in effect, information should be provided separately for each plan.
- For each year for which an income statement is provided, companies should provide this information:
    - (For companies using fair value) a description of the method of determining fair value and a description of the assumptions used.
    - The total compensation cost for share-based payment arrangements, including tax benefits and capitalization of compensation costs.
    - Descriptions of significant modifications and numbers of employees affected.
- On the date of the latest statement of financial position, companies should disclose the total compensation cost related to nonvested awards not yet recognized and the period over which they are expected to be recognized.
- The amount of cash received from exercise of share-based compensation and the amount of cash used to settle equity instruments should be disclosed.
- A description of the company's policy for issuing shares, including the source of the shares.

(b) DISCLOSURE EXAMPLE. Exhibit 23.2 is a footnote disclosure from the 2010 General Electric Annual 10-K disclosure filed with the SEC. One can easily note the extensive disclosure regarding the multiple plans in effect in this large company.

NOTE 16. OTHER STOCK-RELATED INFORMATION

We grant stock options, restricted stock units (RSUs) and performance share units (PSUs) to employees under the 2007 Long-Term Incentive Plan. This plan replaced the 1990 Long-Term Incentive Plan. In addition, we grant options and RSUs in limited circumstances to consultants, advisors and independent contractors (primarily non-employee talent at NBC Universal) under a plan approved by our Board of Directors in 1997 (the consultants' plan). There are outstanding grants under one shareowner-approved option plan for non-employee directors. Share requirements for all plans may be met from either unissued or treasury shares. Stock options expire 10 years from the date they are granted and vest over service periods that range from one to five years. RSUs give the recipients the right to receive shares of our stock upon the vesting of their related restrictions. Restrictions on RSUs vest in various increments and at various dates, beginning after one year from date of grant through grantee retirement. Although the plan permits us to issue RSUs settleable in cash, we have only issued RSUs settleable in shares of our stock. PSUs give recipients the right to receive shares of our stock upon the achievement of certain performance targets.

All grants of GE options under all plans must be approved by the Management Development and Compensation Committee, which consists entirely of independent directors.

(154)

Table of Contents

Stock Compensation Plans

December 31, 2010 (Shares in thousands)	Securities to be issued upon exercise	Weighted average exercise price	Securities available for future issuance
Approved by shareowners			
Options	399,991	$ 20.81	(a)
RSUs	21,468	(b)	(a)
PSUs	700	(b)	(a)
Not approved by shareowners (Consultants' Plan)			
Options	448	29.39	(c)
RSUs	103	(b)	(c)
Total	422,710	$ 20.82	213,047

(a) In 2007, the Board of Directors approved the 2007 Long-Term Incentive Plan (the Plan). The Plan replaced the 1990 Long-Term Incentive Plan. The maximum number of shares that may be granted under the Plan is 500 million shares, of which no more than 250 million may be available for awards granted in any form provided under the Plan other than options or stock appreciation rights. The approximate 105.9 million shares available for grant under the 1990 Plan were retired upon approval of the 2007 Plan. Total shares available for future issuance under the 2007 Plan amounted to 184.8 million shares at December 31, 2010.

(b) Not applicable.

(c) Total shares available for future issuance under the consultants' plan amount to 28.2 million shares.

Outstanding options expire on various dates through December 9, 2020.

The following table summarizes information about stock options outstanding at December 31, 2010.

Stock Options Outstanding

(Shares in thousands)	Outstanding			Exercisable	
Exercise price range	Shares	Average life(a)	Average exercise price	Shares	Average exercise price
Under $10.00	64,595	8.1	$ 9.57	13,061	$ 9.57
10.01-15.00	83,081	8.5	11.97	17,093	11.97
15.01-20.00	104,149	9.4	16.22	173	17.56
20.01-25.00	55	1.9	22.49	55	22.49
25.01-30.00	47,745	4.4	27.62	35,404	27.40
30.01-35.00	49,487	4.1	33.21	46,629	33.16
Over $35.00	51,327	2.3	40.38	45,872	40.57
Total	400,439	6.8	$ 20.82	158,287	$ 29.76

At year-end 2009, options with an average exercise price of $36.94 were exercisable on 147 million shares.

(a) Average contractual life remaining in years.

(155)

Table of Contents

Stock Option Activity

	Shares (in thousands)	Weighted average exercise price	Weighted average remaining contractual term (in years)	Aggregate intrinsic value (in millions)
Outstanding at January 1, 2010	338,163	$ 24.41		
Granted	105,227	16.22		
Exercised	(3,449)	10.65		
Forfeited	(8,223)	15.26		
Expired	(31,279)	46.66		
Outstanding at December 31, 2010	400,439	$ 20.82	6.8	$ 1,312
Exercisable at December 31, 2010	158,287	$ 29.76	4.0	$ 222
Options expected to vest	213,267	$ 15.04	8.7	$ 962

We measure the fair value of each stock option grant at the date of grant using a Black-Scholes option pricing model. The weighted average grant-date fair value of options granted during 2010, 2009 and 2008 was $4.11, $3.81 and $5.26, respectively. The following assumptions were used in arriving at the fair value of options granted during 2010, 2009 and 2008, respectively: risk-free interest rates of 2.9%, 3.2% and 3.4%; dividend yields of 3.9%, 3.9% and 4.4%; expected volatility of 35%, 49% and 27%; and expected lives of six years and eleven months, six years and ten months, and six years and nine months. Risk-free interest rates reflect the yield on zero-coupon U.S. Treasury securities. Expected dividend yields presume a set dividend rate. For stock options granted in 2010, 2009 and the fourth quarter of 2008, we used a historical five-year average for the dividend yield. Expected volatilities are based on implied volatilities from traded options and historical volatility of our stock. The expected option lives are based on our historical experience of employee exercise behavior.

The total intrinsic value of options exercised during 2010, 2009 and 2008 amounted to $23 million, an insignificant amount and $45 million, respectively. As of December 31, 2010, there was $697 million of total unrecognized compensation cost related to nonvested options. That cost is expected to be recognized over a weighted average period of two years, of which approximately $236 million, pre tax, is expected to be recognized in 2011.

Stock option expense recognized in net earnings amounted to $178 million in 2010, $120 million in 2009 and $69 million in 2008. Cash received from option exercises during 2010, 2009 and 2008 was $37 million, an insignificant amount and $353 million, respectively. The tax benefit realized from stock options exercised during 2010, 2009 and 2008 was $7 million, an insignificant amount and $15 million, respectively.

Other Stock-based Compensation

	Shares (in thousands)	Weighted average grant date fair value	Weighted average remaining contractual term (in years)	Aggregate intrinsic value (in millions)
RSUs outstanding at January 1, 2010	25,861	$ 31.98		
Granted	3,245	15.89		
Vested	(6,754)	33.38		
Forfeited	(781)	30.98		
RSUs outstanding at December 31, 2010	21,571	$ 29.16	2.5	$ 395
RSUs expected to vest	19,773	$ 29.24	2.4	$ 362

(156)

Table of Contents

The fair value of each restricted stock unit is the market price of our stock on the date of grant. The weighted average grant date fair value of RSUs granted during 2010, 2009 and 2008 was $15.89, $13.63 and $28.74, respectively. The total intrinsic value of RSUs vested during 2010, 2009 and 2008 amounted to $111 million, $139 million and $274 million, respectively. As of December 31, 2010, there was $334 million of total unrecognized compensation cost related to nonvested RSUs. That cost is expected to be recognized over a weighted average period of two years, of which approximately $147 million, pre tax, is expected to be recognized in 2011. As of December 31, 2010, 0.7 million PSUs with a weighted average remaining contractual term of two years, an aggregate intrinsic value of $13 million and $2 million of unrecognized compensation cost were outstanding. Other share-based compensation expense for RSUs and PSUs recognized in net earnings amounted to $116 million, $127 million and $155 million in 2010, 2009 and 2008, respectively.

The total income tax benefit recognized in earnings for all share-based compensation arrangements amounted to $143 million, $118 million and $106 million in 2010, 2009 and 2008, respectively.

When stock options are exercised and restricted stock vests, the difference between the assumed tax benefit and the actual tax benefit must be recognized in our financial statements. In circumstances in which the actual tax benefit is lower than the estimated tax benefit, that difference is recorded in equity, to the extent there are sufficient accumulated excess tax benefits. At December 31, 2010, our accumulated excess tax benefits are sufficient to absorb any future differences between actual and estimated tax benefits for all of our outstanding option and restricted stock grants.

Exhibit 23.2 ***Continued***

23.6 ACCOUNTING STANDARDS CODIFICATION

FASB Statement No. 123R was the last major stock compensation pronouncement before the Codification project. The Codification covers the elements of accounting for stock compensation in several sections:

- ASC 260, *Earnings per Share*
- ASC 505-50, *Equity-Based Payments to Non-Employees*
- ASC 718, *Compensation—Stock Compensation*
- ASC 815-45, *Derivatives: Contracts in Entity's Own Equity*
- ASC 958, *Not-for-Profit Entities*

ASC 718 is the principal section relating to share-based compensation.

23.7 INTERNATIONAL PERSPECTIVE

IFRS is generally consistent with the fair value approach required for public companies. The comparable IFRS is Statement No. 2, *Share-Based Payment.* However, under IFRS, there is no provision for a simplified method (intrinsic method) for nonpublic entities. One difference is that under GAAP, modifications of awards trigger a new measurement date based on the date of the modification; however, IFRS does not recognize a new measurement of fair value. There are also minor differences in the treatment of tax implications and in the measurement valuation date for exchanges of stock for goods and services from nonemployees. As in many accounting areas, there is a continuing project to reconcile and resolve the differences between GAAP and IFRS.

23.8 SOURCES AND SUGGESTED REFERENCES

Accounting Principles Board. Opinion No. 25, *Accounting for Stock Issued to Employees*. New York: AICPA, 1972. Also see Interpretation of APB Opinion No. 25, *Accounting for Stock Issued to Employees,* New York, AICPA, 1973.

Financial Accounting Standards Board. Statement of Financial Accounting Standards No. 123, *Accounting for Stock-Based Compensation*., Norwalk, CT. Author, 1995.

______. Statement No. 123R. Norwalk, CT. Author, 2004.

______. Statement of Financial Accounting Standards No. 148. *Accounting for Stock-Based Compensation—Transition and Disclosure* Norwalk, CT. Author, 2002.

CHAPTER 24

FAIR VALUE MEASUREMENT

Mark L. Zyla, CPA/ABV, CFA, ASA

Acuitas, Inc.

24.1 INTRODUCTION 2

24.2 WHY THE TREND TOWARD FAIR VALUE ACCOUNTING? 3

(a) The Changing Economy 3
(b) Globalization 4
(c) Relevance and Transparency 4

24.3 HISTORY AND EVOLUTION OF FAIR VALUE 6

(a) Development of Fair Value Concepts 7
(b) Fair Value of Financial Instruments 8
(c) Fair Value Measurement for Nonfinancial Assets and Liabilities 9
(d) Fair Value Measurement and the Economic Crisis 10
  (i) Mark-to-Market Accounting 11
  (ii) Application of Fair Value Accounting in Illiquid Market 11
  (iii) SEC Study on Mark-to-Market Accounting 12
  (iv) The FASB's Credit Crisis Projects 13
(e) Convergence of Fair Value Measurement 14
(f) Future of Fair Value Measurement 14

24.4 FAIR VALUE MEASUREMENTS STANDARDS AND CONCEPTS 15

(a) FASB ASC 820, *Fair Value Measurements and Disclosures* 15
(b) Definition of *Fair Value Measurements and Disclosures* 16
(c) Topic ASC 820, Scope and Scope Exceptions 16
(d) Initial Measurement 16
(e) Fair Value Framework 17
  (i) Asset or Liability 17
  (ii) Transaction 18
  (iii) Principal (or Most Advantageous) Market 18
  (iv) Market Participants 18
  (v) Price 18
  (vi) Highest and Best Use for Nonfinancial Assets 19
  (vii) Application to Liabilities and Instruments Classified in a Reporting Entity's Shareholders' Equity 19
  (viii) Liabilities and Instruments Classified in a Reporting Entity's Shareholders' Equity Held by Other Parties as Assets 20
  (ix) Liabilities and Instruments Classified in a Reporting Entity's Shareholders' Equity Not Held by Other Parties as Assets 20
  (x) Other Factors that Impact the Fair Value of a Liability 20
  (xi) Valuation Techniques 21
  (xii) Cost Approach 21
  (xiii) Market Approach 21
  (xiv) Income Approach 21
  (xv) Multiple Valuation Techniques 22
  (xvi) Calibration 22
  (xvii) Inputs to Valuation Techniques 22
  (xviii) Fair Value Hierarchy 22
  (xix) Measuring Fair Value When the Volume or Level of Activity for an Asset or Liability Has Significantly Decreased 24
  (xx) Identifying Transactions That Are Not Orderly 25

This chapter is adapted from Mark L. Zyla, *Fair Value Measurements: Practical Guidance and Implementation,* 2nd ed. (Hoboken, NJ: John Wiley & Sons, forthcoming), and is used with permission.

(xxi) Using Quoted Prices Provided by Third Parties 25
(f) Disclosures 26
(i) Objectives 26
(ii) Required Disclosures 26
(iii) Private Companies 29

24.5 FAIR VALUE OPTION 29

24.6 AUDITING FAIR VALUE MEASUREMENTS 32

(a) Audit Standards for Fair Value Measurements 33
(b) Auditing Estimates in Fair Value Measurements 34
(c) AU 328, *Auditing Fair Value Measurements and Disclosures* 35
(i) Testing Management's Fair Value Measurements 36
(ii) Testing Management's Significant Assumptions, the Valuation Model, and the Underlying Data 38
(iii) Testing the Reliability of Management's Assumptions 38
(iv) Testing the Data 40
(d) PCAOB Staff Audit Practice Alert No. 2, *Matters Related to Auditing Fair Value Measurements of Financial Instruments and the Use of Specialists* 40
(i) Auditing Fair Value Measurements 41
(ii) Classification within the Fair Value Hierarchy Under FASB ASC 820, *Fair Value Measurements and Disclosures* 41
(iii) Using the Work of a Valuation Specialist 42
(iv) Use of a Pricing Service 42
(e) SEC Audit Guidance 42

24.7 CONCLUSION 43

24.1 INTRODUCTION

Fair value accounting has changed the way financial information is presented. Where once financial statements were based primarily on historical costs, now, under certain circumstances, current fair value is often the basis of measurement for reporting both financial and nonfinancial assets and liabilities. Measuring fair value may require judgment that introduces some subjectivity into financial statements. A trend toward increasing the amount of financial statement information presented or disclosed at fair value persists under U.S. generally accepted accounting standards (GAAP) and international financial reporting standards (IFRS). This trend away from historical costs, which has been the bedrock of traditional accounting, toward fair value accounting has been challenging for preparers, auditors, standards setters, and regulators.

Fair value accounting is a financial reporting approach that requires or permits entities to measure and report assets at the price assets would sell and liabilities at the estimated price that a holder would have to pay in order to discharge the liability. The term *fair value accounting* not only refers to the initial measurement but can also refer to subsequent changes in fair value from period to period and the treatment of unrealized gains and losses in the financial statements. Therefore, fair value accounting affects the reported amounts for assets and liabilities in the balance sheet and affects the reported amounts for unrealized gains or losses shown in the income statement or in the other comprehensive income section of shareholders' equity. In financial reporting, fair value accounting is often applied to financial instruments such as investments in stocks, bonds, an entity's own debt obligations, and derivative instruments like options, swaps and futures. When unadjusted or adjusted market prices are the basis for fair value estimates of financial assets and liabilities, the process is often called mark-to-market accounting.

Fair value accounting is applicable to nonfinancial assets and liabilities as well, but in more limited circumstances. For instance, when an entity is acquired in a business combination, all balance sheet assets and liabilities are recorded at fair value. Subsequent to the acquisition date, the acquired entity's fair value is the basis for testing acquired goodwill for impairment. Likewise, fair value is the benchmark when testing property, plant, and equipment and other amortizable intangible assets for impairment.

Fair value measurement is the process for determining the fair value of financial and nonfinancial assets and liabilities when fair value accounting is required or permitted. Therefore, fair value measurement is broader than mark-to-market accounting. It encompasses estimating fair value based on market prices as well as estimating fair value using valuation models. The Financial Accounting Standards Boards (FASB) Accounting Standards Codification (ASC) 820, *Fair Value Measurements and Disclosures,* provides authoritative guidance for measuring the fair value of assets, liabilities, and equity interests when fair value accounting is required or permitted in other accounting standards.

Advocates of fair value accounting believe that fair value best represents the financial position of the entity and provides more relevant information to the users of the financial information. Detractors believe that fair values are unreliable because they are difficult to estimate. Critics also believe that reporting temporary losses is misleading when they are likely to reverse, and they believe that reported losses adversely affect market prices and market risk.[1] In spite of the criticism, fair value accounting has become more prominent in financial statement presentation and will continue to be a fundamental basis for accounting in the future.

This chapter begins with the history and evolution of fair value accounting. It will discuss some of the trends shaping fair value accounting and the development of fair value concepts, both for financial instruments and nonfinancial assets and liabilities. The economic crisis' impact on the evolution of fair value measurement concepts and standards setters' responses to requests for additional guidance during the crisis is also discussed. And since fair value measurement will continue to evolve, some of the likely future developments will also be covered.

The second section of this chapter discusses the fair value measurement accounting standards found in Financial Accounting Standards Board (FASB) Accounting Standards Codification (ASC) 820, *Fair Value Measurements and Disclosures,* and FASB ASC 825, *Financial Instruments.* The focus is on standards pertaining to the fair value framework and the fair value option. Finally, this chapter will briefly cover the auditing standards specifically applicable to fair value measurement and strategies for auditing fair value measurements in financial reporting.

24.2 WHY THE TREND TOWARD FAIR VALUE ACCOUNTING?

In recent years, there has been an increasing trend toward the use of fair value accounting in financial reporting. Even when fair value accounting is not required and financial statements are prepared using some other measurement basis, there is a likelihood that related disclosures will require the presentation of fair value information. Several factors are influencing the trend toward fair value accounting: the growing economic importance of intellectual property, globalization, and investors' desire for financial statements that are more relevant and transparent.

(a) THE CHANGING ECONOMY. The economy in the United States has undergone tremendous changes over the last quarter century due to a rapid rate of technological innovation. The explosion in the use of personal computers and digital media has created whole industries that did not previously exist. One product of technological innovation that contributed to economic change is the commercialization of the Internet, which resulted in what some call the information revolution. The result of this technological and economic change is that a significant portion of the U.S. economy shifted from bricks-and-mortar businesses to information-based businesses.

This economic change has led to a growing recognition that the value driver of many business entities lies within their intellectual property, not just in their inventory, plant and equipment. Financial statement users also recognize that intellectual property has not been effectively measured under traditional cost-based accounting practices. The reason is that existing accounting principles require internally created intellectual property to be expensed as research and development.

---

[1] Stephen G. Ryan, "Fair Value Accounting: Understanding the Issues Raised by the Credit Crunch," Council of Institutional Investors (July 2008), p. 1, *www.cii.org/UserFiles/file/resource%20center/correspondence/2008/CII%20Fair%20Value%20Paper%20(final)%20%20071108.pdf*

Ocean Tomo, an intellectual capital merchant banking firm, produces an Annual Study of Intangible Asset Market Value that breaks down the Standard & Poor (S&P) 500's equity market value into an implied intangible asset value and tangible asset value. In 2010, tangible and financial assets generated approximately 20 percent of the S&P 500's market value. While tangible and financial assets are reflected on company balance sheets, the remaining 80 percent of value attributable to intangible assets is often not recognized at all. This value gap has become more important in recent years and there is a growing percentage of the S&P 500's market capitalization attributable to intangible assets. Intangible assets comprised only 17 percent of the market capitalization of the S&P 500 in 1975. By 2010, this percentage had increased to 80 percent.[2]

(b) GLOBALIZATION. The International Monetary Fund defines *economic globalization* as "a historical process; the result of human innovation and technological process. It refers to the increasing integration of economies around the world, particularly through the movement of goods, services and capital across borders." Globalization has accelerated since the 1980s as a result of technological advances that made international financial and trading transactions easier and quicker.[3] This increasing globalization of business has created a need for consistent accounting standards across national boundaries.

The FASB and the International Accounting Standards Board (IASB) recognize that users of financial statements would benefit from having one set of international accounting standards that could be used for domestic and international, cross-border financial reporting. As a result, both organizations have been working for several years to jointly create accounting standards and to converge U.S. GAAP with international accounting standards (IAS). According to the FASB, *convergence* refers to both the goal of establishing a single set of high-quality international accounting standards and the path taken to reach that goal, which includes the collaborative efforts "to improve existing U.S. GAAP and International Financial Standards and eliminate the differences between them."[4] Historically, IAS have been more principal based, requiring more fair value measurement than U.S. GAAP, which are considered more rules based, requiring more cost-based measurement. As the accounting standards converge, U.S. GAAP will require more fair value accounting measures.

The history and evolution of fair value measurement encompasses the recent convergence of U.S. GAAP and IAS pertaining to fair value measurement. The five-year joint FASB and IASB project was undertaken to improve and align fair value measurement and disclosure requirements and to respond to the global financial crisis.[5] As originally promulgated, the FASB's Statement of Financial Accounting Standards (SFAS) No. 157, *Fair Value Measurements and Disclosures* influenced the development of International Financial Reporting Standard (IFRS) 7, *Fair Value Measurement.* Convergence has shaped U.S. accounting standards through updates to FASB ASC 820. The FASB's Accounting Standards Update (ASU) 2011-04, *Amendments to Achieve Common Fair Value Measurement and Disclosure Requirements in U.S. GAAP and IFRS,* which was issued in May 2011, eliminated most of the significant remaining differences between U.S. and international accounting standards for measuring fair value.

(c) RELEVANCE AND TRANSPARENCY. An important characteristic of efficient capital markets is that prices are the result of the market's correct assessment of all available information. The FASB recognizes that better financial reporting leads to stronger capital markets by helping investors

[2] "Ocean Tomo's Annual Study of Intangible Asset Market Value—2010," Ocean Tomo Intellectual Capital Equity, *www.oceantomo.com/*.

[3] International Monetary Fund Staff, "Globalization: A Brief Overview" (May 2008), *www.imf.org/external/np/exr/ib/2008/053008.htm*

[4] Financial Accounting Standards Board, "International Convergence of Accounting Standards—Overview," *www.fasb.org/*

[5] FASB News Release, "IASB and FASB Issue Common Fair Value Measurement and Disclosure Requirements," May 12, 2011, *www.fasb.org/cs/ContentServer?c=FASBContent_C&pagename=FASB/FASBContent_C/NewsPage&cid=1176158544944*

make informed decisions. One of the FASB's stated goals is "to set accounting standards that produce financial information useful in helping investors decide whether to provide resources to a company and whether the management of that company has made good use of the resources it already has."[6]

In an effort to make financial reporting more relevant to investors, the FASB has encouraged investors to participate in the accounting standards process by providing comments on discussion papers and exposure drafts that are issued at various stages of the FASB's projects. The FASB has asked interested investors to provide expert advice to the FASB's designated "investor liaison" staff members in conjunction with FASB projects. The goal is to improve the relevance of accounting standards for investors in a cost-effective manner.

Two other investor advisory groups provide input to the FASB from the investor perspective, the Investors Technical Advisory Committee (ITAC) and the Investor Task Force (ITF). The ITAC is focused on providing technical accounting advice and increasing investor participation in standard setting.[7] The ITF is made up of institutional asset managers who analyze various sectors of the economy. The ITF provides advice to the FASB about the impact of various accounting standards proposals on specific industry sectors.[8]

The Securities and Exchange Commission (SEC) is equally committed to advancing high quality accounting standards that are responsive to investors' needs. In testimony before a congressional subcommittee, SEC Director John M. White said:

> An open process that allows standards setters to seek and thoughtfully consider the views of market participants is critical to establishing, maintaining, and continually improving financial accounting and reporting standards. We are committed to high quality accounting standards and a transparent financial reporting system that meets the needs of investors and other market participants.[9]

Transparency in financial reporting is the unbiased, clear, complete presentation of a company's financial position. Information in the management discussion and analysis (MD&A) section of the financial statements about existing risk and uncertainty and about the likely future impact of risk and uncertainty on the company's prospects further promotes transparency. When financial reporting is transparent, investors are better able to make decisions and avoid surprises. On a macroeconomic scale, transparency leads to more efficient allocation of capital and stronger capital markets. In the aftermath of the economic crisis, there was a debate about whether fair value accounting promoted financial statement transparency or whether it caused the meltdown. In a 2008 report to Congress, the SEC found that "investors generally believe that fair value accounting increases financial reporting transparency and facilitates better investment decision-making."[10] The CFA Center for Financial Market Integrity concurs with the SEC's view. It supports fair value as "the most transparent measurement for investors to analyze financial statements," and it said that "fair value is being used as a scapegoat by corporations who have made poor decisions or were not in compliance with accounting standards."[11]

The financial crisis has presented a challenge and an opportunity for the SEC and the FASB to reaffirm their missions and assess their success in achieving their goals. The SEC's mission

---

[6] FASB, "Investors: Your Views are Critical in Helping Us Improve Financial Reporting," *www.fasb.org/*

[7] FASB, Investor Technical Advisory Committee, *www.fasb.org*.

[8] FASB, Investor Task Force, *www.fasb.org*.

[9] John W. White, SEC Director, Division of Corporate Finance, "Testimony Concerning Transparency in Accounting, Proposed Changes to Accounting for Off-Balance Sheet Entities" Before the Subcommittee on, Insurance, and Investment Committee on Banking, Housing and Urban Affairs, United States Senate, September 18, 2008, *www.sec.gov/news/testimony/2008/ts091808jww-jlk.htm*

[10] SEC Press Release, "Congressionally-Mandated Study Says Improve, Do Not Suspend, Fair Value Accounting Standards," December 30, 2008, *www.sec.gov/news/press/2008/2008-307.htm.*

[11] CFA Institute Centre for Financial Market Integrity Press Release, "Fair Value Being Used as a Scapegoat for Bad Decisions, Lack of Compliance," March 17, 2008, *www.cfainstitute.org/about/press/release/Pages/03172008_16466.asp.x*.

is to "protect investors, provide for efficient markets, and to facilitate capital formation."[12] The FASB's mission is "to establish and improve standards of financial accounting and reporting that foster financial reporting by nongovernmental entities that provides decision-useful information to investors and other users of financial reports."[13] The SEC and the FASB have renewed their efforts to ensure greater transparency in financial reporting and its relevance to investors since the financial crisis began and are likely to continue to do so for the foreseeable future.

24.3 HISTORY AND EVOLUTION OF FAIR VALUE

The FASB's Accounting Standards Codification is the single, authoritative source for U.S. GAAP today. In 2009, ASC 820 superseded the original FASB accounting standard SFAS No. 157, which was issued in 2006. In addition, any FASB Staff Positions that amended SFAS No. 157 have also been superseded by ASC 820. FASB ASUs are included in the Codification once they reach their effective date. Those that have not reached their effective date are presented in separate "pending content" sections, adjacent to the subtopic they will replace. ASU 2011-04, *Amendments to Achieve Common Fair Value Measurement and Disclosure Requirements in U.S. GAAP and IFRS,* is effective for all entities with reporting periods beginning after December 15, 2011. The fair value measurement and disclosure requirements contained in ASU 2011-04 have been included in this chapter prospectively.

Fair value accounting is not a new requirement in financial reporting. Fair value has been a standard of measurement in financial reporting for decades. The FASB has issued dozens statements that use fair value as the measurement of value. The concept of value contained in these statements is from a market perspective, not from the perspective of the reporting entity. Therefore, measuring fair value requires financial statement preparers to use judgment and to make assumptions consistent with those made by other market participants. The FASB has also issued a few statements with "fair value–like" measurement standards, such as FASB ASC 718, *Compensation—Stock Compensation.* The main difference between these two measurement standards is that the fair value–like measurement standard does not incorporate an exit price assumption and fair value does. The assumptions underlying the fair value measurement framework of ASC 820 are covered in Section 24.4 of this chapter.

As originally issued in September 2006, SFAS No. 157 (now ASC 820) clarified the concepts related to the measurement of fair value and provided further implementation guidance.[14] According to the FASB, the reason for issuing SFAS No. 157 was to define fair value, establish a framework for measuring fair value, and expand disclosure about fair value measurements.[15] SFAS No. 157 did not introduce any new accounting requirements. Instead, it applied to all existing accounting statements that require assets or liabilities to be presented or disclosed in financial statements at fair value. As originally promulgated, the FASB intended SFAS No. 157 to provide one uniform statement under which the concept of fair value would be more fully explained.

When it was originally issued, SFAS No. 157 became a source of controversy in the United States as soon as it was issued. The banking industry was particularly vocal in its objections to mark-to-market accounting. Many criticized its application to liabilities and preparers felt they needed more guidance to apply the Statement to nonfinancial assets and liabilities. In response to pressures from financial statement preparers and other constituents, the FASB announced that it would delay implementation for nonfinancial assets and liabilities for one year. The announcement came a few days before the statement's original scheduled implementation date. The reason cited by the FASB for the partial implementation was "to allow the Board and constituents additional

[12] Luis A. Aguilar, SEC Commissioner, "Increasing Accountability and Transparency to Investors," Remarks at The SEC Speaks in 2009, February 6, *www.sec.gov/news/speech/2009/spch020609laa.htm*

[13] FASB, "Facts about FASB," *www.fasb.org/facts/index.shtml*

[14] The statement as originally promulgated refers to its historical context.

[15] FASB, Statement of Financial Accounting Standards No.157, *Fair Value Measurements,* paragraph 1.

time to consider the effect of various implementation issues that have arisen, or that may arise, from the application of Statement 157."[16]

Even the partial implementation did not allay all of the controversy. Some critics of fair value accounting claimed that the credit crisis that began in 2008 was exacerbated by financial institutions' implementation of SFAS No. 157. The Statement became fully effective for fiscal years beginning after November 15, 2008, for all items, including financial and nonfinancial assets and liabilities required under existing statements to be measured at fair value.

In order to better understand fair value measurement, this section covers the history and evolution of fair value measurement in financial reporting. It begins with a historical look back at the development of fair value concepts. Then it covers some of the more important milestones related to the development of fair value for financial instruments and fair value measurement for nonfinancial assets and liabilities. The economic crisis shaped fair value measurement and led to the refinement of several accounting standards and concepts as regulators and standards setters responded to the crisis. Convergence of U.S. GAAP and IAS has also shaped fair value measurement concepts. Finally, this section ends by discussing some trends that are likely to influence the future of fair value measurement.

(a) DEVELOPMENT OF FAIR VALUE CONCEPTS. The concept of fair value has been evolving for over a century. In an 1898 U.S. Supreme Court case about railroad rate regulation, *Smyth v. Ames,* the Court referred to the term *fair value* by saying

> In order to ascertain that value, the original cost of constructions, the amount expended in permanent improvements, the amount and market value of its stocks and bonds, the present as compared to the original cost of construction, the probable earning capacity of the property under particular rates prescribed by statute, and the sum required to meet operating expenses, are all matters for consideration, and are to be given such weight as may be just and right in each case. We do not say that there may not be other matters to be regarded in estimating the value of the property.[17]

This reference to fair value alludes to several fair value measurement concepts that are currently in use, such as a cost approach, a market approach, economic value, and the application of judgment to weigh the various indications of value.

The FASB initially considered adopting the definition of *fair market value* and using it to describe fair value in financial reporting. However, the FASB ultimately decided on a unique definition for *fair value;* therefore, the terms *fair value* and *fair market value* are not interchangeable. Fair market value is defined in the *International Glossary of Business Valuation Terms* as

> the price, expressed in terms of cash equivalents, at which property would change hands between a hypothetical willing and able buyer and a hypothetical willing and able seller, acting at arm's length in an open and unrestricted market, when neither is under compulsion to buy or sell and when both have reasonable knowledge of the relevant facts.[18]

Fair market value is the standard of value in all federal and state tax matters. It is often used to value ownership interests in entities, which is consistent with its transaction-based definition. The term *fair market value* has a significant body of interpretive case law, which is the primary reason the FASB decided to adopt a different standard of value with a specific definition for financial reporting.[19]

---

[16] FASB Staff Position (FSP) 157-2, *Effective Date of FASB Statement No. 157,* February 12, 2008, paragraph 1, *www.fasb.org/pdf/aop_FSP_FAS157-2.pdf*

[17] "Book Review: *What Is Fair Value* by Harleigh H. Hartman," *Weekly Review* 3, no. 78 (July–December 1920): 448, digitized at *www/books.Google.com.*

[18] Business Valuation Resources, *International Glossary of Business Valuation Terms 2001, www.bvresources.com/FreeDownloads/IntGlossaryBVTerms2001.pdf*.

[19] Jay E. Fishman, Shannon P. Pratt, and William J. Morrison, *Standards of Value: Theory and Applications* (Hoboken, NJ: John Wiley & Sons, 2007), pp. 21–23.

Fair value is the standard for financial reporting purposes. *Fair value* is defined in the *FASB Master Glossary* as

> the price that would be received to sell an asset or paid to transfer a liability in an orderly transaction between market participants at the measurement date.[20]

While *fair market value* has a rich history with respect to legal and tax matters, the application of fair value to financial reporting is a relatively new development. This section looks at the development of fair value concepts in financial accounting standards from a historical perspective.

One of the first accounting statements requiring the use of fair value in financial reporting was Accounting Principles Board (APB) No. 18, *The Equity Method of Accounting for Investments in Common Stock,* which was issued in 1971. APB No. 18 introduced the equity method of accounting for investments in unconsolidated subsidiaries. Under APB No. 18, a loss would be recognized when the investment's fair value declined below its carrying value and the loss was considered to be other than temporary.[21]

APB No. 29, *Accounting for Nonmonetary Transactions,* introduced in 1973, outlined ways to measure the fair value of nonmonetary transactions. It indicates that the fair value of a nonmonetary transaction should be determined by referring to cash transactions for the same or similar assets, quoted market prices, independent appraisals, and the estimated fair value of the asset or service received. Any determination of fair value using these methods would also have to consider whether the estimated value would be realized.[22]

In 1977, SFAS No. 15, *Accounting by Debtors and Creditors for Troubled Debt Restructurings,* established some important fair value concepts. SFAS No. 15 specifies that fair value is the amount determined through a current sale between a willing buyer and a willing seller, other than in a forced or liquidation sale. It also states:

> Fair value of assets shall be measured by their market value if an active market for them exists. If no active market exists for the assets transferred but exists for similar assets, the selling prices in that market may be helpful in estimating the fair value of the assets transferred. If no market price is available, a forecast of expected cash flows may aid in estimating the fair value of assets transferred, provided the expected cash flows are discounted at a rate commensurate with the risk involved.[23]

SFAS No. 15 established several important criteria for using a market approach and established the use of a discounted cash flow method for measuring fair value. These important concepts persist in financial reporting today.

(b) FAIR VALUE OF FINANCIAL INSTRUMENTS. The FASB has issued several accounting standards that apply to financial instruments including derivatives. One of the first was SFAS No. 2, *Accounting for Certain Marketable Securities.* Issued in 1975, SFAS No. 2 required that marketable securities be carried at the lower of cost or market value. It also established the practice of recording changes in the market value of an entity's noncurrent asset portfolio in a separate component of equity. Therefore, it permitted unrealized losses to bypass the income statement.

---

[20] *FASB Master Glossary, https://asc.fasb.org/glossary&nav_type=left_nav&analyticsAssetName=_left_nav_masterglossary*

[21] Current Text Accounting Standards as of June 1, 1997, General Standards, Section I82.109h, Applying the Equity Method, p. 27719

[22] Current Text Accounting Standards as of June 1, 1997, General Standards, Section N35.111, Nonmonetary Transactions, p. 31985.

[23] SFAS No. 15, *Accounting for Debtors and Creditors for Troubled Debt Restructurings,* June 1977, paragraph 13.

In 1991, SFAS No. 107, *Disclosures About Fair Value in Financial Instruments,* required the fair value disclosure of an entity's financial instruments. The requirement included all financial assets and liabilities, whether recorded or unrecorded in the financial statements.[24]

SFAS No. 115, *Accounting for Certain Investments in Debt and Equity Securities,* was introduced in 1993. It established three categories of investment securities; held-to-maturity debt securities, trading securities and available-for-sale securities. SFAS No. 115 also requires fair value as the standard of measurement for debt and equity securities classified as either trading or available-for-sale. Unrealized changes in the fair value of trading securities are recognized in earnings, while the unrealized changes in the fair value of available-for-sale securities are excluded from earnings and reported in a separate component of shareholders equity.[25]

In 1994, the FASB issued SFAS No. 119, *Disclosure About Derivative Financial Instruments and Fair Value of Financial Instruments.* It required entities that hold or issue derivative financial instruments for trading purposes to disclose the average fair value of those instruments. SFAS No. 119 also required that fair value information be presented without combining, aggregating, or netting the fair value of derivative financial instruments with the fair value of nonderivative financial instruments.[26]

In 2000, the FASB introduced FAS No. 133, *Accounting for Derivative Instruments and Hedging Activities,* which required fair value as the measurement for derivative securities. The accounting treatment for changes in the fair value of derivative instruments depends on their classification as a fair value hedge, a cash flow hedge, a foreign currency hedge, or a derivative instrument not designated as a hedging instrument.[27]

With the issuance of SFAS No. 159, *The Fair Value Option for Financial Assets and Financial Liabilities* in 2007, the FASB expanded fair value measurements for financial instruments, which was consistent with the Board's long-term accounting measurement objectives for financial instruments. The FASB noted in the implementation guidance for SFAS No. 159 that the objective of the Statement is to improve financial reporting, "by providing entities with the opportunity to mitigate volatility in reported earnings caused by measuring related assets and liabilities differently without having to apply complex hedge accounting provisions."[28]

SFAS No. 159 permits entities to choose whether to measure financial assets and liabilities at fair value or whether to retain their current basis of measurement; therefore the fair value option is an election. It can be applied on an instrument-by-instrument basis, and there is no requirement to apply it to all financial assets or liabilities. Once an election is made to measure an instrument at its fair value under SFAS No. 159, the election is irrevocable (unless a new election date occurs). The financial instruments covered by the Statement are fairly broad. The majority of entities electing the fair value option under SFAS No. 159 are in the financial services industry, primarily commercial and investment banks.

A business entity electing the fair value option under SFAS No. 159 is required to report unrealized gains and losses resulting from changes in fair value in earnings at each subsequent reporting date. SFAS No. 159 was superseded by FASB ASC 825 which is covered in more detail in Section 24.4 of this chapter.

(c) FAIR VALUE MEASUREMENT FOR NONFINANCIAL ASSETS AND LIABILITIES. During the technology boom in the late 1990s brought on by the initial commercialization of the Internet, the FASB began a project to update APB Opinion No. 16, *Business Combinations.* The FASB observed that during the 1990s, much of the economic value in mergers and acquisitions was driven by

---

[24] FASB, Summary of Statement No. 107, *www.fasb.org/summary/stsum107.shtml.*

[25] FASB, Summary of Statement No. 115, *www.fasb.org/summary/stsum115.shtml.*

[26] FASB, Summary of Statement No. 119, *www.fasb.org/summary/stsum119..shtml.*

[27] FASB, Summary of Statement No. 133, *www.fasb.org/summary/stsum133.shtml.*

[28] SFAS No. 159, *The Fair Value Option for Financial Assets and Financial Liabilities—Including an Amendment of FASB Statement No. 115,* February 2007, paragraph 1.

technology and other intangible assets owned by the acquired company. Yet these valuable assets were not being fairly presented in the financial statements because under APB No. 16, much of the value of the acquired entity was reported on the balance sheet as goodwill. And under accounting rules at that time, goodwill could be amortized for up to 40 years.

The FASB concluded that purchase price allocation to acquired assets and liabilities under APB No. 16 did not fairly represent the economic substance of business combinations, and that financial statements were not being fairly presented. The Board also concluded that companies had too much leeway in reporting the value of acquired intangible assets. As a result, the FASB made sweeping changes to the accounting standards for business combinations.

On June 29, 2001, the FASB issued SFAS No. 141, *Business Combinations,* which was superseded by SFAS No. 141 (Revised), *Business Combinations* (SFAS No. 141(R)) about six years later as a result of a joint FASB/IASB project. One of the first steps in the FASB and IASB project to converge U.S. GAAP with international accounting standards was to harmonize the accounting standards for business combinations; therefore, the FASB revised SFAS No. 141. The Boards issued common Exposure Drafts, which became SFAS No. 141(R) and IFRS No. 3, *Business Combinations.* The accounting standard for business combinations is now codified in FASB ASC 805, *Business Combinations.*

When it was originally issued, SFAS No. 141(R) introduced the acquisition method, which is based on determining the fair value of all acquired assets and liabilities. The fair values of identifiable acquired assets and liabilities in total may or may not equal the purchase price. When the fair value of all identifiable acquired assets and liabilities is less than the purchase price, the difference represents goodwill. If the fair value of all acquired assets and liabilities is more than the purchase price, a bargain purchase would be indicated.

SFAS No. 141(R) also contained the requirements for the initial recognition of goodwill and other intangible assets in business combinations. The Statement also indicated that SFAS No. 142, *Goodwill and Other Intangible Assets* provides guidance for the subsequent testing of goodwill for impairment and that SFAS No. 144, *Testing for Impairment of Long-Lived Assets,* provides guidance for the subsequent impairment testing for intangible assets subject to amortization. Accounting standards for the subsequent treatment of goodwill and other intangible assets recognized in a business combination are currently codified in ASC 350, *Intangibles—Goodwill and Other,* and ASC 360, *Property, Plant and Equipment.*

In 2001, the FASB issued SFAS No. 142, which provided guidance on determining whether goodwill recorded in a business combination became impaired in subsequent years and it set forth the requirements for the impairment testing. Under SFAS No. 142, goodwill is tested for impairment annually using a two-step test. The first step is to estimate the fair value of the entity or reporting unit by comparing the fair value to its carrying value (book value). If the fair value is *greater* than book value, goodwill is not impaired. If the fair value is *less* than the carrying value, goodwill may be impaired, and a second step is required.

The second step is to estimate the fair values of all of the assets and liabilities of the entity or reporting unit as of the testing date, including the implied fair value of goodwill. This step is similar to the allocation of purchase price under SFAS No. 141(R). The implied fair value of goodwill is then compared to the carrying value of the goodwill. If the fair value of goodwill is less than the carrying value of goodwill, it is considered to be impaired, and the difference must be written off.

The application of fair value measurements to nonfinancial assets and liabilities is most often seen in practice in SFAS No. 141(R) and SFAS No. 142.

(d) FAIR VALUE MEASUREMENT AND THE ECONOMIC CRISIS. Beginning in the latter part of 2006, an increase in the general level of interest rates caused a sharp rise in the delinquency and default rates by subprime rate mortgage borrowers. Most of the underlying subprime mortgages were based on adjustable rates. As interest rose, many borrowers were unable to make the higher interest payments on their mortgages. As a result, the default rates in subprime mortgages increased dramatically.

The rise in interest rates also contributed significantly to a decline in the overall housing market, which compounded the impact of the defaults caused by limited options for sale of the underlying real estate by the defaulter.

As an increasing number of subprime mortgage borrowers began to default, many financial institutions and investment banks holding mortgage-backed securities based on subprime mortgages began to experience uncertainty about the reliability of cash flows from these investments, which further eroded their perceived value. As the level of defaults increased, rating agencies significantly downgraded these subprime mortgage securities. The downgrades caused other investors and lenders to refrain from investing in mortgage-backed securities. The lack of a secondary market created a "liquidity crisis," which began to spread throughout the financial markets. The risk of defaults in the underlying mortgages caused the secondary markets for securitized mortgages to freeze, which impacted a wide range of commercial and investment banks that held these securities.

(i) Mark-to-Market Accounting. At the center of this liquidity crisis was an accounting issue: How should the holders of mortgage securities measure the value of these debt securities for financial reporting? To complicate matters, many of the entities had already elected the fair value option provided by SFAS No. 159, which permitted entities to measure most financial assets and liabilities at their respective fair values in fiscal years beginning after November 15, 2007. The fair value option incorporates the definition of fair value as presented in SFAS No. 157, which includes features such as the fair value hierarchy, market participant assumptions, and the preference for observable inputs.

Among the accounting questions at the center of the financial crisis were these two: What is the fair value of the securitized subprime mortgages that financial institutions and other entities should report on their balance sheet? When the market is considered distressed, what is the appropriate level for disclosure in the fair value hierarchy?

Critics of fair value measurement believed that the credit crisis was made much greater by the mark-to-market accounting of financial institutions that had invested in the securitized subprime debt. The criticism of fair value accounting was based on an apparent difference between the market value of certain securities in distressed markets and the value indicated by holding the securities to maturity. The central issue was whether the fair value of these securities would be the depressed price indicated by the market or the value indicated by the securities' expected future cash flows discounted to the present at a risk-adjusted rate of return.

Many called for suspension or revision of SFAS No. 157 during the economic crisis. However, the Center for Audit Quality reaffirmed its position on the relevance of fair value measurements, saying:

> Suspending fair value accounting during these challenging economic times would deprive investors of critical financial information when it is needed most. Investors have a right to know the current value of an investment, even if the investment is falling short of past or future expectations.[29]

(ii) Application of Fair Value Accounting in Illiquid Market. In response to widespread public criticism of mark-to-market accounting, the SEC Office of the Chief Accountant and FASB Staff released a statement entitled "Clarifications on Fair Value Accounting" on September 30, 2008.[30] The statement responded to several questions raised by the credit crisis.

> Can management's internal assumptions (e.g., expected cash flows) be used to measure fair value when relevant market evidence does not exist?

[29] "Joint Statement of the Center for Audit Quality, the Council of Institutional Investors and the CFA Institute Opposing Suspension of Mark-to-Market Accounting," October 1, 2008.

[30] "SEC Office of the Chief Accountant and FASB Staff Clarifications on Fair Value Accounting, 2008-234," September 30, 2008.

Yes. When an active market for a security does not exist, the use of management estimates that incorporate current market participant expectations of future cash flows, and include appropriate risk premiums, is acceptable.

Are transactions that are determined to be disorderly representative of fair value? When is a distressed (disorderly) sale indicative of fair value?

The results of disorderly transactions are not determinative when measuring fair value. The concept of a fair value measurement assumes an orderly transaction between market participants. An orderly transaction is one that involves market participants that are willing to transact and allows for adequate exposure to the market. Distressed or forced liquidation sales are not orderly transactions, and thus the fact that a transaction is distressed or forced should be considered when weighing the available evidence. Determining whether a particular transaction is forced or disorderly requires judgment.

Can transactions in an inactive market affect fair value measurements?

Yes. A quoted market price in an active market for the identical asset is most representative of fair value and thus is required to be used (generally without adjustment). Transactions in inactive markets may be inputs when measuring fair value, but would likely not be determinative.

On October 10, 2008, the FASB followed the SEC's lead and issued FASB Staff Position 157-3, *Determining the Fair Value of a Financial Asset When the Market for That Asset Is Not Active,* which further clarified assumptions to be used in measuring fair value in circumstances where there may not be a market price. FSP157-3 reinforced the fair value measurement concepts introduced by SFAS No. 157 and reinforced the guidance contained in the SEC's and FASB's joint statement clarifying fair value accounting. Its main points include:

- Determining fair value in a dislocated market depends on the facts and circumstances and may require the use of significant judgment about whether individual transactions are forced liquidations or distressed sales.
- The use of the reporting entity's own assumptions about future cash flows and appropriately risk-adjusted discount rates is acceptable when relevant observable inputs are not available.
- Broker (or pricing service) quotes may be an appropriate input when measuring fair value but are not necessarily determinative if an active market does not exist for the financial assets.[31]

FSP 157-3 was superseded approximately six months later by FSP 157-4, *Determining Fair Value When the Volume and Level of Activity for the Asset or Liability Have Significantly Decreased and Identifying Transactions That Are Not Orderly.*

(iii) SEC Study on Mark-to-Market Accounting. The Emergency Stabilization Act of 2008 required the SEC to conduct a study on "mark-to-market" accounting and to focus on the provisions of SFAS No. 157 that apply to financial institutions. Section 133 of the Act called for a study that would specifically consider:

- The effects of fair value accounting standards on a financial institution's balance sheet
- The impacts of fair value accounting on bank failures in 2008
- The impact of fair value standards on the quality of financial information available to investors
- The process used by the FASB in developing accounting standards
- The advisability and feasibility of modifications to fair value standards
- Alternative accounting standards to those provided in SFAS No. 157

On December 30, 2008, the SEC's Office of the Chief Accountant and Division of Corporate Finance delivered a report to Congress recommending against the suspension of fair value

[31] FSP 157-3, par. 9.

accounting standards. Among key findings, the report notes that investors generally believe fair value accounting increases financial reporting transparency and facilitates better decision making. The report also observes that fair value accounting did not appear to play a meaningful role in the bank failures that occurred in 2008. Rather the report indicated that bank failures in the United States appeared to be the result to growing credit losses, concerns about asset quality, and, in certain cases, eroding lender and investor confidence.[32]

The SEC study on mark-to-market accounting suggested that "additional measures should be taken to improve the application and practice related to existing fair value requirements." The SEC study also recommended that "fair value requirements should be improved through development of application and best practices guidance for determining fair value in illiquid or inactive markets."[33]

(iv) The FASB's Credit Crisis Projects. The FASB added a new project to its agenda in February 2009, in response to the recommendations contained in the SEC study on mark-to-market accounting and based on input from the FASB's Valuation Resource Group. The project was intended to improve the application guidance used to determine fair values and disclosures for fair value estimates. This project initiative evolved into what the FASB refers to as the Credit Crisis Projects, which include:

FSP 157-4 provided additional guidance for measuring fair value in turbulent markets. It was issued in April 2009 in an expedited standards-setting process and in response to pressure from the SEC. The guidance provided by this FASB Staff Position has been incorporated into ASC 820 and is covered in more detail in Section 24.4 of this chapter.

FSP FAS 115-2 and FAS 124-2, *Recognition and Presentation of Other-Than-Temporary Impairments,* provided criteria that indicate when a debt security is permanently impaired and contained new provisions for the recognition of the impairment. This expedited standard was issued simultaneously with FSP 157-4 in April 2009. Current guidance is available at FASB ASC 320, *Investments—Debt and Equity Securities* at 320-10-35-17 to 30.

FSP FAS 107-1 and APB 28-1, *Interim Disclosures about Fair Value of Financial Instruments,* improved the transparency and quality of fair value disclosures and introduced new requirements for disclosures in interim financial statements. This expedited Standard was also issued in April 2009 but has been superseded. Current guidance is available at FASB ASC 320 in the Disclosure Subtopic at 320-10-50.

ASU 2009-05, *Measuring Liabilities at Fair Value,* was originally proposed as FSP 157-c and then as FSP 157-f. This credit crisis issue received a significant amount of attention and public comment. It addresses one of the more contentious aspects of fair value measurement, its application to liabilities. The requirements of ASU 2009-05 have been incorporated into ASC 820 and are discussed in Section 24.4 of this chapter.

ASU 2009-12, *Investments in Certain Entities that Calculate Net Asset Value per Share (or Its Equivalent),* is now part of ASC 820; however, it is not within the scope of this chapter.

ASU 2010-06, *Improving Fair Value Measurements Disclosures,* was issued to improve transparency and to provide more information about the inputs to fair value measurements. The improvements have been incorporated into the disclosures requirements of ASC 820 and are covered further in Section 24.4.

A final credit crisis project with relevance to fair value measurement was *Recoveries of Other-Than-Temporary Impairments (Reversals).* The FASB decided to consider whether to allow an entity to recover, through earnings, a previously recognized other-than-temporary impairment loss on certain financial instruments. The Board decided to consider this topic through its work on the joint FASB/IASB project *Financial Instruments: Improvement to Recognition and Measurement,* which is currently under way.[34]

---

[32] "Congressionally-Mandated Study Says Improve, Do Not Suspend, Fair Value Accounting," *www.sec.gov/news/press/2008/2008-307.htm*

[33] SEC. "Report and Recommendations Pursuant to Section 133 of the Emergency Economic Stabilization Act of 2008: Study on Mark-to-Market Accounting," December 30, 2008.

[34] FASB Project Update, "Recoveries of Other Than Temporary Impairments (Reversals)," *www.fasb.org/otti_reversals.shtml*

(e) CONVERGENCE OF FAIR VALUE MEASUREMENT. In a recent milestone, the FASB and IASB completed their joint project on fair value measurement. The FASB issued ASU 2011-04 and the IASB issued IFRS 13, *Fair Value Measurement,* in an effort to harmonize the concepts surrounding the measurement of fair value and align disclosure requirements. It is important to note that the new guidance does not extend the use of fair value measurement either in the United States or internationally. Instead, it improves the guidance on how fair value should be measured and disclosed in situations where it is already required or permitted in existing accounting pronouncements.[35]

ASU 2011-04 provides clarifications relating to the concepts of highest and best use, the measurement of an entity's equity interest, and qualitative disclosures for unobservable inputs. It also changes the fair value measurement principles for financial instruments managed within a portfolio and for the application of premiums and discounts in the fair value of a reporting unit. In addition, ASU 2011-04 requires additional disclosures for Level 3 measurements, among other disclosures.[36]

IFRS 13 adopted several important fair value measurement concepts from SFAS No. 157, including an exit price assumption, the "principal market" focus, and the exclusion of blockage discounts. In addition, IFRS 13 includes U.S. GAAP fair market value concepts included in subsequent FASB fair value measurement guidance for inactive markets and for measuring liabilities at fair value.[37]

Perhaps the most interesting change brought about by convergence of fair value measurement and the issuance of ASU 2011-04 is that some disclosures have been eliminated for nonpublic companies.[38] The FASB made these changes in response to constituent feedback and in an effort to reduce the reporting burden for private companies. The converged updates to FASB ASC 820 are covered prospectively in Section 24.4.

(f) FUTURE OF FAIR VALUE MEASUREMENT. Convergence of U.S. GAAP with international standards is likely to be approved by the SEC at the end of 2011, and financial reporting standards are likely to continue their parallel courses of harmonized development. Although convergence of fair value measurements has been largely completed, there likely will be future clarifications and harmonization of the few remaining differences.

In contrast, disclosures about fair value measurement likely will take two divergent paths. While there has been a consistent trend toward more disclosure for public companies, which is likely to continue, the same cannot be said for nonpublic companies. In fact, IFRS contain a separate set of reporting Standards for private entities entitled *International Financial Reporting Standards for Small to Medium-sized Entities (IFRS for SMEs).* The self-contained 230-page set of Standards is designed to reduce the financial reporting burden for nonpublic companies. The FASB has decided to follow the IASB's lead and established a Blue Ribbon Panel to address how accounting Standards can best meet the needs of private company financial statement users in the United States.

The panel concluded that the current accounting standards setting system in the United States is deficient in two significant ways.

---

[35] FASB and IASB News Release, "IASB and FASB Issue Common Fair Value Measurement and Disclosure Requirements," May 12, 2011, *www.fasb.org/cs/ContentServer?site=FASB&c=FASBContent_C&pagename=FASB%2FFASBContent_C%2FNewsPage&cid=1176158544944*

[36] FASB Accounting Standard Update No. 2011-04, *Fair Value Measurement* (Topic 820), *Amendments to Achieve Common Fair Value Measurement and Disclosure Requirements in U.S. GAAP and IFRSs,* May 2011, pp. 1–6.

[37] IFRS Project Summary and Feedback Statement, IFRS 13, *Fair Value Measurement,* May 2011, pp. 16–26, *www.ifrs.org/NR/rdonlyres/04E9F096-B1F8-410A-B1E9-2E61003BADFA/0/FairValueMeasurementFeedbackstatement_May2011.pdf*

[38] Podcast:FASB Board Member Russ Golden discusses FASB Accounting Standards Update No. 2011-04: *Fair Value Measurement (Topic 820): Amendments to Achieve Common Fair Value Measurement and Disclosure Requirements in U.S. GAAP and* IFRSs, May 2011, *www.fasb.org/cs/ContentServer?site=FASB&c=Page&pagename=FASB%2FPage%2FSectionPage&cid=1176156828276*

1. Standard setters do not understand decision-useful information from the perspective of private company financial statements users.
2. Standard setters have not weighed the costs and benefits of GAAP for private company financial reporting.

These shortcomings have led to Standards that lack relevance for many users and to Standards with a level of complexity that is a burden for private companies and their certified public accountant practitioners. Fair value measurement and goodwill impairment are two of the current accounting Standards cited by the report as contributing to the problem.

The Blue Ribbon Panel's report considered alternative models and structures for developing accounting standards for private companies. The panel considered a model similar to the IASB's model that has separate International Financial Reporting Standards for Small to Medium-sized Entities (IFRS for SMEs) but rejected a ground-up creation of separate, stand-alone statements for private companies. Instead, the panel decided on and recommended a U.S. GAAP model with exceptions and modifications that respond to the needs of the private company sector. In addition, the panel recommended that a new, separate accounting standards board be created to determine exceptions and modifications to U.S. GAAP.

In an effort to develop pertinent standards that meet constituent needs, the FASB considered the panel's findings in its latest fair value measurement and disclosure guidance in ASU 2011-04 and eliminated some disclosures for private companies. The FASB has also responded to the Blue Ribbon Panel's report, which indicated that constituents have a growing dissatisfaction about the cost of performing goodwill impairment testing. The FASB has proposed accounting Standards changes for goodwill impairment testing that introduce a qualitative "more likely than not" impairment test. If events and circumstances indicate that it is more likely than not that fair value exceeds carrying value, no further testing is required.

24.4 FAIR VALUE MEASUREMENTS STANDARDS AND CONCEPTS

FASB ASC 820, as amended and updated by ASU 2011-04, is the latest FASB guidance on measuring fair value whenever fair value accounting is required or permitted in other accounting standards. The fair value measurement and disclosure requirements amendments contained in ASU 2011-04 are effective for all entities with reporting periods beginning after December 15, 2011. The amended guidance in ASC 820 encompasses all the fair value credit crisis projects that the FASB undertook in the wake of the financial crisis. It encompasses the FASB and the IASB's converged guidance for measuring fair value. The FASB has completed all fair value projects on its project list; therefore, it is unlikely that there will be any significant changes to ASC 820 in the foreseeable future.

This section provides an overview of fair value measurement in U.S. GAAP as provided in ASC 820 and amended for convergence by ASU 2011-04. The overview provides a foundation for understanding the application of fair value measurement in financial reporting and the relevant fair value measurement audit standards in the next section. This section also briefly covers some of the more important fair value option information in FASB ASC 825. ASC references are provided in parentheses throughout this section to help readers locate the FASB's authoritative guidance on fair value measurement.

(a) FASB ASC 820, *FAIR VALUE MEASUREMENTS AND DISCLOSURES*. ASC 820 explains how to measure fair value when it is required or permitted in other ASC topics. It does not establish any new requirements for fair value to be used in financial reporting. ASC 820 states that the objective of a fair value measurement is "to estimate the price at which an orderly transaction to sell the asset or to transfer the liability would take place between market participants at the measurement date under current market conditions." The FASB emphasizes that fair value is a market-based measurement regardless of whether observable market-based transaction information is available. When observable market prices are not available, fair value is measured using a valuation technique that maximizes the use of observable inputs. Fair value pricing assumptions are from the perspective of market participants who are selling an asset or transferring a liability; therefore, the price is assumed to be an exit price. ASC 820 provides a definition of fair value, introduces the fair value framework, and sets out fair value measurement disclosure requirements (ASC 820-10-05-1).

(b) DEFINITION OF *FAIR VALUE MEASUREMENTS AND DISCLOSURES*. According to the FASB's *Master Glossary* (the Glossary), fair value is "the price that would be received to sell an asset or paid to transfer a liability in an orderly transaction between market participants at the measurement date." This definition of fair value is to be applied in all other accounting standards that call for measurement or disclosure at fair value.

The FASB definition of fair value introduced by ASC 820 includes additional concepts, such as the principal or most advantageous market and the concept of market participants, which are unique to fair value measurement for financial reporting.

The objective of a fair value measurement is to estimate a transaction price for the subject asset, liability, or equity instrument. The transaction price is from the perspective of a market participant that owns the asset or owes the liability; therefore, it is considered an exit price. The transaction price must be the result of an orderly transaction between market participants, and it must be the result of current market conditions prevailing at the measurement date.

Market information from observable market transactions may or may not exist for the subject asset or liability. Regardless of the availability of market information, fair value is considered a market-based measurement, not an entity-specific measurement. Therefore, the entity's intent to hold the asset or sell the liability is irrelevant.

If an observable market price is not available for an identical asset or liability, another valuation technique can be used. The goal would be to measure fair value using the same assumptions that a market participant would use to price the asset or liability, including the market participant's assessment of risk. Any valuation technique should maximize the use of observable inputs and minimize the use of unobservable inputs (ASC 820-10-05-1B and 1C).

(c) TOPIC ASC 820, SCOPE AND SCOPE EXCEPTIONS. ASC 820 applies to the measurement of fair value whenever it is required or permitted by another Topic. In some situations, it may not be practical to measure fair value. When it is not practicable to measure the fair value of a financial instrument, the financial instrument is exempt from the requirement. ASC 820 also permits practicability exceptions to fair value measurements for nonmonetary assets, asset retirement obligations, restructuring obligations, and participation rights when their fair value cannot be reasonably determined. As a practical expedient, the fair value of a guarantee can be measured using its transaction (entry) price. The Topic also provides an exception for certain not-for-profit entity transactions when fair value cannot be measured with sufficient reliability (ASC 820-10-15-3).

(d) INITIAL MEASUREMENT. Fair value measurement is based on an exit price assumption. When an entity enters into a transaction to purchase an asset or assume a liability, the price is an entry price. There are some important distinctions between entry prices and exit prices. Sometimes a business may pay more for an asset because it can utilize that asset in a way other businesses cannot. For example, when a business acquires proprietary technology that it can use to enhance its own product line, the proprietary technology may be worth more to the acquirer than to other market participants, and the acquisition price may reflect a potential synergistic use by the acquirer. Subsequently, the entity may not be able to sell the proprietary technology at the same price it paid to acquire the technology; therefore, the exit price would not equal the entry price.

In many cases, the transaction price will equal the exit price and, therefore, will represent the fair value of the asset or liability at initial recognition. In determining whether a transaction price represents the fair value of the asset or liability at initial recognition, the reporting entity must consider factors specific to the transaction and to the asset or liability. Situations where the transaction price may not equal the fair value include forced sales, transactions between related parties, circumstances where transactions costs are included as part of the price, and transactions that take place outside the principal or most advantageous market. When the initial price is required or permitted to be measured at fair value, and when the fair value does not equal the transaction price, a gain or loss is recognized in earnings (ASC 820-10-30-2, 3, and 6).

(e) FAIR VALUE FRAMEWORK. The fair value framework is presented in ASC 820-10-35, under a subtopic entitled *Subsequent Measurement.* The Subtopic provides guidance for the fair value measurement of assets and liabilities in periods after initial measurement. However, the fair value framework also applies to the initial measurement as well as to any subsequent measurement of fair value (ASC 820-10-35-1).

The first section of the fair value framework provides further guidance and clarification about the elements of the fair value definition, including the asset or liability, the transaction, market participants, the price, and application to nonfinancial assets and to liabilities and equity. The fair value framework also covers valuation techniques, inputs to the valuation techniques, and the fair value hierarchy (ASC 820-10-35-2).

(i) Asset or Liability. A fair value measurement under ASC 820 is for a particular asset or liability. The reason provided by the FASB is that assets and liabilities are a primary subject of accounting measurement.[39] The definition of *fair value* also applies to interests that are considered part of the invested capital of the enterprise. Invested capital, or enterprise value, is considered to be shareholder's equity plus interest-bearing debt. Invested capital includes the sources of enterprise financing over the long term.

An example of the application of fair value measurement to individual assets or liabilities is in a business combination, where the assets and liabilities of the acquired entity are measured at individual fair values as of the date of the change of control in the acquisition. An example of the application of fair value measurement to an enterprise value is the fair value measurement of a reporting unit under ASC 350, which is used for testing goodwill for impairment.

When measuring fair value, the characteristics of a particular asset or liability should be considered if a market participant would also consider those characteristics when deciding on a price. The condition and location of the asset and any restrictions on the sale or use of the asset are characteristics that must be considered (ASC 820-10-35-2B).

For example, if an entity owns a share of restricted stock, the restriction is a characteristic of the asset. If the restriction cannot be removed, it would be transferred to other market participants. The fair value of the share would be measured based on the price for an identical, unrestricted share with an adjustment equal to the amount market participants would demand in exchange for accepting the risk associated with the restriction. The amount of the adjustment would depend on the restriction's nature, duration, and impact on market participants (ASC 820-10-55-52).

When considering how restrictions on the use of an asset impact fair value, the key is to determine whether the restriction is specific to the owner or specific to the asset. If a restriction is specific to the owner, it would not be transferred to the market participant. The fair value of the asset would be determined based on its highest and best use, which may be maximized through a transfer to a market participant for use without the restriction. If the restriction stays with the asset, however, the fair value would take the restriction into account (ASC 820-10-55-54).

Another consideration is whether the asset or liability should be measured on a stand-alone basis or in a group of assets or liabilities. The group can be a reporting unit or a business. Whether the fair value measurement should be made on a stand-alone basis or as part of a group depends on the asset or liability's unit of account. According to the Glossary, a unit of account is "the level at which an asset or liability is aggregated or disaggregated in a Topic for recognition purposes." The appropriate unit of account is determined in accordance with the ASC Topic that requires or permits the fair value measurement (ASC 820-10-35-2D).

---

[39] SFAS No. 157, *Fair Value Measurement,* footnote 4.

(ii) Transaction. Fair value measurement assumes the transaction to sell the asset or transfer the liability is an orderly transaction between market participants. It also assumes that the transfer occurs under current market conditions on the measurement date (ASC 820-10-35-3). Under the acquisition method, the fair value of assets acquired and liabilities assumed are measured on the balance sheet at each of their respective values as of the date of change in control in a business combination.

(iii) Principal (or Most Advantageous) Market. One of the assumptions underlying any fair value measurement is that the price is the result of a sale in the principal market, which is defined in the Glossary as "the market with the greatest volume and level of activity for the asset or liability." The principal market is generally presumed to be the same market that the entity usually uses to sell similar assets or transfer similar liabilities, unless there is evidence to the contrary. Because the entity also must have access to the principal market at the measurement date, different entities may have different principal markets. If there is a principal market, the fair value is the price in the principal market, even if there is another market with a better price.

If there is not a principal market for the asset or liability, the fair value measurement is assumed to be the result of a transaction in the most advantageous market. According to the Glossary, the most advantageous market is "the market that maximizes the amount that would be received to sell the asset or minimizes the amount that would be paid to transfer the liability, after taking into account transaction costs and transportation costs." The most advantageous market is also considered from the perspective of the reporting entity.

Two additional clarifications are applicable to the principal (or most advantageous) market assumptions. One is that the reporting entity must be able to access the market in order to measure fair value using a price from that market. That does not mean the entity has to be able to sell the asset or transfer the liability in that market. The second is that there does not have to be an observable market that provides pricing information in order to measure the fair value of an asset or liability. The fair value measurement can be based on an assumed transaction from the perspective of hypothetical market participants (ASC 820-10-35-5 and 6).

(iv) Market Participants. According to the Glossary, market participants are

> buyers and sellers in the principal (or most advantageous) market for the asset or liability that have all the following characteristics:
>
> **a.** They are independent of each other, that is, they are not related parties
> **b.** They are knowledgeable
> **c.** They are able to enter into a transaction for the asset or liability
> **d.** They are willing to enter into a transaction for the asset or liability, that is, they are motivated but not forced or otherwise compelled to do so.

Fair value is based on the assumptions market participants would use to determine the price for an asset or liability. One of those key assumptions is that the market participant is acting in its own best interest. There is no need to identify specific market participants. Instead, the entity should focus on identifying characteristics that distinguish market participants and consider attributes specific to the asset or liability, the principal (or most advantageous) market, and the market participants in that market with whom the reporting entity would likely transact (ASC 820-10-35-9).

(v) Price. *Price* is the key word in the FASB's definition of fair value. It is an exit price based on an orderly transaction in the principal (or most advantageous) market. Price is specific to the measurement date, and it incorporates the current market conditions on that date. Transaction costs cannot be included in the price; however, transportation costs can be included in the measurement. The FASB's decision not to include transaction cost is based on the idea that transaction costs are not part of the asset or liability. Transaction costs are typically unique to the specific transaction and may differ depending on the transaction, not the asset or liability. When location is a characteristic of an asset, however, it is appropriate to include the cost of transportation to the principal (or most advantageous) market in the price (ASC 820-10-35-9A to C).

(vi) Highest and Best Use for Nonfinancial Assets. The Glossary defines the highest and best use for a nonfinancial asset as "[t]he use of a nonfinancial asset by market participants that would maximize the value of the asset or group of assets and liabilities (for example, a business) within which the asset would be used."

Highest and best use is an economic concept that is based on the market participant's ability to generate economic benefits is such a way that it would maximize the value of the asset. The value can be maximized by using the asset on a stand-alone basis, by using it with a group of assets, by using in a business, or by selling it. A sale assumes the highest and best use would be maximized by another market participant.

The highest and best use concept encompasses several assumptions for the underlying asset, including a use that is physically possible, legally permissible, and financially feasible. Therefore, when pricing the asset, market participants would consider the physical characteristics of the asset, any legal restrictions on the use of the asset, and whether the asset would produce the required investment return. Highest and best use is always considered from a market participant's perspective when measuring fair value, even when the entity's use is different. An entity's current use of nonfinancial asset is generally presumed to be its highest and best use, unless there is evidence to the contrary (ASC 820-10-35-10A to C).

An interesting concept recognized by ASC 820 is that a defensive value can be a nonfinancial asset's highest and best use. Defensive value results when acquisitions are made in order to eliminate a competitor or a competing product. The value to the acquirer is the competitive enhancement of its own products and resulting incremental cash flow, not the use of the acquired asset itself. ASC 820 recognizes that value from a defensive acquisition should be measured at the fair value, taking into consideration market participants' highest and best use. Market participants may conclude that the highest and best use would be a defensive use that prevents competitors from gaining access to it. Therefore, defensive value is not inconsistent with a highest and best use assumption (ASC 820-10-35-10D).

The assumption about a nonfinancial asset's highest and best use determines the valuation premise used to measure the asset. The valuation premise applied to the asset can be either on a stand-alone basis or in combination with other assets. If the asset's highest and best use is on a stand-alone basis, the price would be the amount received to transfer the asset to a market participant who would also use the asset on a stand-alone basis. If the asset's highest and best use is in combination with other assets, the price is based on the asset's sale as part of the group of assets to market participants. The group may be a group of assets or a group of assets and liabilities (e.g., a business) (ASC 820-10-35-10E).

(vii) Application to Liabilities and Instruments Classified in a Reporting Entity's Shareholders' Equity. The fair value measurement of a financial or nonfinancial liability rests on the assumptions that the liability is transferred to a market participant on the measurement date, the liability would remain outstanding, and the transferee would fulfill the obligation. Likewise, the fair value measurement of a financial or nonfinancial equity instrument is based on the assumptions that the equity instrument is transferred to a market participant on the measurement date, the instrument would remain outstanding, and the transferee would take on the rights and responsibilities associated with the equity instrument. Therefore, fair value measurement is not made assuming the liability is settled with the counterparty or assuming the equity instrument is canceled.

Observable market information may not exist for liabilities and equity instruments, and contractual or other legal restrictions may prevent their transfer. When that is the case, it is possible that observable market information may exist for the same liability or equity when it is traded as an asset. Corporate bonds are examples of liabilities that trade in observable markets as assets.

When measuring fair value, the use of observable market observations should be maximized and the use of unobservable inputs should be minimized (ASC 820-10-35-16).

(viii) Liabilities and Instruments Classified in a Reporting Entity's Shareholders' Equity Held by Other Parties as Assets. The best indication of a liability's or equity's value is a quoted market price for an identical instrument in an active market. If a quoted price for an identical liability or equity instrument is not available, the next best indication of value is a quoted market price in an active market for an identical instrument that is held by another party as an asset. The fair value of the instrument would then be measured from the perspective of the market participant that holds the debt or equity instrument as an asset. In the absence of an active market, a quoted market price in an inactive market for an identical liability or equity traded as an asset can be used. In the absence of observable market prices for identical instruments traded as assets, the fair value of liabilities and equity instruments can be measured using an income approach, such as a discounted cash flow method, or a market approach using quoted market prices for similar instruments traded as assets. The fair value would be determined from the perspective of a market participant who holds the liability or equity instrument as an asset (ASC 820-10-35-16B to BB).

When using the quoted market price of liability or equity instruments held by another party as an asset to measure fair value, it may be necessary to make adjustments to the quoted market price. Adjustments compensate for factors specific to the asset that are not represented in the liability or equity instrument being measured. Typically adjustments are needed when the quoted price is for a similar but not identical asset or when the unit of account is not the same. For instance, when the credit quality of the instrument held as an asset is not identical to the credit quality of the issuer of the liability being measured, an adjustment would be needed. A liability with a third-party credit enhancement would not have the same unit of account as an otherwise identical asset, and an adjustment would be required. It is interesting to note that the quoted market price of the asset should be adjusted to reflect restrictions on the transfer of the asset when measuring the fair value of the liability (ASC 820-10-35-16D). The converse is not true. Restrictions on the transfer of a liability do not create the need to adjust the transaction price of an identical asset. Those restrictions are assumed to be factored into the transaction price (ASC 820-10-35-18C).

(ix) Liabilities and Instruments Classified in a Reporting Entity's Shareholders' Equity Not Held by Other Parties as Assets. When quoted market prices are not available for similar or identical liabilities and equity instruments, and when they are not available for identical instruments when traded as an asset, fair value of the liability or equity instrument can be measured using another valuation method. The fair value measurement of a liability would be from the perspective of the market participant that owes the liability; the fair value measurement of an equity instrument would be from the perspective of the entity that has issued it. Although the next paragraph discusses the fair value measurement of liabilities, the principles are equally applicable to the fair value measurement of equity instruments.

A discounted cash flow method can be applied from one of two perspectives. The fair value can be measured from the perspective of a market participant that fulfills the obligation, or it can be measured from the perspective of a market participant that issues an identical liability. When assuming the obligation is fulfilled, the discounted cash outflows would include the direct costs to fulfill the obligation and would include compensation for taking on the obligation. The compensation would include a risk premium to compensate for the risk inherent in the cash flows and an amount to cover opportunity costs (i.e., profit). When measured from the perspective of a market participant that issues an identical liability, the fair value would equal the proceeds that a market participant would expect to receive for issuing an instrument with identical terms (i.e., cash flows) and the same credit characteristics (i.e., discount rate) (ASC 820-10-35-16I to J).

(x) Other Factors that Impact the Fair Value of a Liability. Nonperformance risk has a direct impact on the fair value measurement of a liability. According to the Glossary, nonperformance risk is "the risk that an entity will not fulfill an obligation. Nonperformance risk includes, but is not limited to, the reporting entity's own credit risk." Credit risk is the risk that the entity will experience a change in its creditworthiness (ASC 820-10-35-17 to 18).

Credit enhancements, which are third-party guarantees, also impact the nonperformance risk and thus may impact the fair value of the liability. The key to measuring the fair value of a liability with a credit enhancement is to determine the unit of account. If the unit of account excludes the credit enhancement, the liability's fair value would reflect the entity's own credit standing. If the unit of account includes the credit enhancement, the fair value would reflect the third party's credit standing (ASC 820-10-35-18A).

(xi) Valuation Techniques. The guidance for applying valuation techniques to measure fair value emphasizes that the objective "is to estimate the price at which an orderly transaction to sell the asset or to transfer the liability would take place between market participants at the measurement date under current market conditions." The selection of appropriate valuation techniques requires judgment and depends on the particular circumstances, including the availability of sufficient data. Appropriate valuation techniques will maximize the use of observable inputs and minimize the use of unobservable techniques. In some circumstances, it is appropriate to rely on just one valuation technique, particularly if quoted prices in active markets are available. In other situations, multiple valuation techniques can be used to determine multiple indications of value. When assessing multiple indications of value, the reasonableness of the range of values must be considered. "The fair value measurement is the point within that range that is most representative of fair value in the circumstances." Three valuation techniques are widely used to measure fair value: the cost approach, the market approach, and the income approach (ASC 820-10-35-24).

(xii) Cost Approach. According to the Glossary, "the cost approach is a valuation technique based on the amount that currently would be required to replace the service capacity of an asset (often referred to as current replacement cost)."

The notion behind the cost approach is that the fair value of an asset is estimated by the current replacement cost of the asset less any adjustments for obsolescence related to the subject asset. The replacement cost of the asset would equal the amount that it would cost to replace the asset with another asset of comparable utility, as of the measurement date. The cost approach is often used to estimate the value of specific assets, such as a building or machinery and equipment, or certain intangible assets, such as customer relationships or an assembled workforce. Because of its nature, the cost approach is difficult to apply when estimating the fair value of an entire operating business; however, it is not impossible to do so. In financial reporting, the cost method is used most often to estimate the fair value of intangible assets acquired in a business combination under FASB ASC 350.

(xiii) Market Approach. According to the Glossary, the market approach is "a valuation technique that uses prices and other relevant information generated by market transactions involving identical or comparable (that is, similar) assets, liabilities, or groups of assets and liabilities, such as a business."

The market approach estimates fair value by comparing a financial measurement such as an earnings or cash flow for the subject entity to an earnings or cash flow multiple for a similar guideline entity whose shares are transacted in the marketplace. Commonly used financial metrics are multiples of prices to earnings (P/E ratio) or multiples of invested capital to earnings before interest, taxes, depreciation and amortization (EBITDA). Conceptually, the market approach is easy to understand because it estimates fair value based on market transactions for similar assets or business interests. The difficulty in applying the market approach to measure fair value, particularly to intangible assets, is in identifying guideline assets or business interests similar enough to support a determinative comparison.

(xiv) Income Approach. The Glossary says that the income approach includes

> valuation techniques that convert future amounts (for example, cash flows or income and expenses) to a single current (that is, discounted) amount. The fair value measurement is determined on the basis of the value indicated by current market expectations about those future amounts.

Methods under the income approach can be applied to estimate the fair value of an entire entity or reporting unit, or they can be applied to estimate the fair value of a specific asset, particularly an intangible asset. The income approach is generally used to estimate the fair value of a business or an asset of the business, such as an intangible asset based on the risk-adjusted cash flows that the entity or specific intangible asset is expected to generate over its remaining useful life. Several common methods can be used to estimate fair value under the income approach that are based on a discounted cash flow analysis. These methods measure fair value by estimating expected future cash flows that the entity or intangible asset will generate. The sum of these expected cash flows over the life of the entity or asset is discounted to the present at a risk-adjusted rate of return. The discount rate selected for use is commensurate with the risk of actually receiving the cash flows.

(xv) Multiple Valuation Techniques. As a general rule, once valuation techniques are selected, they should be used consistently from period to period. However, there may be circumstances where a change in valuation technique is warranted, such as when new markets develop, when market conditions change, when the availability of information changes, or when valuation techniques improve. There may also be circumstances that indicate a need to change the weights applied to multiple valuation techniques. Or there may be a reason to change the application of adjustments to valuation techniques. These changes are acceptable as long as the objective is to produce a fair value measurement that is equally or more representative of fair value. Changes in valuation techniques or their application are considered to be changes in accounting estimates (ASC 820-10-35-24 to 26).

(xvi) Calibration. A relatively new fair value measurement concept brought about by convergence with IFRS is the calibration of subsequent measurements with the initial measurement. Calibration is applicable in situations where the fair value of the initial measurement is the transaction price (i.e., no gain or loss at initial measurement), and when remeasurement in subsequent periods relies on unobservable inputs. At initial measurement, the valuation technique should be calibrated so that the resulting fair value equals the transaction price. Doing this ensures that current market conditions are reflected in the valuation technique and illuminates situations when adjustments may be needed to capture unique characteristics of the asset or liability that are missed by the valuation technique. Calibration creates a more accurate fair value measurement in subsequent periods because past relationships among unobservable market inputs and observable transaction prices are preserved (ASC 820-10-35-24C).

(xvii) Inputs to Valuation Techniques. Inputs to valuation techniques are either observable or unobservable. Observable inputs are objectively determined price data from exchange markets, dealer markets, brokered markets or principal-to-principal markets. Unobservable inputs are subjective assumptions about how market participants make pricing decisions. According to the Glossary, "Valuation techniques used to measure fair value shall maximize the use of relevant observable inputs and minimize the use of unobservable inputs." Inputs and any adjustments to inputs must be consistent with the characteristics of the asset or liability being measured and consistent with its unit of account. Adjustments such as a control premium or a discount for the lack of control may be needed if a market participant would consider them relevant. A blockage factor, or a discount to reflect the price impact of trading a large block of stock, is not permitted in fair value measurements. As a general rule, quoted prices in active markets are not adjusted when measuring fair value. When market prices are quoted as a bid/ask spread, the price within the range that is most representative of fair value shall be selected. Using a bid price for an asset, an ask price for a liability, a mid-market price convention, or another practical expedient used by market participants are all permitted (ASC 820-10-35-36 to 36D).

(xviii) Fair Value Hierarchy. ASC 820's fair value hierarchy categorizes the inputs to the fair value measurement into three levels. Level 1 inputs are unadjusted prices in active markets for identical assets or liabilities, and they are given the highest priority within the hierarchy and within the fair value measurement itself. Level 2 inputs are observable market inputs that fail to quality as

Level 1 inputs, and Level 3 inputs are unobservable assumptions. Level 3 inputs have the lowest priority. In situations where the fair value measurement of a particular asset or liability is based on inputs from more than one level, the measurement is categorized at the lowest level input that is significant to the overall measurement of the value.

When determining the appropriate fair value hierarchy level, the focus should be on the inputs. Generally, adjustments to inputs should not be taken into consideration when determining the hierarchy level. However, if an observable input is adjusted using an unobservable input and that adjustment is significant to the overall value, the measurement should be categorized in Level 3. It should also be noted that the valuation technique does not determine the hierarchy level. While the availability and reliability of relevant inputs would be considered when selecting a valuation method, it is the inputs, not the valuation method, that determine the hierarchy level. For example, a fair value measurement determined using a discounted cash flow method could be classified as Level 2 or Level 3. The selection of the appropriate level requires judgment and depends on identifying which inputs are more significant to the measurement and where those inputs fall within the hierarchy (ASC 820-10-35-37 to 38).

Level 1 Inputs. According to the Glossary, Level 1 inputs are "quoted prices (unadjusted) in active markets for identical assets or liabilities that the reporting entity can access at the measurement date." As a general rule, when Level 1 inputs are available, they should be used without adjustment because they provide the most reliable evidence about the fair value of a particular asset or liability. The fair value of Level 1assets or liabilities would be equal to the quoted price times the quantity held or owed by the entity. Blockage discounts for large positions should not be applied (ASC 820-10-35-40, 41, and 44).

Level 1 inputs exist for many financial assets and liabilities, and sometimes inputs are available from multiple markets. When there is more than one active market for an asset or liability, the reporting entity must select inputs from the principal market, which is the market with the greatest volume and level of activity for that particular asset or liability. In the absence of a principal market, the entity can select inputs from the most advantageous market. However, the entity must be able to access the market in order to use the inputs in a fair value measurement. *Access* means that it would be possible for the entity to enter into a transaction for that particular asset or liability at that input price, in that market, on the measurement date (ASC 820-10-35-41B).

Level 1 Adjustments. As previously stated, Level 1 inputs should be used without adjustment whenever they are available. However, there are a few exceptions to this general rule. One exception is for entities that use matrix pricing as a practical expedient to price a large number of similar assets, such as investments in bonds. Although prices for identical assets are available, they are not readily accessible. This alternative pricing method results in a measurement that is lower than Level 1. Another exception would be in situations where a quoted price in an active market is not indicative of fair value because of the occurrence of a significant event. For instance, if a publicly traded company makes an announcement after the close of the market, but before the measurement date, the market input may not be indicative of the company's fair value. Any adjustment to the quoted market price would result in a measurement lower than Level 1. A final exception may occur when using the quoted price of an identical instrument traded as an asset to measure the fair value of a liability or equity instrument. Any adjustments required for factors specific to the asset but not present in the liability would result in a measurement lower than Level 1 (ASC 820-10-35-41C).

Level 2 Inputs. Level 2 inputs are defined in the Glossary as "inputs other than quoted prices included within Level 1 that are observable for the asset or liability, either directly or indirectly." Quoted prices for identical assets or liabilities can be categorized as Level 1 or Level 2, depending on whether the market is active (Level 1) or not active (Level 2). Quoted prices for identical assets or liabilities are considered directly observable inputs. Quoted prices for similar assets are always categorized as Level 2 and are considered indirectly observable inputs. Level 2 also includes other inputs that are indirectly observable in markets such as interest rates, yield curves, implied volatilities and credit spreads. One caveat is that the Level 2 input must be observable for the asset or liability's full contractual term (ASC 820-10-35-47 to 48).

Examples of Level 2 inputs for specific assets are:

- *Swaps.* The reference rate, such as the London Interbank Offering Rate (LIBOR), a specific yield curve, or a bank prime rates
- *Options.* The implied volatility rates for the underlying share prices
- *Licensing agreements acquired in a business combination.* Royalty rates for similar agreements with unrelated parties
- *Inventory acquired in a business combination.* Retail market prices and wholesale market prices
- *Buildings.* Valuation multiples based on observable market data, such as price per square foot
- *Reporting units.* Valuation multiples, such as earnings or revenue multiples based on transaction prices for similar businesses (ASC 820-10-55-21)

Level 2 Inputs Adjustments. When measuring the fair value of an asset or liability, it may be necessary to adjust Level 2 inputs for factors specific to the asset or liability, such as its condition or location. Adjustments may also be needed when the asset or liability is not comparable. For instance, a restriction on the transfer of an asset or a different unit of account may affect an asset's comparability. Adjustments may also be needed or based on the volume or level of activity in the market from which the inputs are observed. When adjustments are significant to the fair value measurement of the particular asset or liability, the measurement would be categorized as Level 3 (ASC 820-10-35-50 to 51).

Level 3 Inputs. Unobservable inputs are defined by the Glossary as "inputs for which market data are not available and that are developed using the best information available about the assumptions that market participants would use when pricing the asset or liability." Relevant observable inputs may not be available because there is little to no market activity for the asset or liability as of the measurement date. All unobservable inputs are categorized as Level 3 inputs.

Unobservable inputs are intended to represent an exit price from the perspective of a market participant who owns the asset or owes the liability. They reflect the assumptions that a market participant would use to price the asset or liability. A market participant's assumptions about risk are integral to fair value measurement and include risks inherent in the valuation technique, risks associated with the inputs to that technique, and risks associated with measurement uncertainty.

Unobservable inputs should be developed using the best information available, which may include an entity's own data. When using the entity's own data as a starting point, it would be adjusted when market participants would use different data. Additional adjustments would be necessary for entity-specific synergies not available to other market participants. A reporting entity must consider all information about market participant assumptions that is reasonably available but need not undertake exhaustive efforts (ASC 820-10-35-52 to 54A).

(xix) Measuring Fair Value When the Volume or Level of Activity for an Asset or Liability Has Significantly Decreased. When there has been a significant decrease in the volume or level of activity relative to the normal market activity for an asset or liability, the objective of the fair value measurement does not change. Fair value is an exit price in an orderly market between market participants at the measurement date under current market conditions. When the volume or level of activity has significantly decreased, further analysis must be undertaken to determine whether the quoted market price represents fair value and whether the transaction is orderly.

If the reporting entity determines that a quoted market price does not represent fair value, an adjustment to the quoted market price would be necessary, and the adjustment may be significant.

Other adjustments may also be required when assets are not comparable or when market prices are stale. When a market participant demands a risk premium as compensation for bearing the uncertainty relating to the cash flows of the asset or liability, an adjustment for risk would be needed (ASC 820-10-35-54D to E).

Another factor to consider when the volume or level of activity has changed is whether the entity should change the valuation method for measuring fair value. The entity may also consider whether to add a second technique for measuring fair value. Whenever an entity uses more than one valuation technique, the goal is to determine the point within the range that is the most representative of fair value (ASC 820-10-35-54F).

(xx) Identifying Transactions That Are Not Orderly. Generally, transactions from forced liquidations or distressed sales are not considered to be orderly. When there has been a significant decrease in the volume or level of activity relative to the normal market activity, it does not always mean that the transaction is not orderly. The particular situation must be evaluated further to determine whether the transaction is not orderly after weighing all available evidence. Circumstances that may indicate a transaction is not orderly include:

- Inadequate exposure to the market that does not allow an ample period of time for usual and customary marketing activities for the asset or liability
- A seller that markets the asset or liability to a single market participant
- A distressed seller that is in or near bankruptcy or in receivership
- A forced sale for regulatory or legal reasons
- A transaction price that is an outlier compared to other recent transactions (ASC 820-10-35-54H to I)

When a transaction is not considered to be orderly, little to no weight should be placed on the transaction price, and other indications of fair value should receive more emphasis when measuring fair value. If the transaction is considered to be orderly, the transaction price should be considered. The amount of weight given to the transaction price would depend on such factors as the volume of transactions in the market, the comparability of the market transaction to the subject asset or liability, and the amount of time that has elapsed between the transaction and measurement date.

When the entity cannot conclude whether the transaction is orderly because of insufficient information, the transaction price must be considered. However, less weight would be placed on transaction with inconclusive evidence about whether the transaction is orderly, and more weight would be placed on transactions considered to be orderly. When making its assessment about whether a transaction is orderly, an entity cannot ignore information that is reasonably available, but it need not undertake exhaustive efforts (ASC 820-10-35-54J).

(xxi) Using Quoted Prices Provided by Third Parties. Entities may use quoted prices provided by third parties when measuring fair value if the entity has determined that the third-party prices have been developed in accordance with ASC 820. Pricing services and brokers are typical third-party sources of quoted prices. The entity should consider whether the third-party price represents a binding quote or whether it is an indicative price. More weight would be afforded to a binding quote in the fair value measurement.

When there has been a significant decrease in the volume or level of activity relative to the normal market activity, the entity must evaluate the third-party quotes further. The entity must determine that prices are developed using current information that reflect orderly transactions. Or the third party could develop prices using a valuation technique that reflects market participant assumptions, including risk premiums. The entity should place more weight on third-party prices that reflect transaction prices and less weight on those developed using other valuation techniques (ASC 820-10-35-54K to M).

(f) DISCLOSURES

(i) Objectives. The objective of fair value measurement disclosures is twofold:

1. Disclosures are provided to help financial statement users to assess the valuation techniques and inputs applied to all assets and liabilities measured at fair value after initial recognition.
2. Additional disclosures are presented for recurring measurements made using unobservable, Level 3 inputs so that users can assess the effect of those measurements on earning and other comprehensive income.

Financial statement preparers must disclose sufficient information to meet those objectives. In determining whether disclosures are sufficient, preparers must consider all of these issues;

- The appropriate level of detail
- How much emphasis should be placed on various requirements
- The appropriate level of aggregation or disaggregation, and
- Whether additional information is needed to permit the evaluation of quantitative information (ASC 820-10-50-1 to 1A).

Required disclosures should be presented for each class of asset and liability measured at fair value in the balance sheet after initial recognition. Determining the appropriate classes of assets and liabilities requires judgment and should take into account the nature, characteristics, and risks of the class as well as the hierarchy level where the class would be categorized. As a general rule, asset and liability classes require greater disaggregation than their balance sheet counterparts. Disclosures should also include sufficient information to allow the financial statement user to reconcile the disclosures by class to balance sheet line items (ASC 820-10-50-2B and C).

Another item that entities must disclose is their policy for determining when transfers between levels of the fair value hierarchy occur. The policy should be the same for transfers into a level and for transfers out and should be followed consistently. Some companies recognize transfers on the date of event or change in circumstances. Others recognize all transfers at the beginning or end of the reporting period (ASC 820-10-50-2C).

(ii) Required Disclosures. Quantitative fair value measurement disclosures are required to be presented for all assets and liabilities measured at fair value after their initial measurement. Additional information is required to be presented for assets and liabilities measured at fair value that fall into Level 2 and 3. Exhibit 24.1 provides a graphical summary of the disclosure requirements in ASC 820-10-50-2. The left side shows the hierarchy level to which the disclosure requirements apply. Many disclosures are required regardless of level, and there are additional requirements for Level 2 and Level 3 measurements. When an asset or liability is measured using a measurement basis other than fair value, such as historical cost, the asset or liability may be disclosed in the footnotes at fair value. When that is the case, additional information, such as the hierarchy level, valuation technique, and inputs used in the fair value measurement, must be disclosed as well. Determining which disclosures are required also depends on whether the asset or liability is measured at fair value on a recurring or nonrecurring basis. Many disclosures are required for both recurring and non-recurring measurements. The exhibit shows whether disclosures are required for both recurring and nonrecurring, for recurring measurements only, or nonrecurring measurements only across the top.

Exhibit 24.2 provides an example of disclosures required for all assets measured at fair value. The tabular format shows recurring fair value measurements in the top portion and nonrecurring measurements in the bottom. In the past, recurring and nonrecurring disclosures were presented in separate disclosures. The example in Exhibit 24.3 provides more detail about Level 3 measurements in a roll-forward format. It shows on opening balance and a closing balance for all assets measured at fair value on the reporting dates, and it shows all activity that impacts the fair value measurements during the period. Additional information about the fair value measurement impact on earnings

Topic 820-10-50	Recurring or Nonrecurring	Recurring	Nonrecurring
All assets and liabilities measured at fair value after initial recognition	Description of valuation technique Inputs used in FVM Disclosures for each class of asset/liability FVM at end of reporting period	Transfers between Levels 1 and 2* Reason for transfers* Entity's policy for determining transfers* Transfers in separated from transfers out*	Reason for FVM (i.e., circumstances)
Levels 1, 2, and 3	Level of hierarchy FVM is categorized If highest and best use differs from current use and why		
Level 2	Any change in valuation technique Use of additional valuation technique Reason for change or addition		
Level 3	Any change in valuation technique Use of additional valuation technique Reason for change or addition Quantitative info about unobservable inputs Description of the valuation process including policies and proceedures	Effect of measurement: on earnings and on OCI Reconciliation of opening and closing balances: Including: gains/losses, recognized in earnings, gains/losses in OCI Purchases, sales, issues, and settlements (separately) Transfers in or out of Level 3, separately Income statement line item of gain/loss OCI line item where recognized Reason for transfers in or out of level 3 Company policy for determining transfers Sensitivity analysis of FVM to changes in inputs* Interrelationships among inputs, including their mitigating/magnifying effects on FVM*	
Assets and liabilities disclosed but not measured at FV	Level of hierarchy FVM is categorized Description of valuation technique Inputs used in FVM Any change in valuation technique Use of additional valuation technique Reason for change or addition If highest and best use differs from current use and why.		

Note: All required quantitative disclosures should be presented in tabular format.
*Disclosure not required for nonpublic entities.
Additional disclosures are required for derivative assets and liabilities, liabilities with inseparable third-party credit enhancements, and FVM of investments that calculate net asset value per share.

Exhibit 24.1 Fair Value Measurement Disclosure Summary

		Fair Value Measurements at the End of the Reporting Period Using			
	12/31/X1	Quoted Prices in Active Markets for Identical Assets (Level 1)	Significant Other Observable Inputs (Level 2)	Significant Unobservable Inputs (Level 3)	Total Gains (Losses)
Recurring fair value measurements:					
Trading securities[a]					
Healthcare industry	$ 4,500,000	$ 4,500,000			
Real estate industry	3,900,000	2,750,000	1,150,000		
Other	925,000	925,000			
Total trading securities	$ 9,325,000	$ 8,175,000	$ 1,150,000		
Available-for-sale debt securities					
Mortgage-backed securities	$ 13,575,000			$ 13,575,000	
U.S. Treasury securities	5,235,000	5,235,000		$ 13,575,000	
Total available-for-sale debt securities	$ 18,810,000	$ 5,235,000		$ 13,575,000	
Investments[b]					
Private equity fund	$ 2,135,000			$ 2,135,000	
Venture capital	1,450,000			1,450,000	
	$ 3,585,000			$ 3,585,000	
Total recurring fair value measurements	$ 31,720,000	$ 13,410,000	$ 1,150,000	$ 17,160,000	
Nonrecurring fair value measurements:					
Long-lived assets held and used[c]	$ 20,000,000		$ 35,000,000		$ (15,000,000)
Goodwill[d]	2,000,000			6,000,000	(4,000,000)
Long-lived assets held for sale[e]	1,000,000		16,000,000		(15,000,000)
Total nonrecurring fair value measurements	$ 23,000,000		$ 51,000,000	$ 6,000,000	$ (34,000,000)

Notes:

[a]On the basis of its analysis of the nature, characteristics, and risks of the securities, the reporting entity has determined that presenting them by industry is appropriate.

[b]On the basis of its analysis of the nature, characteristics, and risks of the securities, the reporting entity has determined that presenting them as a single class is appropriate.

[c]In accordance with Subtopic 360-10, long-lived assets held and used with a carrying amount of $50 million were written down to their fair value of $35 million, resulting in an impairment charge of $15 million, which was included in earnings for the period.

[d]In accordance with Subtopic 350-20, goodwill with a carrying amount of $10 million was written down to its implied fair value of $6 million, resulting in an impairment charge of $4 million, which was included in earnings for the period.

[e]In accordance with Subtopic 360-10, long-lived assets held for sale with a carrying amount of $25 million were written down to their fair value of $16 million, less costs to sell of $6 million (or $10 million), resulting in a loss of $15 million, which was included in earnings for the period.

Exhibit 24.2 Example Company Disclosure—Assets Measured at Fair Value

		Investments		
	Mortgage-Backed Securities	Private Equity Fund	Venture Capital	Total
Opening balance	$ 36,500,000	$ 4,000,000	$ 1,575,000	$ 42,075,000
Transfers into Level 3	125,000[a][b]			125,000
Transfers out of Level 3	(6,000,000)[b][c]			(6,000,000)
Total gains or losses for the period				
Included in earnings (or changes in net assets)		(865,000)	500,000	(365,000)
Included in other comprehensive income	(7,050,000)			(7,050,000)
Purchases, issues, sales, and settlements				
Purchases		1,000,000		1,000,000
Issues				
Sales	(10,000,000)		(625,000)	(10,625,000)
Settlements		(2,000,000)		(2,000,000)
Closing balance	$ 13,575,000	$ 2,135,000	$ 1,450,000	$ 17,160,000
Change in unrealized gains or losses for the period included in earnings (or changes in net assets) for assets held at the end of the reporting period		$ (165,000)	$ 500,000	$ 335,000

	Trading Revenues	Other Revenues
Total gains or losses for the period included in earnings (or changes in net assets)	$ 350,000	$ 15,000
Change in unrealized gains or losses for the period included in earnings (or changes in net assets) for assets held at the end of the reporting period	$ 280,000	$ 55,000

Notes:

[a]Transferred from Level 2 to Level 3 because of a lack of observable market data, resulting from a decrease in market activity for the securities.

[b]The reporting entity's policy is to recognize transfers into and out of Level 3 as of the date of the event or change in circumstances that cause the transfer.

[c]Transferred from Level 3 to Level 2 because observable market data became available for the securities.

Exhibit 24.3 Example Company Disclosure—Reconciliation of Fair Value Measurements Categorized Within Level 3 of the Fair Value Hierarchy

and other comprehensive income appears at the bottom of the disclosure. Exhibit 24.4 provides an example of some relatively new disclosures for Level 3 assets. It provides additional information about valuation techniques and inputs used to measure fair value.

(iii) Private Companies. In an effort to respond to constituents' appeal to reduce the reporting burden for smaller companies, the FASB has decided that many fair value measurement disclosures will no longer be required for nonpublic companies. Generally, disclosures relating to transfers between fair value hierarchy levels and disclosures about the sensitivity of measurements to changes in inputs have been eliminated. Exhibit 24.1 indicates the disclosures that have been eliminated for nonpublic companies in a footnote.

24.5 FAIR VALUE OPTION

ASC 825 contains the accounting guidance for the fair value option. The fair value option is an election that companies can make to measure certain items at fair value for financial reporting purposes, which was originally issued in 2006 as SFAS No. 159. The guidance in ASC 825 outlines

	Fair Value at 12/31/X1	Valuation Technique(s)	Unobservable Input	Range (Weighted Averages)
Mortgage-backed securities	$13,575,000	Discounted cash flow	Constant prepayment rate	4%–8% (6%)
			Loss severity	40%–100% (70%)
			Default rate	9%–40% (20%)
Venture capital	1,450,000	Discounted cash flow	Weighted-average cost of capital	12%–16% (15%)
			Long-term growth rate	4%–5% (4%)
			Pretax operating margin	3%–20% (15%)
			Discount for lack of marketability[a]	10%–25% (20%)
			Discount for lack of control[a]	10%–20% (15%)
		Guideline companies	EBITDA multiple[b]	6%–12% (9%)
			Revenue multiple[b]	1%–3% (2%)
			Discount for lack of marketability[a]	10%–25% (20%)
			Discount for lack of control[a]	10%–20% (15%)

Notes:
[a]Represents discounts used when the reporting entity has determined that market participants would take into account these premiums and discounts when pricing investment.
[b]Represents amounts used when the reporting entity has determined that market participants would use such multiples when pricing the investments.

Exhibit 24.4 Example Company Disclosure—Information About Fair Value Measurements Categorized Within Level 3 of the Fair Value Hierarchy

the requirements for making the election and for the presentation and disclosure of accounting information under the election (ASC 825-10-05-5).

The fair value option is applicable to financial instruments, which according to the Glossary encompass both financial assets and liabilities. The Glossary definition also includes the concept that several financial instruments can be linked in a chain under a contract that qualifies as a financial instrument and that the chain ends in the payment of cash or an equity ownership interest. The Glossary defines financial assets as

> cash, evidence of an ownership interest in an equity, or a contract that conveys to one entity a right to do either of the following: 1) receive cash or another financial instrument from a second entity, or 2) exchange other financial instruments on potentially favorable terms with the second entity.

Financial assets arise from contractual agreements between two parties and cannot be imposed by a third party. The definition of a financial liability is the opposite:

> [A] contract that imposes on one entity an obligation to do either of the following; 1) deliver cash or another financial instrument to a second entity, or 2) exchange other financial instruments on potentially unfavorable terms with the second entity.

Any entity can elect to measure financial assets and financial liabilities at fair value. The election is available to a number of other items, such as firm commitments, loan commitments, some insurance contracts, and some warranties. The fair value option is not available for consolidated investments in subsidiaries, consolidated variable interest entities, benefit plan obligations, leases, demand deposits, or the issuer's convertible debt (ASC 825-10-15-4 and 5).

Entities can make a fair value election on election dates, which generally occur on the date the entity first recognizes the item or the date the entity enters into a firm commitment. Election dates may also occur if there is an event or change of status, such as when:

- An asset reported at fair value is transfers to another subsidiary
- Investments become subject to equity accounting

- Subsidiaries or variable interest entities are consolidated or deconsolidated
- Debt is significantly modified
- A business combination occurs (ASC 825-10-25-4 and 5).

The fair value election can be made on the election date on an instrument by instrument basis (with some exceptions as outlined in ASC 825-10-25-7), or it can be made through an existing accounting policy applicable to specific types of financial instruments. Once the election is made, it is irrevocable. The fair value option is applied to entire instruments, never to portions of instruments. A fair value election made by the parent company and applied in consolidation does not have to be applied in to separate company financial statements for the subsidiary. However, if the fair value option is elected by the subsidiary, it is required in separate company financial statements. When several financial instruments are acquired in a single transaction, the fair value option does not have to be applied to all of the financial instruments (ASC 825-10-25-2, 6 and 10).

When there is a change in fair value for an item measured at fair value under the fair value election, the unrealized gain or loss must be reported in earnings (ASC 825-10-35-4). In the statement of financial position, assets and liabilities should be reported so that those measured at fair value are separated from those measured using other measurement attributes. This can be accomplished by presenting them in separate line items or by presenting them in the same line item and parenthetically disclosing the amount measured at fair value (ASC 825-10-45-1 and 2).

Additional disclosures are required for items measured under the fair value option and for derivatives measured at fair value. The disclosures are not required for financial instruments classified as trading securities, life settlement contracts, or servicing rights. The objectives of fair value option disclosures is to promote financial statement comparability between entities that choose different measurement basis for similar assets and liabilities and between the assets and liabilities for a particular entity recorded at different measurement basis. Fair value option disclosures are expected to provide this information:

- Management's reasons for electing or partially electing the fair value option
- How changes in fair value impact earnings for the period
- How certain items would have been measured if the fair value election had not been made (e.g., disclosures about equity investments and nonperforming loans)
- Differences between fair values and contractual cash flows

Disclosures for financial instruments measured at fair value under the fair value election are over and above those required in other ASC Topics, such as ASC 820. Financial statement preparers are encouraged but not required to combine the fair value option disclosures with other fair value disclosures (ASC 825-10-50-24 to 27).

These disclosures are required for each date that a balance sheet is presented in interim or annual financial statements:

- Management's reasons for electing fair value, by item or group of similar items.
- If the fair value option is elected for some but not all items within a group of similar items, disclosures should include a description of the items, the reason for the partial election, and how the group of similar items relates to the balance sheet line item
- For each balance sheet line item that includes fair value option items, disclose how each balance sheet line item relates to major classes of assets and liabilities presented in accordance with disclosures for ASC 820 and disclose the carrying amount of items in that line that are not eligible for the fair value option.
- The difference between the aggregate fair value and the aggregate unpaid principal balance for loans, long-term receivables, and long-term debt instruments
- For loans held as assets, disclose the aggregate fair value of those over 90 days past due, the aggregate value of loans in nonaccrual status, and the difference between the fair value and aggregate unpaid principle on loans over 90 days or in nonaccrual status.

- For investments measured at fair value that would be equity investments absent the fair value option, disclose information about the item as though it were an equity investment (ASC 825-10-50-28).

Additional disclosures are required for each period an annual or interim income statement is presented, including:

- For each income statement line item, the amount of gains and losses included in earnings from changes in fair value
- How interest and dividends are measured and where they are reported in the income statement
- For loans and other receivables held as assets, the gain or loss attributable to changes in instrument specific credit risk and how such gains or losses were determined
- For liabilities with significant changes in instrument specific credit risk the gain or loss attributable to the change in credit risk, qualitative information about the reason for the change, and how gains and losses attributable to changes in credit risk were determined (ASC 825-10-50-30)

Entities must also disclose the methods and significant assumptions used to estimate fair value for fair value option items annually. At the time a fair value election is made, the entity must disclose qualitative information about the nature of the event. Quantitative information about the earnings impact of the initial election on each balance sheet line item must also be disclosed (ASC 825-10-50-31 and 32).

24.6 AUDITING FAIR VALUE MEASUREMENTS

Fair value measurement in financial reporting creates a challenge for auditors. Measuring fair value requires preparers of financial statements to use judgment when selecting appropriate inputs, making adjustments to those inputs, selecting appropriate valuation methods, and making assumptions about future periods. Because of the complexity of fair value measurement, the financial statement preparer may retain an outside valuation specialist to assist with the measurement. The quality of the fair value measurement depends on the preparer's judgment; therefore, auditing measurement also requires judgment.

The role of the auditor is to obtain sufficient competent audit evidence to provide reasonable assurance that fair value measurement is in conformity GAAP. These challenges are faced by auditors in the United States and worldwide as fair value measures become more extensive in financial reporting across the globe. The International Auditing and Assurance Standards Board (IAASB) describes some of the challenges that auditors face in obtaining sufficient competent audit evidence to opine as to the conformity of fair value measurements to accounting standards. Some of the audit challenges recognized by the IAASB include:

- The measurement objective, as fair value accounting estimates are expressed in terms of the value of a current transaction or financial statement items based on conditions prevalent at the measurement date;
- The need to incorporate judgments concerning significant assumption that may be made by others such as valuation specialists engaged by the entity or auditor;
- The availability (or lack thereof) of information or evidence and its reliability;
- The breadth of assets and liabilities to which fair value accounting may be, or is required to be, applied;
- The choice and sophistication of acceptable valuation techniques and models; and
- The need for appropriate disclosure in the financial statements about measurement methods and uncertainty, especially when relevant markets are illiquid.[40]

[40] International Auditing and Assurance Standards Board, Staff Audit Practice Alert, *Challenges in Auditing Fair Value Accounting Estimates in the Current Market Environment,* October 2008.

At the very least, fair value measurement adds an additional layer of complexity to the presentation of financial statements and the audit of those statements.

(a) AUDIT STANDARDS FOR FAIR VALUE MEASUREMENTS. The American Accounting Association' Auditing Standard codified as AU 328, *Auditing Fair Value Measurements and Disclosures,* originally issued as SAS No. 101, was the first auditing standard that specifically addressed fair value measurement and was originally effective for audits of financial statements beginning after June 15, 2003. At the time of its issuance, fair value measurement was required for debt and equity instruments classified as "trading securities" or as "available for sale" in accordance with SFAS No. 115. SFAS No. 119 and SFAS No. 133, *Accounting for Derivative Instruments and Hedging Activities,* issued in 1994 and 2000, respectively, expanded the application of fair value measurement to disclosures and accounting for derivatives. Therefore, when AU 328 was issued, fair value measurement was applicable primarily to financial assets and liabilities.

AU 328 was among the preexisting standards adopted by the Public Companies Auditing Oversight Board (PCAOB) in April 2003. Among other actions, the PCAOB adopted amendments to AU 328 through PCAOB Release No. 2010-004, *Auditing Standards Related to the Auditor's Assessment of and Response to Risk and Related Amendments to PCAOB Standards.* The amendments strengthened and clarified fair value measurement audit requirements. [41] AU 328, as amended, provides the most current PCAOB fair value measurement guidance with respect to the audits of public companies.

The PCAOB also issues Staff Audit Practice Alerts to provide guidance to auditors. Although Staff Audit Practice Alerts are not PCAOB rules, they are a resource to help auditors apply PCAOB standards and laws in certain circumstances. Three Staff Audit Practice Alerts address auditing fair value measurement: Alert No. 2, *Matters Related to Auditing Fair Value Measurements of Financial Instruments and the Use of Specialists,* issued in 2007; Alert No. 3: *Audit Considerations in the Current Economic Environment,* issued in 2008; and Alert No. 4, *Auditor Considerations Regarding Fair Value Measurements, Disclosures and Other-Than-Temporary Impairments,* issued in 2009. Alert No. 2 is the only one of these three alerts with broad guidance about auditing fair value measurements and will be discussed in more detail later in this section.

The American Institute of Certified Public Accountants (AICPA) has issued Clarified SASs in its *Codification of Statements on Auditing Standards* in an effort to streamline existing standards and to converge them with International Standards on Auditing (ISAs). A new clarified Statement on Auditing Standards No. 540, *Auditing Accounting Estimates, Including Fair Value Accounting Estimates and Related Disclosures,* is a combination of two predecessor statements, AU 342, *Auditing Accounting Estimates* (previously SAS No. 57), and AU 328. The new Clarified Statement does not change or expand AU 342 or AU 328, but the guidance has been moved to AU 540.[42] The new combined standard is effective for financial statement periods ending on or after December 15, 2012.[43] The AICPA's Clarified Statement on Auditing Standards AU-C 540, is substantially similar to the IAASB's ISA 540, which has the same title. ISA 540 was effective in countries that adopt ISAs for financial statement periods beginning on or after December 15, 2009.

Auditing fair value measurements and disclosures is discussed in this chapter from the perspective of a U.S. public company; therefore, the PCAOB guidance as set forth in AU 328 and its amendments apply. Some of the guidance in AU 342, a predecessor to AU 328, also applies to the audits of fair value measurements for public companies. While the focus of this chapter is auditing standards for public companies, the guidance is also generally applicable to private companies and international companies in countries that have adopted International Standards for Auditing.

---

[41] *http://pcaobus.org/Rules/Rulemaking/Docket%20026/Release_2010–004_Risk_Assessment.pdf*

[42] Summary of Changes in Requirements from Statements on Auditing Standards (SASs) No. 1 through No. 120 to Clarified SASs, revised April 2011, p11, www.acipa.org.

[43] Morris, Jan Taylor and William Thomas, "Clarified Auditing Standards: The Quiet Revolution," *Journal of Accountancy,* June 2011.

(b) AUDITING ESTIMATES IN FAIR VALUE MEASUREMENTS. An estimate is often the basis for a fair value measurement. Prior to the issuance of AU 328, auditors referred to AU 342 for guidance when auditing estimates that support a fair value measurement. Accounting estimates are defined by AU 342 as "an approximation of a financial statement element, item, or account."[44] The subjective nature of fair value measurement may call for numerous accounting estimates in the measurement process. These measurements are often derived from expectations about future events for which there may not be relevant historical experience.

For public companies, AU 342 outlines management's responsibility for accounting estimates and provides guidance to auditors in "obtaining and evaluating sufficient appropriate evidential matter to support significant accounting estimates ... and evaluating the reasonableness of accounting estimates made by management in the context of the financial statements taken as a whole."[45] Management has the responsibility for making the accounting estimates incorporated in financial statements, including fair value measurements. The Statement points out that

> estimates are based on subjective as well as objective factors and, as a result, judgment is required to estimate an amount at the date of the financial statements. Management's judgment is normally based on its knowledge and experience about past and current events and its assumptions about conditions it expects to exist and courses of action it expects to take.[46]

AU 342 further describes how management should develop a process for preparing accounting estimates. The process does not have to be formal. When applying the process to the measurement of fair value based on accounting estimates, management should be able to provide a reasonable basis for:

- Identifying situations for which accounting estimates are required in the fair value measurement.
- Identifying the relevant factors that may affect the accounting estimate, particularly unobservable inputs.
- Accumulating relevant, sufficient, and reliable data on which to base the estimate. The estimate then may be used in a valuation model using one of the valuation techniques to estimate fair value of the asset or liability.
- Developing assumptions that represent management's judgment of the most likely circumstances and events with respect to the relevant factors.
- Determining the estimated amount based on the assumptions and other relevant factors.
- Determining that the accounting estimate is presented in conformity with applicable accounting principles and that disclosure is adequate.[47]

When determining the process for measuring fair value, giving consideration to the guidance for measuring and disclosing fair value contained in ASC 820 is essential.

When auditing accounting estimates that are inputs to the fair value measurement, the auditor is responsible for evaluating the reasonableness of management's accounting estimate in the context of the financial statements taken as a whole. Since accounting estimates consist of both subjective as well as objective factors, management may have difficulty in establishing appropriate controls over the estimate. Subjective factors may be unobservable inputs, which are defined in the FASB's *Master Glossary* as "inputs for which market data are not available and that are developed using the best information available about the assumptions that market participants would use when pricing the asset or liability."[48] Objective factors may be estimates that are observable in the marketplace.

---

[44] AU 342, *Auditing Accounting Estimates,* section 342.01, *http://pcaobus.org*.

[45] AU 342.01 and 04, *Auditing Accounting Estimates.*

[46] AU 342.03, *Auditing Accounting Estimates.*

[47] AU 342.05, *Auditing Accounting Estimates.*

[48] *FASB Master Glossary, http://asc.fasb.org*.

The Glossary defines observable inputs as "inputs that are developed using market data, such as publicly available information about actual events or transactions that reflect the assumptions that market participants would use when pricing the asset or liability."[49]

The auditor should consider whether management's estimation process involves competent personnel using relevant and reliable data, whether those personnel are part of management or are outside specialists. Even when competent personnel make appropriate use of relevant and reliable data, there is potential for management bias, particularly when subjective factors are included. When planning and performing the audit procedures to evaluate management's accounting estimates, AU 342 suggests that auditors should consider "with an attitude of professional skepticism, both the subjective and objective factors."[50]

(c) AU 328, *AUDITING FAIR VALUE MEASUREMENTS AND DISCLOSURES.* Auditing fair value measurements requires more than just auditing management's estimates. When market prices are not available, management estimates fair value by using valuation techniques, which require inputs based on assumptions that market participants would make when estimating the price of a similar asset or liability. The Auditing Standards Board (ASB) believed that incorporating assumptions that a market participant would use introduced complexity and that auditors needed additional guidance when auditing management's fair value measurement beyond the guidance provided in AU 342 for auditing estimates. The ASB provided this additional guidance through AU 328.

The Statement is now codified in section AU 328 of the PCAOB Professional Standards. The purpose of AU 328 is "to establish standards and provide guidance on auditing fair value measurements and disclosures contained in financial statements."[51] In particular, AU 328 addresses audit considerations relating to the measurement and disclosure of assets, liabilities, and specific components of equity presented or disclosed at fair value in financial statements. These considerations are particularly relevant when fair value measurements change from period to period after the initial measurement of the asset or liability.[52]

AU 328 provides guidance on understanding management's process for developing fair value estimates and evaluating whether the measurement conforms to GAAP. When market prices are not readily available, management must estimate fair value using a valuation technique that relies on unobservable inputs. The inputs to the valuation technique should reflect assumptions that market participants would make, according to ASC 820. Determining appropriate inputs based on market participant assumptions is a unique requirement of fair value measurement that requires judgment.

The need for management to use judgment in financial reporting is a trend that is likely to continue. One reason relates to the convergence of U.S. GAAP with IAS, which have a greater number of accounting standards that require fair value measurements and disclosures. Standards permitting fair value measurements, such the fair value option in ASC 825-10-25, have increased the number of assets and liabilities measured at fair value on a recurring basis in financial reporting. The application of fair value measurement to certain financial statements is also becoming more complex. For instance, applying fair value measurement concepts to FASB ASC 815, *Derivatives and Hedging,* certainly requires a higher level of management expertise and judgment than in the past. The potentially significant and material impact of these fair value measurements to the financial statements as a whole created a need for auditing guidance that is specific to such measurements. AU 328 provides that additional guidance.

AU 328 was designed to provide a general framework for auditing all fair value measurements. The Standard does not provide guidance for auditing specific types of fair value measurement. The general framework begins with understanding management's process for developing the measurement of fair value. After understanding management's process, the auditor tests the entity's fair

[49] AU 342.05, *Auditing Accounting Estimates.*

[50] AU 342.04, *Auditing Accounting Estimates.*

[51] AU 328.01, *Auditing Fair Value Measurements and Disclosures.*

[52] Ibid.

value measurements and disclosures. Audit procedures are used to assess management's assumptions and the suitability of the valuation method and to test the inputs and the valuation model itself. Finally, the auditor makes a determination whether the measurements conform to GAAP.

Management is responsible for the presentation and disclosures of fair value measurements included in the company's financial statements. In order to present the fair value measurement fairly, management should establish an accounting and financial reporting process for:

- Determining when fair value measurements and disclosures are required
- Selecting appropriate methods for measuring fair value from the three basic approaches to valuation
- Identifying and adequately supporting any significant assumptions used in the fair value measurement
- Preparing the valuation internally or with assistance from an outside valuation specialist
- Ensuring that the presentation and disclosure of fair value measurements are in accordance with GAAP[53]

When obtaining an understanding of the entity's process for determining fair value measurements and disclosures, the auditor should consider, for example:

- Controls over the process used to determine fair value measurements, including for example controls over data and the segregation of duties between those committing the entity to the underlying transactions and those responsible for undertaking the valuations.
- The expertise and experience of personnel determining the fair value measurements.
- The role that information technology has in the process.
- The types of accounts or transactions requiring fair value measurements or disclosures (for example, whether the accounts arise from the recording of routine and recurring transactions or whether they arise from non-routine or unusual transactions).
- The extent to which the entity's process relies on a service organization to provide fair value measurements or the data that supports the measurement. When an entity uses a service organization, the auditor must consider the requirements of AU 324, *Service Organizations* (SAS No. 70), as amended.
- The extent to which the entity engages or employs specialists in determining fair value measurements and disclosures.
- The significant management assumptions used in determining fair value.
- The documentation supporting management's assumptions.
- The process used to develop and apply management assumptions, including whether management used available market information to develop the assumptions.
- The process used to monitor changes in management's assumptions.
- The integrity of change controls and security procedures for valuation models and relevant information systems, including the approval processes.
- The controls over the consistency, timeliness, and reliability of the data used in valuation models.[54]

(i) Testing Management's Fair Value Measurements. As with any financial statement assertion, the auditor should test management's fair value measurements and disclosures. The goal is to test management's evidence to see whether it supports the fair value measurement and ensure that the assertion is free from material misstatement. In order to determine if the assertion is free from material misstatement, the auditor should perform substantive tests of the measurement using

---

[53] AICPA, *Auditing Fair Value Measurements and Disclosures: A Toolkit for Auditors,* par. 7, *www.aicpa.org*.

[54] AU 328.12, *Auditing Fair Value Measurements and Disclosures.*

management's audit evidence. These substantive tests of the fair value measurements may include testing management's significant assumptions, testing the valuation model, and testing the underlying data.[55]

According to AU 328.24, auditing a fair value measurement can be complex, and some fair value measurements are much more complicated than others. The level of complexity is due to the nature of the item being measured at fair value and the degree of sophistication of the valuation method itself. For example, when performing goodwill impairment testing under ASC 350, if the equity of a reporting unit is not publicly traded, the fair value of the reporting unit's equity may be estimated by using valuation methods such as the discounted cash flow method or the guideline public company method.

> Complex fair value measurements normally are characterized by greater uncertainty regarding the reliability of the measurement process. This greater uncertainty may be a result of:
>
> - The length of the forecast period
> - The number of significant and complex assumptions associated with the process
> - A higher degree of subjectivity associated with the assumptions and factors used in the process
> - A higher degree of uncertainty associated with the future occurrence or outcome of events underlying the assumptions used
> - Lack of objective data when highly subjective factors are used[56]

Auditing standards for fair value measurement require the auditor to understand management's process for determining fair value measurements and to assess the risk of material misstatement of the fair value measurement. Then the auditor must design audit procedures based on their assessment of management's process and based on the risk of material misstatement. AU 328 provides some examples of situations an auditor might encounter and procedures to consider when auditing fair value measurements.

When the fair value measurement is made at a date other than the financial statement reporting date, the auditor should obtain evidence that management has taken into consideration any differences that may impact the fair value measurement between the date of the fair value measurement and the reporting date. This may occur when an outside valuation specialist conducts the analysis as of a different date due to information constraints or timing constraints for the engagement.

When collateral is an important aspect in the fair value measurement of an investment, the auditor should obtain sufficient appropriate audit evidence that the features of the collateral have been considered by management in estimating its fair value. Certain types of investments in debt instruments measured at fair value have collateral assigned to them. When testing for impairment, possible impairment of the collateral must also be considered. In certain circumstances, the auditor should perform additional procedures, such as a visual inspection of an asset. A detailed inspection of the asset may reveal information about the current physical condition of the asset, which may impact its fair value. In some instances, a thorough inspection or investigation of a security may reveal a restriction as to its marketability, which may affect its value.[57]

When the auditor tests management's fair value measurements, the evaluation process should consider the basis that management used in the fair value measurement. Management's assumptions in the fair value measurement should be reasonable and consistent with information available from the market. If market information is not available, the fair value measurement should be estimated using an appropriate valuation model for that particular asset or liability. In addition, management should incorporate all relevant information available on the date of measurement into the asset or liability's fair value measurement.

---

[55] AU 328.23.

[56] AU 328.24.

[57] AU 328.25.

(ii) Testing Management's Significant Assumptions, the Valuation Model, and the Underlying Data. Once the auditor understands management's process for measuring fair value and has assessed the risk of material misstatement and the complexity of the measurement, the next step is to perform substantive tests of the fair value measurement. Substantive tests can include testing management's assumptions, the valuation model, and underlying data used in the model. Some considerations in auditing fair value measurements are assessing whether:

- Management's assumptions are reasonable and are consistent with assumptions made by market participants.
- Management uses an appropriate valuation model to estimate the fair value measurement.
- Management uses known or knowable market participant assumptions that are available on the measurement date.

One simple indication of the reliability of management's processes is to compare the current fair value measurement to prior periods. Significant swings in value might be evidence that management's process is unreliable. However, the auditor should also take into consideration that the estimate of fair value may be impacted by market or economic changes from the prior period.[58]

(iii) Testing the Reliability of Management's Assumptions. When testing management's assumptions, the auditor should evaluate whether significant assumptions used by management in measuring fair value provide a reasonable basis for the fair value measurements. Assumptions are an essential component of valuation methods, particularly in detailed valuation models. For example, a discounted cash flow analysis is commonly used to measure fair value. A discounted cash flow model incorporates assumptions about expected future cash flows within a discrete forecast period, assumptions about the cash flows after the discrete forecast period, and even more assumptions about the rate of return required to compensate for the uncertainty associated with the future receipt of those cash flows. Auditors should pay particular attention to the assumptions incorporated into a discounted cash flow model and evaluate whether those assumptions are reasonable and whether they are consistent with market participant information.

In evaluating evidence to support the assumptions used in management's fair value measurements, the auditor must consider the source and reliability of the evidence as well as historical and market information related to the evidence. Management should identify assumptions that are significant to the fair value measurement. The auditor then focuses on the evidence that supports the significant assumptions that management has identified. Significant assumptions are those that materially affect the fair value measurement, such as:

- Assumptions that are sensitive to variation or are uncertain in amount or nature. For example, assumptions about a discount rate may be susceptible to significant variation compared to assumptions about long-term growth rates in cash flow.
- Assumptions that may be susceptible to misapplication or bias and can be easily manipulated in the fair value measurement. An example would be the selected royalty rate in the relief from royalty method used to estimate the fair value of a trade name.[59]

When considering the impact of significant assumptions on the fair value measurement, the auditor may ask management to perform sensitivity analysis to help identify critical assumptions. If management cannot identify particularly sensitive assumptions, the auditor should consider performing sensitivity analysis him- or herself to identify those assumptions that may be significant to the measurement.

Assumptions used in fair value measurements should have a reasonable basis individually and when used with other assumptions. An assumption may appear to be reasonable individually but

---

[58] AU 328.26 to 27.

[59] AU 328.33.

many may not be reasonable when used in combination with other assumptions. For example, in a fair value measurement that uses a discounted cash flow valuation method, management may assume that the company's revenue will grow 5 percent each year for the next five years. If the company has historically grown at 5 percent per year, this assumption may appear to be reasonable, at first. However, the forecast may also assume that management is curtailing certain operating expenses and capital expenditures for the next year due to borrowing constraints. The assumption of 5 percent growth may not be reasonable if management does not have the cash available to support growth in revenue as it had in the past.

To test the reasonableness of assumptions in a fair value measurement, the assumptions have to be reasonable individually and in combination with other assumptions. For the fair value measurement to be considered reasonable, AU 328 suggests that assumptions have to be realistic and consistent with these factors as well:

- The general economic environment, the economic environment of the specific industry, and the entity's economic circumstances;
- Existing market information;
- The plans of the entity, including what management expects will be the outcome of specific objectives and strategies;
- Assumptions made in prior periods, if appropriate;
- Past experience of, or previous conditions experienced by, the entity to the extent currently applicable;
- Other matters relating to the financial statements, for example, assumptions used by management in accounting estimates for financial statement accounts other than those relating to fair value measurements and disclosures;
- The risk associated with cash flows, if applicable, including the potential variability in the amount and timing of the cash flows and the related effect on the discount rate.[60]

A fair value measurement generally has two types of assumptions. The first type of assumption is based on historical information, such as the entity's past financial performance. If a company's revenue has grown at 5 percent per year for the past five years, it may be reasonable to forecast 5 percent growth for the next five years. If overall conditions remain consistent with the past, this assumption may be reasonable. However, the reasonableness of this assumption should be considered in conjunction with other assumptions.

The second type of assumption used in a valuation model is not based on historical information but on future projections. In auditing the reasonableness of an assumption, the auditor should consider whether the assumption is consistent with management's plans and projections and whether there are no significant limiting conditions, such as an inability to raise required capital.

In a fair value measurement based on a valuation model, the auditor should first review the model and evaluate whether the model is appropriate. This would require the auditor to evaluate the significant assumptions inherent in the model to be sure they are applicable to the asset or liability being measured. For example, it may be inappropriate to use the guideline company method under the market approach to estimate the fair value of an early-stage equity investment when there are limited revenues to support normalized earnings and cash flow due to the company's stage of development.

Finally, if the auditor believes that the valuation model and the assumptions used in the model are appropriate, the auditor should test the underlying data used in the valuation model. For example, if the guideline company method is used to estimate the fair value of a reporting unit, the auditor should test the data by comparing it to similar data from publicly traded guideline entities. The comparison should test data for accuracy, completeness and relevancy.[61]

---

[60] AU 328.36.

[61] AU 328.38 to 39.

(iv) Testing the Data. Valuation specialists can potentially serve in two capacities and be hired by company management or by the outside auditor firm. Since fair value measurements may require special skill and independent judgment, management often engages an outside valuation specialist to assist with the fair value measurement. The company's auditor may or may not have the skill and knowledge to plan and perform procedures related to audit of management's fair value measurement. Therefore, one of these audit procedures, testing the data used to develop the fair value measurements and disclosures, can be performed by the auditor or by the valuation specialist on the audit team.

In order to test the data used to develop fair value measurements and disclosures and to support management's assertions about fair value measurements, the auditor or valuation specialist may include procedures such as:

- Verifying the source of the data.
- Mathematical recomputation of inputs.
- Reviewing of information for internal consistency.
- Developing independent fair value estimates for corroborative purposes. An independent valuation analysis or "shadow valuation" may use the same valuation technique with different assumption or another valuation technique altogether to test the fair value representation on the financial statements.[62]
- Comparing the methods and assumptions used in the fair value measurement to professional "best practices." Many of the best practices for valuations in financial reporting are being developed by both the AICPA and the Appraisal Foundation.

When the audit team's valuation specialist is asked to test assumptions underlying the fair value measurement, whether they are prepared by management or by management's specialist, the auditor's valuation specialist then will issue what is sometimes referred to as an SAS 73 memo providing their conclusions about the reasonableness of the fair value assertions included in the valuation analysis.

(d) PCAOB STAFF AUDIT PRACTICE ALERT NO. 2, *MATTERS RELATED TO AUDITING FAIR VALUE MEASUREMENTS OF FINANCIAL INSTRUMENTS AND THE USE OF SPECIALISTS.* The PCAOB issued Alert No. 2 in 2007. The PCAOB said the purpose of this alert is to remind auditors of publicly traded companies about their responsibility for auditing fair value measurements of financial instruments. However, the guidance provided in the alert can also be applied to auditing the fair value of nonfinancial assets. The alert also discusses auditor responsibilities under existing standards when auditing the work of management's outside valuation specialists and provides some additional considerations for determining whether a specialist is needed.

Specific factors are likely to increase audit risk related to the fair value of financial instruments. One particularly relevant factor is an unstable or volatile economic environment. The PCAOB specifically asks the auditor to focus on certain areas in the implementations of ASC 820. The alert describes the auditor's responsibilities when management uses the work of an outside valuation specialist. The alert provides additional guidance about the auditor's responsibility to evaluate the appropriateness of using the specialist's work for the fair value measurements. Staff Audit Practice Alert No. 2 has four sections:

1. Auditing fair value measurements
2. Classification within the fair value hierarchy
3. Using the work of valuation specialists
4. Use of a pricing service

[62] AU 328.39 to 40.

(i) Auditing Fair Value Measurements. The PCAOB alert specifically mentions AU 328 as a source for providing guidance to the auditor on evaluating whether the fair value measurement conforms to GAAP. In planning for audit procedures to assess the risk associated with auditing the fair value measurements, the auditor should assess management's process for determining the measurements.

- Consider whether management's inputs into the fair value measurement are "reasonable and reflect, or are not inconsistent with, market information." For example, if management is forecasting significant sales growth during a period where other market participants are not experiencing the same growth, then the auditor should evaluate whether the growth forecast is reasonable under the circumstances at the measurement date.
- Conversely, if management uses historical financial information in the development of an input, the auditor should consider whether the reliance is appropriate for the fair value measurement. Historical information might not be the best indication of future conditions or events. For example, an auditor should evaluate whether a company's use of historical profit margins in a cash flow forecast is justified in an economic environment where sales are declining.
- Evaluate whether management's method for determining fair value measurements are applied consistently. If management uses the same methods and similar assumptions as in the past, then the auditor should consider whether changes in the environment or circumstances affecting the company warrant consistent treatment or whether the methodology or assumptions should be revised. For example, in estimating the fair value of developed technology that was estimated using a relief from royalty method in previous years, the market information may not be as relevant as in previous years. Consequently, the auditor may consider asking management to revise its measurement to include another form of the income approach or to make some other change in the model."[63]

(ii) Classification within the Fair Value Hierarchy Under FASB ASC 820, *Fair Value Measurements and Disclosures.* ASC 820 provides a three-level fair value hierarchy. The purpose of the hierarchy is to provide financial statement users information about the relative reliability of the inputs in a fair value measurement. A particular fair value measurement is classified within the hierarchy based on the lowest-level input that is significant to the fair value measurement in its entirety.

In an article entitled "SFAS No. 157, Fair Value Measurements: Implementation Challenges for the Alternative Investment Industry," Chris Mears says:

> Unfortunately the term "significant" is not defined by the standard. In assessing the significance of a market input, the fund should consider the sensitivity of the fair value to changes in the input used. Assessing the significance of an input will require judgment considering factors specific to the financial instrument being valued. The tone from the top should be one of conservatism in assigning level designations to securities with unobservable inputs.[64]

The article goes on to provide clarifying examples for designating appropriate fair value levels for disclosure. In one example, Level 2 is assigned to a total return swap where the underlying notational position is an actively traded (Level 1) security. The rationale is that the unit of measure is the total return swap, not the underlying stock.

Another example shows how options could be classified as Level 1, 2, or 3 in the fair value hierarchy. Options traded on an exchange in an active market would be classified as Level 1. Those traded on an exchange, but not in an active market, would be Level 2. Options valued using widely accepted models with observable inputs would also be considered Level 2. Finally, options

---

[63] PCAOB, Staff Audit Practice Alert No. 2, *Matters Related to Auditing Fair Value Measurements of Financial Instruments and the Use of Specialists,* December 10, 2007, pp. 4–5.

[64] Chris Mears, "SFAS No. 157, *Fair Value Measurements: Implementation Challenges for the Alternative Investment Industry*," September 2008, p. 3; *www.rko.com/pdfilb/SFAS_157_Fair_Value.pdf*

priced using models with unobservable inputs and significant adjustments and judgments would be assigned to Level 3.[65]

The PCAOB Alert notes that because the risk of material misstatement is higher using lower levels of inputs, different disclosures are associated with each of the three levels of the fair value hierarchy. The auditor should consider whether management has misclassified the level of measurement within the fair value hierarchy.

(iii) Using the Work of a Valuation Specialist. As required in performing an audit, auditors need to honestly evaluate their own skills, knowledge, and ability to plan and perform audit procedures related to fair value measurements. If auditors believe they do not have the necessary skill and knowledge to perform that portion of the audit adequately, they can use the work of an outside specialist. AU 336, *Using the Work of a Specialist,* describes circumstances when an auditor may include a specialist in the audit engagement team. A *specialist* is defined as someone who has specialized skills or knowledge outside of accounting and auditing. If auditors use the work of a specialist as part of the audit process, the auditors have certain responsibilities concerning the uses of the specialist work. Auditors are responsible for obtaining an understanding of the methods and assumptions used by the specialist, making appropriate tests of data provided to the specialist, and evaluating whether the specialist's findings support the related assertions in the financial statements.[66] The specialist's job is to test management's fair value measurements included in the financial statements and in disclosures so that auditors may provide an opinion as to whether those measurements are prepared in conformity with GAAP.

(iv) Use of a Pricing Service. The fair value measurement of complex financial instruments is often determined by using outside pricing services that have developed sophisticated models to price these financial assets and liabilities. When management uses a pricing service to measure fair value, the auditor should first understand the nature of the information used by the pricing service when determining price. The nature of the information would include whether the inputs are observable, meaning they are determined using quoted prices for the same or similar assets or liabilities traded in an active market, or whether the inputs are based on a financial model. If a financial model is used, then the auditor should determine whether the assumptions used by the pricing service are reasonable.

In addition, under ASC 820, the financial model should reflect the price to sell the asset or paid to transfer the liability in the principal market, which is the market with the greatest volume and level of activity. In situations where there is not a principle market, the financial model should reflect prices in the most advantageous market.

If the pricing service valuation is based on actual trades or quotes for the same or similar assets or liabilities, the auditor must consider whether the traded or quoted price would be available to the company, either in the principal market or most advantageous market, if there is no principal market. For example, a pricing service might provide a fair value measurement of an investment-grade corporate bond. The auditor should understand how the pricing service determined the market price for the bond. If the price is based on a market that is not available to the holder of the bond, that price may not be an appropriate measure of fair value under ASC 820.[67]

(e) SEC AUDIT GUIDANCE. The SEC has also provided guidance in auditing fair value measurements. The SEC's Division of Corporation Finance sent a letter in September 2008 to certain public companies identifying a number of disclosure items that should be included when preparing MD&A. Some of the specific items relating to fair value measurement disclosure that the SEC letter described included:

---

[65] Ibid., p. 26.

[66] PCAOB, Staff Audit Practice Alert No. 2, p. 7.

[67] PCAOB, Staff Audit Practice Alert No. 2, pp. 8–9.

- Significant judgments made in classifying a particular financial instrument in the fair value hierarchy
- An explanation of how credit risk is incorporated and considered in the valuation of assets or liabilities
- The criteria used to determine whether the market for a financial instrument is active or inactive
- Which financial instruments are affected by the lack of market liquidity and how the lack of liquidity impacted the valuation techniques used
- If using brokers or pricing services, the extent to which, and how, the information was obtained and was used in developing fair value measurements[68]

24.7 CONCLUSION

The economic environment in the United States and abroad has shaped financial reporting and fair value measurement. Because of technological changes, an increasing portion of our economy's value is attributable to intellectual property. Business entities and financial statement users also recognize that intellectual property drives value and that value is often not reflected in historic cost based financial statements. Another trend, increased globalization, has created a need for IAS, which traditionally have been more principles based than rules based. Convergence of U.S.-based GAAP with IAS is under way with support from the SEC and is substantially complete with respect to fair value measurement. Fair value accounting is generally perceived by constituents as more transparent and more relevant to investment decision making. The SEC and standards setters worldwide are committed to high-quality accounting standards that promote transparency in financial reporting. All three trends—the increased importance of intellectual property, globalization and international convergence of accounting standards, and a focus on relevance and transparency in financial reporting—reinforce the need for additional fair value accounting and disclosure in financial statements.

Guidance for measuring fair value currently appears in ASC 820 and was originally issued in SFAS No. 157 in 2006. SFAS No. 157 did not introduce any new requirements to measure assets and liabilities at fair value, but it provided guidance for applying fair value measurement when required by existing pronouncements. *Fair Value Measurement* has evolved since it was first issued as SFAS No. 157. The economic crisis forced the FASB to reconsider some of the Standard's more controversial aspects, such as measuring fair value in inactive markets, measuring liabilities, and the adequacy of disclosures. Convergence with IAS has also led to a refinement of many of the terms associated with fair value measurement, such as highest and best use, market participants, and exit price. In addition, convergence has shaped required fair value measurement disclosures by requiring more information about the unobservable inputs. However, convergence has also led to a reduction in the required disclosures for nonpublic companies. The issuance of ASU 2011-04, *Amendments to Achieve Common Fair Value Measurement and Disclosure Requirements in U.S. GAAP and IFRSs* marks the end of the FASB's fair value measurement project. Therefore, it appears that the accounting and reporting requirements for fair value measurement will continue to exist in their present form for the foreseeable future.

ASC 820 contains a framework for measuring fair value and provides related disclosure requirements. *Fair value* is defined as the "price that would be received to sell an asset or paid to transfer a liability in an orderly transaction between market participants at the measurement date." Other key concepts are that fair value is an exit price to market participants who are willing and able to transact in the principal market, or in the absence of a principal market in the most advantageous market. Fair value measurement also assumes the highest and best use of the asset by market participants, which depends on the valuation premise (either stand-alone or in-combined use). Inputs

---

[68] "Sample Letter Sent to Public Companies on MD&A Disclosures Regarding the Application of SFAS 157, *Fair Value Measurement,*" *www.sec.gov/divisions/corpfin/guidance/fairvalueltr0908.htm.*

to the fair value measurement can be based on observable market transactions or unobservable data. The input levels from the fair value hierarchy are the basis for disclosure using the fair value hierarchy. Level 1 inputs are unadjusted quoted prices for identical assets or liabilities in active markets, Level 2 inputs are directly or indirectly observable prices for the same or similar assets and liabilities, and Level 3 inputs are unobservable inputs from the entity's own data.

Measuring the fair value of liabilities is based on the assumptions that the liability is transferred to a market participant at the measurement date and that the liability continues with the same level of nonperformance risk. Credit risk is a component of nonperformance risk that must be considered at each measurement date. The entity must also consider its own credit standing when measuring the fair value of a liability. Ironically, an entity can report a gain from a change in the fair value of a liability when it own credit rating deteriorates. The fair value measurement of liabilities was a source of frustration for constituents, particularly during the economic crisis. ASU 2009-05, *Measuring Liabilities at Fair Value,* provided much-needed guidance for applying the fair value hierarchy to liabilities, and that guidance has been incorporated into the FASB's Accounting Standards Codification.

The measurement of fair value is generally accomplished by using one of the three valuation approaches—cost, market, or income—or by using a combination of two or more approaches. The cost approach is based on the amount that would be required to replace the service capacity of the asset. The market approach uses prices and other information from market transactions for identical or similar assets. And the income approach is a valuation technique that converts expected future cash flows to a present value by discounting the cash flows at an appropriate risk-adjusted interest rate.

Certain financial assets and liabilities may be eligible for fair value measurement under ASC 825-10-25, *Fair Value Option.* The option can be applied on an instrument-by-instrument basis, but once made, the election is irrevocable. The option allows entities to simplify the accounting for financial instruments, especially when those instruments are hedged.

Auditing fair value measurements is challenging because many of the inputs are based on assumptions and rely on management's judgment. Auditing management's estimates requires the auditor to evaluate the reasonableness of the judgment in the context of the financial statements as a whole. AU 328 provides a general framework for auditing all fair value measurements. The auditor must assess management's assumptions, assess the suitability of the valuation method, test the inputs, and test the model itself. The PCAOB and the SEC have also provided guidance for auditing fair value measurements.

CHAPTER 25

VALUATION OF ASSETS, LIABILITIES, AND NONPUBLIC COMPANIES

Neil J. Beaton, CPA/ABV/CFF, CFA, ASA

Grant Thornton, LLP

25.1 INTRODUCTION 1

(a) Definition of *Nonpublic Companies* 2
(b) Reasons for a Business Valuation 2

25.2 STANDARDS OF VALUE 2

(a) Fair Market Value 2
(b) Fair Value for Financial Reporting 2

25.3 AUDITING GUIDANCE 3

25.4 BUSINESS VALUATION BASICS 3

25.5 BUSINESS VALUATION METHODS 4

(a) Income Approach 4
(i) Discount Rates 5
(b) Market Approach 7
(c) Asset-Based, or Cost, Approach 9

25.6 DISCOUNTS AND PREMIUMS 9

25.7 WHAT A VALUATION REPORT SHOULD CONTAIN 10

25.8 INTANGIBLE ASSETS—ASC 805/350 ISSUES 10

(a) Determine What Intangible Assets Are Present 10
(b) Determine the Accounting Guidance 12
(c) Determine the Appropriate Methodology to Estimate Fair Value for Financial Reporting Purposes 12
(i) Cost Approach 12
(ii) Market Approach 13
(iii) Income Approach 13

25.9 DOES IT ALL ADD UP? 16

25.10 CREDENTIALS OF A VALUATION ANALYST 16

APPENDIX A BVR'S *GLOSSARY OF BUSINESS VALUATION TERMS, 2009* 17

APPENDIX B ADDITIONAL SOURCES OF STUDY 28

25.1 INTRODUCTION

Beginning in the early 2000s, the accounting environment has created an unprecedented need for accountants to be familiar with, and have a rudimentary understanding of, business valuation theory and implementation. The Financial Accounting Standards Board (FASB) has issued a number of pronouncements relating to business and asset valuation for financial reporting, including the most comprehensive fair value statement, Accounting Standards Codification (ASC) 820, *Fair Value Measurement and Disclosures* (formerly Statement of Financial Accounting Standard (SFAS) No. 157). This chapter focuses on the valuation of assets, liabilities, and nonpublic companies. It must be viewed as a primer only, since there are entire books devoted to the art and science of asset, liability, and business valuation.

(a) DEFINITION OF *NONPUBLIC COMPANIES.* Unlike a public company whose common stock is actively traded and has readily ascertainable value, the common stock of a nonpublic company typically is concentrated in only a few individuals with infrequent trades (if any at all). For that reason, there is no objective means to quantify the value of such shares. Fortunately, a number of professional valuation organizations exist, including the American Institute of Certified Public Accountants (AICPA), that provide training, education, and guidance for business valuation professionals. In addition, a number of excellent books have been written on the subject, allowing the curious or ambitious accountant a means to dig deeper into valuation theory and practice.[1]

(b) REASONS FOR A BUSINESS VALUATION. A number of circumstances trigger the need for valuing the stock of a nonpublic or closely held company. Among the more important situations requiring the valuation of nonpublic stock are estate planning, employee stock ownership plan transactions, granting employee stock options, buy/sell agreements, marital and corporate dissolutions, restructurings, sales, mergers and divestitures, and litigation. In addition, financial reporting requires valuations be performed to identify specific tangible and intangible assets in an acquisition (ASC 805, *Business Combinations*), the testing of goodwill impairment (ASC 350, *Intangibles—Goodwill and Other*) and other listed assets and liabilities (ASC 360, *Property, Plant and Equipment* and ASC 820). Recent FASB pronouncements have included the valuation of derivatives, liabilities and contingent payments.

25.2 STANDARDS OF VALUE

The *International Glossary of Business Valuation Terms* (see Appendix A at the end of this chapter) defines *standard of value* as "the identification of the type of value being utilized in a specific engagement; e.g., fair market value, fair value, and investment value." Common standards of value include these seven:

1. Fair market value
2. Fair value—including statutory and financial reporting definitions
3. Investment value
4. Intrinsic value
5. Book value
6. Liquidation value
7. Fair value in alternate contexts

Of the foregoing, fair market value and fair value for financial reporting are the most prevalent as these standards are promulgated primarily by the Internal Revenue Service and FASB, respectively.

(a) FAIR MARKET VALUE. *Fair market value* is defined as

> the price, expressed in terms of cash equivalents, at which property would change hands between a hypothetical willing and able buyer and a hypothetical willing and able seller, acting at arm's length in an open and unrestricted market, when neither is under compulsion to buy or sell and when both have reasonable knowledge of the relevant facts.

(b) FAIR VALUE FOR FINANCIAL REPORTING. ASC 820 defines *fair value* as the price that would be received to sell an asset or paid to transfer a liability in an orderly transaction between market participants at the measurement date. This definition of fair value is quite close to that of fair market value except for one key difference. The universe of potential buyers and sellers under fair value consists of "market participants" whereas under fair market value, there is no limitation to the hypothetical buyer or seller. To increase consistency and comparability in fair value measurements and related disclosures, the fair value hierarchy prioritizes the inputs to valuation techniques used

---

[1] See Appendix B at the end of this chapter.

to measure fair value into three broad levels. The fair value hierarchy gives the highest priority to quoted prices (unadjusted) in active markets for identical assets or liabilities (Level 1) and the lowest priority to developing fair values from unobservable inputs (Level 3). Quoted market prices in active markets are considered the best evidence of fair value of a security and should be used as the basis the measurement, if available. If quoted market prices are not available, the estimate of fair value should be based on the best information available, including prices for similar securities and the results of using other valuation techniques.

25.3 AUDITING GUIDANCE

Fair values are estimates, and are frequently used in assessing the realizable value of assets and liabilities and indicating whether an allowance or write-down of the asset or liability might be required. SAS (Statement of Auditing Standards) No. 57, *Auditing Accounting Estimates (AU section 342 and AU section 9342),* defines the general responsibilities of management and the auditor with respect to accounting estimates and provides guidance to auditors in obtaining and evaluating sufficient competent evidential matter to support most significant accounting estimates in an audit of financial statements. For audits beginning after June 15, 2003, SAS No. 101, *Auditing Fair Value Estimates and Disclosures,* is effective, setting a higher standard for auditing fair value estimates than other estimates. In broad terms it states:

- *Management* is responsible for making accounting estimates (including estimates related to a business combination or valuation of company stock)
- The *auditor* is responsible for evaluating the reasonableness of accounting estimates made by management in the context of the financial statements as a whole. In that context, the auditor should:
    1. Obtain an understanding of the *events and circumstances* that result in an asset being valued
    2. Evaluate that the *methodology used* to estimate value is appropriate
    3. Evaluate the *assumptions underlying* the methodology used are not unreasonable in the circumstances

The AICPA Toolkit, SAS No. 101, *Auditing Fair Value Measurements and Disclosures (AU section 328 and AU section 9328),* contains substantial guidance to auditors on fair value issues in financial reporting but predates the issuance of ASC 820. Although it provides excellent guidance on auditing fair value, its guidance is not as comprehensive as current accounting pronouncements.

25.4 BUSINESS VALUATION BASICS

A business valuation begins with an understanding of the business at the micro level (operations and finances) and then expands into more macro levels for context (industry, economy, competition). A thorough understanding of the company is required before any meaningful valuation analysis can be performed. This specific knowledge is used to assess the "riskiness" of the company that will impact implied discount rates and the selection of valuation multiples. Revenue Ruling 59-60, an oft-cited treatise on business valuation from the IRS, outlines eight specific business areas an appraiser should consider in a valuation. These areas include:

1. The nature of the business and the history of the enterprise from its inception
2. The economic outlook in general and the condition and outlook of the specific industry in particular
3. The book value of the stock and the financial condition of the business
4. The earning capacity of the company

5. The dividend-paying capacity
6. Whether the enterprise has goodwill or other intangible value
7. Sales of the stock and the size of the block of stock to be valued
8. The market price of stocks of corporations engaged in the same or a similar line of business having their stocks actively traded in a free and open market, either on an exchange or over the counter

Analyzing a company's operating and financial history can help identify past stability or instability, growth trends, operational diversity, and other facts and observations needed to form an opinion of the degree of risk involved in the business. A historical analysis should include, but not be limited to, the nature of the business, its products or services, its operating and investment assets, capital structure, plant facilities, sales records, and management. Similarly, the economic and industry conditions in which a company operates can have a positive or negative impact on value. A historical financial analysis can provide insight into future growth potential as well as place the company's current performance in context. Finally, an analysis of "comparable" or guideline companies is important to gauge the success of the company vis-à-vis its peers.

25.5 BUSINESS VALUATION METHODS

In its most fundamental form, the theory surrounding the value of an asset, a entire business, or an interest in a business depends on the future benefits that will accrue to the particular owner. In short, the value of the asset, business, or business interest depends on an estimate of the future benefits and the required rate of return at which those future benefits are discounted back to the valuation date.

The governing bodies of the major valuation credentialing organizations recognize three fundamental valuation approaches that prevail in the valuation industry and literature:

1. Income approach
2. Market approach
3. Asset-based, or cost, approach

Depending on the circumstance, any of the three approaches or some combination of them may be appropriate.

(a) INCOME APPROACH. The income approach is a general way of determining a value indication of a business, business ownership interest, security, or intangible asset using one or more methods that convert anticipated economic benefits into a present single amount.

The income approach is at the very heart of valuation theory. It involves either capitalizing a single estimate of a company's future expected cash flows or discounting a stream of periodic future cash flows, depending on the stability or instability of the economic income. In either case, events and circumstances internal and external to the company must be considered.

Economic income can mean different things. In a valuation context, economic income is often measured as *free cash flows* that ultimately inure to the benefit of the business owner. Another term sometimes used (particularly in a valuation prepared for gift and estate tax purposes), is *dividend-paying capacity*. Once economic income is forecast, it is then discounted using an expected rate of return that the market requires in order to attract funds to that unique investment opportunity. The result, in general terms, is the value of the enterprise.

So, valuation of an enterprise using the income approach requires two fundamental steps:

1. Measuring the expected future free cash flows that inure to the benefit of the equity or debt owners
2. Converting those free cash flows to a present value using an appropriate cost of capital

Exhibit 25.1 illustrates these concepts.

Tech Co
Valuation Analysis
Discounted Future Cash Flows

Inputs:	
Discount rate	25.00%
Sustainable growth rate	3.00%

	Year 1	Year 2	Year 3	Year 4	Year 5
Discounted Future Earnings:					
Forecasted after-tax earnings	200	350	400	450	500
Add back depreciation	35	40	45	45	45
Deduct capital additions	(50)	(45)	(45)	(45)	(45)
Add (Deduct) working capital change	(55)	(75)	(75)	(75)	(75)
Add (Deduct) long-term debt borrowings/repayments	100	(25)	(25)	(25)	0
Net Forecasted Future Cash Flow	130	270	325	375	425
Discounted	123	204	197	182	165
Five-year sum					870
Terminal value 1,990					771
Implied Value of Equity Capital					1,641

Exhibit 25.1 Illustration of a Discounted Cash Flow Analysis

In this case, management is forecasting that Tech Co will experience earnings increases for the next five years and then is expected to stabilize at a constant growth rate of 3 percent thereafter. Certain adjustments have been made to convert reported earnings to anticipated free cash flows to the equity owner. Typical adjustments include adding back noncash items (such as depreciation), deducting capital expenditures, and adding or deducting changes in working capital during the growth years. The amount of cash forecast to be received by the enterprise from borrowings on long-term debt to sustain operations or used to pay back borrowed amounts are added or subtracted as they are part of free cash flows available to the debt and equity holders.

Each year's cash flow is then discounted at the selected cost of equity, in this case 25 percent, back to the valuation date. Since a going-concern business does not have a defined life, a "terminal value" is computed at the end of year 5. This terminal value may be viewed as the hypothetical sale price of the business in the future based on a perpetual level of cash flow. The terminal value is also discounted back to the valuation date using the 25 percent discount rate and added to the sum of the discounted values of years 1 to 5 to arrive at the implied value of equity capital. Exhibit 25.2 shows a detail of how the terminal value is computed.

(i) Discount Rates. The term *discount rate* is often used interchangeably with *cost of capital,* as they are similar in concept. The discount rate derivation is performed to specifically reflect the appraiser's assessment of risk specific to a company. Under other circumstances apart from the valuation of a company, a discount rate reflects the risk specific to a particular expected future cash flow stream, such as interest on a loan or other debt instrument. In a business valuation, however, the cost of capital is the expected rate of return that the market requires in order to attract investment into the specific business. The fundamental building blocks for building up a discount rate in a business valuation are derived from a modified form of the Capital Asset Pricing Model (CAPM).

Safe rate of interest. Valuators typically select the "safe rate of interest"—U.S. Treasury obligations—as these rates line up with the equity risk premium (to be discussed) derived

Tech Co
Valuation Analysis
Computation of Terminal Value

Inputs:	
Discount rate	25.00%
Sustainable growth rate	3.00%

	Year 5
Discounted Future Earnings:	
Forecasted after-tax earnings	500
Add back depreciation	45
Deduct capital additions	(45)
Add (Deduct) working capital change	(75)
Add (Deduct) long-term debt borrowings/repayments	0
Net Forecasted Future Cash Flow	425
Growth of year 5 cash flow (at sustainable rate)	438
Terminal value ($438/capitalization rate of 22%)	1,990
Discounted Terminal Value (to Valuation Date)	771

Exhibit 25.2 Illustration of Terminal Value Calculation

from studies performed by Morningstar (formerly Ibbotson Associates, Inc.). U.S. Treasury data can be found at *www.federalreserve.gov* under the "Economic Research and Data" link; then go to "Statistical Releases and Historical Data." Morningstar is a commonly-relied-on source for empirical information that is used in building up a discount rate. Morningstar provides equity risk premium data in short-term, intermediate-term, and long-term forms based on data corresponding to Treasury maturities. The safe rate of interest provides for inflation and maturity risk. For most valuations, the consensus in the industry is to use the 20-year U.S. Treasury rate, which matches the Morningstar data calculated in the annually published book *Stocks, Bonds, Bills and Inflation.*

Equity risk premium. Morningstar data are also used to measure the increased risk of holding an equity security over a debt security. To accept this higher risk, an investor demands higher expected returns for investing in equities than for investing in U.S. Treasury obligations. Morningstar tracks the historical average excess return of equities (broad stock market) over U.S. Treasuries as a measure of this risk. This premium is added to the safe rate of interest.

Small stock premium. In addition, Morningstar data are available that measure the increased risk of investing in a smaller company. Studies show that investors demand an additional return for investing in small-capitalization companies. This premium is added to the safe rate of interest and the equity risk premium.

Specific company risk premium. Finally, many business valuation professionals add an additional premium for attributes present or lacking in a subject company. Examples include:

a. Size smaller than the smallest size premium group

b. Industry risk

c. Volatility of returns

d. Leverage

e. Other company-specific factors

Tech Co
Valuation Analysis
Discount Rate Buildup

Long-term U.S. Treasury bond	4.00%
Equity risk premium *(Morningstar)*	7.50%
Equity size premium *(Morningstar)*	6.00%
Company-specific premium, including industry risk (judgmental)	7.50%
Discount Rate	25.00%
Sustainable Growth Rate	3%
Capitalization Rate	22.00%

Exhibit 25.3 Illustration of a Discount Rate Buildup

This premium is added to the safe rate of interest, the equity risk premium, and the small stock premium.

Exhibit 25.3 shows the cost of equity measured for the example above.

Many valuation analysts have refined the equity risk premium with current academic studies and other industry studies, such as the Duff & Phelps Cost of Capital Study, but the Morningstar data are still widely used. Some professionals opt for the "pure" CAPM to estimate the cost of equity capital rather than the buildup method just described. Despite many criticisms, CAPM is still the most widely used model for estimating the cost of equity capital, especially for larger companies.

A third alternative discount rate methodology often used by valuation analysts is the weighted-average cost of capital (WACC). Here the subject company's capital structure (equity and long-term, interest-bearing debt) is taken into account. WACC is used to measure the value of a company's invested capital (equity and long-term debt) so the market value of long-term debt is subtracted from the implied value of invested capital to arrive at the aggregate equity value. This method is particularly useful when the subject's capital structure is different from other companies in that company's industry (more or less highly leveraged) or the valuation is being done on a control basis (from the perspective of a control owner who can change the capital structure to optimize the company's return to both equity and debt holders).

(b) MARKET APPROACH. The market approach is a general way of determining a value indication of a business, business ownership interest, security, or intangible asset by using one or more methods that compare the subject to similar businesses, business ownership interests, securities, or intangible assets that have been sold. Underlying the market approach to valuation is the economic principle of substitution: A prudent investor would not pay more for an investment opportunity than he or she would have to pay for an equally desirable alternative.

The market approach is commonly implemented by (1) selecting a group of peer or "guideline" public companies, (2) analyzing those companies, and (3) selecting one or more multiples from the guideline companies to apply to an economic income stream of the subject company. Referencing the example utilized under the income approach, through discussions with company management at Tech Co and a review of several analysts' reports, five guideline companies were selected. Of course, these companies typically are not identical to Tech Co; they may be many times its size or may have diversified operations, among other differences. Often it is difficult to find companies that are truly comparable because most private company valuations involve companies that are relatively undiversified and small compared to companies that trade on public exchanges. This fact does not render the market method useless, just less compelling as the differences become larger.

Once guideline companies are selected, they are evaluated for comparability with the subject company. Six common financial comparisons are made:

1. Size (generally measured by revenues or assets)
2. Growth (generally measured as compound growth of sales, cash flow, or some other income statement measure)
3. Leverage (generally debt to equity)
4. Profitability (generally measured by gross margin, operating margin, or other intermediate income statement steps depending on the industry)
5. Turnover (generally measured as a percentage of sales to assets or sales to book equity, which also varies by industry)
6. Liquidity (generally measured by current, quick, or similar ratios)

This comparison assists in narrowing the group of selected guideline companies and/or selecting an appropriate multiplier, or multipliers, from among them. A thorough analysis of the differences between the subject company and the guideline companies allows the valuation analyst to make adjustments to the selected multiples before applying them to the subject company's economic income streams. A simple example of what this may look like is shown in Exhibit 25.4.

In this instance, one might use the MCE (Market Capitalization of Equity)/Gross Margin as a multiplier. A revenue multiplier would likely not be selected because revenue multipliers, while still prevalent in some industries, generally become less relevant as companies grow in size or have different cost structures from the guideline companies. The net income multiplier would likely not be selected because, in this case, four of the five companies reported a loss. Often industries have specific multipliers that are commonly used, so familiarize yourself with them and consider their application in those industries that lend themselves to rules of thumb.

Selecting an MCE/Gross Margin multiplier from the range of observed multipliers to apply to Tech Co requires judgment. In exercising this judgment, some of the selected companies may be

Tech Co
Business Valuation Analysis
Guideline Public Company Analysis

($,000 except per share data)	Valuation Ratios Based on Peer Group						
Public Company Stock Symbol:	**AGIL**	**CIMK.OB**	**ITWH**	**MANU**	**NCLM**	**Mean**	**Median**
Market Capitalization of Equity (MCE)							
Price per Share	$ 7.31	$ 0.50	$ 13.75	$ 2.14	$ 13.17		
Shares Outstanding (000)	22,990	7,294	7,550	83,600	34,500		
Market Cap. of Equity	$168,057	$3,647	$103,813	$178,904	$475,065	$185,897	$168,057
Financial Statistics							
Revenues - trailing 12 months	$ 48,431	$2,184	$157,292	$205,637	$ 71,762	$ 97,061	$ 71,762
Gross Margin - trailing 12 months	32,257	1,861	97,021	95,671	47,697	54,901	47,697
Net Income - trailing 12 months	Loss	Loss	Loss	Loss	19,462		
Implied Ratios							
MCE/Revenues	3.47	1.67	0.66	0.87	6.62	2.66	1.67
MCE/Gross Margin	5.21	1.96	1.07	1.87	9.96	4.01	1.96
MCE/Net Income	NA	NA	NA	NA	24.41	24.41	24.41

Exhibit 25.4 Illustration of Market Multiples

weighted more heavily than others or some may be eliminated altogether because they are not very compelling once the financial and nonfinancial comparisons are made.

Assume an MCE/Gross Margin multiplier of 2.5 is selected based on an analysis of the guideline companies. Application of this multiplier to Tech Co's gross margin of $800 results in an implied value for Tech Co's equity of $2,000. The result from the application of the market approach is compared the results of the income or other approaches used, and conclusions about the value of Tech Co can be reached. A weighting scheme, based on the relative strengths of the various valuation approaches, is often employed to derive the most relevant valuation conclusion.

(c) ASSET-BASED, OR COST, APPROACH. The asset-based, or cost, approach is a general way of determining a value indication of an individual asset or business by quantifying the amount of capital required to replace the future service capability of that asset or business. On one hand, the theoretical underpinning of this method is simple: The value of the business equity is the value of the business assets (both tangible and intangible) less the value of the business liabilities (both recorded and contingent). On the other hand, the arduous task of valuing the separate intangibles in a business where the value is not contained in the hard assets makes this approach more costly and cumbersome to apply than the income or market approaches.

An example where the cost approach is used is in the valuation of a real estate holding company. In such a company, there may be very little value in the intangible assets, and the value of real properties can generally be ascertained with reasonable accuracy and cost.

The cost approach does provide a systematic framework of estimating the value of an intangible asset also based on the economic principle of substitution. Accordingly, this approach does have a place in some of the analyses of separate intangibles under ASC 805. For example, the determination of the value of an assembled workforce typically is done through the evaluation of the costs required to hire and train qualified people to do the task necessary in the company being acquired.

25.6 DISCOUNTS AND PREMIUMS

Depending on the purpose of the valuation and the source of information used to derive a company's value, it may be necessary to adjust the concluded value to reach the desired level of value. Two common levels of value are control value and minority value. Most commonly, these adjustments comprise a discount for lack of marketability (DLOM; e.g., when public company guidelines are used to derive a value for a private company) or a discount for lack of control (e.g., when a group of acquired companies are used to derive a value for a minority interest in a private company). Under ASC 820, the concepts of discounts are rare since most valuations under ASC 805 are performed assuming control attributes since the context of ASC 805 is a merger or acquisition. More commonly, a premium for control is encountered under ASC 805 whenever a minority interest valuation methodology is employed, such as the public guideline company methodology described earlier, since that methodology typically results in a minority, marketable value.

The concept underlying the DLOM is straightforward: The marketplace will pay more for an asset that can be liquidated quickly (such as publicly traded common stock) than one that has limited near-term liquidity (such as private company common stock). Here the differences in value are generally measured by empirical evidence that demonstrate discounts for lack of marketability between 0 percent and 90 percent, but generally come in between 35 percent to 45 percent.

Buyers will also typically pay more for an asset that will be controlled by them than for an asset where they have little or no control. These control premiums can be readily observed in the marketplace when an outside acquirer buys out a public company. In such acquisitions, the whole is typically valued higher than the sum of its parts (the individual holdings of the common shareholders). Here too the differences can be quantified by empirical evidence through reference to Morningstar's *MergerStat Review* or other data sources. such as *Pratt's Stats.*

25.7 WHAT A VALUATION REPORT SHOULD CONTAIN

In general, a valuation report should articulate a clear understanding of the company, its industry, and the transaction(s) giving rise to the valuation assignment. That understanding should be consistent with the circumstances under which the valuation is being performed. For example, the valuation of a 10 percent equity interest in a software development company for shareholder buyout purposes should indicate the standard of value and premise of value[2] under which the valuation is to be performed. The report should also set forth the methods and conclusions in a manner sufficiently comprehensive and clear to allow the reader to gain a clear understanding of both the methods used and rationale for those methods and the significant assumptions used and basis for selected assumption inputs.

The AICPA has published standards for licensed certified public accountants to follow when performing a business valuation. The AICPA's Statement on Standards for Valuation Services (SSVS) No. 1, *Valuation of a Business, Business Ownership Interest, Security, or Intangible Asset*. published June 2007, outlines a number of items to include in a well-documented business valuation report:

- Information gathered and analyzed to obtain an understanding of matters that may affect the value of the subject interest
- Assumptions and limiting conditions
- Any restriction or limitation on the scope of the valuation analyst's work or the data available for analysis
- Basis for using any valuation assumption during the valuation engagement
- Valuation approaches and methods considered
- Valuation approaches and methods used, including the rationale and support for their use
- If applicable, information relating to subsequent events considered by the valuation analyst
- For any rule of thumb used in the valuation, source(s) of data used and how the rule of thumb was applied

25.8 INTANGIBLE ASSETS—ASC 805/350 ISSUES

Intangible assets have become an important part of the economy in general and for specific companies in particular. Intangible assets can be developed internally, acquired, or licensed. Each method of attaining those rights has a different method of accounting associated with it. However, the economics underlying these assets are the same, and thus the valuation of these assets follow principles already discussed in this chapter. Identifying a company's intangible assets begins with understanding the company itself. Intangible assets can be found in every area of a company, including operations, marketing, research, administration, distribution, and information technologies. Wherever a competitive advantage exists or rights have been established, you will most likely find intangible assets.

Generally, intangible assets are considered to exist as a separate asset of the company when they stem from contractual rights or from legally defined rights or they can be separated from the business in some form. If they do not have these attributes, they are generally grouped into an amorphous category commonly referred to as goodwill. Advances in the use of real option techniques now assist in the quantification of broader conceptual goodwill, including first-mover advantage, abandonment options, and expansion options.

(a) DETERMINE WHAT INTANGIBLE ASSETS ARE PRESENT. Intangible assets can be categorized according to their characteristics. This can be useful in the valuation process. For example, the category of brand names typically would include trademarks, trade names, trade dress (e.g., the shape of

[2] The premise of value is either going concern or liquidation. Most business valuations are performed under a going-concern premise of value.

a container or color of the packaging), and slogans. A fundamental categorization of intangible assets is based on whether they have a limited life or an indefinite life. Limited-life intangible assets deteriorate due to some form of obsolescence brought on by either environmental changes or legally determined limits. Indefinite-life intangible assets can be renewed indefinitely or can last for an indeterminate period of time, depending on market factors or upkeep. Intangible assets can either indirectly support the business or directly generate revenue. Supporting intangible assets are necessary for sales to occur but do not drive sales; they include an assembled and trained workforce or manufacturing processes. Revenue-generating intangible assets are directly associated with dollars in the door, such as customer contracts, production software, or charging a fee for using a franchised name. Exhibit 25.5 lists some of the most common forms of intellectual property.

- Airport gates and slots
- Architectural drawings
- Assembled workforce
- Backlogs
- Blueprints
- Brand names
- Broadcast rights/licenses
- Certificates of need
- Contracts
- Cooperative ventures
- Copyrights
- Core bank deposits
- Customer contracts
- Customer lists
- Customer relationships
- Databases
- Designs
- Development rights
- Distribution networks
- Distribution rights
- Drawings
- Drilling rights
- Electronic media
- Employment agreements
- Exploration rights
- FCC licenses
- Film libraries
- Formulas
- Franchise agreements
- In-process research and development
- Insurance contracts
- Joint ventures
- Laboratory notebooks
- Landing rights
- Leasehold interests
- Licensing agreements
- Lyrics
- Management contracts
- Manuscripts
- Mask works
- Medical charts and records
- Mineral rights
- Musical compositions
- Noncompetition covenants and contracts
- Patent applications
- Patents
- Patterns
- Permits
- Processes
- Product designs
- Property rights
- Proprietary processes
- Proprietary products
- Proprietary technology
- Publications
- Retail shelf space
- Royalty agreements
- Service marks
- Schematics and diagrams
- Shareholder agreements
- Slogans
- Software
- Subscription lists
- Supplier relationships
- Technical documentation
- Technology rights
- Trade secrets
- Trademarks
- Trade names
- Trade dress

Exhibit 25.5 Commonly Identified Intangible Assets

(b) DETERMINE THE ACCOUNTING GUIDANCE. While a number of generally accepted accounting principle (GAAP) pronouncements deal with intangible assets, three main pronouncements give rise to intangible asset valuations: ASC 805, ASC 350, and ASC 360. Application of these standards requires that both the valuation analyst and the auditor be familiar with the specifics in these pronouncements as well as the other relevant accounting pronouncements.

(c) DETERMINE THE APPROPRIATE METHODOLOGY TO ESTIMATE FAIR VALUE FOR FINANCIAL REPORTING PURPOSES. Once all of a company's intangible assets have been identified (and the applicable GAAP and tax implications are understood), the next step is to value the individual intangible assets. The first step in that process is to determine the most appropriate methodology (or methodologies) to value a specific intangible. As was discussed in the preceding section, there are generally three approaches to valuing intangible assets: the cost approach, the market approach, and the income approach. We will not go over those methodologies again; instead, we focus on their application under ASC 805 and ASC 350. The cost approach considers the cost to recreate a particular asset. It is typically used for intangible assets where there is no direct cash flow generation, such as an assembled workforce. The market approach considers information from sales of similar assets in the open marketplace. This approach is difficult to utilize because it is almost impossible to identify individual sales of intangible assets that are similar enough to the particular intangible asset to be relevant. The income approach is the most robust approach for valuing income-producing intangibles as it focuses on cash flow directly attributable to the intangible asset being valued. The next paragraphs discuss the general methodologies related to valuing intangible assets under ASC 805.

(i) Cost Approach. Under the cost (or asset-based) approach, there are two general methodologies to valuing an intangible asset:

1. Directly estimate current cost to replace the asset at its current stage of obsolescence.
2. Adjust historical expenses to reflect current costs to create the asset.

When determining the current value of an asset under the cost approach, all historical costs must be reviewed and compared against the current state of technology. In addition, the affect of inflation and the time value of money need to be reflected.

Quantifying the impact of functional and technological obsolescence is challenging; often it can be estimated after an understanding is obtained of the facts and circumstances surrounding the intangible asset and its environment. This often begins through discussions with the company's technical staff. For example, the cost approach might be used for valuing software code that is useful only in older computers. Another factor in the consideration of functional and technical obsolescence is quantifying the reduction in value attributable to historical benefits that are no longer available for the particular intangible asset. For example, a chemical plant that relied on a state-of-the-art, two-step chemical process at the time of construction is now disadvantaged since current technology requires only a one-step process. The new one-step process takes 10 percent less energy, thereby creating a cost savings over the older technology. This cost benefit, of course, reduces the value of the older facility by the present value of such anticipated benefits and can be quantified using a discounted cash flow model.

Last, economic obsolescence always must be considered. Simply stated, an asset has become economically obsolete when there are no buyers because there are better alternatives. Whenever the cost of continued use exceeds the benefits, a downward adjustment in the value of the asset should be considered.

Although the cost approach is well recognized among valuation analysts, it does have shortcomings when used in the valuation of intangible assets. While the value of most intangible asset values is measured based on a future benefit that will be derived by that asset, the cost approach is rearward looking and, therefore, ignores future benefits. Furthermore, the cost approach ignores the duration of future economic benefits specific to the intangible asset. For example, a patent has a specific contractual life, but under the cost approach, value is not impacted whether it has only one year or five years left of protection. In addition, the expected trend of future potential economic benefits is lost under the cost approach. Like a photograph compared to a movie, under the cost approach one cannot tell if the asset's past performance was up or down or which direction future performance will take. This is often critical when valuing intangible assets that are based on rapidly changing technology.

Given these shortcomings, the use of the cost approach is limited in valuing intangible assets. As discussed later, the income approach is considerably more robust in capturing the value of intangible assets for purposes of a business combination under ASC 805.

(ii) Market Approach. The market approach has its own set of hurdles to overcome in valuing intangible assets. When applied to intangible assets, the market approach requires the valuation analyst to identify "guideline" transactions (similar to the identification of guideline public companies illustrated earlier). Although one can obtain market research from a number of sources, identifying *relevant* transactions is challenging. Online databases such as *www.royaltysource.com* and publications such as *Licensing Economics Review* provide general data on various market transactions, but their relevance to a particular intangible asset may be difficult to establish. Careful analysis of each potential transaction must be made for relevance, arm's-length determination, and relevant units for comparison.

Application of the market approach also requires that the valuation analyst identify the specific rights which attach to the asset that was transferred in the guideline transaction. These rights could include specified geographic territories, product or market exclusivity, sales channel access, or other unique attributes. Once the rights have been identified and analyzed, the valuation analyst will need to identify the full consideration paid in the transaction, including special financing terms that may mask the "real" price paid. If the transaction is dated—say over a year old—the analyst must also consider environmental changes from the time of the transaction, including economic conditions, industry trends, regulatory changes, and the possible existence of new substitute products. Another consideration that often muddles market transactions is the sale of a group of intangible assets rather than a single asset. If a group of assets is sold, adjustments will need to be considered if the subject asset is a single intangible asset. Unfortunately, adequate information to make such adjustments is often missing.

An example of bundled intangibles under the market approach may be helpful. In an engagement to value a manufacturing plant that utilized proprietary processes, licensed technology and publicly available components were combined in a unique way to produce some widgets. We were able to identify a number of sales of similar plants within the prior two years of the valuation date, so we got excited. However, upon further inspection, key components of the sales were lacking, including the technology that was included in the sale, whether and when licenses for proprietary technology were obtained, and the amount and duration of the licenses. Ultimately, we unable to satisfy ourselves that we had adequate data points to apply the valuation metrics gleaned from these sales to our specific facility.

After discussing the cost and market approaches, it is no wonder the income approach is the most widely used valuation technique in the ASC 805 arsenal. Because most identified intangible assets can be addressed individually through application of the income approach, it is by far the most prevalent of the three approaches in valuing intangible assets.

(iii) Income Approach. Let us now examine the income approach as it is applied to intangible assets. Unlike valuing an entire business using the income approach, as was discussed previously, application of the income approach to a single intangible asset or a bundle of intangible assets requires that the economic benefit generated by each individually identified intangible asset be separately quantified. At the same time, in order to isolate the value of each intangible asset and to avoid double-counting asset values, adjustments need to be made for supporting assets. (Supporting assets include such things as working capital, plant, and equipment as well as the other separately identified intangible assets.) The economic benefit streams so identified should be tested against the market whenever possible as long as the cost to do so is reasonable. Market forces also come into play in considering the duration of the income stream and the economic life of the asset. For example, the economic life of a current version of software will be limited if the company plans to issue new software versions on a periodic basis. In addition to the duration and economic life of the asset, the valuation analyst must identify the specific risks related to that asset's economic benefit stream and determine the appropriate rate of return for the risks associated with that benefit stream.

When assessing the useful life of an asset, determinants, when present, should include:

- Legal life
- Contractual life
- Judicial life
- Functional life
- Economic life
- Analytical life (based on analysis of available data)

These determinants allow for the specific measurement of the duration of cash flows generated by an identifiable intangible asset. Once duration is determined, the economic benefit can be modeled over the asset's useful life. This method enables the analyst to avoid overvaluing the asset by including future benefits that are contractually or otherwise limited.

Specific applications of the income approach that are commonly used in determining the value of intangible assets include these four:

1. *Residual cash flow method* focuses on the present value of cash flows after the consideration of returns for supporting assets (discussed earlier). This method includes both the excess earnings and multiperiod excess earnings methods.
2. *Differential cash flow method* ascertains the difference between the value of the income stream with the asset in place and the value of the income stream without the asset in place.
3. *Relief from royalty method* quantifies the value of owning an asset as based on what it would cost to pay a royalty for use of the asset over the estimated benefit period (sometimes considered a market approach since royalty rates may be estimated from market data).
4. *Options methodology* focuses on contingent aspects of future value and ability to achieve those values.

Another unique factor that comes into play when applying the income approach to the valuation of intangible assets is what is commonly referred to as the *amortization benefit.* An amortization benefit arises as a result of the deductibility, over a 15-year term, of the intangible asset on the company's income tax return. Since most valuations are in consideration of the value if sold, the tax benefit of the 15-year amortization must be added back to capture the full economic benefit of ownership.

There are a number of ways to compute the amortization benefit, but the next formula is a simple and straightforward means to do so:

$$TAB = VBA \times n/[n - ((AF \times t \times (1 + r)\hat{\ }0.5) - 1)]$$

where:

TAB = Tax amortization benefit

VBA = Value before amortization

n = Number of amortization periods in years (15 years in United States; see Internal Revenue Code 197)

AF = Annuity factor(AF = 1/r − 1/r(1 + r)^n)

t = Tax rate

r = Discount rate

As if the foregoing procedures were not enough, one must also assess the useful life of the asset in building a valuation model for specific intangible assets under the income approach. The useful life of an intangible asset to an entity is the period over which the asset is expected to contribute directly or indirectly to the future cash flows of the entity. Some factors set forth in ASC 350 that should be considered in such an analysis include:

- The expected use of the asset by the entity
- The expected useful life of another asset or a group of assets related to the intangible asset
- Any legal, regulatory, or contractual provisions that may limit the useful life
- Any legal, regulatory, or contractual provisions that enable the renewal or extension of the asset's legal or contractual life without substantial costs
- The effects of obsolescence, demand, competition, and other economic factors
- The level of maintenance expenditures required to obtain the expected future cash flows from the asset

Analysts often employ *survivor curves* to assist in determining the remaining useful life of an asset. Although a complete discussion of survivor curves is beyond the scope of this chapter, a number of books discuss these techniques in depth, including *Financial Valuation: Applications and Models* by James R. Hitchener John Wiley & Sons, 2003 and *Valuing Intangible Assets* by Robert F. Reilly and Robert P. Schweihs McGraw-Hill, 1998. Exhibit 25.6 captures the essence of such an analysis in valuing intangible assets.

Once all of these steps have been completed and the identifiable intangible assets have been valued, those values, along with any associated goodwill, need to be allocated to specific reporting units. The allocation process is prescribed by the FASB; however, in many instances it is anything but clear cut. The next guidelines can provide parameters in the allocation process, but a number of Emerging Issues Task Force (EITF) bulletins have addressed specific circumstances related to the attribution of intangible assets to reporting units.

- The asset will be employed in, or the liability relates to, the reporting unit's operations.
- The asset or liability will be considered in determining the reporting unit's fair value.
- All goodwill will be assigned to reporting units in a manner that is reasonable, supportable, and applied consistently.

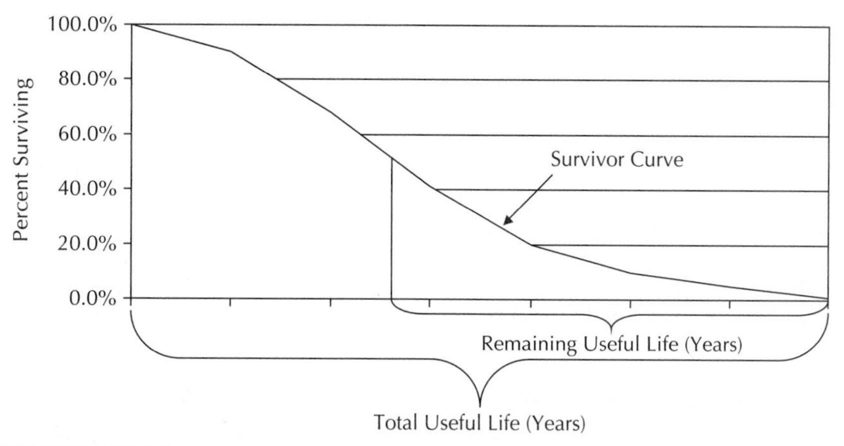

Exhibit 25.6 Illustration of a Survivor Curve

EITF Abstracts, Topic D-101, *Clarification of Reporting Unit Guidance in ASC 350,* provides additional guidance in the identification of reporting units. According to the abstract, in order to be characterized as a separate reporting unit, a business segment must:

- Constitute a business
- Have discrete financial information
- Be reviewed by segment management
- Have similar economic characteristics

25.9 DOES IT ALL ADD UP?

Upon completion of the engagement, it is prudent to perform a reasonableness check of the underlying assumptions and valuation outputs. This also applies when reviewing the valuation analyst's work under an audit engagement for your particular firm. Some questions to ask are:

- Does the forecast correspond to internal budgets or external forecasts by stock analysts?
- Is the current forecast consistent with previous forecasts?
- Do the assumptions in the forecast appear reasonable in relation to historical performance?
- Do the assumptions in the forecast appear reasonable in relation to the performance and structure of the guideline companies?
- Do expectations for the industry and economy generally support management's assumptions?
- Does a discounted cash flow of the forecast reasonably tie out to the value of the reporting unit?
- Does the weighted average of the discount rates of the separate tangible and intangible assets (net of non–interest-bearing liabilities) aggregate to the discount rate for the entire business?

The valuation analyst should address these questions. They are also questions the reviewing party (auditor or the valuation resource) should ask in assessing the valuation analyst's work product.

25.10 CREDENTIALS OF A VALUATION ANALYST

In assessing the credentials of a valuation analyst, professional certifications are a starting point,but not a panacea. The AICPA has established the Accredited in Business Valuation (ABV) credential; the American Society of Appraisers confers the Accredited Senior Appraiser (ASA) and Accredited Member (AM) designations. Other certifying organizations include the National Association of Certified Valuation Analysts, which confers a plethora of designations, and the Institute of Business Appraisers, which confers the Certified Business Appraiser (CBA) designation. A less specific but highly respected credential is the Chartered Financial Analyst (CFA) designation sanctioned by the CFA Institute. These credentials are a starting point as there is no substitute for experience. When assessing the expertise of any valuation analyst, always inquire as to the experience of the individuals actually performing the work.

In addition to professional certifications, it is important that any valuation be performed in accordance with applicable professional standards. The primary standards governing the valuation industry are the Uniform Standards of Professional Appraisal Practice (USPAP) and the SSVS No. 1 promulgated by the AICPA. A compliant valuation report will contain a list of "Contingent and Limiting Conditions" as well as an appraisal certification expressing compliance with USPAP, SSVS No. 1, or both. These Standards can be found under the respective Web sites of the issuing organizations, *www.appraisers.org* for USPAP or *www.aicpa.org* for SSVS No. 1.

APPENDIX A BVR'S *GLOSSARY OF BUSINESS VALUATION TERMS, 2009*

To enhance and sustain the quality of business valuations for the benefit of the profession and its clientele, the American Institute of Certified Public Accountants, American Society of Appraisers, Canadian Institute of Chartered Business Valuators, National Association of Certified Valuation Analysts, and the Institute of Business Appraisers have adopted the definitions for the terms included in this glossary, unless otherwise credited to another source. If another source was used other than the original *International Glossary of Business Valuation Terms 2001*, the source will be noted in parentheses after the term is defined.

The performance of business valuation services requires a high degree of skill and imposes upon the valuation professional a duty to communicate the valuation process and conclusion, in a manner that is clear and not misleading. This duty is advanced through the use of terms whose meanings are clearly established and consistently applied throughout the profession.

If, in the opinion of the business valuation professional, one or more of these terms needs to be used in a manner that materially departs from the enclosed definitions, it is recommended that the term be defined as used within that valuation engagement.

This glossary has been developed to provide guidance to business valuation practitioners by further memorializing the body of knowledge that constitutes the competent and careful determination of value and, more particularly, the communication of how that value was determined.

Departure from this glossary is not intended to provide a basis for civil liability and should not be presumed to create evidence that any duty has been breached.

ABAR (***Accredited in Business Appraisal Review***)—Institute of Business Appraisers designation.

Adjusted Book Value Method—a method within the asset approach whereby all assets and liabilities (including off-balance sheet, intangible, and contingent) are adjusted to their fair market values (NOTE: In Canada on a going concern basis).

Adjusted Net Asset Method—see **Adjusted Book Value Method**.

AIBA (***Accredited by IBA***)—Institute of Business Appraisers designation.

AM (***Accredited Member***)—American Society of Appraisers designation.

Amortization—(1) The paying off of debt in regular installments over a period of time. (2) The deduction of capital expenses over a specific period of time (usually over the asset's life). More specifically, this method measures the consumption of the value of intangible assets, such as a patent or a copyright. (*investopedia.com*)

Appraisal—see **Valuation**.

Appraisal Approach—see **Valuation Approach**.

Appraisal Date—see **Valuation Date**.

Appraisal Method—see **Valuation Method**.

Appraisal Procedure—see **Valuation Procedure**.

Arbitrage Pricing Theory—a multivariate model for estimating the cost of equity capital, which incorporates several systematic risk factors.

ASA (***Accredited Senior Appraiser***)—American Society of Appraisers designation.

Asset (Asset-Based) Approach—a general way of determining a value indication of a business, business ownership interest, or security using one or more methods based on the value of the assets net of liabilities.

AVA (***Accredited Valuation Analyst***)—National Association of Certified Valuation Analysts designation.

Average Revenue Per Unit (ARPU)—a measure of the revenue generated per user or unit. This measure allows for the analysis of a companies revenue generation and growth at the per unit level, which can identify which products are high or low revenue-generators. (*investopedia.com*)

Beta—a measure of systematic risk of a stock; the tendency of a stock's price to correlate with changes in a specific index.

Binomial Options Pricing Model (BOPM)—in finance, the binomial options pricing model (BOPM) provides a generalizable numerical method for the valuation of options. The binomial pricing model uses a "discrete-time framework" to trace the evolution of the option's key underlying variable via a binomial lattice (tree), for a given number of time steps between valuation date and option expiration. Each node in the lattice, represents a possible price of the underlying, at a particular point in time. This price evolution forms the basis for the option valuation. The valuation process is iterative, starting at each final node, and then working backwards through the tree to the first node (valuation date), where the calculated result is the value of the option. (*wikipedia.org*)

Binomial Tree—a graphical representation of possible intrinsic values that an option may take at different nodes or time periods. The value of the option depends on the underlying stock or bond, and the value of the option at any node depends on the probability that the price of the underlying asset will either decrease or increase at any given node. (*investopedia.com*)

Black-Scholes Option Pricing Model—a model of price variation over time of financial instruments such as stocks that can, among other things, be used to determine the price of a European call option. The model assumes that the price of heavily traded assets follow a geometric Brownian motion with constant drift and volatility. When applied to a stock option, the model incorporates the constant price variation of the stock, the time value of money, the option's strike price and the time to the option's expiry. (*investopedia.com*)

Blockage Discount—an amount or percentage deducted from the current market price of a publicly traded stock to reflect the decrease in the per share value of a block of stock that is of a size that could not be sold in a reasonable period of time given normal trading volume.

Book Value—see **Net Book Value**.

Business—see **Business Enterprise**.

Business Enterprise—a commercial, industrial, service, or investment entity (or a combination thereof) pursuing an economic activity.

Business Risk—the degree of uncertainty of realizing expected future returns of the business resulting from factors other than financial leverage. See **Financial Risk**.

Business Valuation—the act or process of determining the value of a business enterprise or ownership interest therein.

BVAL (*Business Valuator Accredited for Litigation*)—Institute of Business Appraisers designation.

Capital Asset Pricing Model (CAPM)—a model in which the cost of capital for any stock or portfolio of stocks equals a risk-free rate plus a risk premium that is proportionate to the systematic risk of the stock or portfolio.

Capitalization—a conversion of a single period of economic benefits into value.

Capitalization Factor—any multiple or divisor used to convert anticipated economic benefits of a single period into value.

Capitalization of Earnings Method—a method within the income approach whereby economic benefits for a representative single period are converted to value through division by a capitalization rate.

Capitalization Rate—any divisor (usually expressed as a percentage) used to convert anticipated economic benefits of a single period into value.

Capital Structure—the composition of the invested capital of a business enterprise, the mix of debt and equity financing.

Cash Flow—cash that is generated over a period of time by an asset, group of assets, or business enterprise. It may be used in a general sense to encompass various levels of specifically defined cash flows. When the term is used, it should be supplemented by a qualifier (for example, "discretionary" or "operating") and a specific definition in the given valuation context.

CBA ***(Certified Business Appraiser)***—Institute of Business Appraisers designation.

CBI ***(Certified Business Intermediary)***—International Business Brokers Association designation.

CBV ***(Chartered Business Valuator)***—Canadian Institute of Chartered Business Valuators designation.

CFA ***(Chartered Financial Analyst)***—CFA Institute designation.

CFF ***(Certified in Financial Forensics)***—American Institute of Certified Public Accountants designation.

CFFA ***(Certified Financial Forensic Analyst)***—National Association of Certified Valuation Analysts designation.

Coefficient of Variation (CV)—a statistical measure of the dispersion of data points in a data series around the mean. It is calculated as follows: Coefficient of Variation = Standard Deviation / Expected Return. The coefficient of variation represents the ratio of the standard deviation to the mean, and it is a useful statistic for comparing the degree of variation from one data series to another, even if the means are drastically different from each other. (*investopedia.com*)

Common Size Statements—financial statements in which each line is expressed as a percentage of the total. On the balance sheet, each line item is shown as a percentage of total assets, and on the income statement, each item is expressed as a percentage of sales.

Company Specific Risk (as defined by *Butler Pinkerton Model™*)—the portion of total risk specific to an individual asset that can be avoided through diversification. (*BVMarket-Data.com*)

Compound Annual Growth Rate (CAGR)—the year-over-year growth rate of an investment over a specified period of time. The compound annual growth rate is calculated by taking the nth root of the total percentage growth rate, where n is the number of years in the period being considered. This can be written as follows: CAGR = [(Ending Value / Beginning Value) ^ (1 / # of years)] – 1. (*investopedia.com*)

Control—the power to direct the management and policies of a business enterprise.

Control Premium—an amount or a percentage by which the pro rata value of a controlling interest exceeds the pro rata value of a non-controlling interest in a business enterprise, to reflect the power of control.

Cost Approach—a general way of determining a value indication of an individual asset by quantifying the amount of money required to replace the future service capability of that asset.

Cost of Capital—the expected rate of return that the market requires in order to attract funds to a particular investment.

CPA/ABV ***(CPA Accredited in Business Valuation)***—American Institute of Certified Public Accountants designation.

Current Ratio—a liquidity ratio that measures a company's ability to pay short-term obligations.

The Current Ratio formula is: Current Ratio = Current Assets / Current Liabilities. Also known as "liquidity ratio," "cash asset ratio" and "cash ratio." (*investopedia.com*)

CVA ***(Certified Valuation Analyst)***—National Association of Certified Valuation Analysts designation.

Debt-Free—*we discourage the use of this term*. See **Invested Capital**.

Depreciation—in accounting, an expense recorded to allocate a tangible asset's cost over its useful life. Because depreciation is a non-cash expense, it increases free cash flow while decreasing reported earnings. (*investopedia.com*)

Discount (Transaction Month) (as defined by the *FMV Restricted Stock Study*™) – the percentage difference between the offer price (the price the restricted stock was purchase for) and the transaction month high-low average. A negative number means that the restricted stock sold in the private placement sold at a premium to the transaction month high-low average for the month. (*BVMarketData.com*)

Discount for Lack of Control—an amount or percentage deducted from the pro rata share of value of 100% of an equity interest in a business to reflect the absence of some or all of the powers of control.

Discount for Lack of Liquidity—an amount or percentage deducted from the value of an ownership interest to reflect the relative absence of liquidity.

Discount for Lack of Marketability—an amount or percentage deducted from the value of an ownership interest to reflect the relative absence of marketability.

Discount for Lack of Voting Rights—an amount or percentage deducted from the per share value of a minority interest voting share to reflect the absence of voting rights.

Discount Rate—a rate of return used to convert a future monetary sum into present value.

Discounted Cash Flow Method—a method within the income approach whereby the present value of future expected net cash flows is calculated using a discount rate.

Discounted Future Earnings Method—a method within the income approach whereby the present value of future expected economic benefits is calculated using a discount rate.

Dividend Yield—a financial ratio that shows how much a company pays out in dividends each year relative to its share price. In the absence of any capital gains, the dividend yield is the return on investment for a stock. Dividend yield is calculated as follows: Annual Dividends Per Share / Price Per Share. (*investopedia.com*)

Earnings Before Interest and Tax (EBIT)—an indicator of a company's profitability, calculated as revenue minus expenses, excluding tax and interest. EBIT is also referred to as "operating earnings," "operating profit" and "operating income," as you can re-arrange the formula to be calculated as follows: EBIT = Revenue – Operating Expenses. Also known as Profit Before Interest & Taxes (PBIT), and equals Net Income with interest and taxes added back to it. (*investopedia.com*)

Earnings Before Interest, Taxes, Depreciation and Amortization (EBITDA)—an indicator of a company's financial performance which is calculated in the following EBITDA calculation: EBITDA = Revenue – Expenses (excluding tax, interest, depreciation and amortization). EBITDA is essentially Net Income with interest, taxes, depreciation, and amortization added back to it. EBITDA can be used to analyze and compare profitability between companies and industries because it eliminates the effects of financing and accounting decisions. However, this is a non- GAAP measure that allows a greater amount of discretion as to what is (and is not) included in the calculation. This also means that companies often change the items included in their EBITDA calculation from one reporting period to the next. (*investopedia.com*)

Economic Benefits—inflows such as revenues, net income, net cash flows, etc.

Economic Life—the period of time over which property may generate economic benefits.

Effective Date—see **Valuation Date**.

Employee Stock Ownership Plan (ESOP)—a qualified, defined contribution, employee benefit (ERISA) plan designed to invest primarily in the stock of the sponsoring employer. ESOPs are "qualified" in the sense that the ESOP's sponsoring company, the selling shareholder and participants receive various tax benefits. ESOPs are often used as a corporate finance strategy and are also used to align the interests of a company's employees with those of the company's shareholders. (*investopedia.com*)

Enterprise—see **Business Enterprise**.

Equity—the owner's interest in property after deduction of all liabilities.

Equity Net Cash Flows—those cash flows available to pay out to equity holders (in the form of dividends) after funding operations of the business enterprise, making necessary capital investments, and increasing or decreasing debt financing.

Equity Risk Premium—a rate of return added to a risk-free rate to reflect the additional risk of equity instruments over risk free instruments (a component of the cost of equity capital or equity discount rate).

Excess Earnings—that amount of anticipated economic benefits that exceeds an appropriate rate of return on the value of a selected asset base (often net tangible assets) used to generate those anticipated economic benefits.

Excess Earnings Method—a specific way of determining a value indication of a business, business ownership interest, or security determined as the sum of a) the value of the assets derived by capitalizing excess earnings and b) the value of the selected asset base. Also frequently used to value intangible assets. See **Excess Earnings**.

Exercise Multiple (as defined by *The BVR/DVA 123R Compliance Calculator*™) – a ratio of the stock price to the contractual strike price at which point it is assumed that the option will be exercised prior to maturity. Industry surveys suggest that the value of this parameter is typically between 1.5 and 2.5. This parameter is typically estimated by calculating the median of ratios of stock prices to strike prices using historical data. (*BVMarketData.com*)

Fair Market Value—the price, expressed in terms of cash equivalents, at which property would change hands between a hypothetical willing and able buyer and a hypothetical willing and able seller, acting at arms length in an open and unrestricted market, when neither is under compulsion to buy or sell and when both have reasonable knowledge of the relevant facts. (NOTE: In Canada, the term "price" should be replaced with the term "highest price.")

Fair Value—the value of the shares immediately before the effectuation of the corporate action to which the shareholder objects using customary and current valuation concepts and techniques generally employed for similar businesses the context of the transaction requiring appraisal, and without discounting for lack of marketability or minority status except, if appropriate, for amendments to the certificate of incorporation pursuant to section 13.02(a)(5). (*Revised Model Business Corporation Act* (RMBCA), American Bar Association (1999))

Fairness Opinion—an opinion as to whether or not the consideration in a transaction is fair from a financial point of view.

Family Limited Partnership (FLP)—a type of partnership designed to centralize family business or investment accounts. FLPs pool together a family's assets into one single family-owned business partnership that family members own shares of. FLPs are frequently used as an estate tax minimization strategy, as shares in the FLP can be transferred between generations, at lower taxation rates than would be applied to the partnership's holdings. (*investopedia.com*)

FASA (*Fellow of the American Society of Appraisers*)—American Society of Appraisers designation.

FCBI (*Fellow Certified Business Intermediary*)—International Business Brokers Association designation.

FCBV (*Fellow of the Canadian Institute of Chartered Business Valuators*)—Canadian Institute of Chartered Business Valuators designation.

FIBA (*Fellow of the Institute of Business Appraisers*)—Institute of Business Appraisers designation.

Financial Risk—the degree of uncertainty of realizing expected future returns of the business resulting from financial leverage. See **Business Risk**.

Fixed Asset Turnover—a financial ratio of net sales to fixed assets. The fixed-asset turnover ratio measures a company's ability to generate net sales from fixed-asset investments—specifically property, plant and equipment (PP&E)—net of depreciation. A higher fixed-asset turnover ratio shows that the company has been more effective in using the investment in fixed assets to generate revenues. The fixed-asset turnover ratio is calculated as: Fixed Asset Turnover = Net Sales / Net Property, Plant and Equipment. (*investopedia.com*)

Forced Liquidation Value—liquidation value, at which the asset or assets are sold as quickly as possible, such as at an auction.

Free Cash Flow—***we discourage the use of this term***. See **Net Cash Flow**.

Going Concern—an ongoing operating business enterprise.

Going Concern Value—the value of a business enterprise that is expected to continue to operate into the future. The intangible elements of Going Concern Value result from factors such as having a trained work force, an operational plant, and the necessary licenses, systems, and procedures in place.

Goodwill—that intangible asset arising as a result of name, reputation, customer loyalty, location, products, and similar factors not separately identified.

Goodwill Value—the value attributable to goodwill.

Gross Profit—a company's revenue minus its cost of goods sold. Gross profit is a company's residual profit after selling a product or service and deducting the cost associated with its production and sale. To calculate gross profit: examine the income statement, take the revenue and subtract the cost of goods sold. Also called "gross margin" and "gross income." (*investopedia.com*)

Gross Profit Margin—a financial metric used to assess a firm's financial health by revealing the proportion of money left over from revenues after accounting for the cost of goods sold. Gross profit margin serves as the source for paying additional expenses and future savings. Also known as "gross margin." Calculated as: Gross Profit Margin = (Revenue – COGS) / Revenue. (*investopedia.com*)

Guideline Public Company Method—a method within the market approach whereby market multiples are derived from market prices of stocks of companies that are engaged in the same or similar lines of business, and that are actively traded on a free and open market.

Holding Period (as defined by the *FMV Restricted Stock Study*™) – to prevent a seller from purchasing unregistered securities with a view to resale, Rule 144 requires a holding period of some length of time. After the initial holding period, unregistered securities could be sold only by complying with certain "dribble out," or volume limit provisions of the Rule. (*BVMarketData.com*)

Implied Minority Discount (as defined by the *Mergerstat®/BVR Control Premium Study*™) – an implied discount computed from the Mergerstat® Unaffected Control Premium. Calculated as: Implied Control Premium = 1 − [1/(1 + Control Premium)]. (Note: The Mergerstat® Unaffected Control Premium is the target company's common stock price per share unaffected by the acquisition announcement and is selected by Mergerstat® after analyzing each transaction). (*BVMarketData.com*)

Income (Income-Based) Approach—a general way of determining a value indication of a business, business ownership interest, security, or intangible asset using one or more methods that convert anticipated economic benefits into a present single amount.

Intangible Assets—non-physical assets such as franchises, trademarks, patents, copyrights, goodwill, equities, mineral rights, securities and contracts (as distinguished from physical assets) that grant rights and privileges, and have value for the owner.

Internal Rate of Return—a discount rate at which the present value of the future cash flows of the investment equals the cost of the investment.

Intrinsic Value—the value that an investor considers, on the basis of an evaluation or available facts, to be the "true" or "real" value that will become the market value when other investors reach the same conclusion. When the term applies to options, it is the difference between the exercise price or strike price of an option and the market value of the underlying security.

Inventory Turnover—a ratio showing how many times a company's inventory is sold and replaced over a period. Generally calculated as: Sales / Inventory. However, it may also be calculated as: Cost of Goods Sold / Average Inventory. The days in the period can then be divided by the inventory turnover formula to calculate the days it takes to sell the inventory on hand or "inventory turnover days." (*investopedia.com*)

Invested Capital—the sum of equity and debt in a business enterprise. Debt is typically a) all interest bearing debt or b) long-term interest-bearing debt. When the term is used, it should be supplemented by a specific definition in the given valuation context.

Invested Capital Net Cash Flows—those cash flows available to pay out to equity holders (in the form of dividends) and debt investors (in the form of principal and interest) after funding operations of the business enterprise and making necessary capital investments.

Investment Risk—the degree of uncertainty as to the realization of expected returns.

Investment Value—the value to a particular investor based on individual investment requirements and expectations. (NOTE: in Canada, the term used is "Value to the Owner.").

Key Person Discount—an amount or percentage deducted from the value of an ownership interest to reflect the reduction in value resulting from the actual or potential loss of a key person in a business enterprise.

Levered Beta—the beta reflecting a capital structure that includes debt.

Limited Appraisal—the act or process of determining the value of a business, business ownership interest, security, or intangible asset with limitations in analyses, procedures, or scope.

Liquidity—the ability to quickly convert property to cash or pay a liability.

Liquidity Discount—see **Discount for Lack of Liquidity**

Liquidation Value—the net amount that would be realized if the business is terminated and the assets are sold piecemeal. Liquidation can be either "orderly" or "forced."

Majority Control—the degree of control provided by a majority position.

Majority Interest—an ownership interest greater than 50% of the voting interest in a business enterprise.

Market (Market-Based) Approach—a general way of determining a value indication of a business, business ownership interest, security, or intangible asset by using one or more methods that compare the subject to similar businesses, business ownership interests, securities, or intangible assets that have been sold.

Market Capitalization of Equity—the share price of a publicly traded stock multiplied by the number of shares outstanding.

Market Capitalization of Invested Capital—the market capitalization of equity plus the market value of the debt component of invested capital.

Market Multiple—the market value of a company's stock or invested capital divided by a company measure (such as economic benefits, number of customers).

Market Value of Invested Capital (MVIC) (as defined by *Pratt's Stats*®) – also known as the selling price, the MVIC is defined by *Pratt's Stats*® as the total consideration paid to the seller and includes any cash, notes and/or securities that were used as a form of payment plus any interest-bearing liabilities assumed by the buyer. The MVIC price includes the non-compete value and the assumption of interest-bearing liabilities and excludes (1) the real estate value and (2) any earnouts (because they have not yet been earned, and they may not be earned) and (3) the employment/consulting agreement values. (*BVMarketData.com*)

Marketability—the ability to quickly convert property to cash at minimal cost.

Marketability Discount—see **Discount for Lack of Marketability**.

MCBA (*Master Certified Business Appraiser*)—Institute of Business Appraisers designation.

Merger and Acquisition Method—a method within the market approach whereby pricing multiples are derived from transactions of significant interests in companies engaged in the same or similar lines of business.

Mid-Year Discounting—a convention used in the Discounted Future Earnings Method that reflects economic benefits being generated at midyear, approximating the effect of economic benefits being generated evenly throughout the year.

Minority Discount—a discount for lack of control applicable to a minority interest.

Minority Interest—an ownership interest less than 50% of the voting interest in a business enterprise.

Multiple—the inverse of the capitalization rate.

Net Book Value—with respect to a business enterprise, the difference between total assets (net of accumulated depreciation, depletion, and amortization) and total liabilities as they appear on the balance sheet (synonymous with Shareholder's Equity). With respect to a specific asset, the capitalized cost less accumulated amortization or depreciation as it appears on the books of account of the business enterprise.

Net Cash Flows—when the term is used, it should be supplemented by a qualifier. See **Equity Net Cash Flows** and **Invested Capital Net Cash Flows**.

Net Income—a company's total earnings (or profit). Net income is calculated by taking revenues and adjusting for the cost of doing business, depreciation, interest, taxes and other expenses. This number is found on a company's income statement and is an important measure of how profitable the company is over a period of time. The measure is also used to calculate earnings per share. Often referred to as "the bottom line" since net income is listed at the bottom of the income statement. In the U.K., net income is known as "profit attributable to shareholders." (*investopedia.com*)

Net Operating Profit After Tax (NOPAT)—a company's potential cash earnings if its capitalization were unleveraged (that is, if it had no debt). NOPAT is frequently used in economic value added (EVA) calculations. Calculated as: NOPAT = Operating Income x (1 – Tax Rate). (*investopedia.com*)

Net Present Value—the value, as of a specified date, of future cash inflows less all cash outflows (including the cost of investment) calculated using an appropriate discount rate.

Net Profit Margin—the ratio of net profits to revenues for a company or business segment - typically expressed as a percentage – that shows how much of each dollar earned by the company is translated into profits. Net profit margins can generally be calculated as: Net Profit Margin = Net Profit / Revenue; where Net Profit = Revenue – COGS – Operating Expenses – Interest and Taxes. (*investopedia.com*)

Net Tangible Asset Value—the value of the business enterprise's tangible assets (excluding excess assets and non-operating assets) minus the value of its liabilities.

Non-Operating Assets—assets not necessary to ongoing operations of the business enterprise. (NOTE: in Canada, the term used is "Redundant Assets.")

Normalized Earnings—economic benefits adjusted for nonrecurring, noneconomic, or other unusual items to eliminate anomalies and/or facilitate comparisons.

Normalized Financial Statements—financial statements adjusted for non-operating assets and liabilities and/or for nonrecurring, noneconomic, or other unusual items to eliminate anomalies and/or facilitate comparisons.

North American Industry Classification System (NAICS)—used by business and government to classify and measure economic activity in Canada, Mexico and the United States. It has largely replaced the older Standard Industrial Classification (SIC) system; however, certain government departments and agencies, such as the U.S. Securities and Exchange Commission (SEC), still use the SIC codes. (*wikipedia.org*)

Operating Profit—the amount of profit realized from a business's own operations, but excluding operating expenses (such as cost of goods sold) and depreciation from gross income. Also known as "earnings before interest and tax" (EBIT). Calculated as: Operating Profit = Revenue – Operating Expenses – Depreciation. (*investopedia.com*)

Operating Profit Margin—a ratio used to measure a company's pricing strategy and operating efficiency. Calculated as: Operating Profit Margin = Operating Income / Revenue. Operating profit margin is a measurement of what proportion of a company's revenue is left over after paying for variable costs of production such as wages, raw materials, etc. A healthy operating margin is required for a company to be able to pay for its fixed costs, such as interest on debt. Also known as "operating margin." (*investopedia.com*)

Orderly Liquidation Value—liquidation value at which the asset or assets are sold over a reasonable period of time to maximize proceeds received.

Outstanding Shares—stock currently held by investors, including restricted shares owned by the company's officers and insiders, as well as those held by the public. Shares that have been repurchased by the company are not considered outstanding stock. (*investopedia.com*)

Premise of Value—an assumption regarding the most likely set of transactional circumstances that may be applicable to the subject valuation; e.g. going concern, liquidation.

Present Value—the value, as of a specified date, of future economic benefits and/or proceeds from sale, calculated using an appropriate discount rate.

Price/Earnings Multiple—the price of a share of stock divided by its earnings per share.

Private Placement—raising of capital via private rather than public placement. The result is the sale of securities to a relatively small number of investors. Investors involved in private placements are usually large banks, mutual funds, insurance companies, and pension funds. (*investopedia.com*)

Portfolio Discount—an amount or percentage deducted from the value of a business enterprise to reflect the fact that it owns dissimilar operations or assets that do not fit well together.

Quick Ratio—an indicator of a company's short-term liquidity. The quick ratio measures a company's ability to meet its short-term obligations with its most liquid assets. The higher the quick ratio, the better the position of the company. The quick ratio is calculated as: Quick Ratio = (Current Assets – Inventories) / Current Liabilities. Also known as the "acid-test ratio" or the "quick assets ratio." (*investopedia.com*)

Rate of Return—an amount of income (loss) and/or change in value realized or anticipated on an investment, expressed as a percentage of that investment.

Redundant Assets—see **Non-Operating Assets**.

Recurring Revenue—the portion of a company's revenue that is highly likely to continue in the future. This is revenue that is predictable, stable and can be counted on in the future with a high degree of certainty. (*investopedia.com*)

Registration Rights Agreement (as defined by the *FMV Restricted Stock Study*™) – even though the resale limitations under Rule 144 have been reduced somewhat over the years, investors still often look for the issuer in a private placement transaction to provide them with a possible liquidity event prior to the end of the holding period. Consequently, investors often require, and issuers often grant, some form of a registration rights agreement to be signed, either as part of the stock purchase agreement or as a separate side agreement thereto. These registration rights provisions typically require the company to do one of two things: (1) register the shares or a portion of the shares within some specified time-frame, at either the company's or the investor's expense ("demand registrations"); or, (2) include the shares or a portion of the shares in any future public offerings that the company makes, if any ("piggyback registrations"). (*BVMarketData.com*)

Report Date—the date conclusions are transmitted to the client.

Replacement Cost New—the current cost of a similar new property having the nearest equivalent utility to the property being valued.

Reproduction Cost New—the current cost of an identical new property.

Required Rate of Return—the minimum rate of return acceptable by investors before they will commit money to an investment at a given level of risk.

Residual Value—the value as of the end of the discrete projection period in a discounted future earnings model.

Restricted Stock—restricted stock, also known as letter stock or restricted securities, refers to stock of a company that is not fully transferable until certain conditions have been met. Upon satisfaction of those conditions, the stock becomes transferable by the person holding the award. Under the securities laws, these conditions are either registration with the U.S. Securities and Exchange Commission (SEC), or fitting into one of the securities exemptions for resale, such as Rule 144. (*wikipedia.org*)

Retained Earnings—the percentage of net earnings not paid out as dividends, but retained by the company to be reinvested in its core business or to pay debt. It is recorded under shareholders' equity on the balance sheet. The formula calculates retained earnings by adding net income to (or subtracting any net losses from) beginning retained earnings and subtracting any dividends paid to shareholders: Retained Earnings = Beginning Retained Earnings + Net Income – Dividends. (*investopedia.com*)

Return on Assets (ROA)—an indicator of how profitable a company is relative to its total assets. ROA gives an idea as to how efficient management is at using its assets to generate earnings. Calculated by dividing a company's annual earnings by its total assets, ROA is displayed as a percentage. (*investopedia.com*)

Return on Equity—the amount, expressed as a percentage, earned on a company's common equity for a given period.

Return on Investment—see **Return on Invested Capital** and **Return on Equity**.

Return on Invested Capital—the amount, expressed as a percentage, earned on a company's total capital for a given period.

Return on Revenue (ROR)—a measure of a corporation's profitability, calculated as net income divided by revenue. (*investopedia.com*)

Revenue—the amount of money that a company actually receives during a specific period, including discounts and deductions for returned merchandise. It is the "top line" or "gross income" figure from which costs are subtracted to determine net income. Revenue is calculated by multiplying the price at which goods or services are sold by the number of units or amount sold. (*investopedia.com*)

Risk-Free Rate—the rate of return available in the market on an investment free of default risk.

Risk Premium—a rate of return added to a risk-free rate to reflect risk.

Rule 144—promulgated by the SEC under the 1933 Act, Rule 144 permits, under limited circumstances, the sale of restricted and controlled securities without registration. In addition to restrictions on the minimum length of time for which such securities must be held and the maximum volume permitted to be sold, the issuer must agree to the sale. If certain requirements are met, Form 144 must be filed with the SEC. Often, the issuer requires that a legal opinion be given indicating that the resale complies with the rule. (*wikipedia.org*)

Rule of Thumb—a mathematical formula developed from the relationship between price and certain variables based on experience, observation, hearsay, or a combination of these; usually industry specific.

Seller's Discretionary Earnings (as defined by *BIZCOMPS®*) – seller's discretionary earnings is defined by BIZCOMPS® as net profit before taxes and any compensation to owner plus amortization, depreciation, interest, other non-cash expense and non-business related expense and normally to one working owner. (*BVMarketData.com*)

Size Premium—size premium is the additional remuneration due to the higher risk and therefore, the higher cost of capital, associated with the smaller size of the company and of the lower trading volume. (*vernimmen.com*)

Special Interest Purchasers—acquirers who believe they can enjoy post-acquisition economies of scale, synergies, or strategic advantages by combining the acquired business interest with their own.

Standard Industrial Classification (SIC)—a United States government system for classifying industries by a four-digit code. (*wikipedia.org*)

Standard of Value—the identification of the type of value being used in a specific engagement; e.g. fair market value, fair value, investment value.

Strike Price—the price at which a specific derivative contract can be exercised. Strike price is mostly used to describe stock and index options, in which strike prices are fixed in the contract. For call options, the strike price is where the security can be bought (up to the expiration date), while for put options the strike price is the price at which shares can be sold. The difference between the underlying security's current market price and the option's strike price represents the amount of profit per share gained upon the exercise or the sale of the option. This is true for options that are in the money; the maximum amount that can be lost is the premium paid. Also known as the "exercise price." (*investopedia.com*)

Sustaining Capital Reinvestment—the periodic capital outlay required to maintain operations at existing levels, net of the tax shield available from such outlays.

Systematic Risk—the risk that is common to all risky securities and cannot be eliminated through diversification. The measure of systematic risk in stocks is the beta coefficient.

Tangible Assets—physical assets (such as cash, accounts receivable, inventory, property, plant and equipment, etc.).

Target Invested Capital (as defined by *Mergerstat®/BVR Control Premium Study™*) – target company's implied total invested capital (TIC) based on the sum of the implied market value of equity (the purchase price per share times total shares outstanding reported in the period prior to the transaction's announcement date) plus the face value of total interest bearing debt and the book value of preferred stock outstanding prior to the announcement date. (*BVMarketData.com*)

Terminal Value. see **Residual Value**.

Total Asset Turnover—this is a measure of how well assets are being used to produce revenue. The total asset turnover ratio is calculated as: Total Asset Turnover = Net Sales / Total Assets. (*investorwords.com*)

Total Beta—total beta is equal to the identity: Beta/R or the standard deviation of the stock/standard deviation of the market (note: the relative volatility). Total Beta captures the security's risk as a stand-alone asset (since the correlation coefficient, R, has been removed from Beta), rather than part of a well-diversified portfolio. Since appraisers frequently value closely-held companies as stand-alone assets, Total Beta is gaining acceptance in the business valuation industry. Appraisers can now use Total Beta in the following equation: Total Cost of Equity (TCOE) = Risk-Free Rate + Total Beta * Equity Risk Premium. Once appraisers have a number of TCOE benchmarks, they can compare/contrast the risk factors present in these publicly-traded benchmarks and the risks in their closely-held company to better defend/support their valuations. (*wikipedia.org*)

Total Cost of Equity (TCOE)—Total Cost of Equity (TCOE) = Risk-Free Rate + Total Beta * Equity risk premium. This equation was developed by Professor Damodaran at NYU. For more information on Total Beta see **Total Beta**. (*BVMarketData.com*)

Transaction Method—see **Merger and Acquisition Method.**

Unlevered Beta—the beta reflecting a capital structure without debt.

Unsystematic Risk—the risk specific to an individual security that can be avoided through diversification.

Valuation—the act or process of determining the value of a business, business ownership interest, security, or intangible asset.

Valuation Approach—a general way of determining a value indication of a business, business ownership interest, security, or intangible asset using one or more valuation methods.

Valuation Date—the specific point in time as of which the valuator's opinion of value applies (also referred to as "Effective Date" or "Appraisal Date").

Valuation Method—within approaches, a specific way to determine value.

Valuation Multiple—see **Valuation Ratio**.

Valuation Procedure—the act, manner, and technique of performing the steps of an appraisal method.

Valuation Ratio—a fraction in which a value or price serves as the numerator and financial, operating, or physical data serves as the denominator.

Value to the Owner—see **Investment Value**.

Vesting Period—In options, the remaining time period during which the option cannot be exercised. (*BVMarketData.com*)

Voting Control—*de jure* control of a business enterprise.

Weighted Average Cost of Capital (WACC)—the cost of capital (discount rate) determined by the weighted average, at market value, of the cost of all financing sources in the business enterprise's capital structure.

Z-Score—a statistical measure that quantifies the distance (measured in standard deviations) a data point is from the mean of a data set. In a more financial sense, Z-score is the output from a credit-strength test that gauges the likelihood of bankruptcy. A Z-score of 0 is equal to a 50% probability of bankruptcy. (*investopedia.com*)

APPENDIX B ADDITIONAL SOURCES OF STUDY

Fannon, N.. *Fannon's Guide to the Valuation of Subchapter S Corporations*. Portland, OR: BVR, 2008.

Hawkins, G., and M. Paschall. *CCH Business Valuation Guide*. Chicago: CCH. Updated annually (2011).

Hitchner, J., ed. *Financial Valuation: Application and Models*, 3rd ed. Hoboken, NJ: John Wiley & Sons, 2003.

Lind, D., W. Marchal, and S. Wathen. *Statistical Techniques in Business and Economics*, 15th ed. New York: McGraw-Hill.

Porter, M.. *Competitive Strategy: Techniques for Analyzing Industries and Competitors.* New York: Free Press, 1998.

Pratt, S.. *Business Valuation Body of Knowledge: Exam Review and Professional Reference*, 2nd ed. Hoboken, NJ: John Wiley & Sons, 2003.

______. *The Market Approach to Valuing Businesses*, 2nd ed. Hoboken, NJ: John Wiley & Sons, 2006.

Pratt, S., and R. Grabowski. *Cost of Capital: Applications and Examples*, 4th ed. Hoboken, NJ: John Wiley & Sons, 2010.

Pratt, S., and A. Niculita. *Valuing a Business*, 5th ed. New York: McGraw-Hill, 2007.

Reilly, R., and Hitchener, J.. *Valuing Intangible Assets*. McGraw-Hill, 1998.

Trugman, Gary. *Understanding Business Valuation: A Practical Guide to Valuing Small to Medium Sized Businesses*, 3rd ed. New York: AICPA, 2008.

AICPA Publications and Pronouncements Related to Business Valuation

American Institute of Certified Public Accountants. Consulting Services Special Report 93-2, *Conflicts of Interest in Litigation Services Engagements*. New York: Author, 1993, Product No. 048563.

______. Consulting Services Practice Aid 96-3, *Communicating in Litigation Services: Reports*. New York: Author, 1996, Product No. 055000.

______. Consulting Services Practice Aid, *Valuing Private Equity Securities in Other Than a Business Combination.* New York:, 2012. Forthcoming.

Frank, P. B., and M. J. Wagner. AICPA Consulting Services Practice Aid 93-4, *Providing Litigation Services*. New York: AICPA, 1993, Product No. 055145.

Menelaides, S., L. Graham, and G. Fischbach. "The Auditor's Approach to Fair Value," *Journal of Accountancy* (June 2003): 73–76.

Miller, W. D. "Assessing Unsystematic Risk: Part I," *CPA Expert* 5, no. 3 (Summer 1999): 1–5.

______. "Assessing Unsystematic Risk: Part II—The Macroenvironment." *CPA Expert* 6, no. 1 (Winter 2000): 1–5.

______. "Assessing Unsystematic Risk: Part III—Market Structure." *CPA Expert* 6, no. 3 (Summer 2001): 1–5.

______. 2002. "Assessing Unsystematic Risk: Part IV—Industry Dynamics." *CPA Expert* 8, no. 1 (Winter 2002): 1–5.

Trugman, G. R. AICPA Consulting Services Practice Aid 93-3, *Conducting a Valuation of a Closely Held Business*. New York: AICPA, 1993, Product No. 055148.

CHAPTER 26

ACCOUNTING FOR DERIVATIVES: A PRIMER

Ira G. Kawaller
Kawaller & Co

26.1 OVERVIEW 1

26.2 DEFINITION OF A *DERIVATIVE* 2

26.3 EXEMPTIONS 3

26.4 EMBEDDED DERIVATIVE INSTRUMENTS 3

26.5 ACCOUNTING TREATMENT 4

- (a) Cash Flow Hedges 4
  - (i) Exposures That Qualify for Cash Flow Hedge Accounting 5
  - (ii) Eligible Risks 5
  - (iii) Prerequisite Requirements 5
  - (iv) Disallowed Situations 6
  - (v) Internal Derivatives Contracts 6
- (b) Fair Value Hedges 6
  - (i) Examples 7
  - (ii) Eligible Risks 7
  - (iii) Prerequisite Requirements 7
  - (iv) Disallowed Situations 8
- (c) Hedges of Net Investments in Foreign Operations 8
- (d) Hedge Effectiveness 8
- (e) Speculative Trades or Trades Not Qualifying for Hedge Accounting 9

26.6 DISCLOSURES 9

- (a) All Reporting Entities 9
- (b) Hedging 9
- (c) Fair Value Hedges 10
- (d) Cash Flow Hedges 10

26.7 INTERNATIONAL FINANCIAL REPORTING STANDARDS AND DERIVATIVES 10

26.8 SOURCES AND SUGGESTED REFERENCES 10

26.1 OVERVIEW

> It would be easy for us to dismiss [derivatives] as [investment products] only sophisticated investors use minimizing any impact to our economy. . . . If we think back to the collapse of Enron, or even farther back to Long-Term Capital Management, we understand how the abuse of derivatives can have a negative impact not only on the parties to the contract, but also on the market and the economy.
>
> *—Rep. Richard Neal, D-Mass., chairman of the House Ways and Means Select Revenue Measures Subcommittee, at a March 5 (2008) hearing on tax treatment of derivatives*

Originally issued as Financial Accounting Statement (FAS) No. 133, *Accounting for Derivative Instruments and Hedging Activities,* the rules for accounting for derivatives and hedging transactions are found under the Accounting Standard Codification (ASC) 815, *Derivatives and Hedging.* This chapter an overview of these rules. It is designed to highlight only the more critical features of the standard, and it may omit relevant guidance for specific situations.

The single inviolate accounting requirement for derivatives is that they must be marked to market and recorded as assets or liabilities on the balance sheet. Beyond that, the accounting treatment will depend on the intended use of the derivative and/or whether specific conditions have been satisfied.

For speculative purposes, derivative gains or losses must be marked to market, and gains or losses are recorded in the current period's income. When hedging exposures associated with the price of an asset, liability, or a firm commitment, accounting for the derivative is the same as it is for speculative uses. In addition, however, the underlying exposure must also be marked to market due to the risk being hedged; and these results must flow through current income as well. This treatment is called a fair value hedge.

A hedge of an upcoming, forecasted event would be a cash flow hedge. For cash flow hedges, derivative results must be evaluated, with a determination made as to how much of the result is effective and how much is ineffective. The ineffective component of the hedge results must be recorded in current income while the effective portion is initially posted to other comprehensive income (OCI) and later reclassified to income in the same time frame in which the forecasted cash flow affects earnings. Importantly, as of this writing, the Financial Accounting Standards Board (FASB) recognizes hedges as being ineffective for accounting purposes only when the hedge effects exceed the effects of the underlying forecasted cash flow, measured on a cumulative basis; however, this asymmetric provision is under consideration and is subject to change.

Finally, the last category qualifying for special accounting treatment is the hedge associated with the currency exposure of a net investment in a foreign operation. Again, the hedge must be marked to market. This time, the treatment requires effective hedge results to be consolidated with the translation adjustment in OCI. Any excess of hedge results relative to the risk being hedged would be recorded in earnings.

26.2 DEFINITION OF A *DERIVATIVE*

According to ASC 815-10-15, a qualifying derivative must satisfy three criteria:

1. It has one or more underlyings and one or more notional[1] amounts or payment provisions or both. These contractual terms determine the amount of the settlement or settlements, and, in some cases, whether or not a settlement is required.

   An *underlying* is a specified security price, or interest rate, commodity price, or other market related variable. For example, a call option enabling an entity to purchase a security in the future at today's price is a derivative. Its value will vary when the stock price increases or decreases. The payment provision is the change in stock price times the number of shares involved.
2. It requires no initial net investment or an initial net investment that is smaller than would be required for other types of contracts that would be expected to have a similar response to changes in market factors.
3. Its terms require or permit net settlement, it can readily be settled net by a means outside the contract, or it provides for delivery of an asset that puts the recipient in a position not substantially different from net settlement.

[1] While the underlying is the variable in a derivative, the notional amount is the fixed amount or quantity that determines the size of the change caused by the movement of the underlying. Examples include the stated principal amount in an interest rate swap, the stated number of bushels in a wheat futures contract, and the contracted amount of euros in a foreign currency forward.

26.3 EXEMPTIONS

Complicating the process for assessing whether any contractual arrangement qualifies as a derivative is the fact the FASB has scoped out a host of situations that might otherwise appear to satisfy the given definition (see Accounting Standards Codification (ASC) 815-10-15). For example:

- Regular-way securities trades, where delivery occurs within the time frame of normal market conventions.
- Normal purchases and normal sales where instruments will be delivered in amounts expected to be used within a reasonable period of time in the normal course of business and where there is a high probability that the contracts will result in physical deliver. Contracts that required periodic cash settlements (e.g., futures contracts) do not qualify for this exception.
- Certain types of insurance are exempt from treatment as a derivative if the payout compensates the insured for an identifiable insurable event other than a change in price.
- Financial guarantee contracts that reimburse for specific losses due to defaults of debtors.
- Off-exchange contracts where settlement amounts are based on (a) climactic, geological, or other physical variables; (b) prices of nonfinancial assets or liabilities on either party to the contract, where the underlying instrument is not readily convertible to cash; or (c) specific volumes of sales or revenues of one of the parties to the contract.
- Derivatives that serve as impediments to sales accounting.
- Contracts (a) indexed to a company's own stock and classified in stockholders' equity; (b) issued by the reporting entity relating to stock-based compensation; or (c) issued as a contingent consideration from a business combination.

26.4 EMBEDDED DERIVATIVE INSTRUMENTS

Embedded derivatives are components of contractual arrangements that, by themselves (i.e., on a stand-alone basis), would satisfy the criteria in the definition of a derivative. Embedded derivatives are often present in structured note contracts and other debt obligations, but they may also be found in such contracts such as leases, purchase agreements, insurance contracts, guarantees, and other tailored arrangements. Embedded derivatives reside in host contracts; and the combined instrument (i.e., the host and the embedded derivative) is referred to as the hybrid instrument. An example of an embedded derivative is a convertible bond. The host security is the debt instrument, and the embedded derivative is the option to convert the bond.

In general, embedded derivatives must be separated from the host contract for accounting purposes. Provided they meet the qualifying criteria for being a derivative under the FASB criteria, embedded derivatives must be accounted for as if they were free-standing derivatives, unless (1) the characteristics and risks of the embedded derivative are clearly and closely related to those of the host, or (2) the hybrid instrument is remeasured at fair value with changes reported in earnings.

According to ASC 815-15-25, if the embedded derivative incorporates a leverage factor or if an investor may not recover substantially all of the initial recorded investment, the embedded derivative would be required to be accounted for separately from the host.

ASC 815-10-15 states that interest-only and principal-only strips are specifically exempted from being treated as derivatives, provided that (1) the original securities from which these derivatives were constructed have no embedded derivatives that would otherwise be covered under FAS 133, and (2) the strips do not contain any features that were not initially a part of the original instrument.

ASC 815-15-10 also states that embedded foreign currency derivatives are exempt from treatment as a derivative if (1) the host is not a financial instrument and settlements are required in the functional currency of any substantial party to the contract, or (2) the settlements are denominated in the currency of the price that is routinely used for international commerce of the underlying good or service.

26.5 ACCOUNTING TREATMENT

The accounting treatment that applies to any given derivatives position may vary, depending on whether the derivative is used as a hedging instrument or not. Even assuming the derivative is intended as a hedge, one cannot simply elect to apply special hedge accounting. The exposure being hedged must qualify as a permissible hedged item, and the intended hedging relationship much be documented as such. If this documentation is not complete as of the trade date of the derivative contract, the hedge could not be applied, and the derivative would have to be marked to market through earnings. Critically, failure to have the documentation in place when the derivative is traded does not preclude drafting this documentation later, at which time hedge accounting could be instituted.

With the determination that the derivative is to be used as a hedge and with all the necessary prerequisites satisfied, the appropriate accounting treatments would depend on the nature of the hedge. Three different types of hedge treatments are cash flow hedges, fair value hedges, and hedges of net investments in foreign operations.

Derivatives that are not intended to serve as hedges—or derivatives that fail to qualify for hedge accounting treatment—must be accorded the regular accounting treatment, which is generally referred to as accounting for speculative derivative transactions.

- When seeking special hedge accounting, hedges must be documented at the inception of the hedge, with the objective and strategy stated, along with an explicit description of the methodology used to assess hedge effectiveness. This documentation must include the identification of the hedged item and the hedging instrument and the nature of the risk being hedged. This documentation must include (among other things) discussion relating to hedge effectiveness.
- A qualifying condition to apply hedge accounting is that derivatives' gains must be expected to be "highly effective at offsetting changes in fair values or cash flows of associated with the risks being hedged. The documentation further requires both a prospective assessment of hedge effectiveness and a retrospective assessment. The former justifies the expectation of high effectiveness before the fact; the latter validates that the hedge performance actually was sufficiently effective, after the fact. Satisfying both assessments is required before hedge accounting is permitted.

(a) CASH FLOW HEDGES. A hedge of an upcoming, forecasted event is a cash flow hedge. To qualify for cash flow hedge treatment, a key requirement is that exposure involves the risk of an uncertain (i.e., variable) cash flow. Derivative results must be evaluated, with a determination made as to how much of the result is effective and how much is ineffective. The ineffective component of the hedge results must be reported in current income, while the effective portion is initially posted to OCI and later reclassified to income in the same time frame in which the forecasted cash flow affects earnings.

For purposes of determining the amount that is appropriate to be posted to OCI, this assessment must be made on a cumulative basis. According to ASC 815-30-35, contributions to earnings are currently required only if the derivative results exceed the cash flow effects of the hedged items. This provision is currently under consideration and subject to change, whereby ineffective earnings amounts would be determined symmetrically, reflecting either excess hedge results or shortfalls.

Cash flow hedge accounting is not automatic. Specific criteria must be satisfied both at the inception of the hedge and on an ongoing basis. If, after initially qualifying for cash flow accounting, the criteria for hedge accounting stop being satisfied, hedge accounting is no longer appropriate. According to ASC 815-30-40, with the discontinuation of hedge accounting, any accumulated OCI would remain there, unless (except in extenuating circumstances) it is probable that the forecasted transaction will not occur by the end of the originally specified time period or within an additional two-month period of time thereafter.

ASC 815-30-40 indicates that reporting entities have complete discretion to undesignate cash flow hedge relationships at will and later redesignate them, assuming all hedge criteria are again (or still) satisfied. This provision is also under consideration and subject to change. While such flexibility affords management the opportunity to most fairly present the financial numbers in economic terms, such flexibility can also lead to accounting manipulation.

(i) Exposures That Qualify for Cash Flow Hedge Accounting. Examples of exposures that qualify for cash flow hedge accounting include:

- Interest rate exposures that relate to a variable or floating interest rates
- Planned purchases or sales of assets
- Planned issuances of debt or deposits
- Planned purchases or sales of foreign currencies
- Currency risk associated with prospective cash flows that are not denominated in the functional currency

(ii) Eligible Risks. The risk being hedge in a designated hedging relation must be explicitly stated in the hedge documentation. The following details explicit risk categories that are permitted to be afforded hedge accounting (ASC topic 815-20-25)

- Currency risk associated with (1) a forecasted transaction in a currency other than the functional currency, (2) an unrecognized firm commitment, or (3) a recognized foreign currency–denominated debt instrument.
- The entire price risk associated with purchases or sales of nonfinancial goods. That is, unless the purchase or sale specifically relates to buying or selling individual components, the full price of the good in question must be viewed as the hedged item.
- For financial instruments, hedgeable exposures include cash flow effects to:
  1. Changes in the full price of the instrument in question
  2. Changes the benchmark rate of interest (i.e., the risk-free rate of interest or the rate associated with swaps based on the London Interbank Offered Rate [LIBOR])
  3. Changes associated with the hedged item's credit spread relative to the interest rate bench mark
  4. Changes in cash flows associated with default or the obligors' creditworthiness
  5. Changes in currency exchange rates

(iii) Prerequisite Requirements. To qualify for cash flow accounting treatment, ASC 815-20-25 states that these prerequisites apply:

- Hedges must be documented at the inception of the hedge, with the objective and strategy stated, along with an explicit description of the methodology used to assess hedge effectiveness.
- Dates (or periods) for the expected forecasted events and the nature of the exposure involved (including quantitative measures of the size of the exposure) must be explicitly documented.
- The hedge must be expected to be "highly effective," both at the inception of the hedge and on an ongoing basis. Effectiveness measures must relate the gains or losses of the derivative to changes in the cash flows associated with the hedged item.
- The forecasted transaction must be probable.
- The forecasted transaction must be made with a different counterparty than the reporting entity.

(iv) Disallowed Situations. According to ASC 815-20-25, cash flow accounting may not be applied under the following circumstances:

- In general, written options may not serve as hedging instruments. An exception to this prohibition (i.e., when a written option may qualify for cash flow accounting treatment) is when the hedged item is a long option.
- In general, basis swaps do not qualify for cash flow accounting treatment unless both of the variables of the basis swap are linked to two distinct variables associated with two distinct cash flow exposures.
- Cross-currency interest rate swaps do not qualify for cash flow hedge accounting treatment if the combined position results in exposure to a variable rate of interest in the functional currency. This hedge *would* qualify, however, as a fair value hedge.
- With held-to-maturity fixed income securities under Statement No. 115, *Accounting for Certain Investments in Debt and Equity Securities*, interest rate risk may not be designated as the risk exposure in a cash flow relationship.
- The forecasted transaction may not involve a business combination subject to Opinion No. 16, *Business Combinations,* and does not involve
  1. A parent's interest in consolidated subsidiaries
  2. A minority interest in a consolidated subsidiary
  3. An equity-method investment
  4. An entity's own equity instruments
- Prepayment risk may not be designated as the hedged item.
- The interest rate risk to be hedged in a cash flow hedge may not be identified as a benchmark interest rate, if a different variable interest rate is the specified exposure—for example, if the exposure is the risk of a higher prime rate, LIBOR may not be designated as the risk being hedged.

(v) Internal Derivatives Contracts. Except in the case when currency derivatives are used in cash flow hedges, derivatives between members of a consolidated group (i.e., internal derivatives) cannot qualify as hedging instruments in the consolidated statement, unless offsetting contracts have been arranged with unrelated third parties on a one-time basis (ASC topic 815-20-25).

For an internal currency derivative to qualify as a hedging instrument in a consolidated statement, it must be used as a cash flow hedge only for a foreign currency forecasted borrowing, a purchase or sale, or an unrecognized firm commitment, , subject to the following conditions:

- The nonhedging counterpart to the internal derivative must offset its net currency exposure with a third party within 3 days of the internal contract's hedge designation date.
- The third-party derivative must mature within 31 days of the internal derivative's maturity date.

(b) FAIR VALUE HEDGES. When hedging exposures associated with the price of an asset, liability, or a firm commitment, the total gain or loss on the derivative is recorded in earnings. In addition, the carrying value of the underlying exposure must be adjusted by an amount attributable to the risk being hedged; and these results flow through current income as well. This treatment is called a fair value hedge. Hedgers may elect to hedge all or a specific identified portion of any potential hedged item.

According to ASC 815-25-40, fair value hedge accounting is not automatic. Specific criteria must be satisfied both at the inception of the hedge and on an ongoing basis. If, after initially qualifying for fair value accounting, the criteria for hedge accounting stop being satisfied, hedge accounting is no longer appropriate. With the discontinuation of hedge accounting, gains or losses of the derivative will continue to be recorded in earnings but no further basis adjustments to the original hedged item would be made.

ASC 815-25-40 states that reporting entities have complete discretion to dedesignate fair value hedge relationships at will and later redesignate them, assuming all hedge criteria remain. As noted earlier, this provision is under reconsideration and subject to change.

(i) Examples. According to ASC 815-25-40, these exposures may qualify for fair value hedge accounting:

- Interest exposures associated with the opportunity cost of fixed rate debt
- Price exposures for fixed rate assets
- Price exposures for firm commitments associated with prospective purchases or sales
- Price exposures associated with the market value of inventory items
- Price exposures on available-for-sale securities.

(ii) Eligible Risks. These are examples of risks that can qualify for fair value hedge accounting (ASC 815-20-25):

- The risk of the change in the overall fair value
- The risk of changes in fair value due to changes in the benchmark interest rates (i.e., the risk-free rate of interest or the rate associated with LIBOR-based swaps), foreign exchange rates, creditworthiness, or the spread over the benchmark interest rate relevant to the hedged item's credit risk
- Currency risk associated with (1) an unrecognized firm commitment, (2) a recognized foreign currency–denominated debt instrument, or (3) an available-for-sale security.

(iii) Prerequisite Requirements. According to ASC 815-20-25, to qualify for fair value accounting treatment these prerequisites must be satisfied:

- Hedges must be documented at the inception of the hedge, with the objective and strategy stated, along with an explicit description of the methodology used to assess hedge effectiveness.
- The hedge must be expected to be "highly effective," both at the inception of the hedge and on an ongoing basis. Effectiveness measures must relate the gains or losses of the derivative to those changes in the fair value of the hedged item that are due to the risk being hedged.
- If the hedged item is a portfolio of similar assets or liabilities, each component must share the risk exposure, and each item is expected to respond to the risk factor in comparable proportions.
- Portions of a portfolio may be hedged if they are:
  1. A percentage of the portfolio
  2. One or more selected cash flows
  3. An embedded option (provided it is not accounted for as a stand-alone option)
  4. The residual value in a lessor's net investment in a direct financing or sale-type lease
- A change in the fair value of the hedged item must present an exposure to the earnings of the reporting entity.

Fair value hedge accounting is permitted when cross-currency interest rate swaps result in the entity being exposed to a variable rate of interest in the functional currency

(iv) Disallowed Situations. ASC 815-20-25 states that fair value accounting may not be applied in these situations:

- In general, written options may not serve as hedging instruments. An exception to this prohibition (i.e., when a written option may qualify for cash flow accounting treatment) is when the hedged item is a long option. Any combinations that include written options and involve the net receipt of premium—either at the inception or over the life of the hedge—are considered to be written option positions.
- Assets or liabilities that are remeasured with changes in value attributable to the hedged risk reported in earnings—for example, nonfinancial assets or liabilities that are denominated in a currency other than the functional currency—do not qualify for hedge accounting. The prohibition does not apply to foreign currency–denominated debt instruments that require remeasurement of the carrying value at spot exchange rates.
- Investments accounted for by the equity method do not qualify for hedge accounting.
- Equity investments in consolidated subsidiaries are not eligible for hedge accounting.
- Firm commitments to enter into business combinations or to acquire or dispose of a subsidiary, a minority interest, or an equity method investee are not eligible for hedge accounting.
- A reporting entity's own equity is not eligible for hedge accounting.
- For held-to-maturity debt securities, the risk of a change in fair value due to interest rate changes is not eligible for hedge accounting. Fair value hedge accounting may be applied to a prepayment option that is embedded in a held-to-maturity security, however, if the entire fair value of the option is designated as the exposure.
- Prepayment risk may not be designated as the risk being hedged for a financial asset.
- Except for currency derivatives, derivatives between members of a consolidated group cannot be considered to be hedging instruments in the consolidated statement, unless offsetting contracts have been arranged with unrelated third parties on a one-time basis.

(c) HEDGES OF NET INVESTMENTS IN FOREIGN OPERATIONS. Special hedge accounting is appropriate for hedges of the currency exposure associated with net investments in foreign operations, which give rise to translation gains or losses that are recorded in the currency translation account (CTA) in shareholders' equity. ASC 815-20-25-66 states that derivatives and nonderivatives (i.e., assets or liabilities denominated in the same currency as that of the net investment) may be designated as hedges of these exposures. According to ASC 815-20-35-1, effective results of such hedges are recognized in the same manner as a translation adjustment. Ineffective portions of hedge results are recognized in earnings.

Hedge accounting for net investments in foreign operations is not automatic. Specific criteria must be satisfied both at the inception of the hedge and on an ongoing basis. If, after initially qualifying, the criteria for hedge accounting stop being satisfied, hedge accounting is no longer appropriate. With the discontinuation of hedge accounting, gains or losses of the derivative will be recorded in earnings.

Reporting entities have complete discretion to hedge relationships at will and later redesignate them, assuming all hedge criteria remain satisfied.

(d) HEDGE EFFECTIVENESS. As noted above, to qualify for special hedge accounting, ASC 815-20-25-79 states that hedge effectiveness must be assessed prospectively (i.e., before the fact) and retrospectively (after the fact, but no less frequently than quarterly). The methods used to for these effectiveness assessments must be defined with the hedge documentation; and these methods must be applied as prescribed. If the entity decides to improve on these methods, the original hedge must be dedesignated and a new hedge relationship needs to be stipulated. According to ASC 815-20-25-81, if the same method is not applied to similar hedges, a justification for using differing methods is required.

Entities may elect to exclude specific components of hedge results from the hedge effectiveness assessment. ASC 815-20-25-82 indicates that allowable excluded items are (1) differences between spot and forward (or futures prices), if the derivative is or contains a forward or futures contract; or (2) the time value or the volatility value of options, if the derivative is or contains an option contract.

As a rule, whenever the underlying exposure relates to a price, interest rate, or currency exchange rate that is not *precisely* identical to the underlying of the associated hedging derivative, some degree of hedge ineffectiveness must be expected. According to ASC 815-20-25-84, however, when entities are able to clearly identify and enter into a hypothetical derivative—that is, a derivative that perfectly offsets the changes in fair values or cash flows of the designated hedged item—they can and should expect the hedge to perform perfectly, generating no earnings impacts attributable to hedge ineffectiveness.

The FASB has not sanctioned any particular methodology for assessing hedge effectiveness, and devising such tests is often nontrivial. Hedging entities are encouraged to discuss their intended approaches with their external auditors prior to initiating any hedging transactions.

(e) SPECULATIVE TRADES OR TRADES NOT QUALIFYING FOR HEDGE ACCOUNTING. The accounting treatment is the same for derivatives intended for speculative purposes or for situations in which the prerequisite hedge criteria are not satisfied. Derivatives are recorded on the balance sheet at fair market value, and gains and losses are realized in earnings. The objective for using the derivative contract(s) must still be disclosed.

26.6 DISCLOSURES

(a) ALL REPORTING ENTITIES. ASC 815-50-10-1 states that all reporting entities that use derivative instruments must disclose:

- Objectives for using each derivative, whether for hedging or for speculation
- The context needed to understand objectives—that is, how the derivative affects the entity's financial position, financial performance, and cash flows
- The location and fair value amounts of derivative reported in the statement of financial performance or the statement of financial position

Qualitative disclosures are encouraged.

(b) HEDGING. ASC 815-50-10-4 states that if derivatives are used in hedging relationships, the next issues must be disclosed:

- Risk management policies must be specified, identifying exposures to be hedged and hedging strategies for managing the associated risks.
- The type of hedging relationship (i.e., fair value, cash flow, net investment in foreign operation) must be identified, if applicable.
- The hedged item must be explicitly identified.
- Ineffective hedge results must be disclosed.
- Any component of the derivatives' results that is excluded from the hedge effectiveness assessment must be disclosed.
- The location and amount of the gains and losses on any related hedged items reported in the statement of financial performance or the statement of financial position must be indicated.

(c) FAIR VALUE HEDGES. According to 815-25-50, there are specific disclosure requirements for fair value hedges, such as disclosing the place on the income statement where derivative gains or losses are reported. When a firm commitment no longer qualifies as a hedged item, the net gain or loss recognized in earnings must be disclosed.

(d) CASH FLOW HEDGES. According to ASC 815-30-50, there are specific requirements for cash flow hedges:

- A description of the conditions that will result in the reclassification of accumulated OCI into earnings and a schedule of the estimated reclassification expected in the coming 12 months must be disclosed.
- The maximum length of time over which hedging is anticipated (except for variable interest rate exposures) must be disclosed.
- Entities must disclose the amount reclassified into earnings as a result of discontinued cash flow hedges because the forecasted transaction is no longer probable.

There are specific requirements for hedges of net investments in foreign operations. Entities must disclose the amount of the derivatives' results that is included in the cumulative translation adjustment during the reporting period.

26.7 INTERNATIONAL FINANCIAL REPORTING STANDARDS AND DERIVATIVES

As is true with most accounting areas of complexity, the march toward international standards is dotted with potholes and issues. While some features of International Accounting Standard (IAS) No. 39, *Financial Instruments: Recognition and Measurement* and U.S. generally accepted accounting principles (GAAP) are shared, some differences will need to be resolved as countries move toward congruence. Generally the IAS tracks GAAP in the criteria used to qualify a hedge, but in a cash flow hedge, U.S. GAAP treats unrealized gains and losses as part of equity (OCI) until realized. Under IAS No. 39, that change in value is recorded as an adjustment to the value of the hedged item. As another example, GAAP does not permit the hedging of a portion of the cash flows, but International Financial Reporting Standards (IFRS) do. These and other differences mean that more thinking on the best accounting in this critically important area[2] is forthcoming.

26.8 SOURCES AND SUGGESTED REFERENCES

American Institute of Certified Public Accountants. *Auditing Derivative Instruments, Hedging Activities, and Investments in Securities. AICPA Audit Guide.* New York, AICPA April 2011.

Banks, E. *Exchange Traded Derivatives*. Hoboken, NJ: John Wiley & Sons, 2002.

Financial Accounting Standards Board. Statement of Financial Accounting Standards No. 133, *Accounting for Derivative Instruments and Hedging Activities*. Stamford, CT: Author, 1998.

______. Statement of Financial Accounting Standards No. 157, *Fair Value Measurement*. Norwalk, CT: Author, 2006.

______. Statement of Financial Accounting Standards No. 159, *The Fair Value Option for Assets and Liabilities*. Norwalk, CT: Author, 2007.

______. Accounting Standards Update (ASU No. 2011-04), *Fair Value Measurement (Topic 820)—Amendments to Achieve Common Fair Value Measurement and Disclosure Requirements in U.S. GAAP and IFRS.* Norwalk, CT: Author, 2011

[2] It is reported that at the end of 2009, there were around $450 trillion in derivative contracts in play. See P. Eavis, "Bill on Derivatives Overhaul Is Long Overdue," *Wall Street Journal,* April 4, 2010.

———. Accounting Standards Update No. 2010-11, *Derivatives and Hedging (Topic 815) Scope Exception Related to Embedded Credit Derivatives.* Norwalk, CT: Author, 2011.

Flavell, R. *Swaps and Other Derivatives*. Hoboken, NJ: John Wiley & Sons, 2010.

Heye, P., "How to Manage Fluctuations in Foreign Currency Rates," *Journal of Accountancy* (April 2011).

Kawaller, I. www.kawaller.com/articles.shtml (link to the extensive published literature and articles by the author of this chapter)

Kolb, R., and J. Overdahl (eds.). *Financial Derivatives: Pricing and Risk Management*. Hoboken, NJ: John Wiley & Sons, 2009.

CHAPTER 27

PENSION PLANS AND OTHER POSTRETIREMENT AND POSTEMPLOYMENT BENEFITS

Jason Flynn, FSA, MAAA
Deloitte Consulting LLP

Timothy Geddes, FSA, MAAA
Deloitte Consulting LLP

Daniel Thomas, EA, MAAA
Deloitte Consulting LLP

27.1 BACKGROUND, ENVIRONMENT, AND OVERVIEW 3

(a) Introduction 3
(b) Development of the Private Pension System 4
(i) The Past 4
(ii) Period of Growth 5
(iii) The Present 5
(c) Plan Administration 5
(d) Evolution of Pension and Postretirement Benefits Accounting Standards 6

27.2 SPONSOR ACCOUNTING 8

(a) Scope of Statement of Financial Accounting Standard No. 87 8
(b) Applicability of Statement of Financial Accounting Statement No. 87 8
(c) Basic Elements of Pension Accounting 9
(i) Attribution 10
(ii) Actuarial Assumptions 10
(iii) Interest Rates 10
(iv) Consistency 11
(v) Actuarial Present Value of Benefits 11
(vi) Measurement Date 12
(d) Net Periodic Pension Cost 13
(i) Service Cost Component 13
(ii) Interest Cost Component 14
(iii) Expected Return on Plan Assets Component 14
(iv) Amortization of Net Gains and Losses Component 14
(v) Amortization of Net Prior Service Cost Component 15
(vi) Amortization of Net Obligation or Net Asset Component 17
(e) Plan Assets 17
(f) Recognition of Liabilities and Assets 17

The material in this chapter is intended to provide an overview of the key concepts in accounting for pension plans and other postretirement benefit plans. While references to specific accounting guidance are used throughout the chapter, it is important to recognize that the chapter is intended to serve as a practical overview and guide to accounting for pension and other benefit plans, from the perspective of actuaries who have served a variety of clients both directly and through support of audit engagements. As discussed in the preface to this *Handbook,* this chapter represents the work and viewpoint of the individual authors and does not represent the opinion of Deloitte Consulting LLP, Deloitte & Touche LLP, or any other portion of the Deloitte U.S. firms.

(g) Interim Measurements 18
(h) Financial Statement Disclosures 18
(i) Public Entity 18
(ii) Nonpublic Entity 19
(iii) Annuity Contracts 23
(i) Defined Contribution Pension Plans 24
(j) Non-U.S. Pension Plans 25
(k) Multiemployer Plans 25
(l) Multiple Employer Plans 26
(m) Funding and Income Tax Accounting 26

27.3 SPONSOR ACCOUNTING FOR NONRECURRING EVENTS 27

(a) Overview 27
(b) Settlement 27
(i) Timing 27
(ii) Gain or Loss 28
(iii) Use of Participating Annuities 28
(c) Curtailment 28
(d) Disposal of a Business 29
(e) Plan Merger, Spinoff, and Termination 29
(f) Termination Benefits 30
(g) Business Combinations 30
(h) Sequence of Measurement Steps 31
(i) Disclosure Requirements for Nonrecurring Events 31
(j) Illustration—Nonrecurring Events 32

27.4 SPONSOR ACCOUNTING FOR NONQUALIFIED PLANS 32

(a) Qualified versus Nonqualified Plans 32
(b) Nonqualified Plan Assets 34
(c) Nonqualified Defined Contribution Plans 34
(d) Nonqualified Defined Benefit Plans 34

27.5 PLAN ACCOUNTING 35

(a) Background 35
(b) Objective and Content of Financial Statements 35
(c) Net Assets Available for Benefits 36
(i) Good-Faith Valuations 36
(ii) Disclosures for Investments 36
(iii) Operating Assets 36
(iv) Contributions Receivable 36
(d) Changes in Net Assets Available for Benefits 36
(e) Actuarial Present Value of Accumulated Plan Benefits 37
(i) Actuarial Assumptions 37
(ii) Disclosures for Actuarial Present Value of Accumulated Plan Benefits 38
(f) Changes in the Actuarial Present Value of Accumulated Plan Benefits 39
(g) Illustrative Plan Financial Statements 39
(h) Additional Financial Statement Disclosures 40
(i) Decision to Prepare Plan Financial Statements 41
(j) Defined Contribution Plans 42
(i) Separate Accounts 42
(ii) Types of Plans 42
(iii) Financial Statements 43
(k) Postretirement Medical Benefit Features of Defined Benefit Pension Plans 43

27.6 ACCOUNTING FOR POSTRETIREMENT BENEFITS OTHER THAN PENSIONS 43

(a) Background 43
(b) Statement of Financial Accounting Standards No. 106 44
(i) Similarities to Statement of Financial Accounting Standards No. 87 44
(ii) Differences from Statement of Financial Accounting Standards No. 87 44
(c) Actuarial Assumptions 46
(d) Nonrecurring Events 46
(e) Disclosures 47

27.7 EMPLOYERS' ACCOUNTING FOR POSTEMPLOYMENT BENEFITS 48

(a) Background 48
(b) Statement of Financial Accounting Standards No. 112 (ASC 712) 48
(i) Application of Statement of Financial Accounting Standards No. 43 (ASC 710) versus Statement of Financial Accounting Standards No. 5 (ASC 450) 48
(ii) Differences in Accrual Accounting 49
(iii) Measurement Issues 49
(iv) Disclosures 51
(v) Illustration 51

27.8 SOURCES AND SUGGESTED REFERENCES 51

27.9 APPENDIX 52

27.1 BACKGROUND, ENVIRONMENT, AND OVERVIEW

(a) INTRODUCTION. The accounting for pensions and other forms of retirement and postemployment benefits underwent dramatic transformation in the 1980s and early 1990s. These changes placed a significant burden on companies and their accountants to understand the intricate concepts of accounting for pension and other types of benefits, assets, obligations, and periodic costs. The accounting applicable to these types of plans continues to evolve, with new standards introduced in 2006 (*Statement of Financial Accounting Standards* [SFASs] No. 157 and No. 158), as the first step in the Financial Accounting Standards Board's (FASB's) project to comprehensively reconsider guidance under SFAS Nos. 87, 88, 106 and 132(R).

This chapter explains the accounting concepts related to pension and other forms of retirement and postemployment benefits and assists the reader in understanding and implementing them. The focus is on the two distinct set of accounting standards that apply to pension and retirement plans: SFAS No. 35, *Accounting and Reporting by Defined Benefit Pension Plans,* and SFAS Nos. 87 and 88, *Employers' Accounting for Pensions* and *Employers' Accounting for Settlements and Curtailments of Defined Benefit Pension Plans and for Termination Benefits.* SFAS No. 35 applies to the preparation of financial statements for the pension plan, as an entity. SFAS Nos. 87 and 88, however, specify the accounting to be followed in the financial statements of the plan sponsor. They also established new standards for measuring a company's annual pension cost and balance sheet pension obligations. Additionally, the intricacies of SFAS No. 106, *Employers' Accounting for Postretirement Benefits Other Than Pensions,* and SFAS No. 112, *Employers' Accounting for Postemployment Benefits,* are explored.

SFAS No. 158, *Employers' Accounting for Defined Benefit Pension and Other Postretirement Plans: An Amendment of FASB Statements No. 87, 88, 106 and 132(R),* revises disclosures about pension and other postretirement benefits. Disclosure requirements are now standardized and presented in one note to the financial statements.

SFAS No. 157, *Fair Value Measurements,* applies under other accounting pronouncements that require or permit fair value measurements. This statement was intended to define fair value, to establish a framework for measuring fair value under U.S. generally accepted accounting principles (GAAP), and to expand the disclosure about fair value measurements.

On July 1, 2009, the FASB Accounting Standards Codification (ASC, or the Codification) became the single source of authoritative nongovernmental U.S. GAAP. The Codification became effective for interim and annual periods ending after September 15, 2009. The FASB indicated that the Codification does not change U.S. GAAP; rather, it restructures U.S. GAAP with the goal to make it easier to find information and, in turn, make it easier to comply with accounting standards.

In general, the Codification is organized by Topics, Subtopics, Sections, and Paragraphs. For example:

Topic 715, *Compensation*

Subtopic 715-30, *Retirement Benefits—Defined Benefit Plans—Pensions*

Section 715-30-25, *Recognition*

Paragraphs 715-30-25-8, *Termination Benefits*

The next table contains a quick-reference guide to the Codification. The remaining sections of this chapter link the original FASB pronouncements with the appropriate sections in the Codification. Reference to the original FASB pronouncements is retained to reflect their historical and topical significance.

	FASB	Primary ASC Topic
Contingencies	SFAS No. 5	ASC 450
Non-Retirement Postemployment Benefits	SFAS No. 112	ASC 712
Retirement Benefits	SFAS No. 87, 88, 106 & 158	ASC 715
Plan Accounting: Defined Benefit Plans	SFAS No. 35	ASC 960
Plan Accounting: Defined Contribution Plans	SOP 94-4	ASC 962
Plan Accounting: Health and Welfare Benefit Plans	SOP 92-6	ASC 965
Fair Value Measurement	SFAS No. 157	ASC 820

The next table provides a more refined presentation of the Codification as it relates to retirement benefits.

Retirement Benefits	ASC Topic/Subtopic
Overall	ASC 715-10
Defined Benefit Plans: General	ASC 715-20
Defined Benefit Plans: Pension	ASC 715-30
Defined Benefit Plans: Other Postretirement	ASC 715-60
Defined Contribution Plans	ASC 715-70
Multiemployer Plans	ASC 715-80

Accounting Updates. The Codification will be updated via Accounting Standards Updates (ASUs). These will be assigned a number that corresponds to the year of the ASU's issuance and its sequential order. ASUs will replace accounting changes that historically were issued as FASB Statements, FASB Interpretations, FASB Staff Positions, or other types of FASB pronouncements.

(b) DEVELOPMENT OF THE PRIVATE PENSION SYSTEM. Before consideration of the accounting requirements specified by SFAS Nos. 35, 87, and 88, some background information regarding the pension system may be useful. It outlines why companies sponsor retirement programs and how plans are changing in response to a changing environment.

(i) The Past. The U.S. private pension system traces its origins to 1875, when the first formal plan was established by a company in the railroad industry. In addition to fostering humanitarian objectives, the early plans were established to achieve a well-defined management goal—to affect the age composition of the workforce. By using such plans, manufacturing firms could ease out older workers who were less productive. Service industries were able to provide promotion opportunities for younger employees. Pension plans typically were established in conjunction with mandatory retirement policies. Tax-driven motives were noticeably absent because there were no meaningful tax incentives until 1942, when corporate tax rates were increased dramatically to finance World War II.

The private U.S. pension system started during the Industrial Revolution. Emerging national companies could not continue their past practice of accommodating aged workers with informal ad hoc policies. One by one, big companies with the financial ability to do so adopted formal retirement arrangements to solve this problem. The list includes the Standard Oil Companies, DuPont, U.S. Steel, and Bell Companies. By 1930, nearly 400 major corporations with more than 4 million workers, representing approximately one-sixth of the private workforce, had adopted formal pension plans.

The seeds of federal regulation were sown before the Great Depression. Many plans were implemented and operated by companies to achieve their goals without regard to employee rights. Courts viewed these contracts as one-sided and issued decisions that construed plans as gratuities.

(ii) Period of Growth. Plan sponsors' motives for providing pensions have become less homogeneous since World War II. During this period of unprecedented economic prosperity, companies responded in droves to increased taxes and union demands (or threats of organization) by establishing plans.

Higher tax rates coupled with federal wage controls that had been imposed to stifle war-related inflation triggered a spurt of growth in plan formation during the 1940s.

The wide-reaching economic prosperity of the 1950s and 1960s had a profound effect on the pension system; coverage almost tripled during this period. Through collective bargaining, unions succeeded in establishing plans in many booming industries. Companies with unfilled orders willingly paid the price of starting a program. In addition, plans were established for nonunion employees to ensure parity with unionized coworkers. In companies without unions, plans were developed to ward off organization drives. As the economic pie grew, one-company workers came to expect that they would be rewarded with a secure retirement for their loyal and long service. They were not disappointed. By the dawn of the congressional debates that culminated in the passage of pension reform legislation in 1974, pension plans had been adopted by virtually all established large and medium-size companies. Pension coverage is still spotty, however, in smaller companies that operate on thin margins.

Small professional corporations maintained a proliferation of pension plans as tax shelters during the 1980s. Accumulation of assets and tax savings for the proprietor(s) is the usual goals of these plans. In many ways, federal pension regulation has been driven by tax authorities' desire to correct perceived abuses in this segment of the pension system.

(iii) The Present. The private system is currently under significant pressure from external forces. Through repeated changes over the past three decades, the federal government is reducing available tax incentives and increasing administrative complexity and, therefore, compliance costs. Foreign competition, corporate restructuring and downsizing, and growing merger activity have caused many companies to rethink their pension policies. Changes in the composition of the labor force are also affecting the makeup of pension programs.

For now, change in plan design and types of plans used for providing retirement income are the only discernible trends in the responses of plan sponsors. Plans such as 401(k) and thrift or matching programs are becoming an increasingly important part of plan sponsors' deferred compensation policies. Younger employees tend to prefer these savings plans because of their visibility, and the predictability of their annual costs appeals to many employers. In response to this preference, some companies changed their traditional defined benefit pension plans to cash balance plans, hybrid defined benefit plans that have features of both traditional defined benefit pension plans and 401(k)-type defined contribution plans. The combination of the great recession and increasingly market-based funding rules has placed significant pressure on traditional defined benefit plans, and many employers have moved to close or completely freeze these legacy plans.

(c) PLAN ADMINISTRATION. Employers still establish plans to affect the age composition of their workforces by providing income security during employees' retirement years. A plan's level of benefit and other important features—such as early retirement provisions—balance the sponsor's management goals and cost tolerance. Once a program is established, its administration is dictated by specific plan language, which in turn is affected significantly by federal law.

The Employee Retirement Income Security Act of 1974 (ERISA) established minimum standards applicable to virtually all employee plans. Certain unfunded nonqualified plans are exempted. Through a succession of amendments since 1974, the original legal standards have been modified and are now considerably more detailed. Employers are not required to start pension plans but, once established, ERISA limits a sponsor's freedom in changing benefits or options. The Internal Revenue Service (IRS) administers most of the minimum standards, including participation, funding, and vesting and accrual of benefits. The Department of Labor (DOL) is responsible for the fiduciary and reporting and disclosure requirements. In addition, the DOL assists participants by investigating alleged infractions and by bringing civil action to enforce compliance, if necessary. The Pension Benefit Guaranty Corporation (PBGC) administers the termination insurance program established by ERISA.

Plan administration can be viewed as three functions: operation, communication, and compliance. Operating a plan in accordance with its terms requires maintaining sufficient data to determine the proper apportionment of benefits to participants, the calculations needed to apply benefits, and an appropriate level of contributions. Communicating information about benefits to participants assists employees' retirement planning and enhances loyalty. Compliance activities include adopting amendments to conform plans to changing federal requirements and to ERISA's reporting and disclosure requirements. The latter include annual and other reporting to the three pension regulatory agencies and to plan participants.

Most defined benefit pension plans are subject to the termination insurance program that was codified by Title IV of ERISA. Covered plans pay annual premiums to the PBGC, which is set as an annual amount per year per participant plus a surcharge applicable to underfunded plans. Within specified time constraints, an employer can terminate a fully funded plan at will. A procedure is prescribed for notifying participants and the PBGC. Underfunded plans maintained by employers in financial distress can transfer responsibility to the PBGC for paying benefits guaranteed by the insurance program.

(d) EVOLUTION OF PENSION AND POSTRETIREMENT BENEFITS ACCOUNTING STANDARDS. SFAS Nos. 35, 87, and 88 were the result of approximately 11 years of deliberations by the FASB. However, the controversies concerning the accounting for pension plans well preceded that. As noted in the introduction to SFAS No. 87, since 1956, pension accounting literature has "expressed a preference for accounting in which cost would be systematically accrued during the expected period of actual service of the covered employees."

In 1966, Accounting Principles Board (APB) Opinion No. 8, *Accounting for the Cost of Pension Plans,* was issued. Within broad limits, annual pension cost for accounting purposes under APB No. 8 was the same as cash contributions for prefunded plans. Over the years, however, actuarial funding methods have evolved that produce different patterns of accumulating ultimate costs; some are intended to produce level costs, other front-end load costs, and still others tend to back-load costs.

In 1980, the FASB issued SFAS No. 35, which established standards of financial accounting and reporting for the annual financial statements of a defined benefit pension plan. The Statement was considered the FASB's first step in the overall pension project. After SFAS No. 35 was issued, the FASB concluded that the contribution-driven standard prescribed by APB No. 8 was no longer acceptable for employer financial reporting purposes. The proliferation of plans and a total asset pool of nearly $1 trillion (and growing) argued for an accounting approach under which reported costs would be more consistent for a company from one period to the next and more comparable among companies.

SFAS No. 87 and its companion SFAS No. 88 were issued in 1985 and were generally effective for fiscal years beginning after December 15, 1986. These Statements now govern the accounting for virtually all defined benefit pension plans. They prescribe a single method for accruing plan liabilities for future benefits that is independent from the way benefits are funded. Standards are prescribed for selecting actuarial assumptions used for calculating plan liability and expense components. Most important, the discount rate used to calculate the present value of future obligations is market driven and follows prevailing yields in the bond markets. Taken together, these changes are intended to improve the quality of pension accounting information, but further refinements are possible. SFAS No. 87 states:

> This Statement continues the evolutionary search for more meaningful and useful pension accounting. The FASB believes that the conclusions it has reached are a worthwhile and significant step in that direction, but it also believes that those conclusions are not likely to be the final step in that evolution.

SFAS No. 106 was issued in 1990 and was generally effective for fiscal years beginning after December 15, 1992. This Statement now governs the accounting for virtually all postretirement benefits other than pensions, but focuses principally on postretirement health care benefits. It prescribes a single method for accruing plan liabilities for future benefits that is independent from the way benefits are funded. Standards are prescribed for selecting actuarial assumptions used for calculating plan liability and expense components. Most important, the discount rate used to calculate the present value of future obligations is market driven and follows prevailing yields in the bond markets. Taken together, these changes are intended to improve the quality of other postretirement benefits accounting information, but further refinements are possible. SFAS No. 106 states:

> This Statement addresses, for the first time, the accounting issues related to measuring and recognizing the exchange that takes place between an employer that provides postretirement benefits and the employees who render service in exchange for those benefits. The Board believes the accounting recognition required by this statement should result in more useful information and representationally faithful financial statements. However, this Statement is not likely to be the final step in the evolution of more useful accounting for postretirement benefit arrangements.

SFAS No. 106 also applies to the settlement of all or a part of an employer's accumulated postretirement benefit obligation (APBO) or curtailment of a postretirement benefit plan and to an employer that provides postretirement benefits as part of a special termination benefits offer. So, while SFAS No. 88 is a separate FASB standard for these special events accounting for pension plans, SFAS No. 106 includes this guidance directly.

SFAS No. 158 was issued in 2006 and was generally effective for fiscal years ending after December 15, 2006, for an employer that is an issuer of publicly traded equity securities (as defined) and for fiscal years ending after June 15, 2007, for an employer that is not. This Statement was intended to improve financial reporting by requiring an employer to recognize the overfunded or underfunded status of a defined benefit pension or postretirement plan (other than a multiemployer plan) as an asset or liability in its statement of financial position and to recognize changes in that funded status in the year in which the change occurs through comprehensive income of a business entity or changes in unrestricted net assets of a not-for-profit organization. This Statement also required an employer to measure the funded status of a plan as of the date of its year-end statement of financial position (with limited exceptions). The FASB issued this Statement to address concerns that prior standards on employers' accounting for defined benefit pension and postretirement plans failed to communicate the funded status of those plans in a complete an understandable way.

SFAS No. 157, *Fair Value Measurements,* was issued in 2006 and was generally effective for fiscal years beginning after November 15, 2007, and interim periods within those fiscal years. This Statement applies under other accounting pronouncements that require or permit fair value measurements. This Statement was intended to define fair value, establish a framework for measuring fair value under U.S. GAAP, and expands the disclosure about fair value measurements. In order to increase consistency and comparability in fair value measurements and related disclosures, a fair value hierarchy was established to prioritize the inputs to the valuation techniques used to measure fair value into three broad levels:

> *Level 1 inputs.* Quoted prices (unadjusted) in active markets for identical assets or liabilities that the reporting entity has the ability to access at the measurement date.
>
> *Level 2 inputs.* Inputs other than quoted prices included within Level 1 that are observable for either the asset or the liability, either directly or indirectly
>
> *Level 3 inputs.* Unobservable inputs for the asset or liability. Unobservable inputs are used to measure the fair value to the extent that observable inputs are not available, thereby allowing for situations in which there is little or no market activity for the asset or liability as of the measurement date.

Projects under the Memorandum of Understanding of the FASB and the International Accounting Standards Board (IASB) are nearing completion, and given the recent Securities and Exchange

Commission (SEC) Staff paper on incorporating International Financial Reporting Standards (IFRS) into the U.S. reporting system, the FASB may consider adding stand-alone projects that would further align U.S. GAAP with IFRS.

On June 16, 2011, IASB issued amendments to International Accounting Standards (IAS) 19 that changes the accounting for defined benefit plans and termination benefits. The objective of this limited scope project was to improve the financial reporting of employee benefits by:

- Requiring changes in defined benefit obligations and in the fair value of plan assets to be reported in a more understandable way
- Eliminating some presentation options allowed under the previous version of IAS 19, thus improving comparability
- Clarifying requirements that have resulted in diverse practices
- Enhancing disclosure about the risks arising from defined benefit plans

The amendments are effective for annual reporting periods beginning on or after January 1, 2013. Retrospective application is generally required in accordance with IAS 8.

Because the June 2011 amendments to IAS 19 eliminated only some of the existing differences between IFRS and U.S. GAAP accounting for retirement programs and, in some cases, created additional discrepancies, defined benefit and defined contribution plan accounting may become an area of focus for the FASB.

See the chart in the appendix to this chapter for a summary of the key differences between U.S. GAAP and IFRS.

27.2 SPONSOR ACCOUNTING

(a) SCOPE OF STATEMENT OF FINANCIAL ACCOUNTING STANDARD NO. 87. The goal of the FASB in issuing SFAS No. 87 was to establish objective standards of financial accounting and reporting for employers that sponsor pension benefit arrangements for their employees. The Statement applies equally to single-employer plans and multiemployer plans as well as pension plans or similar benefit arrangements for employees outside the United States. Any arrangement that is similar in substance to a pension plan is covered by the Statement.

The accounting specified in SFAS No. 87 does not supersede any of the plan accounting and reporting requirements of SFAS No. 35 (see "Plan Accounting" in Section 27.5 of this chapter). It does, however, affect sponsor accounting by superseding the accounting requirements to calculate pension cost as described in APB No. 8, and the disclosure requirements as stated in SFAS No. 36, *Disclosure of Pension Information.*

The Statement does not apply to pension or other types of plans that provide life and/or health insurance benefits to retired employees, although the sponsor of a plan that provides such benefits may elect to account for them in accordance with the provisions of SFAS No. 87. The accounting for the obligations and cost of these other postretirement benefits is the subject of SFAS No. 106 (see "Accounting for Postretirement Benefits Other Than Pensions" in Section 27.6 in this chapter).

(b) APPLICABILITY OF STATEMENT OF FINANCIAL ACCOUNTING STATEMENT NO. 87. In substance, there are two principal types of single-employer pension plans: defined benefit plans and defined contribution plans. SFAS No. 87 applies to both kinds of plans; however, most of the provisions of that statement are directed toward defined benefit plans.

Appendix D of SFAS No. 87 defines these two types of pension plans:

> Defined benefit pension plan—A pension plan that defines an amount of pension benefit to be provided, usually as a function of one or more factors such as age, years of service, or compensation. Any pension plan that is not a defined contribution plan is, for purposes of this Statement, a defined benefit plan.

Defined contribution pension plan—A plan that provides pension benefits in return for services rendered, provides an individual account for each participant, and specifies how contributions to the individual's account are to be determined instead of specifying the amount of benefits the individual is to receive. Under a defined contribution pension plan, the benefits a participant will receive depend solely on the amount contributed to the participant's account, the returns earned on investments of those contributions, and forfeitures of other participants' benefits that may be allocated to such participant's account.

(See ASC 715-30-20—Glossary—for the equivalent ASC definitions)

The paragraphs that immediately follow address the principal accounting and reporting requirements for a sponsor of a defined benefit pension plan. The provisions of SFAS No. 87 that provide standards for other types of pension plans—defined contribution, multiemployer, and multiple employer plans—are discussed in Sections 27.2(i), 27.2(k), and 27.2(m) of this chapter.

It should be noted that cash balance plans, which have characteristics of both defined benefit plans and defined contribution plans, have been the subject of significant FASB discussion and evaluation. In 2002, a group of pension professionals formally requested FASB guidance on the appropriate accounting treatment for cash balance plans. Key questions included whether the plans should be accounted for as defined contribution or defined benefit in nature and the appropriate attribution to apply if the decision were to treat them as defined benefit plans. In 2003, the Emerging Issues Task Force (EITF) formally began considering the issue and assigned it the identification EITF Issue 03-4 (ASC 715-30-15-3).

The EITF has since reached preliminary conclusions with respect to a distinct subset of cash balance plans (i.e., those with fixed interest crediting rates). These plans are to be treated as defined benefit plans and valued according to the traditional unit credit attribution method, which does not reflect future pay increases.

With respect to the remaining group of cash balance plans that use a variable interest crediting rate, the FASB is still deliberating. Preliminary releases indicate that the FASB prefers that these plans record the sum of the hypothetical account balances as the plan liability. This would be more of a defined contribution accounting approach, in that the expense would include the actual allocations made to the account and the actual interest credited as the service cost and interest cost components. Still further, the FASB may expand the scope of this new approach to include all defined benefit plans that pay an immediately available lump sum on termination. On November 10, 2005, the FASB decided to address the issues in this project as part of the broader pension's project that was added to the agenda on that date.

For employers with more than one pension plan, SFAS No. 87 generally applies to each plan separately, although the financial disclosures of the plans in the sponsor's financial statements may be aggregated within certain limitations.

(c) BASIC ELEMENTS OF PENSION ACCOUNTING. The intention of the FASB in adopting SFAS No. 87 was to specify accounting objectives and results rather than the specific computational means of obtaining those results. Accordingly, the Statement permits a certain amount of flexibility in choosing methods and approaches to the required pension calculations.

One of the reasons for the flexibility is that in a defined benefit pension plan an employer promises to provide the employee with retirement income in future years after the employee retires or otherwise terminates employment. The actual amount of pension benefit to be paid usually is contingent on a number of future events, many of which the employer has no control over. These future events are incorporated into the defined benefit plan contract between the employer and employee and form the basis of the plan's benefit formula.

The benefit formula within a pension plan generally describes the amount of retirement income an employee will receive for services performed during employment. Since accounting and financial reporting are intended to mirror actual agreements and transactions, it is logical that sponsor accounting for pensions should follow this contract to pay future benefits—that is the plan's benefit formula. However, two problems arise from this accounting premise: how will the amount and timing of benefit payments be determined, and over what years of service will the cost of those pension benefits be attributed?

(i) Attribution. When drafting SFAS No. 87, the FASB considered whether the determination of net periodic pension cost should be based on a benefit approach or a cost approach. The benefit approach determines pension benefits attributed to service to date and calculates the present value of those benefits. The benefit approach recognizes costs equal to the present value of benefits earned for each period. Even when an equal amount of benefit is earned in each period, the cost being recognized will nevertheless increase as an employee approaches retirement. The cost approach, however, projects the present value of the total benefit at retirement and allocates that cost over the remaining years of service. Under the cost approach, the cost charged in the early years of an employee's service is greater than the present value of benefits earned based on the plan's benefit formula. In the later years of an employee's service, the cost is less than the present value of benefits earned so that the cumulative cost by the time the employee retires will be the same as that under the benefits approach.

As noted previously, accounting is intended to mirror actual agreements. In a defined benefit plan contract, the employer's promise to the employee is specified in terms of how benefits are earned based on service. Accordingly, the benefit approach was selected by the FASB and is the single attribution approach permitted by SFAS No. 87. Specifically, the Statement requires:

- For flat benefit plans, the unit credit actuarial method
- For final-pay and career-average-pay plans, the projected unit credit method

(ii) Actuarial Assumptions. The value of plan benefits that form the basis for determining net periodic pension cost are calculated through use of actuarial assumptions. The discount rate reflects the time value of money. Demographic assumptions help determine the probability and timing of benefit payments—for example, assumptions for mortality, termination of employment, and retirement incidence are used to develop expected payout streams. Demographic assumptions are also utilized to establish certain amortization schedules. Paragraphs 43–45 of SFAS No. 87 and Paragraphs 42–49 of ASC 715-30-35 establish standards for selecting assumptions. Each nonfinancial assumption must reflect the best estimate of future experience for that assumption.

(iii) Interest Rates. Under SFAS No. 87, employers are required to apply two interest rates in measuring plan obligations and computing net periodic pension costs: an expected long-term rate of return on plan assets and an assumed discount rate.

As its name implies, the expected long-term rate of return on assets should reflect the expected long-term yield on plan assets available for investment during the ensuing year as well as the reinvestment that yield in subsequent years.

The discount rate is a snapshot rate determined on the measurement date used for financial reporting. Paragraph 44 of SFAS No. 87 (ASC 715-30-35-43) states:

> Assumed discount rates shall reflect the rates at which the pension benefits could be effectively settled. It is appropriate in estimating those rates to look to available information about rates implicit in current prices of annuity contracts that could be used to effect settlement of the obligation (including information about available annuity rates currently published by the PBGC). In making those estimates, employers may also look to rates of return on high-quality fixed-income investments currently available and expected to be available during the period to maturity of the pension benefits.

SFAS No. 87 was published in 1985. In December 1990, SFAS No. 106 was issued, which stated in Paragraph 186 (ASC 715-60-35-80):

> The objective of selecting assumed discount rates is to measure the single amount that, if invested at the measurement date in a portfolio of high-quality debt instruments, would provide the necessary future cash flows to pay the accumulated benefits when due. Notionally, that single amount,

> the accumulated post-retirement benefit obligation, would equal the current market value of a portfolio of high-quality zero coupon bonds whose maturity dates and amounts would be the same as the timing and amount of the expected future benefit payments.

For SFAS No. 106, the concept of "settling" obligations using annuities is not usually applicable, so the method for selecting discount rates could not use exactly the same method as SFAS No. 87. But both refer to "high-quality" investments. The Chief Accountant of the SEC announced the following in a 1993 letter to the chairman of the EITF at the FASB:

> The SEC staff believes that the guidance that is provided in paragraph 186 of FASB 106 for selecting discount rates to measure the post-retirement benefit obligation also is appropriate guidance for measuring the pension benefit obligation.

Thus, the SEC suggests that SFAS No. 106's method for estimating a discount rate should be used for SFAS No. 87 purposes. Paragraph 186 of SFAS No. 106 can be adapted easily for pension purposes by changing "accumulated postretirement benefit obligation" (APBO) to "projected benefit obligation" (PBO) (ASC 715-30-35-44). The SEC also clarified the term *high quality* in this letter, indicating that any bond receiving one of two highest ratings given by a recognized rating agency (e.g., Moody's Aaa and Aa) would be deemed to be high quality.

(iv) Consistency. The Statement suggests some consistency among the assumptions used to calculate plan liabilities. In practice this means that identical components of financial assumptions generally should be used. For example, the assumed rate of increase in salaries and the rate of increase in Social Security benefits both have an inflation component, so as one increases due to expected inflation, so should the other.

Notwithstanding the preceding paragraph, the Statement does not require an employer to adopt any specific method of selecting the assumptions. Instead, SFAS No. 87 requires the assumptions to be the employer's best estimates. Therefore, it is not deemed a change in accounting principle, as defined in SFAS No. 154, *Accounting Changes and Error Corrections a replacement of APB Opinion No. 20 and FASB Statement No. 3* (ASC 250), if an employer should change its basis of selecting the assumed discount rate, for example, from high-quality bond rates to annuity purchase rates. The change in liabilities due to a change in assumptions goes into "net gain or loss"; hence the amount of net gain or loss is one of the best indicators of the reasonableness of assumptions under the plan. If the assumptions are reasonable, the gains and losses should offset each other in the long term. Therefore, when a plan has a pattern of gains or losses that does not appear to be self-correcting, the assumptions used to measure benefit obligations and net periodic pension cost may be unrealistic. Assumptions that do not appear on the surface to be unreasonable may still be unrealistic if not borne out by experience.

(v) Actuarial Present Value of Benefits. As noted previously, the FASB determined SFAS No. 87 accounting would be based on the plan's contractual arrangement—that the projection of ultimate benefits to be paid under a pension plan should be based on the plan's benefit formula. Accordingly, SFAS No. 87 utilizes two different measurements in estimating this ultimate pension liability—the accumulated benefit obligation (ABO) and the PBO. The ABO comprises two components—vested and nonvested benefits—both of which are determined based on employee service and compensation amounts to date. Benefits are vested when they no longer depend on remaining in the service of the employer. The PBO is equal to the ABO plus an allowance for future compensation levels, that is, a projection of the actual salary upon which the pension benefit will be calculated and paid (i.e., projection of the final salary in a "final-pay" plan). The relationship of these two obligations is reflected in Exhibit 27.1.

Consider the example of a plan that provides a retirement pension equal to 1 percent of an employee's average final five-year compensation for each year of service. The PBO for an employee with five years of service is the actuarial present value of 5 percent of his or her projected average compensation at the expected retirement date; whereas the employee's ABO is determined similarly

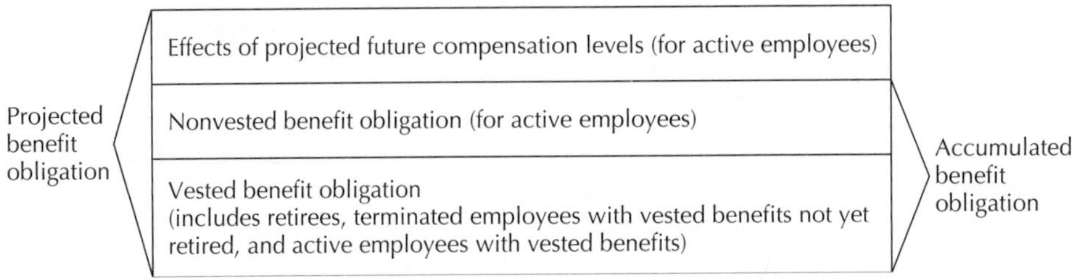

Exhibit 27.1 Relationship of ABO and PBO

but only taking into account his or her average compensation to date. Further, assume that this employee would be 60 percent vested in accrued benefits if service is terminated today; then his or her vested benefit obligation is equal to 60 percent of this employee's ABO.

Unless there is evidence to the contrary, accounting is based on the going-concern concept. Accordingly, the PBO is utilized as the basis for computing the service and interest components of the net periodic pension cost since it is more representative of the ultimate pension benefits to be paid than the ABO.

When evaluating a plan's benefit formula to determine how the attribution method should be applied, SFAS No. 87 specifies that the substance of the plan and the sponsor's history of plan amendments should be considered. For example, an employer that regularly increases the benefits payable under a flat-benefit plan may, in substance, be considered to have sponsored a plan with benefits primarily based on employees' compensation. In such cases, the attribution method should reflect the plan's substance rather than simply conform to its written terms. Similarly, attribution of benefits (and, therefore, recognition of cost) for accounting purposes may differ from that called for in a plan's benefit formula if the formula calls for deferred vesting (backloading) of benefits. This by far is one of the more subjective areas of SFAS No. 87. Obviously, the determination that there is a commitment by the sponsor to provide benefits beyond the written terms of the pension plan's benefit formula requires careful evaluation and consideration.

If an employer has committed to making certain plan amendments, these amendments should be reflected in the PBO even if they have not have been formally written into the plan or if some of the changes may not be effective until a later date. Collectively bargained pension plans often provide for benefit increases with staggered effective dates. Such a plan may provide a monthly pension equal to \$20 per month for each year of service in the first year of a labor contract, \$21 in the second year, and \$22 in the third. Once the contract has been negotiated, the PBO should reflect the \$21 and \$22 benefit multipliers for participants assumed to terminate or retire after the first year of the labor contract.

(vi) Measurement Date. The date as of which the plan's PBO and assets are measured—for purposes of disclosure in the employer's financial statements and determination of pension cost for the subsequent period—is known as the *measurement date.* Although SFAS No. 87 initially contemplated that the measurement date would coincide with the date of the financial statements, an alternative date not more than three months prior to the date of the financial statements was allowed. With the adoption of SFAS No. 158, the FASB required that the measurement date must coincide with the fiscal year-end.

Although most employers have one measurement date each year, some employers remeasure their PBO and select the assumed discount rates on a more frequent basis. The frequency of measurement is part of the employer's accounting methods and may not be changed without proper disclosure of the impact.

Although the PBO disclosed in the financial statements is as of the measurement date, it generally is not necessary to determine the PBO using participant data as of that date. Instead the PBO may be estimated from a prior measurement, provided that the result obtained does not differ materially from that if a new measurement is made using current participant data. The fair value of plan assets, however, should be as of the measurement date.

The period between consecutive measurement dates is known as the *measurement period* and is used for determining the net periodic pension cost. The cost thus determined is used for the related financial reporting period.

(d) NET PERIODIC PENSION COST. Net periodic pension cost represents the accounting recognition of the consequences of events and transactions affecting a pension plan. The amount of pension cost for a specified period is reported as a single net amount in an employer's financial statements. Under SFAS No. 87, net periodic pension cost comprises these six components:

1. Service cost
2. Interest cost
3. Expected return on plan assets
4. Amount of net gain or loss being recognized or deferred
5. Amortization of net prior service cost
6. Amortization of the net obligation or net asset existing at the initial application of the Statement

(i) Service Cost Component. A defined benefit pension plan contains a benefit formula that generally describes the amount of retirement income that an employee will receive for services performed during his or her employment. SFAS No. 87 requires the use of this benefit formula in the measurement of annual service cost. The service cost component of net periodic pension cost is defined by the Statement as the actuarial present value of pension benefits attributed by the pension benefit formula to employee service during a specified period. Under SFAS No. 87, attribution (the process of assigning pension benefits or cost to periods of employee service) generally is based on the benefit formula (i.e., the benefit attribution approach).

A simplified example will help illustrate this concept. Assume that a pension plan's benefit formula states that an employee shall receive, at the retirement age of 65, retirement income of $15 per month for life for each year of credited service. Thus, a pension of $15 per month can be attributed to each year of employee service. The actuarial present value of the $15 monthly pension represents the service cost component of net periodic pension cost. Although it is customary to determine the service cost at the end of the year, an equally acceptable practice is to compute the service cost at the beginning of the year and to add the interest thereon at the assumed discount rate to the interest cost component.

In certain circumstances, the plan's benefit formula does not indicate the manner in which a particular benefit relates to specific services performed by the employee. In this case, SFAS No. 87 specifies that the benefit must be considered to be accumulated in this way (ASC 715-30-35-38):

> If the benefit is includable in vested benefits, the benefit shall be accumulated in proportion to the ratio of total completed years of service as of the present to the total completed years of service as of the date the benefit becomes fully vested. A vested benefit is a benefit that an employee has an irrevocable right to receive. For example, receipt of the pension benefit is not contingent on whether the employee continues to work for the employer.
>
> If the benefit is not includable in vested benefits, the benefit shall be accumulated in proportion to the ratio of completed years of service as of the present date to the total projected years of service. An example of a benefit that is not includable in vested benefits is a death or disability benefit that is payable only if death or disability occurs during the employee's active service.

Some pension plans require contributions by employees to cover part of the plan's overall cost. SFAS No. 87 does not specify how the net periodic pension cost should be adjusted for employee contributions. An often-used approach is to reduce the service cost component directly by the employee contributions, thus possibly resulting in a negative service cost. Under this approach, the plan's PBO encompasses both benefits to be financed by employee contributions and those financed by the employer.

(ii) Interest Cost Component. In determining the PBO of a plan, SFAS No. 87 gives appropriate consideration to the time value of money, through the use of discounts for interest cost. Therefore, the Statement requires that an employer recognize, as a component of net periodic pension cost, interest on the PBO. This interest cost component is equal to the increase in the amount of the PBO due to the passage of time. The accretion of interest on the PBO is based on the assumed discount rate.

Since the assumed discount rate is intended to reflect the interest rate at which the PBO currently could be settled, it is imperative that the discount rate assumption be reevaluated each year to determine whether it reflects the best estimate of current settlement rates. As a rule of thumb, if interest rates are in a period of fluctuation, the discount rate generally should change.

(iii) Expected Return on Plan Assets Component. SFAS No. 87 requires that an employer recognize, as a component of net periodic pension cost, the expected return on pension plan assets [see Section 27.2(e)]. (SFAS No. 87 describes an *actual* return on plan assets component in disclosing the net periodic pension cost. However, the difference between actual and expected return was then put into the net gain or loss, so there is no difference between using expected return on assets versus using actual return on assets plus an offsetting net gain or loss. SFAS No. 158, which amended SFAS No. 87 disclosure requirements, states that expected return is to be disclosed, so that approach is followed here.)

The expected return on plan assets is determined by multiplying the "market-related value of assets" (defined next) by the expected long-term rate of return assumption, and adjusting for interest on contributions and benefit payments expected to be made.

The market-related value of assets (MRVA) is used in determining the expected return on pension plan assets. The MRVA can be either the actual fair value of plan assets or a "calculated" value that recognizes the changes in the fair value of plan assets over a period of not more than five years. Employers are permitted great flexibility in selecting the method of calculating the MRVA. Any method that averages gains and losses over not longer than a five-year period would be acceptable under the Statement, provided it meets two criteria: The method must be both systematic and rational. In fact, changes in the fair value of assets would not have to be averaged but could be recognized in full in the subsequent year's net periodic pension cost, provided that the method is applied consistently to all gains and losses and is disclosed. An employer also may use different methods for determining the MRVA in separate pension plans and in separate asset categories within each plan, provided that the differences can be supported. However, a change in calculating the MRVA (e.g., going from using fair value of assets to a smoothed value, or going from one kind of smoothing to another) would be a change in accounting method under SFAS No. 154 (ASC 250).

The Statement makes no specific allowance for administrative or investment expenses paid directly from the pension fund. These expenses may be reflected in the net periodic pension cost as an offset to the expected return on plan assets and in such case may also be considered in the selection of the expected long-term rate of return on plan assets. If deemed appropriate, administrative expenses may be treated differently from investment expenses and added to the plan's service cost.

(iv) Amortization of Net Gains and Losses Component. SFAS No. 87 broadly defines gains and losses as changes in the amount of either the PBO or pension plan assets that generally result from differences between the estimates or assumptions used and actual experience. Gains and losses may reflect both the refinement of estimates or assumptions and real changes in economic conditions. Hence, the gain and loss component consists of the net difference between the estimates and actual results of two separate pension items: actuarial assumptions related to pension plan obligations (liability gains and losses) and return on plan assets (asset gains and losses).

Liability gains and losses (increases or decreases in the PBO) stem from two types of events: changes in obligation-related assumptions (i.e., discount rate, assumed future compensation levels) and variances between actual and assumed experience (i.e., turnover, mortality). Liability gains and losses generally would be calculated at the end of each year as the difference between the projected value of the year-end pension obligation based on beginning of the year assumptions and the actual year-end value of the obligation based on the end-of-year assumptions.

Asset gains and losses represent the difference between the actual and expected return on plan assets during a period. These gains and losses are entirely experience related. The actual return on pension plan assets is equal to the difference between the fair value of pension plan assets at the beginning and end of a period, adjusted for any contributions and pension benefit payments made during that period. The expected return on pension plan assets is a computed amount determined by multiplying the MRVA by the expected long-term rate of return. The expected long-term rate of return is an actuarial assumption of the average expected long-term interest rate that will be earned on plan assets available for investment during the period.

In order to reduce the potentially volatile impact of gains and losses on net periodic pension cost from year to year, the FASB adopted various smoothing techniques related to the MRVA and the recognition of gains and losses in the calculation of the net periodic pension cost. These techniques are discussed briefly in the next paragraphs.

As noted previously, the MRVA is utilized in the determination of the expected return on pension plan assets. The use of a "calculated" value for the MRVA permits a sponsor to allow asset fluctuations to over time cancel one another out before they are fully included in the determination of the net periodic pension cost.

SFAS No. 87 specifies that the net actuarial gain or loss be deferred and amortized in future periods. Deferred gains and losses (excluding any asset gains and losses that have not yet been reflected in the MRVA) are amortized as a component of net periodic pension cost if they exceed the "corridor." The *corridor* is defined as a range equal to plus or minus 10 percent of the greater of either the PBO or the MRVA. If the cumulative gain or loss, as computed, does not lie outside the corridor, no amount of gain or loss needs to be reflected in net periodic cost for the current period. However, if the cumulative gain or loss does exceed the corridor, only the excess is subject to amortization. To visualize the concept of the corridor, refer to Exhibit 27.2.

The minimum amortization that is required in net periodic pension cost is the cumulative gain or loss that exceeds the corridor divided by the average remaining service period of the active employees expected to receive benefits under the plan. Unlike the amortization of the net prior service cost and net transition obligation, the average remaining service period is redetermined each year for the net gain/loss amortization. The FASB does permit alternative methods of amortization. An employer may decide not to use the corridor method and substitute any alternative amortization method that amortizes an amount at least equal to the minimum. Consequently, an alternative method could recognize the entire amount of the current period's gain or loss in the ensuing period. Any alternative amortization method must be applied consistently from year to year and to both gains and losses, and must be disclosed in the employer's financial statements.

If substantially all of the participants of a pension plan are inactive, the net gain/loss subject to amortization should be amortized over the remaining life expectancy of those plan participants.

The 10 percent corridor is designed to avoid amortization of relatively small and temporary gains and losses arising in any one year that can be expected to offset each other in the long run. It is not intended to exclude a portion of gains and losses from ever being recognized in the sponsor's income statement. If a substantial amount of net gain or loss remains unrecognized from year to year, or increases in size, it may imply that the PBO and net periodic pension cost have been overstated or understated.

(v) Amortization of Net Prior Service Cost Component. Defined benefit pension plans are sometimes amended to provide increased pension benefits to employees. An amendment to a pension plan (or initiation of a pension plan) that grants benefits to employees for services previously rendered generates an increase in the PBO under the plan. This additional PBO is referred to as prior service

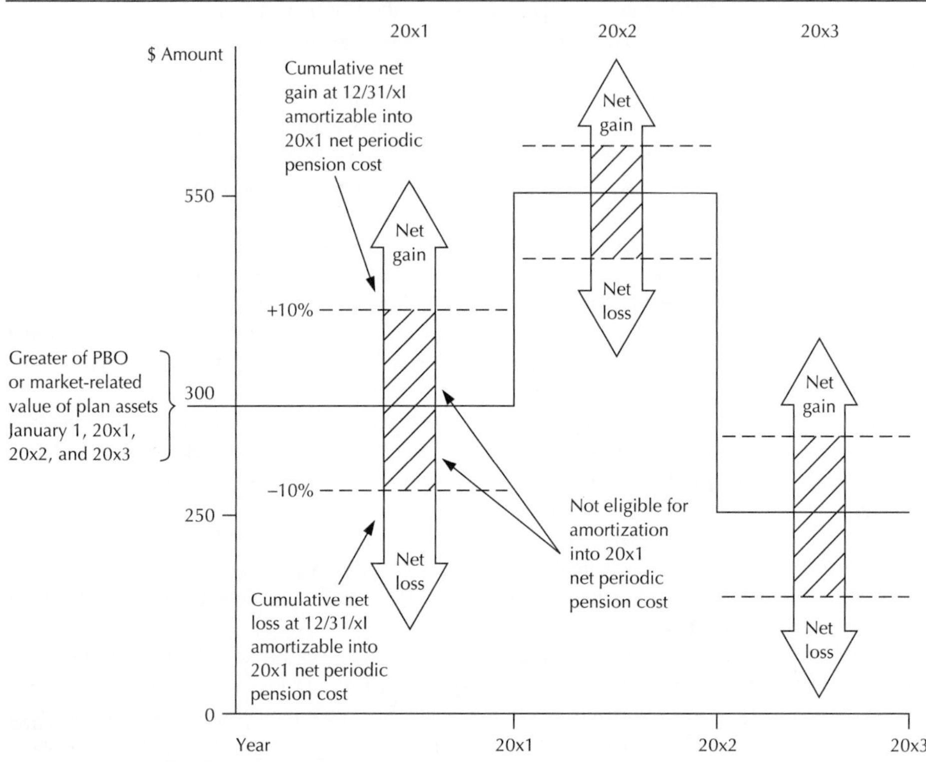

Exhibit 27.2 Illustration of the Corridor

cost. Retroactive pension benefits generally are granted by the employer in the expectation that they will produce future economic benefits, such as increasing employee morale, reducing employee turnover, or improving employee productivity.

Under SFAS No. 87, prior service cost is to be amortized and included as a component of net periodic pension cost. A separate amortization schedule is established for each prior service cost based on the expected future service by active employees who are expected to receive employer-provided benefits under the plan. Instead of a declining amortization schedule, a common practice is to amortize the prior service cost on a straight-line basis over the average future service period. Once this amortization schedule has been established, it will generally not be changed unless the period during which the employer expects to realize future economic benefits has shortened or the future economic benefits have become impaired. Decelerating the amortization schedule is prohibited.

If substantially all of the participants of a pension plan are inactive, the prior service cost from a retroactive amendment should be amortized over the remaining life expectancy of those plan participants.

SFAS No. 87 permits the use of alternative amortization methods that more rapidly reduce the amount of net prior service cost, provided that the alternatives are used consistently. For example, straight-line amortization of net prior service cost over the average future service period of active employees who are expected to receive benefits under the plan is acceptable. The immediate recognition of net prior service cost, however, generally is inappropriate.

As noted previously, a plan amendment can increase the cost of pension benefits and increases the amount of the PBO. However, there are also situations where a plan amendment may decrease the cost of pension benefits, resulting in a decrease in the amount of the PBO. Any decrease resulting from a plan amendment should be applied to reduce the balance of any existing net prior service cost using a systematic and rational method (i.e., LIFO [last-in, first-out], FIFO [first-in, first out], or pro rata, unless such reduction can be related to any specific prior service cost). Any excess is to be amortized on the same basis as increases in net prior service cost.

Once the employer has committed to a plan amendment, the net periodic pension cost for the remainder of the year should reflect the additional service cost, interest cost, and amortization related to the amendment. Remeasurement based on the current discount rate may also be called for. Pension cost for any prior periods should not be restated merely on account of the amendment, even if the amendment may be effective retroactively to a prior date.

(vi) Amortization of Net Obligation or Net Asset Component. The unrecognized net obligation or net asset of a pension plan was determined as of the first day of the fiscal year in which SFAS No. 87 was first applied or if applicable, the measurement date immediately preceding that day. The initial unrecognized net obligation or net asset was equal to the difference between the PBO and fair value of pension plan assets (plus previously recognized unfunded accrued pension cost or less previously recognized prepaid pension cost).

A schedule was set up to amortize the initial unrecognized net obligation or net asset on a straight-line basis over the average remaining service period of employees expected to receive benefits under the plan, except under these circumstances:

- If the average remaining service period was less than 15 years, an employer could elect to use 15 years.
- If the plan was composed of all or substantially all inactive participants, the employer should use those participants' average remaining life expectancy as the amortization period.

(e) PLAN ASSETS. Pension plan assets generally consist of equity or debt securities, real estate, or other investments that may be sold or transferred by the plan, which typically have been segregated and restricted in a trust. In contrast to SFAS No. 35, for purposes of SFAS No. 87, plan assets exclude contributions due but unpaid by the plan sponsor. Also excluded are assets that are not restricted to provide plan benefits such as so-called rabbi trusts in which earmarked funds are available to satisfy judgment creditors.

Pension plan assets that are held as an investment to provide pension benefits are to be measured at fair value as of the date of the financial statements. (This date is defined by the Statement as the measurement date.)

In the context of SFAS No. 87, *fair value* is defined as the amount that a pension plan trustee could reasonably expect to receive from the sale of a plan asset between a willing and informed buyer and a willing and informed seller. The FASB believes that fair value is the appropriate measurement for pension plan assets because it provides the more relevant information in assessing both the plan's ability to pay pension benefits as they become due and the future contributions necessary to provide for unfunded pension benefits already promised.

If an active market exists for a plan investment, fair value is determined by the quoted market price. If an active market does not exist for a particular plan investment, selling prices for similar investments, if available, should be used as a basis for determining fair value. If no active market exists, an estimate of the fair value of the plan investment may be based on its projected cash flow, provided that appropriate consideration is given to current discount rates and the investment risk involved.

Pension plan assets that are used in the actual everyday operations of a plan—buildings, leasehold improvements, furniture, equipment, and fixtures—should be valued at historical cost less accumulated depreciation or amortization.

(f) RECOGNITION OF LIABILITIES AND ASSETS. SFAS No. 158 (ASC 715-20) was issued in 2006 and was generally effective for fiscal years ending after December 15, 2006, for an employer that is an issuer of publicly traded equity securities (as defined) and for fiscal years ending after June 15, 2007, for an employer that is not. This Statement was intended to improve financial reporting by requiring an employer to recognize the overfunded or underfunded status of a defined benefit pension or postretirement plan (other than a multiemployer plan) as an asset or liability in its statement of financial position and to recognize changes in that funded status in the year in which the change occurs through comprehensive income of a business entity or changes in unrestricted net assets of a not-for-profit organization. This Statement also required an employer to measure the funded status of a plan as of the date of its year-end statement of financial position (with limited exceptions).

The funded status of a benefit plan is measured as the difference between plan assets at fair value (with limited exceptions) and the benefit obligation—in its statement of financial position. For a pension plan, the benefit obligation is the projected benefit obligation (PBO); for any other postretirement benefit plan, such as a retiree health care plan, the benefit obligation is the accumulated postretirement benefit obligation (APBO).

These changes eliminated the additional minimum liability that existed under SFAS No. 87 prior to SFAS No. 158.

(g) INTERIM MEASUREMENTS. Generally, the determination of interim pension cost and balance sheet liability or asset should be based on assumptions used as of the previous year-end measurements. If, however, more recent measurements of plan assets and pension obligations are available or, if a significant event occurs that ordinarily would call for such measurements (i.e., a plan amendment), that updated information should be used.

(h) FINANCIAL STATEMENT DISCLOSURES. SFAS No. 158 was released in 2006, amending the disclosure requirements promulgated under SFAS No. 132-R. Additional disclosures in a number of areas were required, and interim reporting was substantially enhanced.

(i) Public Entity. For a public entity sponsoring defined benefit plan(s), all of the next items must be disclosed as of the date of each statement of financial position:

- A reconciliation of the beginning and ending balances of the fair value of assets
- The funded status of the plans and the amounts recognized in the statement of financial position showing separately the assets and current and noncurrent liabilities recognized
- Information about plan assets including
  - Each major category of plan assets
  - Narrative description of investment policies and strategies
  - Narrative description of the basis used to determine the long-term rate of return on assets assumption
  - Disclosure of additional asset categories and additional information about specific assets if that information is useful in understanding the risks associated with each asset category and the overall long-term rate of return on assets
- For a defined benefit pension plan, the ABO
- The benefits expected to be paid in each of the next five fiscal years and in the aggregate for the five fiscal years thereafter
- The contributions expected to be paid to the plan during the next fiscal year
- The amount of the net benefit cost (separated by components)
- Separately, the net gain or loss and net prior service cost or credit recognized in other comprehensive income (OCI) and the reclassification adjustments of OCI for the period as those amounts, including amortization of the net transition obligation or asset, are recognized as components of net period benefit cost
- The amounts in accumulated other comprehensive income (AOCI) that have not been recognized as components of net periodic benefit cost
- The assumed discount rate, rate of compensation increase, and expected long-term rate of return on plan assets used for determining the benefit obligation and the net periodic pension cost

- The assumed health care cost trend rate
- The effect of a 1 percentage-point increase and decrease in the assumed health care cost trend rate on:
  - Aggregate of the service cost and interest cost
  - Accumulated postretirement benefit obligation
- If applicable, the amounts and types of securities of the employer and related parties included in plan assets
- If applicable, any alternative method used to amortize prior service cost or net gains and losses
- If applicable, any substantive commitment used as the basis for accounting for the benefit obligation
- If applicable, the cost of providing special or contractual termination benefits and a description of the nature of the event
- An explanation of any significant change in the benefit obligation or plan assets not otherwise apparent in other disclosures required
- The amounts in AOCI expected to be recognized in net periodic benefit cost during the next fiscal year showing separately the net gain or loss, net prior service cost or credit and net transition obligation or asset
- The amount and timing of any plan assets expected to be returned to the employer during the next fiscal year

For additional detail related to the disclosure requirements for a public entity, see Paragraphs 1–4 of ASC 715-20-50.

The disclosures for all of an employer's defined benefit pension plans may be aggregated. However, if disclosures are aggregated, it is necessary to disclose the aggregate PBO and aggregate fair value of plan assets for plans with PBO in excess of plan assets. In addition, it is necessary to disclose the aggregate ABO and aggregate fair value of plan assets for plans with ABO in excess of plan assets. An employer that sponsors one or more defined benefit pension plans or one or more defined benefit other postretirement plans must provide the disclosure information separately for the pension plans and other postretirement benefit plans.

For interim disclosures, public entities must disclose the next information for its interim financial statements that include a statement of income (ASC 715-20-50-6):

- The net benefit cost recognized
- The amount of the employer's contributions paid, and expected to be paid, during the current fiscal year, if significantly different from amounts previously disclosed

Exhibit 27.3 is a sample annual disclosure for a public entity.

(ii) Nonpublic Entity. A nonpublic entity may elect a "shorter disclosure." A *nonpublic entity* is defined in ASC 715-20 as follows:

> **Nonpublic Entity:** Any entity other than one with any of the following characteristics: FAS 132(R), paragraph E1:
>
> **(a)** Whose debt or equity securities trade in a public market either on a stock exchange (domestic or foreign) or in the over-the-counter market, including securities quoted only locally or regionally.
>
> **(b)** That is a conduit bond obligor for conduit debt securities that are traded in a public market (a domestic or foreign stock exchange or an over-the-counter market, including local or regional markets).
>
> **(c)** That makes a filing with a regulatory agency in preparation for the sale of any class of debt or equity securities in a public market.
>
> **(d)** That is controlled by an entity covered by a., b., or c.

	Pension Benefits		Other Benefits	
	20X3	20X2	20X3	20X2
Change in benefit obligation				
Benefit obligation at beginning of year	$1,246	$1,200	$742	$712
Service cost	76	72	36	32
Interest cost	90	88	55	55
Plan participants' contributions			20	13
Amendments	70		(75)	
Actuarial loss	20		25	
Acquisitions	900		600	
Benefits paid	(125)	(114)	(90)	(70)
Benefit obligation at end of year	2,277	1,068	1,313	742
Change in plan assets				
Fair value of plan assets at beginning of year	1,068	894	206	89
Actual return on plan assets	29	188	5	24
Acquisitions	1,000		25	
Employer contributions	75	100	137	152
Plan participants' contributions			20	13
Benefits paid	(125)	(114)	(90)	(70)
Fair value of plan assets at end of year	2,047	1,068	303	206
Funded status	$(230)	$(178)	$(1,010)	$(536)

Note: Nonpublic entities are not required to provide information in the preceding table; they are required to disclose the employer's contributions, participants' contributions, benefit payments and the funded status.

Amounts recognized in the statement of financial position consist of:

	Pension Benefits		Other Benefits	
	20X3	20X2	20X3	20X2
Noncurrent assets	$227	$127	$0	$0
Current liabilities	(125)	(125)	(150)	(150)
Noncurrent liabilities	(332)	(180)	(860)	(386)
Net amount recognized	$(230)	$(178)	$(1,010)	$(536)

Amounts recognized in accumulated other comprehensive income consist of:

	Pension Benefits		Other Benefits	
	20X3	20X2	20X3	20X2
Net loss (gain)	$94	$18	$(11)	$(48)
Prior service cost (credit)	210	160	(92)	(22)
	$304	$178	$(103)	$(70)

Exhibit 27.3 Sample Disclosure for Public Entity

The accumulated benefit obligation for all defined benefit pension plans was $1,300 and $850 at December 31, 20X3 and 20X2, respectively. Information for pension plans with an accumulated benefit obligation in excess of plan assets:

	December 31	
	20X3	20X2
Projected benefit obligation	$263	$247
Accumulated benefit obligations	237	222
Fair value of plan assets	84	95

Components of net periodic benefit cost and other amounts recognized in other comprehensive income:

	Pension Benefits		Other Benefits	
	20X3	20X2	20X3	20X2
Net Periodic Benefit Cost				
Service cost	$76	$72	$36	$32
Interest cost	90	88	55	55
Expected return on plan assets	(85)	(76)	(17)	(8)
Amortization of prior service cost	20	16	(5)	(5)
Amortization of net (gain) loss	0	0	0	0
Net periodic benefit cost	$101	$100	$69	$74

Other changes in plan assets and benefit obligations recognized in other comprehensive income:

Net loss (gain)	$76	$112	$37	$(48)
Prior service cost (credit)	70	0	(75)	(27)
Amortization of prior service cost	(20)	(16)	5	5
Total recognized in other comprehensive income	126	96	(33)	(70)
Total recognized in net periodic benefit cost and other comprehensive income	$227	$196	$36	$4

The estimated net loss and prior service cost for the defined benefit pension plans that will be amortized from accumulated other comprehensive income into net periodic benefit cost over the next fiscal year are $4 and $27, respectively. The estimated prior service credit for the other defined benefit postretirement plans that will be amortized from accumulated other comprehensive income into net periodic benefit cost over the next fiscal year is $10.

Note: Nonpublic entities are not required to separately disclose components of net periodic benefit cost.

Assumptions:

Weighted-average assumptions used to determine benefit obligations at December 31:

	Pension Benefits		Other Benefits	
	20X3	20X2	20X3	20X2
Discount rate	6.75%	7.25%	7.00%	7.50%
Rate of compensation increase	4.25%	4.50%		

Weighted-average assumptions used to determine net periodic benefit cost for years ended December 31:

	Pension Benefits		Other Benefits	
	20X3	20X2	20X3	20X2
Discount rate	7.25%	7.50%	7.50%	7.75%
Expected long-term rate of return on plan assets	8.00%	8.50%	8.10%	8.75%
Rate of compensation increase	4.50%	4.75%		

Exhibit 27.3 ***Continued***

Entity-specific narrative descriptions of the basis used to determine the overall expected long-term rate of return on assets, as described in paragraph 5(d)(3), would be included here.

Assumed health care cost trend rates at December 31:

	20X3	20X2
Health care cost trend rate assumed for next year	12%	12.5%
Rate to which cost trend rate is assumed to decline (ultimate trend rate)	6%	5%
Year that rate reaches ultimate trend rate	20X9	20X9

Assumed health care cost trend rates have a significant effect on the amounts reported for the health care plans.

A 1-percentage point change in assumed health care cost trend rates would have these effects:

	1-Percentage-Point Increase	1-Percentage-Point Decrease
Effect on total of service and interest cost	$22	$(20)
Effect on postretirement benefit obligation	173	(156)

Note: Nonpublic entities are not required to provide information about the impact of a 1-percentage-point increase and 1-percentage-point decrease in the assumed health care cost trend rates.

Plan Assets:

Company A's pension plan weighted-average asset allocations at December 31, 20X3, and 20X2, by asset category are:

	Plan Assets at December 31	
	20X3	20X2
Asset Category		
Equity securities	50%	48%
Debt securities	30%	31%
Real estate	10%	12%
Other	10%	9%
Total	100%	100%

Entity-specific narrative description of investment policies and strategies for plan assets, including weighted-average target asset allocations (if used as part of those policies and strategies) as described in paragraph 5(d)(2) would be included here.

Equity securities include Company A common stock in the amounts of $80 million (4 percent of total plan assets) and $64 million (6 percent of total plan assets) at December 31, 20X3 and 20X2, respectively.

Company A's other postretirement benefit plan weighted-average asset allocations at December 31, 20X3 and 20X2, by asset category are:

	Plan Assets at December 31	
	20X3	20X2
Asset Category		
Equity securities	60%	52%
Debt securities	30%	27%
Real estate	5%	13%
Other	5%	8%
Total	100%	100%

Exhibit 27.3 ***Continued***

Equity securities include Company A common stock in the amounts of $12 million (4 percent of total plan assets) and $8 million (4 percent of total plan assets) at December 31, 20X3 and 20X2, respectively.

Cash Flow Contributions

Company A expects to contribute $125 million to its pension plan and $150 million to its other postretirement benefit plan in 20X4.

Estimated Future Benefit Payments:

These benefit payments, which reflect expected future service, as appropriate, are expected to be paid:

	Pension Benefits	Other Benefits
20X4	$ 200	$150
20X5	208	155
20X6	215	160
20X7	225	165
20X8	235	170
Years 20X9–20Y3	1,352	984

SFAS No. 157 (ASC 820) requires these additional disclosures with respect to Level 3 inputs used to measure the fair value of assets:

- A reconciliation of the beginning and ending balances, separately presenting changes during the period attributable to:
  1. Total gains or losses for the period (realized and unrealized), segregating those gains or losses included in earnings (or changes in net assets), and a description of where those gains or losses included in earnings (or changes in net assets) are reported in the statement of income (or activities)
  2. Purchases, sales, issuances, and settlements (net)
  3. Transfers in and/or out of Level 3 (e.g., transfers due to changes in the observability of significant inputs)
- The amount of the total gains or losses for the period included in earnings (or changes in net assets) that are attributable to the change in unrealized gains or losses relating to those assets and liabilities still held at the reporting date and a description of where those unrealized gains or losses are reported in the statement of income (or activities).

Exhibit 27.3 ***Continued***

Nonpublic entity disclosure requirements are the same as those for a public entity except that a nonpublic entity is not required to disclose the information required by Paragraphs:

- ASC 715-20-50-1(a-c)
- ASC 715-20-50-1(h)
- ASC 715-20-50-1(m)
- ASC 715-20-50-1(o-r)

For additional detail related to the disclosure requirements for a nonpublic entity, see Paragraph 5 of ASC 715-20-50.

For interim disclosures, nonpublic entities must disclose the next information for interim financial statements for which a complete set of financial statements is presented (see Paragraph 7 of ASC 715-20-50):

- The amount of the employer's contributions paid, and expected to be paid, during the current fiscal year, if significantly different from amounts previously disclosed

(iii) Annuity Contracts. All or part of an employer's obligation to provide pension plan benefits to employees may be effectively transferred to an insurance company by the purchase of annuity contracts. An annuity contract is an irrevocable agreement in which an insurance company unconditionally agrees to provide specific benefits to designated individuals, in return for a fixed consideration or premium. Hence, by purchasing an annuity contract, an employer transfers to the insurer its legal obligation, and the attendant risks, to provide pension benefits. For purposes of SFAS No. 87 (Paragraphs 53–61 of ASC 715-30-35), an annuity contract does not qualify unless the risks and rewards associated with the assets and obligations assumed by the insurance company are actually transferred to the insurance company by the sponsor.

An annuity contract may be participating or nonparticipating. In a participating annuity contract, the insurance company's investment experience with the funds received for the annuity contract are shared, in the form of dividends, with the purchaser (the employer or the pension fund). The purchase price of a participating annuity is ordinarily higher than that for a nonparticipating annuity, with the excess representing the value of the participation right (i.e., expected future dividends). This excess should be recognized as a plan asset.

Benefits covered by annuity contracts are excluded from the benefit obligations of the plan. The annuity contracts themselves are not counted as plan assets, except for the value of any participation rights. If any benefits earned in the current period are covered by annuity contracts, the cost of such benefits is equal to the cost to purchase the annuities less any participation right. That is, if all the benefits attributed by the plan's benefit formula to service in the current period are covered by nonparticipating annuity contracts, the cost of the contracts determines the service cost component of net pension cost for that period.

Annuity contracts issued by a captive insurance company are not considered annuities for the purpose of SFAS No. 87, since the risk associated with the benefit obligations remains substantially with the employer. Similarly, if there is reasonable doubt that the insurance company will meet its obligations under the contract, it is not considered an annuity contract.

Insurance contracts that are not in substance annuity contracts are accounted for as pension plan assets and are measured at fair value. If a contract has a determinable cash surrender value or conversion value, that is presumed to be its fair value.

A pension fund may have structured a portfolio of fixed-income investments with a cash flow designed to match expected benefit payment. Known as a *dedicated bond portfolio,* its purpose is to protect the pension fund against swings in interest rates. For the purposes of SFAS No. 87, a dedicated bond portfolio is not an annuity contract even if it is managed to remove all or most of the investment risk associated with covered benefit payments.

(i) DEFINED CONTRIBUTION PENSION PLANS. A defined contribution pension plan provides for employer contributions that are defined in the plan. A defined contribution plan maintains *individual* accounts for each plan participant and contains terms that specify how contributions are allocated among participants' individual accounts. Pension benefits are based solely on the amount available in each participant's account at the time of retirement. The amount available in each participant's account at the time of retirement is the total of the amounts contributed by the employer, the returns earned on investments of those contributions, and forfeitures of other participants' accounts that have been allocated to the participant's account.

Under SFAS No. 87, the net periodic pension cost of a defined contribution pension plan is the amount of contributions for the period in which services are rendered by the employees. If a plan calls for contributions after an individual retires or terminates, the estimated cost should be accrued during periods in which the individual performs services.

An employer that sponsors one or more defined contribution pension plans discloses the next information separately from its defined benefit pension plan disclosures (see Paragraph 1 of ASC 715-70-50):

- A description of the plan(s) including employee groups covered, the basis for determining contributions, and the nature and effect of significant matters affecting comparability of information for all periods presented
- The amount of pension cost recognized during the period

For the purposes of SFAS No. 87, any plan that is not a defined contribution pension plan is considered a defined benefit pension plan.

(j) NON-U.S. PENSION PLANS. SFAS No. 87 does not make any special provision for non-U.S. pension plans. In some foreign countries, it is customary or required for an employer to provide benefits for employees in the event of voluntary or involuntary severance of employment. In this event, if the substance of the arrangement is a pension plan (i.e., benefits are paid for substantially all terminations), it is subject to the provisions of SFAS No. 87. Paragraphs 65–86 of ASC 715-30-55 discuss aspects of pension plan accounting generally associated with non-US plans.

The discount rate used for valuing liabilities for non-U.S. plans should be based on the yields available on bonds issued in the country where the plan exists. Therefore, companies with international operations may have discount rates for valuing non-U.S. plans that are well above or below the rates used for valuing U.S. liabilities.

In countries where no deep corporate bond market exists, it is typical for government bonds to be considered with a risk premium to approximate corporate bond yields.

There are a number of countries where pension plans adjust inactive participants' benefits periodically for cost of living (during deferral and/or while in payment status). In most cases, these adjustments are, in some way, a function of the prevailing inflation rate. As a result, the explicit assumption with respect to future inflation is more relevant in these countries. The inflation assumption is customarily established after a review of available economic data including, but not limited to, central bank inflation forecasts, other experts' inflation estimates, and the relationship between market yields on inflation adjusted and nominal fixed income securities.

Plans in Puerto Rico or other U.S. territories are typically considered U.S. plans.

(k) MULTIEMPLOYER PLANS. A multiemployer plan is a plan to which more than one employer contributes, usually pursuant to a labor union agreement. Under these plans, contributions are pooled and separate employer accounts do not exist. As a result, assets contributed by one employer may be used to provide benefits to the employees of other participating employers.

SFAS No. 87 provides no change in the accounting for multiemployer plans (ASC 715-80). A participating employer should recognize pension cost equal to the contribution required to the plan for the period. The disclosures required by the Statement for multiemployer plans are similar to those for defined contribution pension plans—a description of the plan, including the employee groups covered and type of benefits provided, and the amount of pension cost recognized in the period.

An underfunded multiemployer plan may assess a withdrawing employer a portion of its unfunded benefit obligations. If this withdrawal liability becomes either probable or reasonably possible, the provisions of SFAS No. 5, *Accounting for Contingencies* (ASC 450), apply.

On September 1, 2010, the FASB issued a proposed Accounting Standards Update (ASU), *Disclosure About an Employer's Participation in a Multiemployer Plan.* The proposed ASU's objective is to improve transparency by amending ASC 715-80 to significantly increase the level of quantitative and qualitative disclosures an employer would be required to make about its participation in multiemployer plans, including the effect on its cash flows. The proposed disclosures would not apply to an employer's participation in multiple-employer plans (e.g., plans that are single-employer plans aggregated to pool plan assets for investment purposes or to reduce the costs of plan administration).

The essential elements of the revised disclosures for employers participating in multiemployer pension plans are summarized next. The final language will not be available until the final ASU is issued by the FASB. (The expected date of publication for the final ASU is September 2011.) For public entities, the enhanced disclosures will be required for annual periods in fiscal years ending after December 15, 2011. For nonpublic entities, the enhanced disclosures will be required for annual periods in fiscal years ending after December 15, 2012.

Essential Elements of the Disclosures

a. For individually material plans:

  1. Plan legal name and Employer Identification Number

  2. Most recent certified funded status, expressed as a "zone status," as required by the Pension Protection Act of 2006. If zone status is not available, an employer should disclose whether the plan was:

    i. Less than 65 percent funded

    ii. Between 65 percent and 80 percent funded

    iii. Greater than 80 percent funded

  3. Expiration date(s) of collective bargaining agreement(s) and any minimum funding arrangements

  4. Indication of whether the employer's contributions represent more than 5 percent of total contributions to the plan

  5. Indication of what plans, if any, are subject to a funding improvement plan

b. Contributions made to each individually material plan and the total contributions made to all other plans in the aggregate

c. A description of the nature and effect of any changes affecting comparability from period to period for each period in which a statement of income is presented

(l) MULTIPLE EMPLOYER PLANS. A multiple employer plan is similar to a multiemployer plan except that it usually does not include any labor union agreement. It is treated under ERISA as a collection of single-employer plans sponsored by the respective participating employers. If separate asset allocation is maintained among the participating employers (even though pooled for investment purposes), SFAS No. 87 applies individually to each employer with respect to its interest and benefit obligations within the plan (ASC 715-30-35-70). If assets are not allocated among the participating employers (e.g., when a number of subsidiaries participate in a plan sponsored by their parent), the organization sponsoring the plan, if one exists, should account for the plan as a single-employer plan, whereas each participating employer should account for this arrangement as a multiemployer plan in its separate financial statements. Disclosure of net periodic pension cost and the reconciliation of the funded status should be for the plan as a whole, with each participating employer further disclosing its own pension cost with respect to this arrangement.

(m) FUNDING AND INCOME TAX ACCOUNTING. SFAS No. 87 does not address funding considerations, other than to recognize that there may be differences between reported net periodic pension cost and funding. Under U.S. pension funding rules, as amended by the Pension Protection Act of 2006, the funding of qualified pension plans utilizes the traditional unit credit funding method (TUC)—similar to the ABO calculation described in SFAS No. 87. The range between the permissible maximum and minimum funding amount may not bracket the net periodic pension cost. This can be caused by the difference in funding method (Projected Unit Credit versus Traditional Unit Credit), amortization periods for unrecognized pension costs and limitation imposed by the tax law on contributions to relatively well-funded plans. In general, the objective of matching the expensing and funding of net periodic pension cost may not be appropriate due to tax, legal, and cash flow considerations. In this regard, companies must continue to provide deferred taxes, where appropriate, for these differences.

The method of accounting for income taxes—particularly the way deferred taxes are calculated—was changed by SFAS No. 109, *Accounting for Income Taxes* (ASC 740). Its focus is on an asset and liability approach, as opposed to an income statement approach. On a simplified basis, deferred taxes are calculated by applying the tax rates enacted for future years to differences between the financial statement carrying amounts and the tax basis of assets and liabilities. These differences are known as *temporary differences.*

Temporary differences frequently arise as a result of differences between the tax basis of pension assets and liabilities and the amounts recognized under SFAS No. 158. For example, assuming that a company funds the pension cost to the extent deductible for tax purposes, a pension asset will be recognized only when the fair value of assets exceeds the benefit obligation, regardless of the amount deductible for tax purposes. A pension liability will be recognized when the benefit obligation exceeds the fair value of assets, regardless of the amount deductible for tax purposes. In addition, settlement gains and losses recognized under SFAS No. 88 will create temporary differences because the transactions generally are not taxable or deductible at the date recognized for financial reporting purposes. Because of the complexities of accounting for pensions, numerous other situations will result in temporary differences.

27.3 SPONSOR ACCOUNTING FOR NONRECURRING EVENTS

(a) OVERVIEW. An integral concept of pension accounting is that certain pension obligations should be recognized in the income statement over time rather than immediately. They include gains and losses from experience different from that assumed, the effects of changes in actuarial assumptions on the pension obligations, the cost of retroactive plan amendments, and any unrecognized net obligation or asset at transition established when the plan first complied with SFAS No. 87. The premise of this delayed recognition is that plan amendments are made in anticipation of economic benefits that the employer may derive over the future service periods of its employees and that gains or losses already incurred may be reversed in the future. When events happen that fundamentally alter or eliminate the premise for delayed recognition, immediate recognition in the income statement of amounts previously recognized through OCI may be required.

Examples of such special events include business combinations, addressed in paragraph 74 of SFAS No. 87 (ASC 715-30-60-6); and settlements, curtailments, and termination benefits, the subjects of SFAS No. 88 (ASC 715-30-05-9), which is effective simultaneously with SFAS No. 87.

(b) SETTLEMENT. To constitute a settlement (ASC 715-30-20), a transaction must (1) be irrevocable, (2) relieve the employer of primary responsibility for a pension benefit obligation, and (3) eliminate significant risks related to the obligations and the assets used to effect the settlement. This is a new accounting concept introduced by SFAS No. 88.

The most common type of settlement is the purchase of nonparticipating annuities for or lump-sum cash payments to plan participants to discharge all or part of the benefit obligation of the plan, which may or may not be connected with a plan termination. (A participating annuity allows the purchaser to participate in the investment performance and possibly other experience—for example, mortality experience—of the insurance company, through dividends or rate credits. It generally costs more than a nonparticipating annuity, which is based on a fixed price.) Although SFAS No. 88 extends condition (2) in the preceding paragraph to include a transaction that relieves the plan of the responsibility for the benefit obligation, that condition is generally not sufficient, for example, if the benefit obligation is transferred to another plan sponsored by the same or a related employer or if the annuities are purchased from a subsidiary of the employer.

(i) Timing. The timing of the settlement recognition depends on when all three qualifying conditions for a settlement have been met. For example, a commitment to purchase annuity is not sufficient to constitute a settlement until the benefit obligation risk has been transferred to the insurance company and the premium for the annuities has been paid in cash or in kind, except for minor adjustments. Although a dedicated portfolio designed to match the estimated benefit payments under the plan may eliminate the investment risk on assets backing those payments, it does not constitute a settlement because the plan continues to be exposed to the mortality risk on those payments and also because the portfolio is not irrevocable.

(ii) Gain or Loss. The maximum gain or loss subject to settlement recognition is the net gain or loss in the plan at the date of settlement, plus any remaining net asset (but not a net obligation) at transition. The magnitude of the PBO to be settled, as determined by the employer prior to the settlement, is generally not the same as the cost to discharge that obligation, such as the premium for the annuities, and must first be set equal to the latter. This adjustment in the PBO generates a gain or loss that is added to net gain or loss before the settlement recognition is done. The amount of the settlement gain or loss is equal to the maximum gain or loss subject to settlement recognition multiplied by the settlement percentage, which is the percentage of the plan's PBO being settled. Computations described in this paragraph are generally performed on a plan-by-plan basis rather than by aggregating all of the employer's plans.

(iii) Use of Participating Annuities. Participating annuities are acceptable instruments to effect a settlement, unless their substance is that the employer remains subject to all or most of the risks and rewards associated with the benefit obligation covered by the annuities or the assets transferred to the insurance company. If the purchase of a participating annuity constitutes a settlement, the maximum gain (but not the maximum loss) must first be reduced by the cost of the participation feature. This means that the participation feature of the annuity contract is excluded from the settlement recognition entirely and its value, which is the present value of the future dividends expected from the insurance company, is carried as a plan asset.

SFAS No. 88 also permits a de minimis exemption from settlement recognition if the total cash and annuity settlements in a year do not exceed the sum of the service cost and interest cost components of the net periodic pension cost, provided this accounting practice is followed consistently from year to year (ASC 715-30-35-82).

(c) CURTAILMENT. A curtailment is an event that significantly reduces the expected years of future service of present employees covered by the plan or eliminates for a significant number of employees covered by the plan the accrual of defined benefit for some or all of their future services. It is possible for an event, such as a window retirement program, to change significantly the benefit obligation but not the total expected future services and, therefore, not to be a curtailment. Unrelated, individually insignificant reductions in future services do not qualify as a curtailment even if they occur in a single year and are significant in aggregate. Conversely, a series of individually insignificant reductions in future services, which are caused by the same event but take place over more than one fiscal year, should be aggregated to determine if the reduction is sufficiently significant to constitute a curtailment.

Examples of curtailment include reduction in workforce, closing of a facility with the employees not employed elsewhere by the employer, disposal of a business segment, window retirement program, termination of a defined benefit plan, or freezing of the benefits thereunder. A process known as *termination/reestablishment,* whereby an employer terminates a defined benefit plan, recovers the surplus plan assets, and then establishes a new plan for the same employees that provides the same overall benefits as the terminated plan when benefits from the terminated plan are taken into account, is not a curtailment because the employer's benefit obligation has not been materially altered. Even if the new plan created through the termination/reestablishment process does not reproduce the same overall benefits, the transaction should be treated as a plan amendment and not a curtailment. Similarly, if the employees are covered by multiple plans and the suspension of their benefit accrual under one plan is wholly or partially balanced by increased benefit accrual under another plan of the same or a related employer (e.g., a supplemental retirement plan providing defined benefits, which is offset by the benefits from the suspended plan), the event should be treated not as a curtailment but as simultaneous amendments to the two plans: one reduces benefits and one increases benefits.

The curtailment gain or loss to be recognized is the sum of the prior service cost recognition and the PBO adjustment, both determined on a plan-by-plan basis rather than by aggregating all of the employer's plans.

According to statements made by the FASB Staff, the prior service cost recognition is intended to be the immediate recognition of any net prior service cost and any remaining net obligation (but not a net asset) at transition that relate to those employees whose services have been curtailed. Since these two items are often not available for specific employees or groups of employees, SFAS No. 88 provides a general rule to compute the prior service cost recognition as the product of any unrecognized net obligation at transition, or any prior service cost related to the entire plan, and the applicable curtailment percentages. The curtailment percentage is the percentage reduction in the remaining expected future years of service associated with the prior service cost or the net obligation at transition; it is determined separately for each prior service cost and the net obligation at transition. To reduce computational complexity, it is common practice to use an alternative curtailment percentage such as the percentage reduction in future years of service of all employees immediately prior to the curtailment, provided that the results would not be materially distorted.

The PBO adjustment can be a gain or a loss. If the curtailment reduces the PBO, the reduction is applied first against any net loss in the plan and the residual amount, if any, is recognized in the income statement as a gain. If the curtailment increases the PBO, the increase is applied first against any net gain and any remaining net asset at transition, and the residual amount, if any, is recognized in the income statement as a loss.

The timing of the curtailment recognition depends on whether the net effect is a gain or a loss. A net gain is recognized when the event has occurred, whereas a net loss is recognized when the event appears probable and its effects are reasonably estimable (ASC 715-30-35-94).

(d) DISPOSAL OF A BUSINESS. When an employer disposes of a business segment, its pension plan may experience a curtailment, due to the termination of some employees' services, and a settlement, if all or part of the benefit obligation is transferred to the purchaser (see Paragraphs 193–197 of ASC 715-30-55). Certain termination benefits, such as severance payments, may also be involved. The effects of such curtailment, settlement, and termination benefits should be determined in accordance with SFAS No. 88 and then included in the gain or loss on the disposal except for the following modifications to the SFAS No. 88 measurements (ASC 715-30-55-134): (1) the curtailment recognition is made regardless of whether the reduction in future services is significant; (2) the de minimis exemption for settlements does not apply; and (3) the difference between any benefit obligation and plan assets transferred to the purchaser is recognized in full as a gain or loss before the settlement percentage is determined. However, if the settlement, by purchasing annuities, for example, could have taken place in the absence of the business disposal, the settlement recognition should not be included in the gain or loss on the disposal (ASC 225-20).

(e) PLAN MERGER, SPINOFF, AND TERMINATION. The merger of two or more pension plans of the same employer does not require any SFAS No. 88 recognition (see Paragraphs 87–92 of ASC 715-30-55). Prior service costs should be amortized as before. The remaining unrecognized net obligations or assets at transition should be netted and amortized over a reasonably weighted average of the remaining amortization periods previously used by the separate plans. The unrecognized net gains or losses should be aggregated and the minimum amortization thereof should reflect the average remaining service period of the combined employee group.

Spinoff of a portion of a pension plan to an unrelated employer, as may happen after the sale of a business segment, should be handled as a settlement unless there is reasonable doubt that the purchaser will meet the benefit obligation and the seller remains contingently liable for it. A settlement does not occur if an employer divides a pension plan into two or more plans all sponsored by it. In that case, any remaining net obligation or asset should be allocated among the plans in proportion to their respective PBOs, as should any unrecognized net gain or loss. Any net prior service cost should be allocated on the basis of the participants in the surviving plans.

If one of these surviving plans is further transferred to a subsidiary, the employer should reduce its funded status by the amount related to the transferred plan and simultaneously record an increase in AOCI by the same amount. The subsidiary, however, should record a corresponding increase its funded status and record a corresponding decrease in its AOCI.

Under SFAS No. 88 the effect of a defined benefit plan termination is accounted for as a combination of a curtailment (i.e., elimination of further benefit accrual, assuming that there is not a successor defined benefit plan) and a settlement (ASC 715-30-55-133). As noted in Section 27.3(c) of this chapter, the termination/reestablishment of a defined benefit plan does not constitute a curtailment, but it may nevertheless require settlement recognition.

Withdrawal from a multiemployer plan may result in additional cost to the employer. The effect of the withdrawal should be recognized when it becomes probable or reasonably possible.

(f) TERMINATION BENEFITS. In 1983, SFAS No. 74, *Accounting for Special Termination Benefits Paid to Employees,* was issued ostensibly to address window retirement programs and shutdown benefits. Although it required recognition of the effects of any changes on the previously accrued expenses for those benefits, no recognition method was defined and compliance with the Statement was not widespread.

SFAS No. 88 superseded SFAS No. 74, and as with that Statement, it deals with both pension and nonpension benefits, such as severance payments, supplemental unemployment benefits, and life and health insurance benefits, regardless of whether they are paid by a plan or directly by the employer. The amount to be recognized is the amount of any immediate payments plus the present value of any expected future payments. The cost of special termination benefits that are offered only for a short period of time should be recognized when the employees accept the offer and the amount can be reasonably estimated. In contrast, contractual termination benefits, which are required by the terms of a plan only if a specified event (such as a plant closing) occurs, should be recognized when it is probable that employees will be entitled to benefits and the amount can be reasonably estimated (see Paragraphs 185–189 of ASC 715-30-55).

Keep in mind that a situation involving termination benefits often also involves a curtailment. The curtailment recognition is first determined using the benefit obligation without the termination benefits. The effect of the termination benefits is then the difference between the benefit obligations determined with and without the termination benefits.

It is not unusual, in the measurement of the PBO and the pension cost of a plan, to assume some probability for events that may give rise to termination benefits. In such a situation, the amount of termination benefits to be recognized under SFAS No. 88 is the difference between the PBO including the termination benefits and that measured without any termination benefit (ASC 715-30-25-11). For example, a plan may permit early retirement after age 55 with a reduced pension but provide an unreduced pension regardless of age in the event of a change in control of the employer. When a change in control occurs, the amount of termination benefit to be recognized for an employee who is age 40 is the difference in the value of his unreduced pension commencing immediately and his reduced pension commencing when he or she will reach age 55. Furthermore, if the situation constitutes a curtailment, the PBO adjustment is the difference between the value of the employee's reduced pension commencing at age 55 and the PBO determined using the regular actuarial assumptions including, if applicable, an allowance for some probability that change-in-control benefits may be invoked. It would likely not be reasonable to treat the entire change in PBO as a gain or loss or to handle the situation solely as a curtailment, merely because the assumptions used to determine the PBO prior to the change of control included some allowance for change-in-control benefits.

(g) BUSINESS COMBINATIONS. SFAS No. 141(R) (ASC 805), issued in June 2001 and revised in 2007, supersedes APB Opinion No. 16 and precludes the use of the pooling-of-interest method for business combinations. Under the Statement, all business combinations must be accounted for under the purchase method. Using the purchase method, the purchaser should record a liability equal to the excess of the acquired PBO over the acquired plan assets or an asset equal to the excess of the acquired plan assets over the acquired PBO. Simultaneous with the recording of such purchase accounting liability (asset), goodwill is increased (decreased) by an equal amount. Once these adjustments have been made, any previously existing unrecognized prior service cost, net obligation, or asset at transition and net gain or loss are eliminated and no further amortization of them will be needed. If the acquired company continues to issue its own separate financial statement after the purchase date, its pension cost may be determined without the purchase accounting adjustment and may therefore be different from the pension cost reported by the parent company on its behalf.

The measurement date for the purchase accounting adjustment is the acquisition date. In determining the PBO at the acquisition date, the effects of certain post-acquisition events should be reflected in the measurement of the PBO. Examples of such events include curtailments (without regard to the significance criterion), termination benefits, and plan amendments that were highly probably at the time of the purchase. To be included in the purchase accounting, these events generally must either occur or be substantially decided on within one year of the acquisition date.

Similar purchase accounting adjustments may also be made for postretirement and postemployment benefits. The restructuring of a company including merger of two or more legal entities generally does not trigger a purchase accounting adjustment for pensions.

(h) SEQUENCE OF MEASUREMENT STEPS. In a year containing one of the unusual events just described, the employer's pension cost comprises (1) the net periodic pension cost for the period prior to the event, determined without regard to the event; (2) the effect of the event such as the curtailment or settlement recognition; and (3) the net periodic pension cost for the period subsequent to the event, fully reflecting the changes resulting from the event. The pre-event pension cost in item (1) is generally based on the assumptions, such as the discount rate, used for the previous year-end measurement. Updated PBO and plan assets are then determined as of the event date as if the event had not taken place, using assumptions that are appropriate at that date, including, if applicable, any adjustment to the PBO to reflect the actual cost of settling any benefit obligation. The funded status, as well as any net prior service cost, net transition obligation or asset, and net gain or loss, is brought up to date. The effect of the event is next determined on the basis of the updated PBO and plan assets. The postevent pension cost in item (3) is based on the PBO, plan assets, net prior service cost, net obligation, or asset at transition and net gain or loss that remain after the event.

In determining the postevent pension cost, the remaining amortization period for any net obligation or asset at transition will generally not be changed even though the amount to be amortized may have. Similarly, the remaining amortization schedule of any net prior service cost will generally remain unchanged, unless the period during which the employer expects to realize future economic benefits from the plan amendment is shorter than originally estimated, or if the future economic benefits have been impaired. Amortization of net gain or loss, however, should reflect the postevent average remaining service period.

In case of multiple events occurring within one fiscal year, the process described in the preceding paragraphs may need to be repeated more than once, taking the events one at a time in chronological order. For simultaneous events, it is permissible to establish the presumed sequence unless there is compelling reason against the logic of that sequence, provided that the same approach is followed consistently in the future. The sequence selected can materially affect the amount of gain or loss to be recognized. It is also possible for events that originated from the situation to be recognized in different fiscal years, for example, when a plan is terminated in one year but the benefit obligation is not settled until the following year.

Gains or losses related to events occurring after the measurement date are generally not recognized in the current period, except when the events relate to a disposal of business segment that is reflected in the current year or when it results from the termination of a pension plan without a successor defined benefit plan. Even if not recognized, the effect of the event should be disclosed if it is material. The preceding statements apply to quarterly financial statements as well.

(i) DISCLOSURE REQUIREMENTS FOR NONRECURRING EVENTS. SFAS No. 158 requires the disclosure of nonrecurring events in these ways:

- The change in PBO due to the nonrecurring event should be included in the reconciliation of PBO from the beginning of the year to the end of the year.
- The change in assets due to the nonrecurring event should be included in the reconciliation of assets from the beginning of the year to the end of the year.
- The amount of gain or loss recognized due to a settlement or curtailment should be included in the disclosure of the amount of net period benefit cost recognized.

- The recognized cost of providing any special or contractual termination benefits should be disclosed, as well as a description of the nature of the event.

Despite the nonrecurring nature of these events, such gain or loss is normally not an extraordinary item as defined in Paragraphs 20–22 of APB Opinion No. 30 (ASC 225-20). One exception is when the gain or loss is related to the disposal of a business segment.

(j) ILLUSTRATION—NONRECURRING EVENTS. Exhibit 27.7 illustrates the application of SFAS No. 88 with respect to settlement, curtailment, and special termination benefits and that of SFAS No. 87 with respect to business combinations accounted for under the purchase method.

27.4 SPONSOR ACCOUNTING FOR NONQUALIFIED PLANS

(a) QUALIFIED VERSUS NONQUALIFIED PLANS. Qualified pension plans present notable tax advantages to both employer and employee as a form of employee compensation. The immediate advantage to the employer is the ability to deduct currently, within limitations, contributions to the plan. The employee on whose behalf the contribution is made does not, however, have to report the amount as gross income until it is made available to him. This deferral of tax has an added advantage since, in the typical case, benefits are not distributed until retirement, when the employee may be in a lower income tax bracket. The long-term and perhaps the most important tax advantage enjoyed by a qualified plan is that the fund or trust that receives and invests the contributions enjoys tax-exempt status. Investments earnings are not taxed until distributed, thus permitting an accelerated rate of growth for the fund.

For a pension plan to be considered qualified for income tax purposes, it must comply with certain Internal Revenue Code (IRC) requirements, not only in the design of the plan but also in its operations. Some of these requirements are:

- The plan must not discriminate in favor of employees who are officers or shareholders or highly compensated.
- Benefits under the plan must be reasonable in amount when considered with other forms of compensation.
- Plan operations must be conducted in accordance with the plan document and trust agreement.
- The pension fund must be exclusively for the benefit of participants and their beneficiaries.
- The plan must comply with certain minimum funding and reporting requirements.

Over the years, these requirements have become increasingly complex and burdensome, adding to the costs of administering qualified plans.

It has always been fairly common for an employer to maintain nonqualified retirement plans or to provide individualized deferred compensation arrangements for a selected group of management and highly compensated employees. There is no precise definition of "highly compensated employees" in this context, and it is not linked to the definition of "highly compensated employees" introduced by the Tax Reform Act of 1986. The primary advantages of such nonqualified arrangements are that (1) the coverage can be limited to only a few selected employees; (2) the benefits can be designed to meet the employer's objectives and the employees' needs without having to worry about the myriad of constraints imposed by ERISA and the Tax Code; and (3) they are exempt from virtually all ERISA reporting and funding requirements except a one-time notice of their existence to the DOL.

During the 1980s, the Tax Code was repeatedly amended to limit the amount of benefit that can be provided by, and the flexibility in the design of, a qualified plan. As a result, nonqualified plans gained increasing importance. Despite these advantages over qualified plans, a nonqualified

Background Information and Assumptions

Company X, which was used to illustrate the application of SFAS No. 87, experienced the following events, all occurring on December 31, 20X3, and in the sequence shown next.

- The PBO for pensioners was $6,000 on December 31, 20X3. Company X purchased participating annuities at a cost of $6,200 to discharge this obligation, $600 of which would be expected to be refunded by the insurance company in the form of dividends in future years.
- Company X closed one of its major manufacturing plants and permanently laid off all its workers. These workers would have represented 20 percent of the future service of all of Company X's employees. The PBO with respect to these laid-off workers was $1,500 before the layoff and only $800 after the layoff, ignoring the special benefits described below.
- For those laid-off employees who were eligible for early retirement, Company X offered unreduced early retirement pensions and an additional supplemental pension up to age 62. If not for the plant closing, these employees would have been entitled to a reduced early retirement pension only and no supplement. The value of the supplements and the waiver of the early retirement reduction was $400.
- Also on December 31, 20X3, Company X acquired Company Y, which sponsored a defined benefit pension plan with a PBO of $1,000 and plan assets worth $1,400.

Effect on Funded Status on December 31, 20X3

	Initial Status	Effect of Settlement[1]	Effect of Curtailment[2]	Special Termination Benefit[3]	Acquisition of Company Y[4]	Revised Status
Projected benefit obligation	$(16,600)	$ 6,200	$ 700	$(400)	$(1,000)	$(11,100)
Plan assets (fair value)	12,150	(5,600)	0	0	1,400	7,950
Funded status	$(4,450)	$ 600	$ 700	$(400)	$ 400	$ (3,150)
Net loss (gain)	967	(728)	(239)	0	0	0
Net prior service cost	1,690	0	(338)	0	0	1,352
Net obligation at date of initial application	2,200	0	(440)	0	0	1,760
Total AOCI	$4,857	$ (728)	$(1,017)	$0	$ 0	$ (266)

[1]Although the price of the annuity contract was $6,200, the cost for SFAS No. 87 purposes is only $5,600 since $600 of future dividends are anticipated. The $600 will be carried as a plan asset.

In accounting for the settlement, these steps are followed:

a. The $16,600 PBO needs to be reevaluated because the PBO for pensioners was discovered to be $5,600 instead of $6,200. The revised PBO, therefore, is $16,000, of which $5,600 was settled through the annuity purchase. The settlement percentage is 35%.

b. The unrecognized net loss is reduced from the $967 before the settlement by the $600 "savings" from the annuity contract, leaving a net loss of $367).

The settlement loss is $128 (i.e., $367 net loss times settlement percentage of 35%). This loss reduces the prepaid pension cost from $407 to $279.

[2]The 20 percent reduction in future services expected from the employee is significant enough to constitute a curtailment under SFAS No. 88.

The curtailment gain/loss consists of two components—the prior service recognition and the PBO adjustment. The curtailment loss is calculated in this way:

The remaining unrecognized prior service cost on December 31, 20X3, is $1,690 and the remaining transition obligation is $2,200 for a total of $3,890. The prior service cost recognition is 20 eprcent (the curtailment percentage) of the $3,890, or a $778 loss.

The PBO is reduced by $700 on account of the plant closing. However, since the plan still carries an unrecognized net loss of $239 at this point, the $700 saving must first be applied to eliminate the $239 unrecognized loss before the remaining $461 may be recognized as a PBO adjustment gain. The net curtailment loss is $317 (the $778 prior service cost less the $461 PBO gain). This $317 loss results in an accrued pension cost of $38. The amortization of the prior service cost ($130 in 20X3) will be $160 in 20X4. The respective remaining amortization periods will nevertheless remain unchanged.

[3]The value of the special benefits ($400) is recognized in full immediately and further increases the accrued pension cost from $38 to $438.

[4]Company Y's plan has an excess of $400, the difference between the plan assets of $1,400 and the PBO of $1,000. The $400 excess (less $228 in deferred tax) is recognized in purchase accounting and added to goodwill.

Exhibit 27.4 Nonrecurring Events

plan suffers from a serious tax disadvantage. Contributions to the plan, if any, are not currently tax deductible to the employer as long as the employees' rights to those contributions are subject to a substantial risk of forfeiture. Instead, the employer may deduct the benefits when they are paid. Moreover, there is no tax shelter for any fund that the employer may have set aside to finance the plan. Investment earnings on such fund are taxed directly to the employer, thus retarding the growth of the fund.

An exception to the preceding paragraph is a plan that is funded through a secular trust (also known as a *vesting trust*). In that case, the employer's contribution is tax deductible to the employer and is taxed as income to the employee when the employee's interest has vested. Investment earnings of the trust are generally taxed to the employer unless distributed to the employee. The use of secular trust as the funding vehicle for a nonqualified plan may subject the plan to the reporting, funding, and other requirements of ERISA and the Tax Code. It is assumed throughout this chapter that the nonqualified plan is not being funded through a secular trust.

(b) NONQUALIFIED PLAN ASSETS. For accounting and tax purposes, any fund that an employer may have set aside to finance a nonqualified plan is treated as an asset of the employer and not as an asset of the plan in the context of SFAS Nos. 87 and 88. Indeed, some plans must be unfunded in order to be exempt from the ERISA funding and reporting requirements. Therefore, such a fund is accounted for like any other general asset of the employer, whereas the cost of the benefits under the plan is determined in accordance with SFAS Nos. 87 and 88 as if there were no plan assets.

In order to improve the security of benefits to the employees, legal devices such as rabbi trusts have been used to prohibit or limit access to the plan fund by the employer or its creditors. Nevertheless, the assets of a rabbi trust are still considered assets of the employer, and the trust accounting is consolidated with the employer's accounting.

(c) NONQUALIFIED DEFINED CONTRIBUTION PLANS. Pure nonqualified defined contribution plans are relatively uncommon. To constitute a defined contribution plan, the employer's obligation must be limited to its contributions to the plan, with the employees receiving benefits based on those contributions plus investment earnings thereon. Since most nonqualified plans are either unfunded or funded indirectly through vehicles such as corporate-owned life insurance, the mechanism to operate a defined contribution generally does not exist. A deferred compensation plan that promises a certain rate of interest on compensations deferred by employees is not a defined contribution plan, unless the promised rate is equal to the actual after-tax rate of return on the compensations deferred by the employees. This situation is not changed if the promised rate is based, for example, on the projected rate of return on certain life insurance policies used to finance the plan.

The employer's cost for a defined contribution plan is equal to its contribution to the plan.

(d) NONQUALIFIED DEFINED BENEFIT PLANS. Both SFAS Nos. 87 and 88 apply to nonqualified plans and to any arrangement that is similar in substance to a pension plan regardless of the form or means of financing. For any other individually designed deferred compensation contract, cost should be accrued in accordance with APB Opinion No. 12 in a systematic and rational manner over the employee's period of active employment, starting from the time the contract is entered into, so that the full cost will have been accrued at the end of the term of active employment (see Paragraphs 9–10 of ASC 710-10-25).

Examples of nonqualified defined benefit plans are:

- Supplemental retirement plans for selected employees providing retirement benefits in addition to the employer's qualified pension plans
- Benefit restoration plans to restore to the employees any benefits that may have been restricted by IRC Section 401(a) or 415, or by Section 401(k) on the maximum amount of compensation that can be deferred
- Deferred compensation or termination indemnity plans promising to credit a rate of interest that is not equal to the after-tax investment return on the assets set aside to finance the plans

Golden parachutes are generally accounted for as severance payments. Change-of-control pension provisions in a pension plan, which provide certain special benefits in the event of a change in control of the employer, are handled as termination benefits under SFAS No. 88.

In applying SFAS Nos. 87 and 88 to a nonqualified plan, four factors should be considered:

1. There is generally no contribution to the plan except for benefits paid to the employees or payments made to purchase annuities because any funds set aside to finance the plan remain assets of the employer.
2. As a result of item 1, the expected return on plan assets is zero (whereas the investment return on any assets or funds that may have been appropriated to finance the plan would have already been reported elsewhere as income to the employer).
3. As noted under item 1, benefit payments are also treated as contributions and, therefore, would reduce the employer's accrued pension cost.
4. A nonqualified plan linked to a qualified plan, such as a supplemental retirement plan providing benefits that are offset by benefits from a qualified pension plan, should nevertheless be accounted for separately from the qualified plan.

27.5 PLAN ACCOUNTING

(a) BACKGROUND. In March 1980, the FASB issued SFAS No. 35, which established U.S. GAAP for the entity defined as a pension plan for the first time. The standard was effective for financial statements for fiscal years beginning after December 15, 1980. SFAS No. 35 was developed only after a great deal of controversy and followed a discussion paper, a public hearing, and two Exposure Drafts over a period of five years. It applies to all plans, including private plans and those of state and local governments. Coming under the standard are defined benefit pension plans that are subject to the financial reporting requirements of ERISA as well as those that are not. It does not apply to plans that are being terminated.

For nongovernmental plans with 100 or more participants as of the beginning of the plan year, a comprehensive annual report (Form 5500) must be filed in accordance with ERISA. The annual report must include these two items:

1. A set of financial statements prepared in accordance with U.S. GAAP, with an audit and opinion by an independent qualified public accountant
2. An actuarial report, including the status of the minimum funding standard account, and opinion by an enrolled actuary

(b) OBJECTIVE AND CONTENT OF FINANCIAL STATEMENTS. Under SFAS No. 35 (ASC 960), the plan itself is the reporting entity, not the trust. The Statement is based on a position that the primary objective of a plan's financial statements is to provide information useful in assessing its present and future ability to pay benefits when due. This objective requires the presentation of information about the economic resources of the plan and a measurement of its participants' accumulated benefits. The Statement leaves unresolved the issue of whether accumulated plan benefits are accounting liabilities of the plan. Therefore, it allows flexibility in presenting the actuarial information by providing that the plan's annual financial statements must include:

- A statement that includes information regarding net assets available for benefits
- A statement that includes information regarding the changes in net assets available for benefits
- Information regarding the actuarial present value of accumulated plan benefits as of the benefit information date (which can either be at the beginning or end of the year)
- Information regarding the effects, if significant, of certain factors affecting the year-to-year change in the actuarial present value of accumulated plan benefits

SFAS No. 35 provides that the actuarial information required under the third and fourth bullet points can be presented in separate statements, in the notes to financial statements, or combined with the other required information on the net assets available for benefits and the year-to-year changes therein (provided the information is as of the same date and/or for the same period).

(c) NET ASSETS AVAILABLE FOR BENEFITS. Plan investments, excluding insurance contracts, must be reported at fair value. Insurance contracts must be reported in accordance with the rules required by certain governmental agencies relating to the plan's annual report filed pursuant to ERISA. Because net assets are the existing means by which a plan can provide benefits, net asset information is necessary to assess a plan's ability to pay benefits when due. Using fair value as the basis to measure a plan's investments provides the most relevant information about resources currently available to pay the participants' benefits. The fair value of an investment is the amount that the plan could reasonably expect to receive for the investment from a current sale between a willing buyer and a willing seller (i.e., not in a forced liquidation sale). If there is an active market for the investment, fair value is measured by the *market price* as of the reporting date.

(i) Good-Faith Valuations. Investments that do not have a quoted market price must be valued "in good faith." In determining a good-faith value, these factors should be considered:

- Quoted market prices for similar investments
- Information about transactions or offers regarding the plan's investment
- Forecast of expected cash flows for that investment

(ii) Disclosures for Investments. Information regarding the plan's investments must be presented in the plan's statement of net assets available for benefits in sufficient detail to identify the general types of investment (e.g., as government securities, short-term securities, corporate bonds, common stocks, mortgages, and real estate). In addition, whether fair values have been measured by quoted price in an active market or determined otherwise must be disclosed.

(iii) Operating Assets. Assets used in the plan's operations must be presented at cost, less accumulated depreciation or amortization. Such assets would include, for example, buildings, equipment, furniture and fixtures, and leasehold improvements. Although the DOL's instructions to Forms 5500 and 5500-C/R require the presentation of all assets at fair value, it is believed that the DOL will not object to this presentation in the financial statements.

(iv) Contributions Receivable. The plan's financial statements should include as contributions receivable all amounts due the plan, as of the reporting date, from the employer, participants, and other sources of funding (e.g., state subsidies or federal grants). These receivables would include amounts due pursuant to formal commitments as well as legal or contractual requirements. For purposes of SFAS No. 35, no interest discount should be applied to the contribution receivable even though the current U.S. funding regulations require the use of discounting.

(d) CHANGES IN NET ASSETS AVAILABLE FOR BENEFITS. The information about a plan's ability to pay benefits when due, provided by its financial statements, is affected whenever transactions or other events affect the net asset or benefit information presented in those statements. Because a plan's ability to pay participants' benefits normally does not remain constant, users of its financial statements are concerned with assessing the plan's ability to pay participants' benefits not only as of a particular point in time but also on a continuing basis. For this reason, they need to know the reasons for changes in the net asset and benefit information reported in successive financial statements.

The FASB concluded, therefore, that plan financial statements should include (1) information regarding the year-to-year change in net assets available for benefits and (2) disclosure of the effects, if significant, of certain factors affecting the year-to-year change in benefit information.

SFAS No. 35 requires presentation of the statement of changes in net assets available for benefits in sufficient detail to permit identification of the significant changes during the year. The statement should include these eight, at a minimum:

1. The net change in fair value for each significant class of investments, segregated as between investments whose fair values have been measured by quoted prices in an active market and those whose fair values have been determined otherwise
2. Investment income, excluding the changes of fair value described in item 1
3. Contributions from employers, segregated as between cash and noncash contributions
4. Contributions from participants
5. Contributions from other identified sources such as state subsidies or federal grants
6. Benefits paid
7. Payments to insurance companies to purchase contracts that are excluded from plan assets
8. Administrative expenses

In presenting this information, gains and losses from investments sold are not segregated from unrealized gains and losses relating to investments held at the plan's year-end.

(e) ACTUARIAL PRESENT VALUE OF ACCUMULATED PLAN BENEFITS. Accumulated plan benefits are future benefit payments that are attributable, under the plan's provisions, to employees' service rendered prior to the benefit information date—the date as of which the actuarial present value of accumulated plan benefits is presented. Accumulated benefits include benefits for retired or terminated employees, beneficiaries of deceased employees, and present employees or their beneficiaries.

The accumulated benefit information may be presented as of the beginning or end of the plan year. If it is presented as of the beginning of the plan year, the prior year statement of net assets available for benefits and changes therein must also be presented. For example, if the plan year end is December 31, 2002, and the statement of accumulated plan benefits is based on a benefit information date of December 31, 2001, statements of net assets available for benefits and of changes therein also would be presented for 2001.

Measurement of accumulated plan benefits is based primarily on the employees' history of pay, service, and other appropriate factors as of the information date. Future salary changes are not considered, nor is a provision for inflation allowed. However, future increases that are guaranteed under a cost-of-living adjustment (COLA) should be estimated. Future years of service are considered only in determining an employee's expected eligibility for benefits of particular types, such as early retirement, death, and disability benefits. To measure the actuarial present value, assumptions are used to adjust the accumulated plan benefits to reflect the time value of money and the probability of payment between the benefit information date and the expected date of payment. An assumption that the plan is ongoing must underlie those assumptions. Benefit information should relate to the benefits reasonably expected to be paid in exchange for employees' service to the benefit information date.

To the extent possible, plan provisions should apply in measuring accumulated plan benefits. If the benefit for each service year is not determinable from the provisions of the plan, the benefit must be considered to accumulate by years of service rendered in proportion to total years required to earn a particular benefit. Normally, plan provisions indicate how to measure accumulated plan benefits. Plan amendments occurring subsequent to the date of the calculation must be excluded from the actuarial computation. In addition, benefits that are guaranteed by a contract with an insurance company (i.e., allocated contracts) are also excluded.

(i) Actuarial Assumptions. The most important decisions in developing the actuarial present value of accumulated plan benefits are in the selection of actuarial assumptions. The interest return assumption is, most likely, the single most important assumption. It is used to discount future benefit payments as well as to determine the anticipated rates of return on current and prospective assets. The concept of a best estimate and the principle of an explicit approach are integral to the rationale used in developing actuarial assumptions.

The concept of a "best estimate" is used by the FASB in discussing the actuarial assumptions in SFAS No. 35, possibly because the term is included in the ERISA certification required of an enrolled actuary. The reason is not critical, but it is important to realize that the best estimate requirement under ERISA is being interpreted in several ways. Its use for plan accounting purposes may be quite different from the best estimate for a funding basis. Paragraphs 1–2 of ASC 960-20-35 dealing with sponsor accounting discuss the concept further.

Although there is no specific discussion of what the FASB intended by "best estimate," there is a discussion in the Statement of what is meant by "explicit approach." It is important to recognize that prior to the Omnibus Budget Reconciliation Act of 1987, the explicit approach, although strongly recommended to actuaries by the American Academy of Actuaries, was not required in developing the ERISA requirements under the minimum funding standard account.

There are economic actuarial assumptions and noneconomic actuarial assumptions. The key issue in developing a plan's economic assumptions is the forecast of long-term inflation. The inflation component should be consistently reflected in all the economic assumptions. For example, if the long-term investment return assumption reflects a 5 percent inflation component, then the estimate of future salary increases should also reflect a 5 percent inflation component. In plan accounting, it is not necessary to develop an assumption for future pay increases or future Social Security benefits. Because very few plans provide for automatic postretirement COLAs, that assumption will seldom be required for plan accounting.

It is clear from SFAS No. 35 that the interest assumption used for accounting purposes will frequently, if not usually, be different from that used for funding (see Paragraphs 5–9 of ASC 960-20-35). The key requirement in developing an interest assumption, and for that matter any other assumption, is to use a sensible rationale. Judgmental elements in the actuary's development of a recommendation should be highlighted and subject to review and approval by the plan's sponsor. Although the result may differ as between sponsor and plan accounting, the same approach can be applied in both instances.

The noneconomic assumptions of mortality, withdrawal, disability, and early (late) retirement are referred to in SFAS No. 35, relating to the probability and timing of benefit payments. They are referred to here as *noneconomic* because they are usually not influenced by the long-term economic forecast, although short-term economic conditions can have a marked impact on withdrawal and early retirement experience. The mortality and disability assumptions are more highly technical. The typical plan sponsor will have to rely more heavily on the actuary's judgment and recommendations when adopting them. The impact of variations in mortality and disability assumptions on the actuarial value of accumulated benefits is not generally very large in any given year, although over the long term, the impact of particularly mortality can influence the cost of the benefit promise substantially. The withdrawal and early retirement assumptions can vary considerably from one organization to another, because they are affected by the personnel practices and business circumstances of the plan sponsor. Accordingly, more input from the plan sponsor is appropriate with respect to these assumptions. The discussion of these assumptions in Section 27.4 applies here as well.

(ii) Disclosures for Actuarial Present Value of Accumulated Plan Benefits. As previously stated, the accumulated benefit information may be presented as a separate financial statement, in a note to the financial statements, or combined with other information in the financial statements. The information must all be located in one place and must be segregated as described next:

- Vested benefits of participants currently receiving benefits
- Other vested benefits
- Nonvested benefits

If employees contribute to the plan, accumulated employee contributions must be disclosed. If applicable, accumulated interest credited on the contributions, including the interest rate, must also be disclosed.

(f) CHANGES IN THE ACTUARIAL PRESENT VALUE OF ACCUMULATED PLAN BENEFITS. The FASB requires disclosure of the effects, if significant, of certain factors affecting the year-to-year change in the benefit information. If the benefit information date is the beginning of the year, the required information regarding the year-to-year change in the benefit information would also relate to the preceding year. Consistent with the requirement for accumulated benefit information, the changes therein also may be presented as a separate financial statement, combined with other information in the financial statements, or in the notes to the financial statements. In addition, the information can be presented either in a reconciliation format or in a narrative format. As a minimum, significant effects of the next factors must be included in the disclosure of the information:

- Plan amendments
- Changes in the nature of the plan, such as a plan spinoff or a merger with another plan
- Changes in actuarial assumptions

Effects that are individually significant should be separately identified.

If only the minimum required disclosure is presented, presentation in a statement format will necessitate an additional unidentified "other" category to reconcile the beginning and ending amounts. Changes in actuarial assumptions are treated as changes in accounting estimates, and therefore previously reported amounts should not be restated.

(g) ILLUSTRATIVE PLAN FINANCIAL STATEMENTS. Exhibits 27.5 through 27.7, taken from ASC 960-205, illustrate the financial statements of a defined benefit pension plan. SFAS No. 35 requires the net asset information to be presented as of the end of the plan year. However, if the information

Year Ended December 31, 20X3	
Investment income	
Net appreciation in fair value of investments	$207,000
Interest	345,000
Dividends	130,000
Rents	55,000
	737,000
Less investment expenses	39,000
	698,000
Contributions	
Employer	780,000
Employees	450,000
	1,230,000
Total additions	1,928,000
Benefits paid directly to participants	740,000
Purchases of annuity contracts	257,000
	997,000
Administrative expenses	65,000
Total deductions	1,062,000
Net increase	866,000
Net assets available for benefits	
Beginning of year	8,146,000
End of year	$9,012,000

Exhibit 27.5 Statement of Changes in Net Assets Available for Benefits
Source: ASC 960-205.

December 31, 20X3	
Actuarial present value of accumulated plan benefits	
Vested benefits	
Participants currently receiving payments	$3,040,000
Other participants	8,120,000
	11,160,000
Nonvested benefits	2,720,000
Total actuarial present value of accumulated plan benefits	$13,880,000

Exhibit 27.6 Statement of Accumulated Plan Benefits
Source: ASC 960-205.

Year Ended December 31, 20X3	
Actuarial present value of accumulated plan benefits at beginning of year	$11,880,000
Increase (decrease) during the year attributable to:	
Plan amendment	2,410,000
Change in actuarial assumptions	(1,050,500)
Benefits accumulated	895,000
Increase for interest due to the decrease in the discount period	742,500
Benefits paid	(997,000)
Net increase	2,000,000
Actuarial present value of accumulated plan benefits at end of year	$13,880,000

Exhibit 27.7 Statement of Changes in Accumulated Plan Benefits
Source: ASC 960-205.

regarding the actuarial present value of accumulated plan benefits is presented as of the beginning of the plan year, the net asset information also must be presented as of that date (i.e., presented as of the end of the current and preceding plan years).

Exhibit 27.5 contains a statement of changes in net assets available for benefits, identifying the significant changes during the plan year. If the information regarding accumulated plan benefits is presented as of the beginning of the plan year, the statement of changes in net assets available for benefits must be presented for two years.

Exhibits 27.6 and 27.7 present a statement of accumulated plan benefits and a statement of changes in accumulated plan benefits. This information can be presented as of a benefit information date that is either the beginning or the end of the plan year. In addition, the information can be presented in a combined statement with the related net asset information or included in the notes to the financial statements. The statement presented in Exhibit 27.7 reconciles the year-to-year change in the actuarial present value of accumulated plan benefits. As an alternative to presenting this information in a statement format, disclosure can be made of only the factors significantly changed in accumulated plan benefits. The information can be disclosed in the notes to the financial statements or presented on the face of the statement of accumulated plan benefits. Factors that usually have a significant effect on accumulated plan benefits include plan amendments, changes in the nature of a plan (e.g., a plan spinoff or merger with another plan), and changes in actuarial assumptions.

(h) ADDITIONAL FINANCIAL STATEMENT DISCLOSURES. Disclosure of the plan's accounting policies must include a description of the methods and significant assumptions used to determine the fair value of investments and the reported value of contracts with insurance companies. In addition, a description of the method and significant actuarial assumptions used to determine the actuarial present value of accumulated plan benefits must be disclosed in the notes to the financial statements. Such disclosure would include any significant changes of methods or assumptions between benefit information dates.

In addition to disclosing significant accounting policies, SFAS No. 35 requires these nine disclosures (ASC 960-20-50):

1. A brief general description of the plan agreement, including vesting and benefit provisions.
2. A description of significant plan amendments made during the year. If significant amendments occur between the latest benefit information date and the plan's year end and therefore were not reflected in the actuarial present value of accumulated plan benefits, disclosure should be made of this matter.
3. A brief general description of the priority order of participants' claims to the assets of the plan in the event of plan termination and benefits guaranteed by the PBGC.
4. Funding policy and any changes in such policy during the plan year.
5. The policy regarding the purchase of contracts with insurance companies that are excluded from plan assets.
6. Tax status of the plan, if a favorable letter of determination has not been obtained or maintained.
7. Identification of individual investments that represent 5 percent or more of the net assets available for benefits.
8. Significant real estate or other transactions between the plan and the sponsor, employers, or employee organizations.
9. Unusual or infrequent events or transactions occurring subsequent to the latest benefit information date but before issuance of the financial statements, such as a plan amendment occurring after the latest benefit information date that significantly increases future benefits that are attributable to employee service rendered before that date.

(i) DECISION TO PREPARE PLAN FINANCIAL STATEMENTS. The number of accounting decisions required to prepare the plan's financial statements is not large.

For many plans, the first and most important decision will be whether to issue a statement at all. Plans subject to ERISA requirements must issue a statement, but public employee plans and ERISA plans with fewer than 100 participants are not required by ERISA to issue statements. The usual reason for not publishing plan financial statements, particularly for smaller employers, will be to avoid the additional expenses of preparing, auditing, and distributing the statement. The usual reasons for publishing statements when not required by ERISA include these four reasons:

1. The employer wishes to present a strong, positive image to employees (or the public) about the administration and financial strength of the plan.
2. The number of participants may not be indicative of the financial values involved. Plan assets could be very significant in relation to the company's net worth.
3. The employer wants to protect the plan's fiduciaries against legal liability.
4. Publication is required by state or local law.

Other reasons for decisions are practical, largely affecting the ease and expense with which financial statements can be prepared. One subtle decision occurs when there have been multiple changes during the year, such as plan amendments and changes in assumptions. The order in which these items are presented can affect the reader's perception of what actually happened during the year. The FASB in SFAS No. 35 commented:

> The Board recognized that the determined effects of factors comprising the net change in the benefit information will vary depending on the order in which the effects are calculated... . Thus, the Board concluded that at this time it would not prescribe an order.

This can be cleared up through footnote disclosures as desired. Some of the practical decisions involved include:

- Whether to use a benefit information date other than year-end. Many plans (if not most) will find it more convenient to use a beginning-of-the-year date. However, that approach does require more information to be furnished regarding both net assets available and changes in such assets during the preceding year. Another approach when the regular actuarial valuation (to determine funding) is performed at the beginning of the year is to value the accumulated benefits at that point, and project to year end, using "reasonable approximation." The FASB makes permissive reference to that type of an approach, provided that the results are substantially the same as those contemplated by SFAS No. 35. For many plans, this approach will produce very acceptable results.
- Whether to make a more complete disclosure of the plan's circumstances. In the interest of doing so, some plan sponsors may wish to present the benefit value information in more than the three minimum categories specified by SFAS No. 35. For example, the other vested benefit category could be expanded to include the value of vested benefits for employees eligible for normal or early retirement.

(j) DEFINED CONTRIBUTION PLANS. Although SFAS No. 35 does not cover defined contribution plans, many of the concepts and principles included are applicable to defined contribution plans. Plan accounting for defined contribution pension plans is discussed in ASC 962. Defined contribution plans require the maintenance of individual accounts for each participant, to record each one's share of the total net assets of the plan. Typically, a defined contribution plan will require a certain contribution from the employer without specifying the amount of benefits to be provided to the participants. The types and amounts of benefits, as well as the eligibility requirements, are frequently determined by the plan's trustees, who can be totally "unrelated" to the employer; in other cases, the employer reserves those rights. Employer contributions are based on a formula that may be a certain rate per hour of work or per unit of production, a function of the employee's contribution, a percentage of the employer's annual profitability, or some other specified method. The employer's obligation here differs from that under a defined contribution plan. With a defined contribution plan, the employer is not obligated to make up any shortfalls in actual versus assumed experience. This can be particularly significant, of course, in the case of the investment experience.

(i) Separate Accounts. Employer contributions, changes in the value of the plan's net assets, and forfeitures, if any, are allocated to individual participant accounts maintained for each participant. In addition, employee contributions, if any, are credited to the account.

(ii) Types of Plans. Defined contribution plans include these four:

1. Profit-sharing plans, which provide for an employer contribution based on current or accumulated profits
2. Money purchase plans, which provide for an employer contribution based on employee compensation, units of production, hours worked, or some criterion other than profits

3. Stock bonus and employee stock ownership plans that are qualified profit-sharing plans that invest substantially all the plan's assets in the stock of the employer company
4. Thrift or savings plans, which provide for periodic employee contributions with matching, in whole or in part, by the employer—usually from current or accumulated profits

(iii) Financial Statements. Financial statements for a defined contribution plan should include a statement of net assets available for benefits and a statement of changes in net assets available for benefits. The disclosures would be similar to those required for a defined benefit pension plan, except for the references to actuarial information (ASC 962-205).

(k) POSTRETIREMENT MEDICAL BENEFIT FEATURES OF DEFINED BENEFIT PENSION PLANS. Assets accumulated under Section 401(h) of the IRC to provide a postretirement medical benefit component to a defined benefit pension plan are not available for pensions. They and the associated liabilities should therefore be presented (see Paragraphs 6–8 of ASC 965-205-45), net, in two places apart from the other amounts in the plan's statement of net assets available for pension benefits: (1) among the assets and (2) among the liabilities. The pension plan's statement of changes in net assets should show only the following related to Section 401(h): (1) qualified transfers to the 401(h) account and (2) any unused or unspent amounts, including allocated income, in the 401(h) account at the end of the year that were qualified transfers of excess pension assets that should have been but were not transferred back to the defined benefit pension plan, or both. Only information concerning pension benefits should be reported as accumulated plan benefits.

The notes to the financial statements of defined benefit pension plans should disclose the nature of the assets related to Section 401(h) and that the assets are available to pay only retiree health benefits. Also, because ERISA requires 401(h) assets to be reported as assets of the defined benefit pension plan in regulatory filings with the U.S. government on Form 5500, a reconciliation of the net assets reported in the plan's financial statements to those reported in Form 5500 should be provided.

27.6 ACCOUNTING FOR POSTRETIREMENT BENEFITS OTHER THAN PENSIONS

(a) BACKGROUND. On December 21, 1990, the FASB issued SFAS No. 106, *Employer's Accounting for Postretirement Benefits Other Than Pensions.* Retiree medical benefits are SFAS No. 106's primary focus, but life insurance and other welfare benefits provided to employees after retirement are also included.

Prior to SFAS No. 106, most employers had recognized the cost of postretirement benefits other than pensions when paid. Under the accounting requirements of SFAS No. 106, postretirement benefits are viewed as a form of deferred compensation that should be recognized on an accrual basis during the periods that the employees render the service needed to qualify for benefits. The specific approach and methodology of SFAS No. 106 (ASC 715-60) closely parallels the pension accounting rules addressed in SFAS Nos. 87 and 88 (ASC 715-30). Their disclosures are similar as well.

The practice of providing postretirement health care benefits took root after the Medicare program was established in 1965. Employers found that, for relatively few dollars, Medicare supplements, as they were called, bought much employee goodwill. The effect of inflation on medical costs, the trend toward earlier retirement, and longer life expectancies have made these benefits increasingly expensive. During recent decades, the cost of medical care has generally risen at twice the average inflation rate for the same period. These dramatic cost increases have prompted many companies to significantly reduce or even eliminate retiree medical benefits. Retiree health care benefits are now found mainly at larger employers, as the escalating costs have made these benefits too costly for most midsize and smaller employers.

Although some employers provide benefits only until retirees reach age 65 and become eligible for Medicare, some programs still provide lifetime benefits. Typically, benefits for retirees are similar to those for active employees, including the ability to cover eligible dependents. Many plans provide the same level of benefits regardless of years of service, while other plans provide incremental benefits to employees retiring with longer service periods. Programs for retirees age 65 and over usually are coordinated with Medicare benefits to help contain costs. Furthermore, retirees are now often required to pay some portion of the cost of these benefits. This cost sharing is one of many methods employers have used to help contain their costs. Another commonly used method is cost caps, where the company establishes a fixed dollar amount above which the retiree will cover all costs.

On March 23, 2010, President Obama signed into law the Patient Protection and Affordable Care Act. Seven days later, the president signed into law a reconciliation measure, the Health Care and Education Reconciliation Act of 2010. The passage of the Patient Protection and Affordable Care Act and the reconciliation measure (collectively, the Act) has resulted in comprehensive health care reform legislation. The effects of the Act on the U.S. economy could be as sweeping as those resulting from the passage of Medicare and Social Security.

Entities will need to identify and plan for changes related to accounting and disclosures that will result from the Act. For example, public entities may need to add disclosures about the positive or negative impact of the Act in their financial statements and management's discussion and analysis (MD&A) in periodic reports (such as Forms 10-K and 10-Q filings) and registration statements.

(b) STATEMENT OF FINANCIAL ACCOUNTING STANDARDS NO. 106. SFAS No. 106 (ASC 715-60) requires employers that provide medical or other affected benefits to follow a prescribed method in determining the annual expense charge for such benefits and to provide extensive disclosures in their financial statements. As noted earlier, much of the guidance in SFAS No. 106 is similar to that in SFAS No. 87, which is covered in detail in Section 27.2. This section focuses on identifying the similarities of the two Statements as well as their key differences.

(i) Similarities to Statement of Financial Accounting Standards No. 87. The measurement of obligations in a postretirement medical plan closely follows SFAS No. 87 methodology. Unlike the pension model, where the monthly benefit is fixed at retirement, future medical benefits depend on the likelihood and cost of future claims. Nonetheless, the basic concept of projecting future cash flows, assigning a probability of payment, and discounting back to the measurement date apply. The discounted value of future benefits forms the basic building blocks for the expense and liability determinations under SFAS No. 106. The attribution of the obligation to an employee's service period under SFAS No. 106 does differ slightly, as is addressed next.

The annual postretirement benefit expense is composed of all of the same components as the SFAS No. 87 net periodic pension expense as outlined in Section 27.2(d). This includes service cost, interest cost, expected return on assets (if funded), and amortization of net transition obligation, net prior service costs, and actuarial gains and losses. With minor exceptions, the measurement of these items is consistent with SFAS No. 87. In particular, most of the allowable amortization methodologies, including the corridor approach for gains and losses, directly follow SFAS No. 87.

The balance sheet liability or asset under SFAS No. 106 is similar to that under SFAS No. 87, which is the funded status of the plan. Under SFAS No. 106, the funded status is the difference between the APBO and the fair value of the plan assets. A balance sheet asset attributable to a postretirement welfare plan is somewhat rare since most postretirement welfare plans are not prefunded.

Many of the actuarial assumptions used to develop SFAS Nos. 87 and 106 liabilities and expense are similar. In particular, the methodology used to develop the SFAS No. 106 discount rate is the same as that described in Section 27.2(c)(iii). Each of the significant actuarial assumptions for SFAS No. 106 is discussed in greater detail later in this section.

(ii) Differences from Statement of Financial Accounting Standards No. 87. While there are many similarities between SFAS No. 106 (ASC 715-60) and SFAS No. 87 (ASC 715-30), there are some important differences. SFAS No. 106 introduces the expected postretirement benefit obligation (EPBO). This represents the discounted value as of the measurement date of all future benefits expected to be paid. SFAS No. 87 does not define an equivalent liability measurement. This differs from the PBO in pension accounting in that the EPBO represents the value of all future postretirement benefits, not just those that have been attributed to employees' service as of the reporting date. The service cost is the portion of EPBO attributed to the current period. The APBO under SFAS No. 106 is determined by apportioning the EPBO over the appropriate attribution period. Therefore, the APBO represents the portion of the EPBO that is attributable to prior service, which is equivalent to the PBO under SFAS No. 87. If an employee has reached his full eligibility date, the APBO would be the same as the EPBO. The concepts are the same but the terminology is slightly different.

SFAS No. 106 also introduces the term *substantive plan* (ASC 715-60-20), which is the plan as understood by the employer and employee, which may differ from the written plan. This can be a significant issue because the employer sometimes communicates to covered employees its intent to change certain plan features, such as the level of employee contributions, in the future. The substantive plan can thus have a value on the measurement date materially different from the plan as written and operated. To the extent the substantive plan differs from the written plan, the substantive plan is the basis for accounting under SFAS No. 106. Therefore, great care should be taken to understand the true nature of the benefit promise the employer has made to its retirees. This is a significant difference from SFAS No. 87, since most pension plans require a formal document that serves as the basis for pension accounting.

The substantive plan has become increasingly more important as employers have made changes to their retiree medical plans to control escalating costs. Specifically, both cost-sharing and cost-cap arrangements are often implemented. These changes can significantly affect the measurement of the plan's obligations, but these measurements are realistic only if the employer implements the cost sharing and caps that have been communicated. To the extent the employer does not implement them, the actual operation of the plan should dictate appropriate accounting treatment.

Unlike SFAS No. 87, SFAS No. 106 gives employers the option of recognizing the entire Transition Obligation immediately in expense as opposed to deferring recognition of the Transition Obligation in expense through the amortization process (see Paragraphs 27–40 of ASC 715-60-35). For employers electing to defer its recognition, SFAS No. 106 allows an amortization period equal to the greater of the average remaining service period for active participants and 20 years. SFAS No. 87 allows deferred recognition of the transition obligation or asset over the greater of the average remaining service period for active participants and 15 years. Both Statements require the use of the average remaining life expectancy of the participants if almost all participants are inactive. Additional amortization of the transition obligation is required if the cumulative cost computed under SFAS No. 106 is less than cumulative benefit payments less any plan assets or unrecognized accrued cost at transition. This provision requires additional amortization for a few mature plans with very high pay-as-you-go costs for the first few years following adoption of the Statement.

The attribution period required by SFAS No. 106 differs slightly from that in SFAS No. 87. As discussed earlier, SFAS No. 87 requires an attribution that accrues the costs from hire date (or service start date) to the expected retirement date, following the accrual pattern specified by the plan formula. SFAS No. 106, in contrast, requires a ratable attribution from hire date (or service start date) to full eligibility date. The end of the attribution period differs for the two Statements.

In many retiree medical plans, employees are eligible to retire with full benefits as early as age 55, assuming they have earned enough service. In this case, SFAS No. 106 would generally require the liability for active employees to be fully accrued by the time they attain age 55. If significant benefits accrue beyond the full eligibility date, as may be the case when additional service provides enhanced benefits, SFAS No. 106 would require an attribution period that is consistent with SFAS No. 87. Overall, SFAS No. 106 generally requires a more rapid accrual of the liability than SFAS No. 87.

As noted, many of the actuarial assumptions used to develop SFAS Nos. 87 and 106 liabilities and expense are similar. Relevant actuarial assumptions, including assumptions that are unique to SFAS No. 106, are discussed in greater detail later in Section 27.6(c) of this chapter.

SFAS No. 158 governs the financial statement disclosure requirements for SFAS No. 87 and SFAS No. 106. The specific disclosure requirements, including a description of the differences for pension and retiree welfare plans, are included later in Section 27.6(e) of this chapter.

Finally, unlike the pension rules under SFAS No. 87, SFAS No. 106 does not require a minimum balance sheet liability.

(c) ACTUARIAL ASSUMPTIONS. Many of the actuarial assumptions necessary to develop the SFAS No. 106 expense and liabilities, such as discount rate, mortality, retirement age, and turnover, are similar to those used for SFAS Nos. 87 and 88. The discount rate for SFAS No. 106 purposes is established using the same discounted cash flow methodology described in SFAS No. 87. In practice, most employers will use the same assumptions for SFAS No. 87 and SFAS No. 106 to the extent the plans cover the same group of employees. However, the nature of the benefits covered by SFAS No. 106 requires the use of some unique actuarial assumptions.

Perhaps the most significant of these assumptions is the assumed per capita claims cost. Unlike pension plans that provide monthly cash payments, retiree medical plans typically promise benefits in the form of medical services. Besides variations due to plan provisions that define the level or richness of benefits provided, claims experience varies significantly by age, sex, occupation, and geographic location. This necessitates the development of an assumed set of per capita health care costs, usually stratified by age and gender. This per capita claims estimate should reflect the provisions of the plan and is typically based on historical claims experience of the employer. Since most plans are integrated with Medicare, assumptions must also be made for post-65 participants as to the portion of their benefits that will be provided by the government.

Another assumption unique to SFAS No. 106 is the medical trend assumption. While some retiree medical plans cap benefits at current levels, the more common approach is to provide uncapped benefits that are subject to medical inflation. As noted, medical inflation has outpaced standard inflation over the past 20 years. Currently, most health care experts expect this trend to continue in the near future. Therefore, the medical trend assumption for most employers reflects a relatively high initial medical trend that decreases each year until it reaches a flat, long-term level. Many employers use different medical trend rates for different benefits that are provided by the plan. In particular, prescription drug inflation has been higher than overall medical trend, and many employers reflect this discrepancy in their assumed trend rates.

There are several other assumptions unique to SFAS No. 106. Since not all employees will elect to be covered by the retiree medical plan, an assumption about the participation level must be made. This is particularly important in plans where retirees must contribute toward the cost of coverage. If these costs become too high, many retirees will decline coverage and rely on Medicare or purchase their own medical coverage. In addition, many retiree medical plans have more than one coverage option, such as a health maintenance organization (HMO), a preferred provider organization (PPO), and an indemnity plan. In such a case, an assumption must be made as to which plan a participant will elect when he or she retires. Actual experience and anticipated employer subsidies must be considered in setting this assumption.

(d) NONRECURRING EVENTS. SFAS No. 88 addresses the special accounting that is required for settlements, curtailments, and special termination benefits related to pension plans. These events may also affect postretirement medical plans. While the treatment for pension and retiree medical plans is quite similar, SFAS No. 106 directly addresses the accounting for settlements and curtailments and the unique issues related to postretirement welfare benefit plans. The Statement defers to SFAS No. 88 for the accounting for special termination and contractual termination benefits.

As discussed earlier, a settlement is an irrevocable commitment that releases the employer from primary responsibility for some or all of the liability. Settlements are fairly rare in postretirement medical plans due to the nature of the benefit promise. Unlike a pension plan that provides that a nonparticipating annuity contract can be purchased to settle the obligation, there are no viable financial instruments that can settle the promise of lifetime medical coverage. The one instance in which settlements can occur with postretirement medical plans is for companies that have instituted cost caps for their retirees and thereby transformed the liability into a fixed monthly annuity. The settlement accounting prescribed by SFAS No. 106 precisely follows SFAS No. 88.

Curtailments occur when the expected years of future service for covered employees is significantly reduced or the future accrual of benefits is eliminated for future service. In general, curtailment accounting under SFAS No. 106 follows the treatment under SFAS No. 88. However, due to the some of the unique aspects of retiree medical benefits, curtailment accounting for these plans can be complex.

For example, assume we have a company that sponsors a retiree medical plan that covers 100 current retirees ($2 million in APBO) and 500 active employees ($3.5 million in APBO). Further assume that the company chooses to eliminate these benefits for all active employees as of some fixed date. This plan change eliminates both past and future accruals. Since these benefits are not protected by minimum vesting requirements similar to those applicable to pension plans, this is a possible scenario. In fact, many companies have taken this approach as a reaction to escalating retiree medical liabilities.

Under this scenario, there is both a negative plan amendment and a curtailment. The negative plan amendment relates to the change in the APBO that is attributable to past service. Curtailment accounting, in contrast, is focused on any portion of the liability attributable to future service. For a retiree medical plan, all of the APBO is attributable to past service. If the plan included retiree life insurance that was based on final average pay, the portion of the APBO attributable to using projected salary increases would be a curtailment gain. For example, assume the life insurance liability is $200,000 based on covered participants current service and salary. However, SFAS No. 106 requires the APBO to be valued using current service and projected salary. Therefore, the total APBO might be $300,000. If this life insurance benefit were eliminated, $200,000 would be treated as a negative plan amendment and $100,000 as a curtailment gain. Since the typical retiree medical plan is not based on salary, the entire APBO is attributable to prior service. Therefore, the entire reduction in APBO is attributed to the negative plan amendment. There is no curtailment gain subject to immediate recognition. The only effect the curtailment might have is the accelerated recognition of existing unrecognized prior service costs or transition obligation. The negative prior service cost from the current plan change is not subject to accelerated recognition. Therefore, in many cases, the elimination of retiree medical benefits for active employees often results in a curtailment that has no immediate income statement effect. The $3.5 million reduction in APBO from the example must be amortized over the average remaining life expectancy of the 100 retirees. Question and Answer 28 from the SFAS No. 106 *Implementation Guide* addresses a similar scenario (see Paragraphs 157–160 of ASC 960-55): "Case C: Negative Plan Amendment and a Curtailment."

(e) DISCLOSURES. As amended by SFAS No. 158, disclosures under SFAS No. 106 are very similar to disclosures under SFAS No. 87. The differences are discussed next.

- One additional assumption must be disclosed: the medical trend assumption. Since the medical trend is assumed to vary over several years, it is acceptable to paraphrase.
- Since the medical trend assumption has a large effect on the benefit obligation, a sensitivity analysis must be performed. This analysis shows the effect on service cost plus interest cost, and the benefit obligation, under a 1 percentage point increase and decrease in the trend assumptions.

See Exhibit 27.3 in Section 27.2(h) for a sample disclosure for a public entity sponsoring a postretirement benefit plan accounted for under SFAS No. 106.

For a nonpublic reporting entity, the disclosures can be considerably shortened, similar to disclosures under SFAS No. 87. The only difference between the formats of disclosures under SFAS No. 87 for nonpublic entities versus SFAS No. 106 for nonpublic entities is that the medical trend rate assumption must be disclosed, using a paragraph similar to the one in Exhibit 27.3.

27.7 EMPLOYERS' ACCOUNTING FOR POSTEMPLOYMENT BENEFITS

(a) BACKGROUND. Issued by the FASB in November 1992, SFAS No. 112, *Employer's Accounting for Postemployment Benefits,* established accounting standards for the estimated cost of benefits provided by an employer to former or inactive employees in the window of time after employment but before retirement (hereafter referred to as *postemployment benefits*). Postemployment benefits include such items as salary continuation, supplemental unemployment benefits, disability-related benefits (including workers' compensation), job training, and the continuation of health care benefits and life insurance coverage.

Prior to the issuance of SFAS No. 112, the accounting for the cost of postemployment benefits varied from employer to employer. Although some employers accounted for these benefits under a form of accrual accounting (e.g., terminal accrual accounting—under which the cost of the benefit is accrued at the time the event giving rise to the payment of benefits occurs), most still used a cash basis to recognize the costs associated with such benefits.

The FASB concluded that GAAP required recognition of postemployment benefits on an accrual basis. It also concluded that two existing Statements, SFAS No. 43, *Accounting for Compensated Absences,* and SFAS No. 5, *Accounting for Contingencies,* specified appropriate accounting for postemployment benefits. However, both these Statements specifically excluded postemployment benefits. Therefore, SFAS No. 112 amended SFAS No. 43 and SFAS No. 5 to include postemployment benefits.

(b) STATEMENT OF FINANCIAL ACCOUNTING STANDARDS NO. 112 (ASC 712). As noted, SFAS No. 112 requires employers to recognize the obligation to provide postemployment benefits under an accrual method of accounting.

(i) Application of Statement of Financial Accounting Standards No. 43 (ASC 710) versus Statement of Financial Accounting Standards No. 5 (ASC 450). The method of accrual accounting required under SFAS No. 112 depends on whether the benefit is covered by SFAS No. 43 or SFAS No. 5. Specifically, postemployment benefits that meet each of the next four conditions should be accounted for in accordance with SFAS No. 43 (ASC 710-10-25-1):

1. The employer's obligation relating to employee's rights to receive compensation for future absences is attributable to employee services already rendered.
2. The obligation relates to rights that vest or accumulate.
3. Payment of the compensation is probable.
4. The amount can be reasonably estimated.

Postemployment benefits covered by SFAS No. 112 that do not meet these conditions should be accounted for in accordance with SFAS No. 5 so long as it is probable that an event causing the liability has occurred and the cost is reasonably estimable.

In practice, the second item above is the most significant in determining whether SFAS No. 5 or SFAS No. 43 accrual accounting is applicable. Since most postemployment benefits do not vest, accumulation is the key factor. In general, the term *accumulate* means that the benefit varies with an employee's service. In other words, a benefit that increases as an employee renders additional service is said to accumulate. A benefit that is independent of an employee's service does not meet this standard, and SFAS No. 5 treatment should be applied.

An example of a plan that would require SFAS No. 43 accrual accounting is a disability plan that pays income continuation benefits for 2 weeks for each year of service an employee has rendered at the time of disability. This plan meets each of the four criteria just described. Conversely, if the plan provided 10 weeks of income continuation regardless of seniority at the time of disability, SFAS No. 5 accounting would apply.

As with all of the Statements described in this chapter, SFAS No. 112 need not be applied to immaterial items. Unlike SFAS Nos. 87 and 106, postemployment benefits are much more likely to fall below the materiality threshold for many employers. This is due to the nature of postemployment benefit plans, which often pay relatively small benefits for short periods of time.

(ii) Differences in Accrual Accounting. For postemployment benefits that are subject to SFAS No. 43, a liability and expense must be accrued for all participants covered by the benefit plan in question. This includes all active employees who are eligible for the benefit as well as participants who are currently in pay status. For active participants, that raises a question regarding attribution. Paragraphs 12 and 13 of SFAS No. 43 (see Paragraphs 2–3 of ASC 710-10-25), which deal with the accrual of the liability, appear to be based on an assumption that accumulating postemployment benefits should accrue uniformly over all service. Looking to SFAS Nos. 87 and 106, as SFAS No. 112 suggests, SFAS No. 43 type benefits should accrue uniformly over all service unless the benefit accrual pattern is strongly front-loaded. In this case, the Statements suggest that the expense accrual pattern should follow the benefit accrual pattern. Therefore, a service-based approach following the pattern of benefit accruals should be applied for the attribution of benefits under SFAS No. 43.

SFAS No. 5 requires a terminal accrual approach. Therefore, income is not charged until both of the next conditions are met:

1. Information available before the financial statements are issued indicates that it is *probable* that a liability has been incurred.
2. The amount of the liability can be reasonably estimated.

The importance of the term *probable* in the conditions just listed is best illustrated with an example. With long-term disability plans, it is often several months between the date a disability occurs and the time at which benefit payments are approved. The time between when the claim is filed and when payment is approved is used to confirm that the disability meets all of the conditions necessary to trigger payment under the terms of the plan. If this adjudication period overlaps a fiscal year-end, SFAS No. 5 requires that a liability be accrued for an employee if the employer believes it is probable that disability payments will be made to the employee in question.

Therefore, the liability for such a plan is equal to the actuarial present value of future benefits for all participants currently in pay status plus the liability attributable to employees who have been injured but whose claims have not been fully adjudicated. Since not every disability claim results in payment, an assumption about the number of disability claims that will result in payment should be made. No liability is accrued for currently healthy active employees under SFAS No. 5.

(iii) Measurement Issues. SFAS No. 112 does not specifically address how to measure an employer's postemployment benefit obligation. However, the FASB urged employers to utilize guidance provided in SFAS Nos. 87 and 106 on the measurement of postretirement benefit obligations. Since most postemployment benefits are structurally similar to pension and other postretirement benefits, employers have generally adopted the methodology and assumptions guidance provided in these two Statements.

For plans subject to SFAS No. 43 accounting, the annual expense determination is similar to that in SFAS Nos. 87 and 106. The expense is made up of several familiar components: service cost, interest cost, amortization of prior service cost, and amortization of actuarial gains and losses. Paragraph 25 of SFAS No. 112 specifically disallowed delayed recognition of the transition obligation. Therefore, all employers were required to record the entire liability at adoption as the effect of a change in accounting principle.

SFAS Nos. 112 and 43 provide little or no explicit guidance on delayed recognition of plan amendments and actuarial gains and losses. While a strict reading of SFAS No. 43 seems to preclude delayed recognition of any portion of the liability, in practice many employers have used the FASB's advice to rely on SFAS Nos. 87 and 106 to support delayed recognition of these two items. When amortization is used, the amortization period is expected future service until expected payment. This produces a fairly short amortization period, thereby reducing the discrepancy between immediate and delayed recognition.

For plans covered by SFAS No. 5, the balance sheet liability is equal to the actuarially determined value of the benefit obligation as of the financial statement date. Therefore, the income statement expense is equal to the amount to reconcile the prior and current year's reserve, adjusting for actual cash payments during the year.

SFAS No. 112 provides no specific guidance on the use of discounting or other assumptions, other than indicating that discounting of postemployment benefit obligations is permitted but not required. SFAS Nos. 43 and 5 are also silent on this issue. As encouraged by paragraph 23 of SFAS No. 112 (ASC 710-10-35-1), employers should look to SFAS Nos. 87 and 106 for guidance in selecting assumptions to the extent they are used. Therefore, employers have used

Reconciliation of Funded Status	
1. Actuarial Liability	
a. Disabled Participants	($12,000,000)
b. Active Participants	($20,000,000)
c. Total	($32,000,000)
2. Fair Value of Assets	$0
3. Funded Status	($32,000,000)
4. Unrecognized Amount at Transition*	$0
5. Unrecognized Net Loss/(Gain)	$6,000,000
6. Unrecognized Prior Service Cost	$0
7. (Accrued)/Prepaid Postemployment Benefit Cost at Year End	($26,000,000)

*SFAS No. 112 did not allow delayed recognition of the transition obligation.

Change in (Accrued)/Prepaid Postemployment Benefit Cost	
1. (Accrued)/Prepaid Postemployment Benefit Cost at Prior Year End	($24,400,000)
2. Expense During Year*	
a. Service Cost	$2,200,000
b. Interest Cost	$2,800,000
c. Amortization of Loss/(Gain)	$600,000
d. Total Expense	$5,600,000
3. Payouts During Year†	$4,000,000
4. (Accrued)/Prepaid Postemployment Benefit Cost at Current Year End	($26,000,000)

*Since SFAS No. 43 applies to this plan, the annual expense is explicitly calculated as the sum of the service cost, interest cost, and amortization of unrecognized actuarial losses. Were this a SFAS No. 5 plan, the annual expense would equal the change in the actuarial reserve, adjusted for benefit payments made during the year.

†Since the plan is unfunded, benefit payments are treated as employer contributions.

Exhibit 27.8 Illustration of SFAS No. 112 Accounting

actuarial assumptions such as discount rates, salary scale, mortality, and disability incidence in measuring the SFAS No. 112 liability. In general, these assumptions are the same as those used for measuring liabilities under SFAS Nos. 87 and 106. One exception is the discount rate for workers' compensation, which is based on yields on risk-free securities. Employers have therefore looked to Treasury security yields instead of high-quality corporate debt in setting the discount rate for these purposes.

(iv) Disclosures. SFAS No. 112 does not include any stringent disclosure requirements. In fact, the Statement requires disclosure only if the obligation for a postemployment benefit plan is not reflected in the financial statements because the amount cannot be reasonably estimated. This may be the case for a postemployment benefit that is triggered by an event that is difficult to predict with any degree of accuracy. Therefore, in practice, employers have not provided detailed financial statement notes like those required under SFAS No. 158 for pension (SFAS No. 87) and other postretirement benefits (SFAS No. 106).

(v) Illustration. An illustration of the key actuarial results for a typical SFAS No. 112 liability is presented next. The plan in question is a long-term disability plan that provides income and medical continuation benefits. The amount of benefit is based on a schedule that takes an employee's service at time of disability into account. Since the benefits "accumulate," the plan is subject to the requirements of SFAS No. 43, and therefore, the reporting on it must reflect a liability for both active and disabled participants.

The reconciliation of funded status is reflected in a manner similar to that for SFAS Nos. 87 and 106 to show the similarities between SFAS No. 112 and these two Statements. However, SFAS No. 112 does not include financial statement note disclosure for this type of plan, so this level of detail need not be presented (see Exhibit 27.8).

27.8 SOURCES AND SUGGESTED REFERENCES

Accounting Standards Executive Committee. Statement of Position 99-2, *Accounting for and Reporting of Postretirement Medical Benefit (401(h)) Features of Defined Benefit Pension Plans*. New York: AICPA, 1999.

Financial Accounting Standards Board. *Accounting Standards Codification—Notice to Constituents (v 4.2) About the Codification*. May 2, 2011.

Financial Accounting Standards Board. Accounting Standards Codification (ASC) Topics. July 1, 2009.

______. ASC 105, *Generally Accepted Accounting Principles*.

______. ASC 225, *Income Statement*.

______. ASC 250, *Accounting Changes and Error Corrections* (FAS 154).

______. ASC 450, *Contingencies* (FAS 5).

______. ASC 712, *Compensation—Nonretirement Postemployment Benefits* (FAS 112).

______. ASC 715, *Compensation—Retirement Benefits* (FAS 87; 88; 106; 112; 132(R); 158).

______. ASC 740, *Income Taxes* (FAS 109/Fn 48).

______. ASC 805, *Business Combinations* (FAS 141(R)).

______. ASC 820, *Fair Value Measurement* (FAS 157).

______. ASC 960, *Plan Accounting—Defined Benefit Pension Plans*.

______. ASC 962, *Plan Accounting—Defined Contribution Pension Plans*.

______. ASC 965, *Plan Accounting—Health and Welfare Benefit Plans*.

Lorenson, Leonard, and Paul Rosenfield. "Vested Benefits—A Company's Only Pension Liability," *Journal of Accountancy* (October 1983).

Munnell, Alicia H. *Economics of Private Pensions*. Washington, DC: Brookings Institution, 1982.

27.9 APPENDIX

On June 16, 2011, the IASB issued amendments to IAS 19 that changes the accounting for defined benefit plans and termination benefits. The objective of this limited scope project was to improve the financial reporting of employee benefits by:

- Requiring changes in defined benefit obligations and in the fair value of plan assets to be reported in a more understandable way
- Eliminating some presentation options allowed under the previous version of IAS 19, thus improving comparability
- Clarifying requirements that have resulted in diverse practices
- Enhancing disclosure about the risks arising from defined benefit plans

The amendments are effective for annual reporting periods beginning on or after January 1, 2013. Retrospective application is generally required in accordance with IAS 8. The table summarizes some of the key differences between U.S. GAAP and IFRS (IAS 19 Revised).

Key Differences Between U.S. GAAP and IFRS (IAS 19 Revised)

Subject	U.S. GAAP (ASC 715)	IFRS (IAS 19 Revised)
Recognition of prior service cost	Prior service costs are amortized over the remaining service period (or life expectancy if all or almost all of the participants are inactive).	Immediately recognized in profit or loss as part of service cost component.
Remeasurement component	Not applicable.	Remeasurement component includes (1) actuarial gains and losses on defined benefit obligation, (2) difference between the actual return on plan assets and interest on plan assets included in the net interest component, and (3) any changes in the effect of the asset ceiling.
Recognition of actuarial gains and losses	An entity may adopt either (1) the deferral method (i.e., corridor approach) and recycle amounts in excess of the corridor through net periodic benefit cost over an amortization period or (2) a systematic method that results in faster recognition.	Immediately recognized through OCI as part of the remeasurement component.
Calculation of the corridor	If an entity applies the deferral method and therefore recognizes actuarial gains and losses outside of the corridor, the lower and upper limits of the corridor are calculated as 10 percent of the greater of the projected benefit obligation or the market-related value of plan assets, which is either the fair value or a calculated value that incorporates asset-related gains and losses over a period of no more than five years.	The corridor approach has been eliminated. All changes in defined benefit obligations and plan assets are recognized immediately when they occur.

Expected return on plan assets	Measurement is based on the market-related value of the plan assets, which is either fair value or a calculated value that incorporates asset-related gains and losses over a period of no more than five years.	Not applicable (implicitly determined by net interest component calculation).
Recognition of gains/losses on a curtailment	A curtailment loss is recognized when it is probable that a curtailment will occur and the effects are reasonably estimable. A curtailment gain is recognized when the relevant employees are terminated or the plan suspension or amendment is adopted, which could occur after the entity is demonstrably committed and a curtailment is announced. The significance test is based on the number of years of service eliminated, not the number of employees.	Gains/losses are recognized as of the earlier the date of curtailment occurs or related restructuring costs or termination benefits are recognized. Amounts are included in past service cost as part of the service cost component.
Disclosure objectives	Not specifically defined.	Disclosures should: • Explain the characteristics and related risks of defined benefit plans. • Identify and explain the amounts in the financial statements. • Describe how defined benefit plans may affect the future cash flows.

CHAPTER 28

NOT-FOR-PROFIT ORGANIZATIONS

Richard F. Larkin, CPA

BDO USA, LLP

28.1 NOT-FOR-PROFIT ACCOUNTING ENVIRONMENT **2**

(a) Current Status of Accounting Principles 2
  (i) Decisions 6
  (ii) AICPA Audit Guides and Other Guidance 7
  (iii) Projects in Process 7
(b) Government Audit Requirements 11

28.2 NOT-FOR-PROFIT ACCOUNTING PRINCIPLES AND REPORTING PRACTICES **11**

(a) Principal Accounting and Reporting Requirements 11
(b) Basis of Accounting: Cash or Accrual 13
(c) Fund Accounting 14
  (i) Relationship of Funds and Classes 14
(d) Reclassifications 15
(e) Appropriations 15
(f) Fixed Assets 16
  (i) Fixed Assets Where Title May Revert to Grantors 17
(g) Depreciation 17
(h) Investments and Investment Income 17
  (i) Investment Income 18
  (ii) Gains and Losses on Investments 18
(i) Contributions 20
  (i) Expendable Support 20
  (ii) Gifts in Kind 22
  (iii) Support Not Currently Expendable 25
  (iv) Transfers of Assets to a Not-for-Profit Organization or Charitable Trust That Raises or Holds Contributions for Others (SFAS No. 136; ASC Topics 958-605 and -20) 30
(j) Taxes 31
(k) Related Organizations 35
  (i) Definition of the *Reporting Entity* 35
  (ii) Pass-Through Gifts 37
(l) Mergers and Acquisitions 39
(m) Cash Flows 41
(n) Governmental versus Nongovernmental Accounting 42

28.3 SPECIFIC TYPES OF ORGANIZATIONS **42**

(a) Voluntary Health and Welfare Organizations 42
  (i) Financial Statements 42
  (ii) Balance Sheet 43
  (iii) Statement of Support, Revenue and Expenses, and Changes in Net Assets 46
  (iv) Statement of Cash Flows 49
  (v) Statement of Functional Expenses 50
(b) Colleges and Universities 50
  (i) Fund Accounting 50
  (ii) Encumbrance Accounting 51
(c) Other Not-for-Profit Organizations 51
  (i) Accounting Principles 51

The author wishes to acknowledge that the exhibits and inspiration for this work were derived from *Financial and Accounting Guide for Not-for-Profit Organizations,* 6th ed., (New York: John Wiley & Sons, 2000) by PricewaterhouseCoopers LLP, Malvern J. Gross Jr., Richard F. Larkin, and John H. McCarthy.

28.4 AUDIT CONSIDERATIONS FOR A NOT-FOR-PROFIT ORGANIZATION 51

(a) General Considerations 51
(b) Internal Control 51
(c) Materiality 51
(d) Taxes 52
(e) Consolidation 52
(f) Compliance Auditing 52
(g) Investments 52
(h) Unique Auditing Areas 53

28.5 SOURCES AND SUGGESTED REFERENCES 53

APPENDIX 28.1: FACTORS TO BE CONSIDERED IN DISTINGUISHING CONTRACTS FOR THE PURCHASE OF GOODS OR SERVICES FROM RESTRICTED GRANTS 55

APPENDIX 28.2: FACTORS TO BE CONSIDERED IN ASSESSING WHETHER CONTRIBUTED SERVICES REQUIRE SPECIALIZED SKILLS 56

APPENDIX 28.3: LIST OF FACTORS TO BE CONSIDERED IN DETERMINING WHETHER AN ORGANIZATION WOULD TYPICALLY NEED TO PURCHASE SERVICES IF NOT PROVIDED BY DONATION 57

APPENDIX 28.4: FACTORS TO BE CONSIDERED IN ASSESSING WHETHER A DONOR HAS MADE A BONA FIDE PLEDGE TO A DONEE 59

APPENDIX 28.5: LIST OF FACTORS TO BE CONSIDERED IN DECIDING WHETHER A GIFT OR PLEDGE SUBJECT TO DONOR STIPULATIONS IS CONDITIONAL OR RESTRICTED 60

APPENDIX 28.6: CONSIDERATION OF WHETHER ITEMS MAY BE REPORTED AS OPERATING OR NONOPERATING 63

APPENDIX 28.7: NOT-FOR-PROFIT ACCOUNTING LITERATURE: CROSS-REFERENCES BETWEEN THE ASC TOPICS AND PREVIOUS GUIDANCE 64

28.1 NOT-FOR-PROFIT ACCOUNTING ENVIRONMENT

Nongovernmental not-for-profit organizations range from the large and complex to the small and simple. They include hospitals, colleges and universities, voluntary social service organizations, religious organizations, associations, foundations, and cultural institutions. All face accounting and reporting challenges. Currently all are covered by authoritative accounting literature. This chapter discusses not-for-profit accounting and reporting conventions and examines accounting pronouncements, auditing concerns, and the regulatory environment applicable to different types of not-for-profit organizations. Health care organizations are covered elsewhere in the *Handbook.*

As this latest edition of the *Handbook* goes to press, there are many issues within our community, including the accounting environment, that require all organizations, including not-for-profits, to adhere to accounting policies and principles with the utmost due diligence required to satisfy scrutinizing donors, the public, the media, and government regulators.

(a) CURRENT STATUS OF ACCOUNTING PRINCIPLES. Not-for-profit accounting has been undergoing a period of profound change. Since 1970, authoritative accounting principles and reporting practices have been established for many types of not-for-profit organizations, and many types of transactions, where no standards existed previously.

During the 1970s, the American Institute of Certified Public Accountants (AICPA) issued Industry Audit Guides for hospitals, for colleges and universities, and for voluntary health and welfare organizations, followed by Statement of Position (SOP) 78-10, *Accounting Principles and Reporting Practices for Certain Nonprofit Organizations.* SOP 78-10 defined accounting principles and reporting practices for all nongovernmental not-for-profit organizations not covered by the three earlier guides. (In 1990, the AICPA issued a new audit and accounting guide, *Audits of Providers of Health Care Service,* to replace the original hospital audit guide.)

These guides and the SOP had a dramatic effect on not-for-profit accounting, as they represented the first authoritative attempt to codify accounting principles and reporting practices for the not-for-profit industry. However, inconsistencies existed among the four guides, and they frequently contradicted one another on key accounting concepts. Also, the accounting principles presented in the guides had limited authority as they constituted generally accepted accounting procedures (GAAP) only until formal standards were set on this subject by the Financial Accounting Standards Board (FASB).

By the early 1980s, persons interested in not-for-profit accounting issues had identified these key areas of accounting that would have to be considered in unifying the diverse not-for-profit accounting practices:

- Reporting entity (when controlled and affiliated organizations should be included in an entity's financial statements)
- Depreciation
- Joint costs of multipurpose activities, particularly those involving a fundraising appeal (on what basis such costs should be divided among the various purposes served)
- Revenue recognition for expendable/restricted receipts (when, in which fund, and how such items should be reported as revenue)
- Display (what format should be used to present financial data)
- Valuation of investments
- Contributions (how these should be valued, when and how they should be reported)
- Grants awarded to others (when these should be accrued and expensed by the grantor)

Before accounting principles could be written, concepts had to be developed. The FASB had originally excluded not-for-profits from concepts development but later started a separate project for not-for-profits. The first concepts statement under this project was issued in 1980. Statement of Financial Accounting Concepts (SFAC) No. 4, *Objectives of Financial Reporting by Nonbusiness Organizations,* proved to be so similar to the corresponding statement for businesses, SFAC No. 1, *Objectives of Financial Reporting by Business Enterprises,* that the FASB started thinking in terms of only one set of concepts. Indeed, SFAC No. 2 was amended to include not-for-profits; SFAC No. 6, *Elements of Financial Statements,* covers both types of entities, although some parts of this Statement deal separately with the two sectors.

The FASB identified five areas in which it planned to develop accounting principles for not-for-profits:

1. Depreciation
2. Contributions
3. The reporting entity
4. Financial statement display
5. Investments

It has issued these Standards that have revolutionized not-for-profit accounting:

- Depreciation is the subject of SFAS No. 93, *Recognition of Depreciation by Not-for-Profit Organizations,* (now codified in Accounting Standards Codification (ASC) Topic 958-360). Effective in 1990, this Statement requires all not-for-profits to depreciate long-lived tangible assets. However, museum collections and similar assets often considered to be inexhaustible need not be depreciated if verifiable evidence of their inexhaustibility is available.
- Accounting for contributions received and made and for museum collections is the subject of FASB Statement No. 116, *Accounting for Contributions Received and Contributions Made* (ASC Topic 958-605), effective beginning in 1995. It requires a number of significant changes to accounting practices previously followed by many not-for-profit organizations. It requires immediate revenue recognition for all unconditional gifts and pledges, regardless of the presence of donor restrictions and regardless of the intended period of payment (pledges payable in future periods will be discounted to PV [PV]). Donors will follow a similar policy for recording expenses and liabilities. Donated services of volunteers will be recorded by charities if certain criteria are met. Museum collection items will be capitalized unless certain criteria are met.

  The requirement for immediate recognition of revenue for purpose and time restricted gifts results from FASB's conclusion in SFAC No. 6 that unspent expendable restricted gifts do not normally meet the definition of a liability (deferred revenue).

- Financial statement format was the subject of initial work by an AICPA task force. FASB issued SFAS No. 117, *Financial Statements of Not-for-Profit Organizations,* (ASC Topic 958-205 to 230) on financial statement format in June 1993. It became effective in 1995, at the same time as the new standard on contributions (previous bullet).

In 1995, the FASB issued Statement of Financial Accounting Standards (SFAS) No. 124, *Accounting for Certain Investments Held by Not-for-Profit Organizations* (ASC Topic 958-320 to 325). Briefly, its requirements are that all marketable securities be reported at current value in the balance sheet and that unrealized losses be reported in the unrestricted class of net assets (absent donor restrictions or law which would require reporting losses in a restricted class). A more detailed summary of this Standard is at Sections 28.2(h and i)

Since these two Statements made the most significant changes in accounting principles for nonprofits, they are discussed separately.

SFAS No. 117, Financial Statements. Statement No. 117 , now codified in ASC Topics 958-205 to 968-230 requires organizations to present aggregated financial data: total assets, liabilities, net assets (fund balances), and change in net assets. Some not-for-profits already did but in the past, many did not do so. Organizations are free to present data disaggregated by classes of net assets (corresponding to funds), but, except for donor-restricted revenue, net assets, and change in net assets, no detail by class is explicitly required.

Three classes of net assets are defined: unrestricted, temporarily restricted, and permanently restricted. Net assets of the two restricted classes are created *only* by donor-imposed restrictions on their use. All other net assets, including board-designated or appropriated amounts, are legally unrestricted and must be reported as part of the unrestricted class, although they may be identified separately within that class as designated if the organization wishes.

Permanently restricted net assets consist mainly of amounts restricted by donors as permanent endowments. Some organizations may also have certain capital assets on which donors have placed perpetual restrictions. Temporarily restricted net assets often contain a number of different types of donor-restricted amounts; these include:

- Unspent purpose-restricted expendable gifts for operating purposes
- Pledges payable in future periods
- Unspent explicitly time-restricted gifts
- Unspent amounts restricted for the acquisition of capital assets
- Certain capital assets
- Unmatured annuity and life income funds
- Term endowments

One requirement that was a significant change for many organizations is the reporting of all expenses in the unrestricted class, regardless of the source of the financing of the expenses. As expendable restricted revenue is reported in the temporarily restricted class, when these amounts are spent, a reclassification (transfer) is made to match the restricted revenue with the unrestricted expenses.

A second requirement is that all capital gains or losses on investments and other assets or liabilities are to be reported in the unrestricted class, no matter which class holds the underlying assets/liabilities, unless there are explicit donor restrictions, or applicable law, which require the reporting of some or all of the capital gains/losses in a restricted class. This practice often has the effect of increasing the reported unrestricted net asset balance (and decreasing the other net asset balances), compared with previous reporting principles.

All organizations must report expenses by functional categories (program, management, fundraising). Voluntary health and welfare organizations must also report expenses by natural categories (salaries, rent, travel, etc.) in a matrix format; other organizations are encouraged to do so. Reporting in functional categories is new for some organizations, mainly those that do not raise significant amounts of contributions from the general public, such as trade associations, country clubs, and many local churches.

What was then a new financial statement for many organizations is a statement of cash flows, showing where the organization received and spent its cash. Cash flows will be reported in three categories: operating flows, financing flows (including receipt of nonexpendable contributions), and investing flows. SFAS No. 95, *Statement of Cash Flows* (ASC Topic 230) had already required this for businesses for several years

Statement No. 95 permits either of two basic methods for preparing the statement of cash flows: the "direct" or the "indirect" method. Briefly, the indirect method starts with the excess of revenues over expenses and reconciles this number to operating cash flows. The direct method reports operating cash receipts and cash disbursements, directly adding these to arrive at operating cash flows. The author believes that the direct method is much more easily understood by readers of financial statements and thus recommends its use.

Much of the information used to prepare a statement of cash flows is derived from data in the other two primary financial statements, some of it from the preceding year's statements. Thus, when planning to prepare this statement for the first time, it is helpful to start a year in advance so that the necessary prior-year data are available when needed.

Appendix C to Statement No. 117 shows sample financial statements, illustrating formats that contain the disclosures required.

SFAS No 116, Contributions. This document established one set of standards for all recipients of contributions, replacing the four different standards in the four AICPA audit guides. It also sets standards for donors of gifts; no explicit standards had existed, except for private foundations. For-profit organizations are also covered by this part of the document.

Certain types of transactions are not considered contributions: transactions that are in substance purchases of goods or services (even though they may be called grants) and transactions in which a recipient of a "gift" is merely acting as an agent or intermediary for, and passes the gift on to, another organization. Unfortunately, there is not much specific guidance for how to distinguish these two situations from real contributions; organizations will have to use judgment on a case-by-case basis. The discussion in Section 28.2(i) in this chapter will help users with these judgments.

SFAS No. 116 also discusses conditional promises to give (pledges). A conditional pledge is one that depends on the occurrence of some specified *uncertain* future event to become binding on the pledgor. Examples of such events are the meeting of a matching requirement by the pledgee or natural or man-made disasters, such as a flood or fire. The mere passage of time is not a condition. Note that the concept of a condition is completely separate from that of a restriction. Conditions relate to events that must occur prior to a pledge becoming binding on the pledgor; restrictions relate to limits on the use of a gift after receipt. Note that a gift or pledge can be both conditional *and* restricted if the donor so stipulates.

Unconditional pledges are recorded at the time verifiable evidence of the pledge is received by the donee. Conditional pledges are not recorded until the condition is met, at which time they become unconditional. Pledges payable in future periods are considered implicitly time restricted and are reported in the temporarily restricted class of net assets until they are due (exceptions are pledges for permanent endowment, which are reported in permanently restricted net assets, and pledges explicitly stated by the donor to be for the current period, which are reported in unrestricted net assets). Long-term pledges are also discounted to their PV to reflect the time value of money (in accordance with Accounting Principles Board (APB) Opinion No. 21). Accretion of the discount to par value is reported as contribution income. An allowance for estimated uncollectable pledges also is set up.

All contributions are reported as revenue, in the class of net assets (unrestricted, temporarily restricted, or permanently restricted) appropriate to any donor restrictions on the gift, at the time of receipt of the gift. The presence or absence of explicit or implicit donor-imposed time or purpose restrictions on the use of a gift do not affect the timing of revenue recognition, only the class of net assets in which they are reported. This principle was a significant change in practice for many organizations, which had previously deferred donor-restricted gifts and all pledges until a later period when the restriction was met or the pledge collected. The effect is to report higher net asset amounts, mainly in the temporarily restricted class, than under previous principles. This principle generated a lot of controversy between those who favored retaining the previous deferral method and advocates of the new Standard.

Accounting by donors for pledges and other contributions follows the same principles with respect to recognition and timing as the donees, although of course the accounting entries are reversed: expense instead of revenue, pledges payable instead of pledges receivable. Also, for-profit donors do not categorize their financial reports into net asset classes, because this concept applies only to not-for-profits.

Reporting the value of donated services of volunteers is required if either of two criteria is met: (1) the services create or enhance nonfinancial assets; or (2) the services require specialized skills, are provided by persons possessing those skills, and typically would otherwise have to be purchased by the recipient if volunteers were not available. If neither criterion is met, the services may not be recorded. Organizations need to consider which of their volunteer services meet either of the two criteria.

Another matter that was controversial during the process of developing SFAS No. 116 was the question of accounting for museum collections. An early FASB proposal was to require capitalization of such assets. After much discussion of the subject, FASB agreed to allow noncapitalization of these items, if certain conditions relating to the items were met and certain footnote disclosures made.

(i) Decisions. Organizations have a number of decisions to make[1] under SFAS Nos. 116 and 117. These are:

Restricted contributions:

- Do we wish to report restricted contributions whose restrictions are met in the same accounting period as that in which they are received as restricted or as unrestricted support?
- Do we wish to adopt a policy which implies that on gifts of long-lived assets, there exists a time restriction which expires over the useful life of the donated assets?

Basic financial statement format:

- What titles do we wish to use for the balance sheet and for the statement of activity? (No particular titles are required or precluded by SFAS No. 117.)
- Do we wish to present additional detail in the statement of financial position of assets and liabilities by class?
- Which of the sample formats for the statement of activities do we wish to follow?
- Do we wish to present a measure of "operations"? (See Appendix 28.6 for further guidance.)
- Do we wish to prepare the statement of cash flows using the direct or the indirect method?
- Do we wish to present comparative financial data for prior year(s)?

Classification of expenses:

- On the face of the statement of activities, do we wish to categorize expenses by functional or by natural classifications? (If expenses are categorized by natural classification in the statement of activities, the functional classification must be shown in a footnote.)
- If we are not required to disclose expenses in natural categories, do we wish to make such disclosure voluntarily?
- What categories (beyond the basic categories of program, management, fundraising, membership development), if any, do we wish to present?
- Do we wish to disclose the fair value of contributed services received but not recognized as revenues?

---

[1] Note that some of these options amount to the selection of an accounting policy. Therefore, they must be followed consistently for all such transactions and in all reporting periods and must be disclosed in a footnote.

Collection items:

- If our organization has assets that meet the definition of collection items in SFAS 116, do we wish to capitalize these assets or not?
- If we have not previously capitalized but now wish to capitalize these items, do we wish to do so retroactively or only prospectively?
- If we choose to capitalize these items retroactively, how do we wish to determine their value for this purpose?
- Do we wish to present nonmonetary information?
- Do we wish to retain our fund accounting system and convert our financial data to the class structure by worksheets prior to preparing the financial statements, or do we wish to convert our entire accounting system to reflect the three-class structure discussed in SFAS No. 117?

(ii) AICPA Audit Guides and Other Guidance. In 1996, the AICPA issued two new Audit Guides, one for health care organizations and one for all other not-for-profit organizations. These guides provide additional implementation guidance for FASB Statements—especially Nos. 116, 117, and 124—as well as other matters affecting not-for-profit organizations. Topics the Guides cover in particular detail include reporting of split-interest gifts and expenses. Its provisions are discussed throughout this chapter. Since that date the AICPA has issued an updated Guide each year to reflect "conforming changes" required as a result of changes in other accounting and auditing standards. As of 2011, the AICPA is in the process of fully revising and updating the Not-for-Profit Guides; a final document is expected within about two to three years.

The AICPA issues Technical Practice Aids (TPAs) to address questions it receives from practitioners. Preparers of not-for-profit organization financial statements should be familiar with the TPAs that are included in the AICPA publication *Technical Practice Aids* at Section 6140.

(iii) Projects in Process. As of late 2011, the FASB has completed work on the five nonprofit-specific projects it had identified in the 1980s. It is considering possible future changes in financial statement format for nonprofits. It is also considering possible changes to the accounting standard-setting process for nonpublic entities, including nonprofits. For the current status of these activities, refer to the FASB Web site at *www.fasb.org*.

The FASB is moving toward changing the accounting for many leases. This project will apply to all organizations, including nonprofits. It plans to require that all leases be accounted for in essentially the way "capital" leases are now—that is, by recording a liability for the PV of future lease payments, offset by an asset representing the right to future use of the property. While this will, in most cases, not change net assets, it may affect an organization's compliance with covenants often contained in debt and grant agreements, such as a requirement to maintain the ratio of debt to net assets at no higher than a stated level. By increasing liabilities (debt) while leaving net assets unchanged, this accounting change for leases may cause some organizations to violate such a covenant.

Another major project under way is about revenue recognition. This project will apply to accounting for business-type transactions and will not affect accounting for contributions. Most business-type transactions normally made by nonprofits, such as tuition, membership dues, performance ticket sales, admissions, patient fees, and the like, are not likely to be much affected by this project. It is possible that accounting for revenue under some government grants with multiple deliverables could be affected.

The FASB and its foreign counterpart, the International Accounting Standards Board, are working together to try to harmonize U.S. and international accounting standards. The existing international standards, known as IFRS (International Financial Reporting Standards), are in use in many foreign countries, and discussions are under way about possibly making them required in the United States as well, but only for public companies. Even if adopted for U.S. public companies, these standards are unlikely to be required for nonprofit organizations any time soon. IFRS currently has no standards specifically applicable to nonprofits.

Consolidations Policy and Procedures. The FASB has been considering a proposed Statement that would require business enterprises and not-for-profit organizations that control other entities to include those subsidiaries in their consolidated financial statements. *Control* would be defined as the nonshared decision-making ability of one entity to direct the policies and management that guide the ongoing activities of another entity so as to increase its benefits and limit its losses from that other entity's activities.

Several years ago, the FASB determined that it had insufficient support to complete this project. FASB members had difficulty agreeing on the definition of control. Accordingly, they suspended work in this area. Not-for-profit organizations cannot expect new guidance in the near future, so the current rules on SOP 94-3 (ASC Topic 958-810) remain applicable.

Fair Value Accounting. A major project of the past few years that is still ongoing involves guidance for measuring the fair value (FV; previously called market value or current value) of assets and liabilities.

Certain accounting standards require nonprofit organizations to use FV for certain transactions and balances; certain other accounting standards permit these organizations to use FV for certain other transactions and balances, as listed in the next table. Determination of FV is governed by Statement of Financial Accounting Standards (SFAS) No. 157, *Fair Value Measurements* (ASC Topic 820), issued in 2006, but note that SFAS No. 157 itself never mandates the use of FV. This section is not a complete discussion of all aspects of SFAS No. 157; it covers those aspects of SFAS No. 157 that are of particular concern or are unique to nonprofit organizations.

Nonprofit Organizations' Use of FV: Items for Which FV Accounting Is Required or Permitted After Initial Recording

Item	Method of Valuation	Comments
Balance sheet: Financial assets and liabilities		
Cash and equivalents	Face value (unless restricted by law, e.g., cash in a foreign country with restrictions on export of currency)	Face value is presumed to be FV
Investment securities covered by SFAS No. 124	Quoted market price (excluding purchase commission and fees, and without any blockage discount)	Already at FV, per SFAS No. 124
Non-SFAS No. 124 investments, except affiliates[a]	Various; also adjust for liquidity constraints, if any	Permitted alternative, per Appendix A to Chapter 8 of the AICPA *Audit Guide*
Investment in affiliates that do not meet criteria for consolidation (SOP 94-3)	Various; also adjust for liquidity constraints, if any	
Derivatives	Amount required to cancel the contract	Already at FV, per SFAS No. 133
Beneficial interests in irrevocable trusts held by a third party	PV of estimated future cash flows, using a current interest rate	Interest rate adjusted each period
Earned income receivable (sales, investment income)	Normally, FV	Discounted if long term
Contributions (pledges) receivable/payable	PV of estimated future cash flows, using a current interest rate	Interest rate adjusted each period
Loans receivable	PV of estimated future cash flows, using a current interest rate adjusted to reflect debtor's risk	Interest rate adjusted each period

(*Continues*)

Item	Method of Valuation	Comments
Loans payable	PV of estimated future cash flows, using a current interest rate adjusted to reflect debtor's risk	Interest rate adjusted each period
Deposits held by/for others	Normally, FV	Discounted if long term
Accounts payable and accrued expenses[b]	Normally, FV	Discounted if long term
Obligations under split-interest agreements	PV of estimated future cash flows, using a current interest rate	Interest rate adjusted each period
Notes and bonds payable	FV, adjusted for debtor's risk	
Statement of Activities:		
Contributions of property other than cash and investments:	(All contributions are initially recorded at FV, per SFAS No. 116)	(For cash and investments, see above)
Unrestricted		
Financial asset	(See above for the type of property)	
Nonfinancial asset	Appraised value	FV used for initial recording only
With a donor restriction as to use	Same as unrestricted, but see right column	See above for discussion
Forgiveness of debt	Carrying value of debt at time of forgiveness (see above)	
Donated service of volunteer	What the organization would otherwise have to pay for the service[c]	
Donated use of property	What the organization would otherwise have to pay for the use of the property[c]	

[a] Nonmarketable equity securities, property, collectables, mortgage notes, partnership interests, and so on.
[b] Other than compensation-related items and most obligations under leases
[c] Since SFAS No. 157 discusses only assets and liabilities, it provides no guidance for measuring the FV of these types of transactions, which do not affect the balance sheet. There is an open question as to whether FV is: (1) the amount the owner of the property or the provider of the service normally charges paying customers for similar property or services, or (2) the amount that the recipient organization would otherwise have paid to acquire the use of property or services of equal utility to the organization. The concept of an exit price cannot be applied since there is no market, real or implied, for such items; they are available only to the organization in question. For example, consider:

	Scenario	One possible method of valuation	Alternative possible method of valuation
Services	Experienced neurosurgeon volunteers to provide routine medical care in a charity clinic	High rate that neurosurgeon normally charges for highly skilled services?	Lower rate charity would otherwise have paid to hire a less experienced doctor?
Services	Experienced neurosurgeon volunteers to help paint church building	High rate that neurosurgeon normally charges for highly skilled medical services?	Much lower rate that church would pay teenager to help with painting?
Property	Property owner allows charity to use lavish property rent free	High rent owner charges for similar property?	Lower rent charity would have paid for less lavish property of equal utility to it?

The overall project objective is to develop a Statement that will establish a framework for applying the fair value measurement (FVM) objective in GAAP. The Statement, which will be developed in phases, will focus on how to measure FV, not what or when to measure at FV. The FASB plans to separately consider what to measure at FV on a project-by-project basis. Related objectives are to improve the consistency and comparability of the measurements, codify and simplify the guidance that currently exists for developing the measurements, and improve disclosures about the measurements.

Paragraph 5 defines FV as "the price that would be received to sell an asset or paid to transfer a liability in an orderly transaction between market participants at the measurement date." This is often called the exit price—that is, what you could sell an asset for, or what you would have to pay to transfer (as opposed to settle) a liability. The definition emphasizes the exchange price notion contained, either explicitly or implicitly, in the definitions of FV previously included in other AICPA and FASB definitions of FV. Consideration must be given to the market in which the asset may be sold or the liability transferred by judging what would be the principal or most advantageous market for the item.

SFAS No. 157 also requires the value to be based on the "highest and best use" of the item, regardless of whether that use is the one intended by the organization. Consider, for example, a donated painting that could be sold by the museum but will not be (assume that the museum does capitalize its collection) or a piece of undeveloped land that will be kept as a park. The fact that it will not be sold is irrelevant; FV is based on what a market participant—that is, a hypothetical buyer—of the painting or the land would pay for it if it were sold,. (But see the discussion following, of when a donor restriction exists that the specific painting or land may not ever be sold.)

Should the recorded FV of SFAS No. 124 securities include the purchase commission? Clearly it will not be recovered on sale (exit); thus it should not be part of the FV. Further, should the FV also be net of the inevitable sales commission, which, of course, will also not be collected in cash upon a future sale (exit)? Probably not, since that cost is an expense of the period of sale.

SFAS No. 157 mentions three valuation techniques:[2]

1. Market for identical or comparable items
2. Future income (discounted) (see also Appendix B to the Statement)
3. Replacement cost

It also mentions three levels of a hierarchy of inputs:

1. Quoted prices in active markets for identical items
2. Observable inputs other than quoted market prices
3. Unobservable inputs

It also gives an example (in an appendix to SFAS 157), of its application in a situation where a donor has placed a restriction on an asset that is donated. If the restriction it irrevocably linked to that particular asset, then the asset value should be adjusted to reflect any diminishment of value due to the restriction. However, if the restriction is linked only to the related net assets, then the value of the property is probably not affected by the restriction.

SFAS No. 157 also requires extensive disclosures about the methods used to determine FVs and changes in FVs, especially for those items valued using level 3 inputs.

Nonprofits are especially likely to need to apply this Statement in connection with:

- Noncash contributions received and made (includes both items that will be capitalized on the balance sheet, and donated services and use of property that flow through the income statement)
- Nonmarketable (so-called alternative) investments

[2] In some cases, two or all three techniques may need to be used in determining fair value.

- Any asset or liability for which the FV option is elected under SFAS No. 159 (ASC Topic 825)
- Assets and liabilities of an acquiree under the rules in SFAS No. 164 (ASC Topic 805)

Balance sheet items for which SFAS No. 159 (ASC Topic 825) is most likely to be elected, and that are likely to require additional effort to determine the FV, are pledges and loans receivable and payable. For long-term receivables and payables discounted to PV under APB Opinion No. 21, the effect of using FV is to unfreeze the interest rate used to compute the discount. Under APB Opinion No. 21, the interest rate is set at the inception of the agreement and is not changed over the life of the agreement; under SFAS No. 157, the interest rate is adjusted each period to a current rate.

Noncash contributions are required to be valued at FV by SFAS No. 116. Even if alternative investments are not reported at FV in the balance sheet, SFAS No. 107 may require disclosure of their FV in a footnote.

Since the issuance of SFAS No. 157, FASB has issued several amendments, involving clarification of the Statement, and disclosures. Several others are under development, including one that would require the use of FV for most financial assets and liabilities (with some exceptions—mainly for pledges, obligations under leases, and employee benefit obligations).

The AICPA has issued a white paper, *Measurement of Fair Value for Certain Transactions of Not-for-Profit Entities,* to help nonprofits measure the FV of these types of transactions:

- Unconditional promises to give cash or other financial assets
- Beneficial interests in trusts
- Split-interest agreements

These items are discussed in more detail in Section 28.2(i).

(b) GOVERNMENT AUDIT REQUIREMENTS. Not-for-profit entities are increasingly subject to audit requirements imposed by government agencies. These requirements are discussed in Subsection 28.4of this chapter.

28.2 NOT-FOR-PROFIT ACCOUNTING PRINCIPLES AND REPORTING PRACTICES

(a) PRINCIPAL ACCOUNTING AND REPORTING REQUIREMENTS. The various accounting standards discussed in this chapter affect the accounting and financial reporting of all types of not-for-profit organizations. A list of the most significant requirements follows.

ACCOUNTING FOR CONTRIBUTIONS

(See SFAS No. 116, SFAS No. 136, and the AICPA *Audit Guide,* codified in ASC Topic 958-605)

- Pledges are recorded when an unconditional promise to give is communicated to the donee.
- A conditional promise to give is not reported until the condition is met. (The distinction between conditional and restricted gifts is not always clear.)
- Pledges are discounted to their PV and are reported net of an allowance for the estimated uncollectable amount.
- All gifts, including pledges and restricted gifts, are reported as revenue when received.
- Donors (including for-profit donors) must follow the same rules as donees (in reverse—an unconditional pledge must be recorded as an expense and a liability when made). (Fundraisers

should take note of this, as it will affect some donors' willingness to make unconditional pledges.)

- Split-interest gifts are essentially treated as pledges (*Audit Guide,* Chapter 6); these include:
  - Gift annuities, remainder annuity trusts, unitrusts, pooled income funds (PIF), lead trusts.
  - Irrevocable trusts held by others are reported in the beneficiary's financial statements.
- Gifts in kind are recorded at FV—including property, use of property, equipment, inventory for sale or use, services by other organizations (including bargain purchases).
- Donated services of individual volunteers are recorded only when specified criteria are met:
  - The services create or enhance nonfinancial assets (building something), OR
  - The services require specialized skills, the volunteer possesses those skills, and the donee would typically have to purchase the services if the volunteer were not available. (In other words, the services involve a significant and central activity of the entity.)
- A pass-through entity may not be able to record gifts as revenue, depending on the circumstances of the gift.
- A museum does not have to capitalize its collection if certain criteria are met.
- New principles apply to transfers of cash or other financial assets from a donor to a recipient organization that agrees to use the assets on behalf of or transfer the assets to a specified beneficiary.
- If the recipient organization and the specified beneficiary are unaffiliated, the recipient organization reports the assets at FV and a liability of equal amount. However, if the donor explicitly grants the recipient organization variance power—unilateral power to redirect the use of the assets to another beneficiary—or if the recipient organization and the specified beneficiary are financially interrelated, the recipient organization reports the FV of the assets as a contribution received.
- A specified beneficiary reports its rights to the assets as an asset at FV while it has rights to the assets, unless the donor explicitly granted the recipient organization variance power. If the beneficiary and the recipient organization are financially interrelated, the beneficiary reports at FV its interest in the net assets of the recipient organization and adjusts that interest for its share of the change in net assets of the recipient organization. However, if the recipient organization is explicitly granted variance power, the specified beneficiary does not report its potential for receipts from the assets held by the recipient organization.

Financial Statement Format

(See SFAS No. 117 and the AICPA *Audit Guide,* codified in ASC Topic 958-205 to 230)

- Required disclosures are: totals of assets, liabilities, net assets, change in net assets.
- Net assets (formerly, fund balance) and revenue are categorized into three classes:
  - **a.** Unrestricted; temporarily restricted; permanently restricted (per donor restrictions only).
  - **b.** Restrictions imposed by nondonors do not change category (e.g., contracts).
  - **c.** Actions of an organization's governing board (such as designating certain assets as quasi-endowment) cannot create legal restrictions, because such actions can always be reversed.
- Required disclosures for each class are: net assets, change in net assets.
- A statement of cash flows is required. (The "direct" method is preferred.)
- All expenses are reported in the unrestricted class.
  - Temporarily restricted net assets are reclassified to match related expenses and the expiration of time restrictions.
- Expenses are reported on a functional basis (program, management, fundraising).
- Revenues and expenses are reported gross, not net (exception: investment management fees).
  - Related items (e.g., sales/cost of sales) may be shown as: gross, deduction, net.

- See Section 28.2(i) for treatment of capital gains/losses.
- Affiliated entities are combined if specified criteria are met (SOP No. 94-3):
  - For-profit affiliate: criteria based on ownership.
  - Not-for-profit affiliate: criteria based on control and economic interest.

ACCOUNTING FOR INVESTMENTS

(See SFAS No. 117 and SFAS No. 124)

- Marketable securities are reported at current market value.
- Capital gains and losses on endowment are reported mostly in the unrestricted class, unless state law or a donor stipulation specifies otherwise.

OTHER MATTERS

- Depreciable assets must be depreciated (see SFAS No. 93).
- Not-for-profits must follow requirements of generally accepted accounting principles (GAAP; see SOP No. 94-2).
- Joint costs of multipurpose activities can be allocated to program functions only if certain criteria are met:
  - Purpose; audience; content, including an explicit call to action other than giving—see SOP No. 98-2, ASC Topic 958-720).
- Contribution rules in SFAS No. 116 do not affect the timing of revenue recognition for advance payments of earned income: dues, fees, sales, season tickets, and so on. These are still deferred until earned.

(b) BASIS OF ACCOUNTING: CASH OR ACCRUAL. Not-for-profit organizations frequently maintain their records on a cash basis, a bookkeeping process that reflects only transactions involving cash. Most commercial organizations, as well as many medium and large not-for-profit organizations, however, keep accounts on an accrual basis. In accrual-basis accounting, income is recognized when earned and expenses are recognized when incurred. For bookkeeping purposes, either basis is acceptable.

Each accounting basis has certain advantages. The principal advantage of cash basis accounting is simplicity—its procedures are easy to learn and easy to execute. Because of this simplicity, a cash-basis accounting system is less complicated and less expensive to maintain than an accrual-basis system. A less complicated system will be easier for a volunteer bookkeeper who does not feel comfortable with the more complicated accrual methods. Because there is often no material difference in financial results between cash- and accrual-basis accounting for small organizations, the incremental cost of an accrual-basis system may be unwarranted. In addition, many not-for-profit organizations think it more prudent to keep their books on a cash basis. Often they do not want to recognize income prior to the actual receipt of cash.

The principal advantage of accrual-basis accounting is that it portrays financial position and results of operations on a more realistic basis—a complex organization with accounts receivable and bills outstanding can present realistic financial results only on the accrual basis. In addition, accrual-basis accounting usually achieves a better matching of revenue and related expenses. Also, many individuals who use the financial statements of not-for-profit organizations, such as bankers, local businesspeople, and board members, often are more familiar with accrual-basis accounting.

Organizations wanting the accuracy of accrual-basis accounting but not wishing to sacrifice the simplicity of cash-basis bookkeeping have alternatives. They can maintain their books on a cash basis and at year-end record all payables, receivables, and accruals. These adjustments would permit presentation of accrual-basis financial statements.

An organization can also keep its books on a cash basis, except for certain transactions that are recorded on an accrual basis. A popular type of modified cash-basis accounting is to record accounts payable as liabilities are incurred but to record income on a cash basis as received.

Another type of modified cash-basis accounting is to record unrealized changes in value of an investment portfolio.

(c) FUND ACCOUNTING. Fund accounting is the process of segregating resources into sets of self-balancing accounts on the basis of either restrictions imposed by donors or designations imposed by governing boards.

In the past, most not-for-profit organizations followed fund accounting procedures in accounting for resources. This was done because many organizations regard fund accounting as the most appropriate means of exercising stewardship over funds. Reporting all the details of funds, however, is not required of all not-for-profit organizations, and in many cases it is not recommended. Fund accounting, if carried to its logical extreme, requires a separate set of accounts for each restricted gift or contribution; this leads to confusing financial statements that often present an organization as a collection of individual funds rather than as a single entity. Today, many not-for-profit organizations are combining funds and eliminating fund distinctions for reporting purposes to facilitate financial statement users' understanding of the organization as a whole.

The FASB Standard on financial reporting (SFAS No. 117) specifically requires the reporting of certain financial information by what it calls "classes" rather than funds.

An infinite variety of funds is possible. To limit the number of funds reported, broad fund classifications may be used. One scheme commonly used today is classification of resources by type of donor restriction. Another criterion for classifying funds is the degree of control an organization possesses over its resources. Under this approach, funds are combined for reporting purposes into two groupings: unrestricted and restricted. A third approach classifies resources on the basis of their availability for current expenditure on an organization's programs. Under this approach, funds are combined into two categories: expendable and nonexpendable.

When resources are classified by type of donor restriction, four fund groupings are commonly used: current unrestricted, current restricted, endowment, and fixed asset funds.

The current unrestricted fund contains assets over which the board has total managerial discretion. This fund includes unrestricted contributions, revenue, and other income and can be used in any manner at any time to further the goals of the organization. For all not-for-profit organizations, "board-designated" funds should be included with current unrestricted funds. Board-designated funds are voluntary segregations of unrestricted fund balances approved by the board for specific future projects or purposes.

Current restricted funds are resources given to an organization to be expended for specific operating purposes.

Endowment funds are amounts donated to an organization with the legal restriction that the principal be maintained inviolate either in perpetuity or for a stated period of time, as well as amounts set aside by the organization's governing board for long-term investment—referred to as quasi-endowment. Investment income on such funds is generally unrestricted and should be reported in the current unrestricted fund. Occasionally endowment gifts stipulate restricted uses for the investment income, and such restricted income should be reported in the appropriate fund.

The fixed asset fund represents the land, buildings, and equipment owned by an organization. Since these assets are usually unrestricted in the sense that the board can employ (or dispose of) them in any manner it wishes to further the goals of the organization, fixed assets need not be reported in a separate fund and may be reported as part of the current unrestricted fund.

(i) Relationship of Funds and Classes. Under SFAS No. 117, organizations must analyze each component of each fund on an individual basis to determine into which class that fund balance (net assets) should be classified. The assessment regarding temporarily and permanently restricted classes is based only on the presence or absence of donor-imposed restrictions. All funds without donor-imposed restrictions must be classified as unrestricted, regardless of the existence of any board designations or appropriations.

The next table shows typical classes into which various types of fund balances normally are classified.

Funds	Unrestricted	Temporarily Restricted	Permanently Restricted
Endowment	Quasi	Term	Permanent
Specific purpose or current restricted	Board designated	Donor restricted	N/A
Loan	Board designated	Donor restricted[a]	Revolving[a]
Split interest (annuity, life income, etc.)	Voluntary excess reserves	Unmatured	Permanent[b]
Fixed asset	Expended;[c] board designated	Donor-restricted unexpended; Expended donated	See note d
General/Operating	Unrestricted	Donor-time restricted	N/A
Custodian	All (on balance sheet only)[e]	N/A	N/A

[a] A permanently restricted loan fund is one where only the income can be loaned, or, if the principal can be loaned, repayments of principal by borrowers are restricted to be used for future loans. A loan fund in which principal repayments are available for any use would be temporarily restricted until the loans are repaid, at which time such amounts would become unrestricted.
[b] For example, an annuity fund that, upon maturity, becomes a permanent endowment.
[c] Expended donor-restricted plant funds will be either unrestricted or temporarily restricted, depending on the organization's choice of accounting principle under paragraph 16 of SFAS No. 116.
[d] Fixed assets could be permanently restricted if a donor has explicitly restricted the proceeds from any future disposition of the assets to reinvestment in fixed assets. Museum collection items received subject to a donor's stipulation that they be preserved and not sold might also be considered permanently restricted, as might undeveloped land restricted in perpetuity as a nature preserve.
[e] Note that because no transactions related to custodian funds are reported in the income statement of the holder of the assets, and because there is never a fund balance amount (assets are always exactly offset by liabilities), reporting of such funds as separate items becomes an issue only when a balance sheet is disaggregated into classes. The logic for reporting the assets and liabilities of custodian funds in the unrestricted class is that such assets are not the result of donor-restricted gifts, which is a requirement for recording items in one of the restricted classes.

(d) RECLASSIFICATIONS. The use of fund accounting necessitates transfers in some situations to allocate resources between funds or classes. Financial statement readers often find it difficult to understand such reclassifications. In addition, if not properly presented, reclassifications may give the impression that an organization is willfully manipulating amounts reported as income.

To minimize confusion and the appearance of deception, transfers must not be shown as either income or expenses of the transferring fund. Reclassifications of the total organization are merely an internal reallocation of resources and in no way result in income or expense recognition.

Columnar statements, which present the activity of each class in separate, side-by-side columns, facilitate clear, comprehensive presentation of reclassifications.

(e) APPROPRIATIONS. Appropriations (or designations) are internal authorizations to expend resources in the future for specific purposes. They are neither expenditures nor legal obligations. When appropriation accounting is followed, appropriated amounts should be set aside in a separate account as part of the unrestricted (or possible temporarily restricted) net assets of an organization.

Appropriation accounting is both confusing and subject to abuse. It is confusing because *appropriation* is an ambiguous term, and many readers do not understand that it is neither a current expenditure nor a binding obligation for a future expenditure. It is subject to abuse because, when treated incorrectly, appropriations can appear to reduce the current year's excess of revenue over expenses to whatever level the board wants. The board can then, at a later date, restore "appropriated" funds to the general use of the organization. (Governments regularly use appropriation accounting for internal reporting, however.)

The use of appropriation accounting is not recommended. If an organization wishes to follow appropriation accounting techniques and wants to conform with GAAP, it must be certain that appropriations are not presented as expenses and that they appear only as part of the net assets of the organization. Expenses incurred out of appropriated funds should be charged as expenses in the year incurred, and the related appropriations should be reversed once an expense has been incurred.

Disclosure in notes is an alternative to appropriation accounting. Under this approach, an organization does not refer to appropriations in the body of its financial statements but instead discloses such amounts only in notes to the financial statements.

Note that it is not logically possible to "appropriate" more net assets that the organization has.

(f) FIXED ASSETS. Treatment of fixed assets sometimes is a perplexing accounting issue for not-for-profit organizations. There are three reasons why some not-for-profit organizations have historically not recorded a value for fixed assets on their balance sheets.

1. Many not-for-profit organizations have not been as interested in matching income and expenses as are businesses. In this case, management has felt no compelling need to record assets and then charge depreciation expense against current income.
2. The principal asset of some not-for-profit organizations is real estate that often was acquired many years previously. In these inflationary times, many organizations do not wish to carry at cost and depreciate assets now worth several times their original purchase price.
3. Many not-for-profit organizations plead poverty as a means of raising funds. By not recording fixed assets, they appear less substantial than they in fact are.

Confusion concerning fixed assets had been heightened by lack of a universally accepted treatment for fixed assets. Historically, there were three common methods for handling fixed assets: immediate write-off, capitalization (with or without depreciation), and write-off followed by capitalization.

Immediate write-off is the simplest method of treating fixed assets and is often used by small organizations and those on a cash basis. Under this method, an organization expenses fixed asset purchases immediately through the statement of income and expenses.

The principal advantage of this approach is simplicity—the bookkeeping complexities of capitalization are avoided, and the amount of excess revenue over expenses reported on the statement of income and expenses more closely reflects the amount of spendable money at the board's disposal.

The major disadvantage of immediate write-off is that the historical costs of an organization's fixed assets are not recorded, and the balance sheet does not present the true net worth of the organization. Another disadvantage is that expensing fixed assets may produce fluctuations in net income that are largely unrelated to operations. Finally, this approach does not conform with GAAP.

A second alternative available to an organization is to capitalize all major fixed asset purchases. Under this approach, significant fixed assets are included on the organization's balance sheet.

The principal advantage of this approach is that it conforms with GAAP and permits an auditor to express an unqualified opinion on an organization's financial statements. It also documents the amount of assets the organization controls, permitting evaluation of management performance, and allows the organization to follow depreciation accounting.

The major disadvantage of capitalization is that it renders financial statements more complex. An unsophisticated statement reader may conclude that an organization has more funds available for current spending than it actually has.

A third alternative is to immediately write off fixed asset purchases on the statement of income and expenses and then capitalize these assets on the balance sheet. This method permits an organization to report expenditures for fixed asset purchases on the statement of income and expenses, thus offsetting any excess of income over expenses that may have been caused by contributions received for fixed assets on its balance sheet.

However, this approach is very confusing, is inconsistent with other accounting conventions, does not permit depreciation accounting in a traditional sense, and does not constitute GAAP. Accordingly, the use of this approach is strongly discouraged.

(i) Fixed Assets Where Title May Revert to Grantors. Some organizations purchase or receive fixed assets under research or similar grants which provide that, at the completion of the grant period, the right of possession of these fixed assets technically reverts to the grantor. If the grantor is not expected to ask for their return, a fixed asset, whether purchased or donated, should be recorded as an asset and depreciated as with any other asset over its useful life (which may be the period of the grant, if it has no alternative use).

(g) DEPRECIATION. Depreciation has been as thorny a problem for not-for-profit organizations as the problem of fixed assets. If an organization capitalizes fixed assets, it is immediately confronted with the question of whether it should depreciate them: that is, allocate the cost over the estimated useful life of the assets.

Depreciation accounting is now a GAAP practice for not-for-profit organizations. SFAS No. 93 (ASC Topic 958-360), requires not-for-profit organizations to record depreciation on depreciable fixed assets. Many arguments in favor of recording depreciation, such as the next ones, are valid for not-for-profit organizations:

- Depreciation is a cost of operations. Organizations cannot accurately measure the cost of providing a product or service (whether funded by contributions or by earned income) or determine a fair price without including this cost component.
- Most organizations replace at least some fixed assets out of recurring income. If depreciation is not recorded, an organization may think that its income is sufficient to cover costs when, in reality, it is not.
- If depreciation is not recorded, income may fluctuate widely from year to year, depending on the timing of asset replacement and the replacement cost of assets.
- Organizations that are "reimbursed" by a government agency for the sale of goods or services must depreciate fixed assets if they wish to recapture all costs incurred.
- Some not-for-profit organizations pay federal income tax on "unrelated business income." Depreciation can and should be reported as an expense to reduce income subject to tax.

Depreciation is computed in the same manner as that used by commercial enterprises. Depreciation is reported as an item of expense on the statement of income and expenses, and accumulated depreciation is reported under the fixed assets caption on the balance sheet.

If fixed asset purchases are capitalized but not written down through regular depreciation charges in the statement of income and expenses, it may be necessary to periodically write down their carrying value so that the balance sheet is not overstated. The preferred method of achieving this is to report the write-down as an expense on the statement of income and expenses and to reduce the asset value on the balance sheet.

(h) INVESTMENTS AND INVESTMENT INCOME. SFAS No. 124 (ASC Topic 958-320 and 205) was issued in 1995. Its requirements include:

Equity securities that have readily determinable fair market values and all debt securities shall be reported at current FV. (SFAS No. 124 does not prescribe accounting for other investments; those are covered in Chapter 8 of the AICPA *Audit Guide* [ASC Topic 958-325].)

- In the absence of donor stipulations or law to the contrary:
  - Capital losses reduce temporarily restricted net assets to the extent that donor-imposed restrictions on net appreciation of the fund have not yet been met.
  - Any remaining loss reduces unrestricted net assets.
  - Gains that restore previous losses are reported in the unrestricted class.

Even when investments are carried at cost, if market value declines "permanently" below cost, the carrying value of these investments should be written down to the market value. This is accomplished by setting up a "provision for decline in market value of investments" in the statement of income and expenses in the same section where realized gains or losses are presented.

(i) Investment Income. Dividends and interest earned on unrestricted investment funds, including board-designated funds, should be reported as income in the unrestricted class.

All investment income earned on donor-restricted endowment funds should initially be reported as income directly in the temporarily restricted class. Then when unrestricted income is appropriated for expenditure, it is reclassified to the unrestricted class. This is required by FASB Staff Position (FSP) No. 117-1, *Endowments of Not-for-Profit Organizations: Net Asset Classification of Funds Subject to an Enacted Version of the Uniform Prudent Management of Institutional Funds Act, and Enhanced Disclosures for All Endowment Funds* (ASC Topic 958-205), and is a change from previous practice. This is discussed further below in Subsection ii below.

Restricted investment income should be reported directly in the appropriate restricted fund. For example, if the donor of an endowment fund gift specifies that the investment income be used for a particular purpose, investment income should be reported directly in the temporarily restricted class (rather than the unrestricted or the permanently restricted class). An exception to this is if the organization has adopted the practice of reporting restricted contributions whose restrictions are met in the same period as received as unrestricted revenue, in which case temporarily restricted investment income is reported the same way. Investment income that is required by the donor to be reinvested in the permanent endowment is reported directly in that class.

(ii) Gains and Losses on Investments. SFAS No. 117 and No. 124 (ASC Topic 958-205 and 225) require organizations to report capital gains on endowment funds in essentially the same way as investment income, with one exception. The exception is that all states (and Washington, DC) have laws regulating the legal status of capital gains on donor-restricted endowments. Accordingly, in accounting for such gains, organizations must consider both donor restrictions (if any) and state law(s) to which the organization is subject.

For investments carried at market, gains and losses are recognized on a continuing basis. While it is permitted to report gains separately from losses and to report realized gains/losses separately from unrealized gains/losses, the author recommends that all gains or losses should be reported together in a single caption: net increase (decrease) in carrying value of investments.

A question may arise as to where in the statement of income and expenses investment income and capital gains/losses should be reported. SFAS No. 117 and No. 124 are quite permissive in this regard (the only requirement is that all income, gains, and losses must be reported above the caption change in net assets), and practice varies. Any of these methods are acceptable:

- All investment return (dividends and interest, and realized and unrealized gains) on one line in the revenue section of the statement of activity. The amount might be negative if major losses have been sustained. (If this happens, a footnote must disclose major components of the amount.)
- Investment income and gains on two or more lines in the revenue section—for example, dividend and interest income, realized gains (losses), unrealized gains (losses).
- Investment income and realized gains (losses) in the revenue section, and unrealized gains (losses) below an operating subtotal.
- Investment income only in the revenue section, and all capital gains (losses) below an operating subtotal.
- All investment return below and operating subtotal
- If the organization uses a total return approach to managing its investments, the expendable return per the client's formula (e.g., 5 percent of asset value) in the revenue section, and the difference between that amount and the actual total return down below an operating subtotal Again, this difference may be negative.

In 2008, FASB Staff Position (FSP) No. 117-1 (ASC Topic 958-205), was issued in response to the adoption of the new Uniform Prudent Management of Institutional Funds Act (UPMIFA) by many states to replace the old UMIFA.

There are two main parts to the document:

1. A conclusion as to net asset classification under UPMIFA
2. Enhanced disclosures that affect all nonprofits, whether they are in a jurisdiction that has adopted UPMIFA or not, and all endowments, whether donor restricted or not

Net Asset Classification. Paragraph 5 of FSP No. 117-1 provides:

> A not-for-profit organization that is subject to an enacted version of UPMIFA shall classify a portion of a donor-restricted endowment fund of perpetual duration as permanently restricted net assets. Consistent with paragraph 14 of FASB Statement No. 116, *Accounting for Contributions Received and Contributions Made,* and paragraph 22 of FASB Statement No. 117, *Financial Statements of Not-for-Profit Organizations,* the amount classified as permanently restricted shall be the amount of the fund (a) that must be retained permanently in accordance with explicit donor stipulations, or (b) that in the absence of such stipulations, the organization's governing board determines must be retained (preserved) permanently consistent with the relevant law.

This may or may not require any reclassification of previous amounts. Note the reference to the governing board's interpretation of the law. Presumably organizations will wish to obtain legal advice on this point.

Paragraph 8 of FSP No. 117-1 provides:

> For each donor-restricted endowment fund for which the restriction described in subsection 4(a) of UPMIFA is applicable, a not-for-profit organization shall classify the portion of the fund that is not classified as permanently restricted net assets as temporarily restricted net assets (time restricted) until appropriated for expenditure by the organization.

This paragraph was a departure from previous practice used by many organizations. It required that some organizations reclassify certain amounts from unrestricted to temporarily restricted net assets (per Paragraph 17 of the document).

Enhanced Disclosures. The proposed disclosures are quite extensive and are set forth in Paragraphs 11 and 12 of FSP No. 117-1:

> 11. At a minimum, an organization shall disclose the following information for each period for which the organization presents financial statements:
>
> **a.** A description of the governing board's interpretation of the law(s) that underlies the organization's net asset classification of donor-restricted endowment funds.
>
> **b.** A description of the organization's policy(ies) for the appropriation of endowment assets for expenditure (its endowment spending policy(ies)).
>
> **c.** A description of the organization's endowment investment policies. The description shall include the organization's return objectives and risk parameters; how those objectives relate to the organization's endowment spending policy(ies); and the strategies employed for achieving those objectives.
>
> **d.** The composition of the organization's endowment by net asset class at the end of the period, in total and by type of endowment fund, showing donor-restricted endowment funds separately from board-designated endowment funds.
>
> **e.** A reconciliation of the beginning and ending balance of the organization's endowment, in total and by net asset class, including, at a minimum, the following line items (as applicable): investment return, separated into investment income (for example, interest, dividends, rents) and net appreciation or depreciation of investments; contributions; amounts appropriated for expenditure; reclassifications; and other changes.

12. In accordance with the requirements of Statements 117 and 124, an organization also shall provide information about the net assets of its endowment funds, including:

a. The nature and types of permanent restrictions or temporary restrictions (paragraphs 14 and 15 of Statement 117)

b. The aggregate amount of the deficiencies for all donor-restricted endowment funds for which the fair value of the assets at the reporting date is less than the level required by donor stipulations or law (paragraph 15(d) of Statement 124).

Appendix C to FSP No. 117-1 contains illustrative disclosures.

Organizations with endowment funds, whether donor restricted or board designated, need to gather the information needed to make these disclosures, as doing so may require changes to how data are accumulated and summarized by an organization's accounting system.

Note that each state's version of UPMIFA should be reviewed for its applicability in that state. Organizations may need to determine to which state's law they are subject. (Depending on the state where they are incorporated and/or the state where a fund or trust is managed, this may not necessarily be the state where their administrative office is located.)

(i) CONTRIBUTIONS. Support for a not-for-profit organization can be received in many different forms. Each of the types of contributions is discussed in this chapter.

(i) Expendable Support

Unrestricted Contributions. Unrestricted gifts, such as cash, pledges, gifts of securities, and gifts of equipment and supplies, are discussed throughout this entire subsection. The general principles discussed here apply to all unrestricted gifts, in whatever form received.

All unrestricted contributions should be reported in the unrestricted class of net assets in a statement of income and expenses or, if a combined statement of income, expenses, and changes in net assets is used, such unrestricted contributions should be shown before arriving at the excess of income over expenses caption. It is *not acceptable* to report unrestricted contributions in a separate statement of changes in net assets or to report such gifts in a restricted class of net assets.

Bargain Purchases. Organizations are sometimes permitted to purchase goods or services at a reduced price that is granted by the seller in recognition of the organization's charitable or educational status. In such cases, the seller has effectively made a gift to the buyer. This gift should be recorded as such if the amount is significant. For example, if a charity buys a widget for $50 that normally sells for $80, the purchase should be recorded at $80, with the $30 difference being reported as a contribution.

It is important to record only true gifts in this way. If a lower price is really a normal discount available to any buyer who requests it, then there is no contribution. Such discounts include quantity discounts, normal trade discounts, promotional discounts, special offers, or lower rates (say, for professional services) to reflect the seller's desire to utilize underused staff or sale prices to move slow-moving items off the shelves.

Current Restricted Contributions. Current restricted contributions are contributions that can be used to meet the current expenses of the organization, although restricted to use for some specific purpose or during or after some specified time. An example of the former would be a gift "for cancer research" (a purpose restriction) and, of the latter, a gift "for your 20XX activities" (a time restriction). In practice, the distinction between restricted gifts and unrestricted gifts is not always clear. In many cases, the language used by the donor leaves doubt as to whether there really is a restriction on the gift.

Current restricted contributions cause reporting problems, in part because the accounting profession took a long time to resolve the appropriate accounting and reporting treatment for these types of gifts. In the past, different types of organizations used different methods of recording such gifts. The resolution arrived at is controversial because many believe it is not the most desirable method of accounting for such gifts.

The principal accounting problem is one of timing and relates to the question of what constitutes "income" or "support" to the organization. Is a gift that can be used only for a specific project or after a specified time "income" to the organization at the time the gift is received, or does this restricted gift represent an amount that should be looked on as being held in a form of escrow until it is expended for the restricted purpose (cancer research in the previous example) or the specified time has arrived (20XX in the previous example)? If it is looked on as something other than income, what is it—deferred income or part of a restricted net asset balance?

If a current restricted gift is considered income or support in the period received—whether expended or not—the accounting is fairly straightforward. It would be essentially the same as for unrestricted gifts, described earlier, except that the gift is reported in the temporarily restricted class rather than in the unrestricted class of net assets. But if the other view is taken, the accounting can become complex.

The approach required by SFAS No. 116 is to report a current restricted gift as income or support in full in the year received, in the temporarily restricted class of net assets. In this approach, gifts are recognized as income as received and expenditures are recognized as incurred. The unexpended income is reflected as part of temporarily restricted net assets.

Observe, however, that in this approach, a current restricted gift received on the last day of the reporting period will also be reflected as income, and this would increase the excess of support over expenses reported for the entire period. Many boards are reluctant to report such an excess in the belief that this may discourage contributions or suggest that the board has not used all of its available resources. Those who are concerned about reporting an excess of income over expenses are therefore particularly concerned with the implications of this approach: A large unexpected current restricted gift may be received at the last minute, resulting in a large excess of income over expenses.

Others, in rejecting this argument, point out that the organization is merely reporting what has happened and to report the gift otherwise is to obscure its receipt. They point out that in reality all gifts, whether restricted or unrestricted, are really at least somewhat restricted and only the degree of restriction varies; even "unrestricted" gifts must be spent to realize the stated goals of the organization, and therefore such gifts are effectively restricted to this purpose even though a particular use has not been specified by the contributor.

There are valid arguments on both sides. This approach is the one that was recommended in the old AICPA *Audit Guide for Voluntary Health and Welfare Organizations;* therefore, it was widely followed. It is now the method used by all not-for-profit organizations if they want their independent auditor to be able to say that their financial statements are prepared in conformity with GAAP.

Grants for Specific Projects. Many organizations receive grants from funders to accomplish specific projects or activities. These grants differ from other current restricted gifts principally in the degree of accountability the recipient organization has in reporting back to the granting organization on the use of such monies. In some instances, the organization receives a grant to conduct a specific research project, the results of which are turned over to the grantor. The arrangement is similar to a private contractor's performance on a commercial for-profit basis. In that case, the grant is essentially a purchase of services. It would be accounted for in accordance with normal commercial accounting principles, which call for the revenue to be recognized as the work under the contract is performed. In other instances, the organization receives a grant for a specific project, and while the grantee must specifically account for the expenditure of the grant in detail and may have to return any unexpended amounts, the grant is to further the programs of the grantee rather than for the benefit of the grantor. This kind of grant is really a gift, not a purchase.

The line between ordinary current restricted gifts and true grants for specific projects is not important for accounting purposes because the method of reporting revenue is now the same for both. What can get fuzzy is the distinction between grants and purchase-of-services contracts. Most donors of current restricted gifts are explicit as to how their gifts are to be used, and often require the organization to report back to them on the use of their gifts. However, restricted gifts and grants usually do not have the degree of specificity that is attached to purchase contracts. Appendix 28.1 contains a list to help readers distinguish between gifts and purchase contracts in practice.

Prepayment versus Cost Reimbursement. Grants and contracts can be structured in either of two forms: In one, the payor remits the amount up front, and the payee then spends that money. In the other, the payee must spend its own money from other sources and is reimbursed by the payor.

In the case of a purchase contract, amounts remitted to the organization in advance of their expenditure should be treated as deferred income until such time as expenditures are made that can be charged against the contract. At that time, income should be recognized to the extent earned. Where expenditures have been made but the grantor has not yet made payment, a receivable should be set up to reflect the grantor's obligation.

In the case of a true grant (gift), advance payments must be recognized as revenue immediately upon receipt, as is the case with all contributions under SFAS No. 116. Reimbursement grants are recognized as revenue as reimbursements become due (i.e., as money is spent that the grantor will reimburse). This is the same method as is used under cost-reimbursement purchase contracts.

Some organizations have recorded the entire amount of the grant as a receivable at the time awarded, offset by deferred grant income on the liability side of the balance sheet. This is no longer appropriate under SFAS No. 116. If the entire grant amount qualifies as an unconditional pledge (see subsection(iii) below), then that amount must be recorded as revenue, not deferred revenue.

Investment Securities. Frequently, an organization will receive contributions that are in the form of investment securities: stocks and bonds. These contributions should be recorded in the same manner as cash gifts. The only problem usually encountered is difficulty in determining a reasonable basis for valuation in the case of closely held stock with no objective market value.

The value recorded should be the fair market value at the date received, determined in accordance with SFAS No. 157 (ASC Topic 820). Marketable stocks and bonds present no serious valuation problem. They should be recorded at their market value on the date of receipt or, if sold shortly thereafter, at the amount of proceeds actually received. However, the phrase *shortly thereafter* refers to a sale within a few days or perhaps a week after receipt. Where the organization deliberately holds the securities for a period of time before sale, the securities should be recorded at their fair market value on the date of receipt. This will usually result in a gain or loss being recorded when the securities are subsequently sold.

For securities without a published market value, the services of an appraiser may be required to determine the FV of the gift. See Section 28.2(h) for further discussion of investments.

(ii) Gifts in Kind

Fixed Assets (Land, Buildings, Equipment), and Supplies. Contributions of fixed assets can be accounted for in one of two ways. SFAS No. 116 permits such gifts to be reported as either unrestricted or temporarily restricted income at the time received. If the gift is initially reported as temporarily restricted, the restriction is deemed to expire ratably over the useful life of the asset: that is, in proportion to depreciation for depreciable assets. The expiration is reported as a reclassification from the temporarily restricted to the unrestricted class of net assets. Nondepreciable assets such as land would remain in the temporarily restricted class indefinitely—until disposed of. (Recognizing the gift as income in proportion to depreciation recognized on the asset is not in conformity with GAAP.)

Supplies and equipment should be recorded at the amount that the organization would normally have to pay for similar items. A value for used office equipment and the like can usually be obtained from a dealer in such items. The valuation of donated real estate is more difficult, and it is usually necessary to get an outside appraisal to determine the value.

Despite some controversy over the subject, Chapter 7 of the AICPA *Audit Guide* specifically requires the recording of a value for contributed inventory expected to be sold by thrift shops and similar organizations at the time the items are received. The amount will be an estimate based on the estimated quantities and quality of goods on hand and known statistics for the percentage of the goods that eventually will be sold for cash (versus recycled or discarded). However, donated items that will be given to others (organizations or individuals) as part of the organization's program (e.g., food, medicine, toys) should be accounted for as inventory until given away.

Museum Collections. SFAS No. 116 makes an exception for recording a value for donated (and purchased) museum collection objects if certain criteria are met and certain disclosures are made. Owners of such objects do not have to record them, although they may if they wish.

Contributed Services of Volunteers. Many organizations depend heavily on volunteers to carry out their programs and sometimes supporting functions. Should such organizations place a value on these contributed services and record them as contributions in their financial statements?

Criteria for Recording. The answer is yes, the contributed services should be valued under certain circumstances. These circumstances exist only when *either* of the next two conditions is satisfied:

1. The services create or enhance nonfinancial assets *or*
2. The services:
   a. Require specialized skills,
   b. Are provided by persons possessing those skills, *and*
   c. Would typically have to be purchased if not provided by donation.

If neither criterion is met, SFAS No. 116 precludes recording a value for the services, although disclosure in a footnote is encouraged.

Creating or Enhancing Fixed Assets. The first criterion is fairly straightforward. It covers volunteers constructing or making major improvements to buildings or equipment. It would also cover things like building sets or making costumes for a theater or opera company and writing computer programs, since the resulting assets could be capitalized on the balance sheet. The criterion says "nonfinancial" assets so as *not* to cover volunteer fundraisers who, it could be argued, are "creating" assets by soliciting gifts.

Specialized Skills. The second criterion has three parts, all of which must be met for recording to be appropriate. The first part deals with the nature of the services themselves. The intent is deliberately to limit the types of services that must be recorded, thus reducing the burden of tracking and valuing large numbers of volunteers doing purely routine work, the aggregate financial value of which would usually be fairly small. SFAS No. 116 gives very little guidance about how to identify, in practice, those skills that would be considered "specialized" as opposed to nonspecialized. There is a list of skills that are considered specialized, but it merely recites a list of obvious professions, such as doctors, lawyers, teachers, and carpenters. What is lacking is an operational definition of specialized that can be applied to all types of services. Appendix 28.2 contains a list to help readers make this distinction in practice.

The second part of the criterion usually causes no problems in practice, as persons practicing the types of skills contemplated should normally possess the skills (if not, why are they performing the services?).

Would Otherwise Purchase. The third part of the criterion is the most difficult of all to consider, as it calls for a pure judgment by management as to what it would do in a hypothetical situation. Would the organization or would it not purchase the services? This is similar to one in SOP 78-10, which stated:

> The services performed are significant and form an integral part of the efforts of the organization as it is presently constituted; the services would be performed by salaried personnel if donated services were not available . . . ; and the organization would continue the activity.

Probably the most important requirement is that the services being performed are an essential part of the organization's program. FASB Concepts Statement No. 6, in distinguishing between revenues and expenses versus gains and losses, describes revenues and expenses as relating to "central and important" activities of the organization while gains and losses result from "incidental or peripheral" activities. Similar logic can be applied here. The key test is whether the organization would hire someone to perform these services if volunteers were not available. Presumably people would be hired to perform central activities but not incidental ones. Also, FASB explicitly says that the financial ability to pay replacements does not determine the judgment. If an activity is central to the mission but cash is not currently available, the organization would go out and raise the money somehow. Appendix 28.2 contains a list to help readers assess this criterion

Basis on Which to Value Services. An additional criterion, which is not explicitly stated in SFAS No. 116 (ASC Topic 958) in connection with donated services, is that there must be an objective basis on which to value these services. It is usually not difficult to determine a reasonable value for volunteer services where the volunteers are performing professional or clerical services. By definition, the services to be recorded are only those for which the organization would in fact hire paid staff if volunteers were not available. This criterion suggests that the organization should be able to establish a reasonable estimate of what costs would be involved if employees had to be hired.

In establishing such rates, it is not necessary to establish individual rates for each volunteer. Instead, volunteers can be grouped into general categories and a rate established for each category.

Some organizations are successful in getting local businesses to donate one of their executives on a full- or part-time basis for an extended period. In many instances, the salary paid by the business to the loaned executive is far greater than the organization would have to pay for hired staff performing the same function. The rate to be used in establishing a value should be the lower rate. This procedure also helps to get around the awkwardness of trying to discern actual compensation. An organization may wish not to record a value unless the services are significant in amount. There is a cost to keep the records necessary to meet the reporting requirements, and unless the resulting amounts are significant, it is wasteful for the organization to record them.

Accounting Treatment. The dollar value assigned to contributed services should be reflected as income in the section of the financial statements where other unrestricted contributions are shown. In most instances, it is appropriate to disclose the amount of such services as a separate line.

On the expense side, the value of contributed services should be allocated to program and supporting service categories based on the nature of the work performed. The amounts allocated to each category are not normally disclosed separately. If volunteers were used for constructing fixed assets, the amounts would be capitalized rather than being charged to an expense category. Unless some of the amounts are capitalized, the recording of contributed services will not affect the excess of income over expenses, since the income and expense exactly offset each other.

The footnotes to the financial statements should disclose the nature of contributed services and the valuation techniques followed.

Use of Facilities. Occasionally a not-for-profit organization will be given use of a building or other facilities either at no cost or at a substantially reduced cost. A value should be reflected for such a facility in the financial statements, both as income and as expense. The value to be used should be the fair market value of facilities that the organization would otherwise rent if the contributed facilities were not available. This means that if very expensive facilities are donated, the valuation to be used should be the lower value of the facilities that the organization would otherwise have rented. Implicit in this rule is the ability to determine an objective basis for valuing the facilities. If an organization is given the use of facilities that are unique in design and have no alternative purpose, it may be impossible to determine what it would have to pay to rent comparable facilities. This often occurs with museums that occupy elaborate government-owned buildings.

Where a donor indicates that the organization can unconditionally use such rent-free facilities for more than a one-year period, the organization should reflect the arrangement as a pledge and record the PV of the contribution in the same way as other pledges.

(iii) Support Not Currently Expendable

Endowment Gifts. Donor-restricted endowment fund contributions should be reported as revenue upon receipt in a restricted class of net assets: temporary in the case of a term endowment gift, otherwise permanent.

Gifts of term endowment are later reclassified to the unrestricted class when the term of the endowment expires. (If, upon expiration of the endowment restriction, the gift is still restricted—likely for some operating purpose—it would not be reclassified until money was spent for that purpose. If upon expiration of the term endowment restriction, the gift becomes permanently restricted, it should be recorded in that class initially.)

Pledges (Promises to Give). A pledge[3] is a promise to contribute a specified amount to an organization. Typically, fundraising organizations solicit pledges because a donor either does not want to or is not able to make a contribution in cash in the amount desired by the organization at the time solicited. In giving, as with consumer purchases, the "installment plan" is a way of life. Organizations find donors are more generous when the payments being contributed are smaller and spread out over a period of time.

A pledge may or may not be legally enforceable. The point is largely moot because few organizations would think of trying to legally enforce a pledge. The unfavorable publicity that would result would only hurt future fundraising. The only relevant criteria are: Will the pledge be collected, and are pledges material in amount?

If these criteria are satisfied, then there are two accounting questions: Should a pledge be recorded as an asset at the time the pledge is received? If the answer is yes, the next question is: When should the pledge be recognized as income?

Recording as an Asset. For many organizations, a significant portion of their income is received by pledge. The timing of the collection of pledges is only partially under the control of the organization. Yet over the years most organizations find they can predict with reasonable accuracy the collectable portion of pledges, even when a sizable percentage will not be collected. Accounting literature requires that unconditional pledges the organization expects to collect be recorded as assets and an allowance established for the portion that is estimated to be uncollectable.

Historically, there was considerable difference of opinion on this subject, but now SFAS No. 116 requires *all* organizations to record unconditional pledges.

Conditions versus Restrictions. The requirement is to record *unconditional* pledges as assets. *Unconditional* means without conditions. What is meant by *conditions*? FASB defines a condition as "a future and uncertain event" that must occur for a pledge to become binding on the pledgor. There are two elements to this definition: future and uncertain. *Future* means it has not happened yet; this is fairly clear. The term *uncertain* is, however, more subject to interpretation. How uncertain? This will be a matter of judgment in many cases.

If a donor pledges to give to a charity "if the sun rises tomorrow," that is not an uncertain event; the sun will rise tomorrow, at a known time. If a donor pledges to give $10,000 to the Red Cross "if there's an earthquake in California," that is very uncertain. (A geologist will say the eventual probability of an earthquake happening is 100 percent, but the timing is completely uncertain.) This latter pledge would be conditional upon an earthquake occurring. Once an earthquake occurs, then the donor's pledge is unconditional (the condition has been removed), and the pledge would be recorded by the Red Cross.

Another example of a condition is a matching pledge (also known as a *challenge grant*). A donor pledges to give an amount to a charity if the charity raises a matching amount from other sources. (The "match" need not be one for one; it can be in any ratio the donor specifies.) In this

---

[3] SFAS No. 116 uses the term *promise to give* to refer to what is more commonly called a *pledge.*

case, the charity is not entitled to receive the donor's gift until it has met the required match. Once it does, it will notify the donor that the pledge is now due.

A third type of donor stipulation sounds like a condition, but it may or may not actually be one. A donor pledges to contribute to a symphony orchestra "if they will perform my favorite piece of music [specified by name]." (A cynical person would call this a bribe.) Yes, this is an uncertain future event, since the piece of music has not yet been performed, but how uncertain is it? If the orchestra might very well have played the piece anyway, then the "condition" is really trivial, and the event would not be considered uncertain. However, if the piece were one that the orchestra would be very unlikely to perform without the incentive represented by the pledge in question, then the event would be considered uncertain and the pledge conditional. In this case, the condition is fulfilled when the orchestra formally places the music on its schedule and so informs the donor.

Note that the concept of a condition is quite different from that of a restriction. Conditions deal with events that must occur before a charity is entitled to receive a gift. Restrictions limit how the charity can use the gift after receipt. Unconditional pledges can be either unrestricted or restricted; so can conditional pledges. Donor stipulations attached to a gift or pledge must be read carefully to discern which type of situation is being dealt with. For example, "I pledge $20,000 *if* you play my favorite music" is conditional but unrestricted (the donor has not said the gift must be used to pay for the performance) whereas "I pledge $20,000 *for* [the cost of] playing my favorite piece of music" is restricted but unconditional. In the latter case, the donor has said the pledge will be paid but can only be used for that performance. The difference in wording is small, but the accounting implications are great. The conditional pledge is not recorded at all until the condition is met; the unconditional restricted pledge is recorded as revenue (in the temporarily restricted class) upon receipt of notification of the pledge. Appendix 28.4 contains a list to help readers determine whether an unconditional pledge actually exists. Appendix 28.5 contains a list to help distinguish conditions from restrictions.

Discounted to PV(Present Value). SFAS No. 116 requires recipients (and donors) of pledges payable beyond the current accounting period to discount the pledges to their PV, using an appropriate rate of interest. Thus, the ability to receive $1,000 two years later is really only equivalent to receiving about $900 (assuming about a 5 percent rate of interest) now, because the $900 could be invested and earn $100 of interest over the two years. The higher the interest rate used, the lower will be the PV of the pledge, since the lower amount would earn more interest at the higher rate and still be worth the full $1,000 two years hence.

The appropriate rate of interest to use in discounting pledges will be a matter of some judgment. In many cases, it will be the average rate the organization is currently earning on its investments or its idle cash. If the organization is being forced to borrow money to keep going, then the borrowing rate should be used. As the time passes between the initial recording of a discounted pledge and its eventual collection, the PV increases since the time left before payment is shorter. Therefore, the discount element must be gradually "accreted" up to par (collection) value. This accretion should be recorded each year until the due date for the pledge arrives. The accretion is recorded as additional contribution income.

Pledges for Extended Periods. There is one limitation to the general rule that pledges be recorded as assets. Occasionally donors will indicate that they will make an open-ended pledge of support for an extended period of time. For example, if a donor promises to pay $5,000 a year for 20 years, would it be appropriate to record as an asset the full 20 years' pledge? In most cases, no; this would distort the financial statements. Most organizations follow the practice of not recording pledges for future years' support beyond a fairly short period. They feel that long-term open-ended pledges are inherently conditional on the donor's continued willingness to continue making payments and thus are harder to collect. These arguments have validity, and organizations should consider very carefully the likelihood of collection before recording pledges for support in future periods beyond, say, 5 or 10 years.

Allowance for Uncollectable Pledges. Not all pledges will be collected. People lose interest in an organization; their personal financial circumstances may change; they may move out of town. This is as true for charities as for businesses, but businesses usually will sue to collect unpaid debts; charities usually will not. Thus another important question is how large the allowance for uncollectable pledges should be. Most organizations have past experience to help answer this question. If, over the years, 10 percent of pledges are not collected, then unless the economic climate changes, 10 percent is probably the right figure to use.

Recognition as Income. The second, related question is: When should an unconditional pledge be recognized as income? As with all types of contributions, GAAP says to record them immediately upon receipt. Conditional pledges are not recorded until the condition is met, at which time they are effectively unconditional pledges. Footnote disclosure of unrecorded conditional pledges should be made.

Further, all pledges are considered implicitly time restricted, by virtue of their being unavailable for use until collected. Like other time-restricted gifts, pledges are reported in the temporarily restricted class of net assets. They are then reclassified to the unrestricted class when the specified time arrives.

This means that even a pledge not payable for 10 years or a pledge payable in many installments is recorded as revenue in full (less the discount to PV) in the temporarily restricted class in the year the pledge is first received. This is a major change from earlier practice, which generally deferred the pledge until the anticipated period of collection.

Sometimes a charity may not want to have to record a large pledge as immediate revenue; it may feel that its balance sheet is already healthy and recording more income would turn away other donors. If a pledge is unconditional, there is no choice: The pledge must be recorded. One way to mitigate this problem is to ask the donor to make the pledge conditional; then it is not recorded until some later time when the condition is met. Of course, there is a risk that the donor may not be as likely ever to pay a conditional pledge as one that is understood to be absolutely binding, so nonprofit organizations should consider carefully before requesting that a pledge be made conditional.

GAAP requires that donors follow the same rules for recognition of the expense of making a gift as recipients do for the income: that is, immediately on payment or of making an unconditional pledge. Sometimes a charity will find a donor reluctant to make a large unconditional pledge but willing to make a conditional pledge. Fundraisers should be aware of the effect of these accounting principles on donors' giving habits as well as on recipients' balance sheets.

Bequests. A bequest is a special kind of pledge. Bequests should never be recorded before the donor dies—not because death is uncertain, but because a person can always change a will, and the charity may get nothing. (There is a special case: the pledge payable upon death. This is not really a bequest, it is just an ordinary pledge, and should be recorded as such if it is unconditional.)

After a person dies, the beneficiary organization is informed that it is named in the will, but this notification may occur long before the estate is probated and distribution made. Should such a bequest be recorded at the time the organization first learns of the bequest or at the time of receipt? The question is one of sufficiency of assets in the estate to fulfill the bequest. Since there is often uncertainty about what other amounts may have to be paid to settle debts, taxes, other bequests, claims of disinherited relatives, and so on, a conservative, and recommended, approach is not to record anything until the probate court has accounted for the estate and the amount available for distribution can be accurately estimated. At that time, the amount should be recorded in the same manner as other gifts.

Thus, if an organization is informed that it will receive a bequest of a specific amount, say, $10,000, it should record this $10,000 as an asset. If instead the organization is informed that it will receive 10 percent of the estate, the total of which is not known, nothing would be recorded yet although footnote disclosure would likely be necessary if the amount could be sizable. Still a third possibility exists if the organization is told that while the final amount of the 10 percent bequest is not known, it will be at least some stated amount. In that instance, the minimum amount would be recorded with footnote disclosure of the contingent interest.

Split-Interest Gifts. The term *split-interest gifts* (also called *deferred gifts*) is used to refer to irrevocable trusts and similar arrangements where the interest in the gift is split between the donor (or another person specified by the donor) and the charity. These arrangements can be divided into two fundamentally different types of arrangements: lead interests and remainder interests. Lead interests are those in which the benefit to the charity "leads," or precedes, the benefit to the donor (or other person designated by the donor). To put this into the terminology commonly used by trust lawyers, the charity is the *life tenant* and someone else is the *remainderman.* The reverse situation is that of the "remainder" interest, where the donor (or the donor's designee) is the life tenant and the charity is the remainderman (i.e., the entity to which the assets become available upon termination; often called the *maturity*) of the trust or other arrangement. There may or may not be further restrictions on the charity's use of the assets and/or the income there from after this maturity.

Under both types of arrangement, the donor makes an initial lump-sum payment into a fund. The amount is invested, and the income during the term of the arrangement is paid to the life tenant. In some cases, the arrangement is established as a trust under the trust laws of the applicable state. In other cases, no separate trust is involved; rather the assets are held by the charity as part of its general assets. In some cases involving trusts, the charity is the trustee; in other cases, a third party is the trustee. Typical third-party trustees include banks and trust companies or other charities, such as community foundations. Some arrangements are perpetual (i.e., the charity never gains access to the corpus of the gift); others have a defined term of existence that will end either on the occurrence of a specified event such as the death of the donor (or other specified person) or after the passage of a specified amount of time.

To summarize to this point, the various defining criteria applicable to these arrangements are:

- The charity's interest may be a lead interest or a remainder interest.
- The arrangement may be in the form of a trust, or it may not be.
- The assets may be held by the charity or held by a third party.
- The arrangement may be perpetual, or it may have a defined term.
- Upon termination of the interest of the life tenant, the corpus may be unrestricted or restricted.

Lead Interests. There are two kinds of lead interests as normally conceived:[4] (1) charitable lead trust and (2) perpetual trust held by a third party.

In both of these cases, the charity receives periodic payments representing distributions of income but never gains unrestricted use of the assets that produce the income. In the first case, the payment stream is for a limited time; in the second case, the payment stream is perpetual.

A *charitable lead trust* is always for a defined term and usually is held by the charity. At the termination of the trust, the corpus (principal of the gift) reverts to the donor or to another person specified by the donor (may be the donor's estate). Income during the term of the trust is paid to the charity; the income may be unrestricted or restricted. In effect, this arrangement amounts to an unconditional pledge, for a specified period, of the income from a specified amount of assets. The current value of the pledge is the discounted PV of the estimated stream of income over the term of the trust. Although the charity manages the assets during the term of the trust, it has no remainder interest in the assets.

[4] It is also possible to consider both a simple pledge and a permanent endowment fund as forms of lead interests. In both cases, the charity receives periodic payments but never gains unrestricted use of the assets that generate the income to make the payments. A pledge is for a limited time; an endowment fund pays forever.

A *perpetual trust held by a third party* is the same as the lead trust, except that the charity does not manage the assets and the term of the trust is perpetual. Again the charity receives the income earned by the assets but never gains the use of the corpus. In effect, there is no remainderman. This arrangement is also a pledge of income, but in this case the current value of the pledge is the discounted PV of a perpetual stream of income from the assets. Assuming a perfect market for investment securities, that amount will equal the current quoted market value of the assets of the trust or, if there is no quoted market value, then the FV, which is normally determined based on discounted future cash flows from the assets.

A variation of this type of arrangement is a trust held by a third party (often a community foundation) in which the third party has discretion as to when and/or to whom to pay the periodic income. Since in this case the charity is not assured in advance of receiving any determinable amount, no amounts should be recorded by the charity until distributions are awarded to the charity by the trustee; these amounts are then recorded as contributions.

Remainder Interests. There are four types of remainder interests:

1. Charitable remainder annuity trust (CRAT)
2. Charitable remainder unitrust (CRUT)
3. Charitable gift annuity (CGA)
4. Pooled income fund (PIF; also referred to as a life income fund)

These arrangements are always for a limited term, usually the life of the donor and/or another person or persons specified by the donor—often the donor's spouse. The donor or the donor's designee is the life tenant; the charity is the remainderman. Again, in the case of a trust, the charity may or may not be the trustee; in the case of a CGA, the charity usually is the holder of the assets. Upon termination of the arrangement, the corpus usually becomes available to the charity; the donor may or may not have placed further temporary or permanent restrictions on the corpus and/or the future income earned by the corpus.

In many states, the acceptance of these types of gifts is regulated by the state government—often the department of insurance—since, from the perspective of the donor, these arrangements are partly insurance contracts, essentially similar to a commercial annuity.

A CRAT and a CRUT differ only in the stipulated method of calculating the payments to the life tenant. An annuity trust pays a stated dollar amount that remains fixed over the life of the trust; a unitrust pays a stated percentage of the then current value of the trust assets. Thus, the dollar amount of the payments will vary with changes in the market value of the corpus. Accounting for the two types is the same except for the method of calculation of the amount of the PV of the life interest payable to the life tenant(s). In both cases, if current investment income is insufficient to cover the stipulated payments, corpus may have to be invaded to do so; however, the liability to the life tenant is limited to the assets of the trust.

A CGA differs from a CRAT only in that there is no trust; the assets usually are held among the general assets of the charity. The annuity liability is a general liability of the charity—limited only by the charity's total assets. Some charities choose (or may be required by state law) to set aside a pool of assets in a separate fund to cover annuity liabilities.

A PIF is actually a creation of the Internal Revenue Code (IRC) Section 642(c)(5), which, together with Section 170, allows an income tax deduction to donors to such funds. (The amount of the deduction depends on the age(s) of the life tenant(s) and the value of the life interest, and is less than that allowed for a simple charitable deduction directly to a charity, to reflect the value that the life tenant will be receiving in return for the gift.) The fund usually is managed by the charity. Many donors contribute to such a fund, which pools the gifts and invests the assets. During the period of each life tenant's interest in the fund, the life tenant is paid the actual income earned by that person's share of the corpus. (To this extent, these funds function essentially as mutual funds.) Upon termination of a life interest, the share of the corpus attributable to that life tenant becomes available to the charity.

Accounting for Split-Interest Gifts. The essence of split-interest gifts is that they are pledges. In some cases, the pledge is of a stream of payments to the charity during the life of the arrangement (lead interests). In other cases, the pledge is of the value of the remainder interest. Calculation of the value of a lead interest is usually straightforward, as the term and the payments are well defined. Calculation of remainder interests is more complicated, since life expectancies are usually involved. Likely the services of an actuary will be needed.

GAAP gives very little guidance specific to split interests. Chapter 6 of the AICPA *Audit Guide* (and ASC Topic 958-30) discusses in detail the accounting for split-interest gifts. Briefly, the assets contributed are valued at their CRAT FV on the date of gift (the same as for any donated assets). The related contribution revenue is usually the PV of the amounts expected to become available to the organization, discounted from the expected date(s) of such availability. (In the case of a remainder interest, it is the actuarially expected death date of the last remaining life tenant.) The difference between these two numbers is, in the case of a lead interest, the PV of the amount to be distributed at the end of the term of the agreement according to the donor's directions; under a remainder agreement, it is the PV of the actuarial liability to make payments to life tenants.

(iv) Transfers of Assets to a Not-for-Profit Organization or Charitable Trust That Raises or Holds Contributions for Others (SFAS No. 136; ASC Topics 958-605 and -20). An intermediary that receives cash or other financial assets should report the assets received and a liability to the specified beneficiary, both measured at the FV of the assets received. An intermediary that receives nonfinancial assets may but need not report the assets and the liability, provided that the intermediary reports consistently from period to period and discloses its accounting policy. A specified beneficiary of a charitable trust agreement having a trustee with a duty to hold and manage its assets for the benefit of the beneficiary should report as an asset its rights to trust assets—an interest in the net assets of the recipient organization, a beneficial interest, or a receivable—unless the recipient organization is explicitly granted variance power in the transferring instrument—unilateral power (power to act without approval from any other party)—to redirect the use of the assets to another beneficiary.

If the beneficiary and the recipient organization are financially interrelated, the beneficiary should report its interest in the net assets of the recipient organization and adjust that interest for its share of the change in the net assets of the recipient organization, similar to the equity method. They are financially interrelated if both of the following factors are present:

1. One has the ability to influence the operating and financial decisions of the other. That may be demonstrated in several ways:
   - The organizations are affiliates.
   - One has considerable representation on the governing board of the other.
   - The charter or bylaws of one limit its activities to those that are beneficial to the other.
   - An agreement between them allows one to actively participate in policy making of the other, such as setting priorities, budgets, and management compensation.
2. One has an ongoing economic interest in the net assets of the other.

If the beneficiary has an unconditional right to receive all or a portion of the specified cash flows from a charitable trust or other identifiable pool of assets, the beneficiary should report that beneficial interest, measuring and subsequently remeasuring it at FV, using a technique such as PV. In all other cases, a beneficiary should report its rights to the assets held by a recipient organization as a receivable and contribution revenue in conformity with the provisions of SFAS No. 116 for unconditional promises to give.

If the recipient organization is explicitly granted variance power by the donor, the beneficiary should not report its potential for future distributions from the assets held by the recipient organization.

In general, a recipient organization that accepts assets from a donor and agrees to use them on behalf of them, or transfer them, or both to a specified beneficiary is not a donee. It should report its liability to the specified beneficiary and the cash or other financial assets received from the donor, all measured at the FV of the assets received. In general, a recipient organization that receives nonfinancial assets may but need not report its liability and the assets, as long as the organization reports consistently from period to period and discloses its accounting policy.

A recipient organization that has been explicitly granted variance power acts as a donee.

A resource provider should report as an asset and the recipient organization should report as a liability a transfer of assets if one or more of these factors is present:

- The transfer is subject to the resource provider's unilateral right to redirect the use of the assets to another beneficiary.
- The resource provider's promise to give is conditional or otherwise revocable or repayable.
- The resource provider controls the recipient organization and specifies an unaffiliated beneficiary.
- The resource provider specifies itself or its affiliate as the beneficiary and the transfer is not an equity transaction, as discussed next.

A transfer of assets to a recipient organization is an equity transaction if all of these factors are present:

- The resource provider specifies itself or its affiliate as the beneficiary.
- The resource provider and the recipient organization are financially interrelated.
- Neither the resource provider nor its affiliate expects payment of the assets, although payment of return on the assets may be expected.

A resource provider that specifies itself as beneficiary should report an equity transaction as an interest in the net assets of the recipient organization or as an increase in a previously reported interest. If a resource provider specifies an affiliate as beneficiary, it should report an equity transaction as a separate line in its statement of activities, and the affiliate should report an interest in the net assets of the recipient organization. A recipient organization should report an equity transaction as a separate line item in its statement of activities.

A not-for-profit organization that transfers assets to a recipient organization and specifies itself or its affiliate as the beneficiary should disclose the following for each period for which a statement of financial position is presented:

- The identity of the recipient organization
- Whether variance power was granted to the recipient organization and, if so, its terms
- The terms under which amounts will be distributed to the resource provider or its affiliate
- The aggregate amount reported in the statement of financial position for the transfers and whether it is reported as an interest in the net assets of the recipient organization or as another asset, such as a beneficial interest in assets held by others or a refundable advance

Exhibit 28.1 illustrates the process that should be followed to determine the proper accounting for such transfers.

(j) TAXES. FASB Interpretation (FIN) 48 (ASC Topic 740-10), *Uncertain Tax Positions,* requires specific consideration of every tax position taken by an organization. Tax positions include consideration of whether an item of income is taxable, whether a deduction is allowable, and whether filing a return is required. Uncertain (less than 50 percent probable of being sustained on audit) positions require disclosure and possibly accrual of a liability.

FIN 48 is *not* inapplicable to nonprofits. Nonprofits do have tax positions, any of which may be uncertain.

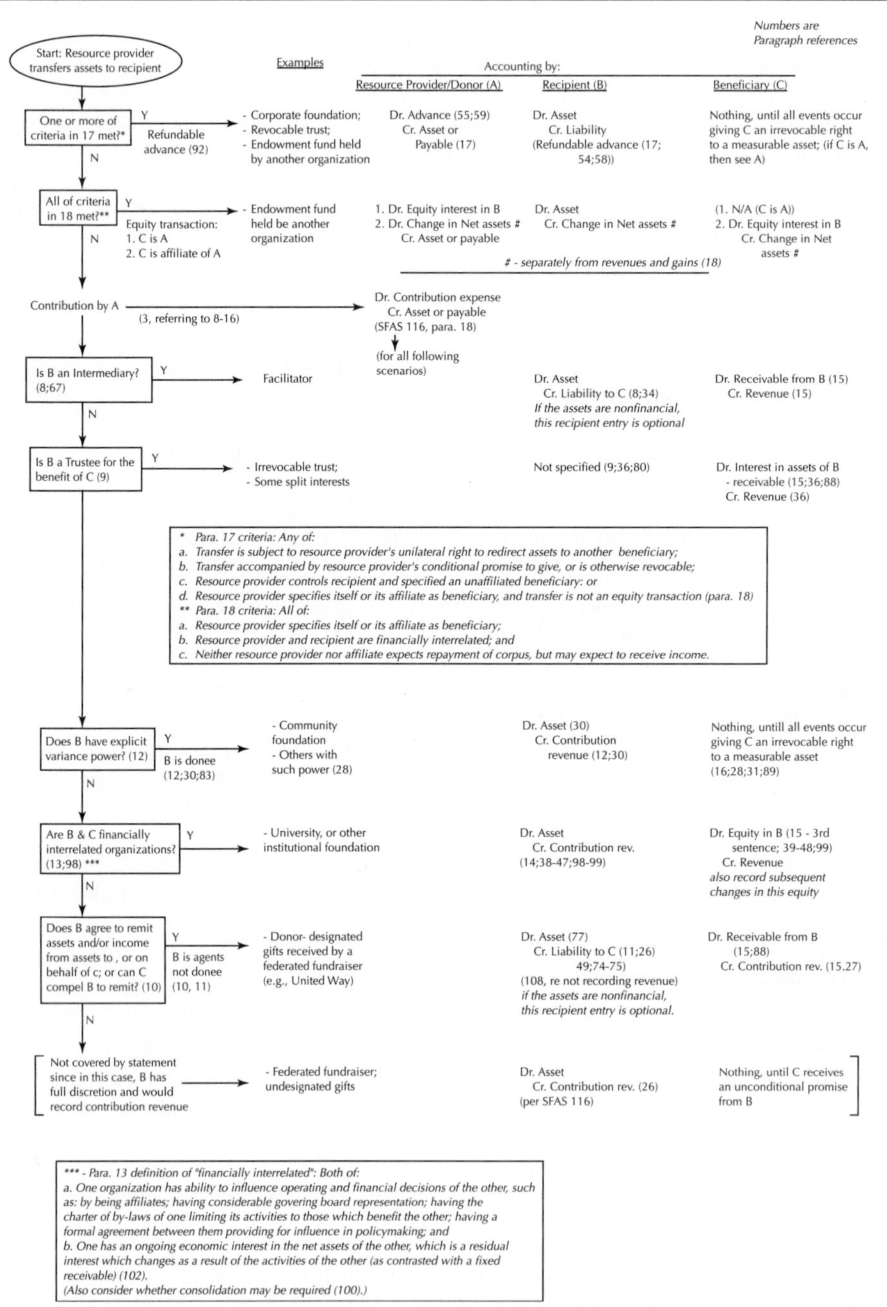

Exhibit 28.1 ASC Topic 958-605; 958-20, *Transfers of Assets to a Not-for-Profit Organization or Charitable Trust that Raises or Holds Contributions for Others*

For nonprofits, there are up to five areas requiring consideration:

1. Tax-exempt status has not been jeopardized
2. Unrelated business income (UBI): characterization and amount of income, and deductible expenses
3. Excise tax on investment income of private foundations
4. Taxable subsidiaries
5. Filing requirements

IRS Form 990 requires inclusion of the FIN 48 footnote from the financial statements. ("Come audit us!")

An overriding tax position for nonprofit organizations is whether they do in fact qualify for tax-exempt status. If there is uncertainty about this position, FIN 48 would apply. Circumstances that might raise questions about continued qualification for tax-exempt status include:

- Private inurement or benefit (consider especially compensation of highly-paid people, insider transactions, loans, asset sales and purchases, etc.)
- Excessive lobbying or political activity
- Failure to meet the "organizational" and "operational" tests (in other words, failure to do what you told the IRS you would do when you applied for exempt status)
- Having so much UBI (as a percentage of total income) that the IRS might assert you are really a business
- Gross violations of other laws and regulations (e.g., repeated failure to file Form 990, discrimination, etc.)

In addition, FIN 48 applies to uncertain tax positions of nonprofit organizations associated with the next three specific situations.

Private Foundation Excise Tax on Net Investment Income, Under IRC Section 4940. Although this is technically an excise tax, it is covered by FIN 48 because it is calculated based on a type of income.

However, FIN 48 will need to be considered only infrequently in these cases, as the applicability and computation of this tax (including deferred amounts) are in most cases not likely to be uncertain. Further, since the tax rate is only 2 percent (1 percent in some cases), any uncertain tax amounts are not likely to be material to a foundation's financial statements.

Two exceptions could be when:

1. The foundation has sold at a gain investment securities that had been donated to it. The basis of the securities used to compute the taxable capital gain is their basis in the hands of the original donor (or, if higher, their value on December 31, 1969, if the securities were owned by the foundation on that date). The foundation may not be readily able to accurately determine this amount.
2. The status of a 501(c)(3) organization as a private foundation versus a public charity under IRC Section 509(a) is open to question. The organization may thus be uncertain whether it is liable for this tax at all.

Tax on UBI Under IRC Section 511. FIN 48 usually will need to be considered in relation to this tax.

The first question the whole rest of this section lists the others is whether the organization has over $1,000 of *net* income, as defined in IRC Section 512(a), from an unrelated trade or business, as defined in Section 513(a). Since there is allowed a specific deduction of that amount, lesser amounts of net income will not result in any tax payable. (There is a $1,000 *gross* income threshold for filing Form 990-T, but if no tax is due, there is no penalty for failure to file this form.)

The next aspects of this tax may give rise to uncertain tax positions:

- Every nonprofit organization (including those not required to file Form 990, such as churches and small organizations) must analyze its sources of gross income and determine which ones the IRS might consider to be UBI.
- Aspects of the IRC definition of UBI that are especially subject to judgment, and thus to uncertainty, include whether an activity is:
  - "Unrelated" to the organization's exempt purpose,
  - Considered a "trade or business," *and*
  - "Regularly carried on."
- So-called passive income (return on investments) is, by law (Section 512(b)), not generally subject to the UBI tax. However, the rules surrounding some types of this income, such as royalties and certain rental income, are complex. There may be uncertainties as to whether an item qualifies as a royalty or whether part or all of rental income is taxable because of certain of its attributes. (Such attributes include whether it: is from debt-financed property; is from rental of personal as opposed to real property; also includes payment for provision of personal services; and is based on a percentage of the net as opposed to gross income of the property).
- Income from certain trade shows conducted by 501(c)(3, 4, 5, and 6) organizations may be excluded from taxable income (Section 513(d)(3)), but only if certain judgmental criteria are satisfied.
- UBI also does not include income from: activities carried on largely by volunteers, selling of donated merchandise, and activities carried on for the convenience of members, students, patients, and so on (Section 513(a)). These definitions are subject to interpretation and may be challenged by the IRS.
- UBI does not include contributions, but in some cases there may be uncertainty as to whether a particular transaction is a contribution or earned income (exchange transaction). (See Appendix 28.1.)
- Once a source of UBI has been identified, then there may be uncertainty in computing the amount of gross income from this source. Besides normal matters of accounting judgment:
  - Advertising income is taxable, but when the affected publications are furnished to dues-paying members of a membership organization, a complex allocation is required to compute the taxable advertising amount and related deductible expenses.
  - There is often some judgment involved in determining amounts of expenses that may be deducted in computing taxable net income. This is especially likely to be the case when allocations of expenses are required, as is usual for personnel costs, occupancy, administrative expenses, and so on.
  - Allocation of occupancy costs is especially subject to IRS challenge if the facility is used for both exempt and nonexempt purposes.
- There are exceptions to most of the rules (and exceptions to the exceptions!).
- If an organization operates in multiple taxing jurisdictions, there may be uncertainty over allocating the taxable income among those jurisdictions.
- If timing differences between book and taxable amounts exist, there may be uncertainties as to the expected timing of the reversal of those differences, and the recoverability of any deferred tax assets.

Tax on Income of a Taxable Subsidiary of a Nonprofit Organization. All of the normal uncertainties affecting for-profit organizations apply here; they are discussed in FIN 48 and elsewhere in professional literature.

(k) RELATED ORGANIZATIONS. Judgment is often required to decide when not-for-profit entities should combine the financial statements of affiliated organizations with those of the central organization. Part of the reason for this is the widely diverse nature of relationships among such organizations, which often creates difficulty in determining when criteria for combination have been met.

(i) Definition of the *Reporting Entity*. There are two issues here with the definition, but they involve the same concepts. First is the question of gifts to affiliated fundraising entities and whether the affiliate should record the gift as its own revenue, followed by gift or grant expense when the money is passed on to the parent organization, or whether it should record the initial receipt as an amount held on behalf of the parent. Such gifts are often called *pass-through gifts* since they pass through one entity to another entity. Second is the broader question of when the financial data of affiliated entities should be combined with that of a central organization for purposes of presenting the central organization's financial statements. If the data are combined, the question of pass-through gifts need not be addressed since the end result is the same regardless of which entity records gifts initially.

The concept underlying the combining of financial data of affiliates is to present to the financial statement reader information that portrays the complete financial picture of a group of entities that effectively function as one entity. In the business setting, the determination of when a group of entities is really just a single entity is normally made by assessing the extent to which the "parent" entity has a controlling financial interest in the other entities in the group. In other words, can the parent use for its own benefit the financial resources of the others without obtaining permission from any party outside the parent? When one company owns another company, such permission would be automatic; if management of the affiliate refused, the parent would exercise its authority to replace management.

In the not-for-profit world, such "ownership" of one entity by another rarely exists. Affiliated organizations are more often related by formal or informal agreements of various sorts or by overlapping governing boards and/or management, but the level of control embodied in such agreements or overlap is usually far short of ownership. The "Friends of the Museum" may exist primarily to support the museum, but in many cases it is a legally independent organization with only informal ties to its "parent." The museum may ask, but the Friends may choose its own time and method to respond. Further, the museum may have no way to legally compel the Friends to do its bidding if the Friends resist.

The issue for donors is, if I give to the Friends, am I really supporting the museum? Or if I am assessing the financial condition of the museum, is it reasonable to include the resources of the Friends in the calculation? Even though the Friends is legally separate, and even though the Friends does not have to turn its assets over to the museum, isn't it reasonable to assume that if the museum got into financial trouble, the Friends would help?

Examples of other types of relationships often found among not-for-profits include:

- A national organization and local chapters, branches, and other affiliates
- An educational institution and student and alumni groups, research organizations, and hospitals
- A religious institution and local churches, schools, seminaries, cemeteries, broadcasting stations, pension funds, and charities

Since each individual relationship may be different, it requires much judgment to decide which entities should be combined and which should not.

While there are rules for businesses to follow, they are based on ownership and thus are not very useful for nonprofits (although they would apply to a not-for-profit in the context of ownership of a for-profit subsidiary).

Rules for not-for-profits are in AICPA SOP 94-3, *Reporting of Related Entities by Not-for-Profit Organizations* (ASC Topic 958-810). These rules focus largely on the question of whether one not-for-profit controls another. This SOP requires:

- When a not-for-profit organization owns a majority of the voting equity interest in a for-profit entity, the not-for-profit must consolidate the for-profit into its financial statements, regardless of how closely related the activities of the for-profit are to those of the not-for-profit.
- If the not-for-profit organization owns less than a majority interest in a for-profit but still has significant influence over the for-profit, it must report the for-profit under the equity method of accounting, except that the not-for-profit may report its investment in the for-profit at market value if it wishes. If the not-for-profit does not have significant influence over the for-profit, it should value its investment in accordance with the applicable audit guide.
- When a not-for-profit organization has a relationship with another not-for-profit in which the "parent" both exercises control over the board appointments of and has an economic interest in the affiliate, it must consolidate the affiliate.
- If the not-for-profit organization has either control *or* an economic beneficial interest, but not both, disclosure of the relationship and significant financial information is required.
- If the parent controls the affiliate by means other than board appointments and has an economic interest, consolidation is permitted but not required. If the affiliate is not consolidated, extensive footnote disclosures about the affiliate are required.

Exhibit 28.2 is designed to help not-for-profits and their accountants decide whether sufficient control exists to require combination.

Following is a list of factors that may be helpful to not-for-profit organizations in deciding whether to combine financial statements of affiliated organizations and to auditors in assessing the appropriateness of the client's combination decision. Many of these factors are not absolutely determinative by themselves but must be considered in conjunction with other factors.

Factors Whose Presence Indicate Control	Factors Whose Presence Indicate Lack of Control
Organization Relationship	
1. A is clearly described as controlled by, for the benefit of, or an affiliate of R in some of these materials: Articles/charter/by-laws Operating/affiliation agreement Fundraising material/membership brochure Annual report Grant proposals Application for tax-exempt status	A is described as independent of R or no formal relationship is indicated.
Governance	
2. A's board has considerable overlap in membership with R; common officers.	There is little or no overlap.
3. A's board members and/or officers are appointed by R or are subject to approval of R's board, officers, or members.	A's board is self-perpetuating with no input from R.
4. Major decisions of A's board, officers, or staff are subject to review, approval, or ratification by R.	A's decisions are made autonomously; or even if in theory subject to such control, R has in fact never or rarely exercised control and does not intend to do so.

Continues

Exhibit 28.2 Factors Related to Control That May Indicate That an Affiliated Organization (A) Should Be Combined with the Reporting Organization (R), if Other Criteria for Combination Are Met

Factors Whose Presence Indicate Control	Factors Whose Presence Indicate Lack of Control
Financial	
5. A's budget is subject to review or approval by R.	Budget not subject to R's approval.
6. Some or all of A's disbursements are subject to approval or countersignature by R.	Checks may be issued without R's approval.
7. A's excess of revenue over expenses or fund balances or portions thereof are subject to being transferred to R at R's request or are automatically transferred	Although some of A's financial resources may be transferred to R, this is done only at the discretion of A's board.
8. A's activities are largely financed by grants, loans, or transfers from R or from other sources determined by R's board.	A's activities are financed from sources determined by A's board.
9. A's by-laws indicate that its resources are intended to be used for activities similar to those of R.	A's by-laws limit uses of resources to purposes that do not include R's activities.
10. A's fundraising appeals give donors the impression that gifts will be used to further R's programs.	Appeals give the impression that funds will be used by A.
Operating	
11. A shares with R many of these operating functions: Personnel/payroll Purchasing Professional services Fundraising Accounting, treasury Office space	Few operating functions are shared; or reimbursement of costs is on a strictly arm's-length basis with formal contracts.
12. Decisions about A's program or other activities are made by R or are subject to R's review or approval.	A's decisions are made autonomously.
13. A's activities are almost exclusively for the benefit of R's members.	Activities benefit persons unaffiliated with R.
Other	
14. A is exempt under IRC Section 501(c) (3) and R is exempt under some other subsection of 501(c), and A's main purpose for existence appears to be to solicit tax-deductible contributions to further R's interest.	A's purposes appear to include significant activities apart from those of R.

Exhibit 28.2 ***Continued***

(ii) Pass-Through Gifts. When one organization (C, in Exhibit 28.3) raises funds for another organization (R, in the exhibit), and either C is not required to be consolidated into R under the rules just listed, or C is consolidated into R but C also issues separate financial statements, the question arises of whether C should record amounts raised by it on behalf of R as its revenue (contribution income) or as amounts held for the benefit of R (a liability). If such amounts are reported by C as a liability, C's statement of revenue and expenses will not ever include the funds raised for R. This issue is of considerable concern to organizations such as federated fundraisers (such as United Ways), community foundations, and other organizations such as foundations affiliated with universities, which raise (and sometimes hold) funds for the benefit of other organizations. SFAS No. 116 (ASC Topic 958-605) indicates that when the pass-through entity has little or no discretion over the use of the amounts raised (i.e., the original donor—D in the exhibit—has specified that C must pass the gift on to R), C should not report the amount as a contribution to it. SFAS No. 136 (ASC Topic 958-605 and -20) clarifies that if a resource provider specifies a third-party beneficiary or beneficiaries and explicitly grants the recipient organization the unilateral power to redirect the use of the assets away from the specified beneficiary or beneficiaries—grants it variance power—the organization acts as a donee and a donor rather than as an agent, trustee, or intermediary and should report the amount provided as a contribution. Exhibit 28.3 lists factors to be considered in assessing whether a pass-through entity should record amounts raised for others as revenue or as a liability.

This list of factors may be helpful to:

- Not-for-profit organizations in deciding whether assets received by them are contributions within the meaning of SFAS No. 116 or are transfers in which the entity is acting as an agent, trustee, or intermediary
- Auditors, in assessing the appropriateness of the client's decision

Usually no one factor is determinative by itself; all relevant factors should be considered together.

D = Original noncharitable donor (individual or business)

C = Initial charitable recipient/donor (sometimes there is more than one charity in the chain)

R = Ultimate charitable or individual recipient

	Factors Whose Presence Indicate Recording by C as Revenue and Expense May Not Be Appropriate	Factors Whose Presence Indicate Recording by C as Revenue and Expense May Be Appropriate
General Factors — Relevant to All Gifts		
1.	D has restricted the gift by specifying that it must be passed on to R.*	D has not restricted the gift in this manner. D specifies a third-party beneficiary or beneficiaries and explicitly grants C the unilateral power to redirect the use of the assets away from the specified beneficiary or beneficiaries—grants it variance power.
2.	C is controlled by D or by R.	C is not controlled by D nor R.
3.	Two or more of D, C, and R are under common control, have overlapping boards or management, share facilities or professional advisors.*	Factor not present.
4.	Even without the intermediation of C, D would still easily be able to make the gift to R.	Without such intermediation, D would not easily be able to make a gift to R. (D is unaware of existence of R or of R's needs, geographic separation, etc.)*
5.	The stated program activities of C and R are similar.	The program activities are not particularly similar.
6.	C has solicited the gift from D under the specific pretense of passing it on to R.*	C has solicited the gift ostensibly for C's own activities.
7.	C does not ever obtain legal title to the assets composing the gift.*	C does at some time obtain legal title to the assets.
8.	D and/or other entities under common control are major sources of support for C.	Factor not present.
9.	R and/or other entities under common control are major destinations for C's charitable resources.	Factor not present.
9a.	Both factors 8 and 9 are present.*	One but not both present.
10.	The "chain" from D to R consists of several Cs.	The chain consists of only one or very few Cs.
11.	Gifts passed from D to C are frequently in exactly the same dollar amount (or very close) as gifts subsequently passed from C to R.*	Factor not present.
12.	Times elapsed between receipt and disbursement of particular amounts by C are short (less than a month).	Times elapsed are relatively long or variable.
13.	C makes pledges to R, payment of which is contingent on receipt of gifts from D.	Factor not present.
14.	C was created only shortly prior to receiving the gift, and/or C appears to have been created specifically for the sole purpose of passing gifts from D on to R.*	Factor not present.

Exhibit 28.3 Factors to Be Considered in Deciding Whether a "Pass-Through" Gift Is Truly Revenue and Expense to Charity (C)

	Factors Whose Presence Indicate Recording by C as Revenue and Expense May Not Be Appropriate	Factors Whose Presence Indicate Recording by C as Revenue and Expense May Be Appropriate
	Factors Especially Relevant to Gifts in Kind	
15.	C never takes physical possession of the gift at an owned or rented facility	C does have physical possession of the items at some time, at a facility normally owned or rented by it.
16.	The nature of the items is not consistent with the program service activities of C as stated in its Form 1023, 990, organizing documents, fundraising appeals, annual report.*	The nature is consistent with C's stated program activities.
17.	The gift was not solicited by C.	C specifically solicited the particular items from D.
18.	The quantity of items is large in relation to the foreseeable needs of C or its donees.	Factor not present.
19.	Factor not present.	Members of the board or staff of C have specific technical or professional expertise about the items and actively participate in deliberations about where to obtain the items and how best to use them.*
20.	D appears to be the only source from which C considers acquiring the item. Same for C/R.	C has several potential or actual sources for the item. Same for R.
21.	C receives numerous types of items dissimilar in their purpose or use.	Factor not present.
22.	C receives items from D and passes them on to R in essentially the same form.	C "adds value" to the items by sorting, repackaging, cleaning, repairing, or testing them.*
23.	C *and* either or both of D and R have little in the way of program services other than distribution of gifts in kind to other charities.	Either C or *both* D and R have significant program services other than distribution of gifts in kind.
24.	The value assigned to the items by D or C appears to be inflated.	Factor not present.
25.	There is a consistent pattern of transfers of items along the same "chain" (D to C to R, etc.).	Factor not present.
26.	Factor not present.	C incurs significant expenses (freight, insurance, storage, etc.) in handling the items.

*Factors considered to be generally more significant.

Exhibit 28.3 ***Continued***

"Economic interest" generally means one or more of four kinds of relationship:

1. Affiliate that raises gifts for the parent
2. Affiliate that holds assets for the parent
3. Affiliate that performs significant functions assigned to it by the parent
4. Parent has guaranteed the debt of or is otherwise committed to provide funds to the affiliate

(l) MERGERS AND ACQUISITIONS. SFAS No. 164 (ASC Topic 958-805) defines two types of combination involving a not-for-profit organization: a merger and an acquisition. Mergers are accounted for on a carryover basis, which is similar to pooling accounting under the old APB Opinion No. 16. Acquisitions are accounted for on an acquisition basis, which is similar to SFAS No. 141(R), now ASC Topic 805.

A determining factor of a merger is the ceding of control by the governing bodies of two (or more) organizations to a new organization. The governing board of the new entity must be newly formed, but establishing a new legal entity is not a requirement.

Other factors, such as relative size, relative dominance of the process and of the combined entity, and relative financial health, can be considered in judging whether control has been ceded but are not themselves determinants of a merger versus an acquisition. All other combinations not meeting the criteria for a merger are accounted for as acquisitions.

The accounting treatment for a combination that is deemed to be a merger is described next.

- Add together the historical financial data of the merging entities as of the merger date (not, as under APB Opinion No. 16, as of the beginning of the fiscal year in which the merger occurs).
- Include in the financial statements of the period of the merger data only since the date of the merger (except that for a public company as defined in FSP 126-1, *Applicability of Certain Disclosures and Interim Reporting Requirements for Obligors for Conduit Debt Securities,* pro forma disclosure is required as if the merger had occurred at the beginning of the fiscal year.) Conform accounting policies, except, because a merger is not a fresh start, it is not an event that permits the election of accounting options that are restricted to the entity's initial acquisition or *recognition of an item (or the reversal of a previous election of an accounting option.* Thus, for example, one merging entity's election of the FV option (SFAS No. 159; ASC Topic 825) for a particular financial asset or liability permits neither the new entity's election of the FV option for *other* financial assets or liabilities nor reversal of a previous election of this option.
- Eliminate effects of any intra-entity transactions.
- Roll all reclassifications, adjustments, and other changes needed to effect a merger into opening balances.
- Since the successor organization after a merger is a new entity, there is no prior period statement of activities or cash flows. An opening balance sheet (statement of financial position) may be presented if desired.

The accounting treatment for a combination that is deemed to be an acquisition is described next.

- Bring in all identifiable assets and liabilities (and any noncontrolling interest) of the acquired entity at their FVs at date of acquisition.
- Some exceptions specific to nonprofits are:
    - Account for collections in accordance with the policy of the acquirer.
    - Do not record conditional pledges.
    - Do not attribute any value to donor relationships.
- An exception for leases: Classify leases (operating versus capital) according to their terms at lease inception, unless they have been modified.
- If the value of the acquired assets exceeds the sum of the acquired liabilities plus any consideration, record the difference as an inherent contribution and report it as a separate credit in the statement of activities.
- If the sum of the liabilities plus consideration exceeds the assets, record the difference as goodwill. If the entity is predominantly supported by contributions and/or investment return, however, write off the goodwill immediately as a separate charge in the statement of activities. *Predominantly supported by* means that contributions and investment return are expected to be significantly more than the total of all other revenues.
- Account for any noncontrolling interests in accordance with SFAS No. 160, *Noncontrolling Interests in Consolidated Financial Statements.*(now ASC Topic 810)
- Account for acquisition-related costs as period expenses, except for debt issuance costs.

SFAS No. 142, *Goodwill and Other Intangibles,* (ASC Topic 350) is made fully effective for not-for-profit entities. Under SFAS No. 142, goodwill is no longer amortized; rather it is tested for impairment.

Various descriptive, quantitative, and qualitative (why the merger/acquisition occurred) disclosures are required.

SFAS No. 164 does not apply to:

- The formation of a joint venture
- The acquisition of assets that do not constitute either a business or a nonprofit activity
- A combination between entities under common control
- An event in which a not-for-profit entity obtains control of another entity but does not consolidate that entity, as permitted or required by AICPA SOP 94-3.

(m) CASH FLOWS. SFAS No. 117 (ASC Topic 958-230) requires the presentation of a statement of cash flows. Exhibit 28.4 illlustrates a sample statement of cash flows, following the example in the Statement.

NATIONAL ASSOCIATION OF ENVIRONMENTALISTS
STATEMENT OF CASH FLOWS
for the Year Ended December 31, 20XX

Operating cash flows:	
Cash received from:	
Sales of goods and services	$ 198,835
Investment income	14,607
Gifts and grants:	
Unrestricted	230,860
Restricted	37,400
Cash paid to employees and suppliers	(265,854)
Cash paid to charitable beneficiaries	(83,285)
Interest paid	(350)
Net operating cash flows	132,213
Financing cash flows:	
Nonexpendable gifts	31,500
Proceeds from borrowing	5,000
Repayment of debt	(5,000)
Net financing cash flows	31,500
Investing cash flows:	
Purchase of building and equipment	(38,617)
Purchase of investments	(60,000)
Proceeds from sale of investments	50,000
Net investing cash flows	(48,617)
Net increase in cash	115,096
Cash: Beginning of year	11,013
End of year	$ 126,109

Reconciliation of Excess of Revenues over Expenses to Operating Cash Flows

Excess of Revenues over Expenses	$ 161,316
Add: Depreciation expense	13,596
Less: Appreciation of investments	(33,025)
Changes in: Receivables	(6,939)
Payables and deferred income	28,765
Nonexpendable contributions	(31,500)
Operating cash flows	$ 132,213

Exhibit 28.4 Statement of Cash Flows, Derived from Data Included in Exhibits 28.5 and 28.6

(n) GOVERNMENTAL VERSUS NONGOVERNMENTAL ACCOUNTING. In 1989, the Financial Accounting Foundation, overseer of the FASB and the Governmental Accounting Standards Board (GASB, its counterpart in the governmental sector; see discussion in Chapter 33), resolved the question of the jurisdiction of each body. A question related to several types of organizations, mainly not-for-profits, that exist in both governmental and nongovernmental forms. These types include institutions of higher education, museums, libraries, hospitals, and others. The issue is whether it is more important to have, for example, all hospitals follow a single set of accounting principles or to have all types of governmental entities do so. This matter was resolved by conferring on GASB jurisdiction over accounting standard setting for all governmental entities.

28.3 SPECIFIC TYPES OF ORGANIZATIONS

This section summarizes the accounting and reporting principles discussed in the FASB Standards, and, the provisions of the AICPA not-for-profit *Audit Guide.* For the most part, the FASB Standards prescribe the same accounting treatment for a given transaction by all types of not-for-profit organizations. One exception to that rule is a requirement that voluntary health and welfare organizations present a statement of functional expenses. (Other types of nonprofits are encouraged, but not required, to do so.) More detailed discussions of certain accounting and reporting standards in the FASB documents can be found in Section 28.2 of this chapter. For example, a full discussion of accounting for contributions is in Section 28.2(i).

(a) VOLUNTARY HEALTH AND WELFARE ORGANIZATIONS. The term *voluntary health and welfare organization* first entered the accounting world with the publication in 1964 of the first edition of the so-called *Black Book, Standards of Accounting and Financial Reporting for Voluntary Health and Welfare Organizations,* published by the National Health Council and the National Social Welfare Assembly. The term has been retained through three successor editions of that book and was used by the AICPA in the title of its *Audit Guide, Audits of Voluntary Health and Welfare Organizations,* first published in 1967 and revised in 1974, and again in 1996. *Voluntary health and welfare organizations* are those not-for-profit organizations that "derive their revenue primarily from voluntary contributions from the general public to be used for general or specific purposes connected with health, welfare, or community services."[5] Note that there are two separate parts to this definition: (1) the organization must derive its revenue from voluntary contributions from the general public; and (2) the organization's mission must involve health, welfare, or community services.

Many organizations fit the second part of this definition but receive a substantial portion of their revenues from sources other than public contributions. For example, an opera company would not be a voluntary health and welfare organization because its primary source of income is box office receipts, although it exists for the common good. A YMCA would be excluded because normally it receives most of its revenues from dues and program fees. A museum would be excluded, even if it were to receive most of its revenue from contributions, since its activities are educational, not in the areas of health and welfare.

(i) Financial Statements. GAAP requires four principal financial statements for voluntary health and welfare organizations. Examples are shown in this chapter. These four statements are:

1. Balance sheet (Exhibit 28.5)
2. Statement of support, revenue and expenses, and changes in net assets (Exhibit 28.6)
3. Statement of cash flows (shown in Exhibit 28.4)
4. Statement of functional expenses (Exhibit 28.7)

The sample financial statements presented are for illustrative purposes only, and variation from the ones presented is permitted, as long as the required disclosure elements are shown.

---

[5] Appendix D (Glossary) of SFAS No. 117.

NATIONAL ASSOCIATION OF ENVIRONMENTALISTS
BALANCE SHEET
December 31, 20XX

	December 31, 20XX					December 31, 20XX
	Current Funds		Endowment Funds	Fixed Asset Funds	Total All Funds	Total All Funds
	Unrestricted	Restricted				
ASSETS						
Current assets:						
Cash	$ 58,392	$17,151	$ 8,416	$ 2,150	$ 86,109	$ 11,013
Savings accounts	40,000				40,000	
Accounts receivable	3,117				3,117	918
Investments, at market	86,195		226,119		312,314	269,289
Pledges receivable	4,509	1,000			5,509	769
Total current assets	192,213	18,151	234,535	2,150	447,049	281,989
Fixed assets, at cost				111,135	111,135	72,518
Less: Accumulated depreciation				(19,615)	(19,615)	(6,019)
Net fixed assets				91,520	91,520	66,499
Total assets	$192,213	$18,151	$234,535	$ 93,670	$538,569	$348,488
LIABILITIES AND NET ASSETS						
Current liabilities:						
Accounts payable	$ 54,181				$ 54,181	$ 25,599
Deferred income	2,516				2,516	2,333
Total current liabilities	56,697				56,697	27,932
Net assets:						
Unrestricted	135,516			$ 93,670	229,186	124,631
Temporarily restricted		$18,151			18,151	5,915
Permanently restricted			$234,535		234,535	190,010
Total	135,516	18,151	234,535	93,670	481,872	320,556
Total liabilities and net assets	$192,213	$18,151	$234,535	$ 93,670	$538,569	$348,488

Exhibit 28.5 Balance Sheet Prepared in Columnar Format

(ii) Balance Sheet. Exhibit 28.5 shows a balance sheet for the National Association of Environmentalists. Although GAAP requires (and illustrates) only a single-column balance sheet showing the totals of assets, liabilities, and net assets (and net assets by class), many organizations will wish to show more detail of assets and liabilities, but not necessarily by class. This is acceptable.

Funds versus Classes. Note that the columns on the balance sheet reflect the funds used for bookkeeping purposes. This is permissible, as long as the net asset amounts for each of the three classes are shown in the net assets section of the balance sheet.

Comparison Column. Exhibit 28.5 shows the totals for the previous year to provide a comparison for the reader. GAAP does not require presentation of a comparison column, but it is recommended, and this author encourages its use.

Designation of Unrestricted Net Assets. While it is a little more awkward to show when the balance sheet is presented in a columnar fashion as in Exhibit 28.5, it is still possible to disclose the composition of the unrestricted net assets of $135,516.

For example, the unrestricted net assets of the National Association of Environmentalists of $135,516 could be split into several amounts, representing the board's present intention of how it

NATIONAL ASSOCIATION OF ENVIRONMENTALISTS
STATEMENT OF SUPPORT, REVENUE AND EXPENSES, AND CHANGES IN NET ASSETS
for the Year Ended December 31, 20XX

	Unrestricted	Temporarily Restricted	Permanently Restricted	Total
Support:				
Contributions and gifts	$174,600	$38,400	$ 10,000	$223,000
Bequests	60,000		21,500	81,500
Total support	234,600	38,400	31,500	304,500
Revenues:				
Membership dues	20,550			20,550
Research projects	127,900			127,900
Advertising income	33,500			33,500
Subscriptions to nonmembers	18,901			18,901
Dividends and interest income	14,607			14,607
Appreciation of investments	30,000		3,025	33,025
Total revenues	245,458		3,025	248,483
Total support and revenues	480,058	38,400	34,525	552,983
Net assets released from restriction	26,164	(26,164)		
Expenses:				
Program services:				
National Environment magazine	110,500			110,500
Cleanup month campaign	126,617			126,167
Lake Erie project	115,065			115,065
Total program services	352,182			352,182
Supporting services:				
Management and general	33,516			33,516
Fundraising	5,969			5,969
Total supporting services	39,485			39,485
Total expenses	391,667			391,667
Excess (deficit) of revenues over expenses	114,555	12,236	34,525	161,316
Other changes in net assets:				
Transfer of unrestricted resources to meet challenge grant	(10,000)		10,000	—
Change in net assets	104,555	12,236	44,525	161,316
Net assets, beginning of year	124,631	5,915	190,010	320,556
Net assets, end of year	$229,186	$ 18,151	$234,535	$481,872

Exhibit 28.6 Income Statement That Meets the Requirements of SFAS No. 117

plans to use this amount. Perhaps $50,000 of it is intended for Project Seaweed and the balance is available for undesignated purposes. The net assets section of the balance sheet would appear:

Net assets:	
Designated by the board for Project Seaweed	$ 50,000
Undesignated, available for current purposes	85,516
	$135,516

As monies are expended for Project Seaweed in subsequent periods, they would be recorded as an expense in the statement of support, revenue and expenses, and changes in net assets. At the same time, the amount of the net assets designated by the board for Project Seaweed would be reduced and the amount "undesignated" would be increased by the same amount.

NATIONAL ASSOCIATION OF ENVIRONMENTALISTS
STATEMENT OF FUNCTIONAL EXPENSES
for the Year Ended December 31, 20XX

		Program Services				Supporting Services		
	Total All Expenses	*National Environment* Magazine	Clean-up Month Campaign	Lake Erie Project	Total Program	Management and General	Fund Raising	Total Supporting
Salaries	$170,773	$ 24,000	$ 68,140	$ 60,633	$152,773	$15,000	$3,000	$18,000
Payroll taxes and employee benefits	22,199	3,120	8,857	7,882	19,859	1,950	,390	2,340
Total compensation	192,972	27,120	76,997	68,515	172,632	16,950	3,390	20,340
Printing	84,071	63,191	18,954	515	82,660	1,161	250	1,411
Mailing, postage, and shipping	14,225	10,754	1,188	817	12,759	411	1,055	1,466
Rent	19,000	3,000	6,800	5,600	15,400	3,000	600	3,600
Telephone	5,615	895	400	1,953	3,248	2,151	216	2,367
Outside art	14,865	3,165	11,700	—	14,865	—	—	—
Local travel	1,741	—	165	915	1,080	661	—	661
Conferences and conventions	6,328	—	1,895	2,618	4,513	1,815	—	1,815
Depreciation	13,596	2,260	2,309	5,616	10,185	3,161	250	3,411
Legal and audit	2,000	—	—	—	—	2,000	—	2,000
Supplies	31,227	—	1,831	28,516	30,347	761	119	880
Miscellaneous	6,027	115	4,378	—	4,493	1,445	89	1,534
Total	$391,667	$110,500	$126,617	$115,065	$352,182	$33,516	$5,969	$39,485

Exhibit 28.7 Analysis of the Various Program Expenses Showing the Natural Expense Categories Making Up Each of the Functional or Program Categories

(iii) Statement of Support, Revenue and Expenses, and Changes in Net Assets. Exhibit 28.6 shows a statement of support, revenue and expenses, and changes in net assets for the National Association of Environmentalists. This is the format shown in SFAS No. 117 (ASC Topic 958-225), with some modifications (to be discussed).

Reporting of Expenses

Functional Classification of Expenses. Exhibit 28.6 shows the expenses of the National Association of Environmentalists reported on a functional basis. This type of presentation requires management to tell the reader how much of its funds were expended for each program category and the amounts spent on supporting services, including fundraising.

This functional reporting is not optional; it must be shown, either in the primary financial statements or in the footnotes.

In many instances, the allocation of salaries between functional or program categories should be based on time reports and similar analyses. Other expenses, such as rent, utilities, and maintenance, will be allocated based on floor space. Each organization will have to develop time and expense accumulation procedures that will provide the necessary basis for allocation. Organizations have to have reasonably sophisticated procedures to be able to allocate expenses between various categories. An excellent reference source is the fourth edition (1998) of *Standards of Accounting and Financial Reporting for Voluntary Health and Welfare Organizations*—commonly called the *Black Book.*

Program Services. Not-for-profit organizations exist to perform particular services either for the public or for the members of the organization. They do not exist to provide employment for their employees or to perpetuate themselves. The *Audit Guide* reemphasizes this by requiring the organization to identify major program services and their related costs. Some organizations may have only one specific program category, but many will have several. Each organization should decide for itself into how many categories it wishes to divide its program activities.

Supporting Services. Supporting services are those expenses that do not relate directly to performing the functions for which the organization was established but nevertheless are essential to the continued existence of the organization.

The statement of support, revenue and expenses, and changes in net assets must clearly disclose the amount of supporting services. These amounts are broken down between fundraising and administrative (management and general) expenses. This distinction between supporting and program services is required, as is the separate reporting of fundraising.

Management and general expenses are probably the most difficult of the supporting categories to define because a major portion of top management's time usually relates more directly to program activities than to management in general. Yet many think, incorrectly, that top management should be classified entirely "management and general." The distinction to be made is between management of one or more programs and management of the organization as a legal entity. The AICPA *Audit Guide* defines *management and general expenses* in this way:

> those that are not identifiable with a single program, fund-raising activity, or membership-development activity but that are indispensable to the conduct of those activities and to an organization's existence. They include oversight, business management, general record keeping, budgeting, financing, soliciting revenue from exchange transactions, such as government contracts and related administrative activities, and all management and administration except for direct conduct of program services or fund-raising activities. The costs of oversight and management usually include the salaries and expenses of the governing board, the chief executive officer of the organization, and the supporting staff. (If such staff spend a portion of their time directly supervising program services or categories of other supporting services, however, their salaries and expenses should be allocated among those functions.) The costs of disseminating information to inform the public of the organization's "stewardship" of contributed funds, announcements concerning appointments, and the annual report, among other costs, should similarly be classified as management and general expenses. The costs of soliciting funds other than contributions, including exchange transactions (whether program-related or not), should be classified as management and general expenses.

The category of fundraising expenses is a very sensitive one because a great deal of negative publicity has been associated with some organizations that appear to have very high fundraising costs. The cost of fundraising includes not only the direct costs associated with a particular effort but a fair allocation of the overhead of the organization, including the time of top management.

Fundraising activities involve inducing potential donors to contribute money, securities, services, materials, facilities, other assets, or time. They include:

- Publicizing and conducting fundraising campaigns
- Maintaining donor mailing lists
- Conducting special fundraising events
- Preparing and distributing fundraising manuals, instructions, and other materials
- Conducting other activities involved with soliciting contributions from individuals, foundations, governments, and others

The financial statements should disclose total fundraising expenses.

Fundraising expenses are normally recorded as an expense in the statement of activity at the time they are incurred. It is not appropriate to defer such amounts. Thus the cost of acquiring or developing a mailing list that has value over more than one year would nevertheless be expensed in its entirety at the time the list was purchased or the costs incurred. The reason for this conservative approach is the difficulty accountants have in satisfying themselves that costs that might logically be deferred will in fact be recovered by future support related thereto. Further, if substantial amounts of deferred fundraising costs were permitted, the credibility of the financial statements would be in jeopardy, particularly in view of the increased publicity surrounding fundraising expenses.

If fundraising is combined with another function, it may be possible to allocate the costs among the functions. In order to allocate any such costs to other than fundraising, criteria of purpose, audience, and content as defined in SOP 98-2, *Accounting for Cost of Activities of Not-for Profit Organizations and State and Local Government Entities that Include Fund Raising,* must be met. These criteria are discussed in the next section.

Organizations soliciting grants from governments or foundations have a cost that is somewhat different from fundraising costs. Where such amounts are identifiable and material in amount, they should be separately identified and reported as a supporting service.

Allocation of Joint Costs of Multipurpose Activities. In 1998, the ACIPA issued SOP 98-2, now included in the *Audit Guide,* and codified in ASC Topic 958-720. This SOP was issued partly in response to criticism of prior standards by charity watchdogs, such as the National Charities Information Bureau and the Philanthropic Advisory Services of the Council of Better Business Bureaus (now merged into the BBB Wise Giving Alliance), and by state attorneys general. Charities were criticized for allocating costs to program that were really fundraising in nature. The greatest criticism was leveled against charities using significant direct mail campaigns that allocated a major portion of those costs to program on the basis that it met the program goal of providing educational literature to recipients.

This SOP provides a clear step-by-step analysis that must be followed in determining whether costs can be allocated to other than fundraising. If any of the criteria of purpose, audience, and content are not met, all costs of the joint activity must be reported as fundraising. This is so even if some of the costs, if incurred in an activity without fundraising, would be properly allocated to program (or management and general) costs. One important change from the previous rules was that education about the cause of an organization does not meet the purpose criterion unless it is part of a call for specific action by the audience that will help accomplish the entity's mission (a "call to action"). Previously, educational information about the cause was routinely allocated to program costs.

The criteria that must be met for allocation are listed next.

- The *purpose* criterion is met if the purpose of the joint activity includes accomplishing program or management and general functions. To accomplish a program function, there must be a specific call for action, as noted in the previous paragraph. The SOP provides a number of examples and tests for judging whether the purpose criterion is met. Note that asking the audience to make contributions is indeed a call for action, but not one that in and of itself directly helps accomplish the organization's mission.

- The *audience* criterion is designed to ensure that the audience is relevant for the non-fundraising purpose of the activity. In particular, there is a rebuttable presumption that the audience criterion is not met if the audience includes prior donors or has been selected based on its ability or likelihood to contribute.
- The *content* criterion requires that the content meet the program or management and general function and that for program purposes there be a call for specific action to help accomplish the entity's mission.

In practice, it has been found that, for some organizations, the call to action is the most difficult part of these criteria to meet. The author suggests that organizations planning to allocate joint costs review their proposed call to action with their auditor before engaging in the activity. Then any deficiency in the proposal can be remedied before the activity occurs.

The SOP does not prescribe or prohibit any specific allocation methods although it does describe some acceptable methods. General cost accounting principles should be used in allocating costs, and they should be consistently applied.

All Expenses Reported as Unrestricted. This was a new requirement in SFAS No. 117 and was a significant change for almost all not-for-profit organizations (except hospitals). In the past, expenses had been reported in the same fund as the revenue that was used to pay for the expenses. Thus, unrestricted revenue, and expenses paid for out of that revenue, were shown together in the unrestricted fund. Current restricted revenue, and the expenses paid for out of that revenue, were in the current restricted fund. (No expenses could ever be paid out of the permanent endowment fund, due to the nature of the restriction of those amounts.)

With the adoption of SFAS No. 117, all expenses, regardless of the origin of the resources used to finance the expenses, are shown in the unrestricted class of net assets; no expenses are in the temporarily restricted class. This is shown in Exhibit 28.6. The method of relating the restricted revenue to the expenses financed out of that revenue is to reclassify an amount of temporarily restricted net assets equal to the expenses to the unrestricted net assets class ($26,164 in the exhibit).

Columnar Presentation. The statement presentation is in a columnar format and, as can be observed in Exhibit 28.6, includes all three classes on one statement. It is also possible to present the information in a single column. In that format, information for the three classes is shown sequentially, including the change in net assets for the class, followed by the total change in net assets for the year. An advantage of such a format is the ease of showing comparative prior-year information for each class; a disadvantage is the inability to present a total column.

It should be noted that this statement provides a complete picture of all activity of this organization for the year—not just the activity of a single class or fund. Further, inclusion of a "total" column on the statement enables the reader to quickly see the overall activity; he or she does not have to add together several amounts to get the complete picture. This represents a major improvement in not-for-profit reporting.

Unrestricted Activity in a Single Column. One of the most significant features of this presentation is that all legally unrestricted revenues and all expenses are reported in the single column representing the unrestricted class of net assets. The use of a single column in which all unrestricted activity is reported greatly simplifies the presentation and makes it more likely that a nonaccountant will be able to understand the total picture of the organization.

Many organizations, of course, will want to continue to keep board-designated accounts within their bookkeeping system. This is fine. But for reporting to the public, all unrestricted amounts must be combined and reported as indicated in Exhibit 28.6.

While not recommended, there would appear to be no prohibition to an organization's including additional columns to the *left* of this total "unrestricted" column to show the various unrestricted board-designated categories of funds that make up the total unrestricted class. However, where an organization does so, it must clearly indicate that the total unrestricted column represents the total unrestricted activity for the year and that the detailed columns to the left are only the arbitrarily subdivided amounts making up this total. An organization is better advised to show such detail in a separate supplementary schedule, if at all.

Where an organization chooses to show its unrestricted class broken into two columns and has only one class with restricted resources, it may be acceptable to eliminate the total unrestricted column in the interest of simplicity. An example of the column headings might be:

Unrestricted			
General Fund	Investment Fund	Temporarily Restricted	Total All Classes

The key to whether this would be acceptable is the extent of activity in the various columns. For example, if the temporarily restricted class in the illustration were relatively minor in amount, the total column would largely reflect the unrestricted class (i.e., the general fund and the investment fund). This is a judgment call.

Temporarily Restricted Column. The "temporarily restricted" column represents those amounts that have been given to the organization for a specified purpose other than for permanent endowment or for use in a specified time period. The amounts reported as revenues in this fund represent the total amount the organization received during the year, not the amount that was actually expended.

Use of Separate Fixed Asset (Plant) Fund. SFAS No. 117 does not mention a separate fixed asset category; rather it includes amounts related to fixed assets in the three classes of net assets discussed earlier. Even though a fixed asset fund is maintained in the organization's bookkeeping system, for external financial reporting purposes, the organization would include most of the amounts of the fixed asset fund in the unrestricted class. This has the additional advantage of reducing the number of columns and eliminating the need for certain reclassifications.

Appreciation of Investments. Appreciation (or depreciation) of investments is shown on the statement of support, revenue and expenses, and changes in net assets. In this instance, the net appreciation of investments was $33,025. Assuming there were no sales or purchases of investments during the year, this amount would have been determined by comparing the market value of the investments at the end of the year with the market value at the beginning of the year. Normally, however, there will be some realized gain or loss during the year. While there is no technical objection to reporting the realized gain or loss separately from the unrealized appreciation (or depreciation), there seems little significance to this distinction.

Operating Statement. A variation on this statement that some may wish to use is to present a subtotal of "operating" revenue in excess of "operating" expenses. This would focus the reader's attention on what the organization considers its core "operations," as distinguished from matters that it considers peripheral or incidental to its operations. SFAS No. 117 (ASC 958-225) permits, but does not require, this presentation. If an organization chooses this presentation, it will decide for itself what it considers to be its operations, versus other activities. Appendix 28.6 contains a list to help organizations decide what they wish to consider as operating versus nonoperating transactions.

(iv) Statement of Cash Flows. A statement of cash flows is a summary of the resources made available to an organization during the year and the uses made of such resources. SFAS No. 117 (ASC Topic 958-230) requires presentation of a statement of cash flows by all not-for-profit organizations.

Exhibit 28.4 shows a statement of cash flows. In some ways it is similar to a statement of cash receipts and disbursements, in that it presents cash received and spent. It differs by grouping transactions into three groups: operating, investing, and financing cash flows. Also, there is less detail of specific types of operating cash flows, since such detail is already shown for revenue and expenses in Exhibit 28.6.

(v) Statement of Functional Expenses. Exhibit 28.7 is a statement that analyzes functional or program expenses and shows the natural expense categories that go into each functional category. It is primarily an analysis to give the reader insight as to the major types of expenses involved. In order to arrive at the functional expense totals shown in the statement of support, revenue and expenses, and changes in net assets, an analysis must be prepared that shows all of the expenses going into each program category. The statement of functional expenses merely summarizes this detail for the reader.

(b) COLLEGES AND UNIVERSITIES. The AICPA *Industry Audit Guide, Audits of Colleges and Universities,* issued in 1973, had been the most authoritative pronouncement on accounting principles and reporting practices for colleges and universities. With the issuance of FASB Statement Nos. 116 and 117, some of the accounting and reporting rules for colleges and universities changed, as discussed throughout this chapter.

(i) Fund Accounting. Fund accounting is a prominent element of college and university accounting. Colleges and universities have historically followed fund accounting procedures. Fund accounting continues to find favor at colleges and universities because many gifts and grants that colleges receive possess external restrictions that must be carefully monitored, and also because many colleges voluntarily set aside some current unrestricted funds as "endowment" to produce future income.

The next six fund groupings are generally used for internal bookkeeping by colleges and universities:

1. *Current funds* are resources available for carrying out the general activities of an institution. In public reporting, current unrestricted funds are usually reported separately from current restricted funds, that is, funds restricted by donors or grantors for specific current purposes.
2. *Loan funds* are resources available for loans to students, faculty, and staff. If only the investment income from restricted endowment funds can be used for loans, only the income should be reported in the loan fund.
3. *Endowment and similar funds* consist of three types of endowment resources:
   a. True endowment, where the donor stipulates that the principal must be maintained inviolate and in perpetuity, and only the income earned thereon may be expended
   b. Term endowment, where the donor stipulates that, upon the passage of time or the incidence of an event, the principal may be used for current operations or specific purposes
   c. Quasi-endowment, where the board of trustees voluntarily retains as principal a portion of current funds to produce current and future income
4. *Annuity and life income funds* are endowment resources of which the college owns only the principal and not the income earned thereon. In accepting an annuity or life income gift, the college agrees to pay the contributor all income earned or a specific amount for a stated period of time. See the discussion of split-interest gifts at Subsection 28.2(i)(iii).
5. *Plant funds* consist of four fund groupings, and separate financial data for each are often reported:
   a. *Unexpended* plant funds are used for plant additions or improvements.
   b. *Renewal and replacement* funds are transferred from current funds for future renewal or replacement of the existing plant. These funds provide for the future integrity of the physical plant.
   c. *Retirement of indebtedness* funds are set aside to service debt interest and principal. It is often appropriate to designate which funds are set aside under mandatory contractual agreements with lenders and which funds are voluntarily designated.
   d. *Investment in plant* records the actual cost of all land, buildings, and equipment owned by the college. Donated plant is recorded at market value at the date of the gift.

6. *Agency funds* are funds over which an institution exercises custodial but not proprietary authority. An example is funds that are owned by a student organization but are deposited with the college.

(ii) Encumbrance Accounting. Encumbrance accounting is not acceptable for financial statements of colleges and universities. It is inappropriate to report, as expenditures or liabilities, commitments for materials or services not received by the reporting date. A portion of the current unrestricted fund may be designated to satisfy purchase orders, provided that the designation is made only in the fund balances (net assets) section of the balance sheet.

(c) OTHER NOT-FOR-PROFIT ORGANIZATIONS

(i) Accounting Principles. Not-for-profit organizations not covered by another AICPA *Industry Audit Guide* were covered by SOP 78-10. Organizations in this group include professional and trade associations, private and community foundations, religious organizations, libraries, museums, private schools, and performing arts organizations. Most accounting principles applicable to these organizations are discussed throughout this chapter.

Subscription and Membership Income. Subscription and membership income should be recognized in the periods in which the organization provides goods or services to subscribers or members. This usually requires deferring such amounts when received and recognizing them ratably over the membership or subscription period. Special calculations, based on life expectancy, are required when so-called life memberships are involved.

Grants to Others. Organizations that award grants should record a grant as a liability and an expense in the period in which the recipient is entitled to the grant. This is usually the period in which the grant is authorized, even though some of the payments may not be made until later periods.

Under SFAS No. 116, grantors account for grants in the same way as grantees—except backward—expense and liability instead of revenue and receivable. See Section 28.2(i) for a discussion of accounting for gifts and pledges.

28.4 AUDIT CONSIDERATIONS FOR A NOT-FOR-PROFIT ORGANIZATION

(a) GENERAL CONSIDERATIONS. An audit of the financial statements of a not-for-profit organization is similar to an audit of a for-profit enterprise, and generally accepted auditing standards should be followed. A not-for-profit organization, however, seeks to provide an optimal level of services rather than to maximize profits, and accordingly, its financial statements focus on the activity and balances of different classes and funds. This in turn influences the conduct of the audit.

(b) INTERNAL CONTROL. Some, especially many smaller, not-for-profit organizations are not able to establish effective internal control. The size of staff may be inadequate to achieve a proper segregation of duties, and the nature of some transactions often precludes sufficient checks and balances. Internal control deficiencies are often mitigated by adoption of procedures, including these five:

1. Involvement of senior management and directors in the operation of the organization
2. Restricting check signing to senior management and directors
3. Implementing effective bank reconciliation procedures
4. Preparing annual budgets and promptly investigating variances from budget estimates
5. Depositing investment securities with independent custodians

(c) MATERIALITY. The issue of what is material is equally important for not-for-profit and for-profit organizations. In for-profit enterprises, evaluating materiality involves considering the effect of alternate accounting treatments and disclosures on decisions by investors, and it relates to net income and earnings per share. These measures are generally not applicable to not-for-profit organizations. Instead, evaluating materiality involves considering the effects of accounting treatments and disclosures on decisions by contributors, and it relates to revenue, expenditures, and the cost of individual programs.

(d) TAXES. Not-for-profit organizations are generally exempt from income taxes and are often exempt from property and sales taxes (but mostly not from payroll taxes). Tax liabilities, however, may arise from tax on unrelated business income, tax on net income resulting from a loss of tax-exempt status, or certain excise taxes applicable to private foundations. Organizations are required to identify all of their tax positions, as described in FIN 48 (ASC Topic 740-10), which is discussed in Section 28.2(j), and assess whether those positions are likely to survive challenge by a taxing authority or would be considered uncertain, in which case disclosure and/or accrual of a liability is required.

(e) CONSOLIDATION. Not-for-profit organizations do not "own" other organizations in the sense that businesses own other businesses. Not-for-profit organizations, however, may exercise effective control over affiliates or related organizations; in such instances, preparation of combined financial statements may be appropriate.

(f) COMPLIANCE AUDITING. In recent years, federal and state governments have become more active in requiring recipients of government money to submit auditor reports on various aspects of financial operations. These usually include opinions on financial data for the organization as a whole and, for government grants, reports on internal controls and compliance with laws and regulations. The exact requirements may differ depending on the type of recipient (college, hospital, etc.), the agency that made the grant, whether the money was received directly or through another level of government, and the amount of money received. It is important for the auditor to ascertain any compliance auditing requirements prior to beginning fieldwork, so that he or she can perform the work necessary to issue the required reports. Specific requirements are contained in a number of different documents including Statement in Auditing Standards (SAS) No. 117 (AU-C[6] Section 801), *Compliance Audits;* the Department of Health and Human Services audit guide, *Guidelines for Audits of Federal Awards to Nonprofit Organizations;* various circulars issued by the Office of Management and Budget (principally A-21, A-110, A-122, A-133); and *Government Auditing Standards,* issued by the Government Accountability Office (generally referred to as the *Yellow Book*). Compliance auditing requirements are also found in the *Office of Management and Budget Compliance Supplement* (revised each year).

Additional guidance for compliance auditing is in the AICPA Audit Guide *Government Auditing Standards and Circular A-133 Audits.* Compliance auditing is discussed further in Chapter 33 of this *Handbook.*

(g) INVESTMENTS. Auditing investments is generally no different in the nonprofit environment from in a for-profit. The auditor needs to become satisfied that the investments: (1) exist, (2) are owned by the organization, and (3) are reported at the proper amount in the balance sheet—which, under SFAS No. 124, for many investments held by nonprofits is "fair value" as discussed in SFAS No. 157 (codified in Topic 320). Satisfaction as to the first two of these issues usually is obtained by confirmation from the investment manager or custodian. Satisfaction as to the value can be more difficult when investments are not publicly traded (so-called alternative investments, such as hedge funds, private placements, partnerships, venture capital funds, funds of funds, real estate, etc.). Even though such alternative investments do not have to be reported at fair value in the balance sheet (although they may be so reported), some larger organizations are required to report

---

[6] Effective for audits ending on or after 12/15/12 the AICPA re-codification of its auditing standards under SAS 122, *Clarification and Recodification*, is effective. AU-C is a temporary designation given the recodified standards to distinguish it from the AU sections which will be phased out.

their fair value in a footnote. Further, auditors normally will want to obtain information about FV to be satisfied that the reported value is not impaired (which would require a write-down to some lower value).

The AICPA has issued an auditing interpretation (AU 9328-1) stating that mere confirmation with an investment manager, fund manager, or trustee is not an adequate procedure for obtaining satisfaction as to FV. The auditor must obtain independent evidence as to the FV of the underlying assets in the investment account, fund, or trust. Doing this may become difficult when, as sometimes happens, the manager or trustee will not reveal—even to the organization—the individual assets being held in the fund or trust. Unless the auditor is able to obtain and audit this information, if such investments are material to the balance sheet, he or she likely will have to report a scope limitation and either qualify the opinion or disclaim an opinion. The AICPA also has issued a practice aid, *Alternative Investments—Audit Considerations,* to assist accountants and auditors with this issue.

(h) UNIQUE AUDITING AREAS. Auditing areas unique to not-for-profit organizations include these:

- *Collections of museums, libraries, zoological parks, and similar organizations.* Auditing considerations include valuation of assets, capitalization, accessions and deaccessions, security, insurance coverage, and observation of inventory. Certain procedures are appropriate even though the collection is not capitalized.
- *Contributions.* Auditing considerations include ascertaining that amounts reported as contributions are properly stated. Audit tests for noncash contributions include testing their assigned value. Auditors are particularly concerned about the possibility that contributions that were intended for the organization may never have been received and recorded. Given that contributions are, by their nature, voluntary, auditors should be aware that performance of a "full inclusion" test is usually more difficult than for other types of revenue.
- *Fees for performance of services, including tuition, membership dues, ticket revenue, and patient fees.* Auditing considerations include confirming that revenue is computed at proper rates, collected, and properly recorded for all services provided.
- *Functional allocation of expenses.* Auditing considerations include appropriateness of allocations among functions, reasonableness of allocation methods, accuracy of computations, and consistency of allocation bases with bases of prior periods. These considerations are especially important when joint costs of multipurpose activities (discussed earlier in 28.3(a)(iii)) are involved.
- *Restricted resources.* Auditing considerations include ascertaining that transactions are for the restricted purpose and are recorded in the proper restricted fund.
- *Grant awards to others.* Auditing considerations include confirming grant awards with recipients and ascertaining that grants are recorded in the proper accounting period.
- *Tax compliance.* Not-for-profits are subject to IRC sections that differ from those regularly applicable to businesses. Auditors must review compliance with these sections. Areas of particular concern are conformity with exempt purpose, unrelated business income, lobbying, status as a public charity (if applicable), and special rules applicable to private foundations.

28.5 SOURCES AND SUGGESTED REFERENCES

American Institute of Certified Public Accountants.[7] *Accounting Trends & Techniques—Not-for-Profit Organizations, Financial Statement Reporting and Disclosure Practices*. New York: Author, updated 2005.

———. *Audit Committee Toolkit: Not-for-Profit Organizations*. New York: Author, 2005.

———. *Audit Risk Alert, Not-for-Profit Entities Industry Developments*. New York: Author, 2011.

———. *Checklists and Illustrative Financial Statements—Not-for-Profit Entities* New York: Author 2011 (annual).

———. *Government Auditing Standards and Circular A-133 Audits.* New York: Author, updated 2011.

[7] Locate AICPA documents at *www.cpa2biz.com/AST/AICPA_CPA2BIZ_Browse/Store/Publications.jsp*

______. Not-for-Profit Organizations Committee, *Audit and Accounting Guide, Not-for-Profit Entities*. New York: Author, 1996, updated 2011.

______. Practice Aid, *Alternative Investments—Audit Considerations.* New York: Author, 2006.

______. Technical Practice Aids, especially Section 6140. 2011 (updated periodically)

______. White Paper, *Measurement of Fair Value for Certain Transactions of Not-for-Profit Entities,* 2011. *www.aicpa.org/interestareas/frc/industryinsights/pages/fv_and_disclosures_nfp.aspx*

Anthony, R. N. *Financial Accounting in Nonbusiness Organizations: An Exploratory Study of Conceptual Issues*. Stamford, CT: Financial Accounting Standards Board, 1978.

Anthony, R. N., and D. W. Young. *Management Control in Nonprofit Organizations*, 3rd ed. Homewood, IL: Richard D. Irwin, 1984.

Blazek, J. *Tax Planning and Compliance for Tax-Exempt Organizations: Forms, Checklists, Procedures*, 5th ed. Hoboken, NJ: John Wiley & Sons, forthcoming.

Cary, W. L., and C. B. Bright. *The Law and the Lore of Endowment Funds—Report to the Ford Foundation*. New York: Ford Foundation, 1969.

Council of Better Business Bureaus Wise Giving Alliance. *Charity Accountability Standards.* Arlington, VA: Author, 2003. *www.bbb.org/us/Standards-Charity/*

Evangelical Joint Accounting Committee. *Accounting and Financial Reporting Guide for Christian Ministries*, rev. ed. San Clemente, CA: Christian Management Association, Author, 2001. *www.ecfa.ws/cgi-bin/category.cgi?item=AFRG&type=store*

______. *Donor-Restricted Gifts Simplified*. Winchester, VA: Author, 2007.

Financial Accounting Standards Board. *Accounting Standards Codification.* Norwalk, CT: Author, 2009. See especially Topic 958, *Not-for-Profit Organizations. www.fasb.org/home*

______. Statement of Financial Accounting Concepts No. 4, *Objectives of Financial Reporting By Nonbusiness Organizations*. Stamford, CT: Author, 1980.

______. Statement of Financial Accounting Concepts No. 6, *Elements of Financial Statements*. Stamford, CT: Author, 1985.

Gross, M. J. Jr., R. Larkin, and J. H. McCarthy. *Financial and Accounting Guide for Not-for-Profit Organizations*, Sixth ed. New York: John Wiley & Sons, 2000.

Gross, M. J. Jr., J. H. McCarthy, and N. E. Shelmon. *Financial and Accounting Guide for Not-for-Profit Organizations*, 7th ed. Hoboken, NJ: John Wiley & Sons, 2005.

Holder, W. W. *The Not-for-Profit Organization Reporting Entity.* New Milford, CT: Philanthropy Monthly Press, 1986.

Hopkins, B. R. *The Law of Fund-Raising*, 4th ed. Hoboken, NJ: John Wiley & Sons, 2009.

______. *The Law of Tax-Exempt Organizations*, 10th ed. Hoboken, NJ: John Wiley & Sons, 2011.

______. *Starting and Managing a Nonprofit Organization: A Legal Guide*, 5th ed. Hoboken, NJ: John Wiley & Sons, 2009.

Hummel, J. *Starting and Running a Nonprofit Organization*, Minneapolis: University of Minnesota Press, 1980.

Larkin, R. F. "Accounting." In *The Nonprofit Management Handbook—Operating Policies and Procedures*. ed. T. D. Connors. New York: John Wiley & Sons, 1993, and 1994 Supplement.

______. "Accounting Issues Relating to Fundraising," In *Financial Practices for Effective Fundraising*, ed. J. M. Greenfield. San Francisco: Jossey-Bass, 1994.

National Assembly, National Health Council. *Standards of Accounting and Financial Reporting for Voluntary Health and Welfare Organizations*, 4th ed. New York: Author, 1998.

National Association of College and University Business Officers. *Financial Accounting and Reporting Manual for Higher Education (FARM).* Washington, DC: Author, updated currently. *www.nacubo.org/documents/FARM_Brochure.pdf*

National Association of Independent Schools. *Business Management for Independent Schools*, 5th ed. Washington, DC: Author, 1997.

United States General Accountability Office. *Government Auditing Standards*. Washington, DC: Author, 2011 Revision. *www.gao.gov/yellowbook*

United States Office of Management and Budget. Circular No. A-21, *Cost Principles for Educational Institutions*. Washington, DC: Author, 2005. *www.whitehouse.gov/sites/default/files/omb/assets/omb/fedreg/2005/083105_a21.pdf*

———. No. A-110, *Uniform Administrative Requirements for Grants and Agreements with Institutions of Higher Education, Hospitals, and Other Nonprofit Organizations.* Washington, DC: Author, 1999. *www.whitehouse.gov/omb/circulars_a110/*

———. No. A-122, *Cost Principles for Nonprofit Organizations*. Washington, DC: Author, 2005. *www.whitehouse.gov/sites/default/files/omb/assets/omb/fedreg/2005/083105_a122.pdf*

———. No. A-133, *Audits of States, Local Governments, and Non-Profit Organizations*. Washington, DC: Author, 2003. *www.whitehouse.gov/sites/default/files/omb/assets/omb/circulars/a133/a133.pdf*

United Way of America. *Accounting and Financial Reporting: A Guide for United Ways and Not-for-Profit Human Service Organizations*, edited by R. D. Sumariwalla and W. C. Levis, rev. 2nd ed. Alexandria, VA: Author, 1989.

———. *Budgeting: A Guide for United Ways and Not-for-Profit Human Service Organizations*. Alexandria, VA: Author, 1975.

———. *Unified Financial Reporting System for Not-for-Profit Organizations.* Alexandria, VA: Author, 2000.

APPENDIX 28.1: FACTORS TO BE CONSIDERED IN DISTINGUISHING CONTRACTS FOR THE PURCHASE OF GOODS OR SERVICES FROM RESTRICTED GRANTS

A list of factors that may be helpful to not-for-profit organizations in deciding how to account for the receipt of payments that might be considered as being either for the purchase of goods or services from the organization, or as restricted-purpose gifts or grants to the organization (as contemplated in par. 3 of SFAS No. 116) is presented next. Auditors also can use these factors in assessing the reasonableness of the client's decision. Additional discussion of this distinction can be found in the instructions to IRS Form 990, Part VIII, lines 1 and 2, and in IRS Regulation 1.509(a)–3(g). Normally no one of these factors is determinative by itself; all relevant factors should be considered together.

Factors Whose Presence Would Indicate Payment Is for the Purchase of Goods or Services	Factors Whose Presence Would Indicate Payment Is a Restricted Grant for a Specific Purpose
Factors related to the agreement between the payor and the payee:	
The expressed intent is for the payee to provide goods/services to the payor, or to other specifically identified recipients, as determined by the payor.	The expressed intent is to make a gift to the payee to advance the programs of the payee.
There is a specified time and/or place for delivery of goods/services to the payor or other recipient.	Time and/or place of delivery of any goods/services is largely at the discretion of the payee.
There are provisions for economic penalties, beyond the amount of the payment, against the payee for failure to meet the terms of the agreement.	Any penalties are expressed in terms of required delivery of goods/services or are limited to return of unspent amounts.
The amount of the payment per unit is computed in a way that explicitly provides for a "profit" margin for the payee.	The payment is stated as a flat amount or a fixed amount per unit based only on the cost (including overhead) of providing the goods/services.
The total amount of the payment is based only on the quantity of items delivered.	The payment is based on a line-item budget request, including an allowance for actual administrative costs.
The tenor of the agreement is that the payor receives approximately equivalent value in return for the payment.	The payor does not receive approximately equivalent value.
The items are closely related to commercial activity regularly engaged in by the payor.	The items are related to the payee's program services.

(*Continues*)

Factors Whose Presence Would Indicate Payment Is for the Purchase of Goods or Services	Factors Whose Presence Would Indicate Payment Is a Restricted Grant for a Specific Purpose
There is substantial benefit to the payor itself from the items.	The items normally are used to provide goods/services considered of social benefit to society as a whole, or to some defined segment thereof (e.g., children, persons having a disease, students), which might not otherwise have ready access to the items.
If the payor is a governmental unit, the items are things the government itself has explicitly undertaken to provide to its citizens; the government has arranged for another organization to be the actual service provider.	The government is in the role of subsidizing provision of services to the public by a nongovernmental organization.
The benefits resulting from the items are to be made available only to the payor or to persons or entities designated by the payor.	The items, or the results of the activities funded by the payment, are to be made available to the general public, or to any person who requests and is qualified to receive them. Determination of specific recipients is made by the payee.
The items are to be delivered to the payor or to other persons or entities closely connected with the payor.	Delivery is to be made to persons or entities not closely connected with the payor.
Revenue from sale of the items is considered unrelated business income (IRC Section 512) to the payee.	Revenue is "related" income to the payee.
In the case of sponsored research, the payor determines the plan of research and the desired outcome, and retains proprietary rights to the results.	The research plan is determined by the payee; desired outcomes are expressed only in general terms (e.g., to find a cure for a disease), and the rights to the results remain with the payee or are considered in the public domain.
The payment supports applied research.	The payment supports basic research.

APPENDIX 28.2: FACTORS TO BE CONSIDERED IN ASSESSING WHETHER CONTRIBUTED SERVICES REQUIRE SPECIALIZED SKILLS

A list of eight factors that may be helpful to recipients of contributed services of volunteers in assessing whether the skills utilized by the volunteers in the performance of their services are considered to be "specialized" follows. These factors may also aid auditors in assessing the appropriateness of the client's judgment. This list is not intended to be used in determining how to value or account for such services. In some cases, no one of these factors is necessarily determinative by itself; all relevant factors should be considered together.

The eight factors whose presence is often indicative that skills are "specialized" are listed next.

1. Persons who regularly hold themselves out to the public as qualified practitioners of such skills are required by law or by professional ethical standards to possess a license or other professional certification, or specified academic credentials. Alternatively, if possession of such license/certification/credentials is optional, the person performing the services does possess such formal certification..
2. Practitioners of such skills are required, by law or professional ethics, to have obtained a specified amount of technical pre-job or on-the-job training, to obtain specified amounts of continuing professional education, to obtain a specified amount of practical work experience, or to complete a defined period of apprenticeship in the particular type of work.

3. Proper practice of the skills requires the individual to possess specific artistic or creative talent and/or a body of technical knowledge not generally possessed by members of the public at large.
4. Practice of the skills requires the use of technical tools or equipment. The ability to use such tools or equipment properly requires training or experience not generally possessed by members of the public at large.
5. There is a union or professional association whose membership consists specifically of practitioners of the skills, as opposed to such groups whose members consist of persons who work in a broad industry, a type of company, or a department of a company. Admission to membership in such organization requires demonstrating one or more of the factors 1, 2, or 3. (Whether the person whose skills are being considered actually belongs to such organization is not a factor in assessing whether the skills are considered to be specialized, although it may be relevant in assessing whether the person possesses the skills.)
6. Practitioners of such skills are generally regarded by the public as being members of a particular "profession."
7. There is a formal disciplinary procedure administered by a government or by a professional association, to which practitioners of such skills are subject, as a condition of offering their skills to the public for pay.
8. Practice of the skills by persons who do so in their regular work is ordinarily done in an environment in which there is regular formal review or approval of work done by supervisory personnel or by professional peers.

APPENDIX 28.3: LIST OF FACTORS TO BE CONSIDERED IN DETERMINING WHETHER AN ORGANIZATION WOULD TYPICALLY NEED TO PURCHASE SERVICES IF NOT PROVIDED BY DONATION

This list of factors may be helpful to not-for-profit organizations, in deciding whether contributed services meet the third part of the criterion in GAAP, and to auditors, in assessing the reasonableness of the client's decision.

No one of these factors is normally determinative by itself; all relevant factors and the strength of their presence should be considered together.

Factors Whose Presence Would Indicate Services Would Typically Need to Be Purchased	Factors Whose Presence Would Indicate Services Would Typically Not Need to Be Purchased
The activities in which the volunteers are involved are an integral part of the reporting organization's ongoing program services (as stated in its IRS Form 1023/4, fundraising material, and annual report), or of management or fundraising activities that are essential to the functioning of the organization's programs.	The activities are not part of the reporting organization's program, or of important management or fundraising activities, or are relatively incidental to those activities; the services primarily benefit the program activities of another organization.
Volunteer work makes up a significant portion of the total effort expended in the program activity in which the volunteers are used.	Volunteer work is a relatively small part of the total effort of the program.
The program activity in which the volunteers function is a significant part of the overall program activities of the organization.	The program activity is relatively insignificant in relation to the organization's overall program activities.
The reporting organization has an objective basis for assigning a value to the services.	No objective basis is readily available.

(Continues)

Factors Whose Presence Would Indicate Services Would Typically Need to Be Purchased	Factors Whose Presence Would Indicate Services Would Typically Not Need to Be Purchased
The organization has formal agreements with third parties to provide the program services that are conducted by the volunteers.	Factor not present.
The reporting organization assigns volunteers to specific duties.	Assignment of specific duties to volunteers is done by persons or entities other than the reporting organization, or the volunteers largely determine for themselves what is to be done within broad guidelines.
The volunteers are subject to ongoing supervision and review of their work by the reporting organization.	The activities of the volunteers are conducted at geographic locations distant from the organization.
The organization actively recruits volunteers for specific tasks.	Volunteers are accepted but not actively recruited, or, if recruited, specific tasks are not mentioned in the recruiting materials.
If the work of the volunteers consists of creating or enhancing nonfinancial assets, the assets will be owned and/or used primarily by or under the control of the reporting organization after the volunteer work is completed. If the assets are subsequently given away by the organization to charitable beneficiaries, the organization decides who is to receive the assets.	The assets will immediately be owned or used primarily by other persons or organizations.
If there were to be a net increase in net assets resulting from the recording of a value for the services (even though, in practice, there usually is not), the increase would better meet the criteria for presentation as revenue, rather than a gain, as set forth in SFAC No. 6, par. 78–79, 82–88, and 111–113.	The net increase would better meet the criteria of a gain rather than revenue.
Management represents to the auditor that it would hire paid staff to perform the services if volunteers were not available.	Management represents that it would not hire paid staff; or it is obvious from the financial condition of the organization that it is unlikely that financial resources would be available to pay for the services.

Auditors are reminded that management representations alone do not normally constitute sufficient relevant evidence to support audit assertions; however, they may be considered in conjunction with other evidence.

Factors particularly relevant in situations where the volunteer services are provided directly to charitable or other beneficiaries of the reporting organization's program services (e.g., Legal Aid Society) rather than to the organization itself:

The reporting organization assumes responsibility for the volunteers with regard to workers' compensation and liability insurance, errors or omissions in the work, and satisfactory completion of the work.	The organization has explicitly disclaimed such responsibility.
The reporting organization maintains ongoing involvement with the activities of the volunteers.	The organization functions mainly as a clearinghouse for putting volunteers in touch with persons or other organizations needing help but has little ongoing involvement.

APPENDIX 28.4: FACTORS TO BE CONSIDERED IN ASSESSING WHETHER A DONOR HAS MADE A BONA FIDE PLEDGE TO A DONEE

A list of factors that may be helpful to donees in assessing whether a pledge (unconditional promise to give, as contemplated in SFAS No. 116 (ASC Topic 958-605)) has, in fact, been made follows. These factors also may help auditors in assessing the appropriateness of the client's judgment. This list of factors is not intended to be used in deciding on proper accounting (for either the pledge asset or the related revenue/net assets) or to assess collectability, although some of the factors may be relevant to those decisions as well. In many cases, no one of these factors is necessarily determinative by itself; all relevant factors should be considered together.

Factors Whose Presence May Indicate a Bona Fide Pledge Was Made	Factors Whose Presence May Indicate a Bona Fide Pledge Was Not Made
1. *Factors related to the solicitation process:*	
a. There is evidence that the recipient explicitly solicited formal pledges.	The pledge was unsolicited, or the solicitation did not refer to pledges.
b. Public announcement[a] of the pledge has been made (by donor or donee).	No public announcement has been made.
c. Partial payment on the pledge has been made (or full payment after balance sheet date).	No payments have yet been made, or payments have been irregular, late, or less than scheduled amounts.
2. *Factors related to the "pledge" itself:*	
a. Written evidence created by the donor clearly supports the existence of an unconditional promise to give.[b]	There is no written evidence;[c] the only written evidence was prepared by the donee, or written evidence is unclear.
b. The evidence includes words such as: promise, agree, will, binding.	
c. The pledge appears to be legally enforceable. (Consult an attorney if necessary.) (Note also factor 4a.)	Legal enforceability is questionable or explicitly denied.
d. There is a clearly defined payment schedule stated in terms of either calendar dates or the occurrence of specified events whose occurrence is reasonably probable.	A payment schedule is not clearly defined, or events are relatively unlikely to occur.
e. The calendar dates or events comprising the payment schedule will (are expected to) occur within a relatively short time[d] after the balance sheet date (or in the case of events, have already occurred).	The time (period) of payment contemplated by the donor is relatively far in the future.
f. The amount of the pledge is clearly specified or readily computable.	The amount is not clear or readily computable.
g. The donor has clearly specified a particular purpose for the gift (e.g., endowment, fixed assets, loan fund, retire long-term debt, specific program service). The purpose is consistent with ongoing done activities.	The purpose is vaguely or not specified, or inconsistent with donee activities.
3. *Factors relating to the donor:*	
a. There is no reason to question the donor's ability or intent to fulfill the pledge.	Collectability of the gift is questionable.
b. The donor has a history of making and fulfilling pledges to the donee of similar or larger amounts.	Factor not present.

(Continues)

Factors Whose Presence May Indicate a Bona Fide Pledge Was Made	Factors Whose Presence May Indicate a Bona Fide Pledge Was Not Made
4. *Factors relating to the donee:*	
a. The donee has indicated that it would take legal action to enforce collection if necessary, or has a history of doing so.	It is unlikely (based on donee's past practices) or uncertain whether the donee would enforce the "pledge."
b. The donee has already taken specific action in reliance on the pledge or publicly[a] announced that it intends to do so.[e]	No specific action has been taken or is contemplated.

[a]The announcement would not necessarily have to be made to the general public; announcement in media circulated among the constituency of either the donor or donee would suffice. Examples include newsletters, fundraising reports, annual reports, a campus newspaper, and so on. In the case of announcements by the donee, there should be a reasonable presumption that the donor is aware of the announcement and has not indicated any disagreement with it.

[b]This factor, if present, normally would be considered determinative.

[c]Oral pledges can be considered bona fide under some circumstances. Clearly, in the case of oral pledges, much greater weight will have to be given to other factors if the existence of a bona fide pledge is to be asserted. Also, the auditor will have to carefully consider what audit evidence can be relied on.

[d]What constitutes a relatively short time has to be determined in each case. The longer the time contemplated, the more weight will have to be given to other factors (especially 2b, 2c, 3a, and 4a) in assessing the existence of a pledge. In most circumstances, periods longer than three to five years would likely be judged relatively long.

[e]Types of specific action contemplated include:

- Commencing acquisition, construction, or lease of capital assets or signing binding contracts to do so
- Making public announcement of the commencement or expansion of operating programs used by the public (e.g., the opening of a new clinic, starting a new concert series, a special museum exhibit)
- Indicating to another funder that the pledge will be used to match part of a challenge grant from that funder
- Soliciting other pledges or loans for the same purpose by explicitly indicating that "x has already pledged"
- Committing proceeds of the pledge in other ways, such as awarding scholarships, making pledges to other charities, hiring new staff, and so on (where such uses are consistent with either the donee's stated purposes in soliciting the pledge or the donor's indicated use of the pledge)
- Forbearing from soliciting other available major gifts (e.g., not submitting an application for a foundation grant) because, with the pledge in question, funding for the purpose is considered complete
- Using pledge as collateral for a loan

APPENDIX 28.5: LIST OF FACTORS TO BE CONSIDERED IN DECIDING WHETHER A GIFT OR PLEDGE SUBJECT TO DONOR STIPULATIONS IS CONDITIONAL OR RESTRICTED

Donors place many different kinds of stipulations on pledges and other gifts. Some stipulations create legal *restrictions* that limit the way in which the donee may use the gift. Other stipulations create *conditions* that must be fulfilled before a donee is entitled to receive (or keep) a gift.

In SFAS No. 116 (ASC Topic 958-605), FASB defines a *condition* as an uncertain future event that must occur before a promise based on that event becomes binding on the promisor. In some cases, it is not immediately clear whether a particular stipulation creates a condition or a restriction. (Some gifts are both conditional and restricted.) Accounting for the two forms of gift is quite different, so it is important to identify the nature of a stipulation be properly in order to categorize the gift properly.

The list of factors in this appendix is to be considered by recipients (and donors) of gifts, in deciding whether a pledge or other gift that includes donor stipulations is conditional or restricted; and by auditors, in assessing the appropriateness of the client's decision.

In many cases, no one of these factors will be determinative by itself; all applicable factors should be considered together.

Factors Whose Presence in the Grant Document, Donor's Transmittal Letter, or Other Gift Instrument or in the Appeal by the Recipient Would Indicate the Gift May Be Restricted	Factors Whose Presence in the Communication from the Donor or the Donee-Prepared Pledge Card Would Indicate the Gift May Be Conditional
Factors related to the terms of the gift/pledge:	
The document uses words such as: If,* subject to,* when, revocable.*	The document uses words such as: must, for, purpose, irrevocable.
Neither the ultimate amount nor the timing of payment of the gift is clearly determinable in advance of payment.	At least one of the amount and/or timing is clearly specified.
The pledge is stated to extend for a very long period of time (over, say, 10 years) or is open-ended (often found with pledges to support a needy child overseas or a missionary in the field).	The time is short and/or specific as to its end.
The donor stipulations in the document refer to *outcomes* expected as a result of the activity (with the implication that if the outcomes are not achieved, the donor will expect the gift to be refunded or will cancel future installments of a multi-period pledge.[1a])* (Such gifts are likely also restricted.)	The donor stipulations focus on the *activities* to be conducted. Although hoped-for outcomes may be implicit or explicit, there is not an implication that achievement of particular outcomes is a requirement.[1b*]
There is an explicit requirement that amounts not expensed by a specified date must be returned to the donor.	There is no such refund provision, or any refund is required only if money is left after completion of the specified activities.
The gift is in the form of a pledge.	The gift is a transfer of cash or other noncash assets.
Payment of amounts pledged will be made only on a cost-reimbursement basis.[(D)]	Payment of the gift will be made up front, or according to a payment schedule, without the necessity for the donee to have yet incurred specific expenses.
The gift has an explicit matching requirement [(D)], or additional funding beyond that already available will be required to complete the activity.	Factor not present.
Factors relating to the circumstances surrounding the gift:	
The action or event described in the donor's stipulations is largely outside the control of the management or governing board of the donee.[2a*]	The action or event is largely within the donee's control.[2b*]
The activity contemplated by the gift is one which the donee has not yet decided to do, and it is not yet certain whether the activity will actually be conducted.*	The donee is already conducting the activity, or it is fairly certain that the activity will be conducted.*
There is a lower probability that the donor stipulations will eventually be met.	There is a higher probability.

(*Continues*)

Factors Whose Presence in the Grant Document, Donor's Transmittal Letter, or Other Gift Instrument or in the Appeal by the Recipient Would Indicate the Gift May Be Restricted	Factors Whose Presence in the Communication from the Donor or the Donee-Prepared Pledge Card Would Indicate the Gift May Be Conditional
As to any tangible or intangible outcomes that are to be produced as a result of the activities, these products will be under the control of the donor. (In such cases, the payment may not be a gift at all; rather it may be a payment for goods or services.)	Any outcomes will be under the control of the donee.

[(D)]Presence of this factor would normally be considered determinative. Absence of the factor is not necessarily determinative.
*Factors that would generally be considered more important.
[1a]Examples of outcomes contemplated by this factor include:

- Successful creation of a new vaccine
- Production of a new television program
- Commissioning a new musical composition
- Establishing a named professorship
- Reduction in the teenage pregnancy rate in a community
- Construction of a new building
- Mounting a new museum exhibit

[1b]Examples of activities contemplated by this factor include (but see Factor 10[§**]):

- Conduct of scientific or medical research
- Broadcasting a specified television program
- Performing a particular piece of music
- Paying the salary of a named professor
- Counseling teenagers judged at risk of becoming pregnant
- Operating a certain facility
- Providing disaster relief

[2a]Examples of events contemplated by this factor include:

- Actions of uncontrolled third parties, for example:
  - Other donors making contributions to enable the donee to meet a matching requirement of this gift
  - A government granting approval to conduct an activity (e.g., awarding a building or land use permit, or a permit to operate a medical facility)
  - An owner of other property required for the activity making the property available to the organization (by sale or lease)
- Natural and man-made disasters
- Future action of this donor (such as agreeing to renew a multiperiod pledge in subsequent periods)
- Future willingness and ability of a donor of personal services to continue to provide those services

Events outside of the donee's control, but which are virtually assured of happening anyway at a known time and place (e.g., astronomical or normal meteorological events), and the mere passage of time, are not conditions.
[2b]Examples of events contemplated by this factor include (but see Factor 10[§**]):

- Eventual use of the gift for the specified purpose (e.g., those listed in Note 1b), or retention of the gift as restricted endowment
- Naming a building for a specified person
- Filing with the donor routine performance reports on the activities being conducted

[§**]There is a presumption here that the right column of Factor 10 applies.

APPENDIX 28.6: CONSIDERATION OF WHETHER ITEMS MAY BE REPORTED AS OPERATING OR NONOPERATING

SFAS 117 (ASC Topic 958-225) leaves it to each organization (if it wishes to present a subtotal of "operating" results) to determine what it considers to be operating versus nonoperating items in a statement of activity. If it is not obvious from the face of the statement what items are included or excluded in the operating subtotal, footnote disclosure of that distinction must be made. Some items that might be considered as nonoperating are listed next. This is not intended to express any preferences, or to limit the types of items that a particular organization might report as nonoperating, but merely to provide a list for consideration of various types of items.

Items Usually Considered Nonoperating in the Current Period

- Extraordinary items
- Cumulative effects of accounting changes
- Correction of errors of prior periods
- Prior period adjustments, generally
- Results of discontinued operations

Items That Many Persons Might Consider Nonoperating in Some Situations

- Unrealized capital gains on investments carried at market value
- Unrelated business income (as defined in IRC Section 512) and related expenses
- Contributions that qualify as "unusual grants," as defined in IRS Regulation Section 1.509(a)–3(c)(3)
- Items that meet some, but not all, of the criteria for extraordinary items, or prior period adjustments

Items That Some Persons Might Consider Nonoperating in Some Situations

- Bequests and other "deferred gifts" (annuity, life income funds, etc.) received
- Gains and losses, generally (as defined in SFAC No. 6, pars. 82–89)
- Sales of goods/services that, although they are not considered unrelated under the IRC, are nevertheless peripheral to the organization's major activities
- Some "auxiliary activities" of colleges
- Revenue and expenses related to program activities not explicitly listed on the organization's IRS Form 1023
- Revenue and expenses directly related to transactions that are reported as financing or investing cash flows in the statement of cash flows; for example, investment income not available for operating purposes, interest expense, write-offs of loans receivable, nonexpendable gifts, adjustment of annuity liability
- Contributions having the characteristics of an "initial capital" contribution to an organization, even though they do not meet the requirements of an extraordinary item or an unusual grant

Notes: The characterization of an item of expense as operating versus nonoperating is not driven by its classification as program, management, or fundraising expense.

In general, expenses should follow related revenue: For example, if contributions are considered operating, then fundraising expenses normally would be also, and vice versa.

APPENDIX 28.7: NOT-FOR-PROFIT ACCOUNTING LITERATURE: CROSS-REFERENCES BETWEEN THE ASC TOPICS AND PREVIOUS GUIDANCE

ASC from previous guidance:[8]

ASC	Subject Matter	Previous Guidance (primarily)
958-		
10	Overall	AAG ch. 1, par. 15.04
20	Financially interrelated entities	SFAS 136
30	Split-interest agreements	AAG ch. 6; DIG B-35
205	Presentation of financial statements	SFAS 117, 124; FSP 117-1
210	Balance sheet	SFAS 117
225	Income statement	SFAS 117, others
230	Statement of cash flows	SFAS 117; AAG ch. 3
310	Receivables	SFAS 116; AAG ch. 5 and others
320	Investments: debt and equity securities	SFAS 124; AAG ch. 8
325	Investments: other	SFAS 124; FSP 124-1; AAG ch. 8
360	Property, plant, and equipment	SFAS 116; FAS 93; AAG ch. 7, 9
405	Liabilities	AAG ch. 10, 11, 13; EITF D-089
450	Contingencies	SFAS 116; AAG ch. 10, 3
470	Debt	AAG ch. 10
605	Revenue recognition	SFAS 116, 136; AAG ch. 5
715	Compensation: retirement benefits	SFAS 87, 88, 106, 132(R), 158
720	Other expenses	SFAS 117; SOP 98-2; AAG ch. 13
805	Combinations	FAS 164
810	Consolidation	SOP 94-3; FSP 94-3-1; EITF 90-15, 96-21; ARB 51
815	Derivatives and hedging	DIG B-35
840	Leases	SOP 94-3; EITF 90-15, 96-21, 97-01

[8]AAG = AICPA Accounting and Audit Guide
DIG = Derivatives Implementation Group
ARB = Accounting Research Bulletin
EITF = Emerging Issues Task Force
FSP = FASB Staff Position
SOP = AICPA Statement of Position

Previous to ASC:

Previous Guidance	Subject Matter	ASC (primarily)
SFAS 87, 88, 106, 132(R), 158	Retirement benefits	958-715
SFAS 93	Depreciation	958-360
SFAS 116	Contributions	958-605
SFAS 117	Financial statement presentation	958-205, 210, 225, 230, 720
FSP 117-1	Endowments	958-205
FAS 124	Investments	958-320, 325, 205
FSP 124-1	Investments	958-325
SFAS 136	Pass-through gifts	958-605, 20
SFAS 157	Fair value	820
SFAS 159	Fair value option	825
SFAS 164	Combinations	958-805
FIN 48	Uncertain tax positions	740-10
ASU 2009-06	Application of FIN 48	740-10-15, 50, 55
DIG B-35	Derivative in a split-interest	958-30, 815
SOP 94-3	Consolidation	958-810
FSP 94-3-1	Consolidation	958-810
SOP 98-2	Joint costs	958-720
AAG-NPO, Chapter:		
1	Introduction	958-10
2	Auditing	(not in ASC)
3	Financial reporting	958-205, 210, 230
4	Cash	958-210
5	Contributions	958-605, 310
6; DIG B-35	Split interest	958-30, 815
7	Other assets	958-605, 360
8	Investments	958-320, 325
9	Property, plant, and equipment	958-360
10	Liabilities	958-405, 450, 720
11	Net assets	958-225
12	Exchange transactions	958-605, 310
13	Expenses	958-720, 225
14	Auditors' reports	(not in ASC)
Para. 15.04 (Exempt status)	Tax	958-10-15-6
Rest of ch. 15	Tax	(not in ASC)
16	Fund accounting	(not in ASC)

CHAPTER 29

COST-VOLUME-REVENUE ANALYSIS FOR NONPROFIT ORGANIZATIONS

JAE K. SHIM, PhD

CALIFORNIA STATE UNIVERSITY, LONG BEACH

29.1 QUESTIONS ANSWERED BY CVR ANALYSIS 2

29.2 ANALYSIS OF REVENUES 2

29.3 ANALYSIS OF COST BEHAVIOR 3

(a) Variable Costs 4
(b) Fixed Costs 4
(c) Types of Fixed Costs: Program-Specific or Common 4

29.4 CVR ANALYSIS WITH VARIABLE REVENUE ONLY 4

(a) Contribution Margin 4
(b) Unit CM 5
(c) CM Ratio 5

29.5 BREAK-EVEN ANALYSIS 5

(a) Graphical Approach in a Spreadsheet Format 6
(b) Determination of Target Surplus Volume 6
(c) Margin of Safety 7
(d) Some Applications of CVR Analysis and What-If Analysis 8

29.6 CVR ANALYSIS WITH FIXED REVENUE ONLY 9

29.7 CVR ANALYSIS WITH VARIABLE AND FIXED REVENUES 10

29.8 PROGRAM MIX ANALYSIS 14

29.9 MANAGEMENT OPTIONS 16

29.10 SOURCES AND SUGGESTED REFERENCES 16

Managers of nonprofit organizations (NPOs) generally are not skilled in financial matters. They often are preoccupied with welfare objectives and ignore the operations efficiency and operating cost controls. There are nine questions that nonprofit financial managers should address in connection with an organization's financial condition and activity:

1. Do we have a profit or a loss?
2. Do we have sufficient reserves?
3. Are we liquid?
4. Do we have strong internal controls?
5. Are we operating efficiently?
6. Are we meeting our budget goals?
7. Are our programs financially healthy?
8. Are we competing successfully?
9. Is our prioritizing of programs and activities reasonable?

By definition, the goal of a nonprofit entity is *not* to earn a profit. Its objective is to render as much suitable service possible while using as little human and physical services possible. Ideally, breaking even should be the goal of an NPO. Breaking even occurs when revenues equal costs. If you generate a surplus, you may not receive the same amount from the funding agency as last year. By operating at a deficit, however, the nonprofit may become insolvent or unable to perform the maximum amount of services. Chances are the nonprofit may not be able to borrow money from the bank as not-for-profit entities often have a weak financial stance. One thing is clear, though: Over the long run, nonprofit entities cannot sustain persistent deficits unless they have large reserves. Even with large reserves, a nonprofit may have to operate below potential. This means the benefit of the nonprofit will not be maximized.

This chapter deals with many planning issues surrounding NPOs. Cost-volume-revenue (CVR) analysis, together with cost behavior information, helps nonprofit managers perform many useful planning analyses. CVR analysis deals with how revenue and costs change with a change in the service level. More specifically, it looks at the effects on revenues from changes in such factors as variable costs, fixed costs, prices, service level, and mix of services offered. By studying the relationships of costs, service volume, and revenue, nonprofit management is better able to cope with many planning decisions.

Break-even analysis, a branch of CVR analysis, determines the break-even service level. The break-even point (the financial crossover point when revenues exactly match costs) does not show up in financial reports, but nonprofit financial managers find it an extremely useful measurement in a variety of ways. It reveals which programs are self-supporting and which are subsidized.

29.1 QUESTIONS ANSWERED BY CVR ANALYSIS

CVR analysis tries to answer four questions:

1. What service level (or units of service) is required to break even?
2. How would changes in price, variable costs, fixed costs, and service volume affect a surplus?
3. How do changes in program levels and mix affect aggregate surplus/deficit?
4. What alternative break-even strategies are available?

29.2 ANALYSIS OF REVENUES

Revenues for nonprofit entities are typically classified into these categories:

- Grants from governments
- Grants from private sources
- Cost reimbursements and sales
- Membership dues
- Public contributions received directly or indirectly
- Donations and pledges
- Legacies, bequests, and memorials
- Program fees
- Other revenue, such as investment income (e.g., interest, dividends)

For managerial purposes, however, each type of revenue is grouped into its fixed and variable parts. Fixed revenues are those that remain unchanged regardless of the level of service. Examples are gifts, grants, and contracts. As an example, in a university setting, donations, gifts, and grants have no relationship to the number of students enrolled. In contrast to fixed revenues, variable revenues are the ones that vary in proportion to the volume of activity. Examples include cost reimbursements and membership fees. Continuing the example of a university setting, the total amount of tuition and fees received varies as the number of students enrolled increases or decreases. Different nonprofit entities may have different sources of revenue: variable revenue only, fixed revenue only, or a combination of both. In this chapter, we discuss all three cases in analyzing break-even and CVR applications.

29.3 ANALYSIS OF COST BEHAVIOR

For external reporting purposes, costs are classified by managerial function, such as payroll, occupancy, office, and so on, and also by programs and supporting services. Exhibit 29.1 presents a model functional classification.

For managerial purposes (i.e., planning, control, and decision making), further classification of costs is desirable. One classification is by behavior. Depending on how costs react or respond to changes in the level of activity, costs may be viewed as variable or fixed. This classification assumes a known high and low volume of service activity called the relative range of activity. The relevant range is the volume zone within which the behavior of variable costs, fixed costs, and prices can be predicted with reasonable accuracy. The relevant range falls between the planned highest and lowest service level for the nonprofit. Within this level of normal activity, the behavior of variable costs, fixed costs, and prices can be predicted with reasonable accuracy. Typical activity measures are summarized in Exhibit 29.2.

IRS Form 990 Line #	Functional Expense Category
26	Salaries and wages
27	Pension plan contributions
28	Other employee benefits
29	Payroll taxes
30	Professional fundraising fees
31	Accounting fees
32	Legal fees
33	Supplies
34	Telephone
35	Postage and shipping
36	Occupancy
37	Equipment rental and maintenance
38	Printing and publications
39	Travel
40	Conferences, conventions, meetings
41	Interest
42	Depreciation, depletion, etc.
43	Other expenses (itemize)

Exhibit 29.1 Internal Revenue Service Form 990 Part II—Statement of Functional Expenses

Nonprofit Types	Units of Service
Hospital or health care	Bed days, patient contact hours, patient days, service hours
Educational	Number of student enrollments, class size, FTE (full-time equivalents), hours
Social clubs	Number of members served

Exhibit 29.2 Measures of the Service Level

IRS Form 990 Line #	Expense Category
	FIXED COSTS
26	Salaries and wages (not hourly employees)
27	Pension plan
28	Other benefits
29	Payroll taxes
30	Fund-raising fees
31	Accounting fees
32	Legal fees
36	Occupancy
37	Equipment rental/maintenance
41	Interest
42	Depreciation
43	Other
	VARIABLE COSTS
33	Supplies
34	Telephone
35	Postage and shipping
38	Printing and publications
39	Travel
40	Conferences, meetings
43	Other

Exhibit 29.3 Fixed–Variable Breakdown of IRS Form 990 Functional Expenses

(a) VARIABLE COSTS. Total variable costs change as the volume or level of activity changes. Examples of variable costs include supplies, hourly wages, printing and publications, and postage and shipping.

(b) FIXED COSTS. Total fixed costs do not change regardless of the volume or level of activity. Examples include property tax, yearly salaries, accounting and consulting fees, and depreciation. Exhibit 29.3 shows the fixed–variable breakdown of Internal Revenue Service (IRS) Form 990 functional expenses.

(c) TYPES OF FIXED COSTS: PROGRAM-SPECIFIC OR COMMON. Fixed costs of nonprofit entities are subdivided into two groups: (1) direct or program-specific fixed costs and (2) common. Direct or program-specific fixed costs are those that can be directly identified with individual programs. These costs are avoidable or escapable if the program is dropped. Examples include the salaries of the staff whose services can be used only in a given program or depreciation of equipment used exclusively for the program. Common fixed costs continue even if an individual program was discontinued. Examples include depreciation of building and property taxes.

29.4 CVR ANALYSIS WITH VARIABLE REVENUE ONLY

For accurate CVR analysis, a distinction must be made between variable costs and fixed costs. In order to compute the break-even point and perform various CVR analyses, the next concepts are important.

(a) CONTRIBUTION MARGIN. The contribution margin (CM) is the excess of total revenue (R) over the variable costs (VC) of the service. It is the amount of money available to cover fixed costs (FC) and to generate surplus. This is symbolically expressed as:

$$CM = R - VC \qquad (29.1)$$

(b) UNIT CM. The unit CM is the excess of the unit price (p) over the unit variable cost (v). This is symbolically expressed as:

$$\text{Unit CM} = p - v$$

(c) CM RATIO. The CM ratio is the CM as a percentage of revenue:

$$\text{CM ratio} = \text{CM/R} = (\text{R} - \text{VC})/\text{R} = 1 - (\text{VC/R}) \tag{29.2}$$

or

$$\text{Unit CM} = (p - v)/p = 1 - (v/p) \tag{29.3}$$

Note: Once you know the contribution margin ratio, then the variable cost ratio is 1 – CM ratio. Similarly, if you know the variable cost ratio (VC/R), the contribution margin ratio is (1 – VC ratio).

Example 29.1

The Los Altos Community Hospital has these data. This information will be used to illustrate the various concepts of contribution margin and contribution margin ratio:

Average revenue per day	=	$ 250		
Variable costs per patient day	=	$ 50		
Total fixed costs	=	$ 650,000		
Expected number of patient days	=	4,000		
		Total	**Per Unit**	**Percentage**
Revenue (4,000 days)		$1,000,000	$250	100%
Less: Variable costs (4,000 days)		200,000	50	20
Contribution margin		$ 800,000	$200	80%
Less: Fixed costs (Annual)		650,000		
Net income		$ 150,000		

Note that unit CM = p – v = $250 – $50 = $200 and CM ratio = unit CM/p = $200/$250 = .8 = 80%

29.5 BREAK-EVEN ANALYSIS

The break-even point represents the level of revenue that equals the total of the variable and fixed costs for a given volume of output service at a particular capacity use rate. Other things being equal, the lower the break-even point, the higher the surplus and the less the operating risk. The break-even point also provides nonprofit managers with insights into surplus/deficit planning. To develop the formula for the break-even units of service, we set:

$$\text{R} = \text{TC (total costs)} \tag{29.4}$$

$$\text{R} = \text{VC} + \text{FC} \tag{29.5}$$

$$px = vx + \text{FC} \tag{29.6}$$

Solving for x yields this formula for break-even sales volume:

$$x = \frac{\text{FC}}{(p - v)} = \frac{\text{Fixed costs}}{\text{Unit CM}}$$

or

$$\text{Break-even point in dollars (R)} = \frac{\text{Fixed costs}}{\text{CM ratio}}$$

Example 29.2

Using the same data given in Example 29.1, the number of break-even patient days and break-even dollars are computed as shown.

$$\text{Break-even point in units} = \text{FC/Unit CM} = \$650,000/\$200 = 3,250 \text{ patient days}$$

$$\text{Break-even point in dollars} = \text{FC/CMratio} = \$650,000/0.8 = \$812,500$$

Or, alternatively,

$$\text{Break-even point in dollars} = 3,250 \text{ patient days} \times \$250 \text{ revenue per patient}$$

$$= 3,250 \times \$250 = \$812,500$$

The hospital therefore needs 3,250 patient days or $ 812,500 revenue to break even.

(a) GRAPHICAL APPROACH IN A SPREADSHEET FORMAT. The graphical approach to obtaining the break-even point is based on the so-called break-even (B-E) chart as shown in Exhibit 29.4. Revenue, variable costs, and fixed costs are plotted on the vertical axis while service volume, x, is plotted on the horizontal axis. The break-even point is the point where the total revenue line intersects the total cost line. The chart can report surplus potentials over a wide range of activity and therefore can be used as a tool for discussion and presentation.

The surplus-volume (S-V) chart as shown in Exhibit 29.5 focuses on how surplus varies with changes in volume. Surplus is plotted on the vertical axis while units of output are shown on the horizontal axis. The S-V chart provides a quick condensed comparison of how alternatives on pricing, variable costs, or fixed costs may affect surplus (or deficit) as volume changes. The S-V chart can be easily constructed from the B-E chart. Note that the slope of the chart is the unit CM.

(b) DETERMINATION OF TARGET SURPLUS VOLUME. CVR analysis can be used to determine the activity levels necessary to attain a target surplus (TS). Once the break-even level of activity is computed, it is useful to determine the level of activity necessary to create a desired surplus. At the break-even point, all fixed costs have been covered.

Therefore, any additional revenue above the break-even level increases the surplus. To calculate the level of service needed to obtain our target surplus, we only need to expand our break-even

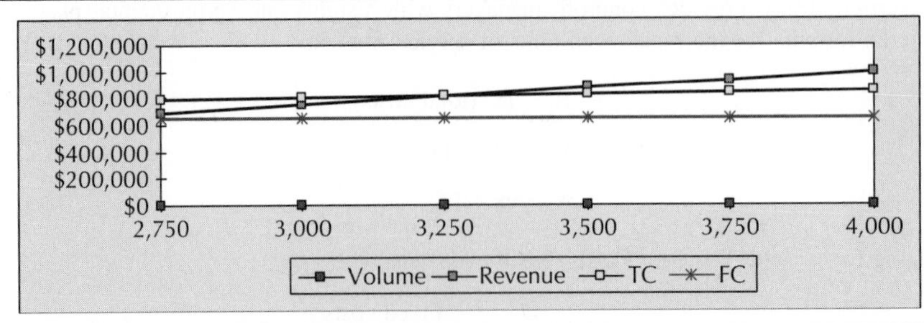

Exhibit 29.4 Break-Even (B-E) Chart—Variable Revenue

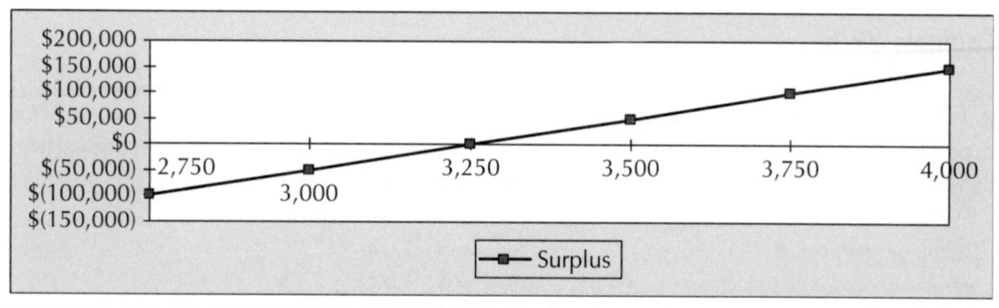

Exhibit 29.5 Surplus-Volume (S-V) Chart—Variable Revenue

formula. All we need to do is expand the numerator of the break-even formula to include the amount of desired surplus in addition to fixed costs. In other words, to achieve our desired increase in surplus, not only must fixed costs be recovered but also the desired increase in surplus.

By expanding the break-even formula to obtain the level of activity for a desired target surplus, the formula becomes:

$$\text{Target income surplus level} = \frac{\text{Fixed costs} + \text{Target surplus}}{\text{Unit CM}} \tag{29.7}$$

Example 29.3

Using the same data given in Example 29.1, assume the hospital wishes to accumulate a surplus of $250,000 per year. Then the target surplus service level would be:

$$\frac{\text{Fixed costs} + \text{Target surplus}}{\text{Unit CM}} = \frac{\$650,000 + \$250,000}{\$200} = 4,500 \text{ patient days}$$

(c) MARGIN OF SAFETY. The margin of safety is a measure of difference between the actual level of service and the break-even level of service. It is expressed as a percentage of expected service level. The margin of safety determines how far the estimated or expected level of service can decline and have the nonprofit still be profitable.

$$\text{Margin of safety} = \frac{\text{Expected level} - \text{Break-even level}}{\text{Expected level}}$$

The margin of safety is used as a measure of operating risk. The larger the ratio, the safer the situation since there is less risk of reaching the break-even point.

Example 29.4

Assume Los Altos Hospital projects 4,000 patient days with a break-even level of 3,250. The projected margin of safety is:

$$\frac{4,000 - 3,250}{4,000} = 18.75\%$$

This means that the hospital's revenue can drop 18.75% before it suffers a deficit.

Example 29.5

A nonprofit college offers a program in management for executives. The program has been experiencing financial difficulties. The dean of the school wants to know how many participants are needed to break even. Operating data for the most recent year are shown next.

Tuition per participant	= $ 7,000	
Variable expense per participant	= $ 4,000	
Total fixed expenses	= $150,000	
Tuition revenue (40 participants @$ 7,000)		$280,000
Less variable expenses (@$4,000)		160,000
Contribution margin		$120,000
Less: Fixed expenses		150,000
Operating deficit		$(30,000)

The break-even calculation is:

$$\$150{,}000/(\$7{,}000 - \$4{,}000) = 50 \text{ participants}$$

Example 29.6

In Example 29.5, the dean of the school is convinced that the class size can be increased to more economic levels without lowering the quality. He is prepared to spend $15,000 per year in additional promotional and other support expenses. The promotional and other support expenses are additional fixed costs. If he spends the $15,000 on promotional expenses, the dean wants to know the new break-even number of participants and how many participants are needed to generate a surplus of $30,000.

If that is the case, the formula to calculate the new break-even point is:

$$(\$150,000 + \$15,000)/\$3,000 = 55 \text{ participants to break even}$$

The formula to calculate the number of participants necessary to generate a target surplus of $30,000 is:

$$[(\$150,000 + \$15,000) + \$30,000]/\$3,000 = 65 \text{ participants}$$

(d) SOME APPLICATIONS OF CVR ANALYSIS AND WHAT-IF ANALYSIS. The concepts of contribution margin and the contribution income statement have many applications in surplus/deficit planning and short-term decision-making. Many what-if scenarios can be evaluated using them as planning tools, especially utilizing a spreadsheet program. Some applications are illustrated in Example 29.7 using the same data as in Example 29.1.

Example 29.7

Assume that the Los Altos Community Hospital in Example 29.1 expects revenues to go up by $250,000 for the next period. How much will surplus increase?

Using the CM concepts, we can quickly compute the impact of a change in the service level on surplus or deficit. The formula for computing the impact is:

$$\text{Change in surplus} = \text{Dollar change in revenue} \times \text{CM ratio}$$

Thus:

$$\text{Increase in surplus} = \$250,000 \times 80\% = \$200,000$$

Therefore, the income will go up by $200,000, assuming there is no change in fixed costs. If we are given a change in service units (e.g., patient days) instead of dollars, then the formula becomes:

$$\text{Change in surplus} = \text{Change in units} \times \text{Unit CM}$$

Example 29.8

Assume the Los Altos Community Hospital in Example 29.1 expects patient days to go up by 500 units. How much will surplus increase? From Example 29.1, the hospital's unit CM is $200. Again, assuming there is no change in fixed costs, the surplus will increase by $100,000, as computed next.

$$500 \text{ additional patient days} \times \$200 \text{ CM per day} = \$100,000$$

Example 29.9

Referring to Example 29.5, another alternative under consideration is to hold the present program without any change in the regular campus facilities instead of in rented outside facilities that are better located. If adopted, this proposal will reduce fixed costs by $60,000. The variable costs will decrease by $100 per participant. Is the move to campus facilities advisable if it leads to a decline in the number of participants by 5?

	Present		Proposed
S (40 × $7,000)	$280,000	(35 × $7,000)	245,000
VC (40 × $4,000)	160,000	(35 × $3,900)	136,500
CM	$120,000		$108,500
FC	150,000		90,000
Surplus	$(30,000)		$ 18,500

The answer is yes, since the move will turn into a surplus.

29.6 CVR ANALYSIS WITH FIXED REVENUE ONLY

In many nonprofit activities, the objectives are not as clear-cut as the objective of profit in commercial business. Furthermore, the relationship between revenue and volume for an NPO is not nearly as well established as is the revenue–volume relationship in business. For example, some

NPOs may have only one source of revenue, which is a lump-sum appropriation. This source does not change with changes in volume. Let FR be fixed revenue, or lump-sum appropriation. At break-even,

$$FR = VC + FC$$

$$FR = vx + FC$$

$$x = (FR - FC)/v$$

$$\text{or Break-even units} = \frac{\text{Fixed revenue} - \text{Fixed costs}}{\text{Unit variable cost}}$$

Example 29.10

A social service agency has a government budget appropriation of $750,000. The agency's main mission is to assist handicapped people who are unable to seek or hold jobs. On the average, the agency supplements each individual's income by $6,000 annually. The agency's fixed costs are $150,000. The agency chief executive officer wishes to know how many people could be served in a given year. The break-even point can be computed as shown.

$$\text{Break-even units} = \text{Fixed revenue} - \frac{\text{Fixed costs}}{\text{Unit variable cost}} = \frac{750,000 - \$150,000}{\$6,000} = 100.$$

The number of people that could be served in a given year is 100.

Exhibits 29.6 and 29.7 display the B-E and S-V charts for this situation.

Nonprofits with a lump-sum appropriation have little incentive to increase their level of service. To do so will either increase a deficit or reduce a surplus (see Exhibit 29.7). Either of these alternatives more than likely will result in a poorer performance evaluation for the program.

Example 29.11

In Example 29.10, assume that the CEO is concerned that the total budget for the year will be reduced by 10 percent to a new amount of 90 percent ($750,000) = $675,000.

The new break-even point is:

$$\text{Break-even units} = \frac{\text{Fixed revenue} - \text{Fixed costs}}{\text{Unit variable cost}} = \frac{\$675,000 - \$150,000}{\$6,000} = 88 \text{ (rounded)}$$

The chief executive's options facing budget cuts can be any one or a combination of three ways: (1) cut the service level as computed above, (2) reduce the variable cost, the supplement per person, and (3) seek to cut down on the total fixed costs.

29.7 CVR ANALYSIS WITH VARIABLE AND FIXED REVENUES

Many NPOs derive two types of revenue: fixed and variable. A lump-sum appropriation may exist to subsidize the activity, and a fee for services may also exist (e.g., state-supported colleges and universities). There are two cases in this situation, however.

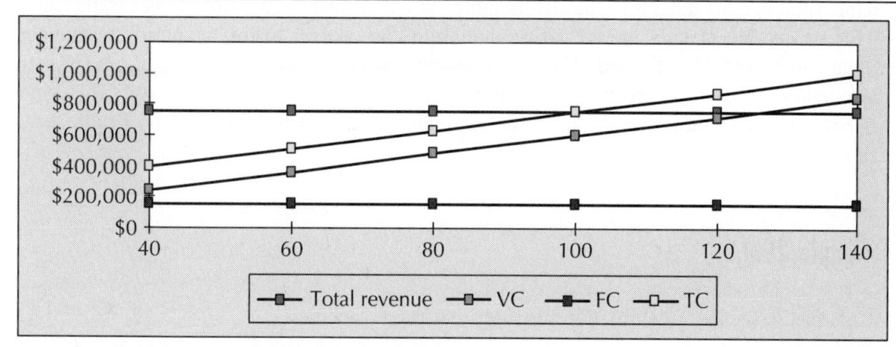

Exhibit 29.6 Break-Even—Fixed Revenue

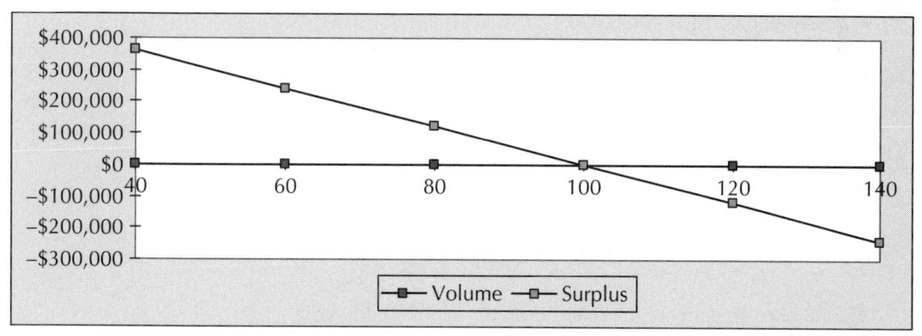

Exhibit 29.7 Surplus-Volume Chart—Fixed Revenue

Case 1: Lump-sum appropriation less than total fixed costs; fee for service greater than unit variable cost of service.

$$\text{Note that R} = \text{FR} + \text{px}$$

$$\text{At break-even, FR} + \text{px} = \text{vx} + \text{FC, where FR} < \text{FC and p} > \text{v}$$

$$\text{x} = \frac{\text{FC} - \text{FR}}{\text{pv}}$$

$$\text{or Break-even units} = \frac{\text{Fixed costs} - \text{Fixed revenue}}{\text{Unit CM}}$$

Case 2: Lump-sum appropriation higher than total fixed costs; fee lower than unit variable cost (subsidized activity) resulting in negative unit CM.

$$\text{Note that R} = \text{FR} + \text{px}$$

$$\text{At break-even, FR} + \text{px} = \text{vx} + \text{FC, where FR} > \text{FC and p} < \text{v}$$

$$\text{x} = \frac{\text{FR} - \text{FC}}{\text{vp}}$$

$$\text{or Break-even units} = \frac{\text{Fixed revenue} - \text{Fixed costs}}{-\text{Unit CM}}$$

In this situation, the fixed revenue covers more than the actual fixed costs. However, the variable costs for service are already more than the nonprofit can charge. In this scenario the number of units that can be served is limited. There is a heavily subsidized unit with a small fee for service to discourage unnecessary use but still making the service available at low cost. This type of appropriate and unit pricing can be used for essential services such as community health services or mass transit.

Example 29.12

ACM, Inc., a mental rehabilitation provider, has these specifics:

- $1,200,000 lump-sum annual budget appropriation to help rehabilitate mentally ill clients
- Monthly charge per patient for board and care = $600
- Monthly variable cost for rehabilitation activity per patient = $700
- Yearly fixed cost = $800,000

The agency manager wishes to know how many clients can be served.

$$\text{Break-even number of patients} = \frac{\text{Fixed revenue} - \text{Fixed costs}}{-\text{Unit CM}} = \frac{1,200,000 - \$800,000}{-(\$600 - \$700)}$$

$$= \frac{\$400,000}{-(-\$10)} = \frac{\$400,000}{\$100} = 4,000 \text{ per year}$$

The number of patients that can be served is 4,000 per year

Exhibits 29.8 and 29.9 display the B-E and S-V charts for variable and fixed revenue.

Note that at the level of service greater than B-E service (i.e., 4,000 units), the service is overused or underpriced (or both) (see Exhibit 29.9). We investigate two what-if scenarios.

Example 29.13

Using the same data as in Example 29.12, suppose the manager of the agency is concerned that the total budget for the coming year will be cut by 10 percent to a new amount of $1,080,000. All other things remain unchanged. The manager wants to know how this budget cut affects the next year's service level. Using the formula yields:

$$\text{Break-even number of patients} = \frac{\text{Fixed revenue} - \text{Fixed costs}}{-\text{Unit CM}} = \frac{\$1,080,000 - \$800,000}{-(\$600 - \$700)}$$

$$= \frac{\$280,000}{-(-\$10)} = 2,800 \text{ Clients per year}$$

The service level will be cut from 4,000 clients to 2,800 clients.

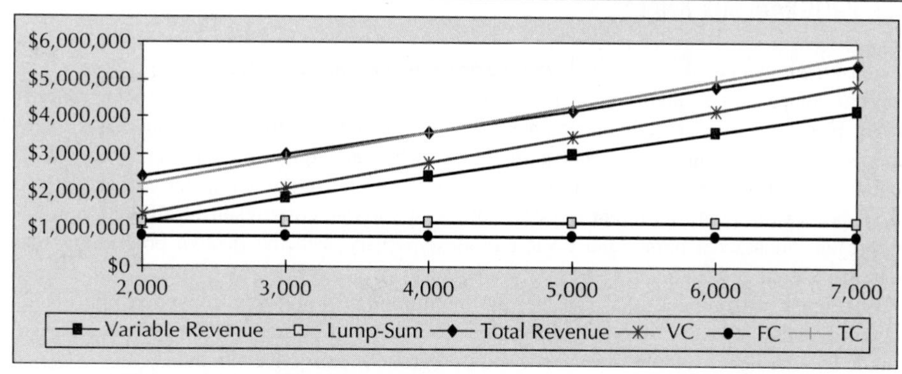

Exhibit 29.8 Break-Even Chart—Variable and Fixed Revenue (Case 2)

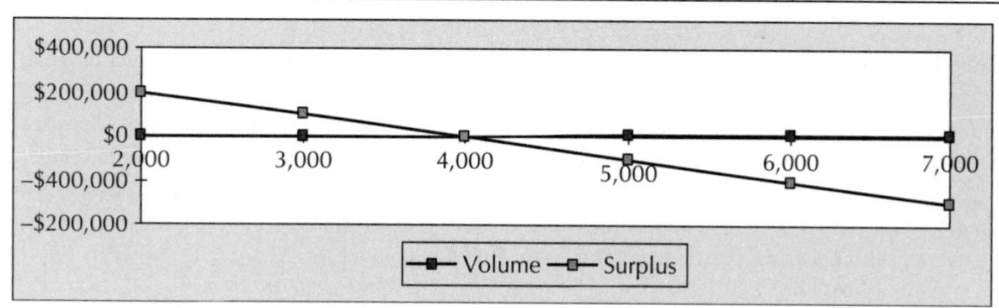

Exhibit 29.9 Surplus-Volume Chart—Variable and Fixed Revenue (Case 2)

Example 29.14

In Example 29.13, suppose that the manager does not reduce the number of clients served despite a budget cut of 10 percent. All other things remain unchanged. How much more does the manager have to charge clients for board and care?

Let p = board and care charge per year and x = 4,000 = number of clients served. The next formula can be used to make this determination:

$$R = \$1,080,000 + 4,000p$$

$$VC + FC = \$700(4,000) + \$800,000$$

$$R + VC + FC$$

$$\$1,080,000 + 4,000p = \$700(4,000) + \$800,000$$

$$4,000p = \$2,800,000 + \$800,000 - \$1,080,000$$

$$4,000p = \$2,520,000$$

$$p = \$630$$

Thus, the monthly board and care charge must be increased to $630.

29.8 PROGRAM MIX ANALYSIS

Previously, our main concern was to determine program-specific break-even volume. However most nonprofit companies are involved in multiservice, multiprogram activities. One major concern is how to plan aggregate break-even volume, surplus, and deficits. Break-even and CVR analysis requires additional computations and assumptions when an organization offers more than one program. In multiprogram organizations, program mix is an important factor in calculating an overall break-even point. Different rates and different variable costs result in different unit CMs. As a result, break-even points and CVR relationships vary with the relative proportions of the programs offered.

By defining the product as a package, the multiprogram problem is converted into a single-program problem. The first step is to determine the number of packages that need to be served to break even. The next example illustrates a multiprogram, multiservice situation.

Example 29.15 (Sheet 1 of 2)

The Cypress Counseling Services is a nonprofit agency offering two programs: psychological counseling (PC) and alcohol addiction control (AAC). The agency charges individual clients an average of $10 per hour of counseling provided under the PC program. The local Chamber of Commerce reimburses the NPO at the rate of $20 per hour of direct service provided under the AAC. The NPO believes that this billing variable rate is low enough to be affordable for most clients and also high enough to derive clients' commitment to the program objectives. Costs of administering the two programs are given next.

	PC	AAC
Variable costs	$ 4.6	$ 11.5
Direct fixed costs	$120,000	$180,000

Example 29.15 (Sheet 2 of 2)

Other fixed costs are common to the two programs, including general and administrative and fundraising of $255,100 per year. The projected surplus for the coming year, segmented by programs, is shown next.

	PC	AAC	Total
Revenue	$ 500,000	$ 800,000	$1,300,000
Program mix in hours	(50,000)	(40,000)	
Less: VC	(230,000)	(460,000)	(690,000)
Contribution margin	$ 270,000	$ 340,000	$ 610,000
Less: Direct FC	(120,000)	(180,000)	(300,000)
Program margin	$ 150,000	$ 160,000	$ 310,000
Less: Common FC			(255,100)
Surplus			$ 54,900

First, based on program-specific data on the rates, the variable costs, and the program mix, we can compute the package (aggregate) value as follows:

Program	P	V	Unit CM	Mix*	Package CM
PC	$10	$4.6	$5.4	5	$27
AAC	20	11.5	8.5	4	4
Package total					$61

***The mix ratio is 5:4 (50,000 hours for PC and 40,000 hours for AAC).**

We know that the total fixed costs for the agency are $555,100. Thus, the package (aggregate) break-even point is:

$$\$555,100/\$61 = 9,100 \text{ packages}$$

The company must provide 45,500 hours of PC (5 × 9,100) and 36,400 hours of AAC (4 × 9,100) to avoid a deficit. To prove,

	PC	AAC	Total
Revenue	$ 455,000(a)	$ 728,000(b)	$1,183,000
Program mix in hours	(45,500)	(36,400)	
Less: VC	(209,300)(c)	(418,600)(d)	(627,900)
Contribution margin	$ 245,700	$ 309,400	$ 555,100
Less: Direct FC	(120,000)	(180,000)	(300,000)
Program margin	$ 125,700	$ 129,400	$ 255,100
Less: Common FC			(255,100)
Surplus			$ 0

(a) 45,500 × $10 (c) 45,500 × $4.60
(b) 36,400 × $20 (d) 36,400 × $11.50

Example 29.16

Assume in Example 29.15 that 56,000 hours of PC services are budgeted for the next period. The NPO wants to know how many hours of AAC services are necessary during that period to avoid an overall deficit. The answer is 29,729 hours, as shown next.

Input Data	PC	AAC
Rates	$ 10	$ 20
Units of service (Hours)	56,000	29,729
Variable cost per unit	$ 4.6	$ 11.5

CONTRIBUTION STATEMENT OF SURPLUS OR DEFICIT

	PC	AAC	Total
Revenue	$560,000	$594,588	$1,154,588
Less: Variable costs	257,600	341,888	599,488
Contribution margin	$302,400	$252,700	$ 555,100
Less: Direct fixed costs	120,000	180,000	300,000
Program margin	$182,400	$ 72,700	$ 255,100
Less: Common fixed costs			255,100
Surplus			$ (0)

29.9 MANAGEMENT OPTIONS

CVR analysis is useful as a frame of reference, as a vehicle for expressing overall managerial performance, and as a planning device via break-even techniques and what-if scenarios. Using CVR, many planning decisions, such as adding or dropping a service, outsourcing, special requests, and changing budget limits, can be made on a sounder basis.

In many practical situations, management will have to resort to a combination of approaches to reverse a deficit, including:

- Selected changes in volume of activity
- Planned savings in fixed costs at all levels
- Some savings in variable costs
- Additional fund drives or grant seeking
- Upward adjustments in pricing
- Cost reimbursement contracts

All of these will have to be mixed to form a feasible planning package. Many nonprofit managers fail to develop such analytical approaches to the economics of their operations. Further, the accounting system is not designed to provide information to investigate CVR relations.

29.10 SOURCES AND SUGGESTED REFERENCES

Shim, J. K. *Cost Accounting for Managers: A Managerial Emphasis*, 7th ed. Los Alamitos, California: Delta Publishing, 2010.

Siegel, J., and J. K. Shim. *Barron's Accounting Handbook*. New York: Barron's, 2010.

CHAPTER 30

FINANCIAL INSTITUTIONS

Zabihollah Zabi Rezaee, PhD, CPA, CMA, CIA, CGFM, CFE, CSOXP, CGRCP, CGOVP

The University of Memphis

30.1 OVERVIEW 3

(a) Changing the Environment 3
(b) Role in the Economy 3
(c) Types of Financial Institutions 4
(i) Banks and Savings Institutions 4
(ii) Mortgage Banking Activities 4
(iii) Investment Companies 5
(iv) Credit Unions 5
(v) Investment Banks 5
(vi) Insurance Companies 5
(vii) Finance Companies 6
(viii) Securities Brokers and Dealers 6
(ix) Real Estate Investment Trusts 6

30.2 BANKS AND SAVINGS INSTITUTIONS 6

(a) Primary Risks of Banks and Savings Institutions 6
(i) Interest Rate Risk 6
(ii) Liquidity Risk 6
(iii) Asset-Quality Risk 7
(iv) Fiduciary Risk 7
(v) Processing Risk 7
(vi) Operating Risk 7
(vii) Market Risk 7
(b) Regulation and Supervision of Banks and Savings Institutions 7
(c) Regulatory Background 10
(i) Office of the Comptroller of the Currency 11
(ii) Federal Reserve Board 11
(iii) Federal Deposit Insurance Corporation 12
(iv) Office of Thrift Supervision 13
(d) Regulatory Environment 13
(e) Federal Deposit Insurance Corporation Improvement Act Section 112 13
(i) The Regulation and Guidelines 13
(ii) Basic Requirements 14
(iii) Holding Company Exception 16
(iv) Availability of Reports 17
(f) Capital Adequacy Guidelines 17
(i) Risk-Based and Leverage Ratios 17
(ii) Tier 1, Tier 2, and Tier 3 Components 17
(iii) Risk-Weighted Assets 18
(iv) Capital Calculations and Minimum Requirements 19
(v) Interest Rate Risk and Capital Adequacy 20
(vi) Capital Allocated for Market Risk 20
(g) Prompt Corrective Action 22
(i) Scope 22
(ii) Regulatory Rating Systems 23
(iii) Risk-Focused Examinations 24
(h) Enforcement Actions 24
(i) Disclosure of Capital Matters 24
(j) Securities and Exchange Commission 25
(i) Background 25
(ii) Reporting Requirements 25
(k) Financial Statement Presentation 26
(i) Income Statements 26
(ii) Balance Sheets 26
(iii) Statements of Cash Flow 26
(iv) Commitments and Off-Balance-Sheet Risk 26
(v) Disclosures of Certain Significant Risks and Uncertainties 26
(l) Accounting Guidance 27
(m) Generally Accepted Accounting Principles versus Regulatory Accounting Principles 27
(n) Loans and Commitments 28
(i) Types of Loans 28
(ii) Accounting for Loans 31

(o) Credit Losses 35
(i) Accounting Guidance 36
(ii) Regulatory Guidance 36
(iii) Allowance Methodologies 37
(p) Loan Sales and Mortgage Banking Activities 38
(i) Underwriting Standards 38
(ii) Securitizations 39
(iii) Loan Servicing 39
(iv) Regulatory Guidance 39
(v) Accounting Guidance 40
(vi) Valuation 40
(q) Real Estate Investments, Real Estate Owned, and Other Foreclosed Assets 40
(i) Real Estate Investments 40
(ii) Former Bank Premises 40
(iii) Foreclosed Assets 40
(r) Investments in Debt and Equity Securities 41
(i) Accounting for Investments in Debt and Equity Securities 42
(ii) Wash Sales 43
(iii) Short Sales 43
(iv) Securities Borrowing and Lending 43
(s) Deposits 45
(i) Demand Deposits 45
(ii) Savings Deposits 45
(iii) Time Deposits 45
(t) Federal Funds and Repurchase Agreements 45
(i) Federal Funds Purchased 45
(ii) Repurchase Agreements 45
(u) Debt 46
(i) Long-Term Debt 46
(ii) Short-Term Debt 46
(iii) Accounting Guidance 47
(v) Taxation 47
(i) Loan Loss Reserves 47
(ii) Mark to Market 48
(iii) Tax-Exempt Securities 49
(iv) Nonaccrual Loans 49
(v) Hedging 49
(vi) Loan Origination Fees and Costs 50
(vii) Foreclosed Property 50
(viii) Leasing Activities 51
(ix) FHLB Dividends 51
(x) Bank-Owned Life Insurance 51
(xi) Original Issue Discount 51
(xii) Market Discount 51
(w) Futures, Forwards, Options, Swaps, and Similar Financial Instruments 51
(i) Futures 52
(ii) Forwards 52
(iii) Options 53
(iv) Swaps 53
(v) Foreign Exchange Contracts 54
(vi) Other Variations 54
(vii) Accounting Guidance 54
(x) Fiduciary Services and Other Fee Income 55
(i) Fiduciary Services 55
(ii) Other Fee Income 55
(y) Electronic Banking and Technology Risks 56

30.3 MORTGAGE BANKING ACTIVITIES 57

(a) Overview 57
(b) Accounting Guidance 57
(c) Mortgage Loans Held for Sale 58
(d) Mortgage Loans Held for Investment 58
(e) Sales of Mortgage Loans and Securities 59
(i) Gain or Loss on Sale of Mortgage Loans 60
(ii) Financial Assets Subject to Prepayment 60
(f) Mortgage Servicing Rights 60
(i) Initial Capitalization of Mortgage Servicing Rights 60
(ii) Amortization of Mortgage Servicing Rights 61
(iii) Impairment of Mortgage Servicing Rights 61
(iv) Fair Value of Mortgage Servicing Rights 61
(v) Sales of Mortgage Servicing Rights 62
(vi) Retained Interests 63
(g) Taxation 63
(i) Mortgage Servicing Rights 63
(ii) Mark to Market 64

30.4 INVESTMENT COMPANIES 65

(a) Background 65
(i) Securities and Exchange Commission Statutes 65
(ii) Types of Investment Companies 65
(b) Fund Operations 66
(i) Fund Accounting Agent 67
(ii) Custodian 67
(iii) Transfer Agent 67
(c) Accounting 67
(d) Financial Reporting 68
(i) New Registrants 68
(ii) General Reporting Requirements 68
(iii) Financial Statements 68

(e) Taxation 69
(f) Filings 69
(g) Investment Partnerships—Special Considerations 70
(h) Offshore Funds—Special Considerations 71

30.5 SOURCES AND SUGGESTED REFERENCES 72

30.1 OVERVIEW

(a) CHANGING THE ENVIRONMENT. The financial institutions industry has changed significantly in the last two decades. The conventional model of providing and receiving financial services has disappeared in the era since the Gramm-Leach-Bliley (GLB) Financial Services Modernization Act of 1999. The continuous wave of consolidations in the financial services industry has resulted in fewer but bigger financial institutions, and they are often perceived as being too big to fail. Financial services and products of banks, insurance companies, mutual funds, and brokerage firms that once were distinguishable and whose roles were separated are now consolidated and converged. Regulatory changes and increased global competition have further blurred the lines among depository institutions, mortgage banking activities, investment companies, credit unions, investment banks, insurance companies, finance companies, and securities brokers and dealers.

Global competition has increased as all types of financial services firms conduct business directly with potential depositors and borrowers. Transactions traditionally executed through depository institutions are now handled by all types of financial institutions. Increased global competition has heightened the depository institutions' desire for innovative approaches to attracting depositors and borrowers worldwide. Financial institutions are seeking higher levels of noninterest income, restructuring banking operations to reduce costs, and continuing consolidation within the industry. Consolidation, convergence, and competition derived primarily from deregulation and technological advances have reshaped the financial services industry. The passage of the GLB Act has accelerated the pace of consolidation and convergence in the financial services industry and has raised some concerns that its implementation has created concentration of economic power that would have made it more difficult for government to effectively oversee the industry's activities and strategies in managing risk. Some overriding reasons for the current financial crises are:

- Ineffective regulation
- Greed and incompetence of executives of troubled financial institutions
- Nature of bank lending and investment
- Inadequate risk assessment
- Conflicts of interest financial services activities

This chapter presents an overview of the financial services industry, its role in the economy, types and nature of financial firms and their regulatory framework, financial activities, and related risks.

(b) ROLE IN THE ECONOMY. Financial services firms play an important role in our economy by financing individual and business projects, lending to individuals and businesses, and investing in capital markets. Financial institutions can promote economic growth and prosperity for the nation, and their inefficiency can cause significant threats and the uncertainty and volatility in the markets, which adversely affect investor confidence worldwide. This lack of public trust and investor confidence has caused once-prominent Wall Street firms to either disappear or reorganize; for example, Bear Stearns merged with JP Morgan Chase; Lehman Brothers went bankrupt; Merrill Lynch was acquired by Bank of America; and Morgan Stanley and Goldman Sachs changed their corporate structures, becoming bank holding companies. It appears that the government facilitates the establishment of giant companies (e.g., AIG, Fannie Mae, Freddie Mac) to promote its social, economic, and political policies. Executives of these giant companies continuously make high-risk decisions, and while they receive outrageous compensation to make these decisions, lawmakers and regulators have failed to hold them accountable for their excessive risk-taking activities and appetite. These companies became too large to fail; in efforts to prevent their collapse, the government steps in to bail them out at the taxpayers' expense. Financial institutions worldwide have lost more than $1.5 trillion on mortgage-related losses during the 2007–2009 global financial crisis. The failed financial institutions of Bear Sterns, Lehman Brothers, AIG, and Merrill Lynch all played a vital role in the recent economic meltdown, as they all engaged in risky mortgage-lending practices, credit derivatives, hedge funds, and corporate loans.

Financial institutions are essential financial intermediaries in the economy in the sense that they provide liquidity transformation and monitoring mechanisms. Financial institutions in their basic role provide a medium of exchange; however, they may also serve as a tool to regulate the economy. In a complex financial and economic environment, the regulation of financial institutions—directly and indirectly—is used to impact economic activity. The Dodd-Frank Act of 2010 was passed to minimize the probability of future financial crisis and systemic distress by empowering regulators to mandate higher capital requirements and to establish a new regulatory regime for large financial firms, by developing regulatory and market structures for financial derivatives and by creating systemic risk assessment and monitoring. Dodd-Frank created a Financial Services Oversight Council (FSOC) that identifies and monitors systematic risk in the financial sector. The FSOC recommends appropriate leverage, liquidity, capital, and risk management rules to the Federal Reserve. The FSOC can practically take control of and liquidate troubled financial services firms if their failure would pose significant threat to the nation's financial stability. Ineffective functioning of financial institutions can be detrimental to the real economy, as evidenced in the recent financial crisis when many U.S. and European banks went bankrupt, had to be rescued by government, or were taken over by other financial institutions.

(c) TYPES OF FINANCIAL INSTITUTIONS. There are many types of financial services firms including commercial banks, investment banks, insurance firms, pension plans, mutual funds and sovereign wealth funds that are vital to the financial markets. The more common types of financial institutions are described in this chapter. In view of the range and diversity within financial institutions, this chapter focuses on three major types of entities/activities: banks and savings institutions, mortgage banking activities, and investment companies.

(i) Banks and Savings Institutions. Banks and savings institutions (including thrifts) continue in their traditional role as financial intermediaries. They provide a link between entities that have capital and entities that need capital while also providing an efficient means for payment and transfer of funds between these entities. Banks also provide a wide range of services to their customers, including cash management and fiduciary services, accepting demand and time deposits, making loans to individuals and organizations, and providing other financial services of documentary collections, international banking, trade financing.

Financial modernization and financial reform legislation (Dodd-Frank Act of 2010) continues to change the way banks and savings institutions conduct business. Banks and savings institutions have developed sophisticated products to meet customer needs and technological advances to support such complex and specialized transactions. Continued financial reform may change the types and nature of permissible banking activities and affiliations.

(ii) Mortgage Banking Activities. Mortgage banking activities include the origination, sale, and servicing of mortgage loans. Mortgage loan origination activities are performed by entities such as mortgage banks, mortgage brokers, credit unions, and commercial banks and savings institutions. Mortgages are purchased by government-sponsored entities, sponsors of mortgage-backed security (MBS) programs, and private companies such as insurance companies, other mortgage banking entities, and pension funds. These financial institutions typically provide the long-term loans to businesses and individuals.

(iii) Investment Companies. Investment companies pool shareholders' funds to provide the shareholders with professional investment management. Typically, an investment company sells its capital shares to the public, invests the proceeds to achieve its investment objectives, and distributes to its shareholders the net income and net gains realized on the sale of its investments. The types of investment companies include management investment companies, unit investment trusts, collective trust funds, investment partnerships, certain separate accounts of insurance companies, and offshore funds. Investment companies have grown significantly in recent years, primarily due to growth in mutual funds.

(iv) Credit Unions. Credit unions are member-owned, not-for-profit cooperative financial institutions, organized around a defined membership. The members pool their savings, borrow funds, and obtain other related financial services. A credit union relies on volunteers (owners and users) who represent the members. Its primary objective is to provide services to its members rather than to generate earnings for its owners. More recently, many credit unions have made arrangements to share branch offices with other credit unions and depository institutions to reduce operating costs. Traditionally, credit unions have owned and managed by several members to provide financial services to its members and now have evolved to thousands of members with multi-billion dollars in assets.

(v) Investment Banks. Investment banks or merchant banks deal with the financing requirements of corporations and institutions. They may be organized as corporations or partnerships. Investment banks are financial institutions that assist corporations and governments in raising capital by underwriting and acting as the agent in the issuance of securities. An investment bank also assists companies involved in mergers and acquisitions and derivatives, and provides ancillary services, such as market making and the trading of derivatives, fixed income instruments, foreign exchange, commodity, and equity securities.

(vi) Insurance Companies. The primary purpose of insurance is the spreading of risks. The two major types of insurance are life, and property and casualty. The primary purpose of life insurance is to provide financial assistance at the time of death. It typically has a long period of coverage. Property and casualty insurance companies provide policies to individuals (personal lines) and to business enterprises (commercial lines). Examples of personal lines include homeowner's and individual automobile policies. Examples of commercial lines include general liability and workers' compensation. Banks, mutual funds, and health maintenance organizations are aggressively trying to expand into products traditionally sold by insurance companies. During the 1990s and early 2000s, the insurance industry benefited from the strong stock and bond markets; however, recent slow premium growth and the increased competition and economic meltdown continued to pressure insurers to reduce costs and improve profitability. Many companies in the insurance sector in particular have been adversely affected by the 2007–2009 financial crisis. Insurance companies that were involved in activities traditionally associated with investment banks, and are designated as savings and loan holding companies (SLHCs) and typically offer leverage and risk-based financial products (security-based swaps) have been deeply impacted by the recent crisis.

Implementation of provisions of Dodd-Frank will have significant effects on insurance companies by impacting their business transactions. The newly established Federal Insurance Office (FIO) is intended to play an important role in overseeing and coordinating insurance activities between the international insurance market and the U.S. insurance market. Nonetheless, the FIO will not be in charge of state regulation of insurance companies. The Dodd-Frank Act directed the Securities and Exchange Commission (SEC) to establish rules and standards for broker-dealers and investment advisors will have a substantial impact on insurance companies. The FIO will oversee all aspects of the insurance industry, including systemic risk, capital standards, consumer protection, and international coordination of insurance regulation.

(vii) Finance Companies. Finance companies are non-banking lenders that do not receive deposits but provide lending and financing services to consumers (consumer financing) and to business enterprises (commercial financing). The more common types of consumer financing include mortgage loans, retail sales contracts, auto loans, debt consolidation loans and insurance service. The more common types of commercial financing include factoring, revolving loans, installment, term and floor plan loans, portfolio purchase agreements, and lease financing. Captive finance entities represent manufacturers, retailers, wholesalers, and other business enterprises that provide financing to encourage customers to buy their products and services. Many captive finance companies also finance third-party products. In the pre-financial crisis era, many mortgage finance companies and diversified finance companies increased their presence by increasing the number of loans made to higher-risk niches at higher yields.

(viii) Securities Brokers and Dealers. Securities brokers and dealers serve in various roles within the securities industry. Brokers, acting in an agency capacity, buy and sell securities, commodities, and related financial instruments for their customers and charge a commission. Dealers or traders, acting in a principal capacity, buy and sell for their own account and trade with customers and other dealers. Broker-dealers perform a wide range of both types of activities, such as assisting with private placements, underwriting public securities, developing new products, facilitating international investment activity, serving as a depository for customers' securities, extending credit, and providing research and advisory services.

(ix) Real Estate Investment Trusts. The new class of real estate investment trusts (REITs), formed since 1991, are basically self-contained real estate companies. They are designed to align the interests of active management and passive investors, generate cash flow growth, and create long-term value. Traditionally, REITs relied on mortgage debt to finance their development and acquisition activities. Recently many REITs have taken advantage of their large market capitalization and strong balance sheets to raise cash by issuing debt on an unsecured basis.

30.2 BANKS AND SAVINGS INSTITUTIONS

(a) PRIMARY RISKS OF BANKS AND SAVINGS INSTITUTIONS. General business and economic risk factors exist for many industries; however, increased competition and consolidation among banks and savings institutions has resulted in the industry's aggressive pursuit of profitable activities. Techniques for managing assets and liabilities and financial risks have been enhanced in order to maximize income levels. Technological advances have accommodated increasingly complex transactions, such as the sale of securities backed by cash flows from other financial assets. Regulatory policy has radically changed the business environment for banks, savings, and other financial institutions. Additionally, there are other risk factors common to most banks and savings institutions, based on their business activities. The Dodd-Frank Act establishes stricter disclosure requirements and restricts banks' risk-taking appetite by encouraging them to redesign their business lines and services. The other primary risk factors are described next.

(i) Interest Rate Risk. Interest rate risk is the risk that adverse movements in interest rates may result in loss of profits since banks and savings institutions routinely earn on assets at one rate and pay on liabilities at another rate. Techniques used to minimize interest rate risk are a part of asset/liability management.

(ii) Liquidity Risk. Liquidity risk is the risk that an institution may be unable to meet its obligations as they become due. An institution may acquire funds short term and lend funds long term to obtain favorable interest rate spreads, thus creating liquidity risk if depositors or creditors demand repayment. The primary function of banks in transforming short-term deposits into long-term loans makes them vulnerable to liquidity risk. Effective liquidity risk management is essential to banks to ensure their ability to meet cash flow obligations. The Basel Committee on Banking Supervision of the Bank for International Settlements (BIS) has released several publications designed to strengthen global capital and liquidity regulations to promote a more resilient global banking sector. The BIS (2010, 2011) has established guidance on managing liquidity risk that provides details on:

- the importance of establishing a liquidity risk tolerance;
- the maintenance of an adequate level of liquidity, including through a cushion of liquid assets;
- the necessity of allocating liquidity costs, benefits and risks to all significant business activities;
- the identification and measurement of the full range of liquidity risks, including contingent liquidity risks;
- the design and use of severe stress test scenarios;
- the need for a robust and operational contingency funding plan;
- the management of intraday liquidity risk and collateral; and
- public disclosure in promoting market discipline.

(iii) Asset-Quality Risk. Asset-quality risk is the risk that the loss of expected cash flows due to, for example, loan defaults and inadequate collateral will result in significant losses. Examples include credit losses from loans and declines in the economic value of mortgage servicing rights, resulting from prepayments of principal during periods of falling interest rates.

(iv) Fiduciary Risk. Fiduciary risk is the risk of loss arising from failure to properly process transactions or handle the custody, management, or both, of financial-related assets on behalf of third parties. Examples include administering trusts, managing mutual funds, and servicing the collateral behind asset-backed securities.

(v) Processing Risk. Processing risk is the risk that transactions will not be processed accurately or timely, due to large volumes, short periods of time, unauthorized access of computerized records, or the demands placed on both computerized and manual systems. Examples include electronic funds transfers, loan servicing, and check processing.

(vi) Operating Risk. Operating risk is the risk that losses can occur from internal failures and external events aside from financial risk. Operating risk is the risk of loss resulting from inadequate or failed internal processes, people, and systems, or from adverse effects of external events. This risk imposes a new capital charge to cover losses associated with operational risk.

(vii) Market Risk. Market risk is a risk that associated with earning volatility that caused by adverse price movements in the bank's principal trading positions. Market risk can be measured in terms of value at risk (VAR).

(b) REGULATION AND SUPERVISION OF BANKS AND SAVINGS INSTITUTIONS. The legal system that governed the financial services industry in the United States was created in response to the stock market crash of 1929 and the resulting Great Depression. Thousands of banks went out of business, and, in response, Congress passed the Glass-Steagall Act in 1933. Glass-Steagall prohibited commingling the businesses of commercial and investment banking. Its intent was to restrict banks from engaging in business activities that allegedly contributed to and accelerated the stock market crash. In the view of legislators, the way to do this was to confine banks to certain strictly defined activities.

In 1945, Congress enacted the McCarran-Ferguson Act as comprehensive legislation governing the insurance industry. McCarran-Ferguson effectively delegated the responsibility for regulating the business of insurance to the states. Since then, the states have maintained autonomy in their regulatory role with relatively minor, but increasing, exceptions. With the Bank Holding Company Act of 1956 and amendments in 1970, Congress limited affiliations between bank and nonbank businesses.

Section 20 of the Glass-Steagall Act took on a life of its own. It limited banks' ability to own subsidiaries principally engaged in securities underwriting. Over time, that section evolved from being considered a prohibition against any securities underwriting to permitting banks to do so through a subsidiary, as long as underwriting revenues did not exceed 25 percent of total revenues of that subsidiary—thus allowing them to meet the not principally engaged test. Over the years, the effective relaxation of those restrictions enabled numerous acquisitions of securities firms by U.S. bank holding companies and by foreign banks.

These barriers also eroded over time through a combination of changes in customer demands and market activities, the increasing use of more sophisticated financial management techniques, advances in technology, regulatory interpretations, and legal decisions. Product innovation played a role, as the industry learned how to rapidly bundle and unbundle risk, creating new securitization products and accessing the capital markets in ways that had not been contemplated under the then-existing regulatory framework.

As banks assumed a larger role in insurance sales, brokerage, and securities underwriting activities, products began to converge in the marketplace, and the perceived benefits from the convergence of these and related activities instilled a new urgency in the effort to modernize and clarify the regulatory framework governing financial services companies.

The GLB Act amended the Bank Holding Company Act to allow a bank holding company or foreign bank that qualifies as a financial holding company to engage in a broad range of activities that are defined by the Act to be financial in nature or incidental to a financial activity, or that the Federal Reserve Board (the Fed), in consultation with the secretary of the Treasury, determines to be financial in nature or incidental to a financial activity. The GLB Act also allows a financial holding company to seek Board approval to engage in any activity that the Fed determines both to be complementary to a financial activity and not to pose a substantial risk to the safety and soundness of depository institutions or the financial system generally. Bank holding companies that do not qualify as financial holding companies are limited to engaging in those nonbanking activities that were permissible for bank holding companies before the GLB Act was enacted.

On July 21, 2010, President Barack Obama signed into law the Dodd-Frank Wall Street Reform and Consumer Protection Act of 2010 (Dodd-Frank), which is considered the most sweeping financial reform since the Great Depression. The Act is named after Senate Banking Committee chairman Christopher Dodd (D-CT) and House Financial Services Committee chairman Barney Frank (D-MA), and its provisions pertain to banks, hedge funds, credit rating agencies, and the derivatives market. Dodd-Frank is about 2,300 pages long, and more than 200 regulations that will arise from the Act have not yet been written. Dodd-Frank authorizes the establishment of an oversight council to monitor systemic risk of financial institutions and the creation of a consumer protection bureau within the Federal Reserve. Dodd-Frank requires the development of over 240 new rules by the SEC, the Government Accountability Office (GAO), and the Federal Reserve to implement its provisions over a five-year period. Dodd-Frank will impact many aspects of the financial services industry, including:

- Foreign banking organizations and foreign nonbank financial companies
- SEC examination and enforcement
- Systemic risk/prudential supervision
- Banks/bank holding companies
- Credit rating agencies
- Non-U.S. asset managers
- Derivatives
- Consumer and mortgage banking
- Alternatives (hedge funds/private equity)
- Large asset managers
- Brokers/dealers
- Insurance companies

Some provisions of the Dodd-Frank Act of 2010 are summarized next.

- Dodd-Frank broadens the supervisory and oversight role of the Fed to include all entities that own an insured depository institution and other large and nonbank financial services firms that could threaten the nation's financial system.
- It establishes a new Financial Services Oversight Council to indentify and address existing and emerging systematic risks threatening the health of financial services firms.
- It develops new processes to liquidate failed financial services firms.
- It establishes an independent Consumer Financial Protection Bureau to oversee consumer and investor financial regulations and their enforcement.
- Dodd-Frank creates rules to regulate over-the-counter (OTC) derivatives.
- It coordinates and harmonizes the supervision, setting, and regulatory authorities of the SEC and the Commodities Futures Trading Commission (CFTC).
- The Act mandates registration of advisers of private funds and disclosures of certain information of those funds.
- It empowers shareholders with a say on pay of nonbonding votes on executive compensation.
- The Act increases accountability and transparency for credit rating agencies.
- It creates a Federal Insurance Office within the Treasury Department.
- It restricts and limits some activities of financial firms, including limiting bank proprietary investing and trading in hedge funds and private equity funds as well as limiting bank swaps activities.
- The Act provides cooperation and consistency with international financial and banking standards.
- It makes permanent the exemption from its Section 404(b) requirement for nonaccelerated filers (those with less than $75 million in market capitalization).
- It requires auditors of all broker-dealers to register with the Public Company Accounting Oversight Board (PCAOB) and gives the PCAOB rulemaking power to require a program of inspection for those auditors.
- It empowers the Financial Stability Oversight Council to monitor domestic and international financial regulatory proposals and developments in order to strengthen the integrity, efficiency, competitiveness and stability of the U.S. financial markets.
- It makes it easier for the SEC to prosecute aiders and abettors of those who commit securities fraud under the Securities Act of 1933, the Securities Exchange Act of 1934, and the Investment Advisers Act of 1940 by lowering the legal standard from knowing to knowing or reckless.
- Dodd-Frank directs the SEC to issue rules requiring companies to disclose in the proxy statement why they have separated, or combined, the positions of chairman and chief executive officer.

In August 2010, the Basel Committee issued its guidance entitled Microfinance Activities and the Core Principles for Effective Banking Supervision. This supervisory guidance highlights the application of the Basel Core Principles for Effective Banking Supervision (BCP) to microfinance activities in order to improve practices on regulating and supervising microfinance activities. The guidance is intended to assist global banking organizations to develop a coherent and comprehensive approach to microfinance supervision that addresses:

- Adequate and specialized knowledge of supervisors to effectively identify and assess risks that are specific to microfinance and microlending
- Proper and effective allocation of supervisory resources to microfinance activities
- Establishment of a regulatory and supervisory framework that is cost effective and efficient.

(c) REGULATORY BACKGROUND. Banks and savings institutions have special privileges and protections granted by government. These incentives, such as credit through the Federal Reserve System and federal insurance of deposits, have not been similarly extended to commercial enterprises. Accordingly, the benefits and responsibilities associated with their public role as financial intermediaries have brought banks and savings institutions under significant governmental oversight. For example, to stabilize the financial system during the financial crisis caused by subprime mortgage in late 2007 and 2008, several bailouts were implemented by the governments in the United States, the United Kingdom, and some western European countries. In the United States, after the government brokered sale of investment banks Bear Stearns and Lehman Brothers, Treasury secretary Paulson and the chairman of the Federal Reserve Ben S. Bernanke proposed a $700 billion bailout for the stabilization of the financial institutions in September 2008.

As a result of the financial repercussions of the Great Depression, the government took certain measures to maintain the stability of the country's financial system. Several new regulatory and supervisory agencies were created to promote economic stability, particularly in the banking industry, and to strengthen the regulatory and supervisory agencies that were in existence at the time. Among the agencies created were the Federal Deposit Insurance Corporation (FDIC), the SEC, the Federal Home Loan Bank Board (FHLBB), and the Federal Savings and Loan Insurance Corporation (FSLIC). The agencies that were strengthened included the Office of the Comptroller of the Currency (OCC) and the Fed. These entities were responsible for designing and establishing policies and procedures for the regulation and supervision of national and state banks, foreign banks doing business in the United States, and other depository institutions. This regulatory and supervisory structure, created during the 1930s, was in place for almost 60 years. In 1989, Congress enacted the Financial Institutions Reform, Recovery and Enforcement Act (FIRREA), which changed the regulatory and supervisory structure of thrift institutions. The FIRREA eliminated the FHLBB and the FSLIC. In their place, it created the Office of Thrift Supervision (OTS) as the primary regulator of the thrift industry and the Savings Association Insurance Fund (SAIF) as the thrift institutions' insurer to be administered by the FDIC.

Even though several of the aforementioned federal agencies have overlapping regulatory and supervisory responsibilities over depository institutions, in general terms, the OCC has primary responsibility for national banks; the Fed has primary responsibility over state banks that are members of the Fed, all financial holding companies and bank holding companies and their nonbank subsidiaries, and most U.S. operations of foreign banks; the FDIC has primary responsibility for all state-insured banks that are not members of the Fed (nonmember banks); and the OTS has primary responsibility for thrift institutions. Exhibit 30.1 lists these regulatory responsibilities.

Bank Classifications*	OTS	OCC	State Banking Department	Federal Reserve	FDIC
National banks		X			
State banks and trust companies					
Federal Reserve members			X	X	
Nonmembers					
FDIC insured			X		X
Noninsured			X		
Bank holding companies				X	
Thrift holding companies	X				
Savings Banks	X			X	X
Savings and Loan Associations	X				

*All national banks are members of the Federal Reserve Board. All national banks and state chartered member banks are insured by the FDIC.

Exhibit 30.1 Supervisor and Regulator

(i) Office of the Comptroller of the Currency. The OCC charters, regulates, and supervises all national banks. It also supervises the federal branches and agencies of foreign banks. Headquartered in Washington, DC, the OCC has six district offices plus an office in London to supervise the international activities of national banks.

The OCC was established in 1863 as a bureau of the U.S. Department of the Treasury. The OCC is headed by the Comptroller, who is appointed by the president, with the advice and consent of the Senate, for a five-year term. The Comptroller also serves as a director of the FDIC and a director of the Neighborhood Reinvestment Corporation.

The OCC's nationwide staff of examiners conducts on-site reviews of national banks and provides sustained supervision of bank operations. The agency issues rules, legal interpretations, and corporate decisions concerning banking, bank investments, bank community development activities, and other aspects of bank operations.

National bank examiners supervise domestic and international activities of national banks and perform corporate analyses. Examiners analyze a bank's loan and investment portfolios, funds management, capital, earnings, liquidity, sensitivity to market risk, and compliance with consumer banking laws, including the Community Reinvestment Act. They review the bank's internal controls, internal and external audit, and compliance with law. They also evaluate bank management's ability to identify and control risk.

In regulating national banks, the OCC has the power to:

- Examine the banks.
- Approve or deny applications for new charters, branches, capital, or other changes in corporate or banking structure.
- Take supervisory actions against banks that do not comply with laws and regulations or that otherwise engage in unsound banking practices. The agency can remove officers and directors, negotiate agreements to change banking practices, and issue cease-and-desist orders as well as civil money penalties.
- Issue rules and regulations governing bank investments, lending, and other practices.

(ii) Federal Reserve Board. The Fed was created by Congress in 1913 by the Federal Reserve Act. The primary role of the Fed as the nation's central bank is to establish and conduct monetary policy as well as to regulate and supervise a wide range of financial activities. The structure of the Fed includes a board of governors, 12 Federal Reserve banks, and the member banks. The board of governors consists of seven members appointed by the president, subject to Senate confirmation. National banks must be members of the Fed. State banks are not required to, but may elect to, become members. Member banks and other depository institutions are required to keep reserves with the Fed, and member banks must subscribe to the capital stock of the reserve bank in the district to which they belong.

Since all national banks are supervised by the OCC, the Fed primarily regulates and supervises member state banks, including administering the registration and reporting requirements of the 1934 Act.

The regulatory and supervisory functions and other services provided by the Fed include:

- Examining the Federal Reserve banks, state member banks, bank holding companies and their nonbank subsidiaries, and state licensed U.S. branches of foreign banks
- Requiring reports of member and other banks
- Setting the discount rate
- Providing credit facilities to members and other depository institutions for liquidity and other purposes
- Monitoring compliance with the money-laundering provisions contained in the Bank Secrecy Act
- Regulating transactions between banking affiliates

- Approving or denying applications by state banks to become members and to branch or merge with nonmember banks
- Approving or denying applications to become bank holding companies and for bank holding companies to acquire bank or nonbank subsidiaries
- Approving or denying applications by foreign banks to establish representative offices, branches, agencies, or bank subsidiaries in the United States
- Supplying currency when needed
- Regulating the establishment of foreign operations of national and state member banks and the operations of foreign banks doing business in the United States
- Enforcing legislation and issuing rules and regulations dealing with consumer protection
- Operating the nation's payment system

The Fed recently undertook several initiatives to mitigate the negative impacts of the financial crisis. These include:

- Extending credit facilities to financial institutions and thus improved market liquidity
- Lowering interest rates to eventually a zero-interest-rate policy by the end of 2008
- Taking several quantitative measures to reduce long-term-interest rates and purchase treasury bonds and Fannie Mae and Freddie Mac MBS
- Increasing deposit insurance limits and guaranteeing bank debt
- Ordering the 19 largest banks holding companies to conduct compensation stress tests to ensure that they had sufficient capital to with stand financial difficulties and be able to raise needed capital

(iii) Federal Deposit Insurance Corporation. The FDIC was created under the Banking Act of 1933. The main reason for its creation was to insure bank deposits in order to maintain economic stability in the event of bank failures. FIRREA restructured the FDIC during 1989 to carry out broadened functions by insuring thrift institutions as well as banks. The FDIC now insures all depository institutions except credit unions.

The FDIC is an independent agency of the U.S. government, managed by a five-member board of directors, consisting of the Comptroller of the Currency, the director of the OTS, and three other members, including a chairman, appointed by the president, subject to Senate confirmation.

The FDIC insures deposits under two separate funds: the Bank Insurance Fund (BIF) and the SAIF. From its BIF, the FDIC insures national and state banks that are members of the Fed. These institutions are required to be insured. Also insured from this fund are state nonmember banks and a limited number of insured branches of foreign banks. (After 1991, foreign bank branches could no longer apply for FDIC insurance.)

From its SAIF, the FDIC insures all federal savings and loan associations and federal savings banks. These institutions are required to be insured. State thrift institutions are also insured from this fund.

Currently, each account, subject to certain FDIC rules, in an insured depository institution is insured to a maximum of $250,000. Other responsibilities of the FDIC include:

- Supervising the liquidation of insolvent insured depository institutions
- Providing financial support and additional measures to prevent insured depository institution failures
- Supervising state nonmember insured banks by conducting bank examinations; regulating bank mergers, consolidations, and establishment of branches; and establishing other regulatory controls
- Administering the registration and reporting requirements of the 1934 Act as applied to state nonmember banks

(iv) Office of Thrift Supervision. In 1989, FIRREA created the OTS under the Department of the Treasury. The OTS regulates federal and state thrift institutions and thrift holding companies. As a principal rule maker, examiner, and enforcement agency, OTS exercises primary regulatory authority to grant federal thrift institution charters, approve branching applications, and allow mutual-to-thrift charter conversions. OTS is headed by a presidentially appointed director. The 12 district Federal Home Loan Banks (FHLBs) continue to be the primary source of credit for thrift institutions.

(d) REGULATORY ENVIRONMENT. The early 1980s were marked by the removal of interest rate ceilings, the applications of reserve requirements to all depository institutions, expanded thrift powers, and related deregulatory actions. However, the failures of a large number of thrift institutions and commercial banks caused legislators in 1989 and 1991 to increase regulatory oversight. Both FIRREA and the Federal Deposit Insurance Corporation Improvement Act of 1991 (FDICIA) were directed toward protection of federal deposit insurance funds through early detection of an intervention in problem institutions with an emphasis on capital adequacy. FIRREA also established the Resolution Trust Corporation (RTC), which took over the conservatorship and liquidation of a large number of failed thrift institutions due to the bankruptcy of the FSLIC. The RTC completed its mission in 1996 at a net cost of approximately $150 billion to the federal government.

In addition to safety and soundness considerations, current banking regulations recognize economic issues, such as the desire for banks and savings institutions to compete successfully with other, less regulated financial services providers and to address social issues, such as community reinvestment, nondiscrimination, and fair treatment in consumer credit, including residential lending. Costs and benefits of regulations are weighed as the approach to regulation of the industry is redefined.

Many provisions of Dodd-Frank are considered to be positive and useful in protecting consumers and investors, including the establishment of a consumer protection bureau and a systemic risk regulator and provisions requiring derivatives to be put on clearinghouses/exchanges. The new Consumer Financial Products Commission (CFPC) will make rules for most retail products offered by banks, such as certificates of deposit and consumer loans. The Dodd-Frank Act requires managers of hedge funds (but not the funds themselves) with more than $150 million in assets to register with the SEC. Some provisions are subject to study and further regulatory actions by regulators, including the so-called Volcker rule to be implemented. Dodd-Frank fails to address the misconception of too-big-to-fail financial institutions, the main cause of the financial crisis—Fannie Mae, Freddie Mac, and the housing agencies and the excessive use of market-based short-term funding by financial services firms.

The Basel Committee on Banking Supervision is intended to strengthen global capital and liquidity regulations to promote a more resilient banking sector with proper ability to absorb shocks arising from financial and economic stress and to improve risk management, governance, transparency, and disclosures. The Basel Committee examines the market failures caused by the recent financial crisis and establishes measures to strengthen bank-level and micro-prudential regulation to address the stability of the global financial system.

(e) FEDERAL DEPOSIT INSURANCE CORPORATION IMPROVEMENT ACT SECTION 112. Regulations implementing Section 36 of the Federal Deposit Insurance Act (FDI Act), as added by Section 112 of FDICIA, became effective July 2, 1993. These regulations imposed additional audit, reporting, and attestation responsibilities on management, directors (especially the audit committee), internal auditors, and independent accountants of banks and savings institutions with $500 million or more in total assets. The reporting requirements were effective for fiscal years ending on or after December 31, 1993. Congress amended the law in 1996 to eliminate attestation reports concerning compliance with certain banking laws; however, management is still required to report on compliance with such laws.

(i) The Regulation and Guidelines. The Dodd-Frank Act of 2010 is aimed at minimizing the probability of future financial crises and systemic distress by empowering regulators to mandate higher capital requirements and establish a new regulatory regime for large financial firms. The Act is intended to provide more cost-effective and efficient regulatory guidelines for financial service firms and other impacted organizations. These regulatory guidelines are presented in Appendix A to the Act. The guidelines often leave discretion to an institution or its board, while simultaneously providing guidance that, if followed, would provide a safe harbor from examiner criticism.

(ii) Basic Requirements. Each FDIC-insured depository institution with assets in excess of $500 million at the beginning of its fiscal year (covered institutions) is subject to requirements concerning its annual report, corporate governance, and audit committee.

Annual Report. Covered institutions must file an annual report, within 90 days of their fiscal year-end, with the FDIC and other appropriate state or federal bank regulators. The annual report must include:

1. Audited financial statements prepared in accordance with generally accepted accounting principles (GAAP) and audited by a qualified independent public accountant (IPA).
2. A management report signed by its CEO and chief financial officer or chief accounting officer containing:
    - A statement of management's responsibilities for:
        - Preparing the annual financial statements
        - Establishing and maintaining an adequate internal control structure and procedures for financial reporting.
        - Complying with particular laws designated by the FDIC as affecting the safety and soundness of insured depositories.
    - Assessment by management of:
        - The effectiveness of the institution's internal control structure and procedures for financial reporting as of the end of the fiscal year.
        - The institution's compliance, during the fiscal year, with the designated safety and soundness laws. Only two kinds of safety and soundness laws must be addressed in the compliance report: (a) federal statutes and regulations concerning transactions with insiders and (b) federal and state statutes and regulations restricting the payment of dividends.
3. An attestation report, by an IPA, on internal control structure and procedures for financial reporting. The institution's IPA must examine, attest to, and report separately on management's assertions about internal controls and about compliance. The attestations are to be made in accordance with generally accepted standards for attestation engagements.

In Financial Institution Letter (FIL) No. 86-94, the FDIC indicated that financial reporting, at a minimum, includes financial statements prepared under GAAP and the schedules equivalent to the basic financial statements that are included in the institution's appropriate regulatory report (e.g., Schedules RC, RI, and RI-A in the Call Report).

On February 6, 1996, the Board of the FDIC amended the procedures that IPAs follow in testing compliance to streamline the procedures and to reduce regulatory burden. Financial services firms must also comply with Sections 302, 906, and 404 of the Sarbanes-Oxley Act of 2002 (SOX) to include executive certifications of both financial statements and internal control over financial reporting in their annual reports files with regulators and submitted to shareholders.

Corporate Governance. The globalization of capital markets and financial institutions demands convergence in regulatory reforms and corporate governance measures and practices. Corporate governance measures are state and federal statutes, judicial deliberations, listing standards, and best practices. In the United States, SOX and financial reform legislation signed into law in July 2010 the Dodd–Frank Wall Street Reform and Consumer Protection Act have established new regulatory reforms for financial institutions. The U.K. corporate governance reforms are specified in the 2003 Combined Code on Corporate Governance.

In October 2010, the Basel Committee issued its Principles for Enhancing Corporate Governance to promote effective corporate governance of financial institutions and banking organizations worldwide. These corporate governance principles address:

- The role of the board
- The qualifications and composition of the board
- The importance of an independent risk management function, including a chief risk officer or equivalent
- The importance of monitoring risks on an ongoing firm-wide and individual entity basis
- The board's oversight of the compensation systems
- The board's and senior management's understanding of the bank's operational structure and risks

The International Federation of Accountants (IFAC) and the United Nations Conference on Trade and Development (UNCTAD) hosted an Accountancy Summit on October 12, 2010. Participants from more than 50 countries collectively supported the next points relevant to convergence in global corporate governance (IFAC, 2010):

> The accountancy profession has a key role to play in strengthening corporate governance and facilitating the integration of governance and sustainability into the strategy, operations, and reporting of an organization.
>
> Boards should be focused on the long-term sustainability of their businesses. As such, corporate governance reform must include strengthening board oversight of management, positioning risk management as a key board responsibility, and encouraging remuneration practices that balance risk and long-term (social, environmental, and economic) performance criteria.
>
> Governance is more than having the right structures, regulation, and principles in place—it is about ensuring that the right behaviors and processes are in place.
>
> Governance mechanisms need to be strengthened at banks and other companies to ensure better oversight of risk management and executive compensation.
>
> More dialogue is needed between policy makers, the accounting profession, and other financial industries to consider how we can work together effectively on a global level.

Audit Committee. Covered institutions must establish an independent audit committee composed of directors who are independent of management. The entire board of directors annually is required to adopt a resolution documenting its determination that the audit committee has met all FDIC-imposed requirements.

The audit committee of any large financial institutions (i.e., total assets of more than $3 billion, measured as of the beginning of each fiscal year) must include members with banking or related financial management expertise, have access to its own outside counsel, and not include any large customers of the institution. If a large institution is a subsidiary of a holding company and relies on the audit committee of the holding company to comply with this rule, the holding company audit committee must not include any members who are large customers of the subsidiary institution. Appendix A to Part 363 of the Federal Deposit Insurance Act provides guidelines in determining whether the audit committee meets these criteria.

The audit committee is required to review with management and the IPA the basis for the reports required by the FDIC's regulation. The FDIC suggests, but does not mandate, additional audit committee duties, including overseeing internal audit, selecting the IPA, and reviewing significant accounting policies.

Each subject institution must provide its independent accountant with copies of the institution's most recent reports of condition and examination; any supervisory memorandum of understanding or written agreement with any federal or state regulatory agency; and a report of any action initiated or taken by federal or state banking regulators.

Recent global financial crises and related economic meltdown underscore the importance of board committees, particularly the audit committee in overseeing managerial function of troubled banks and other financial institutions. Audit committees in the post-SOX world are required to protect investor interests by assuming more effective oversight responsibilities in the areas of internal controls, financial reporting, risk assessment, audit activities, and compliance with applicable laws and regulations. In the post-SOX period, the audit committee selects the bank's external auditor and reviews the company's annual audited financial statements and internal control over financial reporting.

Lawmakers (SOX), regulators (SEC rules), and listing standards of national stock exchanges (New York Stock Exchange, Nasdaq, American Stock Exchange) generally require public committees to have an audit committee, which must be composed of independent directors with no personal, financial, or family ties to management. Rezaee (2007) states that:

- Audit committee members must be independent.
- Audit committee members to select and oversee the issuer's independent account.
- There must be a procedural process for handling complaints regarding the issuer's accounting practice.
- The audit committee is authorized to engage advisors.

Audit committee oversight responsibilities can be grouped into eight categories:

1. *Corporate governance.* The audit committee should protect investor interests by overseeing managerial functions in planning, coordinating, and monitoring bank's financial activities.
2. *Internal controls.* The audit committee should review management and external auditor reports on the effectiveness of internal control over financial reporting.
3. *Financial reporting.* The audit committee should review and oversee executive certifications on the completeness and accuracy of financial statements.
4. *Audit activities.* The audit committee should be in charge of hiring, firing, compensating, and overseeing audit activities as well as reviewing external auditors' reports on financial statements and internal control over financial reporting.
5. *Code of ethics conduct.* The audit committee should review and oversee the design, implementation and enforcement of the bank's code of ethical conduct.
6. *Whistleblower program.* The audit committee should oversee the design and implementation of banks' whistleblower policies and programs to ensure that employees, customers, and others can come forward in reporting bank irregularities, violations of laws, and other concerns without being retaliated against.
7. *Enterprise risk management.* The audit committee should oversee the proper development and functioning of bank risk management in addressing liquidity, interest rate, operating, credit, and other risks presented in the previous sections.
8. *Financial statement fraud.* The audit committee should oversee bank antifraud policies and procedures designed to prevent and detect financial reporting fraud.

(iii) Holding Company Exception. In some instances, FDIC regulation requirements may be satisfied by a bank's or savings association's parent holding company. The requirement for audited financial statements always may be satisfied by providing audited financial statements of the consolidated holding company. The requirements for other reports, as well as for an independent audit committee, may be satisfied by the holding company if:

- The holding company's services and functions are comparable to those required of the depository institution.
- The depository institution has total assets as of the beginning of the fiscal year either of less than $5 billion or equal to or greater than $5 billion and a Capital adequacy, Asset quality,

Management administration, Earnings, and Liquidity (CAMELS) composite rating of 1 or 2. Section 314(a) of the Riegle Community Development and Regulatory Improvement Act of 1994 amended Section 36(i) of the FDI Act to expand the holding company exception to be equal to or greater than $5 billion. The requirement that the institution must have a CAMELS composite rating of 1 or 2 remained unchanged.

The appropriate federal banking agency may revoke the exception for any institution with total assets in excess of $9 billion for any period of time during which the appropriate federal banking agency determines that the institution's exception would create a significant risk to the affected deposit insurance fund.

(iv) Availability of Reports. All of management's reports are made publicly available. The independent accountant's report on the financial statements and attestation report on financial reporting controls is also made publicly available. SOX requires public reporting on:

- The audit committee review of both financial statements and internal control over financial reporting
- Management certifications of accuracy and completeness of financial statements and the effectiveness of internal control over financial reporting
- External auditor report on fair presentation of financial statements and the effectiveness of internal control over financial reporting
- Other financial reports released by management (management Discussion &Analysis, MD&A, earnings guidance).

(f) CAPITAL ADEQUACY GUIDELINES. Capital is one of the primary tools used by regulators to monitor the financial health of insured banks and savings institutions. Statutorily mandated supervisory intervention is focused primarily on an institution's capital levels relative to regulatory standards. The federal banking agencies detail these requirements in their respective regulations under capital adequacy guidelines. The capital adequacy requirements are implemented through quarterly regulatory financial reporting (Call Reports and Thrift Financial Reports (TFRs)).

On September 12, 2010, global bank regulators agreed to require banks to significantly increase their amount of top-quality capital in an attempt to prevent further international financial crisis. The Basel III a global regulatory standard on bank capital liquidity, will require banks to maintain top-quality capital totaling 7 percent of their risk-bearing assets compared to the currently required 2 percent. Effective compliance with Basel III rules, which become effective in January 2019, would require banks to raise substantial new capital over the next several years. The primary objective of Basel III rules is to strengthen global capital standards to ensure sustainable financial stability and growth for banks worldwide. The rules are intended to encourage banks to engage in appropriate risk strategies to ensure their financial health and their ability to withstand financial shocks without government bailout supports. Specifically, Basel III will require banks to: (1) maintain top-quality capital (Tier 1 capital, consisting or equity and retained earnings) up to 4.5 percent of their assets; (2) hold a new separate capital conservation buffer of common equity worth at least 2.5 percent of their assets; and (3) build a separate countercyclical buffer of up to 2.5 percent when their credit markets are booming. The Tier 1 rule will take effect from January 2015, and the requirement for the capital conversation buffer will be phased in between January 2016 and January 2019.

(i) Risk-Based and Leverage Ratios. Capital adequacy is measured mainly through two risk-based capital ratios and a leverage ratio, with thrifts subject to an additional tangible capital ratio.

(ii) Tier 1, Tier 2, and Tier 3 Components. Regulatory capital is composed of three components: core capital or Tier 1, supplementary capital or Tier 2, and for those institutions meeting market risk capital requirements, Tier 3. Tier 1 capital includes elements such as common stock, surplus, retained earnings, minority interest in consolidated subsidiaries and qualifying preferred stock, adjustments for foreign exchange translation, and unrealized losses on equity securities available for sale with readily determinable market values. Tier 2 capital includes, with certain limitations, elements such as general loan loss reserves, certain forms of preferred stock, long-term preferred stock, qualifying intermediate-term preferred stock and term subordinated debt, perpetual debt, and other hybrid debt/equity instruments. Tier 3 capital consists of short-term subordinated debt that meets certain conditions and may be used only by institutions subject to market-risk capital requirements to the extent that Tier 1 and Tier 2 capital elements do not provide adequate Tier 1 and total risk-based capital ratio levels.

Specifically, Tier 3 capital:

- Must have an original maturity of at least two years
- Must be unsecured and fully paid up
- Must be subject to a lock-in clause that prevents the issuer from repaying the debt even at maturity if the issuer's capital ratio is, or with repayment would become, less than the minimum 8 percent risk-based capital ratio
- Must not be redeemable before maturity without the prior approval of the institution's supervisor
- Must not contain or be covered by any covenants, terms, or restrictions that may be inconsistent with safe and sound banking practices.

Tier 2 capital elements individually and together are variously restricted in proportion to Tier 1 capital, which is intended to be the dominant capital component.

Certain deductions are made to determine regulatory capital, including goodwill and other disallowed intangibles, excess portions of qualifying intangibles and deferred tax assets, investments in unconsolidated subsidiaries, and reciprocal holdings of other bank's capital instruments. Certain adjustments made to equity under GAAP for unrealized gains and losses on debt and equity securities available for sale under Financial Accounting Standards Board (FASB) Statement No. 115, mainly unrealized gains, are excluded from Tier 1 and total capital. Portions of qualifying, subordinated debt, and limited-life preferred stock exceeding 50 percent of a bank's Tier 1 capital are also deducted. Any regulatory capital deduction is also made to average total assets for ratio computation purposes. The new market-risk capital guidelines discussed in section vi also contained further capital constraints, by stating that the sum of Tier 2 and Tier 3 capital allocated for market risk may not exceed 250 percent of Tier 1 capital allocated for market risk. Thrift's tangible capital is generally defined as Tier 1 capital less intangibles.

(iii) Risk-Weighted Assets. The capital ratios are calculated using the applicable regulatory capital component in the numerator and either risk-weighted assets or total adjusted on-balance-sheet assets as the denominator, as appropriate. Risk-weighted assets are ascertained pursuant to the regulatory guidelines that allocate gross average assets among four categories of risk weights (0, 20, 50, and 100 percent). The allocations are based mainly on type of asset, type of obligor, and nature of collateral, if any. Gross assets include on-balance-sheet assets, credit equivalents of certain off-balance-sheet exposures, and credit equivalents of certain assets sold with recourse, limited recourse, or that are treated as financings for regulatory reporting purposes.

Credit equivalents of off-balance-sheet exposures are determined by the nature of the exposure. For example, direct credit substitutes (e.g., standby letters of credit) are credit converted at 100 percent of the face amount. Other off-balance-sheet activities are subject to the current exposure method, which is composed of the positive mark-to-market value (if any) and an estimate of the potential increase in credit exposure over the remaining life of the contract. These add-ons are estimated by applying defined credit conversion factors, differentiated by type of instrument and remaining maturity, to the contract's notional value. The nature and extent of recourse impacts the calculation of credit equivalents amounts of assets sold or securitized. In December 2001, the banking agencies issued a final rule amending the agencies' regulatory capital standards to align more closely the risk-based capital treatment of recourse obligations and direct credit substitutes.

The rule also varies the capital requirements for position in securitized transactions and certain other exposures according to their relative credit risk and requires capital commensurate with the risks associated with residual interests.

(iv) Capital Calculations and Minimum Requirements. The capital ratios, calculations, and minimum requirements are presented in Exhibit 30.2.

In summary, Basel III rules set forth tougher capital requirements by providing more restrictive capital definitions, requiring higher risk-weighted assets, capital buffers, and higher minimum capital ratios. These Basel III standards are expected to affect profitability and transformation of the

Capital Ratio	Calculation	Minimum Requirement
Total risk-based ratio:		
Unadjusted	Tier 1 + Tier 2/Risk-weighted assets	≥ 8.0%
Adjusted for marked risk	Tier 1 + Tier 2 + Tier 3/Risk-weighted assets plus market-risk equivalent assets	≥ 8.0%
Tier 1 risk-based ratio	Tier 1/Risk-weighted assets	≥ 4.0%
Tier 1 leverage capital ratio	Tier 1/Average on-balance sheet assets	≥ 4.0%*
Tangible ratio (Thrifts)	Tangible capital/on-balance sheet assets	≥ 1.5%

*3.0% for institutions CAMELS/MACRO rated "1" (overall).

Basel III Accord will require banks to: (1) maintain top-quality capital (tier1 capital, consisting or equity and retained earnings) up to 4.5% of their assets; and (2) hold a new separate "capital conservation buffer" of common equity worth at least 2.5% of their assets; and (3) build a separate "countercyclical buffer" of up to 2.5% when their credit markets are booming. The Tier1 rule will take effect from January 2015 and the requirement for the capital conversation buffer will be phased in between January 2016 and January 2019. The next chart summarizes the Basel III capital requirements.

Calibration of the Capital Framework
Capital requirements and buffers (all numbers in percent)

	Common Equity (after deductions)	Tier 1 Capital	Total Capital
Minimum	4.5	6.0	8.0
Conservation buffer	2.5		
Minimum plus conservation buffer	7.0	8.5	10.5
Countercyclical buffer range	0–2.5		

According to Basel III Accord:
Tier 1 Capital Ratio = 6%
Core Tier 1 Capital Ratio (Common Equity after deductions) = 4.5%
Core Tier 1 Capital Ratio (Common Equity after deductions) before 2013 = 2%, 1st January 2013 = 3.5%, 1st January 2014 = 4%, 1st January 2015 = 4.5%. The transition periods in meeting capital requirements are presented in the next chart.

(*Continues*)

Exhibit 30.2 Capital Ratio Calculations and Minimum Requirements

Annex 2 : Phase-in arrangements (shading indicates transition periods)
(all dates are as of 1 January)

	2011	2012	2013	2014	2015	2016	2017	2018	As of 1 January 2019
Leverage Ratio	Supervisory monitoring			Parallel run 1 Jan 2013–1 Jan 2017 Disclosure starts 1 Jan 2015				Migration to pillar 1	
Minimum Common Equity Capital Ratio			3.5%	4.0%	4.5%	4.5%	4.5%	4.5%	4.5%
Capital Conservation Buffer						0.625%	1.25%	1.875%	2.50%
Minimum Common equity plus capital conservation buffer			3.5%	4.0%	4.5%	5.125%	5.75%	6.375%	7.0%
Phase-in of deductions from CET1 (including amounts exceeding the limit for DTAs, MSR and financials)				20%	40%	60%	80%	100%	100%
Minimum Tier 1 Capital			4.5%	5.5%	6.0%	6.0%	6.0%	6.0%	6.0%
Minimum Total Capital			8.0%	8.0%	8.0%	8.0%	8.0%	8.0%	8.0%
Minimum Total Capital plus conservation buffer			8.0%	8.0%	8.0%	8.625%	9.125%	9.875%	10.5%
Capital instruments that no longer qualify as non-core Tier 1 capital or Tier 2 capital			Phased out over 10-year horizon beginning 2013						
Liquidity coverage ratio	Observation period begins				Introduce minimum standard				
Net stable funding ratio		Observation period begins						Introduce minimum standard	

Source: **Basel III Accord: The new Basel III framework.** ***www.basel-iii-accord.com***

Exhibit 30.2 ***Continued***

business models of many banks as well as other bank activities in regard to stress testing, counterparty risk, and capital management infrastructure. Implementation of provisions of Basel III is expected to demand more standardized risk-adjusted capital requirements that will enable investors to better analyze and compare risk-adjusted performance

In the United State, the Supervisory Capital Assessment Program (SCAP) has increased capital levels by requiring many U.S. banks to increase their capital levels (the current Tier 1 common median for U.S. banks is 9 percent) and providing an adequate transition period of eight years to generate further capital buffers through earnings generation.

(v) Interest Rate Risk and Capital Adequacy. OTS capital rules require that certain savings associations with excessive interest rate risk exposure (as defined) must deduct 50 percent of the estimated decline in its net portfolio value resulting from a 200 basis point change in market interest rates in excess of 2 percent of the estimated economic value of portfolio assets. In August 1995, the banking agencies amended their minimum capital requirements explicitly to include consideration of interest rate risk but did not establish a means for quantifying that risk to a specific amount of additional capital. During 1996, the federal bank regulatory agencies approved a policy statement on sound practices for managing interest rate risk in commercial banks but did not include a standardized framework for measuring interest rate risk. The agencies elected not to pursue a standardized measure and explicit capital charge for interest rate risk due to concerns about the burden, accuracy, and complexity of a standardized measure and recognition that industry techniques for measuring interest rate risk are continuing to evolve.

(vi) Capital Allocated for Market Risk. In September 1996, the federal bank regulatory agencies—the OCC, FDIC, and Fed—amended their respective risk-based capital standards to address market risk. Specifically, an institution subject to the market risk capital requirement must adjust its risk-based capital ratio to take into account the general market risk of all positions located in its trading account and foreign exchange and commodity positions, wherever located and for the specific risk of debt and equity positions located in its trading account. Market risk capital requirements generally apply to any bank or bank holding company whose trading activities equal 10 percent or more of its total assets or whose trading activity equals $1 billion or more. In addition, on a case-by-case basis, an agency may require an institution that does not meet the applicability criteria to comply with the market risk guidelines, if the agency deems it necessary for safety and soundness purposes, or may exclude an institution that meets the applicability criteria.

No later than January 1, 1998, institutions with significant market risk were required to:

- Maintain regulatory capital on a daily basis at an overall minimum of 8 percent ratio of total qualifying capital to risk-weighted assets, adjusted for market risk
- Include a supplemental market-risk capital charge in their risk-based capital calculations and quarterly regulatory reports
- Maintain appropriate internal measurement, reporting, and risk management systems to generate and monitor the basis for the VAR and the associated capital charge

The institution's risk-based capital ratio adjusted for market risk is its risk-based capital ratio for purposes of prompt corrective action and other statutory and regulatory purposes.

Institutions are permitted to use different assumptions and modeling techniques reflecting distinct business strategies and approaches to risk management. The agencies do not specify VAR modeling parameters for internal risk management purposes; however, they do specify minimum qualitative requirements for internal risk management processes as well as certain quantitative requirements for the parameters and assumptions for internal models used to measure market risk exposure for regulatory capital purposes.

There are several models of risk assessment and management, including most widely used models of VAR developed through statistical ideas and probability theories. VAR utilizes a group of related models that share a mathematical framework by measuring the boundaries of risk in a portfolio over short durations. The portfolio can consist of equities, bonds, derivatives, or other financial instruments, and risks can be measured in terms of diversification, leverage, and volatility as a proxy for market risk. VAR takes into consideration both individual risks and firm-wide risks.

Financial institutions use VAR to quantify their risk positions for both internal and external purposes. The extensive use of derivatives by many firms in the late 1990s and the early 2000s encouraged regulators such as the SEC and the Basel Committee to establish rules and guidance to require public quantitative disclosures of market risks in their financial statements. VAR then became the primary model of assessing and managing risks. The Basel Committee even allowed banks to rely on their own internal VAR measures in determining their capital requirements.

Backtesting. Institutions must perform backtests of their VAR measures as calculated for internal risk management purposes. The backtests must compare daily VAR measures calibrated to a one-day movement in rates and prices and a 99 percent (one-tailed) confidence level against the institution's actual daily net trading profit or loss (trading outcome) for each of the preceding 250 business days. The backtests must be performed once each quarter. An institution's obligation to backtest for regulatory capital purposes does not arise until the institution has been subject to the final rule for 250 business days (approximately one year) and, thus, has accumulated the requisite number of observations to be used in backtesting. Institutions that are found not to have appropriate models and backtesting programs or if backtesting results reflect insufficient accuracy likely will be required to incorporate more conservative calculation factors that would result in a higher capital charge for market risk. It has been argued that too much reliance on VAR and its widespread use in determining capital requirement do not consider the important risk of potential financial meltdown.

Basel rules require that bank stress tests consist of:

- The stressed VAR (SVAR), which is computed on a 10-day 99 percent confidence level and three times the 10-day 99 percent stressed VAR will should be maintained
- Model inputs that are calibrated to historical data from a continuous 12-month period of significant financial stress

- Maintenance, on a daily basis, of the capital requirements determined based on the higher of its latest stress VAR number and an average of SVAR numbers calculated over the preceding 60 business days multiplied by the multiplication factor

Risk factors considered in pricing models should also be included in VAR calculations.

(g) PROMPT CORRECTIVE ACTION. The federal banking agencies are statutorily mandated to assign each FDIC-insured depository institution to one of five capital categories, quantitatively defined by the risk-based and leverage capital ratios.

1. *Well capitalized.* The capital level significantly *exceeds* the required minimum level for each relevant capital category.
2. *Adequately capitalized.* The capital level *meets* the minimum level.
3. *Undercapitalized.* The capital level *fails to meet one or more* of the minimum levels.
4. *Significantly undercapitalized.* The capital level is *significantly below one or more* of the minimum levels.
5. *Critically undercapitalized.* The ratio of *tangible equity* (as statutorily defined) *to total assets is 2 percent or less.*

Institutions falling into the last three categories are subject to a variety of prompt corrective actions, such as limitations on dividends, prohibitions on acquisitions and branching, restrictions on asset growth, and removal of officers and directors. Irrespective of the ratios reported, the agencies may downgrade an institution's capital category based on adverse examination findings.

The regulatory capital ratio ranges defining the prompt corrective action capital categories are summarized in Exhibit 30.3.

Federally insured banks and savings institutions are required to have periodic full-scope, on-site examinations by the appropriate agency. In certain cases, an examination by a state regulatory agency is accepted. Full-scope and other examinations are intended primarily to provide early identification of problems at insured institutions rather than as a basis for expressing an opinion on the fair presentation of the institution's financial statements. The Dodd-Frank Act has substantially increased the enforcement oversight function of the SEC and the Federal Reserve Board and their examination programs to regulate the financial services industry effectively.

(i) Scope. The scope of an examination is generally unique to each institution based on risk factors assessed by the examiner. Some examinations are targeted to a specific area of operations, such as real estate lending or trust operations. Separate compliance examination programs also exist to address institutions' compliance with laws and regulations in areas such as consumer protection, insider transactions, and reporting under the Bank Secrecy Act.

Capital Category	Total Risk-Based Ratio		Tier 1 Risk-Based Ratio		Tier 1 Leverage Capital Ratio
Well capitalized	$\geq$ 10%	and	$\geq$ 6%	and	$\geq$ 5%
Adequately capitalized	$\geq$ 8%	and	$\geq$ 4%	and	$\geq$ 4%*
Undercapitalized	< 8%	Or	< 4%	Or	< 4%*
Significantly undercapitalized	< 6%	Or	< 3%	Or	< 3%
Critically undercapitalized	If the ratio of tangible equity (as statutorily defined) to total assets is 2% or less				

*3% for institutions that have a rating of "1" under the regulatory CAMELS, MACRO, or related rating system; that are not anticipating or experiencing significant growth; and that have well- diversified risk.

Exhibit 30.3 Regulatory Capital Categories

(ii) Regulatory Rating Systems. Regulators use regulatory rating systems to assign ratings to banks, thrifts, holding companies, parents of foreign banks, and U.S. branches and agencies of foreign banking organizations. The rating scales vary, although each is based on a 5-point system, with 1 (or A) being the highest rating. The rating systems are presented in Exhibit 30.4. Additionally, in November 1995, the Fed issued Supervision and Regulation Letters (SR) No. 95-51, *Rating the Adequacy of Risk Management Processes and Internal Controls at State Member Banks and Bank Holding Companies.* It states that Federal Reserve System examiners, beginning in 1996, are instructed to assign a formal supervisory rating to the adequacy of an institution's risk management processes, including its internal controls.

The Dodd-Frank Act addresses activities, practices and structure of the nationally recognized statistical rating organizations (NRSROs), better known as credit rating agencies. Specifically, provisions of Dodd-Frank pertaining to NRSROs include:

- Mandating internal control requirements for NRSROs
- Improvements in governance practices of NRSROs
- Addressing potential conflicts of interest of NRSROs
- Imposing new liability exposure on NRSROs
- Requiring new methodology and procedures to be used in credit ratings process
- Requiring more transparent disclosures on credit ratings process
- Increasing SEC oversight of NRSROs

Entity	Assigns Rating	Rating Scale	Rating Components
Banks and Thrifts	OCC, FDIC, OTS, and FRB	**CAMELS** Ratings 1–5	**C**apital adequacy **A**sset quality **M**anagement's performance **E**arnings **L**iquidity **S**ensitivity to Market Risk
Bank holding companies	FRB	**BOPEC** Ratings 1–5	**B**ank's CAMELS rating **O**peration of nonbanking subs **P**arent's strength **E**arnings **C**apital adequacy
Parents of foreign banks with U.S. branches or agencies	FRB	**SOSA*** (**S**trength of **S**upport **A**ssessment) Ratings A–E.	Effectiveness of home country supervision and other country factors Institution-specific issues Ability of parent to maintain adequate internal controls and compliance with procedures in United States
U.S. branches and agencies of foreign banking organizations	FRB, OCC, and FDIC	**ROCA** Ratings 1–5	**R**isk management **O**perational controls **C**ompliance **A**sset quality

*SOSA ratings will not be disclosed to the bank, branch, or home supervisor. Ratings are for U.S. internal supervisory use only.

Exhibit 30.4 Regulatory Rating Systems

(iii) Risk-Focused Examinations. Over the last two decades, the banking agencies have been developing and implementing a risk-focused examination/supervisory program that focuses on the business activities that pose the greatest risks to the institutions and assesses an organization's management systems to identify, measure, monitor, and control its risks. Bank examiners should learn from factors that caused the global financial crisis, pay attention to all types of bank risks, and recognize the importance of risk-focused examination and supervision in preventing further financial crises. It is evidenced the extend, nature and complexity of international financial transactions, in the years preceding the start of financial crisis in 2007, bank supervisors and examiners failed to develop adequate and effective risk-focused techniques to properly deal with the complex situations.

(h) ENFORCEMENT ACTIONS. Regulatory enforcement is carried out through a variety of informal and formal mechanisms. Informal enforcement measures are consensual between a bank and its regulator but are not legally enforceable. Formal measures carry the force of law and are issued subject to certain legal procedures, requirements, and penalties. Examples of formal enforcement measures include ordering an institution to cease and desist from certain practices of violations, removing an officer, prohibiting an officer from participating in the affairs of the institution or the industry, assessing civil money penalties, and terminating insurance of an institution's deposits. As previously discussed, other mandatory and discretionary actions may be taken by regulators under prompt corrective action provisions of the FDI Act. The Dodd-Frank Act has provided more resources and mechanisms for U.S. regulators such as the SEC and the Federal Reserve to more effectively enforce irregularities and violations of securities laws that threaten the health and financial stability of the nation. The Dodd-Frank Act directs regulators to issue more than 240 rules in implementing its provisions such as the Volcker rule, which would ban proprietary trading by those banks that benefit from Fed borrowing privileges and deposit insurance as well as whistleblowing rules in providing incentives and protections for whistleblowers to report violations of securities laws and other irregularities to regulators.

(i) DISCLOSURE OF CAPITAL MATTERS. Beginning in 1996, the American Institute of Certified Public Accountants (AICPA) *Audit Guide for Banks and Savings Institutions* required that GAAP financial statements of banks and savings associations include footnote disclosures of regulatory capital adequacy/prompt corrective action categories. There are five minimum disclosures:

1. A description of the regulatory capital requirements (a) for capital adequacy purposes and (b) established by the prompt corrective action provisions
2. The actual or possible material effects of noncompliance with such requirements
3. Whether the institution is in compliance with the regulatory capital requirements, including, as of each balance sheet date presented:
   a. The institution's required and actual ratios and amounts of Tier 1 leverage, Tier 1 risk-based, total risk-based capital, and, for savings institutions, tangible capital, and (for certain banks and bank holding companies) Tier 3 capital for market risk
   b. Factors that may significantly affect capital adequacy, such as potentially volatile components of capital, qualitative factors, and regulatory mandates
4. The prompt corrective action category in which the institution was classified as of its most recent notification, as of each balance sheet date presented
5. Whether management believes any conditions or events since notification have changed the institution's category, as of the most recent balance sheet date

If, as of the most recent balance sheet date presented, the institution is (1) not in compliance with capital adequacy requirements, (2) considered less than adequately capitalized under the prompt corrective action provisions, or (3) both, the possible material effects of such conditions and events on amounts and disclosures in the financial statements should be disclosed. Additional disclosures may be required where there is substantial doubt about the institution's ability to continue as a going concern.

These disclosures should be presented for all significant subsidiaries of a holding company. Bank holding companies should also present the disclosures as they apply to the holding company, except for the prompt corrective disclosure required by item 4.

As with all footnotes to the financial statements, any management representations included in the footnotes, such as with respect to capital matters, would be subject to review by the independent accountant. Provisions of Dodd-Frank and Basel III rules have significantly increase disclosures of capital requirements for many banks and other financial institutions.

(j) SECURITIES AND EXCHANGE COMMISSION

(i) Background. The SEC was created by Congress in 1934 to administer the Securities Act of 1933 (1933 Act) and the Securities Exchange Act of 1934 (1934 Act). The SEC is an independent agency of the U.S. government, consisting of five commissioners appointed by the president, subject to Senate confirmation.

The 1933 Act requires companies to register securities with the SEC before they may be sold, unless the security or the transaction is exempt. Banks are exempt from the registration requirements of the 1933 Act; however, bank holding companies and their nonbank subsidiaries are not.

(ii) Reporting Requirements. SEC registrants are required to comply with certain industry-specific financial statement requirements set forth in Article 9 for bank holding companies of SEC Regulation S-X. In addition, they must comply with other nonfinancial disclosures required by industry Guide 3for bank holding companies of Regulation S-K.

In 1997, the SEC amended rules and forms for domestic and foreign issuers to clarify and expand existing disclosure requirements for market risk-sensitive instruments. Refer to Financial Reporting Release No. 48, *Disclosure of Accounting Policies for Derivative Financial Instruments and Derivative Commodity Instruments and Disclosure of Quantitative and Qualitative Information about Market Risk Inherent in Derivative Financial Instruments, Other Financial Instruments,* for further discussion. Other SEC guidance is listed in Section 30.5. Additionally, the SEC is undertaking a review of Guide 3 to evaluate potential changes to improve the usefulness of financial institution disclosures.

On December 12, 2001, the SEC issued a financial reporting release, Final Rule (FR) 60, *Cautionary Advice Regarding Disclosure about Critical Policies.* The SEC's Cautionary Advice alerts public companies to the need for improved disclosures about critical accounting policies. FR 60 defines critical accounting policies as those most important to the financial statement presentation and that require the most difficult, subjective, complex judgments.

Perhaps because FR 60 was released late in the year, the management's discussion and analysis (MD&A) disclosures made by registrants in response to FR 60 did not meet the SEC's expectations. As a result, on May 10, 2002, the SEC published a proposed rule, Disclosure in Management's Discussion and Analysis about the Application *of Critical Accounting Policies,* by focusing on the MD&A disclosure about critical accounting estimates that was encouraged in FR 60, but it is much more specific than FR 60 as to the nature of the disclosures and the basis for the sensitivity analysis.

On January 22, 2002, the SEC issued a financial reporting release, FR 61, which provides specific considerations for MD&A disclosures. The SEC issued FR 61 to remind public companies of existing MD&A disclosure requirements and to suggest steps for meeting those requirements in 2001 annual reports. FR 61 focuses on MD&A disclosure about liquidity and off-balance-sheet arrangements (including special-purpose entities [SPE]), trading activities that include non-exchange traded commodity contracts accounted for at fair value, and the effects of transactions with related and certain other parties. These areas have received particular public and regulatory scrutiny following the collapse of Enron. The SEC believes that the quality of information provided by public companies in these areas should be improved. The SEC expects registrants to consider FR 61 when preparing year-end and interim financial reports, effective immediately. Finally, in December 2003, the SEC released its interpretive guidance regarding MD&A, FR 72, which promotes more meaningful disclosure pertaining to overall presentation and content of MD&A by focusing on demands, trends, events, commitments, uncertainties, risk assessment, capital resources and critical accounting policies, methods and estimates.

Dodd-Frank enhances the SEC's oversight function on the financial services industry in five ways by:

1. Providing incentives and protection for witnesses to come forward in reporting violations of the security laws
2. Expanding the types of charges that the SEC can bring against those who help others violate the securities laws with aiding and abetting or secondary liability
3. Giving the SEC additional resources and means to sanction wrongdoers
4. Encouraging cooperation among regulators, such as the PCAOB and foreign securities regulators
5. Requiring disclosure of additional information to the SEC, including requiring foreign auditors to produce workpapers upon request and institutional investors to report on data on their short sales activities on at least a monthly basis.

(k) FINANCIAL STATEMENT PRESENTATION

(i) Income Statements. Banks and savings institutions place heavy emphasis on the interest margin (i.e., the difference between interest earned and the cost of funds). Accordingly, a specialized income statement format has evolved that focuses on net interest income. Supplemental income statement information may be provided separately to show the impact of investing in certain tax-exempt securities. Such taxable equivalent data purports to illustrate income statement data as if such tax-exempt securities were fully taxable.

(ii) Balance Sheets. The balance sheets of banks and savings institutions are not classified into short-term and long-term categories for assets and liabilities but are generally presented in descending order of maturity. Supplemental information is also presented by many banking institutions showing average balances of assets and liabilities and the associated income or expense and average rates paid or earned.

(iii) Statements of Cash Flow. The statements of cash flow are presented in accordance with Statement of Financial Accounting Standards (SFAS) No. 95, *Statement of Cash Flows,* amended by SFAS No. 102, *Statement of Cash Flows—Exemption of Certain Enterprises and Classification of Cash Flows from Certain Securities Acquired for Resale (an Amendment of FASB Statement No. 95),* and SFAS No. 104, *Statement of Cash Flows—Net Reporting of Certain Cash Receipts and Cash Payments and Classification of Cash Flows for Hedging Transactions (an amendment of FASB Statement No. 95).* The amendments permit certain financial institutions, such as banks and savings institutions, to net the cash flows for selected activities such as trading, deposit taking, and loan activities. The FASB, in December 2004, issued revised SFAS No. 123R, *Share-Based Payment.* SFAS No. 123R replaces SFAS No. 123, *Accounting for Stock-Based Compensation.* Among other provisions, SFAS No. 123R amends SFAS No. 95, *Statement of Cash Flows,* requiring firms to report excess tax benefits arising from expensing employee stock options as a financial cash flow rather than an operating cash flow.

(iv) Commitments and Off-Balance-Sheet Risk. Banks and savings institutions offer a variety of financial services, and, accordingly, they enter into a wide range of financial transactions and issue a variety of financial instruments. Depending on the nature of these transactions, they may not appear on the balance sheet and are only disclosed in the footnotes to the financial statements. SFAS No. 105, *Disclosure of Information about Financial Instruments Off-Balance Sheet Risk and Financial Instruments with Concentrations of Credit Risk,* footnote disclosures of off-balance-sheet financial instruments and derivatives provide additional risk-relevant information above and beyond that provided by the balance sheet.

(v) Disclosures of Certain Significant Risks and Uncertainties. AICPA Statement of Position (SOP) No. 94-6, *Disclosure of Certain Significant Risks and Uncertainties,* requires institutions to include in their financial statements disclosures about the nature of their operations and the use of estimates in the preparation of their financial statements.

SOP No. 94-6 also requires disclosure regarding:

- *Certain significant estimates.* Estimates used in the determination of the carrying amounts of assets or liabilities or in gain or loss contingencies are required to be disclosed when information available prior to issuance of the financial statements indicates that (a) it is at least reasonably possible that the estimate of the effect on the financial statements of a condition, situation or set of circumstances that existed at the date of the financial statements will change in the near term due to one or more future confirming events, and (b) the effect of the change would be material to the financial statements.
- SOP No. 94-6 further states that (a) the disclosure should indicate the nature of the uncertainty and include an indication that it is at least reasonably possible that a change in the estimate will occur in the near term and (b) if the estimate involves a loss contingency covered by SFAS No. 5, *Accounting for Contingencies,* the disclosure should also include an estimate of the possible loss or range of loss, or state that such an estimate cannot be made.
- *Current vulnerability due to certain concentrations.* Institutions are required to disclose concentrations, as defined in the Statement, if, based on information known to management prior to issuance of the financial statements, (a) the concentration exists at the date of the financial statements, (b) the concentration makes the institution vulnerable to the risk of a near-term severe impact, and (c) it is at least reasonably possible that the events that could cause the severe impact will occur in the near term
- Provisions of Dodd-Frank and Basel III rules are considered as macroprudential reforms intended to focus on systemic risks. The systemic risk is the risk that banks and other financial institutions may pose on the global financial system. Financial institutions should provide proper disclosure of their systemic risk.

(l) ACCOUNTING GUIDANCE. In addition to the main body of professional accounting literature that comprises GAAP, more specific industry guidance is provided in the industry-specific audit and accounting guides published by the AICPA, specifically *Banks and Savings Institutions* issued in 2000. Additionally, the Emerging Issues Task Force (EITF) of the FASB addresses current issues.

(m) GENERALLY ACCEPTED ACCOUNTING PRINCIPLES VERSUS REGULATORY ACCOUNTING PRINCIPLES Under the Federal Financial Institutions Examination Council (FFIEC), the three federal banking agencies have developed uniform reporting standards for commercial banks that are used in the preparation of the reports of condition and income (Call Reports). The FDIC has also applied these uniform Call Report standards to savings banks under its supervision. Effective with the March 31, 1997, reports, the reporting standards set forth for the Call Reports are based on GAAP for banks. As a matter of law, many banks deviate from GAAP to a more stringent requirement only in those instances where statutory requirements or overriding supervisory concerns warrant a departure from GAAP. The OTS maintains its own separate reporting forms for the savings institutions under its supervision. The reporting form used by savings institutions, known as the TFR, is based on GAAP as applied by savings institutions, which differs in some respects from GAAP for banks.

Certain differences between GAAP and regulatory accounting principles remain after the amendments to the March 1997 Call Report Instructions. Many of these differences remain because the agencies generally default to SEC reporting principles for registrants. The more significant remaining differences between Call Report Instructions and GAAP are related to these areas:

- Impaired collateral-dependent loans
- Pushdown accounting
- Credit losses on off-balance-sheet commitments and contingencies

- Related party transactions
- Application of accounting changes

(n) LOANS AND COMMITMENTS. Loans generate the largest proportion of revenues of most banks and saving institutions. Institutions originate, purchase and sell (in whole or in part), and securitize loans. The parameters used to create the loan portfolio include many of the institution's key strategies, such as credit risk strategy, diversification strategy, liquidity, and interest rate margin strategy. Accordingly, the composition of the loan portfolio varies by institution. The loan portfolio is critical to the institutions' overall asset/liability management strategy.

(i) Types of Loans. Loans are offered on a variety of terms to meet the needs of the borrower and of the institution. The types of loan arrangements normally issued are discussed next.

Commercial Loans. Institutions have developed different types of credit facilities to address the needs of commercial customers. Some of the characteristics that distinguish these facilities are:

- Security (whether the loan is collateralized or unsecured)
- Term (whether the loan matures in the short term, long term, on demand, or on a revolving credit arrangement)
- Variable or fixed interest rates
- Currency (whether the loan is repayable in the local currency or in a foreign currency)

Loan facilities can be tailored to match the needs of commercial borrowers and may include many combinations of specific loan terms. Some of the common general types are described next.

Secured Loans. Collateral (security) to a loan is usually viewed as a characteristic of any type of loan rather than as a loan category itself. Nevertheless, it is not uncommon for institutions to analyze their loan portfolios in part by looking at the proportion of secured credits and the entire balance.

A significant portion of bank lending is not supported by a specific security. The less creditworthy a potential borrower, however, the more likely it becomes that an institution will require some form of collateral in order to minimize its risk of loss.

Loan security is normally not taken with the intention of liquidating it in order to obtain repayment. Maintenance and liquidation of collateral is, in fact, often time consuming and unprofitable for the foreclosing bank. Most loan security takes the form of some kind of fixed or floating claim over specified assets or a mortgage interest in property.

Lines of Credit. Lines of credit, including facilities that are referred to as *revolving lines of credit,* originate with an institution extending credit to a borrower with a specified maximum amount and a stated maturity. The borrower then draws and repays funds through the facility in accordance with its requirements. Lines of credit are useful for short-term financing of working capital or seasonal borrowings. A commitment fee is usually charged on the unused portion of the facility.

Demand Loans. Demand loans are short-term loans that may be called by the institution at any time, hence the term *demand.* Demand loans are often unsecured and are normally made to cover short-term funding requirements. There is usually no principal reduction during the loan term; the entire balance comes due at maturity.

Term Loans. Term loans are often used to finance the acquisition of capital assets such as plant and equipment. Due to their longer term, they involve greater credit risk than short-term advances (all other things being equal). To reduce the credit risk, these loans typically are secured and require amortization of principal over the loan term. Loan agreements often contain restrictive covenants that require the borrower to maintain specified financial ratios and to refrain from defined types of transactions for as long as the loan is outstanding.

Asset-Based Lending. Asset-based lending is a form of revolving line of credit that is related directly to the value of specific underlying assets (typically accounts receivable or inventory). The primary difference between asset-based lending and a simple line of credit is the direct correlation, upon which the institution insists, between the funds advanced and the underlying security. While funds may be advanced on a line of credit up to the approved maximum amount, they may be drawn under an asset-based lending arrangement only to the extent allowed by predetermined formulas related to collateral value. Requests for funds are normally monitored closely, and repayments may be demanded where collateral values fall.

Syndications. A syndicated loan is one where a number of institutions, in a form of joint venture, provide funds they would individually be unwilling or unable to provide. Syndications are used for customers requiring large-scale financing, too great for any single institution to accommodate without distorting its loan portfolio. In addition, consortium banks group together banks from different countries to specialize in and centralize large-scale finance for specific projects.

In a syndicate, its members appoint one or more members as the managing bank. In certain cases, the borrower might appoint the managing bank, in which case the other members commonly appoint an agent bank to act on their behalf. The managing bank is responsible for negotiating with the borrower, preparing the appropriate documentation, collecting the loan funds from the syndicate and disbursing them to the borrower, and collecting amounts due from the borrower and distributing them to the syndicate members.

Apart from the managing bank, the syndicate members will not necessarily have any direct dealings with the borrower, although the borrower is aware of the existence of the syndicate. Credit risk rests with each syndicate member to the extent of its participation.

Participations. Banks sell loans, or part shares in loans, to other financial institutions for a number of reasons, including to: serve large customers whose financing needs exceed their lending ability; diversify their loan portfolios; alter the maturity structure of their loan portfolios; or increase their liquidity. Participation agreements usually specify such matters as the method of payment of proceeds from the borrower, responsibilities in the event of default, and interest in collateral. Loans may be sold with or without recourse and on terms that may or may not agree with those of the underlying loan.

Loans that are participated out (i.e., sold) are normally reported on the seller's balance sheet net of the sold portion (which is reported with other loan assets by the buyer). The fact that another institution has researched and agreed to extend the loan does not reduce the risk of the purchasing bank.

Loans Held for Resale. Loans may be originated by an institution that intends to resell them to other parties. They may be purchased with the intention to resell. The reasons for such transactions vary. Some institutions wish to provide a type of loan service to their customers that they do not wish to retain in their portfolio. Some institutions use loan origination as a source of fee income. Some purchase debt to use as securitization for other instruments that they package and sell to specialized markets.

Real Estate Loans. Real estate loans may be made for commercial or personal purposes, and most banks differentiate their portfolios between the two uses. The rationale for this segregation lies in the fact that while both are classified as real estate lending, the portfolios are subject to different types of risk and/or different degrees of risk. Also, the type and level of expertise required to manage residential and commercial real estate loan portfolios successfully differs, just as the type of financing provided to the homeowner is typically not the same as to an owner or developer of commercial real estate.

Incremental knowledge with respect to the particular financing provided must be obtained and constantly updated to manage commercial real estate property lending successfully. For example, construction loan monitoring, appraisal methods, comparable properties in the area, the status of the economy, use of the property, future property developments, occupancy rates, and projected operating cash flows are all important factors in reaching lending decisions.

Mortgage Loans. Real estate mortgage loans are term loans collateralized by real estate. The loans are generally fairly long term, though some are short term with a large principal (balloon) payment due at maturity. The loan commitments usually involve a fee to be paid by the borrower upon approval or upon closing.

Some institutions originate residential mortgage loans for sale to investors. Under these arrangements, the bank usually continues to service the loans on a fee basis. The sale allows the bank to provide mortgage financing services for its customers without funding a large volume of loans.

Construction Loans. Construction loans are used to finance the construction of particular projects and normally mature at the scheduled completion date. They are generally secured by a first mortgage on the property and are backed by a purchase (or takeout) agreement from a financially responsible permanent lender. They may include the financing of loan interest through the construction period.

Construction loans are vulnerable to a number of risks related to the uncertainties that are characteristic of building projects. Examples of risks associated with construction loans include construction delays, nonpayment of material bills or subcontractors, and the financial collapse of the project contractor prior to project completion.

Construction loan funds are generally disbursed on a standard payment plan (for relatively small, predictable projects) or a progress payment plan (for more complex projects). Extent of completion may be verified by an architect's certification or by evidence of labor and material costs.

In certain construction loans, consideration should be given to accounting for the loan as an investment in real estate if the lender is subject to virtually the same risks and rewards as the owner.

Direct Lease Financing. Leasing is a form of debt financing for fixed assets that, although differing in legal form, is similar to substance to term lending. Like a more conventional loan, the institution's credit concerns in extending lease financing are ones of cash flow, credit history, management, and projections of future operations. The type of property to be leased and its marketability in the event of default or termination of the lease are concerns quite parallel to the bank's evaluation of collateral. In a leasing arrangement, the bank formally owns the property rather than having a lien on it.

Lease financing arrangements may be accounted for either as financings (i.e., as loans) or as operating leases, depending on the precise terms of the transaction and on the applicable accounting principles.

Consumer Loans. Consumer loans—personal loans to individual borrowers—can originate through a bank's own customers (direct loans) or through merchants with whom the borrowers deal (indirect loans). They may relate specifically to the purchase of items that can serve as collateral for the borrowing (e.g., vehicles, mobile homes, boats, furniture) or to other needs that provide no basis for a security interest (e.g., vacations, income tax payments, medical expenses, educational costs). Consumer loans may be made on an installment, single payment, or demand basis. They are often broken down into classifications that describe the purpose of the financing (student loans or home equity loans) or the terms of disbursement and repayment (installment loans, credit card loans, check credit).

Installment Loans. Installment loans are the most common type of consumer credit. Their terms normally include repayment over a specified period of time with fixed minimum periodic (usually monthly) payments. Interest rates are generally fixed on origination but may be variable over the term of the loan. The term is generally determined by the type of purchase being financed and is usually relatively short—10 years or less.

Standby Letters of Credit. A standby letter of credit is a promise made by an institution to provide compensation to a third party on behalf of its customer in the event that the customer fails to perform in accordance with the terms specified by an underlying contract. Standby letters of credit may be available under a credit facility or may be issued for a specified amount with an expiration date. Normally, payment under such agreements depends on performance or lack of performance of some act required by the underlying contract.

Standby letters of credit are typically recorded as contingent liabilities in memorandum records and are offset by customer liability memorandum accounts. In the event that funds are disbursed under a standby letter of credit agreement, the drawing would be recorded as a loan.

Sovereign Risk. Sovereign risk lending involves the granting of credit facilities to foreign governments or to companies based in foreign countries. The facilities are normally denominated in a currency other than the domestic currency of the borrower and are typically used to finance imports or to refinance existing foreign currency debt.

In addition to all of the customary considerations surrounding credit risk, sovereign risk lending involves economic, social, and political considerations that bear on the ability of the borrower to repay foreign currency obligations.

Trade Finance. Trade finance is made up of letters of credit and bankers' acceptances.

Letters of credit are instruments used to facilitate trade (most commonly international trade) by substituting an institution's credit for that of a commercial importing company. A letter of credit provides assurance to a seller that he or she will be paid for goods shipped. At the same time, it provides assurance to the buyer that payment will not be made until conditions specified in the sales contract have been met.

Letter of credit transactions can vary in any number of ways. The issuing and advising institutions may deal with each other through their own local correspondent banks. Some of the documents may flow in different patterns. The requirements for payment and security will certainly vary from transaction to transaction. One of the attractive features of letter of credit financing from the customer's point of view is its flexibility. Facilities can be tailored to individual transactions or groups of transactions.

A *bankers' acceptance* is like a letter of credit in that it provides a seller of goods with a guarantee of payment, thus facilitating trade. The institution's customer is the buyer who, having established an acceptance facility with the bank, notifies the seller to draw up a bill of exchange. The bank accepts that bill (by physically stamping accepted on its face and having an authorized bank officer sign it) and, in so doing, commits itself to disburse funds on the bill's due date.

A banker's acceptance represents both an asset and a liability to the accepting bank. The asset is a receivable from the bank's customer, the buyer in the transaction. The liability is a payable to the holder of the acceptance. The bank's accounting for open acceptances varies from country to country. In some countries, the asset and liability are both reflected on the bank's balance sheet. In others, they are netted against each other and thus become, in effect, off-balance-sheet items. In European Union countries, they appear as memorandum items on the face of the balance sheet.

By substituting its own credit for that of the buying company, the accepting bank creates a financial instrument that is readily marketable. Bankers' acceptances trade as bearer paper on active secondary markets.

Mortgage-Backed Securities. Mortgage-backed securities (MBSs) are asset-backed securities having cash flows backed by the principal and interest payments of a pool of mortgage loans that are made periodically over the lifetime of the underlying loans. Collateralized mortgage obligations (CMOs) are more complex than MBSs and consist of pools of home mortgages backed by government-insured agencies, such as Freddie Mac and Fannie Mae. MBSs and CMOs became popular with investors in the late 1990s and the early 2000s. During the subprime mortgage crisis period in late 2006 and 2007, many investors holding MBSs or CMOs suffered substantial losses because the values of the underlying assets sharply declined.

(ii) Accounting for Loans

Principal. Loans expected to be held until maturity should be reported as outstanding principal, net of charge-offs, specific valuation accounts and any deferred fees or costs, or unamortized premiums or discounts on purchased loans. Total loans should be reduced by the allowance for credit losses.

Loans held for sale should be reported at the lower of cost or fair value determined as of the balance sheet. Mortgage loans held for sale should be reported at the lower of cost or market value in conformity with SFAS No. 65, *Accounting for Certain Mortgage Banking Activities*. Mortgage-backed securities held for sale in conjunction with mortgage banking activities shall be classified as trading securities and reported at fair value in conformity with SFAS No. 115, *Accounting for Certain Investments in Debt and Equity Securities*.

The amount by which the cost exceeds the fair value may be accounted as a valuation allowance. Any change in the valuation allowance maybe included for determining the net income. This may be accounted for the period for which the change is occurring. The fair value of mortgage loans and mortgage backed securities held for sale is essentially determined by the type of loan. The loans are further determined by the next classes:

- *Committed loans*. The investor commitment will form the base for fair values of loans.
- *Uncommitted loans*. The fair value for these loans is based on the market where the mortgage banking entity functions.
- *Uncommitted MBSs*. The fair value for such loans collateralized by a mortgage banking entity's own loans are based on the fair value of the securities.

Interest. Interest income on all loans should be accrued and credited to interest income as it is earned using the interest method. Interest income on certain impaired loans should be recognized in accordance with SFAS No. 114, *Accounting by Creditors for Impairment of a Loan*, as amended by SFAS No. 118, *Accounting by Creditors for Impairment of a Loan-Income Recognition and Disclosures*.

The accrual of interest is usually suspended on loans that are in excess of 90 days past due, unless the loan is both well secured and in the process of collection. When a loan is placed on such nonaccrual status, interest that has been accrued but not collected is reversed, and interest subsequently received is recorded on a cash basis or applied to reduce the principal balance depending on the bank's assessment of ultimate collectability of the loan. An exception to this rule is that many banks do not place certain types of consumer loans on nonaccrual status since they automatically charge off such loans within a relatively short period of becoming delinquent—generally within 120 days.

Loan Fees. Various types of fees are collected by banks in connection with lending activities. SFAS No. 91, *Accounting for Nonrefundable Fees and Costs Associated with Originating or Acquiring Loans and Initial Direct Costs of Leases (an Amendment of FASB Statements No. 13, 60, and 65 and a Rescission of FASB Statement No. 17)*, requires that the majority of such fees and associated direct origination costs be offset. The net amount must be deferred as part of the loan (and reported as a component of loans in the balance sheet) and recognized in interest income over the life of the loan and/or loan commitment period as an adjustment of the yield on the loan. The requirements for cost deferral under this standard are quite restrictive and require direct linkage to the loan origination process. Activities for which costs may be deferred include: (1) evaluating the borrower, guarantees, collateral, and other security; (2) preparation and processing of loan documentation for loan origination; and (3) negotiating and closing the loan. Certain costs are specifically precluded from deferral—for example, advertising and solicitation, credit supervision and administration, costs of unsuccessful loan originations, and other activities not directly related to the extension of a loan.

Loan fees and costs for loans originated or purchased for resale are deferred and are recognized when the related loan is sold.

Commitment fees to purchase or originate loans, net of direct origination costs, are generally deferred and amortized over the life of the loan when it is extended. If the commitment expires, then the fees are recognized in other income on expiration of the commitment. There are two main exceptions to this general treatment:

1. If past experience indicates that the extension of a loan is unlikely, then the fee is recognized over the commitment period.
2. Nominal fees, which are determined retroactively, on a commitment to extend funds at a market rate may be recognized in income at the determination date.

Certain fees, primarily loan syndication fees, may be recognized when received. Generally, the yield on the portion of the loan retained by the syndicating bank must at least equal the yield received by the other members of the syndicate. If this is not the case, a portion of the fees designated as a syndication fee must be deferred and amortized to income to achieve a yield equal to the average yield of the other banks in the syndicate. EITF Issue No. 97-3, *Accounting for Fees and Costs Associated with Loan Syndication's and Loan Participation's after the Issuance of FASB Statement No. 125,* states that loan participation should be accounted for in accordance with the provision of SFAS No. 140 and loan syndications should be accounted for in accordance with the provision of SFAS No. 91.

Purchased loans are recorded at cost net of fees paid/received. The difference between this recorded amount and the principal amount of the loan is amortized to income over the life of the loan to produce a level yield. Acquisition costs are not deferred but are expensed as incurred. AICPA Statement of Position (SOP) 03-3, *Accounting for Certain Loans or Debt Securities Acquired in a Transfer,* was issued in December 2003 which addresses purchased loan with certain deterioration and requires the portion of the acquired or selling institution's allowance relevant to the purchased impaired loans should no longer be added to the acquiring bank's allowance.

Acquisition, Development, and Construction Arrangements. Certain transactions that appear to be loans are considered effectively to be investments in the real estate property financed. These transactions are required to be presented separately from loans and accounted for as real estate investments using the guidance set forth in the AICPA Notice to Practitioners dated February 1986. This notice was reprinted without any change in November 1987 issues as Exhibit I in the Appendix of the AICPA Practice Bulletin. Factors indicating such treatment include six arrangements whereby the financial institution:

1. Provides substantially all financing to acquire, develop, and construct the property (i.e., borrower has little or no equity in the property)
2. Funds the origination or commitment fees through the loan
3. Funds substantially all interest and fees through the loan
4. Has security only in the project with no recourse to other assets or guarantee of the borrower
5. Can recover its investment only through sale to third parties, refinancing, or cash flow of the project
6. Is unlikely to foreclose on the project during development since no payments are due during this period and therefore the loan cannot normally become delinquent

Troubled Debt Restructurings and Impaired Loans. Banks may routinely restructure loans to meet a borrower's changing circumstances. The new loan terms are reflected in the financial statements essentially as if a new loan has been made. However, if a creditor for economic or legal reasons related to the debtor's financial difficulties grants a concession . . . that it would not otherwise consider, then SFAS No. 15, *Accounting by Debtors and Creditors for Troubled Debt Restructurings,* as amended by FASB Statements No. 114; No. 121, *Accounting for Impairment of Long-Lived Assets and Long-Lived Assets to Be Disposed Of;* and No. 144, *Accounting for the Impairment or Disposal of Long-Lived Assets,* applies.

The guidance in the impairment or disposal of Long-Lived Assets Subsections is applicable to the following activities:

A. The transactions relating to the long lived assets to be held and used or to be disposed of, including:

- Capital leases of lessees
- Long-lived assets of lessors subject to operating leases
- Proved oil and gas properties that are being accounted for using the successful-efforts method of accounting
- Long-term prepaid assets

B. The following relates to assets and liabilities which are further considered part of an asset group or a disposal group:

- In case a long lived asset belongs to a group which further includes other assets and liabilities not covered; the guidance will apply to such group. In such scenarios the unit of accounting is its group. If the long lived asset has to held and used, it is classified as an asset group. In case the long lived asset is to be disposed of by sale or otherwise, it is then classified as a disposal group.
- The guidance does not affect the GAAP applicable to those other individual assets and liabilities not covered by the Impairment or Disposal of Long-Lived Assets Subsections that are included in such groups.

The guidance in the impairment or disposal of Long-Lived Assets Subsections of SFAS No.114 (ASC-310) is not applicable to certain transactions. They include the following activities but are not limited to such activities:

- Goodwill
- Intangible assets not being amortized that are to be held and used
- Servicing assets
- Financial instruments, including investments in equity securities accounted for under the cost or equity method
- Deferred policy acquisition costs
- Deferred tax assets

Troubled Debt Restructurings. Troubled debt restructurings may include one or more of these changes:

- Transfers of assets of the debtor or an equity interest in the debtor to partially or fully satisfy a debt
- Modification of debt terms, including reduction of one or more of the following: (1) interest rates with or without extensions of maturity date(s), (2) face or maturity amounts, and (3) accrued interest

Prior to the release of SFAS No. 114, under a SFAS No. 15 restructuring involving a modification of terms, the creditor accumulated the undiscounted total future cash receipts and compared them to the recorded investment in the loan. If these cash receipts exceeded the recorded investment in the loan, no loss or impairment was deemed to exist; however, if the total cash receipts did not exceed the recorded investment, the recorded investment was adjusted to reflect the total undiscounted future cash receipts. For restructurings involving a modification of terms that occurred before the effective date of SFAS No. 114, this accounting still applies as long as the loan does not become impaired relative to the restructured terms. Restructurings involving a modification of terms after the effective date of SFAS No. 114 must be accounted for in accordance with SFAS No. 114.

Impaired Loans. In May 1993, SFAS No. 114 was issued primarily to provide more consistent guidance on the application of SFAS No. 5 loss criteria and to provide additional direction on the recognition and measurement of loan impairment in determining credit reserve levels. The application of this statement was required beginning in 1995.

SFAS No. 114 applies to all impaired loans, uncollateralized as well as collateralized, except:

- Large groups of smaller balance homogeneous loans that are collectively evaluated for impairment, such as credit card, residential mortgage, and consumer installment loans
- Loans that are measured at fair value or at the lower of cost or fair value
- Leases
- Debt securities, as defined in SFAS No. 115

A loan is impaired when, based on current information and events, it is probable (consistent with its use in SFAS No. 5—an area within a range of the likelihood that a future event or events will occur confirming the fact of the loss) that a creditor will be unable to collect all amounts due according to the contractual terms of the loan agreement. As used in SFAS No. 114 and in SFAS No. 5, as amended, all amounts due according to the contractual terms means that both the contractual interest payments and the contractual principal payments of a loan will be collected as scheduled in the loan agreement.

It is important to note that an insignificant delay or insignificant shortfall in the amount of payments does not require application of SFAS No. 114. A loan is not impaired during a period of delay in payment if the creditor expects to collect all amounts due including interest accrued at the contractual interest rate for the period of delay.

SFAS No. 114 provides that the measurement of impaired value should be based on one of these methods:

- Present value of expected cash flows discounted at the loan's effective interest rate
- The observable value of the loan's market price
- The fair value of the collateral if the loan is collateral dependent

The effective rate of a loan is the contractual interest rate adjusted for any net deferred loan fees or costs, premium, or discount existing at the origination or acquisition of the loan. For variable rate loans, the loan's effective interest rate may be calculated based on the factor as it changes over the life of the loan, or it may be fixed at the rate in effect at the date the loan meets the SFAS No. 114 impairment criterion. However, that choice should be applied consistently for all variable rate loans.

All impaired loans do not have to be measured using the same method; the method selected may vary based on the availability of information and other factors. However, the ultimate valuation should be critically evaluated in determining whether it represents a reasonable estimate of impairment.

If the measure of the impaired loan is less than the recorded investment in the loan (including accrued interest, net deferred loan fees or costs, and unamortized premium or discount), a creditor should recognize an impairment by creating a valuation allowance with a corresponding charge to bad-debt expense.

Subsequent to the initial measurement of impairment, if there is a significant change (increase or decrease) in the amount or timing of an impaired loan's expected future cash flows, observable market price, or fair value of the collateral, a creditor should recalculate the impairment by applying the procedures described earlier and by adjusting the valuation allowance. However, the net carrying amount of the loan should at no time exceed the recorded investment in the loan.

Any restructurings performed under the provisions of SFAS No. 15 need not be reevaluated unless the borrower is not performing in accordance with the contractual terms of the restructuring.

EITF Issue No. 96-22, *Applicability of the Disclosures Required by FASB Statement No. 114 When a Loan Is Restructured in a Troubled Debt Restructuring into Two (or More) Loans* (now ASC Topic 310), states that when a loan is restructured in a troubled debt restructuring into two (or more) loan agreements, the restructured loans should be considered separately when assessing the applicability of the disclosures in years after the restructuring because they are legally distinct from the original loan. However, the creditor would continue to base its measure of loan impairment on the contractual terms specified by the original loan agreements.

In-Substance Foreclosures. SFAS No. 114 clarified the definition of in-substance foreclosures as used in SFAS No. 15 by stating that the phrase foreclosure by the creditor in paragraph 34 should be read to mean *physical* possession of debtor's assets regardless of whether formal foreclosure proceedings take place. Further, until foreclosure occurs, these assets should remain as loans in the financial statements.

(o) CREDIT LOSSES. Credit loss estimates are subjective and, accordingly, require careful judgments in assessing loan collectability and in estimating losses.

(i) Accounting Guidance. SFAS No. 114 and SFAS No. 5, are the primary sources of guidance on accounting for the allowance for loan losses. Also, the *Accounting Standards Update 2010-20* released by the FASB mentions the Disclosures about the Credit Quality of Financing Receivables and the Allowance for Credit Losses. In summary, this update offers greater transparency about an entity's allowance for credit losses and the credit quality of its financing receivables. SFAS No. 5 requires that an estimated loss from a contingency should be accrued by a charge to income if both of the next conditions are met:

- Information available prior to issuance of the financial statements indicates that it is probable that an asset had been impaired or a liability had been incurred at the date of the financial statements. It is implicit in this condition that it must be probable that one or more future events will occur confirming the fact of the loss.
- The amount of loss can be reasonably estimated.

SFAS No. 5 states that when a loss contingency exists, the likelihood that the future event or events will confirm the loss or impairment of an asset (whether related to contractual principal or interest) can range from remote to probable. *Probable* means the future event or events are likely to occur; however, the conditions for accrual are not intended to be so rigid that they require virtual certainty before a loss is accrued.

The allowance for loan losses should be adequate to cover probable credit losses related to specifically identified loans as well as probable credit losses inherent in the remainder of the loan portfolio that have been incurred as of the balance sheet date. Credit losses related to off-balance-sheet instruments should also be accrued if the conditions of SFAS No. 5 are met.

Actual credit losses should be deducted from the allowance, and the related balance should be charged off in the period in which it is deemed uncollectable. Recoveries of loans previously charged off should be added to the allowance when received.

SFAS No. 114 addresses the accounting by creditors for impairment of certain loans, as discussed in Subsection 30.2(n)(ii).

(ii) Regulatory Guidance. The regulatory agencies issued the *Interagency Policy on the Allowance for Loan and Lease Losses (ALLL)* in December 1993. The policy statement provides guidance with respect to:

- The nature and purpose of the allowance
- The related responsibilities of the board of directors, management, and the bank examiners
- Adequacy of loan review systems
- Issues related to international transfer risk

The policy statement also includes an analytical tool to be used by bank examiners for assessing the reasonableness of the allowance; however, the policy statement cautions the bank examiners against placing too much emphasis on the analytical tool rather than performing a full and thorough analysis.

The OCC also provides guidance in its *Comptrollers' Handbook, Allowance for Loan and Lease Losses,* issued in June 1996.

In separate releases on July 6, 2001, the SEC and the FFIEC issued guidance on methodologies and documentation related to the allowance for loan losses. In Staff Accounting Bulletin (SAB) No. 102, *Selected Loan Loss Allowance Methodology and Documentation Issues,* the SEC Staff expressed certain of their views on the development, documentation, and application of a systematic methodology as required by FR 28 for determining allowances for loan and lease losses in accordance with GAAP. In particular, the guidance focuses on the documentation the staff normally would expect registrants to prepare and maintain in support of their allowances for loan losses. Concurrent with the release of SAB No. 102, the federal banking agencies issued related guidance through the FFIEC entitled *Policy Statement on Allowance for Loan and Lease Losses (ALLL)*

Methodologies and Documentation for Banks and Savings Institutions. The Policy Statement, developed in consultation with the SEC Staff, provides guidance on the design and implementation of ALLL methodologies and supporting documentation practices. Both SAB No. 102 and the Policy Statement reaffirm the applicability of existing accounting guidance; neither attempts to overtly change GAAP as they relate to the ALLL.

(iii) Allowance Methodologies. An institution's method of estimating credit losses is influenced by many factors, including the institution's size, organization structure, business environment and strategy, management style, loan portfolio characteristics, loan administration procedures, and management information systems.

Common Factors to Consider. Although allowance methodologies may vary between institutions, the factors to consider in estimating credit losses are often similar. Both SAB No. 102 and the Policy Statement require that when developing loss measurements, banks consider the effect of current environmental factors and then document which factors were used in the analysis and how those factors affected the loss measurements. Examples of factors that should be considered are presented next:

- Levels of and trends in delinquencies and impaired loans
- Levels of and trends in charge-offs and recoveries
- Trends in volume and terms of loans
- Effects of any changes in risk selection and underwriting standards, and other changes in lending policies, procedures, and practices
- Experience, ability, and depth of lending management and other relevant staff
- National and local economic trends and conditions
- Industry conditions
- Effects of changes in credit concentrations

Supplemental data, such as historical loss rates or peer group analyses, can be helpful; however, they are not, by themselves, sufficient basis for an allowance methodology.

Portfolio Segments. Another common practice is dividing the loan portfolio into different segments. Each segment typically includes similar characteristics, such as risk classification and type of loan. Segments typically include large problem loans by industry or collateral type and homogeneous pools of smaller loans, such as credit cards, automobile loans, and residential mortgages.

Credit Classification Process. A credit classification process involves categorizing loans into risk categories and is often applied to large loans that are evaluated individually. The categorization is based on conditions that may affect the ability of borrowers to service their debt, such as current financial information, historical payment experience, credit documentation, public information, and current trends. Many institutions classify loans using a rating system that incorporates the regulatory classification system. These definitions are presented next.

Special Mention. Some loans are considered criticized but not classified. Such loans have potential weaknesses that deserve management's close attention. If left uncorrected, these potential weaknesses may result in deterioration of the repayment prospects for the assets or of the institution's credit position at some future date. Special mention loans are not adversely classified and do not expose an institution to sufficient risk to warrant adverse classification.

Substandard. Loans classified as substandard are inadequately protected by the current sound worth and paying capacity of the obligor or of the collateral pledged, if any. Loans so classified must have a well-defined weakness or weaknesses that jeopardize the liquidation of the debt. They are characterized by the distinct possibility that the institution will sustain some loss if the deficiencies are not corrected.

Doubtful. Loans classified as doubtful have all the weaknesses inherent in those classified as substandard, with the added characteristic that the weaknesses make collection or liquidation in full, on the basis of currently existing facts, conditions, and values, highly questionable and improbable.

Loss. Loans classified as loss are considered uncollectable and of such little value that their continuance as bankable assets is not warranted. This classification does not mean that the loan has absolutely no recovery or salvage value but rather that it is not practical or desirable to defer writing off this basically worthless asset even though partial recovery may be effected in the future.

Pools of Smaller-Balance Homogeneous Loans. Loans not evaluated individually are included in pools and loss rates are derived for each pool.

The loss rates to be applied to the pools of loans are typically derived from the combination of a variety of factors. Examples of the factors include historical experience, expected future performance, trends in bankruptcies and troubled collection accounts, and changes in the customer's performance patterns.

Foreign Loans. The Interagency Country Exposure Risk Committee (ICERC) requires certain loans to have allocated transfer risk reserves (ATRRs). ATRRs are minimum specific reserves related to loans in particular countries and, therefore, must be reviewed by each institution. The ICERC's supervisory role is pursuant to the International Supervision Act of 1983. The collectability of foreign loans that do not have ATRRs should be assessed in the same way as domestic loans.

Documentation, Completeness, and Frequency. The institution's allowance methodology should be based on a comprehensive, adequately documented, and consistently applied analysis. The analysis should consider all significant factors that affect collectability of the portfolio and should be based on an effective loan review and credit grading (classification) system. Additionally, the evaluation of the adequacy of the allowance should be performed as of the end of each quarter, and appropriate provisions should be made to maintain the allowance at an adequate level.

SAB No. 102 and the 2001 Policy Statement specifically require, for any adjustments of loss measurements for environmental factors, that banks maintain sufficient *objective* evidence (1) to support the amount of the adjustment and (2) to explain why the adjustment is necessary to reflect current information, events, circumstances, and conditions in the loss measurements.

SAB No. 102 requires that bank methodology in determining ALLL should:

1. Provide a detailed analysis of the loan portfolio performed on a regular basis
2. Consider all loans (whether on an individual or group basis)
3. Identify loans to be assessed for impairment on an individual basis under SFAS No. 114 and segment the remainder of the portfolio into groups of loans with similar risk characteristics for evaluation and analysis under SFAS No. 5
4. Consider all known relevant internal and external factors that may affect loan collectability
5. Be applied consistently but, when appropriate, be modified for new factors affecting ALLL

(p) LOAN SALES AND MORTGAGE BANKING ACTIVITIES. Banks may originate and sell loans for a variety of reasons, such as generating income streams from servicing and other fees, increasing liquidity, minimizing interest rate exposure, enhancing asset/liability management, and maximizing their use of capital.

(i) Underwriting Standards. When loans are originated for resale, the origination process includes not only finding an investor but also preparing the loan documents to fit the investor's requirements. Loans originated for resale must normally comply with specific underwriting standards regarding items such as borrower qualifications, loan documentation, appraisals, mortgage insurance, and loan terms. Individual loans that do not meet the underwriting standards are typically eliminated from the pool of loans eligible for sale. Generally, the originating institutions may be subject to recourse by the investor for underwriting exceptions identified subsequent to the sale of the loans and any related defaults by borrowers.

(ii) Securitizations. Securitization is simply a method of financing a pool of assets intended to generate cash where sellers of assets can transfer part of ownership's risk and benefit to a third party who is willing or has the ability to take the risks. A common method of transforming real estate assets into liquid marketable securities is through securitization. Securitization is where loans are sold to a separate entity that finances the purchase through the issuance of debt securities or undivided interest in the loans. The real estate securities are backed by the cash flows of the loans.

Securitization of residential mortgages has expanded to include commercial and multifamily mortgages, auto and home equity loans, credit cards, and leases. The securitization of mortgage loans is a complex process affected by many players with different incentives that are often conflicting and thus create frictions among players. Ashcraft and Schuermann (2008) identified seven frictions among securitization players;

1. Frictions between the mortgagor and the originator: predatory lending
2. Frictions between the originator and the arranger: predatory borrowing and lending
3. Frictions between the arranger and third parties: adverse selection
4. Frictions between the servicer and the mortgagor: moral hazard
5. Frictions between the servicer and third parties: moral hazard
6. Frictions between the asset manager and investor: principal–agent
7. Frictions between the investor and the credit rating agencies: model error.

The accounting guidance for sales of loans through securitizations is discussed in Section 30.3.

(iii) Loan Servicing. When loans are sold, the selling institution sometimes retains the right to service the loans for a servicing fee, which is collected over the life of the loans as payments are received. The servicing fee is often based on a percentage of the principal balance of the outstanding loans. A typical servicing agreement requires the servicer to perform the billing, collection, and remittance functions as well as maintain custodial bank accounts. The servicer may also be responsible for certain credit losses.

(iv) Regulatory Guidance. Regulatory guidance with respect to loan sales and mortgage banking activities continues to evolve with the increased activity by institutions. In December 1997, the OCC issued regulatory guidance for national banks in its *Comptroller's Handbook: Asset Securitization.* The FDIC Board of Governors of the Federal Reserve System (Board), OCC, and OTS agencies collectively issued guidance regarding correspondent concentration risks for financial institutions. These financial institutions include all banks and their subsidiaries, bank holding companies and their nonbank subsidiaries, savings associations and their subsidiaries, and savings and loan holding companies and their subsidiaries. The guidelines mention the expectations from all banks and their subsidiaries, bank holding companies and their nonbank subsidiaries, savings associations and their subsidiaries, and savings and loan holding companies and their subsidiaries to other institutions. They lay down the guidance to conduct relevant and appropriate due diligence for credit exposures with other financial institutions. The Fed issued a Supervision and Regulation Letter, *Risk Management and Capital Adequacy of Exposures Arising from Secondary Market Credit Activities,* July 11, 1997. In August 2010, the Basel Committee on Banking Supervision issued its *Microfinance Activities and Core Principles for Effective Banking Supervision,* which addresses:

- Efficient allocation of supervisory resources
- Effective evaluation of the risks of microfinance activities through development of specialized knowledge within the supervisory team

- Establishment of proven control and managerial practices relevant to microfinance activities
- Achievement of clarity in the regulations pertaining to microfinance activities

(v) Accounting Guidance. The accounting guidance for purchasing, acquiring, and selling mortgage servicing rights is discussed in Section 30.3.

(vi) Valuation. The accounting guidance addressing the valuation of loans held for sale is discussed in Section 30.3.

(q) REAL ESTATE INVESTMENTS, REAL ESTATE OWNED, AND OTHER FORECLOSED ASSETS. The type and nature of assets included in real estate investments, former bank premises, and other foreclosed assets can vary significantly. Such assets are described next.

(i) Real Estate Investments. Certain institutions make direct equity investments in real estate projects, and other institutions may grant real estate loans that have virtually the same risks and rewards as those of joint venture participants. Both types of transactions are considered to be real estate investments, and such arrangements are treated as if the institution has an ownership interest in the property.

Specifically, GAAP for real estate investments is established in this authoritative literature:

- AICPA SOP 78-9, *Accounting for Investments in Real Estate Ventures*
- SFAS No. 34, *Capitalization of Interest Cost*
- SFAS No. 58, *Capitalization of Interest Cost in Financial Statements That Include Investments Accounted for by the Equity Method*
- SFAS No. 66, *Accounting for Sales of Real Estate*
- SFAS No. 67, *Accounting for Costs and Initial Rental Operations of Real Estate Projects*
- SFAS No. 144, *Accounting for the Impairment or Disposal of Long-Lived Assets*
- SFAS 140, *Accounting for Transfer and Servicing of Financial Assets and Extinguishments of Liabilities*
- International Accounting Standards 39, *Financial Instruments and Standards issued by IASB in 2003*

(ii) Former Bank Premises. Many institutions have former premises that are no longer used in operations. Such former bank premises may be included in real estate owned.

(iii) Foreclosed Assets. Foreclosed assets include all assets received in full or partial satisfaction of a receivable and include real and personal property; equity interests in corporations, partnerships, and joint ventures; and beneficial interests in trusts. However, the largest component of real estate owned by banks and savings institutions is comprised of foreclosed real estate assets. Subprime loans account for the majority of loans in foreclosure. In 2008, about 11 percent of subprime loans were in foreclosure, and this rate is as high as 20 percent in some States as of December 2011.

Guidance on accounting for and reporting of foreclosed assets is established in the next authoritative literature:

- SFAS No. 15, *Accounting by Debtors and Creditors for Troubled Debt Restructurings*
- SFAS No. 144, *Accounting for the Impairment or Disposal of Long-Lived Assets*
- SOP No. 92-3, *Accounting for Foreclosed Assets*

In October 2001, the FASB issued SFAS No. 144. The Statement supersedes FASB Statement No. 121 ; however, it retains the fundamental provisions of that Statement related to the recognition and measurement of the impairment of long-lived assets to be held and used. In addition, the

Statement provides more guidance on estimating cash flows when performing a recoverability test, requires that a long-lived asset (group) to be disposed of other than by sale (e.g., abandoned) be classified as held and used until it is disposed of, and establishes more restrictive criteria to classify as asset (group) as held for sale.

The Statement is effective for year-ends beginning after December 15, 2001 (e.g., January 1, 2002, for a calendar-year entity) and interim periods within those fiscal years. Transition is prospective for committed disposal activities that are initiated after the effective date of the Statement or an entity's initial application of the Statement. The Statement also provides transition provisions for assets held for sale that were initially recorded under previous models (Accounting Principles Board No. 30 or SFAS No. 121) and do not meet the new held for sale criteria within one year of the initial application of the Statement (e.g., December 31, 2002, for a calendar-year-end entity that adopts the Statement effective January 1, 2002). In 2003, the FASB issued SFAS No. 147, *Acquisitions of Certain Financial Institutions,* which amended SFAS Nos. 121 and 144.

(r) INVESTMENTS IN DEBT AND EQUITY SECURITIES. Banks use a variety of financial instruments for various purposes, primarily to provide a source of income through investment or resale and to manage interest rate and liquidity risk as part of an overall asset/liability management strategy.

Institutions purchase U.S. government obligations, such as U.S. Treasury bills, notes, and bonds, in addition to the debt of U.S. government agencies and government-sponsored enterprises, such as the U.S. Government National Mortgage Association (Fannie Mae) and Federal Home Loan Mortgage Corporation (Freddie Mac). Institutions also purchase municipal obligations, such as municipal bonds and tax anticipation notes.

Another common form of investments, which can be tailored to a wide variety of needs, is called *asset-backed securities* (ABSs). ABS values are based on the values of specific assets that back, or get pooled into, the securities. Those assets can include mortgage loans, student loans, credit card payments, auto loans and nearly any other kind of asset that provides a steady flow of payments. Securitization helps expand the availability and lowers the cost of credit for homeowners, consumers, and businesses because as lenders pool the assets into securities and sell them to investors, the lenders then get more money to turn into loans.

For the purpose of categorizing ABSs, each individual ABS should be included in the item that most closely describes the predominant type of asset that collateralizes the security, and this categorization should be used consistently over time. In 2010, the SEC voted to issue new regulatory proposals covering more than $2 trillion of the ABS market. It reasoned that the securitization fostered poor lending practices by encouraging lenders to shift their risk of loss to investors, resulting in investors largely withdrawing from the market when those securities went bad after the U.S. housing bust. Because of the role played by the MBSs in the current financial crisis, the securitized U.S. subprime mortgages are considered to have served as the crisis's immediate trigger. During the financial crisis, ABS holders suffered significant losses, which reveals that many investors are not fully aware of the risk in the underlying mortgages within the pools of securitized assets and over rely on credit ratings assigned by rating agencies. The proposed rules seek to address the problems highlighted by the crisis and to head off the next one, by giving investors the tools they need to accurately assess risk and by better aligning the interests of the issuer with those of the investor.

Banks can hold ABSs as securities, or they can be the issuer of ABSs along with both governmental and private issuers. The ABSs are repaid from the underlying cash flow generated from other financial instruments, such as mortgage loans, credit card receivables, and mobile home loans. ABSs secured by real estate mortgages are often called MBSs.

The level of risk related to ABSs is often related to the level of risk in the collateral. For example, securitized subprime auto loans, experiencing a decline in credit quality, may also cause a reduction in the value of the ABS, if receipt of the underlying cash flow becomes questionable.

ABSs often include a credit enhancement designed to reduce the degree of credit risk to the holder of the ABS security. Examples of credit enhancement include guarantees, letters of credit, overcollateralization, private insurance, and senior/subordinate structures. The degree of protection provided by the credit enhancement depends on the nature of the collateral and the type and extent of the credit enhancement.

ABSs are structured into a variety of products, many of which are complex. Risk variables, such as prepayment risk, changes in prevailing interest rates, and delayed changes in indexed interest rates, make the forecasting of future cash flows more difficult. ABSs with several investment classes may have varying terms such as maturity dates, interest rates, payment schedules, and residual rights, which further complicates an analysis of the investment. CMOs and real estate mortgage investment conduits (REMICs) are two examples of multiclass mortgage securities. The underlying objective of all types of ABSs and mortgage securities is to redistribute the cash flows generated from the collateral to all security holders, consistent with their contractual rights, without a shortfall or an overage.

Banks are generally restricted in the types of financial instruments they may deal in, underwrite, purchase, or sell. Essentially banks may only deal in U.S. government and U.S. government agency securities, municipal bonds, and certain other bonds, notes, and debentures. These restrictions are also limited based on capitalization. The FFIEC policy statement issued in February 1992 addresses the selection of securities dealers, policies and strategies for securities portfolios, unsuitable investment practices, and mortgage derivations. In September 2010, FFIEC announced the availability of data on mortgage lending transactions at 8,124 U.S. financial institutions covered by the Home Mortgage Disclosure Act (HMDA). Covered institutions include banks, savings associations, credit unions, and mortgage companies. The HMDA data cover 2009 lending activity—applications, originations, denials (and other actions such as incomplete or withdrawn applications), and purchases of loans.

(i) Accounting for Investments in Debt and Equity Securities. SFAS No. 115, issued in May 1993, addresses the accounting and reporting for investments in equity securities that have readily determinable fair values and for all investments in debt securities. It superseded SFAS No.12, *Accounting for Certain Marketable Securities,* and related interpretations and amended FASB Statement No. 65, *Accounting for Certain Mortgage Banking Activities,* to eliminate MBSs from its scope. This Statement does not apply to unsecuritized loans. However, after mortgage loans are converted to MBSs, they are subject to its provisions. To reduce the problem with fair-value estimation, the FASB issued SFAS 157 (now FASB ASC Topic 820), which uses different levels of input to assess the value of assets and liabilities.

Held to Maturity. Debt securities for which an institution has both the ability and positive intent to hold to maturity are classified as held to maturity and are carried at amortized cost (Any difference between cost and fair value is recorded as a premium or discount, which is amortized to income using the level yield method over the life of the security).

Trading. Securities that are purchased and held principally for the purpose of selling them in the near term are carried at fair value with unrealized gains and losses included in earnings.

Available for Sale. All other securities are classified as available for sale and carried at fair value with unrealized gains and losses included as a separate component of shareholder's equity.

SFAS No. 115 addresses changes in circumstances that may cause an enterprise to change its intent to hold a certain security to maturity without calling into question its intent to hold other debt securities to maturity in the future.

For individual securities classified as either available for sale or held to maturity, entities are required to determine whether a decline in fair value below the amortized cost basis is other than temporary. If such a decline is judged to be other than temporary, the cost basis of the individual security should be written down to fair value as the new cost basis. The amount of the write-down should be treated as a realized loss and recorded in earnings. The new cost basis must not be changed for subsequent recoveries.

Investment securities are required to be recorded on a trade date basis. Interest income on investment securities is recorded separately as a component of interest income. Realized gains and losses on available-for-sale securities and realized and unrealized gains and losses on trading securities are recorded as a separate component of noninterest income or loss. Upon the sale of an available-for-sale security, any unrealized gain or loss previously recorded in the separate component of equity is reversed and recorded as a separate component of noninterest income or loss.

Discounts and premiums should be accreted or amortized using the interest method in accordance with SFAS No. 91. The interest method provides for a periodic interest income at a constant effective yield on the net investment. The amortization or accretion period should be from the purchase date to the maturity date rather than an earlier call date, except for large numbers of similar loans where prepayments are expected and can be reasonably estimated, such as with certain ABSs.

Transfers among the three categories are performed at fair value. Transfers out of held to maturity should be rare.

(ii) Wash Sales. If the same financial asset is purchased shortly before or after the sale of a security, it is called a *wash sale.* SFAS No. 140 addresses wash sales, stating that unless there is a concurrent contract to repurchase or redeem the transferred financial assets from the purchaser, the seller does not maintain effective control over the transferred assets, and, therefore, the sale should be recorded. SFAS No. 140 provides the accounting guidance for recognizing gains and losses from wash sales, as more fully discussed in Section 30.3.

(iii) Short Sales. An institution may sell a security it does not own with the intention of buying or borrowing securities at an agreed-upon future date to cover the sale. Given the nature of these transactions, such sales should be within the trading portfolio. Obligations incurred in these short sales should be reported as liabilities and recorded at fair value at each reporting date with change in fair value recorded through income. The Dodd-Frank Act directs the SEC to issue rules requiring financial institutions to publicly report on their short sales activities on at least a monthly basis.

(iv) Securities Borrowing and Lending. An institution may borrow securities from a counterparty to fulfill its obligations and may advance cash, pledge other securities, or issue letters of credit as collateral for borrowed securities. If cash is pledged as collateral, the institution that loans the securities typically earns a return by investing that cash at rates higher than the rate paid or rebated back to the institution that borrows the securities. If the collateral is other than cash, the institution that loans the collateral typically receives a fee. Because most securities lending transactions are short term, the value of the pledged collateral is usually required to be higher than the value of the securities borrowed, and collateral is usually valued daily and adjusted frequently for changes in the market price, most securities lending transactions by themselves do not represent significant credit risks. However, other risks exist in securities lending transactions, such as market and credit risks, relative to the maintenance and safeguarding of the collateral. For example, the manner in which cash collateral is invested could present market and credit risk.

SFAS No. 140 (now ASC Topic 310) addresses the accounting for securities lending transactions i.e. for transfers and servicing of financial assets and extinguishments of liabilities a replacement of FASB Statement No. 125. Those standards are based on consistent application of a *financial-components approach* that focuses on control. It provides that if the transferor (institution loaning the securities) surrenders control over those securities, the transfer shall be accounted for as a sale, to the extent that consideration (other than beneficial interest) is received in exchange. SFAS No. 140 states that the transferor has surrendered control over the transferred asset only if *all* three of the next conditions have been met:

1. The transferred assets have been isolated from the transferor—put presumptively beyond the reach of the transferor and its creditors, even in bankruptcy or other receivership (paragraphs 27 and 28).
2. Each transferee (or, if the transferee is a qualifying SPE (paragraph 35), each holder of its beneficial interests) has the right to pledge or exchange the assets (or beneficial interests) it received, and no condition both constrains the transferee (or holder) from taking advantage

of its right to pledge or exchange and provides more than a trivial benefit to the transferor (paragraphs 29–34).

3. The transferor does not maintain effective control over the transferred assets through either (a) an agreement that both entitles and obligates the transferor to repurchase or redeem them before their maturity (paragraph. 47–49) or (b) the ability to unilaterally cause the holder to return specific assets, other than through a cleanup call (paragraphs 50–54).

If all three of these conditions are met, the securities lending transaction shall be accounted for as a sale, in this manner:

- *Institution loaning the securities.* Recognizes the sale of the loaned securities, proceeds consisting of the collateral. Also recognizes the forward repurchase commitment.
- *Institution borrowing the securities.* Recognizes the purchase of the borrowed securities, consideration representing the collateral. Also recognizes the forward resale commitment.

Lending securities transactions accompanied by an agreement that entitles and obligates the institution loaning the securities to repurchase or redeem them before their maturity should be accounted for as secured borrowings. The cash (or securities) received as collateral is considered the amount borrowed, and the securities loaned are considered pledged as collateral against the cash borrowed. Any rebate paid to the institution borrowing the securities is treated as interest on the cash borrowed.

When the transfer is recorded as a sale, the cash (or securities) received in conjunction with loaning securities should be recognized as an asset and a corresponding liability established, recording the obligation to return the cash (or securities).

However, most securities lending transactions are accompanied by an agreement that entitles and obligates the securities lender to repurchase or redeem the transferred assets before their maturity. Such transactions typically will not be reported as sales under SFAS No. 140 because of the obligation of the transferor to repurchase the transferred assets. However, the provisions of SFAS No. 140 relating to the recognition of collateral could require that the transfer of securities and related collateral be recorded. The principal criterion to determine whether the collateral will be required to be recorded is whether the parties to the arrangement have the right to sell or repledge it. If such a right is present, the securities lender records the cash or noncash collateral received as its own asset as well as a corresponding obligation to return it. If the securities lender sells the collateral, it would recognize the proceeds and derecognize the collateral. The securities borrower will typically not record the securities received or an obligation to return them unless they are sold. Additionally, the securities borrower typically will not be required to reclassify the collateral provided, if such collateral is in the form of securities.

Additional guidance on accounting for and reporting of investments in debt and equity securities was established in these documents:

- FASB Technical Bulletin (TB) No. 94-1, *Application of SFAS No. 115 to Debt Securities Restructured in a Troubled Debt Restructuring,* which clarifies that any loan that was restructured in a troubled debt restructuring involving a modification of terms would be subject to SFAS No. 115 if the debt instrument meets the definition of a security.
- SFAS No. 15, *Accounting by Debtors and Creditors for Troubled Debt Restructurings,* which applies to troubled debt restructurings involving debt securities.
- SFAS No. 91, *Accounting for Nonrefundable Fees and Costs Associated with Originating or Acquiring Loans and Initial Direct Costs of Leases,* which specifies that discounts or premiums associated with the purchase of debt securities should be accreted or amortized using the interest method.
- SFAS No. 114, *Accounting by Creditors for Impairment of a Loan (an Amendment, FASB No. 5 and 15),* which addresses troubled debt restructurings involving a modification of terms

of a receivables (i.e., creditor should evaluate the collectability of both contractual interest and contractual principal of all receivables when assessing the need for a loss accrual). This Statement applies to financial statements for fiscal years beginning after December 15, 1994.

(s) DEPOSITS. Generally, the most significant source of a bank's funding is customer deposits. Institutions now offer a wide range of deposit products having a variety of interest rates, terms, and conditions. The more common types of deposits are described next.

(i) Demand Deposits. Customer deposit accounts from which funds may be withdrawn on demand. Checking and negotiable order of withdrawal (NOW) accounts are the most common form of demand deposits. Deposits and withdrawals are typically made through a combination of deposits, check writing, automatic teller machines (ATMs), point-of-sale terminals, electronic funds transfers (EFTs), and preauthorized deposits and payment transactions, such as payroll deposits and loan payments.

(ii) Savings Deposits. Interest-bearing deposit accounts that normally carry with them certain access restrictions or minimum balance requirements. Passbook and statement savings accounts and money market accounts are the most common form of savings accounts. Deposits and withdrawals are typically made at teller windows, ATMs, by ETF, or by preauthorized payment. Money market accounts often permit the customer to write checks, although the number of checks that may be written is limited.

(iii) Time Deposits. Interest-bearing deposit accounts that are subject to withdrawal only after a fixed term. Certificates of deposit (CDs), individual retirement accounts (IRAs), and open accounts are the most common form of time deposits.

CDs may be issued in bearer form or registered form and may be negotiable and nonnegotiable. Negotiable CDs, for which there is an active secondary market, are generally short term and are most commonly sold to corporations, pension funds, and government bodies in large denominations, such as $100,000 to $1 million. Nonnegotiable CDs are generally in smaller denominations, and depositors are subject to a penalty fee if they elect to withdraw their funds prior to the stated maturity.

Individual retirement accounts, Keogh accounts, and self-employed-person accounts (SEPs) are generally maintained as CDs; however, due to the tax benefits to depositors, they typically have longer terms than most CDs.

Brokered deposits are third-party time deposits placed by or through the assistance of a deposit broker. Deposit brokers sometimes sell interests in placed deposits to third parties. Federal law restricts the acceptance and renewal of brokered deposits by an institution based on its capitalization.

(t) FEDERAL FUNDS AND REPURCHASE AGREEMENTS. Federal funds and repurchase agreements are often used as a source of liquidity and as a cost-effective source of funds.

(i) Federal Funds Purchased. Generally, short-term funds maturing overnight bought between banks that are members of the Federal Reserve System. Federal funds transactions can be secured or unsecured. If the funds are secured, U.S. government securities are placed in a custody account for the seller.

(ii) Repurchase Agreements. Repurchase agreements, or repos, occur when an institution sells securities and agrees to repurchase the identical (or substantially the same) securities at a specified date for a specified price. The institution may be a seller or a buyer. Most repo transactions occur with other depository institutions, dealers in securities, state and local governments, and customers (retail repurchase agreements), and involve obligations of the federal government or its agencies, commercial paper, bankers' acceptances, and negotiable CDs. The difference between the sale and repurchase price represents interest for the use of the funds. There are also several types of repurchase agreements, such as collar repurchase agreements, fixed-coupon agreements, and yield-maintenance agreements. The terms of the agreements are often structured to reflect the substance of the transaction, such as a borrowing and lending of funds versus a sale and purchase of securities. Some repurchase agreements are similar to securities lending transactions, whereby the seller may (or may not) have the right to sell or repledge the securities to a third party during the term of the repurchase agreement.

SFAS No. 140 provides the accounting guidance for repurchase agreements. In addition to replacing FASB Statement No. 125 and rescinding FASB Statement No. 127, *Deferral of the Effective Date of Certain Provisions of FASB Statement No. 125,* this Statement carries forward the actions taken by FASB Statement No. 125. In general, SFAS No. 140 uses the three conditions discussed previously in Subsection 30.2(r)(iv), when accounting for repurchase agreements. If all three conditions specified in SFAS No. 140 are met, the seller accounts for the repurchase agreement as a sale of financial assets and a forward repurchase commitment, and the buyer accounts for the agreement as a purchase of financial assets and a forward resale commitment. This Statement was made effective for transfers and servicing of financial assets and extinguishments of liabilities occurring after March 31, 2001, and for the recognition and reclassification of collateral and for disclosures relating to securitization transactions and collateral for fiscal years ending after December 15, 2000.

Government securities dealers, banks, other financial institutions, and corporate investors commonly use repurchase agreements to obtain or use short-term funds. Under those agreements, the transferor (repo party) transfers a security to a transferee (repo counterparty or reverse party) in exchange for cash and concurrently agrees to reacquire that security at a future date for an amount equal to the cash exchanged plus a stipulated interest factor. Repurchase agreements can be effective in a variety of ways. Some repurchase agreements are similar to securities lending transactions in that the transferee has the right to sell the securities to a third party during the term of the repurchase agreement. In other repurchase agreements, the transferee does not have the right to sell the securities during the term of the repurchase agreement.

Two reasons advanced in support of the treatment of repurchase agreements and securities lending transactions as secured borrowings are that (1) those transactions are difficult to characterize because they have attributes of both borrowings and sales and (2) supporting arguments can be found for accounting for those transactions as borrowings or sales. The only supporting arguments cited for the treatment of repurchase agreements and securities lending transactions as secured borrowings that are not equally applicable to certain securitizations are that (1) forward contracts that are fully secured should be treated differently from those that are unsecured and (2) making a change in existing accounting practice would have a substantial impact on the reported financial position of certain entities and on the markets in which they participate.

Also similar to the treatment for securities lending transactions, repurchase agreements where the institution selling the securities maintains effective control over the securities (and thereby not meeting the three sale conditions, described previously, provided by SFAS No. 140) should be accounted for as secured borrowings.

(u) DEBT. Banks and savings institutions use long- and short-term borrowings as a source of funds.

(i) Long-Term Debt. Debentures and notes are the most common form of long-term debt; however, institutions also use long-term mortgages, obligations, commitments under capital leases, and mandatorily redeemable preferred stock to provide long-term funding. Funds are also borrowed through Eurodollar certificates, CMOs, and REMICs; mortgage-backed bonds (MBBs), mortgage-revenue bonds, and FHLB advances. The terms of long-term debt vary; they may be secured or unsecured, and they may be convertible.

(ii) Short-Term Debt. Repurchase agreements and federal funds purchased are the most common form of the short-term debt described earlier. Commercial paper is another common source of short-term funding. Commercial paper is an unsecured short-term promissory note typically issued by bank or savings institution holding companies.

MBBs are any borrowings (other than those from an FHLB) collateralized in whole or in part by one or more real estate loans.

Member institutions may borrow from their regional Federal Reserve Bank in the form of discounts and advances, which are used primarily to cover shortages in the required reserve account and also in times of liquidity problems.

(iii) Accounting Guidance. In general, the accounting for debt is the same for banks and savings institutions as for other enterprises although banks and savings institutions have unclassified balance sheets. SFAS No. 140 provides guidance for transfers of financial assets and extinguishments of liabilities. While few respondents support the reasoning of FASB No. 125, others argue that existing accounting guidance found in the AICPA Statement, *Definition of the Term Substantially the Same for Holders of Debt Instruments, as Used in Certain Audit Guides and a Statement of Position* (now FASB *Accounting Standards Codification* (ASC) No. 105), has proven adequate to constrain the characteristics of assets that are to be reacquired.

(v) TAXATION. Taxation of financial institutions is extremely complex; specific discussion is therefore beyond the scope of this book. However, certain significant factors affecting bank and thrift taxation are discussed next.

(i) Loan Loss Reserves

Banks. Prior to the Tax Reform Act of 1986 (1986 Act), banks were permitted to deduct loan loss provisions based on either the experience method or on a percentage of eligible loans method. Since the mid-198Os, provision for loan losses has been one of the most important factors affecting bank profitability. The federal banking regulators (FDIC, OCC, and Fed) require that all banks include in their financial statements an account named as *allowance for loan losses* (also known as reserves for *loan losses*). When loan losses are recognized (i.e., when a bank decides that some portion of a loan will not be collected and therefore must be *charged off or written down*), the amount of the loss is deducted from the asset category loans and also from reserves for loan losses.

The 1986 Act passed by Congress simplified the tax code and eliminated some deductions quoting its significance in the tax structure of the United States and it modified the Internal Revenue Code (IRC) Section 585, which now allows only a small bank with $500 million or less in average assets (calculated by taking into account the average assets of all other members of an institution's controlled group, if applicable) to calculate an addition to the bad debt reserve using the experience method.

A large bank with over $500 million in assets may not use the reserve method. It is limited to the specific charge-off method under IRC Section 166. If a bank becomes a large bank, it is required to recapture its reserve, usually over a four-year period. A deduction under Section 166 generally is allowed for wholly or partially worthless debt for the year in which the worthlessness occurs. The total or partial worthlessness of a debt is a facts-and-circumstance, loan-by-loan determination. Larger banks may claim losses only when loans are written off. A bank may make a conformity election, however, which provides a presumptive conclusion of worthlessness for charge-offs made for regulatory purposes.

In comparison to GAAP, the specific charge-off method generally results in an unfavorable temporary difference (i.e., the book expense is recognized prior to the tax deduction being allowed) because the actual charge-off of a loan usually occurs later than the time the reserve is established for it. The Act also eliminated the deductibility of nonmortgage consumer interest payments such as interest on credit card balances, automobile loans, and life insurance loans.

Thrifts. Effective for tax years beginning after December 31, 1995, thrift institutions are subject to the same loan loss rules as banks. Thrifts that qualify as small banks (average assets of $500 million or less) can use the experience-based reserve method just described. Thrifts that are treated as large banks must use the specific charge-off method.

A thrift that is treated as either a large or small bank is required to recapture or recognize as income its applicable excess reserves. Such income is generally recognized ratably over a six-year period beginning with the first tax year beginning after 1995.

If a thrift becomes a large bank, the amount of the thrift's applicable excess reserves is generally the excess of (1) the balance of its reserves as of the close of its last taxable year beginning before January 1, 1996, over (2) the balance of its reserves as of the close of its last taxable year beginning before January 1, 1988 (its pre-1988 or base year reserve). Thus, a thrift treated as a large bank generally is required to recapture all post-1987 additions to it bad debt reserves.

In the case of a thrift becoming a small bank, the thrift's applicable excess reserves is the excess of (1) the balance of its reserves as of the close of its last taxable year beginning before January 1, 1996, over (2) the greater of the balance of (a) its pre-1988 reserves, or (b) what the thrift's reserves would have been at the close of its last taxable year beginning before January 1, 1996, had the thrift always used the experience method. Thus, a thrift treated as a small bank may not have any applicable excess reserves (and therefore no recapture) if it had always used the experience method.

A special rule, the residential loan requirement, may allow the six-year recapture period to be delayed for one or two years (i.e., recapture could actually start as late as the first taxable year beginning after 1997). An institution meets the requirement for a taxable year if the principal amount of residential loans made by the institution during the year is not less than its base amount, defined generally as the average of the principal amounts of residential loans made by the institution during the six most recent tax years beginning before January 1, 1996.

A residential loan is generally defined as a loan secured by residential real property, but only to the extent the loan is made to the property owner to acquire, construct, or improve the property. Thus, mortgage refinancing and home equity loans are not considered to be residential loans, except to the extent the proceeds of the loan are used to acquire, construct, or improve qualified real property. Other rules govern the calculation of the base amount for purposes of the requirement.

The residential loan requirement is applicable only for taxable years beginning after December 31, 1995, and before January 1, 1998, and must be applied separately with respect to each such year. Thus, all institutions are required to recapture their applicable excess reserves within the first six, seven, or eight taxable years beginning after December 31, 1995.

(ii) Mark to Market. Contrary to normal realization-based tax accounting principles, IRC Section 475 requires dealers in securities to recognize gain or loss through marking-to-market their securities holdings, unless such securities are validly identified by the taxpayer as excepted from the provisions.

As used in this context, the terms *dealer* and *securities* have very broad application. Virtually all financial institutions are considered dealers in securities for mark-to-market purposes though regulations provide exceptions for certain institutions not engaging in more than de minimus dealer activities. Securities required to be marked (unless validly identified as excepted) include notes, bonds, and other evidences of indebtedness; stock; notional principal contracts; or any evidence of an interest in or a derivative of such security (other than Section 1256(a) contracts); and any clearly identified hedge of such security.

Securities that may be identified as exempted from the mark-to-market provisions are:

- Securities held for investment, and property identified as such for tax purposes.
- Notes and other evidences of indebtedness (and obligations to acquire such) that are acquired or originated by the taxpayer in the ordinary course of a trade or business that are not held for sale.
- Hedges of positions or liabilities that are not securities in the hands of the taxpayer, and hedges of positions or liabilities that are exempt from mark to market under the two foregoing provisions. This does not apply for hedges held as a dealer.

To be exempted from mark to market, the security must be identified by the taxpayer on a contemporaneous basis (generally, day of acquisition) as meeting one of the exceptions.

Whether a security is required to be marked to market for financial accounting purposes is *not* dispositive for purposes of determining whether such security is treated as held for investment or not held for sale.

Some financial institutions identify all or a significant portion of their loans to customers as exempted from the mark-to-market provisions because they intend to hold those loans to maturity. A possible exception are mortgages that are originated for sale (pipeline or warehoused loans), which do not meet the exception criteria and must be marked to market.

(iii) Tax-Exempt Securities. For tax purposes, gross income does not include interest on any obligation of a state or political subdivision thereof (e.g., county, city). Interest on certain nonqualified private activity bonds, unregistered bonds, and arbitrage bonds does not qualify for this exemption.

A deduction is not allowed for interest expense on indebtedness incurred to purchase or carry tax-exempt obligations. Deposit-taking financial institutions (banks and thrifts) are subject to a special two-part formula to determine how much of the total interest expense of an institution is disallowed interest expense.

Interest expense related to tax-exempt obligations acquired after August 1986 is disallowed and is calculated by multiplying total interest expense by the ratio of the tax basis of such obligations to the tax basis of all assets.

Interest expense related to tax-exempt obligations acquired between January 1983 and August 1986 is 20 percent disallowed and is calculated in a manner similar to that just described.

Certain qualified tax-exempt obligations (generally, obligations issued by an entity that will not issue more than $10 million of tax-exempt obligations during the year and that are not private activity bonds) issued after August 1986 are treated as if issued prior to that date (i.e., subject to the 20 percent disallowance rule rather than the 100 percent disallowance rule).

(iv) Nonaccrual Loans. Generally, interest on a loan must be accrued as income unless the taxpayer can demonstrate that the interest is uncollectable at the time of accrual. The tax rule is dependent on the facts and circumstances for the nonaccrual loans at issue. The SFAS No. 114 uses a probable test in determining when a loan is impaired. When it is probable that a creditor will be unable to collect all amounts due according to the contractual terms of the loan agreement, the loan is considered impaired. Use of this analysis may now provide substantiation of the tax treatment for impairment of loans.

(v) Hedging. Financial institutions that are involved in hedging transactions treat the gain or loss from these transactions as ordinary for tax purposes. A hedging transaction must be entered into primarily to manage a taxpayer's risk of interest rate changes, price changes, or currency fluctuations. A taxpayer must also have risk on an overall (or macro) basis. A hedge of a single ordinary asset or liability will be respected if it is reasonably expected to manage the taxpayer's overall risk. Hedges entered into as part of an overall risk reduction program also will qualify.

Fixed to floating hedges (e.g., hedges that convert a fixed-rate liability into a floating-rate liability) may satisfy the risk management requirement if, for example, a taxpayer's income varies with interest rates. In addition, hedges entered into to reverse or counteract another hedging transaction may qualify for ordinary gain or loss treatment. Because tax hedges are permissible only with ordinary property, hedges of mortgage servicing rights generally do not qualify as tax hedges, since mortgage servicing rights are generally capital assets.

Hedges of ordinary liabilities qualify as hedging transactions regardless of the use of the proceeds from the borrowing. Consequently, gain or loss from a hedge of a liability used to fund the purchase of a capital asset will be ordinary. However, recent guidance in the form of final Treasury regulations provide that the purchase or sale of a debt instrument, an equity security, or an annuity contract is not hedging a transaction even if the transaction limits or reduces the taxpayer's risk.

The timing of the gain or loss from a hedging transaction must reasonably be matched with the gain or loss of the item being hedged. This applies to global hedges and other hedges of aggregate risk.

If a taxpayer disposes of a hedged item but retains the hedge, the taxpayer may redesignate the hedge. The taxpayer generally must mark to market the hedge on the date that he or she disposes of the hedged item.

There are detailed contemporaneous identification and record-keeping requirements with which an institution must comply to support its treatment of hedging transactions. Failure to comply could lead to characterization of losses from these transactions as capital losses (which may be used only to offset capital gains).

(vi) Loan Origination Fees and Costs. Loan origination fees are be deferred and recognized over the life of the loan as an adjustment of yield (interest income). Loan origination fees and related direct loan origination costs for a given loan are offset, and only the net amount is deferred and amortized. The practice of recognizing a portion of loan origination fees as revenue in a period to offset all or part of the costs of origination is no longer acceptable.

For financial accounting purposes, SFAS No. 91 requires that all loan origination fees (including loan commitment fees and points) be deferred and generally recognized over the life of the related loan or commitment period as an adjustment of yield. This Statement establishes the accounting for nonrefundable fees and costs associated with originating or acquiring loans and initial direct costs of leases (i.e., association with lending, committing to lend, or purchasing a loan or group of loans). The Statement specifies that loan origination fees must be recognized over the life of the related loan as an adjustment of yield. All loan commitment fees are deferred except for certain retrospectively determined fees; commitment fees meeting specified criteria are recognized over the loan commitment period; all other commitment fees are recognized as an adjustment of yield over the related loan's life or, if the commitment expires unexercised, recognized in income upon expiration of the commitment. Overall, the Statement changes the practice of recognizing loan origination and commitment fees at or prior to inception of the loan.

For tax accounting purposes, loan fees received as cash payments incident to a lending transaction (e.g., points) that represent an amount charged for the use of forbearance of money (rather than payment for services) are deferred. Points received in connection with a lending transaction are applied as a reduction to the issue price of the loan and generally create original issue discount (OID) to be recognized over the life of the loan on a constant yield method. In instances where the OID on a loan is de minimus (as defined in regulations), the de minimus OID is recognized in proportion to principal payments received.

For book purposes, the costs associated with origination of a loan are deferred and recognized over the life of the loan together with the origination fees. For tax purposes, institutions generally deduct these costs currently because to date there has been no published guidance requiring capitalization.

(vii) Foreclosed Property

Banks. Generally, a bank recognizes gain or loss on foreclosure of property securing a loan but is not permitted to deduct any further decrease in or impairment of value. Any decrease in value occurring after foreclosure is recognized when the property is disposed of by the institution. If real property acquired through foreclosure is operated in a trade or business after foreclosure (e.g., as rental property), the institution may deduct depreciation (and other operating expenses) computed in accordance with general tax depreciation provisions.

Thrifts. Effective for taxable years beginning after December 31, 1995, thrift institutions are subject to the same rules as banks.

Under prior law, a special rule treated the acquisition of property by a thrift as a nontaxable event, with no gain or loss recognized at time of foreclosure and no depreciation allowed on the property. A subsequent write-down charge to the bad debt reserve was allowed if the fair market value of the property was less than the tax basis of the loan. Upon final disposition, the gain or loss was credited or charged to the bad debt reserve.

(viii) Leasing Activities. Direct financing activities may qualify as financings for tax purposes. As a result, a bank will be considered the owner of the leased property for tax purposes. Accordingly, rental income and depreciation deductions on the leased asset will be recognized for tax purposes but not for financial reporting purposes. This will result in a difference between book and tax accounting under SFAS No. 109.

(ix) FHLB Dividends. Banks and savings institutions may become members of the FHLB by purchasing stock in individual FHLB member banks. Banks generally become a member of the FHLB for access to additional funding for borrowed funds. The FHLB member banks, of which there are 12, generally pay cash or stock dividends to shareholders, depending on the member bank. Cash dividends paid on FHLB stock that was issued prior to March 28, 1942, are exempt from federal income taxes. This exemption applied even for such stock that was subsequently acquired through merger or otherwise. Cash dividends on FHLB stock issued on or after March 28, 1942, are not exempt from taxation. Stock dividends on FHLB stock are generally not taxable when distributed. These stock dividends create a book/tax difference that is recognized on the sales or redemption of the FHLB shares.

(x) Bank-Owned Life Insurance. Bank-owned life insurance (BOLI) is commonly used by financial institutions for its financial benefits to help fund benefit programs and to offset certain costs typically incurred when losing key employees of the bank. BOLI is life insurance purchased by a financial institution on the lives of specific employees. The economically beneficial aspects of BOLI are tax-free growth in the cash surrender value of the policy and a tax-tree treatment of the death proceeds, which are both realized by the bank as the owner of a given policy. Insurance premiums on life insurance policies are not tax deductible.

(xi) Original Issue Discount. OID rules apply to all debt instruments after July 1, 1982, with certain exceptions. Generally, OID is the excess of what a borrower is obligated to repay when the loan comes due over the amount borrowed. More technically, OID is the excess of the stated redemption price at maturity over its issue price. Under OID rules, the holder of the debt must accrue stated interest under the constant yield method.

(xii) Market Discount. The primary difference between OID and market discount is that purchase of a security at its original purchase versus the secondary market, respectively. Generally, if a debt instrument has declined in value from the time when it was originally issued (other than as a result of principal payments), a purchaser of the bond will acquire it with market discount.

A holder of a market discount may choose between two methods of recognizing accrued market discount. Market discount accrues under a ratable method, in proportion to the payment of principal, unless a constant interest method is elected. The primary difference between market discount and OID is that the borrower is not required to include accrued market discount in taxable income currently but may elect to do so. Instead, the market discount rules require borrowers to recognize accrued market discount only on receipt of the proceeds of a disposition or a principal payment is made.

(w) FUTURES, FORWARDS, OPTIONS, SWAPS, AND SIMILAR FINANCIAL INSTRUMENTS. Futures, forwards, swaps, and options and other financial instruments with similar characteristics (collectively, derivatives) have become important financial management tools for banks. The complexity and volume of derivatives and derivatives trading have increased significantly in recent years. Institutions continue to enhance risk management systems to enable them to monitor the risks involved. Bank regulatory agencies continue to encourage institutions to upgrade policies and procedures, risk measurement and reporting systems, and independent oversight and internal control processes. Senior management has increased its knowledge of the derivative products and how risks are monitored.

Derivatives are receiving considerable attention primarily due to the underlying volatility in the markets, relatively large size of the transactions, and the potential for significant earnings fluctuations. Derivatives have many similar risk characteristics as other credit products, such as credit risk, market risk, legal risk, and control risk. The specific risks in a derivatives portfolio are often difficult to identify due to the complexity of the transactions. For example, two or more basic risks are often used in combination, which may be further complicated by the fact that economic interaction between various positions within an institution (on- and off-balance sheet) may be difficult to assess.

Underlying cash flows for derivatives are often referenced to such items as rates, indexes (which measure changes in specific markets), value of underlying positions in financial instruments, equity instruments, foreign currencies, commodities, or other derivatives.

Derivatives generally can be described as either forward-based or option-based, or combinations of the two. A forward-based contract (futures, forwards, and swap contracts) obligates one party to buy and a counterparty to sell an underlying financial instrument, foreign currency, or commodity at a future date at an agreed-upon price. An option-based derivative (options, interest rate caps, and interest rate floors) are one-sided in that if the right is exercised, only the holder can have a favorable outcome and the writer can have only an unfavorable outcome. Most derivatives are generally combinations of these two types of contracts.

Derivatives traded through an organized exchange typically have standardized contracts, such as futures and certain options, and the risk characteristics are more related to market risk than to credit risk. Alternatively, derivatives traded over-the-counter are customized to meet certain objectives or needs and often vary in structure, such as swaps and forward contracts. Customized derivative products traded privately typically present a greater degree of credit risk and liquidity risk, depending on the counterparty's financial strength, value of the collateral, if any, and the liquidity of the specific instrument.

The complexity of derivative instruments is largely the result of the pricing mechanisms, flexibility and options features, and value calculation formulas. In addition, derivatives can be structured to be more sensitive to general price movements than the cash market instruments from which their value is derived. The types of derivatives products available vary considerably; a brief description of the basic types of contracts is presented next.

(i) Futures. A futures contract is an agreement to make or take delivery of a financial instrument (interest rate instrument, currency, and certain stock indices) at a future date. Most futures contracts are closed out prior to the delivery date by entering into an offsetting contract.

The type of financial instrument delivered depends on the type of futures contract. For example:

- Investment-grade financial instruments, such as U.S. Treasury securities or MBSs are delivered under interest rate futures.
- Foreign currency (in the currency specified) is delivered under foreign currency futures contracts.
- Commodities such as oil, gold bullion, or coffee are delivered under commodities futures contracts.

Buyers and sellers are required to deposit assets (such as cash, government securities, or letters of credit) with a broker. The assets are called a *margin* and are subject to increases and decreases, if losses or gains are incurred on the open position.

(ii) Forwards. A forward contract is a contract between two parties to purchase and sell a specified quantity of a financial instrument, foreign currency, or commodity at a specified price, with delivery and settlement at a specified future date. Such contracts are not traded on exchanges and therefore may have a high degree of credit and liquidity risk. Forward rate agreements are forward contracts used to manage interest rate risk.

(iii) Options. Option contracts provide the purchaser of the option with the right, but not the obligation, to buy (or sell) a specified instrument, such as currencies, interest rate products, or futures. They also put the seller under the obligation to deliver (or take delivery of) the instrument to the buyer of the option but only at the buyer's option.

A premium is typically paid to the seller of the option, representing both the time value of money and any intrinsic value. Intrinsic value, which cannot be less than zero, is derived from the excess of market price for the underlying item in the contract over the price specified in the contract (strike price).

Holders of option contracts can minimize downside price risks because the loss on a purchased option contracts is limited to the amount paid for the option. However, while the profit on written option contracts is limited to the premium received, the loss potential is unlimited because the writer is obligated to settle at the strike price if the option is exercised. Options are often processed through a clearinghouse, which guarantees the writer's performance and minimizes credit risk.

Option-based derivative contracts, such as caps, floors, collars, and swaptions, can be combined to transfer risks form one entity to another. Each type of contract is described next.

- *Interest rate caps* are contracts in which a cap writer, in return for a premium, agrees to make cash payments to the cap holder equal to the excess of the market rate over the strike price multiplied by the notional principal amount if rates go above specified interest rate (strike price). The cap holder has the right, not the obligation, to exercise the option, and if rates move down, the cap holder will lose only the premium paid. The cap writer has virtually unlimited risk resulting from increases in interest rates above the cap rate.
- *Interest rate floors* are contracts in which a floor writer, in return for a premium, agrees to limit the risk of declining interest rates based on a notional amount such that if rates go below a specified interest rate (strike price), the floor holder will receive cash payments equal to the difference between the market rate and the strike price multiplied by the notional principal amount. As with interest rate caps, the floor holder has the right, not the obligation, to exercise the option, and if rates move up, the floor holder will lose only the premium paid. The floor writer has risk resulting from decreases in interest rates below the floor rate.
- *Interest rate collars* are combinations of interest rate caps and interest rate floors (i.e., one held and one written). Such contracts are often used by institutions to lock a floating rate contract into a predetermined interest rate range.
- *Swaptions* are option contracts to enter into an interest rate swap contract at some future date or to cancel an existing swap in the future.

(iv) Swaps. Swaps are contracts between parties to exchange sets of cash flows based on a predetermined notional principal; only the cash flows are exchanged (usually on a net basis) with no principal exchanged. Swaps are used to change the nature or cost of existing transactions—for example, exchanging fixed-rate debt cash flows for floating rate cash flows. Swap contracts are not exchange traded; therefore, they are not as liquid as futures contracts. The principal types of swaps are interest rate swaps and currency swaps. However, there are also basis swaps, equity swaps, commodity swaps, and mortgage swaps. A brief description of seven swaps follows.

1. *Interest rate swaps.* Interest rate swaps are used to manage interest rate risks, such as from floating to fixed or fixed to floating. Periodic fixed payments are made by one party, while another counterparty is obligated to make variable payments, depending on a market interest rate. Master netting agreements are used to permit entities to legally set off related payable and receivable swap contract positions for settlement purposes.
2. *Foreign currency swaps.* Foreign currency swaps are used to fix the value of foreign currency exchange transactions that will occur in the future. Typically, principal is exchanged at inception, interest is paid in accordance with the agreed upon rate and term, and principal is re-exchanged at maturity.

3. *Fixed-rate currency swaps.* Fixed-rate currency swaps occur when two counterparties exchange fixed-rate interest in one currency for fixed-rate interest in another currency.
4. *Basis swaps.* Basis swaps represent a variation on interest-rate swap contracts where both rates are variable but tied to different index rates.
5. *Equity swaps.* Equity swaps occur when counterparties exchange cash flow streams tied to an equity index with a fixed or floating interest.
6. *Commodity swaps.* Commodity swaps occur when counterparties exchange cash flow streams tied to the difference between a commodity's agreed-on price and its variable price, applied to an agreed-on price of the commodity.
7. *Mortgage swaps.* Typical mortgage swaps occur when an investor exchanges interest payments tied to a short-term floating rate, for cash flows based on a generic class of MBSs over a specified period. The cash flows received by the investor include the fixed coupon on the generic class or MBSs and any discount or premium. The notional amount of the mortgage swap is adjusted monthly, based on amortization and prepayment experience of the generic class of MBSs. When the contract expires, the investor may either have to take physical delivery of the mortgages (at a predetermined price) or settle in cash for the difference between the predetermined price and the current market value for the mortgages. Collateral may be posted to reduce counterparty credit risk.

(v) Foreign Exchange Contracts. Foreign exchange contracts are used both to provide a service to customers and as a part of the institution's trading or hedging activities. The bank profits by maintaining a margin between the purchase price and sale price. Contracts may be for current trades (spot contract), future dates (forward contract), or swap contracts. The bank may also enter into these contracts to hedge a foreign currency exposure.

(vi) Other Variations. Other types of derivative products are discussed in Chapter 26 of this *Handbook*.

(vii) Accounting Guidance. The FASB issued Statement No. 133, *Accounting for Derivative Instruments and Hedging Activities,* in June 1998 (now ASC 815). Statement No. 133 provides a comprehensive and consistent standard for the recognition and measurement of derivatives and hedging activities. The first step in considering whether the benefits of a new accounting standard will justify the related costs is to identify the problems in the existing accounting guidance that a new standard seeks to resolve. Hence this Statement resolves the inconsistencies that existed with respect to accounting for derivatives and changes considerably the way many derivatives transactions and hedged items are reported.

This Statement mitigates several issues. It increases the visibility, comparability, and understandability of the risks associated with derivatives by requiring that all derivatives be reported as assets or liabilities and measured at fair value. It reduces the inconsistency, incompleteness, and difficulty of applying previous accounting guidance and practice by providing comprehensive guidance for all derivatives and hedging activities. The comprehensive guidance in this Statement also eliminates some accounting practices, such as synthetic instrument accounting, that had evolved beyond the authoritative literature. This Statement accommodates a range of hedge accounting practices by (1) permitting hedge accounting for most derivative instruments, (2) permitting hedge accounting for cash flow hedges of forecasted transactions for specified risks, and (3) eliminating the requirement in Statement No. 80 that an entity demonstrate risk reduction on an entity-wide basis to qualify for hedge accounting. The combination of accommodating a range of hedge accounting practices and removing the uncertainty about the accounting requirements for certain strategies should facilitate, and may actually increase, entities' use of derivatives to manage risks.

SFAS No. 133 requires all derivatives to be recorded on the balance sheet at fair value and establishes special accounting for these three types of hedges: hedges of changes in the fair value of assets, liabilities, or firm commitments (referred to as *fair value hedges*); hedges of the variable cash flows of forecasted transactions (cash flow hedges); and hedges of foreign currency exposures of net investments in foreign operations. The accounting treatment and criteria for each of the three types of hedges are unique. Changes in fair value of derivatives that do not meet the criteria of one of these three categories of hedges are included in income.

The four basic underlying premises of the new approach are:

1. Derivatives represent rights or obligations that meet the definitions of assets (future cash inflows due from another party) or liabilities (future cash outflows owed to another party) and should be reported in the financial statements.
2. Fair value is the most relevant measure for financial instruments and the only relevant measure for derivatives. Derivatives should be measured at fair value, and adjustments to the carrying amount of hedged items should reflect changes in their fair value (i.e., gains and losses) attributable to the risk being hedged arising while the hedge is in effect.
3. Only items that are assets or liabilities should be reported as such in the financial statements. (The FASB believes that gains and losses from hedging activities are not assets or liabilities and, therefore, should not be deferred.)
4. Special accounting for items designated as being hedged should be provided only for qualifying transactions, and one aspect of qualification should be an assessment of the expectation of the effectiveness of the hedge (i.e., offsetting changes in fair values or cash flows).

See Chapter 26 for further guidance on SFAS No. 133 (ASC 815).

(x) FIDUCIARY SERVICES AND OTHER FEE INCOME

(i) Fiduciary Services. In their fiduciary capacity, banks must serve their clients' interests and must act in good faith at a level absent in most other banking activities. In view of this high degree of fiduciary responsibility, banks usually segregate the responsibilities of the trust department from that of the rest of the bank. This segregation is designed to maintain a highly objective viewpoint in the fiduciary area. Fiduciary services range from the simple safekeeping of valuables to the investment management of large pension funds.

Custodial, safekeeping, and safe deposit activities involve the receipt, storage, and issuance of receipts for a range of valuable assets. This may involve the holding of bonds, stocks, and currency in escrow pending the performance under a contract, or merely the maintenance of a secure depository for valuables or title deeds. As custodian, the bank may receive interest and dividends on securities for the account of customers.

Investment management may be discretionary, whereby the bank has certain defined powers to make investments, or nondiscretionary, whereby the bank may execute investment transactions based only on customers' instructions. The former obviously involves a higher degree of risk to the institution and creates an obligation to make prudent investment decisions.

Other fiduciary services include trust administration, stock and bond registrar, and bank trustee. Trust administration involves holding or management of property, such as pension funds and estates for the benefit of others. Stock and bond registrar and bank trustee functions include the maintenance of records and execution of securities transactions, including changes in ownership and payment of dividends and interest.

Since the assets and liabilities of the trust department of the bank are held in an agency capacity, they are not recorded on the balance sheet of the bank. These activities can, however, generate significant fee income, which is recorded when earned in the statement of income.

(ii) Other Fee Income. Emphasis on fee income-generating activities has increased in response to both the risk-based capital guidelines, which created more pressure to reduce the size of the balance sheet, and a general increase in competition in the financial services industry.

Some of the principal forms of fee-generating activity include:

- *Annuities.* Banks sell fixed and variable annuities.
- *Brokerage.* Banks may arrange for the purchase and sale of securities on behalf of customers in return for a commission.

- *Corporate and advisory services.* These activities involve advice on mergers and acquisitions, capital raising, and Treasury management in return for a fee.
- *Private banking.* This activity involves investment planning, tax assistance, and credit extensions to wealthy individuals.
- *Private placements.* This activity normally involves the placement of securities on a *best efforts* basis as opposed to an underwriting commitment.
- *Underwriting.* Banks may guarantee to purchase certain allowable securities if they are not fully subscribed to in an offering.
- *401(k) plans and mutual funds.* Banks may distribute mutual funds in a 401(k) plan.

Many of the activities, particularly underwriting, are subject to restriction by regulation as to the type of securities that may be transacted, and separately capitalized subsidiaries may be required.

These activities generate fee income that is recorded when earned. Certain activities are conducted in conjunction with credit extension activities, and therefore particular attention is required to ensure that fees generated are appropriately recorded. It is essential to distinguish between fees that may be recorded immediately and fees that are essentially loan origination fees to be accounted for over the life of the loan (SFAS No. 91).

(y) ELECTRONIC BANKING AND TECHNOLOGY RISKS. Conducting banking by personal computer is a growing area for many institutions. The types of transactions customers can perform online has also increased. For example, customers can transfer funds, pay bills, and apply for loans by using electronic banking. The start-up costs of an e-bank are high. Establishing a trusted brand is very costly as it requires significant advertising expenditure in addition to the purchase of expensive technology (as security and privacy is key to gaining customer approval). E-banking services are designed to support the true integration of trade documentation with financing products and cash management on consistent platforms linking banks with corporate customers via multiple channels, from Web-based to fully integrated using Web services or electronic data interchange–related technologies. Advantage should be taken of the current technology as it can help manage fair lending, pricing, fraud detection, and other aspects of compliance and risk.

Transaction/operations risk arises from fraud, processing errors, system disruptions, or other unanticipated events resulting in the institution's inability to deliver products or services. This risk exists in each product and service offered. The level of transaction risk is affected by the structure of the institution's processing environment, including the types of services offered and the complexity of the processes and supporting technology. In most instances, e-banking activities will increase the complexity of the institution's activities and the quantity of its transaction/operations risk. E-banking has unique characteristics that may increase an institution's overall risk profile and the level of risks associated with traditional financial services, particularly strategic, operational, legal, and reputation risks. These unique e-banking characteristics include:

- Speed of technological change
- Changing customer expectations
- Increased visibility of publicly accessible networks (e.g., the Internet)
- Less face-to-face interaction with financial institution customers
- Need to integrate e-banking with the institution's legacy computer systems
- Dependence on third parties for necessary technical expertise
- Proliferation of threats and vulnerabilities in publicly accessible networks

The central authority should define the rules and regulations and share them with all banking organizations in order to reduce the level of risk. The risk can be measured both quantitatively and qualitatively. Information security is essential to a financial institution's ability to deliver e-banking services, protect the confidentiality and integrity of customer information, and ensure that accountability exists for changes to the information and the processing and communications systems. Depending on the extent of in-house technology, a financial institution's e-banking systems can make information security complex with numerous networking and information technology (IT) control issues. Financial institutions should have processes to identify, monitor, and address training needs. Each financial institution should train personnel in the technologies used and the institution's rules governing the use of that technology. Technical training is particularly important for those who oversee the key technology controls, such as firewalls, intrusion detection, and device configuration. Security awareness training is important for all users, including the institution's e-banking customers. Additionally, many institutions are using client/server systems and personal computers, rather than mainframe computers, to process customer transactions and maintain bank records. Accordingly, security and database management controls surrounding these client/servers and personal computers becomes very important.

Information technology (IT) has significantly impacted the financial services industry. IT has enabled transfers between different accounts at the tip of the fingers through the use of mobile and online banking. Banks offer a variety of capabilities with their mobile applications. For example, financial services firms of Citi, Wells Fargo, State Farm's Bank, and J. P. Morgan Chase provide several services such as: remote deposits, initiate or approve wire transfers and outgoing payments for corporate customers, online view transaction details, and other online banking services. Regulatory agencies have issued guidance addressing the safety and soundness aspects of electronic banking and personal computer banking and the security risks associated with the Internet and phone banking.

30.3 MORTGAGE BANKING ACTIVITIES

(a) OVERVIEW. Mortgage banking activities primarily include the origination or purchase, sale, and subsequent long-term servicing of mortgage loans. Mortgage loans are originated or purchased from a variety of sources including applications received directly from borrowers (retail originations) and loans acquired from mortgage brokers or other mortgage lenders (wholesale or correspondent purchases). These loans are then generally sold through the secondary mortgage market to permanent investors or retained by the lender in its own loan portfolio. Typically, loans are sold to permanent investors through conduits, although mortgage loans can also be sold through whole loan sales directly to investors or through public or private securitizations completed by the mortgage banker. Secondary market conduits include government-sponsored entities such as Government National Mortgage Association (GNMA), Federal National Mortgage Association (FNMA), and Federal Home Loan Mortgage Corp (FHLMC), and other private companies involved in the acquisition and securitization of mortgage loans. Loan servicing includes the collection, recording, and remittance to investors of monthly mortgage payments, the maintenance of records relating to the loans, and the management of escrows for taxes and insurance. In return for performing these servicing activities, mortgage servicers earn a fee, which is usually a percentage of the loan's unpaid principal balance. Profits are earned from loan servicing activities if the mortgage banker's cost of performing the servicing of the loans is less than the fee received. The major risks associated with mortgage banking are interest rate risk associated with the loans in the pipeline and warehouse, credit risk associated with loans held for sale or held in portfolio, operational risk associated with performing servicing functions improperly, and prepayment risk associated with mortgage servicing rights.

(b) ACCOUNTING GUIDANCE. The principal accounting guidance for the mortgage banking industry is found in SFAS No. 65, SFAS No. 91, and SFAS No. 140. SFAS No. 140 supersedes SFAS No. 125. SFAS No. 140 is effective for transfers and servicing of financial assets and extinguishments of liabilities occurring after March 31, 2001, and is to be applied prospectively. Earlier or retroactive application is not permitted. The EITF also has addressed several issues related to the accounting for mortgage banking activities. The EITF represents the source of authoritative standards of accounting and reporting, other than those issued by the SEC, to be applied by nongovernmental entities.

An *EITF Update* summarizes issues discussed at meetings held by the EITF, including an overview of both consensuses and consensuses for exposure. Because consensuses and consensuses for exposure are subject to ratification by the FASB, and because some details of the conclusions reached at an EITF meeting are determined during the process of developing the meeting minutes, the contents of the EITF Update are preliminary.

(c) MORTGAGE LOANS HELD FOR SALE. Mortgage loans held for sale represent a mortgage banker's inventory of loans that have been originated or purchased and are awaiting sale to permanent investors. SFAS No. 65 requires that mortgage loans held for sale be reported at the lower of their cost or market value, determined as of the balance sheet date determined on an individual loan or aggregate basis. The excess of cost over market value is required to be accounted for as a valuation allowance with changes in the valuation allowance included in net income of the period in which the change occurs. SFAS No. 91 requires that loan origination fees and direct loan origination costs be deferred until the related loan is sold. Therefore, any net deferred fees or costs should be included in the cost basis of the loan and considered in determining the required valuation allowance at any balance sheet date. Capitalized costs of acquiring the rights to service mortgage loans associated with the purchase or origination of these assets should be excluded from the cost of the mortgage loans for the purposes of determining lower of cost or market. Likewise, the fair value of the servicing rights associated with the loans included in a mortgage banker's loans held for sale classification should be excluded from the determination of lower of cost or market.

The market value of mortgage loans held for sale is determined by type of loan. At a minimum, separate determinations of market value for residential and commercial mortgage loans shall be made. Either the aggregate or individual loan basis may be used in determining the lower of cost or market value for each type of loan under SFAS No. 65. The market value for loans subject to investor purchase commitments is based on those commitment prices. The market value for uncommitted loans held on a speculative basis is based on the market in which the mortgage banker normally operates.

At any balance sheet date, a mortgage banker will also have outstanding rate commitments, which represent commitments made to loan applicants to fund a loan at a locked-in interest rate provided that loan application eventually closes. These rate commitments make up a mortgage banker's pipeline. SFAS No. 65 does not specifically address a mortgage banker's pipeline as being subject to a lower of cost or market determination. However, the pipeline should be evaluated for the impact of any adverse commitments. This may be done in conjunction with the lower of cost or market analysis on loans held for sale. The analysis of the pipeline typically would be done only on those commitments expected to become loans (i.e., close) and not on those loans expected to fall out (i.e., not close). The existence of losses inherent in the pipeline after adjustment for fallout often can be determined by comparing commitment prices to investor delivery prices for similar loans. If any losses are determined to exist in the mortgage banker's pipeline, the loss should be accrued pursuant to SFAS No. 5.

(d) MORTGAGE LOANS HELD FOR INVESTMENT. Mortgage loans can be originated or purchased by a mortgage banker with the intention of holding the loan to maturity, or the loans can be transferred into a mortgage banker's loans held for investment category from a loans held for sale category after it is determined that the loan is unsalable or the mortgage banker decides to retain the loan for investment purposes. SFAS No. 65 requires that mortgage loans held for investment be reported at cost. For mortgage loans transferred into mortgage loans held for investment from loans held for sale, their initial cost basis must be determined as the lower of the loan's cost or market value on the date of the transfer. A mortgage loan must not be classified as held for investment unless the mortgage banker has both the intent and the ability to hold the loan for the foreseeable future or until maturity.

If the ultimate recovery of the carrying amount of a mortgage loan held as a long-term investment is doubtful, and the impairment is considered to be other than temporary, the carrying amount of the loan must be reduced to its expected collectable amount, which then becomes its new cost basis. The amount of the reduction is recorded as a loss. A recovery from the new cost basis is reported as a gain only at the sale, maturity, or disposition of the loan.

As noted, SFAS No. 91 requires that loan origination fees and direct loan origination costs be deferred. For mortgage loans held for investment, any net deferred fees or costs should be included in the cost basis of the loan and amortized into interest income on a level yield method. Under level-yield method, unamortized premiums and discounts are taken into income so as to recognize accounting income less coupon interest plus amortized premium or discount at a constant yield over the life of an investment. It calculates income for each period by multiplying the beginning of period carrying value by the internal rate of return of the investment. The carrying value is then increased by income and reduced by cash flow to get the next period's carrying value.

(e) SALES OF MORTGAGE LOANS AND SECURITIES. Mortgage bankers typically sell the majority of the loans they originate or purchase to third-party investors in order to remove these loans from their balance sheets and provide funds for the continued origination and purchase of future loans. The sale of mortgage loans results in a gain or loss that should be recognized when the mortgage banker has surrendered control over the assets to a purchaser in a manner such that the transfer of the loans can be accounted for as a sale. SFAS No. 140, which provides guidance concerning the transfers and servicing of financial assets and extinguishments of liabilities, states that a transfer of financial assets in which the transferor surrenders control over those financial assets must be accounted for as a sale to the extent that consideration other than beneficial interests in the transferred assets have been received in exchange.

The control over financial assets is deemed to have been surrendered under SFAS No. 140 to the extent that all of the next three conditions have been met:

1. The transferred assets have been isolated from the transferor (i.e., put presumptively beyond the reach of the transferor and its creditors even in bankruptcy).
2. Each transferee has the right to pledge or exchange the transferred assets, and no condition both constrains the transferee from taking advantage of its right to pledge or exchange and provides more than a trivial benefit to the transferor.
3. The transferor does not maintain effective control over the transferred assets through either: (a) an agreement that both entitles and obligates the transferor to repurchase or redeem them before their maturity, or (b) the ability to unilaterally cause the holder to return specified assets, other than through a clean-up call.

The sale of mortgage loans can occur primarily through one of three methods. Loans can be sold (1) through whole loan or bulk transactions to third-party investors where individual loans or groups of loans are transferred; (2) through government-sponsored MBS programs of investors such as FNMA, FHLMC, or GNMA; and (3) through private securitizations where the originator or loan purchaser will securitize and sell directly to third-party investors interests in an underlying pool of mortgage loans.

The most common type of sale utilized by mortgage bankers is the sale of MBSs through programs sponsored by FNMA, FHLMC, and GNMA. These sales are relatively straightforward and generally do not have the complex kinds of terms that could call into question sale treatment for the transfer under SFAS No. 140. Whole loan sales are also generally straightforward and do not present complex SFAS No. 140 sales issues; however, in instances where MBSs or whole loans are sold through private securitizations or on a recourse basis, surrender of control issues under SFAS No. 140 may be encountered.

Depending on the type of structure utilized in a private mortgage loan securitization, including those with terms where significant interests in securitized pools are retained, those with significant continued involvement of the seller in the securitized pool, and those with unusual legal structures, the attainment of sale accounting under SFAS No. 140 may also not be straightforward and may be difficult to assess. Careful consideration should be given to the requirements of SFAS No. 140 to ensure that a sale of the mortgage loans has occurred before a gain or loss on the transaction can be realized.

(i) Gain or Loss on Sale of Mortgage Loans. Upon completion of a transfer of mortgage loans that satisfies the conditions of SFAS No. 140 to qualify as a sale, the mortgage banker allocates the previous cost basis of the loans, including all deferred SFAS No. 91 costs and fees, between interests sold (i.e., the underlying loans) and interests retained (i.e., the loans' servicing rights, or other retained portions of a securitization such as residual spreads, subordinate bonds, and interest-only or principal-only strips) based on the relative fair value of those components on the date of the sale. The allocated basis assigned to interests in the mortgage loans that are sold should then be derecognized, and a gain or loss calculated as the difference between this allocated basis and proceeds received on the sale, net of any assets or liabilities created in the transaction that should be recorded. Newly created assets and liabilities from the sale should be recorded initially at their fair value and accounted for in accordance with current GAAP for similar assets and liabilities. Interests retained in the sale of mortgage loans are recorded initially at their allocated cost basis and subsequently accounted for in accordance with current GAAP for similar assets and liabilities.

(ii) Financial Assets Subject to Prepayment. Interest-only strips, loans, and other receivables and retained interests from sales or securitizations of mortgage loans that can be contractually prepaid or otherwise settled in a way such that the holder would not recover substantially all of its recorded investment are subsequently measured like investments in debt securities and classified as available-for-sale or trading assets under SFAS No. 115.

(f) MORTGAGE SERVICING RIGHTS. A mortgage banking entity may purchase mortgage servicing rights separately, or it may acquire mortgage servicing rights by purchasing or originating mortgage loans and selling or securitizing those mortgage loans with the servicing rights retained. When a mortgage banker purchases or originates mortgage loans, the cost of acquiring those loans includes the cost of the related servicing rights. These servicing rights become separate and distinct assets only when their respective mortgage loans are sold with the servicing rights retained.

SFAS No. 140 provides the primary accounting guidance for mortgage servicing rights and requires that servicing assets and other retained interests in the mortgage loans sold be measured by allocating the previous carrying amount of the mortgage loans (as previously discussed) between the mortgage loans sold and the servicing rights retained, based on their relative fair values at the date of the sale. FASB statement No. or SFAS No. 125 amends and extends to all servicing assets and liabilities the accounting standards for mortgage servicing rights now in FASB Statement No. 65, and supersedes FASB Statement No. 122, *Accounting for Mortgage Servicing Rights.*

Previously, net mortgage servicing rights were recognized as assets, and the amount recognized as net mortgage servicing rights was based on the fair value of certain expected cash inflows, net of expected cash outflows. The expected cash inflows (future servicing revenues) includes a normal servicing fee, expected late charges, and other ancillary revenues. The expected cash outflow (future servicing costs) includes various costs of performing the servicing.

SFAS No. 140 also requires that servicing assets and liabilities be subsequently (1) amortized in proportion to and over the period of estimated net servicing income or loss and (2) assessed for asset impairment or increased obligation based on their fair values.

SFAS No. 140 requires that a mortgage banking enterprise assess its capitalized mortgage servicing rights for impairment based on the fair value of those rights. A mortgage banking enterprise should stratify its mortgage servicing rights based on one or more of the predominant risk characteristics of the underlying loans. Impairment should be recognized through a valuation allowance for each impaired stratum. Each stratum should be recorded at the lower of cost or market value.

(i) Initial Capitalization of Mortgage Servicing Rights. Under SFAS No. 140, each time an entity undertakes an obligation to service mortgage loans, the entity must recognize either a servicing asset or a servicing liability for that servicing contract, unless it retains the underlying mortgage loans as an investment on its balance sheet. If a servicing asset was purchased or assumed rather than undertaken in a sale or securitization of the mortgage loans being serviced, the servicing asset is measured initially at its fair value, presumptively the price paid for the right to service the underlying loans.

Under SFAS No. 140, servicing rights retained in a sale of mortgage loans are initially recorded on the balance sheet at their allocated portion of the total cost of the mortgage loans purchased or originated. The allocation of the total cost basis of the mortgage loans is based on the relative fair values of the mortgage loans and their respective servicing rights.

(ii) Amortization of Mortgage Servicing Rights. SFAS No. 140 requires that amounts capitalized as servicing assets (net of any recorded valuation allowances) be amortized in proportion to, and over the period of, estimated net servicing income. For this purpose, estimates of future servicing revenue include expected late charges and other ancillary revenue, including float. Estimates of expected future servicing costs include direct costs associated with performing the servicing function and appropriate allocations of other costs. Estimated future servicing costs may be determined on an incremental cost basis.

(iii) Impairment of Mortgage Servicing Rights. For the purpose of evaluating and measuring impairment of servicing assets, SFAS No. 140 requires that servicing assets be stratified based on one or more of the predominant risk characteristics of the underlying loans. Those characteristics may include loan type, size, note rate, date of origination, term, and geographic location. Historically, note or interest rate has been the predominant prepayment risk characteristic considered by most mortgage bankers because, in declining interest rate environments, loans have tended to prepay more rapidly with corresponding impairment to the servicing asset.

Impairment is recognized through a valuation allowance for an individual stratum. The amount of impairment recognized is the amount by which the carrying value of the servicing assets in a stratum exceeds their fair value. The fair value of servicing assets that have not been recognized through a sale or securitization must not be used in the evaluation of impairment.

Subsequent to the initial measurement of impairment, the mortgage banking enterprise must adjust the valuation allowance to reflect changes in the measurement of impairment. Fair value in excess of the amount capitalized as servicing assets (net of amortization), however, must not be recognized. SFAS No. 140 does not address when a mortgage banking enterprise should record a direct write-down of servicing assets.

(iv) Fair Value of Mortgage Servicing Rights. A nonpublic entity must make a policy decision of whether to measure all of its liabilities incurred under share-based payment arrangements at fair value or to measure all such liabilities at intrinsic value. Regardless of the method selected, a nonpublic entity must remeasure its liabilities under share-based payment arrangements at each reporting date until the date of settlement. The fair value–based method is preferable for purposes of justifying a change in accounting principle under FASB Statement No. 154, *Accounting Changes and Error Corrections*. Assumptions used to estimate the fair value of equity and liability equipments granted to employees should be determined in a consistent manner from period to period.

The subprime scandals of 2008 can be attributed to many factors, including the improper application of fair value estimates by the real estate appraising industry. The conflicting interest between real estate appraisal firms and real estate brokerage firms provided incentives and opportunities for the appraisals to provide fair value estimates above and beyond reasonable and realistic fair value to get financing needs to close the deal. Banks had all the incentives and opportunities to get the highest fair value estimates to provide subprime loans to customers and then sell the mortgages to mortgage buyers such as Freddie Mac and Fannie Mae, quasi-government corporations established to buy up mortgages from banks. The other factor is banks' securitization vehicles of variable interest entities or SPEs. The appropriate tone set at the top by management regarding corporate culture within which financial reports are produced is vital to the integrity of financial reporting process. When the tone set at the top is lax, fraudulent financial reporting is more likely to occur and not be prevented.

SFAS No. 140 defines the fair value of an asset or a liability as the amount at which that asset or liability could be bought or sold in a current transaction between willing parties (i.e., other than in a forced or liquidation sale). Quoted market prices in active markets are the best evidence of fair value and under SFAS No. 140 are to be used as the basis for the measurement, if available. The FASB and the International Accounting Standards Board both agree pm fair value as an exit price. Both standard setters are trying to converge their accounting standards by 2012. Fair value, or mark to market, accounting has been controversial and blamed for helping exacerbate the financial crisis.

Standard setters have shown some flexibility in allowing financial institutions more discretion in valuing assets such as MBSs in recent years. If a quoted market price is available, the fair value is the product of the number of trading units' times that market price. If quoted market prices are not available, the estimate of fair value is based on the best information available in the circumstances. The estimate of fair value must consider prices for similar assets or liabilities and the results of valuation techniques to the extent available in the circumstances. Examples of valuation techniques include the present value of estimated expected future cash flows using a discount rate commensurate with the risks involved, option-pricing models, matrix pricing, option-adjusted spread models, and fundamental analysis. Valuation techniques for measuring financial assets and liabilities and servicing assets and liabilities must be consistent with the objective of measuring fair value. Those techniques should incorporate assumptions that market participants would use in their estimates of values, future revenues, and future expenses, including assumptions about interest rates, default, prepayment, and volatility. In measuring financial liabilities and servicing liabilities at fair value by discounting estimated future cash flows, an objective is to use discount rates at which those liabilities could be settled in an arm's-length transaction.

Estimates of expected future cash flows, if used to estimate fair value, should be the best estimate based on reasonable and supportable assumptions and projections. All available evidence must be considered in developing estimates of expected future cash flows. The weight given to the evidence should be commensurate with the extent to which the evidence can be verified objectively. If a range is estimated for either the amount or the timing of possible cash flows, the likelihood of possible outcomes must be considered in determining the best estimate of future cash flows.

If it is not practicable to estimate the fair values of assets, the transferor records those assets at zero. If it is not practicable to estimate the fair values of liabilities, the transferor recognizes no gain on the transaction and records those liabilities at the greater of:

- The excess, if any, of (1) the fair values of assets obtained less the fair values of other liabilities incurred, over (2) the sum of the carrying values of the assets transferred
- The amount that would be recognized in accordance with SFAS No. 5, as interpreted by FASB Interpretation No. 14, *Reasonable Estimation of the Amount of a Loss*

SFAS No. 157, *Fair Value Measurements,* categorizes the source of information used in fair value measurements into three levels: (1) Level 1, where there are observable inputs from quoted prices in active markets; (2) Level 2, where there are indirectly observable inputs from quoted prices of comparable items in active markets, identical items in inactive markets, or other market-related information; and (3) Level 3, where there are unobservable, firm-generated inputs in determining fair value.

(v) Sales of Mortgage Servicing Rights. EITF No. 95-5 provides the primary accounting guidance for sales of mortgage servicing rights. It determines of what risks and rewards, if any, can be retained and whether any unresolved contingencies may exist in a sale of mortgage loan servicing rights. The consensus reached in EITF No. 95-5 states that a sale of mortgage servicing rights should be recognized at the date title passes if substantially all risks and rewards of ownership have irrevocably passed to the buyer and any protection provisions retained by the seller are minor and can be reasonably estimated. If a sale is recognized and minor protection provisions exist, a liability should be accrued for the estimated obligation associated with those provisions. The seller retains only minor protection provisions if (1) the obligation associated with those provisions is estimated to be no more than 10 percent of the sales price and (2) the risk of prepayment is retained by the seller for no more than 120 days. The consensus additionally noted that a temporary subservicing agreement in which the seller would subservice the loans for a short period of time after the sale would not necessarily preclude recognizing a sale at the closing date.

(vi) Retained Interests. In certain asset sale or securitizations transactions, the mortgage banker may retain an interest in the transferred assets. Examples of retained interests include servicing assets, interest-only strips, and retained (or residual) interests in securitizations. Historically, excess servicing resulted from the sale of loans where the contractual service fee (the difference between the mortgage rate and the pass-through rate to the investor in the loans, after deducting any guarantee fees) was greater than a normal servicing fee rate. This excess servicing asset was then capitalized separately and subsequently accounted for distinctly from the normal servicing asset recorded. Under SFAS No. 140, the accounting distinction for excess servicing fees was eliminated. In general, under agency servicing contracts, past excess servicing fees represent contractually specified servicing fees as defined under SFAS No. 140 and are combined with servicing rights as a servicing asset. The combined servicing asset will then be subject to the stratified impairment test that was described in Subsection 30.3(f)(iii).

Generally, a servicing fee in excess of a contractually stated servicing fee would only be encountered in an instance where an entity securitizes and sells mortgage loans and creates an interest-only strip above and beyond the compensation allocated to the loan's servicer in the pooling and servicing agreements. If it is determined that an entity's excess servicing fees exceed contractually specified amounts, those amounts would be required to be classified as interest-only strips under SFAS No. 140.

Interest-only strips are rights to future interest income from the serviced assets that exceed contractually specified servicing fees. Interest-only strips are not servicing assets, they are financial assets. These assets should be recorded originally at allocated cost and recorded subsequently as an available-for-sale or trading asset in accordance with SFAS No. 115.

Retained or residual interests in securitizations represents the mortgage banker's right to receive cash flows from the mortgage assets that are not required to:

1. Pay certificate holders their contractual amounts of principal and interest
2. Fund reserve accounts stipulated in the securitization structure
3. Pay expenses of the securitization
4. Make any other payments stipulated in the securitization

Such retained interests must be evaluated for impairment pursuant to EITF No. 99-20, *Recognition of Interest Income and Impairment on Purchased and Retained Beneficial Interests in Securitized Financial Assets.*

(g) TAXATION. Mortgage banks are subject to federal income taxes and certain state and local taxes. The British government now requires all U.K. banks to sign tax avoidance code to ensure that they pay their share of tax at a time of tight budgetary process and public spending. The taxation of mortgage banks is extremely complex; therefore, a discussion in depth is beyond the scope of this *Handbook.* However, certain significant factors of mortgage banking taxation are discussed next.

(i) Mortgage Servicing Rights. The tax treatment of servicing rights changed substantially in 1991 for both mortgage loan originators and subsequent purchasers of mortgage loans. Under Revenue Rule 91-46, a lender selling mortgages while retaining the right to service the loans for an amount in excess of reasonable compensation is deemed to have two types of income resulting from a servicing contract: normal (i.e., reasonable) and excess servicing compensation.

Generally, taxable income for normal servicing is recognized as received (i.e., as asset is not created at the time of loan sale as it is for book purposes); thus, a book-to-tax difference will exist upon sale of the underlying loan to a third party. Income deemed received for excess servicing is included in income on a yield-to-maturity basis.

The Treasury has provided safe harbor amounts offering guidance to what is deemed normal or reasonable compensation. Normal compensation is for the performance of general mortgage services, including a contract requiring the servicer to collect the periodic mortgage payments from the mortgagors and remit these payments to mortgage owners.

The safe harbors establish that compensation for the performance of all services under the mortgage servicing contracts should generally be between 25 and 44 basis points, annually, determined more specifically on the type of residential loans. Guidance as to reasonable compensation on commercial mortgages has not been provided; it is the taxpayer's responsibility to establish and support what is reasonable compensation for the services it performs.

Excess servicing is those funds received in excess of reasonable compensation, thus the term *excess servicing rights.* Excess servicing rights have been determined to represent a stripped coupon, while the underlying mortgage that was sold represents a stripped bond. The fair value of the stripped coupon (i.e., servicing right) is determined based on the relevant facts and circumstances.

The mortgage servicing business is fueled by volume; thus, it is common for a mortgage bank to be an originator of mortgage loans, a purchaser of mortgage loans, and a purchaser of servicing. If both the loan and the servicing right are purchased, and the loan is subsequently sold with servicing retained, tax treatment generally will follow the same treatment as if the seller originated the mortgage loan.

This treatment is significantly different from the purchase of mortgage servicing rights only. Purchased mortgage servicing rights are amortized over 15 years when acquired in connection with a trade or business or over 108 months when a servicing portfolio is acquired separately. Certain restrictions prevent the recognition of loss in value of a servicing portfolio unless the entire portfolio or individually identified loans within a pool of serviced loans are disposed of; thus, taxpayers may have difficulty realizing the loss in value of a servicing portfolio that has significant prepayments until all the underlying mortgages have been paid down.

(ii) Mark to Market. Contrary to normal realization-based tax accounting principles, IRC Section 475 requires dealers in securities to recognize gain or loss through marking-to-market their securities holdings, unless such securities are validly identified by the taxpayer as excepted from the provisions.

As used in this context, the terms *dealer* and *securities* have very broad application. Virtually all financial institutions are considered dealers in securities for mark-to-market purposes though regulations provide exceptions for certain institutions not engaging in more than de minimus dealer activities. Securities required to be marked (unless validly identified as excepted) include notes, bonds, and other evidences of indebtedness; stock; notional principal contracts; or any evidence of an interest in or a derivative of such security (other than Section 1256(a) contracts); and any clearly identified hedge of such security.

Securities that may be identified as exempted from the mark-to-market provisions are:

- Securities held for investment, and property identified as such for tax purposes.
- Notes and other evidences of indebtedness (and obligations to acquire such) that are acquired or originated by the taxpayer in the ordinary course of a trade or business that are not held for sale.
- Hedges of positions or liabilities that are not securities in the hands of the taxpayer, and hedges of positions or liabilities that are exempt from mark to market under the two foregoing provisions. This does not apply for hedges held as a dealer.

To be exempted from mark to market, the security must be identified by the taxpayer on a contemporaneous basis (generally, day of acquisition) as meeting one of the exceptions.

Whether a security is required to be marked to market for financial accounting purposes is *not* dispositive for purposes of determining whether such security is treated as held for investment or not held for sale.

Some financial institutions identify all or a significant portion of their loans to customers as exempted from the mark-to-market provisions because they intend to hold those loans to maturity. A possible exception are mortgages that are originated for sale (pipeline or warehoused loans), which do not meet the exception criteria and must be marked to market.

30.4 INVESTMENT COMPANIES

(a) BACKGROUND. An investment company (referred to as a *fund* or a *mutual fund*) generally pools investors' funds to provide them with professional investment management and diversification of ownership in the securities markets. Typically, an investment company sells its capital shares to the public and invests the net proceeds in stock, bonds, government obligations, or other securities, intended to meet the fund's stated investment objectives. A brief history of investment companies is included in paragraphs 1.07 and 1.08 of the *AICPA Audit and Accounting Guide,* Audits of Investment Companies. One of the more notable distinctions between investment companies and companies in other industries is the extremely high degree of compliance to which registered investment companies must adhere. The *Audit and Accounting Guide* summarizes applicable practices and delivers how-to advice for handling almost every type of financial statement. It describes relevant matters, conditions, and procedures unique to the investment industry, and illustrates treatments of financial statements and reports to caution auditors and accountants about unusual problems. As a financial statement preparer or auditor, it is essential to understand the unique operational, regulatory, accounting, reporting, and auditing aspects of investment companies. AICPA publications provide background on the industry as well as interpretive guidance for both new and existing rules.

(i) Securities and Exchange Commission Statutes. The SEC is responsible for the administration and enforcement of these statutes governing investment companies:

- *Securities Act of 1933.* Governs the content of prospectuses and addresses the public offering and distribution of securities (including debt securities and the capital shares of investment companies).
- *Securities Exchange Act of 1934.* Regulates the trading of securities in secondary markets after the initial public offering and distribution of the securities under the 1933 Act. Periodic SEC financial reporting requirements pursuant to Section 13 or Section 15(d) of the 1934 Act are satisfied by the semiannual filing of Form N-SAR pursuant to Section 30 of the 1940 Act.
- *Investment Advisers Act of 1940.* Requires persons who are paid to render investment advice to individuals or institutions, including investment companies, to register with the SEC and regulates their conduct and contracts.
- *Investment Company Act of 1940.* Regulates registered investment companies and provides extensive rules and regulations that govern record keeping, reporting, fiduciary duties, and other responsibilities of an investment company's management.

(ii) Types of Investment Companies. Three common methods of classification are by securities law definition, by investment objectives, and by form of organization.

Classification by Securities Law Definition. Securities law divides investment companies into three types: management companies, face amount certificate companies, and unit investment trusts. The most common classification is the management company. The term *mutual fund* refers to an open-end management company as described under Section 5 of the 1940 Act. Such a fund stands ready to redeem its shares at net asset value whenever requested to do so and usually continuously offers its shares for sale, although it is not required to do so. A closed-end management company does not stand ready to redeem its shares when requested (although it may occasionally make tender offers for its shares) and generally does not issue additional shares, except perhaps in connection with a dividend reinvestment program. Its outstanding shares are usually traded on an exchange, often at a premium or discount from the fund's underlying net asset value. In addition to open-end and closed-end management companies, there are also management companies that offer the ability for shareholders to redeem their shares periodically on specified dates or intervals.

Other management investment companies include small business investment companies (SBICs) and business development companies (BDCs). Management companies, at their own election, are further divided into diversified companies and nondiversified companies. A fund that elects to be a diversified company must meet the 75 percent test required under Section 5(b)(1) of the 1940 Act. Nondiversified companies are management companies that have elected to be nondiversified and do not have to meet the requirements of Section 5(b)(1).

The 1940 Act also provides for face amount certificate companies, which are rather rare, and unit investment trusts. Unit investment trusts normally are established under a trust indenture by a sponsoring organization that acquires a portfolio (often tax-exempt or taxable bonds that are generally held to maturity) and then sells undivided interests in the trust. Units of the trust may be offered continuously, such as for a trust purchasing treasury securities, but normally do not make any additional portfolio acquisitions. Units remain outstanding until they are tendered for redemption or the trust is terminated.

Separate accounts of an insurance company that underlie variable annuity and variable life insurance products are also subject to the requirements of the 1940 Act. They may be established as management companies or as unit investment trusts. Variable annuities and variable life products are considered to be both securities subject to the 1933 Act and insurance products subject to regulation by state insurance departments.

Classification by Investment Objectives. Investment companies can also be classified by their investment objectives or types of investments—for example, growth funds, income funds, tax-exempt funds, global funds, money market funds, and equity funds.

Classification by Form of Organization. Investment companies can also be classified by their form of organization. Funds may be organized as corporations or trusts (and, to a lesser extent, as partnerships).

Incorporation offers the advantages of detailed state statutory and interpretative judicial decisions governing operations and limited liability of shareholders, and, in normal cases, it requires no exemptions to comply with the 1940 Act.

The business trust, or Massachusetts trust, is an unincorporated business association established by a declaration or deed of trust and governed largely by the law of trusts. In general, a business trust has the advantages of unlimited authorized shares, no annual meeting requirement, and long duration. However, Massachusetts trusts have a potential disadvantage in that there is unlimited liability to the business trust shareholders in the event of litigation or other negative factors. Generally, however, the trust undertakes to indemnify the shareholders against loss.

(b) FUND OPERATIONS. When a new fund is established, it enters into a contract with an investment adviser (often the sponsoring organization) to manage the fund and, within the terms of the fund's stated investment objectives, to determine what securities should be purchased, sold, or exchanged. The investment adviser places orders for the purchase or sale of portfolio securities for the fund with brokers or dealers selected by it. The officers of the fund, who generally are also officers of the investment adviser or fund administrator, give instructions to the custodian of the fund holdings as to delivery of securities and payments of cash for the account of the fund. The investment adviser normally furnishes, at its own expense, all necessary advisory services, facilities, and personnel in connection with these responsibilities. The investment adviser may also act as administrator;

administrative duties include preparation of regulatory filings and managing relationships with other service providers. The investment adviser and administrator are usually paid for these services through a fee based on the value of net assets.

The distributor or underwriter for an investment company markets the shares of the fund—either directly to the public (no-load funds) or through a sales force. The sales force may be compensated for their services through a direct sales commission included in (deducted from) the price at which the fund's shares are offered (redeemed), through a distribution fee (also referred to as a 12b-1 plan fee) paid by the fund as part of its recurring expenses, or in both ways. Rule 12b-1 under the 1940 Act permits an investment company to pay for distribution expenses, which otherwise are paid for by the distributor and not the fund.

A fund has officers and directors (and in some cases, trustees) but generally has no employees, the services it requires being provided under contract by others. Primary servicing organizations are summarized below.

(i) Fund Accounting Agent. The fund accounting agent maintains the fund's general ledger and portfolio accounting records and computes the net asset value per share, usually on a daily basis. In some instances, this service is provided by the investment adviser or an affiliate of the adviser, or a nonaffiliated entity may perform this service. The fund accounting agent, or in some cases a separate administrative agent, may also be responsible for preparation of the fund's financial statements, tax returns, semiannual and annual filings with the SEC on Form N-SAR, and the annual registration statement filing.

(ii) Custodian. The custodian maintains custody of the fund's assets, collects income, pays expenses, and settles investment transactions. The 1940 Act provides for three alternatives in selecting a custodian. The most commonly used is a commercial bank or trust company that meets the requirements of Sections 17 and 26 of the 1940 Act. The second alternative is a member firm of a national securities exchange; the third alternative is for the fund to act as its own custodian and utilize the safekeeping facilities of a bank or trust company. Section 17(f) and Rules 17f-1 and 17f-2 of the 1940 Act provide for specific audit procedures to be performed by the fund's independent accountant when either alternative two or three is used.

(iii) Transfer Agent. The fund's transfer agent maintains the shareholder records and processes the sales and redemptions of the fund's capital shares. The transfer agent processes the capital share transactions at a price per share equal to the net asset value per share of the fund next determined by the fund accounting agent (forward pricing). In certain instances, shareholder servicing—the direct contact with shareholders, usually by telephone—is combined with the transfer agent processing.

(c) ACCOUNTING. The SEC has set forth in Financial Reporting Policies, Section 404.03, *Accounting, Valuation, and Disclosure of Investment Securities,* its views on accounting for securities by registered investment companies.

Because for federal income tax purposes the fund is a conduit for the shareholders, the operations of an investment company are normally influenced by federal income tax to the shareholder. Accordingly, conformity between book and tax accounting is usually maintained whenever practicable under GAAP. In general, investment companies carry securities, which are their most significant asset, at current value, not at historical cost. In such a mark-to-market environment, the deviation between book and tax accounting has no effect on net asset value.

Uniquely, most mutual funds close their books daily and calculate a net asset value per share, which forms the pricing basis for shareholders who are purchasing or redeeming fund shares. SEC Rules 2a-4 and 22c-1 set forth certain accounting requirements, including a 1 cent per share pricing criterion. Because of this daily closing of the books, mutual funds and their agents must maintain well-controlled and current accounting systems to provide proper records for their highly compliance-oriented industry.

The SEC has promulgated extensive rules under each of the statutes that it administers, including these:

- *Article 6 of Regulation S-X (Article 3-18 and Article 12-12).* Sets forth requirements as to the form and content of, and requirements for, financial statements filed with the SEC, including what financial statements must be presented and for what periods.
- *Financial reporting policies.* Section 404 relates specifically to registered investment companies.

(d) FINANCIAL REPORTING

(i) New Registrants. Any company registered under the 1940 Act that has not previously had an effective registration statement under the 1933 Act must include, in its initial registration statement, financial statements and financial highlights of a date within 90 days prior to the date of filing. For a company that did not have any prior operations, this would be limited to a seed capital statement of assets and liabilities and related notes.

Section 14 of the 1940 Act requires that an investment company have a net worth of at least $100,000. Accordingly, a new investment company is usually incorporated by its sponsor with seed capital of that amount.

(ii) General Reporting Requirements. The SEC reporting requirements are outlined in Section 30 of the 1940 Act and the related rules and regulations thereunder, which supersede any requirements under Section 13 or Section 15(d) of the 1934 Act to which an investment company would otherwise be subject. A registered management investment company is deemed by the SEC to have satisfied its requirement under the 1934 Act to file an annual report by the filing of semiannual reports on Form N-SAR.

The SEC requires that every registered management company send to its shareholders, at least semiannually, a report containing financial statements and financial highlights. Only the financial statements and financial highlights in the annual report are required to be audited.

Some funds prepare quarterly reports to shareholders, although they are not required to do so. They generally include a portfolio listing, and in relatively few cases, they include full financial statements. Closed-end funds listed on an exchange have certain quarterly reporting requirements under their listing agreements with the exchange.

(iii) Financial Statements. Article 6 of Regulation S-X deals specifically with investment companies and requires these statements:

- A statement of assets and liabilities (supported by a separate listing of portfolio securities) or a statement of net assets, which includes a detailed list of portfolio securities at the reporting date
- A statement of operations for the year
- A statement of changes in net assets for the latest two years

SFAS No. 95 provides that a statement of cash flows should be included with financial statements prepared in accordance with GAAP. This Statement requires that a statement of cash flows classify cash receipts and payments according to whether they stem from operating, investing, or financing activities and provides definitions of each category. It requires that information about investing and financing activities not resulting in cash receipts or payments in the period be provided separately. A business enterprise that provides a set of financial statements that reports both financial position and results of operations must also provide a statement of cash flows for each period for which results of operations are provided. The information provided in a statement of cash flows, if used with related disclosures and information in the other financial statements, should help investors, creditors, and others to assess:

- The enterprise's ability to generate positive future net cash flows
- The enterprise's ability to meet its obligations, its ability to pay dividends, and its needs for external financing
- The reasons for differences between net income and associated cash receipts and payments
- The effects on an enterprise's financial position of both its cash and noncash investing and financing transactions during the period

Financial statements that show only cash receipts and payments during a short period, such as a year, cannot adequately indicate whether an enterprise's performance is successful. Important uses of information about an entity's financial position include helping users to assess factors such as the entity's liquidity, financial flexibility, profitability, and risk.

SFAS No. 102 exempts investment companies from providing a statement of cash flows, provided certain conditions are met. A statement of changes in net assets should be given even if the statement of cash flows is presented because a statement of changes in net assets shows the changes in shareholders' equity required by GAAP and by Article 6 of Regulation S-X.

(e) TAXATION. Investment companies are subject to federal income taxes and certain state and local taxes. However, investment companies registered under the 1940 Act may qualify for special federal income tax treatment as regulated investment companies (RICs) under the IRC and may deduct dividends paid to shareholders. If a fund fails to qualify as an RIC, it will be taxed as a regular corporation, and the deduction for dividends paid by the fund is disallowed. Subchapter M (Sections 851–855) of the IRC applies to RICs. Chapter 6 of the *Audit Guide* discusses the tax considerations related to RICs.

To qualify as an RIC, the fund must:

- Be a domestic entity registered under the 1940 Act
- Derive 90 percent of its total income from dividends, interest, and gross gains on sales of securities
- Have 50 percent of its assets composed of cash, U.S. government securities, securities of other funds, and other issues, as defined
- Have not more than 25 percent of the value of its total assets invested in the securities (other than U.S. government securities or the securities of other regulated investment companies) of any one issuer or of two or more issuers controlled by the fund that are determined to be engaged in the same or similar trades or businesses

In order for an RIC to use its distributions to offset taxable income, it must distribute at least 90 percent of its net investment company taxable income and net tax-exempt interest income to its shareholders. Also, to avoid a 4 percent nondeductible excise tax, a fund must distribute, by December 31 of each year, 98 percent of its ordinary income measured on a calendar year basis and 98 percent of its net capital gains measured on a fiscal year basis ending October 31. Actual payment of the distribution must be before February 1 of the following year.

(f) FILINGS. SEC registration forms applicable to investment companies include:

- *Form N-8A.* The notification of registration under the 1940 Act.
- *Form N-1A.* The registration statement of open-end management investment companies under the 1940 and the 1933 Acts. (It is not to be used by SBICs, BDCs, or insurance company separate accounts.) The form describes in detail the company's objectives, policies, management, investment restrictions, and similar matters. The form consists of the prospectus, the statement of additional information, and a third section of other information, including detailed information on the SEC required yield calculations. Post-effective amendments on Form N-1A, including updated audited financial statements, must be filed and become effective under the 1933 and 1940 Acts within 16 months after the end of the period covered by the previous audited financial statements if the fund is to continue offering its shares.

- *Form N-SAR.* A reporting form used for semiannual and annual reports by all registered investment companies that have filed a registration statement that has become effective pursuant to the 1933 Act, with the exception of face amount certificate companies and BDCs. BDCs file periodic reports pursuant to Section 13 of the 1934 Act. Management investment companies file the form semiannually; unit investment trusts are only required to file annually. There is no requirement that the form or any of the items be audited. The annual report filed by a management investment company must be accompanied by a report on the company's system of internal accounting controls from its independent accountant. The requirement for an accountant's report on internal accounting controls does not apply to SBICs or to management investment companies not required by either the 1940 Act or any other federal or state law or rule or regulation thereunder to have an audit of their financial statements.
- *Form N-2.* A registration statement for closed-end funds comparable to Form N-1A for open-end funds. Under Rule 8b-16 of the 1940 Act, if certain criteria are met in the annual report of a closed-end fund, the fund may not need to annually update its Form N-2 filing with the SEC.
- *Forms N-1, N-3, N-4, and N-6.* The registration statements for various types of insurance-related products, including variable annuities and variable life insurance.
- *Form N-5.* The registration statement for SBICs, which are also licensed under the Small Business Investment Act of 1958, is used to register the SBIC under both the 1933 Act and the 1940 Act.
- *Form N-14.* The statement for registration of securities issued by investment companies in business combination transactions under the 1933 Act. It contains information about the companies involved in the transaction, including historical and pro forma financial statements.

(g) INVESTMENT PARTNERSHIPS—SPECIAL CONSIDERATIONS. Investment partnerships may be described generally as limited partnerships organized under state law to trade and/or invest in securities. They are sometimes also referred to as *hedge funds,* which has become a generic industry term for an investment partnership (or another nonpublic investment company), although this may be a misnomer depending on the partnership's investment strategy. Investment partnerships, if certain conditions are met, are generally not required to register under the 1940 Act and are also generally not subject to the IRC rules and regulations that apply to RICs.

An investment partnership is governed by its partnership agreement. This is the basis for legal, structural, operational, and accounting guidelines. The majority of the capital in an investment partnership is owned by its limited partners. The general partner usually has a minimal investment in the partnership, if any at all. Limited partners may be a variety of entities, including private and public pension plans, foreign investors, insurance companies, bank holding companies, and individuals. There are legal, regulatory, and accounting and tax considerations associated with each of these types of investors. For example, investment in an investment partnership by pension plans may subject the investment partnership to the rules and regulations of the Employee Retirement Income Security Act of 1974 (ERISA) (generally, investment partnerships will not be subject to ERISA if less than 25 percent of the partnership's capital is derived from pension or other employee benefit plan assets); foreign investors may be subject to foreign withholding taxes; and the number of partners in an investment partnership may subject the investment partnership to registration under the 1940 Act (generally, an investment partnership must have fewer than 100 partners [or must have partners who are all qualified purchasers] to avoid registration under the 1940 Act).

The limited partners are generally liable for the repayment and discharge of all debts and obligations of the investment partnership, but only to the extent of their respective interest in the partnership. They usually have no part in the management of the partnership and have no authority to act on behalf of the partnership in connection with any matter. The general partner can be an individual, a corporation, or other entity. The general partner usually has little or no investment in the investment partnership (often 1 percent of total contributed capital) and is responsible for the day-to-day administration of the investment partnership. The general partner, however, usually has unlimited liability for the repayment and discharge of all debts and obligations of the partnership irrespective of its interest in the partnership. The general partner may also be the investment adviser or an affiliate of the adviser.

Although investment partnerships are generally not investment companies as defined in federal securities laws, they do meet the definition of investment companies as contained in the *Audit Guide*. Accordingly, the *Audit Guide* is generally applicable to investment partnerships. There are, however, certain disclosure requirements in the *Audit Guide* to which most partnerships historically have taken exception and have not followed. The AICPA clarified the appropriate disclosure for partnerships in its issuance of SOP No. 95-2, *Financial Reporting for Nonpublic Investment Partnerships,* as amended by SOP No. 01-1, *Amendment to Scope of Statement of Position 95-2,* which is applicable for fiscal years beginning after December 15, 1994.

A partnership is classified as a pass-through entity for tax purposes, meaning that the partners, not the partnership, are taxed on the income, expenses, gains, and losses incurred by the partnership. The partners recognize the tax effects of the partnership's operations regardless of whether any distribution is made to such partners. This differs from a corporation, which incurs an entity level tax on its earnings and whose owners (stockholders) incur a second level of tax when the corporation's profits are distributed to them.

(h) OFFSHORE FUNDS—SPECIAL CONSIDERATIONS. Offshore funds may be described generally as investment funds set up to permit international investments with minimum tax burden on the fund shareholders. This is achieved by setting up the funds in countries with favorable tax laws and in countries with nonburdensome administrative regulations. Popular offshore locations include Bermuda, the Cayman Islands, and the Netherlands Antilles.

An offshore fund's shares are offered to investors (generally non-U.S.) residing outside the country in which the fund is domiciled. Assuming the offshore fund is not publicly sold in the United States and does not have more than 100 U.S. shareholders (or only qualified purchasers), the offshore fund will not be subject to SEC registration or reporting requirements. Similar to hedge funds, because of the lack of regulatory restrictions, offshore funds often have higher risk investment strategies than U.S. regulated funds.

A major U.S. tax advantage to non-U.S. shareholders of investing in U.S. securities through an offshore fund as opposed to a U.S. domiciled fund is the avoidance of certain U.S. withholding taxes. By investing through the offshore fund, the shareholder avoids withholding taxes on most U.S.-sourced interest income and short-term capital gains, which would be subject to withholding taxes if the amounts were paid to the non-U.S. shareholder through a U.S. domiciled fund. Offshore funds also avoid the U.S. IRC distribution requirements imposed on U.S. funds. This allows for the potential roll-up of income in the fund (i.e., the deferral of income recognition for the shareholder for tax purposes, depending on the tax residence of the shareholder).

Under new 1996 tax legislation, a fund's U.S. administrative and other activities, which were previously required to be performed offshore to comply with IRC Reg. Sec. 1.864–2(c)2 (the Ten Commandments), generally will not create tax nexus for U.S. federal income tax purposes. However, depending on the laws of the particular jurisdiction in which its U.S. activities are conducted, those same U.S. activities may under some circumstances create tax nexus in certain state or local jurisdictions. Careful consideration should be given to the potential state and local tax consequences of onshore activities before any activities that were previously recommended to be conducted outside the United States are brought onshore.

Fund managers and advisers should consider several nontax factors before bringing certain functions onshore. These include:

- Whether the performance of more operations onshore will make it more likely that the fund, manager, and/or advisers can be subject to the jurisdiction of U.S. courts and/or applicable U.S., state, or local laws and regulations
- The regulatory requirements of the fund's domicile (e.g., Luxembourg, Dublin, and Bermuda require administration and certain other functions to be performed locally)

- The investor's desire for confidentiality
- The potential applicability of federal, state, and local tax or other filing requirements
- The potential effect on prospectus disclosure

30.5 SOURCES AND SUGGESTED REFERENCES

Accounting Principles Board. Opinion 30, *Reporting the Results of Operations—Reporting the Effects of Disposal of a Segment of a Business and Extraordinary, Unusual and Infrequently Occurring Events and Transactions.* New York: AICPA, 1973.

Accounting Standards Codification 360, *Property, Plant, and Equipment, Overall, Scope and Scope Exceptions*. Available at *http://asc.fasb.org/link&sourceid=SL2163854-110220&objid=6390208*

American Institute of Certified Public Accountants. Accounting Standards Division, Statement of Position 78-9, *Accounting for Investments in Real Estate Ventures.* New York: Author, 1978.

———. AICPA Practice Bulletin No. 1, *Purpose and Scope of AcSEC Practice Bulletins and Procedures for Their Issuance* (1987), New York: Author, 1987.

———. AICPA Practice Bulletin No. 4, *Accounting for Foreign Debt/Equity Swaps.* New York: Author, 1988.

———. AICPA Practice Bulletin No. 5, *Income Recognition on Loans to Financially Troubled Countries.* New York: Author, 1998.

———. AICPA Practice Bulletin No. 6, *Amortization of Discounts on Certain Acquired Loans.* New York: Author, 1989.

———. *Audit and Accounting Guide,* Banks and Savings Institutions. New York: Author, 1997.

———. *Audits of Investment Companies.* New York: Author, 2001.

———. Statement of Position 92-3, *Accounting for Foreclosed Assets.* New York: Author, 1992.

———. Statement of Position 94-6, *Disclosure of Certain Significant Risks and Uncertainties.* New York: Author, 1994.

———. Statement of Position 95-2, *Financial Reporting for Nonpublic Investment Partnerships.* New York: Author, 1995.

———. Statement of Position 97-1, *Accounting by Participating Mortgage Loan Borrowers.* New York: Author, 1997.

———. Statement of Position 01-1, *Amendment to Scope of Statement of Position 95-2, Financial Reporting for Nonpublic Investment Partnerships.* New York: Author, 2001.

Ashcraft, A. B., and T. Schuermann. *Understanding the Securitization of Subprime Mortgage Credit.* New York: Federal Reserve Bank of New York, Staff Reports, 2008.

Bank for International Settlements (BIS) Basel Committee on Bank Supervision. *Principles for Sound Liquidity Risk Management and Supervision,* 2008. *www.bis.org/publ/bcbs.htm*

Bank for International Settlements (BIS) Basel Committee on Banking Supervision. *Microfinance Activities and the Core Principles for Effective Banking Supervision—Consultative Document,* August 2010. *www.bis.org/publ/bcbs.htm*

Bank for International Settlements (BIS) Basel Committee on Banking Supervision, Basel III: *International Framework for Liquidity Risk Measurement, Standards and Monitoring,* 2011. *www.bis.org/publ/bcbs188.htm*

Bank for International Settlements (BIS) Basel Committee on Banking Supervision: *Principles for Enhancing Corporate Governance,* October 2010. *http://www.bis.org/publ/bcbs176.htm*

Cammarano, N., and J. J. Klink Jr. *Real Estate Accounting and Reporting: A Guide for Developers, Investors, and Lenders*, 3rd ed. New York: John Wiley & Sons, 1995.

Dodd-Frank Wall Street Reform and Consumer Protection Act of 2010, Pub. L. 111-203, 2010.

Financial Accounting Standards Board. EITF Abstracts: A Summary of Proceedings of the FASB Emerging Issues Task Force, EITF Issue No. 84-7, *Termination of Interest Rate Swaps.* Norwalk, CT: Author, 1984.

———. EITF Abstracts: A Summary of Proceedings of the FASB Emerging Issues Task Force, EITF Issue No. 84-14, *Deferred Interest Rate Setting.* Norwalk, CT: Author, 1984.

______. EITF Abstracts: A Summary of Proceedings of the FASB Emerging Issues Task Force, EITF Issue No. 84-36, *Interest Rate Swap Transactions.* Norwalk, CT: Author, 1984.

______. EITF Abstracts: A Summary of Proceedings of the FASB Emerging Issues Task Force, EITF Issue No. 85-6, *Futures Implementation Question.* Norwalk, CT: Author, 1985.

______. EITF Abstracts: A Summary of Proceedings of the FASB Emerging Issues Task Force, EITF Issue No. 86-25, *Offsetting Foreign Currency Swaps.* Norwalk, CT: Author, 1986.

______. EITF Abstracts: A Summary of Proceedings of the FASB Emerging Issues Task Force, EITF Issue No. 86-28, *Accounting Implications of Indexed Debt Instruments.* Norwalk, CT: Author, 1986.

______. EITF Abstracts: A Summary of Proceedings of the FASB Emerging Issues Task Force, EITF Issue No. 87-1, *Deferral Accounting for Cash Securities That Are Used to Hedge Rate or Price Risk.* Norwalk, CT: Author, 1987.

______. EITF Abstracts: A Summary of Proceedings of the FASB Emerging Issues Task Force, EITF Issue No. 87-26, *Hedging of Foreign Currency Exposure with a Tandem Currency.* Norwalk, CT: Author, 1987.

______. EITF Abstracts: A Summary of Proceedings of the FASB Emerging Issues Task Force, EITF Issue No. 88-8, *Mortgage Swaps.* Norwalk, CT: Author, 1988.

______. EITF Abstracts: A Summary of Proceedings of the FASB Emerging Issues Task Force, EITF Issue No. 88-11, *Allocation of Recorded Investment When a Loan or Part of a Loan Is Sold.* Norwalk, CT: Author, 1995.

______. EITF Abstracts: A Summary of Proceedings of the FASB Emerging Issues Task Force, EITF Issue No. 90-17, *Hedging Foreign Currency Risk with Purchased Options.* Norwalk, CT: Author, 1990.

______. EITF Abstracts: A Summary of Proceedings of the FASB Emerging Issues Task Force, EITF Issue No. 91-1, *Hedging Intercompany Foreign Currency Risks.* Norwalk, CT: Author, 1991.

______, EITF Abstracts: A Summary of Proceedings of the FASB Emerging Issues Task Force, EITF Issue No. 91-4, *Hedging Foreign Currency Risk with Complex Options and Similar Transactions.* Norwalk, CT: Author, 1991.

______. EITF Abstracts: A Summary of Proceedings of the FASB Emerging Issues Task Force, EITF Issue No. 93-10, *Accounting for Dual Currency Bonds.* Norwalk, CT: Author, 1993.

______. EITF Abstracts: A Summary of Proceedings of the FASB Emerging Issues Task Force, EITF Issue No. 94-7, *Accounting for Financial Instruments Indexed to, and Potentially Settled in, a Company's Own Stock.* Norwalk, CT: Author, 1994.

______. EITF Abstracts: A Summary of Proceedings of the FASB Emerging Issues Task Force, EITF Issue No. 94-8, *Accounting for Conversion of a Loan into a Debt Security in a Debt Restructuring.* Norwalk, CT: Author, 1994.

______. EITF Abstracts: A Summary of Proceedings of the FASB Emerging Issues Task Force, EITF Issue No. 94-9, *Determining a Normal Servicing Fee Rate for the Sale of an SBA Loan.* Norwalk, CT: Author, 1994.

______. EITF Abstracts: A Summary of Proceedings of the FASB Emerging Issues Task Force, EITF Issue No. 95-2, *Determination of What Constitutes a Firm Commitment for Foreign Currency Transactions Not Involving a Third Party.* Norwalk, CT: Author, 1995.

______. EITF Abstracts: A Summary of Proceedings of the FASB Emerging Issues Task Force, EITF Issue No. 95-5, *Determination of What Risks and Rewards, If Any, Can Be Retained and Whether Any Unresolved Contingencies May Exist in a Sale of Mortgage Loan Servicing Rights.* Norwalk, CT: Author, 1995.

______. EITF Abstracts: A Summary of Proceedings of the FASB Emerging Issues Task Force, EITF Issue No. 95-11, *Accounting for Derivative Instruments Containing Both a Written Option-Based Component and a Forward-Based Component.* Norwalk, CT: Author, 1995.

______. EITF Abstracts: A Summary of Proceedings of the FASB Emerging Issues Task Force, EITF Issue No. 96-1, *Sale of Put Options on Issuer's Stock that Require or Permit Cash Settlement.* Norwalk, CT: Author, 1996.

______. EITF Abstracts: A Summary of Proceedings of the FASB Emerging Issues Task Force, EITF Issue No. 96-2, *Impairment Recognition When a Nonmonetary Asset Is Exchanged or Is Distributed to Owners and Is Accounted the Asset's Recorded Amount.* Norwalk, CT: Author, 1996.

______. EITF Abstracts: A Summary of Proceedings of the FASB Emerging Issues Task Force, EITF Issue No. 96-10, *Impact of Certain Transactions on the Held-to-Maturity Classification under FASB Statement No. 115.* Norwalk, CT: Author, 1996.

———. EITF Abstracts: A Summary of Proceedings of the FASB Emerging Issues Task Force, EITF Issue No. 96-11, *Accounting for Forward Contracts and Purchased Options to Acquire Securities Covered by FASB Statement No. 115.* Norwalk, CT: Author, 1996.

———. EITF Abstracts: A Summary of Proceedings of the FASB Emerging Issues Task Force, EITF Issue No. 96-12, *Recognition of Interest Income and Balance Sheet Classification of Structured Notes.* Norwalk, CT: Author, 1996.

———. EITF Abstracts: A Summary of Proceedings of the FASB Emerging Issues Task Force, EITF Issue No. 96-13, *Accounting for Derivative Financial Instruments Indexed to, and Potentially Settled in, a Company's Own Stock.* Norwalk, CT: Author, 1996.

———. EITF Abstracts: A Summary of Proceedings of the FASB Emerging Issues Task Force, EITF Issue No. 96-14, *Accounting for the Costs Associated with Modifying Computer Software for the Year 2000.* Norwalk, CT: Author, 1996.

———. EITF Abstracts: A Summary of Proceedings of the FASB Emerging Issues Task Force, EITF Issue No. 96-15, *Accounting for the Effects of Changes in Foreign Currency Exchange Rates on Foreign-Currency-Denominated Available-for-Sale Debt Securities.* Norwalk, CT: Author, 1996.

———. EITF Abstracts: A Summary of Proceedings of the FASB Emerging Issues Task Force, EITF Issue No. 96-19, *Debtor's Accounting for a Substantive Modification and Exchange of Debt Instruments.* Norwalk, CT: Author, 1996.

———. EITF Abstracts: A Summary of Proceedings of the FASB Emerging Issues Task Force, EITF Issue No. 96-20, *Impact of FASB Statement No. 125 on Consolidation of Special-Purpose Entities.* Norwalk, CT: Author, 1996.

———. EITF Abstracts: A Summary of Proceedings of the FASB Emerging Issues Task Force, EITF Issue No. 96-22, *Applicability of the Disclosure Required by FASB Statement No. 114 When a Loan Is Restructured in a Troubled Debt Restructuring into Two (or More) Loans.* Norwalk, CT: Author, 1996.

———. EITF Abstracts: A Summary of Proceedings of the FASB Emerging Issues Task Force, EITF Issue No. 96-23, *The Effect of Financial Instruments Indexed to, and Settled in, a Company's Own Stock of Pooling-of-Interests Accounting for a Subsequent Business Combination.* Norwalk, CT: Author, 1996.

———. EITF Abstracts: A Summary of Proceedings of the FASB Emerging Issues Task Force, EITF Issue No. 97-3, *Accounting for Fees and Costs Associated with Loan Syndications and Loan Participations after the Issuance of FASB Statement No. 125.* Norwalk, CT: Author, 1997.

———. EITF Abstracts: A Summary of Proceedings of the FASB Emerging Issues Task Force, EITF Issue No. 97-7, *Accounting for Hedges of Foreign Currency Risk Inherent in an Available-for-Sale Marketable Equity Security.* Norwalk, CT: Author, 1997.

———. EITF Abstracts: A Summary of Proceedings of the FASB Emerging Issues Task Force, EITF Issue No. 97-9, *Effect on Pooling-of-Interests Accounting of Certain Contingently Exercisable Options or Other Equity Instruments.* Norwalk, CT: Author, 1997.

———. Interpretation No. 9, *Applying APB Opinions No. 16 and 17 When a Savings and Loan Association or a Similar Institution Is Acquired in a Business Combination Accounted for by the Purchase Method.* Norwalk, CT: Author, 1976.

———. Interpretation No. 39, *Offsetting of Amounts Related to Certain Contracts.* Norwalk, CT: Author, 1992.

———. Interpretation No. 41, *Offsetting of Amounts Related to Certain Repurchase and Reverse Repurchase Agreements—An Interpretation of APB Opinion No. 10 and a Modification of FASB Interpretation No. 39.* Norwalk, CT: Author, 1994.

———. Statement of Financial Accounting Standards No. 5, *Accounting for Contingencies.* Stamford, CT: Author, 1975.

———. Statement of Financial Accounting Standards No. 15, *Accounting by Debtors and Creditors for Troubled Debt Restructurings.* Stamford, CT: Author, 1977.

———. Statement of Financial Accounting Standards No. 34, *Capitalization of Interest Cost.* Stamford, CT: Author, 1979.

———. Statement of Financial Accounting Standards No. 52, *Foreign Currency Translation.* Stamford, CT: Author, 1981.

———. Statement of Financial Accounting Standards No. 58, *Capitalization of Interest Cost in Financial Statements That Include Investments Accounted for by the Equity Method.* Stamford, CT: Author, 1982.

———. Statement of Financial Accounting Standards No. 65, *Accounting for Certain Mortgage Banking Activities.* Stamford, CT: Author, 1982.

———. Statement of Financial Accounting Standards No. 66, *Accounting for Sales of Real Estate.* Stamford, CT: Author, 1982.

———. Statement of Financial Accounting Standards No. 67, *Accounting for Costs and Initial Rental Operations of Real Estate Projects.* Stamford, CT: Author, 1982.

———. Statement of Financial Accounting Standards No. 72, *Accounting for Certain Acquisitions of Banking or Thrift Institutions (an Amendment of APB Opinion No. 17, an Interpretation of APB Opinions No. 16 and 17, and an Amendment of FASB Interpretation No. 9).* Norwalk, CT: Author, 1983.

———. Statement of Financial Accounting Standards No. 77, *Reporting by Transferors for Transfers of Receivables with Recourse.* Stamford, CT: Author, 1983.

———. Statement of Financial Accounting Standards No. 80, *Accounting for Futures.* Stamford, CT: Author, 1984.

———. Statement of Financial Accounting Standards No. 91, *Accounting for Nonrefundable Fees and Costs Associated with Originating or Acquiring Loans and Initial Direct Costs of Leases (an Amendment of FASB Statements No. 13, 60, and 65 and a Rescission of FASB Statement No. 17).* Stamford, CT: Author, 1986.

———. Statement of Financial Accounting Standards No. 95, *Statement of Cash Flow.* Norwalk, CT: Author, 1987.

———. Statement of Financial Accounting Standards No. 102, *Statement of Cash Flows—Exception of Certain Enterprises and Classification of Cash Flows from Certain Securities Acquired for Resale (an amendment of FASB Statement No. 95).* Norwalk, CT: Author, 1989.

———. Statement of Financial Accounting Standards No. 104, *Statement of Cash Flows—Net Reporting of Certain Cash Receipts and Cash Payments and Classification of Cash Flows from Hedging Transactions (an Amendment of FASB Statement No. 95).* Norwalk, CT: Author, 1989.

———. Statement of Financial Accounting Standards No. 105, *Disclosure of Information about Financial Instruments Off-Balance Sheet Risk and Financial Instruments with Concentrations of Credit Risk.* Norwalk, CT: Author, 1990.

———. Statement of Financial Accounting Standards No. 107, *Disclosures About Fair Value of Financial Instruments.* Norwalk, CT: Author, 1991.

———. Statement of Financial Accounting Standards No. 114, *Accounting by Creditors for Impairment of a Loan (an Amendment of FASB Statements 5 and 15).* Norwalk, CT: Author, 1993.

———. Statement of Financial Accounting Standards No. 115, *Accounting for Certain Investments in Debt and Equity Securities.* Norwalk, CT: Author, 1993.

———. Statement of Financial Accounting Standards No. 118, *Accounting by Creditors for Impairment of a Loan-Income Recognition and Disclosures (an Amendment of FASB Statement 114).* Norwalk, CT: Author, 1994.

———. Statement of Financial Accounting Standards No. 119, *Disclosures about Derivative Financial Instruments and Fair Value of Financial Instruments.* Norwalk, CT: Author, 1994.

———. Statement of Financial Accounting Standards No. 121, *Accounting for the Impairment of Long-Lived Assets and for Long-Lived Assets to Be Disposed Of.* Norwalk, CT: Author, 1995.

———. Statement of Financial Accounting Standards No. 122, *Accounting for Mortgage Servicing Rights.* Norwalk, CT: Author, 1995.

———. Statement of Financial Accounting Standards No. 125, *Accounting for Transfers and Servicing of Financial Assets and Extinguishments of Liabilities.* Norwalk, CT: Author, 1996.

———. Statement of Financial Accounting Standards No. 126, *Exemption from Certain Required Disclosures about Financial Instruments for Certain Nonpublic Entities (an Amendment of FASB Statement No. 107).* Norwalk, CT: Author, 1996.

———. Statement of Financial Accounting Standards No. 127, *Deferral of the Effective Date of Certain Provisions of FASB Statement No. 125 (an Amendment of FASB Statement No. 125).* Norwalk, CT: Author, 1996.

———. Statement of Financial Accounting Standards No. 123R, *Share-Based Payment.* Norwalk, CT: Author, 2004.

———. Statement of Financial Accounting Standards No. 157, *Fair Value Measurements.* Norwalk, CT: Author, 2006.

———. Statement of Financial Accounting Standards No. 91, *Accounting for Nonrefundable Fees and Costs Associated with Originating or Acquiring Loans and Initial Direct Costs of Leases.* Norwalk, CT: Author, December 1986.

______. Statement of Financial Accounting Standards No. 114, *Accounting by Creditors for Impairment of a Loan.* Norwalk, CT: Author, May 1993

______. Statement of Financial Accounting Standards No.115, *Accounting for Certain Investments in Debt and Equity Securities.* Norwalk, CT: Author, May 1993

______. Statement of Financial Accounting Standards No. 133, *Accounting for Derivative Instruments and Hedging Activities.* Norwalk, CT: Author, June 1998

______. Statement of Financial Accounting Standards No. 140, *Accounting for Transfers and Servicing of Financial Assets and Extinguishments of Liabilities.* Norwalk, CT: Author, September 2000.

______ Statement of Financial Accounting Standards No. 157 was codified into FASB Accounting Standard Codification Topic 820, *Fair Value Measurements and Disclosures,* in 2009.

______. Technical Bulletin 85-2, *Accounting for Collateralized Mortgage Obligations.* Norwalk, CT: Author, 1985.

______. Technical Bulletin 94-1, *Application of Statement 115 to Debt Securities Restructured in a Troubled Debt Restructuring.* Norwalk, CT: Author, 1994.

International Federation of Accountants (IFAC). 2010. Accountancy Summit on Corporate Governance Reform Beyond the Global Financial Crisis (October 18, 2010) New York. Available at *http://www.ifac.org/news-events/2010-10/accountancy-summit-corporate-governance-reform-looks-beyond-global-financial-cri*

Rezaee, Z. *Corporate Governance Post-Sarbanes-Oxley: Regulations, Requirements, and Integrated Processes,* Inc. Hoboken, NJ: John Wiley & Sons, 2007.

Sarbanes-Oxley Act of 2002, July 30, 2002. *www.sarbanesoxleysimplified.com/sarbox/compact/htmlact/sec407.html*

Securities and Exchange Commission. Federal Reporting Release No. 23, *The Significance of Oral Guarantees to the Financial Reporting Process.* Washington, DC: Author, 1985.

______. Federal Reporting Release No. 28, *Accounting for Loan by Registrants Engaged in Lending Activities.* Stamford, CT: Author, 1986.

______. Federal Reporting Release No. 36, *Management's Discussion and Analysis of Financial Condition and Results of Operations; Certain Investment Company Disclosures.* Stamford, CT: Author, 1989.

______. Federal Reporting Release No. 48, *Disclosure of Accounting Policies for Derivative Financial Instruments and Derivative Commodity Instruments and Disclosure of Quantitative and Qualitative Information About Market Risk Inherent in Derivative Financial Instruments, Other Financial Instruments.* Stamford, CT: Author, 1997.

______. Federal Reporting Release No. 72. *Interpretation:Commission Guidance regarding Management's Discussion and Analysis of Financial Condition and Results of Operations,* Releases Nos. 33-8350, 34-48960, December 29, 2003. Available at *www.sec.gov/rules/interp/33-8350.htm*

______ Financial Reporting Policies, Section 401, Banks and Holding Companies, Financial Reporting Release No. 1, Section 404.03, Accounting, Valuation, and Disclosure of Investment Securities, *Accounting Series Release No. 118, Accounting for Investment Securities by Registered Investment Companies.* Boston: Warren, Gorham & Lamont, 1995.

______. Regulation S-X, Article 9, *Bank Holding Companies.* SEC 2004. *www.spee.org/images/PDFs/ReferencesResources/Full%20text%20SEC%20Reg%20regsx2.pdf*

______. Securities Act Guide 3, *Statistical Disclosure by Bank Holding Companies.* SEC. *www.sec.gov/about/forms/industryguides.pdf*

______. Staff Accounting Bulletin No. 50, *Financial Statement Requirements in Filings Involving the Formation of a One-Bank Holding Company.* Washington, DC: Author, 1983.

______. Staff Accounting Bulletin No. 56, *Reporting of an Allocated Transfer Risk Reserve in Filings under the Federal Securities Laws.* Washington, DC: Author, 1984.

______, Staff Accounting Bulletin No. 59, *Accounting for Noncurrent Marketable Equity Securities.* Washington, DC: Author, 1985.

______. Staff Accounting Bulletin No. 60, *Financial Guarantees.* Washington, DC: Author, 1985.

______. Staff Accounting Bulletin No. 61, *Allowance Adjustments.* Washington, DC: Author, 1986.

______. Staff Accounting Bulletin No. 69, *Application of Article 9 and Guide 3 to Non-Bank Holding Companies.* Washington, DC: Author, 1987.

———. Staff Accounting Bulletin Nos. 71 and 71A, *Financial Statements of Properties Securing Mortgage Loans*. Washington, DC: Author, 1987. Also see *www.occ.gov/topics/bank-operations/accounting/index-accounting.html*.

———. Staff Accounting Bulletin No. 75, *Accounting and Disclosures by Bank Holding Companies for a "Mexican Debt Exchange" Transaction*. Washington, DC: Author, 1988.

———. Staff Accounting Bulletin No. 82, *Certain Transfers of Nonperforming Assets and Disclosures of the Impact of Assistance from Federal Financial Institution Regulatory Agencies*. Washington, DC: Author, 1989.

———. Staff Accounting Bulletin No. 89, *Financial Statements of Acquired Financial Institutions*. Washington, DC: Author, 1989.

Walter, J. R. Loan Loss Reserve, American Banker issues, *Economic Review*, July/August 1991.

Bank and Savings Institutions' Regulatory Guidance

Selected guidance prepared by the federal bank and savings institutions regulatory agencies is contained in the following documents:

- *Bank Holding Company Supervision Manual*, Federal Reserve System
- *Comptroller's Handbook for Compliance*, OCC
- *Comptroller's Handbook for Fiduciary Activities*, OCC
- *Comptroller's Handbook for National Bank Examiners*, OCC
- *Comptroller's Manual for National Banks*, OCC
- Dodd-Frank Wall Street Reform and Consumer Protection Act of 2010

  The Dodd-Frank Act requires the development of over 240 new rules by the SEC, the GAO, and the Fed to implement its provisions over a five-year period. In addition, the OCC, FDIC, the Fed, OTS, and FFIEC regularly publish various bulletins, advisories, letters, and circulars addressing current issues.
- *FDIC Trust Examination Manual*
- *Federal Banking Law Reporter*, Commerce Clearing House, Inc.
- *Manual of Examination Policies*, FDIC Division of Supervision
- *Commercial Bank Examination Manual*, Federal Reserve System
- *Instructions—Consolidated Reporting of Condition and Income*, FFIEC
- *OCC Bank Accounting Advisory Series*, 3rd ed. (June 1994). Also see *www.occ.gov/topics/bank-operations/accounting/index-accounting.html*
- *Thrift Activities Regulatory Handbook*, OTS

CHAPTER 31

REAL ESTATE AND CONSTRUCTION

Benedetto Bongiorno, CPA, CRE
Natural Decision Systems, Inc

31.1 REAL ESTATE INDUSTRY 2

(a) Overview 2
(b) FASB Accounting Standards Codification 3

31.2 REAL ESTATE TRANSACTIONS 3

(a) Analysis of Transactions 3
(b) Sales of Real Estate 4
(c) Criteria for Sales Recognition 4
(d) Adequacy of Down Payment 5
(i) Size of Down Payment 5
(ii) Composition of Down Payment 6
(iii) Inadequate Down Payment 8
(e) Receivable from the Buyer 9
(i) Assessment of Collectability of Receivable 9
(ii) Amortization of Receivable 9
(iii) Receivable Subject to Future Subordination 10
(iv) Release Provisions 10
(v) Imputation of Interest 10
(vi) Inadequate Continuing Investment 11
(f) Seller's Continued Involvement 11
(i) Participation Solely in Future Profits 11
(ii) Option or Obligation to Repurchase the Property 11
(iii) General Partner in a Limited Partnership with a Significant Receivable 11
(iv) Lack of Permanent Financing 12
(v) Guaranteed Return of Buyer's Investment 12
(vi) Other Guaranteed Returns on Investment—Other than Sale-Leaseback 12
(vii) Guaranteed Return on Investment—Sale-Leaseback 12
(viii) Services Without Adequate Compensation 14
(ix) Development and Construction 14
(x) Initiation and Support of Operations 14
(xi) Partial Sales 16
(g) Sales of Condominiums and Tenants in Common 16
(i) Criteria for Profit Recognition 16
(ii) Methods of Accounting 17
(iii) Estimated Future Costs 18
(h) Retail Land Sales 18
(i) Criteria for Recording a Sale 19
(ii) Criteria for Full Accrual Method 19
(iii) Full Accrual Method 19
(iv) Percentage-of-Completion Method 20
(v) Installment and Deposit Methods 20
(i) Accounting for Syndication Fees 20
(j) Alternate Methods of Accounting for Sales 21
(i) Deposit Method 21
(ii) Installment Method 22
(iii) Cost Recovery Method 22
(iv) Reduced Profit Method 22
(v) Financing Method 22
(vi) Lease Method 23
(vii) Profit-Sharing or Coventure Method 23
(viii) Derecognition Method 23

31.3 CAPITALIZED COST OF REAL ESTATE 24

(a) Capitalization of Costs 24
(b) Preacquisition Costs 24
(c) Land Acquisition Costs 24

(d) Land Improvement, Development, and Construction Costs 24
(e) Environmental Issues 25
(f) Interest Costs 26
(i) Assets Qualifying for Interest Capitalization 26
(ii) Capitalization Period 27
(iii) Methods of Interest Capitalization 27
(iv) Accounting for Amount Capitalized 28
(g) Taxes and Insurance 28
(h) Indirect Project Costs 28
(i) General and Administrative Expenses 29
(j) Amenities 29
(k) Abandonments and Changes in Use 29
(l) Selling Costs 29
(m) Accounting for Foreclosed Assets 30
(i) Foreclosed Assets Held for Sale 30
(ii) Foreclosed Assets Held for Production of Income 30

31.4 ALLOCATION OF COSTS 30

(a) Methods of Allocation 30
(i) Specific Identification Method 31
(ii) Value Method 31
(iii) Area Method 31

31.5 VALUATION ISSUES 31

(a) Accounting for Impairment or Disposal of Long-Lived Assets 32
(i) Real Estate to be Held and Used 32
(ii) Real Estate to Be Disposed of 33
(b) Real Estate Under Development 34
(c) Fair Value Measurements 34
(i) Fair Value Hierarchy 34
(ii) Fair Value Techniques 35

31.6 CONSTRUCTION REVENUE RECOGNITION 35

(a) Authoritative Literature 35
(b) Methods of Accounting 36
(i) Percentage-of-Completion Method 36
(ii) Completed Contract Method 36
(iii) Consistency of Application 36
(c) Percentage-of-Completion Method 37
(i) Revenue Determination 37
(ii) Cost Determination 37
(iii) Revision of Estimates 38
(d) Completed Contract Method 39
(e) Provision for Losses 40
(f) Contract Claims 40

31.7 OPERATIONS OF PROPERTIES IN USE 41

(a) Rental Operations 41
(b) Rental Income 41
(i) Cost Escalation 42
(ii) Percentage Rents 42
(c) Rental Costs 42
(i) Chargeable to Future Periods 42
(ii) Period Costs 43
(d) Depreciation 43
(e) Initial Rental Operations 43
(i) Held in Use 43
(ii) Held for Sale 43
(f) Rental Expense 44

31.8 ACCOUNTING FOR INVESTMENTS IN REAL ESTATE VENTURES 44

(a) Organization of Ventures 44
(b) Accounting 44
(i) Background 44
(ii) Current Status 45
(c) Investor Accounting Issues 45
(d) Accounting for Tax Benefits Resulting from Investments in Affordable Housing Projects 47

31.9 FINANCIAL REPORTING 48

(a) Financial Statement Presentation 48
(i) Balance Sheet 48
(ii) Statement of Income 48
(b) Accounting Policies 49
(c) Note Disclosures 49
(d) Accounting by Participating Mortgage Loan Borrowers 51
(e) Real Estate Investment Trusts 51

31.10 SOURCES AND SUGGESTED REFERENCES 51

(a) Sources by Current Codification 51
(b) Suggested References Prior to Codification 53

31.1 REAL ESTATE INDUSTRY

(a) OVERVIEW. Real estate encompasses a variety of interests (developers, investors, lenders, tenants, homeowners, corporations, conduits, etc.) with a divergence of objectives (tax benefits, security, long-term appreciation, etc.). The industry is also a tool of the federal government's income tax policies (evidenced by the rules on mortgage interest deductions and restrictions on "passive" investment deductions). The real estate industry consists primarily of real estate operating entities (REO), investment real estate investment trusts (REITS), both public and private, and tenants in common (TIC).

Other important forces in the industry include pension funds and insurance companies and large public corporations, whose occupancy (real estate) costs generally are the second largest costs after personnel costs.

After a period of growth spurred by increasing demand for all types of real estate in an expanding economy, the new millennium brought in its wake a series of traumatic events that highlighted the uncertainties inherent in the real estate industry. These included:

- *Collapse of the mortgage debt market.* The sudden dramatic collapse of the CMO market delivered a lasting shock to real estate markets since its financial collapse in 2008.
- *Collapse of the stock market.* The sudden rise and dramatic collapse of the stock market delivered the first shock to real estate markets since the financial collapse of the 1930s. The refinancing market was turned on end as rapid retrenchment left behind a source of capital for real estate.
- *The dramatic rise in tenant closures and bankruptcies.* The reduction of tenant demand dealt a hard blow to an already declining economy and real estate market. It was preceded by a sharp rise in unemployment and severe weakness in financial markets that also curtailed demand for existing and new real estate.

Weak markets will continue to plague the recovery of many real estate markets. The sources and extent of available capital for financings, refinancings, and construction will continue to be a concern. This concern will be centered on the ability and willingness of financing institutions, especially the Wall Street firms, to continue lending in an uncertain and changed market, and lenders will increasingly require creditworthiness or enhancements to reduce to their exposure to real estate risk.

(b) FASB ACCOUNTING STANDARDS CODIFICATION. The Financial Accounting Standards Board (FASB) has completed the Accounting Standards Codification Project. On July 1, 2009, the *FASB Accounting Standards Codification* officially became the single source of authoritative nongovernmental U.S. generally accepted accounting principles (GAAP), superseding existing FASB, American Institute of Certified Public Accountants (AICPA), Emerging Issues Task Force (EITF), and related literature. After that date, only one level of authoritative GAAP exist. All other literature will be considered nonauthoritative FASB has segmented the authoritative literature into various topics, subtopics, sections, and subsections. The topic references in this chapter apply to real estate and incorporate the direct authoritative literature.

31.2 REAL ESTATE TRANSACTIONS

(a) ANALYSIS OF TRANSACTIONS. Real estate transactions generally fall into two categories: real estate as a business combination and real estate as a purchase and sale. Both transactions are generally material to the entity's financial statements. For purchase and sale, "Is the earnings process complete?" is the primary question that must be answered regarding such sales. For business combinations, the question is: "Is the variable interest in the variable interest entity the primary beneficiary?" In other words, have the risks and rewards of ownership been transferred?

Revenue recognition is a priority project that is part of the convergence efforts of the FASB and the International Accounting Standards Board (IASB). On June 24, 2010, the boards jointly issued an exposure draft titled *Revenue from Contracts with Customers* that proposes a new revenue recognition standard which could significantly affect current revenue recognition policies. More changes are expected as a result of the board's redeliberations to be completed during 2011. Although other industries will be impacted more significantly than real estate, constant vigilance will be needed as it regards real estate transactions. In addition, the Private Company Financial Reporting Committee will meet to discuss various topics including revenue recognition.

(b) SALES OF REAL ESTATE. Prior to 1982, guidance related to real estate sales transactions was contained in two AICPA Accounting Guides: *Accounting for Retail Land Sales* and *Accounting for Profit Recognition on Sales of Real Estate.* These guides had been supplemented by several AICPA Statements of Position that provided interpretations.

In October 1982, Statement of Financial Accounting Standards (SFAS) No. 66, *Accounting for Sales of Real Estate,* was issued as part of the FASB project to incorporate, where appropriate, AICPA Accounting Guides into FASB Statements. This Statement adopted the specialized profit recognition principles of the above guides.

The FASB formed the Emerging Issues Task Force Task Force (EITF) in 1984 for the early identification of emerging issues. The EITF has dealt with many issues affecting the real estate industry, including issues that clarify or address Accounting Standard Codification (ASC) 360 (SFAS No. 66).

Regardless of the seller's business, ASC 360 (SFAS No. 66) covers all sales of real estate, determines the timing of the sale and resultant profit recognition, and deals with seller accounting only. This Statement does not discuss nonmonetary exchanges, cost accounting, and most lease transactions or disclosures.

The two primary concerns under ASC 360 are:

1. Has a sale occurred?
2. Under what method and when should profit be recognized?

The concerns are answered by determining the buyer's initial and continuing investment and the nature and extent of the seller's continuing involvement. The guidelines used in determining these criteria are complex and, within certain provisions, arbitrary. Companies dealing with these types of transactions are often faced with the difficult task of analyzing the exact nature of a transaction in order to determine the appropriate accounting approach. Only with a thorough understanding of the substance and details of a transaction can the accountant perform the analysis required to decide on the appropriate accounting method.

(c) CRITERIA FOR SALES RECOGNITION. ASC 360 (SFAS No. 66, pars. 44–50) discussed separate rules for retail land sales (see Section 31.2(h)). The next information is for all real estate sales other than retail land sales. To determine whether profit recognition is appropriate, a test must first be made to determine whether a sale has occurred. Then additional tests are made related to the buyer's investment and the seller's continued involvement.

Generally, real estate sales should not be recorded prior to closing. Since an exchange is generally required to recognize profit, a sale must be consummated. A sale is consummated when all of these conditions have been met:

- The parties are bound by the terms of a contract.
- All consideration has been exchanged.
- Any permanent financing for which the seller is responsible has been arranged.
- All conditions precedent to closing has been performed.

Usually all those conditions are met at the time of closing. However, they are not usually met at the time of a contract to sell or a preclosing.

Exceptions to the "conditions precedent to closing" have been specifically provided for in ASC 360. They are applicable where a sale of property includes a requirement for the seller to perform future construction or development. Under certain conditions, partial sale recognition is permitted during the construction process because the construction period is extended. This exception usually is not applicable to single-family detached housing because of the shorter construction period.

Transactions that should not be treated as sales for accounting purposes because of continuing seller's involvement include situations in which the seller:

- Has an option or obligation to repurchase the property.
- Guarantees return of the buyer's investment.
- Retains an interest as a general partner in a limited partnership and has a significant receivable.
- Is required to initiate or support operations or continue to operate the property at its own risk for a specified period or until a specified level of operations has been obtained.

If the criteria for recording a sale are not met, the deposit, financing, lease, or profit sharing (coventure) methods should be used, depending on the substance of the transaction.

(d) ADEQUACY OF DOWN PAYMENT. Once it has been determined that a sale can be recorded, the next test relates to the buyer's investment. For the seller to record full profit recognition, the buyer's down payment must be adequate in size and in composition.

(i) Size of Down Payment. The minimum down payment requirement is one of the most important provisions in ASC 360 (SFAS No. 66). Appendix A of this pronouncement, reproduced here as Exhibit 31.1, lists minimum down payments ranging from 5 to 25 percent of sales value based on usual loan limits for various types of properties. These percentages should be considered as specific requirements because it was not intended that exceptions be made. Additionally, EITF Consensus No. 88-24, *Effect of Various Forms of Financing under FASB Statement No. 66,* discusses the impact of the source and nature of the buyer's down payment on profit recognition. Exhibit A to EITF No. 88-24 has been reproduced here as Exhibit 31.2.

If a newly placed permanent loan or firm permanent loan commitment for maximum financing exists, the minimum down payment must be the higher of (1) the amount derived from Appendix A or (2) the excess of sales value over 115 percent of the new financing. However, regardless of this test, a down payment of 25 percent of the sales value of the property is usually considered sufficient to justify the recognition of profit at the time of sale.

An example of the down payment test—Appendix A compared to the newly placed permanent loan test—is given next.

ASSUMPTIONS

Initial payment made by the buyer to the seller on sale of an apartment building	$ 200,000
First mortgage recently issued and assumed by the buyer	1,000,000
Second mortgage given by the seller at prevailing interest rate	200,000
Stated sales price and sales value	$1,400,000
115% of first mortgage (1.15 × $1,000,000)	1,150,000
Down payment necessary	$250,000

RESULT

Although the down payment required under Appendix A is only $140,000 (10% of $1,400,000), the $200,000 actual down payment is inadequate because the test relating to the newly placed first mortgage requires $250,000.

The down payment requirements must be related to sales value, as described in ASC 360 (SFAS No. 66, par. 7). Sales value is the stated sales price increased or decreased for other consideration that clearly constitutes additional proceeds on the sale, services without compensation, imputed interest, and so forth.

	Minimum Initial Investment Payment Expressed as a Percentage of Sales Value
Land:	
Held for commercial, industrial, or residential development to commence within two years after sale	20%
Held for commercial, industrial, or residential development after two years	25%
Commercial and industrial property:	
Office and industrial buildings, shopping centers, and so forth:	
Properties subject to lease on a long-term lease basis to parties having satisfactory credit rating; cash flow currently sufficient to service all Indebtedness	10%
Single-tenancy properties sold to a user having a satisfactory credit rating	15%
All other	20%
Other income-producing properties (hotels, motels, marinas, mobile home parks, and so forth):	
Cash flow currently sufficient to service all indebtedness	15%
Start-up situations or current deficiencies in cash flow	25%
Multifamily residential property:	
Primary residence:	
Cash flow currently sufficient to service all indebtedness	10%
Start-up situations or current deficiencies in cash flow	15%
Secondary or recreational residence:	
Cash flow currently sufficient to service all indebtedness	10%
Start-up situations or current deficiencies in cash flow	25%
Single-family residential property (including condominium or cooperative housing)	
Primary residence of buyer	5%[a]
Secondary or recreational residence	10%[a]

[a]As set forth in Appendix A of SFAS No. 66, if collectability of the remaining portion of the sales price cannot be supported by reliable evidence of collection experience, the minimum initial investment shall be at least 60% of the difference between the sales value and the financing available from loans guaranteed by regulatory bodies, such as the FHA or the VA, or from independent financial institutions.

This 60% test applies when independent first mortgage financing is not utilized and the seller takes a receivable from the buyer for the difference between the sales value and the initial investment. If independent first mortgage financing is utilized, the adequacy of the initial investment on sales of single-family residential property should be determined as described in Subsection 31.2(d) (i).

(*Source:* SFAS No. 66, "Accounting for Sales of Real Estate" (Appendix A), FASB, 1982. Reprinted with permission of FASB.)

Exhibit 31.1 Minimum Initial Investment Requirements
Source: SFAS No. 66, *Accounting for Sales of Real Estate* (Appendix A), FASB, 1982. Reprinted with permission of FASB.

Consideration payable for development work or improvements that are the responsibility of the seller should be included in the computation of sales value.

(ii) Composition of Down Payment. The primary acceptable down payment is cash, but additional acceptable forms of down payment are:

- Notes from the buyer (only when supported by irrevocable letters of credit from an independent established lending institution)
- Cash payments by the buyer to reduce previously existing indebtedness
- Cash payments that are in substance additional sales proceeds, such as prepaid interest that by the terms of the contract is applied to amounts due the seller

Situation	Cash Received by Seller at Closing	Components of Cash Received by Seller at Closing: Buyer's Initial Investment	Components of Cash Received by Seller at Closing: Buyer's Independent First Mortgage	Assumption of Seller's Nonrecourse Mortgage
1.	100	20	80	
2.	100	0	100	
3.	20	20		80
4.	0	0		100
5.	20	20		
6.	20	20		
7.	80	20	60	
8.	20	20		60
9.	20	20		
10.	0	0		
11.	0	0		
12.	0	0		
13.	80	0	80	
14.	10	10		
15.	10	10		
16.	90	10	80	
17.	10	10		80
18.	10	10		

Assumptions:
Sales price: $100.
Seller's basis in property sold: $70.
Initial investment requirement: 20%.
All mortgage obligations meet the continuing investment requirements of Statement 66.

Exhibit 31.2 Examples of the Application of the EITF Consensus on Issue No. 88-24
Source: EITF Issue No. 88-24, *Effect of Various Forms of Financing under FASB Statement No. 66* (Exhibit 88-24A), FASB, 1988. Reprinted with permission of FASB.

Examples of other forms of down payment that are not acceptable are:

- Other noncash consideration received by the seller, such as notes from the buyer without letters of credit or marketable securities. Noncash consideration constitutes down payment only at the time it is converted into cash.
- Funds that have been or will be loaned to the buyer builder/developer for acquisition, construction, or development purposes or otherwise provided directly or indirectly by the seller. Such amounts must first be deducted from the down payment in determining whether the down payment test has been met. An exemption from this requirement was provided in paragraph 115 of SFAS No. 66 (ASC 360), which states that if a future loan on normal terms from a seller who is also an established lending institution bears a fair market interest rate and the proceeds of the loan are conditional on use for specific development of or construction on the property, the loan need not be subtracted in determining the buyer's investment.
- Funds received from the buyer from proceeds of priority loans on the property. Such funds have not come from the buyer and therefore do not provide assurance of collectability of the remaining receivable; such amounts should be excluded in determining the adequacy of the down payment. In addition, EITF Consensus No. 88-24 provides guidelines on the impact that the source and nature of the buyer's initial investment can have on profit recognition.

Seller Financing[1]	Assumption Of Seller's Recourse Mortgage[2]	Recognition under Consensus Paragraph	Profit Recognized at Date of Sale[3]		
			Full Accrual	Installment	Cost Recovery
		#1	30		
		#1	30		
		#1	30		
		#1	30		
80(1)		#2	30		
	80	#2	30		
20(2)		#2	30		
20(2)		#2	30		
20(2)	60	#2	30		
	100	#3		0	0
100(1)		#3		0	0
20(2)	80	#3		0	0
20(2)		#3		10	10
90(1)		#3		3	0
	90	#3		3	0
10(2)		#3		20	20
10(2)		#3		20	20
10(2)	80	#3		3	0

[1]First or second mortgage indicated in parentheses.
[2]Seller remains contingently liable.
[3]The profit recognized under the reduced profit method is dependent on various interest rates and payment terms. An example is not presented due to the complexity of those factors and the belief that this method is not frequently used in practice. Under this method, the profit recognized at the consummation of the sale would be less than under the full accrual method, but normally more than the amount under the installment method.

Exhibit 31.2 ***Continued***

- Marketable securities or other assets received as down payment will constitute down payment only at the time they are converted to cash.
- Cash payments for prepaid interest that are not in substance additional sales proceeds.
- Cash payments by the buyer to others for development or construction of improvements to the property.

(iii) Inadequate Down Payment. If the buyer's down payment is inadequate, the full accrual method of accounting is not appropriate, and the deposit, installment, or cost recovery method of accounting should be used.

When the sole consideration (in addition to cash) received by the seller is the buyer's assumption of existing nonrecourse indebtedness, a sale could be recorded and profit recognized if all other conditions for recognizing a sale were met. If, however, the buyer assumes recourse debt and the seller remains liable on the debt, the seller has a risk of loss comparable to the risk involved in holding a receivable from the buyer, and the full accrual method would not be appropriate.

EITF Consensus No. 88-24 states that the initial and continuing investment requirements for the full accrual method of profit recognition of ASC 360 (SFAS No. 66) are applicable unless the seller receives one of the following as the full sales value of the property:

- Cash, without any seller contingent liability on any debt on the property incurred or assumed by the buyer
- The buyer's assumption of the seller's existing nonrecourse debt on the property

- The buyer's assumption of all recourse debt on the property with the complete release of the seller from those obligations
- Any combination of such cash and debt assumption

(e) RECEIVABLE FROM THE BUYER. Even if the required down payment is made, a number of factors must be considered by the seller in connection with a receivable from the buyer. They include:

- Collectability of the receivable
- Buyer's continuing investment—amortization of receivable
- Future subordination
- Release provisions
- Imputation of interest

(i) Assessment of Collectability of Receivable. Collectability of the receivable must be reasonably assured and should be assessed in light of factors such as the credit standing of the buyer (if recourse), cash flow from the property, and the property's size and geographical location. This requirement may be particularly important when the receivable is relatively short term and collectability is questionable because the buyer will be required to obtain financing. Furthermore, a basic principle of real estate sales on credit is that the receivable must be adequately secured by the property sold.

(ii) Amortization of Receivable. Continuing investment requirements for full profit recognition require that the buyer's payments on its total debt for the purchase price must be at least equal to level annual payments (including principal and interest) based on amortization of the full amount over a maximum term of 20 years for land and over the *customary term of a first mortgage* by an independent established lending institution for other property. The annual payments must begin within one year of recording the sale and, to be acceptable, must meet the same composition test as used in determining adequacy of down payments. The customary term of a first mortgage loan is usually considered to be the term of a new loan (or the term of an existing loan placed in recent years) from an independent financial lending institution. In today's lending environment, the terms of the loan have been tightened in both the areas of loan to value and shortened amortization periods.

All indebtedness on the property need not be reduced proportionately. However, if the seller's receivable is not being amortized, realization may be in question and the collectability must be more carefully assessed. Lump-sum (balloon) payments do not affect the amortization requirement as long as the scheduled amortization is within the maximum period and the minimum annual amortization tests are met.

For example, if the customary term of the mortgage by an independent lender required amortizing payments over a period of 15 years, then the continuing investment requirement would be based on such an amortization schedule. If the terms of the receivable required principal and interest payments on such a schedule only for the first five years with a balloon at the end of year 5, the continuing investment requirements are met. In such cases, however, the collectability of the balloon payment should be carefully assessed.

If the amortization requirements for full profit recognition as just set forth are not met, a reduced profit may be recognized by the seller if the annual payments are at least equal to the total of:

- Annual level payments of principal and interest on a maximum available first mortgage
- Interest at an appropriate rate on the remaining amount payable by the buyer

The reduced profit is determined by discounting the receivable from the buyer to the present value of the lowest level of annual payments required by the sales contract, excluding requirements to pay lump sums. The present value is calculated using an appropriate interest rate, but not less than the rate stated in the sales contract.

Assumptions:		
Down payment (meets applicable tests)		$ 150,000
First mortgage note from independent lender at market rate of interest (new, 20 years—meets required amortization)		750,000
Second mortgage notes payable to seller, interest at a market rate is due annually, with principal due at the end of the 25th year (the term exceeds the maximum permitted)		100,000
Stated selling price		$1,000,000
Adjustment required in valuation of receivable from buyer:		
Second mortgage payable to seller	$100,000	
Less: present value of 20 years annual interest payments on second mortgage (lowest level of annual payments over customary term of first mortgage—thus 20 years not 25)	70,000	30,000
Adjusted sales value for profit recognition		$ 970,000

The sales value as well as profit is reduced by $30,000.

In some situations profit will be entirely eliminated by this calculation.

Exhibit 31.3 Calculation of Reduced Profit

The amount calculated would be used as the value of the receivable for the purpose of determining the reduced profit. The calculation of reduced profit is illustrated in Exhibit 31.3.

The requirements for amortization of the receivable are applied cumulatively at the closing date (date of recording the sale for accounting purposes) and annually thereafter. Any excess of down payment received over the minimum required is applied toward the amortization requirements.

(iii) Receivable Subject to Future Subordination. If the receivable is subject to future subordination to a future loan available to the buyer, profit recognition cannot exceed the amount determined under the cost recovery method (see Subsection 31.2(j)(iii)) unless proceeds of the loan are first used to reduce the seller's receivable. Although this accounting treatment is controversial, the cost recovery method is required because collectability of the sales price is not reasonably assured. The future subordination would permit the primary lender to obtain a prior lien on the property, leaving only a secondary residual value for the seller, and future loans could indirectly finance the buyer's initial cash investment. Future loans would include funds received by the buyer arising from a permanent loan commitment existing at the time of the transaction unless such funds were first applied to reduce the seller's receivable as provided for in the terms of the sale.

The cost recovery method is not required if the receivable is subordinate to a previous mortgage on the property existing at the time of sale.

(iv) Release Provisions. Some sales transactions have provisions releasing portions of the property from the liens securing the debt as partial payments are made. In this situation, full profit recognition is acceptable only if the buyer must make, at the time of each release, cumulative payments that are adequate in relation to the sales value of property not released.

(v) Imputation of Interest. Careful attention should be given to the necessity for imputation of interest under Accounting Principles Board (APB) Opinion No. 21, *Interest on Receivables and Payables,* since it could have a significant effect on the amount of profit or loss recognition. As stated in the first paragraph of APB Opinion No. 21: "The use of an interest rate that varies from prevailing interest rates warrants evaluation of whether the face amount and the stated interest rate of a note or obligation provide reliable evidence for properly recording the exchange and subsequent related interest."

If imputation of interest is necessary, the mortgage note receivable should be adjusted to its present value by discounting all future payments on the notes using an imputed rate of interest at the prevailing rates available for similar financing with independent financial institutions. A distinction must be made between first and second mortgage loans because the appropriate imputed rate for a second mortgage would normally be significantly higher than the rate for a first mortgage loan. It may be necessary to obtain independent valuations to assist in the determination of the proper rate.

(vi) Inadequate Continuing Investment. If the criteria for recording a sale have been met but the tests related to the collectability of the receivable as set forth herein are not met, the full accrual method of accounting is not appropriate and the installment or cost recovery method of accounting should be used. These methods are discussed in Section 31.2(j) of this chapter.

(f) SELLER'S CONTINUED INVOLVEMENT. A seller sometimes continues to be involved over long periods of time with property legally sold. This involvement may take many forms, such as participation in future profits, financing, management services, development, construction, guarantees, and options to repurchase. With respect to profit recognition when a seller has continued involvement, the two key principles are:

1. A sales contract should not be accounted for as a sale if the seller's continued involvement with the property includes the same kinds of risk as does ownership of property.
2. Profit recognition should follow performance and in some cases should be postponed completely until a later date.

(i) Participation Solely in Future Profits. A sale of real estate may include or be accompanied by an agreement that provides for the seller to participate in future operating profits or residual values. As long as the seller has no further obligations or risk of loss, profit recognition on the sale need not be deferred. A receivable from the buyer is permitted if the other tests for profit recognition are met, but no costs can be deferred.

(ii) Option or Obligation to Repurchase the Property. If the seller has an option or obligation to repurchase property (including a buyer's option to compel the seller to repurchase), a sale cannot be recognized (ASC 360 (SFAS No. 66, par. 26)). However, neither a commitment by the seller to assist or use his or her best efforts (with appropriate compensation) on a resale nor a right of first refusal based on a bona fide offer by a third party would preclude sale recognition. The accounting to be followed depends on the repurchase terms. EITF Consensus No. 86-6, *Antispeculation Clauses in Real Estate Sales Contracts,* discusses accounting for a sale transaction when antispeculation clauses exist. A consensus was reached that the contingent option would not preclude sale recognition if the probability of buyer noncompliance is remote.

When the seller has an obligation or an option that is reasonably expected to be exercised to repurchase the property at a price higher than the total amount of the payments received and to be received, the transaction is a financing arrangement and should be accounted for under the financing method. If the option is not reasonably expected to be exercised, the deposit method is appropriate.

In the case of a repurchase obligation or option at a lower price, the transaction usually is, in substance, a lease or is part lease, part financing and should be accounted for under the lease method. Where an option to repurchase is at a market price to be determined in the future, the transaction should be accounted for under the deposit method or the profit-sharing method.

(iii) General Partner in a Limited Partnership with a Significant Receivable. When the seller is a general partner in a limited partnership and has a significant receivable related to the property, the transaction would not qualify as a sale. It should usually be accounted for as a profit-sharing arrangement. As a guide, a significant receivable is one that is in excess of 15 percent of the maximum first lien financing that could be obtained from an established lending institution for the property sold.

(iv) Lack of Permanent Financing. The buyer's leveraged investment in the property cannot be evaluated until adequate permanent financing at an acceptable cost is available to the buyer. If the seller must obtain or provide this financing, obtaining the financing is a prerequisite to a sale for accounting purposes. Even if not required to do so, the seller may be presumed to have such an obligation if the buyer does not have financing and the collectability of the receivable is questionable. The deposit method is appropriate if lack of financing is the only impediment to recording a sale.

(v) Guaranteed Return of Buyer's Investment. ASC 360 (SFAS No. 66, par. 28) states: "If the seller guarantees return of the buyer's investment, ... the transaction shall be accounted for as a financing, leasing, or profit-sharing arrangement."

Accordingly, if the terms of a transaction are such that the buyer may expect to recover the initial investment through assured cash returns, subsidies, and net tax benefits, even if the buyer were to default on debt to the seller, or expect to liquidate the debt to the seller from property operations or sale, the transaction is probably not in substance a sale.

(vi) Other Guaranteed Returns on Investment—Other than Sale-Leaseback. When the seller guarantees cash returns on the buyer's investment, the accounting method to be followed depends on whether the guarantee is for an extended or limited period and whether the seller's expected cost of the guarantee is determinable.

Extended Period. ASC 360 (SFAS No. 66) states that when the seller contractually guarantees cash returns on investments to the buyer for an extended period, the transaction should be accounted for as a financing, leasing, or profit-sharing arrangement. An "extended period" was not defined but should at least include periods that are not limited in time or specified lengthy periods, such as more than five years. Specified lengthy periods may be impacted by the buyer's traditional holding period and the terms of the financing, if any.

Limited Period. If the guarantee of a return on the buyer's investment is for a limited period, ASC 360 (SFAS No. 66) indicates that the deposit method of accounting should be used until such time as operation of the property covers all operating expenses, debt service, and contractual payments. At that time, profit should be recognized based on performance (see Section 31.2(j)). A "limited period" was not defined but is believed to relate to specified shorter periods, such as five years or less.

Irrespective of these facts, if the guarantee is determinable or limited, it may be appropriate if the sales price is reduced by the maximum exposure to loss as described next.

Guarantee Amount Determinable. If the amount can be reasonably estimated, the seller should record the guarantee as a cost at the time of sale, thus either reducing the profit or increasing the loss on the transaction.

Guarantee Amount Not Determinable. If the amount cannot be reasonably estimated, the transaction is probably in substance a profit-sharing or coventure arrangement.

Guarantee Amount Not Determinable But Limited. If the amount cannot be reasonably estimated but a maximum cost of the guarantee is determinable, the seller may record the maximum cost of the guarantee as a cost at the time of sale, thus either reducing the profit or increasing the loss on the transaction. Alternatively, the seller may account for the transaction as if the guarantee amount is not determinable. Implications of a seller's guarantee of cash flow on an operating property that is not considered a sale-leaseback arrangement are discussed in Subsection 31.2(f)(x).

(vii) Guaranteed Return on Investment—Sale-Leaseback. A guarantee of cash flow to the buyer sometimes takes the form of a leaseback arrangement. Since the earnings process in this situation has not usually been completed, profits on the sale should generally be deferred and amortized.

Accounting for a sale-leaseback of real estate is governed by ASC 840 (SFAS No. 13), *Accounting for Leases,* as amended by ASC 840 (SFAS No. 28), *Accounting for Sales with Leasebacks,*

ASC 840 (SFAS No. 98), *Accounting for Leases: Sale-Leaseback Transactions Involving Real Estate,* and ASC 360 (SFAS No. 66). ASC 840 (SFAS No. 98) specifies the accounting by a seller-lessee for a sale-leaseback transaction involving real estate, including real estate with equipment. ASC 840 (SFAS No. 98) provides that:

- A sale-leaseback transaction involving real estate, including real estate with equipment, must qualify as a sale under the provisions of ASC 360 (SFAS No. 66 as amended by SFAS No. 98), before it is appropriate for the seller-lessee to account for the transaction as a sale. If the transaction does not qualify as a sale under ASC 360 (SFAS No. 66), it should be accounted for by the deposit method or as a financing transaction (see SFAS No. 66; Subsection 31.2(j)(v)).
- A sale-leaseback transaction involving real estate, including real estate with equipment, that includes any continuing involvement other than a normal leaseback in which the seller-lessee intends to actively use the property during the lease should be accounted for by the deposit method or as a financing transaction.
- A lease involving real estate may not be classified as a sales-type lease unless the lease agreement provides for the transfer of title to the lessee at or shortly after the end of the lease term. Sales-type leases involving real estate should be accounted for under the provisions of ASC 360 (SFAS No. 66).

Profit Recognition. Profits should be deferred and amortized in a manner consistent with the classification of the leaseback:

- If the leaseback is an operating lease, deferred profit should be amortized in proportion to the related gross rental charges to expense over the lease term.
- If the leaseback is a capital lease, deferred profit should be amortized in proportion to the amortization of the leased asset. Effectively, the sale is treated as a financing transaction. The deferred profit can be presented gross but normally is offset against the capitalized asset for balance sheet classification purposes.

In situations where the leaseback covers only a minor portion of the property sold or the period is relatively minor compared to the remaining useful life of the property, it may be appropriate to recognize all or a portion of the gain as income. Sales with minor leasebacks should be accounted for based on the separate terms of the sale and the leaseback unless the rentals called for by the leaseback are unreasonable in relation to current market conditions. If rentals are considered to be unreasonable, they must be adjusted to a reasonable amount in computing the profit on the sale.

The leaseback is considered to be minor when the present value of the leaseback based on reasonable rentals is 10 percent or less of the fair value of the asset sold. If the leaseback is not considered to be minor (but less than substantially all of the use of the asset is retained through a leaseback), profit may be recognized to the extent it exceeds the present value of the minimum lease payments (net of executory costs) in the case of an operating lease or the recorded amount of the leased asset in the case of capital lease.

Loss Recognition. Losses should be recognized immediately to the extent that the remaining cost (net carrying value) exceeds the fair value of the property under the provisions of ASC 820 (SFAS No. 157), *Fair Value Measurements.* Fair value is frequently determined by the selling price from which the loss on the sale is measured. Many sale-leasebacks are entered into as a means of financing or for tax reasons, or both. The terms of the leaseback are negotiated as a package. Because of the interdependence of the sale and concurrent leaseback, the selling price in some cases is not representative of fair value. It would not be appropriate to recognize a loss on the sale that would be offset by future cost reductions as a result of either reduced rental costs under an operating lease or depreciation and interest charges under a capital lease. Therefore, to the extent that the fair value is greater than the sale price, losses should be deferred and amortized in the same manner as profits.

(viii) Services Without Adequate Compensation. A sales contract may be accompanied by an agreement for the seller to provide management or other services without adequate compensation. Compensation for the value of the services should be imputed, deducted from the sales price, and recognized over the term of the contract. See discussion of implied support of operations in Subsection 31.2(f)(x) if the contract is noncancelable and the compensation is unusual for the services to be rendered.

(ix) Development and Construction. A sale of undeveloped or partially developed land may include or be accompanied by an agreement requiring future seller performance of development or construction. In such cases, all or a portion of the profit should be deferred. If there is a lapse of time between the sale agreement and the future performance agreement, deferral provisions usually apply if definitive development plans existed at the time of sale and a development contract was anticipated by the parties at the time of entering into the sales contract.

In addition, ASC 360 (SFAS No. 66, par. 41) provides:

> The seller is involved with future development or construction work if the buyer is unable to pay amounts due for that work or has the right under the terms of the arrangement to defer payment until the work is done.

If the property sold and being developed is an operating property (such as an apartment complex, shopping center, or office building) as opposed to a nonoperating property (such as a land lot, condominium unit, or single-family detached home), Subsection 31.2(f)(x) may also apply.

Completed Contract Method. If a seller is obligated to develop the property or construct facilities and total costs and profit cannot be reliably estimated (e.g., because of lack of seller experience or definitive plans), all profit, including profit on the sale of land, should be deferred until the contract is completed or until the total costs and profit can be reliably estimated. Under the completed contract method, all profit, including profit on the sale of land, is deferred until the seller's obligations are fulfilled.

Percentage-of-Completion Method (Cost-Incurred Method). If the costs and profit can be reliably estimated, profit recognition over the improvement period on the basis of costs incurred (including land) as a percentage of total costs to be incurred is required. Thus, if the land was a principal part of the sale and its market value greatly exceeded cost, part of the profit that can be said to be related to the land sale is deferred and recognized during the development or construction period.

The same rate of profit is used for all seller costs connected with the transaction. For this purpose, the cost of development work, improvements, and all fees and expenses that are the responsibility of the seller should be included. The buyer's initial and continuing investment tests, of course, must be met with respect to the total sales value. Exhibit 31.4 illustrates the cost incurred method.

(x) Initiation and Support of Operations. If the property sold is an operating property, as opposed to a nonoperating property, deferral of all or a portion of the profit may be required under ASC 360 (SFAS No. 66, pars. 28–30). These paragraphs establish guidelines not only for stated support but also for implied support.

Although the implied support provisions do not usually apply to undeveloped or partially developed land, they do apply if the buyer has commitments to construct operating properties and there is stated or implied support.

Assuming that the criteria for recording a sale and the test of buyer's investment are met, the next subsections set forth guidelines for profit recognition where there is stated or implied support.

Stated Support. A seller may be required to support operations by means of a guaranteed return to the buyer. Alternatively, a guarantee may be made to the buyer that there will be no negative cash flow from the project, but may not guarantee a positive return on the buyer's investment. For example, EITF Consensus No. 85-27, *Recognition of Receipts from Made-up Rental Shortfalls,*

Assumptions:

1. Sale of land for commercial development—$475,000.
2. Development contract—$525,000.
3. Down payment and other buyer investment requirements met.
4. Land costs—$200,000.
5. Development costs $500,000 (reliably estimated)—$325,000 incurred in initial year.

Calculation of profit to be recognized in initial year:

Sale of land	$ 475,000
Development contract price	525,000
Total sales price	1,000,000
Costs:	
Land	200,000
Development	500,000
Total costs	700,000
Total profit anticipated	$ 300,000
Cost incurred through end of initial year:	
Land	200,000
Development	$ 325,000
Total	$ 525,000
Profit to be recognized in initial year—525,000 ÷ 700,000 × 300,000 =	$ 225,000

Exhibit 31.4 Percentage of Completion, or Cost-Incurred, Method

considers the impact of a master lease guarantee. The broad exposure that such a guarantee creates has a negative impact on profit recognition.

Implied Support. The seller may be presumed to be obligated to initiate and support operations of the property sold, even in the absence of specified requirements in the sale contract or related document. The next conditions under which support is implied are described in footnote 10 of ASC 360 (SFAS No. 66):

- A seller obtains an interest as general partner in a limited partnership that acquires an interest in the property sold.
- A seller retains an equity interest in the property, such as an undivided interest or an equity interest in a joint venture that holds an interest in the property.
- A seller holds a receivable from a buyer for a significant part of the sales price and collection of the receivable is dependent on the operation of the property.
- A seller agrees to manage the property for the buyer on terms not usual for the services to be rendered and which is not terminable by either seller or buyer.

Stated or Implied Support. When profit recognition is appropriate in the case of either stated or implied support, the next general rules apply:

- Profit is recognized on the ratio of costs incurred to total costs to be incurred. Revenues for gross profit purposes include rent from operations during the rent-up period; costs include land and operating expenses during the rent-up period as well as other costs.
- As set forth in ASC 360 (SFAS No. 66, par. 30):
  Support shall be presumed for at least two years from the time of initial rental unless actual rental operations cover operating expenses, debt service, and other contractual commitments before that time. If the seller is contractually obligated for a longer time, profit recognition shall continue on the basis of performance until the obligation expires.

- Estimated rental income should be adjusted by reducing estimated future rent receipts by a safety factor of $33\frac{1}{3}$ percent unless signed lease agreements have been obtained to support a projection higher than the rental level thus computed. As set forth in ASC 360 (SFAS No. 66, par. 29), when signed leases amount to more than $66\frac{2}{3}$ percent of estimated rents, no additional safety factor is required but only amounts under signed lease agreements can be included.

(xi) Partial Sales. A partial sale includes a sale of:

- An interest in real estate or entity that is in substance real estate
- Real estate where the seller has an equity interest in the buyer (e.g., a joint venture or partnership)
- A condominium unit

Sale of an Interest in Real Estate or Entity That Is in Substance Real Estate. Profit recognition is appropriate in a sale of a partial interest if the transaction is in fact a partial sale of real estate and all the listed conditions exist:

- Sale is to an independent buyer.
- Collection of sales price is reasonably assured.
- The seller will not be required to support the property, its operations, or related obligations to an extent greater than its proportionate interest.
- Buyer does not have preferences as to profits or cash flow. (If the buyer has such preferences, the cost recovery method is required.)

In the case of a sale of a partial interest in real estate, if the conditions set forth in the preceding paragraph are met, profit recognition must reflect an adjustment for the implied presumption that the seller is obligated to support the operations.

Seller Has Equity Interest in Buyer. No profit may be recognized if the seller controls the buyer. If the seller does not control the buyer, profit recognition (to the extent of the other investors' proportionate interests) is appropriate if all other necessary requirements for profit recognition are satisfied. The portion of the profit applicable to the equity interest of the seller/investor should be deferred until such costs are charged to operations by the venture. Again, with respect to a sale of real estate, a portion of the profit relating to other investors' interests may have to be spread as described in Subsection 31.2(f)(x) because there is an implied presumption that the seller is obligated to support the operations.

(g) SALES OF CONDOMINIUMS AND TENANTS IN COMMON. Although the definition of *condominium* varies by state, the term generally is defined as a multiunit structure in which there is fee simple title to individual units combined with an undivided interest in the common elements associated with the structure. The common elements are all areas exclusive of the individual units, such as hallways, lobbies, and elevators.

TIC is also a fee simple interest with undivided interests in the property and not to specific units.

A cooperative is contrasted to a condominium in that ownership of the building is generally vested in the entity, with the respective stockholders of the entity having a right to occupy specific units. Operation, maintenance, and control of the building are exercised by a governing board elected by the owners. This section covers only sales of condominium units.

(i) Criteria for Profit Recognition. The general principles of accounting for profit on sales of condominiums and TIC are essentially those previously discussed for sales of real estate in general.

The next criteria must be met prior to recognition of any profit on the sale of a dwelling unit in a condominium project:

- All parties must be bound by the terms of the contract. For the buyer to be bound, the buyer must be unable to require a refund. Certain state and federal laws require appropriate filings by the developer before the sales contract is binding; otherwise, the sale may be voidable at the option of the buyer.
- All conditions precedent to closing, except completion of the project, must be performed.
- An adequate cash down payment must be received by the seller. The minimum down payment requirements are 5 percent for a primary residence and 10 percent for a secondary or recreational residence.
- The buyer must be required to adequately increase the investment in the property annually; the buyer's commitment must be adequately secured. Typically, a condominium buyer pays the remaining balance from the proceeds of a permanent loan at the time of closing. If, however, the seller provides financing, the same considerations as other sales of real estate apply concerning amortization of the buyer's receivable.
- The developer must not have an option or obligation to repurchase the property.

(ii) Methods of Accounting. Sales of condominium units are accounted for by using the closing (completed contract) method or the percentage-of-completion method. Most developers use the closing method.

Additional criteria must be met for the use of the percentage-of-completion method:

- The developer must have the ability to estimate costs not yet incurred.
- Construction must be beyond a preliminary stage of completion. This generally means at least beyond the foundation stage.
- Sufficient units must be sold to assure that the property will not revert to rental property.
- The developer must be able to reasonably estimate aggregate sales proceeds.

Closing Method. The closing method involves recording the sale and related profit at the time a unit closes. Since the unit is completed, actual costs are used in determining profit to be recognized.

All payments or deposits received prior to closing are accounted for as a liability. Direct selling costs may be deferred until the sale is recorded. Where the seller is obligated to complete construction of common areas or has made guarantees to the condominium association, profit should be recognized based on the relationship of costs already incurred to total estimated costs, with a portion deferred until the future performance is completed.

Percentage-of-Completion Method. The percentage-of-completion method generally involves recording sales at the date a unit is sold and recognizing profit on units sold as construction proceeds. As a result, this method allows some profit recognition during the construction period. Although dependent on estimates, this method may be considered preferable for some long-term projects. A lack of reliable estimates, however, would preclude the use of this method.

Profit recognition is based on the percentage of completion of the project multiplied by the gross profit arising from the units sold. Percentage of completion may be determined by using either of these alternatives:

- The ratio of costs incurred to date to total estimated costs to be incurred. These costs could include land and common costs or could be limited to construction costs. The costs selected for inclusion should be those that most clearly reflect the earnings process.
- The percentage of completed construction based on architectural plans or engineering studies.

Under either method of accounting, if the total estimated costs exceed the estimated proceeds, the total anticipated loss should be charged against income in the period in which the loss becomes evident so that no anticipated losses are deferred to future periods. See further discussion of this method in Section 31.6.

(iii) Estimated Future Costs. As previously mentioned, future costs to complete must be estimated under either the closing method or the percentage-of-completion method. Estimates of future costs to complete are necessary to determine net realizable value of unsold units. Estimated future costs should be based on adequate plans and detail studies and should include reasonable provisions for:

- Unforeseen costs in accordance with sound cost estimation practices
- Anticipated cost inflation in the construction industry
- Costs of off-site improvements, utility facilities, and amenities (to the extent that they will not be recovered from outside third parties)
- Operating losses of utility operations and recreational facilities (Such losses would be expected to be incurred for a relatively limited period of time—usually prior to sale of facilities or transfer to some public authority.)
- Other guaranteed support arrangements or activities to the extent that they will not be recovered from outside parties or be the responsibility of a future purchaser

Estimates of amounts to be recovered from any sources should be discounted to present value as of the date the related costs are expected to be incurred.

Estimated costs to complete and the allocation of such costs should be reviewed at the end of each financial reporting period, with costs revised and reallocated as necessary on the basis of current estimates, as recommended in ASC 970 (SFAS No. 67), *Accounting for Costs and Initial Rental Operations of Real Estate Projects.* How to record the effects of changes in estimates depends on whether full revenues have been recorded or whether reporting of the revenue has been deferred due to an obligation for future performance or otherwise.

When sales of condominiums are recorded in full, it may be necessary to accrue certain estimated costs not yet incurred and also related profit thereon. Adjustments of accruals for costs applicable to such previously recognized sales, where deferral for future performance was not required, must be recognized and charged to costs of sales in the period in which they become known. See Subsection 31.2(g)(ii) for further discussion.

In many cases, sales are not recorded in full (such as when the seller has deferred revenue because of an obligation for future performance to complete improvements and amenities of a project). In these situations, the adjustments should not affect previously recorded deferred revenues applicable to future improvements but should be recorded prospectively in the current and future periods. An increase in the estimate of costs applicable to deferred revenues thus will result in profit margins lower than those recorded on previous revenues from the project. Consistency in the result of gross profit percentages (relative sales value) from period to period are an indicator of adequate development performance and sales.

An exception exists, however, when the revised total estimated costs exceed the applicable deferred revenue. If that occurs, the total anticipated loss should be charged against income in the period in which the need for adjustment becomes evident.

In addition, an increase in estimated costs to complete without comparable increases in market value could raise questions as to whether the estimated total costs of the remaining property exceed the project's net realizable value.

APB Opinion No. 20, *Accounting Changes,* has been interpreted to permit both the cumulative catch-up method and the prospective method of accounting for changes in accounting estimates. It should be noted that ASC 970 (SFAS No. 67, pars. 42–43) requires the prospective method.

(h) RETAIL LAND SALES. Retail land sales, a unique segment of the real estate industry, is the retail marketing of numerous lots subdivided from a larger parcel of land. The relevant accounting guidance originally covered by the AICPA Industry Accounting Guide, *Accounting for Retail Land*

Sales, and now included in ASC 360 (SFAS No. 66), applies to retail lot sales on a volume basis with down payments that are less than those required to evaluate the collectability of casual sales of real estate. Wholesale or bulk sales of land and retail sales from projects comprising a small number of lots, however, are subject to the general principles for profit recognition on real estate sales.

(i) Criteria for Recording a Sale. Sales should not be recorded until:

- The customer has made all required payments and the period of cancellation with refund has expired.
- Aggregate payments (including interest) equal or exceed 10 percent of contract sales price.
- The selling company is clearly capable of providing land improvements and off-site facilities promised as well as meeting all other representations it has made.

If these conditions are met, either the full accrual or the installment method can be used. If the conditions are not met, the deposit method of accounting should be used.

(ii) Criteria for Full Accrual Method. The next tests for the use of full accrual method should be applied on a project-by-project basis:

- The seller has fulfilled the obligation to complete improvements and to construct amenities or other facilities applicable to the lots sold.
- The receivable is not subject to subordination to new loans on the property, except subordination for home construction purposes under certain conditions.
- The collection experience for the project indicates that collectability of receivable balances is reasonably predictable and that 90 percent of the contracts in force six months after sales are recorded will be collected in full. A down payment of at least 20 percent shall be an acceptable indication of collectability.

To predict collection results of current sales, there must be satisfactory experience on prior sales of the type of land being currently sold in the project. In addition, the collection period must be sufficiently long to allow reasonable estimates of the percentage of sales that will be fully collected. In a new project, the developers' experience on prior projects may be used if they have demonstrated an ability to successfully develop other projects with the same characteristics (environment, clientele, contract terms, and sales methods) as the new project.

Collection and cancellation experience within a project may differ with varying sales methods (such as telephone, broker, and site visitation sales). Accordingly, historical data should be maintained with respect to each type of sales method used.

Unless all conditions for use of the full accrual method are met for the entire project, the installment method of accounting should be applied to all recorded sales of the project.

(iii) Full Accrual Method. Revenues and costs should be accounted for under the full accrual method in this way:

- The contract price should be recorded as gross sales.
- Receivables should be discounted to reflect an appropriate interest rate using the criteria established in APB Opinion No. 21.
- An allowance for contract cancellation should be recorded and deducted from gross sales to derive net sales.
- Cost of sales should be calculated based on net sales after reductions for sales reasonably expected to cancel.

(iv) Percentage-of-Completion Method. Frequently, the conditions for use of the full accrual method are met, except the seller has not yet completed the improvements, amenities, or other facilities required by the sales contract. In this situation, the percentage-of-completion method should be applied provided both of these conditions are met:

- There is a reasonable expectation that the land can be developed for the purposes represented.
- The project's improvements have progressed beyond preliminary stages, and there are indications that the work will be completed according to plan. Indications that the project has progressed beyond the preliminary stage include these:
  - Funds for the proposed improvements have been expended.
  - Work on the improvements has been initiated.
  - Engineering plans and work commitments exist relating to the lots sold.
  - Access roads and amenities such as golf courses, clubhouses, and swimming pools have been completed.

In addition, there should be no indication of significant delaying factors such as the inability to obtain permits, contractors, personnel, or equipment, and estimates of costs to complete and extent of progress toward completion shall be reasonably dependable.

The next general procedures should be used to account for revenues and costs under the percentage-of-completion method of accounting:

- The amount of revenue recognized (discounted where appropriate pursuant to APB Opinion No. 21) is based on the relationship of costs already incurred to the total estimated costs to be incurred.
- Costs incurred and to be incurred should include land, interest and project carrying costs incurred prior to sale, selling costs, and an estimate for future improvement costs.

Estimates of future improvement costs should be reviewed at least annually. Changes in those estimates do not lead to adjustment of deferred revenue applicable to future improvements that has been previously recorded unless the adjusted total estimated costs exceed the applicable revenue. When cost estimates are revised, the relationship of the two elements included in the revenue not yet recognized—cost and profit—should be recalculated on a cumulative basis to determine future income recognition as performance takes place. If the adjusted total estimated cost exceeds the applicable deferred revenue, the total anticipated loss should be charged to income. When anticipated losses on lots sold are recognized, the enterprise should also consider recognizing a loss on land and improvements not yet sold.

Future performance costs, such as roads, utilities, and amenities, may represent a significant obligation for a retail land developer. Estimates of such costs should be based on detail estimates, appropriately adjusted for anticipated inflation in the local construction industry, and should include reasonable estimates for unforeseen costs.

(v) Installment and Deposit Methods. If the criteria for the full accrual or percentage-of-completion methods are not satisfied, the installment or deposit method may be used. See Section 31.2(j) for a general discussion of these methods.

When the conditions required for use of the percentage-of-completion method are met on a project originally recorded under the installment method, the percentage-of-completion method of accounting should be adopted for the entire project (current and prior sales). The effect should be accounted for as a change in accounting estimate due to different circumstances and revised estimates. See Subsection 31.2(g)(iii) for further discussion of methodology.

(i) ACCOUNTING FOR SYNDICATION FEES. On February 6, 1992, the AICPA issued Statement of Position Statement of Position (SOP) No.92-1, *Accounting for Real Estate Syndication Income,* which provides guidance on accounting for real estate syndication income.

Syndicators expect to earn fees and commissions from a variety of sources, such as:

- Up-front fees such as lease-up fees, construction supervision fees, and financing fees
- Fees serving as an incentive
- Property management
- Participation in future profit or appreciation

At the time of the syndication, partnerships usually pay cash to the syndicator for portions of their up-front fees. These fees are usually paid from investor contributions or the proceeds of borrowings. Subsequent fees are expected to be paid from operations, refinancing, sale of property, or remaining investor payments.

The SOP states that ASC 360 (SFAS No. 66) applies to the recognition of profit on the sales of real estate by syndicators to partnerships. It concludes that profit on real estate syndication transactions be accounted for in accordance with ASC 360 (SFAS No. 66), even if the syndicator never had ownership interests in the properties acquired by the real estate partnerships.

The SOP states that fees charged by syndicators (except for syndication fees and fees for future services) should be included in the determination of "sales value" in conformity with ASC 360 (SFAS No. 66). It further states that ASC 360 (SFAS No. 66) does not apply to the fees excluded from "sales value." Fees for future services should be recognized when the earning process is complete and collection of the fee is reasonably assured.

This SOP requires that income recognition on syndication fees and fees for future services be deferred if the syndicator is exposed to future losses or costs from material involvement with the properties, partnerships or partners, or uncertainties regarding the collectability of partnership notes. The income should be deferred until the losses or costs can be reasonably estimated.

The SOP requires that for the purpose of determining whether buyers' initial and continuing investments satisfy the requirements for recognizing full profit in accordance with ASC 360 (SFAS No. 66), cash received by syndicators should be allocated to unpaid syndication fees before being allocated to the initial and continuing investment. After the syndication fee is fully paid, additional cash received should first be allocated to unpaid fees for future services, to the extent those services have been performed by the time the cash is received, before being allocated to the initial and continuing investment.

(j) ALTERNATE METHODS OF ACCOUNTING FOR SALES. As previously discussed, in some circumstances the full accrual method is not appropriate and other methods must be used. It is not always clear which method should be used or how it should be applied. Consequently, it is often difficult to determine the appropriate method and whether alternative ones are acceptable.

The methods of profit recognition prescribed where the buyer's initial or continuing investment is inadequate are the deposit, installment, cost recovery, and reduced profit methods.

The methods prescribed for a transaction that cannot be considered a sale because of the seller's continuing involvement are the financing, lease, and profit-sharing (or coventure) methods.

(i) Deposit Method. When the substance of a real estate transaction indicates that a sale has not occurred as a result of the buyer's inadequate investment, recognition of the sale should be deferred and the deposit method used even if it was a legal sale. This method should be continued until the conditions have changed to indicate a sale. For example, when the down payment is so small that the substance of the transaction is an option arrangement, the sale should not be recorded.

All cash received under the deposit method (including down payment and principal and interest payments by the buyer to the seller) should be reported as a deposit (liability). An exception is interest received that is not subject to refund may appropriately offset carrying charges (property taxes and interest on existing debt) on the property. Note also these related matters:

- Notes receivable arising from the transaction should not be recorded.
- The property and any related mortgage debt assumed by the buyer should continue to be reflected on the seller's balance sheet, with appropriate disclosure that such properties and

debt are subject to a sales contract. Even nonrecourse debt assumed by the buyer should not be offset against the related property.

- Subsequent payments on the debt assumed by the buyer become additional deposits and thereby reduce the seller's mortgage debt payable and increase the deposit liability account until a sale is recorded for accounting purposes.
- Depreciation should be continued.

Under the deposit method, a sale is not recorded for accounting purposes until the conditions in ASC 360 (SFAS No. 66) are met. Therefore, for purposes of the down payment tests, interest received and credited to the deposit account can be included in the down payment and sales value at the time a sale is recorded.

If a buyer defaults and forfeits a nonrefundable deposit, the deposit liability is no longer required and may be credited to income. The circumstances underlying the default should be carefully reviewed since such circumstances may indicate deteriorating value of the property. In such a case it may be appropriate to treat the credit as a valuation reserve. These circumstances may require a provision for additional loss. See Section 31.5 for further discussion.

(ii) Installment Method. When the substance of a real estate transaction indicates that a sale has occurred for accounting purposes but that collectability of the total sales price cannot be reasonably estimated (i.e., inadequate buyer's investment), the installment method may be appropriate. However, circumstances may indicate that the cost recovery method is required or is otherwise more appropriate. For example, when the deferred gross profit exceeds the net carrying value of the related receivable, profit may have been earned to the extent of such excess.

Profit should be recognized on cash payments, including principal payments by the buyer on any debt assumed (either recourse or nonrecourse), and should be based on the ratio of total profit to total sales value (including a first mortgage debt assumed by the buyer, if applicable). Interest received on the related receivable is properly recorded as income when received.

The total sales value (from which the deferred gross profit should be deducted) and the cost of sales should be presented in the income statement. Deferred gross profit should be shown as a deduction from the related receivable, with subsequent income recognition presented separately in the income statement.

(iii) Cost Recovery Method. The cost recovery method must be used when the substance of a real estate transaction indicates that a sale has occurred but major uncertainties exist. This may occur when (1) the receivable is subject to future subordination, (2) the seller retains an interest in the property sold and the buyer has preferences, (3) uncertainty exists as to whether all or a portion of the cost will be recovered, or (4) there is uncertainty as to the amount of proceeds. As a practical matter, the cost recovery method can always be used as an alternative to the installment method.

Under the cost recovery method, no profit is recognized until cash collections (including principal and interest payments) and existing debt assumed by the buyer exceed the cost of the property sold. Cash collections in excess of cost should be recorded as revenue in the period of collection.

Financial statement presentation under the cost recovery method is similar to that for the installment method.

(iv) Reduced Profit Method. When the substance of a real estate transaction indicates that a sale has occurred for accounting purposes but the continuing investment criteria for full profit recognition is not met by the buyer, the seller may sometimes recognize a reduced profit at the time of sale (see additional discussion in Subsection 31.2(e)(ii)). This alternative is usually used when the portion of the seller's receivable that is contingent upon some indicator is applied as a reduction of the sales price thereby reducing the full profit, if any, until collection is assured.

(v) Financing Method. A real estate transaction may be, in substance, a financing arrangement rather than a sale. This is frequently the case when the seller has an obligation to repurchase the property or can be compelled by the buyer to repurchase the property. In such a case the financing method must be used.

Accounting procedures under the financing method should be similar to the accounting procedures under the deposit method, with one exception. Under the financing method, the difference between (1) the total amount of all payments received and to be received and (2) the repurchase price is presumed to be interest expense. As such, it should be accrued on the interest method over the period from the receipt of cash to the date of repurchase. As in the deposit method, cash received is reflected as a liability in the balance sheet. Thus, at the date of repurchase, the full amount of the repurchase obligation should be recorded as a liability.

In the case of a repurchase option, if the facts and circumstances at the time of the sale indicate a presumption or likelihood that the seller will repurchase the property, interest should be accrued as if there were an obligation to repurchase. This presumption could result from the value of the property, the property being an integral part of development, or from management's intention. If such a presumption does not exist at the time of the sale transaction, interest should not be accrued and the deposit method is appropriate.

(vi) Lease Method. A real estate transaction may be, in substance, a lease rather than a sale. Accounting procedures under the lease method should be similar to the deposit method, except in these cases:

- Payments received and to be received that are in substance deferred rental income received in advance should be deferred and amortized to income over the presumed lease period. Such amortization to income should not exceed cash paid to the seller.
- Cash paid out by the seller as a guarantee of support of operations should be expensed as paid.

The seller may agree to make *loans* to the *buyer* in support of operations, for example, when cash flow does not equal a predetermined amount or is negative. In such a situation, deferred rental income to be amortized to income should be reduced by all the loans made or reasonably anticipated to be made to the buyer, thus reducing the periodic income to be recognized. Where the loans made or anticipated exceed deferred rental income, a loss provision may be required if the collectability of the loan is questionable.

(vii) Profit-Sharing or Coventure Method. A real estate transaction may be, in substance, a profit-sharing arrangement rather than a sale. For example, a sale of real estate to a limited partnership in which the seller is a general partner or has similar characteristics is often a profit-sharing arrangement. If such a transaction does not meet the tests for recording a sale, it usually would be accounted for under the profit-sharing method. This accounting method should also be followed when it is clear that the buyer and seller are acting in consort for future profits

Under the profit-sharing method, giving consideration to the seller's continued involvement, the seller would be required to account for its share of the operations of the property through the venture's income statement on an equity or consolidated basis.

(viii) Derecognition Method. The FASB has released for public comment proposed Accounting Standards Update (ASU) EITF-100E, *Property, Plant, and Equipment (Topic 360): Derecognition of in Substance Real Estate—a Scope Clarification.* The proposed ASU contains the consensus for exposure reached by the EITF at its June 2011 meeting. The proposal aims to resolve diversity in practice about whether the guidance for the sale and transfer of real estate in ASC 360-20 (formerly Financial Accounting Standard [FAS] No. 66) or the deconsolidation guidance in ASC 810-10 (formerly FAS 160) applies to a parent that ceases to have a controlling financial interest in a subsidiary that is in substance real estate as a result of default on the subsidiary's nonrecourse debt. Under the proposal, the real estate sales guidance would govern these situations.

31.3 CAPITALIZED COST OF REAL ESTATE

(a) CAPITALIZATION OF COSTS. In October 1982, the FASB issued ASC 970 (SFAS No. 67). This Statement incorporates the specialized accounting principles and practices from the AICPA SOPs No. 80-3, *Accounting for Real Estate Acquisition, Development and Construction Costs,* and No. 78-3, *Accounting for Costs to Sell and Rent, and Initial Rental Operations of Real Estate Projects,* and those in the AICPA Industry Accounting Guide, *Accounting for Retail Land Sales,* that address costs of real estate projects. ASC 970 (SFAS No. 67) establishes whether costs associated with acquiring, developing, constructing, selling, and renting real estate projects should be capitalized. Guidance is also provided on the appropriate methods of allocating capitalized costs to individual components of the project.

ASC 970 (SFAS No. 67) also established that a rental project changes from nonoperating to operating when it is substantially completed and held available for occupancy, but not later than one year from cessation of major construction activities.

Costs incurred in real estate operations range from brick-and-mortar costs that clearly should be capitalized to general administrative costs that clearly should not be capitalized. Between these two extremes lies a broad range of costs that are difficult to classify. Therefore, judgmental decisions must be made as to whether such costs should be capitalized.

(b) PREACQUISITION COSTS. Preacquisition costs include payments to obtain options to acquire real property and other costs incurred prior to acquisition such as legal, architectural, and other professional fees, salaries, environmental studies, appraisals, marketing and feasibility studies, and soil tests. Capitalization of costs related to a property that are incurred before the enterprise acquires the property, or before the enterprise obtains an option to acquire it, is appropriate provided all of these conditions are met:

- The costs are directly identifiable with the specific property.
- The costs would be capitalized if the property had already been acquired.
- Acquisition of the property or of an option to acquire the property is probable (i.e., likely to occur). This condition requires that the prospective purchaser is actively seeking acquisition of the property and has the ability to finance or obtain financing for the acquisition. In addition, there should be no indication that the property is not available for sale.

Capitalized preacquisition costs should be included as project costs on acquisition of the property or should be written off to expense when it is probable that the property will not be acquired. The charge to expense should be reduced by the amount recoverable by the recapturing of the preacquistions costs.

(c) LAND ACQUISITION COSTS. Costs directly related to the acquisition of land should be capitalized. These costs include option fees, purchase cost, transfer costs, title insurance, legal and other professional fees, surveys, appraisals, and real estate commissions. The purchase cost may have to be increased or decreased for market adjustment imputation of interest on mortgage notes payable assumed or issued in connection with the purchase, as required under APB Opinion No. 21.

(d) LAND IMPROVEMENT, DEVELOPMENT, AND CONSTRUCTION COSTS. Costs directly related to improvements of the land should be capitalized by the developer. They usually include:

- Land planning costs, including marketing and feasibility studies, direct salaries, legal and other professional fees, zoning costs, soil tests, architectural and engineering studies, appraisals, environmental studies, and other costs directly related to site preparation and the overall design and development of the project

- On-site and off-site improvements, including demolition costs, streets, traffic controls, sidewalks, street lighting, sewer and water facilities, utilities, parking lots, landscaping, and related costs, such as permits and inspection fees
- Construction costs, including on-site material and labor, direct supervision, engineering and architectural fees, permits, and inspection fees
- Project overhead and supervision, such as field office costs
- Recreation facilities, such as golf courses, clubhouse, swimming pools, and tennis courts
- Sales center and models, including furnishings

General and administrative costs not directly identified with the project should be accounted for as period costs and expensed as incurred.

Construction activity on a project may be suspended before a project is completed for reasons such as insufficient funding, sales or rental demand. These conditions may indicate an impairment of the value of a project that is other than temporary, which suggests valuation issues (see Section 31.5).

(e) ENVIRONMENTAL ISSUES. In EITF Issue No. 90-8, *Capitalization of Costs to Treat Environmental Contamination,* the EITF reached a consensus that, in general, costs incurred as a result of environmental contamination should be charged to expense. Such costs include costs:

- To remove contamination, such as that caused by leakage from underground tanks
- To acquire tangible property, such as air pollution control equipment of environmental studies
- Of fines levied under environmental laws

Nevertheless, those costs may be capitalized if recoverable but only if any one of the next criteria is met:

- The costs extend the life, increase the capacity, or improve the safety or efficiency of property owned by the company, provided that the condition of the property after the costs are incurred must be improved as compared with the condition of the property when originally constructed or acquired, if later.
- The costs mitigate or prevent environmental contamination that has yet to occur and that otherwise may result from future operations or activities. In addition, the costs improve the property compared with its condition when constructed or acquired, if later.
- The costs are incurred in preparing for sale that property currently held for sale.

In EITF Issue No. 93-5, *Accounting for Environmental Liabilities,* the EITF reached a consensus that an environmental liability should be evaluated independently from any potential claim for recovery (a two-event approach) and that the loss arising from the recognition of an environmental liability should be reduced only when it is probable that a claim for recovery will be realized.

The EITF also reached a consensus that discounting environmental liabilities for a specific cleanup site to reflect the time value of money is allowed, but not required, only if the aggregate amount of the obligation and the amount and timing of the cash payments for that site are fixed or reliably determinable.

The EITF discussed alternative rates to be used in discounting environmental liabilities but did not reach a consensus on the rate to be used. However, the Securities and Exchange Commission (SEC) Observer stated that SEC registrants should use a discount rate that will produce an amount at which the environmental liability theoretically could be settled in an arm's-length transaction with a third party. That discount rate should not exceed the interest rate on monetary assets that are essentially risk-free (i.e., U.S. Treasury notes) and have maturities comparable to that of the environmental liability. In addition, SEC Staff Accounting Bulletin (SAB) 92, *Accounting and*

Disclosures Relating to Loss Contingencies, requires registrants to separately present the gross liability and related claim recovery in the balance sheet. SAB 92 also requires other accounting and disclosure requirements relating to product or environmental liabilities.

In October 1996, the AICPA issued SOP 96-1, *Environmental Remediation Liabilities.* The SOP has three parts. Part I provides an overview of environmental laws and regulations. Part II provides authoritative guidance on the recognition, measurement, display, and disclosure of environmental liabilities. Part III (labeled as an appendix) provides guidance for auditors. A major objective of the SOP is to articulate a framework for the recognition, measurement, and disclosure of environmental liabilities. That framework is derived from ASC 450 (SFAS No. 5), *Accounting for Contingencies.*

The accounting guidance in the SOP is generally applicable when an entity is mandated to remediate a contaminated site by a governmental agency. However, the SOP does not address these issues:

- Accounting for pollution control costs with respect to current operations, which is addressed in EITF Issue No. 90-8, *Capitalization of Costs to Treat Environmental Contamination*
- Accounting for costs with respect to asbestos removal, which is addressed in EITF Issue No. 89-13, *Accounting for the Costs of Asbestos Removal*
- Accounting for costs of future site restoration or closure that are required upon the cessation of operations or sale of facilities, which is the subject of the FASB's project, *Obligations Associated with Disposal Activities*
- Accounting for environmental remediation actions that are undertaken at the sole discretion of management and that are not undertaken by the threat of assertion of litigation, a claim, or an assessment
- Recognizing liabilities of insurance companies for unpaid claims, which is addressed in ASC 944 (SFAS No. 60), *Accounting and Reporting by Insurance Enterprises*
- Asset impairment issues discussed in ASC 360 (SFAS No. 144), *Accounting for the Impairment or Disposal of Long-Lived Assets,* and EITF Issue No. 95-23, *The Treatment of Certain Site Restoration/Environmental Exit Costs When Testing a Long-Lived Asset for Impairment.*

(f) INTEREST COSTS. Prior to 1979, many developers capitalized interest costs as a necessary cost of the asset in the same way as bricks-and-mortar costs. Others followed an accounting policy of charging off interest cost as a period cost on the basis that it was solely a financing cost that varied directly with the capability of a company to finance development and construction through equity funds. This long-standing debate on capitalization of interest cost was resolved in October 1979 when the FASB published ASC 360 (SFAS No. 34), *Capitalization of Interest Cost,* which provides specific guidelines for accounting for interest costs.

ASC 360 (SFAS No. 34) requires capitalization of interest cost as part of the historical cost of acquiring assets that need a period of time in which to bring them to that condition and location necessary for their intended use. The objectives of capitalizing interest are to obtain a measure of acquisition cost that more closely reflects the enterprise's total investment in the asset and to charge a cost that relates to the acquisition of a resource that will benefit future periods against the revenues of the periods benefited. Interest capitalization is not required if its effect is not material.

(i) Assets Qualifying for Interest Capitalization. Assets qualifying for interest capitalization in conformity with ASC 360 (SFAS No. 34) include real estate constructed for an enterprise's own use or real estate intended for sale or lease. Qualifying assets also include investments accounted for by the equity method while the investee has activities in progress necessary to commence its planned principal operations, but only if the investee's activities include the use of such to acquire qualifying assets for its operations.

Capitalization is not permitted for assets in use or ready for their intended use, assets not undergoing the activities necessary to prepare them for use, assets that are not included in the consolidated balance sheet, or investments accounted for by the equity method after the planned principal operations of the investee begin. Thus land that is not undergoing activities necessary for development is not a qualifying asset for purposes of interest capitalization. If activities are undertaken for developing the land, the expenditures to acquire the land qualify for interest capitalization while those activities are in progress.

(ii) Capitalization Period. The capitalization period commences when:

- Costs for the asset have been incurred.
- Activities that are necessary to get the asset ready for its intended use are in progress.
- Interest cost is being incurred.

Activities are to be construed in a broad sense and encompass more than just physical construction. All steps necessary to prepare an asset for its intended use are included. This broad interpretation includes administrative and technical activities during the preconstruction stage (such as developing plans or obtaining required permits).

Interest capitalization must end when the asset is substantially complete and ready for its intended use. A real estate project should be considered substantially complete and held available for occupancy upon completion of major construction activity, as distinguished from activities such as routine maintenance and cleanup. In some cases, such as in an office building, tenant improvements are a major construction activity and frequently are not completed until a lease contract is arranged. If such improvements are the responsibility of the developer, ASC 970 (SFAS No. 67) indicates that the project is not considered substantially complete until the earlier of (1) completion of improvements or (2) one year from cessation of major construction activity without regard to tenant improvements. In other words, a one-year grace period has been provided to complete tenant improvements.

If substantially all activities related to acquisition of the asset are suspended, interest capitalization should stop and expensed until such activities are resumed. However, brief interruptions in activities, interruptions caused by external factors, and inherent delays in the development process do not necessarily require suspension of interest capitalization.

Under ASC 360 (SFAS No. 34), interest capitalization must end when the asset is substantially complete and ready for its intended use. For projects completed in parts, where each part is capable of being used independently while work continues on other parts, interest capitalization should stop and expensed on each part that is substantially complete and ready for use. Examples include individual buildings in a multiphase or condominium project. For projects that must be completed before any part can be used, interest capitalization should continue until the entire project is substantially complete and ready for use. Where an asset cannot be used effectively until a particular portion has been completed, interest capitalization continues until that portion is substantially complete and ready for use. An example would be an island resort complex with sole access being a permanent bridge to the project. Completion of the bridge is necessary for the asset to be used effectively.

Interest capitalization should not stop when the capitalized costs exceed net realizable value. In such instances, a valuation reserve should be recorded or appropriately increased to reduce the carrying value to net realizable value (see Section 31.3(I)).

(iii) Methods of Interest Capitalization. The basic principle of interest capitalization is that the amount of interest cost to be capitalized should be the amount that theoretically could have been avoided during the development and construction period if expenditures for the qualifying asset had not been made. These interest costs might have been avoided either by forgoing additional borrowing or by using the funds expended for the asset to repay existing borrowings in the case where no new borrowings were obtained.

The amount capitalized is determined by applying an interest rate to the average amount of accumulated capitalized expenditures for the asset during the period. Such expenditures include cash payments, transfer of other assets, or incurrence of liabilities on which interest has been recognized, and they should be net of progress payments received against such capitalized costs. Liabilities such as trade payables, accruals, and retainages, on which interest is not recognized, are not expenditures. Reasonable approximations of net capitalized expenditures may be used.

In general, the interest rate should be based on the weighted average of the rates applicable to borrowings outstanding during the period. If a specific new borrowing is associated with an asset, the rate on that borrowing may be used. If the average amount of accumulated expenditures for the asset exceeds the amounts of specific new borrowings associated with the asset, a weighted average interest rate of all other borrowings must be applied to the excess. Under this alternative, judgment will be required to select the borrowings to be included in the weighted average rate so that a reasonable measure will be obtained of the interest cost incurred that could otherwise have been avoided. It should be remembered that the principle is not one of capitalizing interest costs incurred for a specific asset but of capitalizing interest costs that could have been avoided if it were not for the acquisition, development, and construction of the asset.

The amount of interest cost capitalized in an accounting period is limited to the total amount of interest cost incurred in the period. However, interest cost should include amortization of premium or discount resulting from imputation of interest on certain types of payables in accordance with APB Opinion No. 21 and that portion of minimum lease payments under a capital lease treated as interest in accordance with ASC 840 (SFAS No. 13).

(iv) Accounting for Amount Capitalized. Interest cost capitalized is an integral part of the cost of acquiring a qualifying asset, and therefore its disposition should be the same as any other cost of that asset. For example, if a building is subsequently depreciated, capitalized interest should be included in the depreciable base the same as bricks and mortar.

In the case of interest capitalized on an investment accounted for by the equity method, its disposition should be made as if the investee were consolidated. In other words, if the assets of the investee were being depreciated, the capitalized interest cost should be depreciated in the same manner and over the same lives. If the assets of the investee were developed lots being sold, the capitalized interest cost should be written off as the lots are sold.

(g) TAXES AND INSURANCE. Costs incurred on real estate for property taxes and insurance should be treated similarly to interest costs. They should be capitalized only during periods in which activities necessary to get the property ready for its intended use are in progress. Costs incurred for such items after the property is substantially complete and ready for its intended use should be charged to expense as incurred.

(h) INDIRECT PROJECT COSTS. Indirect project costs that relate to a specific project, such as costs associated with a project field office, should be capitalized as a cost of that project. Other indirect project costs that relate to several projects, such as the costs associated with a construction administration department, should be capitalized and allocated to the projects to which the cost related. Indirect costs that do not clearly relate to projects under development or construction should be charged to expense as incurred. The principal problem is defining and identifying the cost to be capitalized. It is necessary to consider all of the next points:

- Specific information should be available (such as time cards) to support the basis of allocation to specific projects.
- The costs incurred should be incremental costs; that is, in the absence of the project or projects under development or construction, these costs would not be incurred.
- The impact of capitalization of such costs on the results of operations should be consistent with the pervasive principle of matching costs with related revenue.
- The principle of conservatism should be considered.

Indirect costs related to a specific project that should be considered for capitalization include direct and indirect salaries of a field office and insurance costs. Costs that are not directly related to the project should be charged to expense as incurred. An appropriate test for the capitalization of indirect costs is to question the existence of these costs if no project (s) were being developed. If the answer is yes, then they should be expensed as incurred.

(i) GENERAL AND ADMINISTRATIVE EXPENSES. Real estate developers incur various types of general and administrative expenses, including officers' salaries, accounting and legal fees, and various office supplies and expenses. Some of these expenses may be closely associated with individual projects, whereas others are of a more general nature. For example, a developer may open a field office on a project site and staff it with administrative personnel, such as a field accountant. The expenses associated with the field office are directly associated with the project and are therefore considered to be overhead. The developer also may have a number of expenses associated with general office operations that benefit numerous projects and for which specifically identifiable allocations are not reasonable or practicable. Those administrative costs that cannot be clearly related to projects under development or construction should be charged to current operations.

(j) AMENITIES. Real estate developments often include *amenities* such as golf courses, utilities, clubhouses, swimming pools, and tennis courts. The accounting for the costs of these amenities should be based on management's intended disposition, as discussed next:

- *Amenity to be sold or transferred with sales units.* All costs in excess of anticipated proceeds should be allocated as common costs because the amenity is clearly associated with the development and sale of the project. Common costs should include estimated net operating costs to be borne by the developer until they are assumed by buyers of units in the project.
- *Amenity to be sold separately or retained by developer.* Capitalizable costs of the amenity in excess of its estimated fair value on the expected date of its substantial physical completion should be allocated as common costs. The costs capitalized and allocated to the amenity should not be revised after the amenity is substantially completed and available for use. A later sale of the amenity at more or less than the determined fair value as of the date of substantial physical completion, less any accumulated depreciation, should result in a gain or loss in the period in which the sale occurs.

(k) ABANDONMENTS AND CHANGES IN USE. Real estate, including rights to real estate, may be abandoned, for example, by allowing a mortgage to be foreclosed or by allowing a purchase option to lapse. Capitalized costs, including allocated common costs, of real estate abandoned should be written off as current expenses or, if appropriate, to allowances previously established for that purpose. They should not be allocated to other components of the project or to other projects, even if other components or other projects are capable of absorbing the losses.

Donation of real estate to municipalities or other governmental agencies for uses that will benefit the project are not abandonment. The cost of real estate donated should be allocated as a common cost of the project.

Changes in the intended use of a real estate project may arise after significant development and construction costs have been incurred. If the change in use is made pursuant to a formal plan that is expected to produce a higher economic yield (as compared to its yield based on use before change), the project costs should be charged to expense to the extent the capitalized costs incurred and to be incurred exceed the estimated fair value less cost to sell of the revised project when it is substantially completed and ready for its intended use.

(l) SELLING COSTS. Costs incurred to sell real estate projects should be accounted for in the same manner as, and classified with, construction costs of the project when they meet both of these criteria:

- The costs incurred are for tangible assets that are used throughout the selling period or for services performed to obtain regulatory approval for sales.
- The costs are reasonably expected to be recovered from sales of the project or incidental operations.

Examples of costs incurred to sell real estate projects that ordinarily meet the criteria for capitalization are costs of model units and their furnishings, sales facilities, legal fees for the preparation of prospectuses, and semi permanent signs.

ASC 970 (SFAS No. 67) states that other costs incurred to sell real estate projects should be capitalized as prepaid costs if they are directly associated with and their recovery is reasonably expected from sales that are being accounted for under a method of accounting other than full accrual. Costs that do not meet the criteria for capitalization should be expensed as incurred.

Capitalized selling costs should be charged to expense in the period in which the related revenue is recognized as earned. When a sales contract is canceled (with or without refund) or the related receivable is written off as uncollectable, the related unrecoverable capitalized selling costs are charged to expense or to an allowance previously established for that purpose.

(m) ACCOUNTING FOR FORECLOSED ASSETS. Proposed ASU No. EITF-100E deals specifically with the events of foreclosure. It attempts to end some inconsistent application of FASB ASC 360-20-15 and provide clear guidance for dealing with subsidiaries and special-purpose entities that have defaulted on loans used to buy commercial property. FAS No. 66 conditions precedent to foreclosure are applicable.

AICPA SOP 92-3, *Accounting for Foreclosed Assets,* provides guidance on determining the balance sheet treatment of foreclosed assets after foreclosure.

The SOP contains a rebuttable presumption that foreclosed assets are held for sale rather than for the production of income. That presumption may be overcome if (1) management intends to hold a foreclosed asset, (2) laws and regulations as applied permit management to hold the asset, and (3) management's intent is supported by a preponderance of the evidence.

(i) Foreclosed Assets Held for Sale. After foreclosure, foreclosed assets held for sale should be carried at the lower of (a) fair value less estimated costs to sell or (b) net book value. The SOP states that, if the fair value of the asset less the estimated cost to sell is less than the asset's net book value, the deficiency should be recognized as an impairment expense. However, that provision has been superseded by ASC 360 (SFAS No. 144), which prohibits the subsequent restoration of previously recognized impairment losses.

The amount of any senior debt (principal and accrued interest) to which the asset is subject should be reported as a liability at the time of foreclosure and should not be deducted from the carrying amount of the asset.

(ii) Foreclosed Assets Held for Production of Income. After foreclosure, assets determined to be held for the production of income (and not held for sale) should be accounted for in the same way that they would have been had the asset been acquired other than through foreclosure.

31.4 ALLOCATION OF COSTS

After it has been determined what costs are capitalized, it becomes important to determine how the costs should be allocated, because those costs will enter into the calculation of cost of sales of individual units and depreciation. Although a number of methods of allocation can be used in different circumstances, judgment often must be used to make sure that appropriate results are obtained.

(a) METHODS OF ALLOCATION. Capitalized costs of real estate projects should first be assigned to individual components of the project based on specific identification. If specific identification on an overall basis is not practicable, capitalized costs should be allocated as shown next:

- Land costs and all other common costs should be allocated to each land parcel benefited. Allocation should be based on the relative fair value before construction.

- Construction costs should be assigned to buildings on a specific identification basis and allocated to individual units on the basis of relative value of each unit.

In the usual situation, individual sales prices or rental units are available to compute relative values. In rare situations, however, where relative value is impracticable, capitalized costs may be allocated based on the area method/or the relative cost method as appropriate under the circumstances.

The next sections describe the specific identification, value, and area methods of cost allocation.

(i) Specific Identification Method. The specific identification method of cost allocation is based on determining actual costs applicable to each component of real estate. It rarely is used for land costs because such costs usually encompass more than one parcel. However, it frequently is used for direct construction costs because these costs are directly related to the property being sold or held for use. This method should be used wherever practicable.

(ii) Value Method. The relative value method is the method usually used after direct costs have been assigned on a specific identification basis. Under this method, the allocation of common costs should be based on relative fair value (before value added by on-site development and construction activities) of each land parcel benefited. In multiproject developments, common costs are normally allocated based on estimated sales prices net of direct improvements and selling costs. This approach is usually the most appropriate because it is less likely to result in deferral of losses.

With respect to condominium sales, certain units will usually have a higher price because of location. With respect to time-sharing sales, holiday periods such as Easter, Fourth of July, and Christmas traditionally sell at a premium. Depending on the resort location, the summer or winter season will also sell at a premium as compared with the rest of the year. Caution should be exercised to ensure that the relative sales values utilized in cost allocation are reasonable.

(iii) Area Method. The area method of cost allocation is based on square footage, acreage, or frontage. The use of this method will not always result in a logical allocation of costs. When negotiating the purchase price for a large tract of land, the purchaser considers the overall utility of the tract, recognizing that various parcels in the tract are more valuable than others. For example, parcels on a lake front are usually more valuable than those back from the lake. In this situation, if a simple average based on square footage or acreage is used to allocate costs to individual parcels, certain parcels could be assigned costs in excess of their net realizable value.

Generally, the area method should be limited to situations where each individual parcel is estimated to have approximately the same relative value. Under such circumstances, the cost allocations as determined by either the area or value methods would be approximately the same.

31.5 VALUATION ISSUES

FASB issued an exposure draft of a proposed ASU, *Qualitative Test To Determine Impairment,* that would change the goodwill impairment test under U.S. GAAP. The proposal would allow an entity first to assess "qualitatively" whether it is necessary to perform the current two-step goodwill impairment test. Further testing would be required only if an entity determines it is more likely than not that a reporting unit's fair value is less than its carrying amount.

FASB issued ASU 2011-04, *Fair Value Measurement (Topic 820): Amendments to Achieve Common Fair Value Measurement and Disclosure Requirements in U.S. GAAP and IFRS,* and the IASB issued International Financial Reporting Standards (IFRS) No. 13, *Fair Value Measurement* (together, the new guidance). The new guidance results in a consistent definition of fair value and common requirements for measurement of and disclosure about fair value between U.S. GAAP and IFRS. While many of the amendments to U.S. GAAP are not expected to have a significant effect on practice, the new guidance changes some fair value measurement principles and disclosure requirements.

FASB continued its re-deliberations on the classification and measurement of financial instruments and made a number of significant decisions related to financial liabilities and equity investments not accounted for under the equity method. Consistent with its recent decision on financial assets, the Board decided to allow financial liabilities to be measured at amortized cost or fair value depending on an entity's business strategy for the portfolio and the individual instrument's characteristics. In addition, the Board affirmed its prior decision that all equity investments not accounted for under the equity method should be measured at fair value with changes in fair value recognized in net income.

Currently two major pronouncements issued by FASB have a dramatic impact on real estate accounting. FASB issued ASC 360 (SFAS No. 144) and ASC 820 (SFAS No. 157).

(a) ACCOUNTING FOR IMPAIRMENT OR DISPOSAL OF LONG-LIVED ASSETS. FASB issued ASC 360 (SFAS No. 144), *Accounting for the Impairment or Disposal of Long-Lived Assets,* which supersedes SFAS No. 121, *Accounting for the Impairment of Long-Lived Assets and for Long-Lived Assets to Be Disposed Of.* ASC 360 (SFAS No. 144) retains many of the fundamental provisions of SFAS No. 121, particularly that long-lived assets be measured at the lower of carrying amount or fair value less cost to sell.

A major change to previous practice is that the accounting model for long-lived assets to be disposed of by sale applies to all long-lived assets, including discontinued operations, thus superseding provisions of APB Opinion No. 30, *Reporting Results of Operations—Reporting the Effects of Disposal of a Segment of a Business.* Discontinued operations no longer are measured at net realizable value, nor do they include amounts for operating losses that have not yet occurred. However, ASC 360 (SFAS No. 144) retains the requirement in APB Opinion No. 30 to report separately discontinued operations and extends the reporting of discontinued operations to include all components of an entity with operations that can be distinguished from the rest of the entity and that will be eliminated from the ongoing operations of the entity in a disposal transaction. The new reporting requirements are intended to more clearly communicate in the financial statements a change in an entity's business that results from a decision to dispose of operations and, thus, provide users with information needed to better focus on the ongoing activities of the entity.

In another major change from SFAS No. 121, the scope of ASC 360 (SFAS No. 144) does not encompass goodwill. That is, goodwill will not be written down as a result of applying the Statement, but goodwill may be included in the carrying amount of an asset group for purposes of applying the Statement's provisions if that group is a reporting unit or includes a reporting unit. ASC 360 (SFAS No. 144) also does not address impairment of other intangible assets that are not amortized; ASC 350 (SFAS No. 142), *Goodwill and Other Intangible Assets,* issued in July 2001, addresses impairment of goodwill and intangible assets that are not amortized.

(i) Real Estate to be Held and Used. ASC 360 (SFAS No. 144) establishes three steps for recognizing and measuring impairment on long-lived assets and certain identifiable intangibles to be held and used:

1. *Indicators.* The Statement provides a list of indicators that serve as a warning light when the value of an asset to be held and used may have been impaired. The presence of any of the following indicators evidence a need for additional investigation:
   - A significant decrease in the market value of an asset
   - A significant change in the extent or manner in which an asset is used or a significant change in an asset
   - A significant adverse change in legal factors or in business climate that could affect the value of an asset or an adverse action or assessment by a regulator
   - An accumulation of costs significantly in excess of the amount originally expected to acquire or construct an asset

- A current period operating or cash flow loss combined with a history of operating or cash flow losses or a projection or forecast that demonstrates continuing losses associated with an asset used for the purpose of producing revenue
- A current expectation that it is more likely than not (greater than 50 percent likelihood) that an asset will be sold or otherwise disposed of significantly before the end of its previously estimated useful life

The list of indicators is not intended to be all-inclusive. Other events or changes in circumstances may indicate that the carrying amount of an asset that an entity expects to hold and use may not be recoverable.

2. *Gross cash flow analysis.* An entity that detects one or more of the indicators just discussed should evaluate whether the sum of the expected future net cash flows (undiscounted and without interest charges) associated with an asset to be held and used is at least equal to the asset's carrying amount. The FASB imposed a high threshold for triggering the impairment analysis. The selection of a cash flow test based on undiscounted amounts will trigger the recognition of an impairment loss less frequently than would a test based on fair value.
3. *Measurement.* For assets to be held and used, the Statement requires an impairment loss to be measured as the amount by which the carrying amount of the impaired asset exceeds its fair value. The distinction between the recognition process, which uses undiscounted cash flows, and the measurement process, which uses fair value or discounted cash flows, is significant. As a result of a relatively minor change in undiscounted cash flows, the impairment measurement process might kick in, thus causing the balance sheet amount to drop off suddenly in any period in which undiscounted cash flows fall below a long-lived asset's carrying amount. Once assets to be held and used are written down, the Statement does not permit them to be written back up. Thus, a new depreciable cost basis is established after a write-down, and subsequent increases in the value or recoverable cost of the asset may not be recognized until its sale or disposal. In addition, an asset that is assessed for impairment should be evaluated to determine whether a change to the useful life or salvage value estimate is warranted under APB Opinion No. 20. ASC 360 (SFAS No. 144) thus forces entities to immediately record a loss on an impaired asset instead of shortening the depreciable life or decreasing the salvage value of the asset.

(ii) Real Estate to Be Disposed of. ASC 360 (SFAS No. 144) requires long-lived assets held for sale to be reported at the lower of carrying amount or fair value less cost to sell regardless of whether the assets previously were held for use or recently acquired with the intent to sell. The cost to sell generally includes the incremental direct costs to transact the sale, such as broker commissions, legal and title transfer fees, and closing costs. Costs generally excluded from cost to sell include insurance, security services, utility expenses, and other costs of protecting or maintaining the asset. Subsequent upward adjustments to the carrying amount of an asset to be disposed of may not exceed the carrying amount of the asset before an adjustment was made to reflect the decision to dispose of it. A long-lived asset that is classified as held for sale is not depreciated during the holding period.

While SFAS No. 121 required an entity's management to be committed to a disposal plan before it could classify that asset as held for sale, it did not specify other factors that an entity should consider before reclassifying the asset. ASC 360 (SFAS No. 144) lists six criteria that must be met in order to classify an asset as held for sale:

1. Management with the authority to do so commits to a plan to sell the asset (disposal group).
2. The asset (disposal group) is available for immediate sale in its present condition subject only to terms that are usual and customary for sales of such assets (disposal groups). This criterion does not preclude an entity from using an asset while it is classified as held for sale nor does it require a binding agreement for future sale as a condition of reporting an asset as held for sale.

3. The entity initiates an active program to locate a buyer and other actions that are required to complete the plan to sell the asset (disposal group).
4. The entity believes that the sale of the asset (disposal group) is probable (i.e., likely to occur), and, in general, it expects to record the transfer of the asset (disposal group) as a completed sale within one year.
5. The entity actively is marketing the asset (disposal group) for sale at a price that is reasonable in relation to its current fair value.
6. Actions required to complete the plan indicate that it is unlikely that significant changes to the plan will be made or that the plan will be withdrawn.

ASC 360 (SFAS No. 144) requires an asset or group that will be disposed of other than by sale to continue to be classified as held for use until the disposal transaction occurs. As a result, the asset continues to be depreciated until the date of disposal. Dispositions other than by sale include abandonment or a transaction that will be accounted for at the asset's carrying amount, such as an exchange for a similar productive long-lived asset or a distribution to owners in a spinoff.

(b) REAL ESTATE UNDER DEVELOPMENT. For homebuilders and other real estate developers, ASC 360 (SFAS No. 144) classifies land to be developed and projects under development as assets to be held and used until the six criteria for reclassification as held for sale are met (see previous subsection). As a result, unlike assets to be disposed of, such assets are analyzed in light of the impairment indicator list and gross cash flows generated before any consideration is given to measuring an impairment loss. In the absence of such a provision, nearly all long-term projects, regardless of their overall profitability, would be subject to write-downs in their early stages of development, only to be reversed later in the life of the project. Upon completion of development, the project is reclassified as an asset to be disposed of.

(c) FAIR VALUE MEASUREMENTS. ASC 820 (SFAS No. 157) defines *fair value,* and is used in the determination of impairment of real estate. More than 14 accounting standards permit or require fair value; this standard establishes a framework for measuring fair value and expands disclosures how fair value measurements are used.

Real estate fair value is based on exchange price principle. It no longer assumes that the transaction price, entry price, or purchase price represents fair value. *Fair value* is defined as an exit price or sales price in an orderly transaction between market participants. Entry and exit price are often different. In all cases, the transaction price will be equal to an exit price and, therefore, represents a fair value of the asset.

Real estate fair value measurements assume "highest and best use" of the property by independent market participants. Highest and best use of the real estate is measured by market participants that would maximize value and use of the property which may not be the same as the intended use by the reporting company. For example, a company may intend to keep a wooded area for conservation, when the highest and best use would be to use the land for additional housing.

(i) Fair Value Hierarchy. ASC 820 (SFAS No. 157) requires valuation techniques consistent with what is used by the real estate market participant. Inputs to valuation techniques are assumption that market participants would use in pricing the real estate.

The Statement defines three distinct approaches, levels, of which two are based on observable inputs.

Level 1. Quoted prices in active markets for identical assets. Generally, real estate does not fall into this category because of its distinct nature and operating unit.

Level 2. Inputs other than quoted prices that are observable in a market either directly or indirectly. Many observable inputs for real estate fall in this category, such as capitalization rates, market rents, discounts rates, risk-free rates, and sales price per square foot. Generally, the projection of real estate operations using observable inputs to determine fair value would fall under level 3.

Level 3. Inputs that are unobservable in a market either directly or indirectly. Even though real estate valuations are based on observable inputs, the fair value hierarchy within which the fair value is measured falls to the lowest level input which is the projected operations.

(ii) Fair Value Techniques. Real estate valuation techniques are numerous and should be based on observable inputs for the assumptions. The most common technique is the discounted net operating income approach, which generally puts the evaluation method into level 3. Current and future operations are projected and discounted back to the valuation date using current and future market rents and rates of returns.

31.6 CONSTRUCTION REVENUE RECOGNITION

Revenue recognition is a priority project that is part of the convergence efforts of the FASB and the IASB. On June 24, 2010, the Boards jointly issued an exposure draft titled *Revenue from Contracts with Customers* that proposes a new revenue recognition standard which could significantly affect current revenue recognition policies. More changes are expected as a result of the board's redeliberations to be completed during 2011. Although other industries will be impacted more significantly than construction, constant vigilance will be needed regarding construction transactions. The Private Company Financial Reporting Committee also will meet in 2012 to discuss various topics including revenue recognition.

Although most real estate developers acquire land in order to develop and construct improvements for their own use or for sale to others, some develop and construct improvements solely for others. There are also many general contractors whose principal business is developing and constructing improvements for others; rarely, if ever, do they own the land.

This section covers guidelines for accounting for development and construction contracts where the contractor does not own the land but is providing such services for others. The principal issue in accounting for construction contracts is when to record income. Construction contracts are generally of two types: fixed price and cost-plus. Under fixed price contracts, a contractor agrees to perform services for a fixed amount. Although the contract price is fixed, it may be revised frequently as a result of change orders as construction proceeds. If the contract is longer than a few months, the contractor usually receives advances from the customer as construction progresses.

Cost-plus contracts are employed in a variety of forms, such as cost plus a percentage of cost or cost plus a fixed fee. Sometimes defined costs may be limited and penalties provided in situations where stated maximum costs are exceeded. Under cost-plus agreements, the contractor is usually reimbursed for its costs as costs are incurred and, in addition, is paid a specified fee. In most cases, a portion of the fee is retained until the construction is completed and accepted. The method of recording income under cost-plus contracts generally is the same as for fixed price contracts and is described later in Section 31.6(d).

(a) AUTHORITATIVE LITERATURE. In 1955, the AICPA Committee on Accounting Procedures issued Accounting Research Bulletin (ARB) No. 45, *Long-Term Construction-Type Contracts.* This document described the generally accepted methods of accounting for long-term construction-type contracts for financial reporting purposes and described the circumstances in which each method is preferable.

In 1981, the AICPA issued SOP 81-1, *Accounting for Performance of Construction-Type and Certain Production-Type Contracts.* This Statement culminated extensive reconsideration by the AICPA of construction-type contracts. The recommendations set forth provide guidance on the application of ARB No. 45 but do not amend that Bulletin. In 1982, the FASB issued ASC 450 (SFAS No. 6), *Contractor Accounting for* Contingencies., which states that the specialized accounting and reporting principles and practices contained in SOP 81-1 are preferable accounting principles for purposes of justifying a change in accounting principles.

Prior to the issuance of SOP 81-1, authoritative accounting literature used the terms *long term* and *short term* in identifying types of contracts. SOP 81-1 chose not to use those terms as identifying characteristics because other characteristics were considered more relevant for identifying the types of contracts covered. The guidelines set forth next are based largely on SOP 81-1.

(b) METHODS OF ACCOUNTING. The determination of the point or points at which revenue should be recognized as earned and costs should be recognized as expenses is a major accounting issue common to all business enterprises engaged in the performance of construction contracting. Accounting for such contracts is essentially a process of measuring the results of relatively long-term events and allocating those results to relatively short-term accounting periods. Doing this involves considerable use of estimates in determining revenues, costs, and profits and in assigning the amounts to accounting periods. The process is complicated by the need to continually evaluate the uncertainties that are inherent in the performance of contracts and by the need to rely on estimates of revenues, costs, and the extent of progress toward completion.

There are two generally accepted methods of accounting for construction contracts: the percentage-of-completion method and the completed contract method. The determination of the preferable method should be based on an evaluation of the particular circumstances, as the two methods are not acceptable alternatives for the same set of circumstances. The method used and circumstances describing when it is used should be disclosed in the accounting policy footnote to the financial statements.

(i) Percentage-of-Completion Method. The use of the percentage-of-completion approach depends on the ability of the contractor to make reasonably dependable estimates. The percentage-of-completion method should be used in circumstances in which reasonably dependable estimates can be made and in which all of these conditions exist:

- The contract is clear about goods or services to be provided, the consideration to be exchanged, and the manner and terms of settlement.
- The buyer can be expected to pay for the services performed.
- The contractor can be expected to be able to perform his contractual obligations.

The percentage-of-completion method presents the economic substance of activity more clearly and in a more timely manner than does the completed contract method. It should be noted that estimates of revenues, costs, and measurements of performance are the primary criteria for income recognition. Billings alone may have no real relationship to performance and generally are not a suitable basis for income recognition.

(ii) Completed Contract Method. The completed contract method is usually used in circumstances in which an entity's financial position and results of operations would not vary materially from those resulting from the percentage-of-completion method. The completed contract method should be used when reasonably dependable estimates cannot be made or when there are inherent hazards that cause forecasts to be doubtful.

(iii) Consistency of Application. It is possible that a contractor may use one method for some contracts and the other for additional contracts. There is no inconsistency, since consistency in application lies in using the same accounting treatment for the same set of conditions of a contract from one accounting period to another. The method used, and circumstances when it is used, should be disclosed in the accounting policy footnote to the financial statements.

(c) PERCENTAGE-OF-COMPLETION METHOD. The percentage-of-completion method recognizes economic results of contract performance on a timely basis. Financial statements based on the percentage-of-completion method present the economic substance of a company's transactions and events more clearly and more timely than financial statements based on the completed contract method, and they present more accurately the relationships between gross profit from contracts and related period costs. The percentage-of-completion method informs the users of the general-purpose financial statements concerning the volume of a company's economic activity.

In practice, several methods are used to measure the extent of progress toward completion. These methods include the cost-to-cost method, the efforts-expended method, the units-of-delivery method and the units-of-work-performed method. These methods are intended to conform to the recommendations of ARB No. 45 (par. 4), which states:

> that the recognized income be that percentage of estimated total income, either:
>
> **a.** that incurred costs to date bear to estimated total costs after giving effect to estimates of costs to complete based upon most recent information, or
>
> **b.** that may be indicated by such other measure of progress toward completion as may be appropriate having due regard to work performed.

One generally accepted method of measuring such progress is the stage of construction, as determined through engineering or architectural studies.

When using the cost incurred approach, there may be certain costs that should be excluded from the calculation. For example, substantial quantities of standard materials not unique to the project may have been delivered to the job site but not yet utilized. Or engineering and architectural fees incurred may represent 20 percent of total estimated costs whereas only 10 percent of the construction has been performed.

The principal disadvantage of the percentage-of-completion method is that it is necessarily dependent on estimates of ultimate costs that are subject to the uncertainties frequently inherent in long-term contracts.

To determine estimated total income, it is necessary to estimate total revenues and costs. Frequently a contractor can estimate total contract revenue and total contract cost in single amounts. However, on some contracts, a contractor may be able to estimate only total contract revenue and total contract cost in ranges of amounts. In such situations, the most likely amounts within the range should be used, if determinable. If not, the least favorable amounts should be used until the results can be estimated more precisely.

(i) Revenue Determination. Estimating revenue on a contract is an involved process. The major factors that must be considered in determining total estimated revenue include the basic contract price, contract options, change orders, claims, and contract provisions for incentive payments and penalties. All these factors and other special contract provisions must be evaluated throughout the life of a contract in estimating total contract revenue.

(ii) Cost Determination. At any time during the life of a contract, total estimated contract cost consists of two components: costs incurred to date and estimated cost to complete the contract. A company should be able to determine costs incurred on a contract with a relatively high degree of precision. The other component, estimated cost to complete, is a significant variable in the process of determining income earned and is thus a significant factor in accounting for contracts. SOP 81-1 states that these five practices should be followed in estimating costs to complete:

1. Systematic and consistent procedures that are correlated with the cost accounting system should be used to provide a basis for periodically comparing actual and estimated costs.

2. In estimating total contract costs, the quantities and prices of all significant elements of cost should be identified.
3. The estimating procedures should provide that estimated cost to complete includes the same elements of cost that are included in actual accumulated costs; also, those elements should reflect expected price increases.
4. The effects of future wage and price escalations should be taken into account in cost estimates, especially when the contract performance will be carried out over a significant period of time. Escalation provisions should not be blanket overall provisions but should cover labor, materials, and indirect costs based on percentages or amounts that take into consideration experience and other pertinent data.
5. Estimates of cost to complete should be reviewed periodically and revised as appropriate to reflect new information.

(iii) Revision of Estimates. Adjustments to the original estimates of the total contract revenue, cost, or extent of progress toward completion are often required as work progresses under the contract, even though the scope of the work required under the contract has not changed. Such adjustments are changes in accounting estimates as defined in APB Opinion No. 20. Under this Opinion, the cumulative catch-up method is the only acceptable method. This method requires the difference between cumulative income and income previously recorded to be recorded in the current year's income.

Exhibit 31.5 illustrates the percentage-of-completion method.

The amount of revenue, costs, and income recognized in the three periods would be as shown next.

	To Date	Recognized Prior Year (thousands of dollars)	Current Year
Year 1 (25% completed)			
Earned revenue ($9,000,000 × 0.25)	$2,250.0		$2,250.0
Cost of earned revenue ($8,050,000 × 0.25)	2,012.5		2,012.5
Gross profit	$ 237.5		$ 237.5
Gross profit rate	10.5%		10.5%
Year 2 (75% completed)			
Earned revenue ($9,100,000 × 0.75)	$6,825.0	$2,250.0	$4,575.0
Cost of earned revenue ($8,100,000 × 0.75)	6,075.0	2,012.5	4,062.5
Gross profit	$ 750.0	$ 237.5	$ 512.5
Gross profit rate	11.0%	10.5%	11.2%
Year 3 (100% completed)			
Earned revenue	$9,200.0	$6,825.0	$2,375.0
Cost of earned revenue	8,200.0	6,075.0	2,125.0
Gross profit	$1,000.0	$ 750.0	$ 250.0
Gross profit rate	10.9%	11.0%	10.5%

Exhibit 31.5 Percentage of Completion, Three-Year Contract

Source: Adapted from AICPA. Accounting Principles Board Opinion No. 20, *Accounting Changes*, July, 1971, superseded by FASB Statement No. 154, *Accounting Changes and Error Corrections*, Para C1(a), May 2005.

A contracting company has a lump-sum contract for $9 million to build a bridge at a total estimated cost of $8 million. The construction period covers three years. Financial data during the construction period is:

(Thousands of dollars)	Year 1	Year 2	Year 3
Total estimated revenue	$9,000	$9,100	$9,200
Cost incurred to date	$2,050	$6,100	$8,200
Estimated cost to complete	6,000	2,000	—
Total estimated cost	$8,050	$8,100	$8,200
Estimated gross profit	$ 950	$1,000	$1,000
Billings to date	$1,800	$5,500	$9,200
Collections to date	$1,500	$5,000	$9,200
Measure of progress	25%	75%	100%

(d) COMPLETED CONTRACT METHOD. The completed contract method recognizes income only when a contract is completed or substantially completed, such as when the remaining costs to be incurred are not significant. Under this method, costs and billings are reflected in the balance sheet, but there are no charges or credits to the income statement.

As a general rule, a contract may be regarded as substantially completed if remaining costs and potential risks are insignificant in amount. The overriding objectives are to maintain consistency in determining when contracts are substantially completed and to avoid arbitrary acceleration or deferral of income. The specific criteria used to determine when a contract is substantially completed should be followed consistently. Circumstances to be considered in determining when a project is substantially completed include acceptance by the customer, departure from the site, and compliance with performance specifications.

The completed contract method may be used in circumstances in which financial position and results of operations would not vary materially from those resulting from use of the percentage-of-completion method (e.g., in circumstances in which an entity has primarily short-term contracts). In accounting for such contracts, income ordinarily is recognized when performance is substantially completed and accepted. For example, the completed contract method, as opposed to the percentage-of-completion method, usually would not produce a material difference in net income or financial position for a small contractor that primarily performs relatively short-term contracts during an accounting period.

If there is a reasonable assurance that no loss will be incurred on a contract (e.g., when the scope of the contract is ill defined but the contractor is protected by a cost-plus contract or other contractual terms), the percentage-of-completion method based on a zero profit margin, rather than the completed contract method, should be used until more precise estimates can be made.

The significant difference between the percentage-of-completion method applied on the basis of a zero profit margin and the completed contract method relates to the effects on the income statement. Under the zero profit margin approach to applying the percentage-of-completion method, equal amounts of revenue and cost, measured on the basis of performance during the period, are presented in the income statement and no gross profit amount is presented in the income statement until the contract is completed. The zero profit margin approach to applying the percentage-of-completion method gives users of general-purpose financial statements an indication of the volume of a company's business and of the application of its economic resources.

The principal advantage of the completed contract method is that it is based on results as finally determined rather than on estimates for unperformed work that may involve unforeseen costs and possible losses. The principal disadvantage is that it does not reflect current performance when the period of the contract extends into more than one accounting period. Under these circumstances, it may result in irregular recognition of income.

(e) PROVISION FOR LOSSES. Under either of the methods just discussed, provision should be made for the entire loss on the contract in the period when current estimates of total contract costs indicate a loss. The provision for loss should represent the best judgment that can be made in the circumstances.

Other factors that should be considered in arriving at the projected loss on a contract include target penalties for late completion and rewards for early completion, nonreimbursable costs on cost-plus contracts, and the effect of change orders. When using the completed contract method and allocating general and administrative expenses to contract costs, total general and administrative expenses that are expected to be allocated to the contract are to be considered together with other estimated contract costs.

(f) CONTRACT CLAIMS. *Claims* are amounts in excess of the agreed contract price that a contractor seeks to collect from customers or others for customer-caused delays, errors in specifications and designs, unapproved change orders, or other causes of unanticipated additional costs. Recognition of amounts of additional contract revenue relating to claims is appropriate only if it is probable that the claim will result in additional contract revenue and if the amount can be reliably estimated.

These requirements are satisfied by the existence of all the next conditions:

- The contract or other evidence provides a legal basis for the claim.
- Additional costs are caused by circumstances that were unforeseen at the contract date and are not the result of deficiencies in the contractor's performance.
- Costs associated with the claim are identifiable and are reasonable in view of the work performed.
- The evidence supporting the claim is objective and verifiable.

If the foregoing requirements are met, revenue from a claim should be recorded only to the extent that contract costs relating to the claim have been incurred. The amounts recorded, if material, should be disclosed in the notes to the financial statements.

Change orders are modifications of an original contract that effectively change the provisions of the contract without adding new provisions. They may be initiated by either the contractor or the customer. Many change orders are unpriced; that is, the work to be performed is defined, but the adjustment to the contract price is to be negotiated later. For some change orders, both scope and price may be unapproved or in dispute. Accounting for change orders depends on the underlying circumstances and contract conditions, which may differ for each change order depending on the customer, the type of contract, and the nature of the change. Priced change orders represent an adjustment to the contract price and contract revenue, and costs should be adjusted to reflect these change orders.

Accounting for unpriced change orders depends on their characteristics and the circumstances in which they occur. Under the completed contract method, costs attributable to unpriced change orders should be deferred as contract costs if it is probable that aggregate contract costs, including costs attributable to change orders, will be recovered from contract revenues. For all unpriced change orders, recovery should be deemed probable if the future event or events necessary for recovery are likely to occur. Some factors to consider in evaluating whether recovery is probable are the customer's written approval of the scope of the change order, separate documentation for change order costs that are identifiable and reasonable, and the entity's favorable experience in getting change orders (especially as it relates to the specific type of contract and change order being evaluated). The next guidelines should be used in accounting for unpriced change orders under the percentage-of-completion method:

- Costs attributable to unpriced change orders should be treated as costs of contract performance in the period in which the costs are incurred if it is not probable that the costs will be recovered through a change in the contract price.
- If it is probable that the costs will be recovered through a change in the contract price, the costs should be deferred (excluded from the cost of contract performance) until the parties

have agreed on the change in contract price, or, alternatively, they should be treated as costs of contract performance in the period in which they are incurred, and contract revenue should be recognized to the extent of the costs incurred.

- If it is probable that the contract price will be adjusted by an amount that exceeds the costs attributable to the change order and the amount of the excess can be reliably estimated, the original contract price should also be adjusted for that amount when the costs are recognized as costs of contract performance if its realization is probable. However, since the substantiation of the amount of future revenue is difficult, revenue in excess of the costs attributable to unpriced change orders should be recorded only in circumstances in which realization is assured beyond a reasonable doubt, such as circumstances in which an entity's historical experience provides assurance or in which an entity has received a bona fide pricing offer from the customer and records only the amount of the offer as revenue.

If change orders are in dispute or are unapproved in regard to both scope and price, they should be evaluated as claims.

31.7 OPERATIONS OF PROPERTIES IN USE

(a) RENTAL OPERATIONS. Operations of properties in use represent a distinct segment of the real estate industry. Owners are often referred to as *real estate operators.* Properties in use include office buildings, shopping centers, apartments, industrial buildings, and similar properties rented to others. A lease agreement is entered into between the owner/operator and the tenant for periods ranging from one month to many years, depending on the type of property. Sometimes an investor will acquire an existing property or alternatively will have the builder or developer construct the property. Some developers, frequently referred to as *investment builders,* develop and construct income properties for their own use as investment properties.

Currently, ASC 840 (SFAS No. 13) is the principal source of standards of financial accounting and reporting for leases, although FASB and IFRS have it on their agenda to issue new guideline base on the principle of recognizing lease intangibles. Under ASC 840 (SFAS No. 13), a distinction is made between a capital lease and an operating lease. The lessor is required to account for a capital lease as a sale or a financing transaction. The lessee accounts for a capital lease as a purchase. An operating lease, however, requires the lessor to reflect rent income, operating expenses, and depreciation of the property over the lease term; the lessee must record rent expense.

Accounting for leases is discussed in Chapter 15 and therefore is not covered in depth here. Certain unique aspects of accounting for leases of real estate classified as operating leases, however, are covered next.

(b) RENTAL INCOME. Major changes are in the works for leases, such as the recording of the right of use benefits and obligations for each lease with a term of over one year. Until FASB finalizes the new accounting for leases, both from the lessor and lessee recognition perspectives, rental income from an operating lease should be recorded by a lessor as it becomes earned in accordance with the provisions of the lease agreement.

A joint meeting of the IASB and the FASB confirmed that lessors of investment property who reported at fair value would be scoped out of the proposed converged standard that addresses the accounting for leases. These lessors would account for leases as currently reported. Therefore, these lessors would not recognize a receivable for all payments to be received under in-place leases separate from the investment property. The basis of this conclusion is that the fair value of the property includes the present value of payments to be received under in-place leases. In addition, these lessors would continue to report lease revenue over the term of the lease on a straight-line basis.

FASB Technical Bulletin (FTB) No. 85-3, *Accounting for Operating Leases with Scheduled Rent Increases,* provides that the effects of scheduled rent increases that are included in minimum lease payments under ASC 840 (SFAS No. 13) should be recognized by lessors and lessees on a straight-line basis over the lease term unless another systematic and rational allocation basis is more representative of the time pattern in which the leased property is physically employed. Using factors such as the time value of money, anticipated inflation, or expected future revenues to allocate scheduled rent increases is inappropriate because these factors do not relate to the time pattern of the physical usage of the leased property. However, such factors may affect the periodic reported rental income or expense if the lease agreement involves rentals based on contingent events occurring during the lease period, which are excluded from minimum lease payments and accounted for separately under ASC 840 (SFAS No. 13) as amended by ASC 840 (SFAS No. 29).

A lease agreement may provide for scheduled rent increases designed to accommodate the lessee's projected physical use of the property. In these circumstances, FTB No. 88-1, *Issues Relating to Accounting for Leases,* provides for the lessee and the lessor to recognize the lease payments in this way:

1. If rents escalate in contemplation of the lessee's physical use of the leased property, including equipment, but the lessee takes possession of or controls the physical use of the property at the beginning of the lease term, all rental payments, including the escalated rents, should be recognized as rental expenses or rental revenue on a straight-line basis in accordance with paragraph 15 of ASC 840 (SFAS No. 13) and FTB No. 85-3 starting with the beginning of the lease term.
2. If rents escalate under a master lease agreement because the lessee gains access to and control over additional leased property at the time of the escalation, the escalated rents should be considered rental expense or rental revenue attributable to the leased property and recognized in proportion to the additional leased property in the years that the lessee has control over the use of the additional leased property. The amount of rental expense or rental revenue attributed to the additional leased property should be proportionate to the relative fair value of the additional property, as determined at the inception of the lease, in the applicable time periods during which the lessee controls its use.

(i) Cost Escalation. Many lessors require that the lessee pay operating costs of the leased property, such as utilities, real estate taxes, and common area maintenance. Some lessors require the lessee to pay for such costs when they escalate and exceed a specified rate or amount. In some cases, the lessee pays these costs directly. More commonly, however, the lessor pays the costs and is reimbursed by the lessee. In this situation, the lessor should generally record these reimbursement costs as a receivable at the time the costs are accrued, even though they may not be billed until a later date. Since these costs sometimes are billed at a later date, collectability from the lessee should, of course, be considered.

(ii) Percentage Rents. Many retail leases, such as those on shopping centers, enable the lessor to collect additional rents based on the excess of a stated percentage of the tenant's gross sales over the specified minimum rent. While the minimum rent is usually payable in periodic level amounts, percentage rents (sometimes called *overrides*) are usually based on annual sales, often with a requirement for periodic payments toward the annual amount.

ASC 840 (SFAS No. 29, par. 13), *Determining Contingent Rentals,* states: "Contingent rentals shall be includable in the determination of net income as accruable."

(c) RENTAL COSTS. The next considerations help determine the appropriate accounting for rental costs.

(i) Chargeable to Future Periods. All costs, direct or indirect, incurred to rent real estate should be deferred and charged to future periods when they are related to and their recovery is reasonably expected from future operations. Examples include initial direct costs such as commissions, legal fees, costs of credit investigations, costs of preparing and processing documents for new leases acquired, and that portion of compensation applicable to the time spent on consummated leases.

Other examples include costs of model units and related furnishings, rental facilities, semi permanent signs, grand openings, and unused rental brochures, but not rental overhead, such as rental salaries (see the following subsection, "Period Costs").

For leases accounted for as operating leases, deferred rental costs that can be directly related to revenue from a specific operating lease should be amortized over the term of the related lease in proportion to the recognition of rental income. Deferred rental costs that cannot be directly related to revenue from a specific operating lease should be amortized to expense over the period of expected benefit. The amortization period begins when the project is substantially completed and held available for occupancy. Estimated unrecoverable deferred rental costs associated with a lease or group of leases should be charged to expense when it becomes probable that the lease(s) will be terminated.

For leases accounted for as sales-type leases, deferred rental costs must be charged against income at the time the sale is recognized.

(ii) Period Costs. Costs that are incurred to rent real estate projects that do not meet the above criteria should be charged to expense as incurred. ASC 970 (SFAS No. 67) specifically indicates that rental overhead, which is defined in its glossary to include rental salaries, is an example of such period costs. Other examples of expenditures that are period costs are initial indirect costs, such as that portion of salaries and other compensation and fees applicable to time spent in negotiating leases that are not consummated, supervisory and administrative expenses, and other indirect costs.

(d) DEPRECIATION. Under GAAP, the costs of income-producing properties must be depreciated. *Depreciation,* as defined by GAAP, is the systematic and rational allocation of the historical cost of depreciable assets (tangible assets, other than inventory, with limited lives of more than one year) over their useful lives.

In accounting for real estate operations, the most frequently used methods of depreciation are straight-line and decreasing charge methods. The most common decreasing charge methods are the declining balance and sum-of-the-years-digits methods. Increasing charge methods, such as the sinking fund method, are not generally used in the real estate industry in the United States.

The major components of a building, such as the plumbing and heating systems, may be identified and depreciated separately over their respective lives. This method, which is frequently used for tax purposes, usually results in a more rapid write-off.

(e) INITIAL RENTAL OPERATIONS

(i) Held in Use. When a real estate project is substantially complete and held available for occupancy (held in use), the procedures listed here should be followed:

- Rental revenue should be recorded in income as earned.
- Operating costs should be charged to expense currently.
- Amortization of deferred rental costs should begin.
- Full depreciation of rental property should begin.
- Carrying costs, such as interest and property taxes, should be charged to expense as accrued.

If portions of a rental project are substantially completed and occupied by tenants or held available for occupancy and other portions have not yet reached that stage, the substantially completed portions should be accounted for as a separate project. Costs incurred should be allocated between the portions under construction and the portions substantially completed and held available for occupancy.

(ii) Held for Sale. When a real estate project is substantially complete, available for occupancy but held for sale, the procedures listed here should be used:

- Positive rental operations should be recorded as a reduction of the net cost basis.
- Full depreciation of rental property should be suspended.

(f) RENTAL EXPENSE. Rental expense under an operating lease normally should be charged to operations by a lessee over the lease term on a basis consistent with the lessor's recording of income, with the exception of periodic accounting for percentage rent expense, which should be based on the estimated annual percentage rent.

31.8 ACCOUNTING FOR INVESTMENTS IN REAL ESTATE VENTURES

(a) ORGANIZATION OF VENTURES. The joint venture vehicle—the sharing of risk—has been widely utilized for many years in the construction, mining, and oil and gas industries as well as for real estate developments. Real estate joint ventures are typically entered into in recognition of the need for external assistance, for example, financing or market expertise. The most common of these needs is capital formation.

Real estate ventures are organized either as corporate entities or, more frequently, as partnerships. Limited partnerships are often used because of the advantages of limited liability. The venture is typically formed by a small group, with each investor actively contributing to the success of the venture and participating in overall management, and with no one individual or corporation controlling its operations. The venture is usually operated separately from other activities of the investors. Regardless of the legal form of the real estate venture, the accounting principles for recognition of profits and losses should be the same.

(b) ACCOUNTING

(i) Background. Accounting practices in the real estate industry in general and, more specifically, accounting for investments in real estate ventures have varied. The result was lack of comparability and, in some cases, a lack of comprehension. Therefore, the following relevant pronouncements were issued:

- *APB Opinion No. 18.* In response to the wide variation in accounting for investments, the APB, in March 1971, issued Opinion No. 18, *The Equity Method of Accounting for Investments in Common Stock.* This Opinion became applicable to investments in unincorporated ventures, including partnerships, because of an interpretation promulgated in November 1971.
- *AICPA Statement of Position SOP 78-9.* The AICPA recognized the continuing diversity of practice and in December 1978 issued SOP 78-9, *Accounting for Investments in Real Estate Ventures.* This Statement was issued to narrow the range of alternative practices used in accounting for investments in real estate ventures and to establish industry uniformity. The AICPA currently is reconsidering the guidance in SOP 78-9 as part of a broader project, *Equity Method Investments.*
- *ASC 810 (SFAS No. 94).* In response to the perceived problem of off-balance-sheet financing, of which unconsolidated majority-owned subsidiaries were deemed to be the most significant aspect, the FASB issued ASC 810 (SFAS No. 94), *Consolidation of All Majority-Owned Subsidiaries,* in October 1987. ASC 810 (SFAS No. 94) eliminates the concept of not consolidating nonhomogeneous operations and replaces it with the concept that the predominant factor in determining whether an investment requires consolidation should primarily be control rather than ownership of a majority voting interest. This Statement is also applicable to investments in unincorporated ventures, including partnerships.
- *AICPA Notice to Practitioners, ADC Acquisition, Development, and Construction (ADC) Loans, February 1986.* Recognizing that financial institutions needed guidance on accounting for real estate acquisition, development, and construction (ADC) arrangements, the AICPA issued this notice (also known as the *Third Notice*). The notice provides accounting guidance on ADC arrangements that have virtually the same risks and potential rewards as those of joint ventures. It determined that accounting for such arrangements as loans would not be appropriate and provides guidance on the appropriate accounting.
- The SEC incorporated the notice into SAB No. 71, *Views Regarding Financial Statements of Properties Securing Mortgage Loans.* SAB No. 71, and its amendment, SAB No. 71A,

provide guidance to registrants on the required reporting under this notice. Also, EITF Issue Nos. 84-4 and 86-21, as well as SAB No. 71, extend the provisions of this notice to all entities, not just financial institutions.

- *Proposed FASB Interpretation,* Consolidation of Certain Special-Purpose Entities *(SPEs).* The FASB has approved for issuance an Exposure Draft of a proposed Interpretation that establishes accounting guidance for consolidation of SPEs. The proposed Interpretation, *Consolidation of Certain Special-Purpose Entities,* would apply to any business enterprise—both public and private companies—that has an ownership interest, contractual relationship, or other business relationship with an SPE. Under current practice, two enterprises generally have been included in consolidated financial statements because one enterprise controls the other through voting ownership interests. The proposed Interpretation would explain how to identify an SPE that is not subject to control through voting ownership interests and would require each enterprise involved with such an SPE to determine whether it provides financial support to the SPE through a variable interest. Variable interests may arise from financial instruments, service contracts, nonvoting ownership interests, or other arrangements. If an enterprise holds (1) a majority of the variable interests in the SPE or (2) a significant variable interest that is significantly more than any other party's variable interest, that enterprise would be the primary beneficiary. The primary beneficiary would be required to include the assets, liabilities, and results of the activities of the SPE in its consolidated financial statements.

(ii) Current Status. FAS No. 141(R), *Business Combinations,* FIN 46(R), and FAS No. 160, *Noncontrolling Interests in Consolidated Statements,* address financial accounting and reporting for business combinations and supersede APB Opinion No. 16, *Business Combinations,* and FASB Statement No. 38, *Accounting for Preacquisition Contingencies of Purchased Enterprises.* All business combinations in the scope of this Statement are to be accounted for using one method, the purchase method. The standard is now effective for all companies. Although some of the provisions seem straightforward, the impacts are pervasive. The concept of fair value derives important changes to the model including changes in the accounting for partial business combination and step acquisitions. The traditional concepts already mentioned have undergone fundamental change. For example, the standard:

- Expands the definition of a business and business combination
- Requires the recognition of contingent consideration of fair value on the acquisition and requires acquisition related transaction course to be expensed as incurred
- Changes the way certain assets of value
- Requires a retrospective application of measurement, with period adjustments.

Importantly, this new standard may dramatically impact the accounting of real estate ventures. The new standard could increase the number of companies reporting units, change the calculation of goodwill impairment, and cause tax adjustments to be recorded in earnings.

(c) INVESTOR ACCOUNTING ISSUES. The accounting literature already mentioned covers many of the special issues investors encounter in practice. Additional Statements are listed next.

- FASB ASC 323, *Investments—Equity Method and Joint Ventures,* provides equity method accounting guidance for investments in corporate entities that was formerly in APB Opinion No. 18. The Topic specifically applies to investments in corporations, including corporate joint ventures (defined in par. 901.1).
- FASB ASC 325-20, *Investments—Other—Cost Method Investments,* provides cost method accounting guidance for investments in corporate entities that was formerly in APB Opinion No. 18.

- FASB ASC 810, *Consolidation,* provides consolidation accounting guidance for investments in corporate entities and primarily includes guidance formerly in *ARB No. 51, Consolidated Financial Statements* (as amended by SFAS No. 94, *Consolidation of All Majority-Owned Subsidiaries,* and ASC 810 (SFAS No. 160), *Noncontrolling Interests in Consolidated Financial Statements*).
- ASC 810 also includes guidance formerly in FIN 46(R), *Consolidation of Variable Interest Entities,* and SFAS No. 167, *Amendments to FASB Interpretation No. 46(R),* which provide guidance for a situation in which an entity has a controlling financial interest in another entity other than through a majority voting interest.

The major areas of the pending ASC are:

- Investor accounting for results of operations of ventures
- Special accounting issues related to venture losses
- Investor accounting for transactions with a real estate venture, including capital contributions
- Financial statement presentation and disclosures

Initially, the status of the venture should be determined in relation to each joint venture. The next criteria should be evaluated to determine controlling interests as measured by the contractual interest in the venture.

- Is the interest at risk and not sufficient to permit the entity to finance its activities without additional subordinated financial support provided by any parties, including the equity holders?
- Do the investors lack one or more of the next essential characteristics of a controlling financial interest:
  - The direct or indirect ability to make decisions about the entity's activities through voting rights or similar rights
  - The obligation to absorb the expected losses of the entity
  - The right to receive the expected residual returns of the entity
- Do the investors have voting rights that are not proportionate to their economic interests, and the activities of the entity involve or are conducted on behalf of an investor with a disproportionately small voting interest?

A controlling investor should account for its income and losses from real estate ventures under the principles that apply to investments in subsidiaries, which usually require consolidation of the venture's operations. The consolidated net income is to be reported at amounts that include the amounts attributable to both the parent and the noncontrolling interest. It also requires disclosure, on the face of the consolidated statement of income, of the amounts of consolidated net income attributable to the parent and to the noncontrolling interest. Previously, net income attributable to the noncontrolling interest generally was reported as an expense or other deduction in arriving at consolidated net income. It also was often presented in combination with other financial statement amounts. A noncontrolling investor should account for its share of income and losses in real estate ventures by using the equity method. Under the equity method, the initial investment is recorded by the investor at cost; thereafter, the carrying amount is increased by the investor's share of current earnings and decreased by the investor's share of current losses or distributions.

In accounting for transactions with a real estate venture, a controlling investor must eliminate all intercompany profit. When the investor does not control the venture, some situations require that all intercompany profit be eliminated, whereas in others, intercompany profit is eliminated by the investor only to the extent of its ownership interest in the venture. For example, as set forth in AICPA SOP No. 78-9, even a noncontrolling investor is precluded from recognizing any profit on a contribution of real estate or services to the venture. Accounting for other transactions covered by SOP No. 78-9 includes sales of real estate and services to the venture, interest income on loans and advances to the venture, and venture sales of real estate or services to an investor.

With regard to financial statement presentation, a controlling investor is usually required to consolidate venture operations. A noncontrolling investor should use the equity method, with the carrying value of the investment presented as a single amount in the balance sheet and the investor's share of venture earnings or losses as a single amount in the income statement. The proportionate share approach, which records the investor's share of each item of income, expense, asset, and liability, is not considered acceptable except for legal undivided interests.

The material just presented is only a very brief summary of the literature, and there are exceptions to some of those guidelines. In accounting for real estate venture operations and transactions, judgment must be exercised in applying the principles to ensure that economic substance is fairly reflected no matter how complex the venture arrangements.

(d) ACCOUNTING FOR TAX BENEFITS RESULTING FROM INVESTMENTS IN AFFORDABLE HOUSING PROJECTS. The Revenue Reconciliation Act of 1993 provides tax benefits to investors in entities operating qualified affordable housing projects. The benefits take the form of tax deductions from operating losses and tax credits. In EITF Issue No. 94-1, *Accounting for Tax Benefits Resulting from Investments in Affordable Housing Projects,* the EITF reached a consensus that a limited partner in a qualified low-income housing project may elect to use the effective yield method (to be described) if these three conditions are met:

1. The availability of the limited partner's share of the tax credits is guaranteed by a creditworthy entity through a letter of credit, tax indemnity agreement, or other arrangement.
2. The limited partner's projected yield based solely on the cash flows from the guaranteed tax credits is positive.
3. The limited partner's liability for both legal and tax purposes is limited to its capital investment.

Under the effective yield method, the investor recognizes tax credits as they are allocated and amortizes the initial cost of the investment to provide a constant effective yield over the period that tax credits are allocated to the investor. The effective yield is the internal rate of return on the investment, based on the cost of the investment and the guaranteed tax credits allocated to the investor. Any expected residual value of the investment should be excluded from the effective yield calculation. Cash received from operations of the limited partnership or sale of the property, if any, should be included when realized or realizable.

Under the effective yield method, the tax credit allocated, net of the amortization of the investment in the limited partnership, is recognized in the income statement as a component, usually a reduction, of income taxes attributable to continuing operations. Any other tax benefits received should be accounted for pursuant to FASB Statement No. 109, *Accounting for Income Taxes.*

An investment that does not qualify for accounting under the effective yield method should be accounted for under SOP No. 78-9, which requires use of the equity method unless the limited partner's interest is so minor as to have virtually no influence over partnership operating and financial policies. The EITF did not establish a "bright line" as to what percentage ownership threshold is required under SOP No. 78-9 for selecting between the cost and equity methods. The AICPA is currently reconsidering the guidance in SOP No. 78-9 in its project titled *Equity Method Investments.*

If the cost method is used, the excess of the carrying amount of the investment over its residual value should be amortized over the period in which the tax credits are allocated to the investor. Annual amortization should be based on the proportion of tax credits received in the current year to total estimated tax credits to be allocated to the investor. The residual value should not reflect anticipated inflation.

During the deliberations of EITF Issue No. 94-1, the SEC Staff announced that it had revised its position on accounting for investments in limited partnerships. Previously, the SEC had not objected to the use of the cost method for limited partnership investments of up to 20 percent, provided the investor did not have significant influence as defined in APB Opinion No. 18. However, the revised position is that the equity method should be used to account for limited partnership investments, unless the investment is "so minor that the limited partner may have virtually no influence over partnership operating and financial policies." In practice, investments of more than 3 to 5 percent would be considered more than minor. For public companies, this guidance is to be applied to any limited partnership investment made after May 18, 1995. This includes not only the investments in low-income housing projects but all real estate partnerships and any other types of limited partnership investments (such as oil and gas, etc.).

31.9 FINANCIAL REPORTING

(a) FINANCIAL STATEMENT PRESENTATION. Certain matters of financial statement presentation—as opposed to footnote disclosures—are unique to the real estate industry. The financial reporting guidelines in this section are based on the principles set forth in authoritative literature and reporting practice.

(i) Balance Sheet. Real estate companies frequently present nonclassified balance sheets; that is, they do not distinguish between current and noncurrent assets or liabilities. This is because the operating cycle of most real estate companies exceeds one year.

Real estate companies sometimes list their assets on the balance sheet in the order of liquidity, in the same manner as other companies. A more popular method, however, is to list the real estate assets first, to demonstrate their importance to the companies. In either case, real estate assets should be disclosed in the manner that is most demonstrative of the company's operations. These assets are often grouped broadly according to the type of investment or operation:

- Real estate under development
- Real estate held for sale
- Real estate held for use
  - Commercial
  - Residential
  - Retail
  - Industrial

(ii) Statement of Income. Operations are generally classified in a manner consistent with that described for real estate investments. In 1976, the FASB issued SFAS No. 14, *Financial Reporting for Segments of a Business Enterprise,* which states that the financial statements of an enterprise should include certain information about the industry segments of the enterprise. An industry segment is defined in paragraph 10(a) as "a component of an enterprise engaged in providing a product or service or a group of related products and services primarily to unaffiliated customers (i.e., customers outside the enterprise) for profit." Some developers, however, have traditionally considered themselves to be in only one line of business.

In June 1997, the FASB issued ASC 840 (SFAS No. 131), *Disclosures about Segments of an Enterprise and Related Information.* ASC 840 (SFAS No. 131) supersedes SFAS No. 14, although it retains the requirement to report information about major customers. ASC 840 (SFAS

No. 131) adopts a "management approach" to identifying segments and permits entities to aggregate operating segments if certain attributes are present.

(b) ACCOUNTING POLICIES. Because of the alternatives currently available in accounting for real estate developments, it is especially important to follow the guidelines of APB Opinion No. 22, *Disclosure of Accounting Policies.* Paragraph 12 of the Opinion states that disclosures should include the accounting principles and methods that involve any of these items:

> A selection from existing acceptable alternatives.
>
> Principles and methods peculiar to the industry in which the reporting entity operates, even if such principles and methods are predominantly followed in that industry.
>
> Unusual or innovative applications of GAAP (and, as applicable, of principles and methods peculiar to the industry in which the reporting entity operates).

These four accounting policy disclosures are appropriate in the financial statements of a real estate company, as opposed to a manufacturing or service enterprise:

1. *Profit recognition.* The accounting method used to determine income should be disclosed. Where different methods are used, the circumstances surrounding the application of each should also be disclosed. Similarly, a comment should be included indicating the timing of sales and related profit recognition.
2. *Cost accounting.* The method of allocating cost to unit sales should be disclosed (e.g., relative market values, area, unit, specific identification). Financial statement disclosure should include, where applicable, capitalization policies for property taxes and other carrying costs, and policies with respect to capitalization or deferral of start-up or preoperating costs (selling costs, rental costs, and initial operations).
3. *Impairment of long-lived assets.* Real estate held for development and sale, including property to be developed in the future as well as that currently under development, should follow the recognition and measurement principles set forth in SFAS No. 121 for assets to be held and used. A real estate project, or parts thereof, that is substantially complete and ready for its intended use shall be accounted for at the lower of carrying amount or fair value less cost to sell.
4. *Investment in real estate ventures.* Disclosures of these accounting policies should be made:
   - **a.** Method of inclusion in investor's accounts (e.g., equity or consolidation)
   - **b.** Method of income recognition (e.g., equity or cost)
   - **c.** Accounting principles of significant ventures
   - **d.** Profit recognition practices on transactions between the investor and the venture

(c) NOTE DISCLOSURES. The FASB and IFRS boards have tentatively decided to change and increase disclosures.

Some important pending changes are:

- A rollforward of assets arising from the capitalization of costs to obtain and fulfill a contract is required. It will include additions, amortization, and impairments.
- Contract assets and liabilities may be labeled differently in the balance sheet. They may also be combined with other balances and disclosed separately in the footnotes if not material for separate presentation.
- The maturity analysis for remaining performance obligations has been retained, but the Boards are still considering whether to limit the scope to certain types of contracts.

The next list describes current financial statement disclosures that are appropriate in the notes to the financial statements of a real estate developer.

- *Real estate assets.* If a breakdown is not reflected on the balance sheet, it should be included in the footnotes. Disclosure should also be made of inventory subject to sales contracts that have not been recorded as sales and the portion of inventory serving as collateral for debts.
- *Impairment of long lived assets.* A detailed description of the methodology of when and how impairments of real estate are determined should be provided.
- *Inventory write-downs.* Summarized information or explanations with respect to significant inventory write-downs should be disclosed in the footnotes because write-downs are generally important and unusual items.
- *Nonrecourse debt.* Although it is not appropriate to offset nonrecourse debt against the related asset, a note to the financial statements should disclose the amount and interrelationship of the nonrecourse debt with the cost of the related property.
- *Capitalization of interest.* ASC 360 (SFAS No. 34) requires the disclosure of the amount of interest expensed and the amount capitalized.
- *Deferral of profit recognition.* When transactions qualify as sales for accounting purposes but do not meet the tests for full profit recognition and, as a result, the installment or cost recovery methods are used, disclosure should be made of significant amounts of profit deferred, the nature of the transaction, and any other information deemed necessary for complete disclosure.
- *Investments in real estate ventures.* Typical disclosures with respect to significant real estate ventures include names of ventures; percentage of ownership interest; accounting and tax policies of the venture; the difference, if any, between the carrying amount of the investment and the investor's share of equity in net assets and the accounting policy regarding amortization of the difference; summarized information as to assets, liabilities, and results of operations or separate financial statements; and investor commitments with respect to joint ventures.
- *Construction contractors.* The principal reporting considerations for construction contractors relate to the two methods of income recognition: the percentage-of-completion method and the completed contract method.

  When the completed contract method is used, an excess of accumulated costs over related billings should be shown in a classified balance sheet as a current asset and an excess of accumulated billings over related costs should be shown as a current liability. If costs exceed billings on some contracts and billings exceed costs on others, the contracts should ordinarily be segregated so that the asset side includes only those contracts on which costs exceed billings, and the liability side includes only those on which billings exceed costs.

  Under the percentage-of-completion method, assets may include costs and related income not yet billed, with respect to certain contracts. Liabilities may include billings in excess of costs and related income with respect to other contracts.

The next disclosures, which are required for SEC reporting companies, should generally be made by a nonpublic company whose principal activity is long-term contracting: Amounts billed but not paid by customers under retainage provisions in contracts, and indication of amounts expected to be collected in various years

- Amounts included in receivables representing the recognized sales value of performance under long-term contracts where such amounts had not been billed and were not billable at the balance sheet date, along with a general description of the prerequisites for billing and an estimate of the amount expected to be collected in one year
- Amounts included in receivables or inventories representing claims or other similar items subject to uncertainty concerning their determination or ultimate realization, together with a

description of the nature and status of principal items, and amounts expected to be collected in one year

- Amount of progress payments (billings) netted against inventory at the balance sheet date

(d) ACCOUNTING BY PARTICIPATING MORTGAGE LOAN BORROWERS. In May 1997, the AICPA issued SOP 97-1, *Accounting by Participating Mortgage Loan Borrowers*. The SOP establishes the borrower's accounting when a mortgage lender participates in either or both of these items:

- Increases in the market value of the mortgaged real estate project
- The project's results of operations

If a lender participates in the market appreciation of the mortgaged property, the borrower must determine the fair value of the appreciation feature at the inception of the loan. A liability equal to the appreciation feature is recognized with a corresponding charge to a debt discount account. The debt discount should be amortized using the interest method.

Interest expense in participating mortgage loans consists of these items:

- Amounts designated in the mortgage agreement as interest
- Amounts related to the lender's participation in operations
- Amounts representing amortization of the debt discount related to the lender's participation in the project's appreciation

The borrower remeasures the participation liability each period. Any revisions to the participation liability resulting from the remeasurement results in an adjustment to the participation liability via a debit or credit to the related debt discount. The revised debt discount should be amortized prospectively using the effective interest rate.

(e) REAL ESTATE INVESTMENT TRUSTS. REITs generally are formed as trusts, associations, or corporations. They employ equity capital, coupled with substantial amounts of debt financing, in making real estate loans and investments. REITs must distribute substantially all of their taxable income to their shareholders annually in order to retain their favorable tax status (i.e., dividends paid are treated as deductions in arriving at taxable income).

31.10 SOURCES AND SUGGESTED REFERENCES

(a) SOURCES BY CURRENT CODIFICATION. The Codification is a major restructuring of accounting and reporting standards. While the content may reside in new locations within the Codification, the FASB's intent in creating the Codification is that the content accurately represents existing standards

The goal in developing the Codification is to simplify user access to all authoritative GAAP by providing all the authoritative literature related to a particular Topic in one place.

The term *authoritative* includes all nongovernmental-level A–D GAAP that has been issued by a standard setter (levels A-D were previously used to describe the hierarchy of GAAP). The Codification does not include practice, textbooks, articles, and other similar content. The Codification also includes relevant authoritative content issued by the SEC as well as selected SEC Staff interpretations and administrative guidance.

As of July 1, 2009, the Codification will be the single source of authoritative U.S. accounting and reporting standards, other than guidance issued by the SEC. The Codification will supersede all then-existing non-SEC accounting and reporting standards. All other nongrandfathered, non-SEC accounting literature not included in the Codification will become nonauthoritative. All the literature stated in the text, changes, and current updates can be cross referenced to the topics listed next.

(i) 970 Real Estate—General

10 Overall
230 Statement of Cash Flows
323 Investments—Equity Method and Joint Ventures
340 Other Assets and Deferred Costs
360 Property, Plant, and Equipment
470 Debt
605 Revenue Recognition
720 Other Expenses
810 Consolidation
835 Interest

(ii) 972 Real Estate—Common Interest Associations

10 Overall
205 Presentation of Financial Statements
235 Notes to Financial Statements
360 Property, Plant and Equipment
430 Deferred Revenue
605 Revenue Recognition
720 Other Expenses
740 Income Taxes
850 Related Party Disclosure

(iii) 974 Real Estate—Real Estate Investment Trusts

10 Overall
323 Investments—Equity Method and Joint Ventures
605 Revenue Recognition
810 Consolidation
835 Interest
840 Leases

(iv) 976 Real Estate—Retail Land

10 Overall
310 Receivables
330 Inventory
605 Revenue Recognition
705 Cost of Sales and Service

(v) 978 Real Estate—Time-Sharing Activities

10 Overall
230 Statement of Cash Flow
250 Accounting Changes and Error Correction
310 Receivables
330 Inventory
340 Other Assets and Deferred Costs
605 Revenue Recognition
720 Other expenses
810 Consolidation
840 Leases

(b) SUGGESTED REFERENCES PRIOR TO CODIFICATION

Accounting Principles Board. APB Opinion No. 18, *The Equity Method of Accounting for Investments in Common Stock*. New York: AICPA, March 1971.

———. APB Opinion No. 18, Interpretation No. 18-2, *The Equity Method of Accounting for Investments in Common Stock*. New York: Author, November 1971.

———. APB Opinion No. 20, *Accounting Changes*. New York: AICPA, 1971.

———. APB Opinion No. 21, *Interest on Receivables and Payables*. New York: AICPA, August 1971.

———. APB Opinion No. 22, *Disclosure of Accounting Policies*. New York: AICPA, April 1972.

American Institute of Certified Public Accountants. Accounting Research Bulletin No. 43, *Inventory Pricing, Restatement and Revision of Accounting Research Bulletins*. New York: Author, June 1953.

———. Accounting Research Bulletin No. 45, *Long-Term Construction-Type Contracts*. New York: Author, October 1955.

———. *Audit and Accounting Guide for Construction Contractors, Accounting Guide.* New York: Author, 1981.

———. *Guide for the Use of Real Estate Appraisal Information, Accounting Guide.* New York: Author, 1987.

———. Issues Paper, *Accounting for Allowances for Losses on Certain Real Estate and Loans and Receivables Collaterialized by Real Estate*. New York: Author, June 1979.

———. Statement of Position No. 75-2, *Accounting Practices of Real Estate Investment Trusts*. New York: Author, June 27, 1975.

———. Statement of Position No. 78-3, *Accounting for Costs to Sell and Rent, and Initial Real Estate Operations of, Real Estate Projects*. New York: Author, 1978.

———. Statement of Position No. 78-9, *Accounting for Investments in Real Estate Ventures*. New York: Author, December 29, 1978.

———. Statement of Position No. 80-3, *Accounting for Real Estate Acquisition, Development and Construction Costs*. New York: Author, 1980.

———. Statement of Position 81-1, *Accounting for Performance of Construction-Type and Certain Production-Type Contracts*. New York: Author, July 15, 1981.

———. Statement of Position No. 92-1, *Accounting for Real Estate Syndication Income*. New York: Author, 1992.

———. Statement of Position 92-3, *Accounting for Foreclosed Assets*. New York: Author, 1992.

———. Statement of Position 97-1, *Accounting by Participating Mortgage Loan Borrowers*. New York: Author, 1997.

———. Proposed Statement of Position, *Accounting for Certain Costs and Activities Related to Property, Plant, and Equipment*. New York: Author, June 29, 2001.

———. Third Notice to Practitioners, *Accounting for Real Estate Acquisition, Development, and Construction Arrangements*. New York: Author, February 10, 1986.

Financial Accounting Standards Board. *Cost Accounting for Real Estate*. New York, 1983.

———. EITF Issue No. 84-4, *Acquisition, Development, and Construction Loans*. Stamford, CT: Author, 1984.

———. EITF Issue No. 85-27, *Recognition of Receipts from Made-up Rental Shortfalls*. Stamford, CT: Author, 1985.

———. EITF Issue No. 86-6, *Antispeculation Clauses in Real Estate Sales Contracts*. Stamford, CT: Author, 1986.

———. EITF Issue No. 86-21, *Application of the AICPA Notice to Practitioners Regarding Acquisition, Development, and Construction Arrangements to the Acquisition of an Operating Property*. Stamford, CT: Author, 1986.

———. EITF Issue No. 87-9. *EITF Abstracts: A Summary of Proceedings of the FASB Emerging Issues Task Force, Profit Recognition on Sale of Real Estate with Insurance Mortgages on Surety Bonds*. Norwalk, CT: Author, 1988.

———. EITF Issue No. 88-24, *Effect of Various Forms of Financing under Statement of Financial Accounting Standards No. 66*. Norwalk, CT: Author, 1988.

______. EITF Issue No. 94-1, *Accounting for Tax Benefits Resulting from Investments in Affordable Housing Projects*. Norwalk, CT: Author, 1994.

______. Statement of Financial Accounting Standards No. 13, *Accounting for Leases*. Stamford, CT: Author, November 1976.

______. Statement of Financial Accounting Standards No. 14, *Financial Reporting for Segments of a Business Enterprise*. Stamford, CT: Author, 1976.

______. Statement of Financial Accounting Standards No. 28, *Accounting for Sales with Leasebacks (an Amendment of FASB Statement No. 13).* Stamford, CT: Author, 1979.

______. Statement of Financial Accounting Standards No. 29, *Determining Contingent Rentals (an Amendment of FASB Statement No. 13).* Stamford, CT: Author, 1979.

______. Statement of Financial Accounting Standards No. 34, *Capitalization of Interest Cost*. Stamford, CT: Author, October 1979.

______. Statement of Financial Accounting Standards No. 56, *Designation of AICPA Guide and Statement of Position (SOP) 81-1 on Contractor Accounting and SOP 81-2 Concerning Hospital-Related Organizations as Preferable for Purposes of Applying APB Opinion 20*. Stamford, CT: Author, February 1982.

______. Statement of Financial Accounting Standards No. 66, *Accounting for Sales of Real Estate*. Stamford, CT: Author, October 1982.

______. Statement of Financial Accounting Standards No. 67, *Accounting for Costs and Initial Rental Operations of Real Estate Projects*. Stamford, CT: Author, October 1982.

______. Statement of Financial Accounting Standards No. 94, *Consolidation of All Majority-Owned Subsidiaries*. Stamford, CT: Author, October 1987.

______. Statement of Financial Accounting Standards No. 95, *Statement of Cash Flows*. Stamford, CT: Author, November 1987.

______. Statement of Financial Accounting Standards No. 98, *Accounting for Leases*. Norwalk, CT: Author, May 1988.

______. Statement of Financial Accounting Standards No. 121, *Accounting for the Impairment of Long-Lived Assets and for Long-Lived Assets to Be Disposed Of*. Norwalk, CT: Author, March 1995.

______. Statement of Financial Accounting Standards No. 131, *Disclosures About Segments of an Enterprise and Related Information*. Norwalk, CT: Author, 1997.

______. Statement of Financial Accounting Standards No. 142, *Goodwill and Other Intangible Assets*. Norwalk, CT: Author, 2001.

______. Statement of Financial Accounting Standards No. 144, *Accounting for the Impairment or Disposal of Long-Lived Assets*. Norwalk, CT: Author, 2001.

Financial Accounting Standards Board. Financial Interpretation (FIN) 46-R, *Consolidation of Variable Interest Entities: An Interpretation of ARB No. 51,* Author: Norwalk, CT. 2003.

______. Statement of Financial Accounting Standards (FAS) No. 141(R), *Business Combinations.* Norwalk, CT: Author, 2007.

______, FAS 160, *Noncontrolling Interests in Consolidated Statements*. Norwalk, CT: Author, 2007.

______, FAS 144, *Accounting for the Impairment or Disposal of Long-Lived Assets*. Norwalk, CT: Author, 2001.

______, FAS 157, *Fair Value Measurements*. Norwalk, CT: Author, 2006.

______. Technical Bulletin No. 85-3, *Accounting for Operating Leases with Scheduled Rent Increases*. Stamford, CT: Author, November 1985.

______. FASB Technical Bulletin No. 88-1, *Issues Relating to Accounting for Leases*. Norwalk, CT: Author, December 1988.

Klink, J. J. *Investor Accounting for Real Estate Ventures.* New York: Price Waterhouse & Co., 1979.

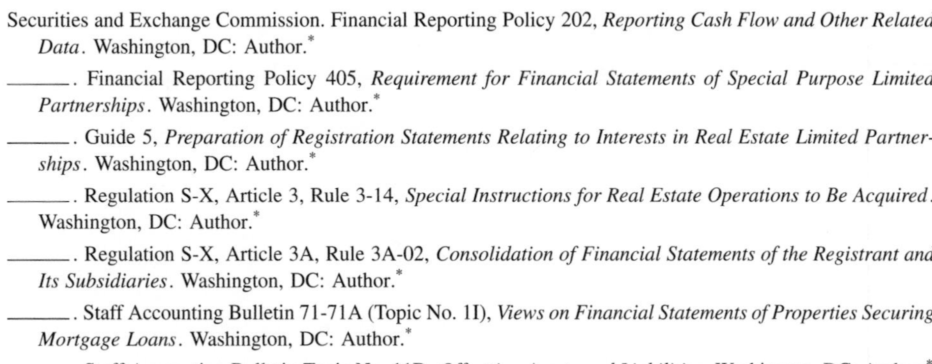

Securities and Exchange Commission. Financial Reporting Policy 202, *Reporting Cash Flow and Other Related Data*. Washington, DC: Author.[*]

______. Financial Reporting Policy 405, *Requirement for Financial Statements of Special Purpose Limited Partnerships*. Washington, DC: Author.[*]

______. Guide 5, *Preparation of Registration Statements Relating to Interests in Real Estate Limited Partnerships*. Washington, DC: Author.[*]

______. Regulation S-X, Article 3, Rule 3-14, *Special Instructions for Real Estate Operations to Be Acquired*. Washington, DC: Author.[*]

______. Regulation S-X, Article 3A, Rule 3A-02, *Consolidation of Financial Statements of the Registrant and Its Subsidiaries*. Washington, DC: Author.[*]

______. Staff Accounting Bulletin 71-71A (Topic No. 1I), *Views on Financial Statements of Properties Securing Mortgage Loans*. Washington, DC: Author.[*]

______. Staff Accounting Bulletin Topic No. 11D, *Offsetting Assets and Liabilities*. Washington, DC: Author.[*]

---

[*] *Note:* Subsequent to publication, the SEC codifies various releases. Readers are urged to consult current codifications under the topics of interest at the SEC website (*www.sec.gov*). The SEC publishes an updated *Financial Reporting Manual,* available at *www.sec.gov/divisions/corpfin/cffinancialreportingmanual.pdf,* which contains sections directed to real estate accounting and presentation issues by topic.

CHAPTER 32

FEDERAL GOVERNMENT ACCOUNTING, BUDGETING, AND AUDITING

David M. Zavada, CPA, MPA
Partner, Kearney & Company

32.1 FEDERAL GOVERNMENT ORGANIZATION 2

32.2 FEDERAL FINANCIAL MANAGEMENT 4

(a) Organizational Roles and Responsibilities Related to Federal Financial Management 5
(i) U.S. Government Accountability Office 6
(ii) Office of Management and Budget 6
(iii) Department of the Treasury 6
(b) Parallel Accounting Bases: Budgetary and Financial Accounting 6
(i) Budgetary (Obligations and Cash) Accounting 7
(ii) Financial (Accrual) Accounting 7
(iii) Comparing and Contrasting Budgetary and Financial Accounting 7

32.3 FEDERAL FINANCIAL REPORTING 8

(a) Federal Accounting and Reporting Today 10
(i) Accelerated Reporting Schedule 11
(ii) Assertions Relating to Internal Control over Financial Reporting 11

32.4 FEDERAL BUDGET PROCESS 11

(a) Federal Budget Defined 11
(b) Phases of the Budget Cycle 12
(i) Phase 1: Budget Formulation 12
(ii) Phase 2: Congressional Action 13
(iii) Phase 3: Budget Execution 14
(iv) Phase 4: Review and Audit 15

32.5 AUDITING IN THE FEDERAL GOVERNMENT 15

(a) Generally Accepted Government Auditing Standards 15
(b) Types of Governmental Audits 16
(i) Audits of Recipients of Federal Financial Assistance 17

32.6 EMERGING ISSUES 18

(a) Achieving a Government-Wide Audit Opinion 18
(b) Developing Information to Support Decision Making 19
(c) Risk Assessment and Prevention-Oriented Controls and Oversight 19
(d) Enhancing Financial Reporting 20

32.7 CONCLUSION 20

APPENDIX A: SELECTED FINANCIAL MANAGEMENT LEGISLATION 21

APPENDIX B: IMPORTANT BUDGETARY ACCOUNTING TERMS 22

Segments of this chapter are adapted in whole or in part from material contained in three books also written by Kearney & Company and published by John Wiley & Sons. These books are: *Federal Accounting Handbook,* 2nd ed. (2006); *Federal Government Auditing* (2005): and *OMB Circular A-123 and Sarbanes-Oxley* (2006). Kearney & Company is a Certified Public Accounting firm located in Alexandria, Virginia, specializing in providing accounting and auditing services to the federal government.

The federal government's spending for fiscal year 2011 was almost $3.8 trillion. The accumulated national debt (debt held by the public) was more than $10.2 trillion. Annual federal outlays accounted for roughly 25 percent of the country's gross national product (GDP) and debt held by the public is on an upward trend now almost 70 percent of GDP. The federal government's financial statements presented on an accrual basis reported gross cost of almost $4 trillion and total liabilities in excess of $17.5 trillion for and as of the end of FY 2011, respectively. Never before has there been a greater time for accountability, credibility and reliability of financial information to inform discussion and decision making.

—Federal Budget for FY 2012, Historical Tables, *Office of Management and Budget, and* Financial Report of the U.S. Government 2011, U.S. Department of the Treasury

The numbers just cited are dramatic and emphasize the massive size, influence and commitments of the federal government. They are also indicative of a growing need to accurately and consistently account for the federal government's financial activities. With so much at stake, accurately measuring and reporting the financial position and condition of the federal government has never been so important. The need for timely and reliable financial information to support budget and program management decisions is essential. The credibility of generally accepted accounting principles (GAAP) and audited financial statements is vital to government integrity, credibility and maintaining confidence.

The federal government's response to the U.S. financial crisis that began in 2008 demonstrated the magnitude of the government's commitments and the underlying role the government plays in maintaining economic stability. From 2008 to 2010, the federal government spent and assumed hundreds of billions of dollars in contingent liabilities to support government-sponsored enterprises, banking, financial services, and other industries to backstop financial markets and avoid further financial calamity. (Source: *Financial Report of the US Government 2010,* US Department of the Treasury.)

This chapter is being written at a time when the U.S. economy is attempting to recover from the effects of that crisis. There is heightened awareness and interest in the financial condition and position of the U.S. government. Public debate and discussion of the long-term fiscal sustainability of spending and revenues at their current rates is increasing, and the president and Congress are engaged in budget discussions. External factors, such as the downgrading of U.S. debt ratings, highlight the need for credible financial management plans and transparent and reliable financial statements.

The federal budget process is the primary management and accountability process in the federal government today. Budget formulation involves identifying policy and budget priorities along with funding justifications. Once enacted, budget execution tracks revenue and spending, primarily on a cash basis. The nature of the budget process subjects it to anecdotal analysis and political agendas, the pace of which has accelerated in the era of instantaneous communication and social media.

Federal accounting is intended to provide another perspective, a perspective that includes actual budgetary and accrual-based financial results, financial position, and condition. For some programs, such as social insurance programs like Medicare and Social Security, it also includes a view of longer-term fiscal sustainability. This view is supported by the credibility and integrity associated with transparent GAAP, generally accepted auditing standards, and an annual independent financial audit. This chapter provides a detailed look at federal accounting and reporting, the budget process, and federal auditing to better understand the current management and accountability framework in place and challenges ahead.

32.1 FEDERAL GOVERNMENT ORGANIZATION

By any measure, the economic impact of the federal government is big. But to say that the federal government is big would be an understatement. It employs millions, owns billions, and spends trillions every year. Not only is the federal government big, but it is also unique. No other entity rivals its size, complexity, or diversity in the types of programs or services delivered. The executive branch manages this activity and is permitted only to implement the will of Congress, as expressed by law. Exhibit 32.1 illustrates the three branches of government: the executive, the legislative, and the judicial branch.

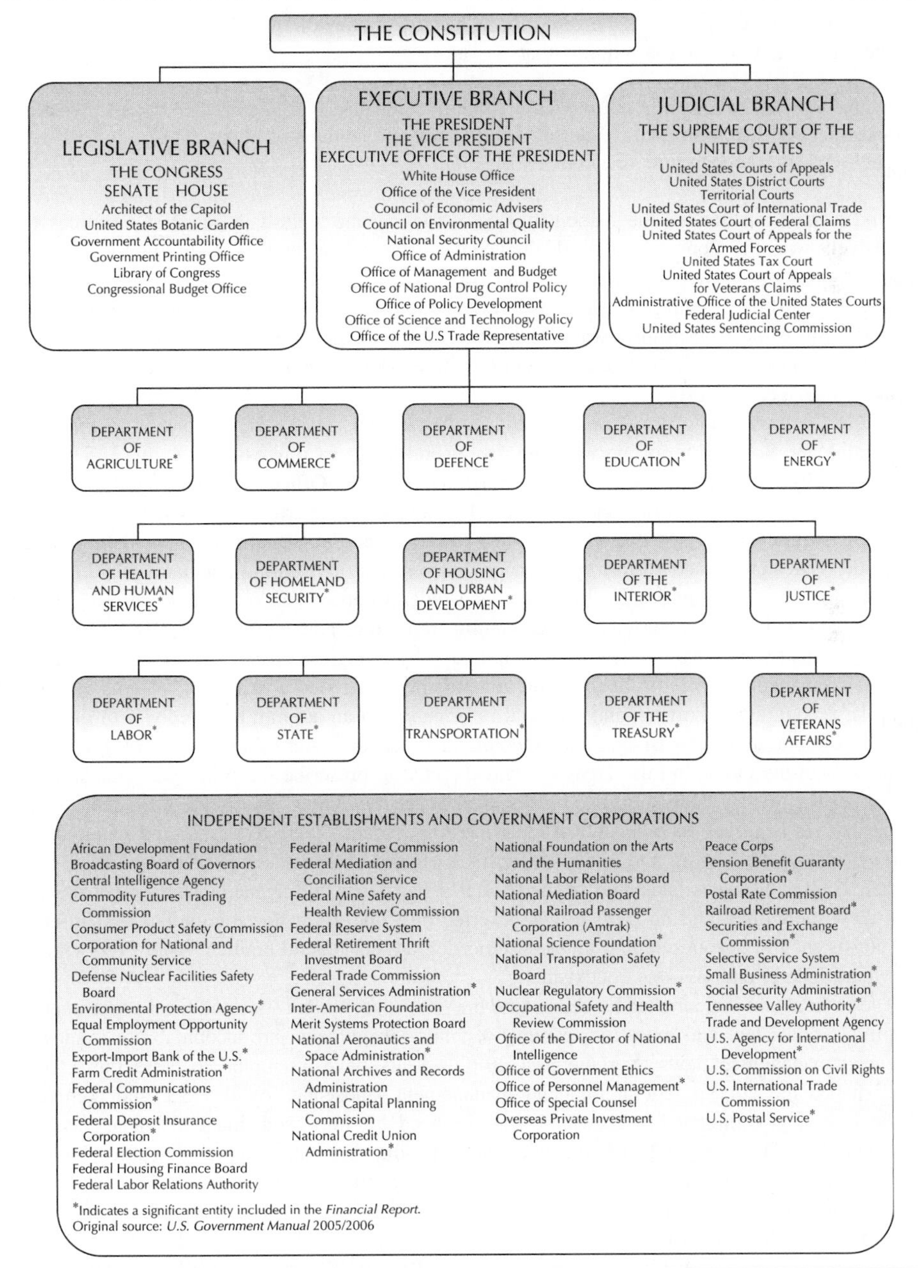

Exhibit 32.1 Federal Government Organization
***Source: Financial Report of the US Government 2010,* US Department of the Treasury.**

32.2 FEDERAL FINANCIAL MANAGEMENT

The nexus of federal financial management is no less than the Constitution itself, which states in Section 8, Clause 1, that

> The Congress shall have the power to lay and collect taxes, duties, imposts, and excises, and to pay the debts and provide for the common defense and general welfare of the United States.

Clause 2 adds that Congress has the authority to "borrow money on the credit of the United States." Furthermore, the Constitution requires that

> No money shall be drawn from the Treasury, but in consequence of appropriations made by law; and a regular statement and account of receipts and expenditures of all public money shall be published from time to time (Section 9, Clause 7).

Under the Constitution, the responsibility for raising and spending financial resources rests exclusively with the Congress of the United States. The federal budget is simply the taxing and spending authority, given by Congress, that forms the financial corpus which must be planned, budgeted, controlled, managed, accounted for, and ultimately reported on by departments and agencies. Since the Constitution was first written, the federal budget process—from the budget formulation phase through the budget execution phase—has been the continuum on which federal financial management rests.

While Congress alone provides the authority to tax and spend, the responsibility for federal accounting and financial reporting was split, by several laws of Congress, among the U.S. General Accountability Office (GAO, a legislative branch agency); the Office of Management and Budget (OMB) and the Department of Treasury (both of which are in the executive branch); and the other federal departments and agencies (i.e., the rest of the executive branch). By laws dating back to 1921, the GAO prescribed forms, systems, procedures, and accounting standards for the federal government. By these same laws, heads of each federal department or agency were required to develop and maintain the systems of accounting, reporting, and internal controls that best met that department's or agency's needs. This approach by Congress spawned a diversity of federal financial management systems, as the many federal entities needed a variety of systems of internal controls, accounting, reporting, and financial information in an attempt to comply with the law.

For example, under the Budget and Accounting Procedures Act of 1950, the GAO, after consultation with the OMB and the Treasury, was directed to prescribe the principles, standards, and related requirements for accounting to be observed by federal entities. But in the same act, Congress stated that the heads of each executive department and agency were to design and maintain their own systems of accounting and internal controls to provide full disclosure of the financial results of their entities. Decades later, half of the federal departments and agencies had not yet complied with these guidelines, and no pressure was exerted by Congress to force compliance. Uniformity and consistency of accounting and financial reporting among federal entities—and even within an individual federal entity—was nonexistent.

The Federal Government had lagged behind the private sector and state and local governments in adopting a consistent and more transparent financial management and accountability framework. Financial management laws over the past 20-plus years have attempted to close this gap and have shaped the current federal financial management landscape. As the size and complexity of the federal government has grown, so has the need for improved financial management and accountability. The enacted legislation chart in Appendix A to this chapter illustrates a gradual shift toward a more sophisticated financial management structure and greater accountability and transparency provided in the budget section of Appendix B.

Today, several laws set overall guidelines and establish detailed uniform federal financial management policy. The Chief Financial Officers Act of 1990 (CFO Act) was landmark legislation in federal financial management creating a financial management structure, leadership, and consistent audited financial reporting; it also paved the way for the development of transparent GAAP. The

CFO Act helped to shift the culture of federal financial management from acquiring and spending resources to a balance that included financial accountability, reporting, and results.

However, unlike commercial accounting and auditing, little is taught or written about this area of accounting in undergraduate accounting curriculums, so there is no technical academic training familiarizing students the unique aspects of federal government accounting and auditing. Key professional associations such as the Association of Government Accountants along with financial management leadership programs at the CFO Academy at the Department of Defense's National Defense University have filled this void by providing ongoing professional development and training opportunities.

The CFO Act gave OMB the main policy responsibility for financial systems and reporting. The Treasury began to support departments and agencies in developing the underlying systems to improve federal accountability. The Treasury also became a more active partner with the OMB in conducting research and experimenting with alternatives to enhance accounting and reporting within departments and agencies government-wide. At about the same time, the U.S. Comptroller General (who heads the GAO), the secretary of the Treasury, and the director of the OMB established the Federal Accounting Standards Advisory Board (or FASAB). The FASAB was instructed to develop and recommend accounting and reporting standards for use by each federal department and agency as well as government-wide. The establishment of the FASAB by its three sponsors, effectively began the process of developing transparent GAAP for the federal government, a process already well established for corporations and state and local governments.

With the mandate of the CFO Act, initiatives to improve financial management moved forward in the 1990s. By 1994, a foundation of accounting and reporting standards, and government-wide systems requirements with which federal departments and agencies must comply were established. Over the next decade, federal agencies worked toward compliance and the goal of an unqualified audit opinion on their financial statements. However, audited federal financial statements were not due to OMB until six months after the end of the fiscal year, and some agencies relied on cumbersome, labor-intensive efforts after fiscal year-end to comply.

In 2005, the OMB accelerated the due date for audited financial statements of major federal agencies and the government-wide statement to November 15 and December 15, respectively. The accelerated reporting shift served as a stress test for federal agency internal controls and transformed federal financial reporting and auditing. The most profound effect being the improvement in underlying internal controls and accounting disciplines enabling agencies to consistently achieve this milestone.

Throughout the last decade, the role of chief financial officers (CFOs) and federal financial management has broadened beyond budget formulation, accounting operations and financial reporting. New laws, such as the Government Performance and Results Act, Improper Payments Information Act, American Recovery and Reinvestment Act (Recovery Act), and Federal Funding Accountability and Transparency Act have placed CFOs at the forefront of implementation efforts. In addition, complex financial systems improvements have required increased attention along with budget exercises, data requests, related to the uncertainty surrounding annual appropriations and the federal budget. CFOs are now key members of federal agency senior leadership actively engaged in all of these areas in an effort to bring greater value, accountability, transparency, and integrity to financial and program operations.

(a) ORGANIZATIONAL ROLES AND RESPONSIBILITIES RELATED TO FEDERAL FINANCIAL MANAGEMENT. Implementation of overall federal financial policy through more detailed regulations, rules, and other publications is dispersed among central agencies as well as executive-branch entities. The three agencies having the preponderance of specific government-wide financial management responsibilities are the GAO, the OMB, and Treasury. For the most part, federal departments and agencies look to these central agencies for coordinated policy, and at times even for procedural guidance. As discussed earlier, these three agencies serve as the sponsors of the FASAB and fund their operations. The roles and responsibilities of GAO, OMB and the Treasury are discussed in the following paragraphs.

(i) U.S. Government Accountability Office. The GAO is an independent agency in the legislative branch and is headed by the comptroller general, an officer appointed by the president with the advice and consent of Congress for a 15-year term and who may not be reappointed. Congress created the GAO with the Budget and Accounting Act of 1921. Over the years, Congress has charged the GAO with many financial management, accounting, reporting, fiscal procedural, and auditing responsibilities.

Congress has declared by law that the GAO shall investigate, government-wide, matters related to the receipt, disbursement, and use of public money. The GAO also is responsible for developing and publishing *Government Auditing Standards,* commonly referred to as the "Yellow Book," which define generally accepted standards for conducting government audits. Routinely GAO audits will assess and report on program performance related to a federal department's goals and objectives, and may consider such issues as the efficiency, economy, and effectiveness of operations. GAO has statutory responsibility for conducting the financial statement audit of certain agencies and for conducting the audit of the government-wide financial statements.

(ii) Office of Management and Budget. Over the years, various laws have given the OMB extensive responsibilities for prescribing regulations and rules governing the federal government's financial management systems of budgeting, accounting reporting and auditing. The CFO Act provided OMB with the authority to take a more definitive executive leadership role in improving federal financial management.

Within OMB, the Office of Federal Financial Management (OFFM) is the lead office for financial management policy. The OFFM is headed by a Controller who is a Presidential appointee. The OMB communicates financial management policy to departments and agencies through a series of OMB Circulars, Bulletins, and Executive Orders that consist of rules, regulations, and directives. Its direction is often quite specific, prescribing what these financial officers shall do, how the prescribed practices are to be followed, and when reporting will be made on the actions taken by federal entities.

(iii) Department of the Treasury. The Treasury is headed by the secretary of the Treasury (not the Treasurer of the United States, who is a subordinate executive within Treasury), and is the official fiscal agency of the federal government, with some of its responsibilities fixed by the Constitution itself. Created in 1789, the Treasury has been given extensive fiscal and accounting responsibilities by Congress and is the primary organization responsible for accounting and reporting on the cash receipts and cash disbursements of the government and on borrowings and the debt of the United States. The Treasury Department also annually produces the *Financial Report of the U.S. Government (Financial Report)* containing the government-wide financial statements.

Like the OMB, the Treasury has its own systems for issuing regulations and rules to departments and agencies—a series of numbered Notices and Circulars for promulgating guidance on specific subjects. The more permanent or continuing guidance is set forth in the *Treasury Financial Manual* issued by Treasury's Financial Management Service bureau

(b) PARALLEL ACCOUNTING BASES: BUDGETARY AND FINANCIAL ACCOUNTING. Federal entities must provide a ready reporting of activities on multiple accounting bases and structures. Federal entities report financial statements on the accrual basis of accounting; but the Treasury requires daily information to support its cash basis accounting. Further, the OMB requires agencies to report on the basis of obligations, and Congress wants reporting structured by appropriations, a format it understands. The different accounting bases and structures can lead to confusion in the way federal financial results are reported.

Broadly, federal accounting is best described under two categories: budgetary accounting and financial accounting. Budgetary accounting is primarily on the cash basis but includes obligations that are budgetary commitments. Financial accounting is akin to the more traditional accrual accounting used in the private sector. Both are described in further detail below.

(i) Budgetary (Obligations and Cash) Accounting. The overall objectives of appropriation budgetary accounting are directed toward fiscal accountability and compliance with the expressed intent of Congress. Implicit features of a federal entity's systems of accounting and controls are checks and balances to ensure that several criteria of a federal appropriation are considered by a federal executive prior to the obligation or expenditure of federal monies and that program execution is consistent with law. As a minimum, all appropriations and budget authorities have three specific compliance considerations:

1. *Timing.* The commitment and, on occasion, the rate of expenditure of appropriated funds must be made during the time period permitted by Congress in legislation.
2. *Purpose.* Appropriated funds may be obligated and expended only for those purposes intended or expressed by Congress in an agency's authorization or appropriation legislation.
3. *Amount.* The total amount of obligations and expenditures may not exceed the appropriation or amount of budgetary authority provided by Congress.

Budgetary accounting is performed on an obligations and cash basis. Budgetary accounting revolves around the receipt, commitment, and outlay of budgetary resources. Budget authority is provided by congressional appropriations, obligations are recorded to reflect a commitment of budgetary resources, and outlays reflect cash disbursed by the government. Appendix B further defines key budgetary terms.

Budgetary accounting guidelines are established by OMB and the Treasury, but specific requirements may also reside in statute. For example, the Federal Credit Reform Act of 1990 directs the full cost of federal credit programs to be budgeted when loan or loan guaranty commitments are entered into by the government. In addition, *OMB Circular A-11, Preparation, Submission and Execution of the Budget,* is updated periodically by OMB and contains specific instructions related to budget formulation and execution. Treasury Department guidance provided in the *Treasury Financial Manual* provides additional assistance for recording budgetary transactions.

Understanding the budgetary accounting process is a prerequisite to appreciating the uniqueness of federal accounting. It is the reporting for the legal, economic, and accounting events and actions, alluded to earlier, that distinguishes federal accounting from the accounting of private sector and other public sector organizations.

(ii) Financial (Accrual) Accounting. Financial accounting for federal agencies is defined by GAAP developed by the FASAB. The financial reporting FASAB has defined is primarily accrual based; however, it includes a Statement of Budgetary Resources prepared on the budgetary basis of accounting. FASAB standards also require forward-looking information to project the long-term fiscal sustainability of key social insurance programs on a separate Statement of Social Insurance prepared by agencies such as the Social Security Administration and the Department of Health and Human Services and government-wide.

To date, the FASAB has developed 41 Statements of Federal Financial Accounting Standards, along with numerous interpretations and technical releases. The FASAB consists of both government and public board members. In addition to the three principal sponsors, the board includes public representatives from the broader accounting and academic community.

Federal accounting standards are developed through a transparent process that includes a public comment period similar to federal regulations. However, as an advisory board, the FASAB can simply recommend accounting standards. The OMB and the GAO hold veto power over accounting standards recommended by the FASAB; however, to date, a veto has never been exercised. The American Institute of Certified Public Accountants (AICPA) designated the FASAB process as determining GAAP for the federal government in 1999. (Source: *FASAB Facts 2010.*)

(iii) Comparing and Contrasting Budgetary and Financial Accounting. Annually, the Treasury Department prepares the government-wide financial statements. By statute (31 USC 331e), the government-wide financial statements are required to be audited by the GAO. The government-wide statements are prepared on an accrual basis of accounting, but include information articulating the relationship

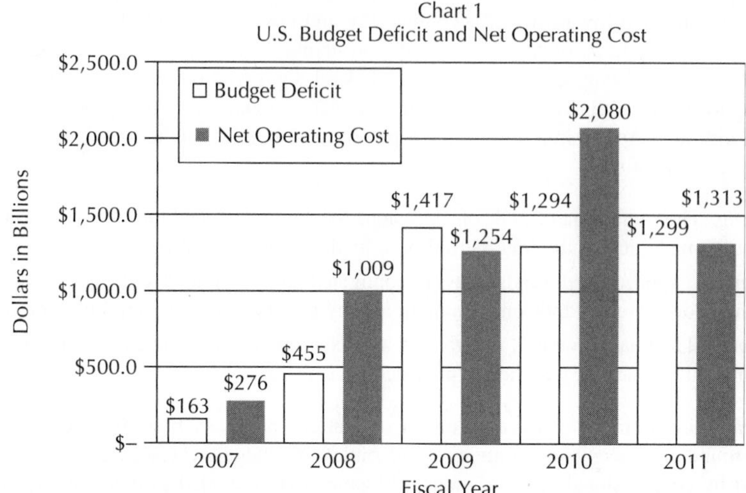

Exhibit 32.2 U.S. Budget Deficit and Operating Cost Trends
Source:* *Citizen's Guide to the 2010 Financial Report of the U.S. Government.* U.S. Department of the Treasury: *www.fms.treas.gov/fr/10frusg/10guide.pdf

to key cash basis numbers like the annual budget deficit. The budget deficit is a measure of total receipts less outlays on a cash basis. Net operating cost, however, reports total government cost on an accrual basis less tax revenue.

Exhibit 32.2 shows key cash and accrual numbers in budget deficit and net operating cost trends from 2007 through 2011 as reported in the *Financial Report of the U.S. Government for Fiscal Year 2011 (Financial Report).* The budget deficit reflects government outlays less receipts on a cash basis, while net operating cost is reflected on an accrual basis. Year-to-year variances are discussed in the *Financial Report* where the effect of costs related to the Government's retirement, benefit and economic recovery programs are explained in detail.

32.3 FEDERAL FINANCIAL REPORTING

Since the enactment of the CFO Act and later laws, annual financial statements are now compiled department- and agency-wide and are independently audited. This section provides context for understanding federal financial statements and discusses the implementation of this reporting requirement.

The FASAB has defined the objectives of federal financial reporting shown in Exhibit 32.3 to address user needs. These objectives are intended to provide a framework for the development of federal accounting standards. As mentioned previously, 41 Statements of Federal Financial Accounting (SFFAS) have been issued by the FASAB to date.

The OMB, in its statement in OMB Circular A-136, *Financial Reporting Requirements,* requires federal agencies to prepare and have audited four principal annual financial statements:

1. The *balance sheet* is needed to present resources, liabilities, and financial status of the entity at a specific point in time, however measured (i.e., budgetary, cash, accrual, etc.), and to show total balances of appropriate assets, liabilities, and equities of a federal organization.
2. A statement of *net cost* is needed to present the various components of the net cost of a reporting entity's operations (i.e., total, gross, or full costs less any exchange revenues).
3. A statement of *changes in net position* reports the beginning net financial position, the items that caused changes in the net position, and the ending net position of a federal entity.

Budgetary Integrity—Federal financial reporting should assist in fulfilling the government's duty to be publicly accountable for monies raised through taxes and other means and for their expenditure in accordance with the appropriations laws that establish the government's budget for a particular fiscal year and related laws and regulations. Federal financial reporting should provide information that helps the reader to determine:

- how budgetary resources have been obtained and used and whether their acquisition and use were in accordance with the legal authorization;
- the status of budgetary resources; and
- how information on the use of budgetary resources relates to information on the costs of program operations and whether information on the status of budgetary resources is consistent with other accounting information on assets and liabilities.

Operating Performance—Federal financial reporting should assist report users in evaluating the service efforts, costs, and accomplishments of the reporting entity; the manner in which these efforts and accomplishments have been financed; and the management of the entity's assets and liabilities. Federal financial reporting should provide information that helps the reader to determine:

- the costs of providing specific programs and activities and the composition of, and changes in, these costs;
- the efforts and accomplishments associated with federal programs and the changes over time and in relation to costs; and
- the efficiency and effectiveness of the government's management of its assets and liabilities.

Stewardship—Federal financial reporting should assist report users in assessing the impact on the country of the government's operations and investments for the period and how, as a result, the government's and the nation's financial condition has changed and may change in the future. Federal financial reporting should provide information that helps the reader to determine whether:

- the government's financial position improved or deteriorated over the period;
- future budgetary resources will likely be sufficient to sustain public services and to meet obligations as they come due; and
- government operations have contributed to the nation's current and future well-being.

Systems and Control—Federal financial reporting should assist report users in understanding whether financial management systems and internal accounting and administrative controls are adequate to ensure that:

- transactions are executed in accordance with budgetary and financial laws and other requirements, consistent with the purposes authorized, and are recorded in accordance with federal accounting standards;
- assets are properly safeguarded to deter fraud, waste, and abuse; and
- performance measurement information is adequately supported.

Exhibit 32.3 Objectives of Federal Financial Reporting
Source:* SFFAC 1, *Objectives of Federal Financial Reporting.

4. A statement of *budgetary resources* provides information on the status of congressional spending authority by those entities whose financing derives, wholly or in part, from congressional budget and spending authority; this is the only financial statement prepared using budgetary accounting.

These are statements of a different character with different content from those appearing in an annual financial report of private sector organizations or other public sector and nonprofit entities. In addition, some agencies are required to prepare a statement of social insurance and a statement of custodial activity, to report on certain unique aspects of programs they operate. Other reporting is dictated by legislation and compliance criteria imposed on a department by the Treasury or the OMB. Additionally, federal GAAP defines a somewhat different set of financial statements for reporting at the government-wide level. These statements are designed to provide a government-wide rather than agency-level view in regard to the overall use of budgetary resources, changes in cash balances, and the relationship between the cash basis budget deficit and accrual basis net operating cost.

(a) FEDERAL ACCOUNTING AND REPORTING TODAY. Federal accounting and reporting today has largely been defined by the CFO Act and related initiatives. Since the enactment of the CFO Act, agencies have focused on improving accounting disciplines and financial controls to the point where they can prepare financial statements and receive an unqualified opinion from an independent auditor on an accelerated reporting schedule. This has been no easy task. To varying degrees, the relative size and complexity of federal agencies along with the variety of nonintegrated financial-related systems that have arisen over many years have added to the challenge.

However, the annual focus on preparing and auditing financial statements has resulted in steady incremental progress toward more reliable budgetary and financial information and improvements in underlying controls as auditor-reported deficiencies have declined. A recent report developed by the federal Chief Financial Officers Council found that:

". . . annual preparation and audit of agency and government-wide financial statements, have contributed to the evolution of reliable, timely, and useful financial information in the Federal Government." (Source: *The Chief Financial Officers Act of 1990—20 Years Later;* Chief Financial Officer's Council and The Counsel of the Inspectors General on Integrity and Efficiency July 2011)

For fiscal year 2011, 21 of the 24 major federal agencies were able to achieve the milestone of an unqualified audit opinion. The results of all agency audits are reflected in Exhibit 32.4. (Source: *Financial Report of the US Government 2011,* p 5.)

CFO Act Agency	Audit Results
Agency for International Development	Unqualified
Department of Agriculture	Unqualified
Department of Commerce	Unqualified
Department of Defense	Disclaimer
Department of Education	Unqualified
Department of Energy	Unqualified
Department of Health and Human Services*	Unqualified
Department of Homeland Security§	Qualified
Department of Housing and Urban Development	Unqualified
Department of Interior	Unqualified
Department of Labor	Unqualified
Department of Justice	Unqualified
Department of State	Qualified
Department of Transportation	Unqualified
Department of Treasury	Unqualified
Department of Veterans Affairs	Unqualified
Environmental Protection Agency	Unqualified
General Services Administration	Unqualified
National Aeronautics and Space Administration	Unqualified
National Science Foundation	Unqualified
Nuclear Regulatory Commission	Unqualified
Office of Personnel Management	Unqualified
Small Business Administration	Unqualified
Social Security Administration	Unqualified

*HHS received a disclaimer of opinion on its 2010 *Statement of Social Insurance.*
§DHS *Balance Sheet* and *Statement of Custodial Activity* were the only statements subject to audit.

Exhibit 32.4 Summary of FY 2011 Financial Statement Audit Results by Agency
Source: Financial Report of the U.S. Government FY 2010.

(i) Accelerated Reporting Schedule. In 2005, the OMB required agencies to begin reporting their audited financial statements within 45 days after the end of the fiscal year. The accelerated reporting schedule has placed an increased emphasis on internal controls to produce reliable information. Prior to the accelerated reporting requirements, agencies took six months or more to produce their audited financial statements. Accelerated financial reporting has transformed federal accounting operations, financial reporting, and auditing within the federal government.

For example, key reconciliations could no longer be delayed until the end of the year; there simply was not enough time. Internal controls needed to be improved to the point where reliable quarterly, and even monthly, information could be produced and audited timely. The approach auditors took to auditing federal financial statements also shifted. Audits became more focused on internal controls to determine if they could be relied on to produce accurate financial statements. Producing audited financial statements on an accelerated schedule is now routine for most federal agencies, representing a significant milestone in federal financial management.

(ii) Assertions Relating to Internal Control over Financial Reporting. Also contributing to the shape of the current landscape of federal financial management is OMB Circular A-123, *Management's Responsibility for Internal Control, Appendix A, Internal Control over Financial Reporting,* (Circular A-123, Appendix A) effective in 2006. The Sarbanes-Oxley Act of 2002, while not applicable to federal entities, served as an impetus for this requirement. By its Circular A-123, Appendix A, the OMB imposed parallel control responsibilities on the management of federal departments and agencies with respect to federal agency financial controls. Specifically, management must annually assert to the effectiveness of internal control over financial reporting. The one important difference is that this circular does not require a separate audit of internal controls over financial reporting since federal audits required internal control testing and reporting.

The effect of OMB Circular A-123, Appendix A, has been significant. It has raised awareness and understanding across the federal government in regard to the importance of financial reporting and internal controls. Major federal agencies now have in place a structured and consistent process that can be used to provide management with evidence to support its assertion over internal control.

OMB Circular A-123, Appendix A, has also served as an overarching requirement within which other financial management improvement efforts can be integrated and leveraged. For example, opportunities exist for independent financial statement auditors to leverage documentation and testing performed by A-123 assessment teams within federal agencies. This would be similar to the way corporate financial statement auditors utilize internal audit resources. Further, the process documentation and testing work performed as part of the A-123 assessment serve as leverage points for streamlining controls and for validating corrective actions. This type of integration and efficiency has yet to be fully realized.

32.4 FEDERAL BUDGET PROCESS

Within the federal government, the budget process is the dominant management and accountability process. It is through the budget process that policy and operational priorities are proposed, debated, and funded by Congress. It is also through the budget process that accountability for program success is determined by either ongoing funding or reductions.

(a) FEDERAL BUDGET DEFINED. Within the federal government, the budget is viewed as more than a guide for planned expenditures. The actual definition of the budget is the legal mandate of Congress to the executive branch to tax, collect, borrow, obligate, and expend money in a prescribed manner, for specified purposes, and within designated time periods. The federal budget, after approval by both houses of Congress, is at one and the same time:

- A listing of the national priorities as determined by the president and Congress for the next year and, in some cases, several years
- Permission for departments and agencies to commence, continue, or cease operating specific government programs and activities

- The legal authority for the government to collect revenues and incur and pay financial obligations
- The financial plan for managing the government during the next fiscal year
- The financial authority that dictates acceptable accounting and reporting policies and procedures

The president's budget articulates and quantifies the president's policy and other priorities. Stated more accurately, this "budget"—the program, initiatives, and estimates of sources of revenues and program spending levels—is a president's proposal or request to Congress. The budget enacted by Congress is often very different from the President's budget. Seldom is a president's request for a budget accepted by Congress without change. When serious disagreements arise between the presidential and congressional view of what the federal budget should be, the ramifications are felt across government. If Congress refused to vote on a budget, the government will shut down; witness the government closures of 1996 and the near shutdown in 2011.

Congress does not approve a president's proposed or requested budget as a single amount. Instead, the amount proposed by the president (now about $3.8 trillion) is broken down and analyzed by several committees and subcommittees of Congress, which eventually approve individual appropriations or provide other forms of budgetary or financing authority. By law, Congress should complete its process and have a total approved budget or financial plan for the entire federal government by October 1 of each year. Once it is finally approved by Congress and accepted by the president, an appropriation or other budgetary authority is then closely managed, monitored, accounted for, and reported on by individual federal entities.

In recent years, Congress has not completed action on all budget requests before the beginning of a fiscal year. In such circumstances, Congress may enact a continuing resolution that provides temporary financing authority for a department to continue operations, usually—but not always—until an appropriation is approved. While under a continuing resolution, the federal entity must conform to certain fiscal restraints.

The execution of the total budget, which is dispersed through many appropriations to many federal entities, is continuously monitored for compliance with congressional intent. Deviations from the budget constitute statutory violations for which there must be a reporting to the president and Congress. For variations considered to be of national importance, Congress may even initiate committee hearings and make these budget issues into events of considerable public prominence.

(b) PHASES OF THE BUDGET CYCLE. The federal budget cycle might be better viewed as a never-ending process rather than as a cycle, which implies an event with a beginning and an end. The process consists of four concurrent phases, not always clearly distinguishable but always present: (1) the budget formulation phase, (2) the congressional action phase, (3) the budget execution phase, and (4) the review and audit phase. Each of these phases are discussed below.

(i) Phase 1: Budget Formulation. The budget formulation phase begins some 15 to 18 months or more before that start of the fiscal year to which it will apply. This phase is a period of continuous exchange of information and decision making by the president, assisted by the OMB, the heads of individual departments and agencies, and special advisers.

In addition, besides being the financial plan of the government, the proposed budget is, as importantly, the culmination of a political process containing key policy initiatives. As this phase nears conclusion, the executive branch prepares to make its oral and written submission to Congress and the general citizenry. Historically, this phase has concluded within the president publicly making a State of the Union message and formally transmitting the proposed or requested budget to Congress shortly after it convenes in the January before the start of the fiscal year.

OMB Role. The OMB is an entity in the Executive Office of the President and has the responsibility of preparing, monitoring and executing federal budgets. The OMB is responsible for providing budget guidance to all federal departments and agencies, compiling budget information, and assisting the president with the analysis and presentation of budget information and with the presentation and defense of the proposed budget before Congress.

The OMB annually issues guidance relating to the preparation and submission of budget estimates to executive branch departments and agencies. The issuance of this guidance is followed by innumerable meetings between the OMB and the entities' executive management. This discussion usually includes a series of internal executive branch budget hearings where department and agency officials describe and justify elements of their OMB budget request. Subsequent to the department and/or agency budget hearings, internal OMB budget reviews are held to inform specific budget and policy decisions that will become part of the president's budget.

Usually in late November, the OMB provides a "passback" to agencies regarding their budget decisions and agencies provide revised budget data consistent with the OMB decisions. On occasions, heads of federal organizations who disagree with the impositions of the OMB make direct appeals to the president. Final budget decisions and data are used to collect, process, and ultimately compile the final budget request that will then be transmitted by the president to Congress.

(ii) Phase 2: Congressional Action. Congress can approve, change, disapprove, or ignore the president's proposed budget. The congressional phase is marked by two sets of hearings: (1) hearings for authorization or continuation of a federal program or activity, and (2) hearings for funding or approval of an appropriation for or financing of the program or activity. The congressional approval of a program, with permission to obligate the federal government and spend federal monies, is what is referred to as an appropriation; that is, the legal or budget authority that makes funds available to individual departments and agencies for spending. The appropriation may be for a single year or several years. In some cases, the congressional budget authority may be permanent, in which case funds become annually available to the department without further congressional action. The congressional phase often is comprised of several types of activities involving many interested parties.

Once congressional consensus is reached, the various appropriations are submitted to the president for review and subsequent approval or veto. Note that the submissions are usually not made to the president as a single package but rather as several appropriation laws—in other words, Congress forwards to the president a host of legislated financing actions that must be aggregated to reach the total spending for the federal government. Key dates related to the congressional budget process are reflected in the following chart.

The Congressional Budget Process Timetable

Date	Action
First Monday in February	President submits budget to Congress.
February 15	Congressional Budget Office submits economic and budget outlook report to Budget Committees.
Six weeks after President submits budget	Committees submit views and estimates to Budget Committees.
April 1	Senate Budget Committee reports budget resolution.
April 15	Congress completes action on budget resolution.
May 15	Annual appropriations bills may be considered in the House, even if action on budget resolution has not been completed.
June 10	House Appropriations Committee reports last annual appropriations bill.
June 15	Congress completes action on reconciliation legislation (if required by budget resolution).
June 30	House completes action on annual appropriations bills.
July 15	President submits mid-session review of his budget to Congress.
October 1	Fiscal year begins.

Source: Bill Heniff, Jr, Congressional Research Service, OC 98-472, March, 2008, The Congressional Budget Process Timetable, and Section 300 of the Congressional Budget Act of 1974, as amended (P.L. 93-344, 2 U.S.C. 631).

CBO Role. The Congressional Budget Office is an agency in the legislative branch accountable to the Congress. CBO provides objective cost estimates, reports and other analysis to the congress in support of the budget process. It has no role in preparing the proposed budget and issues no regulation or guidance concerning the budget process to any executive branch organization. The Congressional Budget Office calculates federal deficit estimates as well as estimates associated with various proposed and enacted legislation.

(iii) Phase 3: Budget Execution. Once passed by Congress and approved by the president, the appropriations and other approved budget authority become the financial operating plan for the federal government for the next fiscal year and ensuing four fiscal years. Thus, the "approved budget" initiates a number of events, necessitating a number of controls, affecting each federal department and agency.

Controlling and Monitoring Congressional Appropriations. From the first Congress, control over appropriations has been a high priority. All early congresses were concerned that agencies not overspend appropriated budgets. The first general appropriation of the United States, in 1789, restricted obligation of the appropriation to the fiscal year for which the appropriation was made. This restriction, unless otherwise stipulated by Congress, has applied to all congressional appropriations since that time.

However, for many years after the adoption of the Constitution, even though that restriction was in place, federal agencies ignored the spending limitations levied by Congress. Agencies often incurred obligations to spend money in excess—or in advance—of congressionally approved appropriations. Further, appropriated funds were commingled or used for purposes far different from those for which Congress had appropriated the money. Agencies would sometimes spend the entire appropriation in the first few months of a new fiscal year, then present Congress with a listing of "coercive deficiencies" that had to be paid. At these times, Congress had essentially lost control, and individual federal entities were financing operations and obligating the federal government in what was technically an illegal manner (i.e., not approved in law by Congress).

Budgetary Controls. The Anti-Deficiency Act of 1870 (ADA) was intended to prevent executive departments and agencies from spending more than was appropriated by congress. In later amendments, the ADA was expanded to include restrictions requiring prior formal apportionment by the OMB of all funds appropriated by congress. An *apportionment* is a distribution (limitation, restriction, or ceiling) made by the OMB of the amounts available to a federal agency in a congressional appropriation or other budgetary authority, into specific amounts that are available for obligations by time period (i.e., generally quarters of the fiscal year) or specific activities, projects, object classes of expenditures, or some combination of these groupings.

The objectives of the federal apportionment process are to (1) prevent obligations of an account (i.e., appropriation or other budget authority) in a manner that would require deficiency or supplemental appropriations and (2) achieve the most effective and economical intended use of amounts made available by Congress. Should an agency either obligate or expend funds in excess of the apportionment limit set by the OMB, it is in violation of the ADA, for which a special reporting must be made to Congress and the president naming the individual federal executives and circumstances involved in the violation.

Budgetary Reporting. After the apportionment requests are approved, departments and agencies must report on budget execution by: (1) making a historical reporting of how, in fact, the apportionments were used; (2) providing a periodic status report for each appropriation or other budgetary authority; and (3) showing the relationship of obligations to outlays and expenditures. In this context, the term *expenditures* is used in reference to checks issued or cash disbursements. This historical accounting of budget execution is completed periodically throughout the year and at year-end by all federal entities.

The form used by departments and agencies during budget execution is the SF-133, *Report on Budget Execution and Budgetary Resources.* The SF-133 provides a status of budgetary resources to include amounts provided, available, obligated, and outlayed by appropriation. Agency annual audited financial statements contain similar information in the Statement of Budgetary Resources (SBR), one of the principal statements. The SBR provides budget execution information for all appropriations within an agency and mirrors the format of the appropriation-level SF-133. It is the only principal financial statement prepared on the budgetary basis of accounting and is annually audited.

(iv) Phase 4: Review and Audit. Federal departments and agencies (by many laws, presidential directives, and OMB and Treasury regulations) are required to establish systems of controls and accounting to ensure that all obligations and disbursements are consistent with the authorizing and appropriation laws of Congress. These federal entities must also establish programs for reviews, evaluations, and audits.

In all departments and agencies, and in several offices of the federal government, the conduct of audits and evaluations is the responsibility of the Offices of Inspectors General. Additionally, the GAO and the OMB regularly make reviews, evaluations, and studies of the manner in which executive branch organizations are complying with the intent of Congress. Federal agencies will also contract with certified public accounting firms for expert assistance during this phase. Audits are described further in Section 32.5.

32.5 AUDITING IN THE FEDERAL GOVERNMENT

Auditing and accounting professionals from various groups are involved with auditing and reporting on the activities of the federal government. Although many of these professionals are employed by the government, many others are employed by independent certified public accounting firms to conduct audits under contracts from federal agencies. The practice of federal auditing encompasses federal agency systems, internal controls, accounting, and financial statements required by federal laws and government regulations as well as the entities receiving federal financial assistance programs in whatever form (e.g., federal subsidies, contracts and grants, loan and loan guarantees, settlement overruns and overhead disputes, and resolution of allowable, unallowable costs, and indirect cost issues).

Audits of all types have played and will continue to play a valuable role in the oversight and management improvement of government programs. Unlike most private sector audits where assurance over financial statements is the primary objective, in government, many federal government audits are undertaken when a problem is suspected or a risk level elevated. In federal financial management as well as other areas, audits are frequently catalysts and provide leverage for management improvements. Annual agency financial and program audits have helped to provide a roadmap and guidepost for ongoing management improvements and the perpetuation of sound accounting disciplines and operations.

(a) GENERALLY ACCEPTED GOVERNMENT AUDITING STANDARDS. In the 1970s, the GAO developed a separate set of audit standards for government entities. GAO's *Government Auditing Standards* define Generally Accepted Government Auditing Standards (GAGAS) and is integrated with the generally accepted auditing standards issued by the AICPA used for private sector corporations. The OMB, in a series of Bulletins and Circulars, provides further audit requirements for financial statement audits, audits of recipients of federal financial assistance, and audit follow-up.

These standards are important to both financial and program accountability in the federal government and state and local governments, organizations, entities, and others involved with, or benefiting from, federal financial assistance. A government audit conducted in accordance with GASAS is:

> "…..an engagement performed by an independent auditor…..
> These standards include (1) ethical principles, (2) general standards,
> such as auditor independence, competence, and

quality control and assurance, and (3) field work and reporting standards . . . and the requirement to obtain sufficient, appropriate evidence."

Source: *Procuring Audit Services in Government: A Practical Guide to Making the Right Decision,* Association of Government Accountants, Jeffrey C. Steinhoff, February, 2009

Most federal government audits conducted under GAGAS are performance audits assessing program efficiency and effectiveness. However, the financial management reforms of the last 20 years have increased the focus on annual financial audits of an entity's financial statements including concurrent assessments of compliance with laws and regulations, and effectiveness of financial controls. The premise is that financial statement audits are important and will continue to be so, but audits of only financial data, as of a specific point in time, provide limited information as to whether an organization is economical or efficient or if its operations even approach operational objectives defined in enabling legislation.

Several organizations, both governmental and nongovernmental, have, by law or otherwise, accrued significant statutory and other authority to prescribe requirements and standards for audits of federal agencies and of financial assistance provided to nonfederal entities through contracts, grants, and other agreements. In addition to laws of Congress establishing audit requirements, other organizations have been instrumental in defining or impacting the scope of federal audits. These organizations are highlighted in Exhibit 32.5.

(b) TYPES OF GOVERNMENTAL AUDITS. When applied to corporate entities, the term *audit* is used primarily in reference to financial statement audits. Such audits are annually made of each required federal department and agency.[1] Additionally, however, during the course of a fiscal year, a far greater number of audits are made under other descriptors, such as *attestation examinations, agreed-upon-procedures, contract and grant audits,* and *performance audits,* to note a few. These special-focus audits are, for the most part, done by auditors of Inspectors General staffs, but a smaller number are also done by independent certified public accountants under contract to federal agencies.

Organization	Role
GAO	Issues auditing standards for all governmental audits. GAO's *Government Auditing Standards,* or "Yellow Book," was first issued in 1972 and most recently revised in August 2011. The Yellow Book provides standards for conducting financial and performance audits and other engagements where an auditor might provide written assurances or attestations other than an audit opinion
AICPA	The American Institute of Certified Public Accountants prescribes the generally accepted auditing standards (GAAS) that form the underlying foundation of the *Government Auditing Standards* used by all auditors when auditing any federal entity or recipient of federal financial assistance. Federal audits must satisfy the GAAS of the AICPA, which include general, fieldwork, and reporting standards, plus the AICPA's Statements on Auditing Standards (SAS).
OMB	By law, Congress delegated responsibilities to OMB for federal accounting, auditing, systems oversight, and other financial management tasks. In exercising these responsibilities, OMB prescribes detailed policies and procedures to be applied in audits of federal executive branch departments, agencies, and their activities, such as applying GAO's *Government Auditing Standards* for all federal agency financial audits. The Single Audit Act of 1984, as amended in 1996, provides OMB the authority to issue audit requirements for state, local and not-for-profit entities receiving federal financial assistance.
Office of the Inspector General (IG)	IGs, sometimes in coordination with the GAO, develop audit and investigation policies, standards, and approaches, and issue mandatory audit guidance relating to audits of federal departments and agencies as well as audits of nonfederal entities receiving varying forms of federal financial assistance. The IG Act of 1978 provides IGs with the authority to conduct all agency audit activities.

Exhibit 32.5 Organizational Roles Related to *Government Auditing Standards*
Source: *Government Auditing Standards,* December 2011 Revision (GAO-12-331G)

[1] Includes the 24 CFO Act agencies and agencies subject to the Accountability of Tax Dollars Act of 2002, as documented by the OMB.

Engagement Type	Engagement Objective	Criteria	Standards Used to Perform Engagement	Who Can Perform	Type of Assurance
Financial Audit	Opinion that the entity's financial statements are presented fairly	Generally Accepted Accounting Principles	GAGAS, including standards issued by the AICPA	GAO, IG, state and local government auditor, or CPA firm	Reasonable Assurance
Attestation Examination	Opinion that management's assertion is stated fairly	Will vary depending on the management assertion	GAGAS, including standards issued by the AICPA for attest engagements	GAO, IG, state and local government auditor, or CPA firm	Reasonable Assurance
Attestation Review	Performance of sufficient work to provide a conclusion (versus an opinion) on a topic or matter	Will vary depending on the audit objective	GAGAS, including standards issued by the AICPA for attest engagements	GAO, IG, state and local government auditor, or CPA firm	Negative Assurance
Attestation Agreed-upon Procedures	Performance of specific procedures defined by management	Will vary depending on the audit objectives	GAGAS, including standards issued by the AICPA for attest engagements	GAO, IG, state and local government auditor, or CPA firm	No Assurance
Performance Audit	Assessment of program efficiency and effectiveness	Will vary depending on the audit objective	GAGAS	GAO, IG, state and local government auditor, or CPA firm	Reasonable Assurance

Exhibit 32.6 Types of Government Audit and Attest Engagements
Source:* AGA Corporate Advisory Group Report No. 19, *Procuring Audit Services in the Government—A Practical Guide to Making the Right the Decision (2009).

Exhibit 32.6 highlights various types of audits and attest engagements used in government, the objective of each engagement types, criteria commonly used, relevant standards, who can perform these audits, and the type of assurance being provided. Most common are financial and performance audits. However, other less common types of engagements may be used where certain circumstance dictate. For example, an attestation examination may be used to provide assurance over an assertion made by management.

(i) Audits of Recipients of Federal Financial Assistance. In the 1950s, problems arose with the manner in which the federal government performed audits of state and local governmental entities and other organizations receiving federal financial assistance. These problems were cataloged by the GAO and government-wide studies and were the subject of numerous congressional committee hearings into the 1980s. Examples of the federal government's problems and the ripple type problems created at the state and local government levels were numerous but fell into a few general categories:

- Excessive duplication of federal audit by many agencies with no coordination or cooperation
- Biased audits reports, since many audits were reported to senior executives under the audit who had the authority to make changes and did change audit reports for the "better"

- Federal resistance to transferring audit responsibility to state and local government auditors despite laws, regulations, and policy statements directing that this be done
- Prohibiting, preventing, or resisting the sharing of federal audit findings with senior executives of other governments, or preventing the public access to such reports

Single Audit Act of 1984, Amended in 1996. Initially passed in 1984 and amended in 1996, the Single Audit Act ordered federal organizations to implement an audit concept whereby recipients receiving \$500,000 or more of federal assistance need undergo only one audit each year. The results of this single audit would then be shared with all organizations having a financial interest in that recipient. Further, the Act declared that audits made in accordance with the Act "shall be in lieu of any financial audit of Federal awards which a non-Federal entity is required to undergo under any other Federal law or regulation." This Act was intended to change the historical focus of federal oversight, eliminating financial and human resource costs related to thousands of duplicative and uncoordinated federal audits and reviews.

The legally defined comprehensive single audit required that:

1. An annual financial statement audit be made of the recipient of federal funds in its entirety.
2. This annual audit include tests and reports made on an entity wide basis, and for each major federal programs basis relative to:
   a. Financial controls and controls to manage the federal assistance programs
   b. Compliance with laws and regulations for major federal award programs

These single audits were required to be made pursuant to GAO's *Government Auditing Standards,* plus the audit procedures and reporting requirements in the OMB regulation, OMB Circular A-133, *Audits of State and Local Governments and Non-Profit Organizations,* as amended.[2]

32.6 EMERGING ISSUES

As federal financial management continues to evolve, issues and challenges continue to emerge. All of the emerging issues discussed in this section are currently cast in the shadow of the federal budget. Addressing the uncertainties surrounding the federal budget is the most prominent financial management emerging issue. It is in these times that accountability, financial integrity, and credibility are even more important. Continuing to accurately account for and monitor federal spending, maintaining sound internal controls, developing useful information to ensure that funds are spent wisely, and maintaining regular independent auditing and oversight are important to maintaining confidence in federal government finances. Other emerging issues are discussed below.

(a) ACHIEVING A GOVERNMENT-WIDE AUDIT OPINION. The most visible indicator of the foundation of internal controls and accounting disciplines in place today within the federal government is the number of agencies with both an unqualified audit opinion and no material internal control weaknesses reported by their independent auditors. Achieving this goal on a government-wide basis is a sign of the financial integrity and credibility of the U.S. government.

At the agency level, achieving this goal required incremental improvements in financial management operations and a sustained multiyear commitment by agency management and their auditors.

[2] When first enacted, the Single Audit Act of 1984 was implemented through two separate OMB Circulars: OMB Circular A-128 for Audits of State and Local Governments and OMB Circular A-133 for Institutions of Higher Education and Nonprofit Entities. In 1997, the OMB Circulars A-128 and A-133 were replaced and superseded by a single circular, OMB Circular A-133, *Audits of States, Local Governments and Non- Profit Organizations,* last amended in June 2007.

Where success has been achieved, management and auditors worked collaboratively year to year to resolve issues and improve accounting processes and internal controls.

Today, challenges remain in some agencies to achieve auditable financial statements. The Department of Defense (DOD) has a budget of more than $600 billion, more than 3 million civilian and military personnel, and worldwide operations. The sheer size, complexity, and number of nonintegrated systems processing financial-related information make achieving auditability challenging. The National Defense Authorization Act of 2010 has set a requirement for the DOD to be auditable by 2017, recently DoD leadership has accelerated this goal for certain financial statements.

Other large agencies have similar challenges; for example, the Department of Homeland Security has the added complexity of being a relatively new federal agency that merged, acquired, and started up new operations. Achieving the milestone of an unqualified audit opinion for these and other agencies will pave the way for an audit opinion on the financial statements of the U.S. government.

(b) DEVELOPING INFORMATION TO SUPPORT DECISION MAKING. Fully accomplishing the intent of the CFO Act entails evolving federal financial management beyond a compliance-focused activity to a more value-added program where decision-useful information is routinely developed. Most agencies have achieved the first step toward this goal: having established a foundation of accounting disciplines and internal controls that routinely produce reliable financial statements. The next step is to leverage the foundation to generate information to better meet the needs of agency leadership and program managers to support budget and program management decisions.

To this end, program cost information is noticeably absent from federal financial management. The development of reliable cost information has been largely centered in agencies where a separate statutory requirement exists or where the agency operates an internal service type fund where fees need to cover the full cost of operations. This pattern continues to hold true today, with only limited areas where cost information is being developed and used. The pressure for this type of information is increasing as the federal budget tightens. Understanding program costs and the relationship of these costs to performance results is essential to achieving the ultimate goals of the CFO Act and to monitoring operational efficiency.

(c) RISK ASSESSMENT AND PREVENTION-ORIENTED CONTROLS AND OVERSIGHT. In 2009, the American Recovery and Reinvestment Act (Recovery Act) became law with the intent to stimulate the nation's economy. The Recovery Act provided $787 billion, most of which to be spent over a two-year period. To oversee the spending of these funds, a special Recovery and Transparency Oversight Board (RATB) was established that worked closely with the vice president, agency Inspectors General, and the GAO. In implementing the Recovery Act, a number of practices emerged that could potentially shape the future of federal financial management. According to the Association of Government Accountants Research Report titled *Redefining Accountability: Recovery Act Practices and Opportunities:*

> In implementing the American Recovery and Reinvestment Act of 2009 (Recovery Act), federal agencies have introduced more aggressive risk management, strengthened oversight, incorporated more detailed financial reporting, and implemented other practices to enhance transparency and accountability over government financial management.... [T[hese practices are innovative—and in some cases unprecedented—and have the potential to shape future government financial management and reporting.
>
> Source: *Redefining Accountability: Recovery Act Practices and Opportunities,* Association of Government Accountants, July 2010, p 4.

Advances in technology along with greater sharing of information helped management and auditors meet these challenges. Comprehensive risk assessments were performed to pinpoint trouble areas, sometimes before a financial transaction occurred. One of the best examples of this is within the RATB operations, where the RATB utilized enhanced data mining, management, and sharing techniques to identify high-risk indicators and patterns. Other early-warning assessments, sometimes referred to flash reports, were issued by agency Inspectors General in an effort to shift their oversight forward to assist in the early identification of risk, supplementing a more traditional after-the-fact audit approach.

Similar risk-based prevention-oriented approaches are being assessed to reduce federal improper payments, estimated to be $125 billion government-wide for FY2010. (Source: Office of Management and Budget, Memorandum M 11-16, April 14, 2011. The practice of leveraging technology to better understand financial risks and prevent fraud, waste, and abuse is an emerging issue.)

(d) ENHANCING FINANCIAL REPORTING. Today, the realm of federal financial information publicly reported is broad. It ranges from detailed transaction-level information reported on multiple government-sponsored Web sites to audited financial statements. As access to information becomes easier, reporting financial information meeting user needs becomes more challenging. Public satisfaction with government financial management information continues to be low. According to an Association of Government Accountants (AGA) survey titled *Public Attitudes Toward Government Accountability and Transparency* conducted in February 2010, the majority of those surveyed were not very satisfied or not at all satisfied with federal financial management information reported. In addition, Congress frequently requests financial information arrayed in ways specific to meet its immediate needs.

Challenges exist in addressing the variety of user needs while balancing costs and benefits and maintaining consistency and integrity, of the information being reported. Addressing this challenge will entail leveraging new technologies to improve access and understanding, while maintaining the internal control, data quality and credibility benefits that are the hallmarks of the audited financial statement process.

32.7 CONCLUSION

Since enactment of the CFO Act in 1990, federal financial management has evolved as a specialized area within accounting and auditing. The CFO Act introduced a series of financial management reforms that modernized federal financial management including the establishment of agency CFOs, audited financial reporting and eventually GAAP; all of which are now part of the broader management and accountability framework at the federal level.

Federal financial management has improved over the years. Audited financial statements, the centerpiece of the CFO Act, are an integral part of the management and accountability framework and have driven the development of a foundation of sound internal controls, fundamental accounting disciplines and more reliable financial data. While much progress has been made, budget uncertainties and a troublesome long-term fiscal outlook, create significant challenges. Continuing to advance federal financial management will require defining and maintaining a strategic focus while managing through these dynamic times. In addition, CFOs will need to equip their organizations to add value by building a greater capacity to develop more useful financial management information and analysis, while achieving efficiencies in their operations. These objectives were central to the financial management reforms of the 1990s and continue to be even more important today.

APPENDIX A: SELECTED FINANCIAL MANAGEMENT LEGISLATION

Selected Laws on Federal Financial Management

1789	United States Constitution	The initial, most basic, legislation making reference to revenues and expenditures of the federal government
1870	Anti-Deficiency Act	Prevented executive departments and agencies from making expenditures in excess of amounts appropriated by Congress
1921	Budget and Accounting Act	The more significant provisions of this Act continue to affect federal financial management policy, systems, controls, and practices to this day
1945	Government Corporation Control Act	Passed to provide for closer Congress scrutiny of government corporations and require that these organizations undergo independent audits by the Comptroller General
1950	Budget and Accounting Procedures Act	Provided Congress with overriding accounting and reporting and more control over federal receipts, expenditures, funds, and property
1951	Supplemental Appropriation Act	Permitted the president to submit annual budget information on a cost basis and to include information on program accomplishments
1955	Public Law 84-863	Changed the federal budgeting and financial process to exert more congressional control over the executive branch
1974	Congressional Budget and Impoundment Act	Established statutory criteria that defined what constitutes a valid obligation against a federal appropriation
1978	Inspector General Act	Established Inspectors General in federal agencies and gave them authority to oversee all audits conducted
1982	Federal Managers Financial Integrity Act	Reflected increased concern by Congress over the adequacy of internal accounting and administrative controls in federal executive agencies.
1990	Federal Credit Reform Act	Required that the president's budget reflect full cost of direct loan and loan guarantee programs, including new direct loan obligations or loan guarantee commitments
1990	Chief Financial Officers Act	Changed significantly the accounting and reporting of the federal government
1993	Government Performance and Results Act, amended in 2010	Required the OMB to submit to Congress a strategic plan of major functions and operations, outcome-related goals and objectives, and a description of skills, technology, and resources required
1994	Government Management Reform Act	Required each federal department and agency to submit, by March 1 of each year, an audited financial statement for the preceding fiscal year showing the financial position and the results of operations
1996	Federal Financial Management Improvement Act	Promoted more useful and reliable financial information through compliance with accounting standards, systems requirements, and the standard general ledger
2003	Improper Payment Information Act, amended in 2010	Required federal agencies to identify, estimate, and reduce improper payments
2002	Accountability for Tax Dollars Act	Extended audited financial statements to government corporations and other executive branch agencies

(Continues)

Selected Laws on Federal Financial Management

2004	Department of Homeland Security Financial Accountability Act	Extended requirements for a CFO and audited financial statements to the newly created department; also required the department to obtain a separate audit opinion over internal control over financial reporting
2006	Federal Funding Accountability and Transparency Act	Required federal agencies to report grant and contract spending information on a government Web site
2009	American Recovery and Reinvestment Act	Provided funding intended to stimulate the economy; introduced similar spending transparency reporting requirements as the Federal Financial Accountability and Transparency Act; established the Recovery Accountability and Transparency Board to oversee and report spending

APPENDIX B: IMPORTANT BUDGETARY ACCOUNTING TERMS

Term	Definition
Budget authority	Legal congressional permission for a department or agency to enter into obligations that bind the federal government and that will require immediate or future outlays of federal funds. Most budget authority exists in the form of congressional appropriations
Contract authority	Provides a department or agency with the legal permission to execute contracts and enter into other obligations before Congress passes an appropriation to provide the funds to pay for them. In these instances, the congressional appropriation provides the cash to pay for these obligations after the liability; that is, Congress appropriates the funds necessary to settle the contract obligations after the fact rather than before contract issuance, which is the more common circumstance.
Apportionment/ reapportionment request	Legal authority provided by the OMB to spend appropriations. The apportionment process is an internal control over the rate or purpose for which appropriated funds are used. Apportionment requests are made by agencies or departments and submitted to the OMB for approval.
Outlay	The amounts of checks issued, interest accrued on the public debt, or other cash disbursements made, including advances to others, net refunds and reimbursements (that is, the net amount of advances made to others after the refunds from the others are subtracted). For budget purposes, the OMB considers the term "outlays" to be interchangeable with "expenditures" and "net disbursements."
Transfers	Legal authorizations to move all or part of an appropriated fund balance to another budgetary account.
Obligated balances	Balances represent the unpaid liabilities and possibly contingent commitments of a federal organization for which services or goods were order but not yet received. For budget reporting purposes, obligated balances include (1) total obligation incurred for which no outlays have been made, plus amount received but not yet earned; less (2) collectable reimbursements/refunds receivable, less (3) unfilled orders within or outside the government.
Unexpended balances	These represent the total of still-outstanding obligations made under an appropriation, plus the balance of an appropriation (or other budgetary authority) not yet obligated, including investments in U.S. securities, if any.
Unobligated balances	The unobligated balance of an appropriation is the total unexpended appropriation or other budgetary authority, less the total of amounts obligated.
Collections	The money received by a government department or agency. It includes the collection of income taxes by the Internal Revenue Service, duties by the Bureau of Customs, and miscellaneous receipts by other federal establishments. For most federal establishments, collections are minimal to nonexistent.

CHAPTER 33

STATE AND LOCAL GOVERNMENT ACCOUNTING

Cynthia Pon, CPA
Macias Gini O'Connell LLP

Richard A. Green, CPA
Macias Gini O'Connell LLP

Caroline H. Walsh, CPA
Macias Gini O'Connell LLP

33.1 INTRODUCTION 2

33.2 NATURE AND ORGANIZATION OF STATE AND LOCAL GOVERNMENT ACTIVITIES 3

(a) Structure of Government 3
(b) Objectives of Government 3
(c) Organization of Government 3
(d) Special Characteristics of Government 4

33.3 SOURCE OF ACCOUNTING PRINCIPLES FOR STATE AND LOCAL GOVERNMENT ACCOUNTING 5

(a) National Council on Governmental Accounting 5
(b) Governmental Accounting Standards Board 5

33.4 GOVERNMENTAL ACCOUNTING PRINCIPLES AND PRACTICES 7

(a) Similarities to Private Sector Accounting 7
(b) Users and Uses of Financial Reports 8
(c) Summary Statement of Principles 10
(i) Accounting and Reporting Capabilities 10
(ii) Government-Wide and Fund Accounting Systems 10
(iii) Types of Funds 11
(iv) Accounting for Capital Assets 12
(v) Valuation of Capital Assets 12
(vi) Depreciation and Impairment of Capital Assets 12
(vii) Accounting for Long-Term Liabilities 12
(viii) Measurement Focus and Basis of Accounting 12
(ix) Budgeting, Budgetary Control, and Budgetary Reporting 13
(x) Transfer, Revenue, Expenditure, and Expense Account Classification 13
(xi) Common Terminology and Classification 13
(xii) Interim and Annual Financial Reports 13
(d) Discussion of the Principles 13
(e) Accounting and Reporting Capabilities 13
(i) Legal Compliance 13
(ii) Reporting Requirements 14
(f) Government-Wide and Fund Accounting Systems 15
(g) Types and Number of Funds 16
(i) Governmental Funds 17

We would like to acknowledge our colleagues, Kevin J. O'Connell and Ernest J. Gini, for their contributions to the previous edition and thank them for their undertaking. We also are indebted to Lynford Graham whose thoughtful feedback helped raise our own understanding of governmental accounting.

(ii) Proprietary Funds 19
(iii) Fiduciary Funds 22
(h) Capital Assets Reporting and Accounting 25
(i) Methods for Calculating Depreciation 26
(ii) Subsidiary Property Records 27
(iii) Disposal or Retirement of Capital Assets 27
(iv) Impairment of Capital Assets 27
(i) Reporting and Accounting for Long-Term Liabilities 27
(j) Measurement Focus and Basis of Accounting 27
(i) Measurement Focus 27
(ii) Basis of Accounting 28
(iii) Revenue Transactions 29
(iv) Expenditure Transactions 29
(v) Reporting on Nonexchange Transactions 30
(k) Budgeting, Budgetary Control, and Budgetary Reporting Accounting 33
(i) Types of Operating Budgets 33
(ii) Budget Preparation 35
(iii) Budget Execution 37
(iv) Proprietary Fund Budgeting 40
(v) Capital Budget 41
(vi) Budgetary Comparison Information 41
(l) Classification and Terminology 41
(i) Classification of Government Fund Revenues 41
(ii) Classification of Government Fund Expenditures 41
(iii) Classifications of Other Transactions 45
(iv) Classifications of Proprietary Fund Revenues and Expenses 45
(v) Classifications of Fund Balance/Equity 46
(m) Financial Reporting 47
(i) Financial Reporting Entity 47
(ii) Basic Financial Statements 49
(iii) Comprehensive Annual Financial Report 61
(iv) Certificate of Achievement Program 63
(v) Popular Reports 63

33.5 BASIC FINANCIAL STATEMENTS REQUIRED FOR SPECIAL-PURPOSE GOVERNMENTS 63

(a) Reporting by Special-Purpose Governments Engaged in Governmental Activities 63
(b) Reporting by Special-Purpose Governments Engaged Only in Business-Type Activities 64
(c) Reporting by Special-Purpose Governments Engaged Only in Fiduciary Activities 64

33.6 ACCOUNTING PRINCIPLES AND PRACTICES—PUBLIC COLLEGES AND UNIVERSITIES 64

33.7 AUDITS OF GOVERNMENTAL UNITS 65

(a) Single Audit Act Amendments of 1996 65
(b) Other Considerations 67
(i) Governmental Rotation of Auditors 67
(ii) Audit Committees 68

33.8 CONCLUDING REMARKS 68

33.9 SOURCES AND SUGGESTED REFERENCES 69

APPENDIX PRONOUNCEMENTS ON STATE AND LOCAL GOVERNMENT ACCOUNTING 69

33.1 INTRODUCTION

Governmental accounting has changed dramatically in recent years in response to changes in the state and local government environment. Subject to greater scrutiny by federal and state agencies and faced with budgetary challenges, governments must also negotiate an ever-increasing level of sophistication required to manage their operations—operations that are on par with the largest and most complex business organizations and are as diverse as airports, hospitals, utilities, schools, and fire protection. Add to that concerns involving deteriorating infrastructure, an aging workforce, public health care, and the spread of terrorism, and it is no surprise that governments are finding themselves addressing increasing demands for public accountability and transparency.

Before discussing the specifics of governmental accounting principles and practices, it is important to have an overall sense of the nature and organization of state and local government activities.

The goal of this chapter is to provide insight on the current governmental accounting landscape and to shed light on future trends to explore. Continued examination is critical in light of the fact that governments are no longer able to be slow adopters, following behind business-related trends and regulations; they must be innovative and proactive in order to secure the quality of their service delivery, now and in the future.

At the end of this chapter is an appendix listing the various State and Local Government accounting pronouncements.

33.2 NATURE AND ORGANIZATION OF STATE AND LOCAL GOVERNMENT ACTIVITIES

(a) STRUCTURE OF GOVERNMENT. For the most part, government is structured on three levels: federal, state, and local. This chapter deals only with state and local governments.

States are specific identifiable entities in their own right, but accounting at the state level is associated more often than not with the individual state functions, such as departments of revenue, retirement systems, turnpike authorities, university systems, and housing finance agencies.

Local governments exist as political subdivisions of states, and the rules governing their types and operation are different in each of the 50 states. There are, however, three basic types of local governmental units: general-purpose local governments (counties, cities, towns, villages, and townships), special-purpose local governments, and authorities.

The distinguishing characteristics of general-purpose local governments are that they:

- Have broad powers in providing a variety of government services (e.g., public safety, fire protection, public works)
- Have general taxing and bonding authority
- Are headed by elected officials

Special-purpose local governments are established to provide specific services or construction. They may or may not be contiguous with one or more general-purpose local governments.

Authorities and agencies are similar to special-purpose governments except that they have no taxing power and are expected to operate with their own revenues. They typically can issue only revenue bonds, not general obligation bonds.

(b) OBJECTIVES OF GOVERNMENT. The purpose of government is to provide the citizenry with the highest level of services possible given the available financial resources and the legal requirements under which it operates. The services are provided as a result of decisions made during a budgeting process that considers the desired level and quality of services. Resources are then made available through property taxes, sales taxes, income taxes, general and categorical grants from the federal and state governments, charges for services, fines, licenses, and other sources. However, there is generally no direct relationship between the cost of the services rendered to an individual and the amount that the individual pays in taxes, fines, fees, and so on.

Governmental units also conduct operations that are financed and operated in a manner similar to private business enterprises, where the intent is that the costs of providing the goods or services be financed or recovered primarily through charges to the users. In such situations, governments have many of the features of ordinary business operations.

(c) ORGANIZATION OF GOVERNMENT. A government's organization depends on its constitution (state level) or charter (local level) and on general and special statutes of state and local legislatures. When governments were simpler and did not provide as many services as they do today, there was less of a tendency toward centralization. The commission and weak mayor forms of governments were common. The financial function was typically divided among several individuals.

As government has become more complex, however, the need for strong professional management and for centralization of authority and responsibility has grown. There has been a trend toward the strong mayor and council-manager forms of government. In these forms, a chief financial officer, usually called the director of finance or controller, is responsible for:

- Maintaining the financial records and preparing financial reports
- Assisting the chief executive officer (CEO) in the preparation of the budget
- Performing treasury functions, such as collecting revenues, managing cash, managing investments, and managing debt
- Overseeing the tax assessment function

Other functions that may report to the director of finance are purchasing, data processing, and personnel administration.

Local governments are also making greater use of the internal audit process. In the past, the emphasis by governmental internal auditors was on pre-audit—that is, reviewing invoices and other documents during processing for propriety and accuracy. The internal auditors reported to the director of finance. Today, however, governmental internal auditors have been removing themselves from the pre-audit function by transferring this responsibility to the department responsible for processing the transactions. They have started to provide the more traditional internal audit function—that is, conducting reviews to ensure the reliability of data and the safeguarding of assets—and to become involved in performance auditing (i.e., reviewing the efficiency and effectiveness of the government's operations). They have also started to report, for professional (as opposed to administrative) purposes, to the CEO or directly to the governing board. Finally, internal auditors are becoming more actively involved in the financial statement audit and single audit of their government.

(d) SPECIAL CHARACTERISTICS OF GOVERNMENT. Several characteristics associated with governments have influenced the development of governmental accounting principles and practices:

- Governments do not have any owners or proprietors in the commercial sense. Accordingly, measurement of earnings attributable or accruing to the direct benefit of an owner is not a relevant accounting concept for governments.
- Governments frequently receive substantial financial inflows for both operating and capital purposes from sources other than revenues and investment earnings, such as taxes and grants.
- Governments frequently obtain financial inflows subject to legally binding restrictions that prohibit or seriously limit the use of these resources for other than the intended purpose.
- A government's authority to raise and expend money results from the adoption of a budget that, by law, usually must balance (e.g., the estimated revenues plus any prior years' surpluses need to be sufficient to cover the projected expenditures).
- The power to raise revenues through taxes, licenses, fees, and fines is generally defined by law.
- Usually restrictions related to the tax base govern the purpose, amount, and type of indebtedness that can be issued.
- Expenditures are usually regulated less than revenues and debt, but they can be made only within approved budget categories and must comply with specified purchasing procedures when applicable.
- State laws may dictate the local government accounting policies and systems.
- State laws commonly specify the type and frequency of financial statements to be submitted to the state and to the government's constituency.
- Federal law—the Single Audit Act of 1984 and as amended in 1996—defines the audit requirements for state and local governments receiving federal awards.

In short, the environment in which governments operate is complex, and legal requirements have a significant influence on their accounting and financial reporting practices.

33.3 SOURCE OF ACCOUNTING PRINCIPLES FOR STATE AND LOCAL GOVERNMENT ACCOUNTING

Governmental accounting principles are not a complete and separate body of accounting principles but rather are part of the whole body of generally accepted accounting principles (GAAP). Since the accounting profession's standard-setting bodies have been concerned primarily with the accounting needs of profit-seeking organizations, these principles have been defined primarily by groups formed by the state and local governments. In 1934, the National Committee on Municipal Accounting published "A Tentative Outline—Principles of Municipal Accounting." In 1968, the National Committee on Governmental Accounting (the successor organization) published *Governmental Accounting, Auditing, and Financial Reporting* (*GAAFR*), which was widely used as a source of governmental accounting principles. The American Institute of Certified Public Accountants (AICPA) Industry Audit Guide, *Audits of State and Local Governmental Units,* published in 1974, stated that the accounting principles outlined in the 1968 *GAAFR* constituted GAAP for government entities.

The financial difficulties experienced by many governments in the mid-1970s led to a call for a review and modification of the accounting and financial reporting practices used by governments. Laws were introduced in Congress, but never enacted, that would have given the federal government the authority to establish governmental accounting principles. The Financial Accounting Standards Board (FASB), responding to pressures, commissioned a research study to define and explain the issues associated with accounting for all nonbusiness enterprises, including governments. This study was completed in 1978, and the Board developed Statement of Financial Accounting Concepts (SFAC) No. 4 for nonbusiness organizations. The Statement defined nonbusiness organizations, the users of the statements, the financial information needs of these users, and the information that is necessary to meet these needs.

(a) NATIONAL COUNCIL ON GOVERNMENTAL ACCOUNTING. The National Council on Governmental Accounting (NCGA) was the successor of the National Committee on Municipal Accounting reconstituted as a permanent organization. One of its first projects was to "restate"—that is, update, clarify, amplify, and reorder—the *GAAFR* to incorporate pertinent aspects of *Audits of State and Local Governmental Units.* The Restatement was published in March 1979 as NCGA Statement No. 1, *Governmental Accounting and Financial Reporting Principles.* Shortly thereafter, the AICPA Committee on State and Local Government Accounting recognized NCGA Statement No. 1 as authoritative and agreed to amend the *Industry Audit Guide* accordingly. This Restatement was completed, and a new guide was published in 1986. Thus NCGA Statement No. 1 became the primary reference source for the accounting principles unique to governmental accounting. However, in areas not unique to governmental accounting, the complete body of GAAP still needed to be considered.

(b) GOVERNMENTAL ACCOUNTING STANDARDS BOARD. In 1984, the Financial Accounting Foundation (FAF) established the Governmental Accounting Standards Board (GASB) as the primary standard setter for GAAP for governmental entities. Under the jurisdictional agreement, GASB has the primary responsibility for establishing accounting and reporting principles for government entities. GASB's first action was to issue Statement No. 1, *Authoritative Status of NCGA Pronouncements and AICPA Industry Audit Guide,* which recognized the NCGA's statements and interpretations and the AICPA's audit guide as authoritative. The Statement also recognized the pronouncements of the FASB issued prior to the date of the agreement as applicable to governments. FASB pronouncements issued after the organization of GASB do not become effective unless GASB specifically adopts them.

The GASB has operated under this jurisdictional arrangement since 1984. However, the arrangement came under scrutiny during the GASB's mandatory five-year review conducted in 1988. The Committee to Review Structure of Governmental Accounting Standards released its widely read report in January 1989 on the results of its review and proposed to the FAF, among other recommendations, a new jurisdictional arrangement and GAAP hierarchy for governments. These two recommendations prompted a great deal of controversy within the industry. The issue revolved around the committee's recommended jurisdictional arrangement for the separately issued financial statements of certain "special entities." (*Special entities* are organizations that can either be privately or governmentally owned and include colleges and universities, hospitals, and utilities). The committee recommended that FASB be the primary accounting standard setter for these special entities when they issue separate, stand-alone financial statements and that GASB be allowed to require the presentation of "additional data" in these stand-alone statements. This arrangement would allow for greater comparability between entities in the same industry (e.g., utilities) regardless of whether the entities were privately or governmentally owned and still allow government-owned entities to meet their "public accountability" reporting objective.

This recommendation and a subsequent compromise recommendation were unacceptable to many and especially to the various public interest groups, such as the Government Finance Officers Association (GFOA), which, 10 months after the committee's report, began discussions to establish a new body to set standards for state and local government. These actions prompted the FAF to consider whether a standard-setting schism was in the interest of the public and the users of financial statements. Based on this consideration, the FAF decided that the jurisdictional arrangement established in 1984 should remain intact.

In response to the jurisdictional arrangement just described, the AICPA issued Statement on Auditing Standards No. 69, *The Meaning of Present Fairly in Conformity with Generally Accepted Accounting Principles in the Independent Auditor's Report,* which creates a hierarchy of GAAP specifically for state and local governments. SAS No. 69 raises AICPA Statement of Positions (SOPs) and audit and accounting guides to a level of authority above that of industry practice. As a result, FASB pronouncements will not apply to state and local governments unless the GASB issues a standard incorporating them into GAAP for state and local government. In September 1993, the GASB issued Statement No. 20, *Accounting and Financial Reporting for Proprietary Funds and Other Governmental Entities That Use Proprietary Fund Accounting.*

Statement No. 20 requires proprietary activities to apply all applicable GASB Statements as well as FASB pronouncements, Accounting Principles Board (APB) Opinions, and Accounting Research Bulletins issued on or before November 30, 1989, unless those pronouncements conflict or contradict with a GASB pronouncement. A proprietary activity may also apply, at its option, all FASB pronouncements issued after November 30, 1989, except those that conflict or contradict with a GASB pronouncement. GASB recently issued Statement No. 62, *Codification of Accounting and Financial Reporting Guidance Contained in Pre-November 30, 1989 FASB and AICPA Pronouncements.* As governments implement Statement No. 62, the option to apply FASB pronouncements issued after November 30, 1989, under Statement No. 20 will be eliminated. However, governments can continue to apply, as other accounting literature, post-November 30, 1989, pronouncements that do not conflict or contradict GASB pronouncements.

The GASB subsequently issued Statement No. 29, *The Use of Not-for-Profit Accounting and Financial Reporting Principles by Governmental Entities,* which amended Statement No. 20 to indicate that proprietary activities could apply only those FASB statements that were developed for business enterprises. The FASB statements and interpretations whose provisions are limited to not-for-profit organizations or address issues primarily of concern to those organizations may not be applied. These actions, along with the increased activity of the FASB in setting standards for not-for-profit organizations, have resulted in increasing differences in GAAP between nongovernmental entities and state and local governments.

These differences also highlight the importance of determining whether a particular entity is a state or local government. While it is obvious that states, cities, and counties are governments, other units of government are less clear. Is a university considered a government if it is supported 70 percent by taxes allocated by the state? What if the percentage is only 15 percent? If a hospital is created by a county but the county has no continuing involvement with the hospital, is the hospital a government? The GASB acknowledged these concerns in the Basis for Conclusions of Statement No. 29 in stating:

> Some respondents believe that the fundamental issue underlying this Statement—identifying those entities that should apply the GAAP hierarchy applicable to state and local governmental entities—will continue to be troublesome until there is an authoritative definition of such "governmental entities." The Board agrees—but does not have the authority to unilaterally establish a definition—and intends to continue to explore alternatives for resolving the issue.

The decision as to whether a particular entity should follow the hierarchy for state and local governments or nongovernmental entities is a matter of professional judgment based on the individual facts and circumstances for the entity in question. The AICPA audit and accounting guide issued in March 2011 for not-for-profit entities provides guidance to distinguish between governmental and nongovernmental organizations. It defines governmental organizations as:

> Public corporations and bodies corporate and politic.... Other organizations are governmental organizations if they have one or more of the following characteristics:
>
> **a.** Popular election of officers or appointment (or approval) of a controlling majority of the members of the organization's governing body by officials of one or more state or local governments;
>
> **b.** The potential for unilateral dissolution by a government with the net assets reverting to a government; or
>
> **c.** The power to enact and enforce a tax levy.

Furthermore, organizations are presumed to be governmental if they have the ability to issue directly (rather than through a state or municipal authority) debt that pays interest exempt from federal taxation. However, organizations possessing only that ability (to issue tax-exempt debt) and none of the other governmental characteristics may rebut the presumption that they are governmental if their determination is supported by compelling, relevant evidence.

33.4 GOVERNMENTAL ACCOUNTING PRINCIPLES AND PRACTICES

(a) SIMILARITIES TO PRIVATE SECTOR ACCOUNTING. Since the accounting principles and practices of governments are part of the whole body of GAAP, certain accounting concepts and conventions are as applicable to governmental entities as they are to accounting in other industries:

- *Consistency.* Identical transactions should be recorded in the same manner both during a period and from period to period.
- *Conservatism.* The uncertainties that surround the preparation of financial statements are reflected in a general tendency toward early recognition of unfavorable events and minimization of the amount of net assets and net income.
- *Historical cost.* Amounts should be recognized in the financial statements at the historical cost to the reporting entity. Changes in the general purchasing power should not be recognized in the basic financial statements.
- *Matching.* The financial statements should provide for a matching, but in government, it is a matching of revenues and expenditures with a time period to ensure that revenues and the expenditures they finance are reported in the same period.
- *Reporting entity.* The focus of the financial report is the economic activities of a discrete individual entity for which there is a reporting responsibility.
- *Materiality.* Financial reporting is concerned only with significant information.
- *Full disclosure.* Financial statements must contain all information necessary to understand the presentation of financial position and results of operations and to prevent them from being misleading.

(b) USERS AND USES OF FINANCIAL REPORTS. Users of the financial statements of a governmental unit are not identical to users of a business entity's financial statements. The GASB Concepts Statement No. 1 identifies three groups of primary users of external governmental financial reports:

1. *Those to whom government is primarily accountable—the citizenry.* The citizenry group includes citizens (whether they are classified as taxpayers, voters, or service recipients), the media, advocate groups, and public finance researchers. This user group is concerned with obtaining the maximum amount of service with a minimum amount of taxes and wants to know where the government obtains its resources and how those resources are used.
2. *Those who directly represent the citizens—legislative and oversight bodies.* The legislative and oversight officials group includes members of state legislatures, county commissions, city councils, boards of trustees, and school boards, and those executive branch officials with oversight responsibility over other levels of government. These groups need timely warning of the development of situations that require corrective action, financial information that can serve as a basis for judging management performance, and financial information on which to base future plans and policies.
3. *Those who lend or participate in the lending process—investors and creditors.* Investors and creditors include individual and institutional investors and creditors, municipal security underwriters, bond-rating agencies (Moody's Investors Service, Standard & Poor's, Fitch Ratings, etc.), bond insurers, and financial institutions.

The uses of a government's financial reports are also different. GASB Concepts Statement No. 1 also indicates that governmental financial reporting should provide information to assist users in (1) assessing accountability and (2) making economic, social, and political decisions by:

- *Comparing actual financial results with the legally adopted budget.* All three user groups are interested in comparing original or modified budgets with actual results to get some assurance that spending mandates have been complied with and that resources have been used for the intended purposes.
- *Assisting in determining compliance with finance-related laws, rules, and regulations.* In addition to the legally mandated budgetary and fund controls, other legal restrictions may control governmental actions. Some examples are bond covenants, grant restrictions, and taxing and debt limits. Financial reports help demonstrate compliance with these laws, rules, and regulations.
  - Citizens are concerned that governments adhere to these regulations because noncompliance may indicate fiscal irresponsibility and could have severe financial consequences such as acceleration of debt payments, disallowance of questioned costs, or loss of grants.
  - Legislative and oversight officials are also concerned with compliance as a follow-up to the budget formulation process.
  - Investors and creditors are interested in the government's compliance with debt covenants and restrictions designed to protect their investment.
- *Assisting in evaluating efficiency and effectiveness.* Citizen groups and legislators, in particular, want information about service efforts, costs, and accomplishments of a governmental entity. This information, when combined with information from other sources, helps users assess the economy, efficiency, and effectiveness of government and may help form a basis for voting on funding decisions.
- *Assessing financial condition and results of operations.* Financial reports are commonly used to assess a state or local government's financial condition, that is, its financial position and its ability to continue to provide services and meet its obligations as they come due.
  - Investors and creditors need information about available and likely future financial resources, actual and contingent liabilities, and the overall debt position of a government to evaluate the government's ability to continue to provide resources for long-term debt service.

- Citizens' groups are concerned with financial condition when evaluating the likelihood of tax or service fee increases.
- Legislative and oversight officials need to assess the overall financial condition, including debt structure and funds available for appropriation, when developing both capital and operating budget and program recommendations.

With the users and the uses of financial reports clearly defined, the GASB developed three overall objectives of governmental financial reporting:

1. Financial reporting should assist in fulfilling a government's duty to be publicly accountable and should enable users to assess that accountability by:
   - **a.** Providing information to determine whether current-year revenues were sufficient to pay for current-year services
   - **b.** Demonstrating whether resources were obtained and used in accordance with the entity's legally adopted budget and compliance with other finance-related legal or contractual requirements
   - **c.** Providing information to assist users in assessing the service efforts, costs, and accomplishments of the governmental entity
2. Financial reporting should assist users in evaluating the operating results of the governmental entity for the year by providing information:
   - **a.** About sources and uses of financial resources
   - **b.** About how the governmental entity financed its activities and met its cash requirements
   - **c.** Necessary to determine whether the entity's financial position improved or deteriorated as a result of the year's operations
3. Financial reporting should assist users in assessing the level of services that can be provided by the governmental entity and its ability to meet its obligations as they become due by:
   - **a.** Providing information about the financial position and condition of a governmental entity. Financial reporting should provide information about resources and obligations, both actual and contingent, current and noncurrent, and about tax sources, tax limitations, tax burdens, and debt limitations.
   - **b.** Providing information about a governmental entity's physical and other nonfinancial resources having useful lives that extend beyond the current year, including information that can be used to assess the service potential of those resources.
   - **c.** Disclosing legal or contractual restrictions on resources and risks of potential loss of resources.

In November 2008, the GASB issued Concepts Statement No. 5, *Service Efforts and Accomplishments Reporting, an Amendment of GASB Concepts Statement No. 2.* Concepts Statement No. 5 includes a clarification that it is beyond the scope of the GASB to establish (1) the goals and objectives of state and local government services, (2) specific nonfinancial measures or indicators of service performance, or (3) standards of, or benchmarks for, service performance. Rather, these decisions should be made by those charged with that responsibility. The Statement provides a rationale for the objective of service efforts and accomplishments (SEA) reporting and identifies the elements of SEA reporting and the qualitative characteristics that SEA reporting should possess. While Concepts Statement No. 5 does not establish SEA reporting requirements, it describes why external reporting of SEA performance information assists users in assessing accountability and in making better informed decisions.

In April 2005, the GASB issued Concepts Statement No. 3, *Communication Methods in General Purpose External Financial Reports That Contain Basic Financial Statements,* which provides a conceptual basis for selecting communication methods to present items of information within general purpose external financial reports that contain basic financial statements. Preparers should select an appropriate communication method to convey information that enhances the consistency, comparability, and understandability of general purpose external financial reports. The hierarchy for selecting communications methods is:

1. Recognition in the basic financial statements
2. Disclosure in notes to basic financial statements
3. Presentation as required supplementary information
4. Presentation as supplementary information

In June 2007, the GASB issued Concepts Statement No. 4, *Elements of Financial Statements,* which establishes definitions for the seven elements of historically based financial statements of state and local governments. These elements are the fundamental components of financial statements. The five statements of financial position elements are defined in this way:

- *Assets* are resources with present service capacity that the government presently controls.
- *Liabilities* are present obligations to sacrifice resources that the government has little or no discretion to avoid.
- A *deferred outflow* of resources is a consumption of net assets by the government that is applicable to a future reporting period.
- A *deferred inflow* of resources is an acquisition of net assets by the government that is applicable to a future reporting period.
- *Net position* is the residual of all other elements presented in a statement of financial position.

The two resource flows elements are defined in this way:

- An *outflow of resources* is a consumption of net assets by the government that is applicable to the reporting period.
- An *inflow of resources* is an acquisition of net assets by the government that is applicable to the reporting period.

Each element's inherent characteristics provide the primary basis for these definitions. Central to these definitions is a resource, which in the governmental context is an item that can be drawn on to provide services to the citizenry. These definitions apply to an entity that is a governmental unit (i.e., a legal entity) and are applicable to any measurement focus under which financial statements may be prepared.

(c) SUMMARY STATEMENT OF PRINCIPLES. Because governments operate under different conditions and have different reporting objectives than commercial entities, basic principles applicable to government accounting and reporting have been developed. These principles are generally recognized as being essential to effective management control and financial reporting. In other words, understanding these principles and how they operate is extremely important to the understanding of governments.

(i) Accounting and Reporting Capabilities. A governmental accounting system must make it possible to both (1) present fairly the basic financial statements in conformity with GAAP, which include both government-wide and fund financial statements with full disclosure, and to provide adequately the required supplementary information, including the management's discussion and analysis (MD&A) and required budgetary comparison information; and (2) determine and demonstrate compliance with finance-related legal and contractual provisions.

(ii) Government-Wide and Fund Accounting Systems. Governmental accounting systems should provide information that permits reporting on a fund basis and provide conversion information that facilitates reporting on a government-wide basis. A *fund* is defined as a fiscal and accounting entity with a self-balancing set of accounts recording cash and other financial resources, together with all related liabilities and residual equities or balances, and changes therein, which are segregated for the purpose of carrying on specific activities or attaining certain objectives in accordance with special regulations, restrictions, or limitations.

Government-wide financial statements should be presented in addition to fund financial statements. These statements should report information about the reporting government as a whole, except for its fiduciary activities. The statements should include separate columns for governmental activities, business-type activities, total activities, and component units, which are legally separate organizations for which the elected officials of the primary government (PG) are financially accountable, or other organizations for which the nature and significance of its relationship with a PG are such that exclusion from the financial statements of the PG would cause them to be misleading. The government-wide financial statements should be prepared using the economic resources measurement focus and the accrual basis of accounting.

(iii) Types of Funds. Three types of funds should be used by state and local governments.

Governmental Funds (Emphasizing Major Funds). These funds consist of:

- *General fund.* To account for all financial resources not accounted for in another fund.
- *Special revenue funds.* To account for the proceeds of specific revenue sources that are restricted or committed to expenditures for specified purposes other than debt service or capital projects.
- *Capital projects funds.* To account for financial resources that are restricted, committed, or assigned to expenditures for capital outlays (other than those financed by proprietary funds and trust funds). Capital outlays include the acquisition or construction of capital facilities and other capital assets.
- *Debt service funds.* To account for financial resources that are restricted, committed, or assigned to expenditures for principal and interest.
- *Permanent funds.* To account for the resources that are restricted to the extent that only the earnings, and not principal, may be used for the benefit of the government or its citizenry.

Proprietary Funds. Proprietary funds consist of:

- *Enterprise funds (emphasizing major funds).* To account for any activity for which a fee is charged to external users for goods or services. Activities are required to be reported as enterprise funds if (1) the activity is financed with debt that is secured solely by a pledge of the net revenues from fees and charges of that activity, (2) laws or regulations require the activity's costs of providing services, including capital costs (such as depreciation or debt service) be recovered with fees and charges, rather than with taxes or similar revenues, or (3) the pricing policies of the activity establish fees and charges designed to recover its costs, including capital costs (such as depreciation or debt service.)
- *Internal service funds.* To account for any activity that provides goods or services to other funds, departments, or agencies of the primary government and its component units, or to other governments, on a cost-reimbursement basis.

Fiduciary Funds. Fiduciary funds consist of:

- *Pension and other employee benefit trust funds.* To account for resources that are required to be held in trust for the members and beneficiaries of defined benefit pension plans, defined contribution plans, other postemployment benefit (OPEB) plans, or other employee benefit plans.
- *Investment trust funds.* To account for the external portion of external investment pools that the government sponsors.

- *Private-purpose trust funds.* To account for all other trust arrangements under which the principal and income benefit individuals, private organizations, or other governments.
- *Agency funds.* To account for resources held by a reporting government in a purely custodial capacity for individuals, private organizations, or other governments.

(iv) Accounting for Capital Assets. A clear distinction should be made between proprietary capital assets and general capital assets. Capital assets related to specific proprietary funds should be accounted for in both the government-wide and proprietary funds statements. All other capital assets of a governmental unit should be accounted for only in the government-wide capital assets account, except for fiduciary fund capital assets that should be accounted for only in the fiduciary fund's statements.

(v) Valuation of Capital Assets. Capital assets should be accounted for at cost or, if the cost is not practicably determinable, at estimated cost. Donated capital assets should be recorded at their estimated fair value at the time received. Intangible assets subject to GASB Statement No. 51 should also be classified as capital assets when they are identifiable. An intangible asset is considered identifiable when either of these conditions are met: (1) the asset is separable (i.e., capable of being separated or divided from the government and sold, transferred, licensed, rented, or exchanged, either individually or together with a related contract, asset, or liability); or (2) the asset arises from contractual or other legal rights, regardless of whether those rights are transferable or separable from the entity or from other rights and obligations.

(vi) Depreciation and Impairment of Capital Assets. While some assets are not depreciated, such as land and intangible assets with indefinite useful lives, most assets are depreciated over their useful lives. An exception is also those assets accounted for using the modified approach, as outlined in GASB Statement No. 34. Depreciation of capital assets should be recorded in the government-wide statement of activities; the proprietary fund statement of revenues, expenses, and changes in fund net assets; and the statement of changes in fiduciary net assets. Capital assets should be evaluated for impairment when events or changes in circumstances suggest that the service utility of a capital asset may have significantly and unexpected decline.

(vii) Accounting for Long-Term Liabilities. Similar to reporting capital assets, a clear distinction should be made between proprietary fund and fiduciary long-term liabilities and general long-term liabilities. Long-term liabilities of proprietary funds should be accounted both in those funds and in the government-wide statement of net assets. All other outstanding general long-term liabilities should be accounted for in the government activities column in the government-wide statement of net assets, except for fiduciary funds long-term liabilities that should be accounted for only in the fiduciary funds' statements.

(viii) Measurement Focus and Basis of Accounting. The modified accrual or accrual basis of accounting, as appropriate, should be used in measuring financial position and changes in financial position.

- Governmental fund revenues and expenditures should be recognized on the modified accrual basis using the current financial resources measurement focus. Revenues should be recognized in the accounting period in which they become available and measurable. Expenditures should be recognized in the accounting period in which the fund liability is incurred, if measurable, except for unmatured long-term indebtedness and other obligations not due for payment in the current period, which should be recognized when mature or due.
- Proprietary fund revenues and expenses should be recognized using the economic resources measurement focus and the accrual basis. Revenues should be recognized in the accounting period in which they are earned and become measurable; expenses should be recognized in the period incurred, if measurable.

- Fiduciary fund revenues/additions and expenses/reductions should be recognized using the economic resources measurement focus and the accrual basis.
- Transfers should be recognized in the period in which the interfund receivable and payable arise.

(ix) Budgeting, Budgetary Control, and Budgetary Reporting. An annual budget should be adopted by every governmental unit. The accounting system should provide the basis for appropriate budgetary control. Budgetary comparisons should be presented for the general fund and for each major special revenue fund that has a legally adopted annual budget.

(x) Transfer, Revenue, Expenditure, and Expense Account Classification. The statement of activities should present activities accounted for in governmental funds by function and activities accounted for in enterprise funds by different identifiable activities.

Governmental fund revenues should be classified by fund and source. Expenditures should be classified by fund, function (or program), organization unit, activity, character, and principal classes of objects.

Proprietary fund revenues and expenses should be classified in essentially the same manner as those of similar business organizations, functions, or activities.

Contributions to term and permanent endowments, contributions to permanent fund principal, other capital contributions, special and extraordinary items, and transfers should each be reported separately.

(xi) Common Terminology and Classification. A common terminology and classification should be used consistently throughout the budget, the accounts, and the financial reports of each fund or activity.

(xii) Interim and Annual Financial Reports. Appropriate interim financial statements and reports of financial position, changes in financial position, and other pertinent information should be prepared to facilitate management control of financial operations, legislative oversight, and, where necessary or desired, external reporting.

A comprehensive annual financial report (CAFR) covering all funds and component units of the governmental reporting entity may be prepared and published, including appropriate government-wide financial statements; fund financial statements; notes to the financial statements; required supplementary information; supplemental combining and individual fund statements and schedules; narrative explanations; and statistical tables.

Basic financial statements may be issued separately from the CAFR. Such statements should include the government-wide and fund financial statements, notes to the financial statements, and any required supplementary information essential to a fair presentation of financial position and changes in financial position and cash flows of proprietary funds.

(d) DISCUSSION OF THE PRINCIPLES. To enable readers to more fully understand the principles, they are discussed next.

(e) ACCOUNTING AND REPORTING CAPABILITIES.

(i) Legal Compliance. Principle 1 of governmental accounting (GASB Codification Section 1100.101) states:

> A governmental accounting system must make it possible both: (a) to present fairly and with full disclosure the funds of the governmental unit in conformity with generally accepted accounting principles; and (b) to determine and demonstrate compliance with finance-related legal and contractual provisions.

Several state and local governments have accounting requirements that differ from GAAP; for example, cash basis accounting is required. When GAAP and legal requirements conflict,

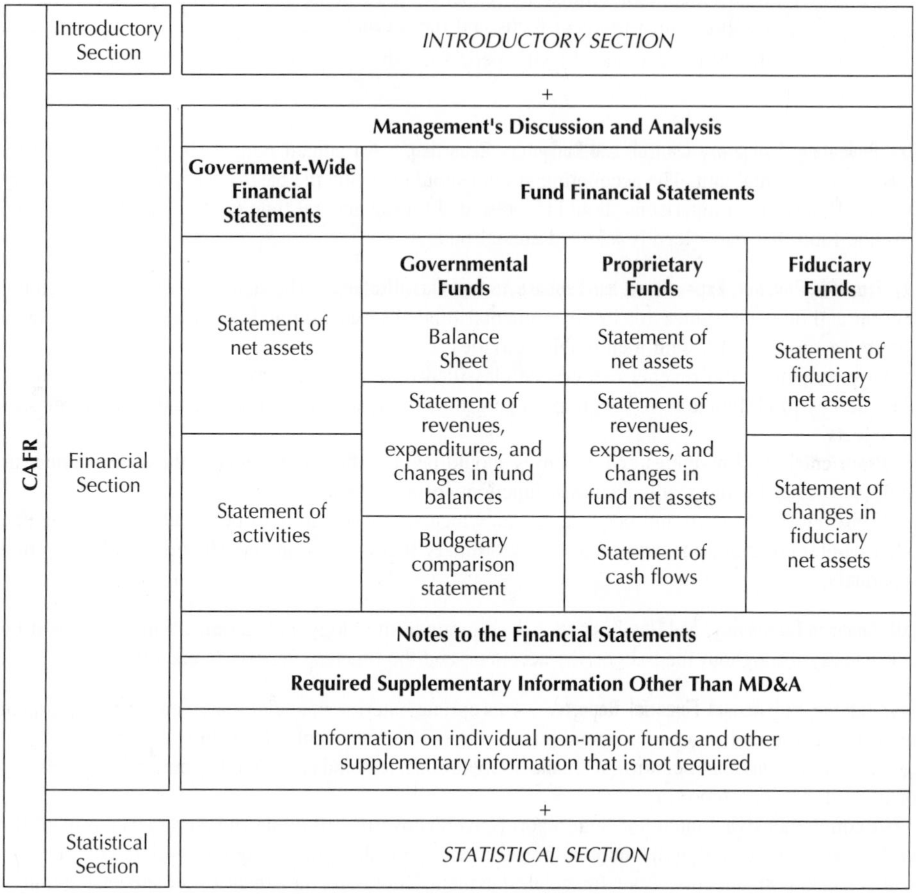

<table>
<tr><td rowspan="13">CAFR</td><td>Introductory Section</td><td colspan="4">INTRODUCTORY SECTION</td></tr>
<tr><td colspan="5">+</td></tr>
<tr><td rowspan="9">Financial Section</td><td colspan="4">Management's Discussion and Analysis</td></tr>
<tr><td>Government-Wide Financial Statements</td><td colspan="3">Fund Financial Statements</td></tr>
<tr><td rowspan="2">Statement of net assets</td><td>Governmental Funds</td><td>Proprietary Funds</td><td>Fiduciary Funds</td></tr>
<tr><td>Balance Sheet</td><td>Statement of net assets</td><td>Statement of fiduciary net assets</td></tr>
<tr><td rowspan="2">Statement of activities</td><td>Statement of revenues, expenditures, and changes in fund balances</td><td>Statement of revenues, expenses, and changes in fund net assets</td><td rowspan="2">Statement of changes in fiduciary net assets</td></tr>
<tr><td>Budgetary comparison statement</td><td>Statement of cash flows</td></tr>
<tr><td colspan="4">Notes to the Financial Statements</td></tr>
<tr><td colspan="4">Required Supplementary Information Other Than MD&A</td></tr>
<tr><td colspan="4">Information on individual non-major funds and other supplementary information that is not required</td></tr>
<tr><td colspan="5">+</td></tr>
<tr><td>Statistical Section</td><td colspan="4">STATISTICAL SECTION</td></tr>
</table>

Exhibit 33.1 Organization of the City and County of San Francisco Comprehensive Annual Financial Report
Source: City and County of San Francisco, California, Comprehensive Annual Financial Report for the Year Ended June 30, 2011, p. 4.

governments should present their basic financial statements in accordance with GAAP and, if the legal requirements differ materially from GAAP, the legally required reports can be published as supplemental data to the basic financial statements or, if these differences are extreme, it may be preferable to publish a separate legal basis report.

However, conflicts that arise between GAAP and legal provisions do not require maintaining two sets of accounting records. Rather, the accounting records typically would be maintained in accordance with the legal requirements but would include sufficient additional information to permit preparation of financial statements in accordance with GAAP.

(ii) Reporting Requirements. Under GASB Statement No. 34, the typical local government's set of basic financial statements comprises three components: (1) *Government-wide* financial statements; (2) *fund* financial statements; and (3) *notes* to the financial statements. Governments will also have other supplementary information in addition to the basic financial statements themselves. An example of how the various elements of a local government's financial statements are related is shown in Exhibit 33.1.

The table in Exhibit 33.2 summarizes the major features of the City and County of San Francisco's financial statements.

	Government-Wide Statements	Fund Financial Statements		
		Governmental	Proprietary	Fiduciary
Scope	Entire entity (except fiduciary funds)	The day-to-day operating activities of the city for basic governmental services	The day-to-day operating activities of the city for business-type enterprises	Instances in which the city administers resources on behalf of others, such as employee benefits
Accounting basis and measurement focus	Accrual accounting and economic resources focus	Modified accrual accounting and current financial resources focus	Accrual accounting and economic resources focus	Accrual accounting and economic resources focus; except agency funds do not have measurement focus
Type of asset and liability information	All assets and liabilities, both financial and capital, short-term and long-term	Current assets and liabilities that come due during the year or soon thereafter	All assets and liabilities, both financial and capital, short-term and long-term	All assets held in a trustee or agency capacity for others
Type of inflow and outflow information	All revenues and expenses during year, regardless of when cash is received or paid	Revenues for which cash is received during the year or soon thereafter; expenditures when goods or services have been received and the related liability is due and payable	All revenues and expenses during year, regardless of when cash is received or paid	All additions and deductions during the year, regardless of when cash is received or paid

Exhibit 33.2 Summary of the Major Features of the City and County of San Francisco's Financial Statements
Source: City and County of San Francisco, California, Comprehensive Annual Financial Report for the Year Ended June 30, 2011, p. 5.

(f) GOVERNMENT-WIDE AND FUND ACCOUNTING SYSTEMS. Principle 2, fund accounting, is used by governments because of (1) legally binding restrictions that prohibit or seriously limit the use of much of a government's resources for other than the purposes for which the resources were obtained, and (2) the importance of reporting the accomplishment of various objectives for which the resources were entrusted to the government.

GASB Codification Section 1100.102 defines a *fund* for accounting purposes as:

> A fiscal and accounting entity with a self-balancing set of accounts recording cash and other financial resources, together with all related liabilities and residual equities or balances, and changes therein, which are segregated for the purposes of carrying on specific activities or obtaining certain objectives in accordance with special regulations, restrictions, or limitations.

Thus a fund may include accounts for assets, liabilities, fund balance or net assets, revenues, expenditures, or expenses. Accounts may also exist for appropriations and encumbrances, depending on the budgeting system used.

A government should report separately on its most important, or "major," funds, including its general fund. A major fund is one whose revenues, expenditures/expenses, assets, or liabilities (excluding extraordinary items) are at least 10 percent of the corresponding totals for all governmental or enterprise funds and at least 5 percent of the aggregate amount for all governmental and enterprise funds. Any other fund may be reported as a major fund if the government's officials believe information about the fund is particularly important to the users of the statements. Other funds should be reported in the aggregate in a separate column. Internal service funds should be reported in the aggregate in a separate column on the proprietary fund statements. Separate fund financial statements should be presented for governmental and proprietary funds.

A government should present a summary reconciliation to the government-wide financial statements at the bottom of the fund financial statements or in a separate schedule. Fund balances for governmental funds should be segregated into nonspendable, restricted, committed, assigned and unassigned categories. Proprietary fund net assets should be reported in the same categories required for the government-wide financial statements. Proprietary fund statements of net assets should distinguish between current and noncurrent assets and liabilities and should display restricted assets.

(g) TYPES AND NUMBER OF FUNDS. Because of the varied nature of activities carried on by government, it is often important to be able to account for certain activities separately from others (i.e., when required by law). Principles 3 and 4 define basic fund types in which to account for various activities of a government. The purpose and operation of each fund type differs, and it is important to understand these differences and why they exist. Every fund maintained by a government should be classified into one of these three fund categories:

1. Governmental funds, emphasizing major funds:
   - The general fund
   - Special revenue funds
   - Capital projects funds
   - Debt service funds
   - Permanent funds
2. Proprietary funds:
   - Enterprise funds, emphasizing major funds
   - Internal service funds
3. Fiduciary funds and similar component units:
   - Pension and other employee benefit trust funds
   - Investment trust funds
   - Private-purpose trust funds
   - Agency funds

The general fund, special revenue funds, debt service funds, capital projects funds, and permanent funds are considered governmental funds since they record the transactions associated with the general services of a local governmental unit (e.g., police, public works, fire prevention) that are provided to all citizens and are supported primarily by general revenues. For these funds, the primary concerns, from the financial statement reader's point of view, are the types and amounts of resources that have been made available to the governmental unit and the uses to which they have been put.

The enterprise funds and internal services funds are considered proprietary funds because they account for activities for which a fee is charged to external users (or in the case of internal service funds to other funds, departments or agencies of the primary government) for goods or services. For enterprise funds, the determination of operating income is often important to establish fees and charges designed to recover costs.

The trust and agency funds are considered fiduciary funds. There are basically three types of trust funds: pension (and other employee benefit) trust funds; investment trust funds and private-purpose trust funds that operate in a manner similar to proprietary funds; and agency funds that account for funds held by a government entity in an agent capacity. Agency funds consist of assets and liabilities only and do not involve the measurement of operations.

Although a government should establish and maintain those funds required by law and sound financial administration, it should set up only the minimum number of funds consistent with legal and operating requirements. The maintenance of unnecessary funds results in inflexibility, undue complexity, and inefficient financial administration. For instance, in the past, the proceeds of specific revenue sources or resources that financed specific activities as required by law or administrative regulation had to be accounted for in a special revenue fund. However, governmental resources restricted to purposes usually financed through the general fund should be accounted for in the general fund, provided that all legal requirements can be satisfied. Examples include state grants received by an entity for special education. If a separate fund is not legally required, the grant revenues and the grant-related expenditures should be accounted for in the fund for which they are to be used.

Another way to minimize funds is by accounting for debt service payments in the general fund and not establishing a separate debt service fund unless it is legally mandated or resources are actually being accumulated for future debt service payments (i.e., for term bonds or in sinking funds).

Furthermore, one or more identical accounts for separate funds should be combined in the accounting system, particularly for funds that are similar in nature or are in the same fund group. For example, the cash accounts for all special revenue funds may be combined, provided that the integrity of each fund is preserved through a distinct equity account for each fund.

(i) Governmental Funds

General Fund. The general fund accounts for the revenues and expenditures not accounted for in other funds and finances most of the current normal functions of governmental units: general government, public safety, highways, sanitation and waste removal, health and welfare, culture, and recreation. It is usually the largest and most important accounting activity for state and local governments. Property taxes are often the principal source of general fund revenues, but substantial revenues may also be received from other financing sources.

The general fund balance sheet is typically limited to current assets and current liabilities. The GASB Codification emphasizes this practice by using the terms *expendable assets* and *current liabilities* when describing governmental funds, of which the general fund is one. Thus the fund balance in the general fund is considered available to finance current operations.

Special Revenue Funds. Special revenue funds account for the proceeds of specific revenue sources that are restricted or committed to expenditure for specified purposes other than debt service or capital projects. The foundation of a special revenue fund is the resources from specific revenue sources. Examples are grant programs funded by a specific grant, highway construction or street maintenance programs funded by gas tax, or housing programs funded by dedicated property taxes.

Debt Service Funds. Debt service funds exist to account for financial resources that are restricted, committed or assigned to expenditure of long-term debt principal and interest other than that which it is issued for and serviced primarily by an enterprise or similar trust fund. A debt service fund is necessary only if it is legally required or if resources are being accumulated for future payment. Although governments may incur a wide variety of debt, the more common types are described below.

Term (or sinking fund) bonds are being replaced by serial bonds as the predominant form of state and local government debt. For term bonds, debt service consists of annual additions of resources being made to a cumulative "investment fund" for repayment of the issue at maturity. The additions, also called *sinking fund installments,* are computed on an actuarial basis, which includes assumptions that certain rates of interest will be earned from investing the resources accumulating in the investment fund. If the actual earnings are less than the planned earnings, subsequent additions are increased; if the earnings are greater than planned, the excess is carried forward until the time of the final addition of the fund. Because term bond principal is due at the end of the bond's term, the expenditure for repayment of principal is recognized at that time.

Debt service on serial bonds, however, generally consists of preestablished principal payments that are due on an annual basis and interest payments based on either fixed or variable rates that are due on a semiannual basis. No sinking fund is involved in the repayment of serial bonds.

The revenues for a debt service fund come from one or more sources, with property taxes being the predominant source. Taxes that are specified for debt service appear as a revenue of the debt service fund. Taxes for general purposes (i.e., not specified but nevertheless used for debt service) are considered to be a transfer to the debt service fund from the fund in which the revenue is recorded, oftentimes the general fund.

Enterprise activity earnings may be another resource for servicing general obligation debt. In these instances, the general obligation debt should be classified as enterprise debt (a liability of the enterprise fund), and the debt service payments should be recorded in the enterprise fund as a reduction of the liability, not in the debt service fund. The debt service transactions would be recorded in the debt service fund only if the enterprise fund was not expected to be responsible for repaying the debt on an ongoing basis. Essentially, if the enterprise fund became unable to service the principal and interest and the general governmental unit assumed responsibility for servicing the debt, then the debt service fund would be used.

In addition, governmental units have been utilizing alternative financing activities including lease-purchase arrangements and issuance of zero-coupon or deep discount debt (e.g., capital appreciation bonds). The issues surrounding lease-purchase arrangements involve legal questions about whether such arrangements constitute debt of a government since they often do not require voter approval prior to incurring the debt. Zero-coupon and deep discount debt issues center on the manner of presenting and amortizing the bond discount amount in the government's financial statements.

In other instances, governmental units have been securitizing specific receivables and future revenues in order to receive cash up-front for current outlays. GASB issued Statement No. 48, *Sales and Pledges of Receivables and Future Revenues and Intra-Entity Transfers of Assets and Future Receivables* to address a divergence in practice as to whether these securitizations should be reported as a revenue or as a liability.

Recently, governments are examining the possibility of issuing debt to fund their unfunded actuarial accrued liability (UAAL) for their other postemployment benefits (OPEB) as has sometimes been done with UAAL for their pension obligations. These are taxable debt issues that are used to fund all or part of a government entity's UAAL. This shifts the liability from one owed to the pension plan to one owed to bondholders and brings the liability onto the government's financial statements. The rationale for issuing this type of debt is to pay down the UAAL to a pension system or other trust and pay a lower interest rate on the bonds compared to the long-term discount rate. Governments should exercise caution when evaluating the possibility of issuing OPEB or pension obligation bonds given the volatility of the computation of the actuarial liabilities, the increase in the government's debt burden and the dependence on a higher rate of earnings on investments.

Quite often, a refunding bond is issued to replace or consolidate prior debt issues. Determining the appropriate accounting principles to apply to refunding bonds depends primarily on whether the bonds are enterprise fund obligations or general obligations. GASB Statement No. 7, *Advance Refundings Resulting in Defeasance of Debt,* outlines the appropriate accounting and reporting principles. For the refunding of debt, the proceeds of the refunding issue become an "other financing source" of the fund receiving the proceeds of the refunding bond (often a debt service fund created to service the original issue or a capital projects fund). Since the proceeds are used to liquidate the original debt, an "other financing use" is also recorded in the debt service or capital projects fund for the amount of proceeds used to pay the remaining principal, interest, and other amounts due on the original debt. Existing resources used to pay remaining debt service on the original debt continue to be reported as debt service expenditures.

If, as a result of the refunding, the liability to the bondholders is satisfied, the refunding is referred to as a *legal defeasance of debt* or *current refunding.* However, refundings often do not result in the immediate repayment of the debt but rather assets are placed in a trust to be used to repay the debt as it matures. These refundings are called *advance refundings* or an *in-substance defeasance.* To qualify for an in-substance defeasance, the proceeds of the refunding bonds are placed in an irrevocable trust and invested in essentially risk-free securities, usually obligations of the U.S. Treasury or other government agencies, so that the risk-free securities, together with any premiums on the defeased debt, and expenses of the refunding operation will be sufficient for the trust to pay off the debt to the bondholders when it becomes due. The accounting for an in-substance defeasance is identical to legal defeasances except that payment is made to a trustee rather than to bondholders. The trustee then pays principal and interest to the bondholders based on the maturity schedule of the bond. In addition, the recording of payments of proceeds to the trustee as another financing use is limited to the amount of proceeds.

Advance refundings of debt follow the accounting principles outlined in GASB Statement No. 23, *Accounting and Financial Reporting for Refundings of Debt Reported by Proprietary Activities.* Statement No. 23 requires that the difference between the reacquisition price and the net carrying amount of the old debt be deferred and amortized as a component of interest expense over the remaining life of the old or the life of the new debt, whichever is shorter.

In addition, GASB Statement No. 7 requires the disclosure of a description of the refunding transaction; the cash flow gain or loss, which is the difference between the total cash outflow of the new debt (i.e., principal, interest, etc.) and the remaining cash outflow of the old debt; and the economic gain or loss, which is the difference between the present values of the cash flows of the new and old debt.

For advance refundings, each year after the defeasance, the footnotes to the financial statements should disclose the remaining amount of debt principal that the trustee has to pay to bondholders.

Capital Projects Funds. The purpose of a capital projects fund is to account for the resources that are restricted, committed, or assigned to expenditure for capital outlays, including the acquisition or construction of capital facilities and other capital assets other than those financed by proprietary funds or for assets that are held in trust for others. Capital outlays financed from general obligation bond proceeds should be accounted for through a capital projects fund.

Accounting for Capital Projects Fund Transactions. Bonds are issued and capital projects are started under a multiyear capital program. In some instances, it is necessary to secure referendum approval to issue general obligation bonds. Obligations are then incurred and expenditures made according to an annual capital projects budget.

When a project is financed entirely from general obligation bond proceeds, the initial entry to be made in the capital projects fund when the bonds are sold is:

Cash	$XXX	
Other financing source—		
Proceeds of general obligation bonds		$XXX

Whereas the proceeds of the bonds are accounted for in the capital projects funds, the liability for the face amount of the bonds is recorded in the government-wide statement of net assets.

If bonds are sold at a premium (i.e., above par value), the premium increases the other financing sources. If the bonds are sold at a discount (i.e., below par value), the discount should be reported as an other financing use. Bond issuance costs either paid out of available funds or withheld from the bond proceeds usually are accounted as debt service expenditures in the capital projects or debt service funds operating statement.

Permanent Funds. Permanent funds should be used to report assets legally restricted so that only earnings, not principal, may be spent for the government's programs (i.e., for the benefit of the government or its citizens).

(ii) Proprietary Funds

Enterprise Funds. Enterprise funds *may be* used to report any activity for which fees are charged to external users in exchange for goods or services. They are *required* to be used if *any one* of the next criteria is met in the context of the activity's principal revenue sources (insignificant activities, such as fees charged for frivolous small-claims suits, are excluded):

- The activity is financed with debt secured solely by a pledge of the net revenues from fees and charges of the activity. (This is met if the debt is secured in part by a portion of its own proceeds.)
- Laws or regulations require that the activity's costs of providing goods or services, including capital costs such as depreciation or debt service, be recovered by its fees and charges, not by taxes or similar revenues.

- The pricing policies of the activity result in fees and charges intended to recover the activity's costs, including capital costs such as depreciation or debt service.

The primary focus of these criteria is on fees charged to external users.

Proprietary (enterprise) activities are frequently administered by departments of the general-purpose government, for example, a municipal water department or a state parks department. They can also be the exclusive function of a local special district, such as a water district, power authority, or bridge and tunnel authority.

User charges are one significant source of enterprise fund resources; revenue bond proceeds are another. Revenue bonds are long-term obligations, the principal and interest of which are paid from the earnings of the enterprise for which the bond proceeds were spent. The enterprise revenues may be pledged to the payment of the debt, and the physical properties may carry a mortgage that is to be liquidated in the event of default.

Revenue bond indentures usually also contain several requirements concerning the use of the bond proceeds, the computation and reporting of revenue bond coverage, and the establishment and use of restricted asset accounts for handling revenue bond debt service requirements. For instance, a revenue bond indenture may require the establishment of various bond accounts including a construction account, operations and maintenance account, current debt service account, future debt service account, and revenue and replacement account. This does not necessarily mean establishing individual accounting funds for each bond issue. Instead, the accounting and reporting requirements can be met through the use of various accounts within an accounting fund.

The revenue bond construction account normally represents cash and investments (including interest receivable) segregated by the bond indenture for construction. Construction liabilities payable from restricted assets should be reported as contracts payable from restricted assets. If there are significant unspent debt proceeds at year-end, the portion of the debt attributable to the unspent proceeds should not be included in the calculation of invested in capital assets, net of related debt. Instead, that portion of the debt should be included as the same net assets component as the unspent proceeds.

A revenue bond operations and maintenance account often is established pursuant to a bond indenture. Resources for this account are provided through bond proceeds and/or operating income or net income. This account generally accumulates assets equal to operating costs for one month. Once this account has been established, additional proceeds from future bond issues generally are necessary only to the extent the costs associated with these expanded operations are expected to increase. This account is normally balanced by a restricted net asset account for revenue bond operations and maintenance.

Bond indentures may also include a covenant requiring the establishment of a restricted account for the repayment of bond principal and interest. Resources for this account also are provided through bond proceeds and/or operating income or net income. Normally, assets accumulated for debt service payments (i.e., principal and interest) due within one year are classified in the revenue bond current debt service account. This account is at least partially associated with the bonds payable—current account and the accrued interest payable account. Any difference between the revenue bond current debt service account not funded with bond proceeds and accrued interest payable should be reported as restricted net assets. When accounts are restricted for debt service payments beyond the next 12 months, a revenue bond future debt service account should be established.

The final restricted account typically established pursuant to a covenant within a bond indenture is the revenue bond renewal and replacement account. Net income is often restricted for payments of unforeseen repairs and replacements of assets originally acquired with bond proceeds. Provided that liabilities have not been incurred for this purpose, the revenue bond renewal and replacement account is balanced by net assets restricted for revenue bond renewal and replacement.

This general rule should be considered when determining the amount of restricted net assets to record: Unless otherwise required by the bond indenture, net assets should only be restricted for amounts of restricted assets in excess of related liabilities and the balance of restricted assets funded by bond proceeds.

Another restricted asset often found in enterprise funds for utility operations is the amount resulting from the deposits customers are required to make to ensure payment of their final charges and to protect the utility against damage to equipment located on the customer's property. These funds are not available for the financing of current operations, and, generally, the amount, less the charges outstanding against the account, must be returned to the customer upon withdrawing from the system. Also, these deposits may, depending on legal and policy requirements, draw interest at some stipulated rate.

In some instances, revenue bonds are also secured by the full faith and credit of the governmental unit. This additional security enables the bonds to obtain better acceptance in the securities market. If the bonds are to be serviced by the enterprise activity, the cash, liability, principal, and interest payments should be accounted for in the enterprise fund. Even if the bonds are secured only by full faith and credit and not by a revenue pledge, but the intention is to use enterprise revenues to service the bonds, they should be accounted for as if they were revenue bonds. If, however, general obligation bond proceeds are used to finance the enterprise activity and there is no intention to service the bonds with enterprise fund resources, the amounts provided to the enterprise fund should be recorded as a transfer from the fund recording the proceeds of the bond, typically, the general fund.

Other sources of contributions also provide significant resources for enterprise activities. Such resources include:

- Capital contributions by other funds or other governmental bodies
- Capital contributions by customers or other members of the general public
- The aforementioned proceeds of a bond issue to be repaid from general fund revenues, federal grants, or state grants
- Connection charges to users of utility services
- Payments by real estate developers for installing utility lines
- Similar receipts

Another resource is the support provided by or to other funds of the government. For instance, an enterprise fund frequently uses the services or commodities of a central facility operated as an internal service fund. Conversely, the general fund departments will use the services of an electric utility fund.

It is important to handle these relationships on a businesslike basis. All services rendered by an enterprise fund for other funds of the government should be billed at predetermined rates, and the enterprise should pay for all services received from other funds on the same basis that is utilized to determine charges for other users. The latter often includes payments in lieu of taxes to the general fund in amounts comparable to the taxes that would have been paid by the enterprise were it privately owned and operated, or an "administrative charge" if the enterprise does not have its own management capacity and instead uses management services provided by the general government. Unless this is done, the financial operations of a government-owned enterprise will be distorted, and valid comparisons of operating results with those for a similar privately owned enterprise cannot be made. However, other considerations, such as the amount of planned idle capacity, have an impact on the comparability of public and private enterprise funds.

Interfund transfers may also occur between an enterprise fund and governmental funds. Operating subsidy transfers from the general fund or special revenue funds are possible. There may also be transfers from an enterprise to finance general fund expenditures.

Finally, there are the nonoperating income and expenses, which are incidental to, or by-products of, the enterprise's primary service function. Nonoperating income consists of such items as interest earnings, rent from nonoperating properties, intergovernmental revenues, and sale of excess supplies. Nonoperating expenses include items such as interest expense and fiscal agents' fees.

Internal Service Funds. Internal service funds finance and account for special activities that are performed and commodities that are furnished by one department or agency of a governmental unit to other departments or agencies of that unit or to other governmental units on a cost-reimbursement basis. The services differ from those rendered to the public at large, which are accounted for in general, special revenue, or enterprise funds. Examples of activities in which internal service funds are established include central motor pools, duplication services, central purchasing and stores departments, and insurance and risk-management activities.

When an internal service fund is established, resources are typically obtained from contributions from other operating funds, such as the general fund or an enterprise fund, or from long-term advances from other funds that are to be repaid from operating income. The entry to be made when the fund is created varies depending on the source of the contributions.

The cost of services rendered and commodities furnished, including labor, depreciation on all capital assets used by the funds other than buildings financed from capital projects, and overhead, are charged to the departments served. These departments reimburse the internal service fund by recording expenditures against their budgeted appropriations. The operating objective of the fund is to recover costs incurred to provide the service, including depreciation. Accordingly, the operations of the fund should not result in any significant profit or loss. Whenever it uses the services of another fund, such as an enterprise fund, the fund pays for and records the costs just as if it had dealt with an outside organization.

Since exact overhead charges are usually not known when bills are prepared, the departments being served are usually billed for direct costs plus a uniform rate for their portion of estimated overhead. Any difference in actual overhead expenses may be charged or credited to the departments at fiscal year-end or adjusted for in a subsequent year. At the end of each fiscal year, net income or loss must be determined. The excess of net billings to the department over costs is closed to the net assets account.

(iii) Fiduciary Funds. The purpose of fiduciary (trust and agency) funds is to account for assets held by a governmental unit in a trustee capacity or as an agent for other individuals, private organizations or other governmental units.

Usually in existence for an extended period of time, trust funds deal with substantial vested interests and involve complex administrative problems. The government's records must provide adequate information to permit compliance with the terms of the trust as defined in the trust document, statutes, ordinances, or governing regulations.

Pension (and Other Employee Benefit) Trust Funds. In the pension (and other employee benefit) trust funds, governments account for resources held for the future retirement and other postemployment benefits (defined benefit and defined contribution) benefit(s) of their employees. The resources of these funds are the members' contributions, contributions from the government employer, and earnings on investments in authorized investments. The expenses are the authorized retirement allowances and other benefits, refunds of contributions to members who resign prior to retirement, and administrative expenses. Professional actuaries make periodic actuarial studies of the retirement systems and compute the amounts that should be provided so that the benefits can be paid as required.

The proper accounting for pension trust funds has been on the GASB's agenda since its creation. The current GASB guidance in effect on pensions and other postemployment employee benefits (OPEB) include: Statement No. 25, *Financial Reporting for Defined Benefit Pension Plans and Note Disclosures for Defined Contribution Plans;* Statement No. 27, *Accounting for Pensions by State and Local Government Employers;* Statement No. 43, *Financial Reporting for Postemployment Benefit Plans Other Than Pension Plans;* Statement No. 45, *Accounting and Financial Reporting by Employers for Postemployment Benefits Other Than Pensions;* and Statement No. 50, *Pension Disclosures—an Amendment of GASB Statements No. 25 and No. 27.* Statements No. 25 and 43 address issues related to accounting by pension and other employee benefit plans and pension and other employee benefit trust funds. Statements No. 27 and 45 addresses accounting and financial reporting for those employers that participate in pension and other employee benefit plans.

Statements No. 25 and 43 describe two basic financial statements for pension (and other employee benefit) plans: the statement of plan net assets and the statement of changes in plan net assets. These two financial statements are designed to provide current information about plan assets and financial activities. Statements No. 25 (as amended by No. 50) and 43 have other requirements for note disclosure that include a brief plan description, a summary of significant accounting principles, and information about contributions, legally required reserves, investment concentrations, funded status of the plan as of the most recent actuarial valuation date, and the actuarial methods and significant assumptions used in the most recent actuarial valuation.

Statements No. 27 and 45 are directed at employers that participate in pension (and other employee benefit) plans and reflect two underlying principles: (1) the pension or OPEB cost recognized should be related to the annual required contribution (ARC) as determined by an actuary for funding purposes; and (2) the actuarial methods and assumptions used by employers should be consistent with those used by the plan in its separate reporting.

In implementing these basic principles, Statements No. 27 and 45 require the ARC to be recognized as pension or OPEB expense in government-wide financial statements and the proprietary funds. Governmental funds will recognize pension expenditure to the extent that the ARC is expected to be liquidated with expendable available resources. If an employer does not contribute the ARC (or has contributed in excess of the ARC), pension or OPEB expense no longer equals the ARC. In these cases, the ARC is adjusted to remove the effects of the actuarial adjustments included in the ARC and to reflect interest on previous under or over funding.

Although Statements No. 27 and 45 try to minimize the differences between accounting for pensions (and other employee benefits) and funding pensions (and other employee benefits), they do place certain limits, or "parameters," on the actuary's modified calculation of the ARC. These parameters are consistent with those established for accounting for the plan itself in Statements No. 25 and 43. These parameters relate to the pension/OPEB obligation, actuarial assumptions, economic assumptions, actuarial cost method, actuarial valuation of assets, and amortization of unfunded actuarial accrued liability.

Statements No. 27 and 45 establish disclosure requirements that vary depending on whether the government merely participates in a pension (and other employee benefits) plan administered by another entity or includes a pension (and other employee benefits) trust fund(s). Disclosure requirements also vary for governments with a pension (and other employee benefits) trust fund based on whether the pension (and other employee benefits) plan issues separate publicly available financial statements. These disclosure requirements generally include a plan description, funding policy, pension or OPEB cost components, actuarial valuation information, and trend data.

Resources accumulated for OPEB should be accounted for in a separate trust fund from resources accumulated for pension benefits.

Since the effective dates of Statements Nos. 25 and 27, there has been significant debate over the theoretical foundations of pension accounting in the public sector. As a result, GASB decided in 2006 that it would perform a comprehensive review of financial reporting by and for pension and postemployment benefit plans in the United States. The project began in earnest in 2008 with a review of existing standards. In June 2011, GASB issued two controversial Exposure Drafts that could fundamentally alter pension accounting rules for state and local governments. The two documents, *Accounting and Financial Reporting for Pensions* and *Financial Reporting for Pension Plans,* would propose significant amendments to the existing pension standards to improve how the costs and obligations associated with the pension benefits that governments provide to their employees are calculated and reported. The Pension Exposure Draft, *Accounting and Financial Reporting for Pensions,* primarily relates to reporting by governments that provide pensions to their employees. A Pension Plan Exposure Draft, *Financial Reporting for Pension Plans,* addresses the reporting by the pension plans that administer those benefits.

The Pension Exposure Draft proposes that governments be required to report in their statement of financial position a net pension liability, which is the difference between the total pension liability and assets (primarily investments reported at fair value) set aside in a qualified trust to pay benefits to current employees, retirees, and their beneficiaries. It also proposes significant changes to how a government would calculate its total pension liability and pension expense. These changes include:

- Immediate recognition of more components of pension expense than is currently required, including the effect on the pension liability of changes in benefit terms, rather than deferral and amortization over as many as 30 years, which is common for funding purposes.

- Use of a discount rate that applies (a) the expected long-term rate of return on pension plan investments for which plan assets are expected to be available to make projected benefit payments, and (b) the interest rate on a tax-exempt 30-year AA-or-higher rated municipal bond index to projected benefit payments for which plan assets are not expected to be available for long-term investment in a qualified trust.
- A single actuarial cost allocation method—"entry age normal"—rather than the current choice among six actuarial cost methods.
- Requiring governments participating in cost-sharing multiple employer pension plans to record a liability equal to their proportionate share of any net pension liability for the cost-sharing plan as a whole.
- Requiring governments in all types of covered pension plans to present more extensive note disclosures and required supplementary information.

The Pension Exposure Draft addresses situations in which another entity contributes to a government's pension plan on behalf of the employer and it also addresses accounting and financial reporting for employers that provide pensions through defined contribution plans.

The Pension Plan Exposure Draft, which addresses financial reporting for plans that are administered through qualified trusts, outlines the basic framework for the separately issued financial reports of defined benefit pension plans. It also details proposed note disclosure requirements for defined contribution pension plans.

GASB expects to release final pension rules in June 2012.

Federal regulators including the U.S. Securities and Exchange Commission (SEC) have recently increased scrutiny of state and local government pension reporting. For example, in August 2010, the SEC for the first time charged a state, the State of New Jersey, with violating federal securities laws. The SEC alleged that the State of New Jersey was negligent in preparing disclosure documents with respect to its municipal bonds, resulting in material misrepresentations and omissions regarding the funding and financial condition of its two largest defined benefit pension plans. New Jersey agreed to settle the SEC case without admitting or denying the agency's findings. In another example, in October 2010, public officials paid fines that were part of an SEC securities fraud suit settlement against certain City of San Diego officials over their roles in the preparation of pension fund disclosures. The suit alleged that the officials knew the city had significant unfunded pension plan and retiree health care benefits liabilities, and that the city was deliberately underfunding its annual pension plan payments so that it could increase employee benefits while deferring costs. The individuals did not admit or deny the SEC allegations but agreed to pay fines.

Lawmakers are also concerned about public sector pensions. Legislation introduced in the U.S. House of Representatives in December 2010 and a companion measure introduced by the U.S. Senate in April 2011 would require state and local governments with public sector pension plans to file annual reports, including funded status information, with the secretary of the U.S. Treasury Department. Failure to file would bar a government from issuing new tax-exempt, tax credit, or direct-pay bonds until it filed its report.

Investment Trust Funds. Investment trust funds should be used by the sponsoring government to report the external part of investment pools, as required by GASB Statement No. 31, paragraph 18.

Private-Purpose Trust Funds. Private-purpose trust funds, such as one used to report escheat property, should be used to report all other trust arrangements under which principal and income benefit individuals, private organizations, or other governments.

Agency Funds. Used by governments to handle cash resources held in an agent capacity, agency funds require relatively simple administration. The typical agency funds used by state and local governments include: (1) tax collection funds, under which one local government collects a tax for an overlapping governmental unit and remits the amount collected less administrative charges to the recipient; and (2) payroll withholdings, under which the government collects the deductions and periodically remits them in a lump sum to the appropriate recipient.

(h) CAPITAL ASSETS REPORTING AND ACCOUNTING. The term *capital assets* includes land, improvements to land, easements, certain rights, buildings, building improvements, vehicles, machinery, equipment, works of art and historical treasures, infrastructure, and all other tangible or intangible assets used in operations and that have initial useful lives beyond a single reporting period. Infrastructure assets are capital assets that are normally stationary and normally can be preserved for a significantly greater number of years than most other capital assets (e.g., roads, bridges, tunnels, drainage systems, water and sewer systems, dams, and lighting systems). Buildings that are not ancillary parts of networks of infrastructure assets are not infrastructure assets.

Purchased capital assets should be reported at their acquisition costs, which should include ancillary charges needed to place the assets in their intended locations and conditions for use. Ancillary charges include costs directly attributable to asset acquisition, such as freight and transportation charges, site preparation costs, and professional fees. Donated capital assets should be reported at their fair values at their times of acquisition plus ancillary charges.

In general, capital assets should be depreciated. They should be reported net of accumulated depreciation in the statement of net assets, with accumulated depreciation reported on the face of the statement or in the notes. Capital assets not depreciated, such as land, intangible assets with indefinite useful lives, and infrastructure assets reported using the modified approach (discussed after the next paragraph) should be reported separately if significant.

Capital assets may also be reported in greater detail, such as infrastructure, buildings and improvements, vehicles, machinery, and equipment. Capital assets should be depreciated over their useful lives based on their net costs less salvage values in a systematic and rational manner unless they are either inexhaustible, such as land and land improvements, or are infrastructure reported using the modified approach. Depreciation, reported in the statement of activities, may be calculated for:

1. A class of assets
2. A network of assets (all the assets that provide a particular kind of service for a government; a network of infrastructure assets may be only one infrastructure asset composed of many components, e.g., a dam composed of a concrete dam, a concrete spillway, and a series of locks)
3. A subsystem of a network (all assets that make up a similar portion or segment of a network of assets, e.g., interstate highways, state highways, and rural roads could each be a subsystem of a network of all the roads of a government)
4. Individual assets

Eligible infrastructure assets—infrastructure assets that are part of a network or subsystem of a network—need not be depreciated but treated by a modified approach if both of the next points are met:

1. The government manages them using an asset management system that has these characteristics:
    - Has an up-to-date inventory of eligible infrastructure assets.
    - Performs condition assessments of the eligible infrastructure assets and summarizes the results using a measurement scale. The assessments must be documented so they can be replicated—based on sufficiently understandable and complete measurement methods so that different measurers using the same methods would reach substantially similar results—performed by the government or by contract.
    - Estimates each year the annual cost to maintain and preserve the eligible infrastructure assets at the condition level established and disclosed by the government.
2. The government documents that the eligible infrastructure assets are being preserved approximately at or above a condition level established and documented by administrative or

executive policy or by legislative action and documented by the government. Adequate documentation requires professional judgment and may vary within governments for different eligible infrastructure assets. Nevertheless, documentation should include:

- Complete condition assessments of eligible infrastructure assets performed consistently at least every three years. Statistical sampling may be used, and eligible infrastructure assets may be assessed on a cyclical basis. A complete assessment on a cyclical basis requires all or statistical samples of all eligible infrastructure assets in the network or subsystem to be assessed.
- The three most recent complete condition assessments provide reasonable assurance that the eligible infrastructure assets are being preserved approximately at or above the condition level established and disclosed by the government. The condition level could be measured either by a condition index or as the percentage of a network of infrastructure assets in good or poor condition.

All expenditures other than for additions and improvements made for eligible infrastructure assets that meet the two requirements and are not depreciated should be reported as expense in the periods incurred. Additions and improvements increase the capacity or efficiency of infrastructure assets; expenditures for them should be capitalized. A change from depreciation to the modified approach should be reported as a change in an accounting estimate.

When and if the requirements to report capital assets by the modified approach are no longer met, they should be depreciated in subsequent periods. The change should be reported as a change in an accounting estimate.

Governments should in general capitalize individual or collections of works of art, historical treasures, and similar assets at their acquisition costs or fair values at the dates of acquisition or donation (estimated if necessary). They are encouraged but not required to capitalize a collection and all additions to the collection, whether donated or purchased, that meets all three of these conditions (but collections capitalized by June 30, 1999, should remain capitalized and additions to them should be capitalized regardless of whether they meet the conditions):

1. The collection is held for public exhibition, education, or research for public service, not financial gain.
2. The collection is protected, kept unencumbered, cared for, and preserved.
3. The collection is subject to an organizational policy that requires that the proceeds from sales of collection items are used to acquire other items for collections.

Governments that receive donations of works of art, historical treasures, and similar assets should report revenues in conformity with GASB Statement No. 33. Governments should report program expense equal to the revenue reported on donated assets added to noncapitalized collections.

Capitalized collections or individual items of works of art, historical treasures, and similar assets that are exhaustible, such as exhibits whose useful lives decreased because of display or educational or research use, should be depreciated over their estimated useful lives. Depreciation is not required for collections or individual items of works of art, historical treasures, and similar assets that are inexhaustible.

(i) Methods for Calculating Depreciation. Governments may use any established depreciation method. It may be based on the estimated useful life of a class of assets, a network of assets, a subsystem, a network, or individual assets. Estimated useful lives may be obtained from general guidelines obtained from professional or industry organizations, information for comparable assets of other governments, or internal information.

A government may use a composite method, applying one rate to calculate depreciation, for example, for similar assets or dissimilar assets of the same class, such as all the roads and bridges of the government. Depreciation is determined as the product of the total cost times the rate. The rate can be determined based on a weighted average or an unweighted average estimate of the useful lives of the assets included. Or it may be based on condition assessment or experience with the useful lives of the group of assets. It is generally used throughout the life of the group of assets, but it should be recalculated if the composition of the assets or the estimate of average useful lives changes significantly.

(ii) Subsidiary Property Records. The maintenance of subsidiary property records aids in the control of fixed assets. The subsidiary records should contain such information as classification code, date of acquisition, name and address of vendor, unit charged with custody, location, cost, fund and account from which purchased, method of acquisition, estimated life, and repair and maintenance data.

(iii) Disposal or Retirement of Capital Assets. In the disposal or retirement of a capital asset, the book value of the asset must be removed from the asset side and the gain or loss must be recorded in the statement of activities or the proprietary fund statements. In governmental fund statements, if the asset is sold, the amount obtained in cash or by evidence of indebtedness should be recorded as another financing source in the appropriate governmental fund.

(iv) Impairment of Capital Assets. Governments should evaluate prominent events or changes in circumstances affecting capital assets to determine whether impairment of a capital asset has occurred. Indicators of impairment include physical damage, enactment or approval of laws or regulations or other changes in environmental factors, technological changes or evidence of obsolescence, changes in the manner or duration of use of a capital asset, and construction stoppage. A capital asset generally should be considered impaired if there is both (1) the decline in service utility of the capital asset is large in magnitude and (2) the event or change in circumstance is outside the normal life cycle of the capital asset.

(i) REPORTING AND ACCOUNTING FOR LONG-TERM LIABILITIES. General long-term liabilities need to be clearly distinguished from fund long-term liabilities. General long-term liabilities are the unmatured principal of bonds, warrants, notes, or other forms of long-term general obligation indebtedness. They may arise from debt issuances, lease–purchase agreements, and other commitments that are not liabilities properly reported in governmental funds. Other general long-term liabilities include capital leases, operating judgments, pensions and other postemployment benefits, special termination benefits, pollution remediation obligations, and landfill closure and postclosure care liabilities that are not due.

General long-term liabilities should be reported in the governmental activities column in the government-wide statement of net assets, not in governmental funds.

Typically, the general long-term debt of a state and local government is secured by the general credit and revenue-raising powers of the government rather than by the assets acquired for specific fund resources. Furthermore, just as general capital assets do not represent financial resources available for appropriation and expenditure, general long-term liabilities does not require current appropriation and expenditure of a governmental fund's current financial resources. Thus, to include it as a governmental fund liability would be misleading for management control and accountability functions for the current period.

(j) MEASUREMENT FOCUS AND BASIS OF ACCOUNTING. The accounting and financial reporting treatment applied to the government-wide financial statements and the fund financial statements is determined by its measurement focus. The *measurement focus* refers to what is being expressed in reporting an entity's financial performance and position. A particular measurement focus is accomplished by considering not only which resources are measured but also when the effects of transactions or events involving those resources are recognized (the basis of accounting). This principle describes the measurement focus and basis of accounting used by governments.

(i) Measurement Focus. The government-wide and proprietary funds financial statements should be prepared using the economic resources measurement focus and the accrual basis of accounting. Assets, liabilities, revenues, expenses, and gains and losses that result from exchange transactions and exchange-like transactions should be reported when the transactions occur. (In an exchange-like transaction, the resources or services exchanged, though related, may not be quite equal or the direct benefits may not be exclusively for the parties to the transactions. Nevertheless, the transactions are similar enough to exchanges to justify treating them as exchanges.) Assets, liabilities, revenues, expenses, and gains and losses that result from nonexchange transactions should be reported as discussed later in this chapter.

The government funds financial statements should be prepared using the current financial resources measurement focus and modified accrual basis of accounting. The operating statements of governmental funds include all transactions that affect current financial resources.

(ii) Basis of Accounting. The basis of accounting determines when revenues, expenditures, expenses, and transfers—and the related assets and liabilities—are recognized in the accounts and reported in the financial statements. Specifically, it relates to the timing of the measurements made, regardless of the measurement focus. For example, whether depreciation is recognized depends on whether expenses or expenditures are being measured rather than on whether the cash, modified accrual, or accrual basis is used.

Cash Basis. Under the cash basis of accounting, revenues and transfers in are not recorded in the accounts until cash is received, and expenditures or expenses and transfers out are recorded only when cash is disbursed.

The cash basis is encountered frequently, but its use is not generally accepted for any governmental unit. With the cash basis, it is difficult to compare expenditures with services rendered, because the disbursements relating to those services may be made in the fiscal period following that in which the services occurred. Also, statements prepared on a cash basis do not show financial position and results of operations on a basis that is generally accepted.

Accrual Basis. Under the accrual basis of accounting, most transactions are recorded when they occur, regardless of when cash is received or disbursed. Items not measurable until cash is received or disbursed are accounted for at that time.

The accrual basis is considered a superior method of accounting for the economic resources of any organization because it results in accounting measurements that are based on the substance of transactions and events, rather than merely on the receipt or disbursement of cash.

Modified Accrual Basis. As indicated previously, the financial flows of governments, such as taxes and grants, typically do not result from a direct exchange for goods or services and thus cannot be accrued based on the completion of the earnings process and an exchange taking place. Governments have thus devised the susceptible-to-accrual concept as the criterion for determining when inflows are accruable as revenue. A revenue is susceptible to accrual when it is both measurable and available to finance current operations. An amount is measurable when the precise amount is known because the transaction is completed, or when it can be accurately estimated using past experience or other available information. An amount is available to finance operations when it is physically available (i.e., collectable within the current period or soon enough thereafter to be used to pay liabilities of the current period).

On the expenditure side, a government's main concern, for governmental funds at least, is to match the financial resources used with the financial resources obtained. Expenditures are generally recognized when payment is due because that is the time they are normally liquidated with expendable available resources.

This adaptation of the accrual basis to the conditions surrounding governmental activities and financing has been given the term *modified accrual.* Modified accrual is currently used in all governmental fund types (i.e., the general fund, special revenue funds, etc.) where the intent is to determine the extent to which provided services have been financed by current resources through the measurement of near-term inflows and outflows of current financial resources.

In proprietary funds, the objective is to determine net income, and the accounting should be essentially the same as commercial accounting. Hence, proprietary funds use the economic resources measurement focus and the accrual basis without the need for modification just described.

(iii) Revenue Transactions. The modified accrual basis of accounting is applied in practice for four different revenue transactions:

1. Property taxes are recorded as revenue when the taxes are levied, provided that they apply to and are collected in the current period or soon enough thereafter to finance the current period's expenditures. The period after year-end generally should not exceed 60 days. The amount recorded as revenue should be net of estimated uncollectable taxes, abatements, discounts, and refunds. (Property taxes that are measurable but not available—and hence not susceptible to accrual—should be deferred and recognized as revenue in the fiscal year they become available.)
2. Taxpayer-assessed income, gross receipts, and sales taxes should be recorded as revenues when susceptible to accrual.
3. Miscellaneous revenues, such as fines and forfeits, athletic fees, and inspection charges, are generally recognized when cash is received because they are usually not measurable and available until they are received.
4. Grants should be recorded when the government has an irrevocable right to the grant. If expenditure of funds is the prime factor for determining eligibility for the grant funds, revenue should be recognized when the expenditure is made provided it meets the availability criteria. Grant revenue that does not meet the availability criteria should be deferred and recognized when it becomes available to pay liabilities of the current period.

Escheat property, which is assets reverted to a governmental entity in the absence of legal claimants or heirs, should be reported in government-wide and fund financial statements generally as an asset in the governmental or proprietary fund to which the property ultimately escheats. If held for individuals, private organizations, or another government, it should be reported in a private-purpose trust fund or an agency fund, as appropriate (or in the governmental or proprietary fund in which escheat property is otherwise reported, with a corresponding liability).

Escheat revenue on escheat property reported in governmental or proprietary funds should be reduced and a governmental or proprietary fund liability reported to the extent that it is probable that escheat property will be reclaimed and paid to claimants. The liability should represent the best estimate of the amount ultimately expected to be reclaimed and paid, giving consideration to such factors as previous and current trends and anticipated changes in those trends. The liability may differ from the amount specified in law to be held separately for payments to claimants.

(iv) Expenditure Transactions. Expenditure transactions under the modified accrual basis are treated in this way:

- If there is no explicit requirement to do otherwise, a governmental fund liability and expenditure should be accrued in the period in which the government incurs the liability. Expenditure transactions include liabilities that normally are paid in a timely manner and in full from available financial resources, such as salaries, professional services, supplies, utilities, and travel. Unpaid, they represent claims against current financial resources and should be reported as governmental fund liabilities.
- Debt principal payments are recorded when due. Debt issue costs paid from debt proceeds, such as underwriter fees, should be reported as expenditures. Issue costs, such as attorneys' fees, rating agency fees, or bond insurance, paid from existing resources, should be reported as expenditures when liabilities for them are incurred.

- Inventory items may be considered expenditures either when purchased (the purchases method) or when used (the consumption method). Under either method, significant amounts of inventory at the end of a fiscal year should be reported as an asset on the balance sheet.
- Expenditures for insurance and similar services extending over more than one accounting period need not be allocated between or among accounting periods, but they may be accounted for as expenditures of the period of acquisition.
- Compensated absences, claims and judgments, special termination benefits, landfill closure and postclosure care costs, and "other obligations" should be recorded as a governmental fund liability when they are is due for payment in the current period.

(v) Reporting on Nonexchange Transactions. Similar to a nonreciprocal transaction discussed in APB Statement No. 4, in a nonexchange transaction, a government of any level other than the federal government gives or receives financial or capital resources, not including contributed services, without directly receiving or giving equal value in exchange. They are discussed in four classes:

1. *Derived tax revenues.* These revenues result from assessments imposed by governments on exchange transactions, such as personal and corporate income taxes and retail sales taxes. Some legislation enabling such a tax provides purpose restrictions, requirements that a particular source of tax be used for a specific purpose or purposes (e.g., motor fuel taxes required to be used for road and street repairs).
2. *Imposed nonexchange revenues.* These revenues result from assessments on nongovernmental entities, including individuals, other than assessments on exchange transactions, such as property taxes, fines, and penalties, and property forfeitures, such as seizures and escheats. Such taxes are imposed on an act committed or omitted by the payer, such as property ownership or the contravention of a law or a regulation that is not an exchange. Some enabling legislation provides purpose restrictions; some also provide time requirements, specification of the periods in which the resources must be used or when their use may begin.
3. *Government-mandated nonexchange transactions.* These transactions occur when a government, including the federal government, at one level provides resources to a government at another level and provides purpose restrictions on the recipient government established in the provider's enabling legislation. Transactions other than cash or other advances that are contingent on fulfillment of certain requirements, which may include time requirements, are called *eligibility requirements.*
4. *Voluntary nonexchange transactions.* These transactions result from legislative or contractual agreements but are not exchanges (unfunded mandates are excluded, because they are not transactions), entered into willingly by two or more parties, at least one of which is a government, such as certain grants, certain entitlements, and donations by nongovernmental entities including individuals (private donations). Providers often establish purpose restrictions and eligibility requirements and require return of the resources if the purpose restrictions or the eligibility requirements are contravened after reporting of the transaction.

Labels such as "tax," "grant," "contribution," or "donation" do not necessarily indicate which of those classes nonexchange transactions belong to and therefore what principles should be applied. Also, labels such as "fees," "charges," and "grants" do not always indicate whether exchange or nonexchange transactions are involved. Principles for reporting on nonexchange transactions depend on their substance, not merely their labels, and determining that requires analysis.

The next expense (or expenditure, for governmental funds) reporting principles for nonexchange transactions apply to both the accrual and the modified accrual basis, unless the transactions are not measurable or are not probable of collection. Such transactions that are not measurable should be disclosed.

Time requirements affect the timing of reporting of the transactions. The effect on the timing of reporting depends on whether a nonexchange transaction is an imposed nonexchange revenue transaction or a government-mandated or voluntary nonexchange transaction. Purpose restrictions do not affect the timing of reporting of the transactions. However, recipients should report resulting net assets, equity, or fund balance as restricted until the resources are used for the specified purpose or for as long as the provider requires the resources to be maintained intact, such as endowment principal.

Award programs commonly referred to as *reimbursement-type* or *expenditure-driven* grant programs may be either government mandated or voluntary nonexchange transactions. The provider stipulates an eligibility requirement that a recipient can qualify for resources only after incurring allowable costs under the provider's program. The provider has no liability and the recipient has no asset (receivable) until the recipient has met the eligibility requirements. Assets provided in advance should be reported as advances (assets) by providers and as deferred revenues (liabilities) by recipients until eligibility requirements have been met.

Assets should be reported from derived tax revenue transactions in the period in which the exchange transaction on which the tax is imposed occurs or in which the resources are received, whichever occurs first. Revenues net of estimated refunds and estimated uncollectable amounts should be reported in the period the assets are reported, provided that the underlying exchange transaction has occurred. Resources received in advance should be reported as deferred revenues (liabilities) until the period of the exchange.

Assets from imposed nonexchange revenue transactions should be reported in the period in which an enforceable legal claim to the assets arises or in which the assets are received, whichever occurs first. The date on which an enforceable legal claim to taxable property arises is generally specified in the enabling legislation, sometimes referred to as the *lien date,* though a lien is not formally placed on the property on that date. Others refer to it as the *assessment date.* (An enforceable legal claim by some governments arises in the period after the period for which the taxes are levied. Those governments should report assets in the same period they report revenues, as discussed next.)

Revenues from property taxes, net of estimated refunds and estimated uncollectable amounts, should be reported in the period for which the taxes are levied, even if the enforceable legal claim arises or the due date for payment occurs in a different period. All other imposed nonexchange revenues should be reported in the same period as the assets unless the enabling legislation includes time requirements. If it does, revenues should be reported in the period in which the resources are required to be used or in which use is first permitted. Resources received or reported as receivable before then should be reported as deferred revenues.

The kinds of eligibility requirements for government-mandated and voluntary nonexchange transactions are listed next.

- The recipient and secondary recipients, if applicable, have the characteristics specified by the provider. For example, under a certain federal program, recipients are required to be states and secondary recipients are required to be school districts.
- Time requirements specified by enabling legislation or the provider have been met (i.e., the period in which the resources are required to be sold, disbursed, or consumed or in which use is first permitted has begun, or the resources are being maintained intact, as specified by the provider).
- The provider offers resources on an "expenditure-driven" basis, and the recipient has incurred allowable costs under the applicable program.
- The offer of resources by the provider in a voluntary nonexchange transaction is contingent on a specified action of the recipient (e.g., to raise a specific amount of resources from third parties or to dedicate its own resources for a specified purpose), and that action has occurred.

Providers should report liabilities or decreases in assets and expenses from government-mandated or voluntary nonexchange transactions, and recipients should report receivables or decreases in liabilities and revenues, net of estimated uncollectable amounts, when all applicable eligibility requirements have been met. (The need to complete purely routine requirements such as filing of claims for allowable costs under a reimbursement program or the filing of progress reports with the provider should not delay reporting of assets and revenues.) Resources transmitted before the eligibility requirements are met should be reported as advances by the provider and as deferred revenue by recipients, except as indicated next for recipients of certain resources transmitted in advance. The exception does not cover transactions in which, for administrative or practical reasons, a government receives assets in the period immediately before the period the provider specifies as the one in which sale, disbursement, or consumption of resources is required or may begin.

A provider in some kinds of government-mandated and voluntary nonexchange transactions transmits assets stipulating that the resources cannot be sold, disbursed, or consumed until after a specified number of years have passed or a specific event has occurred, if ever. The recipient may nevertheless benefit from the resources in the interim (e.g., by investing or exhibiting them). Examples are permanently nonexpendable additions to endowments and other trusts, term endowments, and contributions of works of art, historical treasures, and similar assets to capitalized collections. The recipient should report revenue when the resources are received if all eligibility requirements have been met. Resulting net assets, equity, or fund balance should be reported as restricted as long as the provider's purpose restrictions or time requirements remain in effect.

If a provider in a government-mandated or voluntary nonexchange transaction does not specify time requirements, the entire award should be reported as a liability and an expense by the provider and as a receivable and revenue net of estimated uncollectable amounts by the recipients in the period in which all applicable eligibility requirements are met (applicable period). If the provider is a government, that period for both the provider and the recipients is the provider's fiscal year and begins on the first day of that year; the entire award should be reported as of that date. But if the provider government has a biennial budgetary process, each year of the biennium should be treated as a separate applicable period. The provider and the recipients should then allocate one-half of the resources appropriated for the biennium to each applicable period, unless the provider specifies a different allocation.

Promises of assets voluntarily made to governments may include permanently nonexpendable additions to endowments and other trusts, term endowments, contributions of works of art and similar assets to capitalized collections, or other kinds of capital or financial assets, with or without purpose restrictions or time requirements. Recipients of such promises should report receivables and revenue net of estimated uncollectable amounts when all eligibility requirements are met if the promise is verifiable and the resources are measurable and probable of collection. If the promise involves a stipulation (time requirement) that the resources cannot be sold, disbursed, or consumed until after a specified number of years have passed or a specific even has occurred, if ever, the recipient does not meet the time requirement until the assets are received.

After a nonexchange transaction has been reported in the financial statements, it may become apparent that (1) if the transaction was reported as a government-mandated or voluntary nonexchange transaction, the eligibility requirements are no longer met, or (2) the recipient will not comply with the purpose restrictions within the specified time limit. If it then is probable that the provider will not provide the resources or will require the return of all or part of the resources already provided, the recipient should report a decrease in assets or an increase in liabilities and an expense, and the provider should report a decrease in liabilities or an increase in assets and a revenue for the amount involved in the period in which the returned resources become available.

A government may collect derived tax revenue or imposed nonexchange revenue on behalf of another government, the recipient that imposed the revenue source (e.g., sales tax collected by a state, part of which is a local option sales tax). The recipient should be able to reasonably estimate the accrual-basis information needed to comply with the above-stated requirements for derived tax revenue or imposed nonexchange revenue. However, if a government shares in a portion of the revenue resulting from a tax imposed by another government, it may not be able to reasonably estimate the accrual-basis information or obtain sufficient timely information from the other government needed to comply with the above-stated requirements for derived tax revenue or imposed nonexchange revenue. If it cannot, the recipient government should report revenue for a period in the amount of cash received during the period. Cash received afterward should also be reported as revenue of the period, less amounts reported as revenue in the previous period, if reliable information is consistently available to identify the amounts that apply to the current period.

Revenue from nonexchange transactions reported on the modified accrual basis should be reported in this way:

- Recipients should report derived tax revenue in the period in which the underlying exchange transaction has occurred and the resources are available.
- Recipients should report property taxes in conformity with NCGA Interpretation No. 3, as amended.
- Recipients should report other imposed nonexchange revenue in the period in which an enforceable legal claim has arisen and the resources are available.
- Recipients should report government-mandated nonexchange transactions and voluntary nonexchange transactions in the period in which all applicable eligibility requirements have been met and the resources are available.

(k) BUDGETING, BUDGETARY CONTROL, AND BUDGETARY REPORTING ACCOUNTING

(i) Types of Operating Budgets. Several types of annual operating budgets are used in contemporary public finance. Among the more common are:

- Line item budget
- Program budget
- Performance budget
- Zero-base budget

Line Item Budgeting. Listing the inputs for resources that each organizational unit requests for each line (or object) of expenditure is referred to as *line item budgeting*. This simple approach produces a budget that governing bodies and administrators can understand, based on their own experience. It provides for tight control over spending and is the most common local government budgeting approach, although this popularity is due primarily to tradition.

Line item budgeting is criticized because it emphasizes inputs rather than outputs, analyzes expenditures inadequately, and fragments activities among accounts that bear little relation to purposes of the government. However, all budgeting systems use objects for the buildup of costs and for execution of the budget.

Overcoming criticisms of a line item budgeting system can be accomplished by:

- Improving the budget structure to encompass all funds and organizational units in a manner that enables the total resources available to a particular organizational unit or responsibility center to be readily perceived
- Developing a level of detail for the object categories that permits adequate analysis of proposed expenditures and effective control over the actual expenditures
- Improving the presentation of historical data to stimulate the analysis of trends
- Providing a partial linking of outputs to the objects of expenditures

Program Budgeting. Formulating expenditure requests on the basis of the services to be performed for the various programs the government provides is known as *program budgeting*. A program budget categorizes the major areas of citizen needs and the services for meeting such needs into programs. Goals and objectives are stated for each program, normally in relatively specific, quantified terms. The costs are estimated for the resources required (e.g., personnel and equipment) to accomplish the objective for each program. The governing body can then conduct a meaningful review of budget requests by adding or deleting programs or placing different emphasis on the various programs.

Program budgeting has existed for many years, but relatively few governments have adopted it, partly because line item budgeting is so familiar and comprehensible. Lack of acceptance also results from the difficulty of developing operationally useful program budgets that meet the governmental notion of accountability (i.e., control of the number of employees and other expense items) rather than achievement of results in applying such resources.

The operational usefulness of program budgeting has also been questioned as a result of the complexity of the program structure, the vagueness of goals and objectives, the lack of organizational or individual responsibility for program funds that span several departments or agencies, and the inadequacy of accounting support to record direct and indirect program costs.

Nevertheless, program budgeting can be an extremely effective approach for a government willing to devote the effort. The steps that departments should take to implement the system are:

- Identify programs and the reasons for their existence.
- Define the goals of programs.
- Define kinds and levels of services to be provided in light of budgetary guidelines (council- or CEO-furnished guidelines [e.g., budget priorities, budget assumptions, and budget constraints]).
- Develop budget requests in terms of resources needed, based on program purposes, the budgetary guidelines, the projected levels of services, and the previous years' expenditure levels for the programs.
- Submit budget requests for compilation, review, and approval.

Performance Budgeting. Formulating expenditure requests based on the work to be performed is the primary function of performance budgeting. It emphasizes the work or service performed, described in quantitative terms, by an organizational unit performing a given activity (e.g., number of tons of waste collected by the Sanitation Department and case workload in the Department of Welfare). These performance data are used in the preparation of the annual budget as the basis for increasing or decreasing the number of personnel and the related operating expenses of the individual departments.

The development of a full-scale performance budget requires a strong budget staff, constructive participation at all levels, special accounting and reporting methods, and a substantial volume of processed statistical data. Primarily for these reasons, performance budgeting has been less widely used than line item budgeting.

The approach to developing a performance budgeting system is:

- Decide on the extent to which functions and activities will be segmented into work units and services for formulation and execution of the budget.
- Define the functions in services performed by the government, and assemble them into a structure.
- Identify and assemble or develop workload and efficiency measures that relate to service categories.
- Estimate the total costs of the functions and services.
- Analyze resource needs for each service in terms of personnel, equipment, and so on.
- Formulate the first-year performance budget. (For the first year, set the budget appropriations and controls at a higher level than the data indicate.)
- Perform cost accounting for the functional budget category; initiate statistical reporting of the workload measures; match resources utilized to actual results.

Zero-Base Budgeting. In the preparation of a budget, zero-base budgeting projects funding for services at several alternative levels, both lower and higher than the present level, and allocates funds to services based on rankings of these alternatives. It is an appropriate budgeting system for jurisdictions whose revenues are not sufficient for citizen demands and inflation-driven expenditure increases, where considerable doubt exists as to the necessity and effectiveness of existing programs and services, and where incremental budgeting processes have resulted in existing programs and their funding being taken as a given, with attention devoted to requests for new programs.

Zero-base budgeting can be used with any existing budgeting system, including line item, program, or performance budgeting. The budget format can remain unchanged.

The steps to implement zero-base budgeting are:

- Define decision units (i.e., activities that can be logically grouped for planning and providing each service).
- Analyze decision units to determine alternative service levels, determine the resources required to operate at alternative levels, and present this information in decision packages.
- Rank the decision packages in a priority order that reflects the perceived importance of a particular package to the community in relation to other packages.
- Present the budget to the governing body for a review of the ranking of the decision packages.

(ii) Budget Preparation. The specific procedures involved in the preparation of a budget for a governmental unit are usually prescribed by state statute, local charter, or ordinance. There are, however, certain basic steps:

- Prepare the budget calendar.
- Develop preliminary forecasts of available revenues, recurring expenditures, and new programs.
- Formulate and promulgate a statement of executive budget policy to the operating departments.
- Prepare and distribute budget instructions, budget forms, and related information.
- Review departmental budget requests and supporting work sheets.
- Interview department heads for the purpose of adjusting or approving their requests in a tentative budget.
- Assemble the final tentative budget, including fixing of revenue estimates and the required tax levy.
- Present the tentative budget to the legislative body and the public.
- Conduct a public hearing, with advance legal notice.
- Legislative body adopts final budget.

Revenue and Expenditure Estimates. The property tax has been the traditional basic source of revenue for local government. The amount to be budgeted and raised is determined by subtracting the estimated nonproperty taxes and other revenues, plus the reappropriated fund balance, from budgeted expenditures. This amount, divided by the assessed valuation of taxable property within the boundaries of the governmental unit, produces the required tax rate.

Many jurisdictions have legal ceilings on the property tax rates available for general operating purposes. Additionally, taxpayer initiatives have forced governments to seek new revenue sources. Accordingly, governmental units have turned increasingly to other types of revenue, such as sales taxes; business and nonbusiness license fees; charges for services; state-collected, locally shared taxes; and grants-in-aid from the federal and state governments. Department heads, however, ordinarily have little knowledge of revenue figures. As a result, the primary responsibility for estimating these revenues usually lies with the budget officer and the chief finance officer.

Most governmental units, as a safeguard against excessive accumulation of resources, require that any unappropriated amounts carried over from a previous year be included as a source of financing in the budget of that fund for the succeeding fiscal year. Most controlling laws or ordinances provide for inclusion of the estimated surplus (fund balance) at the end of the current year, although many require that the includable surplus be the balance at the close of the last completed fiscal year.

Departmental estimates of expenditures and supporting work programs or performance data generally are prepared by the individual departments, using forms provided by the central budget agency. Expenditures are customarily classified to conform to the standard account classification of the governmental unit and thus permit comparison with actual performance in the current and prior periods.

Generally, personal services are supported by detailed schedules of proposed salaries for individual full-time employees. Nonsalaried and temporary employees are usually paid on an hourly basis, and the budget requests are normally based on the estimated number of hours of work.

Estimates of materials and supplies and other services, ordinarily quite repetitive in nature, are most often based on current experience, plus an allowance, if justified, for rising costs. Capital outlay requests are based on demonstrated need for specific items of furniture or equipment by individual departments.

In recent years, governmental units, particularly at the county, state, and federal levels, have disbursed substantial sums annually that are unlike the usual current operating expenditures. These sums include welfare or public assistance payments, contributions to other governmental units, benefit payments, and special grants. They are often classified as "other charges." Estimates of these charges are generally based on unit costs for assistance, legislative allotments, requests from outside agencies or governmental units, and specified calculations.

In addition to departmental expenditures, the budget officer must estimate certain nondepartmental or general governmental costs not allocated to any department or organizational unit. Examples include pension costs and retirement contributions, which are not normally allocated, election costs, insurance and surety bonds, and interest on debt.

Although most governments still operate under laws that require the budget to be balanced precisely, an increasing number permit a surplus or contingency provision in the expenditure section of the budget. This is usually included to provide a reserve to cover unforeseen expenditures during the budget year.

The expenditure budget may be approved by a board, commission, or other governing body before presentation to the central budget-making authority.

Presentation of the Budget. To present a comprehensive picture of the proposed fund operations for a budget year, a budget document is prepared that is likely to include a budget message, summary schedules and comparative statements, detailed revenue estimates, detailed expenditure estimates, and drafts of ordinances to be enacted by the legislative body.

The contents of a budget message should set forth concisely the salient features of the proposed budget of each fund and will generally include: (1) a total amount showing amounts of overall increase and decrease; (2) detailed amounts and explanations of the increases and decreases; and (3) a detailed statement of the current financial status of each fund for which a budget is submitted, together with recommendations for raising the funds needed to balance the budget of each fund. It should identify the relationship of the operating budget to the capital program and capital budget, which are submitted separately.

Adoption of the Budget. Most states adopt the budget by the enactment of one or more statutes. Many cities require the formality of an ordinance for the adoption of the budget. In other cases, the budget is adopted by resolution of the governing body.

Appropriations. Because appropriations constitute maximum expenditure authorizations during the fiscal year, they cannot be exceeded legally unless subsequently amended by the legislative body (although some governments permit modifications up to a prescribed limit to be made by the executive branch). Unexpended or unencumbered appropriations may lapse at the end of a fiscal year or may continue as authority for subsequent period expenditures, depending on the applicable legal provisions.

It may be necessary for the legislative agency to adopt a separate appropriation resolution or ordinance, or the adoption of the budget may include the making of appropriations for the items of expenditure included therein. Provision for the required general property tax levy is usually made at this time, either by certifying the required tax rates to the governmental unit that will bill and collect the general property tax or by enacting a tax levy ordinance or resolution.

(iii) Budget Execution. The budget execution phase entails obtaining the revenues, operating the program, and expending the money as authorized. The accounts are usually structured on the same basis on which the budget was prepared. Many governments maintain budgetary control by integration of the budgetary accounts into the general and subsidiary ledgers. The entry is:

Estimated revenues	$XXX	
Appropriations		$XXX

If estimated revenues exceed appropriations, a credit for the excess is made to "budgetary fund balance"; if they are less the appropriations, the difference is debited to "budgetary fund balance."

Individual sources of revenues are recognized in subsidiary revenue accounts. A typical revenue ledger report is illustrated in Exhibit 33.3. This format provides for the comparison, at any date, of actual and estimated revenues from each source.

To control expenditures effectively, the individual amounts making up the total appropriations are recorded in subsidiary expenditures accounts, generally called *appropriation ledgers.* Exhibit 33.4 presents an example of an appropriation ledger. It should be noted that this format provides for recording the budget appropriation and for applying expenditures and encumbrances relating to the particular classification against the amount appropriated at any date.

When the managerial control purposes of integrating the budgetary accounts into the general ledger have been served, the budgetary account balances are reversed in the process of closing the books at year-end. Budgetary accounting procedures thus have no effect on the financial position or changes in financial position of a governmental entity.

Encumbrances. An encumbrance, which is unique to governmental accounting, is the reservation of a portion of an applicable appropriation that is made because a contract has been signed or a purchase order issued. The encumbrance is usually recorded in the accounting system to prevent overspending the appropriation. When the goods or services are received, the expenditure is recorded and the encumbrance is reversed. The entry to record an encumbrance is:

Encumbrances	$XXX	
Reserve for encumbrances		$XXX

The entries that are made when the goods or services are received are:

Reserve for encumbrances	$XXX	
Encumbrances		$XXX
Expenditures	$XXX	
Vouchers payable		$XXX

Many governments report encumbrances that are not liquidated at year-end in the same way as expenditures because the encumbrances are another use of budgetary appropriations. The total amount of encumbrances not liquidated by year-end should be classified in the fund balance category to which the encumbrance relates, such as restricted, committed, or assigned for the subsequent year's expenditures, based on the encumbered appropriation authority carried over.

Allotments. Another way to maintain budgetary control is to use an allotment system. With an allotment system, the annual budget appropriation is divided and allotted among the months or quarters in the fiscal year. A department is not permitted to spend more than its allotment during the period.

NAME OF GOVERNMENTAL UNIT
Budget versus Actual Revenue
by Revenue Source
for Accounting Period June 30, 20XX

Fund Type: The General Fund

Revenues		Budgeted	Actual	Variance
015	Real & per. revenue recognized			
0110	Real & p. prop rev recognized	$459,449,213	$460,004,317	$(555,104)
Revenue class total		459,449,213	460,004,317	(555,104)
020	Motor vehicle & other excise			
0121	M/V taxes—current year	16,000,000	22,727,905	(6,727,905)
0122	M/V taxes—prior 2010	0	2,886,605	(2,886,605)
0123	M/V taxes—2009	0	32,051	(32,051)
0124	M/V taxes—2008	0	45,378	(45,378)
0125	M/V taxes—2007	0	85,393	(85,393)
0126	M/V taxes—2006 and prior	0	2	(2)
0127	Boat excise—current year	15,000	40,414	(25,414)
0128	Boat excise—2010	0	155	(155)
0131	M.V. lessor surcharge	200	60	139
Revenue class total		16,015,200	25,817,963	(9,802,764)
025	Local excise taxes			
0129	Hotel/motel room excise	13,500,000	13,580,142	(80,142)
0130	Aircraft fuel excise	12,400,000	12,960,966	(560,966)
Revenue class total		25,900,000	26,541,108	(641,108)
030	Departmental & other revenue			
0133	Penalties & int—prop. Taxes	1,000,000	1,746,007	(746,007)
0134	Penalties & int.—M/V taxes	525,000	620,124	(95,124)
0135	Penalties & int.—sidewalk	0	115	(115)
0136	Penalties & interest/tax title	5,000,000	3,835,517	1,164,483
0138	Penalties & int./boat excise	0	3	(3)
3101	Data processing services	100	6,849	(6,749)
3103	Purchasing services	50,000	69,038	(19,038)
3104	Recording of legal instruments	150	291	(141)
3105	Registry division—fees	750,000	761,238	(11,238)
3107	City record/sale of publication	10,000	25,353	(15,353)
3108	Assessing fees	1,600	914	686
3109	Liens	400,000	373,410	26,590
3120	City clerk—fees	250,000	231,970	18,030
3130	Election—fees	12,000	10,633	1,367
3140	City council/sale of publication	200	310	(110)
3199	Other general services	35,000	18,691	16,309
3202	Police services	350,000	365,102	(15,102)
3211	Fire services	1,150,000	1,582,355	(432,355)
3221	Civil defense	40,000	161,835	(121,835)
3301	Parking facilities	3,350,000	3,775,810	(425,810)
Revenue class total		$ 12,924,050	$ 13,585,565	$ (661,515)

Exhibit 33.3 Typical Revenue Ledger Report

NAME OF GOVERNMENTAL UNIT
Budget versus Actual Expenditures
and Encumbrances by Activity
for Accounting Period June 30, 20XX

Fund Type: The General Fund

	Expenditures	Budgeted	Actual [1]	Variance
1100 Human services				
011-384-0384	Rent equity board	$ 1,330,977	$ 1,274,531	$ 56,446
011-387-0387	Elderly commission	2,534,005	2,289,549	244,456
011-398-0398	Physically handicapped comm.	180,283	159,768	20,515
011-503-0503	Arts & humanities office	211,916	207,219	4,697
011-740-0741	Vet serv—veterans serv div	2,871,616	2,506,363	365,253
011-740-0742	Vet serv—veterans graves reg	158,270	146,392	11,878
011-150-1505	Jobs & community services	370,053	369,208	845
Activity total		7,657,120	6,953,030	704,090
1200 Public safety				
011-211-0211	Police department	116,850,000	117,145,704	(295,704)
011-221-0221	Fire department	80,594,068	79,587,423	1,006,645
011-222-0222	Arson commission	189,244	175,670	13,574
011-251-0251	Transportation—traffic div	13,755,915	13,707,890	48,025
011-252-0252	Licensing board	542,007	449,825	92,182
011-251-0253	Transportation—parking clerk	7,520,539	7,474,462	46,077
011-261-0260	Inspectional services dept	10,004,470	10,003,569	901
Activity total		229,456,243	228,544,543	911,700
1300 Public works				
011-311-0311	Public works department	64,900,000	60,281,837	4,618,163
011-331-0331	Snow removal	2,250,000	2,360,326	(110,326)
Activity total		67,150,000	62,642,163	4,507,837
1400 Property & development				
011-180-0180	RPD—general administration div	432,740	416,569	16,171
014-180-0183	Real property dept county	1,027,660	354,328	673,332
011-180-0184	RPD—buildings division	6,010,155	6,038,464	(28,309)
011-180-0185	RPD—property division	1,847,650	1,806,427	41,223
011-188-0186	PFD—code enforcement division	504,013	458,984	45,029
011-188-0187	PFD—administration division	4,677,365	4,697,167	(19,802)
011-188-0188	PFD—construction & repair div	3,063,637	2,808,266	255,371
Activity total		$ 17,563,220	$ 16,580,205	$ 983,015

[1]This example actual is presented as a non-GAAP budgetary basis that includes both expenditures plus encumbrances as a budgetary use of resources.

Exhibit 33.4 Typical Appropriation Ledger Report

Interim Reports. The last element in the budget execution process is interim financial reports. These are prepared to provide department heads, senior management, and the governing body with the information needed to monitor and control operations, demonstrate compliance with legal and budgetary limitations, anticipate changes in financial resources and requirements due to events or developments that are unknown or could not be foreseen at the time the budget was initially developed, or take appropriate corrective action. Interim reports should be prepared frequently enough to permit early detection of variances between actual and planned operations, but not so frequently as to adversely affect practicality and economy. For most governmental units, interim reports on a monthly basis are necessary for optimum results. With smaller units, a bimonthly or quarterly basis may be sufficient. With sophisticated data-processing equipment, it may be possible to automatically generate the appropriate information daily.

Governmental units should prepare interim financial reports covering:

- Revenues
- Expenditures
- Cash projections
- Proprietary funds
- Capital projects
- Grant programs

The form and content of these reports should reflect the government's particular circumstances and conditions.

Project Budgets. When debt is issued to finance an entire capital project, it is usually done so at the beginning of the project in an amount equal to the total estimated project cost. Accordingly, a portion of the proceeds may remain unexpended over a considerable period of time. To the maximum extent possible, these excess proceeds should be invested in interest-bearing investments. However, consideration should be given to the federal arbitrage regulations that limit the amount of interest that can be earned from investing the proceeds of a tax-exempt bond issue. If certain limits are exceeded, the bond's tax-exempt status may be lost or severe penalties could be imposed on the issuer.

Project budgets typically are established for capital projects to control costs and to guard against cost overruns. All expenditures needed to place the project in readiness (i.e., indirect as well as direct costs) should be recorded against this budget. The actual expenditures, however, will probably be either less or greater than the amounts authorized. Therefore, in the absence of any legal restrictions, any unspent balance should be transferred to the appropriate sources. If the project was financed only from bond proceeds, the transfer should be to the debt service fund from which the bond issue is to be repaid. If the resources were drawn from more than one source, such as bond proceeds and current revenues, the transfer should be split among the sources in proportion to their contributions. If the expenditures were greater than authorized and a deficit exists, sufficient funds must be transferred to liquidate any commitments.

As construction of the project is completed, the costs should be recorded in the capital account as construction in progress and then transferred to the final building account when construction is completed.

(iv) Proprietary Fund Budgeting. The nature of most operations financed and accounted for through proprietary funds is such that the demand for the goods or services largely determines the appropriate level of revenues and expenses. Increased demand causes a higher level of expenses to be incurred but also results in a higher level of revenues. Thus, as in commercial accounting, flexible budgets prepared for several levels of possible activity typically are better for planning, control, and evaluation purposes than are fixed budgets.

Accordingly, budgets are not typically adopted for proprietary funds. Furthermore, even when flexible budgets are adopted, they are viewed not as appropriations but as approved plans. The budgetary accounts are generally not integrated into the ledger accounts because doing so is considered unnecessary. Budgetary control and evaluation are achieved by comparing interim actual revenues and expenses with planned revenues and expenses at the actual level of activity for the period.

In some instances, fixed dollar budgets are adopted for proprietary funds either to meet local legal requirements or to control certain expenditures (e.g., capital outlay). In such cases, it may be appropriate to integrate budgetary accounts into the proprietary fund accounting system in a manner similar to that discussed for governmental funds.

(v) Capital Budget. Many governments also prepare a capital budget. A capital budget is a plan for capital expenditures to be incurred during a single budget year from funds subject to appropriation for projects scheduled under the capital program. The annual capital budget is adopted concurrently with the operating budgets of the governmental unit, subject to a public hearing and the other usual legal procedures.

The capital budget should not be confused with a capital program or capital project budget. A capital program is a plan for capital expenditures to be incurred over a period of years, usually five or more. The capital project budget represents the estimated amount to be expended on a specific project over the entire period of its construction. The capital budget authorizes the amounts to be expended on all projects during a single year. Controlling this amount is important for the proper use of available funds.

(vi) Budgetary Comparison Information. Under GASB Statement No. 34, the general fund's and the major special revenue funds' budgetary comparison schedules should present: (1) the original appropriated budgets; (2) the final appropriated budgets; and (3) actual inflows, outflows, and balances, stated on the governmental budgetary basis as discussed in NCGA Statement No. 1, paragraph 154. Separate columns may be provided comparing the original budget amounts with the actual amounts, the final budget amounts with the actual amounts, or both. The original budget is the first complete appropriated budget, which may be adjusted by reserves, transfers, allocations, supplementary appropriations, and other legally authorized legislative and executive changes made before the beginning of the reporting year. It also includes appropriation amounts automatically carried over from prior years by law. The final budget is the original budget adjusted by all legally authorized legislative and executive changes whenever signed into law or otherwise legally authorized. Governments may elect to report the budget comparison information in a budgetary comparison statement as part of the financial statements or as required supplementary disclosure (see Exhibit 33.5).

(l) CLASSIFICATION AND TERMINOLOGY. A common terminology and classification should be used consistently throughout the budget, the accounts, and the financial reports of each fund.

(i) Classification of Government Fund Revenues. Governmental fund revenues should be classified by fund and source. The major revenue source classifications are taxes, licenses and permits, intergovernmental revenues, charges for services, fines and forfeits, and miscellaneous. Governmental units often classify revenues by organizational units. This classification may be desirable for purposes of management control and accountability as well as for auditing purposes, but it should supplement rather than supplant the classifications by fund and source.

(ii) Classification of Government Fund Expenditures. There are many ways to classify governmental fund expenditures in addition to the basic fund classification. Function, program, organizational unit, activity, character, and principal class of object are examples. Typically, expenditures are classified by character (current, intergovernmental, capital outlay, and/or debt service). Current expenditures are further classified by function and/or program.

- *Character classification.* Reporting expenditures according to the physical period they are presumed to benefit. The major character classifications are: (1) current expenditures, which benefit the current fiscal period; (2) capital outlays, which are presumed to benefit both the present and future fiscal periods; and (3) debt service, which benefits prior fiscal periods as well as current and future periods. Intergovernmental expenditures is a fourth character classification that is used when one governmental unit makes expenditures to another governmental unit.

	Original Budget	Final Budget	Actual Budgetary Basis	Variance Positive (Negative)
Budgetary Fund Balance, July 1	$ 99,552	$ 312,040	$ 312,040	$ —
Resources (Inflows):				
Property taxes	984,843	984,843	1,061,882	77,039
Business taxes	342,350	342,350	391,057	48,707
Other local taxes:				
Sales tax	98,029	98,029	106,302	8,273
Hotel room tax	157,222	157,222	158,927	1,705
Utility users tax	97,476	97,476	91,683	(5,793)
Parking tax	65,256	65,256	72,739	7,483
Real property transfer tax	110,487	110,487	178,546	68,059
Licenses, permits, and franchises:				
Licenses and permits	8,649	8,649	9,441	792
Franchise tax	14,593	14,593	15,811	1,218
Fines, forfeitures, and penalties	3,794	3,794	6,868	3,074
Interest and investment income	9,540	9,547	8,169	(1,378)
Rents and concessions:				
Garages—Recreation and Park	11,020	11,020	12,361	1,341
Rents and concessions—Recreation and Park	9,564	9,564	8,846	(718)
Other rents and concessions	1,763	1,763	2,196	433
Intergovernmental:				
Federal grants and subventions	236,610	227,983	211,276	(16,707)
State subventions:				
Social service subventions	102,133	102,018	113,790	11,772
Health / mental health subventions	139,204	139,027	99,528	(39,499)
Health and welfare realignment	138,150	138,150	143,225	5,075
Public safety sales tax	63,834	63,834	68,381	4,547
Motor vehicle in-lieu—county	1,711	1,711	5,328	3,617
Other grants and subventions	4,489	8,367	26,220	17,853
Allowance for state revenue reduction	(14,594)	—	—	—
Charges for services:				
General government service charges	45,402	45,402	45,579	177
Public safety service charges	21,291	21,381	22,657	1,276
Recreation charges—Recreation and Park	10,983	10,983	12,564	1,581
MediCal, MediCare and health service charges	68,406	67,677	63,275	(4,402)
Other financing sources:				
Transfers from other funds	114,157	119,027	107,068	(11,959)
Repayment of loan from Component Unit	785	785	—	(785)
Other resources (inflows)	20,677	30,929	8,459	(22,470)
Subtotal—Resources (Inflows)	2,867,824	2,891,867	3,052,178	160,311
Total amounts available for appropriation	2,967,376	3,203,907	3,364,218	160,311

Exhibit 33.5 City and County of San Francisco Budget-to-Actual Comparison Statement for the General Fund
Source: City and County of San Francisco CAFR for the year ended June 30, 2011.

	Original Budget	Final Budget	Actual Budgetary Basis	Variance Positive (Negative)
Charges to Appropriations (Outflows):				
Public Protection				
Adult Probation	$ 11,011	$ 11,155	$ 10,855	$ 300
District Attorney	32,443	31,989	31,897	92
Emergency Communications	38,580	39,651	39,042	609
Fire Department	257,705	262,955	261,647	1,308
Juvenile Probation	31,705	28,863	28,137	726
Police Department	381,997	387,544	386,311	1,233
Public Defender	25,078	25,264	24,670	594
Sheriff	135,182	131,484	130,226	1,258
Superior Court	32,439	32,611	32,609	2
Subtotal—Public Protection	946,140	951,516	945,394	6,122
Public Works, Transportation and Commerce				
Board of Appeals	932	960	839	121
Business and Economic Development	7,363	8,088	8,011	77
General Services Agency - Public Works	18,694	16,715	16,294	421
Subtotal—Public Works, Transportation and Commerce	26,989	25,763	25,144	619
Human Welfare and Neighborhood Development				
Children, Youth and Their Families	28,517	26,575	25,652	923
Commission on the Status of Women	3,288	3,280	3,220	60
County Education Office	78	78	78	—
Environment	1,254	1,896	1,811	85
Human Rights Commission	403	471	273	198
Human Services	621,487	614,649	575,439	39,210
Mayor—Housing/Neighborhoods	1,527	3,673	3,590	83
Subtotal—Human Welfare and Neighborhood Development	656,554	650,622	610,063	40,559
Community Health				
Public Health	519,319	513,625	493,939	19,686
Culture and Recreation				
Academy of Sciences	4,238	4,238	4,016	222
Art Commission	7,587	8,123	8,063	60
Asian Art Museum	7,103	7,116	6,677	439
Fine Arts Museum	11,052	11,448	11,428	20
Law Library	731	737	588	149
Recreation and Park Commission	66,799	68,381	67,911	470
Subtotal—Culture and Recreation	97,510	100,043	98,683	1,360

Exhibit 33.5 ***Continued***

	Original Budget	Final Budget	Actual Budgetary Basis	Variance Positive (Negative)
General Administration and Finance				
Assessor/Recorder	$ 16,759	$ 15,864	$ 15,667	$ 197
Board of Supervisors	10,288	10,248	10,195	53
City Attorney	7,311	9,047	8,883	164
City Planning	19,583	20,285	20,285	—
Civil Service	495	514	514	—
Controller	11,792	19,669	18,756	913
Elections	8,617	9,760	9,760	—
Ethics Commission	4,685	5,879	5,801	78
General Services Agency—Administrative Services	52,155	48,282	48,246	36
General Services Agency—Telecomm. and Info. Services	1,338	1,958	1,857	101
Human Resources	9,255	11,707	10,654	1,053
Mayor	4,041	4,273	4,189	84
Retirement Services	580	542	541	1
Treasurer/Tax Collector	21,100	20,681	19,721	960
Subtotal—General Administration and Finance	167,999	178,709	175,069	3,640
General City Responsibilities				
General City Responsibilities	80,424	88,662	86,477	2,185
Other financing uses:				
Debt Service	1,187	93	93	—
Transfers to other funds	423,550	504,740	501,470	3,270
Budgetary reserves and designations	47,704	6,213	—	6,213
Total charges to appropriations	2,967,376	3,019,986	2,936,332	83,654
Total Sources less Current Year Uses	$ —	$ 183,921	$ 427,886	$243,965
Budgetary fund balance, June 30 before reserves and designations			$ 427,886	
Reserves and designations made from budgetary fund balance, June 30			259,435	
Net Available Budgetary Fund Balance, June 30			$ 168,451	

Exhibit 33.5 ***Continued***

- *Function classification.* Establishing groups of related activities that are aimed at accomplishing a major service or regulatory responsibility. Standard function classifications for current expenditures are:

  General government

  Public safety

  Health and welfare

  Culture and recreation

  Conservation of natural resources

  Urban redevelopment and housing

  Economic development and assistance

  Education

  Miscellaneous

- *Program classification.* Establishing groups of activities, operations, or organizational units that are directed at the attainment of specific purposes or objectives (e.g., protection of property or improvement of transportation). Program classification is used by governmental units employing program budgeting.

- *Organizational unit classification.* Grouping expenditures according to the governmental unit's organization structure. Organizational unit classification is essential to responsibility reporting.
- *Activity classification.* Grouping expenditures according to the performance of specific activities. Activity classification is necessary for the determination of cost per unit of activity, which in turn is necessary for evaluation of economy and efficiency.
- *Object classification.* Grouping expenditures according to the types of items purchased or services obtained (e.g., personnel services, supplies, other services, and charges). Object classifications are subdivisions of the character classification.

Excessively detailed object classifications should be avoided since they complicate the accounting procedure and are of limited use in financial management. The use of a few object classifications is sufficient in budget preparation; control emphasis should be on organization units, functions, programs, and activities rather than on the object of expenditures.

(iii) Classifications of Other Transactions. Certain transactions, although not revenues or expenditures of an individual fund, are increases or decreases in the net assets of an individual fund. These transactions are classified as other financing sources and uses and are reported in the operating statement separately from fund revenues and expenditures. The most common other financing sources and uses are:

- *Proceeds of long-term debt issues.* Such proceeds (including capital leases) are not recorded as fund liabilities, but as proceeds of long-term debt issues; for example, proceeds of bonds and notes expended through the capital project or debt service funds.
- *Transfers.* These are flows of assets such as cash or goods without equivalent flows of assets in return and without a requirement for repayment. They include payments in lieu of taxes that are not payments for, and are not reasonably equivalent in value to, services provided. They should be reported in governmental funds as other financing uses in the funds making transfers and as other financing sources in the funds receiving transfers. They should be reported in proprietary funds after nonoperating revenues and expenses.

Other interfund transactions are:

- *Interfund loans and advances.* These are amounts provided with a requirement for repayment. They should be reported as interfund receivables and payables. They should not be reported as other financing sources or uses in the fund financial statements. If repayment is not expected within a reasonable time, the interfund balances should be reduced and the amount not expected to be repaid should be reported as a transfer from the fund that made the loan to the fund that received the loan.
- If the advance is long term in nature and the asset will not be available to finance current operations, a governmental fund should report the amount as nonspendable in fund balance unless the proceeds from the collection of the advance is restricted, committed or assigned.
- *Interfund services provided and used.* These are sales and purchases of goods and services between funds at prices that approximate their external exchange values. They should be reported as revenues in the seller funds and expenditures or expenses in purchaser funds, except that when the general fund is used to account for risk-financing activity, interfund charges to other funds should be accounted for as reimbursements.
- *Interfund reimbursements.* These are repayments from the funds responsible for particular expenditures or expenses to the funds that initially paid for them. They should not be displayed in the financial statements.

(iv) Classifications of Proprietary Fund Revenues and Expenses. Proprietary fund revenues and expenses should be classified in essentially the same manner as those of similar business organizations, functions, or activities.

(v) Classifications of Fund Balance/Equity. Fund equity is the difference between a fund's assets and its liabilities. The equity reported in the governmental fund balance sheet is called *fund balance.* Financial statements issued prior to the implementation of GASB Statement No. 54, *Fund Balance Reporting and Governmental Fund Type Definitions,* classified the fund balance of its governmental funds as reserved or unreserved. Many governments also designate part of unreserved fund balance. Research conducted by GASB found that there was a lack of consistency among governments in reporting its components of its fund balance, and it was unclear if any of the reserved or designated fund balances are available to help balance a government's budget. This statement is effective for periods beginning after June 15, 2010.

GASB Statement No. 54 changes the reporting classifications of fund balances in governmental funds and provides a more structured classification. GASB created a new hierarchy of fund balance classifications based on the extent to which governments are bound to observe spending constraints imposed on how resources reported in the governmental funds may be used.

The hierarchy of five possible classifications of fund balance (beginning with the most binding constraint) is:

1. Nonspendable fund balance
   - Amounts that cannot be spent due to form (e.g., inventories and prepaid amounts). Also long-term loan and notes receivables and property held for resale would be reported as nonspendable unless the proceeds from these assets are restricted, committed or assigned.
   - Amounts that must be maintained intact legally or contractually (corpus or principal of a permanent fund)
2. Restricted fund balance
   - Amounts constrained for a specific purpose by external parties (i.e., creditors, grantors, contributors, or laws or regulations of other governments), constitutional provisions or enabling legislation.
3. Committed fund balance
   - Amounts constrained for a specific purpose by a government using its highest level of decision-making authority.
   - Requires action by the same group of decision makers to remove or change the constraints placed on the resources.
   - Action to constrain resources must occur prior to year-end; however, the amount can be determined in the subsequent period.
4. Assigned fund balance
   - For all governmental funds other than the general fund, any remaining positive amounts not classified as nonspendable, restricted, or committed.
   - For the general fund, amounts constrained for the intent to be used for a specific purpose by a governing board or a body or official that has been delegated authority to assign amounts.
   - Amounts reported as assigned should not result in a deficit in unassigned fund balance.
5. Unassigned fund balance
   - For the general fund, amounts not classified as nonspendable, restricted, committed, or assigned.
   - The general fund is the only fund that would report a positive amount in unassigned fund balance.
   - For all governmental funds other than the general fund, amount expended in excess of resources that are nonspendable, restricted, committed, or assigned (a residual deficit).

Not all governments will have all five components of fund balance.

The equity reported in the government-wide statement of net assets is called *net assets* and is displayed in three categories:

1. *Invested in capital assets, net of related debt* consists of capital assets, including restricted capital assets, reduced by accumulated depreciation and by any outstanding debt incurred to acquire those assets.
2. *Restricted net assets* reports those net assets with restrictions on their use, either by external or internal factors.
3. *Unrestricted net assets* consists of all other net assets.

Invested in Capital Assets, Net of Related Debt. The amount of this component equals the amount of capital assets, including restricted capital assets, net of accumulated depreciation and less the outstanding balances of bonds, mortgages, notes, or other borrowings attributable to acquiring, constructing, or improving the assets. The portion of debt attributable to significant unspent debt proceeds should be included in the same net assets component as the unspent proceeds (e.g., *restricted for capital projects*).

Restricted Net Assets. Net assets should be reported as restricted if constraints on their use are either:

1. Imposed externally, by creditors, grantors, contributors, or laws or regulations of other governments
2. Imposed by law by constitutional provisions or enabling legislation that both authorizes the government to assess, levy, charge, or otherwise mandate receipt of resources from external providers and includes a legally enforceable requirement to use the resources for only the purposes stated in the legislation

Principal amounts of permanent funds included in restricted net assets should be presented in two components—expendable and nonexpendable. Nonexpendable net assets are those required to be retained in perpetuity.

Unrestricted Net Assets. Unrestricted net assets are other than net assets invested in capital assets, net of related debt, and other than restricted net assets.

Net assets are often *designated* by the management of the government if they do not consider them available for general operations. Such constraints are internal and can be removed or modified by the management. They are not restricted net assets.

The equity reported in the proprietary fund statement of net assets or balance sheet should be labeled either *net assets* or *fund equity,* using the three net asset components discussed for government-wide net assets.

The equity reported in the fiduciary fund statement of fiduciary net assets should be labeled *net assets* but does not require net assets to be categorized into the three components. GASB Statements No. 25 and No. 43 contain specific disclosure requirements for these types of funds.

(m) FINANCIAL REPORTING. Prior to 1979, governments traditionally prepared external financial reports by preparing financial statements for every fund maintained by the government. This often resulted in lengthy financial reports. External financial reporting has evolved to require the presentation of financial statements on a more aggregated basis and the inclusion of legally separate entities that have special relationships.

(i) Financial Reporting Entity. GASB Statement No. 14, *The Financial Reporting Entity,* establishes standards for defining and reporting on the financial reporting entity.

The Statement indicates that the financial reporting entity consists of (a) the PG; (b) organizations for which the PG is financially accountable; and (c) other organizations that, if omitted from the reporting entity, would cause the financial statements to be misleading.

The Statement also outlines the basic criteria for including organizations in or excluding organizations from the reporting entity. All organizations for which the PG is *financially* accountable should be included in the reporting entity. Such organizations include:

- Organizations that make up the PG's legal entity
- Component units; that is, organizations that are legally separate from the PG but:
  - The PG's officials appoint a voting majority of the organization's governing board AND
  - Either the PG is able to impose its will on that organization or there is a potential for the organization to provide specific financial benefits to, or to impose specific financial burdens on the PG.

A legally separate, tax-exempt organization should be reported as a component unit of a reporting entity if all of these criteria are met:

- The economic resources received or held by the separate organization are entirely or almost entirely for the direct benefit of the PG, its component units, or its constituents.
- The PG, or its component units, is entitled to, or has the ability to otherwise access, a majority of the economic resources received or held by the separate organization.
- The economic resources received or held by an individual organization that the specific PG, or its component units, is entitled to, or has the ability to otherwise access, are significant to that PG.

Other organizations should be evaluated as potential component units if they are closely related to, or financially integrated with, the PG. It is a matter of professional judgment to determine whether the nature and the significance of a potential component unit's relationship with the PG warrant inclusion in the reporting entity. Organizations not meeting the preceding criteria are excluded from the reporting entity.

Reporting the inclusion of the various entities comprising the reporting entity can be done using two methods: blending or discrete presentation. Most component units should be included in the financial reporting entity by discrete presentation. Some component units, despite being legally separate entities, are so intertwined with the PG that, in substance, they are the same as the PG and should be blended with the transactions of the PG.

Certain other entities are not considered component units because the PG, while responsible for appointing the organization's board members, is not financially accountable. Such entities are considered related organizations. These related organizations as well as joint ventures and jointly governed organizations should be disclosed in the reporting entity's footnotes.

Reporting Component Units. Discrete presentation of component unit financial information should be included in the government-wide statement of net assets and the statement of activities. However, information on component units that are fiduciary in nature should be included only in the fund financial statements, together with the PG's fiduciary funds. Information required by GASB Statement No. 14 about each major component unit can be given by:

- Presenting each major component unit other than those that are fiduciary in nature in separate columns in the statements of net assets and activities
- Including combining statements of major component units (with nonmajor component units aggregated in a single column) with the reporting entity's basic statements after the fund financial statements, OR
- Presenting condensed financial statements in the notes

The "aggregated total" component unit information, as discussed in GASB Statement No. 14, should be the entity totals derived from the component units' statements of net assets and activities.

(Because component units that are engaged in only business-type activities are not required to prepare a statement of activities, this disclosure should be taken from the information provided in the component unit's statement of revenues, expenses, and changes in fund net assets.)

If component unit information is presented in the notes, this information should be included:

- Condensed statement of net assets:
  - Total assets, distinguishing between capital assets and other assets. Amounts receivable from the PG or from other component units should be reported separately.
  - Total liabilities, distinguishing between long-term debt and other liabilities. Amounts payable to the PG or to other component units should be reported separately.
  - Total net assets, distinguishing between restricted, unrestricted, and amounts invested in capital assets net of related debt.
- Condensed statement of activities:
  - Expenses by major functions and for depreciation expense if separately reported
  - Program revenues by type
  - Net program expense or revenue
  - Tax revenues
  - Other nontax general revenues
  - Contributions to endowments and permanent fund principal
  - Special and extraordinary items
  - Change in net assets
  - Beginning net assets
  - Ending net assets

The nature and amount of significant transactions with the PG and other component units should be reported in the notes for each component unit.

(ii) Basic Financial Statements. As discussed in Section 33.4(e)(ii), the basic financial statements include the financial statements of the governmental activities, the business-type activities, the aggregate discretely presented component units, each major fund, and the aggregate remaining fund information.

The two government-wide financial statements, the statement of net assets and the statement of activities, should report information about the reporting government without displaying individual funds or fund types. The statements should cover the PG and its component units, except for fiduciary funds of the PG and component units that are fiduciary in nature, which should be reported in the statements of fiduciary net assets and changes in fiduciary net assets.

The focus of the government-wide financial statements should be on the PG. The total PG and its discretely presented component units should be distinguished by separate rows and columns. A total column for the government entity and prior year information are optional.

Governmental and business-type activities of the PG should also be distinguished by separate rows and columns. (An activity need not be set out as a proprietary fund if it is not currently reported as such by the management of the government unless it is required to be reported as an enterprise fund, as discussed in Section 33.4(g)(ii)) Governmental and business-type activities are distinguished in general by their methods of financing. Governmental activities are generally financed by taxes, intergovernmental revenues, and other nonexchange-type revenues; they are generally reported in governmental funds and internal service funds. Business-type activities are financed in whole or in part by fees charged for goods or services; they are generally reported in enterprise funds.

These statements measure and report all financial and capital assets, liabilities, revenues, expenses, gains, and losses using the economic resources measurement focus and accrual basis of accounting.

Some amounts reported as interfund activity and balances in the funds should be eliminated or reclassified in aggregating information for the statement of net assets and the statement of activities.

Amounts reported in the funds as interfund receivables and payables should be eliminated in the governmental and business-type activities columns of the PG in the statement of net assets, except for the net residual amount due between the governmental and business-type activities, which should be reported as internal balances. (Amounts reported in the funds as receivable from or payable to fiduciary funds should be reported in the statement of net assets as receivable from and payable to external parties.) Internal balances should be eliminated in the total PG column.

The doubling-up effect of internal service fund activity should be eliminated in the statement of activities. Also, the effects of similar internal events, such as allocations of accounting staff salaries that are, in effect, allocations of overhead expenses from one function to another or within a single function should be eliminated so that the allocated expenses are reported by only the function to which they were allocated. (The effect of interfund services provided and used between functions should not be eliminated.)

Statement of Net Assets. The statement of net assets should report all financial and capital resources and all liabilities, preferably in a format that displays assets less liabilities equal net assets, although the format assets equal liabilities plus net assets may be used. The difference between assets and liabilities should be reported as net assets, not fund balance or equity.

Governments are encouraged to report assets and liabilities in order of their relative liquidity (and subtotals of current assets and current liabilities may be provided). The liquidity of an asset depends on how readily it is expected to be converted to cash and whether restrictions limit the government's ability to use it. The liquidity of a liability depends on its maturity or on when cash is expected to be required to liquidate it. The liquidity of assets and liabilities may be determined by class, although individual assets or liabilities may be significantly more or less liquid than others in the same class, and some may have both current and long-term elements. Liabilities whose average maturities are more than one year should be reported by the amount due within one year and the amount due in more than one year.

As discussed in Section 33.4(l)(v), the three components of net assets are reported as invested in capital assets, net of related debt; restricted, distinguishing between major categories of restrictions; and unrestricted.

Statement of Net Assets Format. The City and County of San Francisco's statement of net assets at June 30, 2011, in Exhibit 33.6 illustrates the statement of net assets format.

Statement of Activities. Some governments have a single function, program, activity, or component unit (together discussed as functions). Most have more than one function. A government with more than one function should present a statement of activities that reports expenses by each function and revenues specifically pertaining to each function, arriving at net expense or net revenue by function. Net expense or net revenue is sometimes referred to as the *net cost* of a function or program and represents the total expenses of the function or program less its program revenues (i.e., charges or fees and fines that derive directly from the function or program and grants and contributions that are restricted to the function or program). That presentation indicates the financial burden (or benefit) each function has on the government's taxpayers and the extent to which each draws on the general revenues of the government or is self-financing. General revenues should be reported after expenses and revenues of the functions, together with contributions to term and permanent endowments, contributions to permanent fund principal, special and extraordinary items, and transfers reported separately, leading to change in net assets for the period.

At a minimum, the statement of activities should present:

- Activities accounted for in governmental funds by function, as discussed in NCGA Statement No. 1, paragraph 112, to coincide with level of detail required in the governmental fund statement of revenues, expenditures, and changes in fund balances.

ASSETS AND DEFERRED OUTFLOWS	Primary Government			Component Units	
	Governmental Activities	Business-Type Activities	Total	San Francisco Redevelopment Agency	Treasure Island Development Authority
Assets:					
Current assets:					
Deposits and investments with City Treasury	$1,353,449	$ 1,114,318	$ 2,467,767	$ —	$2,648
Deposits and investments outside City Treasury	117,177	9,387	126,564	258,689	—
Receivables (net of allowance for uncollectible amounts of $126,939 for the primary government):					
Property taxes and penalties	53,221	—	53,221	9,582	—
Other local taxes	201,006	—	201,006	—	—
Federal and state grants and subventions	294,330	78,080	372,410	—	—
Charges for services	52,832	233,294	286,126	—	2,192
Interest and other	5,864	70,663	76,527	3,572	—
Capital lease receivable from primary government	—	—	—	16,085	—
Due from component unit	3,164	58	3,222	—	—
Inventories	—	75,570	75,570	—	—
Deferred charges and other assets	11,284	10,451	21,735	120	—
Restricted assets:					
Deposits and investments with City Treasury	—	147,470	147,470	—	—
Deposits and investments outside City Treasury	—	129,156	129,156	179,094	—
Grants and other receivables	—	12,303	12,303	3,393	—
Total current assets	2,092,327	1,880,750	3,973,077	470,535	4,840
Noncurrent assets:					
Loans receivable (net of allowance for uncollectible amounts of $530,590 and $336,502 for the primary government and component unit, respectively)	71,346	—	71,346	4,569	—
Advance to component units	24,502	4,027	28,529	—	—
Capital lease receivable from primary government	—	—	—	124,033	—
Deferred charges and other assets	22,737	69,396	92,133	16,307	—
Restricted assets:					
Deposits and investments with City Treasury	—	1,328,362	1,328,362	—	—
Deposits and investments outside City Treasury	77,505	666,179	743,684	—	—
Grants and other receivables	—	19,644	19,644	—	—
Property held for resale	—	—	—	6,081	—
Capital assets:					
Land and other assets not being depreciated	548,024	1,992,041	2,540,065	154,829	—
Facilities, infrastructure, and equipment, net of depreciation	2,766,426	8,944,225	11,710,651	150,474	—
Total capital assets	3,314,450	10,936,266	14,250,716	305,303	—
Total noncurrent assets	3,510,540	13,023,874	16,534,414	456,293	—
Total assets	5,602,867	14,904,624	20,507,491	926,828	4,840
Deferred outflows on derivative instruments	—	63,382	63,382	—	—
Total assets and deferred outflows	$5,602,867	$14,968,006	$20,570,873	$926,828	$4,840
LIABILITIES					
Current liabilities:					
Accounts payable	$ 211,057	$ 167,102	$ 378,159	$ 10,766	$ 434
Accrued payroll	102,912	81,024	183,936	169	—
Accrued vacation and sick leave pay	71,916	49,624	121,540	1,240	—
Accrued workers' compensation	39,662	24,547	64,209	—	—
Estimated claims payable	34,889	36,972	71,861	—	—
Bonds, loans, capital leases, and other payables	306,767	342,627	649,394	49,483	—
Capital lease payable to component unit	16,085	—	16,085	—	—
Accrued interest payable	11,954	37,205	49,159	36,188	—
Unearned grant and subvention revenues	13,350	—	13,350	—	—
Due to primary government	—	—	—	3,188	34
Internal balances	12,517	(12,517)	—	—	—

Exhibit 33.6 City and County of San Francisco Statement of Net Assets (June 30, 2011)
Source: City and County of San Francisco CAFR for the year ended June 30, 2011.

	Primary Government			Component Units	
ASSETS AND DEFERRED OUTFLOWS	**Governmental Activities**	**Business-Type Activities**	**Total**	**San Francisco Redevelopment Agency**	**Treasure Island Development Authority**
Deferred credits and other liabilities	250,759	225,845	476,604	3,049	621
Liabilities payable from restricted assets:					
Bonds, loans, capital leases, and other payables	—	24,348	24,348	—	—
Accrued interest payable	—	30,191	30,191	—	—
Other	—	143,642	143,642	—	—
Total current liabilities	1,071,868	1,150,610	2,222,478	104,083	1,089
Noncurrent liabilities:					
Accrued vacation and sick leave pay	68,705	40,939	109,644	1,210	—
Accrued workers' compensation	183,166	123,639	306,805	—	—
Other postemployment benefits obligation	615,227	448,966	1,064,193	470	—
Estimated claims payable	91,155	61,465	152,620	—	—
Bonds, loans, capital leases, and other payables	2,136,658	8,014,877	10,151,535	1,082,453	—
Advance from primary government	—	—	—	15,334	13,195
Capital lease payable to component unit	124,033	—	124,033	—	—
Accrued interest payable	—	—	—	45,334	—
Deferred credits and other liabilities	1,776	66,732	68,508	3,606	—
Derivative instruments liabilities	—	68,304	68,304	—	—
Total noncurrent liabilities	3,220,720	8,824,922	12,045,642	1,148,407	13,195
Total liabilities	4,292,588	9,975,532	14,268,120	1,252,490	14,284
NET ASSETS					
Invested in capital assets, net of related debt, Note 2(k)	1,910,341	4,481,404	5,993,892	176,464	—
Restricted for:					
Reserve for rainy day	33,439	—	33,439	—	—
Debt service	36,805	62,421	99,226	61,507	—
Capital projects, Note 2(k)	82,315	161,580	223,694	—	—
Community development	59,763	—	59,763	—	—
Transportation Authority activities	1,386	—	1,386	—	—
Building inspection programs	32,112	—	32,112	—	—
Children and families	45,827	—	45,827	—	—
Grants and other purposes	155,152	18,741	173,893	—	—
Unrestricted (deficit), Note 2(k)	(1,046,861)	268,328	(360,479)	(563,633)	(9,444)
Total net assets (deficit)	$1,310,279	$4,992,474	$ 6,302,753	$ (325,662)	$(9,444)

Exhibit 33.6 ***Continued***

- Activities accounted for in enterprise funds by different identifiable activities. An activity is identifiable if it has a specific revenue stream and related expenses and gains and losses that are accounted for separately.

Expenses. All expenses should be reported by function other than special or extraordinary items (see discussion at Special and Extraordinary Items later in this section). At a minimum, direct expenses—those clearly identifiable with a particular function—should be presented. In addition, some or all indirect expenses of the functions may be reported by function, in columns separate from the direct expenses. A column reporting the total of direct and indirect expenses by function may also be presented. Governments that charge functions for centralized expenses need not identify and eliminate such charges. The fact that they are included in direct expenses should be disclosed in the summary of significant accounting policies.

Depreciation expense on capital assets specifically identifiable with functions should be included in their direct expenses. Depreciation expense on shared capital assets should be assigned ratably to the direct expense of the functions benefiting. Depreciation expense on capital assets that serve all functions, such as city hall, need not be included in the direct expense of the functions but may be reported as a separate line in the statement of activities or as part of the general government function. A government that reports unallocated depreciation on a separate line should state on the face of the statement of activities that this item does not include direct depreciation expenses of the various functions.

Depreciation expense for general infrastructure assets should be reported as a direct expense of the function that the government normally associates with capital outlays for and maintenance of infrastructure assets or on a separate line in the statement of activities.

Interest on long-term liabilities should generally be reported as an indirect expense on a separate line in the statement of activities, clearly indicating that it excludes direct interest expenses, if any, reported in other functions. The amount excluded should be disclosed on the face of the statement or in the notes. However, interest should be included in direct expense on borrowings essential to the creation or continuing existence of a program, such as a new, highly leveraged program in its early stages, if excluding it would be misleading.

Revenues. A government obtains revenue essentially from four sources:

1. Entities that buy, use, or directly benefit from the goods or services of programs, including the citizens of the government or others
2. Entities outside the citizens of the government, including other governments, nongovernmental entities, or persons
3. The government's taxpayers, regardless of whether they benefit from particular programs
4. The government itself, for example, from investing

Type 1 is always a program revenue. Type 2 is a program revenue if restricted to specific programs; if unrestricted, type 2 is a general revenue. Type 3 is always a general revenue, even if restricted to specific programs. Type 4 is usually a general revenue.

Program revenues reduce the net cost of program function required to be financed by general revenue. They should be reported separately in three categories: (1) charges for services, (2) program-specific operating grants and contributions, and (3) program-specific capital grants and contributions. To identify the function to which a program revenue pertains, the determining factor for charges for services is which function generates the revenue. For grants and contributions, the determining factor is the function to which the revenues are restricted.

All other revenues are general revenues, including all taxes and all nontax revenues that do not meet the criteria to be reported as program revenues. General revenues should be reported after total net expense of the government's functions.

The next items should be reported separately at the bottom of the statement of activities in the same manner as general revenues, to arrive at the all-inclusive change in net assets for the reporting period:

- Contributions to term and permanent endowments
- Contributions to permanent fund principal
- Special and extraordinary items (see below)
- Transfers between governmental and business-type activities

In the governmental funds operating statement, other financing sources and uses include face amount of long-term debt, issuance premium or discount, certain payments to escrow agents for bond refundings, transfers, and sales of capital assets (unless the sale meets the criteria for reporting as a special item.)

Special and Extraordinary Items. Special items—significant events within the control of management that are either unusual or infrequent as defined in APB Opinion No. 30—should be reported separately at the bottom of the statement of activities. Extraordinary items—significant events that are both unusual and infrequent—should also be reported separately at the bottom of the statement of activities.

Statement of Activities Format. The City and County of San Francisco's statement of activities for the year ended June 30, 2011, illustrates the statement of activities format (see Exhibit 33.7).

Functions/Programs	Expenses	Program Revenues			Net (Expense) Revenue and Changes in Net Assets: Primary Government			Component Units	
		Charges for Services	Operating Grants and Contributions	Capital Grants and Contributions	Governmental Activities	Business-Type Activities	Total	San Francisco Redevelopment Agency	Treasure Island Development Authority
Primary government:									
Governmental activities:									
Public protection	$1,099,791	$ 62,105	$ 138,068	$ —	$ (899,618)	$ —	$ (899,618)	$ —	$ —
Public works, transportation and commerce	239,230	101,846	79,913	49,496	(7,975)	—	(7,975)	—	—
Human welfare and neighborhood development	885,194	56,628	521,029	—	(307,537)	—	(307,537)	—	—
Community health	613,883	64,419	277,484	917	(271,063)	—	(271,063)	—	—
Culture and recreation	318,083	76,528	2,915	7,306	(231,334)	—	(231,334)	—	—
General administration and finance	224,027	37,601	5,187	—	(181,239)	—	(181,239)	—	—
General City responsibilities	84,444	29,316	15,520	—	(39,608)	—	(39,608)	—	—
Unallocated interest on long-term debt	110,142	—	—	—	(110,142)	—	(110,142)	—	—
Total governmental activities	3,574,794	428,443	1,040,116	57,719	(2,048,516)	—	(2,048,516)	—	—
Business-type activities:									
Airport	690,875	607,323	—	24,033	—	(59,519)	(59,519)	—	—
Transportation	905,218	334,140	129,166	164,759	—	(277,153)	(277,153)	—	—
Port	68,661	72,266	557	3,027	—	7,189	7,189	—	—
Water	362,802	288,395	1,810	6,509	—	(66,088)	(66,088)	—	—
Power	119,282	140,035	4,730	—	—	25,483	25,483	—	—
Hospitals	885,294	726,522	67,408	15,036	—	(76,328)	(76,328)	—	—
Sewer	201,629	229,216	482	—	—	28,069	28,069	—	—
Market	1,152	1,655	—	—	—	503	503	—	—
Total business-type activities	3,234,913	2,399,552	204,153	213,364	—	(417,844)	(417,844)	—	—
Total primary government	$6,809,707	$2,827,995	$1,244,269	$271,083	(2,048,516)	(417,844)	(2,466,360)	—	—

Exhibit 33.7 City and County of San Francisco Statement of Activities (Year Ended June 30, 2011)
Source: City and County of San Francisco CAFR for the year ended June 30, 2011.

Functions/Programs	Expenses	Charges for Services	Operating Grants and Contributions	Capital Grants and Contributions	Governmental Activities	Business-Type Activities	Total	San Francisco Redevelopment Agency	Treasure Island Development Authority
		Program Revenues			Net (Expense) Revenue and Changes in Net Assets: Primary Government			Component Units	
Component units:									
San Francisco Redevelopment Agency	$ 246,956	$ 25,029	$ 13,135	$ 3,729				(205,063)	—
Treasure Island Development Authority	12,072	8,563	—	—				—	(3,509)
Total component units	$ 259,028	$ 33,592	$ 13,135	$ 3,729				(205,063)	(3,509)
General Revenues:									
Taxes:									
Property taxes					1,340,590	—	1,340,590	110,166	—
Business taxes					391,779	—	391,779	—	—
Sales and use tax					181,474	—	181,474	—	—
Hotel room tax					209,962	—	209,962	5,550	—
Utility users tax					91,683	—	91,683	—	—
Other local taxes					251,285	—	251,285	—	—
Interest and investment income					17,645	42,299	59,944	1,369	34
Other					58,524	214,993	273,517	6,489	3,670
Transfers - internal activities of primary government					(337,132)	337,132	—	—	—
Total general revenues and transfers					2,205,810	594,424	2,800,234	123,574	3,704
Change in net assets					157,294	176,580	333,874	(81,489)	195
Net assets (deficit) - beginning					1,152,985	4,815,894	5,968,879	(244,173)	(9,639)
Net assets (deficit) - ending					$1,310,279	$4,992,474	$6,302,753	$(325,662)	$(9,444)

Exhibit 33.7 ***Continued***

Basic Financial Statements—Fund Financial Statements

Governmental Fund Balance Statement Format. Exhibit 33.8 presents the balance sheet presentation of the City and County of San Francisco's General Fund, the only major governmental fund of the City and County of San Francisco. Nonmajor funds are aggregated in an "Other" column. Note: the City and County of San Francisco financial statements include optional partial or summarized prior year comparative information.

	General Fund		Other Governmental Funds		Total Governmental Funds	
	2011	2010	2011	2010	2011	2010
ASSETS						
Deposits and investments with City Treasury . .	$386,246	$237,888	$ 938,304	$ 920,171	$1,324,550	$1,158,059
Deposits and investments outside City Treasury	860	203	116,317	144,786	117,177	144,989
Receivables (net of allowance for uncollectible amounts of $95,441 in 2011; $77,793 in 2010):						
Property taxes and penalties	45,278	57,785	7,943	8,539	53,221	66,324
Other local taxes	186,137	171,464	14,869	13,123	201,006	184,587
Federal and state grants and subventions	162,130	132,112	132,200	147,855	294,330	279,967
Charges for services	39,884	36,099	12,814	12,216	52,698	48,315
Interest and other	805	28,313	4,358	4,277	5,163	32,590
Due from other funds	27,833	36,930	8,753	11,410	36,586	48,340
Due from / advance to component unit	16,253	13,486	11,413	10,201	27,666	23,687
Loans receivable (net of allowance for uncollectible amounts of $530,590 in 2011; $519,720 in 2010)	—	—	71,346	72,294	71,346	72,294
Deferred charges and other assets	6,520	5,437	4,348	3,983	10,868	9,420
Total assets	$871,946	$719,717	$1,322,665	$1,348,855	$2,194,611	$2,068,572
LIABILITIES AND FUND BALANCES						
Liabilities:						
Accounts payable	$ 89,882	$117,339	$ 115,476	$ 132,449	$205,358	$ 249,788
Accrued payroll	81,547	75,254	19,400	18,785	100,947	94,039
Deferred tax, grant and subvention revenues	116,330	117,925	66,184	70,043	182,514	187,968
Due to other funds	750	881	41,550	46,897	42,300	47,778
Deferred credits and other liabilities	255,431	216,540	112,976	118,339	368,407	334,879
Bonds, loans, capital leases, and other payables	—	—	167,519	155,035	167,519	155,035
Total liabilities	543,940	527,939	523,105	541,548	1,067,045	1,069,487
Fund balances:						
Nonspendable	20,501	14,874	192	192	20,693	15,066
Restricted	33,439	39,582	831,269	861,188	864,708	900,770
Committed	33,431	4,677	—	—	33,431	4,677
Assigned	240,635	132,645	27,622	27,493	268,257	160,138
Unassigned	—	—	(59,523)	(81,566)	(59,523)	(81,566)
Total fund balances	328,006	191,778	799,560	807,307	1,127,566	999,085
Total liabilities and fund balances	$871,946	$719,717	$1,322,665	$1,348,855	$2,194,611	$2,068,572

Exhibit 33.8 City and County of San Francisco Balance Sheet Governmental Funds
Source: City and County of San Francisco CAFR for the year ended June 30, 2011.

Required Reconciliation to Government-Wide Statements. The amount of net assets reported for a PG in the government-wide statement of net assets usually will differ from the aggregate amount of equity reported in its fund financial position statements since the fund statements are prepared using the current financial resources measurement focus and modified accrual method (see discussion at Section 33.4(j)). There will also be differences between the changes in net assets reported in the various activity statements.

A government should present a summary reconciliation to the government-wide financial statements at the bottom of the fund financial statements or in a schedule. Brief explanations presented on the face of the statements often are sufficient. However, if aggregated information in the reconciliation obscures the nature of the individual elements of a particular reconciling item, a more detailed explanation should be provided in the notes to financial statements.

Exhibit 33.9 presents the reconciliation of the governmental funds balance sheet to the statement of net assets of the City and County of San Francisco. This reconciliation provides summarized explanations that does not describe the nature of the individual elements these reconciling items. As a result, the City and County of San Francisco provides a more detailed explanation in the notes to financial statements.

Reconciling items between the governmental funds balance sheets and the government-wide statement of net assets include the effects of:

- Reporting capital assets at their acquisition cost and depreciating them instead of reporting capital acquisitions as expenditures when incurred
- Adding general long-term liabilities not due and payable in the current period
- Reducing deferred revenue for amounts not available to pay current-period expenditures
- Adding internal service fund net asset balances

Reconciling items between the governmental funds statement of revenues, expenditures, and changes in fund balances and the government-wide statement of activities include the effects of:

- Reporting revenues on the accrual basis
- Reporting annual depreciation expense instead of expenditures for capital outlays
- Reporting long-term debt proceeds in the statement of net assets as liabilities instead of other financing sources
- Reporting debt principal payments in the statement of net assets as reductions of liabilities instead of expenditures

Fund balances—total governmental funds	$1,127,566
Amounts reported for governmental activities in the statement of net assets are different because:	
Capital assets used in governmental activities are not financial resources and, therefore, are not reported in the funds.	3,308,318
Bond issue costs are not financial resources and, therefore, are not reported in the funds.	17,712
Long-term liabilities, including bonds payable, are not due and payable in the current period and therefore are not reported in the funds.	(3,223,191)
Interest on long-term debt is not accrued in the funds, but rather is recognized as an expenditure when due.	(10,190)
Because the focus of governmental funds is on short-term financing, some assets will not be available to pay for current period expenditures. Those assets are offset by deferred revenue in the funds.	287,469
Internal service funds are used by management to charge the costs of capital lease financing, fleet management, printing and mailing services, and information systems to individual funds. The assets and liabilities of internal service funds are included in governmental activities in the statement of net assets.	(197,405)
Net assets of governmental activities	$1,310,279

Exhibit 33.9 City and County of San Francisco Reconciliation of the Governmental Funds Balance Sheet to the Statement of Net Assets (June 30, 2011)

Source: City and County of San Francisco CAFR for the year ended June 30, 2011.

- Reporting other expenses on the accrual basis
- Adding the net revenue or subtracting the expense of internal service funds

For enterprise funds, (1) total enterprise fund net assets should be reconciled to the net assets of business-type activities (however, since both are on the accrual basis, there often are no differences, except for allocation of internal service fund activity to business-type activities), and (2) the total change in enterprise fund net assets should be reconciled to the change in net assets of business-type activities, provided there are differences that require reconciliation.

Reporting Internal Service Fund Balances. Internal service funds are reported as proprietary funds. Nevertheless, their activities, financing goods, and services for other funds, are usually more governmental than business type. Therefore, internal service fund asset and liability balances not eliminated should normally be reported in the governmental activities column of the statement of net assets. However, if enterprise funds are the predominant or only participants in an internal service fund, that fund's residual assets and liabilities should be reported in the business-type activities column.

Disclosure Requirements. Information essential to fair presentation in the financial statements that cannot be displayed on the faces of the statements should be presented in the notes to the financial statements, which should focus on the PG—its governmental activities, business-type activities, major funds, and nonmajor funds in the aggregate. Information about the government's discretely presented component units should be presented as discussed in GASB Statement No. 14, paragraph 63.

General Disclosure Requirements. Governments should provide these added disclosures to the extent applicable in their summaries of significant accounting policies:

- A description of the government-wide financial statements, indicating that fiduciary funds and component units that are fiduciary in nature are not included.
- The measurement focus and basis of accounting used in the government-wide statements.
- The policy for eliminating internal activity in the statement of activities.
- The policy for applying FASB pronouncements issued after November 30, 1989, to business-type activities and to enterprise funds of the PG. (This requirement will no longer be required with the implementation of the codification of FASB and AICPA pronouncements in GASB Statement No. 62 in 2012.)
- The policy for capitalizing assets and for estimating their useful lives. A government that uses the modified approach for reporting eligible infrastructure assets should describe the approach.
- A description of the kinds of transactions included in program revenues.
- A description of the policy for allocating indirect expenses to functions in the statement of activities.
- The government's policy for defining operating and nonoperating revenues of proprietary funds.
- The government's policy on whether to first use restricted or unrestricted resources when an expense is incurred for purposes for which both restricted and unrestricted net assets are available.

Required Note Disclosures and Cash and Investments. A government is subject to numerous GASB disclosures about cash and investments. The required disclosures include:

- A description of how investments are valued including the methods and significant assumptions used to estimate the fair value of investments
- The types of investments authorized by legal or contractual provisions
- The types of investments made during the period but not owned as of the statement of net assets/balance sheet date

- By type of investment, the investments' carrying amounts and fair values at year-end
- The custodial credit risk for uncollateralized deposits with financial institutions and investment securities that are uninsured and unregistered
- The credit and interest rate risks related to investments in debt instruments
- Terms of investments with fair values that are highly sensitive to changes in interest rates
- The concentration of credit risk for amount invested in a separate issuer (except investments held in or guaranteed by the U.S. government) when that amount is at least 5 percent of total investments;
- The foreign currency risk of its investments denominated in a foreign currency
- The assignment of investment income between funds
- Specific information related to investment appreciation and income available for spending on donor-restricted endowments

Required Note Disclosures about Capital Assets and Long Term Liabilities. Details should be disclosed in the notes about capital assets and long-term liabilities of the PG, divided into their major classes and between those associated with governmental activities and those associated with business-type activities. Capital assets not being depreciated should be disclosed separately. This following information should be disclosed about major classes of capital assets:

- Beginning- and end-of-year balances, with accumulated depreciation presented separately from acquisition cost
- Capital acquisitions
- Sales or other dispositions
- Current depreciation expense, including the amounts charged to each of the functions in the statement of activities

Collections of works of art, historical treasures, and similar assets not capitalized should be described and the reasons they are not capitalized should be given. Disclosures as just listed should be given for collections capitalized.

This information should be disclosed about long-term debt and other long-term liabilities, such as compensated absences, claims, and judgments:

- Beginning- and end-of-year balances
- Increases and decreases, presented separately
- The portions of each due within one year
- The governmental funds that typically have been used to liquidate other long-term liabilities

Debt service to maturity separated by principal and interest for each of the succeeding five fiscal years and in at least five-year increments thereafter for all outstanding debt should be disclosed. Interest on variable-rate debt should be calculated using the rate in effect at the financial statement date. The terms that the interest rates change for variable-rate debt should also be disclosed.

Whether to make similar disclosures about capital assets and long-term liabilities of discretely presented component units is a matter of professional judgment, depending on each individual component unit's significance to the total of all discretely presented component units and the component unit's relationship with the PG.

Required Supplementary Information

Management's Discussion and Analysis. An MD&A is an overview and analysis of the government's financial statements. It should provide an objective and easily readable analysis of the government's financial activities based on facts, decisions, or conditions of which management is aware as of the date of the auditor's report. It should discuss the current-year results and compare them with the results of the prior year, including positive and negative aspects.

MD&A requirements are general to encourage effective reporting of only the most relevant information and to avoid boilerplate discussion. The information presented should be confined to the next eight items, including additional details pertaining to those items.

1. A brief discussion of the basic financial statements, including the relationships of the statements to each other and the significant differences in the information they provide. Analyses should be provided to help users understand why measurements and results reported in fund financial statements either reinforce information in government-wide statements or provide additional information.
2. Condensed financial information derived from government-wide financial statements comparing the current year to the prior year. Governments should present the information needed to support their analysis of financial position and results of operations.
3. An analysis of the government's overall financial position and results of operations, addressing both governmental and business-type activities as reported in the government-wide financial statements, to help users assess whether the financial position has improved or deteriorated as a result of the year's operations.
4. An analysis of balances and transactions of the individual funds, including the reasons for significant changes in fund balances or fund net assets and whether restrictions, commitments, or other limitations significantly affect the availability of fund resources for future use.
5. An analysis of significant variations between original and final budget amounts and between final budget amounts and actual budget results for the general fund or its equivalent, including any known reasons for such of those variations that are expected to have a significant effect on future services or liquidity.
6. A description of significant capital asset and long-term debt activity during the year, including a discussion of commitments for capital expenditures, changes in credit ratings, and debt limitations that may affect financing of planned facilities or services.
7. A discussion by governments that use the modified approach to report some or all of their infrastructure assets.
8. A description of facts, decisions, or conditions of which management is aware at the date of the independent auditor's report that are expected to significantly affect financial position or results of operations—revenues, expenses, and other changes in net assets.

In addition to the information required to be presented as required supplementary information (RSI) by GASB Statement Nos. 10, 25, 27, 43, and 45 and other RSI required to be presented by GASB Statement No. 34 includes MD&A, budgetary comparison schedules for governmental funds, and information about infrastructure assets reported using the modified approach (see discussion at 33.4(h)).

Budgetary Comparison Information. Under GASB Statement No. 34, budgetary comparison schedules should present: (1) the original appropriated budgets; (2) the final appropriated budgets; and (3) actual inflows, outflows, and balances, stated on the governmental budgetary basis as discussed in NCGA Statement No. 1, paragraph 154.

Information in a separate schedule or in notes to RSI should be provided that reconciles budgetary information to GAAP information. Notes to RSI should disclose excesses of expenditures over appropriations in individual funds presented in the budgetary comparison, as discussed in NCGA Interpretation No. 6, paragraph 4, as amended by GASB Statement No. 37. (If the budgetary comparison information is included in the basic statements, these disclosures should be in the notes to the financial statements rather than as notes to RSI.)

Modified Approach for Reporting Infrastructure. A government with eligible infrastructure assets (for subsystems, if any) reported using the modified approach should present as RSI these schedules derived from the asset management systems:

- The assessed condition, based on assessments performed at least every three years, for at least the three most recent complete condition assessments, indicating the dates of the assessments

- The estimated annual amount calculated at the beginning of the year to maintain and preserve the assets at or above the condition level established and disclosed by the government compared with the amounts actually reported as expense for each of the past five reporting periods

This information should be disclosed with the schedules:

- The basis for the condition measurement and the measurement scale used to assess and report condition. For example, a basis could be distresses in pavement surfaces. A scale could range from zero for a failed pavement to 100 for pavement in perfect condition.
- The condition level at which the government intends to preserve its eligible infrastructure assets reported using the modified approach.
- Factors that significantly affect trends in the information reported in the schedules, including any changes in the basis for the condition measurement, the measurement scale, or the condition measurement methods used. Also to be disclosed is an estimate of the effect of a change in the condition level at which the government intends to preserve eligible infrastructure assets of the estimated annual amount to maintain and preserve the assets for the current period.

A government that has asset management systems for infrastructure assets that gather the information required under this subsection but do not use the modified approach are encouraged to disclose it as supplementary information.

(iii) Comprehensive Annual Financial Report. The Comprehensive Annual Financial Report (CAFR) differs from the basic financial statements in the level of detail and the quantity of data presented. The additional data are *not* necessary for fair presentation of financial position or changes in financial position in accordance with GAAP, but they are useful and informative for certain readers of a government's financial report. Furthermore, the CAFR may be the vehicle for providing the necessary information for fulfilling the legal and other disclosure requirements of higher levels of government, bondholders, and similar groups. It is also useful in demonstrating management's stewardship responsibilities, since alongside the comparative budgets it presents in more detail the use of the available resources.

The GASB encourages each governmental entity to prepare a CAFR; however, the basic financial statements constitute fair presentation of financial position and the respective changes in financial position and cash flows, where applicable, in accordance with GAAP and could be opined on as such by an independent auditor. The statements would be suitable for inclusion in an official statement for a securities offering and for widespread distribution to users requiring less detailed information about the governmental unit's finances than is contained in the CAFR.

The recommended contents of the general-purpose government's CAFR include:

- *Introductory section*
    - Title page. Contains the title "Comprehensive Annual Financial Report," the name of the governmental unit, the period of time covered, and the names of the principal government officials. Component units that issue separate statements should indicate the PG of which it is a component. A title such as "City Hospital, a Component Unit of City, Any State" is recommended.
    - Table of contents. Identifies the presence and location of each item included in the report.
    - Transmittal letter. Other information from the government's chief finance officer (or CEO) that is not included in the MD&A that and provides basic information about the government and how it operates and other information useful in assessing the government's economic condition. The letter may include, for example: changes in financial policies; discussion of internal controls; significant elements of financial management; budget procedures and current budget; and a preview of the significant developments or changes contemplated in the coming year including economic conditions, outlook, and major initiatives.

- *Financial section*
  - Independent auditor's report.
  - Management's discussion and analysis.
  - Basic financial statements. Includes all required financial statements and related notes as previously described.
  - Required supplementary information. Included when disclosure is required by the GASB.
  - Combining financial statements. Used when a governmental unit has more than one fund of a given type.
  - Individual fund financial statements and schedules. Used when this information is not provided in a separate column in a combining statement or it is desirable to present a level of detail that would be excessive for the BFS or the combining statements. Examples are detail comparisons to budgets that cannot be reflected on the combining statements, comparative data for prior years, or a demonstration of an individual fund's compliance with legal provisions.
  - Schedules necessary to demonstrate compliance. Included when such are required by state law or by a bond covenant.
  - Other schedules desired by the government. Used for reporting particular kinds of information that are spread throughout the numerous financial statements and that can be brought together and presented in greater detail than in the individual statements, or that show the details of a specific amount or amounts presented in the basic financial statements, the combining statements, or the individual fund financial statements.
- *Statistical section*

  Statistical tables cover a period of several years and contain data drawn from more than just the accounting records. Their purpose is to present social, economic, and financial trends, and the fiscal capacity of the governmental unit. The next titles indicate recommended statistical tables for a local general-purpose government's CAFR:
  - Net Assets by Components—Last Ten Fiscal Years
  - Changes in Net Assets—Last Ten Fiscal Years
  - Changes in Fund Balances of Governmental Funds—Last Ten Fiscal Years
  - General Governmental Tax Revenues by Source—Last Ten Fiscal Years
  - Assessed Value and Estimated Actual Value of Taxable Property—Last Ten Fiscal Years
  - Property Tax Rates—Direct and Overlapping Governments—Last Ten Fiscal Years
  - Principal Taxpayers—Current Fiscal Year and Nine Years Ago
  - Property Tax Levies and Collections—Last Ten Fiscal Years
  - Ratios of Outstanding Debt by Type—Last Ten Fiscal Years
  - Direct and Overlapping Governmental Activities Debt
  - Legal Debt Margin Information Last Ten Fiscal Years
  - Pledged-Revenue Coverage Last Ten Fiscal Years
  - Demographic and Economic Statistics—Last Ten Fiscal Years
  - Principal Employers—Current Fiscal Year and Nine Years Ago
  - Full-Time Equivalent Government Employees by Function—Last Ten Fiscal Years
  - Operating Indicators by Function—Last Ten Fiscal Years
  - Capital Asset Statistics by Function—Last Ten Fiscal Years
- *Single Audit Section*

  Although not a required part of a CAFR, some governments include in a separate section the information, including auditor's reports, required by the Single Audit Act Amendments of 1996.

(iv) Certificate of Achievement Program. Governmental units may submit their CAFRs to the GFOA (180 North Michigan Avenue, Chicago, IL 60601) for evaluation in accordance with the standards of financial reporting established by the GASB and the GFOA. If the report substantially adheres to these standards, the government is awarded a Certificate of Achievement for Excellence in Financial Reporting. The certificate is valid only for one year. It may be reproduced in the government's annual report and should be included in the subsequent year's CAFR. Annually, the GFOA publishes a list of the governments that hold valid certificates.

Many governments endeavor to obtain the certificate. They realize that credit rating agencies and others familiar with governmental accounting and financial reporting recognize that governments holding a certificate typically maintain complete financial records and effectively report their financial information to permit detailed analyses to be performed. This characteristic can improve the government's bond rating.

(v) Popular Reports. Governments also prepare popular reports to communicate with persons who are neither interested in a complete set of financial statements nor able to review them. Popular reports are also called *condensed summary data.*

There are three types of popular reports. The first is an aggregation of the data from the financial statements that disregards the distinction among fund types and the different bases of accounting and presents the data as if all the assets, liabilities, equities, revenues, and expenditures (expenses) pertain not to the fund types but to the government as a whole. This results in a presentation similar to that made by corporations and their subsidiaries. In such cases, the government usually eliminates significant interfund transactions before arriving at totals.

The second approach is to visually present the entity's financial information, for instance, by using pie charts or bar graphs. A common presentation is to present one pie to show the composition of revenue by cutting the pie into slices with each slice representing a major revenue source. The size of the slice would reflect the magnitude of the respective revenue source. Similar pie charts can be used to show the major categories of expenditures, the major categories of assets, and the major categories of liabilities.

The third approach is to issue consolidated government-wide financial statements. Such a consolidated approach replaces the funds and government-wide financial statements by a single "fund" that is used to report the financial position and results of operations of the entire oversight unit or reporting entity. Intra-governmental transactions are eliminated in the consolidation process and a single basis of accounting (normally accrual) is used for all transactions.

Consolidated financial statements typically include a balance sheet and an operating statement. Because the accrual basis of accounting is normally used, capital assets are reported and depreciated. Also, long-term obligations are reported.

33.5 BASIC FINANCIAL STATEMENTS REQUIRED FOR SPECIAL-PURPOSE GOVERNMENTS

Special-purpose governments are legally separate entities that are component units or other standalone governments, which are legally separate government organizations that (1) do not have separately elected governing bodies and (2) are not component units, plus joint ventures, jointly governed organizations, and pools.

A special-purpose government that is engaged in more than one governmental program or that has both governmental and business-type activities should meet the reporting requirements for governments that are not special-purpose governments. A special-purpose government is engaged in more than one governmental program if it budgets, manages, or accounts for its activities as multiple programs, such as a school district that provides regular instruction, special instruction, vocational education, and adult education.

(a) REPORTING BY SPECIAL-PURPOSE GOVERNMENTS ENGAGED IN GOVERNMENTAL ACTIVITIES. A special-purpose government engaged in a single governmental activity, such as some cemetery districts, levee districts, assessment districts, and drainage districts, may combine its government-wide financial statements and its fund financial statements in a columnar format that reconciles line items of fund financial information to government-wide information in a separate column on the face of the financial statements rather than at the bottom of the statements or in an accompanying schedule. Otherwise, the special-purpose government may present separate government-wide and fund financial statements and may present its government-wide statement of activities in a different format. For example, it may be presented in a single column that reports expenses first followed by revenues by major sources. The difference, net revenue or expense, should be followed by contributions to permanent and term endowments, special and extraordinary items, transfers, and beginning and ending net assets. The special-purpose government should also present an MD&A and applicable required supplementary information as defined by GASB.

(b) REPORTING BY SPECIAL-PURPOSE GOVERNMENTS ENGAGED ONLY IN BUSINESS-TYPE ACTIVITIES. A government engaged in only business-type activities should present only the financial statement required for enterprise funds:

- MD&A
- Financial statements:
  - Statement of net assets
  - Statement of revenues, expenses, and changes in fund net assets
  - Statement of cash flows
- Notes to financial statements
- Applicable required supplementary information other than MD&A

(c) REPORTING BY SPECIAL-PURPOSE GOVERNMENTS ENGAGED ONLY IN FIDUCIARY ACTIVITIES. A special-purpose government engaged only in fiduciary activities should present just the financial statement required for fiduciary funds:

- MD&A
- Statement of fiduciary net assets
- Statement of changes in fiduciary net assets
- Notes to financial statements
- Applicable required supplementary information other than MD&A

A Public Employees Retirement System (PERS) is a special-purpose government that administers one or more defined benefit pension plans and may also administer other kinds of employee benefit plans, such as defined contribution, deferred compensation, and postemployment health care plans. One that administers more than one defined benefit pension plan or postemployment health care plan should present combining financial statements for all such plans and, if applicable, required schedules for each plan. (A PERS that administers one or more agent multiple-employer plans applies these requirements at the aggregate plan level). It should (1) present a separate column for each plan on the statement of fiduciary net assets and the statement of changes in fiduciary net assets or (2) present combining statements for the plans as part of the basic financial statements.

33.6 ACCOUNTING PRINCIPLES AND PRACTICES—PUBLIC COLLEGES AND UNIVERSITIES

Public colleges and universities should apply the principles discussed in this chapter. The primary guidance for public colleges and universities is GASB Statement No. 35, *Basic Financial Statements—and Management's Discussion and Analysis—for Public Colleges and Universities.*

33.7 AUDITS OF GOVERNMENTAL UNITS

Audits of governmental units with financial statements can be performed in accordance with:

- Generally accepted auditing standards (GAAS)
- *Government Auditing Standards* (the Yellow Book)
- The Single Audit Act Amendments of 1996 and Office of Management and Budget (OMB) Circular A-133

When performing an audit in accordance with GAAS, the guidance contained in the *AICPA Professional Standards* is followed. This is the same guidance followed by auditors when auditing the financial statements of commercial entities; typically it results in the issuance of an opinion on the financial statements and perhaps a management letter. *Government Auditing Standards* (published by the U.S. Comptroller General), establishes the concept of an expanded scope audit that includes both financial and compliance features. According to the Yellow Book, a financial audit can help determine whether:

- The financial statements of an audited entity present fairly the financial position and the results of financial operations in accordance with GAAP
- The entity has complied with laws and regulations that may have a material effect on the financial statements

The Yellow Book incorporates the *AICPA Professional Standards* and sets forth additional standards and requirements, including these six:

1. A review is to be made of compliance with applicable laws and regulations, as set forth in federal audit guides and other applicable reference sources.
2. The auditor reports on the entity's compliance with laws, regulations, contracts, and grant agreements and shall also include material instances of noncompliance and instances or indications of noncompliance or fraud and illegal acts found during or in connection with the audit.
3. The auditors shall report on their consideration of the entity's internal control over financial reporting as part of the financial audit.
   They shall identify as a minimum:
   a. The scope of auditor's work in obtaining an understanding of the internal control over financial reporting.
   b. The significant deficiencies including separate identification of material weaknesses identified as a result of the auditor's work.
4. Auditors performing government audits are required to obtain 80 hours of continuing education that directly enhance the auditor's professional proficiency to perform audits and/or attestation engagements every two years, of which 24 hours should be directly related to government. At least 20 of the 80 hours should be completed in each year of the two-year period.
5. Audit organizations performing government audits are required to establish an internal quality control system and participate in an external quality control review program.
6. The auditor communicates certain information related to the conduct of the audit to those charged with governance or to the individuals with whom they have contracted for the audit.

(a) SINGLE AUDIT ACT AMENDMENTS OF 1996. Many state and local governments are required to obtain a periodic audit of the federal funds they receive—usually once a year. The audits are normally performed by an independent certified public accountant (CPA) or public accountant, or, in some states, by the government's internal audit personnel. A few jurisdictions have an independently elected or appointed auditor who conducts the audit. Single audits are conducted in accordance with GAAS, *Government Auditing Standards,* and the Single Audit Amendments Act of 1996 and its implementing regulation OMB Circular A-133, including its *Compliance Supplement.* These requirements have been updated for fiscal years beginning on or after July 1, 1997, by the Single Audit Amendments Act of 1996.

The objectives of the Act are:

- To improve the financial management of state and local governments with respect to federal financial assistance programs through improved auditing
- To establish uniform requirements for audits of federal financial assistance provided to state and local governments
- To promote the efficient and effective use of audit resources
- To ensure that federal departments and agencies, to the maximum extent practicable, rely on and use audit work performed pursuant to the requirements of the Single Audit Act

Although the single audit builds on the annual financial statement audit currently required by most state and larger local governments, it places substantial additional emphasis on the consideration and testing of internal controls and the testing of compliance with laws and regulations.

The Single Audit Act and OMB Circular A-133 require the auditor to determine whether:

- The financial statements of the government, department, agency, or establishment present fairly its financial position and the results of operations in conformity with GAAP
- The organization has internal and other control structures to provide reasonable assurance that it is managing federal financial assistance programs in compliance with applicable laws, regulations, contracts, and grants
- The organization has complied with laws and regulations that may have a material effect on its financial statements and that may have a direct and material effect on each major federal financial assistance program

Nonfederal entities that expend $500,000 or more in a year in federal awards are subject to a single audit unless they elect (if qualified) to have a program-specific audit conducted. If less than $500,000 is expended, the entity is exempt from federal audit requirements for that year, but records must be retained for review or audit, by, for example the U.S. Government Accountability Office.

The Single Audit Act provides auditors with guidance on the focus of the audit by defining a level of audit work based on the concept of "major" federal programs. OMB Circular A-133 §______.520 provides specific guidance on how to determine what are major federal programs and outlines the three steps required in identifying "major" federal programs. These three steps are:

1. *Identify "Type A" and "Type B" programs.* For most small and medium-size governments, a Type A program is defined as the larger of $300,000 or 3 percent of the total federal *expenditures* for all federal programs. For larger governments whose total federal expenditures exceed $100 million, a Type A program is based on a sliding scale. All programs that are not categorized as a Type A program are "Type B" programs.
2. *Identify "Low Risk Type A" programs by assessing all Type A programs.* Typically, a Low Risk Type A program must have been audited as a "major" program within the last two years and must have no audit findings as defined in §______.510(a). All Type A programs that are not low risk are high risk and must be audited as major programs.
3. *Identify "High Risk Type B" programs if there are one or more Low Risk Type A programs identified.* Auditors have two options in assessing risks in Type B programs:
   a. Complete a risk assessment for all Type B programs that are greater than the Type B floor amount, then classify as major programs one-half of the Type B programs greater than the floor amount identified as high risk with a cap in the number of major programs at the number of Low Risk Type A programs.

b. Complete a risk assessment for some of the Type B programs that are greater than the Type B floor amount until the same number high-risk Type B programs greater equal to the number of Low Risk Type A programs.

If a federal grantor agency formally designates a program to be major, this program must also be audited in addition to the major programs identified in previous steps.

The Single Audit Act and OMB Circular A-133 require the auditor to issue these reports:

- A report on the audit of the basic financial statements of the entity as a whole, or the department, agency, or establishment covered by the audit
- A report on compliance and internal control based on an audit of the basic financial statements
- A report on compliance and internal control over compliance applicable to each major federal award program

In a single audit, the report on the audit of the basic financial statements is typically expanded to include an opinion on the fair presentation of the supplementary schedule of expenditures of federal awards in relation to the audited financial statements.

(b) OTHER CONSIDERATIONS. Most government officials and auditors of governmental units realize that a good audit should furnish more than an opinion on the financial statements. Other services a governmental auditor can provide are:

- Pinpointing the key information upon which decisions should be based and contributing to the presentation of this information in a manner that facilitates decision making
- Uncovering deficiencies in the accounting system and providing suggestions for improving the efficiency and effectiveness of the system
- Obtaining and presenting information useful for marketing securities

Obtaining a qualified auditor, particularly one who can provide the additional services described earlier, requires that the selection be based on qualifications and experience, not solely cost. The National Intergovernmental Audit Forum, in its handbook *How to Avoid a Substandard Audit: Suggestions for Procuring an Audit,* indicates:

> Public entities should never select auditors without considering five basic elements of an effective audit procurement process:
>
> - planning (determining what needs to be done and when),
> - fostering competition by soliciting proposals (writing a clear and direct solicitation document and disseminating it widely),
> - technically evaluating proposals and qualifications (authorizing a committee of knowledgeable persons to evaluate the ability of prospective auditors to effectively carry out the audit),
> - preparing a written agreement (documenting the expectations of both the entity and the auditor), and
> - monitoring the auditor's performance (periodically reviewing the progress of that performance).

This *Handbook* provides detailed information about the five elements of procurement just listed as well as the use of audit committees in a government environment and other useful information about the auditor procurement process.

(i) Governmental Rotation of Auditors. The automatic rotation of auditors after a given number of years is a common practice in many governments; however, it is not always beneficial. Many governments have followed this policy, believing that they will (1) receive a fresh outlook from the audit, (2) spread the work among several firms, and (3) encourage lower fees. What the Government Accountability Office found in its November 2003 *Required Study on the Potential Effects of Mandatory Audit Firm Rotation* is that mandatory audit firm rotation may not be the most efficient way to strengthen auditor independence and improve auditing quality considering the additional financial costs and the loss of institutional knowledge. Automatic rotation may be harmful in that it could deprive the government of the extensive knowledge of the entity developed by the current auditor. It may also impair auditing effectiveness since a new auditor may need to spend considerable time learning the government's system—the government actually may incur more cost since its personnel will need to spend time explaining the organization, systems, and data to the new auditors, and the new auditors will need to spend valuable time reviewing information that is already part of the previous auditor's audit documentation. Although a government should continuously monitor its auditor's performance to ensure that the service obtained is commensurate with the cost, normally an entity should change auditors only because of dissatisfaction with services and not for the sake of receiving a lower fee.

(ii) Audit Committees. In recent years, governments have started establishing audit committees similar to those in the private sector. Audit committees are often comprised of elected officials and top-level management of the government. Governments should consider including an expert in financial accounting and reporting on its audit committee. Some appropriate tasks for a local government's audit committee are:

- Reviewing significant financial information for reliability, timeliness, clarity, appropriateness of disclosure, and compliance with GAAP and legal requirements
- Ascertaining that internal controls are appropriately designed and functioning effectively
- Evaluating independent audit firms and selecting one for approval by the appropriate body
- Overseeing the scope and performance of the independent audit function
- Ensuring that the auditors' recommendations for improvements in internal controls and operating methods receive management's attention and are implemented on a timely basis
- Providing an effective communications link between the auditors and the full governing board

The primary benefit of an audit committee is in assisting the full governing board to fulfill its responsibilities for the presentation of financial information about the governmental unit. There are also secondary benefits: The other parties involved in the issuance of financial information—management and independent and internal auditors—can perform their roles more effectively if an audit committee is involved in the process. Finally, there are advantages for the government's constituencies—in particular, the taxpayers and bondholders.

33.8 CONCLUDING REMARKS

Governmental accounting and reporting is changing and expanding at an increasing rapid rate. Coupling this with public accountability issues, the federal government's pressure for increased audit quality, and the penalties for substandard audit performance results in increasing levels of audit risk.

Government audits, considered low-risk engagements by many, are quickly becoming areas of extremely high risk. Auditing professionals need to recognize the risk associated with government engagements now and in the future before incurring severe penalties or embarrassment. The technical issues involved in government auditing are on a par with those in the commercial environment, but auditors have much less experience and less technical guidance to fall back on.

Dealing with these technical issues requires well-trained, highly motivated individuals; no longer can such audits be left to less experienced members of the team. Dealing with the *real* issues governments are facing (e.g., structural deficits, deteriorating infrastructure, prison overcrowding, increasing pension and other postemployment health care benefits, etc.) requires even more from the individuals in the profession. Like it or not, government accounting and reporting is being thrust into the spotlight and will be scrutinized by a multitude of individuals and groups. It is imperative that individuals in the industry realize this fact and begin now to prepare for the future.

33.9 SOURCES AND SUGGESTED REFERENCES

American Institute of Certified Public Accountants. *AICPA Audit and Accounting Guide: Government Auditing Standards and Circular A-133 Audits*. New York: Author, 2011.

———. *AICPA Audit and Accounting Guide: State and Local Governments*. New York: Author, 2011

———. *AICPA Professional Standards*. New York: Author, 2007.

City and County of San Francisco, California. *Comprehensive Annual Financial Report for the Year Ended June 30, 2011.* 2011.

Financial Accounting Standards Board. Statement of Financial Accounting Concepts No. 4, *Objectives of Financial Reporting by Nonbusiness Organizations*. Stamford, CT: Author, 1980.

———. Statement of Financial Accounting Standards No. 6, *Classification of Short-Term Obligations Expected to Be Refinanced.* Stamford, CT: Author, 1975.

———. Statement of Financial Accounting Standards Board No. 13, *Accounting for Leases*. Stamford, CT: Author, 1975.

Government Accountability Office. *Government Auditing Standards, July 2007 Revision*. Washington, DC: Author, 2003.

———. *Required Study on the Potential Effects of Mandatory Audit Firm Rotation*. Washington, DC: Author, 2003.

Governmental Accounting Standards Board. GASB Statement No. 34, *Basic Financial Statements—And Management's Discussion and Analysis—for State and Local Governments*. Norwalk, CT: Author, 1999.

———. *Codification of Governmental Accounting and Financial Reporting Standards*. Norwalk, CT: Author, 2011.

Government Finance Officers Association. *Governmental Accounting, Auditing and Financial Reporting*. Chicago: Author, 2005.

Ives, M. "The Governmental Accounting Standards Board: Factors Influencing Its Operation and Initial Technical Agenda," *Government Accounting Journal* 49, no. 1 (Spring 2002): 22–27.

Mead, D.M. *What You Should Know About Your Local Government's Finances*. Norwalk, CT: GASB, 2007.

Office of Management and Budget. *Circular No. A-133, Audits of States, Local Governments, and Non-Profit Organizations, June 27, 2003 Revision*. Washington, DC: Author, 2003.

APPENDIX PRONOUNCEMENTS ON STATE AND LOCAL GOVERNMENT ACCOUNTING

	Government Accounting Standard Board	Effective Date
Statement No. 1	Authoritative Status of NCGA Pronouncements and AICPA Industry Audit Guide	On issuance (7/84)
Statement No. 2	Financial Reporting of Deferred Compensation Plans Adopted under the Provisions of Internal Revenue Code Section 457	Superseded by GASB Statement No. 32
Statement No. 3	Deposits with Financial Institutions, Investments (including Repurchase Agreements), and Reverse Repurchase Agreements	Financial statements for periods ending after 2/15/86
Statement No. 4	Applicability of FASB Statement No. 87, "Employers' Accounting for Pensions," to State and Local Governmental Employers	Superseded by GASB Statement No. 27
Statement No. 5	Disclosure of Pension Information by Public Employee Retirement Systems and State and Local Governmental Employers	Financial reports issued for fiscal years beginning after 12/15/86

(Continues)

	Government Accounting Standard Board	Effective Date
Statement No. 6	Accounting and Financial Reporting for Special Assessments	Financial statements for periods beginning after 6/15/87
Statement No. 7	Advance Refundings Resulting in Defeasance of Debt	Fiscal periods beginning after 12/15/86
Statement No. 8	Applicability of FASB Statement No. 93, "Recognition of Depreciation by Not-for-Profit Organizations," to Certain State and Local Governmental Entities	Superseded by GASB Statement No. 35
Statement No. 9	Reporting Cash Flows of Proprietary and Nonexpendable Trust Funds and Governmental Entries that Use Proprietary Fund Accounting	Fiscal periods beginning after 12/15/89
Statement No. 10	Accounting and Financial Reporting for Risk Financing and Related Insurance Issues	Pools—fiscal periods beginning after 6/15/90 Other—fiscal periods beginning after 6/15/93
Statement No. 11	Measurement Focus and Basis of Accounting—Governmental Fund Operating Statements	Fiscal periods beginning after 6/15/94
Statement No. 12	Disclosure of Information on Postemployment Benefits Other than Pension Benefits by State and Local Governmental Employers	Fiscal periods beginning after 6/15/90
Statement No. 13	Accounting for Operating Leases with Scheduled Rent Increases	Leases with terms beginning after 6/30/90
Statement No. 14	The Financial Reporting Entity	Fiscal periods beginning after 12/15/92
Statement No. 15	Governmental College and University Accounting and Financial Reporting Models	Superseded by GASB Statement No. 35
Statement No. 16	Accounting for Compensated Absences	Fiscal periods beginning after June 15, 1993
Statement No. 17	Measurement Focus and Basis of Accounting—Governmental Fund Operating Statements: Amendment of Effective Dates of GASB Statement No. 11 and Related Statements	Immediately
Statement No. 18	Accounting for Municipal Solid Waste Landfill Closure and Post-Closure Care Costs	Fiscal periods beginning after June 15, 1993
Statement No. 19	Governmental College and University Omnibus Statement—An Amendment of GASB Statements No. 10 and 15	Superseded by GASB Statement No. 35.
Statement No. 20	Accounting and Financial Reporting for Proprietary Funds and Other Governmental Entities That Use Proprietary Fund Accounting	Fiscal periods beginning after December 15, 1993
Statement No. 21	Accounting for Escheat Property	Fiscal periods beginning after June 15, 1994
Statement No. 22	Accounting for Taxpayer-Assessed Tax Revenues in Governmental Funds	Superseded by GASB Statement No. 33
Statement No. 23	Accounting and Financial Reporting for Refundings of Debt Reported by Proprietary Activities	Fiscal periods beginning after June 15, 1994

	Government Accounting Standard Board	Effective Date
Statement No. 24	Accounting and Financial Reporting for Certain Grants and Other Financial Assistance	Fiscal periods beginning after June 15, 1995
Statement No. 25	Financial Reporting for Defined Benefit Pension Plans and Note Disclosures for Defined Contribution Plans	Fiscal periods beginning after June 15, 1996; Statement No. 26 must be implemented simultaneously
Statement No. 26	Financial Reporting for Postemployment Healthcare Plans Administered by Defined Benefit Pension Plans	Fiscal periods beginning after June 15, 1996; Statement No. 25 must be implemented simultaneously
Statement No. 27	Accounting for Pensions by State and Local Governmental Employers	Fiscal periods beginning after June 15, 1997
Statement No. 28	Accounting and Financial Reporting for Securities Lending Transactions	Fiscal periods beginning after December 15, 1995
Statement No. 29	The Use of Not-for-Profit Accounting and Financial Reporting Principles by Governmental Entities	Fiscal periods beginning after December 15, 1995
Statement No. 30	Risk Financing Omnibus	Fiscal periods beginning after June 15, 1996
Statement No. 31	Accounting and Financial Reporting for Certain Investments and for External Investment Pools	Fiscal periods beginning after June 15, 1997
Statement No. 32	Accounting and Financial Reporting for Internal Revenue Code Section 457 Deferred Compensation Plans	Earlier of fiscal periods beginning after December 31, 1998, or amendment of the IRC Section 457 Plan
Statement No. 33	Accounting and Financial Reporting for Nonexchange Transactions	Periods beginning after June 15, 2000
Statement No. 34	Basic Financial Statements—and Management's Discussion and Analysis—for State and Local Governments	(1)
Statement No. 35	Basic Financial Statements—and Management's Discussion and Analysis—for Public Colleges and Universities: Amendment of GASB Statement No. 34	(2)
Statement No. 36	Recipient Reporting for Certain Shared Nonexchange Revenues: Amendment of GASB Statement No. 33	Simultaneously with Statement No. 33
Statement No. 37	Basic Financial Statements—and Management's Discussion and Analysis—for State and Local Governments: Omnibus	(3)
Statement No. 38	Certain Financial Statement Note Disclosures Discussion and Analysis-for State and Local Governments	(1)

(Continues)

(1)In three phases, based on total annual revenue in the first fiscal year ending after June 15, 1999; Phase 1: governments with total annual revenues of $100 million or more, fiscal periods beginning after June 15, 2001; Phase 2: governments with total annual revenues of $10 million or more but less than $100 million, fiscal periods beginning after June 15, 2002; Phase 3: governments with total annual revenues of less than $10 million, fiscal periods beginning after June 15, 2003.

(2)Public institutions that are components of another reporting entity should implement the Statement no later than the same year as their primary government. For public institutions that are not components of another reporting entity, this Statement is effective in the three phases indicated in the footnote (1).

(3)Simultaneously with Statement No. 34. For governments that implemented Statement No. 34 before Statement No. 37 was issued, Statement No. 37 is effective for periods beginning after June 15, 2000.

	Government Accounting Standard Board	Effective Date
Statement No. 39	Determining Whether Certain Organizations Are Component Units	Periods beginning after June 15, 2003
Statement No. 40	Deposit and Investment Risk Disclosures—An Amendment of GASB Statement No. 3	Periods beginning after June 15, 2004
Statement No. 41	Budgetary Comparison Schedules—Perspective Differences—An Amendment of GASB Statement No. 34	Simultaneously with Statement 34
Statement No. 42	Accounting and Financial Reporting for Impairment of Capital Assets and for Insurance Recoveries	Periods beginning after December 15, 2004
Statement No. 43	Financial Reporting for Postemployment Benefit Plans Other Than Pension Plans	Effective in three phases based on a government's total annual revenues in the first fiscal year ending after June 15, 1999: for periods beginning after December 15, 2005, 2006 and 2007
Statement No. 44	Economic Condition Reporting—The Statistical Section—An Amendment of NCGA Statement 1	Statistical sections prepared for periods beginning after June 15, 2005
Statement No. 45	Accounting and Financial Reporting by Employers for Postemployment Benefits Other Than Pensions	Effective in three phases based on a government's total annual revenues in the first fiscal year ending after June 15, 1999: for periods beginning after December 15, 2006, 2007 and 2008
Statement No. 46	Net Assets Restricted by Enabling Legislation—An Amendment of GASB Statement No. 34	Periods beginning after June 15, 2005
Statement No. 47	Accounting for Termination Benefits	For termination benefits provided through an existing defined benefit OPEB plan, the provisions of this Statement should be implemented simultaneously with the requirements of Statement 45; for all other termination benefits, this Statement is effective for financial statements for periods beginning after June 15, 2005
Statement No. 48	Sales and Pledges of Receivables and Future Revenues and Intra-Entity Transfers of Assets and Future Revenues	Periods beginning after December 15, 2006
Statement No. 49	Accounting and Financial Reporting for Pollution Remediation Obligations	Periods beginning after December 15, 2007
Statement No. 50	Pension Disclosures—an amendment of GASB Statements No. 25 and No. 27	Periods beginning after June 15, 2007, except for requirements related to the use of the entry age actuarial cost method for the purpose of reporting a surrogate funded status and funding progress of plans that use the aggregate actuarial cost method, which are effective for periods for which the financial statements and RSI contain information resulting from actuarial valuations as of June 15, 2007, or later

	Government Accounting Standard Board	Effective Date
Statement No. 51	Accounting and Financial Reporting for Intangible Assets	Periods beginning after June 15, 2009
Statement No. 52	Land and Other Real Estate Held as Investments by Endowments	Periods beginning after June 15, 2008
Statement No. 53	Accounting and Financial Reporting for Derivative Instruments	Fiscal periods beginning after June 15, 2009
Statement No. 54	Fund Balance Reporting and Governmental Fund Type Definitions	Fiscal periods beginning after June 15, 2010
Statement No. 55	The Hierarchy of Generally Accepted Accounting Principles for State and Local Governments	Immediately
Statement No. 56	Codification of Accounting and Financial Reporting Guidance Contained in the AICPA Statements on Auditing Standards	Immediately
Statement No. 57	OPEB Measurements by Agent Employers and Agent Multiple-Employer Plans	Provisions related to the use and reporting of the alternative measurement method are effective immediately; provisions related to the frequency and timing of measurements are effective for actuarial valuations first used to report funded status information in OPEB plan financial statements for periods beginning after June 15, 2011
Statement No. 58	Accounting and Financial Reporting for Chapter 9 Bankruptcies	Fiscal periods beginning after June 15, 2009; retroactive application is required for all prior periods presented during which a government was in bankruptcy
Statement No. 59	Financial Instruments Omnibus	Fiscal periods beginning after June 15, 2010; earlier application is encouraged
Statement No. 60	Accounting and Financial Reporting for Service Concession Arrangements	Fiscal periods beginning after December 15, 2011; provisions are generally required to be applied retroactively for all periods presented
Statement No. 61	The Financial Reporting Entity: Omnibus—An amendment of GASB Statements No. 14 and No. 34	Fiscal periods beginning after June 15, 2012.
Statement No. 62	Codification of Accounting and Financial Reporting Guidance Contained in Pre-November 30, 1989 FASB and AICPA Pronouncements	Fiscal periods beginning after December 15, 2011; provisions are generally required to be applied retroactively for all periods presented
Statement No. 63	Financial Reporting of Deferred Outflows of Resources, Deferred Inflows of Resources, and Net Position	Starting with the fiscal periods that end December 31, 2012
Statement No. 64	Derivative Instruments: Application of Hedge Accounting Termination Provisions—an Amendment of GASB Statement No. 53	Fiscal periods beginning after June 15, 2011
Interpretation No. 1	Demand Bonds Issued by State and Local Governmental Entities	Fiscal periods ending after June 15, 1985

(*Continues*)

	Government Accounting Standard Board	Effective Date
Interpretation No. 2	Disclosure of Conduit Debt Obligations	Fiscal periods beginning after December 15, 1995
Interpretation No. 3	Financial Reporting for Reverse Repurchase Agreements	Fiscal periods beginning after December 15, 1995
Interpretation No. 4	Accounting and Financial Reporting for Capitalization Contributions to Public Entity Risk Pools	Fiscal periods beginning after June 15, 1996
Interpretation No. 5	Property Tax Revenue Recognition in Governmental Funds	Fiscal periods beginning after June 15, 2000
Interpretation No. 6	Recognition and Measurement of Certain Liabilities and Expenditures in Governmental Fund Financial Statements: An Interpretation of NCGA Statements 1, 4, and 5, NCGA Interpretation 8, and GASB Statement Nos. 10, 16, and 18	Simultaneously with Statement No. 34
Technical Bulletin No. 84-1	Purpose and Scope of GASB Technical Bulletins and Procedures for Issuance	None
Technical Bulletin No. 2003-1	Disclosure Requirements for Derivatives Not Reported at Fair Value on the Statement of Net Assets	Financial statements issued after June 15, 2003
Technical Bulletin No. 2004-1	Tobacco Settlement Recognition and Financial Reporting Entity Issues	June 15, 2004
Technical Bulletin No. 2004-2	Recognition of Pension and Other Postemployment Benefit Expenditures/Expense and Liabilities by Cost-Sharing Employers	Pension transactions: for financial statements for periods ending after December 15, 2004; OPEB transactions: applied simultaneously with the requirements of Statement No. 45
Technical Bulletin No. 2006-1	Accounting and Financial Reporting by Employers and OPEB Plans for Payments from the Federal Government Pursuant to the Retiree Drug Subsidy Provisions of Medicare Part D	On issuance (6/06) except for the portions of answers pertaining specifically to measurement, recognition, or required supplementary information requirements of Statement Nos. 43 or 45; those provisions should be applied simultaneously with the implementation of Statement Nos. 43 or 45
Technical Bulletin No. 2008-1	Determining the Annual Required Contribution Adjustment for Postemployment Benefits	Financial statements for periods ending after December 15, 2008
Concepts Statement No. 1	Objectives of Financial Reporting	None
Concepts Statement No. 2	Reporting Service Efforts and Accomplishments	None
Concepts Statement No. 3	Communication Methods in General Purpose External Financial Reports That Contain Basic Financial Statements	None
Concepts Statement No. 4	Elements of Financial Statements	None
Concepts Statement No. 5	Service Efforts and Accomplishments Reporting—An Amendment of GASB Concepts Statement No. 2	None

	National Council on Government Accounting	Effective Date
Statement No. 1	Governmental Accounting and Financial Reporting Principles	Fiscal years ending after 6/30/80
Statement No. 2	Grant, Entitlement, and Shared Revenue Accounting by State and Local Governments	Fiscal years ending after 6/30/80
Statement No. 3	Defining the Governmental Reporting Entity	Issued 12/81; superseded by GASB Statement No. 14
Statement No. 4	Accounting and Financial Reporting Principles for Claims and Judgments and Compensated Absences	Fiscal years beginning after 12/31/82; ¶20 extended indefinitely by NCGAS 11
Statement No. 5	Accounting and Financial Reporting Principles for Lease Agreements of State and Local Governments	Fiscal years beginning after 6/30/83
Statement No. 6	Pension Accounting and Financial Reporting: Public Employee Retirement Systems and State and Local Government Employers	Superseded by GASB Statement Nos. 25 and 27
Statement No. 7	Financial Reporting for Component Units within the Governmental Reporting Entity	Superseded by GASB Statement No. 14
Interpretation No. 1	GAAFR and the AICPA Audit Guide (Superseded)	Issued 4/86; superseded by NCGAS 1
Interpretation No. 2	Segment Information for Enterprise Funds	Issued 6/80; superseded by GASB Statement No. 34
Interpretation No. 3	Revenue Recognition—Property Taxes	Fiscal years beginning after 9/30/81
Interpretation No. 4	Accounting and Financial Reporting for Public Employee Retirement Systems and Pension Trust Funds (Superseded)	Fiscal years beginning after 6/15/82; superseded by NCGAS 6 and repealed by NCGAI 8
Interpretation No. 5	Authoritative Status of Governmental Accounting, Auditing, and Financial Reporting	Issued 3/82; superseded by GASB Statement No. 34
Interpretation No. 6	Notes to the Financial Statements Disclosure	Prospectively for fiscal years beginning after 12/31/82
Interpretation No. 7	Clarification As to the Application of the Criteria in NCGA Statement, "Defining the Governmental Reporting Entity"	Issued 9/83; superseded by GASB Statement No. 14
Interpretation No. 8	Certain Pension Matters	Fiscal years ending after 12/31/83
Interpretation No. 9	Certain Fund Classifications and Balance Sheet Accounts	Fiscal years ending after 6/30/84
Interpretation No. 10	State and Local Government Budgetary Reporting	Fiscal years ending after 6/30/84
Interpretation No. 11	Claim and Judgment Transactions for Governmental Funds	Issued 4/84; superseded by GASB Statement No. 10

CHAPTER **34**

OIL, GAS, AND OTHER NATURAL RESOURCES

Bill Godshall, CPA

Frazier & Deeter, LLC

34.1 INTRODUCTION 1

34.2 OIL AND GAS EXPLORATION AND PRODUCING OPERATIONS 2

34.3 ACCOUNTING FOR JOINT OPERATIONS 4

(a) Operator Accounting 4
(b) Nonoperator Accounting 5
(c) Other Accounting Procedures 5
(d) Overview of Accounting Standards 5

34.4 ACCEPTABLE ACCOUNTING METHODS 6

(a) Successful Efforts Method 6
(i) Basic Rules 6
(ii) Exploratory versus Development Well Definition 7
(iii) Treatment of Costs of Exploratory Wells Whose Outcome Is Undetermined 7
(iv) Successful Efforts Impairment Test 7
(v) Conveyances 8
(b) Full Cost Method 8
(i) Basic Rules 8
(ii) Exclusion of Costs from Amortization 8
(iii) Full Cost Ceiling Test 9
(iv) Conveyances 10

34.5 ACCOUNTING FOR NATURAL GAS IMBALANCES 10

(a) Sales Method 10
(b) Entitlements Method 10
(c) Gas Balancing Example 11

34.6 HARD-ROCK MINING 11

(a) Mining Operations 11
(b) Sources of Generally Accepted Accounting Principles 13

34.7 ACCOUNTING FOR MINING COSTS 13

(a) Exploration and Development Costs 13
(b) Production Costs 14
(c) Inventory 15
(i) Metals and Minerals 15
(ii) Materials and Supplies 16
(d) Commodities, Futures Transactions 16
(e) Reclamation and Remediation 16
(f) Shutdown of Mines 17
(g) Accounting for the Impairment of Long-Lived Assets 17

34.8 ACCOUNTING FOR MINING REVENUES 18

(a) Sales of Minerals 18
(b) Tolling and Royalty Revenues 18

34.9 SUPPLEMENTARY FINANCIAL STATEMENT INFORMATION—ORE RESERVES 19

34.10 ACCOUNTING FOR INCOME TAXES 19

34.11 FINANCIAL STATEMENT DISCLOSURES 19

34.12 SOURCES AND SUGGESTED REFERENCES 20

34.1 INTRODUCTION

Accounting for oil and gas activities can be extremely complex because the accounting encompasses a wide variety of business strategies and vehicles. The industry's diversity developed in response to the risk involved in the exploration process, the volatility of prices, and the fluctuations in supply and demand for oil and gas. In addition to having a working knowledge of accounting procedures, the oil and gas accountant should be familiar with the operating characteristics of companies involved in oil and gas activities and understand the impact of individual transactions.

Oil and gas activities cover a wide spectrum—ranging from exploration and production activities to the refining, transportation, and marketing of products to consumers. Special accounting rules exist for exploration and production activities. Accounting for refining activities is similar in many ways to other process manufacturing businesses. Likewise, transportation and marketing do not differ significantly from one end product to another. This chapter focuses on the special accounting rules for petroleum exploration and production.

Everything in the preceding paragraph may be said for the mining and processing of minerals except that the accounting rules for mineral exploration and production are not as formalized as for petroleum.

34.2 OIL AND GAS EXPLORATION AND PRODUCING OPERATIONS

Oil- and gas-producing activities begin with the search for prospects—parcels of acreage that management thinks may contain economically viable oil or gas formations. For the most likely prospects, the enterprise may contract with a geological and geophysical (G&G) company to test and assess the subsurface formations and their depths. Three-dimensional (3-D) seismic studies send sound waves thousands of feet below the earth's surface, record the million echoes from underground strata, and use powerful computers to read the echoes to create 3-D electronic images of the underground formations. With these ultrasounds deep into the earth, the enterprise evaluates the various prospects, rejecting some and accepting others as suitable for acquisition of lease rights. (Prospecting may be done before or after obtaining lease rights.)

Specialists called *landmen* may be used to obtain lease rights. A landman is in effect a lease broker who searches titles and negotiates with property owners. Although the landman may be part of the company's staff, oil and gas companies often acquire lease rights to properties through independent landmen. Consideration for leasing the mineral rights usually includes a bonus (an immediate cash payment to the lessor) and a royalty interest retained by the lessor (a specified percentage of subsequent production minus applicable production taxes).

Once the leases have been obtained and the rights and obligations of all parties have been determined, exploratory drilling begins. Because drilling costs run to hundreds of thousands or millions of dollars, many companies reduce their capital commitment and related risks by seeking others to participate in joint venture arrangements. Participants in a joint venture are called *joint interest owners;* one owner, usually the enterprise that obtained the leases, acts as operator. The operator manages the venture and reports to the other, nonoperator participants. The operator initially pays the drilling costs and then bills those costs to the nonoperators. In some cases, the operator may collect these costs from nonoperators in advance.

The operator acquires the necessary supplies and subcontracts with a drilling company for drilling the well. The drilling time may be a few days, several months, or even a year or longer depending on many factors, particularly well depth and location. When the hole reaches the desired depth, various instruments are lowered that "log the well" to detect the presence of oil or gas. The joint interest owners evaluate the drilling and logging results to determine whether sufficient oil or gas can be extracted to justify the cost of completing the well. If the evaluation is negative, the well is plugged and abandoned as a dry hole. If sufficient quantities of crude oil or natural gas (hydrocarbons) appear to be present, the well is completed and equipment is installed to extract and separate the hydrocarbons from the water coming from the underground reservoir. Completion costs are substantial and may even exceed the initial drilling costs.

Before production begins (sometimes even before the well is drilled), the enterprise selects oil and gas purchasers and negotiates sales contracts. To transport the oil or gas from the well, a trunk line may be built to the nearest major pipeline; crude oil also may be stored in tanks at the production site and removed later by truck. The production owner and purchasers prepare and sign division orders, which are revenue distribution contracts specifying each owner's share of revenues. If the division order specifies that the purchaser is to pay all revenues to the operator, the operator must distribute the appropriate amounts to the other joint interest owners and the lessor(s).

The various factors that determine the success or failure of oil and gas exploration activities include many uncertainties. These factors set the oil and gas industry apart from many other capital-intensive industries. Some of these factors include those listed next.

- *Anticipated success of drilling.* Even with the recent technological advances in 3-D seismic, there is still substantial risk of not finding a commercial petroleum reservoir after spending hundreds of thousands of dollars (or more) drilling a well to the target formation. Exploration success is also affected by drilling risks, such as stuck drill pipes, blowouts, and improper completions.
- *Taxation.* A substantial portion of the revenues from the sale of crude oil and natural gas goes directly or indirectly to the federal and state governments in the form of severance taxes, ad valorem taxes, and income taxes. In the late 1970s, Congress enacted the Windfall Profit Tax on domestic crude oil. On August 25, 1988, that tax was repealed for all crude oil removed after that date. After the various taxes, royalties to the landowner, and production costs have been deducted, the producer's income from the sale of crude oil and natural gas may be only a small percentage of gross revenues.
- *Product price and marketability.* U.S. crude oil production meets only half of the country's demand and is readily marketable. The United States imports crude oil from Venezuela, Canada, and other countries. For the past several years, U.S. prices of crude oil have fluctuated widely due to numerous factors including world politics, economic conditions, and technology advances. In the last five years, prices have ranged from a low of about $40 per barrel to a high price of almost $150 per barrel during 2008. Oil prices also vary due to the quality of the oil and the location of the oil field. In a given month, heavy, sour crude oil in California may sell for half or two-thirds the price of light, sweet crude oil produced in Oklahoma.

  Natural gas price volatility also has seen historic levels since the early 2000s. While demand for natural gas is generally seasonal in the United States—high in the winter months for space heating and low in the summer for most areas of the country—the introduction of combined-cycle electric generation has contributed to higher natural gas prices in the summer as these generation plants are used to supplement power needs on a peaking basis. Significant quantities of gas produced in the summer are transported by pipelines to underground formations for temporary storage until the winter season. Such temporary storage helps to reduce the seasonal price fluctuations.

  Because of the volatility in oil and gas prices, a number of price hedging mechanisms have been developed, including futures contracts, long-term hedging arrangements, and product swaps.
- *Timing of production.* How quickly oil and gas are produced directly affects the payback period of an investment and its financial success or failure. The timing of production varies with the geologic characteristics of the reservoir and the marketability of the product. Reservoirs may contain the same gross producible reserves, yet the timing of production causes significant differences in the present value of the future revenue stream.
- *Acreage and drilling costs.* Many U.S. companies are focusing on exploration outside the United States. The United States is a mature exploration area producing 10 percent of the world's oil production from 63 percent of the world's oil wells. The global availability of quality exploration acreage, drilling personnel, and supplies has increased, whereas the related costs have dropped significantly since the boom period of the late 1970s and early 1980s.

34.3 ACCOUNTING FOR JOINT OPERATIONS

Oil- and gas-producing activities are recorded in the same general manner as most other activities that use manual or automated revenue, accounts payable, and general ledger systems. There are significant differences in the data gathering and reporting requirements, however, depending on whether the entity is an operator or a nonoperator for a given joint venture. The two major accounting systems unique to oil- and gas-producing activities are the joint interest billing system and the revenue distribution system. The operator's joint interest billing system must properly calculate and record the operator's net cost as well as the costs to be billed to the nonoperators. Likewise, the revenue distribution system should properly allocate cash receipts among venture participants; this entails first recording the amounts payable to the participants and later making the appropriate payments.

As discussed, joint interest operations evolved because of the need to share the financial burden and risks of oil- and gas-producing activities. Joint operations typically take the form of a simple joint venture evidenced by two formal agreements, generally referred to as an *exploration agreement* and an *operating agreement.* These agreements define the geographic area involved, designate which party will act as operator of the venture, define how revenue and expenses will be divided, and set forth the rights and responsibilities of all parties to the agreement. The operating agreement also establishes how the operator is to bill the nonoperators for joint venture expenditures and provides nonoperators with the right to conduct joint interest audits of the operator's accounting records.

Accounting for joint operations is basically the same as accounting for operations when a property is completely owned by one party, except that in joint operations, revenues and expenses are divided among all of the joint venture partners. The next section discusses accounting for joint operations, first from the operator's standpoint and then from the nonoperators' perspective.

(a) OPERATOR ACCOUNTING. The operator typically records revenue and expenses for a well on a 100 percent, or gross, basis and then allocates the revenue and expenses to the nonoperators based on ownership percentages maintained in the division order and joint interest master files. One approach is to record the full invoice or remittance advice amount and use contra or clearing accounts that set up the amounts due from or to the nonoperators. Recording transactions by means of contra accounts facilitates generation of information that management uses to review operations on a gross basis.

Before drilling and completing a well, the operator prepares an authorization for expenditure (AFE) itemizing the estimated costs to drill and complete the well. Although AFEs are normally required by the operating agreement, they are also useful as a capital budgeting tool in that they are routinely used for all major expenditures by oil and gas companies, even if no joint venture exists. In addition to AFEs, the operator's field supervisor or engineer at the well site prepares a daily drilling report, which is an abbreviated report of the current status and the drilling or completion activity of the past 24 hours. That report may be compared with a drilling report prepared by the drilling company (also called a tour report). Some daily drilling reports indicate estimated cumulative costs incurred to date.

For shallow wells that are quickly and easily drilled, the AFE subsidiary ledger, combined with the daily drilling report, may provide the basis for the operator's estimate of costs incurred but not invoiced. For other wells, however, the engineering department prepares an estimate of cumulative costs incurred through year-end as a basis for recording the accrual and, if material, the commitments for future expenditures.

The operator normally furnishes the nonoperators with a monthly summary billing that shows the amount owed the operator on a property-by-property basis. The summary billing is accompanied by a separate joint operating statement for each property. The joint operating statement contains a description of each expenditure and shows the total expenditures for the property. The statement also shows the allocation of expenditures among the joint interest participants. The operator usually does not furnish copies of third-party invoices supporting items appearing on the joint interest billing, but the third-party invoices can be examined and copied during the nonoperators' audit of the joint account. The operator may also furnish the nonoperators a production report and at a later date remit checks to the nonoperators for their share of production.

(b) NONOPERATOR ACCOUNTING. From the nonoperators' standpoint, the accounting for joint operations is basically the same as that followed by the operator. It is not unusual for a company to act as an operator on some properties and a nonoperator on others. To be able to make comparisons and evaluations that include both types of properties, nonoperators should also record items on a gross basis. A nonoperator should develop a control procedure for reviewing the joint operating statement to determine whether the operator is complying with the joint operating agreement, is billing the nonoperator only valid charges at the appropriate percentages, and is distributing the appropriate share of revenue.

(c) OTHER ACCOUNTING PROCEDURES. The operating agreement may permit the operator to charge the joint venture a monthly fixed fee to cover its internal costs incurred in operating the joint venture. Alternatively, the agreement may provide for reimbursement of the operator's actual costs.

The parties in a joint operation may agree either to share costs in a proportion that is different from that used for sharing revenue or to change the sharing percentages after a specific event takes place. Typically, that event is "payout," the point at which certain venturers have recovered their initial investment or an agreed-on multiple of the investment. All parties involved in joint operations encounter payout situations at some time. Controls must be designed to monitor payout status to ensure that all parties are satisfied that revenues and costs have been properly allocated in accordance with the joint operating agreement.

(d) OVERVIEW OF ACCOUNTING STANDARDS. In June 2009, the Financial Accounting Standards Board (FASB) released Statement of Financial Accounting Standard (SFAS) No. 168, *The FASB Accounting Standards Codification and the Hierarchy of Generally Accepted Accounting Principles.* SFAS No. 168 set the effective date for the use of the Accounting Standards Codification (ASC or Codification). Generally, the Codification became the sole source for generally accepted accounting principles (GAAP) for interim and annual periods ending after September 15, 2009. The primary source for accounting in oil and gas is found in ASC 932, *Extractive Industries—Oil and Gas,* which describes a "successful efforts" method of accounting. Securities and Exchange Commission (SEC) Regulation S-X, Article 4, Section 10 (also referred to as Reg. S-X Rule 4-10), prescribes two acceptable methods for public entities—either the successful efforts method described in ASC 932 or a "full cost" method, as described in the SEC's Reg. S-X Rule 4-10.

Additional guidance and interpretations can be found in SEC Staff Accounting Bulletins (SABs), surveys in industry accounting practices, and petroleum accounting journals and petroleum accounting textbooks. In addition, there is an AICPA *Audit and Accounting Guide, Audits of Entities with Oil and Gas Producing Activities.*

The primary differences between the successful efforts and full cost methods center on costs to be capitalized and those to be expensed. As the name implies, under the successful efforts method, only those costs that lead to the successful discovery of reserves are capitalized, while the costs of unsuccessful exploratory activities are charged directly to expense. Under the full cost method, all exploration efforts are treated as capital costs under the theory that the reserves found are the result of all costs incurred. Both methods are widely used; however, larger companies tend to follow the successful efforts method.

Under income tax law and regulations, all exploration and development costs, except leasehold and equipment costs, generally are expensed as incurred. Petroleum-producing companies with significant refining or marketing activities (called *integrateds* as opposed to independents) must capitalize 30 percent of intangible well costs to be amortized over 60 months. Leasehold costs are expensed by complex depletion deductions that, for independents, can exceed actual costs. Equipment costs are depreciated using accelerated methods. Many independent U.S. oil- and gas-producing companies pay the alternative minimum tax.

34.4 ACCEPTABLE ACCOUNTING METHODS

(a) SUCCESSFUL EFFORTS METHOD

(i) Basic Rules. The next points summarize the major aspects of the successful efforts method of accounting for oil and gas property costs:

- The costs of all G&G studies to find reserves are charged to expense as incurred.
- Lease acquisition costs for unproved properties are initially capitalized. Unproved properties are those on which no economically recoverable oil or gas has been demonstrated to exist. Unproved properties are to be assessed for impairment at least annually.
- If an unproved property becomes impaired because of such events as pending lease expiration or an unsuccessful exploratory well (dry hole), the loss is recognized and a valuation allowance is established to reflect the property's impairment. Two approaches to impairment are used: (1) property by property (typically used by small companies or situations involving significant acreage costs), or (2) a formula approach based on factors such as historical success ratios and average lease terms (typically used by larger companies with a significant number of smaller properties).
- Once proved reserves are found on a property, the property is considered proved and the acquisition costs are amortized on a unit-of-production basis over the property's producing life based on total proved reserves (both developed and undeveloped reserves). Under Reg. S-X Rule 4-10, the definition of *proved reserves* is:

  > Those quantities of oil and gas, which, by analysis of geoscience and engineering data, can be estimated with reasonable certainty to be economically producible—from a given date forward, from known reservoirs, and under existing economic conditions, operating methods, and government regulations—prior to the time at which contracts providing the right to operate expire, unless evidence indicates that renewal is reasonably certain, regardless of whether deterministic or probabilistic methods are used for the estimation.

  The definition states that the economic producibility of a reservoir must be based on existing economic conditions. It specifies that, in calculating economic producibility, a company must use a 12-month average price, calculated as the unweighted arithmetic average of the first-day-of-the-month price for each month within the 12-month period prior to the end of the reporting period, unless prices are defined by contractual arrangements, excluding escalations based on future conditions.
- If both oil and gas are produced from the property, the unit is normally equivalent barrels or thousands of cubic feet (mcfs), whereby gas is converted to equivalent barrels (or barrels are converted to equivalent mcfs) based on relative energy content. A common conversion factor is 5.6 mcf to 1 equivalent barrel.
- For a property containing both oil and gas, the unit may reflect either oil or gas if:
  - The relative property of oil and gas extracted in the current period is expected to continue in the future, *or*
  - The reflected mineral clearly dominates the other for both current production and reserves.
- Carrying costs required to retain rights to unproved properties (delay rentals, ad valorem taxes, etc.) are charged to expense.
- Exploratory wells are capitalized initially as wells in progress and expensed if proved reserves are not found. Successful exploratory wells are capitalized, as are their completion costs (setting casing and other costs necessary to begin producing the well).
- Costs of drilling development wells (even the rare dry ones) are capitalized.
- Costs of successful exploratory wells, along with the costs of drilling development wells on the lease, are amortized on a unit-of-production basis over the property's proved developed reserves on:
  - A property-by-property basis, *or*

  - The basis of some reasonable aggregation of properties with a common geologic or structural feature or stratigraphic condition, such as a reservoir or field.
- Once production has begun, all regular production costs are charged to expense.
- Capitalized interest, under the requirements of ASC 835, would also be capitalized as part of the cost of unevaluated properties during the evaluation phase.

(ii) Exploratory versus Development Well Definition. Because Reg. S-X requires that the costs of dry exploratory wells be charged to expense, whereas the costs of dry development wells are capitalized, it is important to classify wells properly. Reg. S-X Rule 4-10 and the glossary to ASC 932 define the two categories of wells:

> *Development well.* A well drilled within the proved area of an oil or gas reservoir to the depth of a stratigraphic horizon known to be productive.
>
> *Exploratory well.* A well drilled to find and produce oil or gas in an unproved area, to find a new reservoir in a field previously found to be productive of oil or gas in another reservoir, or to extend a known reservoir. Generally, an exploratory well is any well that is not a development well, a service well, or a stratigraphic test well.

These definitions may not coincide with those that have been commonly used in the industry. (Typically, the industry definition of a development well is more liberal than Reg. S-X, Rule 4-10.) This results in two problems:

1. Improper classification of certain exploratory dry holes as development wells. (The problem occurs primarily with stepout or delineation wells drilled at the edge of a producing reservoir.)
2. Inconsistencies between the drilling statistics found in the forepart of Form 10-K (usually prepared by operational personnel) and the supplementary financial statement information required by ASC 932-235-50 (usually prepared by accounting personnel).

(iii) Treatment of Costs of Exploratory Wells Whose Outcome Is Undetermined. As set out next, ASC 932 effectively curtails extended deferral of the costs of an exploratory well whose outcome has not yet been determined.

ASC 932-360-25-10 and 11 state:

> 10. The costs of drilling exploratory wells and the costs of drilling exploratory-type stratigraphic test wells shall be capitalized as part of the entity's uncompleted wells, equipment, and facilities pending determination of whether the well has found proved reserves.
>
> 11. An entity sometimes conducts geological and geophysical studies and other exploration activities on a property owned by another party, in exchange for which the entity is contractually entitled to receive an interest in the property if proved reserves are found or to be reimbursed by the owner for the geological and geophysical and other costs incurred if proved reserves are not found. In that case, the entity conducting the geological and geophysical studies and other exploration activities shall account for those costs as a receivable when incurred and, if proved reserves are found, they shall become the cost of the proved property acquired.

According to ASC 932-260-35-17:

> When the well or wells have been determined to contain proved reserves, the capitalized costs of drilling shall be reclassified as part of the costs of the entity's wells and related equipment and facilities, even though the well may not be completed as a producing well. If proved reserves are not found, the capitalized costs of drilling the well shall be charged to expense.

(iv) Successful Efforts Impairment Test. Guidance for the determination of impairment accounting for oil- and gas-producing properties can be found in ASC 932-360-35, paragraphs 8 through 13. Special guidance is provided for proved properties, unproved properties, and completed exploratory wells.

(v) Conveyances. ASC 932and Reg. S-X Rule 4-10(m) provide rules to account for mineral property conveyances and related transactions. Conveyances of "production payments" repayable in fixed monetary terms (i.e., loans in substance) are accounted for as loans. Conveyances of production payments repayable in fixed production volumes from specified production are deemed to be property sales whereby proved reserves are reduced but the proceeds from sale of a production payment are credited to deferred revenue to be recognized as revenue as the seller delivers future petroleum volumes to the holder of the production payment. Gain or loss is not recognized for conveyances of (1) a pooling of assets in a joint venture to find, develop, or produce oil and gas or (2) such assets in exchange for other assets used in oil- and gas-producing activities. Gain is not recognized (but loss is) for conveyance of a partial property interest when substantial uncertainty exists as to the recovery of costs for the retained interest portion or when the seller has substantial obligation for future performance such as drilling a well. For other conveyances, gain or loss is recognized unless prohibited under accounting principles applicable to enterprises in general.

(b) FULL COST METHOD

(i) Basic Rules. Under Reg. S-X Rule 4-10, oil and gas property costs are accounted for in these ways:

> All costs associated with property acquisition, exploration, and development activities shall be capitalized by *country-wide* cost center. Any internal costs that are capitalized shall be limited to those costs that can be *directly* identified with the acquisition, exploration, and development activities undertaken by the reporting entity for its own account, and shall not include any costs related to production, general corporate overhead, or similar activities.
>
> Capitalized costs within a cost center shall be amortized on the unit-of-production basis using proved oil and gas reserves, as follows:
>
> - Costs to be amortized shall include (A) all capitalized costs, less accumulated amortization, excluding the cost of certain unevaluated properties not being amortized; (B) the estimated future expenditures (based on current costs) to be incurred in developing proved reserves; and (C) estimated dismantlement and abandonment costs, net of estimated salvage values.
> - Amortization shall be computed on the basis of physical units, with oil and gas converted to a common unit of measure on the basis of their approximate relative energy content, unless economic circumstances (related to the effects of regulated prices) indicated that use of revenue is a more appropriate basis of computing amortization. In the latter case, amortization shall be computed on the basis of current gross revenues from production in relation to future gross revenues (excluding royalty payments and net profits disbursements) based on current prices from estimated future production of proved oil and gas reserves (including consideration of changes in existing prices provided for only by contractual arrangements). The effect on estimated future gross revenues of a significant price increase during the year shall be reflected in the amortization provision only for the period after the price increase occurs.
> - In some cases, it may be more appropriate to depreciate natural gas cycling and processing plants by a method other than the unit-of-production method.
> - Amortization computations shall be made on a consolidated basis, including investees accounted for on a proportionate consolidation basis. Investees accounted for on the equity method shall be treated separately.

(ii) Exclusion of Costs from Amortization. Reg. S-X Rule 4-10 allows two alternatives:

1. Immediate inclusion of all costs incurred in the amortization base
2. Temporary exclusion of *all* acquisition and exploration costs incurred that directly relate to unevaluated properties and certain costs of major development projects

Unevaluated properties are defined as those for which no determination has been made of the existence or nonexistence of proved reserves. Costs that may be excluded are all those costs directly related to the unevaluated properties (i.e., leasehold acquisitions costs, delay rentals, G&G, exploratory drilling, and capitalized interest). The cost of exploratory dry holes should be included in the amortization base as soon as the well is deemed dry.

These excluded costs must be assessed for impairment annually, either:

- Individually for each significant property (i.e., capitalized cost exceeds 10 percent of the net full cost pool), *or*
- In the aggregate for insignificant properties (i.e., by transferring the excluded property costs into the amortization base ratably on the basis of such factors as the primary lease terms of the properties, the average holding period, and the relative proportion of properties on which proved reserves have been found previously).

(iii) Full Cost Ceiling Test. The full cost "ceiling test" specified in Reg. S-X Rule 4-10(e)(4) requires that:

> For each cost center, capitalized costs, less accumulated amortization and related deferred income taxes, shall not exceed an amount (the cost center ceiling) equal to the sum of:
>
> (A) The present value of estimated future net revenues computed by applying current prices of oil and gas reserves (with consideration of price changes only to the extent provided by contractual arrangements) to estimated future production of proved oil and gas reserves as of the date of the latest balance sheet presented, less estimated future expenditures (based on current costs) to be incurred in developing and producing the proved reserves computed using a discount factor of ten percent and assuming continuation of existing economic conditions; plus (B) the cost of properties not being amortized pursuant to paragraph (c)(3)(ii) of this section; plus (C) the lower of cost or estimated fair value of unproven properties included in the costs being amortized; less (D) income tax effects related to differences between the book and tax basis of the properties referred to in paragraphs (c)(4)(i)(B) and (C) of this section.
>
> If unamortized costs capitalized within a cost center, less related deferred income taxes, exceed the cost center ceiling, the excess shall be charged to expense and separately disclosed during the period in which the excess occurs. Amounts thus required to be written off shall not be reinstated for any subsequent increase in the cost center ceiling.

Part D, income tax effects, is poorly worded and refers to the income tax effects related to the ceiling components in parts A, B, and C allowing for consideration of the tax bases of oil and gas properties and related depletion carryforwards and related net operating loss carryforwards.

Two other unique aspects of the full cost ceiling test are:

1. *Ceiling test exemption for purchases of proved properties.* A petroleum-producing company might purchase proved properties for more than the present value of estimated future net revenues, causing net capitalized costs to exceed the cost center ceiling on the date of purchase. To avoid the write down, the company may request from the SEC Staff a temporary (usually one year) waiver of applying the ceiling test. The company must be prepared to demonstrate that the purchased properties' additional value exists beyond reasonable doubt. For more details, see SAB No. 47, *Oil and Gas Producing Activities,* Topic 12, D-3a, now part of ASC 932-360.
2. *Effect of subsequent event.* If, after year-end but prior to the audit report date, either (a) additional reserves are proved up on properties owned at year-end, or (b) price increases become known, then such subsequent events may be considered in the year-end ceiling test to mitigate a write down of capitalized costs.

   The avoidance of a writedown must be adequately disclosed, but the subsequent events should not be considered in the required disclosures of the company's proved reserves and standardized measure of discounted future net cash flows relating to such reserves (as further described here in Section 34.11). For more details, see SAB No. 47, Topic 12, D-3b, now part of ASC 932-360.

(iv) Conveyances. Reg. S-X, Rule 4-10(c)(6), provides that accounting for conveyances will be the same as for successful efforts accounting except that sales of oil and gas properties are to be accounted for as adjustments of capitalized costs with no recognition of gain or loss ("unless such adjustments would significantly alter the relationship between capitalized costs and proved reserves"). Exceptions are also made in some circumstances for property sales to partnerships and joint ventures in that (1) proceeds that are reimbursements of identifiable, current transaction expenses may be credited to income and (2) a petroleum company may recognize in income "management fees" from certain types of managed limited partnerships. When a company acquires an oil and gas property interest in exchange for services (such as drilling wells), income may be recognized in limited circumstances.

34.5 ACCOUNTING FOR NATURAL GAS IMBALANCES

Accounting techniques are basically the same whether revenue is generated by selling crude oil or natural gas. However, joint venture participants usually sell their crude oil collectively but may market and sell their shares of natural gas production individually. When a joint venture owner physically takes and sells more or less gas than its entitled share, a "gas imbalance" is created that is later reversed by an equal, but opposite, imbalance or by settlement in cash.

For example, if two joint venture participants each own 50 percent working interests in a well, and one company decides to sell gas on the spot market but the other company declines to sell due to a low spot price (or other factors), the company selling gas will receive 100 percent of revenue after paying the royalty interests. The selling company is in an overproduced capacity with respect to the well. (The company is entitled to 50 percent of the gas after royalties but had received 100 percent.) A gas imbalance can also occur between a gas producer and the gas transmission company that receives the producer's gas but delivers a different volume to the producer's customer.

Gas-producing companies account for gas imbalances under either the sales method or the entitlements method.

(a) SALES METHOD. Under the sales method, the company recognizes revenue and a receivable for the volume of gas sold, regardless of ownership of the property. For example, if Company A owns a 50 percent net revenue interest in a gas property but sells 100 percent of the production in a given month, the company would recognize 100 percent of the revenue generated. In a subsequent month, if Company A sells no gas (and the other owners make up the imbalance), Company A would recognize zero revenue. Company A would reduce its estimate of proved reserves for any future production that it must give up to meet a gas imbalance obligation and increase proved reserves for any additional future production it has a right to receive from other joint venture participants to eliminate an existing gas imbalance.

Although this method is rather simple from a revenue accounting standpoint, it presents other problems. Regardless of the revenue method chosen, the operator will issue joint interest billing statements for expenses based on the ownership of the property. Depending on the gas-balancing situation, the sales method may present a problem with the matching of revenues and expenses in a period. If a significant imbalance exists at the end of an accounting period, the accountant may be required to analyze the situation and record additional expenses (or reduce expenses depending on whether the property is overproduced or underproduced).

(b) ENTITLEMENTS METHOD. Under the entitlements method, the company recognizes revenue based on the volume of sales to which it is entitled by its ownership interest. For example, if Company A owns a 50 percent net revenue interest but sells 100 percent of the production in a given month, the company would recognize 50 percent of the revenue generated. Company A would recognize a receivable for 100 percent of the revenue with the difference being recorded in a payable (or deferred revenue) account. When the imbalance is corrected, the payable account will become zero, thus indicating that the property is in balance.

This method correctly matches revenues and expenses but presents another accounting issue. If a property is significantly imbalanced, Company A may find itself in a position that reserves are insufficient to bring the well back to a balanced condition. If Company A is underproduced in this situation, a receivable (or deferred charge) may be recorded in the asset category that has a questionable realization. In addition, the company is really under- or overproduced in terms of volumes (measured in cubic feet) of gas. A value per cubic foot is assigned based on the sale price at the period of imbalance. If the price is significantly different when the correction occurs, the receivable may not show a zero balance in the accounting records.

(c) GAS BALANCING EXAMPLE

Facts: Company A owns a 50 percent net revenue.
Gas sales for January are 5,000 mcf @ $2.00 per mcf.
Gas sales for February are 5,000 mcf @ $2.00 per mcf.
In January, Company A sells 100 percent of gas production to its purchaser.
In February, Company A sells zero gas to its purchaser.

January Accounting Entries

Under the Sales Method	Debit	Credit
Accounts receivable, gas sales	$10,000	
Gas revenue		$10,000
Under the Entitlements Method		
Accounts receivable, gas sales	$10,000	
Gas revenue		5,000
Payable		5,000

February Accounting Entries

Under the Sales Method	No entries are recorded	
Under the Entitlements Method		
Payable	5,000	
Gas revenue		5,000

34.6 HARD-ROCK MINING

(a) MINING OPERATIONS. The principal difference between hard-rock mining companies and companies involved in oil- and gas-producing activities relates to the nature, timing, and extent of expenditures incurred for exploration, development, production, and processing of minerals.

Generally in the mining industry, a period of as long as several years elapses between the time exploration costs are incurred to discover a commercially viable body of ore and the expenditure of development costs, which are usually substantial, to complete the project. Therefore, the economic benefits derived from a project are long term and subject to the uncertainties inherent in the passage of time. In contrast, the costs related to exploring for deposits of oil and gas are expended generally over a relatively short time. Major exceptions would be offshore and foreign petroleum exploration and development.

Like petroleum exploration and production, the mining industry is capital intensive. Substantial investments in property, plant, and equipment are required; usually they represent more than 50 percent of a mining company's total assets. The significant capital investments of mining companies and the related risks inherent in any long-term major project may affect the recoverability of capitalized costs.

The operational stages in mining companies vary somewhat depending on the type of mineral, because of differences in geological, chemical, and economic factors. The basic operations common to mining companies are exploration, development, mining, milling, smelting, and refining.

Exploration is the search for natural accumulations of minerals with economic value. Exploration for minerals is a specialized activity involving the use of complex geophysical and geochemical equipment and procedures. There is an element of financial risk in every decision to pursue exploration, and explorers generally seek to minimize the costs and increase the probability of success. As a result, before any fieldwork begins, extensive studies are made concerning which types of minerals are to be sought and where they are most likely to occur. Market studies and forecasts, studies of geological maps and reports, and logistical evaluations are performed to provide information for use in determining the economic feasibility of a potential project.

Exploration can be divided into two phases, prospecting and geophysical analysis. *Prospecting* is the search for geological information over a broad area. It embraces such activities as geological mapping, analysis of rock types and structures, searches for direct manifestations of mineralization, taking samples of minerals found, and aeromagnetic surveys. *Geophysical analysis* is conducted in specific areas of interest localized during the prospecting phase. Rock and soil samples are examined, and the earth's crust is monitored directly for magnetic, gravitational, sonic, radioactive, and electrical data. Based on the analysis, targets for trenching, test pits, and exploratory drilling are identified. Drilling is particularly useful in evaluating the shape and character of a deposit. Analysis of samples is necessary to determine the grade of the deposit.

Once the grade and quantity of the deposit have been estimated, the mining company must decide whether developing the deposit is technically feasible and commercially viable. The value of a mineral deposit is determined by the intrinsic value of the minerals present and by the nature and location of their occurrence. In addition to the grade and quality of the ore, such factors as the physical accessibility of the deposit, the estimated costs of production, and the value of joint products and by-products are key elements in the decision to develop a deposit for commercial exploitation.

The *development* stage of production involves planning and preparing for commercial operation. Development of surface mines is relatively straightforward. For open-pit mines, which are surface mines, the principal procedure is to remove sufficient overburden to expose the ore. For strip mines, an initial cut is made to expose the mineral to be mined. For underground mines, data resulting from exploratory drilling are evaluated as a basis for planning the shafts and tunnels that will provide access to the mineral deposit.

Substantial capital investment in mineral rights, machinery and equipment, and related facilities generally is required in the development stage.

Mining breaks up the rock and ore to the extent necessary for loading and removal to the processing location. A variety of mining techniques exists to accomplish this. The drilling and blasting technique is utilized frequently; an alternative is the continuous mining method, in which a boring or tearing machine is mounted on a forward crawler to break the material away from the rock face.

After removal from the mine site, the ore is ready for *milling*. The first phase of the milling stage involves crushing and grinding the chunks of ore to reduce them to particle size. The second milling procedure is concentration, which involves the separation of the mineral constituents from the rock.

Smelting is the process of separating the metal from impurities with which it may be chemically bound or physically mixed too closely to be removed by concentration. Most smelting is accomplished through fusion, which is the liquefaction of a metal under heat. In some cases, chemical processes are used instead of, or in combination with, heating techniques.

Refining is the last step in isolating the metal. The primary methods utilized are fire refining and electrolytic refining. Fire refining is similar to smelting. The metal is kept in a molten state and treated with pine logs, hydrocarbon gas, or other substances to enable impurities to be removed. Fire refining generally does not allow the recovery of by-products. Electrolytic refining uses an electrical current to separate metals from a solution in such a way that by-products can be recovered.

(b) SOURCES OF GENERALLY ACCEPTED ACCOUNTING PRINCIPLES. Accounting and reporting issues in the mining industry are discussed in American Institute of Certified Public Accountants American Institute of Certified Public Accountants (AICPA) Accounting Research Study No. 11, *Financial Reporting in the Extractive Industries* (1969). In 1976, the FASB issued a discussion memorandum, *Financial Accounting and Reporting in the Extractive Industries,* which analyzed issues relevant to the extractive industries. Neither of these attempts, however, culminated in the issuance of an authoritative pronouncement for mining companies. ASC 932 provides established standards of financial accounting and reporting for companies that are engaged in oil and gas exploration, development, and production activities. In 2005, the International Accounting Standards Board (IASB) produced International Financial Reporting Standard (IFRS) No. 6 in an effort to provide the first stage of international accounting standards in the oil and gas and mining industries. However, significant differences still exist between U.S. GAAP and IFRS. The FASB and IASB are working toward a single converged set of global standards, but much work remains before convergence is achieved in the extractive industries.

34.7 ACCOUNTING FOR MINING COSTS

(a) EXPLORATION AND DEVELOPMENT COSTS. Exploration and development costs are major expenditures of mining companies. The characterization of expenditures as exploration, development, or production usually determines whether such costs are capitalized or expensed. For accounting purposes, it is useful to identify five basic phases of exploration and development:

1. Prospecting
2. Property acquisition
3. Geophysical analysis
4. Development before production
5. Development during production

Specific GAAP guidance can be found in ASC 930, *Extractive Activities—Mining.*

Prospecting usually begins with obtaining (or preparing) and studying topographical and geological maps. Prospecting costs, which are generally expensed as incurred, include (1) options to lease or buy property; (2) rights of access to lands for geophysical work; and (3) salaries, equipment, and supplies for scouts, geologists, and geophysical crews.

Property acquisition includes both the purchase of property and the purchase or lease of mineral rights. Costs incurred to purchase land (including mineral rights and surface rights) or to lease mineral rights are capitalized. Acquisition costs may include lease bonus and lease extension costs, lease brokers' commissions, abstract and recording fees, filing and patent fees, and other related expenses.

Geophysical analysis is conducted to identify mineralization. The related costs are generally expensed as exploration costs when incurred. Examples of exploration costs include exploratory drilling, geological mapping, and salaries and supplies for geologists and support personnel.

A body of ore reaches the development stage when the existence of an economically and legally recoverable mineral reserve has been established through the completion of a feasibility study. Costs incurred in the development stage before production begins are capitalized. Development costs include expenditures associated with drilling, removing overburden (waste rock), sinking shafts, driving tunnels, building roads and dikes, purchasing processing equipment and equipment used in developing the mine, and constructing supporting facilities to house and care for the workforce. In many respects, the expenditures in the development stage are similar to those incurred during exploration. As a result, it is sometimes difficult to distinguish the point at which exploration ends and development begins. For example, the sinking of shafts and driving of tunnels may begin in the exploration stage and continue into the development stage. In most instances, the transition from the exploration to the development stage is the same for both accounting and tax purposes.

Development also takes place during the production stage. The accounting treatment of development costs incurred during the ongoing operation of a mine depends on the nature and purpose of the expenditures. Costs associated with expansion of capacity are generally capitalized; costs incurred to maintain production are normally included in production costs in the period in which they are incurred. In certain instances, the benefits of development activity will be realized in future periods, such as when the block-caving and open-pit mining methods are used. In the block caving method, entire sections of a body of ore are intentionally collapsed to permit the mass removal of minerals; extraction may take place two to three years after access to the ore is gained and the block prepared. In an open-pit mine, there is typically an expected ratio of overburden to mineral-bearing ore over the life of the mine. The cost of stripping the overburden to gain access to the ore is expensed in those periods in which the actual ratio of overburden to ore approximates the expected ratio. In certain instances, however, extensive stripping is performed to remove the overburden in advance of the period in which the ore will be extracted. When the benefits of either development activity are to be realized in a future accounting period, the costs associated with the development activity should be deferred and amortized during the period in which the ore is extracted or the product produced.

ASC 915, *Development Stage Enterprises,* states that "an enterprise shall be considered to be in the development stage if it is devoting substantially all of its efforts to establishing a new business" and "the planned principal operations have not commenced" or they "have commenced, but there has been no significant revenue from operations." Although ASC 915 specifically excludes established operating entities in the extractive industries in their exploration and development activities, the definition of a development stage enterprise is helpful in defining the point in time at which a mine's development phase ends and its production phase begins. It is not uncommon for incidental and/or insignificant mineral production to occur before either economic production per the mine plan or other commercial basis for measurement is achieved. Expenditures during this time frame are commonly referred to as *costs incurred in the start-up period.* ASC 720, Section 15, "Start Up Costs," provides guidance for mining companies as to when development stops and commercial operations begin. Start-up activities are defined broadly in ASC 720-15 as

> those one-time activities related to opening a new facility, introducing a new product or service, conducting business in a new territory, conducting business with a new class of customer or beneficiary, initiating a new process in an existing facility, or commencing some new operation.

ASC 720-15 precludes the capitalization of start-up costs that are incurred during the period of insignificant mineral production and before normal productive capacity is achieved.

(b) PRODUCTION COSTS. When the mine begins production, production costs are expensed. The capitalized property acquisition and development costs are recognized as costs of production through their depreciation or depletion, generally on the unit-of-production method over the expected productive life of the mine.

The principal difference between computing depreciation in the mining industry and in other industries is that useful lives of assets that are not readily movable from a mine site must not exceed the estimated life of the mine, which in turn is based on the remaining economically recoverable ore reserves. In some instances, this may require depreciating certain mining equipment over a period that is shorter than its physical life.

Depreciation charges are significant because of the highly capital-intensive nature of the industry. Moreover, those charges are affected by numerous factors, such as the physical environment, revisions of recoverable ore estimates, environmental regulations, and improved technology. In many instances, depreciation charges on similar equipment with different intended uses may begin at different times. For example, depreciation of equipment used for exploration purposes may begin when it is purchased and use has begun, while depreciation of milling equipment may not begin until a certain level of commercial production has been attained.

Depletion (or depletion and amortization) of property acquisition and development costs related to a body of ore is calculated in a manner similar to the unit-of-production method of depreciation.

The cost of the body of ore is divided by the estimated quantity of ore reserves or units of metal or mineral to arrive at the depletion charge per unit. The unit charge is multiplied by the number of units extracted to arrive at the depletion charge for the period. This computation requires a current estimate of economically recoverable mineral reserves at the end of the period.

Often it is appropriate for different depletion calculations to be made for different types of capitalized development expenditures. For instance, one factor to be considered is whether capitalized costs relate to gaining access to the total economically recoverable ore reserves of the mine or only to specific portions.

Usually estimated quantities of economically recoverable mineral reserves are the basis for computing depletion and amortization under the unit-of-production method. The choice of the reserve unit is not a problem if there is only one product; if, however, as in many extractive operations, several products are recovered, a decision must be made whether to measure production on the basis of the major product or on the basis of an aggregation of all products. Generally, the reserve base is the company's total proved and probable ore reserve quantities; it is determined by specialists, such as geologists or mining engineers. Proved and probable reserves typically are used as the reserve base because of the degree of uncertainty surrounding estimates of possible reserves. The imprecise nature of reserve estimates makes it inevitable that the reserve base will be revised over time as additional data becomes available. Changes in the reserve base should be treated as changes in accounting estimates in accordance with ASC 250, *Accounting Changes and Error Corrections.*

(c) INVENTORY. A mining company's inventory generally has two major components: (1) metals and minerals and (2) materials and supplies that are used in mining operations.

(i) Metals and Minerals. Metal and mineral inventories usually comprise:

- Broken ore
- Crushed ore
- Concentrate
- Materials in process at concentrators, smelters, and refineries
- Metal
- Joint and by-products

The usual practice of mining companies is not to recognize metal inventories for financial reporting purposes before the concentrate stage (i.e., until the majority of the nonmineralized material has been removed from the ore). Thus, ore is not included in inventory until it has been processed through the concentrator and is ready for delivery to the smelter. This practice evolved because the amounts of broken ore before the concentrating process ordinarily are relatively small; consequently the cost of that ore and of concentrate in process generally is not significant. Furthermore, the amount of broken ore and concentrate in process is relatively constant at the end of each month, and the concentrating process is quite rapid—usually a matter of hours. In the case of leach operations, generally the mineral content of the ore is estimated and costs are inventoried. However, practice varies, and some companies do not inventory costs until the leached product is introduced into the electrochemical refinery cells.

Determining inventory quantities during the production process is often difficult. Broken ore, crushed ore, concentrate, and materials in process may be stored in various ways or enclosed in vessels or pipes.

Mining companies carry metal inventory at the lower of cost or market value, with cost determined on a last-in, first-out (LIFO), first-in, first-out (FIFO), or average basis.

Valuation of product inventory is also affected by worldwide imbalances between supply and demand for certain metals. Companies sometimes produce larger quantities of a metal than can be absorbed by the market. In that situation, management may have to write the inventory down to its net realizable value; determining that value, however, may be difficult if there is no established market or only a thin market for the particular metal.

Product costs for mining companies usually reflect all normal and necessary expenditures associated with cost centers such as mines, concentrators, smelters, and refineries. Inventory costs comprise not only direct costs of production but also an allocation of overhead, including mine and other plant administrative expenses. Depreciation, depletion, and amortization of capitalized exploration and development costs also should be included in inventory.

If a company engages in tolling (described in Section 34.8(b)), it may have significant production inventories on hand that belong to other mining companies. Usually it is not possible to physically segregate inventories owned by others from similar inventories owned by the company. Memorandum records of tolling inventories should be maintained and reconciled periodically to physical counts.

(ii) Materials and Supplies. Materials and supplies usually constitute a substantial portion of the inventory of most mining companies, sometimes exceeding the value of metal inventories. This is because a lack of supplies or spare parts could cause the curtailment of operations. In addition to normal operating supplies, materials and supplies inventories often include such items as fuel and spare parts for trucks, locomotives, and other machinery. Most mining companies use perpetual inventory systems to account for materials and supplies because of their high unit value.

Materials and supplies inventories normally are valued at cost minus a reserve for surplus items and obsolescence.

(d) COMMODITIES, FUTURES TRANSACTIONS. Mining companies usually have significant inventories of commodities that are traded in worldwide markets. Often these companies enter into long-term forward sales contracts specifying sales prices based on market prices at time of delivery. To protect themselves from the risk of loss that could result from price declines, mining companies often hedge against price changes by entering into futures contracts. Companies sell contracts when they expect selling prices to decline or are satisfied with the current price and want to lock in the profit (or loss) on the sale of their inventory. To establish a hedge when it has or expects to have a commodity (e.g., copper) in inventory, a company sells a contract that commits it to deliver that commodity in the future at a fixed price.

ASC 815, *Derivatives and Hedging,* requires derivative instruments, including those which qualify as hedges, to be reported on the balance sheet at fair value. To qualify for hedge accounting, the derivative must satisfy the requirements of a cash flow hedge, fair value hedge, or foreign currency hedge as defined by ASC 815. ASC 815 provides that certain criteria be met for a derivative to be accounted for as a hedge for financial reporting purposes. These criteria must be formally documented prior to entering the transaction and include risk management objectives and an assessment of hedge effectiveness. Financial instruments commonly used in the mining industry include forward sales contracts, spot deferred contracts, purchased puts, and written calls. Additional financial instruments that should be reviewed for statement applicability include commodity loans, tolling agreements, take or pay contracts, and royalty agreements.

(e) RECLAMATION AND REMEDIATION. The mining industry is subject to federal and state laws for reclamation and restoration of lands after the completion of mining. Historically, costs to reclaim and restore these lands, which can be defined as asset retirement obligations, were recognized using a cost accumulation model on an undiscounted basis. For financial reporting purposes, the environmental and closure expenses and related liabilities were recognized ratably over the mine life using the units-of-production method. ASC 410, *Asset Retirement Obligations,* requires that an asset retirement obligation be recognized in the period in which it is incurred. According to ASC 410, reclamation of a mine at the end of its productive life is an obligating event that requires liability recognition. The asset retirement costs, which include reclamation and closure costs, are capitalized as a component of the long-lived assets of the mineral property and depreciated over the mine life using the units-of-production method. ASC 410 requires that the liability for these obligations be recorded at its fair value using the guidance in FASB Concepts Statement No. 7, *Using Cash Flow Information and Present Value in Accounting Measurements,* to estimate that liability. It also requires that the liability be discounted and accretion expense be recognized using the credit-adjusted risk-free interest rate in effect at recognition date.

Environmental contamination and hazardous waste disposal and clean up is regulated by the Resource Conservation and Recovery Act of 1976 (RCRA) and the Comprehensive Environmental Response, Compensation and Liability Act of 1980 (CERCLA or Superfund). ASC 410 provides accounting guidance for the accrual and disclosure of environmental remediation liabilities. It requires that environmental remediation liabilities be accrued when the criteria of ASC 450, *Contingencies,* have been met. However, if the environmental remediation liability is incurred as a result of normal mining operations and relates to the retirement of the mining assets, the provisions of ASC 410, *Asset Retirement and Environmental Obligations,* probably apply.

(f) SHUTDOWN OF MINES. Volatile metal prices may make active operations uneconomical from time to time, and, as a result, mining companies will shut down operations, either temporarily or permanently. When operations are temporarily shut down, a question arises as to the carrying value of the related assets. If a long-term diminution in the value of the assets has occurred, a write-down of the carrying value to net realizable value should be recorded. This decision is extremely judgmental and depends on projections of whether viable mining operations can ever be resumed. Those projections are based on significant assumptions as to prices, production, quantities, and costs. Because most minerals are worldwide commodities, the projections must take into account global supply and demand factors.

When operations are temporarily shut down, the related facilities usually are placed in a standby mode that provides for care and maintenance so that the assets will be retained in a reasonable condition that will facilitate resumption of operations. Care and maintenance costs usually are recorded as expenses in the period in which they are incurred. Examples of typical care and maintenance costs are security, preventive and protective maintenance, and depreciation.

A temporary shutdown of a mining company's facility can raise questions as to whether the company can continue as a going concern.

(g) ACCOUNTING FOR THE IMPAIRMENT OF LONG-LIVED ASSETS. ASC 360, *Property, Plant and Equipment,* provides definitive guidance on when the carrying amount of long-lived assets should be reviewed for impairment. Long-lived assets of a mining company—for example, plant and equipment and capitalized development costs—should be reviewed for recoverability when events or changes in circumstances indicate that carrying amounts may not be recoverable. For mining companies, factors such as decreasing commodity prices, reductions in mineral recoveries, increasing operating and environmental costs, and reductions in mineral reserves are events and circumstances that may indicate an asset impairment. ASC 360 also establishes a common methodology for assessing and measuring the impairment of long-lived assets. An impairment loss is reported only if the carrying amount of the long-lived asset (asset group) (1) is not recoverable (i.e., if it exceeds the sum of the undiscounted cash flows expected to result from the use and eventual disposition of the asset [asset group], assessed based on the carrying amount of the asset in use or under development when it is tested for recoverability), and (2) exceeds the fair value of the asset (asset group).

For mining companies, cash flows should be based on the proven and probable reserves that are used in the calculation of depreciation, depletion, and amortization. The estimates of cash flows should be based on reasonable and supportable assumptions. For example, the use of commodity prices other than the spot price would be permissible if such prices were based on futures prices in the commodity markets. If an impairment loss is warranted, the revised carrying amount of the asset, which is based on the discounted cash flow model, is the new cost basis to be depreciated over its remaining useful life. A previously recognized impairment loss may not be restored.

34.8 ACCOUNTING FOR MINING REVENUES

(a) SALES OF MINERALS. Generally, minerals are not sold in the raw-ore stage because of the insignificant quantity of minerals relative to the total volume of waste rock. (There are, however, some exceptions, such as iron ore and coal.) The ore is usually milled at or near the mine site to produce a concentrate containing a significantly higher percentage of mineral content. For example, the metal content of copper concentrate typically is 25 to 30 percent, as opposed to between .5 and 1 percent for the raw ore. The concentrate frequently is sold to other processors; occasionally mining companies exchange concentrate to reduce transportation costs. After the refining process, metallic minerals may be sold as finished metals, either in the form of products for remelting by final users (e.g., pig iron or cathode copper) or as finished products (e.g., copper rod or aluminum foil).

Sales of raw ore and concentrate entail determining metal content based initially on estimated weights, moisture content, and ore grade. Those estimates are subsequently revised, based on the actual metal content recovered from the raw ore or concentrate.

The SEC has provided guidance for revenue recognition under GAAP in SAB No. 101, *Revenue Recognition in Financial Statements,* which was issued in December 1999. The Staff noted that accounting literature on revenue recognition included both conceptual discussions and industry-specific guidance. SAB No. 101 provides a summary of the SEC Staff's views on revenue recognition and should be evaluated by mining companies in recording revenues. Revenue should be recognized when these conditions are met:

- A contractual agreement exists (a documented understanding between the buyer and seller as to the nature and terms of the agreed-upon transaction).
- Delivery of the product has occurred (freight on board [FOB] shipping) or the services have been rendered.
- The price of the product is fixed or determinable.
- Collection of the receivable for the product sold or services rendered is reasonably assured.

For revenue to be recognized, it is important that the buyer has to have taken title to the mineral product and assumed the risks and rewards of ownership.

Sales prices often are based on the market price on a commodity exchange, such as the New York Commodity Exchange New York Commodity Exchange or London Metal Exchange London Metal Exchange at the time of delivery, which may differ from the market price of the metal at the time that the criteria for revenue recognition have been satisfied. Revenue may be recognized on these sales based on a provisional pricing mechanism, the spot price of the metal at the date on which revenue recognition criteria have been satisfied. Subsequently the estimated sales price and related receivable should be marked to market through revenue based on the commodity exchange spot price until the final settlement.

(b) TOLLING AND ROYALTY REVENUES. Companies with smelters and refineries may also realize revenue from tolling, which is the processing of metal-bearing materials of other mining companies for a fee. The fee is based on numerous factors, including the weight and metal content of the materials processed. Normally the processed minerals are returned to the original producer for subsequent sale. To supplement the recovery of fixed costs, companies with smelters and refineries frequently enter into tolling agreements when they have excess capacity.

For a variety of reasons, companies may not wish to mine certain properties that they own. Mineral royalty agreements may be entered into that provide for royalties based on a percentage of the total value of the mineral or of gross revenue, to be paid when the minerals extracted from the property are sold.

The accounting for commodity futures contracts depends on whether the contract qualifies as a hedge under ASC 815. In order to qualify for hedging of mineral reserves, management will be required to determine how it measures hedge effectiveness and to formally document the hedging relationship and the entity's risk management objective and strategy for undertaking the hedge. Such documentation will include identification of the hedging instrument, the related hedged item, the nature of the risk being hedged, and how the hedging instrument's effectiveness in offsetting the exposure to changes in the hedged item's fair value attributable to the hedged risk will be assessed. See Chapter 26 for a discussion of the requirements for hedge accounting.

34.9 SUPPLEMENTARY FINANCIAL STATEMENT INFORMATION—ORE RESERVES

ASC 855, *Changing Prices,* eliminated the requirement that certain publicly traded companies meeting specified size criteria must disclose the effects of changing prices and supplemental disclosures of ore reserves. However, Item 102 of SEC Reg. S-K requires that publicly traded mining companies present information related to production, reserves, locations, developments, and the nature of the registrant's interest in properties.

34.10 ACCOUNTING FOR INCOME TAXES

Chapter 17 addresses general accounting for income taxes. Tax accounting for oil and gas production as well as hard rock mining is particularly complex and cannot be fully covered in this chapter. However, two special deductions need to be mentioned: percentage depletion and immediate deduction of certain development costs.

Many petroleum and mining production companies are allowed to calculate depletion as the greater of cost depletion or percentage depletion. Cost depletion is based on amortization of property acquisition costs over estimated recoverable reserves. Percentage depletion is a statutory depletion deduction that is a specified percentage of gross revenue at the well-head (15 percent for oil and gas) or mine for the particular mineral produced and is limited to a portion of the property's taxable income before deducting such depletion. Percentage depletion may exceed the depletable cost basis.

For purposes of computing the taxable income from the mineral property, *gross income* is defined as the value of the mineral before the application of nonmining processes. Selling price generally is determined to be the gross value for tax purposes when the mineral products are sold to third parties prior to nonmining processes. For an integrated mining company where nonmining processes are used, gross income for the mineral generally is determined under a proportionate profits method whereby an allocation of profit is made based on the mining and nonmining costs incurred.

For both petroleum and mining companies, exploration and development costs other than for equipment are largely deductible when incurred. However, the major integrated petroleum companies and mining companies must capitalize a percentage of these exploration and development expenditures, which are then amortized over a period of 60 months. Mining companies must recapture the previously deducted exploration costs if the mineral property achieves commercial production. Property impairments, which are expensed currently for financial reporting purposes, do not generate a taxable deduction until such property is abandoned, sold, or exchanged.

34.11 FINANCIAL STATEMENT DISCLOSURES

ASC 932 details supplementary disclosure requirements for the oil and gas industry, most of which are required only by public companies. Both public and nonpublic companies, however, must provide a description of the accounting method followed and the manner of disposing of capitalized costs. Audited financial statements filed with the SEC must include supplementary disclosures, which fall into four categories:

1. Historical cost data relating to acquisition, exploration, development, and production activity.
2. Results of operations for oil- and gas-producing activities.
3. Proved reserve quantities.

4. Standardized measure of discounted future net cash flows relating to proved oil and gas reserve quantities (also known as SMOG [standardized measure of oil and gas]). For foreign operations, SMOG also relates to produced quantities subject to certain long-term purchase contracts held by a party involved in producing the quantities.

The supplementary disclosures are required of companies with significant oil- and gas-producing activities; *significant* is defined as 10 percent or more of revenue, operating results, or identifiable assets. ASC 932 states that the disclosures are to be provided as supplemental data; thus, they need not be audited. The disclosure requirements are described in detail and examples are provided at the end of ASC 932. If the supplemental information is not audited, it must be clearly labeled as unaudited. However, auditing interpretations (AU 9558, *Required Supplementary Information—Auditing Interpretations* [of AU 558]) require the financial statement auditor to perform certain limited procedures to these required, unaudited supplementary disclosures.

Proved reserves are inherently imprecise because of the uncertainties and limitations of the data available.

Most large companies and many medium-size ones have qualified engineers on their staffs to prepare oil and gas reserve studies. Many also use outside consultants to make independent reviews. Other companies that do not have sufficient operations to justify a full-time engineer engage outside engineering consultants to evaluate and estimate their oil and gas reserves. Usually reserve studies are reviewed and updated at least annually to take into account new discoveries and adjustments of previous estimates.

The standardized measure is disclosed as of the end of the fiscal year. The SMOG reflects future revenues computed by applying unescalated, year-end oil and gas prices to year-end proved reserves. Future price changes may be considered only if fixed and determinable under year-end sales contracts. The calculated future revenues are reduced for estimated future development costs, production costs, and related income taxes (using unescalated, year-end cost rates) to compute future net cash flows. Such cash flows, by future year, are discounted at a standard 10 percent per annum to compute the standardized measure.

Significant sources of the annual changes in the year-end standardized measure and year-end proved oil and gas reserves should be disclosed.

34.12 SOURCES AND SUGGESTED REFERENCES

Brock, H. R., M. Z. Carnes, and R. Justice. *Petroleum Accounting—Principles, Procedures, and Issues*, 6th ed. Denton, TX: Professional Development Institute, 2007.

Council of Petroleum Accountants Societies. Bulletin No. 24, *Producer Gas Imbalances*, as revised. Tulsa, OK: Kraftbilt Products, 1991.

O'Reilly, V. M. *Montgomery's Auditing*, 12th ed. New York: John Wiley & Sons, 1996.

PricewaterhouseCoopers. *Financial Reporting in the Oil and Gas Industry: International Financial Reporting Standards*, 2nd ed. 2011.

Securities and Exchange Commission. Final Rule, "Modernization of Oil and Gas Reporting," effective January 1, 2010.

______. Regulation S-X, Rule 4-10, *Financial Accounting and Reporting for Oil and Gas Producing Activities Pursuant to the Federal Securities Laws and the Energy Policy and Conservation Act of 1975*, as currently amended. Washington, DC: Author, 1995.

______. SEC Staff Accounting Bulletins Topic 12, *Interpretations Relating to Oil and Gas Accounting*. Washington, DC: Author, 1995.

CHAPTER 35

HEALTH CARE ORGANIZATIONS

Martha Garner, CPA
PwC LLP

35.1 THE HEALTH CARE INDUSTRY 2

(a) Overview 2
(b) Not-for-Profit Health Care Entities 2
(c) Governmental Health Care Entities 3
(d) Investor-Owned Health Care Entities 3

35.2 AUTHORITATIVE PRONOUNCEMENTS 3

(a) Generally Accepted Accounting Principles—Private Sector 3
(i) Securities and Exchange Commission Requirements 4
(ii) Definition of "Public" Not-for-Profit Entity 4
(b) Generally Accepted Accounting Principles—Governmental Sector 4
(c) AICPA Audit and Accounting Guide *Health Care Entities* 5
(d) Healthcare Financial Management Association Principles and Practices Board 5

35.3 ACCOUNTING PRINCIPLES 6

(a) Classification and Reporting of Net Assets/Net Position 6
(i) Unrestricted Net Assets/Net Position 6
(ii) Restricted Net Assets/Net Position 6
(iii) Invested in Capital Assets, Net of Related Debt 7
(b) Noncurrent Cash/Claims to Cash 7
(c) Agency Transactions 8
(d) Revenue of Health Care Facilities 8
(e) Patient Service Revenue 10
(i) Estimating Patient Service Revenue Related to Governmental Programs 10
(ii) Reporting Charity Care Provided 13
(iii) Reporting the Provision for Bad Debts 14
(f) Concentration of Credit Risk 14
(g) Contributions 15
(i) General Guidance—Not-for-Profit Entities 15
(ii) Governmental Entities 16
(iii) Contributions Received through Affiliated Fundraising Foundations 17
(iv) Governmental Entities 18
(v) Contributions Established through Trusts 19
(h) Investments 19
(i) Nongovernmental Entities 19
(ii) Governmental Entities 20
(i) Derivatives 21
(i) Not-for-Profit Entities 21
(ii) Governmental Entities 22
(j) Property and Equipment 22
(i) Governmental Health Care Entities 22
(ii) Internal-Use Software Costs 23
(k) Intangible Assets 24
(l) Bonds Payable 24
(i) Refundings and Defeasance 25
(ii) Variable-Rate Demand Bonds 26
(iii) IRS Arbitrage Rebate Liability 27
(iv) Obligated Group Financing Structures 27
(v) Interest during Construction 27
(m) Disclosure of Risks, Uncertainties, and Contingencies 28
(i) Risks and Uncertainties 28
(ii) Illegal Acts Related to Government Programs 28
(iii) Loss Contingencies and Insurance Coverage 29
(n) Reporting Entity Considerations 29
(i) Not-for-Profit Entities 30
(ii) Governmental Entities 32

(iii) Joint Operating Agreements 35
(o) Business Combinations 35
(i) Not-for-Profit Entities 35
(ii) Governmental Entities 36
(p) Deferred Inflows and Outflows of Resources 37

35.4 SPECIAL ACCOUNTING PROBLEMS OF SPECIFIC TYPES OF PROVIDERS 37

(a) Continuing Care Retirement Communities 37
(i) Advance Fees 37
(ii) Obligation to Provide Future Services 39
(iii) Costs of Acquiring Initial Continuing Care Contracts 40
(b) HMOs and Managed Care Entities 41
(i) Revenue 41
(ii) Expense Recognition 42
(iii) Loss Contracts 43
(iv) Risk Pools 44
(v) Stop-Loss Insurance 44
(vi) Acquisition Costs 44
(c) Physician Practice Management Companies 44
(i) Consolidation Requirements 45

35.5 FINANCIAL STATEMENTS 46

(a) Overview of Financial Reporting Models 46
(b) Balance Sheet 47
(i) Not-for-Profit Entities 47
(ii) Governmental Health Care Entities 48
(c) Operating Statement 48
(i) Investor-Owned Entities 48
(ii) Not-for-Profit Entities 49
(iii) Governmental Entities 50
(d) Statement of Changes in Net Assets/Equity 51
(e) Statement of Cash Flows 52
(i) Private Sector Entities 52
(ii) Governmental Entities 52
(f) Segment Reporting 53
(g) Issuance of Financial statements 53
(i) Nongovernmental Entities 53
(ii) Governmental Entities 53

35.6 STATUTORY/REGULATORY REPORTING ISSUES 53

(a) SEC's Role and Authority in the Municipal Securities Market 53
(i) Administration and Enforcement Structure 54
(ii) Disclosure Requirements for Municipal Issuers 54
(iii) EMMA System 57
(iv) Proposed Reforms 57
(b) National Association of Insurance Commissioners 58
(i) Statutory Financial Statements of Health Plans 58
(ii) Risk-Based Capital Requirements 59
(c) Office of Management and Budget Circular A-133 59

35.7 SOURCES AND SUGGESTED REFERENCES 59

35.1 THE HEALTH CARE INDUSTRY

(a) OVERVIEW. Health care in the United States is provided by entities operating in all sectors of the economy. In the private sector, health care entities may be operated by religious organizations, owned by investors seeking a return on their investment, or sponsored by local communities. Public sector health care entities are operated at the federal, state, and local government levels. Consequently, health care providers may be subject to different accounting and reporting standards depending on their ownership and form of organization.

The primary users of health care entities' general-purpose financial statements are providers of capital who make rating and investment decisions in competitive capital markets (including investors in tax-exempt debt securities); private lenders; suppliers of goods and services to the industry with which health care companies maintain credit relationships; stockholders and other owners; government programs, such as Medicare and Medicaid; and regulators such as the Securities and Exchange Commission (SEC), state departments of insurance, and other oversight groups.

(b) NOT-FOR-PROFIT HEALTH CARE ENTITIES. The not-for-profit subsector of the industry consists mainly of health care entities that are organized, sponsored, or operated by communities, religious groups, or private universities and medical schools. The fees charged by these not-for-profit business-oriented health care providers are intended to help the organization maintain its self-sustaining status rather than to maximize profit for an owner's benefit.

Not-for-profit health care entities are usually exempt from federal and state income taxes if they are operated exclusively for religious, charitable, scientific, or educational purposes and if no part of their net earnings inures to the benefit of any private shareholder or individual. However, they may be subject to taxes on income that is derived from activities not related to their tax-exempt purpose. Tax-exempt providers are allowed to generate profits in order to be able to meet financial obligations; improve patient care; expand facilities; and participate in research, training, education, and other activities that advance the entity's charitable purpose.

Although many tax-exempt health care entities may receive support from religious and fraternal organizations, individuals, corporations, and other donors or grantors, most are essentially self-sustaining; that is, they finance their capital needs primarily from the proceeds of debt issues and their operating needs largely from fees they charge for health care services rendered. As a result, accountability to creditors is more of a driving force in matters pertaining to financial statement presentation and disclosure than it is for nonprofit organizations that rely primarily on outside support. Comparability with financial statements of providers in the investor-owned sectors is also important. Consequently, not-for-profit health care providers must keep up with accounting standards of the business sector as well as the not-for-profit sector.

Some entities organized as not-for-profit corporations may be considered governmental entities for accounting purposes rather than not-for-profit entities. This phenomenon is discussed in Section 35.2(b).

(c) GOVERNMENTAL HEALTH CARE ENTITIES. Governmental health care entities are owned and operated by federal, state, city, or county governments or other political subdivisions. The sponsoring government may participate directly in the operation of the facility or there may be little interaction between the facility and the governmental unit. Such entities generally receive varying levels of subsidies from their sponsoring governments. This may range from heavy subsidization to no financial support, depending on the entity's circumstances.

Federally sponsored hospitals include hospitals operated by U.S. Department of Veterans Affairs, military hospitals, federal prison hospitals, and certain long-term specialty hospitals. Federal hospitals follow federal accounting guidelines and are excluded from the scope of this chapter.

(d) INVESTOR-OWNED HEALTH CARE ENTITIES. Investor-owned health care entities may be organized as stock corporations (publicly traded or privately held), partnerships, limited partnerships, professional corporations, or sole proprietorships. Many investor-owned health care entities are SEC registrants and thus are also subject to SEC reporting requirements.

35.2 AUTHORITATIVE PRONOUNCEMENTS

(a) GENERALLY ACCEPTED ACCOUNTING PRINCIPLES—PRIVATE SECTOR. Industry-specific generally accepted accounting principles (GAAP) for investor-owned and not-for-profit health care organizations (HCOs) is housed in Accounting Standards Codification (ASC) Topic 954, *Health Care Entities.* The scope of ASC 954 is the same as the scope of the nongovernmental sections of the American Institute of Certified Public Accountants (AICPA) audit and accounting guide, discussed in Section 35.2(c).

ASC 954 is not the only Codification section that private sector profit HCOs need to be mindful of, however. Unless they are explicitly excluded, they must follow the guidance in all of the ASC's general Topics and Subtopics. When considering the guidance in the general Topics and Subtopics, it may be helpful to determine whether a corresponding industry subtopic exists within ASC 954. For example, when considering the applicability of Topic 320, *Investments—Debt and Equity Securities,* a preparer or auditor could also check the scope section of ASC 954-320, *Health Care Entities—Investment—Debt and Equity Securities,* for additional information.

Not-for-profit HCOs are also subject to most (but not all) of the industry-specific guidance in ASC 958, *Not-for-Profit Entities.* Therefore, the "scope and scope exceptions" subsections of each subtopic within ASC 958 should be consulted for its applicability to not-for-profit HCOs. Some subsections are fully applicable, some are inapplicable, and some are applicable but subject to additional guidance in ASC 954. An example of the latter is a requirement in ASC 954-210, *Health Care Entities—Balance Sheet,* for not-for-profit HCOs to provide information about liquidity of assets and liabilities by presenting a classified balance sheet. That is a narrowing of the general requirement described in ASC 958-210, *Not-for-Profit Entities—Balance Sheet,* regarding how not-for-profit organizations should provide information about liquidity.

(i) Securities and Exchange Commission Requirements. Although many investor-owned HCOs are publicly traded, at this time there are no unique SEC rules pertaining specifically to SEC-registered health care companies.

(ii) Definition of "Public" Not-for-Profit Entity. Some provisions of the FASB ASC differentiate between "public" and "nonpublic" entities with respect to accounting and disclosure requirements. The Financial Accounting Standards Board (FASB) clarified the definition of *public entity* used in numerous pre-Codification FASB standards (and now referenced throughout ASC) to indicate that not-for-profit entities that are obligated for repayment of publicly traded municipal debt securities issued on their behalf are considered "public" for purposes of certain financial reporting requirements. Generally, the rationale behind these requirements is that the entity's financial statements are being utilized in public markets for making decisions about whether to buy, sell, or hold an organization's securities. See further discussion in Section 35.3(l).

(b) GENERALLY ACCEPTED ACCOUNTING PRINCIPLES—GOVERNMENTAL SECTOR. The authoritative definition of *governmental entity* (developed by agreement of the FASB and the Governmental Accounting Standards Board [GASB]) can be found in paragraph 1.08 of the AICPA's audit and accounting guide *Health Care Entities.* Entities are governmental or nongovernmental for accounting and financial reporting purposes based solely on the application of that definition. If a health care entity falls within the scope of this definition, the GAAP it applies will be established primarily by the GASB rather than the FASB.

Many HCOs within the scope of the definition are special hospital districts created by state legislatures. If a majority of the governing board of a health care entity that is incorporated as a not-for-profit corporation is appointed or approved by officials of a state or local government (e.g., by a state university; by a city or county commission), that organization also would be classified as governmental for accounting and financial reporting purposes.

GASB Statement No. 55, *The Hierarchy of GAAP for State and Local Governments,* identifies the sources of accounting principles used by governmental entities in preparing financial statements that are in conformity with GAAP. These principles have a ranking or hierarchy and must be applied as shown next (in descending order of authority).

Category (a). These are officially established accounting principles promulgated by the GASB—that is, GASB Statements and Interpretations.

Category (b). These are principles contained in Technical Bulletins prepared by the GASB Staff as well as accounting principles contained in AICPA industry audit and accounting guides and Statements of Position that are specifically applicable to state and local government entities and that have been cleared by the GASB.

Category (c). Principles contained in AICPA Practice Bulletins that are specifically made applicable to state and local government entities and cleared by the GASB.

Category (d). Principles contained in implementation guides published by the GASB Staff and practices that are widely recognized and prevalent in state and local government.

Until recently, category (a) also included certain statements issued by the FASB or its predecessors that did not conflict with or contradict GASB statements. In 2010, GASB issued Statement No. 62, *Codification of Accounting and Financial Reporting Guidance Contained in Pre-November*

30, 1989 FASB and Accounting Pronouncements, which extracted all relevant nonconflicting, noncontradictory provisions from pre-1989 standards issued by the FASB or its predecessors prior to November 30, 1989, so that the original private sector standards would no longer be needed by GASB entities. Statement No. 62 also eliminated an option that permitted governmental business-type entities (such as HCOs) to elect to apply all nonconflicting, noncontradictory private sector standards issued on or after November 30, 1989. Those changes became effective for financial statements prepared for periods beginning after December 15, 2011.

(c) AICPA AUDIT AND ACCOUNTING GUIDE *HEALTH CARE ENTITIES*. The AICPA's audit and accounting guide *Health Care Entities* (referred to as "the *Guide*" throughout the remainder of this chapter) has been and continues to be the primary industry-specific reference source for discussions of accounting principles and reporting practices for health care entities. A comprehensive revision of the *Guide* was issued in 2011.[1]

The *Guide* applies to all entities whose principal operations involve providing (or agreeing to provide, in the case of prepaid health care arrangements) health care services to individuals. This includes (but is not limited to) hospitals, including specialty facilities such as: psychiatric or rehabilitation hospitals; nursing homes; subacute care facilities; health maintenance organizations (HMOs) and other providers of prepaid health care services; continuing care retirement facilities (CCRCs); home health companies; ambulatory care companies such as clinics, medical group practices, individual practice associations, and individual practitioners; emergency care facilities; surgery centers; outpatient rehabilitation and cancer treatment centers; and integrated health care delivery systems (also called *health networks*) that include one or more of these types of organizations. It also applies to organizations whose primary activities are the planning, organization, and oversight of entities providing health care services, such as parent or holding companies of health care providers. There are some exceptions to this general rule, based on the HCO's ownership characteristics.

- With regard to entities just described that operate in the not-for-profit sector, the *Guide* adds another parameter to the definition: The organization must also derive all or almost all of its revenues from sales of goods and services (e.g., charges to patients). Not-for-profit providers whose primary source of income is contributions—also known as voluntary health and welfare organizations—apply the AICPA's audit and accounting guide *Not-for-Profit Entities* rather than the *Health Care Entities* guide.
- The *Guide* applies to governmental health care entities that report as special-purpose governments engaged only in business-type activities (i.e., whose financial statements are prepared using enterprise fund accounting and reporting). The *Guide* does not apply to other types of governmental health care entities (e.g., long-term institutional care of individuals with certain chronic conditions or mental impairments) that often use governmental fund accounting and financial reporting because charges for goods or services are not their principal source of revenue.

The *Guide* is updated annually for conforming changes (i.e., to incorporate new accounting guidance issued by the FASB or GASB or new auditing guidance issued by the AICPA or PCAOB).

(d) HEALTHCARE FINANCIAL MANAGEMENT ASSOCIATION PRINCIPLES AND PRACTICES BOARD. The Healthcare Financial Management Association (HFMA), a major trade organization that monitors financial issues related to health care providers, sponsors a panel of distinguished individuals who are nationally prominent in the area of health care accounting and financial reporting and who set forth advisory recommendations on emerging health care accounting and reporting issues in the form of Statements and Issues Analyses. Although Statements by this Principles and Practices

[1] The 2011 version of the *Guide* does not contain illustrative financial statements, a departure from previous editions.

Board (P&P Board) have no authoritative standing, they are valuable to the health care community because they can be issued relatively quickly to disseminate consensus opinions, along with views on the issues and relevant background information, regarding issues on which information would not otherwise be available. Information on statements issued by the P&P Board can be obtained from HFMA (*www.hfma.org*).

35.3 ACCOUNTING PRINCIPLES

(a) CLASSIFICATION AND REPORTING OF NET ASSETS/NET POSITION. For purposes of external financial reporting, net assets (i.e., equity) of not-for-profit and governmental HCOs must be classified into appropriate categories. Not-for-profit HCOs use three broad classes of net assets: unrestricted, temporarily restricted, or permanently restricted. For governmental HCOs, the categories are unrestricted, restricted (expendable or nonexpendable), or invested in capital assets, net of related debt. However, the definition of *restricted* for governmental entities differ from that used for not-for-profit entities, as discussed in Subsection 35.3(a)(ii).

Effective for financial reporting periods beginning after December 15, 2011, governmental HCOs will be required to reflect their equity using "net position" categories rather than "net asset" categories. This is a result of the issuance of GASB Statement No. 63, *Financial Reporting of Deferred Outflows of Resources, Deferred Inflows of Resources, and Net Position. Net position* represents net assets (i.e., the difference between assets and liabilities) modified for the effects of deferred inflows of resources and deferred outflows of resources. For more information on this change, see Section 35.3(p).

(i) Unrestricted Net Assets/Net Position. For both not-for-profit and governmental HCOs, unrestricted net assets are the residual component of net assets. For not-for-profit providers, unrestricted net assets represent net assets that are free of any donor-imposed restrictions. Thus, they generally include the net assets associated with the provider's working capital; investment in property, plant, and equipment; and any assets whose use is limited to a particular purpose by other than donor restriction (as discussed in Section 35.3(b)). If a not-for-profit health care entity's interest in any of its consolidated subsidiaries is less than 100 percent, the portion of net assets that is attributable to others (the noncontrolling interest) must be separately reflected, as discussed in Subsection 35.3(n)(i).

For governmental HCOs, *unrestricted net assets* are net assets that do not meet the definition of restricted assets or invested in capital assets, net of related debt. They are the part of net assets that can be used to finance day-to-day operations without constraints established by debt covenants, donor restrictions, irrevocable trusts, and the like. A significant difference from not-for-profit organizations is that the unrestricted category does not include the entity's investment in property plant and equipment or long-term debt used to finance those assets. Effective for financial reporting periods beginning after December 15, 2011, governmental HCOs will replace the "unrestricted net assets" category with a slightly broader "unrestricted net position" category. *Unrestricted net position* refers to unrestricted net assets modified for the effects of any related deferred inflows of resources or deferred outflows of resources.

(ii) Restricted Net Assets/Net Position. Not-for-profit and governmental entities define the concept of *restricted* differently.

For not-for-profit HCOs, assets that are specifically restricted to use for a particular purpose by an external donor or grantor, along with any related obligations, are included in the restricted net assets/net position component. Although donor-imposed restrictions may require individual gifts or grants to be kept separate for record-keeping purposes, as a general rule, they may be grouped for financial reporting purposes. Groupings are determined based on whether the restrictions are temporary or permanent and on the uses for which the resources are intended. The nature of restrictions on donor-restricted resources, if such amounts are material, should be disclosed in the financial statements.

The definition of *restricted* used by governmental entities is broader than the not-for-profit definition, and it applies to both assets and net assets. For governmental HCOs, assets are reported as restricted when limitations on their use change the nature or normal understanding of the availability of the asset. For example, cash and investments held in a separate account that can be used only for specific purposes established by a party external to the organization and that cannot be used to satisfy the organization's general liabilities are considered to be restricted assets. In addition to resources restricted for identified purposes by donors and grantors, a governmental HCO's restricted assets include unexpended debt proceeds held by trustees, bond sinking and debt service reserve funds, and assets set aside to meet statutory reserve requirements. Self-insurance assets held in irrevocable trusts also are considered to be restricted; although the limitation on their use is not externally imposed (because the governmental HCO voluntarily enters into the self-insurance arrangement), the irrevocable nature of the trust creates a legally enforceable restriction on the assets, which have irrevocably been set aside for the payment of future malpractice claims and, therefore, cannot be used to satisfy other obligations of the entity.

GASB's "restricted net assets" category represents restricted assets reduced by liabilities related to those assets. A liability relates to restricted assets if (1) the assets resulted from incurring the liability (e.g., unexpended debt proceeds held by a trustee) or (2) the liability will be liquidated with the restricted assets (e.g., bond sinking fund proceeds that will be used to make payments on a particular debt issue). Major categories of restrictions should be reported on the face of the governmental entity's balance sheet (e.g., "restricted for capital acquisitions").

Effective for financial reporting periods beginning after December 15, 2011, governmental HCOs will replace the "restricted net assets" category with a slightly broader "restricted net position" category. *Restricted net position* is restricted net assets modified for the effects of any associated deferred inflows of resources or deferred outflows of resources.

(iii) Invested in Capital Assets, Net of Related Debt. This net asset class is used only by governmental organizations. In a sense, it represents the extent to which the governmental HCO owns its productive long-term assets outright (versus the extent to which those assets are being financed with debt). Thus, it is calculated as the difference between an entity's capital assets (net of accumulated depreciation) and any related debt used to finance those assets. Effective for financial reporting periods beginning after December 15, 2011, the "invested in capital assets, net of related debt" "net assets" category will be broadened into a "net position" category that incorporates the effects of any deferred inflows of resources and deferred outflows of resources associated with the financing of capital assets.

(b) NONCURRENT CASH/CLAIMS TO CASH. As a general rule, cash (and claims to cash) that meet any of the next criteria must be reported separately and excluded from current assets:

- They are restricted as to withdrawal or use for other than current operations.
- They are designated for expenditures in the acquisition or construction of noncurrent assets.
- They are required to be segregated for liquidation of long-term debt.
- They are required by a donor-imposed restriction that limits their use to long-term purposes (e.g., purchase of capital assets).

However, any portion of such assets that will be used to satisfy debt classified as a current liability in the financial statements should be displayed in current assets rather than in noncurrent assets.

For governmental health care entities, these requirements are established by GASB Statement No. 62, *Codification of Accounting and Financial Reporting Guidance Contained in Pre-November 30, 1989 FASB and Accounting Pronouncements,* par. 31(a). If the types of limitations discussed earlier arise from external sources or are externally imposed, the assets are considered to be "restricted" (and thus will affect the determination of the entity's restricted net assets), as discussed in Subsection 35.3(a)(ii). If instead the limitations are internally imposed by management or board designations, they are not considered restrictions. Apart from considering the need for noncurrent balance sheet classification, GASB does not require restricted assets or board-designated assets to be displayed separately on the face of the balance sheet.

For nongovernmental health care entities, these requirements are established by FASB ASC 954-305-45, *Health Care Entities—Cash and Cash Equivalents: Other Presentation Matters,* and ASC 210, *Balance Sheet.* Many not-for-profit health care entities report these types of assets under the balance sheet caption "assets whose use is limited." The caption includes funds whose use is contractually limited by external parties, such as:

- Unexpended proceeds of debt issues (or other debt financing instruments) that are held by a trustee and that are limited to use in accordance with the requirements of the financing instrument. Typically, this arises when the proceeds of a municipal bond issue must be used for a particular construction or renovation project.
- Funds deposited with a trustee and limited to use in accordance with the requirements of an indenture or similar agreement, such as a bond sinking fund.
- Unexpended proceeds of contributions that are donor-restricted for long-term purposes (e.g., acquisition of property and equipment).
- Other assets limited to use for identified purposes through an agreement with an outside party other than a donor or grantor. Examples include debt service reserve funds required by bond indentures, malpractice self-insurance trust funds (revocable or irrevocable), and assets set aside to meet HMO statutory reserve requirements.

The "assets whose use is limited" caption may also include assets that are designated by the not-for-profit entity's governing board or management for identified purposes. This might include, for example, assets set aside that are designated for plant replacement or expansion (a long-standing industry practice referred to as *funded depreciation*). However, if board- or management-designated assets are reported under this caption, they must be distinguishable from assets whose use is contractually limited by external parties. This distinction is considered important because the board or management retains control and may, at its discretion, subsequently use the funds for other purposes. This distinction may be accomplished through separate disclosure on the face of the balance sheet or in the notes to the financial statements.

A note generally is included in the summary of significant policies (or separately) describing the purpose of the limited-use assets.

(c) AGENCY TRANSACTIONS. Health care entities may act as agents for other parties; as such, they receive and hold assets that are owned by others. An example of this would be patients' or residents' funds. These are funds held by the facility for the patient's or resident's own personal use, such as for purchasing periodicals, making trips outside the facility, or other incidentals. Usually these funds are kept in an account separate from the facility's own cash accounts. In accepting responsibility for these assets, the entity incurs a liability to the owner either to return them in the future or to disburse them as instructed by the owner. Transactions involving agency funds (e.g., disbursements, interest earned) should not have any economic impact on the provider's operations. Consequently, they should not be included in the provider's income statement.

Fundraising foundations may act as agents in accepting donations on behalf of related HCOs. These situations are discussed in Subsection 35.3(g)(iii).

(d) REVENUE OF HEALTH CARE FACILITIES. A unique aspect of health care operations is that revenue transactions primarily involve more parties than the traditional "buyer" and "seller." As many as four parties may be associated with a revenue transaction involving an HCO. These include: (1) the individual who receives the medical care; (2) the physician who orders the required services on behalf of the patient; (3) the health care entity that provides the setting or administers the treatment (e.g., hospital, home health company); and (4) a third-party payer[2] that pays the health care entity, physician, or both on behalf of the patient. The third-party payer may be a government program, such as Medicare or Medicaid, and/or a commercial insurer, such as a managed care plan, a commercial insurance company, a Blue Cross plan, or a preferred provider organization (PPO). In managed care organizations, parties 2, 3, and/or 4 may all be part of the same organization.

The extent to which third-party payers are involved in paying for services varies by type of health care facility. For hospitals, rehabilitation facilities, and home health companies, the majority of services provided are paid for by third-party payers. Such payments are either transacted on a fee-for-service basis (i.e., patient service revenue); or they may be bundled into a capitation payment (described below). In the nursing home sector, roughly half of the patients are considered "private pay" (i.e., the patient or their family pays for the care); for the remainder, Medicaid is the dominant third-party payer (for care provided to low-income individuals). Currently little commercial insurance coverage exists for nursing home care, and Medicare provides very limited nursing home benefits only for short stays. In CCRCs, entrance fees and monthly service fees are paid by the residents themselves, and third-party payer involvement is limited to payment of some services that may be provided in the skilled nursing care portion of the facility.

These types of arrangements are discussed within this chapter:

- Patient service revenue is derived from fees earned in exchange for providing a specific service to a particular patient. This type of revenue is discussed in Section 35.3(e).
- Under capitation arrangements, the provider earns a fixed, predetermined amount per person by *agreeing to* provide covered services to a specific population (e.g., members of a health plan) during a specified time period (usually one month) and is paid a fixed, predetermined amount per member per month regardless of whether any services are actually provided or how expensive those services are. HMOs that arrange for the provision of health care services earn premium revenue in a similar manner. Capitation arrangements and premiums are discussed in Subsection 35.4(b)(i).
- In CCRCs, residents may pay for residential services and amenities (and in many cases, varying amounts of health care services) through a combination of up-front entrance fees plus monthly periodic fees. These types of revenue are discussed in Section 35.4(a).

The financial statements of HCOs that have more than one significant source of revenue (e.g., a hospital that has significant amounts of both patient service revenue and capitation fees) should display those classes of revenue separately.

- Aside from the provision of health care services, a number of other activities are normal in the day-to-day operation of a health care facility. Such income should be accounted for separately from revenue that is derived from providing health care services (or agreeing to provide health care services). Many HCOs (particularly not-for-profit HCOs) report such activities (if material) in a caption such as "other operating revenue." Examples include: sales of medical and pharmacy supplies to employees, physicians, and others
- Proceeds from sales of cafeteria meals and guest trays to employees, medical staff, and visitors
- Proceeds from sales of scrap, used X-ray film, and so on
- Proceeds from sales at gift shops, snack bars, newsstands, parking lots, vending machines, and other service facilities operated by the entity
- Income from education programs
- Rental of facility space

---

[2] Note: the AICPA Guide uses the term "payer" in lieu of the spelling "payor."

- Income from transportation services provided to residents
- Investment income related to operations
- Grants related to operations

(e) PATIENT SERVICE REVENUE.[3] Patient service revenue is derived from fees earned in exchange for providing services to patients. Often such revenue is generically referred to as "fee for service" revenue.

Third-party payers typically do not pay the HCO's established rates for these services. The amount paid may be based on government regulations (for Medicare, Medicaid, and other government programs) or contractual arrangements (for PPOs, Blue Cross plans, HMOs, and commercial insurers). Those regulations or contracts will indicate the basis of payment (i.e., what the provider must do in order to be entitled to revenue under the contract or provider agreement) and the degree of risk that is to be assumed by the provider. Consequently, a thorough understanding of the terms of the provider's arrangements with significant third-party payers is critical to appropriate revenue recognition. Common payment methodologies include (but are not limited to):

- *Fee for specific service.* In these situations, payment is made for the specific services that are provided to the patient; therefore, the provider earns revenue as a result of providing the specific service. Payment may be made based on a predetermined discounted rate (e.g., percent of charges) or a fee schedule agreed to by the provider and the third-party payer.
- *Per diem.* Under a per-diem arrangement, the provider is paid a predetermined flat rate per day of inpatient care, regardless of the level of intensity of the care provided. Therefore, revenue is earned as a result of the patient occupying a bed for a particular day. The Medicare prospective payment system (PPS) for skilled nursing facility services is an example of a per-diem methodology.
- *Per case.* Under a per-case arrangement, the provider is paid a predetermined amount based on the patient's "discharge category." The Medicare PPS for hospital inpatient services is an example of a per-case payment methodology involving diagnosis-related groupings. Medicare's PPS for hospital outpatient services is another per-case methodology based on groupings of procedures performed.
- *Episodic.* Under an episodic payment methodology, the provider is paid a predetermined amount for services provided to patients during an "episode of care" (i.e., a stipulated period of time). Revenue is earned based on the passage of time. Medicare's PPS for home health services is an example of an episodic payment methodology.

The difference between the HCO's established rates and the contractual rates of payment is referred to as the *contractual allowance* or *contractual adjustment.* Because the amounts received from third-party payers bear little relationship to an HCO's established charges, reporting gross charges in the financial statements is not considered meaningful. Consequently, the *Guide* instructs providers to report net patient service revenues (i.e., gross changes less contractual adjustments and other deductions from revenue) in the income statement.

These matters are discussed in Chapter 10 of the *Guide.*

(i) Estimating Patient Service Revenue Related to Governmental Programs

Nature of Retroactive Adjustments. Contracts with governmental payers such as Medicare or Medicaid typically involve a potential for retroactive adjustment. The extent of the potential for retroactive adjustment depends on whether payment rates are determined *prospectively* or *retrospectively.*

Prospective rate setting is a method used to set payment rates in advance of the delivery of health care services. The intent is to establish payment rates before the period to which they

[3]For FASB entities, the requirements discussed in this section may be modified by the FASB/IASB joint revenue recognition project.

A key part of PPS is the categorization of medical and surgical services into diagnosis-related groups (DRGs). The DRGs "bundle" services (labor and nonlabor resources) that are needed to treat a patient with a particular disease or diagnosis. The DRG payment rates cover most routine operating costs attributable to patient care, including routine nursing services, room and board, and diagnostic and ancillary services. The Centers for Medicare & Medicaid Services (the federal government agency responsible for administering the Medicare and Medicaid programs) assigns each DRG a weight based on the average cost to deliver care to a patient with a particular disease or diagnosis. DRG weights are periodically recalibrated based on data captured through Medicare cost reports. At present, there are 499 DRGs, each with a standardized relative weight.

Here is a simplified example of how the payment calculation works. Assume that Sara, a 72-year-old widow, fell and is diagnosed with an open fracture of the left femur that requires surgery. In addition, the physician determines from her medical history that she has non–insulin-dependent diabetes with associated peripheral vascular disorders. Based on those factors, the hospital in which the surgery is performed must assign a DRG to Sara's case. The potential DRG assignments pertaining to femur fracture surgeries are listed in the table. Sara is older than age 17, and she has comorbidities or complications (diabetes). Thus, her diagnosis is classified as DRG 210, which has a relative weight of 1.8817. If the hospital's base payment rate is $20,000, it will receive a flat amount of $37,634 for all care provided to Sara during her stay ($20,000 × 1.8817).

DRG	Description	Relative Weight
210	HIP & FEMUR PROCEDURES EXCEPT MAJOR JOINT AGE >17 WITH COMPLICATIONS OR COMORBIDITIES	1.8817
211	HIP & FEMUR PROCEDURES EXCEPT MAJOR JOINT AGE >17 WITH COMPLICATIONS OR COMORBIDITIES	1.2675
212	HIP & FEMUR PROCEDURES EXCEPT MAJOR JOINT AGE 0-17	1.4162

Exhibit 35.1 How DRGs Work

will apply begins and that are not subject to change. The Medicare Inpatient PPS for short-stay, acute-care hospitals is an example of a prospective methodology. Medicare pays those hospitals a predetermined base payment rate for each admission that is multiplied by a measure (called a diagnosis-related group [DRG] weighting factor) which reflects the nature/acuity of a patient's condition. The DRG weighting factor also is prospectively determined. An example of a DRG payment calculation is provided in Exhibit 35.1.

In contracts that utilize retrospective rate setting, the amount that ultimately will be paid for the service is determined with hindsight. Such contracts involve paying the provider an amount that is based on the costs of providing the services to the Medicare or Medicare beneficiaries during the year. At the time the services are provided, the provider receives interim payments based on an estimated reimbursement rate. After the close of the contract period, a final settlement is determined based the provider's actual costs and charges submitted in a cost report filed after the close of the contract period. (This is referred to as reimbursement on a reasonable-cost basis.)

All institutional health care providers (e.g., hospitals, nursing homes, home health agencies) participating in the Medicare and Medicaid fee-for-service programs are required to submit an annual report cost report covering the revenues, costs, and expenses associated with the services provided by that facility to Medicare beneficiaries or Medicaid recipients. For providers that are reimbursed on a reasonable-cost basis, the cost report is the vehicle used for ultimately determining the amount of payment that the provider is entitled to from the program for a particular contract year. The cost reports are subject to routine audits by government intermediaries, which may result in adjustments to the amounts ultimately determined to be due to (or due from) the provider under the program. Final settlements often are not determined until the government is satisfied (based on the reviews or audits conducted by the program) that the amount paid for the services was appropriate. Often final settlement does not occur until several years after the cost report was filed.

Individual claims (requests for payment) filed by HCOs also are subject to postpayment review to ensure that the payments made were appropriate. Payments for items or services that are found to be not medically necessary, not covered by the program, or that are deemed to be inappropriately coded are subject to recoupment by the government. If the government believes that billing fraud exists, far-ranging government investigations can be launched that can result in recoupments, fines, and penalties. Thus, even rate-setting methods that are described as prospective (e.g., Medicare DRGs) may have the potential for retrospective adjustment related to items such as billing denials or coding changes.

Estimating the Adjustments. As discussed in Subsection 35.3(e)(i), the amount of patient service revenue earned under arrangements with government programs is determined under complex government rules and regulations that subject the organization to the potential for retrospective adjustments in future years. Thus, providers must estimate the amounts that ultimately will be realizable from services provided during a particular contract year (often referred to as a cost-reporting period) and report that amount as revenue. Because several years may elapse before all potential adjustments related to a particular cost-reporting period are known, management must estimate the effects of future program audits, administrative reviews, and billing reviews. Management also must take into account the potential for regulatory investigations that may result in denial of otherwise valid claims for payment. These types of estimation matters are discussed in Statement of Position (SOP) No. 00-1, *Auditing Health Care Third-Party Revenues and Related Receivables.* Although that SOP was issued for use by auditors, it provides helpful guidance to preparers regarding uncertainties inherent in third-party revenue recognition.

Management's estimates relating to third-party revenue are based on subjective as well as objective factors. Estimating these amounts requires judgment that normally is based on management's knowledge of and experience with past and current events and on its assumptions about conditions it expects to exist and courses of action it expects to take. As a result, the extent of management's estimates involving contractual allowances and adjustments may range from relatively straightforward calculations based on information that is readily available, to highly complex judgments based on assumptions as to future events.

All relevant information is used in making these estimates. Approaches vary from entity to entity, depending on individual facts and circumstances. Some entities with significant prior experience may attempt to quantify the effects of individual potential intermediary or other governmental (e.g., Office of Inspector General or Department of Justice) or private payer adjustments, based on detailed calculations and assumptions regarding potential future adjustments. Some may prepare cost report analyses to estimate the effect of potential adjustments. Others may base their estimates on an analysis of potential adjustments in the aggregate, in light of the payers involved, the nature of the payment mechanism, the risks associated with future audits, and other relevant factors. In some cases, the uncertainty surrounding a potential adjustment may be so great (e.g., the potential outcome of a government investigation) that management is unable to make a reasonable estimate of the financial effect for inclusion in the financial statements. In such situations, disclosure regarding such uncertainties should be made in the notes to the financial statements (see Subsection 35.3(e)(i)).

Third-party settlement estimates must be evaluated at each reporting date to determine if any information has come to light that would require revision of the estimates. Future events (e.g., final settlements, ongoing audits and investigations, or passage of time in relation to the statute of limitations) that either occur or fail to occur may differ from management's assumptions about them and therefore require revision of the estimates. Differences between original estimates and subsequent revisions should be included in the statement of operations in the period in which the revisions are made and be disclosed, if material. Such adjustments have the potential to materially affect the health care entity's financial position and results of operations.

Effects of Uncertainty and GAAP. SOP No. 00-1 states that the fairness or reasonableness of financial statement presentation of estimates is not dependent on the outcome of the uncertainty (i.e., management's ability to predict the future with accuracy) but rather on the quality and nature of the evidence supporting management's assertions at the time the estimate is made. The fact that future events may differ materially from management's assumptions or estimates would not necessarily lead to a conclusion that management's estimates were not reasonable or valid at the time they were made, if they were made based on the best information available at the time.

Private-sector GAAP requires that the uncertainties inherent in significant estimates such as third-party settlements be disclosed appropriately in the financial statements. If uncertainties associated with revenue recognition are presented in accordance with ASC 275, *Risks and Uncertainties,* the financial statements of a private-sector entity are presented fairly in conformity with GAAP.

(This guidance is not applicable to governmental entities, although it may be voluntarily applied as "other accounting literature" within the GASB GAAP hierarchy.) This is true even in situations involving material uncertainties. Such disclosures might include the significance of government program revenues to the entity's overall revenues and a description of the complex nature of applicable laws and regulations, indicating that the possibility of future government review and interpretation exists. If a reasonable estimate cannot be made of the outcome of the uncertainty and the circumstances surrounding the uncertainty are adequately disclosed, the financial statements are not deficient from a GAAP perspective. Disclosure, however, is never a substitute for recognition in the financial statements.

(ii) Reporting Charity Care Provided. As a matter of policy, HCOs often render services free of charge (or at discounted rates) to individuals who have little or no means to pay for them. Even though the organization expects no compensation for those services, the related charges must be recorded in the patient accounting system because that typically is the only basis for measuring consumption of resources by those patients.

Because little if any cash flows are expected from these services, charges pertaining to charity care do not qualify for recognition as revenue in a provider's financial statements. The provider is considered to have given away the services rather than having "sold" them. Receivables reported in the balance sheet for health care services and the related valuation allowance similarly should not include amounts related to charity care patients. These prohibitions apply to the face of the financial statements and any note disclosures or supplemental schedules that accompany the provider's financial statements.

Disclosures pertaining to charity care must be provided in the notes to the financial statements of all providers that have a policy of providing charity care to individuals who are unable to pay. (If, as a matter of policy, an entity does not provide charity services, the disclosures are not required.) The disclosure requirements for private-sector entities differ from those for governmental entities. Private-sector entities must disclose:

- *A statement of management's policy with regard to providing charity care.* That information should be included in the entity's "summary of significant accounting policies," along with the fact that charity services do not result in revenue.
- *The estimated cost of the charity care provided and the method used to estimate those costs.* Disclosures of the level of charity care provided must be based on fully loaded estimated costs (i.e., all direct and indirect costs of providing the services), which is consistent with Internal Revenue Service (IRS) Form 990 Schedule H disclosure requirements for not-for-profit hospitals. Costs should be estimated using the best information available. The cost measurement is not required to be based on specific identification or the use of a cost accounting system; management may estimate such costs using "reasonable techniques," such as multiplying a ratio of cost to gross charges by the gross uncompensated charges associated with charity care patients.
- *The value of any funds received to offset or subsidize charity services provided during the period.* This would include, for example, contributions that are donor-restricted for charity care.

Governmental entities must disclose:

- *A statement of management's policy with regard to providing charity care.* That information should be included in the entity's "summary of significant accounting policies," along with the fact that charity services do not result in revenue.
- The level of charity care provided for each of the years covered by the financial statements. The level of care provided may be measured in a variety of ways: the provider's established rates, costs, unit of service statistics (such as patient days or occasions of service), or other statistics. The method used to measure the charity care must also be disclosed since it would be meaningless to assign a dollar value to charity services provided without explaining whether that value represents the facility's charges or costs.

(iii) Reporting the Provision for Bad Debts.[4] For most companies, bad debt expense is a manifestation of credit risk. However, when HCOs (primarily hospitals) provide care to patients who cannot afford to pay for those services, often those services also are written off to bad debt expense.

Hospitals that operate emergency rooms are obligated by law to provide emergency treatment to a patient (customer) regardless of whether they know whether that patient has the ability to pay or will be eligible for third-party coverage. As a result, they often grapple with the inherent difficulty in distinguishing uninsured indigent patients from charity care patients. Often the only difference between the two groups is that those classified as uninsured indigent cannot (or will not) provide the necessary documentation that is required to prove eligibility for charity care (e.g., a pay stub or tax return). As a result, those two demographically similar groups of patients are treated differently for financial reporting purposes. Health care organizations do not recognize revenue for services provided to charity care patients. For services provided to noncharity uninsured indigent patients, they generally will recognize revenues and receivables along with a sizable provision for bad debts. Such bad debts are not a reflection of credit risk (as bad debt expense is typically thought of) but instead are reflective of the questionable quality of the revenues that were recognized.

ASU 2011-07, *Presentation and Disclosure of Net Revenue, Provision for Bad Debts, and the Allowance for Doubtful Accounts,*[5] requires nongovernmental entities that recognize significant amounts of revenue without assessing the patient's ability to pay (such as the hospitals discussed in the previous paragraph) to reflect the provision for bad debts associated with their patient service revenue as a reduction of revenue rather than as an expense. That is, hospitals significantly affected by the "gross-up" of revenue and bad debts associated with services provided to uninsured indigent patients should report their bad debts associated with patient service revenue directly beneath the patient service revenue line on the face of the income statement. This serves two purposes: It flags the uncertainty about the quality of certain revenues reported, and it indicates that the majority of bad debt expense did not arise from a typical extension of credit. Those entities also would be required to provide enhanced disclosure about their policies for recognizing revenue and assessing bad debts. Bad debts associated with revenue-generating activities other than patient service revenue would not reclassified.

Bad debts reported by nongovernmental health care entities that are not affected by this type of gross-up continue to be reported as operating expense.

ASU 2011-07 does not apply to governmental HCOs. Those entities report all bad debt expense as a reduction of revenue in accordance with the GASB financial reporting model, as discussed in Chapter 15 of the *Guide*.

(f) CONCENTRATION OF CREDIT RISK. Geographic concentration of credit risk (as discussed in ASC 825-10-50-20 through 50-21) related to patient accounts receivable is usually an issue for hospitals and physician groups because of the emergency nature of many of the services provided and because they generally tend to treat patients from their local or surrounding communities. An economic event, such as the closing of a large industrial plant, may leave many of the community's residents without insurance. Because an accident or illness requiring an individual to incur hospitalization expense usually is not a matter of choice, many who partake of a provider's services are unable to pay for those services. Hospitals that participate in federal programs cannot deny services to patients who are perceived to be bad credit risks. Therefore, hospitals frequently extend a great deal of unsecured credit. It should be noted that the concentration of credit risk for an individual hospital is different from what it would be for a national multihospital system that includes the individual hospital. When financial statements of individual facilities are consolidated into statements prepared for the entire system, the credit risk is spread over a much larger geographic area and is therefore not as concentrated.

[4]For nongovernmental HCOs, the requirements discussed in this section may be modified by the FASB/IASB joint revenue recognition project.

[5] ASU 2011-07 is required to be applied in years beginning after December 15, 2011.

Some state Medicaid programs are experiencing fiscal problems that may result in inordinately long payment delays or retroactively reduced payment amounts. Such situations may create credit risks for providers with significant concentrations of Medicaid patients or residents.

In the past, concentrations of credit risks have generally been confined to the amount of business or receivables outstanding with governmental payers (Medicare and Medicaid). In recent years, however, Medicare and Medicaid increasingly are contracting with private-sector managed care plans to provide health care services to program beneficiaries on a capitated basis. For providers that treat significant numbers of beneficiaries covered under Medicare or Medicaid risk plans, a concentration of credit risk may therefore exist with the health plan rather than the federal government. Refer to ASC 954-310-50-2 for further discussion.

Prior to adoption of GAS Statement No. 62, governmental entities that elected to apply all nonconflicting, noncontradictory private-sector standards issued on or after November 30, 1989, applied the FASB guidance discussed above. GASB staff informally indicated[6] that the decision on whether governmental entities should discontinue application of this guidance upon adoption of GAS 62 should be based on the prevalent practice in that entity's industry, citing health care as an example. Thus, many governmental health care entities that disclose information pertaining to concentrations of credit risk are likely to continue to apply this guidance as "other accounting literature."

(g) CONTRIBUTIONS. Many HCOs (particularly hospitals) will receive supplemental income from contributions. The applicable accounting and reporting principles for contributions vary depending on whether the health care entity is not for profit or governmental and on whether the contributions are received directly by the health care entity or received indirectly through another party, such as a trust or fundraising foundation (Subsection 35.3(g)(iv))

The classification of contributions is based on the existence or absence of donor-imposed restrictions. Some donor-imposed restrictions permanently limit the entity's use of contributed funds (e.g., a permanent endowment under which the donated assets must be invested in perpetuity and to which the provider is entitled only to the earnings). Those restrictions result in permanently restricted contributions. Other restrictions are temporary in nature, limiting the entity's use of the contributed resources to a specific purpose (e.g., to be used to care for indigent patients; to be used toward purchase of certain equipment) or to use at or after a stipulated time (e.g., a term endowment). Those contributions are classified as temporarily restricted.

As a result, not-for-profit entities classify contributions as unrestricted, temporarily restricted, or permanently restricted. Governmental organizations apply the same concepts using different terminology—for example, unrestricted, restricted-expendable, or restricted-nonexpendable.

(i) General Guidance—Not-for-Profit Entities. As discussed in Section 35.2(c), the *Health Care Entities* guide and ASC 954 "scope out" (i.e., exclude) not-for-profit health care providers whose primary source of revenue is contributions from the general public. However, most not-for-profit HCOs within the scope of the *Guide* usually derive some contribution income. Chapter 11 of the *Guide* discusses contributions.

The "contributions received" subsections of ASC 958-605 provide broad standards regarding the accounting for contributions that apply to all not-for-profit entities; a comprehensive discussion of those standards can be found in Chapter 28 of this *Handbook.* Not-for-profit HCOs apply those standards subject to additional health care–specific guidance in ASC 954-605, discussed in this section.

Unrestricted contributions are reported as increases in unrestricted net assets in the statement of operations. In most cases, the gifts are reported above the performance indicator. However, an unrestricted donation of a long-lived asset (e.g., a donor gives the HCO a parcel of land with no restrictions attached) is reported below the performance indicator.

---

[6] Prior to the effective date of GAS 62, GASB Staff maintained a Web page highlighting the applicability or inapplicability of FASB standards issued after November 30, 1989. This Staff view was communicated on that Web page.

Restricted contributions are reported in the statement of changes in net assets as increases in temporarily restricted or permanently restricted net assets (as appropriate) when received. However, if restrictions are satisfied within the same financial reporting period as the gift is received, not-for-profits can elect an accounting policy of reporting such gifts as unrestricted contributions, as discussed in ASC 958-320-45.

When the donor's stipulations attached to a temporarily restricted contribution have been satisfied (e.g., the equipment has been placed in service, the indigent care has been provided, the time period implicitly or explicitly stipulated by the donor has elapsed), a reclassification is made from temporarily restricted net assets to unrestricted net assets. (If two or more temporary restrictions are imposed on a contribution, the effect of the expiration of those restrictions should be recognized in the period in which the last remaining restriction expires.) The reclassification is reported above the performance indicator in the statement of operations as "net assets released from restriction," unless the restriction pertained to the purchase of long-lived assets.

Contributions of cash that are donor-restricted for the acquisition of long-lived assets generally are reported in the statement of changes in net assets as increases in temporarily restricted net assets. (However, if the asset was purchased and placed in service in the same period as the contribution was received and the entity has a policy of classifying such contributions as unrestricted, it would instead be reported below the performance indicator in the statement of operations.) The expiration of the restriction is reported in the period the asset is placed in service. This is a narrowing of the options available to other types of not-for-profit entities under ASC 958-320 with respect to reporting the release of restriction. The reclassification ("net assets released from restriction") is reported below the performance indicator in the statement of operations.

A few special situations associated with expiration of restrictions are commonly encountered by not-for-profit HCOs.

The first is anecdotally referred to as the "first dollar rule," and it is described in ASC 958-205-45-11. The first dollar rule requires not-for-profit entities to establish an accounting policy of using donor-restricted resources before unrestricted resources. In other words, if a hospital has unexpended contributions that are restricted for purchase of property, plant, and equipment but elects to pay for a particular capital purchase from unrestricted funds (e.g., from board-designated assets set aside for capital replacement), the capital expenditure will nonetheless result in a reclassification from temporarily restricted to unrestricted net assets, even though restricted funds were not used to make the purchase.

Gifts received in the form of promises to give (i.e., pledges) generally are reported as temporarily restricted unless explicit donor stipulations or circumstances surrounding the gift make it clear that the donor intended the gift to be used to support activities of the period in which the pledge was made. Otherwise, it is presumed that donors intend to support activities in the period (or periods) in which the pledge payments become due. Thus, even if a pledge is received that is free of donor-imposed purposes restrictions; it must be reported as temporarily restricted. The time restriction expires in the periods the future payment or payments become due.

Special considerations apply to contributions that are received through affiliated fundraising foundations. These are discussed in Subsection 35.3(g)(iii).

(ii) Governmental Entities. GASB Statement No. 33, *Accounting and Financial Reporting for Nonexchange Transactions,* establishes accounting and financial reporting standards for the timing of recognition of contributions received that involve financial or capital resources. It does not apply to noncapital gifts-in-kind or contributed services.

Statement No. 33 classifies contributions as "voluntary nonexchange transactions." Revenue from voluntary nonexchange transactions should be recognized when all applicable "eligibility requirements" have been met.

Health care organizations may receive contributions that are restricted for specific purposes. Some donor-imposed restrictions permanently limit the organization's use of contributed funds (e.g., a permanent endowment under which the donated assets must be invested in perpetuity and only the investment income may be spent). Those restrictions result in reporting restricted-nonexpendable net position. Other restrictions are temporary in nature, limiting the organization's use of the contributed resources to a specific purpose (e.g., to be used to care for indigent patients; to be used toward purchase of certain equipment). Those contributions are classified as restricted-expendable net position.

The expiration of restrictions (through passage of time or expending funds for the stipulated purpose) is not reflected in the SRECNA. GASB Statement No. 34, *Basic Financial Statements—and Management's Discussion and Analysis—for State and Local Governments,* requires that an amount equal to unexpended restricted contributions at the balance sheet date (less related liabilities, if any) be included in the restricted net position component of the balance sheet, but otherwise restrictions are not recognized in the financial statements. This is a significant difference between governmental and not-for-profit health care entities.

Statement No. 34 also provides guidance on how nonexchange transactions should be displayed in the SRECNA. Contributions (both unrestricted and restricted) are reported as nonoperating revenue unless a restriction relates to a capital purpose (e.g., construction, renovation, equipment purchases, capital debt retirement). Contributions related to capital are reported below nonoperating revenue, as are contributions of or additions to term and permanent endowments.

GASB does not require governmental HCOs that receive restricted resources to apply a policy that is similar to the "first dollar rule" discussed in Subsection 35.3(g)(i). Instead, each entity is required to establish a policy for whether restricted or unrestricted resources will be used first when both sources are available and to disclose that policy in the notes to the financial statements.

If the nonexchange transaction is a term endowment or a permanent endowment, the provider's stipulation that the resources should be maintained intact in perpetuity, for a specified number of years, or until a specific event has occurred (e.g., the donor's death) is a time requirement. In such situations, the time requirement is considered met as soon as the recipient begins to honor the provider's stipulation not to sell, disburse, or consume the resources. The HCO cannot begin to honor the provider's stipulation until the resources are received; therefore, promises to give term or permanent endowments are not recognized in financial statements. The HCO should recognize revenues from term or permanent endowments when the resources are received, provided that all other eligibility requirements have been met. The associated net assets should be reported as restricted for as long as the donor's time requirements (and purpose restrictions, if applicable) remain in effect.

Special revenue recognition considerations related to contributions that are received through affiliated fundraising foundations are discussed in Subsection 35.3(g)(iii).

(iii) Contributions Received through Affiliated Fundraising Foundations. Health care entities may create separate not-for-profit foundations to raise and hold funds for their benefit. The accounting for contributions received through these foundations depends on the nature of the relationship between the organizations and whether the health care entity is not for profit or governmental.

An HCO might be the beneficiary of a fund established on its behalf at a community foundation (a philanthropic institution serving a geographically defined area). Community foundations possess "variance power"—that is, the right to redirect contributions received to a different beneficiary if they deem it appropriate. In those situations, the HCO recognizes contribution income as it receives distributions from, or distributions are unconditionally promised by, the community foundation.

In other cases, health care entities establish foundations to raise and hold funds for their own benefit. For example, ABC Health System might establish the ABC Health Foundation whose mission is to raise funds on behalf of the system's affiliates. When gifts are received by a fundraising foundation that is affiliated with a health care provider, it raises a question: Which entity should report the contribution income—the foundation that received the gift or the health care entity that the gift is intended to benefit? Guidance on these matters is found in the *Transfers of Assets to a Not-for-Profit Entity or Charitable Trust that Raises or Holds Contributions for Others* subsections of ASC 958-605. Some key provisions are highlighted next.

Financially interrelated organizations. Many provider–foundation relationships will meet the definition of financially interrelated organizations[7]—that is, the provider has an ongoing economic interest in the net assets of the foundation, and either the provider has the ability to influence the operating and financial decisions of the foundation or the foundation has the ability to influence the provider in that manner. In these situations, the relationship differs from the typical principal–agent relationship. As a result, ASC 958-605 permits the foundation to recognize the contribution income as an increase in its unrestricted, temporarily restricted, or permanently restricted net assets, as appropriate.

The provider reflects its rights to the resources held on its behalf by reporting an asset (typically captioned "interest in net assets of foundation") that reflects its ongoing economic interest in the foundation's net assets. Periodically, that interest is adjusted to reflect the impact of activity reported in the foundation's statement of activities. (This accounting is similar to the equity method of accounting for investments in noncontrolled entities.). An appendix to Chapter 11 of the *Guide* discusses how the periodic adjustment (an amount analogous to the "equity pickup" reported by an entity using equity method accounting) should be reflected in the provider's statement of operations and statement of changes in net assets.

If the provider has the ability to influence the timing and amount of distributions from the foundation (e.g., if the health care entity controls the foundation or has such a close working relationship with a noncontrolled foundation with it that it can, in essence, access the foundation's assets at will), then the provider should segregate the adjustment into restricted and unrestricted portions that mirror the reporting on the foundation's statement of activities. The unrestricted portion would be reflected as an increase in unrestricted net assets in the statement of operations (reported above or below the performance indicator, as appropriate). The restricted portion would be reported in the statement of changes in net assets as changes in temporarily or permanently restricted net assets, as appropriate. If the provider does not have the ability to influence the timing and amount of distributions from the foundation, an implied time restriction exists. In that situation, the statement of changes in net assets reflects the adjustment as a change in temporarily or permanently restricted net assets.

Not financially interrelated. If the foundation and HCO do not meet the definition of *financially interrelated organizations,* a traditional agency relationship is presumed to exist whenever the foundation receives contributions on behalf of the provider. In those situations, the foundation must reflect its obligation to pass those contributions on to the provider by reporting a liability; it does not recognize contribution income. The provider recognizes a corresponding receivable and contribution revenue.

(iv) Governmental Entities. As a general rule, the amount of contribution revenue recognized by a governmental health care provider will be directly impacted by whether the foundation prepares its financial statements using GASB standards or FASB standards (based on the definition in Section 35.2(b)).

Foundation financial statements that are prepared in accordance with FASB standards will embody FASB's guidance for entities that raise or hold funds for others. As discussed in Subsection 35.3(g)(iii), the determination of whether the foundation recognizes contribution revenue from such transactions depends on whether the organizations are deemed to be "financially interrelated" under ASC 958-20.

If the organizations deemed to be are financially interrelated (e.g., because the health care entity is the sole beneficiary of the foundation's activities), the contribution revenue recognized by the health care entity is limited to the amount of distributions received (or receivable) from the foundation during the reporting period. Although this may appear to result in double-counting contributions—that is, once when the contribution is initially received by the foundation and again when the foundation distributes it to the health care entity—GASB believes that clearly displaying and describing the interentity transactions (on the face of the financial statements and

[7] See ASC 958-20, *Not-for-Profit Entities—Financially-Interrelated Entities.*

in the notes) should minimize any potential for misunderstanding. The foundation reflects those distributions as expense.

If the organizations are not deemed to be financially interrelated, the foundation acts as the health care entity's agent when it solicits and accepts contributions on the health care entity's behalf. In this situation, the foundation reports a liability reflecting its obligation to transfer the contributed resources to the HCO (i.e., due to beneficiary). Statement No. 33, par. 21 requires the health care entity to recognize a corresponding receivable and contribution revenue (or deferred revenue if eligibility requirements have not been met). Thus, all contribution revenue generated by the foundation's activities during the year that meet Statement No. 33's eligibility criteria will be reflected on the HCO's books. When the foundation distributes funds to the health care entity, the health care entity debits cash and credits the receivable; there is no impact on the SRECNA. Statement No. 34, par. 61 requires that amounts payable and receivable between the health care entity and a discretely presented foundation be reported on a separate line in the balance sheet.

When the foundation meets the definition of a governmental entity (and, thus, its financial statements are prepared in accordance with GASB standards), the health care entity will recognize contribution revenue only to the extent that it receives distributions (or receivables) from the foundation. The foundation recognizes contribution income for all gifts received on behalf of the health care entity consistent with the general rule established for pass-through grants in GASB Statement No. 24, *Accounting and Financial Reporting for Certain Grants and Other Financial Assistance.* Due to the extent of a fundraising foundation's financial and administrative involvement with gifts raised, Statement No. 24's "cash conduit" reporting provisions (which are consistent with traditional agency accounting) would rarely if ever be applicable.

(v) Contributions Established through Trusts. Some donors make gifts to HCOs by establishing charitable trusts (or similar agreements) under which providers receive benefits that are shared with other beneficiaries. Examples of such arrangements (termed *split-interest agreements*) include charitable lead trusts, charitable remainder trusts, charitable gift annuities, and pooled life income funds. Recognition and measurement principles for these arrangements are discussed in Chapter 28 of this *Handbook.*

Though not technically a split-interest agreement, perpetual trusts held by third parties are similar, except that the provider is usually the sole beneficiary. Funds contributed to the trust are invested in perpetuity under the terms of the trust, with the provider receiving annually some or all of the income on the trust's assets (i.e., the provider has the irrevocable right to receive the income earned on the trust assets in perpetuity but never receives the assets held in trust). Perpetual trusts held by third parties are quite common among HCOs.

(h) INVESTMENTS

(i) Nongovernmental Entities.[8] Generally speaking, the accounting used by investor-owned health care entities and not-for-profit health care entities for marketable securities (and the investment return thereon) is similar, except that not-for-profit health care entities are not permitted to use a "held to maturity" category in which securities are reported at amortized cost.

The requirements for not-for-profit entities are set forth in ASC 958-320, modified by incremental requirements set forth in ASC 954-320. Because not-for-profit HCOs are required to report a performance indicator, they use an income recognition approach similar to that used by for-profit health care entities. Thus, the incremental guidance in ASC 954-320 tailors the not-for-profit investment reporting model to be as close as possible to the for-profit investment reporting model. Dividends and interest income, realized gains and losses, unrealized gains and losses on marketable securities classified as trading securities, unrealized gains and losses on investments recorded under the fair value option, the net income portion of equity earnings from investments accounted for

[8]The requirements discussed in this section may be modified by the FASB/IASB financial instruments project.

under the equity method, and other-than-temporary impairment losses are all included in the performance indicator. Unrealized gains and losses on marketable securities classified as available for sale, the portion of other-than-temporary impairment losses on debt securities that is related to factors other than credit losses, and any "other comprehensive income" (OCI) portion of equity earnings from investments that are accounted for under the equity method are reported below the performance indicator. The performance indicator also excludes reductions in unrestricted net assets that arise from investment losses on donor-restricted endowment funds, along with subsequent gains that restore the fair value of the assets of the endowment fund to the required level.

Generally speaking, the accounting used by investor-owned health care entities and not-for-profit health care entities for noncontrolling interests alternative investments (investments in financial instruments that do not have a readily determinable fair value) are similar. In that regard, not-for-profit HCOs differ from other types of not-for-profit organizations. Other not-for-profit organizations are permitted to make a fair value election that is not available to not-for-profit health care entities. Other types of investments that are not financial instruments (such as real estate or oil and gas interests) should be reported at the lower of amortized cost or a reduced amount if an impairment in their value is deemed to be other than temporary.

Classification of investment return that is restricted by donors (e.g., net appreciation on donor-restricted endowments that has not yet been appropriated for spending) is reported as an increase or decrease in temporarily or permanently restricted net assets.

Participation in Investment Pools Sponsored by Nonprofits. Two or more nonprofit HCOs may decide to pool their resources for investment purposes. Often such investment pools function similarly to a mutual fund, with participating entities purchasing and selling "units" based on net asset values (NAVs) calculated by the pool sponsor. The investment structure should be carefully analyzed when determining the appropriate accounting to use. While these vehicles sometimes may be structured as formal arrangements with separate legal structures (such as an investment partnership), more often they do not have a formal legal structure, and no legal "security" is created. In the latter situation, the underlying investments of the pool are owned by the sponsor and are held together with the sponsor's own assets.

If the investment pool has a separate legal structure, the not-for-profit HCO accounts for its interest in the pool in accordance with the guidance discussed in Subsection 35.3(h)(i). If no separate legal structure exists, the investing HCO reports an asset and the pool sponsor reports a liability to the investor in accordance with the *Transfers of Assets to a Not-for-Profit Entity or Charitable Trust That Raises or Holds Contributions for Others* subsection of ASC 958-605. For financial reporting purposes, the HCO reports the asset using a caption such as "beneficial interest in investment pool" or "interest in investment pool." Pool participants should not report their pro rata share of the underlying investments owned by the pool.

(ii) Governmental Entities. The principal GASB standard for investment accounting is GASB Statement No. 31, *Accounting and Financial Reporting for Investments and for Certain External Investment Pools.* Generally, the accounting for various types of investments depends on whether they are within the scope of Statement No. 31 (which generally requires fair value accounting).

Under Statement No. 31, all investments in debt securities are carried at fair value. For ownership interests (equity investments), the accounting depends on whether the investment represents a *security.* Statement No. 31 defines a *security* as "a transferable financial instrument that evidences ownership or creditorship." GASB's definition focuses in part on the instrument's transferability; in this respect, it differs from the definition of *security* used in FASB standards. GASB's definition also excludes investments that are transacted directly with another party (such as some limited partnership investments). As a result, certain types of investments that might be considered equity securities under FASB literature are not considered equity securities by GASB.

If the ownership interest meets the definition of a security (e.g., common stock), the level of ownership must be evaluated to determine if the equity method of accounting (described in paragraphs 202-210 of GASB Statement No. 62) must be applied. If application of the equity method is not required, the focus of the evaluation moves to considering whether the security has a readily determinable fair value. If so, it is accounted for at fair value; if not, it is carried at cost subject to impairment.

If the ownership interest does not meet the definition of a security, consideration should be given to whether the underlying investment vehicle meets Statement No. 31's definition of an external investment pool (an arrangement that commingles the monies of multiple investors and invests, on the participants' behalf, in an investment portfolio). If it does, then the ownership interest is accounted for at fair value. If the ownership interest is neither a security nor an interest in an external investment pool, it is carried at cost subject to impairment.

All investment income, including changes in the fair value of investments, is reported in the SRECNA. Realized and unrealized investment gains and losses are displayed together in a single caption. Statement No. 31 prohibits separately displaying realized gains and losses and unrealized gains and losses on the face of the SRECNA. However, it permits disclosure of realized gains and losses in the notes to financial statements provided that certain information about the nature of those amounts and their relationship to the amounts reported in the financial statements also is disclosed.

GASB Statement No. 40, *Deposit and Investment Risk Disclosures,* addresses the disclosures required for investments.

Statement No. 34 also requires certain disclosures for donor-restricted endowments, including the amounts of net appreciation on investments that the governing board can authorize for expenditure and how the amounts are reported in net assets. The entity should also disclose information pertaining to state law regarding the ability to spend net appreciation as well as the policy for authorizing expenditures, such as a spending rate or a total return policy.

If the real estate is held by an endowment, GAS 52, *Land and Other Real Estate Held as Investments by Endowments,* requires that it be reported at fair value with changes in fair value reported as investment income. Nonfinancial investments for which GASB has not issued standards (such as real estate held by a quasi-endowment) are reported at amortized cost and subsequently evaluated for impairment.

More detailed guidance about accounting for investments and investment return in governmental organizations is provided in Chapter 33 of this *Handbook.*

(i) DERIVATIVES

(i) Not-for-Profit Entities. Because a not-for-profit HCO's performance indicator generally is considered analogous to income from continuing operations of a business enterprise, not-for-profit HCOs apply the derivatives accounting requirements in ASC 815, *Derivatives and Hedging,* in the same manner as for-profit enterprises. Thus, derivatives are reported at fair value in the balance sheet. Changes in fair value (and all other derivative gains and losses) are reflected in the statement of operations in the same manner as for-profit enterprises reflect those items in a statement of comprehensive income. That is, any derivative gains or losses included within a for-profit enterprise's income from continuing operations should similarly be included in a not-for-profit HCO's performance indicator, and derivative gains or losses that are excluded from a for-profit enterprise's income from continuing operations (such as items reported in OCI) similarly should be excluded from a not-for-profit HCO's performance indicator. The use of cash flow hedge accounting is explicitly permitted for not-for-profit health care entities that are within the scope of ASC 954 and the *Guide* but not for other types of not-for-profit organizations (because they do not report a performance indicator).

ASC 954-815, *Health Care Organizations—Derivatives and Hedging,* requires not-for-profit HCOs to provide disclosures that are analogous to those required for for-profit enterprises. For example, they must disclose anticipated reclassifications into the performance indicator of gains and losses that have been excluded from that measure and reported in accumulated derivative gain or loss as of the reporting date. They must also separately disclose the beginning and ending accumulated derivative gain or loss that has been excluded from the performance indicator, the related net change associated with current period hedging transactions, and the net amount of reclassifications into the performance indicator.

One of the most common uses of derivatives by HCOs is entering into interest rate swaps in connection with borrowings. For certain interest rate swaps, a shortcut method for evaluating hedge effectiveness is available. However, use of that method is limited to interest rate swaps that reference U.S. Treasury rates or LIBOR (London Interbank Offered Rate) as the "underlying." Many not-for-profit HCOs use swaps whose underlying is the Securities Industry and Financial Markets Association Municipal Swap Index (sometimes referred to as the SIFMA Municipal Swap Index). If the variable leg of a swap is indexed to the SIFMA Municipal Swap Index (or to any rate other than Treasuries or LIBOR), the hedging relationship does not qualify for the shortcut method.

For additional information, see Chapter 5 of the *Guide.*

(ii) Governmental Entities. GASB Statement No. 53, *Accounting and Financial Reporting for Derivative Instruments,* requires almost all derivatives to be reported at fair value on the balance sheet. Accounting for changes in fair value differs based on whether the derivative is used as a hedge against an economic risk or whether it has been entered into for speculative (investment) purposes.

Derivatives used as economic hedges (e.g., an interest rate swap used to protect against changes in interest rates associated with debt) must be evaluated to determine how effectively the hedge is offsetting the risk. If the hedge is effective, hedge accounting *must* be applied; its use is not elective. Changes in the fair value of effective hedges do not impact the statement of revenues, expenses, and changes in net assets (SRECNA); instead, they are reported as deferred inflows or deferred outflows of resources in the statement of net assets. If a hedge becomes ineffective or is terminated, the deferred inflows or outflows are written off, resulting in recognition of a gain or loss in the SRECNA. However, if the termination results from a defeasance of hedged debt, the write-off should be included in the calculation of the gain or loss on the refunding.

If a derivative proves to be ineffective at offsetting risk or was not entered into as an economic hedge, it is considered a derivative entered into for investment purposes. Changes in fair value of "investment derivatives" are reported together with other investment income, gains, and losses in the nonoperating revenue (expense) section of the SRECNA. Those derivatives are subject to the disclosure requirements for investments in Statement No. 40.

For hedging derivatives, governments should disclose their objective for entering into the arrangement, significant terms of the instrument, and risks that it is exposed to (e.g., the possibility that the derivative may be terminated earlier than expected or that the party on the other side of the arrangement will not be able to pay amounts owed to the government).

(j) PROPERTY AND EQUIPMENT. The property and equipment accounts represent the provider's actual investment in plant assets, land, building, leasehold improvements, and equipment. Property that is not used for general operations (such as property held for future expansion or investment purposes) should be presented separately from property used in general operations.

Property and equipment should be recorded at cost or at fair market value if donated. Where historical cost records are not available, an appraisal at historical cost should be made and the amounts recorded in the provider's books.

The amount of depreciation expense should be shown separately (or combined with amortization of leased assets) in the statement of operations. The *Guide* states that the American Hospital Association's "Estimated Useful Lives of Depreciable Hospital Assets" publication may be helpful in determining the estimated useful lives of fixed assets of health care providers.

(i) Governmental Health Care Entities. Governmental providers also are required to disclose their policy for capitalizing assets and for estimating the useful lives of those assets. In addition, GASB Statement No. 34 requires certain information to be presented about major classes of capital assets, including beginning and ending balances, capital acquisitions, sales or other disposition, current-period depreciation expense, and accumulated depreciation.

Statement No. 34 defines *capital assets* to include land, land improvements, easements, buildings, building improvements, vehicles, machinery, equipment, works of art and historical treasures, infrastructure, and all other tangible or intangible assets that are used in operations and that have initial useful lives extending beyond a single reporting period.

Capital assets should be depreciated over their estimated useful lives unless they are either inexhaustible (e.g., land or land improvements) or are noncapitalized collections. Capital assets that are being or have been depreciated should be reported net of accumulated depreciation in the balance sheet. Accumulated depreciation may be reported on the face of the balance sheet or disclosed in the notes. Capital assets that are not being depreciated (e.g., land) should be reported separately if the government has a significant amount of these assets. Depreciation expense should be measured by allocating the net cost of capital assets (less estimated salvage value) over their estimated useful lives in a systematic and rational manner (e.g., straight line, sum of the years' digits, depletion).

Entities are required to provide in-depth information about capital assets in the notes to the financial statements, including a roll-forward schedule detailing the beginning and ending balances of capital assets as well as increases and decreases for the year. Capital assets that are not being depreciated should be disclosed separately from those that are being depreciated. That information should be provided by major classes of capital assets.

Capital Asset Impairment. GASB Statement No. 42, *Accounting and Financial Reporting for Impairment of Capital Assets and for Insurance Recoveries,* establishes standards for reporting the effects of capital asset impairments in financial statements. A capital asset is considered impaired when its service utility has declined significantly and unexpectedly. Statement No. 42 does not require a write-down when the impairment of the assets is considered temporary; only permanent impairments are recognized.

Statement No. 42 also clarifies and establishes accounting requirements for insurance recoveries. Entities are required to evaluate prominent events or changes in circumstances affecting capital assets to determine whether impairment of a capital asset has occurred. Such events or changes in circumstances that may be indicative of impairment include evidence of physical damage, enactment or approval of laws or regulations, or other changes in environmental factors, technological changes or evidence of obsolescence, changes in the manner or duration of use of a capital asset, and construction stoppage.

Impaired capital assets that will no longer be used should be reported at the lower of the carrying value or fair value. For impaired capital assets that will continue to be used, the amount of impairment—the portion of historical cost that should be written off—should be measured by the method that most appropriately reflects the decline in service utility of the capital asset. Statement No. 42 describes three methods for measuring impairment: the restoration cost approach, the service units approach, and the deflated depreciated replacement cost approach.

Impairment losses should be reported as an expense, special item, or extraordinary item per Statement No. 34. The impairment loss should be recognized net of any insurance recovery associated with events or changes in circumstances resulting in impaired capital assets. Restoration or replacement of the capital asset using the insurance recovery should be reported as a separate transaction. Statement No. 42 does not permit the reversal of impairment in future years. A general description, the amount, and the financial statement classification of the impairment loss should be disclosed if it is not otherwise apparent from the face of the financial statements.

(ii) Internal-Use Software Costs. The health care industry is subject to extensive government regulation involving electronic medical records and electronic transfer of patient data. As regulations change, HCOs often will incur costs to upgrade or improve their information systems. An AICPA Technical Practice Aid (TPA) Q&A discusses capitalization of computer systems costs incurred in conjunction with a change in regulatory requirements.[9] The TPA states that costs associated with upgrading and improving an entity's computer systems should be capitalized or expensed in accordance with the guidance set forth in ASC 350-40, *Intangibles—Internal Use Software.* Unless the costs relate to changes that result in "additional functionality" (i.e., they enable the software to

[9] TPA 6400.34, "Accounting for Computer Systems Costs Incurred in Connection with the Health Insurance Portability and Accountability Act of 1996."

perform tasks that it previously could not perform), they should be expensed. Many of the costs associated with regulatory changes relate solely to compliance with the new rules and do not result in additional functionality. For example, changes that merely reconfigure existing data to conform to a new standard or new regulatory requirements would not result in the capability to perform additional tasks, nor would training costs, data conversion costs (except for costs to develop or obtain software that allows for access to or conversion of old data by new systems), and maintenance costs. However, costs of certain changes associated with tasks that the software previously could not perform (e.g., changes that increase the security of data from tampering or alteration or that reduce the ability of unauthorized persons to gain access to the data) may potentially be capitalizable.

(k) INTANGIBLE ASSETS. ASC 350, *Intangibles—Goodwill and Other,* provides guidance for private sector entities with respect to accounting for intangible assets, including evaluating goodwill and other intangible assets for impairment. A comprehensive discussion of these issues is provided in Chapter 14 of this *Handbook.*

For governmental entities, GASB Statement No. 51, *Accounting and Financial Reporting for Intangible Assets,* defines an *intangible asset* as one that lacks physical substance, is nonfinancial in nature, and has an initial useful life extending beyond a single reporting period. "Nonfinancial in nature" means that the asset is not in a monetary form similar to cash or investment securities and that it represents neither a claim or right to assets in a monetary form similar to receivables nor a prepayment for goods or services. Statement No. 51's scope excludes assets initially acquired or created primarily for the purpose of directly obtaining income or profit (e.g., intangibles acquired as investments) and goodwill created through a combination transaction

Statement No. 51's provisions are similar (but not identical) to FASB's intangible assets standard. An intangible asset should be recognized only if it is "identifiable," meaning that the asset either: (a) is capable of being separated or divided and sold, transferred, licensed, rented, or exchanged, either individually or together with a related contract, asset, or liability; or (b) arises from contractual or other legal rights, regardless of whether those rights are transferable or separable from the entity or from other rights and obligations. Intangibles with a limited useful life are amortized over that period. Indefinite-lived intangibles are not amortized but are evaluated for impairment. Statement No. 51 establishes a specified-conditions approach to recognizing intangible assets that are internally generated (including internally generated software). Effectively, outlays associated with the development of such assets should not begin to be capitalized until certain specified criteria are met.

All intangible assets within the scope of Statement No. 51 are considered capital assets under GAS 34 and, thus, are subject to the capital asset impairment and disclosure provisions described in Subsection 35.3(k).

As indicated previously, goodwill is excluded from the scope of Statement No. 51. Until such time as GASB issues guidance on accounting and financial reporting requirements for combination transactions (and, in doing so, addresses issues pertaining to recognition and measurement of goodwill), governmental health care entities should continue to apply private sector goodwill guidance (either ASC 350, *Goodwill and Intangible Assets,* or the goodwill-related guidance in APB Opinion No. 17, *Intangible Assets*).

(l) BONDS PAYABLE. Most institutional not-for-profit and governmental HCOs finance their capital needs largely through the issuance of tax-exempt or taxable municipal bonds.

By and large, the municipal bonds issued by or on behalf of HCOs are revenue bonds (i.e., bonds secured by a pledge of the entity's revenues). Most borrowings involve conduit issuance through a governmental municipal bond financing authority.[10] In these conduit financings, the financing authority (the "issuer") issues the securities and lends the proceeds to the borrowing government (the "conduit borrower"). Although the securities bear the name of the issuer, the issuer has no

---

[10] However, some governmental health care entities have the statutory right to issue municipal bonds directly.

obligation for repayment of the debt; the bondholders' principal and interest will be paid solely from revenue generated by the conduit borrower's bond-financed project. Although technically the health care entity is a "borrower" and not an "issuer" in a conduit municipal financing, for ease of reference the term *issuer* is used generically throughout this section to refer to both issuers and conduit borrowers.

Municipal bonds are issued with either a variable or a fixed interest rate. A fixed-rate bond bears interest at a specified, constant rate. Variable-rate (or floating-rate) bonds bear interest at a rate that is reset from time to time. Some documents provide the ability to change the interest mode (e.g., from auction rate to variable rate). In addition, financing strategies have emerged that allow entities to create "synthetic" fixed- and variable-rate debt by using derivative products. For example, a common financing structure involves "synthetic" fixed-rate debt, which is achieved by initially issuing variable-rate debt and then entering into a floating-to-fixed interest rate swap.

Municipal bonds are issued through negotiated sales, competitive bids, or private placements. In a negotiated sale, the issuer negotiates a price with one or more underwriters. In a competitive bid sale, the securities are sold to one or more underwriters who submitted the best acceptable bid. The underwriters then resell the securities to the public. Municipal bonds issued in negotiated sales or competitive bids are deemed to be *traded in public markets.* In a private placement, the securities generally are sold directly to the investor, usually a bank, and are not considered to trade in public markets.

Whether the bonds trade in public markets or not is an important consideration for entities that apply FASB standards. In some areas, the FASB ASC establishes different accounting or disclosure requirements for entities having debt or equity securities that trade in public markets (referred to as public entities). One area where the ASC provides different guidance for public and nonpublic entities is with respect to the date that financial statements are considered to be issued (see Section 35.5(g)). In addition, certain FASB standards require "public entities" to provide more extensive disclosures than is required for entities that do not have securities trading in public markets. When evaluating a particular standard that contains differential disclosure requirements, it is important to consider whether the use of *public entity* within that standard includes conduit obligors with debt that trades in public markets, or whether it is limited to entities with equity securities that trade in public markets.

The fact that a not-for-profit health care entity with tax-exempt debt might be considered a public entity does not change that organization's status for purposes of applying FASB standards with requirements that are specific to not-for-profit organizations or that explicitly exclude not-for-profit organizations. If the scope of a FASB standard that contains expanded disclosure requirements or additional accounting requirements for public entities explicitly excludes not-for-profit organizations, not-for-profit HCOs would not apply that standard. Additionally, classification as a "public entity" for accounting purposes does not impose SEC or other regulatory filing requirements, nor would it result in a not-for-profit HCO being required to comply with the requirements of the Sarbanes-Oxley Act.

The SEC's mission to protect investors from fraud in connection with securities offerings extends to tax-exempt debt securities. An overview of SEC considerations related to tax-exempt bonds is provided in Section 35.5(a).

(i) Refundings and Defeasance. An HCO may refinance a municipal bond issue by issuing new bonds whose proceeds are used to repay the previously issued bonds (a refunding transaction). The new debt proceeds may be used to repay the old bonds immediately (a current refunding), or the new debt proceeds may be placed with an escrow agent and invested until they are used to pay principal and interest on the old debt at a future time (an advance refunding).

Some bond contracts allow the bonds to be repaid prior to their stated maturity at the option of the issuer. The issuing organization's right to repay the security prior to its scheduled maturity date is referred to as a "call" privilege. Typically, either new debt is issued to pay off the outstanding bonds or, if the bonds were structured as "multimodal"(i.e., the organization has a contractual right to change the interest feature of the bond from one form to another, such as from an auction-based interest rate to a fixed rate), an interest mode conversion option is exercised. Because in most cases a mode conversion involves a call of the old bonds and marketing of new bonds (to new investors as well as existing bondholders), the mode conversion is similar to a traditional refunding. Thus, the same accounting considerations apply to mode conversions as to refundings.

If the HCO would like to retire the debt early but does not have a call privilege, the bond documents might explicitly give it the right to employ a defeasance. In a defeasance, the issuer typically will use some or all of the proceeds of a new bond issue to purchase government securities that are deposited into an escrow account and irrevocably pledged to the payment of the outstanding bonds. The securities and related earnings are sufficient to pay the principal and interest on the bonds when they come due. (In essence, the issuer is substituting collateral on the debt.) Generally, the revenues originally pledged as security on the outstanding securities switch over to become security for payment of the refunding bonds (the new issue) on the date the advance refunding bonds are issued.

Defeasances are categorized as "legal" or "economic." The terms of some bond contracts allow for legal defeasance, which is the termination of the rights and interests of the bondholders and of their lien on the pledged revenues or other security. When the conditions specified in the bond contract for legal defeasance are met, the issuer's obligation for repayment of the bonds is satisfied in full. In other situations (e.g., where the bond contract does not provide a procedure for termination of the bondholders' rights and interests other than through redemption of the bonds), establishing a defeasance escrow makes the pledged revenues available for other purposes without actually effecting a legal defeasance. This is sometimes called an in-substance or economic defeasance. In an economic defeasance, if for some reason the escrowed funds prove insufficient to make future payments on the old debt, the issuer is still legally obligated to make payment on such debt from the pledged revenues.

The accounting considerations associated with defeasance differ based on whether the entity applies FASB or GASB standards. When a defeasance involves an entity that applies FASB standards, liabilities are considered extinguished for accounting purposes only if the not-for-profit debtor is "legally released" from being the primary obligor under the debt. In a legal defeasance, generally the creditor legally releases the debtor from being the primary obligor under the liability; however, the question of whether the debtor has in fact been legally released is a matter of law, and a legal opinion is sometimes required. An in-substance defeasance transaction normally does not meet the derecognition criteria under FASB standards.

GASB entities evaluate defeasance transaction using the guidance in GASB Statement No. 23, *Accounting and Financial Reporting for Refundings of Debt Reported by Proprietary Activities,* and GASB Statement No. 7, *Advance Refundings Resulting in Defeasance of Debt.* GASB's guidance differs from FASB's guidance in three respects.

1. GASB permits derecognition of in-substance defeasances.
2. GASB does not require an evaluation of whether a refinancing is a modification of terms or an extinguishment, as is done in the private sector.
3. GASB entities are required to amortize any gain or loss resulting from a defeasance as an adjustment of interest expense over the shorter of the life of the new bonds or the remaining life of the old bonds. FASB entities recognize gains or losses in income in the period of the extinguishment.

(ii) Variable-Rate Demand Bonds. Although bonds typically often have a stated maturity of many years, careful consideration should be given to classification of the liability as current or noncurrent based on the features of the debt. Bonds that appear to be long term based on their legal maturities might not be considered long term for financial reporting purposes. Careful consideration of the bond agreements and related documents (e.g., bond indenture, loan and trust agreement, liquidity facility, etc.) may be required in order to determine whether debt is classified properly.

The current liability classification is intended to include obligations that, by their terms, are due on demand or will be due on demand within one year from the balance sheet date, even though liquidation may not be expected within that period. Some variable-rate bonds have a demand feature (a "put" or tender option) whereby the bondholder may require the issuer or its remarketing agent to repurchase the bonds, often on short notice. Thus, those variable-rate bonds normally would be classified as current liabilities, despite the fact that their stated maturities could cover many years. However, if the variable-rate demand obligations are supported by a liquidity facility (such as an irrevocable letter of credit from a financial institution) that provides the issuer with the ability to refinance, on a long-term basis, any obligation that may arise if tendered bonds cannot immediately be remarketed to another investor, both FASB and GASB standards permit the debt to be classified as noncurrent if the liquidity facility has two characteristics. First, repayment of draws must extend one year past the balance sheet date. Additionally, the liquidity facility must not expire within one year of the balance sheet date and must not contain any subjective acceleration clauses (clauses that provide the lender with the ability to demand repayment based on criteria that are subjective rather than objective). For GASB entities, the source of this guidance is GASB Interpretation No. 1, *Demand Bonds Issued by State and Local Government Entities.* For FASB entities, it is ASC 470-10, *Debt.*

(iii) IRS Arbitrage Rebate Liability. IRS arbitrage rules (Internal Revenue Code Section 103(c) and related regulations) prohibit the yield realized from the investment of the proceeds of tax-exempt debt from exceeding the interest rate to be paid on such debt. Whenever a provider invests tax-exempt bond proceeds and the ultimate yield is higher than the interest rate on the bonds, the provider may be subject to an arbitrage rebate liability. The earnings in excess of interest expense represent a liability that must be paid to the U.S. Treasury in order for the bonds to maintain their tax-exempt status. The arbitrage rebate liability may be substantial if the bond proceeds are not spent as quickly as planned (e.g., if a provider encounters a delay in a major construction project) or in volatile interest rate environments. The IRS carefully scrutinizes compliance with these rules.

(iv) Obligated Group Financing Structures. In health care tax-exempt financing transactions, it is common practice for health care entities to create a "pool" of assets as a security vehicle. In a master trust indenture financing, a master trustee holds all of the security in the collateral pool, which is defined as the "obligated group." For example, a hospital system may place two or three of its facilities in the obligated group as the asset and revenue base the borrowers look to for security.

Tax-exempt debt agreements that involve an obligated group may require the health care entity to provide audited financial statements for the obligated group, both for use in the initial sale of the bonds and thereafter for compliance with continuing disclosure covenants. If the master trust indenture that created the obligated group excludes entities that are otherwise required to be consolidated under GAAP, then financial statements prepared for the obligated group will constitute an incomplete (i.e., non-GAAP) presentation. (Typically, such statements are required to comply with GAAP in all other respects.) When an auditor is engaged to report on obligated group financial statements which exclude entities that are required under GAAP to be consolidated (but otherwise are in conformity with GAAP), the auditor's report must be restricted to use by specified parties (in this case, the health care entity and other parties to the contract). Audited statements accompanied by a restricted-use auditor's report should not be filed on the Electronic Municipal Market Access (EMMA) database (see Section 35.6(a)(iii)). Similarly, a restricted-use auditor's report cannot be included in an official statement. Generally, the consolidated statements of the complete reporting entity must be used for external reporting purposes, with the obligated group financial information provided in a combining or consolidating schedule presented as other supplementary information: for example, a supplemental schedule with individual columns for each entity in the obligated group, an obligated group subtotal column, an aggregate column for all other entities, and the consolidated total column (similar to the pro forma financials frequently seen in SEC filings).

(v) Interest during Construction. Not-for-profit HCOs apply the guidance in ASC 835-20-30, *The Amount of Interest Cost to be Capitalized in Situations Involving Certain Tax-Exempt Borrowings and Certain Gifts and Grants,* with respect to accounting for interest expense associated with tax-exempt debt used to finance construction. It provides that the capitalized interest cost should be reduced by interest earned on the unexpended bond proceeds during the construction period if the proceeds of the tax-exempt borrowing are externally restricted to finance the acquisition of specified qualifying assets or to service the related debt. Governmental HCOs apply similar guidance that is established by paragraphs 19-20 of GASB Statement No. 62.

(m) DISCLOSURE OF RISKS, UNCERTAINTIES, AND CONTINGENCIES

(i) Risks and Uncertainties. ASC 275, *Risks and Uncertainties,* requires organizations to include disclosures in their financial statements concerning the use of estimates in the preparation of the financial statements as well as information about current vulnerability due to certain concentrations. The disclosures focus primarily on risks and uncertainties that could significantly affect the reported amounts in the near-term or the near-term functioning of the reporting entity. ASC 275 applies to all nongovernmental health care entities.

Examples of estimates that often are significant in HCO financial statements include:

- Provision for contractual allowances
- Estimated third-party settlement reserves
- Provision for bad debts
- Litigation-related accruals and contingencies
- Obligation for future services (CCRC)
- Incurred but not reported (IBNR) accruals involving prepaid health care plans
- Accruals for loss contracts under managed care arrangements
- Estimated risk pool settlements arising from managed care contracting
- Amounts reported for long-term obligations (e.g., pensions and postemployment benefits)

(ii) Illegal Acts Related to Government Programs. In recent years, the federal government and many states have aggressively increased enforcement efforts under Medicare and Medicaid antifraud and abuse legislation. Broadening regulatory and legal interpretations have significantly increased the risk of penalties for providers; for example, broad interpretations of "false claims" laws are exposing ordinary billing mistakes to scrutiny and penalty consideration. As a result, providers may have significant exposure to allegations of fraudulent activity that potentially could entail multimillion-dollar penalties, fines, and settlements. The far-reaching nature of alleged fraud and abuse violations may represent a significant risk and uncertainty that would require disclosure in accordance with ASC 275. If a provider is the target of a government investigation, the need for accruals related to, or disclosure of, contingencies associated with the potential effect of illegal acts must be evaluated.

If the government undertakes an investigation, there are two likely economic consequences to the health care entity:[11] (1) disallowance of certain services previously billed by the entity and paid for by the government; and (2) the imposition of substantial fines or penalties. Consequence (1) is an uncertainty associated with the revenue estimation process discussed in Subsection 35.3(e)(i); it is not a loss contingency within the scope of ASC 450-20. The distinction is important from a financial reporting perspective. To illustrate, consider that management, in making its best estimate of revenue that will be realized under a contract, may believe that it is appropriate to record a valuation allowance for potential billing adjustments in order to avoid reporting revenues that are uncertain of realization, even though the entity is not currently the subject of a government investigation. As a result, a certain amount of revenue will not be recognized. If instead such allowances were accounted for as loss contingencies, the revenue would be recognized but would carry with it an associated loss contingency that might or might not be accruable in the financial statements. Consequence (2) *is* a loss contingency within the scope of ASC 450-20, and management must

[11] There is also the potential for disbarment from participation in the government program, the consequences of which are outside the scope of this discussion.

make provision in the financial statements for, or disclose any contingent liabilities associated with, such fines and penalties.

Another potential economic consequence relates to costs the provider may have to incur in future years to demonstrate its compliance with federal laws. When a provider enters into an agreement with the federal government to settle an investigation, such settlement agreements normally impose an obligation on the provider to engage an independent review organization to test and report on compliance with fraud and abuse requirements each year for the following five years. ASC 954-405-25 addresses whether the expected costs of future audits required as a result of settlement agreements should be accrued as a liability at the time the settlement is agreed to. The staff concluded that a provider should not recognize as liability for the costs of future Medicare compliance audits on the date the settlement is agreed to.

(iii) Loss Contingencies and Insurance Coverage. Due to the nature of their operations, HCOs have significant exposure to risk of loss arising from medical malpractice claims. Additionally, the labor-intensive nature of the business may expose them to risk of losses associated with other types of insured or self-insured arrangements (e.g., worker's compensation or employee health insurance). Organizations often manage such risks using alternatives to traditional occurrence-based coverage, such as retrospectively rated policies, claims-made policies, captive insurance companies, risk-retention groups, or self-insurance arrangements. Accounting and reporting considerations related to these types of exposures and risk financing arrangements are discussed in Chapter 8 of the *Guide.*

Medical malpractice claims typically are the most significant exposure for HCOs. However, the guidance may also be helpful in accounting for other self-insured liabilities, including worker's compensation and employee health insurance. For private sector entities, ASU 2010-24, *Health Care Entities—Presentation of Insurance Claims and Related Insurance Recoveries,* explicitly broadened the scope of the malpractice guidance in ASC 954-450 to be applicable to other similar contingent liabilities.

The *Guide* states that the ultimate costs of malpractice claims should be accrued when the incidents occur that give rise to the claims, if certain criteria are met. These criteria include a determination that a liability has been incurred and an ability to make a reasonable estimate of the amount of the loss. The *Guide* provides guidance in accounting for uninsured asserted and unasserted medical malpractice claims, claims insured by captive insurance companies, claims insured under retrospectively rated or claims-made insurance policies, and claims paid from self-insurance trust funds.

When reporting such transactions in financial statements, private sector HCOs account for the impact of risk transfer differently than do governmental HCOs. Private sector entities reflect the impact of risk transfer by reporting receivables for amounts recoverable from insurers related to insured claims, instead of limiting the amount of liability reported. Governmental HCOs apply a "transfer of risk" model in evaluating the extent to which claims liabilities should be recognized in financial statements.

The risk transfer model applied by governmental health care entities is set forth in GASB Statement No. 10, *Accounting and Financial Reporting for Risk Financing and Related Insurance Issues.* Like ASC 450, *Contingencies,* the general recognition, measurement, and disclosure requirements in Statement No. 10 are based on the requirements of former private sector literature: FASB Statement No. 5, *Accounting for Contingencies,* and FASB Interpretation No. 14, *Reasonable Estimation of the Amount of a Loss.*

Chapter 15 of the *Guide* discusses malpractice contingencies in the context of Statement No. 10.

(n) REPORTING ENTITY CONSIDERATIONS. Investor-owned health care entities follow the same consolidation requirements that are applicable to other for-profit entities. The remainder of this section focuses on consolidation requirements that are applicable to not-for-profit and governmental entities.

(i) Not-for-Profit Entities. Not-for-profit health care entities evaluate relationships with other entities for consolidation using a voting interest model rather than the variable-interest model prescribed in ASC 810-10-15. Chapter 12 of the *Guide* discusses how the voting interest model is applied in evaluating relationships with other not-for-profit organizations, relationships with for-profit investees, and relationships with "special purpose entities." Key considerations are highlighted in the remainder of this section.

Consolidation of Other Not-for-Profit Entities. Not-for-profit health care entities evaluate relationships with other not-for-profit entities for consolidation using the industry-specific voting interest model described in ASC 958-810, *Not-for-Profit Entities—Consolidation.* Under that model, various forms of control that exist dictate the circumstances which would require consolidation. The forms of control described are:

- *Corporate membership.* Nonprofit corporations are prohibited from distributing profits. Therefore, it follows that they characteristically do not have shareholders. Instead, some nonprofit corporations have one or more "members" who vote for directors and on other major corporate decisions, as would shareholders of a for-profit corporation. When nonprofit health care corporations join together in systems, they often do so by a transaction in which the new parent nonprofit corporation becomes the "sole member" of the subsidiary nonprofit corporation. After such a transaction, the sole corporate member generally holds rights and powers equivalent to those of a sole shareholder—for example, the ability to appoint and terminate the board and to make major corporate decisions, such as changing the articles of incorporation or dissolving the corporation.[12]
- When a not-for-profit organization's articles of incorporation designate another not-for-profit organization as its sole corporate member, the member is presumed to possess a controlling financial interest that requires consolidation unless, for some reason, it does not have control (e.g., the articles or bylaws may provide approval or veto rights to a party other than the sole corporate member which are so restrictive that they call into question the member's ability to control).
- *Power to appoint directors.* In other situations, no members exist and the nonprofit's directors have unfettered rights to govern the entity's actions. However, if the nonprofit's bylaws give another organization the right to appoint all (or a majority) its directors,[13] the other organization is deemed to control the nonprofit by virtue of its control of a voting majority of the board (unless unusual circumstances exist which overcome its ability to control).

  For example, assume that the bylaws of Foundation B provide Hospital A with the right to appoint five of its seven board members. In that case, if Hospital A also has an economic interest[14] in Foundation B—for example, a right to Foundation B's net assets if it dissolves—it must consolidate Foundation B. In most cases where an acquisition structure is explicitly designed to give one organization a majority voting interest in the board of another, an economic interest is likely to be present.
- *Control through contract or affiliation agreement.* In still other situations, one nonprofit might control another through means other than corporate membership or the power to appoint

[12] In nonprofit corporations that utilize a membership corporate structure, the governing documents will set forth the right of the board to govern the entities along with the rights bestowed on the corporation's member(s). A sole corporate member's rights involve "reserved powers" that otherwise would normally be held by the board. Typically these rights are limited to decisions on fundamental corporate matters, such as the right to determine who sits on the board of trustees; the right to approve amendments to the articles of incorporation; and the right to approve the dissolution, merger, or sale of the organization. However, in some cases, these rights might be more extensive and include, for example, explicit power over major operational decisions and approval of budgets.

[13] According to ASC 958-810, those appointees do not need to be board members, employees, or officers of the appointing organization in order for a majority voting interest to exist.

[14] The terms *control* and *economic interest* are defined in ASC 958-810.

directors—for example, through rights and powers granted in a contractual agreement. If the controlling nonprofit also has an economic interest in the other nonprofit, consolidation is permitted but not required. If consolidated statements are not presented, the controlling entity must provide certain note disclosures in its financial statements.

If the reporting HCO has either control over another nonprofit or an economic interest, but not both, consolidation is prohibited. Notes to the financial statements should disclose the existence and nature of the relationship and describe and quantify the transactions.

Consolidation of For-Profit Entities. A not-for-profit health care system may own stock, partnership interests, or other ownership interests in for-profit entities.

As previously indicated, not-for-profit entities do not apply the variable interest entities guidance discussed in Chapter 9 of this *Handbook.* Instead, they evaluate the need for consolidation using the framework guidance set forth in the voting interest entities subsection of ASC 810-10. Under the voting interest model, whether the financial statements of a for-profit entity should be consolidated with the reporting entity depends on the nature of control and the legal structure of the entity being evaluated. These are briefly summarized next.

- Under Subtopic ASC 810-10, all majority-owned subsidiaries (i.e., all companies in which a parent has a controlling financial interest through direct or indirect ownership of a majority voting interest) must be consolidated unless control does not rest with the majority owner (as, e.g., where the subsidiary is in legal reorganization or in bankruptcy).
- If the health care entity is the general partner of a for-profit limited partnership (such as a limited liability company [LLC] that has governing provisions that are the functional equivalent of a limited partnership), the health care entity would use the guidance in ASC 810-20 to determine whether the general partner within the group controls and, therefore, should consolidate the limited partnership or similar entity.
- If the health care entity has an investment in an LLC that has governing provisions that are the functional equivalent of a regular corporation, the health care entity would use the guidance in ASB 810-10 to determine whether the reporting entity has a majority voting interest that provides it with a controlling financial interest.
- The *Consolidation of Entities Controlled by Contract* subsections of ASC 810-10 are applied to determine whether a contractual management relationship represents a controlling financial interest. For additional information on this topic as it relates to consolidation by physician practice management entities, see Section 35.4(c).

Consolidation of Special-Purpose Entities. Some not-for-profit HCOs may have relationships with entities that they do not own or control (and, thus, are not subject to evaluation under the voting interest model) but that nonetheless may require consolidation. These are often referred to as special-purpose entities, or SPEs.

According to ASC 958-810, *Not-for-Profit Entities—Consolidation,* if a not-for-profit HCO engages in leasing transactions with a special-purpose leasing entity, it must consolidate the leasing entity if:

- Substantially all of the leasing entity's transactions involve the HCO;
- The residual risks and rewards of the leased assets, and the obligation imposed by any underlying debt of the leasing entity, reside (directly or indirectly) with the HCO through means such as the lease agreement, a guarantee of the SEC's debt, or similar agreement; and
- The leasing entity's owner has not invested capital that is at risk during the term of the lease, or is not independent of the HCO.

Not-for-profit organizations may also engage in transactions with SPEs that do not involve leasing. In practice, the guidance for special-purpose leasing entities is often applied by analogy in evaluating whether to consolidate those entities.

Display of Noncontrolling Interests. When a not-for-profit health care entity owns less than 100 percent of a consolidated for-profit subsidiary, the portion that belongs to the other owners is referred to as the noncontrolling interest.

In addition, situations exist where a not-for-profit health care entity might attribute a portion of the net assets of a consolidated not-for-profit subsidiary to a noncontrolling interest. This sometimes occurs when the HCO has a less-than-complete voting interest in the board of a not-for-profit entity that it consolidates (e.g., the HCO controls five of seven board seats and another organization controls the other two seats). ASC 954-810, *Health Care Entities—Consolidation,* permits recognition of a noncontrolling interest in these situations if the other organization shares in the subsidiary's operating results or has a residual interest in its net assets upon dissolution. This guidance is unique to not-for-profit HCOs; other not-for-profit entities are not permitted to recognize noncontrolling interests in other not-for-profit organizations.

GAAP requires that noncontrolling interests be presented in a certain manner within the financial statements.[15] The consolidated balance sheet must separately display the portion of net assets that belong to outside parties.[16] That amount should be clearly identified and described (e.g., as "noncontrolling ownership interest in subsidiaries") to distinguish it from net assets that belong to the parent.

In addition, the not-for-profit parent must provide a schedule of changes in consolidated net assets attributable to the parent and the noncontrolling interest that reconciles beginning and ending balances of the parent's controlling interest and the noncontrolling interests for each class of net assets for which a noncontrolling interest exists. At a minimum, not-for-profit HCOs must separately disclose the performance indicator and (if present) must separately present discontinued operations, extraordinary items, and any changes in ownership interests.[17] This schedule is provided in the notes to the consolidated financial statements or alternatively, on the face of the statement of changes in net assets.

(ii) Governmental Entities

Governmental Reporting Entity Requirements. GASB Statement No. 14, *The Financial Reporting Entity,* and Statement No. 39, *Determining Whether Certain Organizations Are Component Units,* are the primary sources of guidance that governmental HCOs use to determine what legally separate entities—called *component units*—should be included in the financial reporting entity. Effective for periods beginning after June 15, 2012, this guidance is amended by the issuance of Statement No. 61, *The Reporting Entity—Omnibus.* Certain of those changes are highlighted in Subsection 35.3(n)(ii).

According to Statements 14 and 39, a governmental HCO's financial reporting entity would consist of:

- The reporting government (i.e., the nucleus of the reporting entity).
- Legally separate organizations for which the reporting government is "financially accountable." Generally, a government is financially accountable for legally separate organizations if it has ongoing authority to appoint a voting majority of the organization's governing body (or, in the absence of ongoing authority, the ability to unilaterally abolish an organization that it also created), and either it is able to impose its will on that organization or there is a potential for the organization to provide specific financial benefits to, or impose specific financial burdens on, the primary government. A government also is financially accountable for majority-owned investees in situations where the intent in owning the stock is to directly enhance its ability to provide government service (as opposed to for speculative investment purposes). A reporting government may also be financially accountable for organizations that

[15] ASC 958-810, *Not-for-Profit Entities—Consolidation,* tailors ASC 810's general guidance for reporting noncontrolling interests in subsidiaries to be appropriate for reporting not-for-profit organizations' noncontrolling interests.

[16] ASC 958-810-45-1.

[17] See ASC 958-810-55-25.

are fiscally dependent on it—that is, the reporting government has authority over the other organization's budget, the pricing of its services, or its ability to issue debt.

- Other legally separate organizations whose relationship with the reporting government is of a nature and significance such that its exclusion would cause the reporting government's financial statements to be misleading or incomplete. Organizations that raise and hold economic resources for the direct benefit of the reporting government *must* be reported as a component unit if they meet certain specific criteria (see Subsection 35.3(n)(ii)). Other organizations should be *considered* for inclusion as potential component units if they are closely related to, or financially integrated with, the reporting government; however, it is a matter of judgment as to whether the nature of those relationships warrants inclusion.

Statement No. 14 also provides standards related to how the reporting entity must be displayed in financial statements. Most components units are displayed *discretely* in financial statements—that is, they are shown in a separate column from the reporting government's activities. However, some component units are so intertwined with the reporting government that they must be blended into the reporting government's activities (analogous to consolidation in the private sector). Statement No. 14 limits the use of blending to situations where the component unit and the reporting government have "substantively the same governing body"—in other words, the government has sufficient representation on the component unit's board to effect complete control over it—or to situations where the component unit provides services to or benefit exclusively, or almost exclusively, the reporting government.

Notes to the financial statements should include a description of component units, their relationship to the reporting government, the criteria for including the component unit, and how the component unit is presented.

GASB Statement No. 61. GASB Statement No. 61, *The Reporting Entity—Omnibus,* makes a number of narrow-scope amendments to the governmental reporting entity requirements discussed in Subsection 35.3(n)(ii). Its provisions are effective for periods beginning after June 15, 2012. Certain of these amendments that are of particular interest to governmental HCOs are highlighted next. See Chapter 33 of this *Handbook* for a more comprehensive treatment of Statement No. 61.

Statement No. 61 amends certain of the criteria used in evaluating whether a related organization must be included in the reporting government's financial statements as a component unit. For example, "fiscal dependency" is no longer by itself a sufficient basis for asserting that a reporting government is financially accountable for a related entity. Instead, both "fiscal dependence" and a "financial benefit or burden relationship" must be present. Statement No. 61 also clarifies certain aspects of the analysis associated with application of the "misleading or incomplete" criteria for inclusion of component units. That analysis will focus solely on whether the exclusion of a related entity would make the reporting financial government's statements misleading (in other words, the reference to incomplete is eliminated). Statement No. 61 clarifies that the determination of completeness would normally be based on financial relationships between the organizations, such as a significant benefit or burden relationship with the primary government that is not a temporary arrangement.

Statement No. 61 also amends the guidance pertaining to classification and display of blended component units. Many (but not all) governmental HCOs present component units for which they are financially accountable using a format that is analogous to a consolidated presentation used by private sector HCOs. This means that they treat all entities for which they are financially accountable as blended component units and that they display the resulting group of entities using a single-column presentation. In effect, they are reporting these component units as if they were divisions of the reporting government.

Under Statement No. 61, reporting governments that justified blending of component units using the "substantively the same" criteria can continue to do so only if one of two additional criteria also is present. Either (a) a financial benefit or burden relationship must also exist or (b) management that is responsible for the day-to-day operations of the reporting HCO must also have operational responsibility for the activities of the component unit. (In effect, the component unit is managed as if it were a division of the reporting HCO.) Statement No. 61 will also require that a blended presentation be used for all situations where a component unit's debt will be repaid entirely or almost entirely with the resources of the reporting government. What is more, governmental HCOs that use a single-column presentation for blended component units will be required to provide condensed combining information (including cash flows) for those component units in the notes, similar to the information required for segment reporting.

Not-for-Profit Foundations Associated with Governmental Entities. Legally separate tax-exempt organizations, such as nonprofit foundations, may be established to raise and hold funds on behalf of a governmental HCO. If not-for-profit foundations are considered component units of a governmental entity with which they are affiliated, they are part of the reporting entity and must be included in the governmental entity's financial statements.

Some foundations are component units by virtue of the fact that the primary government is "financially accountable" for them. However, most governmental entities with related fundraising foundations are not "financially accountable" for them. GASB Statement No. 39, *Determining whether Certain Organizations Are Component Units,* amended Statement No. 14 to provide guidance on evaluating component unit reporting in situations where a primary government is not financially accountable for a tax-exempt organization and raises and holds economic resources for its benefit. Under Statement No. 39, such legally separate tax-exempt organizations that meet all of the next three criteria must be included in the reporting entity as a discretely presented component unit, by virtue of the nature and significance of its relationship with the reporting HCO:

1. *Direct benefit.* The economic resources received or held by the foundation are entirely or almost entirely for the direct benefit of the HCO or its component units.
2. *Entitlement/ability to otherwise access.* The HCO or its component units are entitled to, or have the ability to otherwise access, a majority of the economic resources received or held by the foundation. The ability to "otherwise access" is not meant to imply or require that the HCO has control over the foundation or its resources. Rather, it is a broader concept that may be demonstrated in several ways, for example:
   a. The HCO or its component units historically may have received (directly or indirectly) a majority of the economic resources provided by the foundation.
   b. The foundation previously may have received and honored requests to provide resources to the HCO.
   c. The foundation is "financially interrelated" with the HCO under FASB Statement No. 136.
3. *Significance.* The resources of the foundation to which the HCO or its component units are entitled/have the ability to otherwise access are significant to the HCO. Significance can also be evaluated in terms of the economic resources that are raised and distributed to the government during a period, according to Statement No. 39's Appendix C.

When all three of these criteria are met, a foundation is deemed to be a component unit of the HCO's reporting entity. If any of the criteria are not met, Statement No. 39 requires the primary government to further evaluate whether, as a matter of professional judgment, the tax-exempt organization is financially integrated or otherwise so closely related with it that component unit reporting is warranted under Statement No. 14's "misleading to exclude" standard. While it is likely that such component units would be discretely presented, there is no requirement to do so; instead, an analysis would be required under the general blending versus discrete display requirements of Statement No. 14. In Statement No. 39's *Basis for Conclusions,* the Board emphasizes that exercise of professional judgment is the central consideration in applying the "misleading-to-exclude" standard.

Typically, discrete presentation involves displaying the component unit financial data as a separate column (or columns) in a side-by-side presentation with the financial data of the primary government. However, the financial statements of foundations that are deemed to be component units under Statement No. 39's criteria typically are prepared in accordance with FASB standards rather than GASB standards. In such situations, the foundation's statements may be presented on separate pages (e.g., the foundation's balance sheet is presented on the page following the HCO's balance sheet; the foundation's operating statement is presented on the page following the HCO's operating statement; etc.). If a side-by-side presentation is desired, the foundation's financial statements can be converted to a GASB presentation format. Appendix E of Statement No. 39 provides illustrative financial statements that demonstrate how information presented in a private sector financial statement format can be recast so that it is "compatible" with the reporting government's financial statement format and, thus, can be presented on the same page. This does not, however, also require conversion of the underlying accounting principles used in preparation of the foundation's financial statements to GASB accounting principles.

Statement No. 39 does not require disclosure of the differences between the FASB accounting principles used in preparing the nonprofit organization's financial statements and GASB accounting principles. Appendix E of the statement illustrates an optional disclosure of a policy note addressing such differences.

For each discretely presented component unit resulting from application of Statement No. 39, the notes to the HCO's financial statements should include a brief description of the component unit, its relationship to the HCO, a discussion of the criteria for including the component unit, and how the component unit is reported.

(iii) Joint Operating Agreements. Not-for-profit HCOs may pursue alternatives to a merger or acquisition transaction when evaluating approaches to combining or coordinating their services, operations, and resources. For example, they may enter into a venture in which they combine all or certain aspects of their operations but retain their separate identities.

If the venture is conducted as a separate legal entity (such as a stock corporation, partnership, limited partnership or LLC), the HCO would account for its interest in the venture using the accounting described in Subsection 35.3(h)(i).

If the venture is not conducted in a separate legal entity, the HCO would account for its interest in accordance with ASC 808, *Collaborative Arrangements.* Revenues generated and costs incurred by the venture participants should be reported in the appropriate line items in each participant's statement of operations. A line item such as "collaboration revenue" or "collaborative expenses" would be used to report "sharing" payments made between the venture participants. The equity method of accounting should not be used.

(o) BUSINESS COMBINATIONS. ASC 805, *Business Combinations,* addresses financial accounting and reporting for business combinations involving investor-owned health care entities. ASC 805 is discussed in Chapter 8 of this *Handbook.*

Guidance pertaining to combinations involving not-for-profit or governmental health care entities is highlighted next.

(i) Not-for-Profit Entities. The scope of ASC 958-805, *Business Combinations—Not-for-Profit Entities,* includes combinations of two or more not-for-profit entities as well as transactions in which a not-for-profit entity acquires a for-profit organization. Acquisition of a not-for-profit entity by a for-profit organization is accounted for using ASC 805.

In developing the guidance in ASC 958-805, the FASB assumed that the general framework set forth in ASC 805 generally would apply, with any departures justified by specific differences in the nature of not-for-profit combination transactions. The key difference identified is that a combination accounted for under ASC 805 is presumed to be a bargained exchange—a transaction in which each party sacrifices and receives commensurate value—whereas not-for-profit combinations often are motivated by public interest reasons that consider the mission and programs of the entities. Many not-for-profit transactions involve no cash consideration; if consideration is involved, it often does not represent the fair value of the acquiree.

One significant difference is that ASC 805 requires that an acquiree be designated for every transaction. Under ASC 958-805, some combinations are accounted for as mergers. Ceding of control by all parties to a new entity is the sole definitive criterion for identifying a merger. Similarly, one entity obtaining control over another entity is the sole definitive criterion for an acquisition.

A merger is accounted for using the "carryover method" (combining the assets and liabilities of the combining entities at the merger date at their carryover bases, adjusted as necessary to conform the respective accounting policies). Operations of the new entity are reported from the merger date forward consistent with the FASB's view that, in a merger, a new entity (i.e., one with no previous operations) has emerged from the formerly separate organizations.

Combinations that are not mergers are acquisitions. An acquisition is an event that results in initial inclusion of a not-for-profit or business entity in a not-for-profit parent's consolidated financial statements. In a not-for-profit health care acquisition, the value of the acquired entity is measured by adding together the fair values of the identifiable assets acquired and subtracting the fair values of the liabilities assumed and the consideration transferred (if any). In the simplest form of acquisition transaction (i.e., where no cash consideration is involved), if the fair value of the acquired entity's assets exceed its liabilities, a special type of contribution income ("inherent contribution") is recognized for the difference. The portion of an inherent contribution that increases unrestricted net assets is reported above the performance indicator in the statement of operations. The portion of an inherent contribution that increases temporarily restricted or permanently restricted net assets is reported in the statement of changes in net assets.

If, however, the fair value of the liabilities exceeds the fair value of the acquired entity's assets, in most cases the excess represents goodwill that is reported on the health care entity's balance sheet. However, if the acquired entity's predominant source of support is contributions and investment return, the excess is accounted for as an expense that is reported above the performance indicator in the statement of operations.

(ii) Governmental Entities. Historically, governmental health care entities have applied private sector guidance in accounting for business combinations. Although GASB Statement No. 62 technically will eliminate all private sector guidance for accounting for combinations from the governmental GAAP hierarchy in periods beginning after December 15, 2011, its basis for conclusions (par. 534) directs governmental entities to "continue their current practice" of accounting for and reporting of government combinations (i.e., either ASC 805 as described or its predecessor, Accounting Principles Board Opinion No. 16, *Business Combinations*) until GASB issues a standard addressing those matters. GASB has a government combinations project on its current technical agenda, with issuance of a final standard targeted for 2013. Thus, until GASB's project on accounting for combinations is completed, governmental entities continue to apply private sector guidance as described next.

Governmental HCOs that applied the provisions of GASB Statement No. 20, par. 7 prior to the adoption of Statement No. 62 apply the provisions of FASB ASC 805, *Business Combinations,* to purchase transactions. All other governmental HCOs account for purchase transactions in accordance with APB Opinion No. 16. Applicable GASB statements, where available, should be used in assigning amounts to identifiable assets acquired and liabilities assumed (e.g., Statement No. 13 for operating leases with scheduled rent increases, Statement No. 16 for compensated absences, Statement No. 27 for pension liabilities, Statement No. 31 for investments within its scope, and Statement No. 45 for other postemployment benefit liabilities). Accounting for intangible assets acquired in business combinations is discussed in Section 35.3(k).

For change-of-control transactions that do not involve an exchange of consideration, prevalent practice is to apply accounting that is similar to the pooling-of-interests method described in APB Opinion No. 16. That is, there is no revaluation of the assets acquired and liabilities assumed; assets and liabilities are carried forward at the same basis as they were carried on the books of the combining entities, and the financial statements of the combined entities should be restated for all periods presented, as if the combining entities had always been operated as a single entity.

(p) DEFERRED INFLOWS AND OUTFLOWS OF RESOURCES. Two of the financial statement elements used in GASB's conceptual framework have no counterparts within FASB's conceptual framework. According to GASB Concepts Statement No. 4, *Elements of Financial Statements,* a *deferred outflow of resources* is "a consumption of resources of net assets by the government that is applicable to a future reporting period." Similarly, a *deferred inflow of resources* is "an acquisition of net assets by the government that is applicable to a future reporting period."

GASB's derivative standard (Statement No. 53) was the first to make use of these financial statement elements, and the implementation of that standard surfaced many questions on the presentation and display of these items in the balance sheet. In particular, uncertainty existed as to whether they should be included in (or alternatively, excluded from) the net assets section of the balance sheet. As defined in Concepts Statement No. 4, *net assets* represent the difference between assets and liabilities. However, Concepts Statement No. 4 also says that deferred outflows of resources are not an asset, and deferred inflows of resources are not a liability.

GASB Statement No. 63, *Financial Reporting of Deferred Outflows of Resources, Deferred Inflows of Resources, and Net Position,* was issued in response to requests for guidance on these important presentation matters. Effective for years beginning after December 15, 2011, Statement No. 63 replaces the "net assets" section of the balance sheet with a new residual section called "net position." The "net position" section represents net assets modified for the effects of deferred inflows and deferred outflows of resources. Similarly, the current requirement to provide information about three categories of net assets was replaced with a requirement to provide information on three categories of net position: *net investment in capital assets, restricted,* and *unrestricted.*

In August 2011, GASB issued an exposure draft that proposes to apply the deferred outflows of resources and deferred inflows of resources elements to a broader range of items. The proposed statement, *Reporting Items Previously Recognized as Assets and Liabilities,* would require certain items currently being reported as assets and liabilities to instead be reported as a different type of financial statement element—that is, revenue, expense, deferred inflow of resources, or deferred outflow of resources. For example, debt issue costs, which currently are reported in balance sheets as an asset, would instead be reported as an expense of the period in which they are incurred. Another example is gain or loss on debt refunding, which currently is deferred and deducted from or added to the liability. Under the proposal, the gain or loss would be reported as a deferred outflow or deferred inflow of resources that is reported separately from the liability. Issuance of a final standard is expected in 2012.

35.4 SPECIAL ACCOUNTING PROBLEMS OF SPECIFIC TYPES OF PROVIDERS

(a) CONTINUING CARE RETIREMENT COMMUNITIES. CCRCs provide or guarantee residential and health care services for persons who may reside in apartments, other living units, or a nursing center. They are usually characterized by an obligation to provide future services and some sort of up-front payment on the part of the resident, part of which may be refundable. Unique accounting issues pertaining to CCRCs include accounting for advance fees, accounting for the obligation to provide future services and the use of facilities to current residents, and accounting for costs of acquiring continuing-care contracts. These matters are discussed in Chapter 14 of the *Guide.*

(i) Advance Fees.[18] As explained in FASB ASC 954-605-05-10, a CCRC may require several different payment methods for services and the use of facilities. Generally, payment of an advance fee (also called an *entrance fee*) is required before a resident acquires a right to reside in an apartment or a residential unit.

[18]The requirements discussed in this section may be modified by the FASB/IASB joint revenue recognition project.

Nonrefundable Advance Fees. Some contracts do not allow any of the advance fee to be refunded upon the resident's death or withdrawal. According to the *Guide,* these nonrefundable fees represent payment for future services to be provided over the life of the resident (unless the contract terms state otherwise). Therefore, nonrefundable fees are initially reported as deferred revenue when received and then amortized into income over the resident's remaining life expectancy (or the contract term, if it is shorter). The period of amortization would be adjusted annually based on the actuarially determined estimated remaining life expectancy of each individual (or joint and last survivor life expectancy of each pair of residents occupying the same unit).

Generally, the deferred revenue is amortized using the straight-line method, except in certain circumstances where costs are expected to be significantly higher in the later years of residence. In those cases, a method that reflects the timing of the costs of the expected services may be used. The amortization method used should be disclosed in a note to the financial statements.

Upon the death or withdrawal of a resident, any remaining unamortized deferred revenue associated with the contract should immediately be recognized as revenue.

Refundable Advance Fees. Frequently, continuing care contracts provide for some or a resident's entire advance fee to be refunded if the resident dies or decides to move out of the facility. In most cases, a refundable advance fee is reported as a liability. However, certain forms of refundable fee arrangements are permitted to be deferred and amortized into income over future periods. These are contracts where the refundable amount declines over time and contracts where the amount of refund payable is limited to the proceeds of reoccupancy.

Refundable amount declines over time. In some contracts, the refundable amount diminishes as time passes. For example, the amount of entrance fee that is refundable might decline by 2% per month during the first 50 months the resident resides in the facility. After the 50th month, the entrance fee becomes fully nonrefundable. In those situations, the entrance fee would initially be reported as deferred revenue when received and amortized into income in the same manner as nonrefundable entrance fees. However, at each financial reporting date, a portion of the unamortized deferred revenue should be reclassified and reported in the financial statements as "refunds payable." The amount of the reclassification would be the amount that the facility estimates it will actually be called on to refund based on its historical experience (or, for a newer facility, the experience of comparable facilities). This estimate typically is made on a portfolio basis (e.g., 2% of the overall unamortized entrance fees for the residents who still have refund provisions remaining), and it typically is a fraction of the contractual refund obligation that exists at the reporting date (i.e., the amount that contractually is refundable to each resident who is still in the refundable phase of the contract at a specific reporting date). In these situations, ASC 954-430-25-1 requires that the gross amount of contractual refund obligation be disclosed.

Refund amount is potentially limited by the amount of proceeds received upon reoccupancy of the unit. Most refundable fee contracts stipulate that entrance fees will be refunded only if and when the contract holder's unit is relet to a new resident (who pays a new entrance fee). However, if the contract also stipulates that in the event the entrance fee received from the new resident is lower than the amount of entrance fee otherwise refundable to the contract holder, the CCRC is allowed to account for the refundable fee as deferred revenue (instead of a liability) and amortize it into income *over the remaining useful life of the facility.* In this narrow fact pattern, the refund is in essence a transaction between residents, and the current resident bears the risk of having a limitation on the amount otherwise refundable if the unit resells for a lesser amount than he or she paid or the risk of no refund if the unit does not resell. These concepts are illustrated by the transactions reflected for Residents C and D in ASC 954-430-55-3. In order to use deferred revenue accounting in these situations, the limitation on the refund must be stated in the contract, and it must be management's policy or practice to comply with that limitation.

The basis and method of amortization should be consistent with the method for calculating depreciation and should be disclosed in the notes to the financial statements.

No liability for the refund amount exists until the unit is in fact resold. At that time, the liability will be paid from the proceeds of the unit's resale. If the amount received from the new resident is greater than the amount to be refunded to the former resident, the excess also should be considered deferred revenue (provided that the resale contract also contains a provision that refundability is potentially limited to the proceeds received from reoccupancy).

Balance Sheet Classification. According to ASC 954-210, CCRCs are not required to prepare a classified balance sheet. Instead, they may sequence assets according to their nearness of conversion to cash and may sequence liabilities according to their nearness of maturity and resulting use of cash. Nonetheless, many CCRCs opt to utilize a classified balance sheet.

Among CCRCs that present a classified balance sheet, diversity in practice exists based on whether the CCRC is an SEC registrant. Historically, the predominant industry practice has been to present the estimated liability for the refundable portion of entrance fees and deferred revenue as a noncurrent liability. Particularly in situations where refunds decline over time (as discussed in Subsection 35.4(a)(i), the estimate of the amount refundable is often an amount that is substantially less than the facility's contractual obligation to make refunds, because, based on historical experience, only a small percentage of the legal obligation will actually ever be required to be refunded.

The diversity arose when the SEC required a CCRC registrant that was following the predominant practice to restate its classification of refundable advance fees from noncurrent to current, because, under the terms of its resident agreements, residents could elect to withdraw from the CCRC on 90 days' notice (thus triggering payment of a refund). The SEC's view was that the refundable advance fees constitute "puttable" debt that should be classified as current under ASC 470-10-45.

FASB considered adding a project to its agenda to provide authoritative guidance on the balance sheet classification issue but decided against it due to concerns about the interaction of this issue with the joint FASB/IASB revenue recognition project (discussed in Chapter 12 in this *Handbook*), among others things. The Board recognized and acknowledged that that in the absence of guidance from FASB, the diversity in practice will continue.

(ii) Obligation to Provide Future Services.[19] CCRCs generally commit to provide services and the use of facilities to residents for the rest of their lives. Annually, the CCRC needs to assess its contractual arrangements with existing residents to determine whether the expected future revenues from those contracts will be sufficient to cover the costs of providing services and use of facilities over the rest of the residents' lives.

In addition to any advance fees paid, many CCRCs require residents to pay periodic fees that may be increased, if necessary. CCRCs that have no restrictions on their ability to cover future costs, and those that have a history of profitable operations, may not encounter problems in this area. More likely to be affected are CCRCs that have contracts which restrict the amount of periodic fee increases and those having contracts that only require residents to pay an advance fee. In this situation, no additional funds can be required to be paid, regardless of how long a resident lives or if the resident requires more services than anticipated.

If the estimated costs of future services are determined to exceed anticipated revenues, the CCRC has entered into a loss contract. Losses resulting from such contracts—that is, the obligation to provide future services and use of facilities—should be recorded in the period in which they are determined to exist. In determining the loss, contracts should be grouped by type, such as "contracts with a limit on annual increases in fees" and "contracts with unlimited fee increases."

At the time of initial determination that a loss exists, the CCRC would record a liability and make a corresponding charge to income. ASC 954-440-55 provides this formula for calculating the liability:

- Present value of future net cash flows
- Minus the balance of unamortized deferred revenue
- Plus depreciation of facilities to be charged related to the contracts
- Plus unamortized costs of acquiring the related initial continuing-care contracts, if applicable

[19]The requirements discussed in this section may be modified by the FASB/IASB joint revenue recognition project.

For purposes of determining the present value of future net cash flows, the *Guide* defines *cash inflows* as revenue contractually committed to support the residents and inflows resulting from monthly fees, including anticipated increases in accordance with contract terms. *Cash outflows* are defined as operating expenses, including interest expense but excluding selling and general and administrative expenses. Cost increases resulting from inflation should be factored into the amount of operating expenses included in the computation. The difference between cash inflows and cash outflows should be discounted to present value. The expected inflation rate and other factors should be taken into account in determining the discount rate to be used.

A formula for determining the depreciation of facilities to be charged to current residents is also provided. Basically, the purpose of this formula is to exclude from the loss computation any depreciation allocable to revenue-producing service areas.

For both the net present value of cash flows and the depreciation of facilities, the computation should be made on a resident-by-resident basis within each contract group, using the resident's remaining life expectancy. The life spans used should be the same as those used in calculating the amortization of deferred revenue.

Each year, the liability should be recalculated. Increases or decreases in the liability would be reported in the income statement as a separate line item, "change in obligation to provide future services and use of facilities," with appropriate note disclosure. In the balance sheet, the obligation to provide future services should be presented separately as a long-term liability, if it is material.

The notes to the financial statements should include a description of the obligation to provide future services, the carrying amount of the liability that is presented at present value (if it is not separately disclosed in the balance sheet), and the interest rate used to discount the liability.

(iii) Costs of Acquiring Initial Continuing Care Contracts.[20] Most CCRCs regard the costs of obtaining contracts to initially fill a new facility as an investment that will result in future revenues from amortization of advance fees or from future periodic fees, in some cases. ASC 954-340-25-1 through 25-2 provides guidance on whether "costs of acquiring initial continuing care contracts" (as specifically defined in the glossary of the *Guide*) should be capitalized or expensed. The glossary states that these are costs incurred to originate a contract that result from and are essential to acquire initial contracts and are incurred through the date of substantial occupancy but no later than one year from the date of completion of construction. They include:

a. The costs from activities in connection with soliciting potential initial residents (such as model units and their furnishings, sales brochures, semipermanent signs, tours, and grand openings). However, these costs do not include advertising, interest, administrative costs, rent, depreciation, or any other occupancy or equipment costs.

b. Sales salaries incurred in connection with the activities described in (a).

c. The costs of processing the contracts, such as evaluating the prospective resident's financial condition; evaluating and recording guarantees, collateral, and other security arrangements; negotiating contract terms; preparing and processing contract documents; and closing the transaction.

d. The portion of an employee's compensation and benefits that relates to the initial contract acquisitions.

The costs of acquiring initial continuing-care contracts that are described in item (a) and are expected to be recovered from future contract revenues should be capitalized in accordance with ASC 970-340, *Real Estate—Other Assets and Deferred Costs,* and amortized to expense on a straight-line basis over the average expected remaining lives of the residents under the contract or the contract term, if shorter. Such costs incurred after a CCRC is substantially occupied or one year following completion should be expensed when incurred. Costs that are described in item (b)

[20]The requirements discussed in this section may be modified by the FASB/IASB joint revenue recognition project.

should be expensed, and costs that are described in items (c) and (d) should be accounted for in conformity with the guidance in ASC 720-15, *Start-up Costs.*

Advertising cost is not a component of "costs of acquiring initial continuing-care contracts." Advertising cost incurred in connection with acquiring initial continuing-care contracts should be accounted for in conformity with the guidance in ASC 720-35, *Advertising Costs.*

(b) HMOs AND MANAGED CARE ENTITIES. Prepaid health care plans provide or arrange for the delivery of health care services to a specified group of individuals in exchange for a fixed, predetermined fee. The most common form of prepaid HCO is the HMO.

Some have questioned the need for developing specific guidance for prepaid health care plans when GAAP for insurance companies might be applied to certain similar transactions entered into by those entities. The fundamental difference noted in the accounting guidance for the two industries is that prepaid health care plans undertake to provide (or arrange for the provision of) health care services in addition to their role as a third-party payer. Because ASC 944, *Financial Services—Insurance,* applies only to contracts that involve payment for health care services (instead of contracts that extend to the provision of health care services), specialized guidance was needed. That guidance is discussed in Chapter 13 of the *Guide,* as highlighted next.

(i) Revenue. Health plan premiums are the primary source of revenue for HMOs. In exchange for receipt of premiums, the HMO provides or arranges for provision of covered services to plan members, either by using its own facilities and physicians or by sending members to facilities, physicians, or other companies with which it has contractual relationships. Payment arrangements with those parties may be based on services provided, or they may involve subcontracting provision of certain types of services to specialty managed care companies. Often these subcontracting arrangements are paid for on a capitation basis; that is, the specialty managed care company is paid a fixed, predetermined amount per member per month, similar to the premium revenue earned by the HMO.

Under capitation arrangements, the provider earns revenue by *agreeing to* provide covered services to a specific population (e.g., members of a health plan) during a specified time period (usually one month), regardless of whether any services are actually provided or how expensive those services are. The provider is paid a fixed, predetermined amount per member per month.

Capitation revenue is similar to premium revenue earned by HMOs; it is not patient service revenue. Therefore, revenue under capitation contracts should be reported in the period that plan members are entitled to receive health care services. Capitation payments are generally made at the beginning of each month and obligate the provider to render covered services during that month. Therefore, revenue earned under capitation contracts should be recorded by the provider on a month-to-month basis. If capitation payments are received in advance of the month to which they relate, they must be reported as deferred revenue until they are earned. If the provider's accounting system records patient charges and establishes patient receivables as services are rendered, valuation allowances or adjustments must be recorded so only the amount of capitation revenue is reported in the financial statements.

The reporting of revenues as gross or net also is a significant issue for specialty managed care organizations that have capitation arrangements with HMOs and, in turn, subcontract services to other providers. In those situations, the question is whether the specialty managed care organization's statement of operations should reflect gross revenues and expenses related to the managed care contract or instead reflect the net amount in income in a caption such as "network management fees earned."

ASC 605-45-45, *Principal–Agent Considerations,*[21] addresses situations in which an entity should recognize revenue based on (a) the gross amount billed to the customer because it has earned revenue from the sale of goods or services, or (b) the net amount retained (i.e., the amount billed to

[21] The requirements discussed in this section may be modified by the FASB/IASB joint revenue recognition project.

the customer less the amount paid to a supplier) because, in substance, it has earned a commission or fee from the supplier. While ASC 605-45-15-4 states that it excludes transactions involving insurance and reinsurance premiums, that exclusion pertains to contracts within the scope of ASC 944, *Financial Services—Insurance,* rather than the prepaid health care arrangements addressed in ASC 954.

ASC 605-45-45 concludes that the determination of gross versus net revenue reporting is a matter of judgment that depends on the relevant facts and circumstances, and that each entity's specific facts and circumstances should be evaluated against the next list of indicators that would point toward either gross or net reporting:

INDICATORS OF GROSS REVENUE REPORTING

Entity is the primary obligor in the arrangement (i.e., responsible for fulfillment, including acceptability of the product or service provided).

Entity has general inventory risk (for sales of products) or is obligated to compensate individual service providers for work performed (for sales of services).

Entity has latitude in establishing price for the product or service.

Entity adds value by changing the nature of the product or by performing part of the service.

Entity has discretion in supplier selection.

Entity is involved in the determination of product or service specifications.

Entity has credit risk.

INDICATORS OF NET REVENUE REPORTING

Supplier (rather than the entity) is the primary obligor in the arrangement.

Amount the entity earns is a fixed portion of the overall transaction price (i.e., a set dollar amount per transaction; a stated percent of amount billed).

Supplier (rather than the entity) has credit risk.

While some of these indicators are stronger than others, no single indicator would provide a presumption that gross or net treatment was appropriate. The relative strength of all indicators present should be considered.

(ii) Expense Recognition. Insurance accounting would require that the costs of the patient's entire expected course of treatment be estimated and reported as an expense of the period in which the diagnosis is made. This is because the event that triggers an insurance company to recognize claims expense is the occurrence of a particular accident or illness ("insured event"). However, the event that triggers an HMO to recognize claim expense is the provision of health care services to an enrolled member, not the occurrence of an accident or illness. In order to achieve a proper matching of the HMO's revenues and expenses, as a general rule the costs of providing health care services to HMO members should be reported in the periods in which those services are actually rendered. This is true even if the subscriber is being treated for an illness that requires long-term treatment. It is not appropriate to estimate and accrue the expense of the entire spell of illness in the period in which the diagnosis is made. However, in certain situations, it is appropriate for HMOs to accrue the costs of health care services, as described next.

Contractual or regulatory obligations. In situations where the contract or prevailing regulations obligate the HMO to continue to provide care to members after the end of the premium period, the HMO will have to accrue the total costs of these hospitalization services. An example would be if the HMO is contractually obligated to continue to provide coverage for hospital stays that are "in progress" at the end of the premium period.

IBNR accruals. Incurred but not reported accruals must be estimated and reserves recorded for services that have been rendered by providers but not reported to the HMO as of the financial statement date. This will include recurring claims from the HMO's contracted providers, claims from specialists, and claims arising from situations in which a subscriber requires medical care outside of the HMO's service area (such as while traveling). In such cases, the HMO should accrue the costs of any services rendered during the fiscal period for which payment has not been made as of the close of the fiscal period, even if the subcontracting provider has not yet billed the HMO for those services.

The IBNR reserve is one of the key risk areas for an HMO, not only because it has a major effect on an HMO's financial statements but also because it serves as one of the early warning signals of utilization problems. An HMO's finance personnel must work closely with utilization management and contacting personnel to analyze cost and utilization data, which is essential to conducting lag schedule analyses and formulating the reserves.

Termination of contract. Another situation in which an accrual of health care costs might be required is when a contract between an HMO and an employer is terminated. For instance, a staff model HMO might contract with a major industrial corporation to establish a medical clinic on or near the premises of a plant. In a staff model HMO, the costs of providing health care services to the plant's employees are relatively fixed, because the clinic's physicians and support personnel are generally salaried employees. If the contract with the corporation is terminated, expenses associated with the clinic that the HMO will be unable to avoid, such as guaranteed salaries, rent, or depreciation, should be accrued net of any related anticipated revenues.

(iii) Loss Contracts.[22] If an HMO's premiums are set too low, or if utilization by plan members is higher than expected, the HMO may sustain an economic loss in fulfilling a particular contract. In those situations, losses should be accrued when the HMO's projected health care costs and maintenance costs pertaining to a particular group of contracts exceed the anticipated premium revenues and stop-loss insurance recoveries under those contracts.[23]

To determine whether a loss accrual is necessary, an HMO will need to analyze the unexpired contracts in force at the end of each reporting period. Contracts should be grouped in the manner discussed in this section and the aggregate health care costs, maintenance expenses, premium revenue, and stop-loss recoveries projected for the contracts in each group. The costs considered should include fixed costs as well as variable costs; in other words, the computation should include costs that would be incurred regardless of whether a particular contract is in force (such as staff physician's salaries and costs attributable to facilities owned by the HMO). The costs considered should also include all direct costs of the contracts along with indirect costs identifiable with or allocable to the contracts, as is customary in any type of contract accounting. Generally this requires inclusion of all HMO costs other than general and administrative, selling, marketing, and interest. If the aggregate expenses for the contract period are expected to exceed the aggregate revenues for the contract period, the amount of the excess should be accrued as a loss on that group of contracts. Furthermore, if any of the contracts in a "loss group" have guaranteed renewal provisions and the HMO is constrained by statutory requirements or community rating practices from increasing the premiums charged on those contracts, the HMO should also accrue any losses it expects to incur attributable to the guaranteed renewal periods.

The groupings used for loss determination correspond with the groupings used by the HMO in establishing its premium rates. For HMOs that use community rating (i.e., one premium rate is established for all members in a given enrollment population; e.g., a particular geographic area or actuarial class), the contracts grouped together for loss determination would be those considered to be part of the same enrollment "pool" for premium determination. HMOs that are experience-rated would group their contracts along the same lines as are used for rate-setting purposes, such as by type of employer. (In an experience-rated HMO, members covered by each contract constitute a separate population base for rate-setting purposes; therefore, premiums are based on the actual or anticipated health care costs of each contract.)

---

[22]The requirements discussed in this section may be modified by the FASB/IASB joint revenue recognition project.

[23] ASC 954-450, *Health Care Entities—Contingencies.*

Similar considerations would apply to providers that enter into unprofitable capitation contracts. The provider would record losses on those contracts if future costs, including contract-related administrative costs (e.g., medical records, claims processing, billing) are expected to exceed future revenues from the contract plus any anticipated stop-loss recoveries.

(iv) Risk Pools.[24] Risk pools provide a vehicle for sharing favorable and unfavorable experiences among participants in a managed care contract (and by creating incentives for physicians and hospitals to control utilization of services). The type of incentive offered by the HMO may be positive (gain-sharing pool) or negative (loss-sharing pool), or may combine both positive and negative incentives (combined risk-sharing pool). Risk pool settlements retroactively determine the amount of fees a health care provider ultimately will be paid under a managed care contract; therefore, the settlements affect the amount of revenue that should be recognized in the provider's financial statements and the amount of health care expense that should be recognized by the HMO. The HMO should accrue risk pool settlements payable to physicians, hospitals, and other providers based on relevant factors such as experience to date.

Risk pool estimated settlements receivable or payable should be accrued periodically based on relevant factors such as experience to date such that interim financial statements will not be materially understated or overstated.

In situations where settlements are due from providers under risk-sharing arrangements, a receivable will exist. Whether this receivable can be collected may be a significant item for HMOs, because the amounts can be large relative to net income. It is not uncommon for HMOs ultimately to write such receivables off. Alternatively, some HMOs "recover" the receivable over a period of years by withholding payments from compensation to providers calculated at greater than market rates. Receivables of this nature should be presented net of an allowance for uncollectibles; that allowance may be difficult to estimate due to the factors already discussed. Such receivables may be disclosed separately, if they are material.

(v) Stop-Loss Insurance. HMOs often purchase stop-loss insurance (also called excess-of-loss reinsurance) to protect themselves against the risk of loss incurred in the process of satisfying the claims of HMO subscribers. HMOs should report stop-loss insurance premiums as a health care cost. Stop-loss insurance recoveries should be reported as a reduction of the related premium expense; they should not be reported as revenue. Amounts recoverable (i.e., receivable) from insurers under stop-loss policies should be reported as assets, reduced by appropriate valuation allowances; it is not appropriate to offset such amounts against amounts payable for health care costs.

(vi) Acquisition Costs.[25] HMOs incur certain costs in connection with writing contracts and obtaining new members. These costs may be general in nature, such as marketing staff salaries, general promotional literature, and other advertising; or they may be directly related to the acquisition of specific contracts, such as the costs of specialized brochures and advertising and commissions paid to agents or brokers. Advertising costs should be accounted for in accordance with ASC 720-35. All other acquisition costs should be expensed as incurred (ASC 954-720-25-6).

(c) PHYSICIAN PRACTICE MANAGEMENT COMPANIES. Physician practice management companies (PPMs) are corporations that seek to amass physician or dental practices into large groups. The unique accounting and reporting issues of PPMs arise primarily from the prohibitions in many states against the corporate practice of medicine.

Broadly speaking, the intent of the corporate practice of medicine doctrine is to ensure that only licensed professionals deliver medical care and that laypersons and entities not influence

---

[24]The requirements discussed in this section may be modified by the FASB/IASB joint revenue recognition project.

[25]The requirements discussed in this section may be modified by the FASB/IASB joint revenue recognition project.

treatment decisions. As a result of this doctrine, most states regulate to some degree the form of entity in which a physician or dentist may practice. Typically, state laws permit a medical professional to conduct a medical practice only as an individual, as a member of a partnership, or as an employee of a professional corporation (i.e., a corporation in which all the shareholders are medical professionals). Although the form of the prohibitions varies from state to state, generally a business corporation comprised of laypersons is not allowed to practice medicine or to employ a physician to provide professional medical services. (A typical exception allows hospitals to employ physicians because hospitals are formed for the specific purpose of treating patients and providing health care services and are themselves licensed entities.)

In states that prohibit the corporate practice of medicine, a PPM cannot legally own the stock of a medical or dental practice. In those cases, the PPM is unable to acquire a controlling financial interest in the practice through purchasing an ownership interest. Instead, the PPM might execute a long-term management services agreement (MSA) under which the physicians or dentists convey rights involving the practices that are similar to those that would be obtained through outright ownership. In exchange, the PPM pays a lump sum up front for the rights to manage the practice for the term of the agreement (typically 25–40 years).

If the terms of the arrangement are stringent enough to provide the PPM with a controlling financial interest, then for accounting and financial reporting purposes, the PPM is deemed to have acquired the practice. PPMs that use this model characterize their primary business as providing medical care, and the top line of the income statement will be the revenue derived by the medical practices from patient care.

If the terms of the arrangement do not convey a controlling financial interest to the PPM, the PPM has purchased an intangible asset (the long-term rights to manage the practice). PPMs that utilize this model characterize their operations as a management company to which the physicians are outsourcing the business functions associated with running the practice. In those situations, the income statement begins by reporting the management fees the PPM earns under the MSAs. Exhibit 35.2 compares the income statement presentation formats under the two models.

(i) Consolidation Requirements. In evaluating situations where long-term MSAs convey rights that are similar to those that would be obtained through outright ownership, the PPM first considers whether the *Variable Interest Entities* (VIE) subsections of ASC 810, *Consolidation,* apply. If so, then that guidance is used to determine whether the PPM should consolidate the assets and operations of the medical practice. This guidance is discussed further in Chapter 9 of this *Handbook.*

If the VIE guidance does not apply, the PPM assesses the need for consolidation based on the *Consolidation of Entities Controlled by Contract* subsections of ASC 810-10. Briefly, that guidance states that a PPM can establish a controlling financial interest in a medical entity solely through the terms of contractual arrangements if, for the *requisite period of time,* the PPM has both *control* over the medical entity and a *financial interest* in the medical entity. ASC 810-10-55 provides a decision tree illustrating the basic analysis required.

Format A: Provider of Medical Care		**Format B: Management Company**	
Net medical practice revenue	$85,000	Management services revenue	$52,000
Expenses:			
Physician salaries	(30,000)		
Provision for uncollectible accounts	(3,000)		
Clinic costs	(49,000)	Clinic costs	(49,000)
Net Income	$ 3,000	Net Income	$ 3,000

Exhibit 35.2 Income Statement Presentation

Requisite period of time. The first threshold is that the contractual agreement between the PPM and the medical entity must be for a period of 10 years or more (or for the remaining legal life of the medical entity, if shorter) and may not be terminable by the medical entity except in the event of gross negligence, fraud, or other illegal activities, or bankruptcy of the PPM. The evaluation should be based on substance as opposed to form. Thus, both the original stated contract term and any renewal or cancellation provisions must be considered. For example, an agreement having an initial stated term of 5 years, with one 5-year renewal option exercisable solely at the discretion of the PPM, meets the requirement because it is in substance a 10-year contract.

Control. Generally, the most effective way for the PPM to obtain control of the practice is to structure the arrangement using a "nominee shareholder" model. In those arrangements, a majority of the practice's outstanding voting equity instruments is owned by a licensed medical professional (the nominee shareholder of the practice) who, in turn, executes various legal agreements with the PPM. Among other things, those agreements place restrictions on the nominee shareholder's ability to transfer the stock of the medical entity. They also permit the PPM to change the nominee shareholder at any time, at its sole discretion and without cause, with no more than nominal cost or other significant adverse impact for either the PPM or the managed practice. Due to the high level of control the PPM exerts over the nominee shareholder physician's role and responsibilities, an automatic presumption exists that the control criterion is met. However, the presumption is rebutted if the PPM has granted rights to others (either through a management agreement or through its nominee) such that it does not have exclusive decision-making authority.

If the nominee shareholder model is not used, the threshold for attaining control is much higher. The MSA must provide the PPM with exclusive authority over all decision making related to: (1) total compensation of the licensed medical professionals as well as the ability to establish and implement guidelines for their selection, hiring, and termination; and (2) ongoing major or central operations of the medical entity, other than the dispensing of medical services (e.g., scope of services, pricing of services, negotiation and execution of contracts, and establishment and approval of operating and capital budgets). In many states, certain aspects of these requirements would likely run afoul of the corporate practice of medicine doctrine. Thus, it is difficult to meet the criteria for control in other than a nominee–shareholder arrangement.

Financial interest. To meet the financial interest criterion, the MSA must provide the PPM with the equivalent of a transferable financial interest in the managed medical entity. If a nominee shareholder model is used, as discussed, the PPM is presumed to have a financial interest in the medical entity, as long as it has the power (at will, and for no or nominal compensation) to reset the terms of its financial interest in the physician practice so that is has an interest that is unilaterally salable or transferable and that interest provides the PPM with the right to receive both as ongoing fees and as proceeds from the sale of its interest an amount that fluctuates based on the performance of the practice.

If, however, the nominee shareholder method is not employed, the PPM must demonstrate through other means that that it has a significant financial interest in the practice that: (1) is unilaterally salable or transferable by the PPM; and (2) provides the PPM with the right to receive both as ongoing fees and as proceeds from the sale of its interest an amount that fluctuates based on the performance of the practice.

35.5 FINANCIAL STATEMENTS

(a) OVERVIEW OF FINANCIAL REPORTING MODELS. Investor-owned and not-for-profit health care providers generally prepare four financial statements:

1. Balance sheet
2. Income statement/statement of operations
3. Statement of changes in stockholders' equity/statement of changes in net assets
4. Statement of cash flows

As discussed in Chapter 28 of this *Handbook,* the financial statement presentation subsections of ASC 958 set forth the broad standards of financial reporting with which all not-for-profit organizations must comply. However, not-for-profit health care providers must apply those standards in accordance with additional guidance contained in ASC 954.

The primary reason for these differences is that ASC 958 allows more flexibility in financial reporting than traditionally has existed within the health care industry. For example, it does not require not-for-profit organizations to present a separate operating statement with a performance measure. The additional guidance in ASC 954 restricts some of that flexibility in order to create a not-for-profit financial reporting format that is similar (but not identical) to that used by investor-owned entities. Chapter 3 of the *Guide* contains a comprehensive discussion of the not-for-profit health care financial reporting model.

Governmental health care entities are required to follow the financial reporting requirements prescribed by GASB Statement No. 34, *Basic Financial Statements—and Management's Discussion and Analysis—for State and Local Governments* (discussed more comprehensively in Chapter 33 in this *Handbook*). Within that model, most governmental HCOs are considered "special purpose governments engagement in business-type activities." The financial statements required for those entities consist of:

- Statement of net assets (balance sheet)
- Statement of revenues, expenses, and changes in net assets (SRECNA)
- Statement of cash flows

In addition, management's discussion and analysis (MD&A) must be provided as "required supplementary information." Financial reporting considerations for governmental HCOs are also described in Chapter 15 of the *Guide.*

The reporting model used by governmental health care entities often entails the preparation of financial statements that use a single column presentation (rather than the multicolumn format required for many other types of governments). If a governmental health care entity elects or is required to accounts for its activities in multiple funds, the statements must disaggregate information for "major" funds by presenting them in separate columns, with a separate column provided for all nonmajor funds in the aggregate. Regardless of whether an entity uses single-column or multicolumn reporting for its own operations, any discretely presented component units must be displayed in an additional column.

An AICPA practice aid, *Health Care Entities: Checklists and Illustrative Financial Statements,* provides illustrative financial statements for investor-owned, tax-exempt, and governmental HCOs. Those statements illustrate the application of the reporting practices discussed in the *Guide* and in ASC 954. Specific types of HCOs are presented, but only to illustrate a wide diversity of reporting practices. It is not intended that these illustrations represent either the only types of disclosure or the only statement formats that would be appropriate. More or less detail should appear in the financial statements or notes, depending on the circumstances. Examples of financial statements of not-for-profit and governmental health care entities can also be found in the MSRB's EMMA database (see Subsection 35.6(a)(iii)) and on Web sites of many large HCOs.

(b) BALANCE SHEET. The balance sheet reporting requirements for investor-owned health care providers are similar to those for other types of investor-owned service providers. Special considerations related to preparation of balance sheets for not-for-profit and governmental health care entities are discussed next.

(i) Not-for-Profit Entities. Not-for-profit health care entities prepare balance sheets in accordance with the general requirements applicable to not-for-profit organizations, subject to additional health care–specific guidance contained in ASC 954-210, *Health Care Entities—Balance Sheet.* The additional guidance in ASC 954 restricts some of the reporting flexibility that is allowed for other not-for-profit organizations. For example, not-for-profit health care entities (with the exception of some CCRCs) must provide liquidity information by preparing a classified balance sheet; other not-for-profit organizations have additional options for reporting this information.

The primary difference from the balance sheet of investor-owned health care entities is the equity section. The not-for-profit health care entity will report unrestricted, temporarily restricted, and permanently restricted net assets instead of stock, retained earnings, and accumulated other comprehensive income.

ASC 958-810, *Not-for-Profit Entities—Consolidation,* tailors the general FASB ASC requirements for reporting noncontrolling interests in subsidiaries (discussed in Chapter 9 of this *Handbook*) to the not-for-profit reporting model. Noncontrolling interests in the equity (net assets) of consolidated subsidiaries should be reported in the consolidated balance sheet as a separate component of the appropriate net asset class. ASC 958-810-55 provides a comprehensive illustration of this reporting.

(ii) Governmental Health Care Entities. A governmental provider's balance sheet may be prepared using either the traditional balance sheet format or a net assets format (assets less liabilities equal net assets). The equity section of the balance sheet is structured into three broad classes of net assets: unrestricted; invested in capital assets, net of related debt (i.e., capital assets reduced by accumulated depreciation and by any outstanding debt incurred to acquire, construct, or improve those assets); and restricted (differentiated between expendable and nonexpendable). Major categories of restrictions should be reported on the face of the balance sheet (e.g., "restricted for capital acquisitions").

The "restricted net assets" category represents restricted assets reduced by liabilities related to those assets. Because the definition of *restricted* in the governmental financial reporting model is broader than the definition of *restricted* in the not-for-profit financial reporting model, a governmental HCO's restricted net assets category includes a broader array of resources than the restricted net assets classification used by not-for-profit HCOs. While both models require resources restricted for identified purposes by donors and grantors to be reported as restricted, the governmental restricted net asset category also includes unexpended debt proceeds held by trustees, bond sinking and debt service reserve funds, assets set aside to meet statutory reserve requirements, and assets held in irrevocable self-insurance trusts, among others. For additional information on the restricted net assets category (including considerations related to calculating the amounts to be reported in that category), see Chapter 33 in this *Handbook.*

Similar to not-for-profit health care entities, the *unrestricted* net asset category includes net assets that are board- or management-designated for specific purposes (e.g., plant replacement and expansion).

Effective for financial reporting periods beginning after December 15, 2011, GASB Statement No. 63, *Financial Reporting of Deferred Outflows of Resources, Deferred Inflows of Resources, and Net Position*, substitutes the concept of "net position" for the concept of "net assets" currently used in balance sheets. This is to accommodate the relatively new financial statement elements "deferred inflows of resources" and "deferred outflows of resources" that are discussed in Section 35.3(p). "Net position" is net assets (i.e., the difference between assets and liabilities) modified for the effects of deferred inflows of resources and deferred outflows of resources.

As modified by Statement No. 63, a balance sheet must report "deferred outflows of resources" in a separate section following assets. Similarly, "deferred inflows of resources" would be reported in a separate section following liabilities.

(c) OPERATING STATEMENT. An AICPA practice aid, *Health Care Entities: Checklists and Illustrative Financial Statements,* provides illustrative operating statements for investor-owned, not-for-profit, and governmental health care entities that illustrate the reporting conventions discussed in the *Guide.*

Similarities and differences among these three reporting models are highlighted in the next sections.

(i) Investor-Owned Entities. The income statement reporting requirements for investor-owned health care providers are similar to those for other types of investor-owned service providers.

(ii) Not-for-Profit Entities. Not-for-profit health care entities prepare operating statements in accordance with the general not-for-profit requirements of ASC 958-225, subject to additional healthcare-specific guidance contained in ASC 954-225, to be discussed.

Not-for-profit HCOs subdivide the nonprofit statement of activities into two separate statements—a statement of operations (which reports detailed information pertaining to the change in unrestricted net assets for the period) and a statement of changes in net assets (which reflects all changes in temporarily and permanently restricted net assets, along with changes in unrestricted net assets). The result is similar (but not identical) to the statement of comprehensive income prepared by investor-owned entities.

The statement of operations must also include a subtotal that displays the results of operations for the period. The *Health Care Entities* guide and ASC 954-225, *Health Care Entities—Income Statement,* refer to this subtotal as the "performance indicator." This terminology is used because FASB deemed the term *net income* inappropriate for describing the earnings measure in the not-for-profit environment. The performance indicator is the functional equivalent of income from continuing operations reported by a for-profit enterprise. Thus, elements of revenues and expenses that would be included in income from continuing operations by a for-profit entity must similarly be included in the performance indicator of a not-for-profit health care entity. The performance indicator typically is identified in the statement of operations using a caption such as "excess of revenues over expenses," and its nature and composition should be described in the notes to the financial statements.

The principal difference between the performance indicator and net income of a business enterprise is that extraordinary items, discontinued operations, and (where explicitly provided for in the transition provisions of newly issued FASB standards) certain changes in accounting principle are reported below the performance indicator, whereas an investor-owned entity would include them in net income. Otherwise, the two measures should be consistent, except for items that clearly are not applicable (e.g., investor-owned health care enterprises typically would not report contribution income).

If an "income from operations" subtotal is presented above the performance indicator and its composition is not apparent from the details provided on the face of the statement, note disclosure should be made regarding the nature of the measure. However, any restrictions imposed by FASB on items that must be included within an operating income subtotal reported by investor-owned entities (e.g., an impairment loss on assets held for use) must also be complied with by not-for-profit health care entities.

Items reported below the performance indicator in the statement of operations are regarded as the functional equivalent of other comprehensive income (OCI) in a for-profit enterprise. In addition to transactions that are explicitly required by the FASB ASC to be reported in or reclassified from OCI (such as unrealized gains and losses from other than trading securities and certain derivative transactions), this category of the statement of operations includes:

- Equity transfers involving other entities that control the reporting entity, are controlled by the reporting entity, or are under common control with the reporting entity
- Contributions of (and assets released from donor restrictions related to) long-lived assets
- Extraordinary items, discontinued operations, and cumulative effect of a change in accounting principle that are required by FASB standards to be included in change in net assets of the period (as discussed previously)
- Reductions in unrestricted net assets that arise from investment losses on donor-restricted endowment investments, along with investment gains that restore the fair value of the assets of the endowment fund to the required level

Functional Reporting Expenses. ASC 958-225, *Not-for-Profit Entities—Income Statement,* requires that all expenses be reported as decreases in unrestricted net assets. In addition, expenses should be reported by functional categories, either on the face of the statement or in notes to the financial statements. The *Health Care Entities* guide encourages the use of "natural" expense classifications (e.g., salaries and wages, employee benefits, supplies) on the face of the statement of operations, with disclosure of functional details in the notes. The *Guide* also states that the extent of classification and subclassification of expenses by function depends on many factors, such as the nature and complexity of the HCO. Some organizations may present only two categories: health services and general and administrative. Others may present additional distinctions, such as physician services, research, and teaching. Any functional allocations made should be based on full cost allocation.

Noncontrolling Interests. When consolidated financial statements of a not-for-profit entity include noncontrolling interests, ASC 958-810 tailors the general guidance in ASC 810 on reporting changes in equity attributable to the parent and the noncontrolling interest to accommodate the not-for-profit financial reporting model. Generally, the not-for-profit parent must provide a schedule of changes in consolidated net assets attributable to the parent and the noncontrolling interest that reconciles beginning and ending balances of the parent's controlling interest and the noncontrolling interests for each class of net assets for which a noncontrolling interest exists. When the not-for-profit parent is an HCO that applies ASC 954 and the *Guide,* it must separately disclose the performance indicator and, if present, must separately present discontinued operations, extraordinary items, and/or changes in ownership interests. In most cases, that schedule will appear in the notes rather than on the face of the statement of operations (although not-for-profit HCOs are not precluded from displaying it on the face of the statement of operations if they desire).

(iii) Governmental Entities. The operating statement prepared by governmental HCOs is the "Statement of revenues, expenses, and changes in net assets" (SRECNA).

Significant differences exist between the SRECNA and the operating statements prepared by private sector entities. One difference is the absence of a performance measure in the SRECNA that corresponds to either net income of an investor-owned entity or to the performance indicator reported by a not-for-profit entity. In the GASB financial reporting model for business-type entities, a primary focus is on the operating income or loss subtotal, which indicates the extent to which the entity is self-sustaining from fees charged for its services or, alternatively, the extent to which it is dependent on investment income or subsidies for carrying out its mission.

Another difference is that governmental entities do not have a concept of OCI similar to that used by private sector HCOs. Under GASB, certain items that would be considered OCI under the FASB model (e.g., gains and losses on hedging derivatives) are instead deferred and reported on the balance sheet using the captions "deferred inflows of resources" or "deferred outflows of resources," as appropriate. This is discussed further in Section 35.3(p).

Yet another difference is that the SRECNA's focus is on the change in *total* net assets rather than changes in *classes of* net assets. As a result, no reclassifications from restricted to unrestricted funds are reported when restrictions are released (as is done in not-for-profit financial reporting).

The SRECNA follows a prescribed format that distinguishes between operating and nonoperating revenues and expenses and provides an intermediate total for operating income or loss. (This is another difference from private sector reporting, where use of a "nonoperating" category is permitted but not required.) The prescribed sequence (with totals and subtotals displayed in boldface) is:

Operating revenues (reported by major source)

Total operating revenues (required subtotal)

Operating expenses (detailed)

Total operating expenses (required subtotal)

Operating income/loss (required subtotal)

Nonoperating revenues/expenses (detailed)

Income before other revenues, expenses, gains, losses, and transfers

Capital contributions

Additions to term and permanent endowments

"Special items"

Extraordinary items

Transfers

Increase (decrease) in net assets

Net assets—beginning of period

Net assets—end of period

Classification of items as operating or nonoperating is determined by how the related transactions are classified in the statement of cash flows. Transactions associated with cash flows that are classified as noncapital financing, capital financing, or investing in the statement of cash flows typically would not be classified as "operating" in the SRECNA. Examples of items that are required to be classified as nonoperating using this approach are contributions received (which are reported in the statement of cash flows as either capital or noncapital financing activity), interest expense (capital or noncapital financing activity), and interest income (investing activity). Under the SRECNA's all-inclusive format, restricted contributions (other than capital contributions) and restricted investment income are reported together with unrestricted contributions and unrestricted investment income in the nonoperating revenue section. Each organization must establish a policy that defines operating revenues and expenses based on these parameters and disclose that policy in the notes to the financial statements.

Capital contributions, contributions to term and permanent endowments, extraordinary items, special items, and transfers are reported separately below nonoperating revenues/expenses. The criteria for reporting extraordinary items are based on the criteria used by private sector entities. A "special item" is a significant transaction or other event that meets one (but not both) of the criteria for classification as an extraordinary item. Further, in order to be classified as a special item, the transaction must be within the control of management; similar transactions that are beyond the control of management may not be reported as special items.

At present, the presentation of discontinued operations is not explicitly addressed in Statement No. 34. GASB is expected to provide guidance on this topic during 2012 in connection with its technical agenda project on government combinations (see Section 35.3(o)(ii)).

(d) STATEMENT OF CHANGES IN NET ASSETS/EQUITY. Investor-owned health care entities prepare a statement of changes in equity in the same manner as other for-profit enterprises. Governmental HCOs do not utilize this particular statement, due to the all-inclusive nature of the SRECNA.

Not-for-profit health care entities prepare a statement of changes in net assets that reports all changes that have occurred during the reporting period within each category of net assets (unrestricted, temporarily restricted, permanently restricted). This includes contributions received that are subject to donor-imposed restrictions; investment returns (including unrealized gains and losses) that are restricted by donors or by law; and releases of donor-imposed restrictions. If another not-for-profit organization was acquired during the period, the statement of changes in net assets would report any inherent contribution received that increases temporarily or permanently restricted net assets. Required subtotals include the change in temporarily restricted net assets, the change in permanently restricted net assets, the change in unrestricted net assets (typically at a highly aggregated level rather than at the level of detail reported in the statement of operations), and the change in net assets for the entity as a whole.

This statement may be prepared on a stand-alone basis, or it may be combined with the statement of operations (in which case, the result is a "statement of operations and changes in net assets").

According to ASC 958-225, no expenses may be reported within the temporarily or permanently restricted categories of the statement of changes in net assets. However, reporting of losses within those categories is permissible.

(e) STATEMENT OF CASH FLOWS

(i) Private Sector Entities. For the most part, all private sector HCOs apply the same principles in preparing a cash flow statement (ASC 230-10, *Statement of Cash Flows*). Some differences between not-for-profit cash flow statements and investor-owned cash flow statements exist; these are highlighted next.

- As discussed in Section 35.3(b) of this chapter, some not-for-profit HCOs report cash and investments that are restricted or designated for long-term purposes in a noncurrent balance sheet caption called "assets whose use is limited." For cash flow reporting purposes, such amounts would not be included in "cash and cash equivalents."
- The reconciliation of cash flows from operations differs between investor-owned entities and not-for-profit entities. Not-for-profit entities reconcile net cash flows from operating activities to the "total change in net assets" reported in the statement of changes in net assets, while investor-owned entities reconcile to "net income (loss)."
- Because not-for-profit entities must reconcile cash flows from operations to change in total net assets (rather than to net income), the reconciliation will involve certain items that are not dealt with in cash flow statements prepared for investor-owned companies.
  - Additional adjustments will be required for noncash transactions, such as unrealized gains and losses on certain investments, investment returns restricted by donor or law, undistributed portions of changes in interest in financially interrelated foundations, and the effective portion of fair value changes of cash flow hedging derivatives.
  - Equity transfers (i.e., transfers of cash between related not-for-profit HCOs) will be adjusted out of operating cash flows and "transferred" to the financing category.
  - Receipts from contributions and investment income that by donor stipulation are restricted for the purposes of acquiring, constructing, or improving property, plant, equipment, or other long-lived assets or establishing or increasing a permanent endowment or term endowment—a transaction that is unique to not-for-profit organizations—will need to be adjusted out of operating cash flows and "transferred" to the financing category

(ii) Governmental Entities. Governmental providers follow the guidance in GASB Statement No. 9, *Reporting Cash Flows of Proprietary and Nonexpendable Trust Funds and Governmental Entities That Use Proprietary Fund Accounting,* in preparing their statement of cash flows. That statement's requirements differ from FASB's requirements in these ways:

- The direct method of presenting operating cash flows must be used, with a reconciliation provided of operating cash flows to operating income (loss).
- The GASB cash flow statement has four categories: operating, investing, capital financing, and noncapital financing. The capital financing category is used for acquiring and disposing of capital assets, borrowing money for acquiring capital assets, and repaying the amounts borrowed. All other financing is classified as noncapital.
- Some transactions are classified differently by the GASB than they are by the FASB. For example, fixed assets are classified as capital financing activities under GASB Statement No. 9 but are considered to be investing activities under the FASB guidance.
- GASB Statement No. 9, par. 8 provides that a statement of cash flows should explain the change in *all* cash and cash equivalents, regardless of any restrictions on their use. Not-for-profit organizations, however, must exclude any cash classified as noncurrent (e.g., cash included in the noncurrent "assets whose use is limited" caption) from cash and cash equivalents.

Additional information on governmental cash flow reporting requirements is provided in Chapter 33 of this *Handbook.*

(f) SEGMENT REPORTING. Segment reporting requirements vary widely within the health care industry. Not-for-profit HCOs are not required to report information by segments and, thus, do not apply the guidance in ASC 280, *Segment Reporting,* that is applied by investor-owned HCOs.

GASB's definition of *segment* differs from the private sector definition; GASB's focus is on ensuring the availability of information about activities financed by revenue-backed debt. Under GASB, a *segment* is an identifiable activity (or grouping of activities) reported as or within an enterprise fund or a stand-alone entity that has a revenue stream pledged in support of bonds or other debt instruments, *and* an external party requires that activity's revenues, expenses, gains and losses, assets, and liabilities to be accounted for separately. Segment disclosures are not required if: (a) the activity is not financed with revenue-backed debt; (b) the requirement to report separately is not imposed by an external party; or (c) separate reporting is required for only a portion of the activity's transactions (e.g., only the revenues and expenses).

(g) ISSUANCE OF FINANCIAL STATEMENTS

(i) Nongovernmental Entities. ASC 855, *Subsequent Events,* prescribes the date of issuance for financial statements (and, thus, the date through which management must evaluate subsequent events). The guidance in ASC 855 differs based on whether an organization is an SEC registrant, a conduit municipal bond obligor whose bonds trade in public markets, or a private company that is not distributing information to investors.

Many not-for-profit HCOs are conduit bond obligors whose securities are traded in public markets (see Section 35.3(l)). Thus, they are presumed to be widely distributing information to investors and, like SEC registrants, are considered to have issued statements as of the date the first wide distribution occurs. Often that will be the date that the financial statements are filed electronically with the MSRB's EMMA repository (see Subsection 35.6(a)(iii)). Conduit bond obligors that do not have publicly traded debt (i.e., those whose bonds are privately placed) are not subject to these requirements; instead, they use an "available to be issued" issuance date, as is required for other private companies.

(ii) Governmental Entities. The GAAP guidance related to management's evaluation of events occurring after the balance sheet date but before issuance of the financial statements is set forth in GAS Statement No. 56, *Codification of Accounting and Financial Reporting Requirements Contained in the AICPA Statements on Auditing Standards.* Subsequent events are defined similarly to ASC 855; however, there is no requirement to disclose the date through which subsequent events have been evaluated and no specification of a financial statement "issuance date" through which subsequent events must be evaluated.

35.6 STATUTORY/REGULATORY REPORTING ISSUES

(a) SEC'S ROLE AND AUTHORITY IN THE MUNICIPAL SECURITIES MARKET. Many not-for-profit and governmental HCOs finance their capital needs through the issuance of tax-exempt or taxable municipal bonds. Certain types of governmental entities can issue municipal bonds directly. Other governmental entities (and all not-for-profit entities) utilize conduit municipal bond financings. In a conduit financing, the bonds are issued by a governmental financing agency, which then loans the proceeds to the health care entity. Although technically the health care entity is a "borrower" and not an "issuer" in conduit financings, for ease of reference, the term *issuer* is used generically throughout the remainder of this section in discussing the SEC rules that pertain to issuers and conduit borrowers alike.

The SEC does not possess regulatory authority over municipal bond issuers. Instead, it derives its powers over the municipal market by virtue of its ability to regulate municipal broker-dealers. Tax-exempt bond issuers generally are exempt from most provisions of the federal securities laws (i.e., they are not required to file Form 10Ks or register their securities like registered companies) but are not exempt from the sections that prohibit misleading statements or omitting material facts from the disclosure made in primary offering documents (official statements) and continuing disclosure documents. Those antifraud provisions apply to a municipal issuer whenever it releases information to the public that is reasonably expected to reach investors and the trading markets. Whenever an issuer releases an official statement, files other information pursuant to a Rule 15c2-12 contract, or otherwise speaks to investors, the antifraud provisions come into play. (Rule 15c2-12 is discussed in Subsection 35.6(a)(ii)).

The fact that an investor may decide whether to buy an issuer's bonds based on the disclosure provided by that issuer is at the heart of federal securities law and the antifraud provisions. When the courts apply the antifraud provisions, an omitted fact is material if there is a substantial likelihood that the disclosure of the omitted fact would have been viewed by reasonable investors as having significantly altered the total mix of information made available.

Material misstatements or omissions in official statements, annual reports, or material event reports may be the basis for claims of securities fraud under Rule 10b-5 of the Exchange Act (which applies to disclosures intended to influence markets) and other federal or state securities laws, or action by the SEC or private plaintiffs (bondholders or other investors), with substantial potential liability for issuers or other obligated persons. The SEC takes very seriously its obligation to protect investors in the municipal securities markets from fraud. As discussed next, there are numerous instances in which the SEC's enforcement division has taken action with respect to municipal bond issues for which disclosure documents contained material misstatements or omissions of material facts. The latter includes knowingly filing disclosure information that is stale and misleading (i.e., disclosure that is no longer representative of an entity's financial condition due to financial deterioration).

(i) Administration and Enforcement Structure. The Office of Municipal Securities (OMS) is the focal point within the SEC for all matters related to municipal securities. It coordinates all activity related to Rule 15c2-12 and the 1994 Interpretive Release (discussed at Subsection 35.6(b)(ii)), advises the commission on policy matters relating to the municipal bond market, and provides technical assistance in the development and implementation of major SEC initiatives in the municipal securities area. In addition, OMS assists the Division of Enforcement and other SEC offices and divisions on a wide array of municipal securities matters. OMS works closely with municipal securities industry participants to educate them about risk management issues and foster a thorough understanding of the commission's policies. OMS maintains a Web page of helpful information specifically directed to municipal securities issues and conduit obligors (*www.sec.gov/info/municipal.shtml*).

The SEC's Division of Enforcement maintains a specialized enforcement unit that focuses on municipal securities and public pensions. The municipal securities unit has significant resources at its disposal, including a staff of attorneys charged solely with investigating and trying municipal and public pension fund cases, along with significant technology and administrative support. A compendium of enforcement proceedings against municipal issuers over the past several decades can be found on the SEC's Web site at *www.sec.gov/info/municipal/mbonds/omstoc.shtml*.

The SEC and the IRS have entered into a memorandum of understanding (MOU) in which they agreed to work more closely to monitor and regulate the municipal bond market. The IRS has the power to revoke tax exemption of bonds if they are used to commit fraud or generate arbitrage. The MOU reflects the commitment both agencies have in using all means possible to ensure the municipal bond market operates in accordance with all the laws that govern it. The two agencies pledged to work cooperatively to identify issues and trends related to tax-exempt bonds in the municipal securities industry and to develop strategies to enhance performance of their respective regulatory responsibilities and will also share information as appropriate regarding market risks, practices, and events related to municipal securities, among other things.

(ii) Disclosure Requirements for Municipal Issuers

SEC Rule 15c2-12. The securities law requirements pertaining to municipal securities are set forth in SEC Rule 15c2-12, *Municipal Securities Disclosure.* Under Rule 15c2-12, issuers have a duty to make disclosures about new bonds at the time of issuance (through the official statement). Further, most issuers must agree to provide certain financial information and operating data each year thereafter and to provide notices of the occurrence of certain significant events for as long as the bonds remain outstanding.

The SEC does not have the ability to regulate the form or content of these disclosure filings (i.e., there is nothing comparable to Regulation S-X for the municipal market). However, in 1994 the SEC published its views with respect to the disclosure obligations of participants in the municipal securities markets in an Interpretive Release, *Statement of the Commission Regarding Disclosure Obligations of Municipal Securities Issuers and Others* (Securities Act Release No. 7049, Exchange Act Release No. 33741, March 9, 1994). The Interpretive Release complements Rule 15c2-12 by providing the SEC's views pertaining to disclosure both at the time of the initial offering and on an ongoing basis. Commission staff view the Interpretive Release as essential reading for all municipal market participants in understanding their responsibilities under the federal securities laws. An updated version of the Interpretive Release is expected to be issued in 2012. Additionally, the SEC makes its views known through routine communications, speeches, and enforcement actions.

Disclosure at the Time of Issuance. An *official statement* is a document prepared by or on behalf of an issuer in connection with a new issue of municipal securities that describes the essential terms of the bonds. Generally, it will be the most comprehensive source for information on the specific terms of a particular bond issue. In some respects, the official statement is analogous to the prospectus for a corporate equity or debt offering. As indicated earlier, in contrast to a prospectus in the corporate securities market. There are no regulatory requirements regarding the contents of an official statement. Rule 15c2-12 requires, for most offerings of municipal securities, that an underwriter receive and review an official statement that contains: information concerning the terms of the proposed issue; financial information or operating data about the issuer or other relevant parties; and a description of the undertaking to provide continuing disclosures in connection with the securities.

In general, an official statement will provide a description of the terms of the bonds, including such features as:

- The interest rate (or, if the interest rate is variable, the manner in which it is determined)
- The timing and manner of payment of the interest on and the principal of the bonds
- The minimum denomination in which the bonds may be sold
- Whether the bonds can be redeemed by the issuer prior to maturity and, if so, on what terms
- Whether the investor has the right to require the issuer to repurchase the bonds at their face value
- The sources from which the issuer has promised to make payment on the bonds
- Whether any bond insurance, letter of credit, or other guarantees have been provided for repayment
- The consequences of a payment or nonpayment default by the issuer

In addition, financial and/or operating data regarding the issuer of the securities or any other parties who are principally responsible for repayment of the bonds is generally provided, together with descriptions of any covenants undertaken by the issuer or such other party intended to protect the investor's financial interests. The official statement also typically includes summaries of the material terms of the principal legal documents binding the issuer with respect to the bonds as well as a copy of the legal opinion of bond counsel relating to the legality of the issue and tax treatment of the bonds for federal income tax purposes.

The issuer of the securities is ultimately responsible for the contents of the official statement, although the issuer is often assisted by the underwriter, financial advisor, and legal counsel in the preparation of the document. The underwriter is responsible for reviewing the official statement in connection with a new issue.

Copies of official statements for most bond offerings since 1990 are available on EMMA (see Subsection 35.6(a)(iii)).

Disclosure Subsequent to Issuance. Potential investors in a new securities offering have a wealth of financial and operational data available through the official statement. Subsequent to sale of the new issue, it is equally important for existing and prospective investors to have access to ongoing financial and operating information about the issuer so that they can make informed decisions about whether to hold, sell, or buy that security. In 1994, the SEC amended Rule 15c2-12 to require, as a condition of issuance of debt securities, that the issuer agree to implement a system of continuing disclosure that remains in effect as long as the bonds are outstanding. (A copy of the SEC release concerning this amendment to SEC Rule 15c2-12 can be accessed at *www.sec.gov/rules/final/adpt6.txt*.)

At the core of this system is the continuing disclosure agreement (sometimes referred to as a 15c2-12 agreement). This is a covenant under which the issuer agrees to provide certain specified information to bondholders and beneficial owners throughout the life of the bond issue. The terms of the issuer's continuing disclosure agreement are spelled out in the indenture or bond resolution and also are summarized in the official statement.

The continuing disclosure required of municipal issuers is much less prescriptive than the system of periodic reporting required of publicly traded companies. The primary elements are (1) annual reporting of financial and operating information and (2) reporting of significant events. Quarterly reporting is encouraged but not required (unless agreed to in the continuing disclosure covenant for a particular issue, as is often the case in health care offerings). All continuing disclosure information must be filed with the EMMA system (see Subsection 35.6(a)(iii)).

Annual Financial Information. There is no prescribed reporting format (similar to the 10-K) for submission of the annual financial and operating information. The specific list of items to be included in the annual report will be agreed on by the parties to the financing transaction and enumerated in the continuing disclosure agreement and in an appendix to the official statement. The financial information and operating data to be provided will mirror the financial information and operating data that appeared in the official statement. For example, if anticipated cash flow information was provided in the official statement, cash flow data reflecting actual operations must be provided on an annual basis throughout the life of the bond issue.

There is no statutory due date for the filing of annual financial information, as there is with 10-K filings. Instead, the filing deadline is contractually agreed to in the continuing disclosure agreement. The SEC strongly recommends that the information be made available within six months after the close of the issuer's fiscal year, but this is not mandated, and the reporting date may be any time within one year. If an issuer fails to file information by the agreed-on deadline and subsequently issues an official statement for new bonds, it must disclose its failure to file in that official statement. Failure to disclose this information constitutes a material omission in the official statement.

The annual report does not have to be submitted all at once, in a single document; it may be submitted as a single document or as separate documents comprising a package.

Significant Events Reporting. In addition to receiving regularly scheduled periodic information, such as audited financial statements, investors need timely disclosure of events that occur in the interim that materially reflect on the creditworthiness of municipal securities issuers or on the terms of their securities. Thus, the continuing disclosure agreement also requires the issuer to file disclosures related to significant events (similar to 8-K filings) within 10 days of their occurrence. Events that must be disclosed are described next.

REPORTABLE EVENTS NOT SUBJECT TO MATERIALITY THRESHOLD

Principal and interest payment delinquencies

Unscheduled draws on debt service reserves reflecting financial difficulties

Unscheduled draws on credit enhancements reflecting financial difficulties

Substitution of credit or liquidity providers, or their failure to perform

Adverse tax opinions or events affecting the tax-exempt status of the security (including issuance by the IRS of proposed and final decisions about whether the bond can be taxed)

Defeasances

Rating changes

Tender offers

Bankruptcy, insolvency, receivership or similar event

Notices of failures to provide annual financial information on or before the date specified in the written agreement

REPORTABLE EVENTS SUBJECT TO A MATERIALITY THRESHOLD

Appointment of successor/additional trustee or the change of name of a trustee

Modifications to rights of security holders

Optional or unscheduled bond calls

Matters affecting collateral (i.e., release, substitution, or sale of property securing repayment of the securities)

Consummation of merger, consolidation, or acquisition involving an obligated person or the sale of substantially all of the assets of an obligated person, other than in the ordinary course of business, the entry into definitive agreement to undertake such an action, or the termination of a definitive agreement relating to any such action, other than pursuant to its terms

As noted, for certain of these events, disclosure must be made regardless of whether the issuer considers the event to be "material." For others, event disclosure is required only if the specified event is deemed by the issuer to be material. While there have been numerous definitions of *materiality* and much discussion of how the term relates to municipal issuers, the most common definitions center on any information that a reasonable investor might consider significant in an investment decision. It does not have to be an event that all investors would consider significant. In many cases, common sense is the best guide to the definition of *materiality*. The rule clearly leaves to municipal issuers the responsibility to determine materiality, although of course there may be consequences if their determination is later questioned.

(iii) EMMA System. Rule 15c2-12 requires all continuing disclosure information to be filed with the Electronic Municipal Market Access system operated by the Municipal Securities Rulemaking Board (MSRB). EMMA is an Internet-based centralized database (*www.emma.msrb.org*) that provides free public access to disclosure and transaction information about municipal bond issues. From a single Web page, users are able to access the original offering document, continuing disclosure information, real-time pricing information, and any advance refunding documents associated with a particular bond issue. EMMA also permits users to sign up for free alerts as new disclosure documents are filed for a particular bond issue.

All information filed with EMMA must be in an electronic (PDF) format that is word-searchable (i.e., preferably native PDF or PDF normal files). Filings are made through secure, password-protected accounts. The registration and continuing disclosure submission process is described in the *EMMA Dataport Manual for Continuing Disclosure Submissions*. The disclosure submission process used by underwriters for primary offering documents is described in a similar manual. Issuers can choose between two submission methods: (1) an Internet-based upload to the EMMA Web site or (2) for high-volume filers, a direct computer-to-computer connection to the MRSB.

(iv) Proposed Reforms. At present, neither the SEC nor any other federal regulator has the authority to regulate the type, quality, and timeliness of disclosure investors receive related to municipal securities. However, that could change in light of recent actions taken by both the SEC and Congress.

SEC officials have often stated that investors who buy municipal securities should have access to the same quality and quantity of information as those who buy equity securities. They also have stated that for issuers, access to the public market comes with certain obligations and responsibilities. During 2010, the SEC launched a nationwide inquiry into the municipal market. As part of that inquiry, public hearings were held in 2010 and 2011 to solicit input and gather information for a report that will recommend specific statutory and regulatory changes in the SEC's authority to regulate the municipal market. The SEC's report is expected to be issued in 2012.

Congress is also independently considering the need for reform of the market. The Dodd-Frank Wall Street Reform and Consumer Protection Act requires the Government Accounting Office (GAO) to: (1) complete a study that compares the amount, frequency, and quality of disclosures provided by issuers of municipal securities with the amount and frequency of disclosures provided by SEC registrants (taking into account the differences between those types of entities); (2) evaluate the costs and benefits of requiring issuers of municipal bonds to provide additional financial disclosures for the benefit of investors; and (3) make recommendations relating to disclosure requirements for municipal issuers, including consideration of expanding the SEC's statutory authority. The GAO's report must be submitted to Congress by mid-2012.

(b) NATIONAL ASSOCIATION OF INSURANCE COMMISSIONERS

(i) Statutory Financial Statements of Health Plans. Most health plans that provide insurance coverage and bear financial risk are regulated by their states. Generally speaking, regulated insurers are required annually submit to the state a set of audited financial statements that are prepared using that state's prescribed or permitted statutory accounting practices.

The National Association of Insurance Commissioners (NAIC) is the U.S. standard-setting and regulatory support organization created and governed by the chief insurance regulators from the 50 states, the District of Columbia, and U.S. territories. Among other things, the NAIC is responsible for creating the statutory accounting principles on which statutory financial reporting is based. These Statements of Statutory Accounting Principles (SSAPs) are the highest level of requirements used in preparing statutory financial statements. They are codified in the NAIC's *Accounting Practices and Procedures Manual.* An updated version of the manual is issued each year reflecting revisions or additions to SSAPs and interpretations of SSAPs. States generally require health plans to comply with the manual's provisions in preparing their statutory financial statements; however, state laws, regulations, and administrative rules that differ from the guidance provided in the manual preempt the guidance in the manual.

Various SSAPs issues that specifically address issues related to regulated health plans include:

- SSAP No. 25, *Accounting for and Disclosures about Transactions with Affiliates and Other Related Parties*
- SSAP No. 35, *Guaranty Fund and Other Assessments*
- SSAP No. 47, *Uninsured Plans*
- SSAP No. 50, *Classifications and Definitions of Insurance or Managed Care Contracts in Force*
- SSAP No. 54, *Individual and Group Accident and Health Contracts*
- SSAP No. 55, *Unpaid Claims, Losses and Loss Adjustment Expenses*
- SSAP No. 66, *Retrospectively Rated Contracts*
- SSAP No. 73, *Health Care Delivery Assets—Supplies, Pharmaceuticals and Surgical Supplies, Durable Medical Equipment, Furniture, Medical Equipment and Fixtures, and Leasehold Improvements in Health Care Facilities*
- SSAP No. 84, *Health Care Receivables and Receivables Under Government Insured Plans*
- SSAP No. 85, *Claim Adjustment Expenses* (amends SSAP No. 55)
- SSAP No. 87, *Capitalization Policy* (amends SSAP No. 73, among others)
- SSAP No. 96, *Settlement Requirements for Intercompany Transactions* (amends SSAP No. 25)

While these standards are particularly relevant to health plans, all other SSAPs must be considered that are appropriate to the particular health plan.

(ii) Risk-Based Capital Requirements. State laws generally require insurers to maintain minimum levels of capital or surplus. The risk-based capital (RBC) formula is one of the tools used by regulators to evaluate the financial health of regulated entities, including health plans. A separate RBC formula exists for each of the primary insurance types: life, property/casualty, and health. The RBC formula generally consists of these principal risk elements: affiliated investment risk, asset risk, underwriting risk, credit risk, and general business risk. Based on the outcome of the RBC formula, a health plan may be classified into one of four regulatory action levels. In order of increasingly stringent level of regulatory response, these are: company action level, regulatory action level, authorized control level, and mandatory control level. At a minimum, the company action-level event requires the filing of an RBC plan that details conditions leading to the event and proposals of corrective action with the state insurance commissioner. State laws vary regarding compliance with the RBC formula and required actions to be taken by the health plan. Additional information can be found on the NAIC Web site at *www.naic.org*.

(c) OFFICE OF MANAGEMENT AND BUDGET CIRCULAR A-133. Health care entities that receive federal awards from a government agency may be subject to audits in accordance with the Single Audit Act Amendments of 1996 and Office of Management and Budget (OMB) Circular A-133, *Audits of Institutions of Higher Education and Other Nonprofit Organizations.* Federal awards may take the form of grants, contracts, loans, loan guarantees, property, cooperative agreements, interest subsidies, and insurance or direct appropriations. Medicare payments to a nonfederal entity for providing patient care services to Medicare beneficiaries are not considered federal awards under OMB Circular A-133. Medicaid payments to a subrecipient for providing patient care services to Medicaid-eligible individuals are not considered federal awards under OMB Circular A-133, unless a state requires the funds to be treated as expended federal awards because reimbursement is on a cost-reimbursement basis.

35.7 SOURCES AND SUGGESTED REFERENCES

American Institute of Certified Public Accountants. *Health Care Entities: Industry Audit and Accounting Guide.* New York: Author, 2001.

______. *Checklists and Illustrative Financial Statements for Health Care Organizations*. New York: Author, 2011.

______. *Health Care Entities* (Section 6400). *Technical Practice Aids*. New York: Author, 2011.

Healthcare Financial Management Association. *www.hfma.org*

CHAPTER 36

REGULATED UTILITIES

Darin W. Kempke, CPA

KPMG Partner, Power and Utility Audit Sector Leader

36.1 NATURE AND CHARACTERISTICS OF REGULATED UTILITIES 2

(a) Introduction to Regulated Utilities 2
(b) Descriptive Characteristics of Utilities 3

36.2 HISTORY OF REGULATION 4

(a) *Munn v. Illinois* 4
(b) *Chicago, Milwaukee & St. Paul Railroad Co. v. Minnesota ex rel. Railroad & Warehouse Comm* 4
(c) *Smyth v. Ames* 4

36.3 REGULATORY COMMISSION JURISDICTIONS 5

(a) Federal Regulatory Commissions 5
(b) State Regulatory Commissions 6

36.4 TRADITIONAL RATE-MAKING PROCESS 6

(a) How Commissions Set Rates 6
(b) Rate-Making Formula 6
(c) Rate Base 7
(d) Rate Base Valuation 7
(i) Original Cost 7
(ii) Fair Value 8
(iii) Weighted Cost 8
(iv) Judicial Precedents—Rate Base 8
(e) Rate of Return and Judicial Precedents 8
(f) Operating Income 9
(g) Alternative Forms of Regulation 11
(i) Price Ceilings or Caps 11
(ii) Rate Moratoriums 12
(iii) Sharing Formulas 12
(iv) Regulated Transition to Competition 12
(v) Revenue Decoupling 13
(vi) Non–Fuel Rate Trackers/Riders 13
(vii) Formula Rates 14

36.5 INTERRELATIONSHIP OF REGULATORY REPORTING AND FINANCIAL REPORTING 14

(a) Accounting Authority of Regulatory Agencies 14
(b) Securities and Exchange Commission and Financial Accounting Standards Board 15
(c) Relationship Between Rate Regulation and Generally Accepted Accounting Principles 15
(i) Historical Perspective 15
(ii) Addendum to Accounting Principles Board Opinion No. 2 16

36.6 ACCOUNTING STANDARDS CODIFICATION 980, *REGULATED OPERATIONS* 16

(a) Scope of ASC Topic 980 16

Along with key members of the KPMG power and utility team: Robert Bergbauer (advisory partner and regulatory leader), Steve Rathjen (audit partner), Tim McCann (audit partner), Kevin Hughes (audit partner),Chet Williams (audit partner), Rod Andersen (tax partner and federal tax leader). John Lathrop (audit partner), Jason Harris (audit partner) David Ellerbeck (audit partner), Scott Heiser (audit senior manager), Michael Kraehnke (partner, department of professional practice), Yunyoung Shin (senior manager, department of professional practice), and John Kunasek (advisory partner and KPMG power and utilities overall industry leader).

Mr. Kempke also wishes to acknowledge the work completed on previous versions of this chapter by Benjamin A. McKnight III, Alan D. Felsenthal, and Robert W. Hriszko, all formerly of Arthur Andersen LLP.

(b) Amendments to Accounting for Regulated Operations 17
(c) Overview of Accounting for Regulated Operations 17
(d) General Standards 18
  (i) Regulatory Assets 18
  (ii) Regulatory Liabilities 18
(e) Specific Standards 19
  (i) Allowance for Funds Used During Construction 19
  (ii) Intercompany Profit 20
  (iii) Accounting for Income Taxes 20
  (iv) Refunds 20
  (v) Deferred Costs Not Earning a Return 20
  (vi) Examples of Application 20

36.7 ASC TOPIC 980-360-35, *COST DISALLOWANCES* 21

(a) Significant Provisions 21
  (i) Accounting for Cost Disallowances of Newly Completed Plant 21
  (ii) Accounting for Plant Abandonments 21
  (iii) Income Statement Presentation 21

36.8 ASC TOPIC 980-340, *OTHER ASSETS AND DEFERRED COSTS* 22

(a) Significant Provisions 22
  (i) Accounting for Phase-in Plans 22
  (ii) Financial Statement Classification 23
  (iii) Allowance for Funds Used During Construction 23
  (iv) Interrelationship of Phase-in Plans and Disallowances 23
  (v) Financial Statement Disclosure 23

36.9 DISCONTINUATION OF RATE-REGULATED ACCOUNTING: ASC TOPIC 980-20 24

(a) Factors Leading to Discontinuing Application of ASC Topic 980 24
(b) Regulatory Assets and Liabilities 25
(c) Plant, Equipment, and Inventory 25
(d) Regulatory Assets 25
(e) Income Taxes 26
(f) Investment Tax Credits 27
(g) Income Statement Presentation 27
(h) Reapplication of ASC 980 27

36.10 OTHER SPECIALIZED UTILITY ACCOUNTING PRACTICES 27

(a) Utility Income Taxes and Income Tax Credits 27
  (i) Interperiod Income Tax Allocation 27
  (ii) Flow-Through 28
  (iii) Provisions of the Internal Revenue Code 30
  (iv) Concept of Tax Incentives 30
  (v) Tax Legislation 31
  (vi) ASC Topic 740, Accounting for Income Taxes 32
  (vii) Investment Tax Credit 34
(b) Revenue Recognition—Alternative Programs 35
(c) Accounting for Postretirement Benefits Other Than Pensions 37
(d) Other Financial Statement Disclosures 38
  (i) Purchase Power Contracts 38
  (ii) Financing Through Construction Intermediaries 38
  (iii) Jointly Owned Plants 39
  (iv) Decommissioning Costs and Nuclear Fuel 39
  (v) Securitization of Stranded Costs, Including Regulatory Assets 40
  (vi) Expanded Footnote Disclosure 41
(e) Other Current Utility Topics 42

36.11 SOURCES AND SUGGESTED REFERENCES 43

Note: For clarity purposes, the GAAP references (SFAS, APB, etc.) in the chapter have been included along with the new GAAP references (ASC Topics) under the FASB Codification project, which concluded in 2010.

36.1 NATURE AND CHARACTERISTICS OF REGULATED UTILITIES

(a) INTRODUCTION TO REGULATED UTILITIES. Many types of business have their rates for providing services set by the government or other regulatory bodies; consider utilities, insurance companies, transportation companies, hospitals, and shippers. The enterprises addressed in this chapter are limited to electric, gas, telephone, and water (and sewer) utilities that are primarily regulated on an individual cost-of-service basis. Effective business and financial involvement with the utility industry requires an understanding of what a utility is, the regulatory compact under which all utilities operate, and the interrelationship between the rate decisions of regulators and the resultant accounting effects.

(b) DESCRIPTIVE CHARACTERISTICS OF UTILITIES. Regulated utilities are similar to other businesses in that there is a need for capital and, for private sector utilities, a demand for investor profit. Utilities are different in that they are dedicated to public use—they are obligated to furnish customers service on demand—and the services are considered to be necessities. Many utilities operate under monopolistic conditions. A regulator sets their prices and grants an exclusive service area or franchise territory, which usually serves a relatively large number of customers. Consequently, a high level of public interest typically exists regarding the utility's rates and quality of service.

Only a utility that has a monopoly of supply of service can operate at maximum economy and, therefore, provide service at the lowest cost. Although portions of utilities (electric generation, transmission, and providers as well as natural gas transportation and providers) have been deregulated in numerous jurisdictions, distribution continues to be regulated under a monopoly. Duplicate plant facilities would result in higher costs. This is particularly true because of the capital-intensive nature of utility operations (i.e., a large capital investment is required for each dollar of revenue).

Because there is an absence of free market competitive forces such as those found in most business enterprises, regulation is a substitute for these missing competitive forces. The goal of regulation is to provide a balance between investor and consumer interests by substituting regulatory principles for competition. This means regulation is designed to:

- Provide consumers with adequate service at the lowest price
- Provide the utility the opportunity, but not a guarantee, to earn an adequate return so that it can attract new capital for development and expansion of plant to meet customer demand
- Prevent unreasonable prices and excessive earnings
- Prevent unjust or undue discrimination among customers, commodities, and locations
- Insure public safety

To meet the goals of regulation, regulated activities of utilities typically include these six areas:

1. Service area
2. Rates
3. Accounting and reporting
4. Issuance of debt and equity securities
5. Construction, sale, lease, purchase, and exchange of operating facilities
6. Standards of service and operation

This chapter covers the historical development of regulated utilities as monopoly service providers and the regulation of their rates as a substitute for competition. Although in many jurisdictions the historical practices of regulation continue, regulated utilities are increasingly operating in a deregulated, competitive environment. Certain industry segments have been more affected than others by the judicial, legislative, and regulatory actions, as well as technological changes, that have produced this shift. These industry segments include long-distance telecommunications services, natural gas production and transmission, and electric generation. The shift has had a dramatic effect on the operations of utilities and the related accounting. (See Section 36.6.) Continued unbundling of costs and revenues for utilities and deregulation of portions of the business provide both opportunities and risks to utilities.

36.2 HISTORY OF REGULATION

Some knowledge of the history of regulation is essential in order to understand utilities. Companies that are now regulated utilities find themselves in that position because of a long sequence of political events, legislative acts, and judicial interpretations.

Rate regulation of privately owned business was not an accepted practice during the early history of the United States. This concept has evolved because important legal precedents have established not only the right of government to regulate but also the process that government bodies must follow to set fair rates for services. The background and the facts of *Munn v. Illinois* [94 U.S. 113 (1877)] are significant and basic to the development of rate making since the case established a U.S. legal precedent for the right of government to regulate and set rates in cases of public interest and necessity.

(a) *MUNN V. ILLINOIS.* In 1871, the Illinois State Legislature passed a law that prescribed the maximum rates for grain storage and that required licensing and bonding to ensure performance of the duties of a public warehouse. The law reflected the popular sentiment of midwestern farmers at that time against what they felt was a pricing monopoly by railroads and elevators. Munn and his partner, Scott, owned a grain warehouse in Chicago. They filed a suit maintaining that they operated a private business and that the law deprived them of their property without due process.

The case ultimately reached the U.S. Supreme Court. The Court decided that, when private property becomes "clothed with a public interest," the owner of the property has, in effect, granted the public an interest in that use and "must submit to be controlled by the public for the common good." The Court was impressed by Munn and Scott's monopolistic position while furnishing a service practically indispensable to the public.

From the precedent of *Munn,* railroads, a water company, a grist mill, stockyards, and finally gas, electric, and phone companies were brought under public regulation. Thus, when utilities finally came into existence in the twentieth century, the framework for regulation already was in place and did not have to be decided by the courts. When state legislatures began to set up utility commissions, it was the *Munn* decision that established beyond question their right to do so.

(b) *CHICAGO, MILWAUKEE & ST. PAUL RAILROAD CO. V. MINNESOTA EX REL. RAILROAD & WAREHOUSE COMM.* A second important case that began to establish the principle of "due process" in rate making is *Chicago, Milwaukee & St. Paul Railroad Co. v. Minnesota ex rel. Railroad & Warehouse Comm.* [134 U.S. 418 (1890)]. In this case, the courts first began to address the issue of standards of reasonableness in regulation. The U.S. Supreme Court decided that a Minnesota law was unconstitutional because it established rate regulation but did not permit a judicial review to test the reasonableness of the rates. The Court found that the state law violated the due process provisions of the Fourteenth Amendment because the utility was deprived of the power to charge reasonable rates for the use of its property, and if the utility was denied judicial review, then the company would be deprived of the lawful use of its property and, ultimately, the property itself.

(c) *SMYTH V. AMES.* A third important case, *Smyth v. Ames* [169 U.S. 466 (1898)], established the precedent for the concept of "fair return upon the fair value of property." It should be noted that *fair value* in this context is not in reference to accounting definitions of fair value under Accounting Standards Codification (ASC) Topic 820 and that there is no current remeasurement of fair value at a later period in U.S. regulation. During the 1880s, the State of Nebraska passed a law that reduced the maximum freight rates that railroads could charge. The railroads' stockholders brought a successful suit that prevented the application of the lowered rates. The state appealed the case to the U.S. Supreme Court, which unanimously ruled that the rates were unconstitutionally low by any standard of reasonableness.

In its case, the state maintained that the adequacy of the rates should be tested by reference to the present value, or reproduction cost, of the assets. This position was attractive to the state because the current price level had been declining. The railroad was built during the Civil War, a period that was marked by a high price level and substantial inflation, and the railroad believed that its past costs merited recognition in a "test of reasonableness."

In reaching its decision, the Court began the formulation of the "fair value" doctrine, which prescribed a test of the reasonableness and constitutionality of regulated rates. The Supreme Court's opinion held that a privately owned business was entitled to rates that would cover reasonable operating expenses plus a fair return on the fair value of the property used for the convenience of the public.

The *Smyth v. Ames* decision also established several rate-making terms still in use today. This was the first attempt by the courts to define rate-making principles. These four terms include:

1. *Original cost of construction*—The cost to acquire utility property
2. *Fair return*—The amount that should be earned on the investment in utility property
3. *Fair value*—The amount on which the return should be based
4. *Operating expenses*—The cost to deliver utility services to the public

Each of these three landmark cases, especially *Smyth v. Ames,* established the inability of the legislative branch to effectively establish equitable rates. They also demonstrated that the use of the judicial branch is an inefficient means of accomplishing the same goal. In *Smyth v. Ames,* the U.S. Supreme Court, in essence, declared that the process could be more easily accomplished by a commission composed of persons with special skills and experience and the qualifications to resolve questions concerning utility regulation.

36.3 REGULATORY COMMISSION JURISDICTIONS

A view of the overlays of regulatory commissions is helpful in understanding their unique position and responsibilities.

(a) FEDERAL REGULATORY COMMISSIONS. The interstate activities of public utilities are under the jurisdiction of several federal regulatory commissions. The members of all federal regulatory commissions are appointed by the executive branch and are confirmed by the legislative branch. The judicial branch can review and rule on decisions of each commission. This form of organization represents a blending of the functions of the three separate branches of government.

- The Federal Communications Commission (FCC), established in 1934 with the passage of the Communications Act, succeeded the Federal Radio Commission of 1927. At that time the FCC assumed regulation of interstate and foreign telephone and telegraph service from the Interstate Commerce Commission, which was the first federal regulatory commission (created in 1887). The FCC prescribes for communications companies a uniform system of accounts (USOA) and depreciation rates. It also states the principles and standard procedures used to separate property costs, revenues, expenses, taxes, and reserves between those applicable to interstate services under the jurisdiction of the FCC and those applicable to services under the jurisdiction of various state regulatory authorities. In addition, the FCC regulates the rate of return carriers may earn on their interstate business.
- The Federal Energy Regulatory Commission (FERC) was created as an agency of the cabinet-level Department of Energy in 1977. The FERC assumed many of the functions of the former Federal Power Commission (FPC), which was established in 1920. The FERC has jurisdiction over the transmission and sale at wholesale of electric energy in interstate commerce. The FERC also regulates the transmission and sale for resale of natural gas in interstate commerce and establishes rates and prescribes conditions of service for all utilities subject to its jurisdiction. The entities must follow the FERC's USOA and file with the FERC a Form 1 (electric) or Form 2 (gas) annual report.

- The Securities and Exchange Commission (SEC) was established in 1934 to administer the Securities Act of 1933 and the Securities Exchange Act of 1934. The powers of the SEC are restricted to security transactions and financial reporting and disclosures, not operating standards. The SEC also administered the Public Utility Holding Company Act of 1935 (the 1935 Act), which was passed because of financial and services abuses in the 1920s and the stock market crash and subsequent depression of 1929 to 1935. Under the 1935 Act, the SEC was given powers to regulate the accounting, financing, reporting, acquisitions, allocation of consolidated income taxes, and parent–subsidiary relationships of electric and gas utility holding companies. The Energy Policy Act of 2005 includes the repeal of the 1935 Act, which was effective on February 8, 2006, and eliminated significant federal restrictions on the scope, structure, and ownership of electric companies. However, the repeal is accompanied by the transfer of certain authority to the FERC and state regulatory commissions.

(b) STATE REGULATORY COMMISSIONS. All 50 states and the District of Columbia have established agencies to regulate rates. State commissioners are either appointed or elected, usually for a specified term. Although the degree of authority differs, they have authority over utility operations in intrastate commerce. Each state commission sets rate-making policies in accordance with its own state statutes and precedents. In addition, each state establishes its prescribed forms of reporting and systems of accounts for utilities. However, most systems of accounts at the state level are modifications of the federal USOAs.

36.4 TRADITIONAL RATE-MAKING PROCESS

(a) HOW COMMISSIONS SET RATES. The process for establishing rates probably constitutes the most significant difference between utilities and enterprises in general. Unlike an enterprise in general, where market forces and competition establish the price a company can charge for its products or services, rates for utilities generally are determined by a regulatory commission after much debate among regulators, the company and outside public interest groups (intervenors). The process of establishing rates is described as rate making. The administrative proceeding to establish utility rates is typically referred to as a rate case or base rate proceeding. Utility rates, once established, generally will not change without another rate case.

The establishment of a rate for a utility on an individual cost-of-service basis typically involves two steps. The first step is to determine a utility's general level of rates that will cover operating costs and provide an opportunity to earn a reasonable rate of return on the property dedicated to providing utility services. This process establishes the utility's required revenue (often referred to as the revenue requirement or cost of service). The second step is to design specific rates in order to eliminate discrimination and unfairness from affected classes of customers. The aggregate of the prices paid by all customers for all services provided should produce revenues equivalent to the revenue requirement.

(b) RATE-MAKING FORMULA. This first step of rate regulation, on an individual cost-of-service basis, is the determination of a utility's total revenue requirement, which can be expressed as a rate-making formula, which involves five areas:

$$\text{Rate Base} \times \text{Rate of Return} = \text{Return (Operating Income)}$$
$$\text{Return} + \text{Operating Expences} = \text{Required Revenue (Cost of Service)}$$

1. *Rate base.* The amount of investment in utility plant devoted to the rendering of utility service upon which a fair rate of return may be earned.
2. *Rate of return.* The rate determined by the regulatory agency to be applied to the rate base to provide a fair return to investors. It is usually a composite rate that reflects the carrying costs of debt, dividends on preferred stock, and a return provision on common equity.

3. *Return.* The rate base multiplied by rate of return.
4. *Operating expenses.* Merely the costs of operations and maintenance associated with rendering utility service. Operating expenses include:
   a. Depreciation and amortization expenses
   b. Production fuel and gas for resale
   c. Operations expenses
   d. Maintenance expenses
   e. Income taxes
   f. Taxes other than income taxes
5. *Required revenue.* The total amount that must be collected from customers in rates (often referred to as the utility's revenue requirement). The new rate structure should be designed to generate this amount of revenue on the basis of current or forecasted levels of usage.

(c) RATE BASE. A utility earns a return on its rate base. Each investor-supplied dollar is entitled to such a return until the dollar is remitted to the investor. Some of the items generally included in the rate base computation are utility property and plant in service, a working capital allowance, and, in certain jurisdictions or circumstances, plant under construction. Generally, nonutility property, abandoned plant, plant acquisition adjustments, and plant held for future use are excluded. Deductions from rate base typically include the reserve for depreciation, accumulated deferred income taxes (ADITs), which represent cost-free capital, certain unamortized deferred investment tax credits, and customer contributions in aid of construction including government grants related to plant. Exhibit 36.1 provides an example of the computations used to determine a rate base.

(d) RATE BASE VALUATION. Various methods are used in valuing rate base. These methods apply to the valuation of property and plant and include these three:

1. Original cost
2. Fair value
3. Weighted cost

(i) Original Cost. The original cost method, the most widely used method, corresponds to accounting principles generally accepted in the United States (GAAP), which require historical cost data for primary financial statement presentation. In addition, all regulatory commissions have adopted

Net Investment Rate Base

	In Millions
Plant in service	$350
Less reserve for depreciation	(100)
Net plant in service	250
Add:	
Working capital allowance	3
Construction work in progress	33
Deduct:	
Accumulated deferred income taxes	(14)
Advances in aid of construction/Grant	(2)
Net investment rate base	$270

Exhibit 36.1 Example of a Utility Rate Base Computation

the USOA, requiring original cost for reporting purposes. Original cost is defined in the FERC's USOA as "the cost of such property to the person first devoting it to public service." This method was originally adopted by various commissions during the 1930s, at which time inflation was not a major concern.

(ii) Fair Value. The fair value method is defined as not the cost of assets but rather what they are really worth at the time rates are established. Three methods of computing fair value are most often used:

1. *Trended cost.* Utilizes either general or specific cost indices to adjust original cost
2. *Reproduction cost new.* A calculation of the cost to reproduce existing plant facilities at current costs
3. *Market value.* Involves the appraisal of specific types of plant

(iii) Weighted Cost. The weighted cost method for valuation of property and plant is used in some jurisdictions as a compromise between the original cost and the fair value methods. Under this method, some weight is given to both original cost and fair value. Regulatory agencies in some weighted-cost jurisdictions use a 50/50 weighting of original cost and fair value, whereas others use 60/40 or other combinations.

(iv) Judicial Precedents—Rate Base. In a significant rate base case, *Federal Power Commission v. Hope Natural Gas Co.* [320 U.S. 591 (1944)], the original cost versus fair value controversy finally came to a head. A number of important points came out of this case, including the doctrine of the end result. The U.S. Supreme Court's decision did not approve original cost or fair value. Instead, it said a rate-making body can use any method, including no formula at all, so long as the end result is reasonable. It is not the theory but the impact of the theory that counts.

(e) RATE OF RETURN AND JUDICIAL PRECEDENTS. The rate of return is the rate determined by a regulator to be applied to the rate base to provide a fair return to investors. In the capital market, utilities must compete against nonregulated companies for investors' funds. Therefore, a fair rate of return to common equity investors is critical.

Different sources of capital with different costs are involved in establishing the allowed rate of return. Exhibits 36.2 and 36.3 show the computations used to determine the rate of return.

The cost of long-term debt and preferred stock is usually the "embedded" cost (i.e., long-term debt issues have a specified interest rate, whereas preferred stock has a specified dividend rate). Computing the cost of equity is more complicated because there is no stated interest or dividend rate. Several methods have been used as a guide in setting a return on common equity.

Cost of Capital and Rate of Return

	In Millions
Capitalization	
Stockholder's equity:	
Common stock ($8 par value, 5 million shares outstanding)	$ 40
Other paid-in capital	45
Retained earnings	55
Common stock equity	140
Long-term debt (6.75% average interest rate)	130
	$270

Exhibit 36.2 Example of a Utility Capitalization Structure

	In Millions	Capitalization Ratios	Annual Cost Rate	Weighted Cost
Long-term debt	$130	48%	6.75%	3.24%
Common stock equity	140	52	13.00	6.76
Cost of capital	$270	100%		10.00%

Exhibit 36.3 Computation of the Overall Rate Of Return

These methods reflect different approaches, such as earnings/price ratios, discounted cash flows, comparable earnings, and perceived investor risk.

The cost of each class of capital is weighed by the percentage that the class represents of the utility's total capitalization.

Two important cases provide the foundation for dealing with rate of return issues: *Bluefield Water Works & Improvement Co. v. West Virginia Public Service Comm.* [262 U.S. 679 (1923)] and the *Hope Gas* case. The important rate of return concepts that arise from these cases include these five concepts:

1. A company is entitled to, but not guaranteed, a return on the value of its property.
2. Return should be equal to that earned by other companies with comparable risks.
3. A utility is not entitled to a return such as that earned by a speculative venture.
4. The return should be reasonably sufficient to:
   a. Assure confidence and financial soundness of the utility.
   b. Maintain and support its credit.
   c. Enable the utility to raise additional capital.
5. Efficient and economical management is a prerequisite for profitable operations.

(f) OPERATING INCOME. Operating income for purposes of establishing rates is computed based on test-year information, which is normally a recent or projected 12-month period. In either case, historic or projected test-year revenues are calculated based on the current rate structure in order to determine if there is a revenue requirement deficiency. The operating expense information generally includes most expired costs incurred by a utility. As illustrated in Exhibit 36.4, the

Cost of Service Income Statement—Test Year (12 Months Ended 12/31/XX)	
	In Millions
Operating revenue	$310
Operating expenses	
Commercial	45
Maintenance	45
Traffic	49
General and administrative	61
Depreciation	60
General taxes	20
Income taxes	10
Total operating expenses	290
Operating income	$ 20

Exhibit 36.4 Example of a Utility Operating Income Computation

Rate-Making Formula and Revenue Requirement Calculation

(Rate of Return × Rate Base) + Operating Expenses = Revenue Requirement

Revenue Requirement Calculation:			In Millions
Test-Year Operating Revenues			$310
Test-Year Operating Expenses Other Than Income Taxes		$280	
Interest Expense Required ($270 × 3.24%)		9	
Equity Return Required ($270 × 6.76%)	$18		
Income Tax Conversion Factor (1–40% Tax Rate)	.6		
Equity Return and Income Taxes		30	
Revenue Requirement			319
Revenue Requirement Deficiency			$ 9

Exhibit 36.5 Example of the Revenue Requirement Computation Based on Exhibits 36.1 Through 36.4

operating expense information, after reflecting all necessary pro forma adjustments, determines operating income for rate-making purposes.

Above-the-line and *below-the-line* are frequently used expressions in public utility, financial, and regulatory circles. The above-the-line expenses on which operating income appears are those that ordinarily are directly included in the rate-making formula; below this line are the excluded expenses (and income). The principal cost that is charged below the line is interest on debt since it is included in the rate-making formula as a part of the rate-of-return computation and not as an operating expense. The inclusion or exclusion of a cost above the line is important to the utility since this determines whether it is directly includable in the rate-making formula as an operating expense.

A significant consideration in determining the revenue requirement is that the rate of return computed is the rate after income taxes (which are a part of operating expenses). In calculating the revenue required, the equity return component of operating income (the equity return) (equity rate of return times rate base) deficiency must be grossed up for income taxes. This is most easily accomplished by dividing the equity return deficiency by the complement of the applicable income tax rate. For example, if the operating income deficiency is $5,000 and the income tax rate is 40 percent, the required revenue is $5,000/.6, or $8,333. By increasing revenues $8,333, income tax expense will increase by $3,333 ($8,333 × 40 percent), with the remainder increasing equity return by the deficiency amount of $5,000. This concept is illustrated as part of an example revenue requirement calculation based on the information presented in Exhibit 36.5. Exhibit 36.6 shows a proof of the revenue requirement calculation.

When the rate-making process is complete, the utility will set rate tariffs to recover $319 million. At this level, future revenues will recover $292 million of operating expenses (including income taxes of $12 million) and provide a return of $27 million. This return equates to a 10 percent earnings level on rate base. The $27 million operating income will go toward paying $9 million of

Proof of Revenue Requirement Calculation	In Millions
Revenue Requirement	$319
— Operating Expenses Other Than Taxes	(280)
— Interest Expenses	(9)
Taxable Income	30
— Income Tax @ 40%	(12)
Equity Return ($270 × 6.67%)	$ 18

Exhibit 36.6 Shortcut Computation of the Utility Revenue Requirement

interest on long-term debt ($130 million × 6.75 percent) and leaving net income for the common equity holders of $18 million—which approximates the desired 13 percent return on common equity of $140 million. However, the rate-making process provides only the opportunity to earn at that level. If future sales volumes, operating costs, or other factors change, the utility will earn more or less than the allowed amount. It is that struggle between "allowed" and "actually earned" that creates continual assessment by the utility, the regulators, and the consumers. Alternative forms of regulation have been introduced in an attempt to balance these concerns. Electric utilities in particular have faced many issues with alternative generation (wind, biomass, solar), environmental concerns (coal, emissions, and nuclear generation), and overall competition and price of power both for physical and capacity that is monitored, priced, and contracted in some cases every 15 minutes in regional independent transmission systems (RTOs or ISOs) across the United States.

(g) ALTERNATIVE FORMS OF REGULATION. As a result of changing market conditions and growing competition, alternative forms of regulation began to emerge in the late 1980s. There are many new and different forms of regulation, but they all generally share a common characteristic. Utilities are provided an opportunity to achieve and retain higher levels of earnings compared with traditional regulation. It is believed that this opportunity will fundamentally change the incentives under regulation for cost reductions and productivity improvement. Alternative forms of regulation also are intended, in some cases, to provide needed pricing flexibility for services in competitive markets.

Examples of alternative forms of regulation include:

- Price ceilings or caps
- Rate moratoriums
- Sharing formulas
- Regulated transition to competition
- Revenue decoupling
- Non–fuel rate trackers/riders
- Formula rates

(i) Price Ceilings or Caps. Price caps are essentially regulation of the prices of services. This contrasts with rate-of-return or cost-based regulation under which the costs and earnings levels of services are regulated.

The fundamental premise behind price cap regulation is that it provides utilities with positive incentives to reduce costs and improve productivity because shareholders can retain some or all of the resulting benefits from increased earnings. Under rate-of-return regulation, assuming simultaneous rate making, customers receive all of the benefits by way of reduced rates.

Typical features of price cap plans are these three:

1. A starting point for prices that is based on the rates that were previously in effect under rate of return regulation. Under some plans, adjustments may be made to beginning rates to correct historical pricing disparities with the costs of providing service.
2. The ability to subsequently adjust prices periodically up to a cap measured by a predetermined formula.
3. The price cap formula usually includes three components: the change in overall price levels, an offset for productivity gains, and exogenous cost changes.

   The change in overall price levels is measured by some overall inflation index, such as the Gross National Product—Price Index or some variation of the Consumer Price Index.

   The productivity offset is a percentage amount by which a regulated utility is expected to exceed the productivity gains experienced by the overall population measured by the inflation index. The combination of a change in price levels less the productivity offset can produce positive or negative price caps. As an example, if the change in price levels was

+5.5 percent, and the productivity offset was 3.3 percent, a utility could increase its prices for a service by +2.2 percent.

There are also provisions to add or subtract the effects of exogenous cost changes from the formula. *Exogenous changes* are defined as those beyond the control of the company. *Endogenous changes* are those assumed to be included in the overall price level change. Examples of exogenous items in certain jurisdictions might include changes in GAAP, environmental laws, or tax rates. Each regulatory jurisdiction's price cap plan may differ somewhat as to the definition of exogenous versus endogenous cost changes.

In their purest form, price caps are applied to determine rates, and the company retains the actual level of earnings the rates produce. However, most price cap plans also include backstop mechanisms. These include sharing earnings above a certain level with customers or for increasing rates if actual earnings fall below a specified level. Some plans also permit adjustment of rates above the price cap, subject to full cost justification and burden of proof standards.

(ii) Rate Moratoriums. Rate moratoriums are simply a freeze in prices for a specified period of time. In effect, rate moratoriums function like a price cap where the productivity offset is set equal to the change in price levels, yielding a price cap of zero percent. Most rate moratorium plans have provisions to adjust prices for specified exogenous cost changes, although the definition of exogenous may be even more restrictive than under price cap plans.

(iii) Sharing Formulas. Sharing formulas are often paired with traditional rate-of-return regulation as an interim true-up mechanism between rate proceedings or added to price cap or rate moratorium plans as a backstop.

Sharing usually involves the comparison of actual earnings levels (determined by applying the traditional regulatory and cost allocation processes) with an authorized rate of return. Earnings above specified intervals are shared between shareholders and customers based on some formula.

Sharing is accomplished in a variety of ways. Five of the more common forms are:

1. One-time cash refunds or bill credits to customers
2. Negative surcharges on customer bills for a specified time period
3. Adjustments to subsequent price cap formulas
4. Infrastructure investment requirements
5. Capital recovery offsets

(iv) Regulated Transition to Competition. Prior to the 2000–2001 energy crisis in California and the western United States, regulators in a number of states had adopted, or were in the process of adopting, legislation to change the traditional approach to the regulation of the generation portion of electric utility operations. The objective of this change was to provide customers with the right to choose their electricity supplier.

In simple terms, this legislation provides for a transition period from cost-based to market-based regulation. During this transition period, customers obtain the right to choose their electricity supplier at market price. Customers might also be charged a transition surcharge during the transition, which is intended to provide the electric utility with recovery of some or all of its electric generation stranded costs.

Stranded costs are often synonymous with high-cost generating units. However, they are more broadly defined to include other assets or expenses that, when recovered under traditional cost-based regulation, cause rates to exceed market prices. These costs can include regulatory assets and various obligations, such as for plant decommissioning, fuel contracts, or purchase power commitments.

At the end of the transition period, customers are able to purchase electricity at market prices from their chosen supplier, and the electric utility is limited to providing transmission and distribution services at regulated rates.

The transition to retail competition in the electric supply sector paralleled a similar, but earlier, transition in the natural gas industry. FERC Order 436 in 1985 required natural gas pipelines to provide open access to transportation services, enabling gas distribution utilities and large gas consumers to negotiate prices directly with producers and contract separately for transportation. In 1992 FERC issued Order 636, which mandated the unbundling of sales services from transportation services, allowing customers to choose suppliers and opening gas retail markets to competition.

(v) Revenue Decoupling. A significant portion of a utility's revenue requirement (including return) is typically recovered each month through volumetric charges under traditional utility rate design. Therefore, changes in weather and/or customer growth patterns can affect actual earned returns. Some regulatory policy analysts have contended that the traditional regulatory ratemaking framework removes incentives (or may even provide disincentives) for utilities to invest in conservation programs to help their customers use energy more efficiently. In response to this, a significant number of states have recently approved the use of revenue decoupling mechanisms, primarily for natural gas distribution utilities.

Decoupling refers to the disassociation of a utility's profits from throughput or its sales of the commodity delivered by the utility. Instead, a rate of return is aligned with meeting revenue targets (usually on a per-customer basis to allow for growth) and rates are trued up or down to meet that target at the end of the adjustment period (typically annually). In theory, this makes the utility indifferent to selling or delivering less product, removing perceived disincentives to fund energy efficiency programs for customers.

To date, the American Gas Association reported that 17 states had approved revenue decoupling, with approval decisions pending in another 5 states. From a regulatory policy perspective, decoupling should in theory lower a utility's risk profile since revenue targets and associated returns are trued-up annually. Interestingly, there has so far been no observed direct relationship between the approval of revenue decoupling and lower ROE awards commensurate with the perceived reduction in risk.

(vi) Non–Fuel Rate Trackers/Riders. Regulatory lag is a critical issue facing many utilities today. This *lag* refers to the gap between the time a utility incurs a cost and when they ultimately receive recovery of the cost. Regulatory lag can occur even in a scenario where a utility may file frequent or periodic rate cases since a full base rate proceeding can take 6 to 12 months to complete. In a volatile cost environment, this "normal" time lag may still produce a significant mismatch between cost and recovery.

As part of the industry restructuring or transition to competition that occurred in many states, base rates were often frozen for a period of time, and some utilities agreed to specific "stay-out" provisions which prohibited them from filing a new base rate case within a multiyear period. In response to this, a number of jurisdictions have recently approved the use of non–fuel rate trackers, riders, or other surcharge mechanisms as a way of reducing or addressing the impact of regulatory lag on a utility's financial condition.

Similar in design and operation to periodic fuel adjustment clauses that have been in use for many years, these trackers allow a utility to forecast a specific cost over a recovery period (typically quarterly, semiannually, or annually) and design a rate surcharge that, in theory, should match recovery to cost. Since that match is never perfect, the tracker usually contains a provision requiring the utility to file a periodic reconciliation or true-up to assess actual under-recoveries or over-recoveries as an input to determining the future tracker charge. The state regulatory authority has an opportunity to review and approve these filings and the resulting tracker levels.

From a regulatory policy perspective, these non–fuel trackers have been approved with the objectives of reducing regulatory lag, sending more accurate and timely price signals to customers by better matching cost recovery with cost incurrence and streamlining the timeliness and efficiency of the regulatory rate-setting process. Trackers have been approved to recover costs associated with pensions, environmental compliance and storms, as well as larger capital programs such as specific construction projects, infrastructure modernization initiatives, and smart grid program implementation costs.

(vii) Formula Rates. In an effort to streamline the regulatory rate review process, the FERC and a limited number of states have recently approved the use of formula rates. *Formula rates* refer to a process whereby the regulator specifies the cost components that form the basis of the rates a utility charges its customers. Once initial rate design is set, the utility is subsequently permitted to adjust those rates quarterly or annually according to preset formulas that reference actual cost levels in periodic filings made to the commission (e.g., FERC Form 1 filings for electric utilities).

The use of the formula rates approach with specific filing requirements and expedited commission review procedures is intended to reduce regulatory lag by streamlining and shortening the usual cycle time associated with full base rate proceedings. FERC has utilized formula rates for interstate electric transmission services, while some states, such as Mississippi and Louisiana, have implemented formula rate programs for certain electric distribution utilities they regulate.

36.5 INTERRELATIONSHIP OF REGULATORY REPORTING AND FINANCIAL REPORTING

(a) ACCOUNTING AUTHORITY OF REGULATORY AGENCIES. Regulatory agencies with statutory authority to establish rates for utilities also prescribe the regulatory or statutory accounting that their jurisdictional regulated entities must follow. Accounting may be prescribed by a USOA, by periodic reporting requirements, or by accounting orders.

Because of the statutory authority of regulatory agencies over both accounting and rate setting of regulated utilities, some regulators, accountants, and others believe that the agencies have the final authority over the form and content of general financial statements published by those utilities for their investors and creditors. This is believed to be the case even when the financial statements provided to shareholders, based on regulatory accounting requirements, would not be in accordance with GAAP.

Actually, this issue has not arisen frequently because regulators have usually reflected changes in GAAP in the accounting requirements that they prescribe. For example, the USOA of the FERC has GAAP as its foundation, with departures being permitted but very limited as necessary, because of departures from GAAP in rate making. But the general willingness of regulators to conform to GAAP does not answer the question of whether a regulatory body has the final authority to prescribe the accounting to be followed for the financial statements included in the annual and other reports to stockholders or outsiders, even when such statements are not prepared in accordance with GAAP.

The landmark case in this area is the *Appalachian Power Co. v. Federal Power Commission* [328 F.2d 237 (4th Cir.), *cert. denied,* 379 U.S. 829 (1964)]. The FPC (now the FERC) found that the financial statements in the annual report of the company were not in accordance with the accounting prescribed by the FPC's USOA. The FPC was upheld at the circuit court level in 1964, and the Supreme Court denied a writ of certiorari. The general interpretation of this case has been that the FPC had the authority to order that the financial statements in the annual report to stockholders of its jurisdictional utilities be prepared in accordance with the USOA, even if not in accordance with GAAP.

During subsequent years, the few differences that have arisen have been resolved without court action, so it is not clear just what authority the FERC or other federal agencies may now have in this area. The FERC has not chosen to contest minor differences, and one particular utility, Montana Power Company, met the issue of FPC authority versus GAAP by presenting, for several years, two balance sheets in its annual report to shareholders. One balance sheet was in accordance with GAAP, which reflected the rate making prescribed by the state commission, and one balance sheet was in accordance with the USOA of the FPC, which had ordered that certain assets be written off even though the state commission continued to allow them in the rate base. The company's auditors stated that the first balance sheet was in accordance with GAAP and that the second balance sheet was in accordance with the FPC USOA.

Regulated utilities generally file regulatory/statutory reports with regulators (both federal and state), which include financial statements prepared in accordance with accounting requirements of the regulator. These financial statements may not be fully in accordance with GAAP (depending on what regulatory adjustments are required, such as equity method accounting for nonregulated investments in which the utility consolidates for GAAP purposes but does not for FERC purposes). However, the SEC has ruled that the company must follow GAAP when preparing financial statements included in filings with the SEC. As a result, many regulated utilities prepare financial statements both in accordance with the requirements of the regulator and in accordance with GAAP. Each of these financial statements is designed to meet the needs of the regulator and the users it represents.

(b) SECURITIES AND EXCHANGE COMMISSION AND FINANCIAL ACCOUNTING STANDARDS BOARD. The Financial Accounting Standards Board (FASB) has no financial reporting enforcement or disciplinary responsibility. Enforcement with regard to entities whose shares are traded in interstate commerce arises from SEC policy articulated in Accounting Series Release (ASR) No. 150, which specifies that FASB standards (and those of its predecessors) are required to be followed by registrants in their filings with the SEC. Thus, the interrelationship between the FASB and the SEC operates to achieve, virtually without exception for an entity whose securities trade in interstate commerce, the presentation of financial statements that reflect GAAP. Although this jurisdictional issue is neither resolved nor disappearing, it appears that the SEC currently exercises significant, if not controlling, influence over the general-purpose financial statements of all public companies, including regulated utilities.

(c) RELATIONSHIP BETWEEN RATE REGULATION AND GENERALLY ACCEPTED ACCOUNTING PRINCIPLES

(i) Historical Perspective. Rate making on an individual cost-of-service basis is designed to permit a utility to recover its costs that are incurred in providing regulated services. Individual cost of service does not guarantee cost recovery. However, there is a much greater assurance of cost recovery under individual cost-of-service rate making than for enterprises in general. This likelihood of cost recoverability provides a basis for a different application of GAAP, which recognizes that rate making can affect accounting.

As such, a rate regulator's ability to recognize, not recognize, or defer recognition of revenues and costs in established rates of regulated utilities adds a unique consideration to the accounting and financial reporting of those enterprises. This unique economic dimension was first recognized by the accounting profession in paragraph 8 of Accounting Research Bulletins (ARB) No. 44, now ASC Topic 360 (Revised), *Declining-Balance Depreciation:*

> Many regulatory authorities permit recognition of deferred income taxes for accounting and/or rate-making purposes, whereas some do not. The committee believes that they should permit the recognition of deferred income taxes for both purposes. However, where charges for deferred income taxes are not allowed for rate-making purposes, accounting recognition need not be given to the deferment of taxes if it may reasonably be expected that increased future income taxes, resulting from the earlier deduction of declining-balance depreciation for income-tax purposes only, will be allowed in the future rate determinations.

A year later, in connection with the general requirement to eliminate intercompany profits, paragraph 6 of ARB No. 51, now ASC Topic 810-10-45, *Consolidated Financial Statements,* concluded:

> Many regulatory authorities permit recognition of deferred income taxes for accounting and/or rate-making purposes, whereas some do not. The committee believes that they should permit the recognition of deferred income taxes for both purposes. However, where charges for deferred income taxes are not allowed for rate-making purposes, accounting recognition need not be given to the deferment of taxes if it may reasonably be expected that increased future income taxes, resulting from the earlier deduction of declining-balance depreciation for income-tax purposes only, will be allowed in the future rate determinations.

(ii) Addendum to Accounting Principles Board Opinion No. 2. In 1962, the Accounting Principles Board (APB) decided to express its position on applicability of GAAP to regulated industries. The resulting statement, initially reported in the *Journal of Accountancy* in December 1962, later became APB Opinion No. 2, which is now included in ASC Topic 740, *Accounting for the Investment Credit* (the Addendum), and provided that:

1. GAAP applies to all companies, regulated and nonregulated.
2. Differences in the application of GAAP are permitted as a result of the rate-making process because the rate regulator creates economic value.
3. Cost deferral on the balance sheet to reflect the rate-making process is appropriately reflected on the balance sheet only when recovery is clear.
4. A regulatory accounting difference without rate-making impact does not constitute GAAP. The accounting must be reflected in rates.
5. The financial statements of regulated entities other than those prepared for regulatory filings should be based on GAAP with appropriate recognition of rate-making consideration.

The Addendum provided the basis for utility accounting for almost 20 years. During this period, utilities accounted for certain items differently from enterprises in general. For example, regulators often treat capital leases as operating leases for rate purposes, thus excluding them from rate base and allowing only the lease payments as expense. In that event, regulated utilities usually treated such leases as operating leases for financial statement purposes. This resulted in lower operating expenses during the first few years of the lease.

Also, utilities capitalize both debt and equity components of funds used during construction, which is generally described as an allowance for funds used during construction (AFUDC). The FASB, under Accounting Standards Codification (ASU) 835-20, ASC Topic 835, *Capitalization of Interest,* allows nonregulated companies to capitalize only the debt cost. Because property is by far the largest item in most utility companies' balance sheets and because they do much of their own construction, the effect of capitalizing AFUDC can be very material to both the balance sheet and the statement of income.

Such differences, usually concerning the timing of recognition of a cost, were cited as evidence that the Addendum allowed almost any accounting treatment if directed by rate regulation. There was also some concern that the Addendum applied to certain industries that were regulated, but not on an individual cost-of-service basis. These as well as other issues ultimately led to the FASB issuing Statement of Financial Accounting Standards (SFAS) No. 71, ASC Topic 980, *Accounting for the Effects of Certain Types of Regulation,* which attempted to provide a clear conceptual basis to account for the economic impact of regulation, to emphasize the concept of one set of accounting principles for all enterprises, and to enhance the quality of financial reporting for regulated enterprises.

36.6 ACCOUNTING STANDARDS CODIFICATION 980, *REGULATED OPERATIONS*

(a) SCOPE OF ASC TOPIC 980. ASC Topic 980 specifies criteria for the applicability of the Standard by focusing on the nature of regulation rather than on specific industries. As stated in ASC Topic 980-10-15-2:

> The guidance in the Regulated Operations Topic applies to general-purpose external financial statements of an entity that has regulated operations that meet all of the following criteria:
>
> 1. The entity's rates for regulated services or products provided to its customers are established by or are subject to approval by an independent, third-party regulator or by its own governing board empowered by statute or contract to establish rates that bind customers.
> 2. The regulated rates are designed to recover the specific enterprise's costs of providing the regulated services or products.

3. In view of the demand for the regulated services or products and the level of competition, direct and indirect, it is reasonable to assume that rates set at levels that will recover the entity's costs can be charged to and collected from customers. This criterion requires consideration of anticipated changes in levels of demand or competition during the recovery period for any capitalized costs.

Based on these criteria, ASC Topic 980 provides guidance in preparing general-purpose financial statements for most investor-owned, cooperative, and governmental utilities.

The FASB's sister entity, the Governmental Accounting Standards Board (GASB), has been empowered to set pervasive standards for government utilities to the extent applicable, and, accordingly, financial statements issued in accordance with GAAP must follow GASB standards. However, in the absence of an applicable pronouncement issued by the GASB, differences between accounting for a transaction under GASB or other FASB pronouncements and treatment of the transaction for rate-making purposes should be accounted for in accordance with ASU Topic 980.

(b) AMENDMENTS TO ACCOUNTING FOR REGULATED OPERATIONS. After the issuance of SFAS No. 71 (now ASC Topic 980), the FASB became concerned about the accounting being followed by utilities (primarily electric companies) for certain transactions. Significant economic events were occurring, including these three:

1. Disallowances of major portions of recently completed plants
2. Very large plant abandonments
3. Phase-in plans

All of these events in one way or another prevented utilities from recovering costs currently and, in some instances, did not allow recovery at all. As a result, the FASB amended the accounting for regulated operations with SFAS No. 90, *Regulated Enterprises—Accounting for Abandonments and Disallowances of Plant Costs,* now ASC Topic 980-360-35, and SFAS No. 92, *Regulated Enterprises—Accounting for Phase-in Plans,* now ASC Topic 980-340. Also, SFAS No. 144, *Accounting for the Impairment or Disposal of Long-Lived Assets,* now ASC Topic 360-10-35, amended accounting for regulated operations to require a continuing probability assessment for the recovery of regulatory assets. Each of these amendments has been incorporated into ASC Topic 980.

Due to the increasing level of competition and deregulation faced by all types of rate regulated enterprises, the FASB issued SFAS No. 101, *Regulated Enterprises—Accounting for the Discontinuation of Application of FASB Statement 71,* now ASC Topic 980-20. ASC Topic 980-20 addresses the accounting to be followed when the application of ASC Topic 980 is discontinued. Related guidance is also set forth in the FASB's Emerging Issues Task Force (EITF) Issue No. 97-4, Deregulation of the Pricing of Electricity—Issues Related to the *Application of FASB Statements No. 71, Accounting for the Effects of Regulation, and No. 101, Regulated Enterprises—Accounting for the Discontinuation of Application of FASB Statement No. 71.* The requirements of SFAS No. 101 and EITF Issue No. 97-4 have also been included in ASC Topic 980-20-35.

(c) OVERVIEW OF ACCOUNTING FOR REGULATED OPERATIONS. The major issues addressed in ASC Topic 980 concern:

- Effect of rate making on GAAP
- Evidence criteria for recording regulatory assets and liabilities
- Application of GAAP to utilities
- Proper financial statement disclosures

ASC Topic 980 sets forth general standards of accounting for the effects of regulation. In addition, specific standards are derived from the general standards and various examples of the application of the general standards are presented.

(d) GENERAL STANDARDS. In ASC Topic 980, the FASB recognized that a principal consideration introduced by rate regulation is the cause-and-effect relationship of costs and revenues—an economic dimension that, in some circumstances, should affect accounting for regulated enterprises. Thus, a regulated utility should capitalize a cost (as a regulatory asset) or recognize an obligation (as a regulatory liability) if it is probable that, through the rate-making process, there will be a corresponding increase or decrease in future revenues. Regulatory assets and liabilities should be amortized over future periods consistent with the related increase or decrease, respectively, in future revenues.

(i) Regulatory Assets. ASU Topic 980-340-25-1 states that the "rate action of a regulator can provide reasonable assurance of the existence of an asset." All or part of an incurred cost that would otherwise be charged to expense should be capitalized if:

- It is probable that future revenues in an amount approximately equal to the capitalized cost will result from inclusion of that cost in allowable costs for rate-making purposes.
- Based on available evidence, it is probable that future revenue will be provided to permit recovery of the previously incurred cost rather than to provide for expected levels of similar future costs.

This general provision is not totally applicable to the regulatory treatment of costs of abandoned plants and phase-in plans. The accounting accorded these situations is also specified in ASC Topic 980 *Regulated Operations* and is discussed in Section 36.7. Also ASC Topic 980-715-25 addresses regulatory assets created in connection with differences between ASC Topic 715-60, costs for postretirement benefits other than pensions and other postretirement benefit costs included in rates.

With these exceptions, ASC Topic 980 requires a rate-regulated utility to capitalize a cost that would otherwise be charged to expense if future recovery in rates is probable. *Probable,* as defined in ASC Topic 450, *Contingencies,* means likely to occur, a very high probability threshold. If, however, at any time the regulatory asset no longer meets the above criteria (bullets one and two) , the cost should be charged to earnings. Thus, ASC Topic 980 mandates a probability of future recovery test to be met at each balance sheet date in order for a regulatory asset to remain recorded.

The terms *allowable costs* and *incurred costs,* as defined in ASC Topic 980-340-20, also required further attention. The two terms were often applied interchangeably so that, in practice, the provisions of ASC Topic 980-340-25-1 were interpreted to permit the cost of equity to be deferred and capitalized for future recovery as a regulatory asset. The FASB concluded in ASC Topic 980-340-25-5 that equity return (or an allowance for earnings on shareholders' investment) is not an incurred cost that would otherwise be charged to expense. Accordingly, such an allowance must not be capitalized pursuant to ASC Topic 980-340-25-1.

An incurred cost that does not meet the asset recognition criteria in ASU Topic 980-340-25-1 at the date the cost is incurred should be recognized as a regulatory asset when it meets those criteria at a later date. ASC Topic 980-340-35-2 provides for previously disallowed costs that are subsequently allowed by a regulator to be recorded as an asset, consistent with the classification that would have resulted had the cost initially been included in allowable costs. This provision covers plant costs as well as regulatory assets. Additionally, ASC Topic 980-340-35-1 requires the carrying amount of a regulatory asset recognized pursuant to the criteria in ASU Topic 980-340-25-1 to be reduced to the extent the asset has been subsequently disallowed from allowable costs by a regulator.

(ii) Regulatory Liabilities. The general standards also recognize that the rate action of a regulator can impose a liability on a regulated enterprise, usually to the utility's customers.

These are three typical ways in which regulatory liabilities can be imposed:

1. A regulator may require refunds to customers (revenue collected subject to refund).
2. A regulator can provide current rates intended to recover costs that are expected to be incurred in the future. If those costs are not incurred, the regulator will reduce future rates by corresponding amounts.

3. A regulator can require that a gain or other reduction of net allowable costs be given to customers by amortizing such amounts to reduce future rates.

ASC Topic 980-405-40-1 states that "actions of a regulator can eliminate a liability only if the liability was imposed by actions of the regulator." The practical effect of this provision is that a utility's balance sheet should include all liabilities and obligations that an enterprise in general would record under GAAP, such as for capital leases, pension plans, compensated absences, and income taxes.

(e) SPECIFIC STANDARDS. ASC Topic 980 also sets forth specific standards for several accounting and disclosure issues.

(i) Allowance for Funds Used During Construction. ASC Topic 980-835-25-1 allows the capitalization of AFUDC, including a designated cost of equity funds, if a regulator requires such a method, rather than using ASC Topic 835-20 for purposes of capitalizing the carrying cost of construction.

Rate regulation has historically provided utilities with two methods of capturing and recovering the carrying cost of construction:

1. Capitalizing AFUDC for future recovery in rates
2. Recovering the carrying cost of construction in current rates by including construction work in progress in the utility's rate base

The computation of AFUDC is generally prescribed by the appropriate regulatory body. The predominant guidance has been provided by the FERC. The FERC has defined AFUDC as "the net cost for the period of construction of borrowed funds used for construction purposes and a reasonable rate on other funds when so used." The term *other funds,* as used in this definition, refers to equity capital.

The FERC formula for computing AFUDC is comprehensive and takes into consideration these five items:

1. Debt and equity funds
2. The levels of construction
3. Short-term debt
4. The costs of long-term debt and preferred stock are based on the traditional embedded cost approach, using the preceding year-end costs
5. The cost rate for common equity is usually the rate granted in the most recent rate proceeding

In allowing AFUDC, the FERC recognizes that the capital carrying costs of the investments in construction work in progress are as much a cost of construction as other construction costs, such as labor, materials, and contractors.

In contrast to regulated utilities, nonregulated companies are governed by a different standard, ASC Topic 835-20. Under the FASB guidelines:

> [T]he amount of interest to be capitalized for qualifying assets is intended to be that portion of interest cost incurred during the assets acquisition periods that theoretically could have been avoided (for example, by avoiding additional borrowings or by using the funds expended for the assets to repay existing borrowings) if expenditures for the assets had not been made.

Furthermore, ASC Topic 835-20 allows only debt interest capitalization and does not recognize an equity component.

The specific standard in ASC Topic 980-835-35-1 states that capitalization of such financing costs can occur only if, "after construction is completed, the resulting capitalized costs, including the allowance for funds used during construction, is the basis for depreciation and unrecovered investment for rate-making purposes."

The FASB also concluded in ASC Topic 980-835-25-2 that:

> [I]f the specific criteria in 980-835-35-1 are met but an allowance for funds used during construction is not capitalized because its inclusion in the cost that will become the basis for future rates is not probable, the regulated utility may not alternatively capitalize interest cost in accordance with ASC Topic 835-20.

(ii) Intercompany Profit. ASU Topic 980-810-45-1 provides that intercompany profits on sales to regulated affiliates should not be eliminated in general-purpose financial statements if the sales price is reasonable and it is probable that future revenues allowed through the rate-making process will approximately equal the sales price.

(iii) Accounting for Income Taxes. Originally in paragraph 18 of SFAS No. 71 (now ASC Topic 980), the FASB recognized that, in some cases, a regulator flows through the tax effects of certain timing differences as a reduction in future rates. In such cases, if it is probable that future rates will be based on income taxes payable at that time, SFAS No. 71 did not permit deferred taxes to be recorded in accordance with APB Opinion No. 11, *Accounting for Income Taxes.*

In February 1992, SFAS No. 71 was amended by SFAS No. 109 (now ASC Topic 740) and paragraph 18 was replaced by this one:

> A deferred tax liability or asset shall be recognized for the deferred tax consequences of temporary differences in accordance with FASB Statement No. 109, *Accounting for Income Taxes.*

(iv) Refunds. ASC Topic 980 addresses the accounting for significant refunds. Examples include refunds granted gas distribution utilities from pipelines and telephone refunds occurring where revenues are estimated in one period and trued up at a later date or where revenues are billed under bond pending settlement of a rate proceeding.

For refunds recognized in a period other than the period in which the related revenue was recognized, disclosure of the effect on net income and the years in which the related revenue was recognized is required if material. ASC Topic 980 provides presentation guidance that the effect of such refunds may be disclosed by displaying the amount, net of income tax, as a line item in the income statement but not as an extraordinary item.

Adjustments to prior quarters of the current fiscal year are appropriate for such refunds, provided all of the next three criteria are met:

1. The effect is material (either to operations or income trends).
2. All or part of the adjustment or settlement can be specifically identified with and is directly related to business activities of specific prior interim periods.
3. The amount could not be reasonably estimated prior to the current interim period but becomes reasonably estimable in the current period.

This treatment of prior interim periods for utility refunds is one of the restatement exceptions contained in paragraph 13 of SFAS No. 16, *Prior Period Adjustments,* now ASC Topic 250-10.

(v) Deferred Costs Not Earning a Return. ASC Topic 980 requires disclosure of costs being amortized in accordance with the actions of a regulator but not being allowed to earn a return during the recovery period. Disclosure should include the remaining amounts being amortized (the amount of the nonearning asset) as well as the remaining recovery period.

(vi) Examples of Application. ASC Topic 980 contains examples of the application of the general standards to specific situations. These examples, along with the basis for conclusions, are an important aid in understanding the provisions of ASC Topic 980 and the financial statements of utilities.

Items discussed include:

- Intangible assets
- Accounting changes

- Early extinguishment of debt
- Accounting for contingencies
- Accounting for leases
- Revenue collected subject to refund
- Refunds to customers
- Accounting for compensated absences
- Asset retirement and environmental obligations

36.7 ASC TOPIC 980-360-35, *COST DISALLOWANCES*

(a) SIGNIFICANT PROVISIONS. The provisions of ASC Topic 980-360-35 (formerly SFAS No. 90, *Regulated Enterprises—Accounting for Abandonments and Disallowance of Plant Costs*) are limited to the narrow area of accounting for abandonments and disallowances of plant costs and not to other assets, regulatory or otherwise.

(i) Accounting for Cost Disallowances of Newly Completed Plant. When a *direct disallowance* of a newly completed plant is probable and estimable, a loss should be recorded, dollar for dollar, for the disallowed amount. After the write-down is achieved, the reduced asset forms the basis for future depreciation charges.

An indirect disallowance occurs when, in certain circumstances, no return or a reduced return is permitted on all or a portion of the new plant for an extended period of time. To determine the loss resulting from an indirect disallowance, the present value of the future revenue stream allowed by the regulator should be determined by discounting at the most recent allowed rate of return. This amount should be compared with the recorded plant amount and the difference recorded as a loss. Under this discounting approach, the remaining asset should be depreciated consistent with the rate making and in a manner that would produce a constant return on the undepreciated asset equal to the discount rate.

(ii) Accounting for Plant Abandonments. In the case of abandonments, when no return or only a partial return is permitted, at the time the abandonment is both probable and estimable, the asset should be written off and a separate new asset should be established based on the present value of the future revenue stream. The entities' incremental borrowing rate should be used to measure the new asset. During the recovery period, the new asset should be amortized to produce zero net income based on the theoretical debt, and interest should be assumed to finance the abandonment. Federal Technical Bulletin No. 87-2, *Computation of a Loss on an Abandonment,* now included in ASC Topic 980-360-35, supports discounting the abandonment revenue stream is calculated using an after-tax incremental borrowing rate.

(iii) Income Statement Presentation. Abandonments and cost disallowances under Staff Accounting Bulletin (SAB) No. 72 (currently cited as SAB Topic 10E) and now ASC Topic 980-360-S99 concludes that the effects of applying ASC Topic 980-300-35 should not be reported as an extraordinary item. ASC Topic 980-360-S99 states that such charges should be reported gross as a component of other income and deductions and not shown net of tax. The next presentation complies with these requirements:

Operating income	$XX
Other income (expense)	
Allowance for equity funds used during construction	XX
Disallowed plant cost	(XX)
Income tax reduction for disallowed plant cost	XX
Interest income	XX
Income taxes applicable to other income	XX
Income before interest charges	$XX

36.8 ASC TOPIC 980-340, *OTHER ASSETS AND DEFERRED COSTS*

(a) SIGNIFICANT PROVISIONS. A phase-in plan, as defined in ASC Topic 980-340 (formerly SFAS No. 92, *Regulated Enterprises—Accounting for Phase-in Plans*), is a method of rate making that meets each of these three criteria:

1. Adopted in connection with a major, newly completed plant of the regulated enterprise or one of its suppliers or a major plant scheduled for completion in the near future
2. Defers the rates intended to recover allowable costs beyond the period in which those allowable costs would be charged to expense under GAAP applicable to enterprises in general
3. Defers the rates intended to recover allowable costs beyond the period in which those rates would have been ordered under rate-making methods routinely used prior to 1982 by that regulator for similar allowable costs of that utility

The phase-in definition includes virtually all deferrals associated with newly completed plant, such as rate levelization proposals, alternative methods of depreciation (such as a sinking fund approach), rate treatment of capital leases as operating leases, and other schemes to defer new plant costs to the future. ASC Topic 980-340 specifically states that it applies to rate-making methods developed for "major newly completed plant of the regulated enterprise or of one of its suppliers." Accordingly, ASC Topic 980-340 must be considered with respect to purchase power contracts.

Under the accounting provisions of ASC Topic 980-340, cost deferral under a phase-in plan is not permitted for plant/fixed assets on which substantial physical construction had not been performed before January 1, 1988. Consequently, for a major, newly completed plant that does not meet the January 1, 1988, cutoff date, post–in-service deferrals for financial reporting purposes are limited to a time frame that ends when rates are adjusted to reflect the cost of operating the plant. This limitation, along with the restriction on modifying an existing phase-in plan, as discussed next, are the most important ASC Topic 980-340 provisions today.

As indicated, ASC Topic 980-340 applies to the costs of a major, newly completed plant. There are situations in which a regulator subsequently starts to defer rates intended to recover allowable plant costs after return on and recovery of such costs have been previously provided. One example of this situation would occur when a regulator orders a future reduction in the depreciation rate (and rates charged to customers) of a 15-year-old nuclear generation plant, to factor in a potential 20-year license extension. Assuming that the new depreciation rate adopted by the regulator cannot be supported under GAAP (perhaps because the utility does not believe a license extension will occur), a regulatory deferral of plant costs (i.e., regulatory depreciation expense would be less than depreciation for financial reporting purposes) would result.

If the rate order was issued in connection with a major, newly completed plant, the guidance presumes that the regulatory deferral of the "old" plant is equivalent to the regulatory deferral of the "new" plant. Thus, ASC Topic 980-340 must be applied. And, under that Statement, because the regulatory action results in a phase-in plan as defined in ASC Topic 980-340, no costs can be deferred for financial reporting purposes.

However, if the new rate order was not issued in connection with a major, newly completed plant and it is clear that the regulatory deferral relates only to "old" plant, ASC Topic 980-340 would not apply. Any deferral for financial reporting purposes must meet the requirements of SFAS No. 71, paragraph 9, for establishing and maintaining a regulatory asset. That determination should consider, that the existence of such regulatory cost deferrals calls into question the applicability of ASC Topic 980-20.

(i) Accounting for Phase-in Plans. If the phase-in plan meets all of the criteria required by ASC Topic 980-340, all allowable costs that are deferred for future recovery by the regulator under the plan should be capitalized for financial reporting as a separate asset. If any of the following criteria is not met, none of the allowable costs that are deferred for future recovery by the regulator under the plan should be capitalized.

- The plan has been agreed to by the regulator.
- The plan specifies when recovery will occur.
- All allowable costs deferred under the plan are scheduled for recovery within 10 years of the date when deferrals begin.
- The percentage increase in rates scheduled for each future year under the plan is not greater than the percentage increase in rates scheduled for each immediately preceding year.

When an existing phase-in plan is modified or a new plan is ordered to replace or supplement an existing plan, the listed criteria should be applied to the combination of the modified plan and the existing plan. Thus, the 10-year period requirement, from when cost deferral commences until all costs are recovered, cannot be extended. If the recovery period is modified beyond 10 years, recorded costs under the phase-in plan should be immediately charged to earnings.

(ii) Financial Statement Classification. From a financial statement viewpoint, costs deferred should be classified and reported as a separate item in the income statement in the section relating to those costs. For instance, if capital costs are being deferred, they should be classified below the line. If depreciation or other operating costs are being deferred, the "credit" should be classified above the line with the operating costs. Allowable costs capitalized should not be reported net as a reduction of other expenses. Amortization of phase-in plan deferrals typically should be above the line (similar to recovering AFUDC via depreciation). This income statement presentation is consistent with guidance provided by the SEC Staff in the Official Minutes of the Emerging Issues Task Force Meeting from the open meeting held on February 23, 1989.

(iii) Allowance for Funds Used During Construction. ASC Topic 980-340 clarifies that AFUDC equity can be capitalized in general-purpose financial statements only during construction or as part of a qualifying phase-in plan. Thus, it is clear that, after January 1, 1988, AFUDC equity cannot be capitalized in connection with short-term rate synchronization deferrals. It should also be noted that, in connection with the adoption of ASC Topic 980-340, such deferrals can be recorded only when it is probable—based on ASC Topic 450-20 (SFAS No. 5)—that such costs will be recovered in future rates. This is consistent with the discussion on ASC Topic 980-360 relating to capitalizing AFUDC.

(iv) Interrelationship of Phase-in Plans and Disallowances. Amounts deferred pursuant to ASC Topic 980-340 should also include an allowance for earnings on stockholders' investments. If the phase-in plan meets the criteria in ASC Topic 980-340 and the regulator prevents the enterprise from recovering either some amount of its investment or some amount of return on its investment, a disallowance occurs that should be accounted for in accordance with ASC 980-360-35.

(v) Financial Statement Disclosure. A utility should disclose in its financial statements the terms of any phase-in plans in effect during the year. If a phase-in plan exists but does not meet the criteria in ASC Topic 980-340, the financial statements should include disclosure of the net amount deferred for rate-making purposes at the balance sheet date and the net change in deferrals for rate-making purposes during the year for those plans. In addition, the nature and amounts of any allowance for earnings on stockholders' investment capitalized for rate-making purposes but not capitalized for financial reporting are to be disclosed.

36.9 DISCONTINUATION OF RATE-REGULATED ACCOUNTING: ASC TOPIC 980-20

The continuing applicability of ASC Topic 980 has been receiving more and more attention recently, particularly with price cap regulation in the telecommunications industry and market-based or other alternative forms of pricing taking place in the pipeline and electric industries. Virtually every major telecommunications company that historically applied ASC Topic 980 has discontinued applying it. Also, electric companies, including some of the largest in the industry, in various regulatory jurisdictions have discontinued application of ASC Topic 980 for the generation portion of their operations as a result of the industry undergoing various fundamental changes. However, the changes are being revisited by many electric companies and their regulators due to continued changes in and dynamics of the industry. As a result, some companies have reapplied or are currently evaluating whether to reapply ASC Topic 980.

It is important that companies carefully review *both the current and anticipated future* rate environment to determine continued applicability of ASC Topic 980. In ASC Topic 980-20-40-6, a segment of a rate-regulated enterprise's operations that is subject to a deregulation transition period should cease no later than the time when the legislation is passed or a rate order is issued and the related effects are known.

(a) FACTORS LEADING TO DISCONTINUING APPLICATION OF ASC TOPIC 980. ASC Topic 980-20-15-2 gives several examples that may cause an enterprise to no longer meet the criteria for applying ASC Topic 980. Because virtually all regulated utilities are experiencing one or more of the examples cited, it is important to evaluate the continuing application of ASC Topic 980 at each balance sheet date (more frequently if a utility has a significant amount of rate orders or actions).

Causes cited in ASC Topic 980-20 include: deregulation, a change from cost-based rate making to another form of regulation, increasing competition that limits the ability to recover costs, and regulatory actions that limit rate relief to a level insufficient to recover costs. Other stress signs that may indicate that ASC Topic 980 is no longer applicable include these eight:

1. Increasing amounts of regulatory assets, including systematic underdepreciation of assets and deferral of costs
2. Regulatory assets being consistently amortized over long periods, particularly if such assets relate to ongoing operating costs
3. Substantial regulatory disallowances
4. Increasing amounts of deferred costs not earning a return
5. Chronic excess capacity (e.g., generating capacity and/or readily available supplies) resulting in nonearning assets
6. Rates for services or per 1,000 cubic or kilowatt-hour that are currently, or forecasted to be in the future, higher than those of neighboring entities and/or alternative competitive energy sources
7. Significant disparity among the rates charged to residential, commercial, and industrial customers and rate concessions for major customers or segments
8. Stress accumulation and/or the actions of others to discontinue application of ASC Topic 980, making the specialized regulatory accounting model no longer creditable

These examples provide warning signs and are not meant as hard-and-fast rules. Instead, considerable judgment is required to determine when an enterprise ceases to meet the criteria of ASC Topic 980. However, we believe that two trigger points generally indicate that an enterprise no longer meets the criteria of ASC Topic 980:

1. The current form of rate regulation results in an extended rate moratorium or a regulatory process that precludes the enterprise for an extended period (generally in excess of five years) from adjusting rates to reflect the utility's cost of providing service.

2. The regulatory process results or is expected to result in the utility earning significantly less (generally 250 to 300 basis points) than its allowed or a reasonable current rate of return for an extended period of time (more than one year); however, the interpretation of these differences of actual return to allowed return require professional judgment.

(b) REGULATORY ASSETS AND LIABILITIES. Once a utility concludes that all or a part of a company's operations no longer qualifies for rate regulated accounting under ASC Topic 980, it should discontinue application of accounting for regulation Statement and report the resulting discontinuation by eliminating from its balance sheet the effects of any actions of regulators that had been previously recognized as assets and liabilities pursuant to ASC Topic 980 but would not have been recognized as assets and liabilities by enterprises in general. The guidance in ASC Topic 980-20 indicates that all regulatory-created assets and liabilities should be written off unless the right to receive payment or the obligation to pay exists as a result of past events and regardless of expected future transactions.

Some examples of such regulatory-created assets and liabilities include:

- Deferred storm damage
- Energy efficiency costs
- Deferred plant abandonment loss
- Receivables or payables to future customers under purchased gas or fuel adjustment clauses (unless amounts are receivable or payable regardless of future sales)
- Deferred gains or losses or reacquisition of debt
- Revenues subject to refund as future sales price adjustments

(c) PLANT, EQUIPMENT, AND INVENTORY

> The carrying amounts of plant, equipment, and inventory measured and reported pursuant to ASC Topic 980 should not be adjusted unless those assets are impaired (as measured by enterprises in general), in which case the carrying amounts of those assets should be reduced to reflect that impairment.

The carrying amount of inventories measured and reported pursuant to ASC Topic 980 would not be adjusted—to eliminate, for example, intercompany profit—absent loss recognition by applying the "cost or market, whichever is lower" rule set forth in ASC Topic 330-10-35.

Reaccounting is required for true regulatory assets that have been misclassified as part of plant, such as postconstruction cost deferrals recorded as part of plant, and for systematic underdepreciation of plant in accordance with rate-making practices.

(d) REGULATORY ASSETS. In recent years, the SEC Staff has focused on electric utility restructuring and its effect on financial reporting. As a result, the appropriateness of the continuing application of ASC Topic 980 became a serious issue during the late1990s and early 2000s. Specifically, the SEC Staff challenged the continued applicability of ASC Topic 980 by registrants in states where plans transitioning to market-based pricing/competition for electric generation were being formulated.

The SEC Staff concerns initially resulted from enacted legislation in California that provided at that time for transition to a competitive electric generation market. These concerns led to the identification of several unresolved issues concerning when ASC Topic 980 should be discontinued and how ASC Topic 980-20 should be adopted. ASC Topic 980-20-35-6 to 980-20-35-9 provide the guidance discussed next.

The first issue addresses when an enterprise should stop applying ASC Topic 980 to the separable portion of its business whose product or service pricing is being deregulated. However, this issue was limited to situations in which final legislation is passed or a rate order is issued that has the effect of transitioning from cost-based to market-based rates. In such situations, should ASC Topic 980 be discontinued at the beginning or the end of the transition period?

The EITF concluded that when deregulatory legislation or a rate order is issued that contains sufficient detail to reasonably determine how the transition plan will affect the separable portion of the business, ASC Topic 980 should be discontinued for that separable portion. Thus, ASC Topic 980 should be discontinued at the beginning (not the end) of the transition period.

Once ASC Topic 980 is no longer applied to a separable portion of an enterprise, the financial statements should segregate, via financial statement display or footnote disclosure, the amounts contained in the financial statements that relate to that separable portion.

The scope of this section was limited to a specific circumstance in which deregulatory legislation is passed and a final rate order issued. The section did not address the broader issue of whether the application of ASC Topic 980 should cease prior to final passage of deregulatory legislation or issuance of a final rate order.

Based on this guidance, once it becomes probable that the deregulation legislative and/or regulatory changes will occur and the effects are known in sufficient detail, ASC Topic 980-20 should be adopted.

If the start of the transition period is delayed and uncertainty exists because of an appeal process, it seems reasonable that the application of ASC Topic 980 should continue until the completion of such process and the change to market-based regulation becomes probable. However, if or when it is probable that the appeal will be denied and the change to market-based regulation ultimately enacted, the adoption of ASC Topic 980-20 should not be delayed.

Regulatory assets and regulatory liabilities that originated in the separable portion of an enterprise to which ASC Topic 980-20 is being applied should be evaluated on the basis of where (i.e., the portion of the business in which) the regulated cash flows to realize and settle them will be derived. *Regulated cash flows* are rates that are charged customers and intended by regulators to be for the recovery of the specified regulatory assets and settlement of the regulatory liabilities. They can be, in certain situations, derived from a levy on rate-regulated goods or services provided by another separable portion of the enterprise that meets the criteria for application of ASC Topic 980.

Accordingly, if such regulatory assets and regulatory liabilities have been specifically provided for via the collection of regulated cash flows, they are not eliminated until:

- They are recovered by or settled through regulated cash flows, OR
- They are individually impaired or the regulator eliminates the obligation, OR
- The separable portion of the business from which the regulated cash flows are derived no longer meets the criteria for application of ASC Topic 980.

The source of cash flow approach adopted in the second consensus should be used for recoveries of all costs and settlements of all obligations for which regulated cash flows are specifically provided in the deregulatory legislation or rate order. This is not limited to regulatory assets and regulatory liabilities that are recorded at the date ASC Topic 980-20 is applied.

For example, a regulatory asset should also be recorded for the loss on the sale of an electric generating plant or the loss on the buyout of a purchased power contract that is recognized after ASC Topic 980-20 is applied to the generation portion of the business, if it is specified for recovery in the legislation or a rate order, and a separable portion of the enterprise that meets the criteria for application of ASC Topic 980 continues to exist.

(e) INCOME TAXES. An apparent requirement of ASC Topic 980 when rate regulated accounting is discontinued is that net-of-tax AFUDC should be displayed gross along with the associated deferred income taxes. This requirement is based on the notion that the net-of-tax AFUDC presentation is pursuant to industry practice and not ASC Topic 980. The interaction of this requirement under ASC Topic 980-20 treatment of excess deferred income taxes and the transition provision in ASC Topic 740 must be considered in connection with discontinuing the application of regulated accounting under ASC Topic 980.

(f) INVESTMENT TAX CREDITS. A utility might consider changing its method of accounting for investment tax credits in connection with adopting ASC Topic 980-20 (SFAS No. 101). Paragraph 11 of APB Opinion No. 4, *Accounting for the Investment Credit,* included in ASC Topic 740-10-50-20, as well as the Revenue Act of 1971 and U.S. Treasury releases, have required specific, full disclosure of the accounting method followed for Income Tax Credit (ITC)—either the flow-through method or the deferral method. Paragraph 16 of APB Opinion No. 20, *Accounting Changes,* now under ASC Topic 250-10, specifies that the previously adopted method of accounting for ITC should not be changed after the ITC has been discontinued or terminated. Therefore, the method of accounting used for ITC reported in financial statements when the Tax Reform Act of 1986 was signed, and such credits were discontinued, must be continued for those tax credits. Paragraph 4 of Accounting Interpretations of APB No. 4, now under ASC Topic 740-10-50-20, indicates that the preceding guidance would apply to old ITC, even if a new similar credit were later enacted.

(g) INCOME STATEMENT PRESENTATION. The net effect of these adjustments should be included in income of the period of the change.

(h) REAPPLICATION OF ASC 980. In its original standard SFAS No. 101, now ASC Topic 980-20, the FASB concluded that the accounting for the reapplication of ASC Topic 980-10 was beyond the scope of ASC Topic 980-20. As mentioned previously, several companies have reapplied ASC Topic 980-10, including some registrants that precleared their accounting with the SEC Staff.

When facts and circumstances change so that a utility's regulated operations meet all of the criteria set forth in paragraph 5 of ASC Topic 980, that Topic should be reapplied to all or a separable portion of its operations, as appropriate.

Reapplication includes adjusting the balance sheet for amounts that meet the definition of a regulatory asset or regulatory liability in ASC Topic 980-340-25-1 and ASC Topic 980-405-25-1, respectively. AFUDC should commence to be recorded if it is probable of future recovery, consistent with ASC Topic 980-835-25. Plant balances should not be adjusted for any difference that resulted from capitalizing interest under ASC 360-10-30 instead of AFUDC while ASC Topic 980 was discontinued. Instead, a regulatory asset should be recorded if supportable. As provided for in SFAS No. 144, now ASC Topic 360-10-35, previously disallowed costs that are subsequently allowed by a regulator should be recorded as an asset, consistent with the classification that would have resulted had these costs initially been allowed.

In practice, the net effect of the adjustments to reapply ASC Topic 980 have been classified as an extraordinary item in the income statement.

36.10 OTHER SPECIALIZED UTILITY ACCOUNTING PRACTICES

(a) UTILITY INCOME TAXES AND INCOME TAX CREDITS. Income tax expense is important to utilities because it generally is one of the largest items in the income statement and usually is a key factor in the determination of cost of service for rate-making purposes. Deferred income taxes represent a significant element of internally generated funds and a major financing source for the extensive construction programs that utilities have historically experienced. In addition, the complexity of the Internal Revenue Code (IRC) and of the various regulations to which utilities are subject causes a significant amount of controversy. As a result, the method of accounting for income taxes—"normalization" versus "flow-through" rate making—is often a specific issue in rate proceedings. The rate-making method is an important area of concern to analysts and can be a factor in establishing the cost of equity and new debt offerings.

(i) Interperiod Income Tax Allocation. GAAP, under SFAS No. 109, now ASC Topic 740, requires that a "provision for deferred taxes" be made for the tax effect of most of differences between income before income taxes and taxable income. This practice of interperiod tax allocation is referred to in the utility industry as normalization.

The term *normalization* evolved because income taxes computed for accounting purposes on the normalization basis would cause reported net income to be a "normal" amount had the utility not adopted, for example, a particular tax return method for a deduction that created the tax-book difference. Under the deferred tax or normalization concept, the taxes that would be payable, except for the use of the tax return deduction that created the tax-book difference, are merely deferred, not saved. For example, when tax depreciation exceeds book depreciation in the early years of property life, deferred taxes are charged to expense with a contra credit to a liability account. In later years, when the tax write-offs are lower than they otherwise would be, the higher taxes when payable are charged against this reserve. To illustrate the concept, assume these facts:

	Year 1	Year 2	Year 3
Revenues	$1,000	$1,000	$1,000
Other expenses	600	600	600
Book depreciation	200	200	200
Tax depreciation	300	200	100
Tax rate	34%	34%	34%

Exhibit 36.7 sets forth how normalized (deferred) tax accounting would be recorded in Year 1 for the tax and book depreciation difference of $100.

(ii) Flow-Through. *Flow-through* is a concept wherein the reductions in current tax payments from tax deductions, such as created by using accelerated depreciation, are flowed through to customers via lower cost-of-service and revenue requirements. Under this approach, income tax expense is equal to the currently payable amount only. No recognition (deferred taxes) is given to the tax effect of differences between book income before income taxes and taxable income. Under a "partial" allocation approach, deferred taxes are provided on certain differences but are ignored on others.

The principal argument used by those who support flow-through accounting is that a provision for deferred taxes does not constitute a current cost, and therefore such a deferment should not be made. Income tax expense for the year should include only those taxes legally payable with respect to the tax return applicable to that year, and any provision in excess of taxes payable represents "phantom" taxes or "customer-contributed capital." Further, when property additions are growing, and if no changes were made to the tax law, deferred tax provisions in the aggregate would continue to grow and would never turn around (or reverse); thereby the tax timing differences are, in fact, "permanent differences."

Deferred Tax Accounting

	Income Statement	Tax Return	Timing Difference
Revenue	$1,000	$1,000	$ —
Depreciation	(200)	(300)	100
Other expenses	(600)	(600)	—
Income before taxes	$ 200	$ 100	$100
Federal income taxes:			
Payable currently (34% × $100)	$ 34	$ 34	
Deferred (34% × $100)	34		$ 34
Total	$ 68		
Operating income	$ 132		

Exhibit 36.7 Illustration of "Normalized" Tax Accounting

Exhibit 36.8 sets forth the initial effect of flow-through tax accounting in Year 1 for the tax and book depreciation difference of $100.

Although Exhibit 36.8 shows a "bottom-line" effect of the elimination of deferred tax expense, such accounting is not acceptable. GAAP requires deferred tax accounting with ASC Topic 980 (SFAS No. 71), permitting departures only when regulators actions affect revenues. To be acceptable, therefore, the regulator would lower revenue requirements due to the omission of deferred tax expense as an element of the utility's cost of service for rate-making purposes. The action of the regulator in this case is to defer a cost that will be recoverable through increased rates in the future.

As previously discussed, utility regulators determine operating income first and then add allowable expenses to derive operating revenue. In Exhibit 36.7, $132 is presumed to be the result of multiplying rate base by rate of return. The same operating income of $132 in the normalization example would be developed first under the flow-through concept and, with the elimination of deferred tax expense of $34, only $948 of revenue would be required to produce the $132 of operating income under flow-through. The proper application of flow-through is shown in Exhibit 36.9.

This $52 reduction in revenues (by eliminating only $34 of deferred tax expense) is caused by the tax-on-tax effect, which is discussed under the rate-making formula in Section 36.4. In short,

Flow-Through Accounting Assuming No Decrease in Customer Rates

	Income Statement	Tax Return	Timing Difference
Revenue	$1,000	$1,000	$ —
Depreciation	(200)	(300)	$100
Other expenses	(600)	(600)	—
Income before taxes	$ 200	$ 100	$100
Federal income taxes:			
Payable currently (34% × $100)	$ 34	$ 34	
Deferred (34% × $0)	—		$ —
Total	$ 34		
Net income	$ 166		

Exhibit 36.8 Illustration of Flow-Through Accounting with No Effect on Customer Rates

Flow-Through Accounting Assuming Decrease in Customer Rates

	Income Statement	Tax Return	Timing Difference
Revenue	$948	$948	$ —
Depreciation	(200)	(300)	$100
Other expenses	(600)	(600)	—
Income before taxes	$148	$ 48	$100
Federal income taxes:			
Payable currently (34% × $48)	16	16	
Deferred	—		—
Total	$ 16		
Net income	$132		

Exhibit 36.9 Illustration of Flow-Through Accounting with a Decrease in Rates

Comparison of Normalization and Flow-Through

	Normalization				Flow-Through			
	Year 1	Year 2	Year 3	Total	Year 1	Year 2	Year 3	Total
Revenues	$1,000	$1,000	$1,000	$3,000	$(948)	$1,000	$1,052	$3,000
Depreciation	(200)	(200)	(200)	(600)	(200)	(200)	(200)	(600)
Other expenses	(600)	(600)	(600)	(1,800)	(600)	(600)	(600)	(1,800)
Income before income taxes	200	200	200	600	148	200	252	600
Income taxes								
Payable currently	34	68	102	204	16	68	120	204
Deferred taxes	34	—	(34)	—	—	—	—	—
	68	68	68	204	16	68	120	204
Operating income	$ 132	$ 132	$ 132	$ 396	$ 132	$ 132	$ 132	$ 396

Exhibit 36.10 Illustration of Normalization versus Flow-Through Differences

the elimination of the deferred tax expense results in a direct reduction of revenues, causing current tax expense also to be reduced. This effect is the primary reason so much attention is focused on normalization versus flow-through rate making for income taxes.

The comparison of the normalization and flow-through concepts in Exhibit 36.10 illustrates that operating income continues to be $132 under both methods and that the $52 of savings in revenue requirement in Year 1 due to flow-through is offset by $52 of higher rates in Year 3. For simplicity, this example ignores the rate base reducing effects of deferred taxes.

The comparison illustrates the principal argument for normalization: that revenues are at a level, or normal, amount, whereas revenue varies greatly under flow-through. Advocates of normalization note that normalization distributes income tax expense to time periods, and therefore to customers' revenue requirements, consistently with the costs (depreciation) that are affecting income tax expense. As the rate-making process necessarily involves the deferral of costs such as plant investment and distribution of these costs over time, normalization is used to produce a consistent determination of income tax expense.

Normalization also recognizes that the "using up" of tax basis of depreciable property (or using up an asset's ability to reduce taxes) creates a cost. This cost should be recognized as the tax payments are reduced. Basing tax expense solely on taxes payable without recognizing the cost of achieving reductions in tax payments is not consistent with accrual accounting. Although flow-through rate making ignores this current cost, this cost does not disappear any more than the nonrecognition of depreciation for rate making would make that cost disappear.

(iii) Provisions of the Internal Revenue Code. Complicating the regulatory treatment and financial reporting of income taxes for utilities are significant amounts of deferred income taxes that are "protected" under provisions of the IRC. That is, normalization is required with respect to certain tax and book depreciation differences if the utility is to remain eligible for accelerated depreciation. A historical perspective of tax incentives and tax legislation, as they relate to the utility industry, is helpful in understanding why the regulatory treatment of income tax is of such importance.

(iv) Concept of Tax Incentives. The first significant tax incentive that was generally available to all taxpayers was a provision of the 1954 Code that permitted accelerated methods of depreciation. Prior to enactment of this legislation, tax depreciation allowances were generally limited to those computed with the straight-line method, which is traditionally used for financial reporting and rate-making purposes. The straight-line method spread the cost of the property evenly over its estimated useful life. The accelerated depreciation provisions of the 1954 Code permitted taxpayers to take greater amounts of depreciation in the early years of property life and lesser amounts in later years.

Although accelerated methods permit taxpayers to recover capital investments more rapidly for tax purposes, deductions are limited to the depreciable cost of property. Thus, only the timing, not the ultimate amount, of depreciation is affected.

Because utilities are capital intensive in nature, accelerated depreciation provisions generate significant amounts of tax deferrals. Additionally, other sources of deferred taxes can be relatively small in some industries but are magnified in the utility industry because of its large construction programs. Among the major differences, generally referred to as basis differences, are interest, pensions, and taxes capitalized as costs of construction for book purposes but deducted currently (as incurred) as expenses for tax purposes. Once again, it is the timing, not the ultimate cost, that is affected.

Accelerated methods and lives were intended by the U.S. Congress to generate capital for investment, stimulate expansion, and contribute to high levels of output and employment. The economic benefit to the taxpayer arising from the use of accelerated depreciation and capitalized costs is the time value of the money because of the postponement of tax payments. The availability of what are effectively interest-free loans, obtained from the U.S. Treasury, reduces the requirements for other sources of capital, thereby reducing capital costs. Prior to the Tax Reform Act of 1986, these capitalized overheads represented significant deductions for tax purposes. However, subsequent to that Act, such amounts are now capitalized into the tax basis of the asset and depreciated for tax purposes as well. Thus, the benefits that once resulted from basis differences have, to a large extent, been eliminated.

(v) Tax Legislation. A brief history of the origin of accelerated tax depreciation and the intent of the U.S. Congress in permitting liberalized depreciation methods is helpful in understanding the regulatory and accounting issues related to income taxes.

Tax Reform Act of 1969. The accelerated tax depreciation methods initially made available to taxpayers in 1954 were without limitations in the tax law as to the accounting and rate-making methods used for public utility property. However, in the late 1960s, the U.S. Treasury Department and Congress became concerned about larger-than-anticipated tax revenue losses as a result of rate regulatory developments. Although both Congress and the Treasury realized that accelerated tax deductions would initially reduce Treasury revenues by the tax effect, they had not anticipated that flow-through would about double (at the then 48 percent tax rate) the Treasury's tax loss because of the tax-on-tax effect. Depending on the exact tax rate, about one-half the reduction in payments to the Treasury came from the deduction of accelerated depreciation and the other one-half from the immediate reduction in customer rates from the use of flow-through. It was this second one-half reduction of Treasury revenues that was considered unacceptable. Furthermore, immediate flow-through of these incentives to utility customers negated the intended congressional purpose of the incentives themselves. It was the utility customers who immediately received all of the benefit of accelerated depreciation. Accordingly, the utility did not have all the Treasury "capital" that was provided by Congress for investment and expansion.

Faced with larger-than-anticipated Treasury revenue losses, Congress enacted the Tax Reform Act of 1969 (TRA '69). By adding Section 167(1), it limited the Treasury's exposure to revenue losses by making the accelerated depreciation methods available to public utility properties only if specific qualifying standards as to accounting and ratemaking were met. Although Section 167(1) did not dictate to state regulatory commissions a rate-making treatment they should follow with respect to the tax effects of accelerated depreciation, the Act provided that:

- If a utility had not used accelerated depreciation prior to 1970, it would not be allowed to use accelerated tax depreciation in the future unless it normalized for rate-making and accounting purposes.
- Utilities that had been using accelerated tax depreciation and were normalizing for accounting and ratemaking purposes would not be allowed to use accelerated depreciation in the future unless they continued to normalize for accounting and rate-making purposes.

- Companies that were currently on a flow-through basis were allowed to continue on a flow-through basis in the future. However, an election was offered to such companies by which they could elect to be in a position where they would lose accelerated depreciation on future expansion additions unless they were normalizing for rate-making and accounting purposes with respect to such future expansion property additions.

Revenue Act of 1971. The Revenue Act of 1971, signed into law on December 10, 1971, codified the asset depreciation range (ADR) system for determining depreciation for tax purposes. Under ADR, lives were shortened, thereby accelerating tax depreciation even further. The ADR regulations prescribed the same standards regarding normalization versus flow-through rate making as were set forth in TRA '69.

Economic Recovery Act of 1981. The Economic Recovery Act of 1981, signed into law on August 31, 1981, continued to allow acceleration of depreciation tax deductions and included normalization rules for public utility property with respect to depreciation under the ACRS. Normalization is mandatory under the Act for accelerated depreciation taken on all public utility property placed in service after December 31, 1980.

Tax Reform Act of 1986. The Tax Reform Act of 1986 (TRA '86) reduced the acceleration of depreciation tax deductions and continued normalization requirements for public utility property. In addition, the maximum federal tax rate for corporations was reduced from 46 to 34 percent. This reduction in the federal tax rate not only reduces tax payments currently being made but will also reduce future tax payments (assuming continuation of the present tax rate) that result from the reversal of previously recorded deferred tax amounts—effectively forgiving a portion of the loan from the U.S. Treasury.

Section 203(e) of TRA '86 provided that deferred taxes related to certain depreciation method and life differences on public utility property in excess of the new 34 percent statutory rate be used to reduce customer rates using the average rate assumption method. This method generally requires the development of an average rate determined by dividing the aggregate normalized timing differences into the accumulated deferred taxes that have been provided on those timing differences. As the timing differences begin to reverse, the turnaround occurs at this average rate. Under this method, the so-called excess in the reserve for deferred taxes is reduced over the remaining life of the property.

If a regulatory commission requires reduction in the deferred tax balance more rapidly than under this method, book depreciation must be used for tax purposes. There is no provision in TRA '86 for any protection of other deferred taxes, such as book/tax basis differences, life differences on pre-ADR assets, salvage value on ADR assets, repair allowance, and so on. In addition, the deferred taxes on depreciation method and life differences provided at rates in excess of 46 percent are not protected under the average-rate assumption method.

Job Creation and Worker Assistance Act of 2002 (and Subsequent Acts). The Job Creation and Worker Assistance Act of 2002 (JCWA) included a provision allowing for an immediate expensing of 30 percent of qualified property. Generally, qualified property includes Modified Accelerated Cost Recovery System property with a recovery period of 20 years or less that meets certain criteria including specific acquisition and placed in service date requirements, This so-called bonus depreciation provision has been modified and extended as part of subsequent legislation with the bonus depreciation amount being extended to 50 percent and ultimately as much as 100 percent (through the 2010 Tax Relief, Unemployment Insurance Reauthorization and Job Creation Act) of qualifying property cost.

The bonus depreciation deductions are subject to the general normalization requirements applicable to other forms of accelerated depreciation.

(vi) ASC Topic 740, *Accounting for Income Taxes.* ASC Topic 740 (SFAS No. 109) shifts the focus of income tax accounting from the income statement to an asset and liability approach. ASC Topic

740 retains the requirement to record deferred taxes whenever income or expenses are reported in different years for financial reporting and tax purposes. However, it changes the way companies compute deferred taxes by requiring deferred tax assets and liabilities to be adjusted whenever tax rates or other provisions of the income tax law change. This is referred to as the *liability method* of providing deferred income taxes. ASC Topic 740 also requires utility companies to record tax liabilities for all temporary differences (defined as differences between the book and tax bases of assets and liabilities recorded on their respective balance sheets), even those that have previously been flowed through. For many utilities, these amounts are significant.

As a result of adopting ASC Topic 740, utilities adjusted their ADIT(Accumulated Deferred Income Taxes) balances to the level obtained by multiplying the statutory tax rate by existing temporary differences. Because this amount may be more or less than what has been permitted to be recovered through the rate-making process, regulatory assets or liabilities have also been recorded for financial reporting purposes. These regulatory assets and liabilities represent the future recovery or reduction in revenues as a result of previous income tax policies of regulatory commissions.

To illustrate the unique effects of utilities adopting ASC Topic740, two significant transactions will be described: recording of amounts previously flowed through as a reduction in customer rates and the effects of a change in tax rates.

1. *Recording of amounts previously flowed through.* ASC Topic 740 requires utilities to record accumulated deferred taxes using the liability approach for all temporary differences whether normalized or flowed through. Accordingly, ASC Topic 740 supersedes paragraph 18 of SFAS No. 71 (now ASC Topic 980). Furthermore, the FASB has concluded that the asset (liability) created by a regulatory promise to allow recovery (or require a settlement) of flow-through amounts is best measured by the expected cash flow to be provided as the temporary difference turns around and is recovered (settled) in rates. Thus, a regulatory asset or liability is established at the revenue requirement level, taking into account the tax-on-tax impact. In the Statement, these regulatory assets/liabilities are characterized as "probable future revenue/probable reduction in future revenue."

   The corresponding ADIT liability represents the income taxes that would result in connection with recovering both the temporary difference itself and the newly recorded regulatory asset. Accordingly, the computation of the amount to be recorded for prior flow-through is:

   Temporary differences flowed through
   × Gross-up (tax-on-tax) factor
   × Tax rate
   Dr. Regulatory asset/Cr. ADIT liability

   ASC 740 requires the regulatory asset and ADIT liability to be displayed separately for general-purpose financial reporting.

2. *Effects of a change in tax rates.* Under the liability method in SFAS No.109, ASC Topic 740, the ADIT liability is reported at the enacted settlement tax rate. Thus, deferred tax liabilities or assets established at rates in excess of the current statutory rate (35 percent) should be reduced to that level. Utilities are required to record the reduction in the ADIT liability but presumably will not recognize the reduction in the results of operations immediately because:

   a. The average rate assumption method provision contained in TRA '86 prohibits excess deferred taxes related to protected depreciation differences from being used to reduce customer rates more rapidly than over the life of the asset giving rise to the difference. Under this method, the excess in the deferred tax reserve is not reduced until the temporary differences giving rise to deferred taxes begin to turn around.

   b. Regulators may adopt a similar methodology for nonprotected excess deferred taxes.

   For these reasons, the credit to offset the reduction in the ADIT liability required by the liability method should be reclassified by regulated utilities as a separate liability. Consistent with the asset recovery scenario discussed previously, the FASB measures this separate liability as the cash flow impact of settling the specific liability (i.e., the future reduction in the revenue requirement). Accordingly, a gross-up factor must be applied to the excess deferred tax liability. The concept is illustrated with the next skeleton entry:

Temporary differences
× Enacted tax rate
Required ADIT liability
– Existing deferred taxes on temporary difference
Excess deferred taxes
× Gross-up factor
Dr. ADIT liability/Cr. Other liabilities

Other temporary differences that will result in the recording of ADIT and regulatory assets/liabilities are unamortized ITC balances (see the next subsection), amounts recorded on a net-of-tax basis (ASC Topic 740 prohibits such presentations), and AFUDC equity (previously recorded on an after-tax basis). Considering the large amounts of construction activity, the AFUDC-equity ADIT and regulatory assets may be significant.

At the time of adoption, ASC Topic 740 set forth transitional guidance whereby a single temporary difference between the book and tax bases of plant in service could be computed and the net effect recorded on the balance sheet.

The important concept to consider is that ASC Topic 740, in and of itself, did not alter rate-making/revenue requirements, and therefore ASC Topic 980 (SFAS No. 71) requires regulatory assets/liabilities for differences in the recognition of the timing of income tax expense via that process. Thus, flow-through of tax expense may continue for regulatory purposes, but ASC Topic 740 will require financial statements to report the deferred income tax liability with an offsetting regulatory asset to recognize that such cost will be recovered at a future date.

(vii) Investment Tax Credit. The accounting and rate-making aspects of the ITC are discussed separately because the economics and the effect are different from those of the acceleration in the write-off of costs for tax purposes. The ITC represents a permanent savings in taxes rather than a deferral. Although the tax credit should be used to reduce expense, the accounting and rate-making question is not one of flow-through but rather is a question as to which year's tax expense should be reduced and the benefit passed on to utility customers.

Accounting for ITC. Based on APB Opinion Nos. 2 and 4 (now under ASC Topic 740-10-50-20), the two accounting methods in use are to:

1. Flow the tax reduction through to income over the life of the property giving rise to the investment tax credit (service-life method), OR
2. Reduce tax expense in the current year by the full amount of the credit (initial year flow-through method).

Tax Legislation and Regulatory Treatment. The IRC requires the service-life method in order for many utilities to claim ITC. In 1964, in connection with the investment credit, Congress specifically established certain rate-making requirements, stating that federal regulatory agencies could not use the investment credit to reduce cost of service except over the service life of the related property. Congress also extended the practice of including rate-making requirements in the tax law when it enacted the job development tax credit in 1971 and provided that, except where a special election was made by a limited number of eligible companies, the benefits of the job development credit were to be shared between consumers and investors and that the consumers' share was to be passed on to them over the life of the property.

If the rate making and the accounting are not in accordance with the irrevocable election made by the company pursuant to the 1971 Act, the utility taxpayer can be denied ITC. The four available options were:

1. No portion of the investment credit would be used to reduce cost of service for rate purposes, but the unamortized credit could be used to reduce rate base (general rule).
2. The rate-making authority could reduce the cost of service for no more than the annual amortization of the investment credit over the book life of the property giving rise to the credit, and the unamortized balance of the credit could not be used to reduce rate base (ratable flow-through).
3. Utilities that were flow-through for accelerated depreciation under the standards of the Tax Reform Act of 1969 were permitted to elect to continue to follow the flow-through method for the investment credit. This election does not preclude the use of a service-life method of amortization of the credit if the regulatory commission agreed.
4. If the appropriate regulatory agency declared that there was a shortage of supply, companies in the natural gas or steam heat business would lose the credit if the rate-making body either reduced the cost of service or reduced the rate base.

With few exceptions, electric utilities, gas distribution companies, and telephone companies are now on the service-life amortization method for all or most of the investment credit, in most cases using the rate-making method covered by option 2 just discussed. Natural gas pipeline companies elected option 4, the shortage-of-supply option. As a result, no element of the credit could be passed on to customers. They were in the same position as nonregulated companies and could use either the initial year flow-through or service-life method for accounting purposes. However, in 1986, the FERC determined that there was no longer a shortage of gas supply and these companies would follow option 1 for any credits subsequently realized.

The 1986 Act repealed the ITC, generally effective for property placed in service after December 31, 1985. The Act requires that a utility continue follow its present method of accounting for amortizing the ITC. For failure to continue its present method, a utility will be forced to recapture the greater of (1) ITC for all open years or (2) unamortized ITC of the taxpayer or ITC not previously restored to rate base.

However, certain types of energy property, including solar, wind, and other types of renewable energy property, are eligible for ITC under Section 48(a). ITC can be claimed in lieu of production tax credits claimed under Section 45. The American Recovery and Reinvestment Act of 2009 (ARRA) extended the ITC provisions for qualifying renewable energy property and added a new incentive, Treasury grants taken in lieu of tax credits. The grant program is intended to mirror the ITC in most respects, including the application of normalization requirements.

(b) REVENUE RECOGNITION—ALTERNATIVE PROGRAMS. There are various financial reporting issues related to the accounting by rate-regulated utilities for the effects of certain alternative revenue programs adopted in a number of regulatory jurisdictions. Although the specific objectives of various recent programs are intended to address relatively new regulatory policies, the basic form and economic substance of the related regulatory treatment has been around for many years. The major alternative revenue programs currently in use include these three:

1. *Weather normalization clauses.* These clauses operate in a manner similar to fuel adjustment clauses and are designed to protect both rate payers and shareholders from the effects of significant changes in unit sales due to weather. Amounts billed or refunded are generally computed by multiplying the difference between actual units sold and units included in the rate-making process times base rates (excluding variable fuel costs). The intent of such a clause is to recover nonfuel cost of service (incurred costs) and return (including equity). These clauses are also being used currently with decoupling revenue mechanisms.

2. *Operating/plant performance measurements.* These programs are designed to hold a utility's management accountable and to effectively reward or penalize shareholders for meeting or not meeting established performance measurements. The reward or penalty can be a specific amount or an amount based on an increase or decrease in the return allowed by the regulator. The amount is usually based on performance for a specific measurement and period (typically an annual period) and billed or refunded to customers prospectively after regulatory review.
3. *Demand side management* (DSM). Many utility companies have implemented various load management and conservation programs that are designed to address capacity shortages, potential peak demand reductions, money-saving opportunities for customers, and environmental concerns. Such programs include:
    - Payments made to customers to assist in installation of cost-effective electric load reduction measures
    - Incentives paid to customers for proven conservation and load management measures
    - Retrofit programs directed at large customers to remodel or update operating equipment
    - Numerous projects to reduce individual customer energy use (such as bill credits for more efficient lighting and water heaters, energy-efficient appliances, residential weatherization, and insulation)
    - Developing standby generation
    - Interruptible service rates

DSM programs reduce sales so regulators are taking various actions to remove this disincentive by:

- Permitting recovery of and return on program costs
- Permitting compensation for lost revenues
- Granting bonuses or incentives for meeting goals and objectives

These programs typically enable the regulated utility to adjust rates in the future (usually as a surcharge applied to future billings) in response to past activities, transactions, or completed events.

In practice, accounting for amounts due to customers has not been an issue. These amounts represent refunds of revenues collected during the measurement period and are accounted for as contingent liabilities or regulatory liabilities that meet the conditions for accrual under ASC Topic 450-20 (SFAS No. 5) or ASC Topic 980 (paragraph 11 of SFAS No. 71), respectively.

The primary accounting question for these programs is whether the economic substance of regulatory actions should be accrued and recorded as assets for financial reporting purposes when it is probable that amounts for program costs and revenue shortfalls will be recovered from customers and no other event is required in the future other than billing. Financial reporting issues related to this question include: (1) the limitations on accruing equity return or profit under ASC Topic 980 (SFAS No. 71); (2) distinguishing between an incurred and allowable (equity) cost under ASC Topic 980 (SFAS No. 71) and situations in which the deferral/capitalization of such costs create regulatory assets for financial reporting purposes; and (3) distinguishing regulatory assets from GAAP assets.

At its May 21, 1992, meeting, the EITF addressed Issue No. 92-7, now under ASC Topic 980-605-25, *Accounting by Rate-Regulated Utilities for the Effects of Certain Alternative Revenue Programs,* and reached a consensus that once the specific events permitting billing of the additional revenues under a program have been completed, the regulated utility should recognize the additional revenues if all of the next three conditions are met:

1. The program is established by an order from the utility's regulatory commission that allows for automatic adjustment of future rates. Verification of the adjustment to future rates by the regulator would not preclude the adjustment from being considered automatic.

2. The amount of additional revenues for the period is objectively determinable and is probable of recovery.
3. The additional revenues will be collected within 24 months following the end of the annual period in which they are recognized.

For purposes of applying the consensus, the conditions for accruing revenue effectively determine what accounting model is being followed for asset recognition: a GAAP-based model as followed by enterprises in general or an ASC Topic 980 (SFAS No. 71) model. Accordingly, if the conditions of ASC Topic 980-605-25 (Issue No. 92-7) are met, an asset with many of the characteristics of a GAAP receivable is recorded. In situations where revenue is not accruable as a GAAP asset, ASC Topic 980 (paragraph 9 of SFAS No. 71) should be followed to the extent that probable future revenue is being provided to recover a specific *incurred cost* and a regulatory asset exists.

(c) ACCOUNTING FOR POSTRETIREMENT BENEFITS OTHER THAN PENSIONS. In December 1990, the FASB issued SFAS 106, now ASC Topic 715-60, which concludes that postretirement benefits other than pensions, commonly referred to as *OPEB costs,* represent deferred compensation that should be accounted for on an accrual basis.

Regulators have historically provided regulated utilities rate recovery of OPEB costs on a pay-as-you-go basis. Since ASC Topic 715-60 was issued, most regulators have allowed ASC Topic 715-60 expense, or some level of funding above pay as you go, for rate-making purposes. Others, such as the FERC, have specifically issued a policy statement adopting ASC Topic 715-60-based regulatory treatment for OPEB costs. However, a few regulatory jurisdictions have indicated that they will continue to limit cost recovery through rates to pay as you go or to some other regulatory treatment that will result in significant deferrals of OPEB costs for future recovery in rates. In situations where ASC Topic 715-60 is not adopted for regulatory purposes, regulatory asset recognition, for the annual difference between ASC Topic 715-60 costs and costs allowable in rates, would be appropriate only if future rate recovery of the regulatory asset is *probable,* as defined in ASC Topic 450.

In order to provide authoritative guidance as to the appropriate accounting and what constitutes sufficient evidence that a regulatory asset exists, the EITF created ASC Topic 980-715.

The EITF reached a final consensus for ASC Topic 980-715 that a regulatory asset related to ASC Topic 715-60 costs should not be recorded in a regulated utility's financial statements if the regulator continues to *limit inclusion* of OPEB costs in rates to a pay-as-you-go basis. Several EITF members noted that the application of ASC Topic 980 for financial reporting purposes requires that a rate-regulated enterprise's rates be designed to recover the specific enterprise's costs of providing the regulated service or product and that enterprise's cost of providing a regulated service or product includes ASC Topic 715-60 costs.

Further, the EITF reached a final consensus in ASC Topic 980-715 that a rate-regulated enterprise *should not* recognize a regulatory asset for financial reporting purposes for the difference between ASC Topic 715-60 costs and OPEB costs included in the regulated utility's rates unless the company (a) determines that it is *probable* that future revenue in an amount at least equal to the deferred cost (regulatory asset) will be recovered in rates and (b) meets *all* four of these criteria:

1. The regulated company's regulator has issued a rate order, including a policy statement or a generic order applicable to enterprises within the regulator's jurisdiction, that allows the deferral of ASC Topic 715-60 costs and subsequent inclusion of those deferred costs in rates.
2. Annual ASC Topic 715-60 costs, including *normal* amortization of the transition obligation, should be included in rates within approximately five years of ASC Topic 715-60 adoption. The change to full ASC Topic 715-60 in rates may take place in multiple steps, but the deferral period should not exceed approximately 5 years.

3. The combined deferral and recovery period approved by the regulator should not exceed approximately 20 years. If a regulator approves a total deferral and recovery period of more than 20 years, a regulatory asset should not be recognized for any costs not recovered by the end of the approximate 20-year period.
4. The percentage increase in rates scheduled under the regulatory recovery plan for each future year should be no greater than the percentage increase in rates scheduled under the plan for each immediately preceding year. This criterion is similar to that required for phase-in plans in paragraph 3(d) of ASC Topic 980-340-25. The EITF observed that recovery of the regulatory asset in rates on a straight-line basis would meet this criterion.

(d) OTHER FINANCIAL STATEMENT DISCLOSURES.

(i) Purchase Power Contracts. Many utilities enter into long-term contracts for the purchase of electric power in order to meet customer demand. The SEC's SAB Topic 10D sets forth the disclosure requirements related to long-term contracts for the purchase of electric power. This release states:

> The cost of power obtained under long-term purchase contracts, including payments required to be made when a production plant is not operating, should be included in the operating expenses section of the income statement. A note to the financial statements should present information concerning the terms and significance of such contracts to the utility company including date of contract expiration, share of land output being purchased, estimated annual cost, annual minimum debt service payment required and amount of related long-term debt or lease obligations outstanding.

Purchasers of power under contracts that specify a level of power to be made available for a specific time period usually account for such contracts as purchase commitments with no recognition of an asset for the right to receive power and no recognition of a liability for the obligation to make payments (i.e., the contracts are accounted for as executory agreements). However, some power purchase contracts may have characteristics similar to a lease in that the contract confers to the purchaser the right to use specific property, plant, and equipment.

The determination of whether a power purchase contract is a lease should be based on the substance of the contract using the guidance set forth in ASC Topic 840-10, *Determining Whether an Arrangement Contains a Lease.* The fact that an agreement is labeled a power purchase agreement is not conclusive. If a contract "conveys the right to use property, plant, and equipment," the contract should be accounted for as a lease. Other power purchase contracts could be accounted for as executory agreements with disclosure as required by SFAS ASC Topic 440, *Disclosure of Long-Term Obligations,* or as derivative contracts under ASC Topic 815.

Many utilities manage the risk of change in the price of fuel for generation, such as natural gas or coal, with long-term contracts or derivative instruments, such as futures, forwards, and options. While these derivatives may qualify for hedge accounting if properly documented, many utilities do not designate the derivative as a hedge for accounting purposes. This situation will generally occur when the regulator allows the benefit or cost associated with the settlement of the derivative to be netted with fuel cost and passed back to or recovered from the rate payer. In this case, utilities will record the fair value of the derivative on the balance sheet with changes in the fair value reported as a regulatory asset or liability.

(ii) Financing Through Construction Intermediaries. Utilities using a construction intermediary should include the intermediary's work in progress in the appropriate caption of utility plant on the balance sheet. SAB Topic 10A requires the related debt to be disclosed and included in long-term liabilities. Capitalized interest included as part of an intermediary's construction work in progress should be recognized as interest expense (with an offset to AFUDC-debt) in the income statement.

A note to the financial statements should describe the organization and purpose of the intermediary and the nature of its authorization to incur debt to finance construction. The note should also disclose the interest rate and amount of interest capitalized for each period in which an income statement is presented.

(iii) Jointly Owned Plants. SAB Topic 10C also requires a utility participating in a jointly owned power station to disclose the extent of its interests in such plant(s). Disclosure should include a table showing separately for each interest the amount of utility plant in service, accumulated depreciation, the amount of plant under construction, and the proportionate share. Amounts presented for plant in service may be further subdivided into subcategories, such as production, transmission, and distribution. Information concerning two or more generating plants on the same site may be combined if appropriate.

Disclosure should address the participant's share of direct expenses included in operating expenses on the income statement (e.g., fuel, maintenance, other operating). If the entire share of direct expenses is charged to purchased power, disclosure of this amount, as well as the proportionate amounts related to specific operating expenses on the joint plant records, should be indicated.

A typical footnote is:

(x) Jointly Owned Electric Utility Plant

Under joint ownership agreements with other state utilities, the company has undivided ownership interests in two electric generating stations and related transmission facilities. Each of the respective owners was responsible for the issuance of its own securities to finance its portion of the construction costs. Kilowatt-hour generation and operating expenses are divided on the same basis as ownership with each owner reflecting its respective costs in its statements of income. Information relative to the company's ownership interest in these facilities at December 31, 20XX, is as follows:

	Unit 1	Unit 2
Utility plant in service	$XXX,XXX	$XX,XXX
Accumulated depreciation	$XXX,XXX	$XX,XXX
Construction work in progress	$ XX,XXX	$ XX
Plant capacity—Mw	XXX	XXX
Company's share	XX%	XX%
In-service date	1974	1981

(iv) Decommissioning Costs and Nuclear Fuel. The term *decommissioning* means to safely remove nuclear facilities from service and reduce residual radioactivity to a level that permits termination of the Nuclear Regulatory Commission (NRC) license and release of the property for unrestricted use. The NRC has issued regulations requiring affected utilities with nuclear generation to prepare formal financial plans providing assurance that decommissioning funds in an amount at least equal to prescribed minimums will be accumulated prospectively over the remaining life of the related nuclear power plant. The NRC minimum is based on decontamination of the reactor facility but not demolition and site restoration. The amounts are based on generic studies; they represent the NRC's estimate of the minimum funds needed to protect the public safety and are not intended to reflect the actual cost of decommissioning. Companies making annual sinking fund contributions are required by the NRC to maintain external trust funds. ASC Topic 825, *Disclosure About Fair Value of Financial Instruments,* and ASC Topic 320, *Accounting for Certain Investments in Debt and Equity Securities,* should be reviewed with respect to decommissioning trusts.

Financial reporting considerations related to nuclear decommissioning costs are addressed in ASC Topic 410, *Accounting for Asset Retirement Obligations.* Generally, the estimated decommissioning obligation for nuclear power plants had been recognized over the life of the plant as a component of depreciation. ASC Topic 410 changed this practice. Instead, an amount for an asset retirement obligation, such as for the decommissioning of a nuclear power plant, is recognized when it is incurred and displayed as a liability. The asset retirement cost is capitalized as part of the plant asset's carrying amount and subsequently allocated to expense over that asset's useful life. ASC Topic 410 includes special provisions for entities that apply ASC Topic 980. Differences between amounts collected through rates and amounts recognized in accordance with ASC Topic 410 were recognized as regulatory assets and liabilities if the requirements of ASC Topic 980 were met.

(v) Securitization of Stranded Costs, Including Regulatory Assets. In connection with the electric industry restructuring efforts that occurred in a number of states, regulatory mechanisms were established to mitigate potential stranded costs. The legislative or regulatory framework for moving to a competitive marketplace included provisions when issued for the affected companies to securitize or "monetize" all or a portion of their stranded costs through the issuance of debt securities that would provide the utility with a lower cost of capital than that to which they were previously exposed. Generally, such provisions establish a separate unbundled revenue stream from the current bundled stream, surcharge, or tariff that would be the source of recovery from a company's rate payers for the stranded costs. Companies securitize their rights to impose such revenue stream, surcharge, or tariff by receiving cash flows from investors in exchange for future cash flows to be collected from customers. The utility would issue debt obligations in an amount equal to its stranded costs (or portion thereof). The resulting debt obligations would be nonrecourse since the company would sell the stranded costs to a credit-enhanced, bankruptcy remote special-purpose entity or trust established to finance the purchase through the sale of state-authorized debt. Collections of the tariff by the company would be passed through to holders of the debt as periodic payments of interest and principal.

The potential benefits to a company from securitizing stranded costs include the opportunity to improve credit quality and to use the proceeds to reduce leverage and fixed charges, or fund the termination of uneconomic contracts. The expectation is that monetizing the stranded costs would result in lower rates for consumers since higher cost of capital is effectively replaced by traditional utility debt with lower cost.

In February 1997, the SEC's Office of Chief Accountant provided financial reporting guidance to California's utility registrants for proceeds received in connection with a stranded cost securitization. The SEC Staff concluded that the proceeds received should be classified as either debt or deferred revenue based on the guidance in ASC Topic 470-10-25, *Debt.*

ASC Topic 470-10-25 reached a consensus that the presence of any one of six specifically identified factors independently creates a rebuttable presumption that classification of the proceeds as debt is appropriate. The facts and circumstances of stranded cost securitization transactions will typically result in the presence of one or more of the factors. Thus, securitization proceeds are generally expected to be classified as debt for financial reporting purposes.

ASC Topic 470-10-25 also concluded that amounts recorded as debt should be amortized under the interest method. Generally, this will result in an increasing amount of stranded cost recognition in the income statement during the securitization period. This occurs because the amount recognized will equal the principal portion (on a mortgage basis) of the tariffed debt service cost that is billable to customers and recorded as revenue during each period.

In connection with providing classification guidance, the SEC Staff also concluded that regulatory assets are not financial assets. This is supported by ASC Topic 860-55-8, *Transfers and Servicing,* and SFAS No. 166, *Accounting for Transfers of Financial Assets—an Amendment of FASB No. 140*-FASB Statement Appendix C paragraph 6. Further, the legislation that provides for the securitization of regulatory assets simply allows the utility's regulator to impose a surcharge or tariff on electricity sold in the future. The law, however, does not transpose regulatory assets into financial assets. The basis for the SEC Staff's conclusion is that the resulting law creates an enforceable right (which is a right imposed on one party by another, such as a property tax) and not a contractual right. The SEC Staff, after consulting with the FASB Staff, concluded that the FASB specifically limited financial assets to a contractual right, which is essentially a subset of an enforceable right. Thus, enforceable rights that are not contractual rights do not meet the definition of a financial asset under ASC Topic 860-55-8. However, beneficial interests in a securitization trust that holds nonfinancial assets, such as securitized stranded costs, would be considered financial assets by third-party investors, unless that third party must consolidate the trust pursuant to the provisions of ASC Topic 810-10-55 and other prevailing consolidation guidance.

The SEC Staff also concluded that the proceeds received by the utility do not represent cash for assets sold, but cash received for future services. This approach seems to preclude accounting for this type of a transaction as any kind of a sale outside of ASC Topic 860-55.

Although the preceding conclusion is based on the facts and circumstances of a specific transaction, the SEC Staff indicated that it is doubtful whether this type of transaction could be altered enough to get a different answer.

(vi) Expanded Footnote Disclosure. The current relevance of ASC Topic 980, *Regulated Operations,* is an often-discussed financial reporting topic for rate-regulated enterprises. In SEC Staff comment letters, rate-regulated registrants are typically requested to discuss and quantify the effect on the company's financial statements of the application of ASC Topic 980. Some key items that would make such discussions and disclosures meaningful include:

- Background and scope of the regulations and regulatory jurisdictions that oversee the entity(ies)
- Periods covered by the current rate design and orders including any significant pending filings with the respective commissions or jurisdictions
- Deregulation and resulting competition for a variety of services
- Discounting of approved tariffs
- New rate designs, such as demand-side designs or new forms of regulation that are not based on the cost of providing utility service
- Actual and expected discontinuations of application of ASC Topic 980

Based on current FASB requirements and SEC comments, a regulated entity should consider discussing these issues in disclosures as they relate to the entity's recorded regulatory assets and liabilities under FASB ASC Topic 980:

- Quantitative summary of the regulatory assets and liabilities recorded on the balance sheet
- General background and basis of the assets and liabilities including the authority (i.e., order or precedent) that gave rise to the item
- Discussion on the recovery period of the asset and return earned; for regulatory items (typically assets) with no return, a discussion that states there is no return and the amortization period of those items
- Any uncertainties that may exist within the different regulatory assets and liabilities
- For entities with regulated operations in several jurisdictions: disclosure of the regulatory items by jurisdiction/location is recommended

An excerpt of a sample footnote disclosure for an entity that follows the guidance within ASC Topic 980 is presented next. Typically a company would discuss the basics of its regulatory accounting within the summary of significant accounting policies footnote and would discuss the specifics of the regulatory assets and liabilities in a separate regulatory footnote.

Note 1: Summary of Significant Accounting Policies

Regulatory Assets and Liabilities:

The Company is subject to the provisions of FASB ASC 980, *Regulated Operations,* and accounts for the effects of regulation through the application of regulatory accounting to its operating utilities since their rates:

- are established by a third-party regulator with the authority to set rates that bind customers;
- are cost-based;
- can be charged to and collected from customers.

An enterprise meeting all of these criteria capitalizes costs that would otherwise be charged to expense (regulatory assets) if the rate actions of its regulator make it probable that those costs will be recovered in future revenue. Regulatory accounting is applied only to the parts of the business that meet the above criteria. If a portion of the business applying regulatory accounting no longer meets those requirements, previously recorded net regulatory assets are removed from the balance sheet in accordance with GAAP.

A company typically would include an example breakdown as shown below of their regulatory assets and if material regulatory liabilities within either their summary of significant accounting policies footnote or within the separate regulatory footnote. Also, a company would typically then in some format explain and discuss the basis and other disclosure considerations as noted above for each of the material regulatory assets/liabilities.

Regulatory assets on the balance sheets are comprised of the following:

	20XX	20XX
Deferred income taxes	$ XX,XXX	$ XX,XXX
Transition costs	(X,XXX)	(X,XXX)
Energy efficiency costs	XX,XXX	XX,XXX
Customer shopping incentives	XX,XXX	X,XXX
Lost on reacquired debt	XX,XXX	X,XXX
Plant costs	XX,XXX	XX,XXX
Postretirement benefit costs	XX,XXX	XX,XXX
Nuclear plant decommissioning	X,XXX	—
Storm damage costs	XXX	X,XXX
Transmission costs	X,XXX	X,XXX
Over-recovered fuel adjustment clause	(X,XXX)	(X,XXX)
	$XXX,XXX	$XXX,XXX

(e) OTHER CURRENT UTILITY TOPICS. As noted, the industry has gone through a number of changes over the past decade with the increase in deregulation, renewable energy, rate mechanisms, and environmental pressures. State and federal political pressure on the use of renewable energy has prompted expanded sources of power and energy on a scale not seen before in the United States. Solar fields and wind farms have increased dramatically since 2008 in conjunction with federal grant and incentive programs to build alternative and/or renewable energy. Most U.S. electric utilities are either involved in the construction, investment, and ownership of these assets or have agreed to purchase power from them. The Environmental Protection Agency and state governments have increased their awareness and desire to eliminate perceived hazardous pollutants (carbon, sulfur dioxide, nitrous oxide, and mercury) that are emitted or created by coal generation. Such actions have prompted large environmental spends on coal plant scrubbers and changes in types of fuel (coal type: PRB low or high sulfur, etc.) used. States have recently used an emission credit system to create a cap and trade platform for the long-term reduction of emissions. Large reserves of natural gas found in shale regions have driven the current price of natural gas very low. Given the large supply and the cleaner nature of burning of gas versus coal, numerous decisions on capital, plant recovery, plant conversions (coal to gas), and reduction of coal facilities are occurring. The transmission and distribution systems of the United States need to be repaired and upgraded; but that will take substantial funding to complete. The cost of utility services to maintain a network, meet new environmental requirements, fulfill renewable energy requirements, and replace existing dated infrastructure (pipes, wires, etc.) will have a profound effect on future rates and utility services for years to come. Whether the utility owns the generation or the reserves or simply contracts to get them, it is likely that costs will be borne all involved. Reliability, sustainability, and a fair return to investors is and will continue to be a challenge. Finally, technology and knowledge management have increased substantially. The introduction of smart meters which allow a utility and in some cases the individual user of electricity or gas to see usage on a 15 minute or less basis and the technology and knowledge that can be gleamed from such items will help transform the next decade of utility decision making. Serving customers better through energy-efficient means will most likely be a driver in the next decade.

36.11 SOURCES AND SUGGESTED REFERENCES

Accounting Principles Board. Opinion No. 4, *Accounting for the "Investment Credit"* (ASC 740-10-50-20, *Investment Tax Credit Recognition Policy*). New York: Author, 1964.

______. Opinion No. 11, *Accounting for Income Taxes* (ASC 740, *Income Taxes*). New York: AICPA, 1967.

______. Opinion No. 20, *Accounting Changes* (ASC 250-10, *Accounting for Changes and Error Corrections*). New York: AICPA, 1971.

______. Opinion No. 30, *Reporting the Results of Operations—Reporting the Effects of Disposal of a Segment of a Business, and Extraordinary, Unusual and Infrequently Occurring Events and Transactions* (ASC 225-20-45, *Criteria for Presentation as Extraordinary Items*). New York: AICPA, 1973.

Amble, J. L., and J. M. Cassel. *A Guide to Implementation of Statement 87 on Employers' Accounting for Pensions.* Stamford, CT: FASB, 1986.

American Institute of Certified Public Accountants. Accounting Research Bulletin No. 44, *Declining-Balance Depreciation*—(now ASC 360-10, *Property, Plant, and Equipment*). New York: Author, July 1958.

______. Accounting Research Bulletin No. 51, *Consolidated Financial Statements* (ASC 810-10, *Consolidation—Overall*). New York: Author, August 1959.

Financial Accounting Standards Board. ASC Topic 815 Derivatives and Hedging. FASB., Norwalk Conn. Codification date 2009)

______,ASC 715-30, *Defined Benefit Plans—Pension.* FASB. Norwalk Conn. Codification Date 2009.

______, Discussed FAS 102, *Official Minutes of the Emerging Issues Task Force Meeting* (ASC 230-10, *Statement of Cash Flows*). Norwalk, CT: Author, February 23, 1989.

______. Emerging Issues Task Force, Issue No. 92-12, *Accounting for OPEB Costs by Rate-Regulated Enterprises* (ASC 980-715, *Compensation-Retirement Benefits*). Norwalk, CT: Author, January 1993.

______. Emerging Issues Task Force, Issue No. 92-7, *Accounting by Rate-Regulated Utilities for the Effects of Certain Alternative Revenue Programs* (ASC 980-605-25, *Revenue Recognition*). Norwalk, CT: Author, July 1992.

______. Emerging Issues Task Force, Issue No. 93-4, *Accounting for Regulatory Assets* (ASC 980-340, *Recognition of Regulatory Assets*). Norwalk, CT: Author, March 1993.

______. Emerging Issues Task Force, Issue No. 97-4, *Deregulation of the Pricing of Electricity—Issues Related to the Application of FASB Statements No. 71, "Accounting for the Effects of Regulation," and No. 101, "Regulated Enterprises—Accounting for the Discontinuance of Application of FASB Statement No. 71"* (ASC 980-20-35, *Discontinuation of Rate-Regulated Accounting—Subsequent Measurement*). Norwalk, CT: Author, May-- July 1997.

______. Emerging Issues Task Force, Issue No. 01-8, *Determining Whether an Arrangement Contains a Lease* (ASC 840-10, *Leases—Overall*). Norwalk, CT: Author, May 2003.

______. Statement of Financial Accounting Standards No. 5, *Accounting for Contingencies* (ASC 450-20, *Loss Contingencies*). Stamford, CT: Author, 1975.

______. Statement of Financial Accounting Standards No. 16, *Prior Period Adjustments* (ASC 250-10, *Accounting for Changes and Error Corrections*). Stamford, CT: Author, 1977.

______. Statement of Financial Accounting Standards No. 34, *Capitalization of Interest Cost* (ASC 835-30, *Capitalization of Interest*). Stamford, CT: Author, 1979.

______. Statement of Financial Accounting Standards No. 71, *Accounting for the Effects of Certain Types of Regulation* (ASC 980-10/20, *Regulated Operations—Overall/Discontinuation of Rate-Regulated Accounting*). Stamford, CT: Author, 1982.

______. Statement of Financial Accounting Standards No. 90, *Regulated Enterprises—Accounting for Abandonments and Disallowances of Plant Costs* (ASC 980-360-35, *Property, Plant, and Equipment—Subsequent Measurement*). Stamford, CT: Author, 1986.

______. Statement of Financial Accounting Standards No. 92, *Regulated Enterprises —Accounting for Phase-in Plans* (now ASC 980-340, *Other Assets and Deferred Costs*). Stamford, CT: Author, 1987.

______. Statement of Financial Accounting Standards No. 101, *Regulated Enterprises—Accounting for the Discontinuation of Application of FASB Statement No.* 71 (now ASC 980-20, *Discontinuation of Rate-Regulated Accounting*). Norwalk, CT: Author, 1988.

______. Statement of Financial Accounting Standards No. 106, *Employers' Accounting for Postretirement Benefits Other Than Pension* (now ASC 715-60, *Compensation–Retirement Benefits: Other Postemployment Benefit Plans*). Stamford, CT: Author, December 1990.

———. Statement of Financial Accounting Standards No. 109, *Accounting for Income Taxes* (now ASC 740, *Income Taxes*). Norwalk, CT: Author, February 1992.

———. Statement of Financial Accounting Standards No. 143, *Accounting for Asset Retirement Obligations* (now ASC 410-20, *Asset Retirement Obligations*). Norwalk, CT: Author, June 2001.

———. Statement of Financial Accounts Standards No. 144, *Accounting for the Impairment or Disposal of Long-Lived* Assets (now ASC 360-10-35, *Property, Plant, and Equipment—Subsequent Measurement*). Norwalk, CT: Author, August 2001.

———. Technical Bulletin No. 87-2. *Computation of a Loss on an Abandonment* (now ASC 980-360-35, *Property, Plant, and Equipment—Subsequent Measurement*). Stamford, CT: Author, December 1987.

Securities and Exchange Commission. Staff Accounting Bulletin No. 19, Topic 10J, *Interpretation Describing Disclosure Concerning Expected Future Costs of Storing Spent Nuclear Fuel and of Decommissioning Nuclear Electric Generating Plants*. Washington, DC: Author, January 1978.

———. Staff Accounting Bulletin No. 28, *Financing by Electric Utilities Through Use of Construction Intermediaries* (ASC 980-810-S99, *Regulated Operations—Consolidation SEC Materials*). Washington, DC: Author, December 1978.

———. Staff Accounting Bulletin No. 72, *Utilities—Classification of Disallowed Costs or Costs of Abandoned Plants* (ASC 980-360-S99, *Regulated Operations—Property, Plant, and Equipment SEC Materials*). Washington, DC: Author, November 1987.

CHAPTER 37

PRODUCERS OR DISTRIBUTORS OF FILMS

Francis E. Scheuerell, Jr., CPA

Navigant Consulting

37.1 HISTORY OF GUIDANCE 1

37.2 REVENUE REPORTING 2

- (a) Basic Revenue Reporting Principles 2
- (b) Detailed Revenue Reporting Principles 3
  - (i) Persuasive Evidence of an Arrangement 3
  - (ii) Delivery 3
  - (iii) Availability 3
  - (iv) Fixed or Determinable Fee 3
  - (v) Barter Revenue 4
  - (vi) Modifications of Arrangements 4
  - (vii) Returns and Price Concessions 4
  - (viii) Licensing of Film-Related Products 4
  - (ix) Present Value 5

37.3 COSTS AND EXPENSES 5

- (a) Film Costs—Capitalization 5
- (b) Film Costs—Amortization and Participation Cost Accruals 5
- (c) Ultimate Revenue 6
- (d) Ultimate Participation Costs 7
- (e) Film Costs Valuation 7
- (f) Subsequent Events 8
- (g) Exploitation Costs 8
- (h) Manufacturing Costs 8

37.4 PRESENTATION AND DISCLOSURE 8

37.1 HISTORY OF GUIDANCE

In 1974, the American Institute of Certified Public Accountants (AICPA) issued Industry Accounting Guide, *Accounting for Motion Picture Films,* and Statement of Position (SOP) No. 79-4, *Accounting for Motion Picture Films,* which provided specialized reporting principles for the industry. In 1981, the Financial Accounting Standards Board (FASB) extracted those specialized principles and presented them in its Statement No. 53, *Financial Reporting by Producers and Distributors of Motion Picture Films.* Between 1981 and 2000, the origin of the majority of a film's revenue expanded from distribution to movie theaters and free television to those outlets plus, for example, home video, satellite and cable television, and pay-per-view television, and international revenue has become more significant. As the origins of film revenue expanded during this time period, so did diversity in practice expand in applying the requirements of Statement No. 53. As a result of industry changes and the issues in applying Statement No. 53, the FASB asked the Accounting Standards Executive Committee (AcSEC) to develop an SOP to replace that Statement.

In response, AcSEC issued SOP 00-2, *Accounting by Producers or Distributors of Films,* in June 2000, effective for fiscal years beginning after December 15, 2000, and the FASB simultaneously rescinded its Statement No. 53 in its Statement No. 139, *Rescission of FASB Statement No. 53 and Amendments to FASB Statements No. 63, 89, and 121.* This chapter presents the accounting guidance in SOP 00-2. Subsequently, the guidance in SOP 00-2 is now in FASB Accounting Standards Codification (Codification or ASC), Topic 926, *Entertainment Films.*

The guidance applies to all types of films and to all producers or distributors that own or hold rights to distribute or exploit films. Films includes feature films, television specials, television series, or similar products (including animated films and television programming) that are sold, licensed, or exhibited, whether produced on film, videotape, digital, or other video recording format. However, the guidance in SOP 00-2 does not apply to the

- Creating and distributing of recorded music products (however, the cost of acquiring music rights for use in a film is within the scope of SOP 00-2 (ASC 926))
- Reporting by cable television
- Reporting by broadcasters
- Accounting for internal use software
- Software revenue recognition
- Accounting for the film and software costs associated with developing entertainment and educational software products.

37.2 REVENUE REPORTING

(a) BASIC REVENUE REPORTING PRINCIPLES. A film producer or distributor obtains revenue from sale or licensing of its films.

An arrangement to license a single film or multiple films transfers a single right or a group of rights to distributors, theaters, exhibitors, or others exclusively or nonexclusively in a particular market and territory under terms that may vary significantly among different contracts. License fees are commonly fixed in amount or based on a percentage of the customer's revenue, which may include a nonrefundable minimum guarantee payable in advance or over the license period. Direct control over the distribution of a film may remain with the producer or may be transferred to a distributor, exhibitor, or other licensee.

A producer or distributor should report revenue from a sale or licensing arrangement of a film when all of these five conditions are met:

1. Persuasive evidence exists of a customer's sale or licensing arrangement.
2. The film is complete and has been delivered or is available for immediate and unconditional delivery in accordance with the terms of the arrangement.
3. The arrangement's license period has begun and the customer can begin its exploitation, exhibition, or sale.
4. The arrangement fee is fixed or determinable.
5. Collection of the arrangement fee is reasonably assured.

A producer or distributor should defer recognizing revenue until all of the conditions are met. A producer or distributor that reports a receivable for advances currently due before the date revenue is to be reported or that receives cash payments before that date should also report an equivalent liability for deferred revenue until all of the above listed conditions have been met. Even if a producer or distributor sells or otherwise transfers such a receivable to a third party, the producer or distributor should not recognize revenue before meeting all of the preceding revenue recognition conditions. Amounts scheduled to be received in the future based on an arrangement for any form of distribution, exploitation, or exhibition should be reported as a receivable only when they are currently due or when the above listed conditions have been met, if earlier.

(b) DETAILED REVENUE REPORTING PRINCIPLES

(i) Persuasive Evidence of an Arrangement. The persuasive evidence of a licensing arrangement needed to report revenue is provided solely by legally enforceable documentation (e.g., contract) that states, at a minimum, the license period, the film or films covered, the rights transferred, and the consideration to be exchanged. Revenue should nevertheless not be reported if there is significant doubt about the obligation or ability of either party to perform under the terms of the arrangement.

Verifiable evidence required is, for example, a purchase order or an online authorization. It should include correspondence from the customer that details the mutual understanding of the arrangement or evidence that the customer has acted in accordance with the arrangement.

(ii) Delivery. A producer or distributor should not recognize revenue before delivery is complete if the licensing arrangement requires physical delivery of a product to the customer or if the arrangement is silent about delivery.

However, it is not uncommon for a licensing arrangement not to require immediate or direct physical delivery of a film to the customer but instead provide the customer with immediate and unconditional access to a film print held by the producer or distributor or provide authorization to the customer to order a film laboratory to make the film immediately and unconditionally available for the customer's use—known as a *lab access letter*. If the film is complete and available for immediate delivery, the requirement for delivery has been met.

A licensing arrangement may require a producer or distributor to change the film significantly after it is first available to a customer. If so, revenue should be reported only after those changes are made. Significant changes are additive to the film (i.e., the producer or distributor is required to create new or additional content, e.g., by reshooting a scene or creating additional special effects). Insertion or addition of preexisting film footage, adding dubbing or subtitles, removing offensive language, reformatting to fit a broadcaster's screen dimensions, and adjustments to allow for the insertion of commercials are examples of insignificant changes in this sense.

Costs incurred for significant changes should be added to film costs (discussed later in this chapter in Section 37.3(a)) and later reported as expense when the related revenue is reported. Costs expected to be incurred for insignificant changes should be accrued and reported as expense if revenue is reported before those costs are incurred.

(iii) Availability. Some arrangements may have a specific date that a customer may begin its first exploitation, exhibition, or sale of a film. For example, the imposition of a street date on the initial date on which home video products may be sold or rented defines the date on which a customer's exploitation rights begin. In this instance, the producer or distributor should report revenue no sooner than the street date. If conflicting agreements place restrictions on the initial exploitation, exhibition, or sale of a film by a customer in a particular territory or market, the producer or distributor should report revenue no sooner than the date the restrictions lapse and meeting all of the previously listed revenue recognition conditions.

(iv) Fixed or Determinable Fee. A fee based on a licensing arrangement for a single film that provides for a flat fee is considered fixed and determinable, and the producer or distributor should recognize the fee as revenue when the other conditions for recognizing revenue have been met.

A producer or distributor should allocate a flat fee arrangement on multiple films, including films not yet completed, to each individual film, by market and territory, based on relative fair values of the rights to exploit each film under the arrangement. Allocations to films not yet completed should be based on the amounts refundable if the producer or distributor does not complete and deliver the films. The allocations should not be adjusted later. The producer or distributor should recognize as revenue the amount allocated to an individual film when all of the conditions for recognizing revenue have been met for the film by market and territory. If the producer or distributor cannot determine the relative fair values, the fee is not fixed or determinable and the producer or distributor should not recognize revenue until meeting all of the previously listed revenue recognition conditions.

Quoted market prices are usually not available to determine fair value for this purpose. The producer or distributor should estimate the fair value of a film by using the best information available in the circumstances, with the objective to arrive at an amount it believes it would have received had the arrangement granted the same rights to the film separately. A discounted cash flow model may be used, in conformity with paragraphs 39 to 71 of FASB Statement of Concepts No. 7, *Using Cash Flow Information and Present Value in Accounting Measurements,* which provide guidance on the traditional and expected cash flow approaches. The rights granted for the film under the arrangement, such as the length of the license period and limitations on the method, timing, or frequency of exploitation, should be observed.

The contract's fee may be based on a percentage or share of the customer's revenue from exhibition or other exploitation of a film, in which case it is a variable fee. The producer or distributor should report revenue as the customer exhibits or exploits the film if the other conditions for reporting revenue have been met.

If the customer guarantees and pays or agrees to pay the producer or distributor a nonrefundable minimum amount applied against a variable fee on films that are not cross-collateralized—part of an arrangement in which the exploitation results for multiple films are aggregated—the producer or distributor should recognize the minimum guaranteed amount as revenue when all the other conditions for revenue reporting have been met. If they are cross-collateralized, the minimum guarantee for each film cannot be objectively determined and should be recognized as revenue as the customer exhibits or exploits the film when all the other conditions for recognizing revenue have been met.

(v) Barter Revenue. Some licensing arrangements with television station customers provide that the stations may exhibit films in exchange for advertising time for the producers or distributors. The exchanges should be reported in conformity with ASC Subtopic 845, *Nonmonetary Transactions.*

(vi) Modifications of Arrangements. If all of the conditions for reporting revenue are met by an existing arrangement and the parties agree to extend the time for the arrangement, reporting revenue depends on whether a flat fee or a variable fee is involved. The producer or distributor should recognize the fee as revenue in conformity with the principles stated earlier for flat fees or variable fees.

Any other kind of change to a licensing arrangement—for example, the arrangement is changed from a fixed fee to a smaller fixed fee with a variable component—should be reported on as a new licensing arrangement, in conformity with the guidance in this section. The producer or distributor should consider the original arrangement terminated and accrue and expense associated costs and reverse previously reported revenue for refunds and concessions, such as a provision to accept a license fee rate below market.

(vii) Returns and Price Concessions. A producer or distributor should report revenue on an arrangement that includes a right of return or if its past practices allow for returns in conformity with ASC 605-15-25, which includes the requirement for the producer or distributor to be able to reasonably estimate the future returns.

Contractual provisions or the producer's or distributor's customary practices may involve price concessions (e.g., "price protection") in which the producer or distributor lowers the prices to the customer on product it previously bought based on a lowering of its wholesale prices. If so, the producer or distributor should provide related allowances when it reports revenue. If it cannot reasonably and reliably estimate future concessions or if there are significant uncertainties about whether it can maintain its prices, the fee is not fixed or determinable, and it should report revenue no sooner than it can estimate concessions reasonably and reliably.

(viii) Licensing of Film-Related Products. A producer or distributor should report revenue from licensing arrangements to market film-related products no sooner than the film is released.

(ix) Present Value. Revenue should be calculated based on the present value of the license fee as of the date it is first reported in conformity with ASC 835-30-25.

37.3 COSTS AND EXPENSES

Costs incurred by producers and distributors to produce a film and bring it to market include film costs, participation costs, exploitation costs, and manufacturing costs.

(a) FILM COSTS—CAPITALIZATION. A separate asset should be reported at cost for films in development or in inventory. Interest costs should be reported in conformity with ASC Topic 835.

The production overhead component of film costs includes allocable costs of persons or departments with exclusive or significant responsibility for the production of films. Production overhead should not include administrative and general expenses, charges for losses on properties sold or abandoned (i.e., no full-cost method for films), or the costs of certain overall deals as follows.

In an overall deal, a producer or distributor compensates a producer or other creative individual for the exclusive or preferential use of that party's creative services. The producer or distributor should report as expense the costs of overall deals it cannot identify with specific projects over the period the costs are incurred. The producer or distributor should report a reasonable proportion of costs of overall deals as specific project film costs to the extent that the costs are directly related to the acquisition, adaptation, or development of specific projects. The producer or distributor should not allocate to specific project film costs amounts it had previously reported as expense.

The costs to prepare for the production of a particular film of adaptation or development of a book, stage play, or original screenplay to which a producer or distributor has film rights should be added to the cost of the particular film.

Properties in development should be periodically reviewed to determine whether they likely will ultimately be used in the production of films. When a producer or distributor determines that a property will not be used or disposed of, it should charge to the statement of operations any loss involved, including allocable amounts from overall deals, as discussed earlier. A property should be presumed to be subject to disposal (whether by sale or abandonment) if the film has not been set for production within three years of the time of the first capitalized transaction. In the film industry, *set for production* means that management has implicitly or explicitly authorized and committed to funding the production of a film, active preproduction has begun, and principal photography is expected to begin within six months. The amount of loss charged to the statement of operations is the excess of the fair value of the project over the carrying amount. If management has not committed to a plan to sell the property, the rebuttable presumption is that the film will be abandoned; as a result, the fair value of the property is zero.

In addition to the preceding guidance for film costs, the following applies to an episodic television series. Ultimate revenue for an episodic television series can include estimates from the initial market and secondary markets, as discussed further in the Ultimate Revenue section below. Costs for a single episode in excess of the amount of revenue contracted for the episode should not be capitalized until the producer or distributor can establish estimates of secondary market revenue, as discussed further in Section 37.3(c). Costs over this limit should be reported as expense and not subsequently restored as capitalized costs. Costs capitalized for an episode should be reported as expense as it reports revenue for the episode. When the producer or distributor can estimate secondary market revenue, as discussed further in Section 37.3(c), it should capitalize subsequent film costs as discussed in that section and should evaluate the carrying amount for impairment as discussed further in Section 37.3(e).

(b) FILM COSTS—AMORTIZATION AND PARTICIPATION COST ACCRUALS. A producer or distributor should amortize film costs and accrue expense for participation costs using the individual-film-forecast-computation method. That method amortizes costs or accrues expenses in this ratio: the current period actual revenue divided by estimated remaining unreported ultimate revenue as of the beginning of the current fiscal year. Unamortized film costs as of the beginning of the current fiscal year and ultimate participation costs not yet reported as expense are each multiplied by that fraction. Without changes in estimates, this method yields a constant rate of profit over the ultimate period for each film before exploitation costs, manufacturing costs, and other period expenses. A producer or distributor should report a liability for participation costs only if it is probable that it will have to pay to settle its obligation under the terms of the participation agreement. At each reporting date, accrued participation costs should be at least the amounts the producer or distributor has to pay as of that date. Amortization of capitalized film costs and reporting of participation costs as expenses should begin when the film is released and revenue reporting on it begins.

With no revenue from third parties that is directly related to the exhibition or exploitation of a film, the producer or distributor should make a reasonably reliable estimate of the portion of unamortized film costs that is representative of the utilization of the film in its exhibition or exploitation. The producer or distributor should report those amounts as expense as it exhibits or exploits the film. Consistent with the objective of the individual film-forecast-computation methods, all revenue should bear a representative amount of the amortization of film costs during the ultimate period.

Results may vary from estimates, of course. A producer or distributor should revise estimates of ultimate revenue and participation costs as of each reporting date to recognize the most current information available. When it is necessary to revise the estimate, the producer or distributor should adjust the denominator that recognizes only ultimate revenue from the beginning of the fiscal year of change. In other words, any subsequent changes to ultimate revenue are treated prospectively as of the beginning of the year of change. Also, revenue for the current year is not affected by the change in estimate. The producer or distributor should apply the revised ratio to the net carrying amount of unamortized film costs and to the film's ultimate participation costs not reported as expense as of the beginning of the fiscal year. The producer and distributor should report the difference between expenses determined using the new estimates and amounts previously reported as expense during the fiscal year in the income statement in the period, such as the quarter in which the estimates are revised.

A producer or distributor should consider multiple seasons of an episodic television series that meets the conditions to include estimated secondary market revenue in ultimate revenue (discussed in Section 37.3(c)) as a single product, with multiple seasons of the series combined for purposes of applying the individual film-forecast-computation method.

(c) ULTIMATE REVENUE. Ultimate revenue for the denominator of the individual-film-forecast-computation method fraction should include estimates of revenue expected to be recognized by the producer or distributor from the exploitation, exhibition, and sale of the film in all markets and territories, subject to these limitations:

- For other than episodic television series, the period covered by the ultimate revenue estimate should not exceed 10 years following the film's initial release. For episodic television series, the ultimate revenue period should not exceed 10 years from the date of delivery of the first episode or, if still in production, 5 years from the date of delivery of the most recent episode, if later. For previously released films acquired as part of a film library (individual films whose initial release dates were at least 3 years before the acquisition date), the period should not exceed 20 years from the date of acquisition.
- For episodic television series, a producer or distributor should include in ultimate revenue estimates of secondary market revenue for produced episodes only if it can show by experience or industry norms that the episodes already produced plus those for which a firm commitment exists and are expected to be delivered can be licensed successfully in the secondary market.
- A producer or distributor should include in ultimate revenue estimated revenue from a particular market or territory only if there is persuasive evidence that there will be revenue or if the producer or distributor can show a history of earning revenue in that market or territory. In addition, ultimate revenues should include estimated revenue from newly developing territories only if an existing arrangement provides persuasive evidence that the producer or distributor will realize such revenue in those developing areas.

- Ultimate revenue should include estimated revenue from licensing arrangements with third parties to market film-related products only if there is persuasive evidence that an arrangement for the particular film exists (e.g., a signed contract with a nonrefundable minimum guarantee or a nonrefundable advance) or if the producer or distributor can show a history of earning revenue from that kind of arrangement.
- Ultimate revenue should include estimated revenue of the portion of the wholesale or retail revenue from a producer's or distributor's sale of peripheral items, such as toys and apparel attributable to the exploitation of themes, characters, or other contents related to a film only if the producer or distributor can show a history of earning revenue from that kind of exploitation in similar kinds of films, such as, but not limited to, the portion of such revenue that it would earn by having rights granted under licensing arrangements with third parties. However, estimated revenue should not include the entire amount of wholesale or retail revenue from a producer's or distributor's sale of peripheral items.
- Ultimate revenue should not include estimated revenue from unproven or undeveloped technologies.
- Ultimate revenues should not include wholesale promotion or advertising reimbursements; such amounts should be offset against exploitation costs.
- Ultimate revenue should not include estimated revenue related to the sale of film rights for periods after those stated in the first bullet point.
- Ultimate revenue should not be discounted to its present value, except as required by ASC 835-30-25, and should not include projections for inflation. Foreign currency estimates should be based on current rates.

(d) ULTIMATE PARTICIPATION COSTS. A producer or distributor uses estimates of unaccrued (i.e., not yet expensed) ultimate participation costs in the individual-film-forecast-computation method to arrive at current period participation cost expense. The unaccrued ultimate participation costs are determined using assumptions consistent with the producer's or distributor's estimates of film costs, exploitation costs, and ultimate revenue, limited as discussed in the last section. If the recognized participation costs liability exceeds the estimated unpaid ultimate participation costs for an individual film at any reporting date, a producer or distributor should reduce the excess with an offsetting credit to unamortized film costs. If an excess liability exceeds unamortized film costs for that film, it should be recognized as income.

A producer or distributor should continue to accrue associated participation costs as revenue is recognized, even after a film costs are fully amortized.

(e) FILM COSTS VALUATION. A producer or distributor should assess whether the fair value of a complete or incomplete film is less than its unamortized film costs, for example, if the following events or changes in circumstances occur:

- An adverse change in the expected performance of the film before it is released
- Actual costs are substantially more than budgeted costs
- The completion or release schedule is substantially delayed
- The release plans change; for example, the initial release pattern is reduced
- Resources or funding to complete the film and market it effectively become insufficient
- Performance after release does not meet expectations before release.

If the producer or distributor concludes that the fair value of a film (reduced for any future exploitation costs yet to be incurred) is less than its unamortized film costs, it should recognize the difference as an impairment loss in the income statement. The resulting fair value of the film becomes the adjusted cost basis for subsequent accounting purposes. The write-off should not subsequently be restored. A producer or distributor would continue to account for exploitation costs incurred after recognizing an impairment loss as discussed in Section 37.3(g).

In determining the current fair value of a film, discounted cash flows may be used based on existing contractual arrangements without consideration of the limitations discussed earlier in Section 37.3(c). As a result, a producer or distributor should considering these factors:

- The film's performance in prior markets
- The public's perception of the film's story, cost, director, or producer
- Historical results of similar films
- Historical results of the cast, director, or producer on prior films
- The running time of the film.

The determination of a film's fair value should incorporate estimates of necessary future cash outflows such as, but not limited to, costs to complete and exploitation and participation costs necessary to generate a film's cash inflows. The most likely cash inflows and outflows should be used, probability weighted by period using the mean or average by period.

The discount rate should reflect the risks associated with the film, and therefore these rates should not be used: the producer's or distributor's incremental borrowing rate, liability settlement rates, and weighted cost of capital. In addition to the time value of money, expectations should be incorporated about possible variations in the amount or timing of the most likely cash flows. Also incorporated should be an element to reflect the price market participants would seek for bearing the uncertainty in such an asset, and other factors, sometimes unidentifiable, including illiquidity and market imperfections.

(f) SUBSEQUENT EVENTS. For films released before or after the reporting date for which evidence of the possible impairment of unamortized film costs occurs after the reporting date but before the financial statements are issued or are available to be issued (as discussed in ASC 855-10-25), a rebuttable presumption exists that the conditions leading to the impairment existed at the reporting date. In such situations, a producer or distributor should adjust financial statements for the effect of any changes in estimates resulting from the use of the subsequent evidence. A producer or distributor can overcome the rebuttable presumption if it can demonstrate that the conditions leading to the impairment did not exist at the reporting date.

(g) EXPLOITATION COSTS. Advertising costs should be reported in conformity with ASC Subtopic 720-35 (SOP 93-7). All other exploitation costs, including marketing costs, should be recognized as an expense when incurred.

(h) MANUFACTURING COSTS. Manufacturing or duplication costs of products for sale, such as videocassettes and digital video discs, should be recognized as an expense on a unit-specific basis when the related revenue is recognized. At each reporting date, inventories of such products should be evaluated for net realizable value and obsolescence, and needed adjustments should be recognized as expense. The cost of theatrical film prints should be recognized as expense over the period benefited.

37.4 PRESENTATION AND DISCLOSURE

If the reporting entity presents a classified balance sheet, it should classify film costs as noncurrent on the face of the balance sheet. In any event, a reporting entity should disclose the following in its notes to financial statements:

- The portion of the costs of its completed films expected to be amortized in the upcoming operating cycle, presumed to be 12 months
- The operating cycle if other than 12 months

- The components of film costs for films released, completed and not released, in production, or in development or preproduction, separately for theatrical films and direct-to-television products
- The percentage of unamortized film costs for released films other than acquired film libraries expected to be amortized within 3 years of the reporting date; if less than 80 percent, additional information should be provided, including the period over which 80 percent will be reached
- The amount of remaining unamortized costs, the method of amortization, and the remaining amortization period for acquired film libraries
- The amount of accrued participation liabilities expected to be paid during the upcoming operating cycle
- The methods of reporting revenue, film costs, participation costs, and exploitation costs

Cash outflows for film costs, participation costs, exploitation costs, and manufacturing costs should be reported as operating activities in the statement of cash flows. Amortization of film costs should be included in the reconciliation of net income to net cash flows from operating activities.

CHAPTER 38

ESTATES AND TRUSTS

Philip M. Herr, JD, CPA, PFS
AXA Equitable Life Insurance Company

Elizabeth Lindsay-Ochoa , JD, LLM (Taxation)
AXA Equitable Life Insurance Company

38.1 ESTATES—LEGAL BACKGROUND 2

(a) Executing a Will 2
(b) Will Provisions 2
(c) Rules Under Intestacy 3
(d) Domicile 3
(e) Probate Procedures: Will 4
(f) Probate Procedures: Failure of Executor 4
(g) Probate Procedures: Intestacy 5
(h) Settlement of Small Estates 5
(i) Fiduciary Responsibilities 5
(i) Executor versus Administrator 5
(ii) General Duties of Representatives 5
(iii) Preliminary Administration 5
(iv) Specific Duties of Representatives 6
(v) Possession of Assets 6
(vi) Probate versus Nonprobate Assets 6
(vii) Personal Property Exemptions 6
(viii) Real Property 6
(ix) Inventory of Assets 7
(x) Valuation of Assets 8
(xi) Management of Estate Funds 8
(xii) Payments of Debts 8
(xiii) Advertising for Creditors 8
(xiv) Order of Debt Payment 9
(xv) Source of Funds for Debt Payment 9
(xvi) Administration Expenses 10
(xvii) Distribution of Estate Assets 10
(xviii) Payment of Legacies 10
(xix) Abatement of Legacies 10
(xx) Deductions from Legacies 11
(xxi) Lapsed Legacies 11
(xxii) Advancement and Hotchpot 11
(xxiii) Surviving Spouse's Right of Election Against the Will 11
(xxiv) Disclaimers 11
(xxv) Decree of Distribution and Postdecree Procedure 12
(xxvi) Funding of Trusts 12
(j) Powers of Estate Representative 12
(i) Executor versus Administrator 12
(ii) Will Powers Not Conferred by Statute 12
(iii) Will Powers versus Statutory Powers 13
(k) Commissions of Representatives 13
(l) Taxation of Estates 13
(i) Final Individual Income Taxes 13
(ii) Federal Estate Tax 14
(iii) State Estate and Inheritance Taxes 17
(iv) Generation-Skipping Transfer Tax 17
(v) Estate Income Taxes 18

38.2 ACCOUNTING FOR ESTATES 19

(a) Governing Concepts 19
(i) Accounting Period 19
(ii) Principal and Income 19
(iii) Treatment of Liabilities 19
(b) Record-Keeping System 19
(i) Journals 19
(ii) Operation of a Going Business 19
(iii) Final Accounting 20
(c) Reports of Executor or Administrator 20

38.3 TRUSTS AND TRUSTEES—LEGAL BACKGROUND 21

(a) Nature and Types of Trusts 21
(i) Limitations on Private Trusts 21
(ii) Revocation of Trusts 21
(b) Appointment and Removal of Trustees 22
(i) Choice of Trustee 22
(ii) Methods of Appointment 22
(iii) Acceptance or Disclaimer 22
(iv) Resignation of Trustee 22
(v) Removal of Trustee 23
(c) Powers and Duties of Trustees 23
(i) General Powers 23
(ii) Duties 23
(d) Proper Trust Investments 24
(e) Trustee's Personal Liabilities and Liability for Acts of Cotrustee 25
(f) Guardians 26
(g) Testamentary Trustee 26
(h) Compensation of Trustees 26
(i) Rights of Beneficiary 26
(j) Distinction Between Principal and Income 27
(i) Receipts of Principal 27
(ii) Disbursements of Principal 28
(iii) Receipts of Income 28
(iv) Disbursements of or Charges to Income 29
(k) Principal and Income—Special Problems 29
(i) Unproductive Property 29
(ii) Accruals 29
(iii) Dividends 30
(iv) Premium and Discount on Bonds 31
(v) Depreciation and Depletion 31
(l) Tax Status of Trust 31
(m) Termination of Trust 32

38.4 ACCOUNTING FOR TRUSTS 32

(a) General Features 32
(i) Accounting Period 32
(ii) Recording Principal and Income 32
(iii) Accounting for Multiple Trusts 33
(iv) Treatment of Liabilities 33
(b) Record-Keeping System 33
(i) Journals 33
(ii) Principal and Income Accounts 33
(iii) Opening Books of Account 33
(iv) Amortization of Bond Premium or Discount 33
(v) Depreciation 34
(vi) Payments of Expenses 34
(c) Trustees' Reports 34

38.5 SOURCES AND SUGGESTED REFERENCES 34

38.1 ESTATES—LEGAL BACKGROUND

(a) EXECUTING A WILL. A *will* is a revocable instrument whereby a person makes a disposition of his property to take effect at death. A prudent person should secure legal advice upon reaching the age of majority (age 18 in many states). If the attorney deems it advisable, such person should execute a will. In the will, the testator (maker) should spell out in detail who is to inherit his or her property upon his or her death. The testator may also name a person to administer the estate and select a guardian (a protector of the body and property of his or her children, if any). A will can be very simple or very complex depending on the extent of the testator's property and desires. To be valid, the will must be properly executed according to state law. Such state laws normally require a maker of sound mind to declare that the document is his or her last will and testament and to sign it in the presence of at least two disinterested witnesses, who also sign. Such witnesses, called *subscribing witnesses,* may later be called on to testify about the maker's appearance of mental competence at the time of the execution of the will.

(b) WILL PROVISIONS. Every will provision must be adhered to by the executor and the courts unless it is contrary to law or against public policy.

A typical will provides for:

- A statement revoking all prior wills and codicils.
- An instruction to pay all just debts, expenses of administration, funeral expenses, and sometimes final burial instructions. (However, these instructions are better left in a letter of instruction left with a close family member or friend in case the will should be found after the funeral.)

- General bequests or legacies of money or property to named individuals payable out of the general assets of the estate.
- Devises of real property to specified individuals.
- Specific bequests or legacies of specific property. They fail or lapse if the property does not exist at the testator's death.
- Demonstrative bequests or legacies. These are gifts of money or property payable out of a particular fund; if the fund is insufficient, the balance becomes a general legacy.
- Provisions concerning disposal of the residuary estate. The residuary estate is all property not otherwise provided for in the will.
- The duties and powers of the executor (described later in this section).
- The naming of fiduciaries (executors, trustees, guardians, committees for incompetents) and their successors; and, often, the exemption of having to post a fidelity bond.
- Definitions of terms used in the will.
- Provisions apportioning federal and state death taxes among the various classes of beneficiaries (marital versus nonmarital, specific versus residuary, charitable versus noncharitable).
- Simultaneous death provision that provides who shall be presumed to have survived whom as between the testator and other beneficiaries taking under the will.
- The terms of any testamentary trusts that might be established under the will (i.e., for a minor beneficiary).
- Signature of testator and subscribing witnesses, which may also be notarized in an attempt to "self-prove" the will.

(c) RULES UNDER INTESTACY. *Intestacy* is defined as the state or condition of dying without having made a valid will or without having disposed by will of a part of the deceased's property. Thus, it arises not only when the deceased died without having made a will but also if the will is invalid or if it contains ineffective or no provisions concerning the disposal of the residuary estate.

When an intestacy is present, state law provides who is to receive the property. In effect, state statutes make a will for the deceased. The plan of distribution of the property, sometimes called *intestate succession* or *laws of descent and distribution,* is strictly defined by state statute and is based on degree of relationship to the deceased. New York State, for example, provides that if a decedent dies without a will and leaves a wife and two children that are from both of them, the wife receives $50,000 and one-half of the residuary estate and the children share the other one-half. Under the same circumstances, Oregon gives the spouse the entire estate. Distribution plans under state laws vary even more if a spouse or children do not survive the decedent. It could result, for example, in a surviving parent, who may have made lifetime gifts to the decedent for the parent's own estate planning purposes, receiving those assets back. Distribution plans under intestacy do not take into account financial needs or close bonds of a decedent to certain relatives. It may result in relatives with whom a decedent has had no contact for many years inheriting a portion of the property. Absence of a will can result in fights over the appointment of administrators and in custody battles over the guardianship of minor children and their property. The failure to make a will should be a conscious decision of an informed individual to allow state law to make it for him or her and not a result of ignorance or procrastination.

(d) DOMICILE. Generally most states take the position that the property of a person domiciled in a state at the time of death is subject to court jurisdiction (and the estate and inheritance tax) of that state. *Domicile* is defined as the place where a person has a true, fixed, and permanent home to which, whenever absent, the person has the intention of returning.

In addition, states generally also claim court jurisdiction over (and estate and inheritance tax on) real and tangible personal property located within their boundaries for persons domiciled outside the state at the time of their death.

These two concepts often force an executor or administrator to bring court proceedings in more than one state. Proceedings brought outside the state of domicile are called *ancillary proceedings.* The distribution by the executor or administrator of ancillary property is governed by the state law of the property's location.

Sometimes more than one state claims that a decedent was domiciled in that state at the time of death. Such a situation can lead to expensive litigation and excessive estate or inheritance tax. People with dual residences should clearly establish which state they consider to be their domicile. This can be done by consistency in such evidence of domicile as voter registration, automobile registration, state income tax returns, declaration in will, and positions taken in documents executed during life.

Separate issues arise if the decedent is not a U.S. citizen. If the decedent was a resident alien, his or her estate will be administered and taxed as if a U.S. citizen. The executor or administrator, however, should determine whether the United States has an estate tax treaty with the decedent's country of citizenship, especially if the decedent owned assets in that country, and review the laws of that country to determine if any death taxes are owed to that country. If the surviving spouse is not a U.S. citizen and is married with a U.S. citizen spouse, the executor or administrator must carefully review the estate tax rules relating to this situation. For example, the regular marital deduction rules do not apply. A marital deduction is permitted only if the will provides for a qualified domestic trust or if the spouse elects to become a U.S. citizen.

If the decedent is not a U.S. citizen and not a resident alien, the estate taxation and administration of the estate take on a whole new complexion. The issue of domicile becomes extremely important and could have a major impact on the U.S. taxation of the estate as well as the number of ancillary international proceedings that may have to be conducted. A situation like this behooves an executor or administrator to seek expert advice and counsel.

(e) PROBATE PROCEDURES: WILL. The courts having jurisdiction over decedents' estates have different names. Some states call such a court a probate court; others, a surrogate court or an orphan's court. Often the same court governs both decedents leaving wills and those dying without wills.

Most wills are drafted by an attorney; however, a holographic will is written entirely in the decedent's handwriting. Most state statutes recognize these wills and impose only minimal requirements to establish their validity. Two universal requirements are that the will be executed with testamentary intent and be signed by the testator. A holographic will need *not* be witnessed to be valid in certain states. A court's determination of whether a holographic will is valid becomes part of the probate process.

A codicil to a will, or will codicil, is an amendment to or modification of an otherwise valid will. Testators will often use a codicil to make minor or modest changes instead of going through the whole process of redrafting the entire will. Testator may make handwritten changes or amend their own will. This may be a misconception on their part since a codicil must meet certain statutory requirements of its own and must be executed in the same manner as a will (i.e., signed by the testator and two or more witnesses). In any event, a codicil becomes part of the last will and testament document.

After a decedent's will has been located, it should be presented to the court for probating (i.e., proving it valid). The named executor (executrix if a female), if qualified and willing to act, is issued letters testamentary (i.e., a document authorizing him or her to act on behalf of the estate. In some states, temporary letters are issued with formal letters issued at a later date.

(f) PROBATE PROCEDURES: FAILURE OF EXECUTOR. If the executor named in the will is unqualified because of such factors as age, competency, or residency, any named successor if qualified is allowed to take the executor's place. Should all successors fail to qualify or refuse the appointment, any beneficiary of the estate may petition the court for appointment. State laws generally provide an order of priority, the appointment going first to a qualified surviving spouse, then to qualified children (sometimes in age order), then to qualified grandchildren, and so on.

The person who qualifies and accepts the appointment is called an *administrator* (or administratrix) CTA (*cum testamento annexo,* i.e., "with the will annexed"). The administrator CTA has the same duties and powers as an executor and looks to the will for authority to act.

(g) PROBATE PROCEDURES: INTESTACY. The death of a person without a will necessitates the appointment of an administrator. As mentioned, appointments are made by interested parties petitioning the court and the court appointing the first person who can qualify in the order of priority outlined under state law. Letters of administration are issued after compliance with the governing statutes. The administrator must distribute the estate in accordance with the laws of intestacy of the state in which he or she is appointed.

(h) SETTLEMENT OF SMALL ESTATES. Most state statutes provide special rules for the settlement of small estates with either no court administrative involvement or some form of an abbreviated procedure. The definition of *small* depends on the gross value of the estate. These values can be as low as $5,000 to $15,000, or as high as $50,000 to $60,000. Utilization of these special rules results in greatly reduced administration costs and a quicker settlement of the estate.

(i) FIDUCIARY RESPONSIBILITIES

(i) Executor versus Administrator. Although the executor's powers and duties come primarily from the will and secondarily from state law if the will is silent, the administrator of a person dying intestate must look solely to state law for authority to act.

The term *personal representative* or simply *representative* as used in this section encompasses both executors and administrators. The term *fiduciary* includes executors, administrators, guardians, and trustees.

(ii) General Duties of Representatives. Duties of a representative, stated generally, are to collect the decedent's assets, pay creditors, account for all income and expenses, and distribute the assets remaining according to the provisions of the will or in accordance with state law in the absence of will provisions.

In the performance of these duties, the personal representative must use the "reasonable man" rule; that is, duties must be exercised with the prudence a reasonable person would exercise with his or her own property. The representative does not guarantee estate assets against loss. However, the representative is responsible for acting reasonably and can be asked to make good estate losses should he or she fail to act reasonably. Since the representative is not required to possess the expertise of an accountant, attorney, or investment counselor (although a decedent may often name such a professional in the will), a representative acting in a "reasonable" manner should determine whether the will or state law authorizes the retention of such advisers whenever necessary.

(iii) Preliminary Administration. Often a death is sudden and unexpected. Determining whether the decedent left a will is sometimes a problem. Finding it and determining whether it is the last will executed may be even bigger problems. A careful search must be made of the decedent's personal papers. If the decedent had an attorney, accountant, banker, or insurance broker, that person may be helpful in ascertaining the existence of a will and locating it. The importance of the will lies not only in carrying out the decedent's plan for distribution of assets but also in determining the persons named as executors, trustees, and guardians of minors or others incapable of caring for themselves. Administration of the estate must begin, however, at the moment of death. There are too many important acts, such as carrying out the decedent's instructions for bodily organ donations, arranging for the funeral, and safeguarding valuable or perishable assets, to await the location of the will or formal appointment of a representative. Someone must take responsibility at once. Should it later turn out that another person was named executor or appointed administrator, an orderly transition of authority can be made.

(iv) Specific Duties of Representatives. Twelve other specific duties of the personal representative are to:

1. Arrange to have all estate assets inventoried and title transferred to the name of the executor or administrator.
2. Obtain possession of the decedent's important papers and personal property and arrange for safekeeping.
3. Arrange for adequate insurance coverage for estate assets.
4. Collect all debts owed to the decedent and litigate if necessary.
5. Arrange for an appraisal of all estate assets by qualified appraisers before distributing any assets.
6. Keep clear and accurate records of all estate receipts and disbursements. This is necessary for tax returns and for accountings to courts and beneficiaries.
7. Determine whether assets coming under the control of representatives are sufficient to meet both claims against the estate and legacies allowed by will and/or state law.
8. Review cash requirements to pay legacies, taxes, debts, and administration expenses, and determine whether assets are sufficiently liquid to pay such claims as they become due.
9. Arrange for the preparation of any payment of tax due on the decedent's final income tax returns, federal estate return, state or foreign estate or inheritance tax returns, and estate income tax returns.
10. Advertise for creditors (publish notification of decedent's death, allowing statutory period for claim presentation), and pay all valid claims against the estate.
11. Pay legacies at times specified under state law, and distribute the remainder of the estate after payment of all debts and administration expenses to persons directed by will or by state law in the absence of will direction.
12. Prepare interim and/or final accountings for beneficiaries and courts as required by state law.

A graphic outline of the administration of a decedent's estate is presented in Exhibit 38.1.

(v) Possession of Assets. After the appointment of the administrator or executor, the next step is to assemble the property belonging to the estate. The representative is required to exercise due diligence in the discovery of assets and must take all proper legal steps to obtain possession of them.

(vi) Probate versus Nonprobate Assets. Probate assets are those assets whose disposition is controlled by the decedent's will. Nonprobate assets pass to the designated beneficiary by either operation of law (i.e., joint tenancy with right to survivorship, tenants by the entirety) or by operation of contract (i.e., designated beneficiary of an insurance policy, qualified retirement plan, or other form of deferred compensation). Although the value of nonprobate assets is includable in the decedent's gross estate for tax purposes, the administrator or executor is not responsible for the collection of these assets. However, the estate representative's cooperation in assisting a beneficiary obtain possession of these assets is a usual occurrence.

(vii) Personal Property Exemptions. Personal property of the deceased passes directly to the personal representative of the decedent. However, certain items of personal property must be exempted by statute for the benefit of the family of the decedent.

(viii) Real Property. Title to real property passes directly to the heirs, or devisees, and such property does not ordinarily come under the control of the representative unless left to the estate by will, sold by order of the court to pay valid obligations of the estate, or administered by the representative as a requirement of state law. If real estate does come under the control of the representative, it is

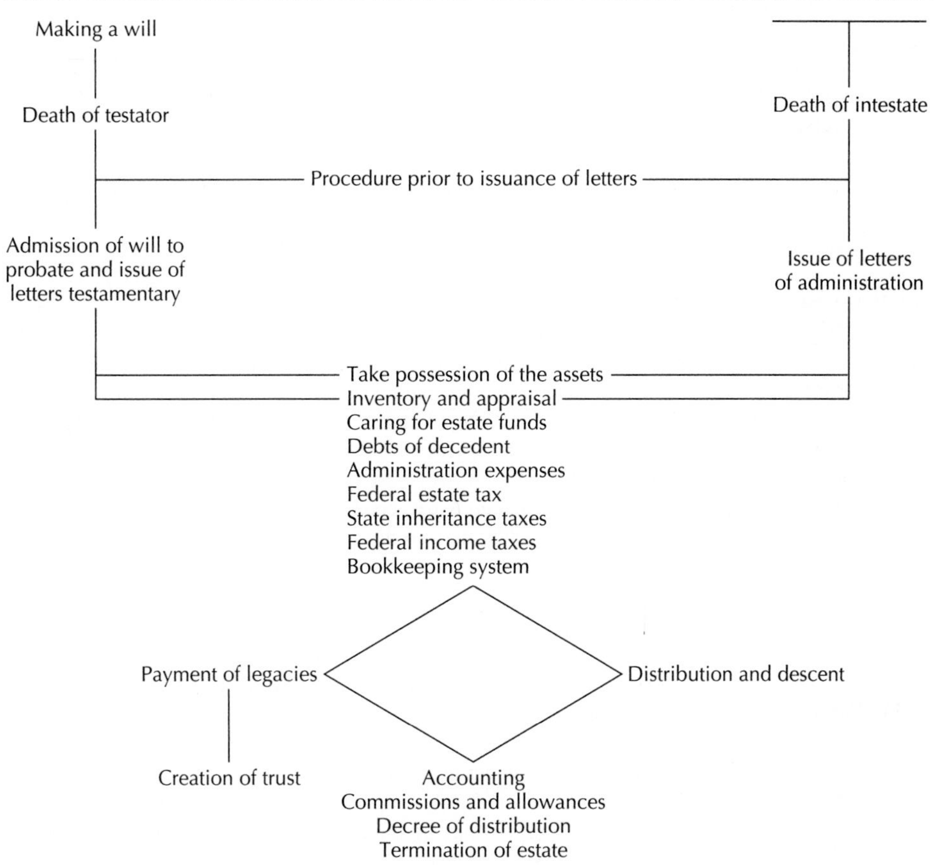

Exhibit 38.1 Outline of the Administration of Decedent's Estate

handled in the same manner as personal property. In some states, the representative may manage the real estate and collect rents during the period of administration. The balance due on a land contract receivable is personal property of the estate, although the title to the land passes to the heirs and is retained by them until the contract is paid.

(ix) Inventory of Assets. A detailed inventory of all assets taken over, which will form the basis of the accounting of the representative, should be prepared and filed with the court. Schedules should be prepared of all:

- Cash on hand and on deposit
- Furniture, fixtures, and articles of personal use
- Claims against others (choices in action)
- Contract rights that do not involve personal services
- Unpaid fees, commissions, and salaries
- Life insurance policies payable to the estate
- Interest in partnerships
- Unpaid dividends of record as of the date of death, or other accrued income
- Leases
- Other personal property owned by the decedent

The inventory does not include goods or money held by the decedent for others. Claims canceled by will are included in the inventory, as are articles exempted for the decedent's family and articles of no apparent value. No liabilities are mentioned in the inventory, and assets pledged to secure a loan are listed without deduction for the amount of the loan. Accruals are to be computed up to midnight following the death of the decedent.

(x) Valuation of Assets. The asset values are usually set by appraisers appointed by the court and will presumably be the market values at the time of death. The executor should keep a copy of the inventory and incorporate its details into the bookkeeping system.

(xi) Management of Estate Funds. Generally, the function of the administrator or executor of an estate is to liquidate, whereas the role of the trustee or guardian is to manage. Nonetheless, the administrator or executor may have important managerial functions to perform. Perishable goods, speculative investments, and burdensome property should be disposed of promptly. Unless forgiven in the will, every effort should be made to collect all claims due the estate. Articles of a personal nature are usually distributed among legatees or next of kin at their inventory value but may be sold if such a distribution is not feasible.

All estate funds should be kept in a separate bank account in the name of the representative, with an indication of the fiduciary relationship, and should not be commingled with those of the representatives (except in the case of a trust company). All disbursements should be made by check. Interest should be secured on bank balances if possible. Stock certificates in the name of the decedent should be transferred to the name of the representative in his or her fiduciary capacity. Adequate insurance should be carried against fire, theft, public liability, and other risks. In general, the representative may be considered a fiduciary under state law. To avoid personal liability for loss of funds and property, the representative must care for the assets as diligently as if they were his or her own, as a reasonably prudent person.

An executor or administrator may not be under legal compulsion to invest the funds of the estate, but it is certainly good business practice to make interim investments in guaranteed obligations, such as short-term U.S. securities or bank savings certificates or savings accounts if significant amounts of cash are accumulated for taxes, expenses, or future distribution. If investments are made, the representative must be guided by the procedure required of trustees (see later discussion in Section 38.3(d)).

The representative is not justified in continuing to operate a business owned by the decedent unless authorized to do so by the will. In the case of a closely held business, either a corporation or partnership, the representative will be guided by the provisions, if any, in the partnership, limited liability company, or shareholder agreement. The terms of a buy-sell agreement may obligate and bind the representative to sell the decedent's business interest to either the surviving shareholders or partners, or to the corporation or partnership itself. In the absence of any such agreements or provisions, the business should be liquidated by the surviving partners.

(xii) Payments of Debts. The administrator or executor has a duty to satisfy him- or herself as to the validity of the claims made against the estate and should interpose objections to any doubtful claims. A judgment cannot be rejected. A doubtful claim may be settled by a reasonable compromise in good faith. A partial payment of a debt barred by the statute of limitations does not revive the debt.

The representative is not required to pay any debt or make any distribution of assets until the expiration of a statutory period of time. If any payment or distribution is made during the period, the representative may be held responsible for the remaining assets not being sufficient to meet the remaining liabilities.

(xiii) Advertising for Creditors. The representative is permitted to advertise for creditors and should do so for personal protection. Notices are inserted in one or more newspapers published in the county requesting persons who have claims to present them with supporting affidavits and vouchers within a specified time, usually six months. Claims not yet due should be presented for proof so that funds will be set aside for their payment.

(xiv) Order of Debt Payment. When the list of debts is completed and presented to the court, the solvency or insolvency of the estate can be determined. If the estate is solvent, the order of payment is immaterial, but if the liabilities are in apparent excess of the value of the assets, a statutory order must be followed. The next order of payment is, according to Stephenson and Wiggins, representative:[1]

1. Debts that by law have a special lien on property to an amount not exceeding the value of the property
2. Funeral expenses
3. Taxes
4. Debts due to the United States and to the state
5. Judgments of any court of competent jurisdiction, within the state, docketed and in force, to the extent to which they are a lien on the property of the deceased person at death
6. Wages due to any domestic servant or mechanical or agricultural laborer for a period of not more than one year immediately preceding the death
7. Claim for medical services within 12 months preceding death
8. All other debts and demands

(xv) Source of Funds for Debt Payment. Unless the will directs otherwise, six assets of the estate are used in the listed order in the payment of debts:

1. Personal property not bequeathed
2. Personal property bequeathed generally
3. Personal property bequeathed specifically
4. Realty not devised
5. Realty devised generally
6. Realty devised specifically

The sale, lease, or mortgaging of real estate to provide funds for the payment of debts must, in the absence of a provision to the contrary in the will, follow a petition to the court for permission to so use the realty, and the court must approve of the disposition made by the representative. Property descended to heirs is usually used before that distributed by will. Land sold by an heir or devisee before the estate is settled is subject to a possible claim for unpaid debts of the estate. All dower or curtsy rights (statutory rights for surviving wife or husband) and estates for life or years are adjusted, and heirs or devisees must be reimbursed if any assets are subsequently discovered from which the debts could have been paid.

In many instances, if the decedent was an owner of a closely held business, he or she may have entered into some form of a buy-sell agreement with co-owners. The agreement usually provides that the executor shall sell the decedent's interest in the business to one or more co-owners, or to the business entity itself, at the price set forth therein in exchange for cash. Depending on the arrangement, the buy-sell agreement will be referred to as either a *cross purchase* or *entity redemption* (or corporate stock redemption) agreement. The decedent's agreement to be bound by the terms of the agreement contractually binds the executor to sell the decedent's interest in the business pursuant to the terms of the agreement. This sales price also works to establish the estate tax value of the business interest in the gross estate.

---

[1] G. T. Stephenson and N. Wiggins, *Estates and Trusts,* 5th ed. (New York: Appleton-Century-Crofts, 1973).

The decedent, anticipating a need to provide liquidity for the estate, may have established and funded an irrevocable life insurance trust. In this arrangement, the trust applies for a life insurance policy on the decedent's life. The trustee is both the owner and beneficiary of the policy. Upon the decedent's death, the trustee collects the insurance proceeds. While neither the trustee nor the executor is contractually bound to do so, the trustee usually purchases assets from the estate, hence providing the needed liquidity. This technique also eliminates the need for the executor to sell assets in a rush at liquidation, or "estate sale," prices.

The executor should be sure to review the decedent's personal papers thoroughly, and interview the surviving spouse and business associates or partners, to determine the existence of a buy-sell agreement or irrevocable life insurance trust.

(xvi) Administration Expenses. Reasonable and necessary outlays made by the representative in collecting and distributing assets will be allowed by the court. The representative is personally liable for amounts disallowed. The compensation of the representative, court costs, and an allowance for preparing the accounting are allowed specifically when an accounting is made. Attorney's fees, accountant's fees, fire insurance premiums, necessary repairs to property, collection costs, and other ordinary expenses will be allowed. The character and amount of the estate and the complications of the particular situation will govern the decisions of the courts as to the reasonableness or necessity of a particular expenditure.

Most states statutorily regulate attorney's fees by prescribing a set fee schedule based on the size of the probate estate. Should an attorney's fee exceed the statutory maximum, he or she will need to seek the court's approval. In many instances, the estate's attorney may also be one of the executors or the sole executor. This may entitle the attorney/executor to both a fee and a commission; however, the attorney/executor will have to keep detailed records of time spent and duties performed in order to sustain dual compensation.

(xvii) Distribution of Estate Assets. After making appropriate provisions for the payment of all claims against the estate, the personal representative proceeds to distribute the remaining assets according to the instructions in the will or in compliance with the laws of descent and distribution.

(xviii) Payment of Legacies. Legacies are usually payable one year after the death of the testator. General legacies ordinarily draw interest after that date and should be charged with interest for payments prior to the due date. General legacies to the testator's dependent children usually bear interest from the date of death. If the estate appears to be solvent, the executor may pay or deliver legacies at any time but should, for his or her own protection, take a bond from the legatee providing for a refund to the estate in case the assets prove to be inadequate to meet the prior claims. Otherwise a suit in equity may be necessary to recover the improper payments.

(xix) Abatement of Legacies. If there are insufficient assets to meet the debts and other prior claims, the legacies are reduced or abated. A complete revocation is referred to as an *ademption.* The four rules governing priority in the abatement of legacies are:

1. A specific legacy takes priority over a general legacy. If the testator bequeaths specific shares of stock to A and $5,000 in cash to B, B's legacy will be diminished or, if necessary, entirely wiped out before the stock left to A is resorted to.
2. A legacy for the support of the testator's widow or children, who are not otherwise adequately provided for, takes priority over legacies to strangers or more distant relatives.
3. In most states, the personal assets of the estate will be used for the payment of debts before resorting to the real estate. As a result, the bequests of money or personal property may be diminished or wiped out, although the devisees of the real property are not affected.
4. Subject to the foregoing rules, all legacies are reduced pro rata in case of a deficiency.

If the will directs that real estate be sold to pay debts, the sale will take place before any legacies are abated.

(xx) Deductions from Legacies. There may be certain required deductions from legacies, the most common one being state inheritance taxes. A debt due by a legatee to the testator should be deducted, but a debtor who becomes a legatee is not entitled to retain funds applicable to the payment of all charges and legacies.

(xxi) Lapsed Legacies. A legacy is said to have "lapsed" if the legatee dies before the testator, and the assets involved revert to the undistributed or residuary portion of the estate. An exception is sometimes made when the deceased legatee is a child or other near relative who has left surviving children; the children then receive the legacy.

The children would receive the legacy on either a per stripes or per capita basis. *Per stripes* means that the children of a deceased parent receive an equal share of the deceased parents' share. *Per capita* means that the children of a deceased parent receive their own share. For example: A's will leaves everything to spouse or A's children should spouse predecease. A's spouse and one adult child predecease A. A is survived by a second adult child (B) and the predeceased child's two children (C and D). A per stripes distribution would leave 50 percent to B and 25 percent to each of C and D. A per capita distribution would leave $33\frac{1}{3}$ percent to B, C, and D.

(xxii) Advancement and Hotchpot. An *advancement* is a transfer of property by a parent to a child in anticipation of the share of the estate the child would receive if the parent died intestate. If a person indicates in his or her will that the advances are to be part of the child's legacy, these advances are considered as part of the corpus of the estate and must be taken into account in making the final distribution. An allowance to a widow for the support of the family is not an advance, nor is it a direct charge against items devised or bequeathed to her.

If there is no will and the advancement exceeds the child's distributable shares of the estate, the legatee is entitled to no further distribution but is not required to return the excess; if the advancement is less than the child's share, he or she is entitled to the difference. *Hotchpot,* or collation, is the bringing together of all the estate of an intestate with the advancements made to the children in order that it may be divided in accordance with the statutes of distribution. Generally speaking, hotchpot has been discontinued under state intestacy rules.

(xxiii) Surviving Spouse's Right of Election Against the Will. Should a decedent's will completely disinherit a surviving spouse or provide less than a certain percentage of the estate to him or her, the spouse may petition the court to elect to receive a specified percentage of the estate, normally ranging between 30 and 50 percent, "against the will" (e.g., in lieu of the existing dispositive will provisions). The right to make this election will vary among the states depending on whether the probated will was executed before the marriage or during the marriage between the decedent and surviving spouse.

(xxiv) Disclaimers. It is often recommended that an intended legatee or beneficiary forfeit, give up, or disclaim an estate distribution. In other words, the legatee or beneficiary waives his or her right to receive all or part of an interest in an estate asset or distribution of assets. The effect of a proper disclaimer is that the intended legatee or beneficiary is presumed to have predeceased the decedent, and the asset is distributed to the contingent legatee or beneficiary. Disclaimers are governed both by state statute and the Internal Revenue Code (IRC) in Sections 2046 and 2518. The requirements of both must be carefully observed in order to obtain the desired result. In general, these four steps must be observed:

1. The disclaimer must be made in writing.
2. It must be received by the executor and filed with the surrogate or probate court that has jurisdiction of the estate within nine months of the date of death.
3. The intended legatee or beneficiary must renounce all right, title, and interest in the item(s) and must not have received, or be deemed to have received, any economic benefit of the assets being disclaimed.

4. The disclaimed interest must pass to someone other than the disclaiming legatee or beneficiary, and he or she may not direct to whom the asset will pass in lieu of him- or herself.

(xxv) Decree of Distribution and Postdecree Procedure. The principal distribution of estate properties is made after the issuance by the court of a decree of distribution. Upon the filing of an acceptable final accounting (see Section 38.2) and the expiration of the time for objections by interested parties, the court approves the accounting, allows the expenses of preparing the accounting and the representative's commission, and issues a decree that disposes of the balance of the estate according to the will or according to the statutes of descent and distribution in that jurisdiction.

The representative distributes the estate assets according to the decree, pays his or her commission, settles any other expenses allowed in the decree, closes the books, presents vouchers to the court, and asks for a discharge from his or her responsibilities and for the cancelation of his or her bond.

(xxvi) Funding of Trusts. It is not uncommon for part of the estate to be distributed to a testamentary trust or to a preexisting *inter vivos* trust. The distribution to the trust may make up part of a marital, residuary, or charitable bequest. A testamentary trust may also be funded to hold assets for a minor beneficiary. The appointment and approval of the trustee(s) and the distribution of the estate assets to the trust would be included in the courts' decree described above in section 38.1(xxv).

(j) POWERS OF ESTATE REPRESENTATIVE

(i) Executor versus Administrator. The personal representative's powers, as distinguished from duties, are those acts that he or she is authorized, rather than required, to perform. As previously mentioned, the powers of an executor or administrator CTA are outlined in the will and are often broader than those allowed to an administrator of an intestate, who must look solely to statutory authority.

The most common statutory and will clause powers of the personal representative are to:

- Invest and reinvest estate assets
- Collect income and manage the estate property
- Sell estate property as he or she sees fit
- Mortgage property (in some states)
- Deliver and execute agreements, contracts, deeds, and other instruments necessary to administer the estate

Most properly drawn wills reproduce the statutory powers and add additional desired powers not granted by statute.

(ii) Will Powers Not Conferred by Statute. Using New York State law as outlined by Harris as an example, the 10 powers listed next, when included in a will of a New York decedent, would grant additional powers not conferred by statute.[2] These 10 powers would not be available to an executor unless enumerated in the will (and are never available to an administrator of an intestate):

1. To distribute the estate immediately after death. Many states require the executor to delay any distribution for as much as one year after letters testamentary are issued.
2. To hold property without regard to the limitations imposed by law on the proper investment of estate assets.
3. To make "extraordinary repairs" to estate assets. New York allows the representative to make only "ordinary repairs"; he or she has to secure the permission of all beneficiaries and

[2] H. I. Harris, *Estates Practice Guide,* 4th ed. (Rochester, NY: Lawyer's Co-Operative Publishing, 1984), November 1994 Supplement.

possibly of the court to make "extraordinary repairs," such as replacing a heating system on real estate administered by the estate.

4. To charge the cost of agents such as attorneys, accountants, and investment advisers as estate expenses.
5. To continue a business of decedent.
6. To keep funds uninvested or invested in nonincome-producing assets.
7. To abandon, alter, or demolish real estate.
8. To borrow on behalf of the estate and give notes or bonds for the sums borrowed, and to pledge or mortgage any property as security for the borrowing.
9. To pay all necessary or proper expenses and charges from income or principal, or partly from each as the fiduciary deems advisable. (This important power will be expanded on in the discussion of income and principal of trusts. See Section 38.3(j))
10. To do all acts not specifically mentioned as if the fiduciary were the absolute owner of the property.

(iii) Will Powers versus Statutory Powers. It is important to remember that state law is looked to only where the will is silent. Any will provision will be adhered to, even if it is broader or more restrictive than statutory powers, unless such provision is contrary to law or public policy.

(k) COMMISSIONS OF REPRESENTATIVES. Many states make executors' and administrators' commissions statutory. However, with an executor, the first step is to look to the will. Testators may specifically provide the amount of commission or prohibit commissions for fiduciaries. These will provisions will be adhered to, although several states allow an executor to renounce the will provisions and receive statutory commissions. Other states force the executor to renounce the appointment and petition to be appointed administrator, thereby becoming eligible for the statutory commissions of an administrator. Some states do not have statutory commission rates, leaving the awarding of commissions to the court's discretion.

It is important to bear in mind that commissions are allowed only on the probate assets (i.e., assets that come under the administration of the personal representative). As mentioned, real property does not generally come under the control of the representative and thus is not usually a probate asset. When real property is a probate asset, the representative is entitled to commissions. In several states, specific bequests and the income thereon are treated as nonprobate and thus noncommissionable assets. In addition, if an asset is secured by a liability, only the net equity should enter into the commission base.

Sometimes a will provides for more than one executor. State law must then be examined to determine whether each is entitled to statutory commission or whether one such commission must be shared.

(l) TAXATION OF ESTATES

(i) Final Individual Income Taxes. One of the responsibilities of the personal representative is to file any unfiled federal and state income tax returns as well as final income tax returns for the short taxable year that ends on the date of death of the decedent. If the deceased left a surviving spouse, the personal representative can elect to file a joint federal tax return for the year of death. A joint return will normally be prepared on the cash basis for the calendar year, including the decedent's income only through the date of death and the income of the surviving spouse for the full calendar year. An election in the final return to accrue medical expenses unpaid at death that are paid within one year of death may be made. Accrued interest on U.S. Government Series E Bonds owned by the decedent may be included as income in the final federal income tax return. The representative should secure expert tax advice before making these or various other available elections.

Unused capital loss carryforwards and unused charitable contribution carryforwards of a decedent are no longer deductible after the final year. Unused passive activity losses are allowed on the final return to the extent they exceed the estate tax value over the decedent's adjusted basis.

If a joint return is being filed, the tax shown on the return must be allocated between the decedent and the surviving spouse. The allocation will take into account the decedent's withholding tax and his or her actual payments of estimated tax, leaving the estate of the decedent with either an asset (representing overpayment of taxes) or a liability (representing underpayment of taxes). If the surviving spouse had income or paid some portion of the tax, he or she would owe the estate or be entitled to reimbursement from it, depending on the relationship of his or her tax payments to the separate tax liability on his or her income.

If the surviving spouse is a same-sex spouse in a state that recognizes same-sex marriage, any federal tax forms will have to be filed as individuals because of the federal Defense of Marriage Act. State taxes are filed as joint tax returns. Additionally, if there is property in another state, the representative will need to see if that state recognizes same-sex marriage to see what appropriate tax forms need to be filed.

(ii) Federal Estate Tax. Decedents with gross estates valued at over $5 million[3] are required to file a Federal Estate Tax Return, Form 706, regardless of the fact that there may be no federal estate tax liability. The federal estate tax is a tax on the value of the decedent's gross estate less certain deductions. Generally, the tax is paid from the estate property and reduces the amount otherwise available to the beneficiaries. Therefore, in the absence of specific directions in a will or trust, taxes are generally apportioned to the property that causes a tax. If property passes without tax because of a marital or charitable deduction, no taxes are chargeable to the property.

The gross estate for tax purposes includes all of the decedent's property as defined in the IRC, not merely probate property. Next are listed seven examples of property that is part of the gross estate for estate tax purposes, though not part of the probate estate and thus not accounted for in the representative's accounting:

1. Specifically devised real property
2. Jointly owned property passing to the survivor by operation of law
3. Life insurance not payable to the estate when the decedent possessed "incidents of ownership," such as the right to borrow or change the beneficiary of the policy, and policies transferred within three years of death
4. Lump-sum distributions from retirement plans paid to someone as a result of surviving the decedent
5. Gift taxes paid by the decedent within three years of death
6. Fair market value of the principal of any revocable "living" trust of which the decedent was the grantor or settlor
7. Fair market value of the principal of any irrevocable trust in which the decedent, as grantor or settlor, had retained any rights to income, or over the beneficiaries' rights to the use, enjoyment, or possession of the trust principal

In putting a value on the gross estate for estate tax purposes, the representative has an election to value the estate as of the date of death or an alternative date. The alternative date is either six months after the date of death or at disposition of an asset if sooner. If the election to use the alternative date is not made, all property must be valued as of the date of death; if the alternative date is elected, all property must be valued at the alternative valuation date or dates. Alternate valuation is available only if there is a reduction in estate taxes.

Deductions from the gross estate to arrive at the taxable estate include administration expenses (if an election has not been made to deduct them on estate income tax returns), funeral expenses,

[3] This is the filing threshold effective for decedents dying on or after January 1, 2012 under the Tax Relief, Unemployment Reauthroitazion, and Job Creation Act of 2010.

debts of the decedent, bequests to charitable organizations, and a marital deduction for property passing to a surviving spouse.

The 1976 Tax Reform Act unified estate and gift tax rates by provisions for a unified table to be applied both to taxable gifts made after 1976 and to taxable estates for persons dying after 1976. In computing estate taxes on the taxable estate, gifts made after 1976 are added to the taxable estate and the unified tax is recomputed with credit given for the gift tax previously paid on such gifts. This computation has the effect of treating gift taxes paid as only payments on account of future estate and gift tax brackets. A marital deduction is now available for 100 percent of property passing to the surviving spouse. The property may be left in trust with income to the spouse for life, together with either a general power of appointment or limited power of appointment. The latter may qualify for the marital deduction if the representative makes a Qualified Terminable Interest Property (QTIP) election with the return. Eventually, the property would be taxable in the surviving spouse's estate, and the tax thereon would be payable from the property.

Estates are also allowed an unlimited charitable deduction for bequests left directly to charities. A prorated charitable deduction is allowed for a split-interest bequest to charity either in the form of a remainder interest or an income interest.

The Tax Reform Act of 1997 added a new exclusion or deduction. Effective for decedents dying after December 31, 1997, decedents who owned a "qualified family owned business interest" or family farm may be eligible for this new estate tax exclusion. The amount of the exclusion is correlated with the unified credit, so that in any one year the combination of the taxable estate equivalent of the unified credit and the family-owned business exclusion total $1.3 million. The eligibility rules to qualify for this new exclusion are complex and extensive; therefore, they must be closely reviewed before assuming that an estate will be able to avail itself of this exclusion.

A unified credit is allowed against the computed estate tax. The unified credit is subtracted from the taxpayer's estate or gift tax liability. However, the amount of the credit available at death will be reduced to the extent that any portion of the credit is used to offset gift taxes on lifetime transfers. The amount of the credit is equivalent to a taxable estate of $600,000. Therefore, a decedent can have a taxable estate of up to $600,000 before any estate tax is due.

The Tax Reform Act of 1997 increased the unified credit over a period of years. Beginning in 1998, the taxable estate equivalent to the credit was increased to $625,000; and will increase as follows through 2006: 1999, $650,000; 2000 and 2001, $675,000; 2002 and 2003, $700,000; 2004, $850,000; 2005, $950,000; and 2006, $1,000,000.

The Economic Growth and Tax Relief Reconciliation Act of 2001 (EGTRRA), signed into law June 7, 2001, made broad, sweeping changes to several areas of the tax law, including the estate, generation-skipping transfer, and gift taxes. In short, the estate and generation-skipping transfer taxes are phased out from 2002 to 2009 and eventually repealed in 2010. The current law, however, "sunsets" on December 31, 2010, and becomes effective again as it did back in 2001. The gift tax is not repealed; however, the rates decrease to 35 percent by 2010. A brief description of the changes made by EGTRRA (while they last) is presented next.

The highest tax rate for all three transfer taxes will reduce in this way from 2002 through 2009:

2002: 50 percent	2005: 47 percent
2003: 49 percent	2006: 46 percent
2004: 48 percent	2007–2009: 45 percent

In 2010, the gift tax is cut to 35 percent while the other two transfer taxes are zero percent (i.e., repealed). In 2011, the rates return to the 2001 level of 55 percent when the law sunsets. The unified tax credit, or applicable exclusion amount, for the estate tax increases from 2002 through 2009 in this way:

2002–2003: $1 million	2006–2008: $2 million
2004–2005: $1.5 million	2009: $3.5 million

The unified credit, or applicable exclusion amount, returns to the 2001 level of $1 million in 2011.[4] The unified credit, or applicable exclusion amount, is increased to and remains at $1 million in 2002. This remains constant through 2010, until it returns to the pre-EGTRRA levels.

The qualified family-owned business deduction that was added to the law by the Tax Reform Act of 1997 (discussed earlier) was repealed in its entirety in 2004. It reappears, however, when the law sunsets.

In 2010, Congress passed the Tax Relief, Unemployment Reauthorization, and Job Creation Act of 2010 (TRA 2010). This act allows executors to elect no estate tax for those who died in the 2010 tax year, which allows for the election of the rules under the previous EGTRRA, or to allow the new estate tax law to apply. Therefore, when a person died in 2010, his or her estate or trust has right to choose if the old law or new law applies to the estate. The election to opt out of the estate tax needs to be made on the estate tax return.

This is a unique opportunity for the fiduciaries of estates and trusts of decedents who died in 2010 to elect to follow the law that is most beneficial to their estate or trust. Generally, the fiduciary will need to decide whether to choose the estate tax and receive a the full step-up in basis rather than electing out of the new estate tax law to the carry over basis system. This choice can be important, depending on the size of the estate and for other matters, such as if the decedent owned a life estate in property.

Of course, other considerations will have to be made in deciding which law to apply, as each case must be considered separately. Accordingly, each estate or trust should be closely examined to determine the most advantageous law to apply. Additionally, because Congress acted so late in the year, the federal estate tax return in 2010 is due no earlier than nine months after date of enactment.

TRA 2010 also gives a $5 million unified credit for both 2011 and 2012 with a 35 percent rate. The 2012 rate may be indexed for inflation. If Congress does not pass new legislation, this Act is set to sunset in 2013, with unified credit rates at the 2001 rates.

A significant planning change for clients in TRA 2010 is that individuals who die in 2011 or 2012 will not only have a $5 million exemption available (reduced by any lifetime gifts), but also have the ability to have any unused portion passed on to the surviving spouse. In fact, a deceased client may not need to even have $5 million in assets to pass $5 million of unused exemption on to a surviving spouse. This is known as the portability of the exemption or unified credit amount.

Careful planning is still required. The unused exemption amount is available to the surviving spouse only if an election is made and the amount is calculated on the timely filed estate tax return of the deceased spouse. This means that even if the deceased spouse does not have an estate tax, a federal estate tax return must be filed in order to use the portability. This may catch clients with smaller estates who may not necessarily think they need to file an estate tax return. During this time of portability, it may be wise to always file a form 706 Estate Tax return to preserve the unused exemption in case the surviving spouse comes into a windfall.

Several other credits may be allowed against the computed estate tax. Most common is a credit for state estate and inheritance taxes (described next). Depending on the nature, situs, and other aspects of certain assets included in the gross estate, these other credits may be allowed against the computed estate tax: prior transfers, foreign death taxes, death taxes on remainders, and recovery of taxes claimed as credits.

Filing of the Form 706 is due nine months after the decedent's date of death. The executor or administrator may request a five-month extension of time to file the return. If any tax is due with the return, an estimated payment of said tax is due nine months from the date of death, with any balance due with the filing of the return.

While payment of the estate tax cannot normally be extended, IRC Section 6166 provides relief for certain estates. Should the estate assets include an interest in a closely held business

[4] The estate tax unified credit exclusion, which was $675,000 in 2001 was scheduled to increase by steps to $1,000,000 in 2006.

that exceeds 35 percent of the adjusted gross estate, an election by the executor or administrator would permit the deferral and payment of the estate tax that is attributable to the inclusion of the closely held business interest in the estate in installments over several years. The requirements of this Code section are strict; therefore, the executor or administrator should carefully consider all available options, advantages, and consequences of making this election.

One of these options, available to closely held corporations, is an IRC Section 303 stock redemption. If funds are available, the corporation may redeem stock held by the executor or administrator equal to an amount that may not exceed the sum of the estate taxes, outstanding debts, and administration expenses. While this option does not serve to defer the payment of estate taxes, it may be used in conjunction with or in lieu of the deferred payments under Section 6166 described earlier.

(iii) State Estate and Inheritance Taxes. The estate tax in some states, such as New York, take the form of a tax on the right to transmit wealth that is similar to the federal estate tax. In other states, such as New Jersey, an inheritance tax is applied to one's right to receive a portion of a decedent's estate. The state inheritance taxes are paid from estate funds by the representative, who will therefore withhold an appropriate amount from each legacy or establish a claim against those beneficiaries responsible for the tax by the terms of the will or by state law. Kinship of the beneficiary to the decedent is usually the controlling factor in determining exemptions and tax rates, with close relatives being favored.

Other states, such as Florida, assess an estate tax based on the amount of credit for state death taxes claimed on the federal estate tax return.

Almost all states provide for the tax to be at least equal to the federal credit for state death taxes if total inheritance taxes are less.

EGTRRA reduces the state death tax credit by 25 percent in 2002, 50 percent in 2003, and 75 percent in 2004. In 2005, the credit is repealed and replaced with a deduction for state death taxes actually paid. This will require almost every state to enact some form of conforming legislation to coordinate its statute with the federal changes.

The timing of the state's estate or inheritance tax return and payment of any taxes may differ from the federal rules. An executor or administrator should be acquainted with these rules to avoid penalty and interest assessments. A state return may be required to be filed even though no federal return is required even if no state tax is due.

(iv) Generation-Skipping Transfer Tax. The Tax Reform Act of 1986 revised and imposed a new generation-skipping transfer tax on most transfers made to individuals two generations (i.e., grandchildren) down from the donor or decedent. Most transfers prior to 1987 are exempt. Direct transfers or distributions from trusts to individuals two generations down will be subject to the tax if the transfer exceeds the allowable exemption.

A donor/decedent has a lifetime exemption of $1 million. Effective for decedents dying after December 31, 1998, the Taxpayer Relief Act of 1997 provides that the $1 million exemption amount will be indexed for cost-of-living adjustments in $10,000 increments. Transfers in excess of this amount to grandchildren are subject to a flat tax in addition to the estate and gift tax. This flat tax is imposed at the highest marginal estate and gift tax rate, which is currently 55 percent. Consequently, it is conceivable that transferring $100 could cost $110 in estate/gift and generation-skipping taxes. The law is relatively new and complex. Therefore, knowledge of the law and planning is important in order to minimize the impact of the tax.

In 2001, the lifetime exemption was indexed up to $1,060,000. It will continue to be indexed for inflation in 2002 and 2003. For 2004 through 2009, the lifetime exemption is equal to the unified credit or applicable exclusion amount. The tax is repealed for 2010 and then returns to the 2001 levels. The tax rate is changed in the same manner as the estate tax rates discussed earlier. In addition, some of the substantive rules were liberalized effective for transfers made after December 31, 2000.

In 2011 and 2012, the exemption is $5 million with a 35 percent flat tax. The exemption is subject to increases for inflation. This exemption is scheduled to sunset to 2001 rates (indexed for inflation) in 2013.

(v) Estate Income Taxes. The representative may be responsible for filing annual federal income tax returns for the estate for the period beginning the day after the date of death and ending when the estate assets are fully distributed. The returns are generally prepared on a cash basis and can be prepared on a fiscal-year, rather than a calendar-year, basis. Such an election is made with the filing of the initial return and is often done to cut off taxable income in the first year of the estate. Maintenance of books on a fiscal-year basis and filing the request for an extension of time to file the return will also establish the fiscal year. If returns are not timely filed, the estate will then be required to file on a calendar-year basis.

A federal income tax return is due if the estate earns gross income of $600 or more per year. A $600 exemption is allowed in computing the income subject to federal income taxes. Administration expenses, such as executor's commission and legal and accounting fees, may be deducted if the representative does not elect to take these expenses on the federal estate tax return. If the estate distributes net income (gross income less expenses), such distributable net income is taxed to the recipient, and the estate is allowed a corresponding deduction in computing its taxable income. Any remaining taxable income after deductions for exemption, expenses, and distributions is taxed at a rate specified in a table to be used exclusively for estates and trusts.

The income tax basis of estate assets are stepped up to their estate tax value. Therefore, should the executor or administrator sell any assets to raise cash, the assets' estate tax value is used to determine whether any gain or loss is realized upon the sale. There are, however, certain assets includable in the estate whose income tax basis carries over from the decedent. These assets are called *income* in respect of a decedent (IRD) and are described in IRC Section 691. Examples of IRD include:

- Proceeds of U.S. savings bonds in excess of decedent's purchase price
- Individual retirement accounts
- Tax-sheltered annuities and regular annuities
- Deferred compensation
- Final paychecks and other remittances of compensation

Certain IRD give rise to income taxation upon receipt, while others do not cause taxation until they are redeemed or otherwise liquidated. Should an item of IRD be paid directly to an estate beneficiary or be distributed to the beneficiary from the estate, the same rules regarding income tax basis apply. An offsetting deduction is available to the executor or beneficiary who must recognize IRD in his or her gross income. The deduction is equal to that item's attributable share of the estate tax its inclusion in the estate has caused.

EGTRRA has modified the income tax rules relating to the step-up in basis discussed earlier beginning in 2010. To make up for the loss of revenue from the estate tax repeal, a new carryover basis regime will become effective. Under this regime, property acquired from a decedent will have a basis equal to the lesser of the decedent's basis or the fair market value of the property on the date of the decedent's death. A total $4.3 million of property may, however, still qualify to use the current step-up in basis rules. Up to $3 million of property passing to a surviving spouse, plus up to an aggregate of $1,300,000 of property passing to any beneficiaries will qualify for a step-up in basis. These new rules sunset after 2010, resulting in the modified carryover basis rules ending and the current step-up in basis rules being reinstated in 2011. Because of carry over basis, better records are needed in order to accurately reflect tax basis in the assets.

Estates must now make quarterly estimated tax payments in the same manner as individuals, except that an estate is exempt from making such payments during its first two taxable years. Accordingly, the penalties for underpayment of income tax are applicable to fiduciaries.

Some states also tax the income of estates, and the representative must see to it that such state statutes are complied with.

38.2 ACCOUNTING FOR ESTATES

(a) GOVERNING CONCEPTS. The general concepts governing the accounting for decedents' estates are for the most part similar to those applicable to trusts, but there are some differences. The underlying equation expressing the accounting relationship is assets equal accountability. However, the representative is concerned *not* with the long-term management of property for beneficiaries but rather with the payment of debts and the orderly realization and distribution of the estate properties. The collection and the distribution of income are incidental to the main function of the estate's fiduciary.

Whenever an estate accounting is prepared, a reconciliation of the gross estate as finally determined for estate tax purposes should be made with the schedule of principal received at the date by the representative. Every difference should be explainable.

(i) Accounting Period. The accounting period of the estate is determined by the dates set by the fiduciary or by the court for intermediate and final accountings; nevertheless, the books must be closed at least once a year for income tax purposes.

(ii) Principal and Income. Unless otherwise provided for, the rules outlined in Section 38.3(j) for the trustee should generally be followed by the representative in the allocation of receipts and disbursements to principal and income. Such distinctions, although not called for under the will, are frequently mandated by requirements of estate, inheritance, and income tax laws and regulations.

(iii) Treatment of Liabilities. The representative picks up only the inventory of assets of the decedent at the inception of the estate. Claims against the estate, after presentation and review, are paid by the representative and are recorded as debts paid. The payment of such debts reduces in proportion the accountability of the representative.

(b) RECORD-KEEPING SYSTEM. No special type of bookkeeping system is prescribed by law, but a complete record of all transactions must be kept with sufficient detail to meet the requirements of the courts and of the estate, inheritance, and income tax returns. Much of the information may be in memorandum form outside of the formal accounting system.

The federal estate tax law requires information regarding assets beyond those ordinarily under the control of the representative (e.g., real estate). Such information must be assembled in appropriate form by the representative, who has responsibility for the estate tax return.

(i) Journals. A single multicolumn journal is usually sufficient for recordkeeping. It should incorporate cash receipts, cash disbursements, and asset inventory adjustments. Further, it is important to note and keep track of the distinction between principal and income.

(ii) Operation of a Going Business. If the decedent was the individual proprietor of a going business and if the court or the will instructs the administrator or executor to continue the operation of the business, the bookkeeping procedure becomes somewhat complicated. The books of the business may be continued as distinct from the general estate books, or the transactions of the business may be combined with other estate transactions in one set of records. The best procedure, if the business is of at least moderate size, is to keep the operations of the business in a separate set of books and to set up a controlling accounting in the general books of the executor or administrator.

As soon as the representative takes charge of the business, the assets should be inventoried and the books closed, normally as of the date of death. The liabilities should be transferred to the list of debts to be paid by the representative, leaving the assets, the operating expenses and income, and the subsequently incurred liabilities to be recorded in the books of the company. An account should be opened in the books of the business for the representative that will show the same amount as the controlling account for the business in the books of the representative.

(iii) Final Accounting. The "final" accounting is the report to the court of the handling of the estate affairs by the representative, if required. It presents, among other things, a plan for the distribution of the remainder of the assets of the estate and a computation of the commission due the representative for his services. If the court approves the report, it issues a decree putting the proposals into effect.

(c) REPORTS OF EXECUTOR OR ADMINISTRATOR. The form of the reports of the fiduciary will vary according to the requirements of the court and to the character of the estate. In general, however, the representative "charges" him- or herself with all of the property received and subsequently discovered plus gains on realizations, and "credits" (or discharges) him- or herself with all disbursements for debts paid, expenses paid, legacies distributed, and realization losses. Each major item in the charge and discharge statement should be supported by a schedule showing detailed information. At any time during the administration of the estate, the excess of charges over credits should be represented by property in the custody of the fiduciary. It may be necessary to show the market value of property delivered to a legatee or trustee at the date of delivery, in which case the investment schedule will show the increase or decrease on distribution of assets as well as from sales. The income schedule, when needed, should be organized to show the total income from each investment, the expenses chargeable against income, and the distribution of the remainder.

Exhibit 38.2 is typical of the charge-and-discharge statement, each item being supported by a schedule.

ESTATE OF JOHN SMITH
Charge-and-Discharge Statement
A. L. White, Executor
From April 7, 20XX, to December 15, 20XX

First, as to Principal:			
The Executor charges himself as follows:			
With amount of inventory at the date of death, April 7, Schedule A		$xxx	
With amount of assets discovered subsequent to date of death, Schedule B		xxx	
With gain on realization of assets, Schedule C		xxx	
			$xxx
The Executor credits himself as follows:			
With loss on realization of assets, Schedule C		$xxx	
With amount paid for funeral and administrative expenses, Schedule D		xxx	
With amount paid on debts of the estate, Schedule F		xxx	
With distributions to legatees, Schedule G		xxx	
			xxx
Leaving a balance of principal, Schedule C, of			$xxx
Second, as to Income:			
The Executor charges himself as follows:			
With amount of income received, Schedule H		$xxx	
The Executor credits himself as follows:			
With amount of administrative expenses chargeable to income, Schedule D	$xxx		
With distribution of income to legatees, Schedule I	xxx	xxx	
Leaving a balance of income, Schedule J			Xxx
Leaving a balance of principal and income of			$xxx
Balance of principal and income to be distributed to those entitled thereto, subject to the deduction of the Executor's commissions, legal fees, and the expenses of this accounting, Schedule K.			

Exhibit 38.2 Sample Charge-and-Discharge Statement

38.3 TRUSTS AND TRUSTEES—LEGAL BACKGROUND

(a) NATURE AND TYPES OF TRUSTS. The trust relationship exists whenever one person holds property for the benefit of another. The trustee holds legal title to the property for the benefit of the beneficiary, or *cestui que trust.* The person from whom trust property is received is known as the *grantor, donor, settlor, creator,* or *trustor.*

An express trust is one in which the trustee, beneficiary, subject matter, and method of administration have been explicitly indicated. An implied trust may be created where language of an instrument indicates the desirability of a trust but does not specify the details or when the trust relationship is assumed in order to prevent the results of fraud, breach of trust, or undue influence. The terms *constructive, resulting,* and *involuntary* trust are sometimes applied to such situations.

A testamentary trust is one created by a will. A living trust, or *trust inter vivos,* is created to take effect during the grantor's lifetime. Trusts are sometimes created by court order, as in the case of a guardianship.

A private trust is created for the benefit of particular individuals, while a public or charitable trust is for the benefit of an indefinite class of persons.

A simple trust directs the trustee to distribute the entire net income of the trust to the named beneficiary. A complex trust gives the trustee the discretionary authority to distribute or accumulate the trust net income to or on behalf of the named beneficiary. In some instances, the trust may start off as complex and then convert to a simple trust upon the happening of a specified event (i.e., the beneficiary's attainment of age 21 or 25).

A grantor trust exists when both the grantor and beneficiary are the same individual. A grantor trust may be implied if the grantor retains sufficient rights or controls over disposition of trust income and/or principal.

When a grantor establishes an irrevocable trust *inter vivos* and transfers assets to it, the grantor has made a completed gift of the property transferred for income, gift, and estate tax purposes. Should the grantor retain any of the rights enumerated in IRC Sections 671 to 679, however, the grantor will be continue to be treated as the grantor or owner of the trust property for income tax purposes only. The grantor will be taxed on the income of the trust instead of the trust or trust beneficiaries (even if they receive a distribution of this trust income). This is referred to as an *intentionally defective grantor trust* (IDGT) and can be used as an effective estate and financial planning tool.

A trust may include a spendthrift clause that prohibits the beneficiary from assigning his or her interest before receiving it or prevents creditors from enforcing their claims against the income or principal of a trust fund, or both.

Trusts are often used for business purposes, as when property is transferred by a deed of trust instead of a mortgage, when trustees are appointed to hold title and perform other functions under a bond issue, or when assets are assigned to a trustee for the benefit of creditors. Bankruptcy and insolvency are discussed in Chapter 39.

(i) Limitations on Private Trusts. A public trust may be established for an indefinite period, but a trust may not suspend indefinitely the power of anyone to transfer the trust property. The common law rule, otherwise known as the *rule against perpetuities,* limits the duration of a private trust to 21 years after the death of an identifiable individual living at the time the interest was created ("life in being". Another common limitation in certain states is "two lives in being" at the origin of the trust. Many states have extended the time limit or abolished the rule against perpetuities.

Accumulation of the income of a trust is also restricted by state law. A common provision, for example, is that in the case of a trust created for the benefit of a minor, the income can be accumulated only during the minority of the beneficiary. Even the income of a charitable trust cannot be accumulated for an "unreasonable" period.

(ii) Revocation of Trusts. A completed trust cannot be revoked without the consent of all the beneficiaries unless the right to revoke has been expressly reserved by the grantor. Trusts are therefore sometimes classified as revocable or irrevocable.

(b) APPOINTMENT AND REMOVAL OF TRUSTEES. In general, anyone competent to make a will or a contract is competent to create a trust. The trustee must be one who is capable of taking and holding property and who has the legal capacity and natural ability to execute the trust.

(i) Choice of Trustee. The decedent's will usually names the trustee for a testamentary trust. A grantor who is establishing an *inter vivos* trust will usually appoint one or more of these to act as trustee: a relative; a professional adviser (i.e., attorney, accountant, broker); a business associate; or an institutional entity, such as a bank or trust company. Each type of trustee has its pros and cons; however, the most important concern is not to choose a trustee that will cause adverse income tax consequences.

(ii) Methods of Appointment. Seven of the means by which trustees are appointed are:

1. *By deed or declaring of trust.* The creator of the trust names the trustees in the instrument.
2. *By will.* The same person may be both executor and trustee under a will, but this dual capacity should be clearly indicated.
3. *By agreement.*
4. *By the court.* The court will appoint a trustee when a trust may fail for lack of a trustee, when a trustee refuses to serve or has died, or when a vacancy from any cause exists and no other means have been provided for filing the vacancy.
5. *By implication of law.*
6. *By self-perpetuating boards.* When vacancies occur, they are filed by the remaining members of the board.
7. *By the exercise of a power of appointment.* The instrument creating the trust may give the remaining trustees, beneficiaries, or any other person the power to appoint a trustee to fill a vacancy. Specific instructions should be included in the instrument as to the situation establishing a vacancy, the persons who may be appointed, and the manner of making the appointment.

(iii) Acceptance or Disclaimer. Acceptance of an appointment as trustee may be made by positive statement, by qualifying as executor if the appointment is by will, by the acceptance of property of the trust, or by other acts from which acceptance may be presumed. An individual may refuse to accept an appointment as a trustee and should execute and deliver a disclaimer expressing rejection of the appointment.

(iv) Resignation of Trustee. According to the Restatement of the Law of Trusts 2d (1 Trusts A.L.I. 234):

> A trustee who has accepted the trust cannot resign except (a) with the permission of a proper court; or (b) in accordance with the terms of the trust; or (c) with the consent of all the beneficiaries, if they have capacity to give such consent.

Restatement 3d states:

> A trustee who has accepted the trust can properly resign:
>
> **(a)** in accordance with the terms of the trust;
> **(b)** with the consent of all beneficiaries; or
> **(c)** upon terms approved by a proper court.

In states that have enacted the Uniform Trust Code Section 705, it goes further:

> **(a)** A trustee may resign:
>
> **(1)** upon at least 30 days' notice to the qualified beneficiaries, the settlor, if living, and all cotrustees; or
> **(2)** with the approval of the court.

It is best to check with your state to determine the law it follows.

(v) Removal of Trustee. The court has power to remove a trustee and appoint a successor under certain circumstances. Asher cites, among others, these six grounds upon which trustees have been removed:

1. Failure to exercise discretion
2. Self-dealing
3. Failure to keep proper accounts, and mingling with trustee's own funds
4. Incompetency and neglect of duty
5. Conversion of trust property
6. Refusal to obey orders of the court[5]

(c) POWERS AND DUTIES OF TRUSTEES. The powers of trustees are obtained both from the provisions and implications of the instrument creating the trust and from the general laws pertaining to the trust relationship. The instrument may either expand or restrict the general powers, except that it may not relieve the trustee from liability for gross negligence, bad faith, or dishonesty. The powers of a trustee may be either (1) imperative or mandatory or (2) permissive or discretionary. In other words, the powers must either be exercised definitely and positively within a given length of time or upon the occurrence of some contingency, or they may be exercised at the discretion of the trustee.

(i) General Powers. The nine general powers of a trustee, which include all necessary incidental powers, are:

1. To take and retain possession of the trust property
2. To invest trust funds so as to yield a fair income
3. To sell and reinvest when necessary
4. To sell and convey real estate when necessary to carry out the provisions of the trust
5. To release real estate so that it may earn income
6. To pay for repairs, taxes, and other such expenses in connection with trust property
7. To sue or defend suits when necessary
8. To make contracts that are necessary to carry out the purposes of the trust
9. To pay over and distribute the trust property to those entitled to it

The trustee secures possession of the trust property and holds title in his or her own name. All debtors should be notified of the change in ownership of claims against them in order to hold them directly liable to the trustee. All debts due the trust estate should be collected promptly. Trust property must be kept separate from the property of anyone else. The trustee will be liable for any loss occurring as a result of the mingling of funds or other property. An exception is usually made when a trust company is acting as trustee; it may deposit cash in trust funds with itself or may mingle various trust funds and deposit same with designated depositories.

(ii) Duties. Asher and Scott outline 14 duties of the trustee:[6]

1. To administer the trust as long as he or she continues as trustee.
2. To administer the trust solely in the interest of the beneficiary (the duty of loyalty as a fiduciary).
3. Not to delegate to others the performance of acts that the trustee sought personally to perform.
4. To keep clear and accurate accounts.

---

[5] M. Asher, A. W. Scott, and W. F. Fratcher, *Scott and Ascher on* Trusts, 5th ed. (New York: Aspen Publishers, 2011), supplement.

[6] Ibid.

5. To give to beneficiaries upon their request complete and accurate information as to the administration of the trust.
6. To exercise such care and skill as a person of ordinary prudence would exercise in dealing with his or her own property; and if the trustee possesses greater skill than that of an ordinary prudent person, he or she must exercise that skill.
7. To take reasonable steps to secure control of trust property and to keep control of it.
8. To use care and skill to preserve the trust property. The standard of care and skill is that of a person of ordinary prudence.
9. To take reasonable steps to realize on claims that he or she holds in trust and to defend claims of third persons against the trust estate.
10. To keep the trust property separate from his or her own property and separate from property held upon other trusts; and to designate trust property as property of the trust.
11. To refrain in ordinary circumstances from lending trust money without security.
12. To invest trust funds so that they will be productive of income.
13. To pay the net income of the trust to the beneficiary at reasonable intervals; and if there are two or more beneficiaries, to deal with them impartially.
14. Where there are several trustees, it is the duty of each of them, unless otherwise provided by the trust instrument, to participate in the administration of the trust, and each trustee must use reasonable care to prevent the others from committing a breach of trust.

(d) PROPER TRUST INVESTMENTS. The trustee is under a duty to invest funds in such a way as to receive an income without improperly risking the loss of the principal. The only general rule as to investment is that the trustee is under a duty to make such investments as a prudent person would make of his or her own property, having primarily in view the preservation of the estate and the amount and regularity of the income to be derived. In some states ("legal-list" states), the legislatures tell trustees in what they must or may invest funds unless the terms of the trust otherwise provide.

Eight kinds of investments that are almost universally condemned are:

1. Purchase of securities on margin
2. Purchase of speculative shares of stock
3. Purchase of bonds selling at large discount because of uncertainty of repayment at maturity
4. Purchase of securities in new and untried enterprises
5. Use of trust property in the carrying on of a trade or business, even though it is not an untried enterprise
6. Purchase of land or other things for the purpose of resale, unless authorized by the terms of the trust
7. Purchase of second and other junior mortgages
8. Making unsecured loans to individuals or firms or corporations.

Three types of investments that are almost universally permitted include:

1. Bonds of the United States or of the state or of a municipality thereof
2. First mortgages on land
3. Corporate bonds of a high-investment grade

In 1990, the American Law Institute adopted the Uniform Prudent Investor Act (the UPIA) and published it in the third edition of the *Restatement of the Law of Trusts.* The UPIA was amended, in part, in 2008. It incorporates a prudent investor rule that has since been adopted by a significant majority of the states in a form that is similar to, or somewhat comparable to, the scope of these new rules. The Restatement embodies three main themes:

1. Although it is thought that a trustee may not delegate any of his or her duties, other than certain ministerial duties, this position is relaxed in that a trustee should, or even must, delegate investment authority to skilled professionals, should the trustee lack the required expertise or experience to properly manage the assets within the trust.
2. The costs incurred by the trustee in performing his or her duties must be reasonable.
3. A trustee is charged with the responsibility for maintaining the trust portfolio so as to keep pace with inflation. In other words, trustees should invest for the maximum total return on investment without regard for distinctions between principal and income. This is referred to as *modern portfolio theory,* permitting trustees to invest for capital appreciation as well as current income in the form of interest, dividends, rents, and so forth.

(e) TRUSTEE'S PERSONAL LIABILITIES AND LIABILITY FOR ACTS OF COTRUSTEE. Trustees are liable to the beneficiary for failure to fulfill their duties under the statutes, general rules of equity, or the provisions of the trust indenture.

Trustees must be particularly circumspect in all matters affecting their own property or benefit. They are personally liable for torts committed by themselves or their agents and, unless the agreement states otherwise, they are personally liable on all contracts made on behalf of the trust.

Trustees are not responsible for loss by theft, embezzlement, or accident if they have taken all the precautions that a careful person takes in guarding their own property and if they are strictly following their line of duty as trustees. If a trustee is not insolvent and mixes trust property with his or her own, the beneficiary may take the whole, leaving the trustee to prove his or her own part. If the trustee is insolvent, the beneficiary shares with the other creditors unless definite property can be identified as belonging to the trust. Interest will be charged against trustees who have mingled trust funds with their own. If bank deposits are made in the individual names of trustees, they will be treated as a guarantor of the solvency of the bank, even though they use care in their choice of the bank and have not in any way misused the funds.

In general, a trustee is not liable for losses caused by the default or negligence of a co-trustee unless he or she has cooperated with the trustee who is at fault or has known of the trustee's misconduct and has not taken any steps to prevent it. If, however, each trustee should have interested him- or herself in the matter in question, such as the proper investment of funds, each would be responsible even though he or she took no part in or knew nothing of the misconduct. All trustees should act together in handling the trust property and should apply to the court for instructions in case they cannot agree. Unanimity is usually required for all important decisions in the case of private trusts, but a majority of a board of trustees may act for a charitable trust.

In certain circumstances, a trustee may become personally liable for the unpaid estate taxes of a decedent under the theory of transferee liability. Ordinarily, the beneficiary of an estate or trust is ultimately liable for any unpaid estate or gift taxes due on the transfer. The liability is equal to the value of the property received by the recipient as of the date of transfer.

A review of IRC Sections 6324 and 6901, primarily, is in order. For example, the trustee of an *inter vivos* trust that is included in the gross estate for estate tax purposes could result in the trustee being personally liable, as opposed to the beneficiaries, for payment of any attributable estate taxes. Certain trust distributions trigger the generation-skipping transfer tax, requiring the trustee to pay this tax. As a result of this possibility, trustees should consider maintaining a reserve until they are satisfied that all such taxes are satisfied. Upon making distributions, trustees should also consider requesting that the beneficiaries indemnify the trustees for any taxes that may be assessed against them.

If a trust possesses insufficient assets to pay all its debts, federal law requires it to first satisfy any federal tax deficiencies before any other debt. Trustees who fail to abide by this requirement will subject themselves to personally liability for the amount of the unpaid tax deficiency under IRC Section 3713(b). When there are insufficient assets to pay a federal tax obligation as a result of the trustee's actions, the IRS may collect the tax obligation directly from the trustee without regard to transferee liability.[7] If the IRS determines a trustee to be personally liable for the tax deficiency, it will be required to follow normal deficiency procedures in assessing and collecting the tax under IRC Section 6212.

(f) GUARDIANS. If a person is incompetent to manage his or her own property because of a disability such as infancy or mental incompetency, a guardian will be appointed by the probate or other appropriate court. The court must approve the appointment of a guardian by will. A guardian is a trustee in the strictest sense of the term. He or she is directly under the supervision of the court. If possible, only the income from the property should be used for the maintenance and education of the beneficiary; permission must be granted by the court before the principal can be used for this purpose. Any sale of real estate must be authorized by the court. A guardian should have the authorization of the court or the direction of a will before paying money to a minor or to anyone for the minor; otherwise, the guardian may be compelled to pay the amount again when the minor becomes of age.

(g) TESTAMENTARY TRUSTEE. The work of the trustee appointed by a will begins when the executor sets aside the trust fund out of the estate assets. One person may serve as both executor and trustee under a will.

The testamentary trustee has slightly more freedom in handling the funds than does the executor, and his or her responsibility may be made less rigorous by provisions of the will. The testamentary trustee holds, invests, and cares for the property, and disposes of it or its income as directed by the will. A trustee should have specific authority of a will or the court, or the consent of everyone interested, before carrying on a business. If there are several executors, one can act alone, but trustees must act jointly.

(h) COMPENSATION OF TRUSTEES. Trustees are usually allowed compensation for their work, either by provision of the trust instrument or by statute. The statutory provision is usually a graduated percentage of the funds handled.

A trustee is entitled to be repaid expenditures reasonably and properly incurred in the care of trust property. The compensation is usually allocated to principal and income in accordance with the specific provision of the indenture or as provided by statute or rules of law.

(i) RIGHTS OF BENEFICIARY. Beneficiaries have an equitable title to the trust property (i.e., they can bring suit in a court of equity to enforce their rights and to prevent misuse of the property by the trustee). Unless the instrument by which the trust is created provides otherwise, beneficiaries, if of age, can sell or otherwise dispose of their equitable estate in the property.

Beneficiaries have the right to inspect and take copies of all papers, records, and data bearing on the administration of the trust property and income that are in the hands of the trustee. Beneficiaries may have an accounting ordered whenever there is any reason for suspicion, or any failure to allow inspection or to make satisfactory reports and statements. Whenever it seems advisable, a court of equity will order an accounting.

Beneficiaries may have an injunction issued to restrain the trustee from proceeding with any unauthorized action, if such action will result in irremediable damage. Beneficiaries may present a petition to the court for the removal of a trustee but must be able to prove bad faith, negligence, lack of ability, or other such cause for the removal. The trustee is entitled to a formal trial.

Beneficiaries can, if it is possible to do so, follow the trust property and have it subjected to the trust, even if a substitution has been made for the original property, unless it comes into the hands of an innocent holder for value. If the trust property cannot be traced or is in the hands of an innocent holder for value, beneficiaries may bring action against the trustee in a court of equity for breach of trust.

If the beneficiaries are of age and mentally competent, they may approve or ratify acts of the trustee that would otherwise be a violation of the trustee's duties or responsibilities.

---

[7] See *United States v. Whitney,* 654 F.2d 607 (9th Cir. 1981).

(j) DISTINCTION BETWEEN PRINCIPAL AND INCOME. Probably the most difficult problem of the trustee is differentiating between principal (corpus) and income. The intention of the creator of the trust is binding if it can be ascertained, but in the absence of instructions to the contrary, the general legal rules must be followed.

Generally, the life tenant (the present beneficiary) is entitled to the net income and the remainderman (the future beneficiary) is entitled to the principal, as legally determined. The *principal* is the property itself that constitutes the trust fund, and the *income* is the accumulation of funds and other property arising from the investment or other use of the trust principal. Increases or decreases in the value of the assets that constitute the trust fund affect only the principal. The income determined under these rules is not always the same as taxable income or income as determined by generally accepted accounting principles (GAAP). The life tenant is entitled to receive only the net income from all sources for the entire term of his or her tenancy. He or she is not allowed to select the income from only those investments that are lucrative.

The existing rules regarding principal and income are based on the Uniform Principal and Income Act of 1962 (UPAIA). These rules are, to a great extent, at odds with a trustee's ability to comply with the modern portfolio theory contained in the Uniform Prudent Investor Act described earlier. As one commentator noted, the incompatibility of the UPIA and UPAIA were reconciled in 1997 by the National Conference of Commissioners on Uniform State Laws. The revised UPAIA accomplishes

> this result by way of an adjustment power conferred upon trustees, pursuant to which the trustee is empowered to allocate traditional trust accounting income (e.g., interest, dividends, rents) to principal and perhaps more importantly, to allocate to income what is typically considered principal. Thus, a trustee can increase the amount currently distributable to a beneficiary, for example, by allocating capital appreciation to income. Some states (New York, New Jersey, Delaware, and Missouri) added an alternative approach to their respective adoptions of the new UPAIA: an optional unitrust provision. Instead of being limited to the annual accounting income actually realized by the trust in any year, the current beneficiary of a unitrust is entitled to an amount equal to a fixed percentage of the value of the trust's assets determined annually. As a result, the trustee is free to invest for total return absent the need to produce sufficient income to satisfy the current beneficiary. By adopting the unitrust alternative, the trustee is relieved of the obligation to determine each year whether an equitable adjustment is warranted. In addition, the unitrust approach provides the current beneficiary with the certainty of knowing what he or she is entitled to each year instead of having to await the trustee's possible exercise of its discretionary adjustment power.

All of the statutes give testators and grantors the ability to opt out of the statutory language by defining how they want principal and income to be recognized and charged. The UPAIA in effect in a given state is operative only if the trust document or will is silent. The U.S. Treasury Department and Internal Revenue Service have recognized this new trend in trust accounting and have issued Proposed Treasury Regulation Section 1.643(a) through (d).

The following four sections describes the principal and income rules under the UPAIA of 1962. Although most states have now enacted the UPIA, trustees are advised to seek to professional counseling to determine whether the 1962 or 1997 revised rules are in effect in their respective state.

(i) Receipts of Principal. Ten receipts of cash or other property have been held to be part of the corpus of the trust and therefore to belong to the remainderman or persons entitled to the corpus:

1. Interest accrued to the beginning of the trust. Bond coupons are not apportioned in the absence of a statute providing for such a division.
2. Rent accrued to the beginning of the trust. Under the common law, rent was not apportioned according to the time expired.
3. Excess of selling price of trust assets over their value in the original inventory or over its purchase price. Appreciation, in general, belongs to the trust corpus.

4. The value of assets existing at the time the original inventory was taken but not included in the inventory.
5. Dividends (see discussion in Subsection 28.3(k)(iii)).
6. Proceeds of the sale of stock rights.
7. Profit from the completion of executory contracts of a decedent.
8. Profits earned prior to the beginning of the trust on the operations of a partnership or sole proprietorship.
9. Insurance money received for a fire that occurred prior to the date of the beginning of the trust, or after that date if the property is in the hands of the trustee for the benefit of the trust in general.
10. If trust property is mortgaged, the proceeds may be said to be principal assets, although there is no increase in the equity of the remainderman.

(ii) Disbursements of Principal. The next 12 payments, distribution, and exhaustion of assets have been held to be chargeable to the corpus:

1. Excess of the inventory value or purchase price of an asset over the amount realized from its sale.
2. Payment of debts owed, including accruals, at the date of the beginning of the trust.
3. Real estate taxes assessed on or before the date of the beginning of the trust. In the case of special assessments made during the administration of the trust, the remainderman may pay the assessment and the life tenant may be charged interest thereon annually during the life of the trust, or else some other equitable adjustment will be made between them.
4. Any expenditures that result in improvements of the property, except those made voluntarily by a life tenant for his or her own benefit, and all expenditures on newly acquired property that are necessary to put it into condition to rent or use.
5. Wood on the property that the life tenant uses for fuel, fences, and other similar purposes. The life tenant may operate mines, wells, quarries, and so on, that have been opened and operated on the property.
6. Losses due to casualty and theft of general trust assets.
7. Expenses of administration except those directly pertaining to the administration of income. For example, legal expenses incurred in defending the trust estate are chargeable to principal; however, the expenses of litigation in an action to protest only the income are payable out of income.
8. Trustees' commissions in respect to the receipts or disbursements out of principal. Commissions computed on income are ordinarily payable out of income.
9. Brokerage fees and other expenses for changing investments should generally be chargeable to principal, since they are a part of the cost of purchase or sale.
10. Income taxes on gains made from disposition of principal assets (capital gains).
11. Carrying charges on unproductive real estate, unless the terms of the trust direct the trustee to retain the property even though it is unproductive.
12. Cost of improvements to property held as part of the principal.

(iii) Receipts of Income. Six receipts have been held to be income and to belong to the life tenants or persons entitled to the income:

1. Interest, rent, and so on, accruing after the date of the beginning of the trust. The proceeds of a foreclosed mortgage may be apportionable between principal and income. Interest includes the increment in securities issued at a discount.
2. Increase in value of investments made by the trustee from accumulated undistributed income.

3. Dividends (see discussion in Subsection 38.3(k)(iii)).
4. Crops harvested during the trust.
5. Royalties or other income from operation of mines, quarries, or wells that were made productive prior to the beginning of the trust, or were developed or leased in cooperating with the remainderman.
6. Net profit from the operation of a business.

(iv) Disbursements of or Charges to Income. Eight items have been held to be chargeable against the income of the trust:

1. Interest payable, accruing during the life of the trust
2. Any expenses incurred in earning or collecting income, caring for trust property, or preserving its value, and an appropriate share of administration fees and expenses
3. Income tax except those levied on gains from sale of principal assets
4. Premiums on trustee's bond
5. Provision for amortization of wasting property, including leasehold interests, royalties, oil and gas wells, machinery, and farm implements (see discussion of depreciation in Subsection 38.3(k)(v))
6. Provision for amortization of improvements to trust property when such improvements will not outlive the duration of the trust
7. Losses of property due to the negligence of the life tenant
8. Losses due to casualty and theft of income assets

(k) PRINCIPAL AND INCOME—SPECIAL PROBLEMS. The distinction between principal and income also involves a consideration of such problems as unproductive property, accruals, dividends, bond premium and discount, and depreciation and depletion.

(i) Unproductive Property. When the trustee is required to sell unproductive property and the sale is delayed, the net proceeds of the sale should be apportioned between principal and income. The net proceeds are allocated by determining the sum that, with interest thereon at the current rate of return on trust investments, would equal the net proceeds, and the sum so determined is treated as principal and the balance as income (Restatement of Trusts 2d, § 241). Apportionment between principal and income is generally applicable to real estate, but it has been applied in the case of personal property also. It does not matter whether the property is sold at a gain or a loss.

(ii) Accruals. There are two dates at which the matter of accruals becomes significant. The first is the date at which the trust begins. Income and expenses accrued at that date belong to the corpus of the estate. The second date is the one when the life interest terminates. Income and expenses accrued at that date belong to the life tenant or his estate.

Larsen summarizes the general rule of accrual as applied to certain items, from which the next list is taken:

1. *Interest.* Interest accrued on receivables and investments at the date the trust is established is considered part of the trust corpus. Exceptions are interest on (a) savings accounts when the interest is paid only if the deposit remains until the end of the interest period, and (b) coupon bonds when the payment is contingent upon the owner presenting the coupon, in which case the date of receipt is controlling. Similar rules apply to the accrual of interest expense.
2. *Rent.* The accrual of rent prior to the beginning of the trust is considered by many states as a portion of a trust corpus. Any rent accruing between the date of the establishment of the trust and the termination of the tenancy belongs to the income beneficiary. Rent expense is handled similarly.

3. *Dividends.* Ordinary cash dividends are not divisible. If the dividend is declared and the date of record has passed before the trust is created, the dividend is a part of the corpus. Otherwise it is considered income to the trust. A stock dividend is treated in the same manner in many states . . . . [For a discussion of special treatment of cash and stock dividends under the Massachusetts and Pennsylvania rules, see the next subsection.]
4. *Property taxes.* Taxes which have been levied on trust property prior to the beginning of the trust are charges against the principal. Any taxes assessed on the basis of trust property held for the benefit of the income beneficiary are chargeable against income. Special assessments made during the administration of the trust are usually paid by the remainderman, although in some cases where the assessment is for improvements that benefit the life tenant, a part or all of the assessment may be charged against income. When the assessment is paid from the corpus, interest on the funds advance may be charged against income.
5. *Profits.* Income earned by a partnership or proprietorship does not accrue. The income that is earned prior to the creation of the trust is considered a part of the principal of the trust. In many cases a partnership is dissolved upon the death of a partner, and there may be no income earned after the trust is established. In the event that the business continues by specific direction of the grantor or provision of the partnership agreement, any income earned after the trust is created is income of the trust.
6. *Executory contracts.* Any profits earned on the completion of an executory contract by the trustee is an addition to the principal of the trust.
7. *Livestock and crops.* Any livestock born during the tenancy under the trust is considered income, except to the extent that the herd must be maintained as directed by the grantor, in which case the increase must be divided between principal and income in a manner which honors this intention. If the principal includes land, any crops harvested during this tenancy are considered income of the trust.
8. *Premium returns.* Any return of premium or dividend on insurance policies which was paid prior to the creation of the trust is a part of the principal. This is considered realization of assets.
9. *Royalties.* Royalties or other income from the operation of mines or other natural resource deposits which were made operative before the trust was created or which were developed in cooperation with the remainderman are income to the trust.[8]

(iii) Dividends. The determination of whether a dividend is principal or income involves a consideration of applicable state laws. Ordinary cash dividends declared during the period of the trust belong to the income beneficiary. An ordinary stock dividend is usually regarded as income except in states that follow the Massachusetts rule. This rule holds that all cash dividends are treated as income and that stock dividends are entirely principal.

Some states follow the Pennsylvania rule, which holds that, in regard to extraordinary dividends, it is not the form of the dividend but its source that determines whether and to what extent it is income or principal. Generally, under this rule, extraordinary dividends are income if declared out of earnings accruing to the corporation during the period of the trust, but they are principal if declared out of earnings accruing prior to the creation of the trust. Thus, if such dividends cause the book value of the corporation's stock to be reduced below the book value that existed at the creation of the trust, that portion of the dividend equivalent to the impairment of book value is principal and only the remainder is income. The present Pennsylvania law provides that stock dividends of 6 percent or less "shall be deemed income" unless the instrument provides to the contrary.

Although there is still wide diversity among the courts and state statutes in the apportionment of corporate distributions, Asher and Scott point out that the recent trend has been in favor of the Massachusetts rule.[9] The Uniform Principal and Income Act (Uniform Laws Annotated, Vol. 7B, § 5) follows the essence of the Massachusetts rule in treating cash and other property dividends as income and stock dividends as principal.

---

[8] E. J. Larsen, *Modern Advanced Accounting,* 10th ed. (New York: Shepard's/McGraw-Hill, 2006). Chapter 15.

[9] Asher and Scott.

(iv) Premium and Discount on Bonds. The necessity of accumulating bond discount or amortizing bond premium in order to determine the correct interest income still gives rise to a great deal of confusion in trust and estate administration. In general, it appears that most courts support the amortization of premium on bonds purchased by the trustee, but there has been little or no support of the accumulation of discount. Any difference between the inventory value and the face value of the bonds taken over by the trustee is usually treated as an adjustment of principal.

In the event of redemption before maturity, it has been held that the proper procedure is to amortize the premium to the date of redemption; the unamortized balance is a loss borne by principal. If a bonus is received, it should be credited to principal.

Asher and Scott suggest:

> It might well be held that the whole matter [of amortizing premium and discount] should be left to the discretion of the trustee, and if he is not guilty of an abuse of discretion in unduly favoring some of the beneficiaries at the expense of the others, the court should not interpose its authority. This, of course, is the result reached where such discretion is expressly conferred upon the trustee by the terms of the trust.[10]

(v) Depreciation and Depletion. In determining whether provision must be made for depreciation and depletion, it is essential to consider carefully the intentions and wishes of the trustor. If the trustor intended to give the full, undiminished income to the life tenant even though the principal would thereby be partially or completely exhausted, no deduction from income for depletion or depreciation is allowed. If, however, there is an expressed or implied intention to preserve the principal intact, the trustee is required to withhold from income an amount sufficient to maintain the original property of the trust.

When the trustor's intentions regarding the receipts from wasting property cannot be determined from the trust instrument, then, according to Asher and Scott, the inference is that the trustor did not intend that the life beneficiary should receive the whole income at the expense of the principal. Thus, when the trustee holds wasting property, including royalties, patents, mines, timberlands, machinery, and equipment, he is under a duty to make a provision for amortization of such property. The general rule has been applied to new buildings erected and improvements made by the trustee; however, the courts have generally held that buildings that were part of the trust estate at the beginning of the trust need not be depreciated. The courts have, in effect, refused to treat the buildings as wasting property.

The trend appears to be in the direction of adopting principles of depreciation followed in accounting practice. For example, the position taken in Section 13 of the Revised Uniform Principal and Income Act is that, with respect to charges against income and principal, there shall be:

> a reasonable allowance for depreciation under generally accepted accounting principles, but no allowance shall be made for depreciation of that portion of any real property used by a beneficiary as a residence or for depreciation of any property held by the trustee on the effective date of this Act for which the trustee is not then making an allowance for depreciation.

(l) TAX STATUS OF TRUST. Unless the trust qualifies as an exempt organization (charitable, educational, etc.), or unless the income of the trust is taxable to the grantor (revocable, or grantor retains substantial dominion and control), the income of the trust is subject to the federal income tax in a manner similar to the case of an individual. In general, the trust is treated as a conduit for tax purposes and is allowed a deduction for its income that is distributed or distributable currently to the beneficiaries. The trust may also be subject to state income taxes, personal property taxes, and so on. A tax service should be consulted for the latest provisions and rulings as to deductions, credits, rates, and filing requirements.

---

[10] Ibid.

It is important to note that although trusts and estates are taxed similarly, there are two major differences. Trusts must be operated on a calendar-year basis, whereas estates may operate on a fiscal year, usually tied to the decedent's date of death. Second, trusts must pay estimated taxes in the same fashion as individuals. Estates, however, are exempt from this requirement, but only for their first two tax years.

The impact of the Revenue Reconciliation Act of 1993 (RRA) substantially compressed the income tax rates applicable to trusts and estates. Indexed from its original level effective for tax years beginning in 1993, trusts reach the top 38.6 percent marginal bracket at $9,200 of taxable income in 2002. In 2011, the 35 percent bracket is reached at taxable income over $11,350. Compare this to married individuals filing jointly, for example, where the 35 percent top marginal bracket is not reached until taxable income exceeds $379,150. That is quite a disparity. Trustees of existing trusts need to consider their responsibility to take this disparity into consideration when reviewing the mix of assets in the current trust portfolio and when exercising their discretion to make discretionary distributions of income. In certain cases, where older trusts were established with a different rate structure in mind, and where state law permits, a trustee may want to consider bringing a court proceeding to reform the terms of the trust accordingly. If the settlor is still alive, all of the beneficiaries are adults, and trust is irrevocable, it may be possible under state law, as it is in New York, to revoke the trust and create a new one if the gift tax cost is not excessive.

(m) TERMINATION OF TRUST. A trust may be terminated by the fulfillment of its purpose or by the expiration of the period for which the trust was created. A trust may also be terminated under a power reserved by the grantor or by the consent of all beneficiaries unless continuance of the trust is necessary to carry out a material purpose for which it was created.

When the trust is terminated, the trustee is discharged when he or she has transferred the property to those entitled to it according to the terms of the trust instrument. The trustee, to protect him- or herself, may secure a formal release of all claims from all who receive any of the property and are competent to consent, may require a bond of indemnity from the beneficiaries, or may refuse to act without a decree of court.

38.4 ACCOUNTING FOR TRUSTS

(a) GENERAL FEATURES. Generally, accounting for a trust is the same as accounting for an estate. The emphasis for a trust, however, is that principal or corpus versus income should be properly distinguished. Two interests—that is, current or life versus future or remainder—usually serve different parties. One party may have a current or income interest whereas another party holds a future or remainder interest. Therefore, allocation between principal and income is important. See discussion at Section 38.3(j) for an update on these issues.

(i) Accounting Period. The accounting period for a trust depends somewhat on the nature of the trust and the provisions of the trust instrument. Reports may be required by the court or may be submitted to other interested parties at various intervals during the life of the trust.

(ii) Recording Principal and Income. A careful distinction must be made between principal (corpus) and income in recording the transactions. The legal theory seems to be that the principal of a trust is not a certain amount of monetary value but is a certain group of assets that must be capable of isolation from the assets that compose the undistributed income. Actual separation of cash and investments is difficult because of such factors as accrued interest and amortization of bond premium and discount. Ordinarily it is sufficient to keep one account for cash and one for each type of investment, and to indicate the claims of the principal and income in the total.

Accounts should be kept with the beneficiaries to show the amounts due and paid to each.

The trustee should keep records that will meet both the requirements of the income tax law and regulations and the law relating to principal and income. There are apt to be conflicts at various points in the determination of taxable income and of income belonging to the life tenant. The only solution is to keep sufficiently detailed records so that all of the information is available for both purposes. In some cases, it may be necessary to prepare reconciliation schedules in order to keep a record of the differences between the income tax calculation of net income and the application of trust accounting principles of accounting income.

(iii) Accounting for Multiple Trusts. Several trusts may be created by a single instrument, such as trusts originating through the provisions of a will, and a single trustee may have to keep accounts so as to be able to prepare a report of the administration of the estate as a whole and also a separate report of each trust.

(iv) Treatment of Liabilities. In some cases, trust property will be encumbered with an unpaid mortgage or other obligation of which the trustee must keep a record. It is also possible that in handling the business of the trust some liabilities will be incurred. These are usually current in character, and the entry made at the time of payment, charging the amount to an asset or expense account, is usually sufficient.

(b) RECORD-KEEPING SYSTEM. The bookkeeping system requirements for the trust, like those for any other enterprise, vary with the complexity of the situation. Trustees should keep a complete record of all transactions relating to the trust in order to protect themselves, to make reports to the court, to prepare income tax returns, and to give the beneficiaries of the trust an adequate accounting. No special type of bookkeeping system is prescribed by law, but a complete record of all transactions must be kept in such a way that the reports required by the courts can be prepared. All records should be kept in permanent form and should be carefully preserved and filed for possible future reference.

(i) Journals. In a comparatively simple situation, one multicolumn journal may be satisfactory, but in most cases, a set of various journals should be kept.

(ii) Principal and Income Accounts. It is necessary to distinguish carefully between principal and income in the administration of trusts. The trust principal account and the undistributed trust income account record the net worth or capital of the trust. It usually is necessary to analyze those accounts for income tax purposes, just as equity is analyzed in corporation accounts to obtain all of the information required for the income tax return. There may be some conflicts between income as defined by the law relating to the administration of trusts and taxable income as defined by the income tax law and regulations.

(iii) Opening Books of Account. If an inventory has been filed with the court, such as an executor's or guardian's inventory, trustees must record the same values in their accounts. If no such inventory was filed, trustees should have one prepared that will serve as the basis of their property accounting. Whenever possible, the inventory should contain the same values as those required for income tax purposes in determining the gain or loss from the sale of property. In any case, a record of such values must be available.

(iv) Amortization of Bond Premium or Discount. When bonds are taken over in the inventory at more or less than their face value, the difference between the inventory value and the amount received at maturity is ordinarily treated as a loss or gain on realization; but when bonds are purchased at a premium or discount, the difference between the amount paid and the amount to be received at maturity should be treated as an adjustment of the interest earned and should be written off during the remaining life of the bond. If the amount is not large, the straight-line method may be used (i.e., the total premium or discount is divided by the number of remaining interest payments to obtain the amount to be written off at each interest date). If the amount is large, amortization tables may be used in which the effective rate of interest is applied to the present value of the bond to obtain the income due to the life tenant.

(v) Depreciation. Except for buildings forming part of the inventory at the date of origin of the trust or in trusts where contrary provisions were intended by the grantor, wasting assets, including buildings and equipment, should be preserved by reflecting depreciation as a charge to income, if allowed by the trust instrument or state law. Many states have no provision for depreciation.

If all of the trust income is distributed to beneficiaries without regard for depreciation, the entire periodic deduction for depreciation is taken for income tax purposes by the beneficiaries, and the trustee has no occasion to record depreciation in his or her records. In all instances, the trustee should be guided by the provisions of the trust instrument or state law in the handling of depreciation.

(vi) Payments of Expenses. A distinction must be made between expenses chargeable to principal and income. In the absence of direction in the instrument, the fiduciary should rely on state law as to allocation of trust expenses. Generally if an expense is recurring each year, it is usually charged to income. It could also be allocable one-half to principal and one-half to income. If an expense is attributable to corpus, it should be charged to principal. If the expense was to maintain and collect income, then it should be charged to income. For example, capital gains are allocated to principal, and the income tax paid by the trustee on capital gains should also be charged to principal; however, when a bank assesses an annual fee for a custody account, the custody fee could be charged to income or split 50/50 between income and principal.

(c) TRUSTEES' REPORTS. Trustees' reports vary in form and in frequency according to the nature and provisions of the trust, and whether it is being administered under the jurisdiction of a court. Moreover, the form of the report varies among jurisdictions. Before preparing the report, the accountant should ascertain from the court whether a particular form is required. The valuations to be used must always be the same as those appearing on the inventory unless specific permission has been granted to change them. If assets have been written off as worthless, they must nevertheless appear in the new inventory without value.

If income and principal cash accounts have been properly maintained, the balance of the undistributed income would be represented by an equal amount of cash in the bank. If specific investments have been made with the intention that the funds used were still to be considered as undistributed income, the assets acquired should be shown as assets belonging to the trust income account.

The reports consist primarily of an analysis of the principal and income accounts. In addition, a statement showing the changes in the investments, an inventory of the property at the date of the report, and supporting schedules of various items will be required. A reconciliation of cash receipts and disbursements is also often prepared.

38.5 SOURCES AND SUGGESTED REFERENCES

Asher, M., A. W. Scott, and W. F. Fratcher. *Scott and Ascher on Trusts*, 5th ed. New York: Aspen Publishers. 2011.

Denhardt, J. G. Jr., and J. W. Denhardt. *Complete Guide to Trust Accounting and Trust Income Taxation*. Englewood Cliffs, NJ: Prentice-Hall, 1977.

Denhardt, J. G. Jr., and J. D. Grider. *Complete Guide to Estate Accounting and Taxes*, 4th ed. Englewood Cliffs, NJ: Prentice-Hall, 1988.

———. *Complete Guide to Fiduciary Accounting*. Englewood Cliffs, NJ: Prentice-Hall, 1981.

"Effect of Death on an Individual's Income Tax Attributes," *Federal Taxes Weekly Alert*, November 16, 1995.

Executors and Administrators, 31 Am Jur 2d (rev.), Rochester, NY: Lawyer's Cooperative Publishing, 1989, April 1995 Cumulative Supplement.

Ferguson, M. Carr, J. J. Freeland, and M. L. Ascher, *Federal Income Taxation of Estates, Trusts and Beneficiaries*, 2nd ed. Boston: Little, Brown, 1993.

Gillett, M. R., and J. D. Stafford. "Steps to Prepare and File Estate Tax Returns Effectively," *Estate Planning* (May/June 1995). Warren Gorham & Lamont.

Harris, A. C. "Proper Disposition if IRD Items Can Produce Tax Savings," *Estate Planning* (September/October 1994). Warren Gorham & Lamont.

Harris, H. I. *Estates Practice Guide*, 4th ed. Rochester, NY: Lawyer's Cooperative Publishing, 1984, November 1994 Supplement.

Harrison, L. S. "Coordinating Buy-Outs and Installment Payment of Estate Tax," *Estate Planning* (May/June 1995). Warren Gorham & Lamont.

Herr, P. M., and S. M. Etkind. "When and How an Interest in a Tax Shelter Should Be Disposed of Before Death," *Estate Planning* (September/October 1990). Warren Gorham & Lamont.

Larsen, E. J. *Modern Advanced Accounting*, 10th ed. New York: Shephards McGraw-Hill, 2005.

Nossman, W. L., J. L. Wyatt Jr. and J. R. McDaniel. Trust *Administration and Taxation*, rev. 2nd ed. New York: Matthew Bender, 1988, August 1995 Cumulative Supplement.

Peschel, J. L. and E. D. Spurgeon. *Federal Taxation of Trusts, Grantors and Beneficiaries,* 2nd ed. New York: Warren Gorham & Lamont, 1989, 1995 Cumulative Supplement.

Restatement 2nd Trusts. American Law Institute, 1959.

Restatement 3rd Trusts (Prudent Investor Rule) §§ 227–229. American Law Institute, 1990.

Sages, R. A. "The Prudent Investor Rule and the Duty Not to Delegate," *Trust & Estates* (May 1995).

Schlesinger, S. J., and F. T. Weingast. "Income Taxation of Estates and Trust: New Planning Ideas," *Estate Planning* (May/June 1995). Warren Gorham & Lamont.

Share, L. A. "Domicile Is Key in Determining Transfer Tax of Non-Citizens," *Estate Planning* (January/February 1995). Warren Gorham & Lamont.

Stephens, R. B., et al. *Federal Estate and Gift Taxation*, 6th ed. New York: Warren, Gorham & Lamont, New York, 1991, 1995 Cumulative Supplement No. 3.

Stephenson, G. T., and N. Wiggins. *Estates and Trusts*, 5th ed. New York: Appleton-Century-Crofts, 1973.

Tractenberg, B. D. "Transferee Liability Can Reach Trustee as Well as a Beneficiary," *Estate Planning* (September/October 1994). Warren Gorham & Lamont.

Trusts & Estates Staff. "Uniform Laws Provide a Road Map for Estate Planners," *Trust & Estates* (May 1994).

Trusts. 76 Am Jur 2 d (rev.). Rochester, NY: Lawyer's Cooperative Publishing, 1992, April 1995 Cumulative Supplement.

Turner, G. M. *Trust Administration and Fiduciary Responsibility*. New York: Shephards McGraw-Hill, 1994.

Uniform Principal and Income Act. *American Laws Annotated,* Vol. 7.

Uniform Probate Code. *American Laws Annotated*, Vol. 8, 8A and 8B.

Uniform Trust Code ,

Waggoner, L. W. "The Revised Uniform Probate Code," *Trust & Estates* (May 1994).

CHAPTER 39

BANKRUPTCY

Grant W. Newton, PhD, CPA, CIRA
Pepperdine University

39.1 OVERVIEW 2

39.2 ALTERNATIVES AVAILABLE TO TROUBLED COMPANIES 2

(a) Out-of-Court Settlements 2
(b) Assignment for Benefit of Creditors 3
(c) Bankruptcy Court Proceedings 3
(i) Title 11—Bankruptcy Code 3
(ii) Chapter 7—Liquidation 4
(iii) Chapter 12—Adjustment of Debt of a Family Farmer with Regular Annual Income 4
(iv) Prepackaged/Prenegotiated Chapter 11 Plans 6
(d) Accountant's Services in Proceedings 6

39.3 GENERAL PROVISIONS OF BANKRUPTCY CODE 7

(a) Filing of Petition 7
(b) Timing of Petition—Tax Considerations 7
(c) Accounting Services—Data Required in the Petition 8
(d) Adequate Protection and Automatic Stay 9
(i) Relief from the Stay 10
(ii) Accounting Services—Determining Equity in Property 10
(e) Executory Contracts and Leases 10
(i) Limitations on Executory Contracts 11
(ii) Accounting Services—Rejection of Executory Contracts 11
(f) Avoiding Power 11
(g) Preferences 12
(i) Exceptions to Preferential Transfers 12
(ii) Accounting Services—Search for Preferential Payments 13
(h) Fraudulent Transfers 14
(i) Leveraged Buyout as a Fraudulent Transfer 14
(ii) Accounting Services—Search for Fraudulent Transfers 14
(i) Postpetition Transfers 14
(i) Adequate Value Received 14
(ii) Accounting Services—Preventing Unauthorized Transfers 15
(j) Setoffs 15
(i) Early Setoff Penalty 15
(ii) Accounting Services—Setoffs 15
(k) Reclamation 15
(l) U.S. Trustee 16

39.4 HANDLING OF CLAIMS UNDER CHAPTER 11 16

(a) Proof of Claims 16
(b) Undersecured Claims 16
(c) Administrative Expenses 17
(d) Priorities 17
(e) Processing of Claims 18

39.5 OPERATING UNDER CHAPTER 11 19

(a) Use of Property 19
(i) Cash Collateral 19
(ii) Accounting Services—Assisting Debtor in Providing Information to Secured Lender 19
(b) Obtaining Credit 20
(c) Appointment of Trustees 20
(d) Appointment of Examiner 21

(i) Functions of Examiner 21
(ii) Accountants as Examiners 22
(e) Operating Statements 22
(f) Reporting in Chapter 11 22
(i) Balance Sheet 23
(ii) Statement of Operations 23
(iii) Statement of Cash Flows 24

39.6 CHAPTER 11 PLAN 25

(a) Classification of Claims 25
(b) Development of Plan 26
(c) Disclosure Statement 27
(i) Definition of Adequate Information 27
(ii) Content 27
(d) Confirmation of Plan 28
(e) Confirmation Requirements 29
(f) Accounting Services—Assistance to Debtor 30
(i) Liquidation Value of Assets 30
(ii) Projections of Future Operations 30
(iii) Reorganization Value 30
(iv) Pro Forma Balance Sheet 31
(v) Reorganization Model 31
(g) Accounting Services—Assistance to Creditors' Committee 31
(i) Assistance in the Bargaining Process 31
(ii) Evaluation of Debtor's Projections 32
(iii) Reorganization Value 32
(iv) Review of Plan and Disclosure Statement 32
(h) Accounting for the Reorganization 33
(i) Requirements for Fresh Start Reporting 33
(ii) Allocation of Reorganization Value 34
(iii) Disclosure Requirements 34
(iv) Reporting by Debtors Not Qualifying for Fresh Start 35
(i) Accounting for the Impairment of Long-Lived Assets Under Chapter 11 35

39.7 REPORTING REQUIREMENTS IN BANKRUPTCY CASES 36

(a) Litigation Services 36
(b) Disclosure Requirements 37
(c) Operating Reports 37
(d) Investigative Services 38
(e) Financial Projections 39

39.8 SOURCES AND SUGGESTED REFERENCES 40

39.1 OVERVIEW

This chapter contains a brief description of the Bankruptcy Code, a discussion of the services that can be rendered by the accountant, and an introduction to the problems faced by accountants working in the bankruptcy area.

39.2 ALTERNATIVES AVAILABLE TO TROUBLED COMPANIES

The debtor's first alternatives to resolve the debtor's financial problems are to locate new financing, to merge with another company, or to find some other basic solution to its situation that avoids the necessity of discussing its problems with representatives of creditors. If none of these alternatives is possible, the debtor may be required to seek a remedy from creditors, either informally (out of court) or with the help of judicial proceedings.

(a) OUT-OF-COURT SETTLEMENTS. The debtor may request a meeting with a few of the largest creditors and one or two representatives of the small claimants to effect an informal agreement. The function of such a committee may be merely to investigate, consult, and give advice to the debtor, or it may involve actual supervision of the business or liquidation of the assets. An informal settlement usually involves an extension of time (a moratorium), a pro rata settlement (composition), or a combination of the two. The details of the plan are worked out between the debtor and creditors, the latter perhaps represented by a committee. Such extralegal proceedings are most successful when there are only a few creditors, adequate accounting records have been kept, and past relationships have been amicable. The chief disadvantage of this remedy is that there is no power to bind those creditors who do not agree to the plan of settlement.

(b) ASSIGNMENT FOR BENEFIT OF CREDITORS. A remedy available under state law to a corporation in serious financial difficulties is an assignment for the benefit of creditors. In this instance, the debtor voluntarily transfers title to its assets to an assignee, which then liquidates them and distributes the proceeds among the creditors. Assignment for the benefit of creditors is an extreme remedy because it results in the cessation of the business. This informal liquidation device (although court-supervised in many states) is like the out-of-court settlement devised to rehabilitate the debtor, in that it requires the consent of all creditors or at least their agreement to refrain from taking action. The appointment of a custodian over the assets of the debtor gives creditors the right to file an involuntary bankruptcy court petition.

Proceedings brought in the federal courts are governed by the Bankruptcy Code. Normally it is necessary to resort to such formality when suits have been filed against the debtor and its property is under garnishment or attachment or is threatened by foreclosure or eviction.

(c) BANKRUPTCY COURT PROCEEDINGS. Bankruptcy court proceedings are generally the last resort for the debtor whose financial condition has deteriorated to the point where it is impossible to acquire additional funds. When the debtor finally agrees that bankruptcy court proceedings are necessary, the liquidation value of the assets often represents only a small fraction of the debtor's total liabilities. If the business is liquidated, the creditors get only a small percentage of their claims. The debtor is discharged of its debts and is free to start over; however, the business is lost and so are all the assets. Normally, liquidation proceedings result in large losses to the debtor, the creditors, and the business community in general. Chapter 7 of the Bankruptcy Code covers the proceedings related to liquidation. Another alternative under the Bankruptcy Code is to seek some type of relief so that the debtor, with the help of the bankruptcy court, can work out agreements with creditors and be able to continue operations. Chapters 11, 12, and 13 of the Bankruptcy Code provide for this type of operation.

(i) Title 11—Bankruptcy Code. Title 11 U.S. Code contains the bankruptcy law. The Code is divided into nine chapters:

Chapter 1	General Provisions
Chapter 3	Case Administration
Chapter 5	Creditors, the Debtor, and the Estate
Chapter 7	Liquidation
Chapter 9	Adjustment of Debts of a Municipality
Chapter 11	Reorganization
Chapter 12	Adjustment of Debts of a Family Farmer with Regular Income
Chapter 13	Adjustment of Debts of an Individual with Regular Income
Chapter 15	Ancillary and Other Cross-Border Cases

Chapters 1, 3, and 5 apply to all proceedings under the Code except Chapter 9, where only specified sections of Chapters 1, 3, and 5 apply. A case commenced under the Bankruptcy Code—Chapters 7, 9, 11, 12, or 13—is referred to as a *Title 11* case. Chapter 13, which covers the adjustment of debts of individuals with regular income, is beyond the scope of this presentation because it can be used only by individuals with unsecured claims of less than $360,475 (through March 31, 2013) and secured claims of less than $1,081,400 (through March 31, 2013). The dollar amount of the debt limits for a Chapter 13 petition (as well as dollar amounts for other purposes) are to be increased to reflect the change in the Consumer Price Index for All Urban Consumers on April 1 every third year. The amounts are to be rounded to the nearest $25 multiple. The next three-year-period adjustment will be made on April 1, 2013. Provisions relating to Chapter 11 are discussed in detail in a separate section.

Chapter 15 was added by the 2005 Act to provide effective mechanisms for relief to foreign debtors in the United States. Chapter 15 encourages fair and efficient administration of cross-border insolvencies protecting the interests of both creditors and debtors as well as other interested entities.

(ii) Chapter 7—Liquidation. Chapter 7 is used only when the corporation sees no hope of being able to operate successfully or to obtain the necessary creditor agreement. Under this alternative, the corporation is liquidated and the remaining assets are distributed to creditors after administrative expenses have been paid. An individual debtor may be discharged from liabilities and entitled to a fresh start. A corporation's debt is not discharged.

The decision as to whether rehabilitation or liquidation is best also depends on the amount that can be realized from each alternative. The method resulting in the greatest return to the creditors and stockholders should be chosen. The amount received from liquidation depends on the resale value of the firm's assets minus the costs of dismantling and legal expenses. The value of the firm after rehabilitation must be determined (net of the costs of achieving the remedy). The alternative leading to the highest value should be followed.

Financially troubled debtors often attempt an informal settlement or liquidation out of court; if it is unsuccessful, they will then initiate proceedings under the Bankruptcy Code. Other debtors, especially those with a large number of creditors, may file a petition for relief in the bankruptcy court as soon as they recognize that continuation of the business under existing conditions is impossible.

As soon as the order for relief has been entered, the U.S. trustee appoints a disinterested party from a panel of private trustees to serve as the interim trustee. The functions and powers of the interim trustee are the same as those of an elected trustee. Once an interim trustee has been appointed, the creditors meet to elect a trustee that will be responsible for liquidating the business. If a trustee is not elected by the creditors, the interim trustee may continue to serve in the capacity of the trustee and carry through with an orderly liquidation of the business.

The objective of the trustee is to liquidate the assets of the estate in an orderly manner. Once the property of the estate has been reduced to money and the security claims have been satisfied to the extent allowed, then the property of the estate is distributed to the holders of the claims in the order specified by the Bankruptcy Code. The first order, of course, is priority claims; when they have been established, the balance goes to unsecured creditors. After all the funds have been distributed, the remaining debts of an individual are discharged. As mentioned earlier, if the debtor is a corporation, the debts are not discharged. Thus it is necessary for the corporation to cease existence. Any funds subsequently coming into the corporate shell would be subject to attachment.

(iii) Chapter 12—Adjustment of Debt of a Family Farmer with Regular Annual Income. To help farmers resolve some of their financial problems, Congress passed Chapter 12 of the Bankruptcy Code. It became effective November 26, 1986, and was scheduled to expire several times. On a few occasions, the legislation expired before Congress extended it for an additional time period. The 2005 Act provided for Chapter 12 to be permanent and was expanded to include fisherman with regular income.

Prior to Chapter 12, a family farmer in need of financial rehabilitation had to file either a Chapter 11 or 13 petition. Most family farmers, because they have too much debt to qualify, cannot file under Chapter 13 and are limited to Chapter 11. Many farmers have found Chapter 11 needlessly complicated, unduly time-consuming, inordinately expensive, and, in too many cases, unworkable. Chapter 12 is designed to give family farmers an opportunity to reorganize their debts and keep their land. According to legislative history, Chapter 12 gives debtors the protection from creditors that bankruptcy provides while, at the same time, it prevents abuse of the system and ensures that farm lenders receive a fair repayment.

In order to file a petition, an individual or an individual and spouse engaged in farming operations must have total debt that does not exceed $3,792,650 (through March 31, 2013), and at least

50 percent of noncontingent, liquidated debts (excluding debt from principal residence unless debt arose out of family operations) on the date the petition is filed must have arisen out of farming. Additionally, more than 50 percent of the petitioner's gross income for the taxable year prior to the filing of the petition must be from farming operations.

A corporation or partnership may file if more than 50 percent of the outstanding stock or equity is owned by a family and:

- More than 80 percent of the value of its assets consists of assets related to farming operations.
- The total debts do not exceed $3,792,650 and at least 50 percent of its noncontingent, liquidated debts on the date the case is filed arose out of farming operations.
- The stock of a corporation is not publicly traded.

Similar provisions apply to family fisherman except that the aggregate debt limit is $1,757,475 (through March 31, 2013) and at least 80 percent of the debt is from commercial fishing operations.

Only the debtor can file a plan in a Chapter 12 case. The requirements for a plan in Chapter 12 are more flexible and lenient than those in Chapter 11. In fact, only four requirements are set forth in Section 1205 of the Bankruptcy Code.

1. The debtor must submit to the supervision and control of the trustee all or such part of the debtor's future income as is necessary for the execution of the plan.
2. The plan must provide for full payment, in deferred cash payments, of all priority claims unless the creditors agree to a different treatment.
3. Where creditors are divided into classes, the same treatment must apply to all claims in a particular class unless the holder of a claim or interest agrees to less favorable treatment.
4. Less than full payment of domestic support obligations that are a priority claim may be provided for in the plan, if all of the debtor's disposable income over a five-year period is used to make the payments required under the plan. (This requirement was added by the 2005 Act.)

The plan can alter the rights of secured creditors with an interest in real or personal property, but there are a few restrictions. To alter the right of the secured claim holder, the debtor must satisfy one of these three requirements:

1. Obtain acceptance of the plan.
2. Provide in the plan that the holder of such claim retain the lien and as of the effective date of the plan provide that the payment to be made or property to be transferred is not less than the amount of the claim.
3. Surrender the property securing such claim.

If a holder of an allowed unsecured claim does not accept the plan, then the court may not approve the plan unless the value of the property to be distributed is equal to at least the amount of the claim and the plan provides that all of the debtor's projected disposable income to be received within three years, or longer if directed by the court, after the first payment is made will be a part of the payments under the plan.

To facilitate the operation of the business and the development of a plan, Section 1206 of the Bankruptcy Code allows family farmers to sell assets not needed for the reorganization prior to confirmation without the consent of the secured creditor, provided the court approves such a sale.

The income tax effects of transactions proposed in a Chapter 12 plan could affect the feasibility of the plan in some cases. Section 1231(b) allows bankruptcy courts to authorize the proponents of Chapter 12 plans to request determinations of the federal state and local income tax effects of the proposed plan. The determination is limited to questions of law. Section 1231(b) also provides that in the event of an actual controversy, the court may declare the tax effects of a proposed plan after the earlier of the date on which the governmental unit responds to the request or 270 days after the request.

The Service issued Rev. Proc. 2006-52[1] to provide guidance for the Chapter 12 debtor to follow in asking the bankruptcy court to determine the tax effect of the plan. First the regulation provides that if a Chapter 12 plan proponent is authorized by the bankruptcy court to request a determination of the income tax effects of a proposed plan, then a request must first be filed with the Internal Revenue Service. The written request must be filed with the Centralized Insolvency Operation, PO Box 21126, Philadelphia, PA 19114 (marked "Request for Determination of Tax Effects of Chapter 12 Plan").

(iv) Prepackaged/Prenegotiated Chapter 11 Plans. Before filing a Chapter 11 plan, some debtors develop a plan and obtain approval of the plan by all impaired classes of claims and interests. The court may accept the voting that was done prepetition provided that the solicitation of the acceptance (or rejection) was in compliance with applicable nonbankruptcy laws governing the adequacy of disclosure in connection with the solicitation. For example, in the case of a public company, the proponent of the plan would be required to follow the guidelines issued by the Securities and Exchange Commission (SEC). If no nonbankruptcy law is applicable (i.e., nonpublic company), then the solicitation must have occurred after or at the time the holder received adequate information as required under Section 1125 of the Bankruptcy Code.

It is often necessary for a Chapter 11 plan to be filed for several reasons, including these three:

1. Income from debt discharge is taxed in an out-of-court workout to the extent that the debtor is or becomes solvent. While some tax attributes may be reduced in a bankruptcy case, the gain from debt discharged is not taxed.
2. A larger percent of the net operating loss may be preserved if a Chapter 11 petition is filed. For example, the provisions of Sections 382(l)(5) and 382(l)(6) of the Internal Revenue Code (IRC) dealing with net operating losses apply only to bankruptcy cases.
3. A smaller percentage of creditor approval is needed in Chapter 11. Only two-thirds of the dollar amount of debt represented by those creditors voting and a majority in number in each class are necessary in Chapter 11. However, for any out-of-court workout to succeed, the percentage accepting the plan must be much greater. For example, some bond indenture agreements provide that amendments cannot be made unless all holders of debt approve the modifications. Since it is difficult, if not impossible, to obtain 100 percent approval, it is necessary to file a bankruptcy plan to reduce interest or modify the principal of the bonds.

Since the professional fees and other costs, including the cost of disrupting the business, of a prepackaged plan are generally much less than costs of a regular Chapter 11 bankruptcy, a prepackaged bankruptcy may be the best alternative.

The use of a *prenegotiated plan* is common among public companies today. A prenegotiated plan is a modification of the prepackaged bankruptcy in that the voting is completed after the petition has been filed rather than before the plan is filed. In a prenegotiated plan, the debtor reaches an agreement with the major creditors and then files a plan either at the time or shortly after the Chapter 11 petition is filed. For public companies, the filing of the petition before voting allows all documents related to the plan to be filed with the bankruptcy court and eliminates the need to follow the SEC requirements in the voting process.

(d) ACCOUNTANT'S SERVICES IN PROCEEDINGS. One of the first decisions that must be made at an early meeting of the debtor with bankruptcy counsel and accountants is whether it is best to liquidate (under provisions of state law or Bankruptcy Code), to attempt an out-of-court settlement, to seek an outside buyer, or to file a Chapter 11 petition. To decide which course of action to take, it is also important to ascertain what caused the debtor's current problems, whether the company will be able to overcome its difficulties, and, if so, what measures will be necessary. Accountants

[1] 119.1 2006-48 I.R.B. 995.

may be asked to explain how the losses occurred and what can be done to avoid them in the future. To help with this determination, it may be necessary to project the operations over at least the next quarter, often referred to as a 13-week forecast, and to indicate the areas where steps will be necessary in order to earn a profit.

For existing clients, the information needed to make a decision about the course of action to make may be obtained with limited additional work; however, for a new client, it is necessary to perform a review of the client's operations to determine the condition of the business. Once the review has been completed, the client normally must decide to liquidate the business, attempt an informal settlement with creditors, or file a Chapter 11 petition, unless additional funds can be obtained or a buyer for the business is located. For example, where the product is inferior, the demand for the product is declining, the distribution channels are inadequate, or other similar problems exist that cannot be corrected, either because of the economic environment or management's lack of ability, it is normally best to liquidate the company immediately.

The decision whether a business should immediately file a Chapter 11 petition or attempt an out-of-court settlement depends on several factors. Among them are these eight:

1. Size of company
   a. Public
   b. Private
2. Number of creditors
   a. Secured
   b. Unsecured
   c. Public
   d. Private
3. Complexity of matter
   a. Nature of debt
   b. Prior relationships with creditors
4. Pending lawsuits
5. Executory contracts, especially leases
6. Impact of alternatives selected
7. Nature of management
   a. Mismanagement
   b. Irregularities
8. Availability of interim financing

39.3 GENERAL PROVISIONS OF BANKRUPTCY CODE

(a) FILING OF PETITION. A voluntary case is commanded by the debtor's filing of a bankruptcy petition under the appropriate chapter.

An involuntary petition can be filed by three or more creditors (if 11 or fewer creditors, only one creditor is necessary) with unsecured claims of at least $14,425 (through March 31, 2013) and can be initiated only under Chapter 7 or 11. An indenture trustee may be one of the petitioning creditors. The court allows a case to proceed only if (1) the debtor generally fails to pay its debts as they become due, provided such debts are not the subject of a bona fide dispute; or (2) within 120 days prior to the petition a custodian was appointed or took possession. The latter excludes the taking of possession of less than substantially all property to enforce a lien.

(b) TIMING OF PETITION—TAX CONSIDERATIONS. The timing for filing the petition is important. For example, if the debtor delays filing the petition until the creditors are about to force the debtor into bankruptcy, the debtor may not be in a position to effectively control its destiny. If the petition is filed when the problems first develop and while the creditors are reasonably cooperative, however, the debtor is in a much better position to control the proceeding. If possible, it is best to file the petition near the end of the month or, even better, near the end of the quarter, to avoid a separate closing of the books.

Tax factors should also be considered in deciding when to file the petition. For example, if a debtor corporation that has attempted an unsuccessful out-of-court settlement decides to file a petition, the tax impact of the out-of-court action should be considered. If, in the out-of-court agreement, the debtor transferred property that resulted in a gain and a substantial tax liability, it would be best for the debtor to file the petition after the end of the current taxable year. By taking this action, the tax claim is a prepetition tax claim and not an administrative expense. If the tax claim is a prepetition claim, interest and penalties stop accruing on the day the petition is filed and the debtor may provide in the plan for the deferral of the tax liability up to six years. If the tax claim is an administrative expense, penalties and interest on any unpaid balance will continue to accrue and the provision for deferred payment of up to six years does not apply.

(c) ACCOUNTING SERVICES—DATA REQUIRED IN THE PETITION. The accountant must supply the attorney with certain information necessary for filing a Chapter 11 petition. This would normally include these items:

- *List of largest creditors.* A list containing the names and addresses of the 20 largest unsecured creditors, excluding insiders, must be filed with the petition in a voluntary case. Some petitions for public companies have expanded the list to include up to 40 creditors. In an involuntary situation, the list is to be filed with the petition in a voluntary case. In an involuntary petition, the list is to be filed within two days after entry of the order for relief. See Bankruptcy Rule 1007 and Bankruptcy Form 4.
- *List of creditors.* The debtor must file with the court a list of the debtor's creditors of each class, showing the amounts and character of any claims and securities and, so far as is known, the name and address or place of business of each creditor and a notation whether the claim is disputed, contingent, or unliquidated as to amount, when each claim was incurred and the consideration received, and related data.
- *List of equity security holders.* It is necessary to provide a list of the debtor's security holders of each class showing the number and kind of interests registered in the name of each holder and the last known address or place of business of each holder.
- *Schedules of assets and liabilities.* The schedules that must accompany the petition (or filed within 15 days after the petition is filed—unless the court extends the time period) are sworn statements of the debtor's assets and liabilities as of the date the petition is filed under Chapter 11. These schedules consist primarily of the debtor's balance sheet broken down into detail, and the accountant is required to supply the information generated in the preparation of the normal balance sheet and its supporting schedules. The required information is supplied on Schedules A through C, which include a complete statement of assets, and Schedules D through F, which are a complete statement of liabilities. Schedule G requires the debtor to list all executory contracts and unexpired leases. It is crucial that this information be accurate and complete because the omission or incorrect listing of a creditor might result in a failure to receive notice of the proceedings, and consequently the creditor's claim could be exempted from a discharge when the plan is later confirmed. Also omission of material facts may be construed as a false statement or concealment.
- *Statement of financial affairs.* The statement of affairs, not to be confused with an accountant's usual use of the term, is a series of detailed questions about the debtor's property and conduct. The general purpose of the statement of affairs is to give both the creditors and the court an overall view of the debtor' operations. It offers many avenues to begin investigations into

the debtor's conduct. The statement (Official Form No. 7) consists of 25 questions to be answered under oath concerning these areas:

1. Income from employment or operation of business
2. Income other than from employment or operation of business
3. Payments to creditors
4. Suits, executions, garnishments, and attachments
5. Repossessions, foreclosures, and returns
6. Assignments and receiverships
7. Gifts
8. Losses
9. Payments related to debt counseling or bankruptcy
10. Other transfers
11. Closed financial accounts
12. Safe deposit boxes
13. Setoffs
14. Property held for another person
15. Prior address of debtor
16. Spouses and former spouses
17. Environmental issues
18. Nature, location, and name of business
19. Books, records, and financial statements
20. Inventories
21. Current partners, officers, directors, and shareholders
22. Former partners, officers, directors, and shareholders
23. Withdrawals from a partnership or distributions by a corporation
24. Tax consolidation group
25. Pension funds

- *Exhibit "A" to the petition.* This is a thumbnail sketch of the financial condition of the business listing total assets, total liabilities, secured claims, unsecured claims, information relating to public trading of the debtor's securities, and the identity of all insiders.

The debtor must also file any additional reports or documents that may be required by local rules or by the U.S. trustee.

(d) ADEQUATE PROTECTION AND AUTOMATIC STAY. A petition filed under the Bankruptcy Code results in an automatic stay of the actions of creditors. The automatic stay is one of the fundamental protections provided the debtor by the Bankruptcy Code. In a Chapter 7 case, it provides for an orderly liquidation that treats all creditors equitably. For business reorganizations under Chapter 11, 12, or 13, it provides time for the debtor to examine the problems that forced it into bankruptcy court and to develop a plan for reorganization. As a result of the stay, no party, with minor exceptions, having a security or adverse interest in the debtor's property can take an action that will interfere with the debtor or his or her property, regardless of where the property is located, until the stay is modified or removed. Section 362(a) provides a list of eight kinds of acts and conduct subject to the automatic stay.

Under Section 362 of the Bankruptcy Code, a tax audit, a demand for a tax return, or the issuance of a notice and demand for payment for such assessment is not considered a violation of the automatic stay.

The stay of an act against the property of the estate continues, unless modified, until the property is no longer the property of the estate. The stay of any other act continues until the case is closed or dismissed, or the debtor is either granted or denied a discharge. The earliest occurrence of one of these events terminates the stay.

(i) Relief from the Stay. The court may grant relief after notice and hearing, by terminating, annulling, modifying, or conditioning the stay. The court may grant relief for cause, including the lack of adequate protection of the interest of the secured creditor. With respect to an act against property, relief may be granted under Chapter 11 if the debtor does not have any equity in the property and the property is not necessary for an effective reorganization.

Section 361 identifies three acceptable ways of providing adequate protection.

1. The trustee or debtor may be required to make periodic cash payments to the entity entitled to relief as compensation for the decrease in value of the entity's interest in the property resulting from the stay.
2. The entity may be provided with an additional or replacement lien to the extent that the value of the interest declined as a result of the stay.
3. The entity may receive the indubitable equivalent of its interest in the property.

The granting of relief when the debtor does not have any equity in the property solves the problem of real property mortgage foreclosures where the bankruptcy court petition is filed just before the foreclosure takes place. It was not intended to apply if the debtor is managing or leasing real property, such as a hotel operation, even though the debtor has no equity, because the property is necessary for an effective reorganization of the debtor.

The automatic stay prohibits a secured creditor from enforcing its rights in property owned by the debtor until the stay is removed.

The Supreme Court held in *In re Timbers of Inwood Forest Associates* [484 U.S. 365 (1988)] that creditors having collateral with a value less than the amount of the debt are not entitled to interest during the period that their property is tied up in the bankruptcy proceeding.

If relief from the stay is granted, a creditor may foreclose on property on which a lien exists, may continue a state court suit, or may enforce any judgment that might have been obtained before the bankruptcy case.

(ii) Accounting Services—Determining Equity in Property. The accountant may assist either the debtor or the creditor in determining the value of the collateral to help determine if there is any equity in the property. As a result of the *Timbers* decision, the court is more closely considering the prospects for successful reorganization. In cases where there is considerable question about the ability of the debtor to reorganize, courts are now allowing the stay to be removed, providing there is no equity in the property. The debtor, creditors' committee, or secured creditor(s) may ask accountants to provide evidences as to the ability of the debtor to reorganize.

(e) EXECUTORY CONTRACTS AND LEASES. Section 365(a) provides that the debtor or trustee, subject to court approval, may assume, assign, or reject any executory contract or unexpired lease of the debtor. For nonresidential real property leases, the debtor must make a decision to assume, assign, or reject the lease within 120 days after the petition is field. Only a 90-day extension will be granted, unless the landlord agrees to a larger extension. This limitation of 210 days, added by the 2005 Act, has made it more difficult for large retail companies to reorganize successfully under Chapter 11. If a lease is not assumed by the end of the time period, it is presumed that the lease is rejected. A decision regarding all other leases must be made prior to confirmation of a plan in Chapter 11. In the case of a Chapter 7 petition, the decisions must be made regarding the assumption or rejection of all leases within 60 days, unless an extension is granted.

Executory contracts are contracts that are "so far unperformed that the failure of either [the bankrupt or nonbankrupt] to complete performance would constitute a material breach excusing the performance of the other."[2] This definition seems to have been adopted by Congress in the statement that "executory contracts include contracts under which performance remains due to some extent on both sides."[3] However, before a contract can be assumed, Section 361 indicates that the debtor or trustee must:

- Cure the past defaults or provide assurance they will be promptly cured.
- Compensate the other party for actual pecuniary loss to such property or provide assurance that compensation will be made promptly.
- Provide adequate assurance of future performance under the contract or lease.

(i) Limitations on Executory Contracts. To be rejected, the contract must still be an executory contract. For example, the delivery of goods to a carrier before the petition is filed, under terms that provide that the seller's performance is completed upon the delivery of the goods to the carrier, would not be an executory contract in Chapter 11. Furthermore, the seller's claim would not be an administrative claim. If, however, the terms provide that the goods are received on delivery to the buyer, the seller under Uniform Commercial Code Section 2–705 would have the right to stop the goods in transit and the automatic stay would not preclude such action. If the goods are delivered, payment for such goods would be an administrative expense.

The damages allowable to the landlord of a debtor from termination of a lease of real property are limited to the greater of one year or 15 percent of the remaining portion of the lease's rent due not to exceed three years after the date of filing or surrender, whichever is earlier. This formula compensates the landlord while not allowing the claim to be so large as to hurt other creditors of the estate. The damages resulting from the breach of an employment contract are limited to one year following the date of the petition or the termination of employment, whichever is earlier.

(ii) Accounting Services—Rejection of Executory Contracts. The accountant may render several services relating to the rejection of executory contracts, including these three:

1. Estimating the amount of the damages that resulted from the lease rejection for either the debtor or landlord
2. Evaluating for the landlord the extent to which the debtor has the ability to make the payments required under the lease
3. Assisting the debtor in determining (or evaluating for the creditor's committee) the leases that should be rejected

To the extent possible, this assessment should be made at the beginning of the case to help reduce the expenses of administration during the Chapter 11 case. Amounts paid for rent for the period after filing petition to the date of rejection are considered administrative expenses. Each lease needs to be analyzed to determine if there is equity in the lease or if the debtor needs it to successfully reorganize.

(f) AVOIDING POWER. The Bankruptcy Code grants to the trustee or debtor in possession (DIP) the right to avoid certain transfers and obligations incurred. For example, Section 544 allows the trustee to avoid unperfected security interest and other interests in the debtor's property. Thus, if the creditor fails to perfect a real estate mortgage, the trustee may be able to avoid that security interest and force the claim to be classified as unsecured rather than secured.

The trustee needs these powers and rights to ensure that actions by the debtor or by creditors in the prepetition period do not interfere with the objective of the bankruptcy laws, to provide for

---

[2] See Vern Countryman, "Executive Contracts in Bankruptcy," *Minnesota Law Review* 57 (1973): 439, 460.

[3] See S. Rep. No. 95–989, 95th Cong., 2nd Sess. (1977).

a fair and equal distribution of the debtor's assets through liquidation—or rehabilitation, if this would be better for other creditors involved.

In addition the trustee has the power to avoid preferences, fraudulent transfers, and postpetition transfers.

(g) PREFERENCES. A preferential payment as defined in Section 547 of the Bankruptcy Code is a transfer of any of the property of a debtor to or for the benefit of a creditor, for or on account of an antecedent debt made or suffered by the debtor while insolvent and within 90 days before the filing of a petition initiating bankruptcy proceedings, when such transfer enables the creditor to receive a greater percentage of payment than it would receive if the debtor were liquidated under Chapter 7. Insolvency is presumed during the 90-day period. A transfer of property to an insider between 90 days and one year before the filing of the petition is also considered a preferential payment. An officer, director, or person in control of the corporation would be considered an insider. Action to recover a preferential payment received by a third party that benefited an officer or other insider may only be taken against the officer or other insider and not against the third party. For example, if a president paid off a loan that he personally guaranteed six months before the petition was filed, the payment would be recoverable as a preference from the president, but not from the bank. Preferences include the payment of money, a transfer of property, assignment of receivables, or the giving of a mortgage on real or personal property.

A preferential payment is not a fraud but rather a legitimate and proper payment of a valid antecedent debt. The voidability of preferences is created by law to effect equality of distribution among all the creditors. The 90-day period (one year for transactions with insiders) prior to filing the bankruptcy petition has been arbitrarily selected by Congress as the time period during which distributions to the debtor's creditors may be redistributed to all the creditors ratably. During this period, a creditor who accepts a payment is said to have been preferred and may be required to return the amount received and later participate in the enlarged estate to the pro rata extent of its unreduced claim.

(i) Exceptions to Preferential Transfers. Section 547(c) contains eight exceptions to the power the trustee has to avoid preferential transfers. Five of the assumptions are discussed next.

1. *Contemporaneous exchange.* A transfer intended by the debtor and creditor to have a contemporaneous exchange for new value given to the debtor and that is in fact a substantially contemporaneous exchange is exempted. The purchase of goods or services with a check would not be a preferential payment, provided the check is presented for payment in the normal course of business.
2. *Ordinary course of business or according to ordinary business terms.* This exemption protects payments of debts that were incurred in the ordinary course of business or according to ordinary business terms from being considered a preference. Prior to the 2005 Act, both conditions—ordinary course of business and ordinary business terms—were necessary before an exception from recovery was granted.
3. *Purchase money security interest.* This exception exempts security interests granted in exchange for enabling loans when the proceeds are used to finance the purchase of specific personal property. For example, a debtor borrowed $75,000 from a bank to finance a computer system and subsequently purchased the system. The "transfer" of this system as collateral to the bank would not be a preference provided the proceeds were given after the signing of the security agreement, the proceeds were used to purchase the system and the security interest was perfected within 20 days after the debtor received possession of the property.
4. *New value.* This exception provides that the creditor is allowed to insulate from preference attack a transfer received to the extent that the creditor replenishes the estate with new value. For example, if a creditor receives $10,000 in preferential payments and subsequently sells to the debtor, on unsecured credit, goods with a value of $6,000, the preference would be

only $4,000. The new credit extended must be unsecured and can be netted only against a previous preferential payment, not a subsequent payment.

5. *Inventory and receivables.* This exception allows a creditor to have a continuing security interest in inventory and receivables (or proceeds) unless the position of the creditor is improved during the 90 days before the petition. If the creditor is an insider, the time period is extended to one year. An improvement in position occurs when a transfer causes a reduction in the amount by which the debt secured by the security interest exceeds the value of all security interest for such debt.

   A two-point test is to be used to determine if an improvement in position occurred: The position 90 days (one year for insiders) prior to the filing of the petition is compared with the position as of the date of the petition. If the security interest is less than 90 days old, then the date on which new value was first given is compared to the position as of the date of the petition. The extent of any improvement caused by transfers to the prejudice of unsecured creditors is considered a preference.

   To illustrate this rule, assume that on March 1, the bank made a loan of $700,000 to the debtor secured by a so-called floating lien on inventory. The inventory value was $800,000 at that date. On June 30, the date the debtor filed a bankruptcy petition, the balance of the loan was $600,000 and the debtor had inventory valued at $500,000. It was determined that 90 days prior to June 30 (date petition was filed), the inventory totaled $450,000 and the loan balance was $625,000. In this case there has been an improvement in position of $75,000 ($600,000 – $500,000) – ($625,000 – $450,000), and any transfer of a security interest in inventory or proceeds could be revoked to that extent.

(ii) Accounting Services—Search for Preferential Payments. The trustee or DIP will attempt to recover preferential payments. Section 547(f) provides that the debtor is presumed to be insolvent during the 90-day period prior to bankruptcy. This presumption does not apply to transfers to insiders between 91 days and one year prior to bankruptcy. This presumption requires the adverse party to come forth with some evidence to prove the presumption. The burden of proof, however, remains with the party in whose favor the presumption exists. Once this presumption is rebutted, insolvency at the time of payment is necessary, and only someone with the training of an accountant is in a position to prove insolvency. The accountant often assists the debtor or trustee in presenting evidence showing whether the debtor was solvent or insolvent at the time payment was made. In cases where new management is in charge of the business or where a trustee has been appointed, the emphasis is often on trying to show that the debtor was insolvent in order to recover the previous payments and increase the size of the estate. The creditors' committee likewise wants to show that the debtor was insolvent at the time of payment to provide a larger basis for payment to unsecured creditors. Of course, the specific creditor recovering the payment looks for evidence to indicate that the debtor was solvent at the time payment was made.

Any payments made within the 90 days preceding the bankruptcy court filing and that are not in the ordinary course of business should be reviewed very carefully to see if the payments were preferences. Suspicious transactions would include anticipations of debt obligations, repayment of officers' loans, repayment of loans that have been personally guaranteed by officers, repayment of loans made to personal friends and relatives, collateral given to lenders, and sales of merchandise made on a countra account basis.

Business debts of less than $5,850 (through March 31, 2013) are not recoverable. If the amount is less than $11,725 (through March 31, 2013), actions must be filed in the federal district where the business is located.

In seeking to find voidable preferences, the accountant has two crucial tasks: to determine the earliest date on which insolvency can be established within the 90-day period (one year for insiders) and to report to the trustee's attorney questionable payments, transfers, or encumbrances that have been made by the debtor after that date. It is then the attorney's responsibility to determine the voidable payments. However, the accountant's role should not be minimized, for it is the accountant who initially determines the suspect payments. See Newton for a discussion of the procedures to follow in a search for preferences.[4]

(h) FRAUDULENT TRANSFERS. Fraudulent transfers and obligations are defined in Section 548 and include transfers that are presumed fraudulent regardless of whether the debtor's actual intent was to defraud creditors. A transfer may be avoided as fraudulent when made within two years prior to the filing of the bankruptcy petition, if the debtor made such transfer or incurred such obligation with actual intent to hinder, delay, or defraud existing or real or imagined future creditors. Also avoidable are constructively fraudulent transfers where the debtor received less than a reasonably equivalent value in exchange for such transfer or obligation and (1) was insolvent on the date that such transfer was made or such obligation was incurred, or became insolvent as a result of such transfer or obligation; (2) was engaged in business, or was about to engage in business or a transaction, for which any property remaining with the debtor was an unreasonably small capital; or (3) intended to incur, or believed that the debtor would incur, debts that would burden the debtor's ability to pay as such debts matured.

Under Section 544 of the Bankruptcy Code, fraudulent transfers may also be recovered under state law for payments made between one and six years. Section 546 provides that any action to recover a preference or a fraudulent transfer under Section 548 through the Bankruptcy Code or under Section 544 through state law must commence the action within two years after the order for relief or if a trustee is appointed during the second year after the petition is filed within one year after the trustee is appointed.

In the determination of fraudulent transfers, insolvency is defined by Section 101(32) as occurring when the present fair salable value of the debtor's property is less than the amount required to pay its debts. The fair value of the debtor's property is also reduced by any fraudulently transferred property, and for an individual, by the exempt property under Section 522.

(i) Leveraged Buyout as a Fraudulent Transfer. A fraudulent transfer may occur in a leveraged buyout (LBO). For example, in a LBO transaction where the assets of the debtor were used to finance the purchase of the debtor's stock and the debtor became insolvent, operated with an unreasonably small capital, or incurred debt beyond the ability to repay, a fraudulent transfer may have occurred. Note that the transfer may have been made without adequate consideration because the debtor corporation received no benefit from the proceeds from the loan that were used to retire former stockholder's stock.

(ii) Accounting Services—Search for Fraudulent Transfers. It is important for the accountant to ascertain when a fraudulent transfer has in fact occurred because it represents a possible recovery that could increase the value of the estate. It can, under certain conditions, prevent the debtor from obtaining a discharge. To be barred from a discharge as the result of a fraudulent transfer, the debtor must be an individual, and the proceedings must be under Chapter 7 liquidation or the trustee must be liquidating the estate under a Chapter 11 proceeding.

In ascertaining if the debtor has made any fraudulent transfers or incurred fraudulent obligations, the independent accountant would carefully examine transactions with related parties within the year prior to the petition or other required period, look for the sale of large amounts of fixed assets, review liens granted to creditors, and examine all other transactions that appear to have arisen outside the ordinary course of the business.

(i) POSTPETITION TRANSFERS. Section 549 allows the trustee to avoid certain transfers made after the petition is filed. To be avoidable, transfers must not be authorized either by the court or by an explicit provision of the Bankruptcy Code.

(i) Adequate Value Received. The trustee can avoid transfers made under Section 303(f) and 542(c) of the Bankruptcy Code even though authorized. Section 303(f) authorizes a debtor to continue

---

[4] Grant W. Newton, *Bankruptcy and Insolvency Accounting,* 7th ed. (Hoboken, NJ: John Wiley & Sons, 2010).

operating the business before the order for relief in an involuntary case. Section 549 does, however, provide that a transfer made prior to the order for relief is valid to the extent of value received. Thus, the provision of Section 549 cautions all persons dealing with a debtor before an order for relief has been granted to evaluate the transfers carefully. Section 542(c) explicitly authorizes certain postpetition transfers of real property of the estate made in good faith by an entity without actual knowledge or notice of the commencement of the case.

(ii) Accounting Services—Preventing Unauthorized Transfers. To prevent unauthorized transfers, the accountant should see that these three procedures are operative:

1. Establishing procedures to ensure that prepetition debt payments are made only with proper authorization
2. Designating an individual to handle all requests for prepetition debt payments
3. Acquainting accounting personnel with techniques that might be used to obtain unauthorized prepetition debt payments

(j) SETOFFS. *Setoff* is that right existing between two parties to net their respective debts where each party, as a result of unrelated transactions, owes the other an ascertained amount. The right to setoff is an accepted practice in the business community today. When one of the two parties is insolvent and files a bankruptcy court petition, the right to setoff has special meaning. Once the petition is filed, the debtor may compel the creditor to pay the debt owed and the creditor may in turn receive only a small percentage of the claim—unless the Bankruptcy Code permits the setoff.

The Bankruptcy Code gives the creditor the right to offset a mutual debt, providing both the debt and the credit arose before the commencement of the case. Major restriction on the use of setoff prevents the creditor from unilaterally making the setoff after a petition is filed. The right to setoff is subject to the automatic stay provisions of Section 362 and the use of property under Section 363. Thus, a debtor must obtain relief from the automatic stay before proceeding with the setoff. This automatic stay and the right to use the amount subject to setoff are possible only when the trustee or DIP provides the creditor with adequate protection. If adequate protection—normally in the form of periodic cash payments, additional or replacement collateral, or other methods that will provide the creditor with the indubitable equivalent of its interest—is not provided, then the creditor may proceed with the offset as provided in Section 553.

(i) Early Setoff Penalty. Section 553(b) contains a penalty for those creditors who, when they see the financial problems of the debtor and threat of the automatic stay, elect to offset their claim prior to the petition. The Code precludes the setoff of any amount that is a betterment of the creditor's position during the 90 days prior to the filing of the petition. Any improvement in position may be recovered by the DIP or trustee. The amount to be recovered is the amount by which the insufficiency on the date of offset is less than the insufficiency 90 days before the filing of the petition. If no insufficiency exists 90 days before the filing of the petition, then the first date within the 90-day period where there is an insufficiency should be used. *Insufficiency* is defined as the amount by which a claim against the debtor exceeds a mutual debt owing to the debtor by the holder of such claim. The amount recovered is considered an unsecured claim.

(ii) Accounting Services—Setoffs. In addition to developing a schedule that helps determine the amount of the penalty, the accountant may assist in determining the amount of debt outstanding.

(k) RECLAMATION. One area where the avoiding power of the trustee is limited is in a request for reclamation. Section 546(c) provides that under certain conditions, the creditor has the right to reclaim goods if the debtor received the goods while insolvent during the 45 days prior to the filing of the petition. To reclaim these goods, the seller must demand in writing, within 20 days after the petition was filed. If the seller does not make a timely demand for reclamation, the seller has the right to an administrative expense claim for goods delivered within 20 days prior to bankruptcy.

(l) U.S. TRUSTEE. Chapter 30 of Title 28, U.S. Code, provides for the establishment of the U.S. trustee program. The attorney general is responsible for appointing one U.S. trustee in each of the 21 regions, and one or more assistant U.S. trustees perform the supervisory and appointing functions formerly handled by bankruptcy judges. They are the principal administrative officers of the bankruptcy system. The judicial districts of Alabama and North Carolina are not part of the U.S. Trustee program. In these districts, some of the functions performed by the U.S. trustee in other districts are assigned to an administrator in the bankruptcy court.

The U.S. trustee establishes, maintains, and supervises a panel of private trustees that are eligible and available to serve as trustee in cases under Chapter 7 or 11. Also, the U.S. trustee supervises the administration of the estate and the trustees in cases under Chapters 7, 11, 12, or 13. The intent is not for the U.S. trustee system to replace private trustees in Chapters 7 and 11. Rather, the system should relieve the bankruptcy judges of certain administrative and supervisory tasks and thus help to eliminate any institutional bias or the appearance of any such bias that may have existed in the prior bankruptcy system.

The U.S. trustees are responsible for the administration of cases. They appoint the committees of creditors with unsecured claims and also appoint any other committees of creditors or stockholders authorized by the court. If the court deems it necessary to appoint a trustee or examiner, a U.S. trustee makes this appointment (subject to court approval) and also petitions the court to authorize such an appointment.

U.S. trustees monitor applications for compensation and reimbursement for officers and accountants and other professionals retained in the case, raising objections when deemed appropriate. Other responsibilities include monitoring plans and disclosure statements, creditors' committees, and the progress of the case.

39.4 HANDLING OF CLAIMS UNDER CHAPTER 11

A claim antedating the filing of the petition that is not a priority claim or that is not secured by the pledge of property is classified as an unsecured claim. Claims where the value of the security interest is less than the amount of the claims are divided into a secured and an unsecured part.

(a) PROOF OF CLAIMS. A proof of claim or interest is deemed filed in a Chapter 11 case provided the claim or interest is listed in the schedules filed by the debtor, unless the claim or interest is listed as disputed, contingent, or unliquidated. A creditor is thus not required to file a proof of claim if it agrees with the debt listed in the schedules. It is, however, advisable for creditors to file a proof of claim in most situations. Creditors who for any reason disagree with the amount admitted on the debtor's schedules, such as allowable prepetition interest on their claims, or creditors desiring to give a power of attorney to a trade association or lawyer, should always prepare and file a complete proof of claim. Special attention must also be devoted to secured claims that are undersecured.

(b) UNDERSECURED CLAIMS. Section 506 provides that if a creditor is undersecured, the claim will be divided into two parts. The first part is secured to the extent of the value of the collateral or to the extent of the amount of funds subject to setoff. The balance of the claim is considered unsecured. The value to be used to determine the amount of the secured claim is, according to Section 506(a), to "be determined in light of the purpose of the valuation and of the proposed disposition or use of such property, and in conjunction with any hearing on such disposition or use or on a plan affecting such creditors' interest." Bankruptcy Rule 3012 provides that any party in interest may petition the court to determine the value of a secured claim.

Thus, the approach used to value property subject to a lien for a Chapter 7 may be different from that for a Chapter 11 proceeding. Even within a Chapter 11 case, property may be valued differently. For example, fixed assets that are going to be sold because of the discontinuance of operations may be assigned liquidation values, whereas assets that will continue to be used by the debtor may be assigned going concern values. Although courts have to determine value on a case-by-case basis, it is clear that the value is to be determined in light of the purpose of the valuation and the proposed disposition or use of the property.

Section 1111(b) allows a secured claim to be treated as a claim with recourse against the debtor in Chapter 11 proceedings (i.e., where the debtor is liable for any deficiency between the value of the collateral and the balance due on the debt) whether the claim is nonrecourse by agreement or by applicable law. This preferred status terminates if the property securing the loan is sold under Section 363 or is to be sold under the terms of the plan, or if the class of which the secured claim is a part elects application of Section 1111(b)(2).

Another available section under Section 1111(b) is that a class of undersecured creditors can elect to have its entire claim considered secured. A class of creditors will normally be only one creditor. For example, in Chapter 11 cases where most of the assets are pledged, very little may be available for unsecured creditors after paying administrative expenses. Thus, the creditor might find it advisable to make the Section 1111(b)(2) election. If, however, there will be a payment to unsecured creditors of approximately 75 cents per dollar of debt, the creditor may not want to make this election.

The purpose of the election is to provide adequate protection to holders of secured claims where the holder is of the opinion that the collateral is undervalued. Also, if the treatment of the part of the debt that is accorded unsecured status is so unattractive, the holder may be willing to waive his unsecured deficiency claims. The class of creditors making this election has the right to receive full payment for its claims over time. If the members of the class do not approve the plan, the court may confirm the plan as long as the plan provides that each member of the class receives deferred cash payments totaling at least the allowed amount of the claim. However, the present value of these payments as of the effective date of the plan must be at least equal to the value of the creditors' interest in the collateral. Thus, a creditor who makes the election under Section 1111(b)(2) has the right to receive full payment over time, but the value of that payment is required only to equal the value of the creditor's interest in the collateral.

(c) ADMINISTRATIVE EXPENSES. The actual, necessary costs of preserving the estate, including wages, salaries, and commissions for services rendered after the commencement of the case, are considered administrative expense. Any tax including fines or penalties is allowed unless it relates to a tax-granted preference under Section 507(a)(8). Compensation awarded a professional person, including accountants, for postpetition services is an expense of administration. Expenses incurred in an involuntary case subsequent to the filing of the petition but prior to the appointment of a trustee or the order for relief are not considered administrative expenses. They are, however, granted second priority under Section 507. Administrative expenses of a Chapter 11 case that is converted to Chapter 7 are paid only after payment of Chapter 7 administrative expenses.

Section 503(b)(9) grants administrative expense status for "the value of any goods received by the debtor within 20 days before the date of commencement of a case under this title in which the goods have been sold to the debtor in the ordinary course of such debtor's business." As a result of this provision, more prepetition planning is required on the part of debtors to avoid placing orders for goods associated with product lines or stores that will be shutdown at, or immediately after, the filing of the petition.

(d) PRIORITIES. Section 507 provides for these 11 priorities:

1. Allowed unsecured claim for prepetition domestic support obligations
2. Administrative expenses
3. Unsecured claims in an involuntary case arising after commencement of the proceedings but before an order of relief is granted
4. Wages earned within 180 days prior to filing the petition (or the cessation of the business) to the extent of $11,725[5] per individual

[5] The dollar amounts for priority claims will be adjusted every three years to reflect the changes in the Consumer Price Index for All Urban Consumers. The next adjustment will be made on April 1, 2013.

5. Unsecured claims to employee benefit plans arising within 180 days prior to filing petition limited to $11,725 times the number of employees covered by the plan less the amount paid in item 4 and the amount previously paid on behalf of such employees
6. Unsecured claims of grain producers against a grain storage facility or of fishermen against a fish storage or processing facility to the extent of $5,775 (through March 31, 1013)
7. Unsecured claims of individuals to the extent of $2,600 (through March 31, 2013) from deposits of money for purchase, lease, or rental of property or purchase of services not delivered or provided
8. Claims for debts to a spouse or former spouse or child for alimony, maintenance, or support payments
9. Unsecured tax claims of governmental units:
   a. Income or gross receipts tax, provided tax return was due (including extension) within three years prior to filing petition; tax is assessable after commencement of the case; or tax was assessed within 240 days before petition was filed, exclusive of any time during which an offer in compromise was outstanding during the 240-day period plus 30 days and any time a stay of proceeding against collections was in effect in a prior case during the 240-day period, plus 90 days
   b. Property tax last payable without penalty within one year prior to filing petition
   c. Withholding taxes
   d. Employment tax on wages, and so forth, due within three years prior to the filing of the petition
   e. Excise tax due within three years prior to the filing of the petition
   f. Customs duty on merchandise imported within one year prior to the filing of the petition
   g. Penalties related to a type of claim above in compensation for actual pecuniary loss
10. Allowed unsecured claims based on any commitment by the debtor to the federal depository institutions' regulatory agency (or predecessors to such agency), to maintain the capital of an insured depository institution
11. Allowed claims for personal injury or death resulting from the use of a motor vehicle or vessel if the operator was intoxicated

Priority claims in a Chapter 11 case must be provided for in the plan.

(e) PROCESSING OF CLAIMS. Several accounting firms and other businesses have developed models to handle the processing of claims of both small and large debtors. Some of their features include these six:

1. Capture of all the various formats of claims needed by the bankruptcy court
2. Information needed for management to review and evaluate each claim
3. Mailing lists and labels
4. Creditor statements
5. Online update and inquiry capability
6. Modeling and decision analysis capability that enables management to evaluate settlement alternatives efficiently

One system uses a multifield database to help debtors deal with the complexities of a bankruptcy. Creditors' files can be sorted in terms of classes of creditors, priorities of claims, and so on, and then alphabetically within these categories. Notices sent to creditors include all the necessary information, such as the amount of a claim and its current status. Ongoing information that changes over time is constantly updated. This could include the extent to which proofs of claim differ from the recorded debt, the assessment of market values of collateral pledged as security, other assets that are not pledged as security, distributions made during the course of a Chapter 11 case, and changes to or withdrawals of claims. Automatically prepared and mailed notices keep creditors current on the proceedings of a case. The system, through automatic mailings, answers telephone inquiries as they are entered.

39.5 OPERATING UNDER CHAPTER 11

No order is necessary under the Bankruptcy Code for the debtor to operate the business in Chapter 11. Sections 1107(a) and 1108 grant the debtor all the rights, powers, and duties of a trustee, except the right to compensation under Section 330 and provide that the trustee may operate the business unless the court directs otherwise. Thus, the debtor will continue to operate the business unless a party in interest requests that the court appoint a trustee. Until action is taken by management to correct the problems that caused the adverse financial condition, the business will most likely continue to operate at a loss. If the creditors believe new management is necessary to correct the problem, they will press for a change in management or the appointment of a trustee.

In most large bankruptcies as well as in many smaller cases, the management is replaced, often by turnaround specialists, who have particular expertise in taking over troubled companies. They often eliminate the unprofitable aspects of the company's operations, reduce overhead, and find additional financing as part of the turnaround process. Once the plan has been confirmed, turnaround specialists frequently move on to other troubled companies. In small cases where management is also the stockholders, creditors are apt to be uncomfortable with existing management, which may have created the problems.

(a) USE OF PROPERTY. The debtor or trustee must be able to use a secured party's collateral, or in most situations there would be no alternative but to liquidate the business. Section 363(c) gives the trustee or debtor the right to use, sell, or lease property of the estate in the ordinary course of business without a notice and a hearing. As a result of this provision, the debtor may continue to sell inventory and receivables and use raw materials in production without notice to secured creditors and without court approval. The use, sale, or lease of the estate's property other than in the ordinary course of business is allowed only after notice and an opportunity for a hearing. Under Section 363 of the Bankruptcy Code, companies, with court approval, may sell all of a large percent of the assets of the company. As noted below in Section 39.6(b) of this chapter, the sale of all or a large percentage of the debtor's assets is viewed as a very viable option to the development of a plan.

(i) Cash Collateral. One restriction on the use of the property of the bankruptcy estate is placed on the trustee or debtor where cash collateral is involved. Cash collateral is cash, negotiable instruments, documents of title, securities, deposit accounts, or other cash equivalents where the estate and someone else have an interest in the property. Also included would be the proceeds of noncash collateral, such as inventory and accounts receivable and proceeds, products, offspring, and rents, profits, or property subject to a security interest, if converted to proceeds of the type defined as cash collateral, provided the proceeds are subject to the prepetition security interest.

To use cash collateral, the creditor with the interest must consent to its use or the court, after notice and hearing, must authorize its use. The court may authorize the use, sale, or lease of cash collateral at a preliminary hearing if there is a reasonable likelihood that the DIP will prevail at the final hearing. The Bankruptcy Code also provides that the court is to act promptly for a request to use cash collateral.

(ii) Accounting Services—Assisting Debtor in Providing Information to Secured Lender. In many cases, a company cannot operate unless it can obtain use of its cash collateral. For example, cash in bank accounts subject to setoff or collections from pledged receivables and inventory prior to the filing of the petition are not available for use until the company obtains the consent of the appropriate secured creditor or of the court.

Thus, an immediate concern of many companies that need to file a Chapter 11 petition is how to procure enough cash to operate for the first week or so after filing the petition. Often the best way to obtain the use of the cash is to get approval from the secured creditor prior to the filing of the petition. Accountants can work with the debtor in putting together information for the secured lender that may result in the pledge of additional property or an extension of a receivable or inventory financing agreement for the release of cash to allow operation of the business once the petition is filed.

(b) OBTAINING CREDIT. In most Chapter 11proceedings, the debtor must obtain additional financing in order to continue the business. Although the debtor was allowed to obtain credit under prior law, the power granted to the debtor under the Bankruptcy Code is broader. Section 364(a) allows the debtor to obtain unsecured debt and to incur unsecured obligations in the ordinary course while operating the business. This right is automatic unless the court orders otherwise. Also, the holder of these claims is entitled to first priority as administrative expenses.

If the debtor is unable to obtain the necessary unsecured debt under Section 364(a), the court may authorize the obtaining of credit and the incurring of debt by granting special priority for claims. These priorities may include:

- Giving priority over any or all administrative expenses
- Securing the debt with a lien on unencumbered property
- Securing the debt with a junior lien on encumbered property

DIP financing may be obtained from the existing lender or from a new lender. Most all major banks are involved in DIP financing as well as several other financial entities, including funds that are established to make loans to companies in Chapter 11 and on emergence from Chapter 11. At times, existing creditors will lend to the Chapter 11 debtor in order to prevent other lenders from obtaining a position that may be superior to that of the existing lender. The bankruptcy court may allow the debtor to prime the position of the existing lender. However, for the court to authorize the obtaining of credit with a lien on encumbered property that is senior or equal to the existing lien, the debtor must not be able to obtain credit by other means and the existing lien holder must be adequately protected.

Credit obtained other than in the ordinary course of business must be authorized by the court after notice and a hearing. Where there is some question whether the credit is related to the ordinary course of business, the lender should require court approval.

The number of 363 sales has recently increased compared to the number of plans approved. Banks and other financial institutions are less willing to lend funds for the time period necessary for businesses to reorganize, but may be willing to provide funds for a shorter period while the debtor implements a 363 sale. Additionally, creditors appear to be less patient today than they were in the 1980s and early 1990s, asking debtors to sell the business or in some cases filing a motion asking the court to provide for a 363 sale.

Asset sales are not restricted to the middle market or smaller cases. For example, companies like Polaroid (received $56.5 million cash for assets of its Identification Systems Business Division), Fruit of the Loom (business operations purchased by Berkshire Hathaway, Inc.), and LTV Corporation (sold its integrated steel assets to WL Ross & Co.) completed significant asset sales as a part of their Chapter 11 filing.

(c) APPOINTMENT OF TRUSTEES. The Bankruptcy Code provides that a trustee can be appointed in certain situations based on facts in the case and not related to the size of the company or the amount of unsecured debt outstanding. The trustee is appointed only at the request of a party in interest after a notice and hearing. A party in interest includes the debtor, the trustee (in other contexts), creditors' or stockholders' committees, creditors, stockholders, or indenture trustees. Also, a U.S. trustee, while not a party in interest, may petition the court for an appointment of a trustee.

Section 1104(a) states that a trustee be appointed:

1. For cause, including fraud, dishonesty, incompetence, or gross mismanagement of the affairs of the debtor by current management, either before or after the commencement of the case, or similar cause, but not including the number of holders of securities of the debtor or the amount of assets or liabilities of the debtor; or
2. If such appointment is in the interest of creditors, any equity security holders, and other interests of the estate, without regard to the number of holders of securities of the debtor or the amount of assets or liabilities of the debtor.

The U.S. trustee is responsible for the appointment of the trustee from a panel of qualified trustees, once the appointment has been authorized by the court. It also appears that the U.S. trustee would have the right to replace trustees who fail to perform their functions properly.

The Bankruptcy Code, as originally enacted, provided that in a Chapter 7 case, the interim trustee appointed by the U.S. trustee would serve as the trustee unless a trustee is elected by a majority of at least 20 percent of the unsecured creditors voting in an election at a meeting of creditors under Section 341 of the Bankruptcy Code. In most Chapter 7 cases, the interim trustee serves as the trustee. The Bankruptcy Reform Act of 1994 modified Section 1104 of the Bankruptcy Code to provide that on request of a party in interest (made within 30 days after the court authorized the appointment of a trustee), the U.S. trustee must call a meeting of unsecured creditors for the purpose of electing a Chapter 11 trustee. This change has encouraged the U.S. trustee to seek input from creditors before making trustee appointments.

(d) APPOINTMENT OF EXAMINER. Under the Bankruptcy Code, the trustee's major functions are to (1) operate the business and (2) conduct an investigation of the debtor's affairs. Under certain conditions, it may be best to leave the current management in charge of the business, without resolving the need for the investigation of the debtor. The Code provides for the appointment of an examiner to perform this function. Section 1104(b) states that if a trustee is not appointed:

> on request of a party in interest, and after notice and hearing, the court shall order the appointment of an examiner to conduct such an investigation of the debtor as is appropriate, including an investigation of any allegations of fraud, dishonesty, incompetence, misconduct, mismanagement, or irregularity in the management of the affairs of the debtor of or by current or former management of the debtor, if
>
> 1. Such appointment is in the interest of creditors, any equity security holders, and other interests of the estates; or
> 2. The debtor's fixed, liquidated, unsecured debts, other than debts for goods, services, or taxes, or owing to an insider, exceed $5 million.

(i) Functions of Examiner. The function of the examiner is to conduct an investigation into the actions of the debtor, including fraud, dishonesty, mismanagement of the financial condition of the debtor and the operation of the business, and the desirability of the continuation of such business. The report is to be filed with the court and given to any creditors' committee, stockholders' committees, or other entities designated by the court. In addition to these two provisions, Section 1106(b) also states that an examiner may perform other functions as directed by the court. In some cases, the court has expanded the role of the examiner. For example, the bankruptcy judges may prefer to see additional controls exercised over the management of the debtor but may not see the need to incur the costs of the appointment of a trustee. These functions are assigned to the examiner.

(ii) Accountants as Examiners. Accountants may serve as examiners, and in some regions U.S. trustees have expressed a preference for appointing accountants in certain situations. Where a financial investigation is needed, an accountant may be the most qualified person to perform as an examiner. In many cases where the role of the examiner has been expanded, accountants were serving as examiners.

(e) OPERATING STATEMENTS. Several different types of reports are required while the debtor is operating the business in a Chapter 11 reorganization proceeding. The nature of the reports and the time period in which they are issued depend to some extent on local rules and on the type of internal controls of the debtor and the extent to which large losses are anticipated.

Districts establish local bankruptcy rules that generally apply to all cases filed in that particular district. These rules cover some of the procedural matters that relate to the handling of a bankruptcy case, including appearance before the court, forms of papers filed with the court, assignment of case, administration of case, employment of professionals, and operating statements. The rules for the filing of operating statements have become primarily the responsibility of the U.S. trustee and, as a result, the specific procedures for these statements are those of the U.S. trustee.

One statement required by all regions is an operating statement—profit and loss statement. This statement may include, in addition to the revenue and expense accounts needed to determine net income on the accrual basis, an aging of accounts payable (excluding prepetition debts) and accounts receivable, status of payments to secured creditors, analysis of tax payments, analysis of insurance payments and coverage, and summary of bankruptcy fees that have been paid or are due.

The U.S. trustee also requires cash receipts and disbursement statements. In some cases, it may be necessary to prepare this statement for each bank account of the debtor. For example, the U.S. trustee for the central district of California requires that the debtor, in addition to the regular account, establish separate accounts for payroll and taxes. Separate cash receipts and disbursement statements are also required for each account.

The U.S. trustee office is in the process of developing uniform standards for operating reports that would apply to all regions.

An independent accountant may assist the debtor in the preparation of these monthly operating reports. See Section 39.7(c) in this chapter.

(f) REPORTING IN CHAPTER 11. In November 1990, the American Institute of Certified Public Accountants (AICPA) issued Statement of Position (SOP) No. 90-7, *Financial Reporting by Entities in Reorganization Under the Bankruptcy Code,* which represents the first major pronouncement to be issued on financial reporting by companies in bankruptcy. The SOP applies to any company that files a Chapter 11 petition after December 31, 1990. In addition, the provisions regarding fresh start reporting apply to any entity that has its plan confirmed after June 30, 1991. SOP No. 90-7 is now Accounting Standards Codification (ASC) 852.

SOP No. 90-7 (ASC 852) was designed to eliminate some of the significant divergences in accounting for bankruptcies and to increase the relevance of financial information provided to debtors, creditors, stockholders, and other interested parties who make decisions regarding the reorganization, especially the reorganization plan, of the debtor. The SOP (ASC 852) applies to financial reporting by companies that have filed Chapter 11 petitions and expect to reorganize as going concerns, and to companies that emerge from Chapter 11 under confirmed plans. It does not apply to companies that are restructuring their debt outside of Chapter 11 or to those that adopt Chapter 11 plans of liquidation. It deals with how to report the activities of the Chapter 11 company during the reorganization proceeding and how to report the emergence of the company from Chapter 11.

A major objective of financial statements issued by the debtor in Chapter 11 should be to reflect the financial evolution of the debtor during the proceeding. Thus, for financial statements issued in the year the petition is filed and in subsequent years, a distinction should be made between transactions and events directly associated with the reorganization, as opposed to those related to the ongoing operations of the business. This principle is reflected in several significant areas of the financial statements.

(i) Balance Sheet. Paragraphs 23 to 26 of SOP No. 90-7 (ASC 852-10-45-2 to 45-7; 852-210-10-60-3) provide specific guidance for the preparation of the balance sheet during the reorganization.

Liabilities subject to compromise should be separated from those that are not and from postpetition liabilities. Liabilities that are subject to compromise include unsecured claims, undersecured claims, and fully secured claims that may be impaired under a plan. Paragraph 23 (ASC 852-10-45-2) indicates that if there is some uncertainty as to whether a secured claim is undersecured or will be impaired under the plan, the entire amount should be included with prepetition claims subject to compromise.

In view of this provision, it is expected that most prebankruptcy claims will be reported initially as liabilities subject to compromise. There are a number of reasons for this. For example, at the time the balance sheet is prepared, the collateral may not have been appraised. Also, it might be determined as the case progresses that estimated cash flows from property are less than anticipated. All security interests may not have been fully perfected. Due to these and other factors, it is not unusual for claims that appeared fully secured at the onset of a case to be found to be compromised during the proceedings.

Paragraph 26 of SOP No. 90-7 (ASC 852-10-45-7) also indicates that circumstances arising during the reorganization may require a change in the classification of liabilities between those subject to compromise and those not subject to compromise.

The principal categories (such as priority claims, trade debt, debentures, institutional claims, etc.) of the claims subject to compromise should be disclosed in the notes to the financial statements. Note that the focus of the reporting requirement is on providing information about the nature of the claims rather than whether the claims are current or noncurrent.

Liabilities that are not subject to compromise consist of postpetition liabilities and liabilities not expected to be impaired under the plan. They are reported in the normal manner and thus should be segregated into current and noncurrent categories if a classified balance sheet is presented.

Liabilities that may be affected by the plan should be reported at the amount expected to be allowed even though they may be settled for a lesser amount. For example, once the allowed amount of an existing claim is determined or can be estimated, the carrying value of the debt should be adjusted to reflect that amount. Paragraph 25 of SOP No. 90-7 (ASC 852-10-45-6) provides that debt discounts or premiums as well as debt issue costs should be viewed as valuations of the related debt. When the allowed claim differs from the net carrying amount of the debt, the discount or premium and deferred issue costs should be adjusted to the extent necessary to report the debt at the allowed amount of the claim. If these adjustments are not enough, then the carrying value of the debt will be adjusted. The gain or loss resulting from the entries to record these adjustments is to be reported as a reorganization item as described on the next page.

Prepetition claims that become known after the petition is filed, such as a claim arising from the rejection of a lease, should also be reported on the basis of the expected amount of the allowed claim and not at an estimate of the settlement amount. Paragraph 48 of SOP No. 90-7 (ASC 852) suggests that these claims should be reported at the amount allowed by the court because that is the amount of the liability until it is settled and the use of the allowed amount is consistent with the amounts at which other prepetition liabilities are stated.

Financial Accounting Standards Board (FASB) Statement No. 5, *Accounting for Contingencies* (ASC 450[6]) applies to the process of determining the expected amount of an allowed claim. Claims that are not subject to reasonable estimation should be disclosed in the notes to the financial statements based on the provisions of ASC 450. Once the accrual provisions of ASC 450 are satisfied, the claims should be recorded.

(ii) Statement of Operations. The objective of reporting during the Chapter 11 case is to present the results of operations of the reporting entity and to clearly separate those activities related

[6] This ASC was issued by the FASB codifying the Statements of Financial Accounting Standards, Accounting Principles Board Opinions, Statements of Positions, and other previously issued statements of principles and concepts.

to the normal operations of the business from those related to the reorganization. Thus, revenues, expenses (including professional fees), realized gains and losses, and provisions for losses resulting from the Chapter 11 reorganization and restructuring of the business should be separately reported. According to paragraph 27 of SOP 90-7 (ASC 852-10-45-9), items related to the reorganization (except for the reporting of discontinued operations which are already reported separately) should be reported in a separate category within the income (loss) from operations section of the statement of operations. Appendix A in SOP 90-7 (ASC 852-10-55-3) contains an example of the form to use for operating statements issued during a Chapter 11 case. The part of the operating statement that relates to the reporting of reorganization items is shown next.

Earnings before reorganization items and income tax benefits	47
Reorganization items:	
Loss on disposal of facility	(60)
Professional fees	(50)
Provision for rejected executory contracts	(10)
Interest earned on accumulated cash resulting from Chapter 11 proceeding	1
	(119)
Loss before income tax benefit and discontinued operations	$ (72)

Note that the reader of the statement of operations is able to determine the amount of income generated from continuing operations without the impact of the reorganization being reflected in these totals. While determining the part of income that relates to ongoing operations will involve some judgment on the part of management, a reasonable estimate of the segregation will be much more beneficial to the reader than including all items in the same category, as is current practice.

These five provisions relate to the operating statements:

1. Gains or losses as a result of restructuring or disposal of assets directly related to the reorganization are reported as a reorganization item (unless the disposal meets the requirement for discontinued operations). The gains or losses include the gain or loss on disposal of the assets, related employee costs, and other charges related to the disposal of assets or restructuring of operations. Note that the reporting of a reduction in business activity does not result in reclassification of revenues or expenses identified with the assets sold or abandoned, unless the transaction is classified as a disposal of a discounted business under FASB Statement No. 144, *Accounting for the Impairment or Disposal of Long-Lived Assets* (ASC 360).
2. Professional fees are expensed as incurred and reported as a reorganization item.
3. Interest income that was earned in Chapter 11 that would not have been earned but for the proceeding is reported as a reorganization item.
4. Interest expense should be reported only to the extent that it will be paid during the proceeding or to the extent that it may be allowed as a priority, secured, or unsecured claim. The extent to which the reported interest expense differs from the contractual rate should be reflected in the notes to the operating statement or shown parenthetically on the face of the operating statement. (The SEC prefers the latter.) Under current practice, some debtors have accrued interest even though this procedure has been somewhat questionable. This practice ceased under the new SOP (now ASC 852).
5. Income from debt discharge (forgiveness) in a Chapter 11 case where fresh start reporting is required should be shown as an reorganization item unless it meets the conditions for an extraordinary item under Accounting Principles Board (APB) Opinion No. 30, paragraph 26 (ASC 225-20-45-16) dealing with unusual items and infrequently occurring items.

(iii) Statement of Cash Flows. Paragraph 31 of SOP 90-7 (ASC 852-10-45-13) indicates that reorganization items should be disclosed separately within the operating, investing, and financing categories of the statement of cash flows. SOP 90-7 (ASC 852) also indicates that reorganization items related to operating cash flows are better reflected if the direct method is used to prepare the statement of cash flows. An example of the statement of cash flows issued during a Chapter 11 case using the direct approach is found in Appendix A of SOP 90-7 (ASC 852-10-55-3).

SOP 90-7 (ASC 852) indicates that if the indirect method is used, the details of the operating cash receipts and payments resulting from the reorganization should be disclosed in a supplementary schedule or in the notes to the financial statement. The footnote or supplementary schedule should include the information from the reorganization section of the statement of cash flows that is presented earlier.

It would also be acceptable to reflect this information in the cash flow statement, as shown next:

Net loss	$(118)
Adjustment to determine net cash provided by operating items before reorganization items:	
Depreciation	
Loss on disposal of facility	60
Provision for rejection of executory contracts	10
Loss on discontinued operations	56
Increase in postpetition liabilities and other liabilities	250
Increase in accounts receivable	(180)
Reorganization items	49
Net cash provided by operating activities before reorganization items	147
Reorganization items	
Interest received on cash accumulated because of the Chapter 11 proceeding	1
Professional fees paid for services rendered in connection with the Chapter 11 proceeding	(50)
Net cash provided by reorganization items	(49)
Net cash provided by operating activities	$ 98

Any reorganization items included in financing and investing activities should also be disclosed separately.

39.6 CHAPTER 11 PLAN

The accountant advises and gives suggestions to the debtor and attorney in drawing up a plan. Section 1121 of the Bankruptcy Code provides that only the debtor may file a plan of reorganization during the first 120 days of the case (unless a trustee has been appointed). This period may be extended; however, the 2005 Act provides that the time period may not be extended beyond 18 months after the petition was filed. This breathing period permits the debtor to hold lawsuits and foreclosures in status quo and to determine economic causes of its financial predicament while developing a plan. Using the schedules of assets and liabilities, statement of affairs, and past and projected financial statements, the debtor and its accountant examine the liabilities of the debtor and the value of the business and explore sources of funding for the plan such as enhanced profitability, partial liquidation, issuing debt securities, or outside capitalization. They outline the classes of debt that cannot be deferred or reduced and negotiate with the rest.

(a) CLASSIFICATION OF CLAIMS. Section 1122 provides that claims or interests can be divided into classes provided each claim or interest is substantially similar to the others of such class. In addition, a separate class of unsecured claims may be established consisting of claims that are below or reduced to an amount the court approves as reasonable and necessary for administrative convenience. For example, claims of less than $10,000, or those creditors who will accept $10,000 as payment in full of their claim, may be placed in one class, and the claimants will receive the lesser of $10,000 or the amount of their claim. All creditors or equity holders in the same class are treated the same, but separate classes may be treated differently.

Generally, all unsecured claims, including claims arising from rejection of executory contracts or unexpired leases, are placed in the same class except for administrative expenses. They may, however, be divided into different classes if separate classification is justified. The Bankruptcy Code does not require placing all claims that are substantially the same in the same class.

Courts have stated that Section 1122(a) "does not require that similar claims must be grouped together, but merely that any group created must be homogeneous."

(b) DEVELOPMENT OF PLAN. The items that may be included in the plan are listed in Section 1123. Certain items are listed as mandatory and others are discretionary. The seven mandatory provisions are:

1. Designate classes of claims and interests.
2. Specify any class of claims or interest that is not impaired under the plan.
3. Specify the treatment of any class of claims or interest that is impaired under the plan.
4. Provide the same treatment for each claim or interest in a particular class unless the holders agree to less favorable treatment.
5. Provide adequate means for the plan's implementation, such as:
   - Retention by the debtor of all or any part of the property of the estate.
   - Transfer of all or any part of the property of the estate to one or more entities.
   - Merger or consolidation of the debtor with one or more persons.
   - Sale of all or any part of the property of the estate, either subject to or free of any lien, or the distribution of all or any part of the property of the estate among those having an interest in such property of the estate.
   - Satisfaction or modification of any lien.
   - Cancelation or modification of any indenture or similar instrument.
   - Curing or waiving any default.
   - Extension of a maturity date or a change in an interest rate or other term of outstanding securities.
   - Amendment of the debtor's charter.
   - Issuance of securities of the debtor, or of any entity involved in a merger or transfer of the debtor's business for cash, for property, for existing securities, or in exchange for claims or interests, or for any other appropriate purpose.
6. Provide for the inclusion in the charter of the debtor, if the debtor is a corporation, or of any corporation referred to in item 5, of a provision prohibiting the issuance of nonvoting equity securities, and providing, as to the several classes of securities possessing voting power, an appropriate distribution of such power among such classes, including, in the case of any class of equity securities having a preference over another class of equity securities with respect to dividends, adequate provisions for the election of directors representing such preferred class in the event of default in the payment of such dividends.
7. Contain only provisions that are consistent with the interests of creditors and stockholders and with public policy with respect to the selection of officers, directors, or trustee under the plan.

In addition to these requirements, the plan may also include these five provisions:

1. Impair or leave unimpaired any class of unsecured or secured claims or interests.
2. Provide for the assumption, rejection, or assignment of executory contracts or leases.

3. Provide for settlement or adjustment of any claim or interest of the debtor or provide for the retention and enforcement by the debtor of any claim or interest.
4. Provide for the sale of all of the property of the debtor and the distribution of the proceeds to the creditors and stockholders.
5. Include any other provision not inconsistent with the provisions of the Bankruptcy Code.

In determining the classes of creditors' claims or stockholders' interests that must approve the plan, it is first necessary to determine if the class is impaired. Section 1124 states that a class of claims or interest is impaired under the plan unless the plan leaves unaltered the legal, equitable, and contractual rights of a class, cures defaults that led to acceleration of debts, or pays in cash the full amount of their claims.

(c) DISCLOSURE STATEMENT. A party cannot solicit the acceptance or rejection of a plan from creditors and stockholders affected by the plan unless they receive a written disclosure statement containing adequate information as approved by the court. Section 1125(b) requires that the court must approve this disclosure statement, after notice and a hearing, as containing adequate information.

(i) Definition of Adequate Information. Section 1125(a) states that *adequate information* means information of a kind, and in sufficient detail, as far as is reasonably practicable in light of the records, that would enable a hypothetical reasonable investor typical of holders of claims or interests of the relevant class to make an informed judgment about the plan. This definition contains two parts. First it defines adequate information, and then it sets a standard against which the information is measured. It must be the kind of information that a typical investor of the relevant class, not one that has special information, would need to make an informed judgment about the plan.

Section 1125(a)(1) provides that adequate information need not include information about other possible proposed plans.

(ii) Content. As noted, the information disclosed in the statement should be adequate to allow the creditor or stockholder to make an informed judgment about the plan. The next seven items describe the types of information that might be included.

1. *Introduction.* The statement should provide information about voting on the plan as well as background information about the debtor and the nature of the debtor's operations.
2. *Management.* It is important to identify the management that will operate the debtor on emergence from bankruptcy and to provide a summary of their background.
3. *Summary of the plan of reorganization.* Typical investors want to receive a description of the terms of the plan and the reasons the plan's proponents believe a favorable vote is advisable.
4. *Reorganization value.* Included in the disclosure statement should be the reorganization value of the entity that will emerge from bankruptcy. One of the first, as well as one of the most difficult, steps in reaching agreement on the terms of a plan is determining the value of the reorganized entity. Once the parties—debtor, unsecured creditors' committee, secured creditors, and shareholders—agree on the reorganization value, this value is then allocated among the creditors and equity holders. Thus, before determining the amount that unsecured creditors, secured creditors, or equity holders will receive, it is necessary to determine the reorganization value. An unsecured creditors' committee or another representative of creditors or equity holders is generally unable, and often unwilling, to agree to the terms of a plan without any knowledge of the emerging entity's reorganization value. It also appears that if this value is needed by the parties that must agree on the terms of a plan, it is also needed by each unsecured creditor to determine how to vote on the plan.

   Paragraph 37 of SOP 90-7 (ASC 852-10-5-15) states that while the court determines the adequacy of information in the disclosure statement, entities that expect to adopt fresh start reporting should report information about the reorganization value in the disclosure statement. The reporting of this value should help creditors and shareholders make an informed judgment about the plan.

SOP 90-7 (ASC 852) suggests that the most logical place to report the reorganization value in the pro forma balance sheet that shows the financial position of the entity as though the proposed plan was confirmed.

5. *Financial information.* Among several types of information that may benefit creditors and stockholders considerably in assessing the potential of the debtors' business are:
   - Audited reports of the financial position as of the date the petition was filed or as of the end of a recent fiscal year, and the results of operations for the past year
   - A detailed analysis by the debtor of its properties, including a description of the properties, the current values, and other relevant information
   - A description of the obligations outstanding with identification of the material claims in dispute

   If the nature of the company's operations is going to change significantly as a result of the reorganization, historical financial statements for the past two to five years are of limited value.

   In addition to the historical financial statements, it may be useful to present a pro forma balance sheet showing the impact that the proposed plan, if accepted, will have on the financial condition of the company. Included should be the source of new capital and how the proceeds will be used, the postpetition interest obligation, lease commitments, financing arrangements, and so forth.

   To provide the information needed by creditors and stockholders for effective evaluation of the plan, the pro forma statement should show the reorganization value of the entity. Thus the assets would be presented at their current values, and, if there is any excess of the reorganization value (going-concern value) over individual assets, this value would be shown. Liabilities and stockholder's equity should be presented at their discounted values based on the assumption that the plan will be confirmed. If appraisals of the individual assets have not been made, it appears appropriate to reflect the differences between the book value and reorganization value as an adjustment to the asset side of the pro forma balance sheet.

   If the plan calls for future cash payments, the inclusion of projections of future operations will help the affected creditors make a decision as to whether they believe the debtor can make the required payments. Even if the plan calls for no future cash payments, it may still be advisable to include the financial information in the disclosure statement that will allow creditors and stockholders to see the business's potential for operating profitably in the future. These projections must, of course, be based on reasonable assumptions, and the assumptions must be clearly set forth in the projections accompanying the disclosure statement.

6. *Liquidation values.* Included in the disclosure statement should be an analysis of the amount that creditors and equity holders would receive if the debtor were to be liquidated under Chapter 7. In order to effectively evaluate the reorganization alternative, the creditors and equity holders must know what they would receive through liquidation. Also, the court, in order to confirm the plan, must ascertain, according to Section 1129(a)(7), that each holder of a claim or interest who does not vote in favor of the plan must receive at least an amount that is equal to the amount that would be received in a Chapter 7 liquidation.

   Generally, it is not acceptable to state that the amount provided for in the plan exceeds the liquidation amount. The presentation must include data to support this type of statement.

7. *Special risk factors.* In any securities that are issued pursuant to a plan in a Chapter 11 proceeding, certain substantial risk factors are inherent. It may be advisable to include a description of some of the factors in the disclosure statement.

(d) CONFIRMATION OF PLAN. Prior to the confirmation hearing on the proposed plan, the proponents of the plan will seek its acceptance. Once the results of the vote are known, the debtor or other proponent of the plan will request confirmation of the plan.

The holder of a claim or interest, as defined under Section 502, is permitted to vote on the proposed plan. Voting is based on the classification of claims and interests. A major change from prior law is that the acceptance requirements are based on those actually voting and not on the total value or number of claims or interests allowed in a particular class. The secretary of the Treasury is authorized to vote on behalf of the United States when the United States is a creditor or equity security holder.

A class of claim holders has accepted a plan if at least two-thirds in amount and more than one-half in number of the allowed claims for that class that are voted are cast in favor of the plan. For equity interests, it is necessary only that votes totaling at least two-thirds in amount of the outstanding securities in a particular class that voted be cast for the plan. The majority in number requirement is not applicable to equity interests.

(e) CONFIRMATION REQUIREMENTS. Section 1129(a), which contains the requirements that must be satisfied before a plan can be confirmed, is one of the most important sections of the Bankruptcy Code. The 13 provisions follow

1. *The plan complies with the applicable provisions of Title 11.* Section 1122 concerning classification of claims and Section 1123 on the content of the plan are significant sections.
2. *The proponents of the plan comply with the applicable provisions of Title 11.* Section 1125 on disclosure is an example of a section that is referred to by this requirement.
3. *The plan has been proposed in good faith and is not by any means forbidden by law.*
4. *Payments are disclosed.* Any payment made or to be made for services, costs, and expenses in connection with the case or plan has been approved by, or is subject to the approval of, the court as reasonable.
5. *There is disclosure of officers.* The proponent of the plan must disclose the persons who are proposed to serve after confirmation as director, officer, or voting trustee of the reorganized debtor. Such employment must be consistent with the interests of creditors and equity security holders and with public policy. Also, names of insiders to be employed and the nature of their compensation must also be disclosed.
6. *Regulatory rate has been approved.* Any governmental regulatory commission that will have jurisdiction over the debtor after confirmation of the plan must approve any rate changes provided for in the plan.
7. *The plan satisfies the best-interest-of-creditors test.* It is necessary for the creditors or stockholders who do not vote for the plan to receive as much as they would if the business were liquidated under Chapter 7.
8. *The plan has been accepted by each class.* Each class of creditors or stockholders impaired under the plan must accept the plan. Section 1129(b), however, provides an exception to this requirement: the "cram down."

   This section allows the court under certain conditions to confirm a plan even though an impaired class has not accepted it. The plan must not discriminate unfairly, and it must be fair and equitable with respect to each impaired class of claims or interest that has not accepted the plan. The Code states conditions for secured claims, unsecured claims, and stockholder interests that would be included in the "fair and equitable" requirement. It should be noted that because the word *includes* is used, the meaning of fair and equitable is not restricted to these conditions.[7]
9. *Priority claims have been satisfied.* This requirement provides that priority claims must be satisfied with cash payment as of the effective date of the plan unless the holders agree to a different treatment. An exception to this general rule is allowed for taxes. Taxes must be paid over a period of six years from date of assessment with a present value equal to the amount of the claim.

[7] A discussion of the cram down provision is found in Section 5.33 of Newton's *Bankruptcy and Insolvency Accounting.*

10. *At least one class accepts the plan.* If a class of claims is impaired under the plan, at least one class that is impaired, other than a class of claims held by insiders, must accept the plan.
11. *Plan is feasible.* Confirmation of the plan is not likely to be followed by liquidation or by the need for further financial reorganization unless the plan provides for such liquidation or reorganization.
12. *Payment of fees.* The filing fees and quarterly fees must be paid or provided in the plan that they will be paid as of the effective date of the plan.
13. *Retiree benefit continuation.* The plan must provide, as of the effective date, for the continuation of all retiree benefits as defined under Section 1114 and at the level established under Section 1114.

(f) ACCOUNTING SERVICES—ASSISTANCE TO DEBTOR. Accountants can provide considerable services to their client relating to the formulation of the plan, some of which are described in the next subsections.

(i) Liquidation Value of Assets. Section 1129(a)(7) provides that each holder of a claim must either accept that plan or receive or retain interest in property of a value that is at least equal to the amount that would have been received or retained if the debtor were liquidated under Chapter 7. Accountants can help the debtor establish these values.

(ii) Projections of Future Operations. Section 1129(a)(11) contains the feasibility standard of Chapter 11 requiring that confirmation of the plan of reorganization is not likely to be followed by liquidation or further reorganization (unless contemplated). The accountant may assist the debtor or trustee to formulate an acceptable plan by projecting the ability of the debtor to carry out and perform the terms of the plan. To establish feasibility, the debtor must project the profitability potential of the business. Where the plan calls for installment payments, the accountant may be requested to prepare or review projected budgets, cash flow statements, and statements of financial position. The creditors must be assured by the projected income statement and cash flow statement that the debtor will be in a position to make the payments as they become due. The forecast of the results of operations and financial position should be prepared on the assumption that the proposed plan will be accepted, and the liability and asset accounts should reflect the balance that would be shown after all adjustments are made relative to the debt forgiveness. Thus, interest expense is based on the liabilities that will exist after the discharge occurs.

(iii) Reorganization Value. Not only are cash projections needed for the feasibility test as mentioned in the previous paragraph, but they are an important part of the negotiation process. The creditors want to receive the maximum amount possible in any Chapter 11 plan and often want the payment in cash as of the effective date of the plan. The creditors realize, however, that if their demands are beyond the ability of the debtor to make payments, the plan will not work and they will not receive the payments provided for in the plan. Cash flow projections assist both parties in developing reasonable conclusions regarding the value of the entity emerging from Chapter 11. In some reorganizations, there is considerable debate over cash flow projections and the discount rate to be used in determining the value of the debtor's continuing operations, to which must be added the amount to be realized on the sale of nonoperating assets plus excess working capital. Once the debtor and its creditors' committee can agree on the basic value of the entity, it is easier to negotiate the terms of the plan.

During the formulation of the plan, the accountant can assist the debtor considerably by helping to determine the reorganized value of the debtor or to assess the valuation of an investment banker or other specialists. If the accountant develops the cash projections supporting the valuation, he or she will be precluded from being independent for SEC purposes. Once the debtor has determined an estimate of the value of the entity that will emerge from bankruptcy, the accountant can provide assistance to the debtor in negotiating the terms of the plan with the creditor.

(iv) Pro Forma Balance Sheet. Also of considerable help in evaluating a plan is a pro forma balance sheet showing how the balance sheet will look if the plan is accepted and all provisions of the plan are carried out. By using reorganization models or simulation models, the pro forma balance sheet may be prepared based on several possible courses of action that the debtor could take. The pro forma balance sheet illustrates the type of debt equity position that would exist under different alternatives.

This pro forma balance sheet should reflect the debts at discounted values. Assets are generally presented at their historical cost values unless the debtor has made a decision to apply the concept of quasi reorganization. A pro forma balance sheet that reflects the reorganized values of the entity is of considerable benefit to the debtor in developing the terms for a plan.

Once the terms of the proposed plan have been finalized, the pro forma balance sheet based on historical values reflecting these terms is generally included in the disclosure statement that must be submitted prior to or at the time votes are solicited on the plan. The pro forma balance sheet reflecting reorganized values, however, provides information for the creditors and stockholders that is much more relevant in making an informed judgment about how to vote on the plan.

(v) Reorganization Model. Accountants can develop a model to help the debtor in developing a plan. The outcome of a reorganization plan depends on a variety of assumptions, including the creditors' willingness to accept different mixes of cash and securities, economic trends, possible sources for financing continuing operations or acquisitions, and many other factors. Using a model, these assumptions can be altered one at a time with all else held constant, and the possible courses of action can be analyzed according to the needs of management. Using this technique, creditors or the debtor can identify potential problem areas and request clarifications. Once these clarifications have been received and entered into the system, a new set of comparisons is made, and the process is repeated until both sides are satisfied that the most favorable course is being pursued. Breakdowns of reorganization plans by computer models allow debtors and creditors to focus on the financial data most relevant to the case at hand.

(g) ACCOUNTING SERVICES—ASSISTANCE TO CREDITORS' COMMITTEE. The following subsections describe several of the services that the accountant can render for the creditors' committee or for a committee of equity holders.

(i) Assistance in the Bargaining Process. One of the basic functions performed by the creditors' committee is to negotiate a settlement and then make its recommendation to the other creditors. The accountant should be familiar with the bargaining process that goes on between the debtor and the creditors' committee in trying to reach a settlement. Bargaining can be both vigorous and delicate. The debtor bargains, perhaps, for a settlement that consists of a small percentage of the debt, demanding only a small immediate cash outlay, with payments to be made in the future. The debtor may want the debts outstanding to be subordinated to new credit or may ask that the agreement call for partial payment in preferred stock. The creditors want a settlement that represents a high percentage of the debt and consists of a larger cash down payment with the balance to be paid as soon as possible. In cases where there is very little cash available for debt repayment on confirmation, unsecured creditors may be interested in obtaining most of the outstanding stock of the company. In the past 20 years, the creditors of public companies have received an increasing interest in the ownership of the debtor. It is not unusual for the creditors to own all of the outstanding stock of the emerging entity. The shareholders of failed LBOs and other highly leveraged firms often receive no equity interest in the reorganized entity.

The services that the accountant may render for the creditors' committee in the negotiations with the debtor vary significantly depending on several factors, including the size of the debtor, the experience of the members of the creditors' committee, the nature of the debtor's operations, and the creditors' committee confidence in the debtor and in the professionals—especially attorneys and accountants—who are helping the debtor. In most cases, to varying degrees, the committee depends on the accountant to help evaluate the debtor's operations, the information provided about those operations, and the terms of a proposed plan. Often accountants may be engaged to investigate selected aspects of the debtor's operations and to obtain an overall understanding of the debtor's problems and possible solutions.

(ii) Evaluation of Debtor's Projections. Of primary significance to a creditors' committee is determining whether the projections and forecasts submitted by the debtor are realistic. The representatives of the largest unsecured creditors on the committee typically are not accountants and thus may need assistance in evaluating the financial data prepared by the debtor. The accountant for the creditors' committee may be in a strong position to evaluate the debtor's projections and to make recommendations. The intention is not to perform an audit of such data but rather to review the information to determine whether the projections can be supported to some extent by hard evidence. The level of involvement by the accountant for the creditors' committee will vary, depending on the sophistication of the company or of the financial people who prepared the data. In some cases, the review could be limited to a discussion of the data with those who prepared the projections, to determine whether the forecasts seem to make sense. In other situations, however, the accountant may find that the preparation of this information has been somewhat loose or vague. In these circumstances, the accountant for the committee may need to get involved in the preparation or to perform a review of the appropriate accounting records to see whether the basic underlying data have some foundation in fact.

(iii) Reorganization Value. In some cases, accountants for the creditors' committee develop their own models of the debtor's operations. Cash flow projections can then be prepared for determining the reorganized entity's value. Operational changes made by the debtor are entered in the model as are proposed sales or other major actions, providing a basis for the committee's response to the debtor's proposals. Evaluation by the creditors' committee focuses on the impact these actions will have on the value of the reorganized entity and on the amount of potential settlement.

(iv) Review of Plan and Disclosure Statement. As noted earlier, the accountant for the debtor provides advice and assistance in the formulation of a plan of reorganization in a Chapter 11 proceeding and a plan of settlement in an agreement out of court. An important function of an accountant employed by the creditors is to help evaluate the proposed plan of action. In a Chapter 11 case where the debtor has not proposed a plan within 120 days, a proposed plan has not been accepted within 180 days after the petition was filed, or where the trustee has been appointed, the accountant may assist the creditors in developing a plan to submit to the court. The accountant is able to provide valuable assistance to the committee because of familiarity with the financial background, nature of operations, and management of the company gained during the audit. In committee meetings, a great deal of discussion goes on between the committee members and the accountant concerning the best settlement they can expect and how it compares with the amount they would receive if the business were liquidated.

The creditors are interested in receiving as much as possible under any reorganization plan. The accountant may work with the creditors' committee to see that the amount proposed under the plan is reasonable and fair based on the nature of the debtor's business. First, it must be determined that the plan provides for at least as much as would be received in Chapter 7 liquidation. Second, the creditors must leave for the debtor enough assets to operate the business after reorganization. If a reasonable basis does not exist for future operations, the judge may not confirm the plan because it is not feasible.

If an audit has not been performed, the accountant for the creditors' committee must rely on the information contained in the disclosure statement and in other reports that have been issued. Thus, the content of the disclosure statement may be most important. Also, since the disclosure statement serves as the basic report used by the creditors to evaluate the plan, it is critical that it be properly prepared and contain the type of information that allows the creditors to effectively evaluate the proposed plan.

The accountant for the creditors' committee may be asked to evaluate the disclosure statement. If, in the accountant's opinion, it does not contain adequate information, the deficiencies may be conveyed to the debtor informally (normally through creditors' committee counsel) prior to submission of the plan to the court, or an objection to the content of the statement may be raised at the disclosure hearing.

In evaluating the information in the disclosure statement, the accountant for the creditors' committee may be asked to review the financial statements contained in the disclosure statement or others that were issued by the debtor. Special consideration must be made in reviewing pro forma and liquidation statements of financial condition. The pro forma statement provides the creditors with an indication of the debtor's likely financial condition if the plan is accepted. This statement should show that the creditors will receive more if they accept the plan than they would receive if the debtor were liquidated. The pro forma statement also should demonstrate that the plan is feasible in that, after satisfying the provisions of the plan, the debtor retains an asset base with which to operate. In reviewing the pro forma statement prepared by the debtor, special consideration must be given to the analysis of the assumptions used to prepare it and to the evaluation of the value of the assets (which may differ from book values). If the pro forma statements are based on historical costs, the accountant for the creditors' committee may want to restate them to reflect the reorganized values of the entity. The creditors' committee will be able to evaluate the terms of the plan more effectively if it can compare the terms to pro forma statements containing the reorganized value of the entity rather than historical values.

Liquidation statements show what the unsecured creditors would receive if the business were liquidated. The assumptions used in the adjustments to book values must be evaluated carefully. The accountant for the creditors' committee may be asked to review statements of this nature and to provide advice as to the reasonableness of the analysis. There may be a tendency for the debtor to understate liquidation values in order to make the terms of the plan more appealing to the unsecured creditors.

(h) ACCOUNTING FOR THE REORGANIZATION. SOP 90-7 (ASC 852) explains how the debtor emerging from Chapter 11 should account for the reorganization both when fresh start reporting should be adopted and when it is not allowed. Fresh start reporting requires the debtor to use current values (going-concern or reorganization values) in its balance sheet for both assets and liabilities and to eliminate all prior earnings or deficits.

(i) Requirements for Fresh Start Reporting. The two conditions that must be satisfied before fresh start reporting can be used are:

1. The reorganized value of the emerging entity immediately before the confirmation of the plan is less than the total of all postpetition liabilities and allowed claims.
2. Holders of existing voting shares immediately before confirmation retain less than 50 percent of the voting share of the emerging entity.

Paragraph 36 of SOP 90-7 (ASC 852-10-45-19) indicates that the loss of control contemplated by the plan must be substantive and not temporary. Thus, the new controlling interest must not revert to the shareholders existing immediately before the plan was confirmed. For example, a plan that provides for shareholders existing prior to the confirmation to reacquire control of the company at a subsequent date may prevent the debtor from adopting fresh start reporting.

Debtors that meet both of the preceding conditions will report the assets and liabilities at their going-concern (reorganization) values. *Reorganization value* is defined as the "fair value of the entity before considering liabilities and approximates the amount that a willing buyer would pay for the assets of the entity immediately after the restructuring." The focus in determining the reorganization value is on the value of the assets. Normally the value is determined by discounted future cash flows. However, the value from the discounting of cash flows is defined as enterprise value. To get from enterprise value to reorganization value, current liabilities (ignoring current portion of funded debt) are added to the enterprise value.[8] The reorganization value of the entity

[8] If the appraiser reduced the enterprise by the amount of cash or excess cash, this amount should also be added with current liabilities to determine reorganization value.

may be determined by several approaches depending on the circumstances.[9] In most cases, it is not the responsibility of the accountant to determine the reorganization value of the debtor but to report in the financial statements the value that is determined through the negotiations by the debtor, creditors' and stockholders' committees, and other interested parties.

Professionals involved in bankruptcy cases have been aware of the limited usefulness of book values for some time. For example, market values are required in the schedules that are filed with the bankruptcy court, and fair market values of assets are determined under Section 506 of the Bankruptcy Code for assets pledged.

Reorganization values will be used only when both conditions for a fresh start are satisfied. For example, fresh start reporting will not be used by most nonpublic companies because in most cases there is no change of ownership. Thus, the provisions of SOP 90-7 (ASC 852) will apply primarily to public companies.

(ii) Allocation of Reorganization Value. For entities meeting the criteria just discussed (reorganization value less than liabilities and old shareholders own less than 50 percent of voting stock of the emerging entity), fresh start reporting will be implemented in these three ways:

1. The reorganization value is to be allocated to the debtor's assets based on the market value of the individual assets. The reorganization value is to be allocated to the debtor's assets based on the market value of the individual assets. The allocation of value to the individual assets should generally follow the guidelines of FASB Statement No. 141 (ASC 805). Any part of the reorganization value not attributable to specific tangible assets or identifiable intangible assets should be reported as an intangible asset (goodwill) and is not amortized but, in accordance with FASB Statement No. 142 (ASC 350), will be written down if impaired. Goodwill will be tested for impairment at a level of reporting referred to as a *reporting unit* at least annually and more often if an event occurs that would more likely than not reduce the carrying value of a reporting unit below its carrying value. FASB Statement No. 142 (pars. 19–20) (ASC 350-20-35-4 and 13) indicates that a two-step impairment test should be used (a) to identify potential goodwill impairment and (b) to measure the amount of the impairment loss to be recognized.
2. Liabilities that survive the reorganization should be shown at present value of amounts to be paid determined at appropriate current interest rates. Thus, all liabilities will be shown at their discounted values. (The practice of discounting debt has not always been followed in the past.)
3. Deferred taxes are to be reported in conformity with generally accepted accounting principles. Benefits realized from preconfirmation net operating loss carryforwards should be used to first reduce reorganization value in excess of amounts allocable to other intangibles. Once the balance of the intangible assets is exhausted, the balance is reported as a direct addition to the additional paid-in capital.

SOP 90-7 (ASC 852) indicates that three basic entries are needed to record the adoption of fresh start reporting in the accounts:

1. Entries to record debt discharge
2. Entries to record exchange of stock for stock
3. Entries to record the adoption of fresh start reporting and to eliminate the deficit

(iii) Disclosure Requirements. Paragraph 39 of SOP 90-7 (ASC 852-10-50-7) indicates that when fresh start reporting is adopted, the notes to the initial financial statement should disclose:

- Adjustments to the historical amounts of individual assets and liabilities
- The amount of debt forgiven

---

[9] Newton, *Bankruptcy and Insolvency Accounting.*

- The amount of prior retained earnings or deficit eliminated
- Significant matters relating to the determination of reorganization value

According to SOP 90-7 (ASC 852), some of the other significant matters that should be disclosed include:

- The method or methods used to determine reorganization value and factors such as discount rates, tax rates, the number of years for which cash flows are projected, and the method of determining terminal value
- Sensitive assumptions (those assumptions about which exists a reasonable possibility of the occurrence of a variation that would significantly affect measurement of reorganization value)
- Assumptions about anticipated conditions that are expected to be different from current conditions, unless otherwise apparent

(iv) Reporting by Debtors Not Qualifying for Fresh Start. Debtors that do not meet both of the conditions for adopting fresh start reporting should state any debt issued or liabilities compromised by confirmed plans at the present values of amounts to be paid. Thus, the debtor will no longer have the option to elect to discount or not to discount debt issued in a Chapter 11 case.

These provisions apply only to Chapter 11 cases. However, in out-of-court workouts where liabilities are generally restated, it will be difficult to justify accounting for issuance of new debt in a manner different from the discounting procedure described in SOP 90-7 (ASC 852).

(i) ACCOUNTING FOR THE IMPAIRMENT OF LONG-LIVED ASSETS UNDER CHAPTER 11. Companies that qualify for fresh start reporting will value all of the assets at their fair value. If a company does not qualify for fresh start reporting, the provisions of FASB Statement No. 144 (ASC 360) must be followed. FASB Statement No. 142 (ASC 350), as described, provides guidance for the reporting of the impairment of goodwill.

The accounting for impairment of assets follows a three-step approach for financial statement recognition and valuation:

1. *Evaluate conditions.* Initially, the person who prepares the financial statements considers whether conditions exist that indicate an inability to fully recover the carrying amount of an asset held and used.
2. *Review for impairment.* If such conditions exist, the company will look for possible impairment by estimating the future cash flows from the asset. The estimated cash flows are undiscounted and without interest.
3. *Recognition of loss (determination of trigger).* If the sum of the estimated future cash flows is less than the asset's carrying amount, generally an impairment loss must be recognized in earnings.

The loss from impairment of the assets will be the difference between the carrying amount and the fair value of the assets. For example, assume that a manufacturing facility is potentially impaired by use of the plant to manufacture a product different from the original design for plant use. This change in the nature of the product was caused by technological advancements in the industry. The company reviews for impairment by estimating the expected future net cash flows for the asset undiscounted and without interest. For example, if the carrying value of the plant is $3 million and the further cash flows are less than $3 million, then the asset is impaired. For example, if the future cash flows were expected to be $2.5 million and the fair value of the plant was determined to be $1.7 million, a loss of $1.3 million would be reflected even though the difference between the cash flows and the carrying value of the plant is only $.5 million. This process is viewed as one only of cost allocation; as a result, subsequent increases in the value of the asset may not be reflected in the accounts.

The rules described here also apply to assets that will be disposed of. Prior practice allowed the entity to reflect these assets to be disposed of at their net realizable value; if there was an increase in their value, a gain was reflected in the accounts to the extent of a previous write-down. This practice will no longer be allowed, except in a case in which FASB Statement No. 144 (ASC 360). In the case of disposition of assets associated with discontinued operations, under FASB Statement No. 144 (ASC 360) the assets will continue to be measured at their realizable value. At the time a bankruptcy petition is filed, it may appear that assets are impaired and carrying value should be materially reduced. However, with the filing of the petition, there will be a complete analysis of the viability of the business and of the various segments of the business. Until the assessment is complete, the company should avoid the impulse to materially reduce the carrying value of assets.

39.7 REPORTING REQUIREMENTS IN BANKRUPTCY CASES

Accountants often issue various types of reports and schedules as part of services rendered in the bankruptcy and insolvency area. These services include the preparation of operating reports, evaluation or development of a business plan, valuation of the business, and search for preferences. Many of the reports or schedules produced would generally be classified as financial statements. Because financial statements are issued, the accountant must determine if a compilation, review, or audit report must be issued, or if the service that generated the statements is exempted from professional standards related to compilation of financial statements from the records and the attestation standards. This issue has involved considerable controversy among accountants who practice in the bankruptcy and insolvency area.

(a) LITIGATION SERVICES. When the accountant begins an engagement involving bankruptcy or insolvency issues, a decision needs to be made as to application of the attestation standards. Section 9100.48 of *Attestation Engagements Interpretation,* "Applicability of Attestation Standards to Litigation Services," excludes litigation services that "involve pending or potential formal legal or regulatory proceedings before a trier of fact in connection with the resolution of a dispute between two or more parties." Guidance in this area is provided by the AICPA's Management Consulting Division, in *Consulting Services Special Report 03-1,* "Litigation Services and Applicable Professional Standards" (CSSR 03-1). This report concludes in paragraph 76/105.03 that "[b]ankruptcy, forensic accounting, reorganization, or insolvency services, as practiced by certified public accountants (CPA's), generally are acceptable as forms of litigation services."

CSSR 03-1 notes that the role of the accountant in a litigation engagement is different from the role in an attestation services engagement. When involved in an attestation engagement, the CPA firm expresses "a conclusion about the reliability of a written assertion of another party." In the performance of litigation services, the accountant helps to "gather and interpret facts and must support or defend the conclusions reached against challenges in cross-examination or regulatory examination and in the work product of others."

Appendix G of CSSR 03-1 describes the delivery of reorganization services to include items such as these:

- Preparing or reviewing valuations of the debtor's business
- Analyzing the profitability of the debtor's business
- Preparing or reviewing the monthly operating reports required by the bankruptcy court
- Reviewing disbursements and other transactions for possible preference payments and fraudulent conveyances
- Preparing or reviewing the financial projections of the debtor
- Performing financial advisory services associated with mergers, divestitures, capital adequacy, debt capacity, and so forth
- Consulting on strategic alternatives and developing business plans
- Providing assistance in developing or reviewing plans of reorganization or disclosure statements[10]

[10] CSSR 03-1 notes that the words *review* and *reviewing* are not intended to have the same meaning as they do in the AICPA Statements on Standards for Accounting and Review Services.

CSSR 03-1 then concludes that bankruptcy services similar to those listed above that are provided by CPAs generally are accepted as a form of litigation services. Appendix G of CSSR 03-1 provides that:

> This acceptance is due to many fundamental and practical similarities between bankruptcy services and the consulting services associated with other forms of litigation. Bankruptcy law, as promulgated by the Bankruptcy Code and case law, is applied by bankruptcy judges and lawyers to resolve disputes between a debtor and its creditors (for example, distribution of the debtor's assets). Bankruptcy cases frequently include actions related to claims for preferential payments and fraudulent conveyances; negligence of officers, directors, or professionals engaged by the debtors; or other allegations common to commercial litigation. The bankruptcy court has the power and authority to value legal claims and resolve such common litigation as product liability, patent infringement, and breach of contract. The decisions of bankruptcy judges can be appealed as can the decisions of other courts.

According to CSSR 03-1, these guidelines should also apply to services rendered in an out-of-court workout, as described in the following paragraph from Appendix G:

> Out-of-court restructuring holds the potential for litigation. Therefore, the settlement process is generally conducted with the same scrutiny, due diligence, and intense challenge as that of a formal court-administered process. Furthermore, bankruptcy services provided by CPAs are typically not three-party attest services (the three parties in attest services are the asserter, the attester, and the third party). Instead, affected parties have the opportunity to question, challenge, and provide input to the bankruptcy findings and process.

For services to be exempted, they must be rendered in connection with the litigation, and the parties to the proceeding must have an opportunity to analyze and challenge the work of the accountant. For example, when the CPA expresses a written conclusion about the reliability of a written assertion by another party, and the conclusions and assertions are for the use of others who will not have the opportunity to analyze and challenge the work, the professional standards would apply. Also, when the CPA is specifically engaged to perform a service in accordance with the attestation standards or accounting services standards (SAARS), professional standards are applicable.

(b) DISCLOSURE REQUIREMENTS. If it is determined that the analysis or report that will be issued comes under the guidelines as a form of litigation services, it is advisable to explain both the association and the responsibility, if any, through a transmittal letter or a statement affixed to documents distributed to third parties. Appendix 71/B of CSSR 93-1 suggests this format for a statement that would explain the association of the CPAs and their responsibility, if any:

> The accompanying schedules (projected financial information; debt capacity analysis; liquidation analysis) were assembled for your analysis of the proposed restructuring and recapitalization of ABC Company. The aforementioned schedules were not examined or reviewed by independent accountants in accordance with standards promulgated by the AICPA. This information is limited to the sole use of the parties involved (management; creditors' committee; bank syndicate) and is not to be provided to other parties.

If it is determined that the service does not qualify as litigation service, any financial statements that might be issued from the services rendered should be accompanied with an accountant's report based on the compilation of the financial statements. Prior to the issuance of a compilation report, the format and nature of the report must be cleared with the firm administrator.

(c) OPERATING REPORTS. Another area where there is considerable uncertainty is in the issuance of operating reports. All regions of the U.S. trustee require monthly operating reports be submitted to the court as well as annual operating reports. Among those items that were listed in CSSR 03-1 that might fall under litigation services was the preparation or review of the monthly operating reports required by the bankruptcy court. These reports, especially for larger public companies, are often prepared in accordance with generally accepted accounting principles, including SOP 90-7 (ASC 852). For example, in the region of New York, Connecticut, and Vermont, the U.S. trustee has issued guidelines that require the statements to conform to SOP 90-7 (ASC 852). Other U.S. trustees have on request by the accountant allowed the statements to be prepared in the format that conforms to the manner in which the accountant normally prepares monthly financial statements. Additionally, the accountant is asked to prepare supplemental data not generally presented in monthly financial statements such as an aging schedule of postpetition payables and a schedule of postpetition taxes paid and accrued.

As noted in CSSR 03-1, the professional standards would apply under two conditions:

1. When the CPA expresses a written conclusion about the reliability of a written assertion by another party, and the conclusions and assertions are for the use of others who will not have the opportunity to analyze and challenge the work
2. When the CPA is specifically engaged to perform a service in accordance with the attestation standards or accounting services standards

In most situations, the second requirement—specifically engaged to perform attestation or compilation services—is not satisfied. Thus, based on this condition, the professional standards would not apply. Certified public accountants are generally engaged to prepare the operating reports that the U.S. trustee and the bankruptcy court require and not specifically to perform an audit or review of the financial records or even compile the financial statements in accordance with the professional standards.

It is the first requirement—expressing a written conclusion about the reliability of a written assertion by another party who will not have the opportunity to analyze and challenge the work—that needs further consideration by the profession. While no specific hearing is scheduled to review the reports, creditors or other parties in interest might raise objections to the content of the reports. Objections to the operating reports have been raised, but rarely. The preparation or the review of monthly operating reports that are required by the court is one of the items listed in the services that are rendered by accountants in the performance of reorganization services. CSSR 03-1 notes that "[b]ankruptcy services provided by CPAs generally are accepted as a form of litigation services."

Since operating reports are considered a form of litigation services, a compilation report should not be issued on the reports. Rather, the following statement should be included in a transmittal letter or affixed to the operating reports:

> The accompanying operating reports for the month of were assembled for your analysis of the proposed restructuring of the ABC Company under Chapter 11 of the Bankruptcy Code. The aforementioned operating reports were not examined or reviewed by independent accountants in accordance with the standards promulgated by the AICPA. This information is limited to the sole use of the parties in interest in this Chapter 11 case and is not to be provided to other parties.

If, however, it is determined in a particular engagement that professional standards are applicable and the CPA is associated with the financial statements, then a compilation report should be issued based on the prescribed form as set forth in SAARS No. 3. As noted, prior to the issuance of a compilation report the format and nature of the report must be reviewed for conformity to applicable standards.

(d) INVESTIGATIVE SERVICES. Preference analysis or other special investigative services performed in a bankruptcy proceeding, receivership or out-of-court settlement, are considered litigation services. As a result, the accountant is not required to issue an agreed-on procedures report. This would not preclude the professional from issuing a report that described the procedures performed and the results ascertained from the performance of the stated procedures. For example, using the preceding format, a report issued to a trustee based on an analysis of preferences might be worded:

> The accompanying analysis of preferential payments was assembled (or prepared) for your analysis (or consideration) in conjunction with the proposed reorganization under Chapter 11 of the Bankruptcy Code. The aforementioned analysis of preferential payments was not examined or reviewed by independent accountants in accordance with standards promulgated by the AICPA. This information is limited to the sole use of the trustee in this Chapter 11 case and is not to be provided to other parties.

(e) FINANCIAL PROJECTIONS. Section 200.3 of the AICPA Statements on Standards for Attestation Engagements states that the standards for prospective financial statements do not apply for engagements involving prospective financial statements used solely in connection with litigation support services. CSSR 03-1 clearly indicates that prospective financial information qualifies as a litigation service. CSSR 03-1 states that parties-in-interest can challenge prospective financial information during negotiations or during bankruptcy court hearings often dealing with the plan's feasibility and adequacy of disclosure. Projections that are included in a disclosure statement would not be subject to the attestation standards since there is a hearing on the disclosure statement and the court must approve the disclosure statement before votes for the plan can be solicited. Parties-in-interest have an opportunity to challenge the prospective information included. Any projections provided for the debtor or for the creditors' committee that is used in the negotiations of the plan would also not fall under the attestation standards.

CSSR 03-1 does, however, indicate that in situations where the users of the prospective financial information cannot challenge the CPA's work, the attestation standards apply. CSSR 03-1 suggests that the attestation standard might apply in situations where exchange offers are made to creditors and stockholders with whom the company has not negotiated or who are not members of a creditor group represented by a committee. Section 200.3 of the AICPA Statements on Standards for Attestation Engagements indicates that if the prospective financial statements are used by third parties that do not have the opportunity to analyze and challenge the statements, the litigation exception does not apply.

Section 200.2 of the AICPA Statements on Standards for Attestation Engagements indicates that when an accountant submits, to the client or to others, prospective financial statements that he or she has assembled (or assisted in assembling) or reports on prospective financial statements that might be expected to be used by third parties, a compilation, examination, or agreed-on procedures engagement should be performed. Thus, for prospective financial statements that do not qualify for the litigation exception, the engagement must be in the form of a compilation, examination, or agreed-on procedures if the accountant is associated with the financial statements.

The determination of the reorganization or liquidation values to be included in the disclosure statement or to be used by the debtor or creditors' committee in the negotiations of the terms of a plan, as well as other services that involve financial projections, would fall under the litigation exception. If it is determined that the report regarding the issuance of financial projections would not fall under litigation services, the format and nature of the report must be reviewed for conformity to applicable standards.

This wording might be in the transmittal letter or in a statement affixed to the documents:

> The accompanying projected financial statements (or information) were assembled for your analysis of the proposed restructuring and reorganization of under Chapter 11 of the Bankruptcy Code. The aforementioned statements were not examined or reviewed by independent accountants in accordance with standards promulgated by the AICPA. This information is limited to the sole use of and is not to be provided to other parties.

39.8 SOURCES AND SUGGESTED REFERENCES

American Institute of Certified Public Accountants. Accounting Standards Executive Committee, Statement of Position (SOP) No. 90-7, *Financial Reporting by Entities in Reorganization Under the Bankruptcy Code* (ASC 852, *Reorganization*). New York: Author, 1990.

Behrenfield, W. H., and A. R. Biebl. "Bankruptcy/Insolvency." In *The Accountant's Business Manual*., New York: AICPA, 1989.

Countryman, V. "Executory Contracts in Bankruptcy," *Minnesota Law Review* 57 (1973): 439, 460.

Financial Accounting Standards Board.Statement of Financial Accounting Standards No. 5, *Accounting for Contingencies* (ASC 450). Stamford, CT: Author, 1975 (ASC 450 *Contingencies*).

______. Statement of Financial Accounting Standards No. 141F, *Business Combinations* (SC 805). Norwalk, CT: Author, 2001 (ASC 805 *Business Combinations*).

______. Statement No. 144, *Accounting for the Impairment or Disposal of Long-Lived Assets* (ASC 360). Norwalk, CT: Author, 2001 (ASC 360 *Property, Plant, and Equipment*).

______. Statement of Financial Accounting Standards No. 142, *Goodwill and Other Intangible Assets* (ASC 350). Norwalk, CT: Author, 2001 (ASC 350 *Intangibles - Goodwill and Other*).

______. Statement of Financial Accounting Standards No. 15, *Accounting by Debtors and Creditors for Troubled Debt Restructurings* (ASC 310 and 470). Stamford, CT: Author, 1977 (ASC 310 *Receivables* and ASC 470 *Debt*).

King, L. P., ed. *Collier Bankruptcy Manual*. New York: Matthew Bender, 1994.

Newton, G. W. *Bankruptcy and Insolvency Accounting*, 7th ed. Hoboken, NJ: John Wiley & Sons, 2010.

______. *Corporate Bankruptcy: Tools, Strategizing, and Alternatives.* Hoboken, NJ: John Wiley & Sons, 2002.

Patterson, G. F., Jr., and G. Newton. "Accounting for Bankruptcies: Implementation SOP 90-97 (ASC 852)," *Journal of Accountancy* 46 (April 1993).

Securities and Exchange Commission. Staff Accounting Bulletin No. 73, "'Push Down' Basis of Accounting for Parent Company Debt Related to Subsidiary Acquisitions." Washington, DC: Author, 1987.

______. Staff Accounting Bulletin No. 78, "Views Regarding Certain Matters Relating to Quasi-Reorganizations, Including Deficit Eliminations." Washington, DC: Author, 1988. (See ASC 852.)

CHAPTER 40

DETECTING FRAUD

W. Steve Albrecht
Brigham Young University

Conan C. Albrecht
Brigham Young University

40.1 INTRODUCTION 1

40.2 TYPES OF FRAUD 2

40.3 FIGHTING FRAUD: AN OVERVIEW 2

40.4 FRAUD DETECTION: THE EARLIEST APPROACHES 3

40.5 FRAUD DETECTION: THE RED-FLAG APPROACH 3

40.6 MANAGEMENT AND THE BOARD OF DIRECTORS 5

(a) Understanding Management and Director Backgrounds 6
(b) Understanding Management and Director Motivations 7
(c) Understanding the Degree of Influence of Key Members of Management and the Board of Directors 7

40.7 RELATIONSHIPS WITH OTHERS 7

(a) Relationships with Financial Institutions 9
(b) Relationships with Related Parties 10
(c) Relationships with Auditors 10
(d) Relationships with Lawyers 10
(e) Relationships with Investors 10
(f) Relationships with Regulatory Bodies 11

40.8 ORGANIZATION AND INDUSTRY 11

40.9 FINANCIAL RESULTS AND OPERATING CHARACTERISTICS 12

40.10 STRATEGIC FRAUD DETECTION 14

40.11 CONCLUSION 16

40.1 INTRODUCTION

Fraud is different from most crimes in that it is seldom observed. Traditional crimes usually leave evidence that can be seen. For example, if a bank is robbed, there are usually witnesses, physical money is missing, and the entire episode is often captured on video. Similarly, the discovery of a body that is obviously the victim of murder leaves little question about whether a crime has been committed. With fraud, however, it is not usually obvious that a crime has been committed. Only fraud symptoms or indicators, called *red flags,* are observed. In addition, often these red flags can be caused by nonfraud factors, such as unintentional control weaknesses or missing documents, so significant investigation is required before investigators can know for certain that fraud has occurred.

To detect fraud, managers, auditors, employees, and examiners must learn to recognize these red flags and pursue them until sufficient evidence has been collected. Investigators must discover whether the symptoms resulted from actual fraud or were caused by other factors. Unfortunately, in many cases, many fraud symptoms go unnoticed, and even symptoms that are recognized are often not vigorously pursued.

40.2 TYPES OF FRAUD

Before discussing the detection of fraud, it is important to discuss the different types of frauds. Statement on Auditing Standards (SAS) No. 99 discusses two types of fraud: (1) fraudulent financial reporting and (2) misappropriation of assets. *Fraudulent financial reporting* includes manipulation of the financial statements as intentional misrepresentation in or omission of material events, transactions or other information; intentional misappropriation of generally accepted accounting principles (GAAP); or falsification or manipulation of accounting records or documents. *Misappropriation of assets* includes the theft of assets, such as cash, from an organization by its employees, vendors, customers, or others. In addition to these two types, there are many other types of fraud, including investment scams, identity theft, telemarketing fraud, bankruptcy fraud, money laundering, and others. In this chapter, we focus our discussion on fraudulent financial reporting and misappropriations.

40.3 FIGHTING FRAUD: AN OVERVIEW

The three primary activities in fighting fraud are:

1. *Fraud prevention:* deterring or preventing fraud from occurring
2. *Fraud detection:* finding fraud predication, defined as searching for and discovering red flags (indicators or symptoms)
3. *Investigating fraud:* once predication is present, following up on discovered red flags to determine if they represent actual fraud and, if so, determining who committed the fraud, how much was taken, which accounts were manipulated, and other elements of the fraud

Accountants can be involved in all three of these activities. For example, one of the best ways to prevent fraud is through the implementation of effective internal controls. Preventive and detective controls eliminate or reduce the opportunities for fraud—making fraud harder to commit and conceal. Accountants, through Section 404 and other control work, are highly involved in establishing, testing, and evaluating the adequacy of internal controls.

All accountants should be involved in fraud detection. Whether accountants are performing tax-related, systems-related, consulting, or auditing work, they should always be alert for fraud symptoms or red flags. Although they are not expected to be fraud experts or forensic accountants, all accountants should understand fraud symptoms and be able to recognize when additional investigation is necessary.

Fraud investigation involves following up on fraud predication to determine whether fraud has actually occurred and, if it has, who the perpetrators were, how much was taken or manipulated, how the fraud was concealed, why the fraud occurred, and what the impact of the fraud was on the organization and its financial statements. Fraud investigation is usually time consuming and is performed by forensic accountants, fraud examiners, investigators, and attorneys. Of the three fraud activities (prevention, detection, and investigation), it is usually fraud detection that is most difficult but most important to perform. Even though extremely effective controls and other preventive approaches deter fraud, some fraud will still occur because perpetrators will intentionally work around the system or will perpetrate collusive fraud involving forgery that is hard to prevent. If fraud symptoms or red flags are not recognized, fraud investigation cannot occur. Only when there is predication, based on fraud detection, can fraud investigation determine whether red flags were caused by fraud or by other factors.

40.4 FRAUD DETECTION: THE EARLIEST APPROACHES

Historically, most frauds were detected by luck or chance. Fraud symptoms were not categorized or made explicit in the literature, and there were no proactive approaches to detect fraud. Fraud was investigated if someone with knowledge or suspicion provided a tip or if the fraud became so egregious that other symptoms were recognized. In fact, most fraud detection studies, such as those performed by the Association of Certified Fraud Examiners[1] or KPMG,[2] find that fraud is still most commonly detected through luck, tips, or other factors outside the auditor's direct control.

The most effective way to find fraud through tips or complaints is to have an effective whistle-blowing system, as required of public companies by the Sarbanes-Oxley Act of 2002. Although whistleblowing systems often generate spurious claims, effective systems provide opportunities for those with knowledge of actual or suspected fraud to come forward with information.

40.5 FRAUD DETECTION: THE RED-FLAG APPROACH

Recent accounting standards and fraud literature, however, have focused on the red-flag approach to detecting fraud. With this approach, examples and categories of fraud symptoms are proposed, and accountants and auditors are cautioned to watch for these symptoms in their work. No specific type of fraud is predicted or hypothesized, but if symptoms are observed, they are investigated to determine if fraud is the cause.

Fraud symptoms can be separated into six groups:

1. Analytical anomalies
2. Accounting anomalies
3. Internal control weaknesses
4. Extravagant lifestyles
5. Unusual behavior
6. Tips and complaints

These six categories of symptoms are inclusive of all types of frauds, regardless of type. Obviously, some symptoms are more common with specific types of fraud. For example, lifestyle symptoms are more relevant for fraud perpetrated for personal gain, such as employee or vendor fraud against organizations, than for financial statement fraud. However, every fraud symptom can be categorized as one of these six types, regardless of whether the fraud being examined is financial statement fraud (usually perpetrated on behalf of an organization) or irregularities (usually perpetrated against an organization). Next are descriptions of the six red-flag types:

1. *Analytical symptoms.* Analytical anomalies are amounts, ratios, or other factors that are out of the ordinary or otherwise unusual. Analytical symptoms include:
   a. Amounts that are too high or too low or that are increasing too fast or too slow
   b. Events that are unusual or do not make sense within the context of the business

---

[1] *www.acfe.com/fraud-resources.aspx*

[2] *www.amr.kpmg.com/aci/fraud_risk.asp#KPMGReleases2009FraudSurvey*

c. Actions taken by the wrong people or at the wrong time
d. Financial statement ratios that are unusual

In short, anything that is unusual or unexpected is an analytical anomaly.

2. *Accounting or documentary symptoms.* These anomalies are organizational records that are not appropriate or that are questionable. Examples include photocopies where an original should exist, a ledger that does not balance, altered or forged documents, stale items on bank reconciliations, missing records, fraudulent documents hidden on computers, and email, memoranda, or correspondence between co-conspirators. Accounting or documentary anomalies can be paper or electronic, formal or informal.
3. *Internal control symptoms.* Internal control weaknesses include the overriding or absence of internal controls. Fraud occurs only when there is a complete fraud triangle, comprised of:

   a. Perceived pressure
   b. Perceived opportunity
   c. Some way to rationalize the fraudulent actions as acceptable

   The absence or overriding of an internal control creates a real or perceived opportunity that often completes the fraud triangle. When accountants see control weaknesses or the overriding of internal controls, they should not only remediate the control but also determine if it has been abused.
4. *Lifestyle symptoms.* When people commit fraud—especially when they steal assets—they rarely save what they misappropriate. Almost always, they use the stolen funds to meet the financial need that created the perceived pressure; they then continue to steal and spend to enhance their lifestyle. Sudden lifestyle changes, such as purchases of new cars, homes, boats, cabins, or other large, expensive items; spending lavishly on travel or other things; or giving of extravagant gifts are often excellent fraud symptoms, especially of irregularities. Remember, it is not high spending that is the symptom but rather the *change* in spending patterns.
5. *Behavioral symptoms.* Most fraud perpetrators are first-time offenders. As a result, they usually feel tremendous guilt about their actions and fear getting caught. These feelings of guilt and fear are addressed with changed behavior. For example, people who were nice and congenial may suddenly become irritable or difficult. (The opposite can also be true.) People who used to come to work late may start arriving early and staying late. Remember, it is not personal behavioral idiosyncrasies that represent symptoms; rather, it is *changes* in behavior.
6. *Tips and complaints.* Tips and complaints are excellent indicators of possible fraud. The receipt of a tip does not automatically mean that there is fraud. It is important to know what motivated the tip or complaint. Sometimes tips or complaints are forwarded to get even with someone, to get someone in trouble, to camouflage or defer attention from someone else, or for other personal reasons. Often, however, tips signal real fraud and are a great source of predication.

To correctly identify fraud, accountants must understand the context in which the symptom was observed. Fraud symptoms are real symptoms only in context, meaning that the same observation could be taken as a symptom for one person but not by another, because of the differing context or knowledge of the two individuals.

Although the symptoms just described relate to all types of fraud, to better understand how these symptoms relate to financial statement fraud, accountants must clearly understand the operations and nature of the organization they are examining, as well as the nature of the industry and the organization's competitors. Accountants must have a good understanding of the organization's management and its motivations. It is important to understand how the company is organized and have an awareness of relationships the company has with other parties, including the influence that each of those parties has on the client and its officers.

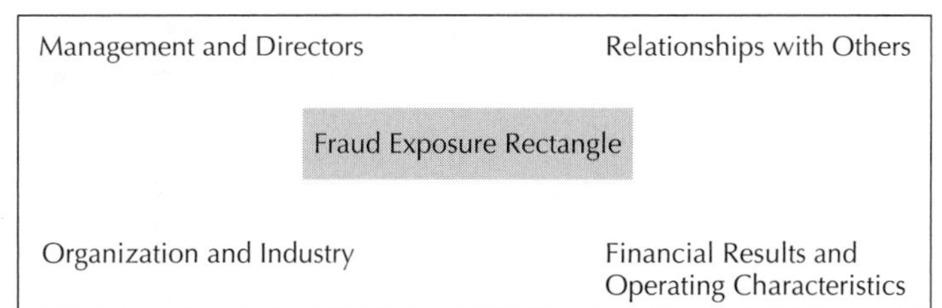

Exhibit 40.1 Fraud Exposure Rectangle

Fraudulent financial statements are rarely detected solely by analyzing the financial statements. Rather, financial statement fraud is usually detected when the information in the financial statements is compared with (1) the real-world referents those numbers are supposed to represent, (2) the context in which management is operating and being motivated, and (3) how the financial statements compare with past financial statements and with those of similar organizations. Fraud is often detected by focusing on the changes in reported assets, liabilities, revenues, and expenses from period to period or by comparing company performance to industry norms. In most financial statement fraud cases, for example, each period's financial statements look correct when viewed as stand-alone statements. It is only when changes in assets and revenues from period to period are examined, and when assets and revenues reported in the financial statements are compared with past periods and with other organizations and physical assets, that it can be determined that the financial statements are incorrect.

The exposure rectangle shown in Exhibit 40.1 is useful in thinking about financial statement fraud symptoms. The first corner of the rectangle represents the management and directors of the company. The second corner represents the relationships the company has with other entities. The third corner represents the nature of the organization you are examining and the industry in which that organization operates. The fourth corner represents the financial results and operating characteristics of the organization.

Although accountants have traditionally focused almost entirely on the financial statements and results of operations to perform generally accepted accounting standards (GAAS) audits and detect financial statement fraud, each of these four areas presents fraud exposures that must be examined.

40.6 MANAGEMENT AND THE BOARD OF DIRECTORS

Top management, including the chief executive officer (CEO) and chief financial officer (CFO), is almost always involved when financial statement fraud occurs. Unlike embezzlement and misappropriation, financial statement fraud is usually committed by the highest individuals in an organization, and most often it occurs on behalf of the organization as opposed to against the organization. Because members of management are usually involved, the organization's management and the directors must be investigated to determine their exposure to and motivation for committing fraud. Fraud is not committed by financial statements; rather, it is perpetrated by management or other top officers or directors. In detecting financial statement fraud, accountants must gain an understanding of management and their motivations; this understanding is at least as important as understanding the financial statements. In particular, three aspects of management should be investigated:

1. Management backgrounds
2. Management motivations
3. Management influence in making decisions for the organization

With respect to backgrounds, you should understand what kinds of organizations and situations managers and directors have been associated with in the past. With today's computerized interconnections and databases (e.g., the World Wide Web), it is easy to conduct simple searches on individuals. One way to perform such searches is to type the individual's name into Google or another search engine. The search engine will list all the references to the person's name, including past proxy statements and 10-Ks the person has been affiliated with, newspaper articles about the person, articles written by the person, positions held, and so forth. More in-depth searches can be done with pay-for-use sites such as LexisNexis, and many other online services. If Web searches prove insufficient, it does not cost very much to hire a private investigator to perform custom research on members of management.

It is also important to know what motivates directors and managers. Are their personal assets tied up in the organization? Are they under pressure to deliver unrealistic results? Is their compensation primarily performance based? Do they have a habit of guiding Wall Street to higher and higher expectations? Have they grown through acquisitions or internally? Are there debt covenants or other financial measures that must be met? Are managers' jobs at risk? These questions are examples of what must be asked and answered to properly understand management's motivations. Many financial statement frauds have been perpetrated because management needed to report positive or high income to support stock prices, show positive earnings for a public stock or debt offering, or report profits to meet regulatory or loan restrictions.

Finally, management's ability to influence decisions for the organization must be understood, because perpetrating fraud is much easier when one or two individuals have primary decision-making power than when an organization has a more democratic leadership. Most people who commit financial statement fraud are first-time offenders, and being dishonest the first time is difficult for them. Therefore, it is much more difficult for two or even three individuals to conduct dishonest acts simultaneously. When decision-making ability is spread among several individuals, or when the board of directors takes an active role in the organization, fraud is much more difficult to perpetrate. Most financial statement frauds do not occur in large, historically profitable organizations. Rather, they occur in smaller, public or private organizations where one or two individuals have almost total decision-making control, in companies that have experienced very rapid growth, or where the board of directors and audit committee do not take an active role in financial matters. (Note that new corporate governance standards have made it very difficult for board members to remain aloof of the financial matters of their companies.) An active board of directors and/or audit committee that gets involved in the major decisions of the organization can do much to deter management fraud. In fact, it is for this reason that National Association of Securities Dealers Automated Quotations (Nasdaq) and New York Stock exchange (NYSE) corporate governance standards require that the majority of board members be independent and that some of the key committees, such as audit and compensation, be comprised entirely of independent directors.

Once members of management decide to commit fraud, the particular schemes used are usually determined by the nature of their business operations. In searching for red flags, some of the key questions that must be asked about management and the directors are as described in the following subsections.

(a) UNDERSTANDING MANAGEMENT AND DIRECTOR BACKGROUNDS

1. Have any of the key executives or board members been associated with other organizations in the past? If so, what was the nature of those organizations and relationships?
2. Were key members of management promoted from within the organization or recruited from the outside?
3. Have any key members of management had past regulatory or legal problems, either personally or with organizations they have been associated with?
4. Have there been significant changes in the makeup of management or the board of directors?
5. Has there been a high turnover of management and/or board members?
6. Do any members of management or the board have criminal backgrounds?

7. Are there any other issues related to the backgrounds of key members of management and the board of directors?
8. Are the majority of the board members independent?
9. Is the chairman of the board separate from the CEO?
10. Does the company have independent audit, compensation, and nominating committees?

(b) UNDERSTANDING MANAGEMENT AND DIRECTOR MOTIVATIONS

1. Do any of the key executives have personal worth tied up in the organization?
2. Is management under pressure to meet earnings or other financial expectations, or does management commit to analysts, creditors, and others to achieve what appear to be unduly aggressive forecasts?
3. Is management's compensation primarily performance based (bonuses, stock options, etc.)?
4. Are there significant debt covenants or other financial restrictions that management must meet?
5. Is the job security of any key member of management at serious risk?
6. Is the organization's reported financial performance decreasing?
7. Is management excessively interested in maintaining or increasing the entity's stock price?
8. Does management have an incentive to use inappropriate means to minimize reported earnings for tax reasons?
9. Are there any other significant issues related to the motivations of managers and board members?

(c) UNDERSTANDING THE DEGREE OF INFLUENCE OF KEY MEMBERS OF MANAGEMENT AND THE BOARD OF DIRECTORS

1. Which key members of management and the board of directors have the most influence?
2. Are there one or two key people who have dominant influence in the organization?
3. Is the management style of the organization autocratic or democratic?
4. Is the organization's management centralized or decentralized?
5. Does management use ineffective means of communicating and supporting the entity's values or ethics, or do they communicate inappropriate values or ethics?
6. Does management fail to correct known reportable conditions in internal control on a timely basis?
7. Does management set unduly aggressive financial targets and expenditures for operating personnel?
8. Does management have too much involvement in or influence over the selection of accounting principles or the determination of significant estimates?
9. Are there any other significant issues related to the degree of influence of key members of management and the board of directors?

40.7 RELATIONSHIPS WITH OTHERS

Financial statement fraud is rarely perpetrated without the help of other real or fictitious organizations. Enron's fraud was conducted primarily through what is known as *special-purpose* or *variable interest entities* (SPEs)—business interests formed solely to accomplish some specific tasks. SPEs are not of themselves illegal but were used in Enron's case to hide debt, manipulate income, hide losses, and conduct other illegitimate activities.

Though relationships with all parties should be examined to determine if they present management fraud opportunities or exposures, relationships with financial institutions, related organizations and individuals, external auditors, lawyers, investors, and regulators should always be carefully considered. Relationships with financial institutions and bondholders are especially important because they indicate the extent to which the company is leveraged. Examples of the kinds of questions that should be asked about debt relationships include:

- Is the company highly leveraged, and with which financial institutions?
- What assets of the organization are pledged as collateral?
- Is there debt or other restrictive covenants that must be met?
- Do the banking relationships appear normal, or are there strange relationships with financial institutions, such as using institutions in unusual geographical locations?
- Are there relationships between the officers of the financial institutions and your client organization?

Relationships with related organizations and individuals (related parties) should be examined, because structuring non-arm's-length and often unrealistic transactions with related organizations and individuals is one of the easiest ways to perpetrate financial statement fraud. These kinds of relationships are usually identified by examining large or unusual transactions, often occurring at strategic times (i.e., at the end of a period) that make the financial statements look better. The kinds of relationships and events that should be examined include:

- Large transactions that result in revenues or income for the organization
- Sales or purchases of assets between related entities
- Transactions that result in goodwill or other intangible assets being recognized in the financial statements
- Transactions that generate nonoperating, rather than operating, income
- Loans or other financing transactions between related entities
- Any transaction that appears to be unusual or questionable for the organization, especially transactions that are unrealistically large

Analysis of the relationship between a company and its auditors is important for several reasons. If there has been an auditor change, there is probably a good reason for the change. Auditing firms do not easily give up clients, and the termination of an auditor-auditee relationship is most often caused by failure of the client to pay, an auditor-auditee disagreement, fraud or other problems suspected by the auditor, or the auditee's belief that the auditor's fees are too high. Although some of these reasons, such as high fees, may not signal a potential fraud problem, auditor-auditee disagreements, failure to pay an audit fee, and suspected problems can all suggest a financial statement fraud problem. The fact that an auditor was dismissed or resigned, together with the difficulty of discovering financial statement fraud for a first-time auditor, is cause for concern any time there is an auditor change. In examining a company for possible financial statement fraud, it is important to know who its auditor is and how long that relationship has existed.

Relationships with lawyers pose even greater risks than relationships with auditors. Auditors are supposed to be independent and must resign if they suspect that financial results may not be appropriate; in contrast, lawyers are usually advocates for their clients. Lawyers will often follow and support their clients until it is obvious that fraud has occurred. In addition, lawyers usually have information about a client's legal difficulties, regulatory problems, and other significant occurrences. Like auditors, lawyers rarely give up a profitable client unless something is obviously wrong. Thus, a change in legal firms without an apparent reason is often a cause for concern. Unlike a change of auditors, for which an 8-K must be filed for public companies, a change of lawyers requires no such reporting.

Relationships with investors are important because financial statement fraud is often motivated by a debt or equity offering to investors. In addition, knowledge of the number and kinds of investors (public or private company, major exchange or small exchange, institutional or individual, etc.) can often provide an indication of the degree of pressure on and public scrutiny of the management of the company and its financial performance. If an organization is publicly held, usually investor groups or investment analysts follow the company very closely; often they can provide information or indications that something is wrong with the company. For example, "short" investors are always looking for bad news about an organization that will make its stock go down. If they suspect that something is not right, they will often contact management or even the auditors (or press) to vent their concerns. Investor groups often focus on information very different from that used by auditors, and sometimes the fraud symptoms are more obvious to them than they are to auditors, especially auditors who focus solely on the financial statements. Short sellers have a unique perspective that has allowed them to discover financial statement frauds. Because short sellers often focus on bad news, there have been instances in which they were the first ones to put the pieces of the fraud puzzle together. With Enron, for example, the first one to come forward with negative information about the company was Jim Chanos of Kynikos Associates, a highly regarded firm specializing in short selling, who stated publicly in early 2001 that "no one could explain how Enron actually made money." He noted that Enron had completed transactions with related parties that "were run by a senior officer of Enron" and assumed it was a conflict of interest. (Enron would not answer questions about LJM and other partnerships.) Then, in its March 5, 2001, issue, *Fortune* magazine ran a story about Enron that stated: "To skeptics, the lack of clarity raises a red flag about Enron's pricey stock ... [t]he inability to get behind the numbers combined with ever higher expectations for the company may increase the chance of a nasty surprise. Enron is an earnings-at-risk story." Unfortunately, investors kept ignoring this bad news until late in 2001, when a misguided earnings release led skeptics to start selling the stock. The company declared bankruptcy in late 2001.

Finally, accountants must understand a client's relationship with regulators. If a client is a publicly held company, accountants should find out whether the Securities and Exchange Commission (SEC) has ever issued an enforcement release against it; whether the Public Company Accounting Oversight Board, through its inspection of certified public accounting firms, has focused on the company; or whether the Internal Revenue Service (IRS) or another government agency is investigating or has disputes with the company. For example, in its report pursuant to Section 704 of the Sarbanes-Oxley Act, the SEC stated that during the five-year period from July 31, 1997, to July 30, 2002, it had filed 515 enforcement actions involving 869 named parties, 164 entities, and 705 individuals. Accountants also need to know if all annual, quarterly, and other reports have been filed on a timely basis. If a client is in a regulated industry, such as banking, it is important to discover the nature of its relationship with the corresponding regulatory bodies, such as the Federal Deposit Insurance Corporation, Federal Reserve, and Office of the Controller of the Currency. Are there any problematic issues related to those bodies? Does the organization owe any back taxes to the federal or state government or to other taxing districts? Because of the recourse and sanctions available to taxing authorities, organizations usually do not fall behind on their payments unless something is wrong or the organization is having serious cash-flow problems. The next subsections present some of the questions that should be asked about a company's relationships with others when searching for red flags.

(a) RELATIONSHIPS WITH FINANCIAL INSTITUTIONS

1. With what financial institutions does the organization have significant relationships?
2. Is the organization highly leveraged through bank or other loans?
3. Are there loan or debt covenants or restrictions that pose significant problems for the organization?
4. Do the banking relationships appear normal, or are there unusual attributes about the relationships (strange geographical locations, too many banks, etc.)?
5. Do members of management or the board have personal or other close relationships with officers of any of the major banks used by the company?
6. Have there been significant changes in the financial institutions used by the company? If so, why?

7. Are there significant bank accounts or subsidiary or branch operations in tax-haven jurisdictions for which there appears to be no clear business justification?
8. Have critical assets of the company been pledged as collateral on risky loans?
9. Are there any other questionable financial institution relationships?

(b) RELATIONSHIPS WITH RELATED PARTIES

1. Are there significant related-party transactions not in the ordinary course of business or with related entities not audited or audited by another firm?
2. Are there large or unusual transactions at or near the end of a period that significantly improve the reported financial performance of the company?
3. Are there significant receivables or payables between related entities?
4. Has a significant amount of the organization's revenues or income been derived from related-party transactions?
5. Is a significant part of the company's income or revenues derived from one or two large transactions?
6. Are there any other questionable related-party relationships?
7. Have relationships with other entities resulted in the reporting of significant amounts of nonoperating income?

(c) RELATIONSHIPS WITH AUDITORS

1. Have there been frequent disputes with the current or predecessor auditors on accounting, auditing, or reporting matters?
2. Has management placed unreasonable demands on the auditor, including unreasonable time constraints?
3. Has the company placed formal or informal restrictions on the auditor that inappropriately limit the auditor's access to people or information or ability to communicate effectively with the board of directors or the audit committee?
4. Is there domineering management behavior in dealing with the auditor, especially involving attempts to influence the scope of the auditor's work?
5. Has there been an auditor change? If so, for what reason?
6. Are there any other questionable auditor relationships?

(d) RELATIONSHIPS WITH LAWYERS

1. Has there been significant litigation involving the company in matters that could severely and adversely affect the company's financial results?
2. Has there been an attempt to hide litigation from the auditors or others?
3. Has there been a change in outside counsel? If so, for what reasons?
4. Are there any other questionable lawyer relationships?

(e) RELATIONSHIPS WITH INVESTORS

1. Is the organization in the process of issuing an initial or secondary public debt or equity offering?
2. Are there any investor-related lawsuits?
3. Are there any problematic or questionable relationships with investment bankers, stock analysts, or others?
4. Has there been significant short selling of the company's stock? If so, why?
5. Are there questionable investor relationships?

(f) RELATIONSHIPS WITH REGULATORY BODIES

1. Does management display a significant disregard for regulatory authorities?
2. Has there been a history of securities law violations or claims against the entity or its senior management alleging fraud or violations of securities laws?
3. Have any 8-Ks been filed with the SEC? If so, for what reasons?
4. Are there any new accounting, statutory, or regulatory requirements that could impair the financial stability or profitability of the entity?
5. Are there significant tax disputes with the IRS or other taxing authorities?
6. Is the company current on paying its payroll taxes and other payroll-related expenses, and is the company current on paying other liabilities?
7. Are there any other questionable relationships with regulatory bodies?

40.8 ORGANIZATION AND INDUSTRY

Perpetrators sometimes mask financial statement fraud by creating an organizational structure that makes it easier to hide fraud. The attributes of an organization that can act as red flags include such things as an unduly complex organizational structure, an organization without an internal audit department, a board of directors with no or few outsiders on the board or audit committee, an organization in which one or a small group of individuals control related entities, an organization that has offshore affiliates with no apparent business purpose, an organization that has made numerous acquisitions and has recognized large merger-related charges, or an organization that is new. Accountants should gain an understanding of who the owners of an organization are. Sometimes silent or hidden owners are using the organization for illegal or other questionable activities.

The study sponsored by the *Committee of Sponsoring Organizations*[3] of the attributes of firms committing financial statement fraud concluded:

> The relatively small size of fraud companies suggests that the inability or even unwillingness to implement cost-effective internal controls may be a factor affecting the likelihood of financial statement fraud (e.g., override of controls is easier). Smaller companies may be unable or unwilling to employ senior executives with sufficient financial reporting knowledge and experience.
>
> The concentration of fraud among companies with under $50 million in revenues and with generally weak audit committees highlights the importance of rigorous audit committee practices even for smaller organizations. In particular, the number of audit committee meetings per year and the financial expertise of the audit committee members may deserve closer attention.
>
> Investors should be aware of the possible complications arising from family relationships and from individuals (founders, CEO/board chairs, etc.) who hold significant power or incompatible job functions.

The industry of the organization must also be carefully examined. Some industries are riskier than others. For example, in the 1980s, the savings and loan (S&L) industry was extremely risky—to the extent that some accounting firms would not audit an S&L client. More recently, technology companies, especially dot.com-type Internet companies with new and unproven business models, and telecom companies have been extremely risky. With any company, however, the organization's performance relative to that of similar organizations in the same industry should be examined. The next kinds of questions should be asked to understand the exposure to management fraud:

1. Does the company have an overly complex organizational structure involving numerous or unusual legal entities, managerial lines of authority, or contractual arrangements without apparent business purpose?

[3] *www.theiia.org/iia/index.cfm?doc_id=97.*

2. Is there a legitimate business purpose for each separate entity of the business?
3. Is the board of directors comprised primarily of officers of the company or other related individuals?
4. Is the board of directors passive, or active and independent?
5. Is the audit committee comprised primarily of insiders or outsiders?
6. Is the audit committee passive, or active and independent?
7. Does the organization have an independent and active internal audit department?
8. Does the organization have offshore activities without any apparent business purpose?
9. Is the organization a new entity without a proven history?
10. Have there been significant recent changes in the nature of the organization?
11. Is there adequate monitoring of significant controls?
12. Is there an effective accounting and information technology staff and organization?
13. Is there a high degree of competition or market saturation, accompanied by declining margins?
14. Is the client in a declining industry with increasing business failures and significant declines in customer demand?
15. Are there rapid changes in the industry, such as high vulnerability to rapidly changing technology or rapid product obsolescence?
16. Is the performance of the company similar or contrary to that of other firms in the industry?
17. Are there any other significant issues related to organization and industry?

40.9 FINANCIAL RESULTS AND OPERATING CHARACTERISTICS

Much can be learned about exposure to financial statement fraud by closely examining management and the board of directors, relationships with others, and the nature of the organization. Investigation of these three elements is always a good idea, but it usually involves the same procedures for all kinds of financial statement frauds, whether the accounts manipulated are revenue accounts, asset accounts, liabilities, expenses, or equities. What differs from fraud scheme to fraud scheme are the kinds of exposures and red flags identified by the financial statements and operating characteristics of the organization. In examining financial statements to assess fraud exposures, a nontraditional approach to the financial statements must be taken. Fraud symptoms are most often manifested through changes in the financial statements. For example, financial statements that contain large changes in account balances from period to period are more likely to contain fraud than financial statements that exhibit only small, incremental changes in account balances. A sudden, dramatic increase in receivables, for example, is often a signal that something is wrong. In addition to changes in financial statement balances and amounts, the footnotes to the financial statements should be studied. Many times the footnotes strongly hint that fraud is occurring, but auditors and others do not clearly understand what is contained in the footnotes.

When assessing fraud exposure through financial statements and operating characteristics, the balances and amounts must be compared with those of similar organizations in the same industry, and the real-world referents to the financial statement amounts must be determined. If, for example, an organization's financial statements report that the company has \$2 million of inventory, then the inventory has to be located somewhere. Depending on the type of inventory it is, it should require a certain amount of space to store it, forklifts and other equipment to move and ship it, and people to manage it. Are the financial statement numbers realistic, given the actual inventory that is on hand?

Using financial relationships to assess fraud exposures requires that accountants know the nature of the client's business, the kinds of accounts that should be included, the kinds of fraud that could occur in the organization, and the kinds of symptoms those frauds would generate. For example, the major activities of a manufacturing company could probably be subdivided into sales and collections, acquisition and payment, financing, payroll, and inventory and warehousing. Accountants should break an organization down into various activities or cycles such as these and then, for each cycle, identify the major functions performed, the major risks inherent in each function, the kinds of abuse and fraud that could occur, and the kinds of symptoms those frauds would generate. An examiner can then use proactive detection techniques to determine if there is a likelihood of fraud in those cycles. This proactive approach is similar to hypothesis testing done by researchers: Auditors repetitively hypothesize that a type of fraud might be occurring and investigate whether symptoms in the financial statements support each hypothesis. Some of the critical questions that must be asked about financial statement relationships and operating results when searching for red flags are listed next.

1. Are there unrealistic changes or increases in financial statement account balances?
2. Are the account balances realistic given the nature, age, and size of the company?
3. Do actual physical assets exist in the amounts and values indicated on the financial statements?
4. Have there been significant changes in the nature of the organization's revenues or expenses?
5. Do one or a few large transactions account for a significant portion of any account balance or amount?
6. Are there significant transactions near the end of the period that positively affect the results of operations, especially transactions that are unusual or highly complex or that pose substance-over-form questions?
7. Do financial results appear consistent on a quarter-by-quarter or month-by-month basis, or are there unrealistic amounts in a subperiod?
8. Is there an inability to generate cash flows from operations while reporting earnings and earnings growth?
9. Is there significant pressure to obtain additional capital necessary to stay competitive, considering the financial position of the entity—including the need for funds to finance major research and development or capital expenditures?
10. Are reported assets, liabilities, revenues, or expenses based on significant estimates that involve unusually subjective judgments or uncertainties or that are subject to potential significant change in the near term in a manner that may have a financially disruptive effect on the entity (i.e., ultimate collectibility of receivables, timing of revenue recognition, realizability of financial instruments based on the highly subjective valuation of collateral or difficult-to-assess repayment sources, or significant deferral of costs)?
11. Is there unusually rapid growth or profitability, especially compared with that of other companies in the same industry?
12. Is the organization highly vulnerable to changes in interest rates?
13. Are there unrealistically aggressive sales or profitability incentive programs?
14. Is there a threat of imminent bankruptcy, foreclosure, or hostile takeover?
15. Is there a high possibility of adverse consequences on significant pending transactions, such as a business combination or contract award, if poor financial results are reported?
16. Is there a poor or deteriorating financial position when management has personally guaranteed significant debts of the entity?
17. Does the firm continuously operate on a crisis basis or without a careful budgeting and planning process?
18. Does the organization have difficulty collecting receivables or have other cash flow problems?
19. Is the organization dependent on one or two key products or services, especially products or services that can quickly become obsolete? Do other organizations have the ability to adapt more quickly to market swings?

20. Do the footnotes contain information about difficult-to-understand issues?

21. Are there adequate disclosures in the footnotes?

22. Are there questionable or suspicious factors relating to financial results or operating characteristics?

40.10 STRATEGIC FRAUD DETECTION

The red-flag approach to fraud detection just described typically begins with an anomaly or indication that something is not right, such as anonymous tips, unusual financial statement relationships, or control overrides. The red flags observed provide predication that fraud may exist. Management, auditors, or fraud examiners then investigate the indicators to determine whether the red flags observed represent real fraud or are being caused by other factors. This approach can be viewed as an inductive method: It begins with anomalies brought to someone's attention or found proactively (without a specific fraud in mind) and continues by researching additional events and data until it is determined that fraud may be causing the indicators.

Developments in technology and the widespread use of electronic databases to record transactions have made it possible to reverse the traditional red-flag approach; that is, now it is possible to focus first on specific types of fraud and move forward to determine whether indicators or red flags of those specific frauds exist. It is possible to specifically target different types of frauds, analyze entire populations, and proactively detect fraud before traditional indicators become egregious enough to be observed or predication exists. This strategic approach to fraud detection is a proactive approach that targets industry- and company-specific fraud anomalies and patterns and mines data for indicators of specific fraud types. Exhibit 40.2 describes the six steps involved in the strategic fraud detection model.

Step 1. Understand the business. Strategic fraud detection starts with an understanding of the business or unit being examined. Because each business environment is different—even within the same industry or firm—strategic fraud detection is an analytical process. The same fraud detection procedures cannot be applied generically to all businesses or even to different units of the same organization. Rather than rely on generic fraud detection methods or generic queries, strategic fraud examiners must gain intimate knowledge of each specific organization and its processes. Having a detailed understanding of the business

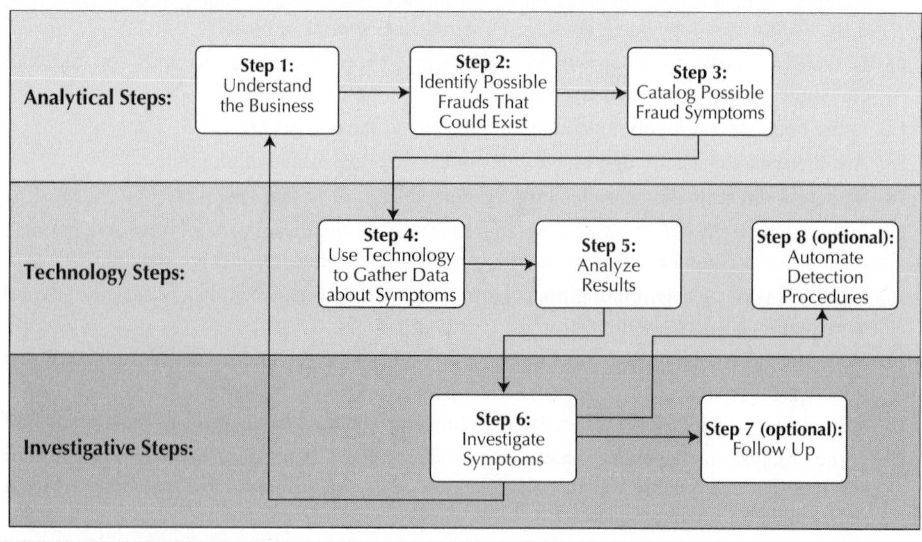

Exhibit 40.2 Strategic Fraud Detection

process underlies the entire strategic fraud detection process. Understanding processes in an organization or unit is similar to performing an analysis as part of a business process reengineering project.

Step 2. Identify possible frauds that could exist. Once accountants feel confident that they understand the business, they must determine what possible frauds could occur in the operation being examined. This risk assessment step requires an understanding of the nature of different frauds, how they occur, and what symptoms they exhibit. The fraud identification process begins by conceptually dividing the business unit into its individual functions. For example, accountants might decide to focus directly on the manufacturing plant, the collections department, or the purchasing function. In this step, people knowledgeable about the business functions (internal auditors, managers, security directors, etc.) are interviewed. Accountants ask questions such as: Who are the players? What types of employees, vendors, or contractors are involved? How do insiders and outsiders interact with each other? What types of fraud could be committed against the company or on behalf of the company? How could employees or management acting alone commit fraud? How could vendors or customers acting alone commit fraud? How could vendors or customers working in collusion with employees commit fraud? What motivations are there to commit fraud on behalf of the organization or against the organization? During this stage, accountants should brainstorm potential frauds by type and participant. The likely occurrence of the various frauds is considered, and a laundry list of frauds that will be considered is developed.

Step 3. Catalog possible fraud symptoms for each type of fraud. This step in strategic fraud detection involves careful consideration of whether variations of the six types of symptoms discussed earlier could be present in the cataloged frauds identified in Step 2. A matrix, tree diagram, or mind map should be created that correlates specific symptoms with specific possible frauds. For example, fraud involving kickbacks from vendors to buyers might be characterized as shown in Exhibit 40.3. This step is extremely important because it makes operational the list of frauds hypothesized in the previous step.

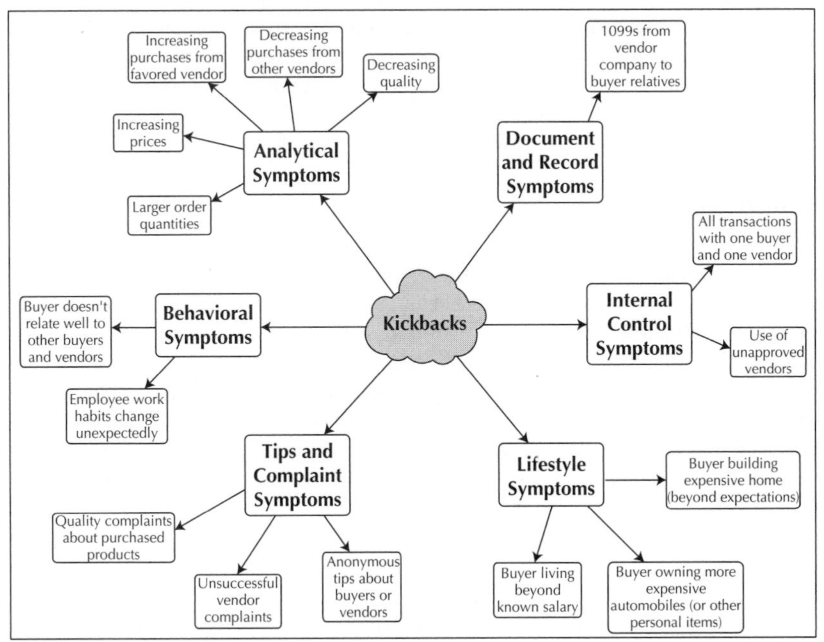

Exhibit 40.3 Example of Strategic Fraud Detection with Kickbacks

Step 4. Use technology and other means to gather data about symptoms. Once symptoms are defined and correlated with specific frauds, data are extracted from corporate databases, online Web sites, interviews, and other sources. Traditional fraud-search procedures prescribe sampling data, but it is preferable to run fraud-detection queries against full transaction populations. Summarization or sampling limits the power of the detection process. Sampling can miss important transactions within which fraud has been hidden.

Because of the large size of typical organizational data stores, many queries are actually composed of several extractions combined with algorithms programmed in scripting languages. Small scripts, quickly written and executed, allow accountants to analyze large numbers of transactions and perform repeated analyses. For example, ACLScript, the scripting language within ACL, provides significantly more power to the user than using ACL from the menu options alone. Other popular scripting languages include IDEAScript (IDEA), Visual Basic (Microsoft Excel or Access), PowerScript (PowerBuilder), and Python.

Step 5. Analyze and refine results. Once relevant data are retrieved, they are compared against expectations and models. These algorithms examine records and highlight anomalies, unknown values, suggestive trends, or outliers that can then be analyzed directly by examiners. These algorithms must be company- and data-specific to be valuable. Data analysis techniques, such as time trending, regression, CUSUM, fuzzy text matching, stratification and summarization, z-score distancing and comparisons, time axis standardization, and relation matching, should be used for analysis. (Discussion of these and other appropriate techniques is important but beyond the scope of this chapter.)

Although specific analyses are unique to the business being examined and the type of fraud being searched for, most searches include time series models. This is because fraud is often discovered by examining changes over time. Historical patterns within the data, rather than outside factors, often set the standard against which data are measured. Sharp and unexpected increases in spending, purchases, labor, or even account balances often signal possible fraud. Generated norms that allow the data to speak for themselves are often useful to determine whether observed values are anomalies or fall within expected ranges.

Step 6. Investigate symptoms. Once anomalies are highlighted and determined to be indicators of fraud, they are investigated using either traditional or strategic approaches. The advantage to the strategic approach, however, is that now the investigation is targeted and specific. Based on the strategic red flags observed, fraud examiners can now, in a cost-effective way, focus their investigation efforts.

40.11 CONCLUSION

It is no longer necessary to wait until fraud symptoms become so egregious as to be observed to detect fraud. Fraud can now be detected either through inductive search for red flags or through deductive, strategic fraud detection. Once fraud occurs, there are no winners. Everyone, including the victim organization, the perpetrators, the auditors, and others, loses. These losses are minimized if fraud can be detected early. Every accountant should understand both the importance of fraud detection and the nature of fraud symptoms. Frauds will never be eliminated completely, but those who understand the nature of fraud and how to detect its occurrence will minimize their losses and, it is hoped, avoid expensive lawsuits, negative exposure, and financial losses.

CHAPTER 41

FORENSIC ACCOUNTING IN LITIGATION CONSULTING SERVICES, INVESTIGATIONS, AND COMPLIANCE MATTERS

Yogesh Bahl, CPA, MBA
Deloitte Financial Advisory Services LLP

Frank Hydoski, PhD
Deloitte Financial Advisory Services LLP

41.1 INTRODUCTION 2

(a) Comparing Litigation Consulting Services to Attest Services 2

41.2 ACCOUNTANT'S ROLE IN DISPUTE RESOLUTION PROCEEDINGS 3

(a) U.S. Legal System: General Information 3
(i) Adversarial Process 3
(ii) Stages in a Civil Suit 3
(iii) Alternative Dispute Resolution 4
(iv) Required Proofs 4
(b) Accountant's Role in the Litigation Process 5
(i) Testifying Expert 5
(ii) Nontestifying Consultant 5
(iii) Case Analysis and Planning 6
(iv) Discovery 6
(v) Settlement Analysis 6
(vi) Pretrial 7
(vii) Trial 7
(viii) Credentials and Certifications 7
(c) Federal Rules of Evidence 8
(i) Federal Rule of Evidence 702 8
(ii) Effect of *Daubert v. Merrell Dow Pharmaceuticals* 8
(iii) Federal Rule of Civil Procedure 26 8
(d) Types of Services 9
(i) Damage Calculations 9
(ii) Arbitration 10
(iii) Bankruptcy 11
(e) Calculating Damages 12
(i) General Concepts 12
(ii) Measuring Damages 12
(iii) Mitigation 13
(iv) Present Value and Inflation 13
(v) Income Taxes 13
(f) Support for Opinions 14
(i) Sources of Information 14
(ii) Reliance on Others 14
(iii) Documentation 14
(g) Testimony 14
(i) Giving Deposition Testimony 14
(ii) Giving Trial Testimony 15

41.3 ACCOUNTANT'S ROLE IN INVESTIGATIONS AND COMPLIANCE MATTERS 16

(a) Corporate Investigations 16
(i) General/White Collar 16
(ii) Securities Violations 17

The information contained in this chapter does not necessarily represent the views of Deloitte Financial Advisory Services LLP.

(b) Anti–Money Laundering 18
(i) AML Technology 20
(c) Foreign Corrupt Practices Act Violations 20
(d) Antifraud Programs and Controls 21
(i) AFPC Service Types 21
(e) Licensing and Contract Investigations 22
(f) Forensic Technology 23
(i) Computer Forensics 23
(ii) Data Analysis 24

41.4 GLOBALIZATION IMPACT 25
(a) International Financial Reporting Standards 25
(b) U.K. Anticorruption and Bribery Laws 25

41.1 INTRODUCTION

Forensic accounting can be defined as the application of accounting principles, theories, and discipline to facts and hypotheses at issue in a legal, investigatory, or compliance context. The legal context is generally litigation, but any dispute resolution proceeding (e.g., arbitration or mediation) is a candidate for the application of forensic accounting, as are a number of other contexts, including investigations involving accounting issues, information or systems, and regulatory and corporate compliance matters.

Litigation consulting services can include forensic accounting but also involve any professional assistance nonlawyers provide to lawyers in the litigation process in connection with pending or potential formal legal or regulatory proceedings before a trier of fact in connection with the resolution of a dispute between two or more parties. A trier of fact can be a court, regulatory body, or government authority; its agents; a grand jury; or an arbitrator of a dispute. Litigation consulting services also include the application of specialized disciplines to the issues involved in a matter in order to express an expert opinion that would help the trier of fact reach an informed conclusion.

Forensic accounting and litigation consulting services apply to both civil and criminal litigation. The principal focus of this chapter is civil litigation because it is by far the most frequent dispute resolution proceeding in which the professional accountant will be involved. However, this chapter also focuses on corporate investigations, compliance and other contexts in which forensic accountants are increasingly involved.

Although some may want to use the terms *forensic accounting, dispute analysis, litigation support,* and *litigation consulting* as synonyms, a distinction should be made. For purposes of this chapter, *forensic accounting* involves the exploration of accounting issues, information, or systems and refers to the disciplined process used in gathering facts and understanding issues prior to a dispute resolution proceeding, or in the course of an investigation, or in relation to the compliance matters this chapter describes. In addition, *litigation consulting services* refers to the assistance provided during a dispute resolution proceeding in the case, for example, of expert jury consulting.

(a) COMPARING LITIGATION CONSULTING SERVICES TO ATTEST SERVICES. The role of the practitioner in a litigation consulting engagement is different from that in an attestation engagement, where the certified public accountant (CPA) can express different levels of opinion about the reliability of a written assertion of another party. In a litigation consulting engagement, the practitioner provides his or her individual opinion around the facts at issue in the case, usually to opine on liability or damage amounts.

In an attestation engagement, the audience is composed of all persons relying on the accountant's report, whereas in a litigation consulting engagement, the audience for the litigation consulting practitioner's opinion and work product is generally limited to the trier of fact and the parties to the dispute who have the opportunity to evaluate and question the practitioner's conclusions, support for the conclusions, and methodology.

This chapter provides a brief description of litigation consulting matters relevant to accountants and explains their role in them. It also describes the role of accountants in a number of other contexts, including investigations, compliance, and technology. In this chapter, although the terms *accountant, practitioner, CPA,* and *litigation consultant* are used in various ways to describe an accountant who is providing forensic accounting and litigation consulting services, it should be noted that distinctions between service providers are often made, particularly with those who are licensed as CPAs and those who are not. The chapter includes a description of the types of cases in which accountants typically get involved, the types of services accountants usually provide, and a discussion of the professional standards relevant to litigation consulting services. Subsection 41.2(d)(iii) gives a brief overview of bankruptcy, while Chapter 39 discusses bankruptcy in detail. Section 41.2(g) provides examples of how to prepare and deliver deposition and trial testimony. Discussions of some of the issues related to expert testimony in this chapter are extended in Chapter 43. Additionally, Chapter 42 provides insight into the tools and techniques of modern textual forensic analysis. Finally, Chapter 40 provides an overview of the subject of fraud.

41.2 ACCOUNTANT'S ROLE IN DISPUTE RESOLUTION PROCEEDINGS

(a) U.S. LEGAL SYSTEM: GENERAL INFORMATION

(i) Adversarial Process. In civil disputes, it is generally up to the parties (i.e., the plaintiff and defendant), not the court, to initiate and prosecute litigation, to investigate the pertinent facts, and to present proof and legal argument to the adjudicative body. The court's function, in general, is limited to adjudicating the issues that the parties submit to the court, based on the proofs presented by the parties.

(ii) Stages in a Civil Suit. Civil suits have four basic stages, barring appeal, which are the same for virtually all adversarial proceedings, whether in a federal, state, or administrative court:

1. *Pleadings.* A lawsuit is started by a complaint that is filed with the clerk of the trial court and served on the defendants. The complaint lays out the facts and causes of action alleged by the plaintiff. The defendants may file a motion to dismiss (arguing that the defendant is not legally liable even if the alleged facts are true) or an answer to the complaint. The answer may contain a denial of the allegations or an affirmative defense (e.g., statute of limitations has expired). The defendant also may file a counterclaim that presents a claim by the defendant (counterplaintiff) against the plaintiff (counterdefendant).
2. *Pretrial discovery.* The purpose of pretrial discovery is to narrow the issues that need to be decided at trial and to obtain evidence to support legal and factual arguments. It is essentially an information-gathering process. Evidence is obtained in advance to facilitate presentation of an organized, concise case as well as to prevent any surprises at trial. This sharing of information often will result in the settlement of the case before trial.
   - The first step in discovery typically involves the use of interrogatories and document requests. Interrogatories are sets of formal written questions directed by one party in the lawsuit to the other. They are usually broad in nature and are used to fill in and amplify the fact situation set out in the pleadings. Interrogatories are also used to identify individuals who may possess unique knowledge or information about the issues in the case. Requests for production of documents identify specific documents and records that the requesting party believes are relevant to its case and that is in the possession of and controlled by the opposing party. The opposing party is required to produce only the specific documents requested. Accordingly, when drafting these requests, care must be taken to be as broad as possible so as to include all relevant documents but narrow enough to be descriptive. It is not unusual for more than one set of interrogatories and document requests to be issued during the course of a lawsuit. The accountant is often involved in developing interrogatories and document requests on financial and business issues.
   - Depositions are the second step in the discovery process. They are the sworn testimony of a witness recorded by a court reporter. During the deposition, the witness may be

asked questions by the attorneys for each party to the suit. The questions and answers are transcribed, sworn to, and signed. The testimony will allow the party taking the deposition to better understand the facts of the case and may be used as evidence in the trial. The accountant may be heavily involved at this stage, both in being deposed and in developing questions for the deposition of opposing witnesses.

3. *Trial.* The third stage of the litigation/adversarial process is the trial. It is the judicial examination and determination of issues between the parties to the action. In a jury trial, the trial begins with the selection of a jury. The attorneys for each party then make opening statements concerning the facts they expect to prove during the trial. Then the plaintiff puts forth its case, calling all of the witnesses it believes are required to prove its case. Each witness will be subject to direct examination and then cross-examination by the opposing party's attorney. After the plaintiff has called all of its witnesses and presented all of its evidence, the defendant will then present its case in the same manner. The plaintiff then has an opportunity to present additional evidence to refute the defendant's case in a rebuttal. The defendant can respond in a surrebuttal. Finally, each party has the opportunity to make a closing statement before the court.
4. *Settlement.* At any time in the litigation process, the parties can attempt to settle the dispute without the intervention of the court. This can be accomplished by participating in settlement discussions or by using alternative methods of dispute resolution.

(iii) Alternative Dispute Resolution. Alternative dispute resolution can encompass mediation, arbitration, facilitation, and other ways of resolving disputes focused on effective communication and negotiation rather than using adversarial processes such as the courtroom. Two basic types of alternative dispute resolution exist. There are nonbinding methods, such as mediation, negotiation, or facilitation, which assist in reaching, but do not impose, a resolution of the dispute. There are also more binding methods, such as arbitration or adjudication, in which a neutral decision maker rules on the issues presented. Combinations of these methods also exist. Alternative dispute resolution is often used because it is the vehicle prescribed in an agreement or contract for the resolution of a dispute.

The U.S. Constitution and most state constitutions provide for the right of trial by jury in most cases. This right does not have to be exercised, and many cases are tried without a jury (i.e., a bench trial where the judge is the trier of fact). In most states and in federal courts, one of the parties must request a jury or the right is presumed to be waived.

(iv) Required Proofs. In order for a plaintiff to succeed in a claim for damages, it must satisfy three different but related proofs: liability, causation, and amount of damages if applicable. If the burden of proof is not met on any one of these, the claim will fail.

1. *Liability.* The plaintiff must prove that one of its legal rights has been transgressed by the defendant. The plaintiff will present evidence attempting to prove that the actions of the defendant were in violation of the plaintiff's legal rights. Similarly, the defendant will present evidence in an effort to prove that the plaintiff's rights were not violated, or at least were not violated by the defendant.
2. *Causation.* If the plaintiff proves that the defendant has violated one of its legal rights, it must be shown that this violation resulted in some harm to the plaintiff. Here attorneys for the plaintiff and defendant will try to prove or disprove the nexus between the defendant's actions and some harm to the plaintiff.
3. *Damages.* After presenting the evidence relating to the liability and causation issues, the parties' next step in most cases is to prove damages. Damages are one of a number of remedies that may be available to a prevailing plaintiff. Other types of remedies include specific performance (performance of the act that was promised), injunctions (an order by the court forbidding or restraining a party from doing an act), and restitution (the return

of goods, property, or money previously conveyed). Damages are the only type of remedy discussed in this chapter. The general principle in awarding damages is to put the plaintiff in the same position it would have been in if its legal rights had not been transgressed. There are three main categories of damages: compensatory, consequential, and punitive.

4. *Compensatory damages* compensate the injured party only for injuries or losses actually sustained and proved to have arisen directly from the violation of the plaintiff's rights. *Consequential damages* are foreseeable damages that are caused by special circumstances beyond the action itself; they flow only from the consequences or results of an action. *Punitive damages* are intended to penalize the guilty party and to make an example of the party to deter similar conduct in the future; they are awarded only in certain types of cases (e.g., fraud). The quantification of damages is primarily a question of fact. The burden of proving the damage amount normally falls on the plaintiff. Although accountants can be used in cases in which damages are not an issue, accountants are most frequently used in cases in which damages are an issue. The calculation of damages often involves a series of scenarios and the quantification of each can involve complex algorithms. Accountants can utilize the skills sets of econometric and/or data analytics professionals to assist in building data models to accommodate these scenarios. In addition, it is important not to forget that the damages model needs to include the nuances specific to the industry involved in the case.

(b) ACCOUNTANT'S ROLE IN THE LITIGATION PROCESS. Typically the accountant is hired by attorneys representing either the plaintiff or the defendant. In some cases, however, an accountant may be engaged directly by one of the parties to the action. No matter who engages the accountant, he or she may play a number of possible roles. A litigation consulting practitioner can work as a testifying expert, a consultant, a trier of fact (e.g., an arbitrator), a special master (working for the court), or a court-appointed neutral party (an expert not for the parties to the dispute but to the court as a neutral party). A detailed discussion of the role of the testifying expert and the consultant is presented next.

(i) Testifying Expert. Frequently, the accountant's purpose in the case will be to develop and render an opinion regarding financial or accounting issues. Ordinarily, only facts and firsthand knowledge can be presented by witnesses at trial. The only exception to this rule is the testimony of experts, which can include an expression of the expert's opinions.

According to the courts and the law, experts are those who are qualified to testify authoritatively because of their education, special training, and experience. A professional accountant can qualify as an expert in issues relating to accounting and financial data.

The accountant as expert may be asked to develop and present evidence in support of any or all of the required proofs. For example, the accountant can review and offer an opinion as to the adequacy of the work performed by another accountant in a professional liability suit (proof of liability).The accountant might review the financial records and the business environment of a company to determine whether a bank's withdrawal of credit caused the company to go out of business (proof of causation). Most commonly, the accountant will be asked to provide an opinion regarding the economic loss suffered by the plaintiff in the case or to rebut the damages alleged by the plaintiff on behalf of the defendant (proof of damages).

(ii) Nontestifying Consultant. In certain situations, the accountant will be asked to be a consultant rather than a testifying expert. The accountant will take on more of an advisory role and will not provide testimony. The work the accountant performs for the attorney as a consultant is generally protected by the attorney's work product privilege and as such is not discoverable by the opposing party. For this reason, accountants are often engaged initially as consultants. Doing this enables the attorney to explore avenues and conduct analyses from which he or she might want to shield the testifying expert. However, once the accountant has been designated as an expert, all work products may be subject to discovery. It is critical for any accountant to work closely with the attorney to understand the processes that must be maintained to safeguard the consulting, as opposed to the expert, role. In certain circumstances, courts have pierced through the veil of the consulting role to suggest that the consultant's work, particularly in circumstances where the consultant has worked closely with the expert, should be made available to opposing parties.

(iii) Case Analysis and Planning. In the role as either testifying expert or nontestifying consultant, the litigation consulting practitioner can provide valuable assistance throughout the litigation process.

In many circumstances, the accountant can be of use to the attorney before the complaint is even filed. The accountant can help the attorney understand the accounting, financial, and economic issues involved in the case and can also help assess the potential value of the claim by providing an estimate of the amount of damages. In certain cases, the accountant may actually help to identify causes of action to be included in the complaint.

Once a case has been filed, the accountant can help the attorney understand and evaluate critical accounting, financial, and economic issues and assist with the formulation of an appropriate strategy. Strategy formulation is a continual process; as new information is received and additional issues uncovered, the overall strategy is revised. During the planning phase, the accountant will help evaluate alternative approaches and help the attorney determine the most reasonable approach to take based on all available information. At the same time, the accountant will assess the strengths and weaknesses of the opponent's case. The accountant's involvement in this phase will help the attorney to focus on those issues that have the greatest impact on proving the case.

(iv) Discovery. Discovery is the information-gathering stage of the litigation process. During discovery, each party attempts to identify and obtain all the information and documents necessary to prove its case. The accountant's initial assistance may be in formulating specific accounting and financially oriented questions to be included in interrogatories. The accountant will also assist in drafting document requests by identifying in a very specific manner the types of documents (particularly accounting records and reports) that would be of interest and that the opposing party is likely to have retained. The more specific the requests are, the more likely the response will be useful. The accountant will also be able to assist the attorney with the preparation of responses to the opposing party's interrogatories and document requests.

A significant role that the litigation consulting practitioner can play during the discovery phase is in the review and analysis of the documents. During this review, the litigation consulting practitioner can identify key documents that are helpful or harmful to the parties that have retained him or her. It is also during this phase that the litigation consulting practitioner identifies documents requiring further explanation that can be provided during deposition. Depending on the legal forum in which the case is being tried, expert reports are usually drafted, issued, and exchanged with the opposing party during or just after the discovery phase.

Depositions provide each side with an opportunity to elicit relevant facts and to identify weaknesses in an opponent's argument. The accountant can be helpful in this area by assisting the attorney in identifying subjects to be explored and in developing specific deposition questions, especially when financial executives or experts are being deposed. Frequently, an attorney will request the accountant to be present at these key depositions. Here the accountant can help the attorney understand and interpret the deponent's responses and help formulate follow-up questions to probe more deeply into the subject area. Having the accountant present at the deposition will enable the attorney to better understand and consider the financial issues.

The accountant who will be a testifying expert may be subject to deposition by the opposing attorney. The opposition will attempt to gain a thorough understanding of the accountant's analysis and conclusions and, when possible, identify weaknesses and lay the groundwork for attack at trial. Subsection 41.2(g)(i) presents a description of the deposition process.

(v) Settlement Analysis. Settlement negotiations can occur at any point during the litigation process. They can be greatly facilitated by the use of an accountant. The accountant can be instrumental in helping evaluate existing alternatives and terms as well as in proposing other strategic approaches. The accountant's evaluation may involve analyses of (1) the economic value and feasibility of various strategies or (2) the strengths and weaknesses of the positions of the two sides.

When assisting with the determination of value and evaluation of feasibility, the accountant can estimate potential damages under various scenarios and help assess the probability of occurrence for each, thereby giving the attorney a better understanding of the risks involved.

Just as important, the accountant can help evaluate the true economic value of various settlement alternatives and assist in determining possible tax effects of each. This will enable the attorney and client to make a more informed decision regarding settlement options and perhaps offer alternatives that benefit both parties. The accountant can also assist with an analysis of the relative strengths and weaknesses of both the plaintiff's and the defendant's positions, thereby helping the attorney strengthen his or her bargaining position and anticipate potential problems.

(vi) Pretrial. When preparing for trial, the accountant can assist the attorney with:

1. Preparation of courtroom graphics, presentations, and exhibits
2. Preparation of witnesses for trial testimony
3. Preparation for the cross examination of opposing witnesses
4. Fine-tuning the overall case strategy

(vii) Trial. If the case does not settle, the final role of the accountant will be to assist during the trial itself. The accountant's testimony in court is a key part of this role. In testimony, the accountant, as expert, presents the opinions developed as a result of his or her information gathering, review, and analysis. It is imperative that the accountant present opinions in a straightforward, cogent, and concise manner. Subsection 41.2(g)(ii) describes the course of direct testimony and suggests ways that could enhance the effectiveness of the testimony.

Although opinion testimony is of paramount importance at the trial stage, the accountant can play other valuable roles. For example, the accountant can be of tremendous value to attorneys during the cross-examination of opposing experts and financial witnesses. The accountant can work with the attorney to prepare cross-examination questions in an effort to challenge the statements made during testimony or the credibility of the witness. The accountant will be important in this phase because of his or her ability to help formulate accounting and financially oriented questions designed to be difficult for the witness to evade or deflect. More important, the accountant will be able to assess the responses and provide follow-up questions to close the loop on important issues.

(viii) Credentials and Certifications. Experts or consultants in a litigation case bring their skills and past experience to the table. Increasingly, individuals are obtaining professional certifications to reflect those attributes. Along with increased societal and regulatory attention to fraud, as evidenced in the passage of the Sarbanes-Oxley Act of 2002 (SOX), various professional organizations are increasingly offering professional certifications in forensic and fraud-related subject matters. Fraud-specific specialty certifications, in most instances, are obtained as a supplement to the widely recognized designation of CPA, but holding a CPA designation may not be a prerequisite to holding other certifications.

One of the better-recognized certifications is the Certified Fraud Examiner (CFE) designation of the 40,000-member Association of Certified Fraud Examiners (ACFE). The American Institute of Certified Public Accountants (AICPA) also established the credential of Certified in Financial Forensics (CFF). The CFF is granted exclusively to CPAs who specialize in forensic accounting. The AICPA and ACFE have been working together for some years to leverage expertise and develop joint training programs. The American College of Forensic Examiners Institute (ACFEI) offers certifications such as the Certified Forensic Consultant (CFC) and Certified Forensic Accountant (Cr.FA) as well as specialized certifications in homeland security and certain aspects of forensic medical practice. The National Association of Certified Valuation Analysts (NACVA) supports the business valuation, litigation consulting, and fraud deterrence disciplines. It offers the Certified Forensic Financial Analyst (CFFA) and Certified Fraud Deterrence Analyst (CFD) credentials. The Forensic CPA Society, founded in 2005, offers a Forensic Certified Public Accountant certification to those CPAs passing an examination who also demonstrate relevant practical experience. Other certification organizations also exist.

Most certifications require candidates to pass a written examination and have prerequisite experience requirements and annual continuing education requirements. They also require adherence to a code of professional ethics.

(c) FEDERAL RULES OF EVIDENCE

(i) Federal Rule of Evidence 702. Many witnesses who testify during litigation are fact witnesses. A fact witness can provide testimony based on what he or she has seen, heard, or otherwise observed. A fact witness may not offer opinions. By contrast, an expert witness by reason of education or specialized experience possesses superior knowledge about a subject and as such may offer opinions at trial. An accountant may testify as an expert witness if his or her opinion will assist the trier of fact in understanding the evidence or determining the issues in a case.

Federal Rule of Evidence 702 governs the admissibility of expert opinion testimony. Rule 702 states that "if scientific, technical, or other specialized knowledge will assist the trier of fact to understand the evidence or to determine a fact in issue, a witness qualified as an expert by knowledge, skill, experience, training, or education, may testify thereto in the form of an opinion or otherwise."

(ii) Effect of *Daubert v. Merrell Dow Pharmaceuticals*. In *Daubert v. Merrell Dow Pharmaceuticals,* 113 S. Ct. 2796 (1993) (*Daubert*), the Supreme Court addressed the rules pertaining to the admission of expert testimony.

Since 1923, based on *Frye v. United States,* 293 F.1013 (D.C. Cir 1923), the federal courts applied a test (the general acceptance test) by which scientific expert opinions should be admitted into evidence. Under this standard, an opinion was admitted only if it was based on generally accepted methodology within the industry.

In the *Daubert* decision, the Supreme Court determined that in order for expert witness opinions to be admitted under Rule 702, they did not have to meet the *Frye* general acceptance test and clarified that Rule 702 does not establish general acceptance as a criteria for admissibility. The *Daubert* decision clarified the trial court's role in determining the admissibility of expert testimony. In doing so, the court need not determine whether the methodology meets the general acceptance test; instead, the court must assess the validity of the methodology used and the applicability of that methodology to the specific facts of the case. Discussions of issues of expert testimony are extended in Chapter 43.

(iii) Federal Rule of Civil Procedure 26. If the accountant has been engaged to serve as a testifying expert witness, he or she must become aware of the effect of Rule 26 of the Federal Rules of Civil Procedure, which deals with the procedure for written disclosure of expert testimony.

Pursuant to Rule 26, the identity of one side's potential testifying experts, as well as information about the expected testimony, must be voluntarily disclosed at the outset of a case, without receipt of a formal discovery request.

In addition, Rule 26 provides that the expert prepare and sign a written report. This report must be disclosed to the other parties before the expert will be allowed to testify at trial. Unless the date by which disclosure of the written report must be made is decided by the trial judge, rules of the local court, or agreement of the parties, the report must be disclosed at least 90 days before the date of trial. If an expert is retained solely to rebut the testimony of an opposing expert, the report of the rebuttal witness must be disclosed within 30 days of the disclosure of the other expert's report.

Generally, the expert witness will not be permitted to testify at trial to his or her opinions unless the opinions are contained in the expert witness's written report. Therefore, the content of the expert's report should contain all of his or her opinions and the bases for the opinions. In addition, once the expert's report is disclosed to the other side, any changes to the report must be disclosed before the commencement of trial.

Rule 26 requires that the expert's report contain:

- A complete statement of the opinion to be expressed and the bases and reasons therefore
- The data or other information the witness considered in forming the opinions

- Any exhibits to be used as a summary of or as support for the opinions
- Qualifications of the witness, including a list of publications the witness authored within the preceding 10 years
- The compensation to be paid to the witness for the study and testimony
- A list of all other cases in which the witness has testified as an expert at trial or in deposition within the preceding four years
- Signature of the expert

Pursuant to Rule 26, once the expert's written report required by Rule 26 has been disclosed, the opposing side has the right to take the deposition of any person who has been identified as an expert whose opinions may be presented at trial.

The accountant who is engaged as an expert witness in a matter to be tried in a federal court should ascertain the current status of Rule 26 in the applicable federal district and discuss compliance with Rule 26 with the counsel retaining him.

It is important to point out that the Federal Rules of Civil Procedure give local courts the option of not complying with certain provisions, including the provisions of Rule 26 just discussed. The accountant should consult with the retaining attorney to ascertain whether the case is to be tried in federal or local court and the local rules that apply to the case.

(d) TYPES OF SERVICES

(i) Damage Calculations. The following types of services are relevant to damage calculations.

- *Patent infringement.* These cases typically involve unauthorized or unreported use or sale of licensed intellectual property, transfer pricing errors, inaccurate allocation of sales value to the patented components, and other erroneous deductions. Damages are in the form of lost royalties. Determining revenue loss may involve steps such as conducting interviews, examining sales records, pricing, freight, parts, and other types of deductions, and testing sales, production, and inventory for underreporting.
- *Breach of contract.* Typically, the plaintiff has a contract with the defendant that the defendant is accused of breaching. For example, the contract may call for the defendant to buy a certain quantity of product for a certain price. The defendant, however, fails to make the required purchases. Or the defendant may be accused of breaching a warranty on its goods or services. The accountant may be asked to quantify the damages suffered by the plaintiff as a result of the breach. Usually the damages are measured by lost profits (i.e., the additional profits the plaintiff would have earned but for the defendant's breach). Among the issues the accountant may address are lost revenues, avoided costs, available capacity, and possible mitigating actions, including sale of the product to others.
- *Business interruption.* A business interruption claim may arise from an accident, fire, flood, strike, or other unexpected event. It may even arise from a contract or warranty claim where the defendant's breach has caused the plaintiff to suspend operations. Typically, these claims are filed by a business against its insurance carrier, though a claim against the entity causing the event is possible. In a business interruption case, the plaintiff claims the event caused the business to suffer losses. Often the accountant is asked to quantify the loss. Elements to be considered may include lost profits, loss of tangible assets, loss of intangible assets (including goodwill), loss of an entire business or business line, cost to repair or reestablish the business, cost of downtime, or cost of wasted effort (time spent fixing the problem instead of generating operating profits).
- *Antitrust.* The plaintiff in antitrust litigation may be either the government or a private party. The government usually brings suit to oppose a merger or to break up a monopoly. Government suits are usually not for monetary damages. Experts in these suits, particularly in liability issues involving monopolistic practices, relevant market share, and the like, are often economists, not accountants. In a private suit, the plaintiff accuses the defendant of

violating antitrust laws, resulting in injury to competition, including (or especially) injury to the plaintiff. The accountant's role again may be the computation of lost profits. A company may be accused of violating antitrust laws by selling the same goods at different prices to different parties in the same channel of distribution. This ostensibly discriminatory pricing may be refuted if the defendant can show that the price differences are justified by differences in cost of production, service, freight, and so on. An accountant may conduct these cost justification studies.

- Accusations of predatory pricing also fall under the antitrust laws. The defendant in a predatory pricing case is accused of pricing so low that competitors lose money and are driven out of business. Once the competition is eliminated, the defendant presumably raises prices and enjoys monopoly profits. One legal standard for predatory pricing is pricing below cost of production. Depending on the law, the standard may be either incremental costs or fully allocated costs. An accountant may help establish or refute this claim by studying product pricing and production costs and measuring the resulting profit margins.
- *Personal injury.* Personal injury cases stem from automobile accidents, slip-and-falls, and the like. Typically, damage components include medical expenses, pain and suffering, lost earnings, and loss of consortium to the injured party's spouse. The accountant is usually involved in the calculation of lost earnings and in calculations regarding the interest components of the judgment. For identification of the issues involved, see Section 41.2(e).

(ii) Arbitration. Arbitration is a form of alternative dispute resolution that is binding on the parties involved. An impartial arbitrator listens to the evidence presented and renders a decision. Disputes in connection with a purchase and sale agreement are common candidates for arbitration. These can arise for a variety of reasons, such as disagreements related to purchase price adjustments based on a closing date balance sheet or some other financial measure; representation and warranty provisions involving financial information; transition services and related cost-sharing provisions; and earnout provisions or other deferred payment mechanisms that generally depend on future operations or earnings results. Many of these issues involve questions of fact and how those facts should be reflected in financial statements prepared in accordance with generally accepted accounting principles (GAAP) or another basis of accounting.

Buy–sell agreements may also contain a component of compensation to the seller in the form of an earnout that is typically based on future performance and attaining certain mutually agreed-on financial metrics. Disputes frequently result over the contractual wording and earnout measurement mechanisms when the company, according to the buyer's calculation, does not meet earnout targets and, therefore, the seller does not receive any or all of the potential earnout compensation that was anticipated. An accountant may be helpful in assisting both buyers and sellers in offering strategic advice during the drafting of earnout provisions as well as evaluating the relevant financial results to establish whether any or all of the earnout has been attained.

Because certain accounting issues disputed in a postclosing purchase price dispute may also be at issue in an earlier balance sheet that is subject to representations and warranties of the seller, these same issues might be disputed in a different forum under a breach of representation or warranty claim. While these disputes are often decided in a litigation context as opposed to private arbitration, the skills and experience of professionals are also highly applicable in these matters. The accounting issues in a dispute may or may not include some of the same issues involved in a postclosing purchase price adjustment. However, in addition to accounting and financial reporting, numerous other issues can arise in a breach case, including:

- The manner in which the purchase price was established by the buyer
- The nature and extent of due diligence by the buyer
- The reliance and causation issues that may stem from any alleged accounting errors
- The damages alleged by the buyer

Addressing such issues may involve analyzing the underlying records, researching complex accounting questions, or interpreting contractual modifications of GAAP, or another relevant basis for accounting. The accountant may provide consultation to the buyer, seller, or the arbitrator him- or herself or may render expert opinions in breach of representation litigation matters. The accountant may be asked to assist with:

- Evaluating the accounting transactions and policies and practices that underlie a balance sheet transaction and assisting in identifying relevant and appropriate GAAP or other applicable accounting standards, including any contractual adjustments required by the buy–sell agreement.
- Identifying potential issues that a party may choose to pursue in an objection to a closing statement forming the basis of a purchase price adjustment.
- Helping guide the arbitration process in terms of the quantity and quality of documents to be shared, the extent of interviews of witnesses, or the number of submissions by the parties.
- Assisting the buyer or the seller in documenting positions regarding the disputed issues and preparing one or more rebuttals. Although there is no standard format for these written submissions, professionals experienced with such disputes can help to convey the underlying issues and facts with clarity and express a party's view with persuasiveness. Crafting submissions that are articulate, well organized, and responsive to the facts and circumstances is critical to success.
- Providing expert testimony as needed. Because many buy–sell agreement disputes are resolved in ad hoc arbitration where the arbitrator is also an expert in accounting, formal expert testimony is not always necessary to explain a party's position. However, expert testimony may be necessary in some disputes, particularly where parties have brought the issues before a court of law. The accountant may be called in to explain the nature of certain provisions, such as typical purchase price adjustment provisions, to distinguish unusual financial features of the contract, or to explain the nature of underlying evidence and related facts and help judges and juries understand complex accounting and industry issues.

(iii) Bankruptcy. Bankruptcy matters may require an accountant's services for many different tasks. The role of the accountant and scope of services to be performed are influenced by the size of the company and by whether the accountant is working for the trustee, debtor in possession, secured creditors, or the creditors' committee(s).

Accountants for the debtor in possession may be asked to prepare analyses supporting the solvency or insolvency of the debtor, which may affect creditors' claims, recoveries, or security interests. Such accountants may also be involved in preparing prospective financial information filed with the U.S. Trustee's Office or used in negotiating plans of reorganization with the parties of interest. Another important role may require making analyses to support a debtor's use of cash collateral as well as analyses showing that adequate protection is available to the secured creditor.

An accountant for the creditors' committee, in addition to reviewing any analyses prepared for the debtor, will have additional responsibilities. The accountant initially may be asked to determine the cause for the business failure and may need to determine quickly whether the debtor's operation may be further depleting the assets available for creditors. The creditors' accountants may also need to investigate the conduct of the debtor. The scope and depth may vary significantly based on the relationship and confidence the creditors have with existing management. At a minimum, analyses to determine possible preferential payments, fraudulent conveyances, and insider transactions are usually performed. The roles, definitions, and exceptions to preferences and fraudulent conveyances are detailed in the Bankruptcy Code as well as in Newton.[1]

The work required to establish liability in bankruptcy cases revolves around the question of whether the debtor is liable for debts and/or claims expressed by various parties and classes of claimants. However, liability issues in bankruptcy have the benefit of explicit rules in the

[1] Grant W. Newton, *Bankruptcy and Insolvency Accounting*. 7th Ed. (Hoboken, NJ: John Wiley & Sons, 2010).

Bankruptcy Code (Title 11 USC, more specifically, Subsections 543–549). These sections of the Bankruptcy Code detail the powers of a trustee to avoid transfers that defraud, hinder, or delay creditors, give preferential treatment to certain creditors, or do not give the bankrupt person or entity fair value for the transfer. Since these Code sections define the scope of the trustee's power, an accountant engaged by the trustee should first read and understand the relevant provisions before planning the work. In addition, an accountant should obtain an understanding of certain sections of the Uniform Commercial Code and in particular the Uniform Fraudulent Transfer Act of the state in which the business is situated. The location of the business may influence the scope of the work since the time period under the bankruptcy statute allows for recovery only one year prior to the bankruptcy, whereas state laws vary from three to ten years.

Once the appropriate time period and scope have been determined, the accountant needs to review all material transactions to gain an understanding of the economic benefit of the exchange to the bankrupt party, including all monetary and nonmonetary exchanges. In addition, the accountant needs to determine the timing and explanation for any liens or other security interest granted or recorded during the time period. This review should include any asset sales, purchases, foreclosures, and tax assessments. Transactions between related entities or commonly controlled entities or their affiliates must be reviewed. In a bankruptcy case, the accountant is trying to develop any evidence that might show fraud or fraudulent intent.

A preferential payment analysis covers a review of transactions within 90 days for noninsiders and one year for insiders prior to filing for bankruptcy protection wherein a creditor is paid for an antecedent debt at a time the debtor is insolvent and such payment is not in the ordinary course of business. The definition of *insolvency* for this purpose is the fair value of assets compared with the fair value of liabilities—a balance sheet approach. *Ordinary course of business* is not defined except by reference to case precedents. For example, if creditors are routinely paid in 90 days but certain creditors get paid just before bankruptcy within 30 days, such payments are probably not in the ordinary course of business.

Certain leveraged buyouts (LBOs) have encountered financial difficulty shortly after consummation, and some creditors have used various security law and bankruptcy law theories to unwind these transactions and seek recoveries from selling shareholders, secured creditors, and others.

The accountant's work in helping establish or defend liability is critical. Analyses that show the cash flow of the entity before and after the LBO help establish whether sufficient capital or working capital was available to the company. Changes in a company's borrowing, especially where a significant amount of assets have been recently pledged, also illustrate the potential damage to unsecured creditors. The accountant's ability to distinguish operating losses caused by the form and structure of the buyout from losses due to the economy or other competing companies will also assist counsel in determining whether the LBO can be attacked as a fraudulent transfer. For a more detailed discussion on bankruptcy matters and issues, please refer to Chapter 39 of this *Handbook.*

(e) CALCULATING DAMAGES

(i) General Concepts. In proving liability, the plaintiff must demonstrate that the defendant's actions were in violation of the plaintiff's legal rights. In moving from liability to causation, the plaintiff must demonstrate that the illegal actions caused injury to the defendant; only then can damages be calculated. In discussing damages, accountants rely on the concept of the *but-for world.* The but-for world is the economic and physical environment that would have existed but for the actions of the defendant. In other words, it is the *undamaged* world, in contrast to the *actual,* damaged world that did occur and in which the defendant allegedly performed the claimed illegal acts.

(ii) Measuring Damages. Depending on the case, there are many standards by which damages are measured, including these four:

1. Lost profits (past profits, prospective profits, or both, including increased costs)
2. Lost asset value (the appraised value of identified assets, including goodwill, or other intangibles)

3. Lost personal earnings (wages, salary, etc.)
4. Lost royalties or licensing fees (amounts due for use of the plaintiff's assets or rights) or share of profits pursuant to participation agreements

In most cases, these approaches are all attempts to compute the difference between the but-for world and the actual world. That is, they attempt to measure the difference between what should have happened and what actually did happen.

Lost profits are the most common standard for business cases. Valuations are used in both business disputes and marital dissolution proceedings. Personal earnings are the damages standard for the economic component of personal injury suits. Other components are medical costs and pain and suffering. Reasonable royalty is used in intellectual property disputes, especially patent cases.

(iii) Mitigation. A plaintiff has the obligation to mitigate damages. This means that the plaintiff must take reasonable steps to minimize the damages suffered. More specifically, the courts (and damages experts or consultants) will compute damages as if the plaintiff mitigated, whether the mitigation really occurred or not.

In many cases, reasonable mitigation occurred, and the expert or consultant may look at the difference between what should have occurred and what did occur as the measure of damages. After all, the plaintiff's recovery through litigation is uncertain, and plaintiff has every incentive to reduce their damages. However, if reasonable mitigation did not occur, the accountant should consider what adjustments may be necessary.

(iv) Present Value and Inflation. Time is a factor in most damage claims. A violation typically occurs sometime prior to the loss suffered by the plaintiff; the loss can continue into the future (e.g., lost earnings in a personal injury case); the trial can occur either after the entire loss has been suffered or prior to the full recovery from the effects of the violation; and the award may not be paid until sometime after the trial. Thus, a damage award must compensate the plaintiff for both past and future losses, but it must be made in full at the present time. This requires that the accountant accumulate both past and future lost profits to the present. This accumulation is accomplished by discounting the projected lost profits to the date of violation using a rate of interest and compounding the resulting amount to the present at some prejudgment interest rate. The choice of discount rate depends on the circumstances. A nominal discount rate (such as the Treasury bill rate, the prime rate, or another market rate) includes both a real rate of interest and an inflation premium. If the damages into the future are computed in constant (uninflated) dollars, then discounting at a real rate (net of inflation) may be appropriate. If inflation has been built into the projected damage figures, a nominal interest rate is correct. In either case, the appropriate discount rate should include an adjustment for risk.

For more on determining the present value of a damage award, see Kabe and Blonder.[2]

(v) Income Taxes. Under the law, some damage awards are taxable to the recipient, whereas others are tax-free. In computing damages, the goal is to properly account for taxes so the plaintiff is in the same position as it would have been if the liability act had never occurred.

If the award is taxable, then the damages should be computed on a before-tax basis. The plaintiff then receives the damage award, pays taxes, and is in the proper after-tax position. If the amount is tax-free, only the after-tax amount should be assessed as damages.

Complications arise in the two areas: (1) if prejudgment interest is due, and (2) if tax rates have changed from the damage date to the payment date. As discussed, prejudgment interest is computed on the after-tax amount, since that is the amount the plaintiff would have had to invest. However, if the award is taxable, the damages must be expressed in pretax dollars. A reasonable approach

[2] Elo R. Kabe and Brian L. Blonder, "Discounting Concepts and Damages," in *Litigation Services Handbook,* 1996 Suppl., ed. Roman L. Weil, Michael J. Wagner, and Peter B. Frank (New York: John Wiley & Sons, 1996).

is to compute the entire award, including damages and interest, in after-tax dollars. Then gross up the award by the tax rate in the year of payment. When the plaintiff receives this amount and pays tax on it, plaintiff will be in the proper after-tax position. This approach, although accurate, has been relatively untested in court.

A similar situation arises if tax rates have changed. If pretax damages are used, the change in tax rates will result in an incorrect after-tax award. A reasonable approach is again to compute the after-tax amounts, then gross up the award for the current tax rate.

(f) SUPPORT FOR OPINIONS

(i) Sources of Information. The accountant acting as expert witness should have adequate data to authoritatively support opinions or conclusions. The data should be of high reliability since the accountant is subject to cross-examination.

There are two primary sources for data: the litigating parties (either the plaintiff or the defendant) and external sources, such as industry publications, economic statistics, and so on. The former is obtained through the discovery phase discussed previously. The latter is discussed here.

Many reference books list sources of business information. Also, computer databases are widely available and eliminate the need for data entry as the information can be downloaded into a computer file.

Often an accountant may need to call on other specialists or persons knowledgeable in the particular industry. These specialists may be found within a different practice area of the accountant's firm, or the accountant may need to obtain assistance from specialists outside his or her firm.

(ii) Reliance on Others. The accountant as an expert witness may rely on the work of employees as well as personal research or sources in forming his or her opinion. Federal Rule of Evidence No. 703 describes permissible bases on which expert testimony may be founded. These include: (1) information acquired through firsthand observation; (2) facts observed by, or presented to, the expert witness at the trial or at the hearing; and (3) data considered by the expert witness outside of court. Rule 703 permits an expert to rely on facts that are not normally admissible in evidence if they are of a type reasonably relied on by experts in the field. *Reasonably relied on* means *trustworthy*. *Type relied on* is left to the discretion of the trial judge. In turn, the judge may question the accountant-witness as to the appropriate degree of reliance.

(iii) Documentation. All materials prepared, accumulated, or referred to by the accountant acting as an expert witness in a case may have to be made available to the opposing side. At the outset, the attorney and accountant should develop a clear understanding of exactly what the accountant will be preparing and retaining for the engagement.

Then the accountant should carefully control the content of supporting documentation, collect relevant materials, and avoid collecting materials that are irrelevant to forming an opinion. Preparing documentation should be an ongoing process, as the accountant may not be able to remove anything after receiving a subpoena. All work products of an expert may be discoverable and could be thoroughly scrutinized by the opposing party. Any errors, inconsistencies, and irrelevant materials may form the basis for an effective challenge to the testimony of the accountant.

(g) TESTIMONY

(i) Giving Deposition Testimony. A deposition of an expert witness is part of the discovery process in which counsel seeks to fulfill several major objectives. The most obvious objective is to find out what opinions the expert is going to offer at trial, and why. A deposition is also an opportunity to commit the expert to sworn testimony that can be used later for impeachment purposes, should the expert try to change his or her opinion. Additionally, counsel will use the deposition to assess the expert's effectiveness as a witness and the strength of the case for purposes of settlement negotiation and development of trial strategy. Consequently, expert depositions may be more important than the trial testimony and should be regarded with due respect.

Adequate preparation is crucial to giving an effective deposition. Naturally, a thorough review of the expert's opinions and underlying support is in order. The expert should also review any prior writings and testimony for previous positions that may be construed as contradictory. Being caught unaware in an apparent contradiction can have a debilitating effect on the credibility of a deponent's testimony. The expert should know the information and sources relied on, the various analyses performed, the opinions reached, and the strengths as well as the weaknesses of the case. Above all, the expert should tell the truth.

Finally, the expert witness should insist on a detailed predeposition briefing with counsel. This briefing should include a conclusion regarding disclosure strategy. If the objective is to cause a settlement to occur, a complete disclosure of all the strengths of the case should be made. If the case is likely to proceed to trial, then a restrictive approach may be called for. For example, counsel may instruct the expert to be careful to answer the questions asked by opposing counsel very directly and to avoid volunteering any related issues.

(ii) Giving Trial Testimony. The following are phases of testimony in a trial situation.

- *Direct testimony.* The objective of direct testimony is to present an opinion in a manner such that it will be understood and believed by the judge and jury or other trier of fact. The testimony will begin by reviewing the witness's qualifications, which provide the prerequisite skill and training enabling the witness to provide the court with expert testimony. Opposing counsel will then have the opportunity to voir dire the expert and to challenge his or her qualifications as an expert. The judge will then decide whether the court will qualify the accountant as an expert. The expert's opinions then will be solicited. It is imperative that the expert not appear to be an advocate for the plaintiff or defendant but rather appear fair and unbiased. The job of advocacy should be reserved for the attorney. Violation of this precept will tend to undermine the expert's credibility. Finally, the basis for the expert's opinion will be presented. The engagement scope is reviewed, including who retained the expert and why, documents reviewed, interviews conducted, the engagement team, manner of supervision and time spent, compensation, and any engagement scope limitations imposed. Next, the methodology employed is explained, which leads to the conclusions and opinions reached. Typically, any weaknesses are acknowledged and explained in a preemptive fashion to reduce potential damage on cross-examination. The key to persuasive and effective testimony is communication. The expert's position may be a technical marvel, but it is worthless if the jury does not understand the testimony or is not convinced. Therefore, the expert should speak plain English and avoid technical accounting and financial jargon. Concepts should be explained by way of common, everyday occurrences. Condescending or patronizing speech is usually deemed inappropriate. The expert's job is to educate the jury and the court in an interesting fashion. This job can be facilitated by the use of and reference to trial exhibits. Trial exhibits are used to lead the jury, court, and the expert himself through the basis of the opinion, as well as to keep everyone's attention focused. As with the language used in testimony, the exhibits should be kept clear and simple so the point is clear and memorable. In many jurisdictions, the jury cannot take notes, and visual exhibits can be an effective way to impress the point or conclusion upon the jurors' memories.
- *Cross-examination.* The purpose of cross-examination is to cast doubt on or, if possible, undermine the expert witness's credibility and testimony. One of the simpler ways to accomplish this objective is through impeachment. Consequently, a thorough review of prior testimony, writings, and the deposition transcript is required. The expert must make sure not to be on record as holding a view that is or appears to be contrary to the one he is now presenting, or he or she must be able to provide an explanation.
- *Redirect examination.* The purpose of redirect examination is to rehabilitate points made by the witness and clarify responses and mischaracterizations. It is generally counterproductive to a witness's credibility to argue with opposing counsel or to resist answering questions that, to the jury, appear reasonable and straightforward. An evasive witness generally is a less credible witness. The expert is back in friendly hands during redirect, and this is the time to mitigate any real or perceived damage. During the redirect examination, the attorney will typically

select two or three areas where additional explanation is necessary to counter the points made on cross-examination. This is the witness's opportunity to clearly explain why the points made during cross-examination are irrelevant and have no bearing on the expert's opinion.

41.3 ACCOUNTANT'S ROLE IN INVESTIGATIONS AND COMPLIANCE MATTERS

Forensic accountants are increasingly involved in a wide variety of client issues and projects that go far beyond litigation and litigation consulting. Most prominently, accountants have a key role in conducting corporate investigations and in using many of the tools developed in the litigation support context to do so. However, accountants are also involved in compliance investigations and compliance consulting. For example, forensic accountants are often involved in antibribery investigations, anti–money laundering investigations and consulting, and antifraud consulting. They are also deeply involved in other corporate issues, such as the protection of intellectual property. Finally, due to the penetration of technology in the corporate world, accountants have helped lead the way in developing the field of forensic technology. Today, forensic accounting and forensic technology are intertwined.

(a) CORPORATE INVESTIGATIONS

(i) General/White Collar. Corporate investigations make up a growing field within the area of forensic accounting and cover a wide range of cases. Examples of fraud and white-collar crime cases are schemes by executives, employees, and customers to siphon funds from financial institutions for their personal use, check kiting, lapping, computer fraud, embezzlement, defense procurement fraud, costing fraud, schemes involving kickbacks, income tax frauds, charity and religious frauds, money laundering, insider trading cases, and fraudulent bankruptcy actions. Additional examples include investigations of *boiler-room* operations that solicit funds from investors based on promises of high investment return and Ponzi arrangements in which there are no real profits; instead, funds from new investors are used to pay investment returns to existing investors, giving the impression of profits.

The accountant's work in this area centers on investigating what happened and helping companies and their attorneys evaluate potential liability. After the investigation is completed, the accountant may be asked to quantify the amount of the loss attributable to the allegation.

The accountant will typically review and analyze many types of data, including correspondence, e-mail, text messages, blogs, journal entries, financial statements, and financial schedules. Many times the accountant commences his or her investigation with little or no detail as to the extent of the situation and must put the pieces of a puzzle together. Doing this involves developing and testing hypotheses throughout the investigation. Therefore, when reviewing documents and other data, it is important to keep an open mind and not dismiss any reasonable possibilities. Very often, an investigation in one area will lead to other problem areas.

Most corporate investigations take place in an adversarial environment. This is especially true in cases involving white-collar crime or fraud. The forensic accountant may conduct or assist the attorney in conducting interviews of relevant parties. Often the forensic accountant or attorney is attempting to obtain information from the persons who are the subject of the investigation and who may be attempting to conceal their activities. As such, the forensic accountant should maintain a high level of professional skepticism throughout the investigation.

Since the forensic accountant's investigation, work product, and findings may form the basis of evidence in a litigation case or prosecution, it is critical to understand the importance of obtaining and preserving evidence and seek guidance from the retaining attorney about such matters whenever necessary. In addition, the forensic accountant may have to coordinate his or her efforts with those of law enforcement officials who may have an interest in the matter.

The circumstances of each engagement are unique, and the forensic accountant or retaining attorney may need to engage other specialists or experts. Computer forensic specialists are frequently used in these types of cases to extract data from computer drives or to search the contents of computer disks using keyword searches. Private investigators can also be of great assistance in performing detailed background checks or surveillance of potential suspects.

In white-collar crime cases where Ponzi schemes are suspected, the accountant will want to document how the enterprise was structured and to develop organizational charts and flowcharts. Tracing transactions from the receipt of investor funds to their ultimate investment or disposition will be required. Analyses that illustrate the lack of any positive cash flow other than by raising additional investor funds can be useful to the attorney in proving liability. Documenting the flow of all cash transactions or custodial arrangements is within the accountant's scope. Today, visual analytics (including geospatial analytics) are often used to depict the flow of cash transactions. Working with data analytic professionals, the accountant can summarize the work performed and results found to date in a visual format; doing so often can provide more information in a shorter amount of time than the typical text representation.

The accountant should also analyze cash disbursements to see whether any patterns indicating self-dealing emerge and to help identify possible related entities or personal use or benefit of company assets. Unusual expenses should be vouched, and particular attention should be devoted to traditionally sensitive areas, such as travel and entertainment expenses. While some suspicious transactions are easily detected, such as employee fraud schemes involving payments to fake vendors, many illegal activities involve disguised transactions. Still, it is likely that things like paid bills and supporting evidence will be fairly self-explanatory.

In the case of a penny stock fraud scheme, the accountant may shift greater attention to the financial results and reports to shareholders, press releases, and the like to determine whether there is evidence that such public information is incorrect or inaccurate. Income recognition abuses or improper capitalization of expenses are typical categories of abuses used by penny stock promoters to misstate the operating results and mislead investors. In addition, the accountant should analyze key contracts, employment agreements, and other consulting arrangements. A timeline analysis that reflects all key "publicized events" should be developed and used to help determine whether such events did occur. The timeline can be used to analyze whether, in the same time frame, all acquisitions or dispositions of assets and other financial transactions were accounted for properly.

(ii) Securities Violations. Lawsuits in the area of securities violations usually involve alleged violations of the federal acts, specifically Sections 11 and 12(2) of the Securities Act of 1933 and Section 10(b) of the Securities Exchange Act of 1934. These sections are concerned with making false or misleading public statements about a company or omitting a material fact (either in a prospectus or in public statements, including financial statements), resulting in an alleged overvaluing of the company's stock. Plaintiffs claim that, but for the misleading statements, they would not have bought the stock or they would have bought the stock at a lower price. These lawsuits are often brought against officers, directors, investment bankers, lawyers, accountants, and others who may have been party to the misstatements.

Accountants may be accused of being involved in the liability, causation, and damages portions of securities cases. Involvement with liability issues is most common when there are allegations that the alleged fraud on the market was caused by the issuance of financial statements that were materially misstated or by the absence of important disclosures in the financial statements. On other occasions, an accounting firm may be a defendant accused of violating Section 10(b)5 by failing to perform an audit in accordance with generally accepted auditing standards (GAAS) and/or by giving a clean opinion to financial statements that do not conform to GAAP. Cases involving public company audits dated after the effective date of Public Company Accounting Oversight Board (PCAOB)[3] Auditing Standard No. 1, *References in Auditor's Reports to Standards of the Public Company Auditing Oversight Board,* will reference the standards of the PCAOB in lieu of GAAS. In these types of cases and investigations, the forensic accountant will review the auditor's workpapers and other relevant materials to analyze the adequacy of the audit of the financial statements within the context of the applicable professional standards.

[3] The PCAOB (*www.pcaobus.org*) is a nonprofit organization created by the Sarbanes-Oxley Act of 2002 to oversee the auditors of public companies.

The causation and damages phases of securities cases are closely linked. They consist of determining whether the information had any impact on the stock price and quantifying the losses suffered by the plaintiff investors as a result. Typically, the type of analysis performed by a forensic accountant involves determining what the stock price would have been if the proper information had been released at the proper time. The methods for doing this are beyond the scope of this chapter; see de Silva, Low, and Nells for a treatment of this subject.[4]

(b) ANTI–MONEY LAUNDERING. Money laundering is the criminal practice of illegally filtering money (or lawfully derived money intended to be used for illicit purposes) through a series of transactions to break the trail of ownership. Money laundering is a diverse and often complex process and most often plays a fundamental role in facilitating the ambitions of drug traffickers, terrorists, organized criminals, insider traders, and tax evaders as well as many others who need to avoid the kind of attention that "sudden" wealth brings. A professional money launderer is typically limited only by the breadth of his or her imagination. No business, whether it takes cash or operates under a strict no-cash policy, is immune from becoming the unwitting accomplice of the money launderer.

Accountants' anti–money laundering (AML) and Bank Secrecy Act (BSA) responsibilities vary depending on the clients they serve and the services they perform. In general, accountants and auditors who serve the financial services industry are the most affected by the AML/BSA requirements of their respective clients. Accountants providing services for clients—acting in a fiduciary capacity, for example—also need to be concerned about not running afoul of the money laundering criminal statutes by unknowingly participating in a money laundering scheme. The *willful blindness* theory of criminal liability could apply as well, as will be discussed, but an attorney should always be consulted on these issues.

Financial institutions, and certain other businesses such as casinos, broker-dealers, and others, are required under the BSA and USA Patriot Act to implement and maintain a program of controls to deter and detect money laundering and terrorist financing. These programs typically include:

- *Policies and procedures* to establish how an organization's AML controls are implemented, assigning responsibility for monitoring and maintaining controls, and helping ensure timely reporting of suspicious activity.
- *Know your customer (KYC) procedures and customer information program (CIP)* requirements that establish the process for understanding who the organization's customers are, what information is required to adequately identify the customer, as well as assessing the customer's risk profile and risk to the organization.
- *Transaction monitoring,* a key component of an effective AML program. Transaction monitoring is typically automated, either on a real-time (i.e., as transactions are occurring), or batched (e.g., daily, weekly, monthly, etc.) basis. Transaction monitoring seeks to identify unusual and/or potentially suspicious activity by applying a set of defined AML scenarios or rules against the transaction activity for each customer.
- *Suspicious activity reporting (SAR).* Once identified, suspicious activity must be reported within a specified number of days following identification. The Financial Crimes Enforcement Network (FinCEN), a department of the U.S. Treasury, is responsible for receiving and analyzing all SAR filings for all U.S. financial institutions.

In the course of providing accounting services to clients or in conducting an audit for a financial institution or a client, an accountant may find it necessary to:

- Exercise due diligence when performing client acceptance activities. Launderers may seek assistance from accounting professionals without the accountants fully realizing it. A client

[4] Harinda de Silva, Nancy N. Low, and Tara N. Nells, "Securities Act Violations: Estimation of Damages," in *Litigation Services Handbook: The Role of the Accountant as Expert,* ed. Roman L. Weil, Michael J. Wagner, and Peter B. Frank (New York: John Wiley & Sons, 1995).

may ask an accountant to wire funds to and from various bank accounts without giving any reasonable explanation, to make cash deposits in different financial institutions with amounts just under the $10,000 reporting requirement, or issue checks to clients or their vendors in return for cash.

- Perform audit procedures pursuant to the Financial Accounting Standards Board Statement of Auditing Standards (SAS) No. 54, *Illegal Acts by Clients,* to determine whether money laundering has taken place and to obtain a more detailed understanding of the questionable transactions, the business reasons behind the transactions, and the parties involved.
- Analyze findings in previous examination reports, in areas other than BSA compliance, for adequacy of internal controls and audit procedures. If prior internal control audits have significant or a large number of findings, this may be indicative of deficiencies in the AML compliance program.
- Report money laundering activities to the client's board of directors (Board) if the accountant believes that money laundering has occurred under the Private Securities Litigation Reform Act of 1995. The board is required to notify the Securities and Exchange Commission (SEC) within one day of being notified by the accountant. The Act further requires accountants to notify the SEC if the board does not do so.
- Express a qualified or adverse opinion on the financial statements if the accountant believes the consequences of money laundering have not been properly accounted for or disclosed in the company's financial statements in accordance with SAS No. 54.
- Resign if a client refuses to accept the auditor's modified report.
- Advise clients who become subject to asset forfeiture.
- Provide remediation advice to clients regarding Internal Revenue Service (IRS) Form W-8, acceptance of and reliance upon which has been disallowed by the IRS due to incompleteness or lack of appropriate treaty status claimed. Additionally, accountants may be called on to advise clients who may have incorrectly filed or failed to appropriately file IRS Form 8300 (Currency Transactions). Such advice might involve counseling or consulting with the client's legal counsel (for internal auditors) or other specialists.
- Estimate increased contingent liabilities for clients who become subject to AML-related litigation, particularly criminal actions.
- Advise on accrual methods for presumptive legal and regulatory penalties and fines.
- Seek professional advice whenever appropriate and consult with the client's legal counsel (for internal auditors) or other specialists.

Accountants may become inadvertently exposed to potential money laundering activities through the processing and evaluating of their clients' financial records and activities. Accountants are often viewed as "gatekeepers" for their clients' financial transactions and need to conduct appropriate risk-based due diligence. Accountants should consider attending periodic training on money laundering–related issues, including preventive techniques, and courses of action in cases where the clients are suspected to be involved in money laundering. One of the most effective steps an accountant can take to understand how the accounting profession can work with clients to help prevent money laundering is to become familiar with the Bank Secrecy Act and the USA PATRIOT Act. Additionally, accountants and auditors who focus on the financial services industry should have an awareness of the AML self-regulatory mechanisms proposed by industry organizations,[5] previous enforcement actions, and regulatory penalties.

Accountants should also be aware of the willful blindness concept and should always consult an attorney on this issue. *Willful blindness* means attempting to avoid criminal or civil liability for a wrongful act by intentionally putting oneself in a position to be unaware of facts that would render one otherwise liable. The government may charge accountants as accomplices to a money

[5] The New York Stock Exchange and the National Association of Securities Dealers, now collectively FINRA.

laundering crime. If the government is not able to prove the accountants' actual knowledge of criminal activities, the government may use the willful blindness argument sometimes employed by prosecuting attorneys.

(i) AML Technology. The accountant should leverage AML technology to support an organization's money laundering risk management undertaking. Such technology includes:

- Account behavior and transaction-monitoring software systems that capture suspicious data
- Systems that provide for analysis, investigation, and resolution
- Systems that produce SAR and currency transaction reports as well as monitor Office of Foreign Assets Control obligations and compliance with other sanctions programs

These technologies can provide organizations with the capability to effectively monitor the behavior of millions of client accounts and complex financial real-time and transactional activity, to identify potential unusual activity that may need further investigation, and to ensure the subsequent and timely reporting of suspicious activity to FinCEN or other jurisdictional regulatory authorities. In addition, these systems can provide an organization with the ability to define various types of potential suspicious activities based on customers' type of business, country of incorporation, transaction type, product, channel, time, and other dimensions that may be applicable to the business.

Because of the nature of the technologies in use, consultation with forensic technology specialists is generally required.

(c) FOREIGN CORRUPT PRACTICES ACT VIOLATIONS. In recent years, with the increasing globalization of business, U.S. regulators have focused on the conduct of businesses. Although it dates back from the post-Watergate era, the Foreign Corrupt Practices Act of 1977 (FCPA) has been the focal point for investigations of companies and for actions being taken by the U.S. Department of Justice (DOJ) and the SEC. The increasing number of FCPA investigations has been considerable over the past several years, resulting in potentially high civil penalties. Official corruption investigations have also been spurred, during the latter part of 2007 and in 2008, by some foreign governments taking actions in antibribery matters that parallel the types of investigations coming from the United States.

The FCPA's most critical parts are discussed next.

- The *antibribery provision* covers a wide array of prohibited actions by any U.S. individual or organization, as well as non-U.S. persons and entities within U.S. jurisdiction, including paying, offering to pay, or authorizing payments to foreign officials in order to secure an improper business advantage. In other words, companies, their employees, and their agents are prohibited from offering or authorizing anything of value, directly or through third parties, to foreign officials for the purpose of obtaining or retaining business. The Act is both a criminal statute enforced by the DOJ and a civil statute enforced by the SEC.
- The *accounting requirements*—also known as the books and records provisions—apply to public companies that are "issuers" of securities under the Exchange Act of 1934. The accounting provisions require that issuers (including foreign issuers) accurately record payments in their books and records detailing their financial transactions. The accounting provisions apply to U.S. issuers' domestic and foreign majority-owned subsidiaries.
- The *internal controls provision* requires companies to establish and maintain a system of internal controls that provide reasonable assurances that transactions are properly authorized and recorded and that companies do not make inappropriate payments to foreign officials. Companies must also make a good-faith effort to use their influence to cause entities (domestic and foreign) in which they hold a minority interest to devise and maintain an adequate system of controls.

Because the individuals involved with transactions that violate the FCPA often know the transaction is illegal, they will likely take precautions to hide the transaction, misrecord it, or move it off the financial records completely. Typical controls and processes rely on the accurate disclosure of the nature of a transaction, the truth of the underlying document, or primary approval. These assumptions may not be appropriate and may not catch what is purposely hidden. A different focus from normal internal audit or investigatory procedures may be called for as a result. Sifting through transactions looking for bribes has a needle-in-a-haystack aspect and makes sampling less effective than it is in an audit context. Not only do transactions need to be reviewed more comprehensively, but the investigator also needs to be aware of the ways in which bribes often are masked.

The forensic accountant's role in the course of an investigation into potential FCPA violations often includes analyzing electronic and hardcopy financial records and assisting counsel in conducting interviews of relevant personnel to help identify whether schemes exist and to understand how the schemes work, assess the scope of the violations, and report on findings. Accountants might also be called in to help their clients respond to specific allegations or requests that might not relate to wrongdoing on their part.

To review company records for the presence of schemes, accountants must inspect payable records, and especially journal entries regarding payables, including the text for such entries and words that mask the true purpose of the transaction (e.g., referring to a bribe as a *tuition payment*), employee expense records and reimbursements, and e-mails and other forms of corporate communication. Forensic accountants who typically do this work have at their disposal a wealth of knowledge about how schemes work and therefore a number of specific tests they employ to determine whether instances of schemes are present in transactions. Because the records of most companies are electronic these days, the forensic accountant usually works closely with forensic technologists who have developed deep knowledge of the major accounting systems and techniques for exploring the data in these systems.

(d) ANTIFRAUD PROGRAMS AND CONTROLS. With the advent of Auditing Standard (AS) No. 2, updated in AS No. 5, and the related SOX Section 404 guidance, the need for companies to implement an effective Antifraud Programs and Controls Framework (AFPC) has been reemphasized, particularly for public companies. For example, it is now clear that management has a responsibility to assess fraud risks for their organization utilizing "sound and thoughtful judgments that reflect a company's individual facts and circumstances."[6] An overall risk assessment that does not appropriately consider specific fraud risks to the organization is not compliant with current legislation and regulation. Further, current legislation and regulations emphasize the use of a top-down risk-based approach in the design and implementation of entity-level controls, the intent being that appropriately designed entity-level controls can reduce process-level testing.

A focus of the accountant as AFPC consultant is to understand whether corporate management is fulfilling its responsibilities and duties in a manner that reflects the underlying spirit, guidance, and requirements under AS No. 5, SAS No. 99, and SOX Section 404. Delivery of AFPC consulting services requires specialized training and experience. The practitioner must develop a thorough understanding of the client's antifraud program and make determinations as to the effectiveness of the program in terms of preventing and detecting fraud.

(i) AFPC Service Types. AFPC services generally fall into three broad categories that can be tailored to meet the needs of the engagement:

1. Assisting management with its design and implementation of an AFPC program or its components
2. Assessing the design and operating effectiveness of an organization's existing AFPC framework in order to aid management in meeting its responsibilities under SOX Section 404

[6] Securities and Exchange Commission, 17 CFR Part 241, *Commission Guidance Regarding Management's Report on Internal Control over Financial Reporting under Section 13(a) or 15(d) of the Securities Exchange Act of 1934; Final Rule,* p. 15.

3. Assisting the audit engagement team in assessing the design and operating effectiveness of an audit client's AFPC framework, in connection with assurance services, as required under SAS No. 99 and AS No. 5

The accountant can add value to the AFPC process by assisting clients in several specific ways, including:

- Assessing the client's antifraud programs and controls in each of the five main COSO (Committee of Sponsoring Organizations of the Treadway Commission; *www.coso.org*) areas, including:
  1. *Control environment.* Assessing the effectiveness of oversight provided by the audit committee and the board, evaluating the code of conduct/ethics, assessing the effectiveness of the whistleblower hotline and incident reporting within the entity, assessing the effectiveness of the entity's investigation and remediation processes, assessing the client's hiring and promotion procedures in terms of fraud risk and other control environment considerations
  2. *Risk assessment.* Evaluating the client's approach and fraud risk assessment, assisting in the client's fraud risk assessment implementation, and providing training in the fraud risk assessment process
  3. *Control activities.* Considering the linkage of control activities the entity has identified as being antifraud in nature and assessing the effectiveness of those controls
  4. *Information and communication.* Assessing the client's approach to fraud training, assessing knowledge and records management around fraud, evaluating data and system security and antifraud measures
  5. *Monitoring.* Evaluating the effectiveness and extent of monitoring activities by management and internal audit
- Assisting in the company's fraud risk assessment
- Providing fraud awareness training to client personnel

For non–Section 404 attest clients, especially those considering a future initial public offering, the AFPC team can also add value by conducting a formal assessment of the client's antifraud programs and controls with the goal of providing a road map of required steps toward SOX readiness.

(e) LICENSING AND CONTRACT INVESTIGATIONS. Protecting company assets, particularly intellectual property, and securing the global supply chain has become a strategic initiative for companies entering into contracts with other entities through joint ventures; profit sharing; patent, trademark, and copyright licensing; or distribution transactions. Corporations may have entered into production/distribution agreements with an international partner or into licensing contracts with global manufacturers of consumer products. In these situations, effective management of revenues and costs involving other entities can help protect a company's return on investment and bottom-line profits. In addition, specific industry knowledge is particularly important with respect to investigations involving contracts among the parties.

An accountant may be called in to assist in these matters by providing services, including:

- Conducting investigations to help clients evaluate whether they have been paid properly pursuant to their agreements and, if not, providing analyses to help quantify potential discrepancies
- Providing forensic services aimed at detecting and quantifying:
  - Unpaid royalties, understated joint venture profits, and unreported revenue streams
  - Inaccurate calculations of royalties payable
  - Overstatements of joint venture costs

- Helping clients understand financial implications related to licensing, co-promotion, and joint venture partners and the interpretations of financial calculations in the relevant agreements
- Assisting in evaluating business transactions, helping to identify potential transaction partners, and assessing the relative merits of various forms of compensation, including up-front payments, ongoing royalties, cross-licenses, and strategic partnerships
- Assisting in developing processes that could help reduce the risk of revenue loss and identify unauthorized use of licensed intellectual property
- Facilitating or assisting settlement negotiations regarding financial aspects of the agreements and damage calculations
- Helping develop the financial, accounting, and auditing provisions in licensing/profit sharing/distribution agreements
- Helping clients establish royalty rates for various technologies

(f) FORENSIC TECHNOLOGY. Business records today are largely kept in electronic form. Most companies generate and maintain corporate correspondence, corporate policies and procedures, compliance and governance records, records of transactions, manufacturing records, accounting ledgers, employee records, records of services, and so on in computerized format. The information forensic accountants need to do their work, whether the context is dispute resolution or investigations, is therefore increasingly electronic. An entire business dispute or multimillion-dollar litigation may hinge on identifying when a single piece of data was generated—or altered or deleted—by whom, and under what circumstances, or on a demonstration that no data were altered or deleted. Similarly, anti–money laundering investigations and investigations based on corruption allegations require the ability to sift through huge numbers of transactions to confirm or disconfirm the presence of money laundering transactions or bribes—the proverbial needle-in-a-haystack problem. Not only must various forms of computer technology be available to the forensic accountant to perform tests and development opinions, but forensic accountants must be skilled in how to most effectively used the technology. Simply put, the accountant must have the ability to acquire the information in a forensically sound manner and to analyze it. With the growing number of international and domestic data privacy and security regulations, forensic accountants and data management professionals need to identify and understand such regulations before obtaining, transferring, or processing data. Inasmuch as the web of data privacy laws is quickly growing very complex, it may be advisable to seek outside assistance in this regard,

(i) Computer Forensics. Computer forensics is the science of retrieving and chronicling evidence located on computers, disks, tapes, thumb drives, voicemail systems—any form of electronically stored information for use as evidence in a court of law, or in an investigation, or in a compliance context. The practice of computer forensics includes the use of formal, accepted techniques for collecting, analyzing, and presenting suspect data in court, concentrating on rules of evidence, the legal processes, the integrity and perpetuity of evidence, reporting of facts, and the preparation and presentation of expert testimony. The same disciplined collection techniques are used in investigations where the key issues are the same—demonstrating that there was no bias in the collection of information, that the information was not altered in the collection process, and that the chain of custody was maintained.

A wealth of information may be recoverable from computer hard drives and backup tapes, including active, deleted, hidden, lost, or encrypted files or file fragments. Even files that were created but never saved may be recovered. In addition to collecting information for litigation consulting and investigations, computer forensic specialists are also called on to analyze information technology systems for evidence of potential malfeasance, such as information deletion, policy violations, or unauthorized access. The process used by a computer forensic specialist often involves taking an image or exact replica of the hard drive, which is preserved in a locked, fireproof safe for evidentiary and chain-of-custody purposes. Diagnostic software tools are then run against copies of the image to search for the existence of relevant files. Paper documents still play a significant role in many litigation matters. Computer forensics may also be used to compare paper documents with their electronic counterparts to help determine whether the document has been altered.

After collecting information, computer forensics professionals can then look for e-mails, documents, spreadsheet files, Web downloads, and other electronic data that may have been deleted or encrypted or may exist only in fragments. Such bits and pieces of data can have tremendous value in an investigation.

An accountant may be tasked with leading cases or investigations involving computer forensics or may assist counsel in the investigatory process of preserving, collecting, processing, and reviewing data. The accountant's role may include providing assistance with:

- Identifying the "trigger" that initiated the investigation (e.g., a document, an e-mail, a spreadsheet) and ensuring that the computer or information technology systems involved are secured to prevent tampering or deleting evidence.
- Defining the scope and timeline of the investigation, considering complexities such as locations involved, global regions, type of accounting systems in use, language barriers, and the like. Because the very act of investigating often can reveal more layers of data and avenues to explore, scope creep is a common problem. Tightly defining the project parameters and specific tasks to be accomplished can help control creep.
- Identifying and prioritizing individuals involved, particularly the custodians (i.e., owners or creators) of data in question, and interviewing them as needed.
- Engaging and consulting with computer forensics specialists to collect data and verify that the collection was done correctly and that a defensible chain of custody was maintained.
- Providing micro or macro financial analyses as needed, such as analyzing recovered files or assessing the situation in the context of the organization's broader financial picture.

(ii) Data Analysis. After data are collected, computer technology is also required to analyze them. Data analysis takes two principal forms: (1) Textual information is put into discovery databases so it can be explored by the forensic accountant and other members of the litigation or investigation team. The process and role of such databases is discussed fully in Chapter 42; (2) numeric information, such as accounting transaction data, is usually put into relational database management systems so that it can be ordered into patterns. Various analyses can be performed on the data, such as date analysis or analysis by type of transaction, or the database can be searched for particular types of transactions, such as those that may be in violation of the FCPA requirements. The data analysis component of litigation and investigations often can help put together pieces of the litigation puzzle by searching, analyzing, and modeling data obtained as part of the discovery process. Data can be obtained from various sources including accounting systems (such as SAP, Oracle Financials, etc.), manufacturing systems, human resource and payroll systems, billing systems, customer relationship management systems, spreadsheets, and more. Individuals' personal files and folders are also open to scrutiny.

Leveraging data analysis to support the accounting investigation can yield several advantages, including the ability to:

- Extract and restore data from the original (native) format, which reduces the risk of working with potentially manipulated data.
- Maintain and process data in a secure environment.
- Summarize data for reconciliation to financial or system reports to check for completeness.
- Use visual analytic techniques to explore data points visually and depict investigation results. This can include dashboard-type reports, interactive graphs, and social networking diagrams.
- Search and analyze the entire population of data for anomalies to identify a smaller set of exceptions for detailed review.

- Piece together data from different sources to create a coherent understanding of past transactions (e.g., bringing contract, payment, shipping, and banking records together to identify the full history of transactions).
- Obtain faster access to information by electronically processing large volumes of data, given that speed and accuracy are essential in a litigation case.
- Perform advanced keyword and pattern searches, including handling foreign languages.
- Compare data from various systems potentially in different formats (e.g., matching vendor names, addresses, bank accounts, etc., from the payables ledger to the employee master and payroll system) to identify potential nonobvious relationships among parties.
- Build complex data models to analyze patterns, predict behavior, and efficiently reperform various analyses by manipulating the data parameters to test different scenarios.

The forensic accountant plays an active role in the data analysis process, particularly in defining tests, performing various forms of data reconciliation (such as reconciling general ledger data to the financial statements), assisting with the development of keywords for searching, developing anomaly detection tests in AML and FCPA contexts, and reviewing and interpreting analysis results for potentially responsive or hot transactions.

Given the specialized skills required to manipulate various database systems, understand the client's business processes, load the data into a platform for analysis, and develop and generate programs for analysis, it is advisable for the forensic accountant to work closely with a practitioner who specializes in data analysis. The background of such professionals typically includes an understanding of relational database systems, knowledge of financial information, and appropriate computer programming skills.

41.4 GLOBALIZATION IMPACT

(a) INTERNATIONAL FINANCIAL REPORTING STANDARDS. Increasingly, forensic accountants must focus on globalization, including in regard to accounting principles. International Financial Reporting Standards (IFRS) is a single set of accounting principles that is more focused on objectives and principles and less reliant on detailed rules than U.S. GAAP. With more than 100 countries and approximately 40 percent of the Global Fortune 500 companies already using IFRS, and with the SEC expected to push for allowing U.S. multinationals to use IFRS,[7] this expanded use of IFRS will be an important challenge for the accounting profession. In addition, U.S. public companies likely will have the option of using either IFRS or U.S. GAAP. IFRS requires more use of professional judgment and provides less detailed, principles-based guidance. It focuses on reflecting "economic reality." Many U.S. public companies will face the challenge of converting their books and records and financial reporting obligations to IFRS and may face future litigation issues as a result. In addition, any other litigation issues currently accounted for under U.S. GAAP will translate into IFRS issues.

(b) U.K. ANTICORRUPTION AND BRIBERY LAWS. The Serious Fraud Office is an agency of Her Majesty's Government in the United Kingdom. It was established in 1988 to assist in enforcement of the Criminal Justice Act 1987. The mandate of the agency has been to investigate and prosecute serious and complex crimes. It does this through special powers afforded it by the Criminal Justice Act.

In 2010, U.K. Parliament passed the Bribery Act, which, while similar in nature to the U.S. Foreign Corrupt Practices Act, has distinct differences. The Act delegates the decision to prosecute to the director of those agencies that report to the attorney general. At the time of writing, those

---

[7] Foreign registrants can already use IFRS for filings.

agencies are the Serious Fraud Office and the Crown Prosecution Services. The Crown Prosecution Services is primarily a prosecution agency and relies heavily on the nation's police forces to assist. The Serious Fraud Office is unique as it is the only U.K. law enforcement agency that carries out both investigations and prosecutions.

One key difference between the FCPA and the U.K. Bribery Act is the scope and reach of the Bribery Act. The Act provides for wide extraterritorial jurisdiction, which enables prosecution of alien persons or corporations with only a "close connection"[8] to the United Kingdom. Similarly, the Act does not provide for facilitation payments; in fact, guidance issued by the director of the Serious Fraud Office clearly states that any such payments are illegal. Penalties under this Act are unlimited fine and/or up to 10 years' imprisonment.

[8] A person has a close connection with the United Kingdom if, at the time of the act in questions the person was a British citizen, a British overseas territories citizen, a British Overseas citizen, a person who under the British Nationality Act 1981 was a British subject, a British protected person within the meaning of that Act, an individual ordinarily resident in the United Kingdom, a body incorporated under the law of any part of the United Kingdom, or a Scottish partnership.

CHAPTER 42

INTRODUCTION TO E-DISCOVERY

Jack Moorman
PricewaterhouseCoopers LLP

Greg Schaffer
PricewaterhouseCoopers LLP

42.1 COMPUTERS? NOW, THAT CHANGES EVERYTHING! 2

42.2 SHIFT TO DIGITAL DATA STORAGE AND COMMUNICATION 2

42.3 INCREASING DATA VOLUMES 2

42.4 INCREASED VALUE OF DIGITAL DATA 3

42.5 GOING AFTER EVIDENCE 3

42.6 THE LEGAL SETTING 3

42.7 TODAY'S USE OF ELECTRONIC DISCOVERY TECHNIQUES 6

42.8 MORE/BETTER SUBSTANTIVE INFORMATION (METADATA) 6

42.9 AUDIT TRAILS (TRAFFIC DATA) 7

42.10 FASTER/BETTER/CHEAPER 7

42.11 ROLE OF COMPUTER FORENSICS 8

42.12 EVIDENCE PRESERVATION 8

42.13 PHYSICAL IMAGING VERSUS LOGICAL BACKUPS 8

42.14 FORENSIC RECORDKEEPING 9

42.15 ACQUISITION NOTES 10

42.16 CHAIN-OF-CUSTODY DOCUMENTATION 10

42.17 ANALYSIS WORKPAPERS 11

42.18 GET THE "WHOLE ENCHILADA" 11

42.19 EVIDENCE DISCOVERY 12

- (a) De-Duplication 12
- (b) Data Sorting 13
  - (i) Date/Time 13
  - (ii) Owner/Author 14
  - (iii) File Types/Extension 14

42.20 DATA SEARCHING 14

- (a) Key Word Searches 15
- (b) Known File Searches (Hash Values) 15

42.21 DELETED/SLACK/UNALLOCATED SPACE 15

42.22 CONCLUSION 16

This chapter was minimally updated for this edition by the editor. It is scheduled to be revised and fully updated in the next *Supplement* to the 12th Edition of the *Handbook*.

42.1 COMPUTERS? NOW, THAT CHANGES EVERYTHING!

At the beginning of the information age, computers were not likely targets for the interests of lawyers or courtrooms. Indeed, their use was so cumbersome that only the most complex mathematical problems were addressed via these room-size, punch-card-reading behemoths. These machines "crunched numbers" and were not particularly useful for anything else. Needless to say, the integration of computers into society has come a very long way. While visionaries and science fiction writers continue to imagine a world in which computers are even more intertwined with the day-to-day lives of human beings, it is evident that the business world is utterly dependent on computers today.

Whether you support this reality (carrying cell phone, personal digital assistant, and wireless network card clipped to your belt or tucked in your purse) or eschew it (clinging to the dictation and shorthand world only recently abandoned by the rest of us), one thing is clear: There is no turning back. Although the predictions of a paperless world have never quite come to pass, the computer has changed the way society conducts its business in fundamental ways. These changes make it nearly impossible to run the world without the assistance of silicon chips, keyboards, and hard drives (or the next generation of computing technology that is likely to replace these devices with something that is faster, better, and cheaper).

42.2 SHIFT TO DIGITAL DATA STORAGE AND COMMUNICATION

With the advent of computers, one of the key changes has been the shift to digital storage of virtually everything we create. One hundred years ago the intellectual property of our societies was primarily stored on a single medium: paper. Moreover, it was stored in the most analog of analog forms: handwriting. Handwriting is distinct and variable from person to person. The ability to read and correctly understand every word in a letter, for instance, especially one that had traveled for weeks from one location to another, was questionable at best.

Today we can store and reliably reproduce virtually any form of intellectual property, from music to photographs to manuscripts to handwritten notes, in a digital format that can be reliably and perfectly reproduced at virtually any location on the globe almost instantly. Ben Franklin, a forward thinker in his time, could not have imagined the possibility, but today's four-year-olds, armed with broadband access to the Internet and a parent on business travel, cannot imagine a world without such wonders.

And because we can perform these acts, once considered miracles or magic, with such ease, we do take advantage of the technologies that are available to us, eagerly and often. For example, statistics from the Radicati Group (April 2010) estimate the number of emails sent per day to be around 294 billion.[1] Studies have shown that as much as 93 percent of a modern society's intellectual output is stored digitally.

42.3 INCREASING DATA VOLUMES

It is not just the storage and distribution of data that have changed; it is also our access to it. Imagine what would have been necessary years ago if you wanted to maintain ready access to the amount of data stored on an average desktop computer on sale at any office supply store in United States today (say with a 40-gigabyte hard drive). First, you would have needed a warehouse. Forty gigabytes of data are roughly equivalent to 6 million printed pages.[2] Your basic small-town library probably does not store as much information in analog form. Second, like that library, you would need a staff of employees to index, catalog, and maintain the data over time. Now imagine the data stored on a small business's network of 40 personal computers (PCs) and 3 servers. Your

---

[1] *http://email.about.com/od/emailtrivia/f/emails_per_day.htm*

[2] Based on Microsoft Word document format.

small-town library is now more like the entire library system of a major metropolitan city. And now consider the data stored on a Fortune 100 company's network with literally tens of thousands of desktop and laptop computers and thousands of servers, many with huge storage arrays of disk drives. The U.S. Library of Congress, with its analog collection of more than 120 million items on approximately 530 miles of bookshelves, would never fill this much storage space.[3]

The simple truth is that, as a society, we are pack rats, retaining as much as we can within the limits of our storage capacity. As that capacity has increased through the availability of ever-cheaper digital storage technologies, our tendency not to throw things away has taken over. The bottom line is that we could not manage the data we have stored today without the benefit of the digital technologies we have developed for that storage.

42.4 INCREASED VALUE OF DIGITAL DATA

It should not be surprising to learn that the value of our digital data is enormous. In our increasingly service-oriented economy, our ideas are often more valuable than the things they are designed to enable. Imagine the mining company that develops new methodologies for extracting ore from stone but owns very little ore-bearing land. The methodology, stored as zeros and ones on a hard drive thousands of miles away from any precious gems, may be worth far more than the inventing company's mining results. And this scenario is repeated time and again in American businesses in every sector of the economy.

42.5 GOING AFTER EVIDENCE

With so much valuable information stored on computer systems, and so much of our vital communications passing through computer networks, it is no surprise that our massive communication and storage networks are the target of attorneys looking for proof to support their positions when businesses find themselves in complex commercial disputes. Lawyers increasingly engage in electronic discovery for a simple, straightforward reason: because that is where the data are. And it is not just more of the same data once available to counsel in analog form. Electronically stored information has some special properties that in many ways make it a better source of proof. An understanding of the tools and techniques of computer forensics practitioners can provide an attorney with a wealth of information to review that would otherwise be unavailable. And in a litigation setting, more information is generally a good thing (especially if the information is about the other side).

42.6 THE LEGAL SETTING

The Federal Rules of Civil Procedure (FRCP) make it clear that this wealth of information is generally discoverable but provide certain limitations. For instance, Rule 26(b)(1) of the FRCP specifies that "any matter, not privileged, that is relevant to the claim or defense of any party" is discoverable. Rule 34 provides a mechanism, "the discovery request," that permits service by one party on another of a request for documents:

> Any party may serve on any other party a request (1) to produce and permit the party making the request, or someone acting on the requestor's behalf, to inspect and copy, any designated documents.

---

[3] Of course, today the Library of Congress also stores a sizable amount of digital data on its own very extensive computer network.

The definition of what constitutes a document was extended to include electronic documents in the 1970 amendments to Rule 34 of the FRCP.[4] Indeed; the federal courts have been in agreement for years that electronic data are discoverable. For instance, in 1995 the Federal District Court for the Southern District of New York wrote: "it is black letter law that computerized data is discoverable if relevant";[5] as early as 1985, the Federal District Court for the Central District of Utah had declared that "information in computers should be [as] freely discoverable as information not stored in computers";[6] and the Federal District Court for the Southern District of Indiana reiterated this point in 2000: "[C]omputer records ... are documents discoverable under Fed. R. Civ. P. 34."[7] Although discoverable, electronic documents face the same limitations under the FRCP as do paper documents. Rule 26(b)(2) limits discovery where:

> (i) the discovery sought is unreasonably cumulative or duplicative, or is obtainable from some other source that is more convenient, less burdensome, or less expensive; (ii) the party seeking discovery has had ample opportunity by discovery in the action to obtain the information sought; or (iii) the burden or expense of the proposed discovery outweighs its likely benefit, taking into account the needs of the case, the amount in controversy, the parties' resources, the importance of the issues at stake in the litigation, and the importance of the proposed discovery in resolving the issues.

As the three sections of FRCP 26(b)(2) clearly indicate, a host of factors come into play when making and responding to a discovery request. Suffice it to say that the common law duty to preserve evidence that may be relevant to pending or threatened litigation provides fertile ground for the requesting side to seek to preserve and discover evidence through preservation orders, motions to compel, motions for sanctions, and so on. This places a burden on the responding side, but respondents can attack the request on several fronts, such as relevancy, unreasonably cumulative or duplicative, overly broad, and unduly burdensome. Oftentimes, this leads to legal haggling that can take weeks, months, or years to play out. However, the courts are becoming increasingly sophisticated in dealing with electronic discovery requests and disputes. As a practical matter, there is broad consensus that "the preservation and production of electronic data and documents" should be discussed by the parties, and agreements reached to the extent possible, during their conference under Rule 26(f), if not sooner.[8]

One of the key issues being addressed in cases involving digital evidence regards the question of cost shifting; which party should bear the expenses associated with various aspects of the electronic discovery process? As United States District Judge Shira A. Scheindlin wrote in *Zubulake v. UBS Warburg LLC,* 2003 U.S. Dist. LEXIS 12643 (S.D.N.Y. July 24, 2003), the "presumption is that the responding party must bear the expense of complying with discovery requests," and requests that run afoul of the Rule 26(b)(2) proportionality test may subject the requesting party to protective orders under Rule 26(c), "including orders conditioning discovery on the requesting party's payment of the costs of discovery." A court will order such a cost-shifting protective order only on a motion

---

[4] The Advisory Committee Notes for the 1970 amendments to the FRCP reflect the inclusive nature of the term *document:* The inclusive description of "documents" is revised according with changing technology. It makes clear that Rule 34 applies to electronic data compilations from which information can be obtained only from detection devices, and that when data can, as a practical matter, be made usable by the discovering party only through the respondent's devices, respondent may be required to use his devices to translate the data into usable form.

[5] *Anti-Monopoly, Inc. v. Hasbro, Inc.,* 94 CIV 2120, 1995 WL 649934, at *2 (S.D.N.Y. Nov. 3, 1995).

[6] *Bills v. Connect Corp.,* 108 F.R.D 459 (C.D. Utah 1985).

[7] *Cf. Simon Property Group L. P. v. my Simon,* 194 F.R.D. 639, 640 (S.D. Ind. 2000).

[8] *Observations on "The Sedona Principles,"* John L. Carroll and Kenneth J. Withers. Item 61 at *www.thesedonaconference.org/content/miscFiles/publications_html*. Also see current reference: The Sedona Conference® International Principles on Discovery, Disclosure & Data Protection: Best Practices, Recommendations & Principles for Addressing the Preservation & Discovery of Protected Data in U.S. Litigation (European Union Edition, Public Comment Version, December 2011), at *www.thesedonaconference.org/*

of the responding party to a discovery request, and for good cause shown.[9] In *Zubulake,* Judge Scheindlin distinguished accessible electronic data from *inaccessible* data and held that cost shifting is "potentially appropriate only when *inaccessible* data is sought."[10] *Zubulake* sets forth a seven-factor test to determine if costs should be shifted to the requesting party when inaccessible data are sought in discovery. In doing so, Judge Scheindlin reversed the trend (as she saw it[11]) of cost shifting to favor the responding party as articulated in *Rowe Entertainment, Inc. v. William Morris Agency, Inc.*[12] The cornerstone of the seven-factor test in *Zubulake* is the marginal utility test announced in *McPeek v. Ashcroft:*

> The more likely it is that the backup tape contains information that is relevant to a claim or defense, the fairer it is that the [responding party] search at its own expense. The less likely it is, the more unjust it would be to make the [responding party] search at its own expense. The difference is "at the margin."[13]

Employment of the seven-factor test should reduce the frequency of fishing-expedition electronic discovery requests since the costs of such endeavors are more likely to be shifted to the requesting party. However, before the court can apply the test, it must have a factual basis on which to opine. In determining that basis, the court may consider, as in *Zubulake,* sampling a subset of the available universe of electronic data or other measures intended to determine the probative value of the requested materials and the likely costs of comprehensive retrieval, review, and production.[14]

Zubulake further points out that inaccessible data (i.e., backup tapes) can be quite expensive to restore, but once restored, they should be considered as readily accessible as any other data. Consequently, *Zubulake* also establishes this rule:

> The responding party should always bear the cost of reviewing and producing electronic data once it has been converted to an accessible form.[15]

Thus, under *Zubulake,* cost shifting is generally not appropriate where the responding party has ready access to information in databases, e-mail systems, or other on-line electronic storage mechanisms. And post-*Zubulake,* accessible data presumably includes e-mails and other files restored from less accessible media such as backup tape, even when such restoration was conducted for purposes of e-discovery in another litigation matter. Since Judge Scheindlin is considered knowledgeable in the area and is from the influential Southern District of New York, *Zubulake* is likely to influence other courts.[16] This will also have a significant impact on the electronic discovery marketplace, making the subject of this chapter all the more topical. Since there is no end in sight

---

[9] *Zubulake v. UBS Warburg LLC,* 2003 U.S. Dist. LEXIS 12643 (S.D.N.Y. July 24, 2003), also quoting *Oppenheimer Fund, Inc. v. Sanders,* 437 U.S. 340, 358 (1978).

[10] See *Zubulake I,* 2003 WL 21087884, at *12 ("A court should consider cost-shifting only when electronic data is relatively inaccessible, such as in back-up tapes.").

[11] See *Zubulake I,* 2003 WL 21087884, at *7 ("Courts must remember that cost-shifting may effectively end discovery, especially when private parties are engaged in litigation with large corporations. As large companies increasingly move to entirely paper-free environments, the frequent use of cost-shifting will have the effect of crippling discovery in discrimination and retaliation cases. This will both undermine the 'strong public policy favoring resolving disputes on their merits,' and may ultimately deter the filing of potentially meritorious claims.").

[12] 205 F.R.D. 421, 429 (S.D.N.Y.), *aff'd* 2002 WL 975713 (S.D.N.Y. May 9, 2002).

[13] 202 F.R.D. 31, 34 (D.D.C. 2001).

[14] See *Zubulake I,* Id. at *13.

[15] *Zubulake v. UBS Warburg LLC,* 2003 U.S. Dist. LEXIS 12643 (S.D.N.Y. July 24, 2003), at 26.

[16] Indeed, a recent Federal District Court opinion from the Northern District of California, (*Open TV vs. Liberate Technologies,* C 02 0655 JSW (MEJ), decided November 18, 2003) adopted and applied the *Zubulake* seven-factor test to determine if cost shifting should be applied to a request for production of computer source code stored in electronic form.

to the need for electronic discovery services, there will likely be a continued push for better, faster, and cheaper[17] electronic discovery tools and a need for best practices standards.

42.7 TODAY'S USE OF ELECTRONIC DISCOVERY TECHNIQUES

Today the use of electronic discovery techniques is still generally limited to certain classes of cases, typically those that do not suffer from what is sometimes referred to as the *reciprocity is hell* problem. The fact is that a lack of understanding of the costs and benefits of modern forensic processes has led many lawyers to believe that making an electronic discovery request is like launching a thermonuclear attack against your opponent. In other words, they believe their opponent will respond in kind, leading to mutually assured destruction through huge processing costs. This has meant that most electronic discovery requests today are being made by government prosecutors, regulatory agencies, and class action plaintiff's counsel. These are parties that generally do not have significant relevant electronically stored data that can be requested by their opponents. It also means that the requests are usually quite broad, since these litigants are not concerned about in-kind responses. In the end, this situation has perpetuated the perception that electronic discovery is expensive and dangerous in the typical company versus company litigation.

The truth is that electronic discovery has come a long way. As the case law makes clear, and as this chapter highlights, there are significant amounts of information to be gained through electronic discovery that are not available anywhere else. Moreover, the processes and procedures employed by computer forensic practitioners today can dramatically reduce the overall cost of the discovery process, especially in large cases. Finally, as many attorneys who have dipped their toes into the electronic discovery waters have learned, "there's gold in them there pools."

42.8 MORE/BETTER SUBSTANTIVE INFORMATION (METADATA)

Metadata are prime examples of the benefits of working with electronic evidence. Imagine two litigators working the same case, one based only on paper evidence, one working with the original electronic files that were the source of the paper documents found in the company's files. There can be little question which lawyer will have the better set of data to work with.

When computers store information for later retrieval, the operating systems necessarily create certain data about the stored information in order to facilitate ongoing processing. Such information typically includes the name of the file being stored (e.g., alternateAR.xls), the date the file was created and last modified, and the size of the file.

Many programs automatically add other metadata to the file, such as the type of file being stored, the location the file was stored to, the name of the author, the name of the person who last saved the file, and the number of revisions the file has gone through. Some programs also allow users to add their own metadata to a file, such as a document title, the subject of the file, the name of the author of the document, the name of the manager responsible for the document, and the name of the company that owns the document.

Some programs permit a user to assign metadata to a document in order to facilitate later retrieval. This type of metadata can include assignment of the document to a particular category (i.e., "supplier contract" or "workflow protocol"), inclusion of searchable key words, or a description of the document's contents.

In addition to these explicit types of metadata, there are other variations that are less obvious. For example, spreadsheets and databases can contain complex mathematical formulas and links among fields that are responsible for calculation of the numbers that appear in various cells. Typically the printed spreadsheet will show only the result of the calculation, not the formula that was used to calculate the result. Similarly, modern word processing documents can contain links and references

[17] See Section 42.10.

to various types of other electronic files, such as pictures, charts, spreadsheets, and sound files. These linked files may be stored in the same location as the main document or halfway around the world on another computer linked by a proprietary network or the Internet. The printed document may show the content of the other files without revealing that the content is not part of the printed document at all, but rather just linked data. The electronic document will necessarily contain the code needed to connect to the data in the linked files and may give an investigator pointers to additional sources of relevant information. This in turn may lead to additional witnesses, such as the author of the linked document in the remote—and heretofore undisclosed—location.

The key thing about all of this metadata, or data about the files, is that none of it typically appears on the page when the files are printed to paper or converted to an image format such as a TIFF or PDF file.[18] There can be no question that access to this additional information will be useful to anyone investigating alleged misconduct.

42.9 AUDIT TRAILS (TRAFFIC DATA)

In addition to the metadata created at the file level, many computer systems generate significant amounts of traffic data when information is manipulated within a computer or across a computer network. This traffic data, often referred to as *audit trails,* can be particularly useful when trying to tie activity back to a particular user or set of users. Imagine finding a smoking-gun document describing a planned fraud sitting out on a network file server accessible to 50 employees in a particular department. An analysis of the metadata associated with the file may give clues as to its authorship, but network traffic data (if it is being stored) may indicate which user account was responsible for storing the document to that location.

Many types of traffic data may be available to an investigator. For example, most general ledger systems can be configured to record the user name associated with the last change to any value in the system. Some systems allow users to record the user names responsible for every change to a value over time. Similarly, many e-mail systems retain information about the dates and times associated with transmissions of each e-mail and attachment. Some of these systems also record the date and time of message deletions. Operating systems may maintain dates associated with accessing, moving, or deleting files. All of this information can be extremely useful during the course of an investigation into a legal dispute.

It is important to note, however, that traffic data can only take an investigation so far. It is sometimes said that the last inch in a cyber investigation, or computer-enhanced investigation, is the hardest. What we mean by this is that electronic audit trails may indeed lead an investigator back to a particular computer as having been responsible for a given set of activity (e.g., a particular change to a general ledger system). But this does not tell you who was sitting at the keyboard of that computer at the moment the change was made. Proving who was there—making the one-inch jump from keyboard to fingers—is often the hardest part of a cyber investigation and often requires the application of traditional gumshoe and forensic accounting techniques.

42.10 FASTER/BETTER/CHEAPER

Even without the metadata and traffic data, electronic files have one huge advantage over paper documents when conducting discovery. Simply put, a computer can search, sort, and manipulate an electronic document in a fraction of the time necessary for a human to perform the same tasks. In a case involving hundreds of thousands or millions of pages of printed materials, human review and searching for specific information can be tedious and imprecise work. But computer searches

[18] The tagged image file format (TIFF) is a widely used format for storing image data. The Portable Document Format (PDF) was developed by Adobe Corporation to allow efficient electronic distribution of large documents.

across the same volume of electronic files can reliably discover every instance of a particular word or combination of words in short order. Similarly, a computer can instantly sort a large volume of information by date, file name, author, storage location, or any number of other criteria, thereby lifting the cream to the top of an investigator's stack of documents for review.

42.11 ROLE OF COMPUTER FORENSICS

Computer forensics refers to the process of preserving and analyzing electronically stored information for presentation in a legal proceeding. Over the past 10 years, computer forensics has evolved from an arcane hobby of an eclectic group of law enforcement officers to a growing litigation support industry where it was once necessary for practitioners to cobble together collections of various disk utilities and shareware programs to perform specific computer forensic tasks, there are now relatively mature software suites that integrate and automate some of the most common computer forensic operations. But in the end, forensics is not just about the tools. It is about process, documentation, and the ability to demonstrate that a given result is accurate, reliable, and repeatable.

42.12 EVIDENCE PRESERVATION

One of the key goals of the computer forensic process is the preservation of evidence. Computer data have certain unique and paradoxical properties. These data are simultaneously very hard to fully destroy and very easy to manipulate. Once again a comparison to paper is illuminating. Imagine the existence of two sets of very incriminating documents. One set consists of a notepad containing handwritten notes on paper and the other is a collection of documents stored on a thumb drive. Which set is most easily destroyed? Which is most easily modified?

There can be no question that destruction of the paper documents will be easier. Place the pad in a barbecue, apply lighter fluid, apply match. It is as simple as that. As long as the notes had not been copied, destruction is complete. Do the same to the thumb drive and you still have many questions to consider: What computer(s) was used to create and store the files before they were placed on the disk? Were those computers' hard drives backed up to some other storage media? Were the files ever printed or copied to other locations (on a network or through an e-mail attachment)? Have those printed or forwarded materials also been located and destroyed?

The question of modification is also fairly easy to answer. Attempting to reliably alter a handwritten document in a manner that will escape all detection is relatively difficult. Handwriting analysis and forensic analysis of inks and paper are all mature technologies well understood by science and the courts. But electronic files consist of zeros and ones, long lists of binary markings stored on some type of electrical, optical, magnetic, or other media. Bits are bits. Changes are often hard to detect unless you have taken some steps to lock down the data and verify that it has not been changed.

The forensic process is designed to do precisely that: It takes preexisting data and preserves them in a reliable fashion so that litigants and courts can confidently make use of them at a later time.

42.13 PHYSICAL IMAGING VERSUS LOGICAL BACKUPS

Once the goal of the computer forensic process is understood, the advantages of physical imaging of electronic storage media over the logical backing up of data become clear. *Physical imaging* is the term used to describe the process of making a full bit-for-bit copy of all of the data on a given piece of storage media. It is the equivalent of copying every page in a legal pad, including pages that have no writing, pages that are only partially full, pages from the back end of a note for which the front end was ripped out for copying, and pages that have been slashed through (marked for deletion). This is distinguished from a *logical backup,* in which only the pages containing the full text of the documents being actively used by the owner of the pad would be copied and everything else would be ignored.

This simple explanation makes plain why a litigator should prefer to have access to a physical image. The simple fact is that the files the user has chosen to retain are not the only potential pieces of evidence on the legal pad, and the same is true on a hard drive. Because of the way modern computer operating systems work, hard drives and other storage media often contain significant amounts of data in addition to the active files being retained by the user. The drive is likely to contain full versions of files the user has chosen to delete. It is also likely to contain bits and pieces of deleted files captured within the slack space of existing active files.

Most computer users today have heard of the concept of slack space but do not have a detailed understanding of how data from deleted files comes to be stored in "slack." This process is fairly straightforward. Imagine again that your legal pad is a computer hard drive. Imagine that you have a rule that only one active note can be placed on each page. Imagine also that you are an efficient user of legal pads and do not like to waste storage space, so you reuse pages by "deleting" old notes with a slash mark and writing new notes on pages containing deleted notes to the extent there is room to do so. This is almost exactly what a computer does when storing and "deleting" files. Slack space is simply the space in a cluster (a cluster being a legal pad page in our analogy) that is not being used by the active file (note) that is stored on that cluster. Any data previously stored on that cluster beyond the end-of-file marker[19] for the active file is data "stored in slack." The computer, being efficient, does not overwrite these data but simply ignores them. A forensic expert does just the opposite.

But a logical backup of the hard drive or other storage media does not contain any of the data beyond the logical size of each active file, and therefore analysis of file slack, unallocated disk areas (containing erased but recoverable data), or deleted directory entries is impossible based on a logical backup. Conversely, a physical image of a drive preserves all of the data in slack and allows an investigator to view material that may have been "deleted" months or years before the examination is conducted. Moreover, there is little incremental cost involved in preparing a physical image. Today software and hardware tools exist that allow for very efficient and cost-effective imaging. Whereas imaging an average-size hard drive in 2000 typically took four to six hours of computer time, the much larger drives used today (2011) can often be imaged in minues.[20] It is likely that the time necessary to image drives will continue to shrink as new and better imaging tools become available.

This is not to suggest that a physical image must be made in every case. The volume of data that can be stored on modern hard drives can present an analysis challenge. Searches across hundreds of gigabytes of data (or terabytes in some cases) can take days and result in millions of search hits unless the search criteria used are carefully tailored to focus in on very specific categories of information. In such cases analysis of only the logical user-created files and deleted but fully recoverable materials (exclusive of slack space, unallocated space, and system files) may be more appropriate. In other cases the likelihood of discovering material from slack and unallocated space may be remote (e.g., when the data on a device was recently restored from a logical backup). In such cases the incremental cost of making and examining a physical image may not be justified.

42.14 FORENSIC RECORDKEEPING

It is not good enough to simply create physical images of the relevant data. It is also necessary to adequately document (to the greatest extent possible) what data were imaged, from which

---

[19] Or beyond the logical size of the active file in file types that do not use end-of-file markers.

[20] How Long Does it Take to Clone a Hard Drive? at *www.ehow.com/how-does_5207765_long-clone-hard-drive_.html*

machines, at what point in time, and by what methodology. Without such documentation there is the potential for an opposing party in a legal dispute to launch a collateral attack against the results of any analysis of the data by challenging the authenticity of the evidence. This is particularly important to keep in mind during the early stages of an investigation when companies are often inclined to ask their information technology (IT) staff to "take a quick look" at computers expected to contain relevant information. Unless the IT staff member is trained in forensic procedures and has access to the necessary forensic hardware and software tools, a "quick look" can result in significant damage to otherwise useful evidence. Stated differently, the reliability of the evidence collected could be called into question.

42.15 ACQUISITION NOTES

During the process of acquiring data for forensic analysis (whether via physical imaging of media, creation of logical backups, or the simple collection of backup tapes from system administrators), examiners typically record information about the acquisition process. This information generally includes details about the computer the data were collected from, such as the make, model, and serial number of the PC, laptop, server, or other device. It should also include information about the media itself, such as the type, size, and serial number of the drive or disk. Examiners often photograph the evidence as well.

It is also important to document information about the equipment used to store the copy of the data to be examined by the forensic specialist (if for no other reason than to be able to find the image or logical copy at a later point in time). Other information typically retained from the acquisition process includes the date and time of the acquisition and the name of the examiner.

Examiners also often retain notes about the acquisition process, especially to the extent that a problem with the hardware or software resulted in a deviation from normal processes. For example, if the examiner's normal process involves booting the target computer to a forensic boot disk[21] but the CD ROM drive or USB on the computer is not functional, an alternative process would need to be deployed (or a repair would need to be implemented). If all other drives in the case were imaged via a boot disk and this one drive was imaged via another process, opposing counsel might try to attack the deviation from procedure. This is far less likely to be an effective attack against the evidence if the acquisition paperwork notes the reason for the deviation and documents the alternative process used. Such notes can be especially helpful when counsel seeks to introduce evidence found through a forensic process several years after the actual acquisition at a time when the original examiner is no longer available to testify.

Many modern computer forensic software and hardware tools automate the process of collecting much of this information by extracting some of the data directly from the media and allowing the examiner to input some of the data as part of the acquisition process. Collecting and storing the acquisition data directly in the forensic software is a significant improvement over legacy processes in that retention of the evidentiary data will necessarily result in retention of the associated acquisition information.

42.16 CHAIN-OF-CUSTODY DOCUMENTATION

In addition to notes about the acquisition, it is important that the forensic examiner maintain information about the chain of custody of the evidence once it comes into his or her possession. As noted, electronic evidence is easily altered. It is therefore important to be able to establish that the evidence was maintained in a forensically sound manner. This is accomplished through

---

[21] A boot disk stores the files necessary to start up a computer and its operating system, whereas a forensic boot disk starts up a computer and enables access without changing data on the target computer's hard drives.

chain-of-custody documentation that tracks the movement and storage of the data from the time of acquisition until the time of trial.

In addition to traditional chain-of-custody paperwork, technology has also provided a means to ensure that the data acquired by a forensic examiner were not changed while in storage. Many of the forensic software programs in wide use today provide a means for "hashing" the data found on a particular piece of media and using the hash value as a means of detecting any change in the data over time. Hashing a file or set of data simply involves applying a mathematical formula to the data and storing the resultant hash value. Because the formula operates on every bit of data in the target set, even a one-character change in the data will result in a change in the hash value.

By comparing a hash value calculated at the time of acquisition with a hash value calculated at the time the data are being analyzed, an examiner can ensure (to a very significant degree of probability) that no changes to the data have occurred in the intervening period. Thus, use of a hash value can serve as a means of quickly detecting any alteration or corruption of the data collected and can serve to authenticate the data and their analysis.

42.17 ANALYSIS WORKPAPERS

In addition to acquisition and chain of custody documentation, most computer forensic examiners will prepare various reports during the course of their examination. Such reports can take a wide range of forms including printouts of data recovered from the target media, timeline charts of relevant files, notes detailing searches conducted and analysis performed, and various reports from the forensic software tools.

While there are no strict rules regulating what types of workpapers should be created during the course of a forensic examination, as a general rule, the notes should be sufficient to allow an examiner to repeat the processes that resulted in the discovery of critical evidence.

Obviously computer forensics is not just about preserving the evidence. It is also about analyzing the evidence and discovering relevant materials. But before data analysis can begin, some preliminary considerations are important.

42.18 GET THE "WHOLE ENCHILADA"

To the greatest extent possible (and practical), computer forensic investigations should be conducted on all available relevant data rather than a mere subset of the data. Although this can be difficult, it is nonetheless potentially very important. For instance, consider what happened in a capital murder case in California. The electronic source file for a press release and related memorandum that had been issued by the police department was important to the case but could not be readily located. Prior to the forensic search, but after the memo and release had been written, the police department's network file server had been upgraded. The replacement file server did not contain a copy of the press release. Fortunately, forensic examiners determined that the old file server was sitting in a warehouse and had not been used in over three years. The server was reassembled and started, and the press release was found. Interestingly, the fact that the active server contained a file with the same name in the same path, but with drastically different contents from the original memo, indicates that a cover-up may have been attempted.

During the initial interviews on a case, an effort should be made to identify all potential sources of relevant information. Although a decision may be made to limit the analysis of certain data sets in the first instance, preservation of all relevant data should be a goal. Failure to identify relevant data sets can literally have life-and-death consequences.

Similarly, a good forensic examiner should verify, whenever possible, the answers to questions provided by IT staff. Consider the case of the class action lawsuit where members of the class had to be identified from the defendant's proprietary database system. The defendant's programmer modified an existing computer program to extract the list of potential class members.

When the program code was later reviewed by a forensic examiner, it was discovered to contain documentation that seemed to indicate that records were inadvertently being bypassed by a section of the code. Testing revealed that the program had indeed ignored hundreds of thousands of rows of the database, and the class list was ultimately revised.

Another example of the need to independently confirm IT staff assumptions comes from a case involving a key executive who had deleted many e-mail and calendar entries from his mail file. Examining the mail file showed a reference to another copy of his e-mail file on a different server. The forensic examiner was told that this alternate server did not store any mail files. When IT was asked to inspect the server anyway, it was determined that there was indeed one mail file on the server, the executive's. Apparently, the server had been a migration or fail-over[22] server for this particular user at one time. The file had not been updated by the executive's deletion activity and consequently contained documents that were several years old, including some of the data erased from the active mail server. This discovery assisted the forensic team to identify messages that had recently been deleted by the user.

There is one additional point to be mentioned about these processes before we discuss the analysis process itself. Many attorneys and investigators would like to be able to review all of the electronic data relevant to a case in a single unified process. They would prefer to find, sort, search, and review e-mail and attachments, word processing documents, spreadsheets, presentation slides, and financial data all from a single computer terminal. While we are closer to this goal today than ever before, this is still generally not practical in most cases.

The reason is that the electronic files associated with certain types of data do not lend themselves to the same processes as simple word processing or spreadsheet files. For example, e-mail messages are generally not stored as distinct files but instead are aggregated into a data store generally thought of as the user's "mailbox." Searches across all of the files on a user's hard drive will hit very often on these e-mail data stores, but that is generally useless to the investigator because he or she is interested in *which* e-mail contained the relevant data. The only way to answer that question is to parse the e-mail file and search across all the individual e-mail messages and attachments. The same problem exists with respect to compressed volumes such as ZIP and TAR files,[23] databases, and various other file types.

As a practical matter, generally the processing of electronic data necessarily happens on parallel tracks, with e-mail and other special file types being handled separately from other simpler file types. Within each track, similar (but not identical) processes are performed. In some cases the results of these separate processing streams can eventually be brought together into a unified review or presentation tool. But the exigencies of modern litigation practice, combined with the very large volumes of data associated with electronic discovery, often dictate that data reviews begin as soon as any data are available rather than waiting for multiple processes to be completed.

42.19 EVIDENCE DISCOVERY

While the analysis process deployed in each case tends to depend on the facts at issue, the nature of the available evidence, and the resources of the examining party, most computer forensic investigations involve undertaking at least some of the processes described next.

(a) DE-DUPLICATION. One of the problems for forensic examiners is that multiple copies of various materials may be recovered as part of the investigative process. Because of the expense involved in reviewing such duplicative materials, de-duplication of the recovered data sets is often the first order of business after the data have been copied and the acquisition documentation has been completed.

---

[22] A fail-over server is a server on standby to step in for a primary server in the event that the primary server fails.

[23] ZIP is a file format where the files are compressed (referred to as zipped). Using a file compression program (e.g., PKZip for DOS, or Winzip for Windows), a ZIP file could be created from one or more original files. TAR is a Unix archive file format. TAR files may also be compressed.

One might suspect that de-duplication would be a straightforward process; however, several variations of the process need to be considered before the work can begin. First the examiner must decide what qualifies as a duplicate. Do all of the fields of data need to match exactly, or should two e-mail messages be considered duplicates if the subject and body are identical without regard to the date and routing information? If you require all of the data to match exactly, then any message with a bcc will appear at least twice since the bcc field will only show up in the bcc recipient's mailbox and not in the other recipients'. Similarly, if the time stamp is off by a second, the message will appear more than once in the review data.

Second, the practitioner must decide which universe of documents should be subjected to de-duping. Consider an investigation involving the e-mail of 25 employees, one e-mail server, and four sets of backup tapes. There are likely to be at least six sets of data available for each employee (four sets of mail from the backup tapes, one set from each individual's office computer, and one from the active server), and there could be many more depending on a variety of variables (i.e., data from one or more additional laptop or desktop computers, BlackBerry devices, pagers, e-mail-enabled cell phones, home PCs, etc.).

De-duplication of these data could proceed based on the entire universe of data (so that each message would be reviewed by investigators only once), or across the data related to each user (so that each message would appear only once in each user's mailbox but might be reviewed up to 25 times by investigators if all 25 targets received a copy of the same message), or across a subset of the entire universe (e.g., all employees from a certain department).

Each of these choices has advantages and disadvantages. De-duplication across the entire universe of messages may be the most efficient process in terms of limiting the amount of time it will take to review the data, but it also poses challenges. If the reviewers are divided into teams, with each team focusing on the activities of one of the targets (a typical arrangement) and only one copy of a message sent to seven people will appear in the review data, then which team will see the message? Should one target be considered the prime suspect such that all messages sent to him or her and other targets will appear only in his or her data? And if so, won't this make the review of the other targets' data nonsensical since many of the messages will appear out of context with all duplicated messages not appearing in the secondary subject's data set? As a practical matter, these issues require the examiner and the entire investigative team to map out their approach in advance and choose a process that is consistent with the particular project's needs.[24]

De-duplication can dramatically reduce the cost of reviewing a large data set. In one investigation, 5 terabytes (and nearly 21 million files) of e-mail and user file data recovered from backup tapes was reduced to less than 900 gigabytes of data (and less than 5 million files) through the de-duplication process, thereby cutting the attorney review time by over 75 percent.

(b) DATA SORTING. Although the ability to sort investigative data is mundane, it can also be essential to the project goal, especially when millions of e-mail messages or pages of file documents must be reviewed. Data sorting allows the investigator to separate the data into more manageable subsets for review and analysis.

(i) Date/Time. Date and time sorts are the most common forms of data sorting in investigations. The key factor to keep in mind when sorting computer data is that many dates may be associated with a single document or data point. It is important to understand exactly what a particular date means before drawing conclusions about the data. In a typical Windows environment, you may find up to five dates associated with each file (file created, last accessed, last written, deleted, entry modified). All of these dates will not necessarily be available for each file. And each date has a different meaning. Without going into detail, the general meaning of these date references are described next.

- *File created date.* This is a record of when a particular file was created at the particular location where it is found. Thus a file created on a thumb drive just before Christmas in

[24] Some of these concerns can be obviated if all of the reviewers have access to the same centralized and duplicated database, but this is not always possible or practical.

December 2011 may have a file created date in January 2012 if it is found by investigators on the desktop hard drive to which it was copied "after the holidays."

- *Last accessed date.* This date refers to the last time the file was accessed, either by viewing, dragging, or even right clicking. A file does not have to be changed for the last accessed date to change. It is important to note that certain automated processes, such as backup routines and virus checking software, can change last accessed dates.
- *Last written date.* This date refers to the last time that a file was opened, changed, and saved. Merely accessing the file without making changes will not change the last written date.
- *Entry modified date.* Some file systems (notably New Technology Filing System (NTFS) and Linux) can store the date when a file's size last changed. Changes to the file that do not affect its size will not change the entry modified date.

It is important to note that different programs may use different criteria when assigning dates of various types. It may therefore be necessary to research the particulars of a given set of dates if timing is important to an investigation.

(ii) Owner/Author. As noted, many programs either automatically insert author information or allow users to input author information into the metadata associated with files. It is often helpful to sort documents subject to an investigation by author. It is, however, important to understand the limitations of reliance on the author data.

First, if the data are input automatically every time a document is created, then every document produced on a certain person's computer will indicate that he or she is the author of the documents. But what if another person was using that computer for some reason? It is also possible that a computer initially issued to one employee was later assigned to another individual without changing the default author setting.

Sometimes a document created by one user becomes a form for documents created by many other users. In this circumstance the author information for all of the documents created from the form will reflect the original author of the form.

If the author information is input manually, there are obvious potential manipulation possibilities.

(iii) File Types/Extension. It is often very useful to sort the data found on a computer by file type or extension. This allows the investigator to segregate all of the word processing documents, spreadsheets, presentation slides, and other user-created files from program files, dynamic link libraries, and system files. It is important, however, to understand that users can attempt to hide documents by adding false extensions to make a spreadsheet look like an executable program (or any other file type).

Forensic practitioners can get around this problem by performing what is called a *signature analysis* on the files. Many programs require that certain specific programming codes be placed in the initial bytes of data in files used by the program. These codes are sometimes referred to as *file signatures.* Forensic tools can search for these bits of code and compare them to the file extensions used in the file name. If the code does not match the file extension, the software can report a file signature mismatch. Moreover, if the file signature is of a known file type, the software may be able to report what the file actually is (as opposed to what the file extension falsely suggests it is).

While file signature analysis cannot guarantee that all relevant materials will be reviewed by investigators, it will increase the likelihood that user-created files are found and reviewed.

42.20 DATA SEARCHING

Searching the data collected is obviously one of the most basic steps in the investigative process, and there are a variety of ways to conduct such searches. Some of the most basic ones are discussed next.

(a) KEY WORD SEARCHES. Key word searching is the most basic type of search that can be conducted across a set of electronic data. It simply involves asking the computer to look for a string of characters appearing in a certain order. Some programs index all of the data on a particular piece of media in order to expedite the search process and allow the investigator to perform complex Boolean[25] searches based on multiple key words, word proximity, and other criteria. Other tools allow searches based on various wildcards and variations.

There are two key things to keep in mind when conducting key word searches. First, computers are precise. They will only find *exactly* what you tell them to look for within the data set. A search for "Robert P. Smith" will not find "Robert Smith," "Bob P. Smith" or "Robert.P.Smith@aol.com." You can fashion searches that will find these variants, but doing so requires precision and a clear understanding of the search syntax of the particular program being used by the investigator.

For instance, in an investigation for a large distributor, over 4 terabytes of e-mail and user files from personal computers, file servers, and e-mail servers were collected and had to be searched for relevant documents. Users did not use private or home directories on the corporate network but had instead saved the majority of their files in common or group directories accessible to a large number of people. This resulted in having to search several million files. Complex search terms were used instead of single key words. This helped to identify the most relevant documents quickly. Out of the several million initial files, 200,000 files were identified as relevant in a 10-week span.

Second, it is important to keep in mind that certain terms are almost useless as key words. Virtually any search term of four characters or less will result in massive false positive (unintended matches returned from search) results. This does not mean that such searches should never be run if you have the human resources necessary to separate the wheat from the chaff, but longer, more complex searches will likely be more fruitful.

(b) KNOWN FILE SEARCHES (HASH VALUES). In some cases it may be possible to search large sets of data very efficiently without using key words at all. If an investigator is looking for a known electronic file within a set of data (e.g., a memo that an executive claims he or she never received), a hash value search may be the best way to proceed.

Hash values are unique numbers calculated by performing a fixed mathematical formula or algorithm against all of the data in a file. The resulting "hash" of the file is a very long unique value that identifies the file and can be used to search for additional copies of the file within a large data set.

Hashing every file in a large data set will allow an investigator to identify a known file by searching for its hash value. Once the hash values are calculated, this type of search is much faster than searching through the file data itself.

Hash values are also useful for identifying identical files within a data set. An investigator merely needs to sort the data by hash value to find files that are identical even though the file names may be different. (Hash values generally are calculated on the file data only, not on the associated metadata, such as file names and dates.) This method is particularly useful for identifying all copies of an incriminating file even if a user has changed the file name.

One caveat about hash values is that they will identify two files as identical only if the contents of the files are absolutely the same. If one comma, space, or letter is changed within the file, the hash value will also change.

42.21 DELETED/SLACK/UNALLOCATED SPACE

Up to this point our discussion has centered on active files stored on a computer system, backup tape, server, or other electronic media. One of the beauties of computer forensics is that an investigator is not limited to examining these active files. When files are "deleted" from a computer

[25] English mathematician George Boole developed a logical combinatorial system (as Boolean algebra) that represents symbolically relationships (as those implied by the logical operators AND, OR, and NOT) between entities.

hard drive, the operating system typically just removes references to the data in the file system. The actual file data typically are not removed from the drive until the operating system needs the space to store other data. Although this "unallocated" space generally cannot be seen using normal operating system tools (e.g., Windows Explorer), it can be seen, searched, and sorted by computer forensic tools. Some data in unallocated space will be fully recoverable as if they were never deleted. Other data may consist of file fragments that have been partially overwritten. While such data may not be fully recoverable, they may still provide clues about the computer user's activities.

Such tools can also search through the space at the end of files between the end-of-file marker and the end of the cluster in which the active file data resides. This slack space that is not being used by any active file may contain bits of data from files long ago marked for deletion from the hard drive. Forensic tools can search for and find data stored in these spaces that might otherwise go undetected.

However, there are several potential limitations to the use of data discovered in slack and unallocated space.

1. It may not always be possible to attribute dates to such information accurately because the normal operating system dates will not typically be available.
2. Highly fragmented data found in slack or unallocated space may be hard to place in context. Therefore, drawing conclusions about the data may be difficult in some cases.
3. It may be hard to attribute data found in slack or unallocated space to a particular user, especially if the computer being examined was used by more than one person.

Notwithstanding these potential limitations, the ability to review data that has been marked for deletion by a user is one of the key advantages of a forensic approach to the review of electronic data. Just knowing that a user attempted to erase certain files prior to the investigation may provide significant clues to the investigative team.

42.22 CONCLUSION

Many of the computer forensic techniques described in this chapter were considered exotic just a few years ago, but today they have become routine practices in major investigations. Given our society's dependence on computers, it is reasonable to anticipate that five years from now these procedures will necessarily be performed in virtually every large litigation matter and many smaller ones as well. We can also anticipate that new and better tools and techniques will be brought to bear over time. Indeed, the only constant in computer forensics is rapid change. By making use of the most up-to-date practices and procedures, it is hoped that investigators can stay one step ahead of those who are up to no good.

CHAPTER **43**

FINANCIAL EXPERT WITNESS CHALLENGES AND EXCLUSIONS: RESULTS AND TRENDS IN FEDERAL AND STATE CASES SINCE *KUMHO TIRE*

Lawrence F. Ranallo, CPA
PricewaterhouseCoopers LLP

Keith R. Ugone, PhD
Analysis Group, Inc.

43.1 INTRODUCTION 1

43.2 METHODOLOGY AND OVERVIEW OF OBSERVATIONS AND CONCLUSIONS 3

43.3 EXPERT WITNESS CHALLENGES AND EXCLUSIONS: 2000–2002 7

43.4 REASONS FINANCIAL EXPERTS WERE EXCLUDED: RELEVANCE, RELIABILITY, AND QUALIFICATIONS 9

43.5 EXCLUSION OF PLAINTIFF FINANCIAL EXPERTS 9

43.6 TYPES OF FINANCIAL EXPERTS EXCLUDED 11

43.7 JUNE 30, 2003 UPDATE: OBSERVATIONS 12

43.8 SUMMARY AND CONCLUSIONS 13

43.9 FINAL COMMENTS RELEVANT TO THE CERTIFIED PUBLIC ACCOUNTANT DESIGNATION 13

43.1 INTRODUCTION

Complex business disputes often require complex financial expert witness testimony. Depending on the nature of the case or the cause of action, financial expert witness testimony could cover a very broad range of accounting, financial, and economic topics. These topics might include historically based analyses, such as the insolvency date of a business or the past profitability of a business. Alternatively, the financial expert witness might testify regarding certain counterfactuals, such as the profitability of a business in the absence of an alleged wrongful act. Finally, a financial expert

We wish to thank Sharon Freeman, Na Dawson, and Aijun Besio for research assistance. The information contained in this chapter does not represent the views of either PricewaterhouseCoopers, LLP, or Analysis Group, Inc.

witness might even testify on economic causation issues, including the impact of market-related events (i.e., industry downturns or increased competition) on the profitability of a business.[1]

Hence, depending on the facts and circumstances of a business dispute, financial expert witnesses could have a number of interwoven important roles. The financial expert witness could provide the trier of fact with guidance as to the economic harm the plaintiff may have suffered. Alternatively, the financial expert witness could provide guidance as to the existence/nonexistence of a financial causal linkage between the alleged wrongful conduct and the claimed economic harm.[2] A certified public accountant (CPA), a financial analyst, an economist, or a statistician, depending on the facts and circumstances of the dispute, could be equally well qualified to render these types of opinions.

The requirements for expert witness qualification in federal cases are provided in certain federal rules, and, since 1993, in the *Daubert* case and its case progeny.[3] The requirements for expert witness qualification in state cases vary by jurisdiction; some states follow the *Daubert* criteria while other states apply requirements similar to the older *Frye* criteria.[4]

Rule 702 of the Federal Rules of Evidence provides for the admissibility of expert testimony in this way:

> If scientific, technical, or other specialized knowledge will assist the trier of fact to understand the evidence or to determine a fact in issue, a witness qualified as an expert by knowledge, skill, experience, training, or education, may testify thereto in the form of an opinion or otherwise, if (1) the testimony is based upon sufficient facts or data, (2) the testimony is the product of reliable principles and methods, and (3) the witness has applied the principles and methods reliably to the facts of the case.[5]

In its *Daubert* opinion, the Supreme Court established four now commonly cited nonexclusive criteria for the admissibility of scientific and technical expert testimony. These criteria were developed to assist the trial judge to "make a preliminary assessment of whether the testimony's underlying reasoning or methodology is scientifically valid and properly can be applied to the facts at issue."[6] The criteria are:

1. Whether the theory or technique in question can be (and has been) tested
2. Whether the theory or technique has been subjected to peer review and publication
3. Whether the theory or technique has a known or potential error rate and the existence and maintenance of standards concerning its operation
4. Whether the theory or technique has attracted widespread acceptance within a relevant scientific community

---

[1] This list is illustrative only and is not intended to be all-inclusive. It is quite common for financial experts to testify on these or similar subjects in securities-related matters, antitrust matters, intellectual property matters, breach of contract disputes, purchase price disputes, and loss of earnings matters, among others.

[2] Here we make a distinction between economic or financial causation versus legal causation (e.g., whether a wrongful act occurred).

[3] See, for example, *William Daubert, et ux., etc., et al. v. Merrell Dow Pharmaceuticals, Inc. (92–102),* 509 U.S. 579 (1993), and *Kumho Tire Company, Ltd., et al. v. Patrick Carmichael, etc., et al.* (97–1709), 526 U.S. 137 (1999).

[4] See *Frye v. United States,* 292 F. 1013 (1923). See also, for example, the Supreme Court of Texas case captioned *E.I. du Pont de Nemours and Company, Inc. v. C. R. Robinson and Shirley Robinson* (94–0843), 923 S.W.2d 549 (1995).

[5] Rule 702, Federal Rules of Evidence (Including Amendments Effective December 1, 2000), 2000–2001 Edition, p. 113. As implied by Rule 702, the expert witness must use a reliable methodology and a methodology that fits the facts and circumstances of the case.

[6] *Daubert,* 113 Supreme Court Reporter, 509 U.S. 579, p. 2790.

The *Kumho Tire* case in 1999 clarified that the nonexclusive *Daubert* criteria were also applicable to financial experts such as CPAs, financial analysts, economists, and statisticians, among others, in federal cases.

Consequently, financial expert witnesses must be aware of the criteria being used to judge the admissibility of their work and opinions. Since *Kumho Tire,* there has been a particular focus on how courts have applied the *Daubert* criteria to financial experts—especially since financial experts are often used in the liability aspects of cases involving accounting and auditing issues and are used for damage quantification and related economic causation issues.

43.2 METHODOLOGY AND OVERVIEW OF OBSERVATIONS AND CONCLUSIONS

In this chapter we present our findings from an analysis of *published opinions* of federal and state cases relating to challenges and exclusions of financial expert witnesses over the 2000 to 2002 time period (i.e., post-*Kumho Tire*). It is important to note that our search criteria included published opinions that referenced the *Kumho Tire* case decision explicitly—which we used as a primary indicator of matters likely to involve challenges to nonscientific experts such as CPAs, financial analysts, economists, and statisticians (see Exhibit 43.1).[7] Our sample included 895 challenges identified through published opinions meeting these criteria.[8] Financial experts were named in 165 of these 895 challenges, with 68 financial experts being excluded either in whole or in part.[9]

Several interesting conclusions can be drawn from the opinions reviewed, including these:

- *The number of challenges to experts of all types is increasing.* In 2000, there were 250 challenges to expert witnesses in general.[10] This number increased to 289 in 2001 and 356 in 2002. This trend is to be expected. The exclusion of a litigant's expert is often devastating to that party's case. Hence, challenging the admissibility of an expert's opinion is an increasingly utilized weapon in the arsenal of opposing counsel.
- *Once challenged, the rate at which financial experts are excluded in whole or in part is decreasing.* Based on our sample of cases, 22.0 percent of the challenges in 2000 involved financial expert witnesses. The corresponding figures in 2001 and 2002 were 15.2 percent and 18.5 percent, respectively. Hence, the relative proportion of challenges between financial and nonfinancial expert witnesses has not changed appreciably between 2000 and 2002.[11] Interestingly, however, the percentage of financial experts excluded in whole or in part (once challenged) over this same time period declined from 54.5 percent to 40.9 percent to 30.3 percent. While at first this result may appear paradoxical, we believe it is the natural result of the increased emphasis on challenging the admissibility of the opposing financial expert's opinions. Two forces are creating this result. To the extent a *Daubert* challenge is a strategy increasingly utilized by opposing counsel, the quality of challenges and the likelihood of exclusion may not be as high at the margin when increasing numbers of challenges are made.[12] In addition, to the extent it is likely a financial expert has to withstand both a *Daubert* challenge and cross-examination, financial experts are more inclined (at the margin) to perform higher-quality investigations, to use generally accepted methodologies, and to use

[7] Although broader search criteria would identify additional cases in federal and state jurisdictions, the expert challenges identified using the stated search criteria provided interesting and meaningful insights into certain trends regarding challenges to financial expert witness testimony since *Kumho Tire.*

[8] We conducted research on cases citing *Kumho Tire* (526 U.S. 137) in the LexisNexis federal and state court cases database.

[9] Some identified published opinions addressed the proposed testimony of more than one expert.

[10] Using the *Kumho Tire* search criteria previously described.

[11] The purpose of this chapter is to identify and discuss certain observations and trends relating to expert witness challenges and exclusions. We have not analyzed whether statistically significant differences exist between certain percentages we report.

[12] Restated, in the aggregate, it is likely there are diminishing returns to *Daubert* challenges.

	Total Challenges	Federal Challenges*		State Challenges**	
		Number	% Total	Number	% Total
2000					
Expert witness challenges	250	196	78.4%	54	21.6%
Financial expert witness challenges	55	47	85.5%	8	14.5%
2001					
Expert witness challenges	289	254	87.9%	35	12.1%
Financial expert witness challenges	44	38	86.4%	6	13.6%
2002					
Expert witness challenges	356	295	82.9%	61	17.1%
Financial expert witness challenges	66	63	95.5%	3	4.5%
2000–2002 Grand Total					
Expert witness challenges	**895**	**745**	**83.2%**	**150**	**16.8%**
Financial expert witness challenges	**165**	**148**	**89.7%**	**17**	**10.3%**

Notes:

*Federal courts searched included the U.S. Supreme Court, various circuit courts, Court of International Trade, Claims Court, Administrative and Agency Court, U.S. Tax Court, National Labor Relations Board, and Military Justice court.

**State courts searched included state courts, state supreme courts, and state appellate courts.

Exhibit 43.1 Jurisdiction Analysis (Cases Citing *Kumho Tire v. Carmichael*) Annual, 2000–2002

methodologies that fit the facts and circumstances of the particular matter. In other words, financial experts have appropriately responded to the incentives created by the likelihood of a *Daubert* challenge. Diminishing returns to financial expert witness challenges and financial expert witness response to the *Daubert* environment have caused the percentage of financial experts excluded in whole or in part to decline.

- *Plaintiff-side financial experts are challenged and excluded more frequently than defense-side financial experts.* Based on our sample of cases, plaintiff financial experts are two to three times as likely to be challenged relative to defense financial experts. In 2000, 76.4 percent of financial expert challenges involved plaintiffs' financial experts. The corresponding figures in 2001 and 2002 were 68.2 percent and 71.2 percent, respectively. These trends carry over to actual exclusions as well. In 2000, 79.3 percent of financial expert exclusions were plaintiff financial experts. This number increased to 83.3 percent in 2001 and 90.0 percent in 2002. Again, in many respects, these results are not surprising. For one thing, a defendant can survive without its financial expert witness better than a plaintiff can survive without its financial expert witness. (The plaintiff needs a financial expert to put forth a claimed damages figure, whereas a defendant could always just cross-examine the plaintiff's financial expert without putting its own expert on the witness stand.) Hence, at the margin, there is a greater incentive to challenge the plaintiff's financial expert than the defendant's financial expert. In addition, the plaintiff's financial expert often is building or constructing a damage model, while the defendant's financial expert is often just evaluating the work of the plaintiff's financial expert. In terms of pure numbers, the plaintiff's financial expert has many more assumptions and inputs to justify relative to defendant's financial expert, leading to a greater likelihood of a challenge. For the same reason, there is a greater likelihood the plaintiff's financial expert will ultimately be excluded in whole or in part.

The rate of challenges to accountants/CPAs as testifying experts appears to be lower than that for other types of financial experts. The success rate of excluding accountants/CPAs is lower as well.[13] Of the 165 challenges to financial experts, 18 related to accountants/CPAs, 41 related to economists, and 17 related to statisticians.[14] Only 3 of the accountants/CPAs were excluded in whole or in part, while 21 of the economists and eight of the statisticians were excluded in whole or in part. Care should be exercised when interpreting these figures, however. These figures should not be interpreted as meaning a financial expert with a CPA is necessarily less susceptible to challenges and exclusions relative to financial experts with a PhD in economics, for example. To the contrary, these figures are likely the product of (1) the nature of the engagements traditionally assigned to different types of financial experts, (2) the data that may be available to properly conduct the required analysis in the engagements traditionally assigned to different types of financial experts, and (3) the degree to which the required testimony deviates from the interpretation of historical data toward projecting business performance under an alternative set of conditions. CPAs, in certain types of engagements, may be assessing accounting rules, using accounting rules to support their opinions, or opining on issues relating to the actual past performance of a business. In contrast, the majority of the challenges and exclusions relating to economists pertained to antitrust cases. (See Exhibit 43.2.) Defining a relevant market and/or hypothesizing as to prices, output, market shares, and profits in the absence of an alleged monopolization may place the economist at greater risk of challenge and possible exclusion than an accountant/CPA functioning as a financial expert in matters that do not involve these components. Hence, we believe that the nature of the cases

---

[13] While some courts identified the expert in question as a CPA, others simply identified the expert as an accountant. Consequently, the statistics reported in this chapter may include both CPAs and non-CPA accountants.

[14] The remaining financial experts were classified as "other financial experts" in our analysis. In some challenges, not enough information was reported to identify these "other financial experts" as CPAs, economists, or statisticians. In other challenges, "other financial experts" included financial analysts and appraisers, among others.

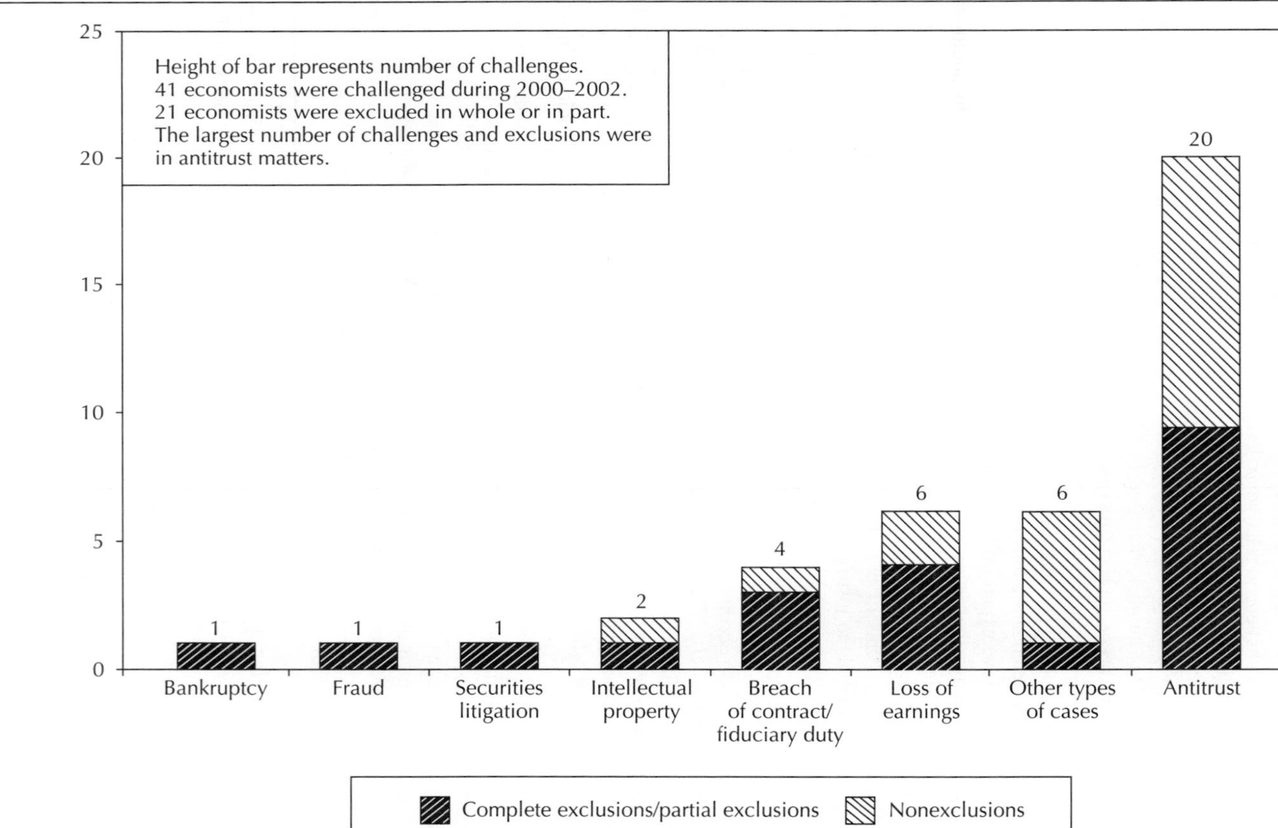

Exhibit 43.2 Challenges and Exclusions of Economists by Case Type, 2000–2002

Type of Expert	Number of Challenges*	Partial Exclusions	Complete Exclusions	Total Number of Exclusions	Exclusions as a Percent of Challenges
Financial experts	165	19	49	68	41.2%
Nonfinancial experts**	730	78	258	336	46.0%
Total	**895**	**97**	**307**	**404**	**45.1%**

Note:
*Multiple experts could be challenged in the same case.
**Nonfinancial experts include medical doctors, engineers, forensic scientists, psychologists, and psychiatrists, among others.

Exhibit 43.3 Expert Witness Challenges (Cases Citing *Kumho Tire v. Carmichael*), January 2000–December 2002

and the required analyses explain the different exclusion rates of CPAs and economists rather than alternative explanations.[15]

Other details to our study are presented in the remainder of this chapter, followed by additional conclusions.

43.3 EXPERT WITNESS CHALLENGES AND EXCLUSIONS: 2000–2002

Exhibit 43.3 reports the number of challenges relating to the admissibility of financial and nonfinancial expert witnesses over the January 2000 through December 2002 time period. The results of these challenges are also reported in Exhibit 43.3. Our investigation indicates that:

- Of the 895 challenges identified using our search criteria, financial experts were challenged a total of 165 times (18.4 percent) while nonfinancial experts were challenged 730 times (81.6 percent).
- When financial experts were challenged, their testimony was excluded in whole or in part in 68 cases, or 41.2 percent of the time.[16] In contrast, testimony of nonfinancial experts was excluded in whole or in part in 336 cases, or 46.0 percent of the time.[17]
- Financial and nonfinancial experts have their testimony excluded entirely at a higher rate than excluded in part. Our investigation reveals that 72.1 percent of the financial expert exclusions and 76.8 percent of the nonfinancial expert exclusions were in whole rather than in part.

Based on these data, once challenged, financial and nonfinancial experts appear to be excluded in roughly the same proportions.

[15] It is interesting to note the reasons given for the exclusion of the three accountants/CPAs discussed in the text. In *In re: Bonham* (2000 Bankr. Lexis 727), a bankruptcy court judge excluded the CPA "based on substantial factual mistakes, speculation, innuendo, and inferences which are not supported by full explanations and analysis." In *United States v. Sparks* (2001 U.S. App. Lexis 8002), the circuit court judge upheld the exclusion of an accountant "because there was no indication of authenticity [of documents relied on], however, [the accountant's] testimony, which was based on those documents, did not 'rest on a reliable foundation' and had to be excluded under Rule 702. *Daubert,* 509 U.S. at 597." In *United States v. Rockwell Space Operations* (2002 U.S. Dist. Lexis 6650), the district court judge wrote, "As a consequence, the accuracy of [the CPA's] damage assessment is entirely dependent upon the accuracy and the credibility of [the plaintiff's] non-expert and unreliable estimates. [The CPA's] opinion is not reliable because it was built upon a faulty foundation: the uncorroborated and unreliable estimates of [the plaintiff]." [Bracketed terms have been added for clarity.]

[16] Financial experts were excluded in whole 49 times and excluded in part 19 times.

[17] Nonfinancial experts were excluded in whole 258 times and excluded in part 78 times.

Type of Expert	Number of Challenges*	Partial Exclusions	Complete Exclusions	Total Number of Exclusions	Exclusions as a Percent of Challenges
2000					
Financial experts	55	7	23	30	54.5%
Nonfinancial experts**	195	26	64	90	46.2%
Subtotal	**250**	**33**	**87**	**120**	**48.0%**
2001					
Financial experts	44	5	13	18	40.9%
Nonfinancial experts**	245	28	91	119	48.6%
Subtotal	**289**	**33**	**104**	**137**	**47.4%**
2002					
Financial experts	66	7	13	20	30.3%
Nonfinancial experts**	290	24	103	127	43.8%
Subtotal	**356**	**31**	**116**	**147**	**41.3%**

Note:
*Multiple experts could be challenged in the same case.
**Nonfinancial experts include medical doctors, engineers, forensic scientists, psychologists, and psychiatrists, among others.

Exhibit 43.4 Expert Witness Challenges (Cases Citing *Kumho Tire Co. v. Carmichael*) Annual, 2000–2002

Exhibit 43.4 presents the annual number of challenges and rate of exclusions of financial and nonfinancial expert witnesses over the 2000 to 2006 time period. Based on annual data:

- The number of challenges of experts has trended upward. The total number of expert challenges increased by 15.6 percent in 2001 (from 250 in 2000 to 289 in 2001) and increased by 23.2 percent in 2002 (from 289 in 2001 to 356 in 2002).
- Financial expert challenges have stayed relatively steady as a percentage of the total number of challenges over this three-year period. In 2000, 55 of the 250 challenges (22.0 percent) were challenges of financial experts. In 2002, 66 of the 356 challenges (18.5 percent) were challenges of financial experts.
- The rate at which financial experts have been excluded, once challenged, has declined from 54.5 percent in 2000 to 40.9 percent in 2001 to 30.3 percent in 2002.[18] As discussed previously, this is likely the result of two forces. At the margin, with increases in the number of challenges, the likelihood of a successful challenge to a financial expert witness may be less. Also, at the margin, the quality of work prepared by financial expert witnesses may have improved in response to increased scrutiny stemming from tightened admissibility guidelines. Both of these forces likely explain the decline in the exclusion rate over the 2000 to 2006 time period.[19]

Interestingly, based on the data in Exhibit 43.4, it appears as if a crossover has occurred with respect to the rate of exclusions of financial and nonfinancial expert witnesses once challenged.

[18] The rate at which nonfinancial experts have been excluded, once challenged, increased slightly in 2001 and then declined in 2002. However, the rate at which nonfinancial experts have been excluded did not decline to the same extent in 2002 as compared to the figures for financial experts.

[19] Analysis of future exclusions will provide insights as to whether the exclusion rate has reached its steady state or equilibrium level. While not part of this study, the case filings mix could also impact the exclusion rate of financial experts over time.

Whereas in 2000, when challenged, financial experts were excluded at a higher rate than nonfinancial experts, by 2002, nonfinancial experts were excluded, in whole or in part, at a higher rate. In 2000, 54.5 percent of the challenges of financial experts resulted in a partial or complete exclusion, declining to 30.3 percent in 2002. In contrast, 46.2 percent of the challenges of nonfinancial experts resulted in a partial or complete exclusion in 2000, declining only slightly to 43.8 percent in 2002.

43.4 REASONS FINANCIAL EXPERTS WERE EXCLUDED: RELEVANCE, RELIABILITY, AND QUALIFICATIONS

We next determined the reasons financial experts were excluded or partially excluded.[20] This analysis was done in the context of the Rule 702 focus on the qualifications of the proposed expert as well as the relevance and reliability of the planned testimony. When financial experts are excluded, it is more likely to be as a result of the lack of reliability in the planned testimony than as a result of relevance issues or the qualifications of the expert. While multiple reasons were often given for the exclusions of the financial experts studied, reliability was mentioned in over 80 percent of the exclusions, relevance was mentioned in half of the exclusions, and qualifications were mentioned in a quarter of the exclusions. Finally, when financial expert testimony is determined to be unreliable, it is more likely to be a result of problems with the quantity or validity of the data used by the expert than with any of the *Daubert* criteria.

43.5 EXCLUSION OF PLAINTIFF FINANCIAL EXPERTS

Exhibits 43.5, 43.6, and 43.7 present analyses of challenges and exclusions by the party engaging the financial expert. Our analysis of the data shows:

- Of the 165 financial expert challenges identified, 119 (or 72.1 percent) were engaged by the plaintiff. (See Exhibit 43.5.) Thus, it is more likely that a financial expert will be challenged when engaged by the plaintiff than the defendant.
- The number of challenges of plaintiff financial experts relative to defense financial experts has remained consistent in each year. (See Exhibit 43.6.) At least two out of every three challenges to financial experts are plaintiff side in each year.

	Number of Challenges	Plaintiff's Financial Expert	Percent Plaintiff	Defendant's Financial Expert	Percent Defendant
Partially excluded	19	17	89.5%	2	10.5%
Completely excluded	49	40	81.6%	9	18.4%
Not excluded	97	62	63.9%	35	36.1%
Total	**165**	**119**	**72.1%**	**46**	**27.9%**

Exhibit 43.5 Plaintiff and Defendant Financial Expert Challenges, January 2000–December 2002

[20] Based on a reading of the published opinions reviewed, reasons for the exclusion of financial experts were categorized as relating to relevance issues, reliability issues, and/or qualification issues. A particular expert may have been excluded for more than one reason.

- Once challenged, plaintiff financial experts are more likely to be excluded in whole or in part than defense financial experts. (See Exhibit 43.7.) Although 72.1 percent of the challenges are plaintiff side, 83.8 percent of the exclusions or partial exclusions are plaintiff side. In contrast, while 27.9 percent of the challenges are defense side, only 16.2 percent of the exclusions in whole or in part are defense side.

Notably, while the rate at which financial experts are excluded is declining (as previously discussed), such observations are not quite descriptive of the rate at which plaintiff financial experts are excluded (once challenged) relative to defendant financial experts.

The data reported in Exhibit 43.6 suggests that plaintiff financial experts are consistently challenged at a rate two to three times that of defendant financial experts. Annually, over the 2000 to 2006 time period, 68.2 percent to 76.4 percent of the challenges to financial experts were to the plaintiff's financial expert. The data reported in Exhibit 43.7 suggests that plaintiff financial experts are consistently excluded at a rate four to nine times that of defendant financial experts. Annually, over the 2000 to 2006 time period, 79.3 percent to 90.0 percent of the exclusions of financial experts were to the plaintiff's financial expert.

Exhibits 43.6 and 43.7 combined demonstrate that plaintiff and defendant financial experts have experienced declines in the proportion of exclusions, once challenged. However, the percentage of plaintiff financial experts excluded in whole or in part has not declined to the same extent as defense financial expert exclusions. In 2000, 24 exclusions occurred relating to the 42 plaintiff financial expert challenges (57.1 percent). In 2002, 18 exclusions occurred relating to the 47 plaintiff financial expert challenges (38.3 percent). In comparison, in 2000, 6 of 13 challenged defendant financial experts were excluded (46.2 percent). This figure was reduced to 2 of 19 challenged defendant financial experts being excluded in 2002 (10.5 percent).

	Number of Challenges	Plaintiff's Financial Expert	Percent Plaintiff	Defendant's Financial Expert	Percent Defendant
2000	55	42	76.4%	13	23.6%
2001	44	30	68.2%	14	31.8%
2002	66	47	71.2%	19	28.8%
Total	**165**	**119**	**72.1%**	**46**	**27.9%**

Exhibit 43.6 Plaintiff and Defendant Financial Expert Challenges, Annual, 2000–2002

	Number of Challenges	Plaintiff's Financial Expert	Percent Plaintiff	Defendant's Financial Expert	Percent Defendant
2000	30	24	79.3%	6	20.7%
2001	18	15	83.3%	3	16.7%
2002	20	18	90.0%	2	10.0%
Total	**68**	**57**	**83.8%**	**11**	**16.2%**

Note: Includes partial and complete exclusions.

Exhibit 43.7 Plaintiff and Defendant Financial Expert Exclusion, Annual, 2000–2002

43.6 TYPES OF FINANCIAL EXPERTS EXCLUDED

Next we looked at the composition of financial expert challenges and exclusions in the context of the particular financial expertise involved. While the pool of financial experts identified in cases is diverse,[21] we have separately analyzed the challenges and exclusions of economists, statisticians, and accountants/CPAs. These data are reported in Exhibit 43.8. Note that because our analysis is focused only on those cases in which a challenge was made in federal and state cases referring to *Kumho Tire,* it is not possible to calibrate the rate of a particular expert exclusion to the many other cases in which a financial expert is not challenged and provides testimony. However, we have found:

- Among financial experts, accountants/CPAs appear to be among the least frequently challenged financial experts.
- Among financial experts, accountants/CPAs appear to have the lowest proportion of exclusions. Out of 68 financial expert exclusions in whole or in part, only 3 CPAs have been excluded. In contrast, each of the other categories of financial experts—economists, statisticians, and other financial experts—has a higher percentage of exclusions when challenged than accountants/CPAs.

However, as previously discussed, care must be exercised when interpreting these figures. The empirical data presented does not support the proposition that when two functionally different but equally qualified experts are being considered for retention, and the nature of the assignment is such that the talents of either type of expert are appropriate, the CPA will have a lower probability of being challenged or excluded.

To the contrary, the figures just reported are likely the product of (1) the nature of the engagements traditionally assigned to different types of financial experts, (2) the data that may be available to properly conduct the required analysis in the engagements traditionally assigned to different types of financial experts, and (3) the degree to which the required testimony deviates from the interpretation of historical data toward projecting business performance under an alternative set of conditions. Hence, we believe it is frequently the nature of the cases and the required analyses that explain the different exclusion rates of CPAs and economists rather than alternative explanations.

Type of Expert	Number of Challenges	Completely/Partially Excluded	% Being Completely/Partially Excluded
Accountant/CPA	18	3	16.7%
Economist	41	21	51.2%
Statistician	17	8	47.1%
Other financial	89	36	40.4%
Total	**165**	**68**	**41.2%**

Note: Includes partial and complete exclusions.

Exhibit 43.8 Financial Expert Challenges and Exclusions by Expert Type, January 2000–December 2002

[21] *Financial experts* in this context refers to economists, statisticians, accountants/CPAs, appraisers, finance professors, and so on.

43.7 JUNE 30, 2003 UPDATE: OBSERVATIONS

The trends identified over the three-year survey period largely continued in the six-month period ended June 30, 2003, with some important exceptions. Reported next are notable results in the first six months of 2003.

- Financial expert testimony was wholly or partially excluded in 24 situations (or 55.8 percent of the financial expert challenges). The exclusion rate in the first six months of 2003 was greater than the exclusion rate for the year 2002.
- For these financial expert exclusions, there are a higher number of partial exclusions (17 cases) than complete exclusions (7 cases). This is a reversal of prior trends.
- The reliability of the financial expert's opinion (based on the underlying facts and data considered and the methodology used to formulate an opinion) was again the predominant reason for exclusion. Deficiencies relating to the reliability of the proposed testimony were cited in nearly 80 percent of the 24 exclusions. The qualifications of the financial expert were cited in only 1 exclusion.
- Of 43 total challenges, 30 (or 69.8 percent) were directed to plaintiff financial experts. Of these 30 challenges, plaintiff financial experts were excluded 63.3 percent of the time. This is in contrast to defense financial experts, who were excluded in 38.5 percent of the challenges reviewed.
- Accountants/CPAs did not fare as well in the first six months of 2003. Whereas only 4 of the 43 financial expert challenges related to accountants or CPAs, all 4 of such experts were wholly or partially excluded, more than the total number of exclusions for this type of expert in all of the prior three years surveyed.[22]

---

[22] The reasons for these four exclusions follow. *In re: EZ Dock, Inc. v. Schafer Sys* (2003 U.S. Dist. Lexis 3634), the circuit court judge determined that "In his expert report, ... [the CPA] has not himself formed an opinion as to the existence of a 'two supplier' market; he has simply adopted Wortley's opinion regarding the nature of the market.... His proposed opinions regarding the existence of a demand for the patented product and the absence of non-infringing alternative products is 'not based upon sufficient facts or data' as required by Rule 702." In *In re: Valentino v. Proviso Twp.* (2003 U.S. Dist. Lexis 11574), the circuit judge found that [the CPA] "stated he thought this analysis was widespread knowledge; however, neither [plaintiff's] response to the motion nor [the CPA's] subsequent affidavit makes mention of anything to support his assertion that his borrowing history analysis is widespread knowledge or a reliable method to determine the borrowing ability of a Township." In *In re: Space Maker Designs, Inc. v. Weldon F. Stump and Company, Inc.* (2003 U.S. Dist. Lexis 3941), the district judge found that "Expert reports should be 'detailed and complete' so as 'to avoid the disclosure of 'sketchy and vague' expert information." *Sierra Club* (995 F. 2d 571-Sierra Club v. Babbitt). Under the terms of the Agreed Amended Scheduling Order, Defendants were required to file a complete statement of all opinions to be expressed and the basis and reasons therefore. [The CPA's] expert report falls short of that standard." As to the CPA's licenses, the court found: "None of those licenses make him qualified to opine on economic trends and their likely effect on profits." In *In re: JRL Enterprises, Inc. v. Procorp Associates, Inc.* (2003 U.S. Dist. Lexis 9397), the district court found that the expert's calculations were based solely on projections found in the agreement. The district court noted that the expert performed no market analysis to verify the reasonableness or accuracy of the projections in the DA Agreement. 1998 U.S. Dist. LEXIS 15414 at *1. The court found that this failure established that the expert's calculations could not be evaluated for accuracy. Furthermore, the court found that the expert had failed to establish that the expert's numbers had any basis in reality. The court found that "the expert had failed to offer any evidence of general acceptance, or known rate of error for his methods; finally, the court said that the plaintiff had shown no evidence that the expert's calculations were anything more than an exercise in arithmetic based on inherently unreliable values. 1998 U.S. Dist. LEXIS 15414 at *4." [Bracketed terms have been added for clarity.] Footnote citations have been removed.

43.8 SUMMARY AND CONCLUSIONS

In summary, certain observations and trends stand out in the analysis of federal and state cases from 2000 to 2002 where the admissibility of the financial expert witness's opinions has been challenged:

- The number of challenges to experts of all types is increasing.
- Once challenged, the rate at which financial experts are excluded in whole or in part decreased over the 2000 to 2002 time period.
- Plaintiff financial experts are challenged and excluded more frequently than defense financial experts.
- The rate of challenges to accountants/CPAs as testifying experts appears to be lower than that for other types of financial experts. The success rate of excluding accountants/CPAs is lower as well.[23]

43.9 FINAL COMMENTS RELEVANT TO THE CERTIFIED PUBLIC ACCOUNTANT DESIGNATION

As discussed, we believe it is the nature of the cases and the required analyses that explain the different exclusion rates of CPAs and other financial experts rather than alternative explanations. However, it is worth mentioning, admittedly with a mix of both fact and intuition, that because the CPA designation is well established and well known, it may be qualifying in *certain types* of litigation roles and cases. While the designation is not a sine qua non for the admissibility of testimony, the accreditation of a CPA—which embodies completion of defined education, examination, experience, and annual continuing education requirements—is an established basis for qualification of the financial expert in a suitable litigation context.[24]

CPAs are often chosen for certain defined types of roles in a litigation context that are customarily and commonly within the province of CPAs. For example, the historical cost focus of accountants/CPAs is conducive to the evaluation of historical accounting data in a litigation context. This may be a factor explaining the lower rate of challenges and exclusions of CPAs relative to non-CPAs who conduct analyses outside of traditional historical accounting analyses.

Finally, CPAs may benefit from the professional standards to which they must adhere when faced with a *Daubert* challenge. Since the *Daubert* criteria include peer review and general acceptance of a methodology, the CPA can turn to the codified professional standards of the American Institute of Certified Public Accountants (AICPA) and other standard-setting organizations, among other information, as a basis on which professional opinions may be drawn. Such accounting standards have heretofore been the result of an established process that largely includes focused research, public input, exposure of issues and standards for open comment, and expert deliberative decision making by members of panels and boards.

In a litigation context, the CPA is able to rely not only on generally accepted accounting principles but also on the standards defined by the AICPA related to audit, consulting (including litigation or business valuation services), or attestation engagements to perform the analysis needed to support opinions relating to liability or economic damages. In contrast, other types of financial experts, though highly skilled and trained, do not have a set of technical standards as codified as those of CPAs. Of course, as a cautionary note, the protections these standards provide the CPA are applicable only to CPAs who are retained on matters where these standards play a role or are relevant to the nature of the inquiry being made. To the extent statistical, economic, or econometric analyses are required, the standards on which a CPA often relies may not be as directly relevant.

---

[23] Subject to the caveats discussed in this chapter.

[24] This is not true in all types of litigation contexts. For example, a CPA designation would not provide a shield to a *Daubert* challenge if a CPA was attempting to opine on relevant market issues in an antitrust case.

INDEX

Accounting. *See also specific types of accounting, e.g.:* Forensic accounting
as CPA service, 1.10(b)(ii)
management, 2.1(b)
tax, 2.1(b)
U.S. standards for, 1.2
Accounting basis, *see* Basis of accounting
Accounting Principles Board (APB):
dissolution of, 2.2(c)(iii)
generally, 2.2(c)
and investment credit, 2.2(c)(ii)
postulates/principles of, 2.2(c)(i)
and Seidman Committee, 2.2(c)(ii)
Accounting Research Bulletins (ARB), 2.2(b)(ii)
Accounting Standards Codification (ASC) Topic 350 (*Intangibles*):
after June 30, 2001, goodwill acquired, 14.11(a)
equity method goodwill, 14.11(d)
previously recognized goodwill, 14.11(c)
Accounting Standards Codification (ASC) Topic 740 (*Income Taxes*):
annual computation of taxes, 17.2(c)(ii)
basic objectives/principles of, 17.2(c)
business combinations, 17.2(e)(iii)
disclosure, 17.4(b), 17.4(c)
Emerging Issues Task Force:
discussions on income taxes, 17.2(b)(iii)
implementation issues addressed by, 17.2(e)(vi)
and FASB special report, 17.2(b)(ii)
financial reporting:
disclosure, 17.4(b), 17.4(c)
intraperiod tax allocation, 17.4(a)
statement presentation and disclosure, 17.4(b)
generally, 17.1(b)(iv)
interim period tax:
determination of, 17.5(c)
estimated annual effective tax rate, 17.5(b)
generally, 17.5(a)
special issues, 17.5(d)
leveraged leases, 17.2(e)(ii)
measurement of deferred tax liabilities/assets, 17.2(d)(iv)
and pre-codification literature, 17.2(b)(i)
primary guidance, 17.2(b)
quasi reorganizations, 17.2(e)(iv)
recognition of deferred tax liabilities/assets:
of change in valuation allowance, 17.2(d)(iii)
generally, 17.2(d), 17.2(d)(i)
of valuation allowance, 17.2(d)(ii)
regulated companies, 17.2(e)(i)
scope of, 17.2(a)
subsidiary, separate financial statements of, 17.2(e)(v)
and tax laws vs. financial accounting standards, 17.2(c)(i)
Accounting Standards Codification (ASC) Topic 740–10 (*Accounting for Uncertainty in Income Taxes*):
balance sheet presentation, 17.3(h)
consolidated/combined financial statements, 17.3(b)(i)
derecognition, 17.3(f)
disclosures for external reporting:
pass-through entities, 17.3(i)(iii)
tabular reconciliation of unrecognized tax benefits, 17.3(i)(i)
tax-exempt entities, 17.3(i)(iii)
uncertain tax position statement (Schedule UTP), 17.3(i)(ii)

Accounting Standards Codification (ASC) Topic (*Continued*)
generally, 17.3(a)
interest and penalties, 17.3(g)
and IRS access to tax accrual workpapers, 17.3(j)
measurement:
generally, 17.3(e)
subsequent, 17.3(f)
measurement-cumulative probability approach, 17.3(e)(ii)
recognition:
derecognition, 17.3(f)
generally, 17.3(e), 17.3(e)(i)
subsequent, 17.3(f)
scope of, 17.3(b)
subsequent recognition/measurement, 17.3(f)
tax position, 17.3(c)
unit of account, determining, 17.3(d)
Accounting Standards Codification (ASC) Topic 820 (*Fair Value Measurements and Disclosures*):
fair value measurements:
generally, 24.4(a)
scope and scope exceptions, 24.4(c)
and PCAOB Staff Audit Practice Alert No. 2, 24.6(d)(ii)
Accounting Standards Codification (ASC) Topic 980 (*Regulated Operations*):
amendments, 36.6(b)
construction, allowance for funds used during, 36.6(e)(i), 36.8(a)(iii)
cost disallowances (Topic980–360–35):
abandonments, plant, 36.7(a)(ii)
income statement presentation of, 36.7(a)(iii)
newly completed plants, 36.7(a)(i)
discontinuation of rate-regulated accounting (Topic980–20):
assets/liabilities, regulatory, 36.9(b), 36.9(d)
factors leading to, 36.9(a)
generally, 36.9
income statement presentation, 36.9(g)
income taxation, 36.9(e)
investment tax credit, 36.9(f)
plant, equipment, and inventory, 36.9(c)
and reapplication of ASC 980, 36.9(h)
general standards:
assets, regulatory, 36.6(d)(i)
liabilities, regulatory, 36.6(d)(ii)
major issues addressed in, 36.6(c)
other assets and deferred costs (Topic980–340):
construction, allowance for funds used during, 36.8(a)(iii)
disallowances, phase-in plans vs., 36.8(a)(iv)
financial statement classification, 36.8(a)(ii)
financial statement disclosure, 36.8(a)(v)
phase-in plans, 36.8(a)(i), 36.8(a)(iv)
provisions of, 36.8(a)
scope of, 36.6(a)
specific standards:
application examples, 36.6(e)(vi)
construction, allowance for funds used during, 36.6(e)(i)
deferred costs not earning a return, 36.6(e)(v)
income taxation, 36.6(e)(iii)
intercompany profit, 36.6(e)(ii)
refunds, 36.6(e)(iv)
Accounts payable:
as current liability:
trade creditors, 18.3(c)
Acquisition method (business combinations):
acquired company, determining cost of:
acquisition date, 8.3(b)(vi)
fair value of acquired company, 8.3(b)(v)
fair value of consideration given, 8.3(b)(i)
fair value of consideration transferred, 8.3(b)(ii)
generally, 8.3(b)
stock options of acquiree, 8.3(b)(iii)
stock options of acquiror, 8.3(b)(iv)
acquiring company, identification of, 8.3(a)
allocation period, 8.3(j)
contingencies:
assets/liabilities arising from, 8.3(h)
earnings, based on, 8.3(d)(i)
security prices, based on, 8.3(d)(ii)
contingent consideration in:
adjustments, 8.3(d)(iv)
earnings, 8.3(d)(i)
earnings per share, 8.3(d)(iii)
generally, 8.3(d)
securities prices, 8.3(d)(ii)

direct costs of business combination:
acquiree, costs incurred by, 8.3(c)(i)
discretionary costs, 8.3(c)(iv)
employee costs, 8.3(c)(ii), 8.3(c)(iii)
generally, 8.3(c)
plant closing costs, 8.3(c)(ii)
disclosures:
in financial statements, *see subhead:* financial statement disclosures
SEC filings, 8.3(o)
effective date, 8.3(q)
employee-related costs:
payments to employees, 8.3(c)(iii)
severance, 8.3(c)(ii)
financial statement disclosures:
acquired securities, classification of, 8.3(n)(ii)
interim financial information, 8.3(n)(ii)
pro forma disclosure, 8.3(n)(i)
intangible assets:
artistic-related, 8.3(f)(iii)
contract-based, 8.3(f)(iv)
customer-related, 8.3(f)(ii)
generally, 8.3(f)
marketing-related, 8.3(f)(i)
technology-based, 8.3(f)(v)
leveraged buyouts, *see* Leveraged buyouts
minority interests:
exchange of ownership interests, 8.3(e)(i)
generally, 8.3(e)
simultaneous common control mergers, 8.3(e)(ii)
purchase method vs., 8.3(p)
pushdown accounting:
exceptions, 8.3(i)(ii)
generally, 8.3(i)
with parent company debt, 8.3(i)(i)
recognition/measurement of assets and liabilities:
costs to complete, 8.3(g)(iv)
deferred taxes; identifiable intangible assets with no tax basis, 8.3(g)(xiv)
excess of fair value of acquired net assets over cost, 8.3(g)(ii)
fair value of liabilities at acquisition date, 8.3(g)(xii)
fair value when less than 100 percent acquired, 8.3(g)(xvi)
goodwill amortization, tax deductibility of, 8.3(g)(xv)
income tax effects on purchase price allocation, 8.3(g)(xiii)
last-in, first-out (LIFO) inventories, 8.3(g)(iii)
leases, 8.3(g)(vi)
long-lived assets classified as held for sale, 8.3(g)(viii)
noncurrent assets, 8.3(g)(v)
normal profit margin, 8.3(g)(iv)
pensions, purchase price of, 8.3(g)(ix)
postemployment benefits of acquiree, 8.3(g)(xi)
postretirement benefits of acquiree, 8.3(g)(x)
purchase price allocation, income tax effects on, 8.3(g)(xiii)
recognition and measurement principle, 8.3(g)(i)
research and development (R&D) acquired, 8.3(g)(vii)
SEC concerns, 8.3(g)(xvii)
selling costs, 8.3(g)(iv)
recording date, 8.3(l)
reverse acquisitions:
consideration transferred in, 8.3(a)(ii)
generally, 8.3(a)(i)
SAB No. 61, 8.3(k)
SEC filings, disclosures in, 8.3(o)
stages, combination achieved in, 8.3(m)(i)
without transfer of consideration, 8.3(m)(ii)
AFPC, *see* Antifraud Programs and Controls Framework
American Institute of Certified Public Accountants (AICPA):
auditing standards:
clarity/convergence of, 1.10(a)(ii)
generally, 1.10(a)
risk assessment, 1.10(a)(i)
technical assistance, provision of, 1.10(a)(iii)
CPA services:
accounting, 1.10(b)(ii)
auditing, 1.10(b)(i)
consulting, 1.10(b)(iv)
generally, 1.10(b)
special investigations, 1.10(b)(iv)
tax services, 1.10(b)(iii)
valuation, 1.10(b)(iv)
financial statement disclosure requirements, 4.8(a)(vii)

American Institute of Certified Public Accountants (AICPA): (*Continued*)
- generally, 1.7, 1.10
- health care organizations, 35.2(c)
- not-for-profit organizations, 28.1(a)(ii)
- Uniform CPA Examination, 1.10(c)

Antifraud Programs and Controls Framework (AFPC):
- generally, 41.3(d)
- service types of, 41.3(d)(i)

APB, *see* Accounting Principles Board
ARB, *see* Accounting Research Bulletins
ASC, *see* Accounting Standards Codification
Assets:
- acquisition method (business combinations), *see* Acquisition method (business combinations), *subhead:* recognition/measurement of assets and liabilities
- on balance sheet:
  - current assets, 4.3(a)(i)
  - generally, 4.3(a)
  - noncurrent assets, 4.3(a)(ii)
- capital assets (state/local government accounting):
  - depreciation of, 33.4(c)(vi), 33.4(h)(i)
  - disposal/retirement of, 33.4(h)(iii)
  - generally, 33.4(c)(iv), 33.4(h)
  - impairment of, 33.4(c)(vi), 33.4(h)(iv)
  - subsidiary property records, 33.4(h)(ii)
  - valuation of, 33.4(c)(v)
- depreciation of, *see* Depreciation
- fair value measurements of:
  - liabilities vs. assets, 24.4(e)(i)
  - nonfinancial assets, 24.3(c), 24.4(e)(vi)
- on Form 8-K, 5.6(a)(i)
- generally, 4.3(a)
- health care organizations:
  - changes in net assets/equity, statement of, 35.5(d)
  - intangible assets, 35.3(k)
  - net assets/net position, 35.3(a)
- intangible, *see* Intangible assets
- long-term assets, 10.4(c)
  - capitalization analysis, 10.4(c)(ii)
  - capitalization table, 10.4(c)(iii)
  - debt ratios, 10.4(c)(iv)
  - fixed asset turnover ratio, 10.4(c)(i)
  - off-balance-sheet obligations, 10.4(c)(vi), 10.4(c)(vii)
  - preferred stock ratios, 10.4(c)(v)
  - property analysis, 10.4(c)(viii)
- measurement of deferred tax assets, 17.2(d)(iv)
- not-for-profit organizations:
  - depreciation of assets by, 28.2(g)
  - fixed assets, 28.2(f), 28.2(f)(i)
- pension plans:
  - expected return, 27.2(d)(iii)
  - generally, 27.2(e)
  - net assets available for benefits, 27.5(c), 27.5(c)(i)
  - recognition, 27.2(f)
- on personal financial statements:
  - closely held business, 22.3(h)
  - estimated current value, 22.3(a)
  - future interests, 22.3(l)
  - intangible assets, 22.3(k)
  - life insurance, 22.3(g)
  - limited partnership interests, 22.3(d)
  - listing of assets/liabilities on, 22.1(d)
  - marketable securities, 22.3(c)
  - options on other than marketable securities, 22.3(f)
  - personal property, 22.3(j)
  - precious metals, 22.3(e)
  - real estate, 22.3(i)
  - receivables, 22.3(b)
- realization of (partnerships), 20.5(a)
- recognition of deferred tax assets:
  - of change in valuation allowance, 17.2(d)(iii)
  - generally, 17.2(d), 17.2(d)(i)
  - of valuation allowance, 17.2(d)(ii)
- valuation of, *see* Valuation

AU 328 (*Auditing Fair Value Measurements and Disclosures*):
- assumptions, testing reliability of, 24.6(c)(iii)
- data, testing of, 24.6(c)(iv)
- fair value measurements, testing, 24.6(c)(i)
- generally, 24.6(c)
- significant assumptions, testing, 24.6(c)(ii)
- underlying data, testing, 24.6(c)(ii)
- valuation model, testing, 24.6(c)(ii)

Audits and auditing:
- AICPA standards:
  - clarity/convergence of, 1.10(a)(ii)
  - generally, 1.10(a)
  - risk assessment, 1.10(a)(i)

technical assistance, provision of, 1.10(a)(iii)
as CPA service, 1.10(b)(i)
of fair value, 25.3
of fair value measurements:
AU 328 guidance, 24.6(c)
estimates in, 24.6(b)
generally, 24.6
PCAOB Staff Audit Practice Alert No. 2, 24.6(d)
standards for, 24.6(a)
in federal government:
generally, 32.5
Generally Accepted Government Auditing Standards (GAGAS), 32.5(a)
government-wide audit opinion, achievement of, 32.6(a)
recipients of federal financial assistance, 32.5(b)(i)
by GAO:
compliance audits, 1.12(b)
financial statement audits, 1.12(a)
operational audits, 1.12(c)
of not-for-profit organizations:
compliance auditing, 28.4(f)
consolidation of financial statements, 28.4(e)
generally, 28.4(a)
government requirements, 28.1(b)
and internal control, 28.4(b)
investments, 28.4(g)
materiality, 28.4(c)
taxes, 28.4(d)
unique areas, 28.4(h)
of personal financial statements, 22.10
role of, in U.S. economy, 1.1
of state/local governmental units:
committees, audit, 33.7(b)(ii)
generally, 33.7
governmental rotation of auditors, 33.7(b)(i)
Single Audit Act Amendments (1996), 33.7(a)
U.S. standards, 1.8
Average capital ratio, 20.2(c)

Balance sheet:
ASC Topic 740–10 on, 17.3(h)
assets on:
current assets, 4.3(a)(i)
generally, 4.3(a)
noncurrent assets, 4.3(a)(ii)
banks and savings institutions, 30.2(k)(ii)
bond discounts/premiums on, 18.4(g)
Chapter 11 bankruptcy reporting, 39.5(f)(i), 39.5(f)(iv)
current liabilities classification on, 18.3(l)(i)
elements of, 10.4(a)
generally, 4.3
health care organizations:
generally, 35.5(b)
governmental health care entities, 35.5(b)(ii)
not-for-profit entities, 35.5(b)(i)
international standards and, 4.10(b)
liabilities on:
current liabilities, 4.3(b)(i)
and current ratio, 4.3(b)(iii)
generally, 4.3(b)
noncurrent liabilities, 4.3(b)(ii)
and working capital, 4.3(b)(iii)
not-for-profit organizations, 28.3(a)(ii)
partnerships:
initial balance sheet, 20.1(f)
liquidation, 20.5(d)
real estate on, 31.9(a)(i)
revenue-related disclosures on:
generally, 12.7(b)
installment receivables, 12.7(b)(ii)
interest on receivables, 12.7(b)(iii)
single-payment accounts receivable, 12.7(b)(i)
segregation of compensating cash balances on, 11.2(f)(ii)
shares of stock on, 19.2(g), 19.3(e)(ii)
stockholders' equity on:
contributed equity, 4.3(c)(i)
generally, 4.3(c)
retained earnings, 4.3(c)(ii)
subclassifications, 4.3(c)(iii)
treasury stock on, 19.5(b)
Balance sheet analysis:
liquidity analysis:
activity ratios, 10.4(b)(ii)
analytical ratios, 10.4(b)(i)
generally, 10.4(b)
long-term assets and liabilities:
capitalization analysis, 10.4(c)(ii)
capitalization table, 10.4(c)(iii)
debt ratios, 10.4(c)(iv)

Balance sheet analysis: (*Continued*)
fixed asset turnover ratio, 10.4(c)(i)
generally, 10.4(c)
off-balance-sheet obligations, 10.4(c)(vi), 10.4(c)(vii)
preferred stock ratios, 10.4(c)(v)
property analysis, 10.4(c)(viii)
Bankruptcy:
alternatives to:
assignment for benefit of creditors, 39.2(b)
generally, 39.2
out-of-court settlements, 39.2(a)
automatic stay:
equity in property, determination of, 39.3(d)(ii)
generally, 39.3(d)
relief from, 39.3(d)(i)
avoiding power, 39.3(f)
bankruptcy court proceedings:
accounting services in, 39.2(d)
generally, 39.2(c)
Chapter 7 bankruptcy (liquidation), 39.2(c)(ii)
Chapter 11 bankruptcy, *see* Chapter 11 bankruptcy
Chapter 12 bankruptcy (debt adjustment for family farmers with regular annual income), 39.2(c)(iii)
dispute resolution proceedings, 41.2(d)(iii)
executory contracts:
generally, 39.3(e)
limitations on, 39.3(e)(i)
rejection of, 39.3(e)(ii)
filing of petition for, 39.3(a)
fraudulent transfers:
generally, 39.3(h)
leveraged buyouts as, 39.3(h)(i)
search for, 39.3(h)(ii)
leases:
generally, 39.3(e)
limitations on, 39.3(e)(i)
petition for:
data required in, 39.3(c)
filing of, 39.3(a)
timing of, 39.3(b)
postpetition transfers:
and adequate value received, 39.3(i)(i)
generally, 39.3(i)
unauthorized transfers, prevention of, 39.3(i)(ii)
preferential payments:
exceptions, 39.3(g)(i)
generally, 39.3(g)
search for, 39.3(g)(ii)
reclamation, requests for, 39.3(k)
reporting requirements:
disclosure requirements, 39.7(b)
financial projections, 39.7(e)
generally, 39.7
investigative services, 39.7(d)
litigation services, 39.7(a)
operating reports, 39.7(c)
setoffs:
early setoff penalty, 39.3(j)(i)
generally, 39.3(j), 39.3(j)(ii)
Title 11 of U.S. Code provisions, 39.2(c)(i)
U.S. trustee, appointment of, 39.3(l)
Banks and savings institutions:
capital adequacy guidelines for:
assets, risk-weighted, 30.2(f)(iii)
calculations, 30.2(f)(iv)
generally, 30.2(f)
interest rate risk, 30.2(f)(v)
market risk, 30.2(f)(vi)
minimum requirements, 30.2(f)(iv)
ratios, risk-based and leverage, 30.2(f)(i)
Tier 1/2/3 components, 30.2(f)(ii)
capital matters, disclosure of, 30.2(i)
corrective action with:
examinations, risk-focused, 30.2(g)(iii)
generally, 30.2(g)
regulatory rating systems and, 30.2(g)(ii)
scope, 30.2(g)(i)
credit losses:
accounting guidance, 30.2(o)(i)
allowance methodologies, 30.2(o)(iii)
regulatory guidance, 30.2(o)(ii)
debt/equity securities, investments in:
accounting for, 30.2(r)(i)
borrowing and lending, securities, 30.2(r)(iv)
generally, 30.2(r)
short sales, 30.2(r)(iii)
wash sales, 30.2(r)(ii)
debt incurred by:
accounting guidance, 30.2(u)(iii)
long-term debt, 30.2(u)(i)
short-term debt, 30.2(u)(ii)

deposits:
  demand, 30.2(s)(i)
  savings, 30.2(s)(ii)
  time, 30.2(s)(iii)
and derivatives:
  accounting guidance, 30.2(w)(vii)
  foreign exchange contracts, 30.2(w)(v)
  forwards, 30.2(w)(ii)
  futures, 30.2(w)(i)
  generally, 30.2(w)
  options, 30.2(w)(iii)
  swaps, 30.2(w)(iv)
disclosure:
  of capital matters, 30.2(i)
  of risks/uncertainties, 30.2(k)(v)
electronic banking, risks of, 30.2(y)
enforcement actions, 30.2(h)
federal funds purchased, 30.2(t)(i)
fee income:
  from fiduciary services, 30.2(x)(i)
  miscellaneous forms of, 30.2(x)(ii)
fiduciary services offered by, 30.2(x)(i)
financial statement presentation for:
  balance sheets, 30.2(k)(ii)
  cash flow, statements of, 30.2(k)(iii)
  commitments/off-balance-sheet risk, 30.2(k)(iv)
  income statements, 30.2(k)(i)
  risks/uncertainties, disclosure of, 30.2(k)(v)
and GAAP vs. regulatory accounting principles, 30.2(m)
generally, 30.1(c)(i)
industry guidance, sources of, 30.2(l)
loans:
  accounting for, 30.2(n)(ii)
  credit losses with, *see subhead:* credit losses
  nonaccrual loans, taxation of, 30.2(v)(iv)
  taxation of loan loss reserves, 30.2(v)(i)
  types of, 30.2(n)(i)
loan sales:
  accounting guidance, 30.2(p)(v)
  loan servicing, 30.2(p)(iii)
  regulatory guidance, 30.2(p)(iv)
  securitizations, 30.2(p)(ii)
  underwriting standards, 30.2(p)(i)
  valuation, 30.2(p)(vi)
real estate, bank-owned:
  foreclosed assets, 30.2(q)(iii), 30.2(v)(vii)
  former bank premises, 30.2(q)(ii)
  investments, 30.2(q)(i)
  taxation of, 30.2(v)(vii)
regulation of:
  environment, regulatory, 30.2(d)
  Federal Deposit Insurance Corporation (FDIC), 30.2(c)(iii)
  Federal Reserve Board (Fed), 30.2(c)(ii)
  generally, 30.2(c)
  Office of the Comptroller of the Currency (OCC), 30.2(c)(i)
  Office of Thrift Supervision (OTS), 30.2(c)(iv)
regulation/supervision of, 30.2(b)
repurchase agreements, 30.2(t)(ii)
risk factors with:
  asset-quality risk, 30.2(a)(iii)
  electronic banking, 30.2(y)
  fiduciary risk, 30.2(a)(iv)
  generally, 30.2(a)
  interest rate risk, 30.2(a)(i)
  liquidity risk, 30.2(a)(ii)
  market risk, 30.2(a)(vii)
  operating risk, 30.2(a)(vi)
  processing risk, 30.2(a)(v)
and Section 112 of FDIC Improvement Act (FDICIA):
  generally, 30.2(e)
  guidelines, 30.2(e)(i)
  holding company exception, 30.2(e)(iii)
  reports, availability of, 30.2(e)(iv)
  requirements, 30.2(e)(ii)
and Security and Exchange Commission (SEC):
  background, 30.2(j)(i)
  reporting requirements of, 30.2(j)(ii)
taxation of:
  FHLB dividends, 30.2(v)(ix)
  foreclosed property, 30.2(v)(vii)
  hedging, 30.2(v)(v)
  leasing activities, 30.2(v)(viii)
  life insurance, bank-owned, 30.2(v)(x)
  loan loss reserves, 30.2(v)(i)
  loan origination fees/costs, 30.2(v)(vi)
  market discount, 30.2(v)(xii)
  mark to market, 30.2(v)(ii)
  nonaccrual loans, 30.2(v)(iv)
  original issue discount, 30.2(v)(xi)
  tax-exempt securities, 30.2(v)(iii)
technology, risks of, 30.2(y)

Basis of accounting:
for income taxes, 17.1(b)
for not-for-profit organizations, 28.2(b)
for personal financial statements, 22.1(d)
for state/local government accounting:
expenditure transactions, 33.4(j)(iv)
generally, 33.4(c)(viii), 33.4(j)(i), 33.4(j)(ii)
nonexchange transactions, 33.4(j)(v)
revenue transactions, 33.4(j)(iii)
Board of directors:
fraud by:
backgrounds, 40.6(a)
degree of influence, 40.6(c)
generally, 40.6
motivations, 40.6(b)
and Sarbanes-Oxley Act, 5.1(e)(i)
Bonds:
balance sheet, discount and premium in, 18.4(g)
blocks issued at different rates, 18.5(e)
conversion of:
accrued interest, 18.6(l)
generally, 18.6(j)
induced conversion, 18.6(k)
convertible, 18.4(b)(i)
discount on, 18.5(d)
with issuer option to settle for cash upon conversion, 18.11(a)(v)
with premium put, 18.11(a)(i)
defaulted, 18.6(c)
defined, 18.4(a)
discount, bond:
amortization of, 18.5(c)
in balance sheet, 18.4(g)
convertible bonds, 18.5(d)
issue of bonds, 18.4(e)(ii)
origin, 18.4(e)(i)
warrants, bonds with, 18.5(d)
issuance of:
authority, 18.4(c)
blocks at different rates, 18.5(e)
bond discount, 18.4(e)(i), 18.4(e)(ii)
business combinations, allocation of costs in, 18.4(e)(iv)
between interest dates, 18.4(e)(v)
premium, 18.4(e)(i), 18.4(e)(ii)
price, determination of, 18.4(f)
recording issue of bonds, 18.4(e)
segregation of costs, 18.4(e)(iii)
steps, 18.4(d)
maturity of:
payment at, 18.6(a)
redemption before, 18.6(f)
settlement after, 18.6(b)
premium, bond:
amortization of, 18.5(c)
in balance sheet, 18.4(g)
issue of bonds, 18.4(e)(ii)
origin, 18.4(e)(i)
serial, 18.4(b)(ii)
interest rates, 18.5(f)
and sinking funds, 18.4(b)(ii)
subscription rights and warrants sold with, 18.6(m)
types of, 18.4(b)
with warrants, 18.5(d)
Bond interest:
accrual of, 18.5(a)
amortization of premium or discount, 18.5(c)
payment of, 18.5(b)
bonds held by trustee, 18.5(b)(ii)
treasury bonds, 18.5(b)(i)
serial bonds, 18.5(f)
treasury bonds, 18.5(b)(i)
trustee, bonds held by, 18.5(b)(ii)
Bond redemption:
creditors:
classification of obligations by, 18.6(d)
compositions with, 18.6(e)
extinguishment of debt:
gains and losses from, 18.6(f)(i)
noncash, 18.6(f)(ii)
before maturity, 18.6(f)
payment at maturity, 18.6(a)
redemption before maturity, 18.6(f)
refunding, payment by, 18.6(h)(i)
reissue of treasury bonds, 18.6(g)
settlement after maturity, 18.6(b)
sinking funds, use of, 18.6(h)
treatment of treasury bonds, 18.6(g)
Bond refunds, 18.6(i)
Break-even analysis:
generally, 29.5
graphical approach to, 29.5(a)
margin of safety, 29.5(c)
target surplus volume, 29.5(b)
Broadcasting:
generally, 14.6(d)
licenses, revoked or nonrenewed, 14.6(d)(ii)

rights, 14.6(d)(i)
Budgets and budgeting:
federal government accounting:
accounting, budgetary, 32.2(b), 32.2(b)(i), 32.2(b)(iii), 32 (App B)
budget process, 32.4(a)
congressional action, 32.4(b)(ii)
execution of budget, 32.4(b)(iii)
formulation of budget, 32.4(b)(i)
Office of Management and Budget (OMB), 32.2(a)(ii)
review/audit of budget, 32.4(b)(iv)
inventory control, 13.7(a)(iv)
state/local government accounting:
capital budgets, 33.4(k)(v)
comparisons, budgetary, 33.4(k)(vi)
execution of budget, 33.4(k)(iii)
generally, 33.4(c)(ix)
operating budgets, 33.4(k)(i)
preparation of budget, 33.4(k)(ii)
proprietary fund budgeting, 33.4(k)(iv)
Business combinations:
acquisition method of accounting for, *see* Acquisition method
and ASC Topic 740 (*Income Taxes*), 17.2(e)(iii)
consolidated financial statements, 9.1(b)
defined, 8.2
direct costs of:
acquiree, costs incurred by, 8.3(c)(i)
discretionary costs, 8.3(c)(iv)
employee costs, 8.3(c)(ii), 8.3(c)(iii)
generally, 8.3(c)
plant closing costs, 8.3(c)(ii)
generally, 8.1
health care organizations:
governmental entities, 35.3(o)(ii)
not-for-profit entities, 35.3(o)(i)
identifying, 8.2(a)
IFRS No. 3 on, 8.4(i)
intangible assets, acquisition of, 14.2(a)
issuance of bonds; allocation of costs, 18.4(e)(iv)
leases, 15.10(f)
leveraged buyouts, *see* Leveraged buyouts
pension plans, nonrecurring events with, 27.3(g)
purchase of; inventory valuation method, 13.5(h)
Business valuation:
cost approach:
generally, 25.5(c)
with intangible assets, 25.8(c)(i)
and credentials of valuation analyst, 25.10
and discount rates, 25.5(a)(i)
and discounts/premiums, 25.6
generally, 25.4
income approach:
generally, 25.5(a)
with intangible assets, 25.8(c)(iii)
intangible assets:
accounting guidance for, 25.8(b)
cost approach, 25.8(c)(i)
determining existence of, 25.8(a)
generally, 25.8
income approach, 25.8(c)(iii)
market approach, 25.8(c)(ii)
methodology, choice of, 25.8(c)
market approach:
generally, 25.5(b)
with intangible assets, 25.8(c)(ii)
methods of:
asset-based (cost) approach, 25.5(c)
generally, 25.5
market approach, 25.5(b)
reasonableness check in, 25.9
reasons for, 25.1(b)
terminology, 25 (App A)
and valuation report, 25.7

Capitalized costs, real estate, *see* Real estate capitalized costs
Capital leases:
accounting for, 15.4(a)
disclosures for, 15.4(b)
example:
amortization, lessee, 15.4(c)(iv)
classification of lease, 15.4(c)(ii)
inception, accounting at, 15.4(c)(iii)
minimum payments, 15.4(c)(i)
payments, 15.4(c)(i), 15.4(c)(v)
Cash:
accounting for, 11.1(b)
characteristics of, 11.1(a)
classification of, 11.2(b)
and concentration of credit risk:
disclosure, fair value, 11.2(h)(i)
generally, 11.2(h)
control over, 11.1(b)

Cash: (*Continued*)
defined, 11.2(a)
disclosure issues with:
concentration of credit risk, 11.2(h)(i)
lines of credit, unused, 11.2(g)(ii)
importance of, 11.1(a)
overdrafts, bank, 11.2(d)
presentation of, 11.2(b)
restricted, 11.2(c)
unused lines of credit:
disclosure with, 11.2(g)(ii)
fees paid for future credit availability, 11.2(g)(i)
generally, 11.2(g)
Cash balances:
compensating:
disclosure, 11.2(f)(i)
generally, 11.2(f)
segregation of, on balance sheet, 11.2(f)(ii)
foreign balances, 11.2(e)
misrepresentation of, 11.1(c)
Cash flow analysis:
comparing cash flows, 10.5(b)
direct vs. indirect methods of, 10.5(a)
Cash flows, comparing, 10.5(b)
Cash flows, statement of, *see* Statement of cash flows
Certified Public Accountants (CPAs):
accounting services, 1.10(b)(ii)
auditing services, 1.10(b)(i)
consulting services, 1.10(b)(iv)
generally, 1.10(b)
special investigations, 1.10(b)(iv)
tax services, 1.10(b)(iii)
valuation services, 1.10(b)(iv)
Chapter 11 bankruptcy:
claims under:
administrative expenses, 39.4(c)
priorities, 39.4(d)
processing of claims, 39.4(e)
proof of claims, 39.4(a)
undersecured claims, 39.4(b)
creditors' committee, assistance to:
bargaining process, 39.6(g)(i)
debtor's projections, evaluations of, 39.6(g)(ii)
plan and disclosure statement, review of, 39.6(g)(iv)
reorganization value, 39.6(g)(iii)
debtor, assistance to:
liquidation value of assets, 39.6(f)(i)
pro forma balance sheet, 39.6(f)(iv)
projections of future operations, 39.6(f)(ii)
reorganization model, 39.6(f)(v)
reorganization value, 39.6(f)(iii)
disclosure statement:
adequate information, definition of, 39.6(c)(i)
content of, 39.6(c)(ii)
generally, 39.6(c)
examiner, appointment of:
accountants as examiners, 39.5(d)(ii)
functions of examiner, 39.5(d)(i)
generally, 39.5(d)
operating under:
credit, obtaining, 39.5(b)
examiner, appointment of, *see subhead:* examiner, appointment of
generally, 39.5
operating statements, 39.5(e)
trustees, appointment of, 39.5(c)
use of property, *see subhead:* use of property
plan under:
claim classification, 39.6(a)
confirmation of plan, 39.6(d)
confirmation requirements, 39.6(e)
disclosure statement, *see subhead:* disclosure statement
generally, 39.6
long-lived assets, impairment of, 39.6(i)
plan development, 39.6(b)
prepackaged/prenegotiated plans, 39.2(c)(iv)
reorganization under:
allocation of reorganization value, 39.6(h)(ii)
debtors not qualifying for fresh start, reporting by, 39.6(h)(iv)
disclosure requirements, 39.6(h)(iii)
fresh start reporting, requirements for, 39.6(h)(i)
reporting in:
generally, 39.5(f)
statement of cash flows, 39.5(f)(iii)
statement of operations, 39.5(f)(ii)
use of property:
cash collateral, 39.5(a)(i)
generally, 39.5(a)

secured lender, providing information to, 39.5(a)(ii)
Closely held business, valuation of, 22.3(h)
Colleges, public, 33.6
Committee on Accounting Procedure:
  Accounting Research Bulletins (ARB), 2.2(b)(ii)
  failures of, 2.2(b)(iii)
  generally, 2.2(b)
  statement of principles, lack of, 2.2(b)(i)
Compensation, stock-based, *see* Stock-based compensation
Comprehensive income, on income statement, 4.4(d)(iv)
Computers. *See also* E-discovery
  and forensic technology, 41.3(f)(i)
  generally, 42.1
  software, as intangible asset, 14.6(f)
Conceptual framework (FASB):
  Accounting Principles Board (APB) and:
    dissolution of, 2.2(c)(iii)
    generally, 2.2(c)
    and investment credit, 2.2(c)(ii)
    postulates/principles of, 2.2(c)(i)
    and Seidman Committee, 2.2(c)(ii)
  assets and liabilities, defining:
    generally, 2.2(d), 2.2(d)(i), 2.3(a)(iii)
    matching, 2.2(d)(ii), 2.2(d)(iii)
    nondistortion, 2.2(d)(ii), 2.2(d)(iii)
    what-you-may-call-its, 2.2(d)(ii), 2.2(d)(iii)
  as body of concepts, 2.3(a)
  Committee on Accounting Procedure and:
    Accounting Research Bulletins (ARBs), 2.2(b)(ii)
    failures, 2.2(b)(iii)
    generally, 2.2(b)
    lack of statement of principles, 2.2(b)(i)
  as decision-making tool, 2.3(a)(i)
  functions of, 2.3(a)(iv)
  generally, 1.4(e), 2.2, 2.3
  historical background, 2.2(d)(i)
  initiation of, 2.2(d)(iv)
  and representation of real world, 2.3(a)(ii)
  Special Committee on Cooperation with Stock Exchanges and:
    "accepted principles of accounting," 2.2(a)(i)
    generally, 2.2(a)
    recommendations, 2.2(a)(ii)
    and SEC, 2.2(a)(iii)
    and Securities Exchange Act, 2.2(a)(iii)
Consolidated financial statements:
  about, 9.1
  and business combinations, 9.1(b)
  combined statements, 9.1(e)
  disclosures with, 9.1(a)(iv)
  and equity method, 9.1(d)
  equity method vs., 9.3(a)
  historical summary of pronouncements, 9.4(a)
  intercompany amounts on, 9.1(a)(ii)
  policy, consolidation, 9.1(a)(i)
  purpose of, 9.1(a), 9.1(f)
  Regulation S-X and, 5.4(d)
  SEC rules and regulations:
    disclosures, miscellaneous, 9.1(g)(iii)
    intercompany items and transactions, 9.1(g)(ii)
    reporting entity, selection of, 9.1(g)(i)
  and translation, 9.1(c)
  and variable interest entities, 9.1(a)(iii)
Construction:
  ASC Topic 980 and, 36.6(e)(i), 36.8(a)(iii)
  costs of, 31.3(d)
  health care organizations, 35.3(l)(v)
  in progress, 16.13(b)
  property under, 16.9(b)
  real estate transactions; continued involvement of seller, 31.2(f)(ix)
  regulated utilities, 36.10(d)(ii)
  sale and leaseback transactions, 15.10(h)(i)
Construction revenue recognition:
  accounting methods:
    completed contract, 31.6(b)(ii), 31.6(d)
    consistent application of, 31.6(b)(iii)
    generally, 31.6(b)
    percentage-of-completion, *see subhead:* percentage-of-completion method
  authoritative literature on, 31.6(a)
  claims, 31.6(f)
  completed contract method, 31.6(b)(ii), 31.6(d)
  generally, 31.6
  losses, provision for, 31.6(e)
  percentage-of-completion method:
    cost determination, 31.6(c)(ii)
    estimates, revision of, 31.6(c)(iii)

Construction revenue recognition: (*Continued*)
generally, 31.6(b)(i), 31.6(c)
revenue determination, 31.6(c)(i)
Consulting (by CPAs), 1.10(b)(iv)
Contingencies. *See also* Loss contingencies
business combinations:
assets/liabilities arising from, 8.3(h)
earnings, based on, 8.3(d)(i)
security prices, based on, 8.3(d)(ii)
current liabilities:
generally, 18.3(i)
likelihood of, 18.3(i)(i)
types of, 18.3(i)(ii)
Control, internal, *see* Internal control
Corporation(s):
advantages of, 19.1(b)
certificate of incorporation, 19.1(d)
defined, 19.1(a)
owners' interests in, 19.1(c)
Corrections to income statement, 4.4(d)(v)
Cost behavior analysis:
fixed costs, 29.3(b), 29.3(c)
generally, 29.3
program-specific vs. common fixed costs, 29.3(c)
variable costs, 29.3(a)
Cost-volume-revenue (CVR) analysis for nonprofit organizations:
break-even analysis:
generally, 29.5
graphical approach to, 29.5(a)
margin of safety, 29.5(c)
target surplus volume, 29.5(b)
cost behavior analysis:
fixed costs, 29.3(b), 29.3(c)
generally, 29.3
program-specific vs. common fixed costs, 29.3(c)
variable costs, 29.3(a)
examples, 29.5(d)
with fixed revenue only, 29.6
program mix analysis, 29.8
questions answered by, 29.1
revenue analysis, 29.2
usefulness of, 29.9
with variable and fixed revenues, 29.7
with variable revenue only:
CM ratio, 29.4(c)
contribution margin, 29.4(a)
unit CM, 29.4(b)
CPAs, *see* Certified Public Accountants
Creditors:
advertising for (estates), 38.1(i)(xiii)
assignment for benefit of, 39.2(b)
Chapter 11 bankruptcy:
bargaining process, 39.6(g)(i)
debtor's projections, evaluations of, 39.6(g)(ii)
plan and disclosure statement, review of, 39.6(g)(iv)
reorganization value, 39.6(g)(iii)
classification of obligations by, 18.6(d)
compositions with, 18.6(e)
debtor–creditor relationship (partnerships), 20.2(d)(iv)
financial statement analysis by, 10.1(b)(ii)
obligations callable by, 18.3(a)(iii)
trade, 18.3(c), 18.3(e)
Current liabilities:
accounts payable, 18.3(c)
accrued expenses, 18.3(f)
accrued payroll, 18.3(f)(ii)
commissions and fees, 18.3(f)(iv)
federal income taxes, 18.3(f)(v)
interest payable, 18.3(f)(i)
property taxes, 18.3(f)(vi)
rent, 18.3(f)(vii)
vacation pay, 18.3(f)(iii)
advances from officers and employees, 18.3(g)
balance sheet classification of, 18.3(l)(i)
contingencies:
accrual of, 18.3(i)(iii)
assessments, 18.3(i)(vii)
disclosure of, 18.3(i)(v)
environmental liabilities, 18.3(i)(x)
estimating amounts to accrue, 18.3(i)(iv)
generally, 18.3(i)
general reserves for, 18.3(i)(viii)
likelihood of, 18.3(i)(i)
litigation and claims, 18.3(i)(vii)
types of, 18.3(i)(ii)
uninsured risks, 18.3(i)(vi)
vulnerability from concentrations, 18.3(i)(xi)
warranty obligations, 18.3(i)(ix)
deferred revenue, 18.3(h)(i)
defined, 18.3(a)
demand notes, 18.3(a)(iv)
dividends payable, 18.3(h)

exit or disposal activity obligations:
contract termination costs, 18.3(j)(ii)
disclosure of, 18.3(j)(v)
financial statement presentation, 18.3(j)(iv)
generally, 18.3(j)
miscellaneous costs, 18.3(j)(iii)
one-time termination benefits, 18.3(j)(i)
financial statement presentation:
balance sheet, 18.3(l)(i)
exit or disposal activity obligations, 18.3(j)(iv)
separate statement or note, 18.3(l)(ii)
foreign currencies, translation into, 18.3(k)
generally, 4.3(b)(i)
long-term obligations:
approaching maturity, 18.3(a)(i)
subjective acceleration clause, 18.3(a)(v)
notes payable:
bank loans, 18.3(d)
trade creditors, 18.3(e)
obligations callable by creditor, 18.3(a)(iii)
short-term obligations to be refinanced, 18.3(a)(ii)
trade creditors:
accounts payable, 18.3(c)
notes payable, 18.3(e)
types of, 18.3(b)
various, 18.3(l)(ii)
Current ratio, 4.3(b)(iii)
CVR analysis, *see* Cost-volume-revenue analysis

Debt. *See also* Bankruptcy
acquisition of PP&E by issuance of, 16.2(a)(ii)
banks and savings institutions, incurred by:
accounting guidance, 30.2(u)(iii)
long-term debt, 30.2(u)(i)
short-term debt, 30.2(u)(ii)
estates, payment of debts by:
generally, 38.1(i)(xii)
order of payment, 38.1(i)(xiv)
source of funds for, 38.1(i)(xv)
extinguishment of (bond redemption), 18.6(f)(i), 18.6(f)(ii)
family farmers with regular annual income (bankruptcy), 39.2(c)(iii)
on financial statements:
debt and equity investments, 4.8(b)(i)
generally, 4.8(b)(iv)
long-term debt, 4.8(b)(iv), 18.7
health care organizations; provision for bad debts, 35.3(e)(iii)
increasing-rate, 18.11(a)(ii)
indexed debt instruments, 18.11(a)(iii)
partnerships, debtor–creditor relationship in, 20.2(d)(iv)
restructurings, troubled debt, 18.10(a)
warrants issued with, 19.6(b)(i)
Debt analysis (finance companies):
asset protection ratios, 10.8(b)
capitalization, 10.8(f)
generally, 10.8
liquidity, 10.8(e)
loan spreads, 10.8(d)
operating agreement, 10.8(a)
reserve and loss ratios, 10.8(c)
Debt ratios, 10.4(c)(iv)
Debt securities:
after acquisition, accounting for:
available-for-sale securities, 11.4(c)(iii)
generally, 11.4(c)
held-to-maturity securities, 11.4(c)(i)
trading securities, 11.4(c)(ii)
transfers between categories, 11.4(c)(iv)
defined, 11.4(a)
disclosures with, 11.4(e)
generally, 11.4(a)
impairment of, 11.4(d)
initial recognition/measurement of:
available-for-sale securities, 11.4(b)(iii)
generally, 11.4(b)
held-to-maturity securities, 11.4(b)(i)
trading securities, 11.4(b)(ii)
Depreciation:
composite, 16.11(b)(ii)
group, 16.11(b)(i)
property, plant and equipment, *see* Property, plant and equipment depreciation
Depreciation methods:
changing, 16.10(f)
decreasing-charge:
double-declining-balance method, 16.10(c)(iii)
fixed-percentage-of-declining-balance method, 16.10(c)(ii)
generally, 16.10(c)
sum-of-digits method, 16.10(c)(i)

Depreciation methods: (*Continued*)
  generally, 16.10
  interest:
    annuity method, 16.10(d)(i)
    sinking-fund method, 16.10(d)(ii)
  for partial periods, 16.10(e)
  straight-line, 16.10(a)
  usage:
    productive-output method, 16.10(b)(ii)
    service-hours method, 16.10(b)(i)
Derecognition, 17.3(f), 31.2(j)(viii)
Derivatives:
  accounting treatment of, 26.5
  cash flow hedges:
    disallowed situations, 26.5(a)(iv)
    disclosures for, 26.6(d)
    eligible risks, 26.5(a)(ii)
    generally, 26.5(a)
    internal derivatives contracts, 26.5(a)(v)
    prerequisites, 26.5(a)(iii)
    qualifying exposures, 26.5(a)(i)
  disclosures for:
    all reporting entities, 26.6(a)
    cash flow hedges, 26.6(d)
    fair value hedges, 26.6(c)
    hedging relationships, 26.6(b)
  embedded, 26.4
  fair value hedges:
    disallowed situations, 26.5(b)(iv)
    disclosures for, 26.6(c)
    examples of, 26.5(b)(i)
    generally, 26.5(b)
    prerequisite requirements with, 26.5(b)(iii)
    risks qualifying as, 26.5(b)(ii)
  generally, 26.1
  hedges:
    cash flow hedges, *see subhead:* cash flow hedges
    disclosures for, 26.6(b)
    effectiveness of, 26.5(d)
    fair value hedges, *see subhead:* fair value hedges
    foreign operations, net investments in, 26.5(c)
    nonqualifying trades, 26.5(e)
    speculative trades, 26.5(e)
  and IFRS, 26.7
  qualifying criteria for:
    exemptions to, 26.3
    generally, 26.2

Disclosure(s). *See also* AU 328 (*Auditing Fair Value Measurements and Disclosures*)
  in annual report to stockholders, 5.4(q)
  bankruptcy:
    adequate information, definition of, 39.6(c)(i)
    content of disclosure statement, 39.6(c)(ii)
    generally, 39.6(c), 39.6(h)(iii), 39.7(b)
    plan and disclosure statement, review of, 39.6(g)(iv)
  banks and savings institutions:
    capital matters, 30.2(i)
    risks/uncertainties, 30.2(k)(v)
  for capital leases, 15.4(b)
  of capital structure:
    generally, 19.9
    preferred stock, 19.9(a)
  of cash:
    and concentration of credit risk, 11.2(h)(i)
    lines of credit, unused, 11.2(g)(ii)
  compensating cash balances, 11.2(f)(i)
  consolidated financial statements, 9.1(a)(iv)
  of contingencies, 18.3(i)(v)
  of debt securities, 11.4(e)
  for derivatives:
    all reporting entities, 26.6(a)
    cash flow hedges, 26.6(d)
    fair value hedges, 26.6(c)
    hedging relationships, 26.6(b)
  employee stock options, 19.6(c)(ii)
  with equity method, 9.3(d)
  of equity securities, 11.5(f)
  of exit or disposal activity obligations, 18.3(j)(v)
  fair value measurements:
    nonpublic companies, exemption for, 24.4(f)(ii)
    objectives, 24.4(f)(i)
    required disclosures, 24.4(f)(ii)
  film producers and distributors, 37.4
  on financial statements, *see* Financial statements, *subhead:* disclosure requirements
  foreign operations; translation, 9.2(i)
  health care organizations:
    fraud related to government programs, 35.3(m)(ii)
    loss contingencies, 35.3(m)(iii)
    municipal securities market, 35.6(a)(ii)
    risks/uncertainties, 35.3(m)(i)

with intangible assets, 14.10
leases:
capital, 15.4(b)
direct financing, 15.6(b)
examples, 15.11
leveraged, 15.8(b)
sales-type, 15.6(b)
lessee, 15.3(b)
of liabilities, 18.1(d), 18.3(j)(v)
of loans, 11.3(f)
of long-term liabilities:
guarantee obligations, 18.8(k)(iv)
unconditional purchase obligations, 18.8(j)
pension plans:
actuarial present value of benefits, 27.5(e)(ii)
annuity contracts, 27.2(h)(iii)
generally, 27.2(h)
miscellaneous disclosures, 27.5(h)
net assets available for benefits, 27.5(c)(ii)
nonpublic entities, 27.2(h)(ii)
nonrecurring events, 27.3(i)
public entities, 27.2(h)(i)
statement of net assets, 27.5(c)(ii)
postemployment benefits, 27.7(b)(iv)
postretirement benefits, 27.6(e)
professional concerns with, 4.8(d)
real estate notes, 31.9(c)
regulated utilities:
construction intermediaries, financing through, 36.10(d)(ii)
expanded footnote disclosures, 36.10(d)(vi)
jointly owned plants, 36.10(d)(iii)
nuclear decommissioning costs, 36.10(d)(iv)
purchase power contracts, 36.10(d)(i)
stranded costs, securitization of, 36.10(d)(v)
Regulation S-X requirements:
compensating balances, 5.4(l)(i)
generally, 5.4(g)
income tax expense, 5.4(k)
short-term borrowings, 5.4(l)(ii)
sources of, 5.4(h)
subsidiary, disclosure by, 5.4(i)
translation; foreign operations, 9.2(i)
Discontinued operations, 4.4(d)(iii)
Dispute resolution proceedings, accountant's role in:
damage calculation:
generally, 41.2(e)(i)
income taxation, 41.2(e)(v)
inflation, 41.2(e)(iv)
measurement, 41.2(e)(ii)
mitigation, 41.2(e)(iii)
present value, 41.2(e)(iv)
and Federal Rules of Evidence:
Daubert v. Merrell Dow Pharmaceuticals, 41.2(c)(ii)
Federal Rule of Civil Procedure 26, 41.2(c)(iii)
Federal Rule of Evidence 702, 41.2(c)(i)
in litigation process:
case analysis and planning, 41.2(b)(iii)
credentials/certifications, related, 41.2(b)(viii)
discovery, 41.2(b)(iv)
generally, 41.2(b)
nontestifying expert, 41.2(b)(ii)
pretrial tasks, 41.2(b)(vi)
settlement analysis, 41.2(b)(v)
testifying expert, 41.2(b)(i)
trial, 41.2(b)(vii)
opinions, support for:
documentation, 41.2(f)(iii)
information sources, 41.2(f)(i)
reliance on others, 41.2(f)(ii)
services offered:
arbitration, 41.2(d)(ii)
bankruptcy, 41.2(d)(iii)
damage calculations, 41.2(d)(i)
testimony:
depositions, 41.2(g)(i)
at trial, 41.2(g)(ii)
and U.S. legal system:
adversarial process, 41.2(a)(i)
alternative dispute resolution, 41.2(a)(iii)
civil suits, stages of, 41.2(a)(ii)
required proofs, 41.2(a)(iii)
Dividends:
as ancillary revenue, 12.6(a)
as current liability, 18.3(h)
on ESOPs, 19.6(d)(iii)
expected, 23.3(a)(ii)
FHLB, 30.2(v)(ix)
preferred, 10.2(c)(vi)
on preferred stock, 19.2(c)(iii)
principal and income from; trusts, 38.3(k)(iii)

Dividends: (*Continued*)
as retained earnings:
cash dividends, 19.7(g)
closely held corporations, 19.7(h)(iii)
declaration dates, 19.7(f)
generally, 19.7(e)
large stock dividends, 19.7(h)(ii)
liquidating dividends, 19.7(k)
property dividends, 19.7(i)
reasons for declaration, 19.7(h)(v)
record date, 19.7(h)(iv)
scrip or liability dividends, 19.7(j)
small stock dividends, 19.7(h)(i)
stock dividends, 19.7(h)

Economy, financial statements and, 1.1(b)(i)
E-discovery:
audit trails, 42.9
computer forensics, role of, 42.11
and computers, 42.1
data:
compiling, 42.18
increased volumes of, 42.3
metadata, 42.8
storage/communication of, 42.2
traffic, 42.9
value of, 42.4
data searching:
generally, 42.20
via hash value, 42.20(b)
via key word, 42.20(a)
data sorting:
by date/time, 42.19(b)(i)
by file type/extension, 42.19(b)(iii)
generally, 42.19(b)
by owner/author, 42.19(b)(i)
and de-duplication, 42.19(a)
deleted files, 42.21
evidence:
electronic vs. paper, 42.8
finding, 42.5
preserving, 42.12, 42.13
legal setting of, 42.6
metadata, 42.8
physical imaging vs. logical backups, 42.13
recordkeeping, forensic:
acquisition notes, 42.15
analysis workpapers, 42.17
chain-of-custody documentation, 42.16
generally, 42.14
and slack space, 42.21
speed and low cost of, 42.10
techniques for, 42.7
and unallocated space, 42.21
Employees:
advances from, 18.3(g)
costs, employee-related, 8.3(c)(ii), 8.3(c)(iii)
Employee stock options, 19.6(c)
disclosure requirements, 19.6(c)(ii)
share-based payments, 19.6(c)(i)
Employee stock ownership plans (ESOPs), 19.6(d)
accounting for, 23.2(d)
dividends on, 19.6(d)(iii)
purchase of shares by, 19.6(d)(i)
redemption of, 19.6(d)(ii), 19.6(d)(iv)
release of shares, 19.6(d)(ii)
Equipment, *see* Property, plant and equipment (PP&E)
Equity method:
about, 9.3
application of:
Bundle A, 9.3(c)(i)
Bundle B, 9.3(c)(ii)
Bundle C, 9.3(c)(iii)
generally, 9.3(c)
profit/loss, intercompany, 9.3(c)(iv)
proportional consolidation, 9.3(c)(vi)
special considerations, 9.3(c)(v)
and consolidated financial statements, 9.1(d)
consolidation vs., 9.3(a)
disclosures with, 9.3(d)
historical summary of pronouncements, 9.4(c)
with joint ventures, 9.3(b)(ii)
with significant influence via common stock ownership, 9.3(b)(iii)
with unconsolidated subsidiaries, 9.3(b)(i)
Equity securities. *See also* Stock
after acquisition, accounting for, 11.5(c)
disclosures with, 11.5(f)
generally, 11.5(a)
impairment of, 11.5(d)
initial recognition/measurement of, 11.5(b)
transfers between categories of, 11.5(e)
ESOPs, *see* Employee stock ownership plans
Estates:
accounting for:
governing concepts, 38.2(a)
liabilities, treatment of, 38.2(a)(iii)

period, accounting, 38.2(a)(i)
principal and income, 38.2(a)(ii)
administrator:
executor vs., 38.1(i)(i)
reports of, 38.2(c)
assets:
distribution of, 38.1(i)(xvii)
inventory of, 38.1(i)(ix)
possession of, 38.1(i)(v)
probate vs. nonprobate, 38.1(i)(vi)
valuation of, 38.1(i)(x)
debts, payment of, *see subhead:* payment of debts
and domicile, 38.1(d)
executor:
administrator vs., 38.1(i)(i)
failure of, 38.1(f)
reports of, 38.2(c)
fiduciary responsibilities:
advancements, 38.1(i)(xxii)
assets, *see subhead:* assets
creditors, advertising for, 38.1(i)(xiii)
debts, payments of, *see subhead:* payment of debts
decree of distribution, 38.1(i)(xxv)
disclaimers, 38.1(i)(xxiv)
estate funds, management of, 38.1(i)(xi)
and executor vs. administrator distinction, 38.1(i)(i)
exemptions, personal property, 38.1(i)(vii)
expenses, administration, 38.1(i)(xvi)
hotchpot, 38.1(i)(xxii)
legacies, *see subhead:* legacies
postdecree procedure, 38.1(i)(xxv)
preliminary administration, 38.1(i)(iii)
real property, 38.1(i)(viii)
representatives' duties, 38.1(i)(ii), 38.1(i)(v)
special duties of representatives, 38.1(i)(iv)
and surviving spouse's right of election against will, 38.1(i)(xxiii)
trusts, funding of, 38.1(i)(xxv)
income taxes:
estate, 38.1(l)(v)
final individual, 38.1(l)(i)
intestacy, 38.1(c), 38.1(g)
legacies:
abatement of, 38.1(i)(xix)
deductions from, 38.1(i)(xx)
lapsed, 38.1(i)(xxi)
payment of, 38.1(i)(xviii)
payment of debts:
generally, 38.1(i)(xii)
order of payment, 38.1(i)(xiv)
source of funds for, 38.1(i)(xv)
probate procedures:
failure of executor, 38.1(f)
intestacy, 38.1(g)
will, 38.1(e)
record-keeping system for:
final accounting, 38.2(b)(iii)
generally, 38.2(b)
going business, operation of, 38.2(b)(ii)
journals, 38.2(b)(i)
reports of executor/administrator, 38.2(c)
representatives of:
commissions of, 38.1(k)
and executor vs. administrator distinction, 38.1(j)(i)
fiduciary duties, 38.1(i)(ii), 38.1(i)(v)
special duties, 38.1(i)(iv)
and will powers not conferred by statute, 38.1(j)(ii)
and will powers vs. statutory powers distinction, 38.1(j)(iii)
small, 38.1(h)
taxation of:
federal estate tax, 38.1(l)(ii)
generation–skipping transfer tax, 38.1(l)(iv)
income taxes, estate, 38.1(l)(v)
income taxes, final individual, 38.1(l)(i)
state estate tax, 38.1(l)(iii)
state inheritance tax, 38.1(l)(iii)
will:
execution of, 38.1(a)
probate procedures, 38.1(e)
provisions of, 38.1(b)
surviving spouse's right of election against, 38.1(i)(xxiii)
European Union:
Council Directives, 1.16(a)
generally, 1.16
recent developments, 1.16(b)
Expert witness challenges and exclusions:
causes of exclusion:
qualifications of expert, 43.4
relevance, 43.4
reliability, 43.4

Expert witness challenges and exclusions: (*Continued*)
CPAs and, 43.9
generally, 43.1
methodology, 43.2
plaintiff expert exclusion, 43.5
rates of exclusion, 43.3
trends, 43.7, 43.8
types of experts excluded, 43.6

Fair market value:
defined, 25.2(a)
Fair value:
of acquired company, 8.3(b)(v)
auditing guidance with, 25.3
of consideration given, 8.3(b)(i)
of consideration transferred, 8.3(b)(ii)
disclosures, in MD&A, 6.1(d)(ii)
excess of fair value of acquired net assets over cost, 8.3(g)(ii)
for financial reporting, 25.2(b)
of liabilities at acquisition date, 8.3(g)(xii)
when less than 100 percent acquired, 8.3(g)(xvi)
Fair value accounting:
factors in growth of:
economic changes, 24.2(a)
globalization, 24.2(b)
relevance, 24.2(c)
transparency, 24.2(c)
generally, 24.1
in illiquid market, 24.3(d)(ii)
Fair value measurement(s):
of assets vs. liabilities, 24.4(e)(i)
auditing of:
AU 328 guidance, 24.6(c)
estimates in, 24.6(b)
generally, 24.6
PCAOB Staff Audit Practice Alert No. 2, 24.6(d)
SEC guidance, 24.6(e)
standards for, 24.6(a)
convergence of, 24.3(e)
and Credit Crisis Projects, 24.3(d)(iv)
defined, 24.1, 24.4(b)
disclosures:
nonpublic companies, exemption for, 24.4(f)(ii)
objectives of, 24.4(f)(i)
required, 24.4(f)(ii)
economic crisis and, 24.3(d)
and fair value hierarchy, 24.4(e)(xviii)
and fair value option, 24.5
FASB ASC 820 and:
generally, 24.4(a)
scope and scope exceptions, 24.4(c)
for financial instruments, 24.3(b)
and framework for fair value, 24.4(e)
future of, 24.3(f)
highest and best use for nonfinancial assets, 24.4(e)(vi)
historical background:
development of concepts, 24.3(a)
generally, 24.3
in illiquid market, 24.3(d)(ii)
initial measurement, 24.4(d)
liabilities and instruments classified in reporting entity's shareholder's equity:
generally, 24.4(e)(vii)
held by other parties, 24.4(e)(viii)
not held by other parties, 24.4(e)(ix)
liability, miscellaneous factors that impact fair value of, 24.4(e)(x)
market participants and, 24.4(e)(iv)
mark-to-market accounting:
generally, 24.3(d)(i)
SEC study on, 24.3(d)(iii)
most advantageous market, 24.4(e)(iii)
nonfinancial assets, highest/best use for, 24.4(e)(vi)
for nonfinancial assets/liabilities, 24.3(c)
non-orderly transactions, 24.4(e)(xx)
price and, 24.4(e)(v)
principal market, 24.4(e)(iii)
with significant decrease in volume/level of activity, 24.4(e)(xix)
standards and concepts for, 24.4
third parties, using quoted prices from, 24.4(e)(xxi)
transactions and, 24.4(e)(ii)
valuation techniques:
calibration, 24.4(e)(xvi)
cost approach, 24.4(e)(xii)
generally, 24.4(e)(xi)
income approach, 24.4(e)(xiv)
inputs to, 24.4(e)(xvii)
market approach, 24.4(e)(xiii)
use of multiple valuation techniques, 24.4(e)(xv)

FCPA, *see* Foreign Corrupt Practices Act of1977
Federal Accounting Standards Advisory Board (FASAB), 1.6
Federal government:
audits in:
generally, 32.5
Generally Accepted Government Auditing Standards (GAGAS), 32.5(a)
government-wide audit opinion, achievement of, 32.6(a)
recipients of federal financial assistance, 32.5(b)(i)
budgetary accounting by:
financial vs., 32.2(b)(iii)
generally, 32.2(b), 32.2(b)(i)
terminology, 32 (App B)
budget process:
congressional action on, 32.4(b)(ii)
defined, 32.4(a)
execution of, 32.4(b)(iii)
formulation of, 32.4(b)(i)
review/audit of, 32.4(b)(iv)
decision-making support, development of, 32.6(b)
financial accounting by:
budgetary vs., 32.2(b)(iii)
generally, 32.2(b), 32.2(b)(ii)
financial management by:
Department of the Treasury, 32.2(a)(iii)
generally, 32.2, 32.2(a)
Government Accountability Office (GAO), 32.2(a)(i)
legislation, 32 (App A)
Office of Management and Budget (OMB), 32.2(a)(ii)
financial reporting by:
accelerated reporting schedule, 32.3(a)(i)
assertions relating to internal control over, 32.3(a)(ii)
enhancement of, 32.6(d)
generally, 32.3, 32.3(a)
generally, 32
organization of, 32.1
parallel accounting bases in, 32.2(b)
prevention-oriented controls, 32.6(c)
risk-assessment controls, 32.6(c)
Federal Rules of Evidence:
Daubert v. Merrell Dow Pharmaceuticals, 41.2(c)(ii)
Federal Rule of Civil Procedure 26, 41.2(c)(iii)
Federal Rule of Evidence 702, 41.2(c)(i)
Film producers and distributors:
accounting guidance history, 37.1
costs/expenses:
amortization, 37.3(b)
capitalization, 37.3(a)
costs valuations, 37.3(e)
exploitation costs, 37.3(g)
manufacturing costs, 37.3(h)
participation costs, 37.3(b)
subsequent events, 37.3(f)
ultimate participation costs, 37.3(d)
ultimate revenue, 37.3(c)
disclosure issues, 37.4
presentation issues, 37.4
revenue reporting by:
availability of film, 37.2(b)(iii)
barter revenue, 37.2(b)(v)
delivery of film, 37.2(b)(ii)
fixed/determinable fee, 37.2(b)(iv)
generally, 37.2(a)
licensing of film-related products, 37.2(b)(viii)
modifications of arrangements, 37.2(b)(vi)
persuasive evidence of arrangement, 37.2(b)(i)
present value, 37.2(b)(ix)
price concessions, 37.2(b)(vii)
returns, 37.2(b)(vii)
Financial accounting:
objective of, 1.1(a)
role of, in U.S. economy, 1.1
Financial accounting and reporting:
conceptual framework:
generally, 2.2
initiation of, 2.2(d)(iv)
FASB and, 2.1(a)
income taxes, *see* Income taxes, *subhead:* financial reporting of
management accounting vs., 2.1(b)
purpose of, 2.1
tax accounting vs., 2.1(b)
Financial Accounting Standards Board (FASB):
Accounting Standards Codification (ASC) topics of, *see under* Accounting Standards Codification
Concepts Statements of:

Financial Accounting Standards Board (FASB): (*Continued*)
accounting information, qualitative characteristics of, 2.3(b)(ii)
cash flow information, use of, 2.3(b)(v)
financial reporting objectives, 2.3(b)(i)
financial statement elements, 2.3(b)(iii)
generally, 2.3(a), 2.3(b)
measurement, 2.3(b)(iv)
present value, 2.3(b)(v)
recognition, 2.3(b)(iv)
conceptual framework of, *see* Conceptual framework (FASB)
criticism of standards, 1.4(g)
due process procedures, 1.4(d)
fair value measurements, 24.4(a), 24.4(c)
generally, 1.4
and general purpose external financial accounting and reporting, 2.1(a)
guarantee obligations, 18.8(k)(i)
historical background, 1.4(a)
leases, 15.12
not-for-profit organizations, 28.1(a)(iii)
publications, 1.4(c)
real estate, 31.1(b)
regulated utilities, 36.5(b)
revenue recognition, 12.3(c), 12.4(d)
standards overload and, 1.4(f)
structure, 1.4(b)
Financial institution(s). *See also* Banks and savings institutions; Investment companies; Mortgage banking activities
credit unions, 30.1(c)(iv)
economic role of, 30.1(b)
finance companies, 30.1(c)(vii)
industry changes, 30.1(a)
insurance companies, 30.1(c)(vi)
investment banks, 30.1(c)(v)
real estate investment trusts, 30.1(c)(ix)
securities brokers/dealers, 30.1(c)(viii)
types of, 30.1(c)
Financial position, statement of, *see* Balance sheet
Financial reporting:
fair value for, 25.2(b)
by federal government:
accelerated reporting schedule, 32.3(a)(i)
assertions relating to internal control over, 32.3(a)(ii)
enhancement of, 32.6(d)
generally, 32.3, 32.3(a)
by investment companies:
financial statements, 30.4(d)(iii)
new registrants, 30.4(d)(i)
requirements, 30.4(d)(ii)
Financial reporting system:
participants in, 1.1(c)
Financial statements. *See also specific financial statements, e.g.:* Balance sheet
and accrual accounting, 4.2(b)(v)
analysis of, *see* Financial statement analysis
as approximate measures, 4.2(b)(ii)
articulation of, 4.7
ASC Topic 740–10 and, 17.3(b)(i)
ASC Topic 740 and, 17.2(e)(v)
ASC Topic 980 and, 36.8(a)(ii), 36.8(a)(v)
banks and savings institutions:
balance sheets, 30.2(k)(ii)
cash flow, statements of, 30.2(k)(iii)
commitments/off-balance-sheet risk, 30.2(k)(iv)
income statements, 30.2(k)(i)
risks/uncertainties, disclosure of, 30.2(k)(v)
business combinations:
acquired securities, classification of, 8.3(n)(ii)
interim financial information, 8.3(n)(ii)
pro forma disclosure, 8.3(n)(i)
consolidated, *see* Consolidated financial statements
disclosure requirements:
accounting policies, 4.8(a)(i)
AICPA recommendations, 4.8(a)(vii)
capital structure, 4.8(b)(v)
contingent liabilities, 4.8(a)(v)
debt, 4.8(b)(iv)
debt and equity investments, 4.8(b)(i)
doubt about continued existence, 4.8(a)(iv)
earnings per share, 4.8(c)(ii)
generally, 4.8(a), 4.8(b)
interim reporting, 4.8(c)(iii)
inventories, 4.8(b)(ii)
long-term debt, 4.8(b)(iv)
plant assets and depreciation, 4.8(b)(iii)
publicly held companies, 4.8(c)
related party transactions, 4.8(a)(ii)
risks/uncertainties, significant, 4.8(a)(vi)
segment disclosure, 4.8(c)(i)

subsequent events, 4.8(a)(iii)
elements of, 2.3(b)(iii)
exit or disposal activity obligations, 18.3(j)(iv)
explanatory notes/disclosures on, 4.2(b)(vi)
external users of, 10.1(a)
Form 8-K and, 5.6(a)(iii)
GAO and, 1.12(a)
generally, 4.1
general-purpose, 4.2(b)(iv)
health care organizations:
generally, 35.5(a)
governmental entities, 35.5(g)(ii)
NAIC and, 35.6(b)(i)
nongovernmental entities, 35.5(g)(i)
historical orientation of, 4.2(b)(iii)
intangible assets on:
generally, 14.9(a)
goodwill, 14.9(b)
integrated analysis of, 10.6
international standards and:
balance sheet, 4.10(b)
cash flow statement, 4.10(b)
generally, 4.10
income statement, 4.10(c)
inventory on, 13.8
investment companies, 30.4(d)(iii)
limitations of:
content influence by management, 4.9(d)
estimation, 4.9(c)
flexibility vs. uniformity, 4.9(f)
generally, 4.9
historical orientation, 4.9(b)
judgment, 4.9(c)
stable monetary unit assumption, 4.9(a)
unrecorded items, 4.9(e)
limited partnerships, 20.6(d)(i), 20.6(d)(ii)
long-term debt on, 4.8(b)(iv), 18.7
and market efficiency, 1.1(b)(ii)
natural resources on:
disclosures, 34.11
ore reserves, supplementary information on, 34.9
not-for-profit organizations:
audits, 28.4(e)
voluntary health and welfare organizations, 28.3(a)(i)
pension plans:
content of statements, 27.5(b)
decisions related to, 27.5(i)
defined contribution plans, 27.5(j)(iii)
example, 27.5(g)
historical background, 27.5(a)
objective of statements, 27.5(b)
personal, *see* Personal financial statements
property, plant and equipment (PP&E) on:
construction in progress, 16.13(b)
fully depreciated/idle assets, 16.13(d)
general requirements, 16.13(a)
impairment of value, 16.13(e)(i)
retirement, gain/loss on, 16.13(c)
segment information, 16.13(f)
prospective, *see* Prospective financial statements
real estate transactions:
balance sheet, 31.9(a)(i)
statement of income, 31.9(a)(ii)
Regulation S-X and, 5.4(d), 5.4(f)
and sound economy, 1.1(b)(i)
as sources of information, 4.2(b)(i), 10.1(c)
statement of cash flows:
financing activities, 4.6(c)
generally, 4.6
investing activities, 4.6(b)
operating activities, 4.6(a)
statement of stockholders' equity, 4.5
stock-based compensation on, 23.5(a)
stockholders' equity on, 19.8(b)
users of:
creditors, 10.1(b)(ii)
equity investors, 10.1(b)(i)
external users, 10.1(a)
generally, 10.1(b)
Financial statement analysis:
by creditors, 10.1(b)(ii)
depreciation, 10.3(c)
discontinued operations, 10.3(f)
earnings per share, 10.3(q)
by equity investors, 10.1(b)(i)
expense deferrals, 10.3(d)
extraordinary gains/losses, 10.3(f)
financial company debt analysis:
asset protection ratios, 10.8(b)
capitalization, 10.8(f)
generally, 10.8
liquidity, 10.8(e)
loan spreads, 10.8(d)
operating agreement, 10.8(a)
reserve and loss ratios, 10.8(c)
fixed income analysis:

Financial statement analysis: (*Continued*)
earnings protection, 10.7(a)
generally, 10.7
foreign operations, 10.3(h)
framework for, 10.1(d)
income statements, *see* Income statement analysis
integrated analysis, 10.6
interim results, 10.3(m)
and international reporting:
foreign issuers in United States, 10.3(n)(ii)
International Accounting Standards Board, 10.3(n)(i)
inventory, 10.3(b)
investments, 10.3(o)
key ratios for, 10.9
mergers and acquisitions, 10.3(i)(iii), 10.3(j)
postemployment benefits:
actuarial assumptions affecting, 10.3(i)(ii)
generally, 10.3(i)
mergers and acquisitions, impact of, 10.3(i)(iii)
OPEB disclosures, analysis of, 10.3(i)(i)
prices, changing, 10.3(g)
pushdown accounting, 10.3(k)
quality of earnings, 10.3(a)
revenue recognition, 10.3(e)
segment data, 10.3(l)
stock compensation plans, 10.3(p)
unusual items, 10.3(f)
Fixed asset turnover ratio, 10.4(c)(i)
Fixed income analysis:
earnings protection, 10.7(a)
generally, 10.7
Foreclosure:
assets, foreclosed:
generally, 31.3(m)
held for income, 31.3(m)(ii)
held for sale, 31.3(m)(i)
bank-owned real estate, 30.2(q)(iii), 30.2(v)(vii)
taxation of foreclosed property, 30.2(v)(vii)
Foreign Corrupt Practices Act of 1977 (FCPA):
accountant, role of, 41.3(c)
internal accounting control, 5.1(h)(ii)
payments to foreign officials, 5.1(h)(i)
Foreign currency translation, *see* Translation
Forensic accounting:
defined, 41.1
dispute resolution, *see* Dispute resolution proceedings, accountant's role in
impact of globalization on:
anticorruption and bribery laws (United Kingdom), 41.4(b)
International Financial Reporting Standards (IFRS), 41.4(a)
investigations and compliance matters, *see* Investigations and compliance matters, accountant's role in
litigation consulting vs. attest services, 41.1(a)
Form 8-K:
acquisition/disposition of assets, 5.6(a)(i)
certifying accountant, changes in, 5.6(a)(ii)
Item 2.01, 5.6(a)(i)
Item 4.01, 5.6(a)(ii)
Item 4.02, 5.6(a)(iii)
non-reliance on previous financial statements, 5.6(a)(iii)
requirements of, 5.6(a)
Form 10-K:
certifications, 5.4(p)(vi)
generally, 5.4
Part I of, 5.4(p)(i)
Part II of, 5.4(p)(ii)
Part III of, 5.4(p)(iii)
Part IV of, 5.4(p)(iv)
signatures, 5.4(p)(v)
structure of, 5.4(p)
Form 10-Q:
generally, 5.5
Part I of, 5.5(a)(i)
Part II of, 5.5(a)(ii)
signatures, 5.5(a)(iii)
Fraud:
detection of:
early approaches, 40.4
red-flag approach, 40.5
strategic approach to, 40.10
via financial results, 40.9
via operating characteristics, 40.9
fighting, 40.3
generally, 40.1
industry-specific, 40.8
by management/board of directors:
backgrounds, 40.6(a)
degree of influence of, 40.6(c)
generally, 40.6
motivations of, 40.6(b)

and relationships with others:
auditors, 40.7(c)
financial institutions, 40.7(a)
generally, 40.7
investors, 40.7(e)
lawyers, 40.7(d)
regulatory bodies, 40.7(f)
related parties, 40.7(b)
types of, 40.2
via organizational structure, 40.8

GAAP, *see* Generally Accepted Accounting Principles
GAO, *see* Government Accountability Office
Gas, natural, *see* Natural resources
GASB, *see* Governmental Accounting Standards Board
Generally Accepted Accounting Principles (GAAP):
banks and savings institutions, 30.2(m)
health care organizations:
governmental sector, 35.2(a)
private sector, 35.2(a)
IASB and, 3.2
income taxation, 17.6(c)(i), 17.6(c)(ii)
mining, 34.6(b)
personal financial statements, 22.11(e)
regulated utilities:
APB Opinion No. 2, 36.5(c)(ii)
historical background, 36.5(c)(i)
General purpose external financial accounting and reporting, *see* Financial accounting and reporting
Gold, on personal financial statements, 22.3(e)
Goodwill:
and ASC 350 effective date/transition provisions:
after June 30, 2001, goodwill acquired, 14.11(a)
equity method goodwill, 14.11(d)
previously recognized goodwill, 14.11(c)
bankruptcy, entities emerging from, 14.7(b)(ix)
and equity method investments, 14.7(b)(viii), 14.11(d)
fair value measurements of, 14.7(b)(ii)
impairment testing of:
and fair value vs. carrying amount, 14.7(b)(i)
generally, 14.7(b)(iii)
in noncontrolling interest, 14.7(b)(vi)
by subsidiary, 14.7(b)(v)
initial valuation of, 14.7(a)
reporting unit:
disposal of, 14.7(b)(vii)
generally, 14.7(b)(iv)
subsequent accounting for, 14.7(b)
Government Accountability Office (GAO):
compliance audits, 1.12(b)
financial statement audits, 1.12(a)
generally, 1.12, 32.2(a)(i)
operational audits, 1.12(c)
Governmental Accounting Standards Board (GASB):
generally, 1.5
jurisdiction issues with, 1.5(b)
structure, 1.5(a)
Governmental health care entities:
balance sheet, 35.5(b)(ii)
business combinations involving, 35.3(o)(ii)
cash flows, statement of, 35.5(e)(ii)
contributions to, 35.3(g)(ii)
derivatives accounting with, 35.3(i)(ii)
financial statements, issuance of, 35.5(g)(ii)
generally, 35.1(c)
investments in, 35.3(h)(ii)
operating statement, 35.5(c)(iii)
property and equipment, 35.3(j)(i)
reporting entity considerations with, 35.3(n)(ii)

Health care organizations:
agency transactions involving, 35.3(c)
authoritative pronouncements:
AICPA *Health Care Entities* guide, 35.2(c)
GAAP, *see subhead:* GAAP
HFMA Principles and Practices Board, 35.2(d)
balance sheet:
generally, 35.5(b)
governmental health care entities, 35.5(b)(ii)
not-for-profit entities, 35.5(b)(i)
bonds payable:
construction, interest during, 35.3(l)(v)
generally, 35.3(l)
and IRS arbitrage rebate liability, 35.3(l)(iii)

Health care organizations: (*Continued*)
obligated group financing structures, 35.3(l)(iv)
refundings/defeasance, 35.3(l)(i)
variable-rate demand bonds, 35.3(l)(ii)
business combinations:
governmental entities, 35.3(o)(ii)
not-for-profit entities, 35.3(o)(i)
cash and claims to cash, noncurrent, 35.3(b)
cash flows, statement of:
governmental entities, 35.5(e)(ii)
private sector entities, 35.5(e)(i)
changes in net assets/equity, statement of, 35.5(d)
continuing care retirement communities:
advance fees, 35.4(a)(i)
future services, obligation to provide, 35.4(a)(ii)
generally, 35.4(a)
initial continuing care contracts, acquisition of, 35.4(a)(iii)
contributions to:
generally, 35.3(g)
governmental entities, 35.3(g)(ii), 35.3(g)(iv)
not-for-profit entities, 35.3(g)(i)
via fundraising foundations, 35.3(g)(iii)
via trusts, 35.3(g)(v)
credit-risk concentration and, 35.3(f)
and deferred inflows/outflows of resources, 35.3(p)
derivatives accounting:
governmental entities, 35.3(i)(ii)
not-for-profit entities, 35.3(i)(i)
disclosures:
fraud related to government programs, 35.3(m)(ii)
loss contingencies, 35.3(m)(iii)
risks/uncertainties, 35.3(m)(i)
financial statements:
generally, 35.5(a)
governmental entities, 35.5(g)(ii)
nongovernmental entities, 35.5(g)(i)
GAAP:
governmental sector, 35.2(a)
private sector, 35.2(a)
governmental entities, *see* Governmental health care entities
HMOs and managed care entities:
acquisition costs, 35.4(b)(vi)
expense recognition, 35.4(b)(ii)
generally, 35.4(b)
loss contracts, 35.4(b)(iii)
revenue, 35.4(b)(i)
risk pools, 35.4(b)(iv)
stop-loss insurance, 35.4(b)(v)
industry overview, 35.1(a)
intangible assets, 35.3(k)
investments in:
governmental entities, 35.3(h)(ii)
nongovernmental entities, 35.3(h)(i)
investor-owned entities, 35.1(d)
managed care entities, *see subhead:* HMOs and managed care entities
municipal securities market and:
administration/enforcement structure, 35.6(a)(i)
disclosure requirements for issuers, 35.6(a)(ii)
EMMA system, 35.6(a)(iii)
reforms, proposed, 35.6(a)(iv)
SEC's role/authority in, 35.6(a)
NAIC and:
risk-based capital requirements, 35.6(b)(ii)
statutory financial statements of health plans, 35.6(b)(i)
net assets/net position:
generally, 35.3(a)
invested in capital assets, net of related debt, 35.3(a)(iii)
restricted, 35.3(a)(ii)
unrestricted, 35.3(a)(i)
not-for-profit entities, *see* Not-for-profit health care entities
OMB Circular A-133 and, 35.6(c)
operating statement:
generally, 35.5(c)
governmental entities, 35.5(c)(iii)
investor-owned entities, 35.5(c)(i)
not-for-profit entities, 35.5(c)(ii)
patient service revenue:
bad debts, provision for, 35.3(e)(iii)
and charity care, 35.3(e)(ii)
generally, 35.3(e)
and governmental programs, 35.3(e)(i)
physician practice management companies:
consolidation requirements, 35.4(c)(i)
generally, 35.4(c)
property and equipment:
generally, 35.3(j)

governmental health care entities, 35.3(j)(i)
software costs, internal-use, 35.3(j)(ii)
reporting entity considerations:
governmental entities, 35.3(n)(ii)
joint operating agreements, 35.3(n)(iii)
not-for-profit entities, 35.3(n)(i)
revenues:
generally, 35.3(d)
patient service revenue, *see subhead:* patient service revenue
SEC requirements; private sector, 35.2(a)(i)
segment reporting, 35.5(f)
Hedges:
cash flow hedges:
disallowed situations, 26.5(a)(iv)
disclosures for, 26.6(d)
eligible risks, 26.5(a)(ii)
generally, 26.5(a)
internal derivatives contracts, 26.5(a)(v)
prerequisites, 26.5(a)(iii)
qualifying exposures, 26.5(a)(i)
disclosures for, 26.6(b)
effectiveness of, 26.5(d)
fair value hedges:
disallowed situations, 26.5(b)(iv)
disclosures for, 26.6(c)
examples of, 26.5(b)(i)
generally, 26.5(b)
prerequisite requirements with, 26.5(b)(iii)
risks qualifying as, 26.5(b)(ii)
foreign operations, net investments in, 26.5(c)
nonqualifying trades, 26.5(e)
speculative trades, 26.5(e)

IASB, *see* International Accounting Standards Board
IASs, *see* International Accounting Standards
IFAC, *see* International Federation of Accountants Council
Impairment:
of debt securities, 11.4(d)
of equity securities, 11.5(d)
of loans:
generally, 11.3(c)
measurement guidelines, 11.3(c)(i)
of long-lived assets:
disposed of, real estate to be, 31.5(a)(ii)
generally, 31.5(a)
held/used, real estate to be, 31.5(a)(i)
mortgage servicing rights, 30.3(f)(iii)
property, plant and equipment (PP&E):
assets to be disposed of, 16.3(c), 16.13(e)(iii)
assets to be held and used, 16.3(b), 16.3(b)(i), 16.3(b)(ii), 16.13(e)(ii)
financial statement presentation, 16.13(e)(i)
pronouncements, authoritative, 16.3(a)
state and local government accounting, 33.4(c)(vi), 33.4(h)(iv)
Impairment testing:
of goodwill:
and fair value vs. carrying amount, 14.7(b)(i)
generally, 14.7(b)(iii)
noncontrolling interest, 14.7(b)(vi)
by subsidiary, 14.7(b)(v)
long-lived assets, 39.6(i)
natural resources, 34.4(a)(iv), 34.7(g)
Income. *See also* Revenue
debt adjustment for family farmers with regular annual, 39.2(c)(iii)
of estates, 38.2(a)(ii)
fee income of banks:
from fiduciary services, 30.2(x)(i)
miscellaneous forms of, 30.2(x)(ii)
foreclosed assets held for production of, 31.3(m)(ii)
investment, 28.2(h)(i)
lessor's recognition of, 15.8(a)(iv)
loans as, 11.3(c), 11.3(c)(ii)
from rental operations:
and cost escalation, 31.7(b)(i)
generally, 31.7(b)
percentage rents, 31.7(b)(ii)
stockholders' equity and reporting comprehensive, 19.8(d)
and translation, 9.2(g), 9.2(g)(i), 9.2(g)(ii)
from trusts:
accounts and recordkeeping, 38.4(b)(ii)
accrual of, 38.3(k)(ii)
bond discounts/premiums, 38.3(k)(iv)
charges to income, 38.3(j)(iv)
depletion and, 38.3(k)(v)
depreciation and, 38.3(k)(v)
disbursements of income, 38.3(j)(iv)
disbursements of principal, 38.3(j)(ii)

Income (*Continued*)
distinguishing principal from income, 38.3(j)
dividends, 38.3(k)(iii)
generally, 38.3(j)
receipts of income, 38.3(j)(iii)
receipts of principal, 38.3(j)(i)
recording, 38.4(a)(ii)
unproductive property, sale of, 38.3(k)(i)
utility rates and operating, 36.4(f)
Income statement:
comprehensive income on, 4.4(d)(iv)
corrections to, 4.4(d)(v)
discontinued operations on, 4.4(d)(iii)
expenses on, 4.4(b)
extraordinary items on, 4.4(d)(i)
generally, 4.4
international standards and, 4.10(c)
presentation issues with, 4.4(c)
revenue-related disclosures on, 12.7(a)
revenues on, 4.4(a)
special issues, 4.4(d)
unusual gains/losses on, 4.4(d)(ii)
Income statement analysis:
cost and expense:
analytical adjustments, 10.2(c)(iii)
classification of costs, 10.2(c)(i)
fixed charges, 10.2(c)(v)
generally, 10.2(c)
margin analysis, 10.2(c)(ii)
operating leverage, 10.2(c)(iv)
preferred dividend coverage, 10.2(c)(vi)
earnings power, 10.2(a), 10.2(e)
income taxes, 10.2(d)
risk, 10.2(a)
sales and revenue:
comparative trend analysis, 10.2(b)(iv)
components of sale trends, 10.2(b)(iii)
generally, 10.2(b)
trend analysis, 10.2(b)(i)
variability, 10.2(b)(ii)
Income taxes:
accounting basis for, 17.1(b)
accrued expenses, 18.3(f)(v)
ASC Topic 980 and:
discontinuation of rate-regulated accounting, 36.9(e)
specific standards, 36.6(e)(iii)
deferred; intangible assets, 14.8
dispute resolution, 41.2(e)(v)
estates, 38.1(l)(i), 38.1(l)(v)
FASB ASC 740 and, *see* Accounting Standards Codification (ASC) Topic 740 (*Income Taxes*)
financial reporting of:
disclosure, 17.4(b), 17.4(c)
intraperiod tax allocation, 17.4(a)
statement presentation and disclosure, 17.4(b)
financial statement presentation, 10.2(d)
future, on long-term liabilities, 18.8(i)
IAS 12 (*Income Taxes*):
generally, 17.6(b)
and U.S. GAAP, 17.6(c)(i), 17.6(c)(ii)
IFRS and:
convergence, 17.6(a)(i)
convergence project, 17.6(a)(ii)
fair value, deferred tax on property remeasured at, 17.6(a)(iii)
generally, 17.6(a)
IAS 12 (*Income Taxes*), *see subhead:* IAS 12 (*Income Taxes*)
for interim periods:
determination of tax, 17.5(c)
estimated annual effective tax rate, 17.5(b)
generally, 17.5(a)
special issues, 17.5(d)
natural resources, 34.10
partnerships and, 20.2(f)
of pension plans, 27.2(m)
on personal financial statements:
computation of provision for, 22.5(b)
disclosures, 22.5(d), 22.5(e)
as liability, 22.4(d)
provision for, 22.5(a)
and tax basis, 22.5(c)
purchase price (business combinations), 8.3(g)(xiii)
recognition of:
accounting guidance, 17.1(c)(vii)
ASC Topic 740 and, *see* Accounting Standards Codification (ASC) Topic 740 (*Income Taxes*), *subhead:* recognition of deferred tax liabilities/assets
asset transfers, 17.1(c)(v)
basic problem with, 17.1(a)
basis for, 17.1(b)
delay/reconsideration, 17.1(b)(iii)

foreign nonmonetary assets, 17.1(c)(vi)
general approach to, 17.1(c)(i)
goodwill exceptions, 17.1(c)(iv)
leveraged lease exceptions, 17.1(c)(iv)
liability method for, 17.1(b)(ii), 17.1(b)(iii)
methods for, 17.1(b)(i), 17.1(b)(ii), 17.1(b)(iii)
and uncertainty of tax position, 17.1(c)(ii)
valuation allowances and, 17.1(c)(iii)
regulated utilities:
accounting for income taxes (ASC Topic 740), 36.10(a)(vi)
flow-through, 36.10(a)(ii)
generally, 36.10(a)
incentives, tax, 36.10(a)(iv)
Internal Revenue Code provisions, 36.10(a)(iii)
interperiod allocation, 36.10(a)(i)
investment tax credit, 36.10(a)(vii)
legislation, tax, 36.10(a)(v)
Regulation S-X and, 5.4(k)
on stock-based compensation, 23.4(e)
and translation, 9.2(h)(i)
Independent auditors:
coordinating with, 7.8
responsibilities of, 7.5
Intangible assets:
acquisition of:
in business combinations, 14.2(a)
with other assets, 14.2(b)
separately, 14.2(b)
advertising, 14.5(p)
and ASC 350 effective date/transition provisions:
after June 30, 2001, assets acquired, 14.11(a)
equity method goodwill, 14.11(d)
generally, 14.11
previously recognized goodwill, 14.11(c)
previously recognized intangible assets, 14.11(b)
transitional disclosures, 14.11(e)
copyrights:
amortization of, 14.5(b)(ii)
capitalization amounts for, 14.5(b)(i)
generally, 14.5(b)
customer and supplier lists:
amortization of, 14.5(c)(ii)
capitalizable amounts for, 14.5(c)(i)
generally, 14.5(c)
and deferred income taxes, 14.8
defined, 14.1
determining useful life of, 14.4(a)
disclosures with, 14.10
financial statement presentation of:
generally, 14.9(a)
goodwill, 14.9(b)
franchises, 14.5(d)
generally, 14.1
goodwill, *see* Goodwill
initial valuation of:
acquired intangible assets, 14.3(a)
and cost allocation, 14.3(a)(i)
court opinions, 14.3(a)(iii)
intangibles as distinct from goodwill, 14.3(a)(vi)
SEC/PCAOB issues with, 14.3(a)(ii)
by tech-transfer practitioners, 14.3(a)(iv)
Wall Street transactions, 14.3(a)(v)
internal controls over:
improvement of, 14.2(h)(ii)
practical approaches, 14.2(h)(iii)
internally developed, 14.2(c), 14.3(b)
leases, favorable:
amortization of, 14.5(e)(ii)
capitalization amounts for, 14.5(e)(i)
generally, 14.5(e)
management of:
and internal controls, 14.2(h)(ii), 14.2(h)(iii)
and Sarbanes-Oxley Act, 14.2(h)(i)
not subject to amortization, 14.4(c)
organization costs, 14.5(f)
patents:
amortization of, 14.5(a)(ii)
capitalizable amounts for, 14.5(a)(i)
generally, 14.5(a)
recognition of:
on acquisition of subsidiary, 14.2(d)
goodwill, when applying equity method, 14.2(e)
registration costs, 14.5(g)
research and development:
acquired in-process, 14.5(j)
arrangements, 14.5(i)
costs of, 14.5(h)
royalty and license agreements, 14.5(k)
secret formulas and processes, 14.5(l)
in specialized industries:

Intangible assets: (*Continued*)
airlines, 14.6(a)
banking and thrifts, 14.6(b)
broadcasting, 14.6(d)
cable television, 14.6(e)
computer software, 14.6(f)
extractive industries, 14.6(g)
films, producers/distributors of, 14.6(h)
generally, 14.2(g)
mortgage banking, 14.6(c)
public utilities, 14.6(i)
record and music industry, 14.6(j)
timber industry, 14.6(k)
specific guidance on, 14.2(f)
start-up activities, 14.5(m)
subject to amortization, 14.4(b)
tooling costs, 14.5(n)
trademarks and trade names:
amortization of, 14.5(o)(ii)
capitalizable amounts for, 14.5(o)(i)
generally, 14.5(o)
valuation of, *see subhead:* initial valuation of
Web site development costs, 14.5(q)
Interest:
on ancillary revenue, 12.6(b)
bond:
accrual of, 18.5(a)
and amortization of premium/discount, 18.5(c)
issuance of bonds, 18.4(e)(v)
payment of, 18.5(b)
serial bonds, 18.5(f)
capitalization, interest, 16.2(c)
on income tax owed, 17.3(g)
as liability, 18.2
payable, interest, 18.3(f)(i)
pension plans:
interest cost, 27.2(d)(ii)
interest rates, 27.2(c)(iii)
on receivables, 12.7(b)(iii)
Interest rate risk, 30.2(a)(i), 30.2(f)(v)
during construction; health care organizations, 35.3(l)(v)
imputation of (real estate), 31.2(e)(v)
real estate capitalized costs:
amount capitalized, accounting for, 31.3(f)(iv)
generally, 31.3(f)
methods of capitalization, 31.3(f)(iii)
period, capitalization, 31.3(f)(ii)
qualifying assets, 31.3(f)(i)
Internal control:
audit standards for:
documentation, 7.6(b)
generally, 7.6
independent auditors, 7.6(d)(i), 7.6(d)(ii), 7.6(f)
internal auditors, use of, 7.6(d)
and management's assessment, 7.6(a)
material weaknesses, determination of, 7.6(e)
scope of test work, 7.6(c)
defined, 7.2
independent auditors:
company's internal control work, use of, 7.6(d)(i)
coordinating with, 7.8
others' work, use of, 7.6(d)(ii)
responsibilities of, 7.5
working with, 7.6(f)
management certifications of, 7.4
required reports:
annual requirements, 7.3(a)
disclosure controls/procedures, 7.3(b)(i)
effective dates, 7.3(a)(i)
quarterly requirements, 7.3(b)
Sarbanes-Oxley Act:
effectiveness, 7.1(a)
generally, 7.1
top-down/risk-based approach for evaluating:
generally, 7.7
principles, 7.7(a)
International Accounting Standards (IASs):
case for adopting unified, 3.3
generally, 3.7
impediments to standards implementation, 3.8
myths/misconceptions about, 3.9
International Accounting Standards Board (IASB). *See also* International Financial Reporting Standards
board membership, 1.14(d)
formation of, 3.5
GAAP, transition to international, 3.2
generally, 1.14, 3.1, 10.3(n)(i)
historical background, 1.14(a), 3.4
International Financial Reporting Interpretations Committee, 1.14(f)

processes of, 3.6
purpose of, 3.3
and reporting, 10.3(n)(i)
Standards Advisory Council, 1.14(e)
standards and interpretations of, 3.7
structure, 1.14(b)
structure of, 3.5
trustees, 1.14(c)
International Federation of Accountants Council (IFAC):
generally, 1.17
governance, 1.17(b)
International Federation of Accountants Board, 1.17(c)(i)
International Standards on Auditing, 1.17(d)
membership, 1.17(a)
standing committees, 1.17(c)(ii)
International financial accounting and auditing institutions, role of, 1.13
International Financial Reporting Standards (IFRSs):
acceptance by foreign private issuers, 1.14(g)(ii)
generally, 1.14(g)
procedures for development of, 1.14(g)(i)
International Organization of Securities Commissions (IOSCO), 1.15
International standards:
financial statements:
balance sheet, 4.10(b)
cash flow statement, 4.10(b)
generally, 4.10
inventory, 13.9
liabilities, 18.13
reporting, 10.3(n)(i)
stock-based compensation, 23.7
Inventory:
as asset, 13.2(a)
consignment, 13.3(c)
contract production, 13.3(f)
control procedures:
analysis of variances, 13.7(a)(v)
budgets, 13.7(a)(iv)
generally, 13.7(a)
physical safeguards, 13.7(a)(i)
quantities, control of, 13.4(d)
reconciliations, 13.7(a)(iii)
specified, 13.7(b)
standard costs, use of, 13.7(a)(v)
written policies, 13.7(a)(ii)
costs, flow of, *see subhead:* flow of costs
defined, 13.2(b)
financial statement disclosure requirements, 13.8
flow of costs:
alternative assumptions, 13.6(f)
average cost, 13.6(d)
first-in, first-out (FIFO), 13.6(b)
generally, 13.6(a)
last-in, first-out (LIFO), *see subhead:* last-in, first-out (LIFO)
specific identification, 13.6(e)
generally, 13.1
international standards on, 13.9
last-in, first-out (LIFO):
dollar-value method, 13.6(c)(ii)
double-extension technique, 13.6(c)(iii)
generally, 13.6(c), 13.6(c)(viii)
link-chain technique, 13.6(c)(iv)
new items, 13.6(c)(vii)
retail LIFO method, 13.6(c)(v)
specific goods method, 13.6(c)(i)
valuing the current-year layer, 13.6(c)(vi)
manufacturing:
finished goods, 13.3(b)(iii)
generally, 13.3(b)
raw materials, 13.3(b)(i)
supplies, 13.3(b)(iv)
work in process, 13.3(b)(ii)
miscellaneous, 13.3(i)
objectives of accounting for, 13.2(c)
periodic system of determining quantity of:
cutoff periodic system, 13.4(b)(ii)
generally, 13.4(b)
physical count procedure, 13.4(b)(i)
perpetual system of determining quantity of:
cutoff perpetual system, 13.4(c)(ii)
generally, 13.4(c)
recordkeeping procedures, 13.4(c)(i)
products maturing in more than one year, 13.3(g)
quantities, determining:
generally, 13.4(a)
periodic system, 13.4(b)
perpetual system, 13.4(c)
repossessed, 13.3(e)
retail–wholesale, 13.3(a)
spare parts, 13.3(h)
trade-in, 13.3(d)

Inventory valuation methods:
above cost, 13.5(d)
business combination, purchase of, 13.5(h)
control procedures, 13.5(i)
cost method:
direct labor component, 13.5(a)(iv)
direct material component, 13.5(a)(iii)
flow of costs, *see* Inventory, *subhead:* flow of costs
generally, 13.5(a)
job-order costing, 13.5(a)(i)
overhead allocation, 13.5(a)(vi)
overhead component, 13.5(a)(v)
process costing, 13.5(a)(ii)
current-year layer, valuation of, 13.6(c)(vi)
gross margin, 13.5(g)
lower cost or market valuation method:
generally, 13.5(b)
LIFO considerations with, 13.5(b)(i)
net realizable value, 13.5(f)
replacement cost, 13.5(e)
retail method, 13.5(c)
Investigations and compliance matters, accountant's role in:
Antifraud Programs and Controls Framework (AFPC):
generally, 41.3(d)
service types of, 41.3(d)(i)
contract investigations, 41.3(e)
corporate investigations:
generally, 41.3(a)(i)
securities violations, 41.3(a)(ii)
white-collar crime, 41.3(a)(i)
Foreign Corrupt Practices Act violations, 41.3(c)
generally, 41.3
licensing investigations, 41.3(e)
money laundering, anti–:
generally, 41.3(b)
technology, 41.3(b)(i)
special investigations by CPAs, 1.10(b)(iv)
technology, forensic:
computer, 41.3(f)(i)
data analysis, 41.3(f)(ii)
generally, 41.3(f)
Investment companies:
accounting for securities by, 30.4(c)
financial reporting for:
financial statements, 30.4(d)(iii)
new registrants, 30.4(d)(i)
requirements, 30.4(d)(ii)
fund operations:
accounting agent, role of, 30.4(b)(i)
custodian, role of, 30.4(b)(ii)
generally, 30.4(b)
transfer agent, role of, 30.4(b)(iii)
generally, 30.1(c)(iii)
historical background:
generally, 30.4(a)
SEC statutes, 30.4(a)(i)
offshore funds, 30.4(h)
partnerships, investment, 30.4(g)
SEC filings, 30.4(f)
taxation of, 30.4(e)
types of, 30.4(a)(ii)
Investment credit, 2.2(c)(ii)
IOSCO, *see* International Organization of Securities Commissions

Joint ventures, 20.8. *See also* Real estate ventures
accounting for investments in, 20.8(c)
defined, 20.8(a)
equity method with, 9.3(b)(ii)
health care organizations, 35.3(n)(iii)
natural resources:
alternate procedures, 34.3(c)
generally, 34.3
nonoperator accounting, 34.3(b)
operator accounting, 34.3(a)
standards, 34.3(d)

Land:
and capitalized costs:
land acquisition costs, 31.3(c)
land improvement and development costs, 31.3(d)
cost of:
carrying charges, 16.2(d)(iii)
generally, 16.2(d)
interest, 16.2(d)(ii)
purchase options, 16.2(d)(i)
leases involving:
land and buildings, 15.9(b)(ii)
land and equipment, 15.9(b)(iii)
land only, 15.9(b)(i)
retail land sales:
full accrual method, 31.2(h)(ii), 31.2(h)(iii)

- generally, 31.2(h)
- installment and deposit methods, 31.2(h)(v)
- percentage-of-completion method, 31.2(h)(iv)
- recording of sale, 31.2(h)(i)

Lease(s):
- advantages of leasing, 15.1(a)
- and asset retirement obligations, 15.10(i)
- assignment of lease or property subject to lease as sales-type or direct financing lease, 15.7
- and bankruptcy:
  - generally, 39.3(e)
  - limitations, 39.3(e)(i)
- build-to-suit, 15.10(h)(ii)
- business combinations, 8.3(g)(vi)
- and business combinations, 15.10(f)
- capital:
  - accounting for, 15.4(a)
  - amortization, lessee, 15.4(c)(iv)
  - classification of lease, 15.4(c)(ii)
  - disclosures for, 15.4(b)
  - example, 15.4(c)
  - inception, accounting at, 15.4(c)(iii)
  - minimum payments, 15.4(c)(i)
  - payments, 15.4(c)(i), 15.4(c)(v)
- changes to provisions of, 15.10(d)
- direct financing:
  - accounting for, 15.5(a)
  - disclosure requirements, 15.6(b)
  - example, 15.5(b)
  - sale/assignment of lease or property subject to lease as, 15.7
  - sales-type lease vs., 15.6
- disadvantages of leasing, 15.1(b)
- disclosure, examples of, 15.11
- extension of, 15.10(e)
- FASB guidance updates, 15.12
- favorable, as intangible asset:
  - amortization of, 14.5(e)(ii)
  - capitalization amounts for, 14.5(e)(i)
  - generally, 14.5(e)
- lessee, classification by, 15.2(b)
- lessor, classification by, 15.2(c)
- leveraged:
  - accounting for, 15.8(a)
  - characteristics of, 15.8(a)(i)
  - disclosures with, 15.8(b)
  - generally, 17.1(c)(iv), 17.2(e)(ii)
  - investment, lessor accounting for, 15.8(a)(iii)
  - lessee accounting, 15.8(a)(ii)
  - recognition of income, lessor, 15.8(a)(iv)
- long-term, 18.8(c)
- operating:
  - example, 15.3(d)
  - lessee accounting for, 15.3(a)
  - lessee disclosures for, 15.3(b)
  - lessor accounting for, 15.3(c)
- pronouncements related to, 15.2
- provisions, changes to, 15.10(d)
- real estate:
  - and characteristics of real estate, 15.9(a)
  - government unit/authority, facilities owned by, 15.9(c)
  - land and buildings, 15.9(b)(ii)
  - land and equipment, 15.9(b)(iii)
  - land only, 15.9(b)(i)
  - part of a building, 15.9(b)(iv)
- related party leases, 15.10(b)
- renewal of, 15.10(e)
- residual value, changes in, 15.10(g)
- sale and leaseback transactions:
  - build-to-suit leases, 15.10(h)(ii)
  - construction, lessee involvement with, 15.10(h)(i)
  - generally, 15.10(h)
  - lessee accounting, 15.10(h)(iv)
  - lessor accounting, 15.10(h)(v)
  - miscellaneous issues with, 15.10(h)(iii)
  - for real-estate, 15.10(h)(vi)
  - special-purpose entities, 15.10(h)(iii)
- sale–leaseback arrangements, 31.2(f)(vii)
- sale of leased departments, sale of, 12.3(h)(iv)
- sale of lease or property subject to lease as sales-type or direct financing lease, 15.7
- sales-type:
  - accounting for, 15.6(a)
  - direct financing lease vs., 15.6
  - disclosure requirements, 15.6(b)
  - example, 15.6(c)
  - sale/assignment of lease or property subject to lease as, 15.7
- subleases:
  - generally, 15.10(c)
  - lessor, original, 15.10(c)(iii)
  - non-relief of obligation, original lessee's, 15.10(c)(ii)

Lease(s): (*Continued*)
relief of obligation, original lessee's, 15.10(c)(i)
technical terms defined, 15.2(d)
termination of, 15.10(e)
third parties, participation by, 15.10(a)
unique characteristics of, 15.2(a)
Leveraged buyouts:
accounting for the transaction, 8.4(d), 8.4(h)
carrying amount:
determination of, 8.4(f)
limitation of, 8.4(g)
change in control with:
generally, 8.4(e)
no change in control, 8.4(e)(iii)
objective criteria, 8.4(e)(i)
subjective criteria, 8.4(e)(ii)
defined, 8.4(a)
historical background, 8.4(c)
IFRS No. 3 on, 8.4(i)
structure:
financing arrangements of, 8.4(b)(iii)
generally, 8.4(b)
legal form, 8.4(b)(i)
management participation in, 8.4(b)(ii)
tax considerations and, 8.4(b)(iv)
Leveraged leases, 17.2(e)(ii)
Liability(-ies):
accounts payable, *see* Accounts payable
acquisition method (business combinations), *see* Acquisition method (business combinations), *subhead:* recognition/measurement of assets and liabilities
asset-securitization transactions, 18.11(b)
on balance sheet, 10.4(c)
convertible bonds with issuer option to settle for cash upon conversion, 18.11(a)(v)
convertible bonds with premium put, 18.11(a)(i)
credit balances vs., 18.1(a)(ii)
current, *see* Current liabilities
and current ratio, 4.3(b)(iii)
defined, 18.1(a)
derivative financial instruments indexed to company's own stock, 18.11(a)(iv)
disclosures of:
fair value of financial instruments, 18.1(d)
executory contracts as, 18.1(a)(i)
extinguishment of, 18.10(b)
and fair value accounting, 18.12
fair value measurements of:
assets vs. liabilities, 24.4(e)(i)
nonfinancial liabilities, 24.3(c)
financial instruments classified as both equity and:
generally, 18.9(a)
mandatorily redeemable financial instruments, 18.9(a)(i)
measurement of, 18.9(b)
obligations to issue a variable number of shares, 18.9(a)(iii)
obligations to repurchase the issuer's equity shares, 18.9(a)(ii)
presentation and disclosure of, 18.9(c)
financing instruments, accounting for, 18.11(a)
generally, 4.3(b)
increasing-rate debt, 18.11(a)(ii)
indexed debt instruments, 18.11(a)(iii)
interest as, 18.2
international standards, U.S. vs., 18.13
long-term:
capitalization analysis, 10.4(c)(ii)
capitalization table, 10.4(c)(iii)
debt ratios, 10.4(c)(iv)
fixed asset turnover ratio, 10.4(c)(i)
generally, 10.4(c)
off-balance-sheet obligations, 10.4(c)(vi), 10.4(c)(vii)
preferred stock ratios, 10.4(c)(v)
property analysis, 10.4(c)(viii)
measurement of, 18.1(c)
measurement of deferred tax liabilities, 17.2(d)(iv)
noncurrent, 4.3(b)(ii)
offsetting, against assets, 18.1(b)
on personal financial statement, 22.1(d)
recognition of deferred tax liabilities:
of change in valuation allowance, 17.2(d)(iii)
generally, 17.2(d), 17.2(d)(i)
of valuation allowance, 17.2(d)(ii)
restructurings, troubled debt, 18.10(a)
and working capital, 4.3(b)(iii)
Loans:
capital stock, notes received for, 11.3(e)
disclosures with, 11.3(f)
generally, 11.3(a)
impairment of:

generally, 11.3(c)
measurement guidelines, 11.3(c)(i)
measurement of, 11.3(b)
recognition of:
generally, 11.3(b)
income recognition, 11.3(c), 11.3(c)(ii)
troubled debt restructuring, 11.3(d)
Loan sales:
accounting guidance, 30.2(p)(v)
loan servicing, 30.2(p)(iii)
regulatory guidance, 30.2(p)(iv)
securitizations, 30.2(p)(ii)
underwriting standards, 30.2(p)(i)
valuation, 30.2(p)(vi)
Local governments, *see* State and local governments
Long-term assets:
on balance sheet, 10.4(c)
capitalization analysis, 10.4(c)(ii)
capitalization table, 10.4(c)(iii)
debt ratios, 10.4(c)(iv)
fixed asset turnover ratio, 10.4(c)(i)
off-balance-sheet obligations, 10.4(c)(vi), 10.4(c)(vii)
preferred stock ratios, 10.4(c)(v)
property analysis, 10.4(c)(viii)
Long-term liability(-ies):
asset retirement obligations, 18.8(g)
borrowings on open account, 18.8(f)
deferred compensation contracts, 18.8(h)
deferred revenue obligations, 18.8(d)
disclosure of, 18.8(j), 18.8(k)(iv)
expense accruals, long-term, 18.8(e)
guarantee obligations:
disclosure, 18.8(k)(iv)
FASB Interpretation No. 45, 18.8(k)(i)
initial recognition, 18.8(k)(ii)
subsequent accounting, 18.8(k)(iii)
income taxes, future, 18.8(i)
installment purchase contracts, 18.8(b)
leases, long-term, 18.8(c)
mortgages and long term notes, 18.8(a)
forfeiture of real-estate subject to nonrecourse mortgage, 18.8(a)(ii)
related party transactions, 18.8(a)(i)
pension plans, 18.8(h)
unconditional purchase obligations, disclosure of, 18.8(j)
Loss contingencies:
health care organizations, 35.3(m)(iii)
retained earnings, 19.7(o)

Maintenance and repairs:
property, plant and equipment (PP&E):
accounting alternatives, 16.4(b)(i)
extraordinary repairs, 16.4(b)(ii)
generally, 16.4(b)
Management accounting, financial accounting and reporting vs., 2.1(b)
Management Discussion and Analysis (MD&A):
capital resources disclosures, 6.1(d)(ii)
concentrations, vulnerability due to, 6.3(e)
critical accounting estimates, 6.2(b)
disclosures, 6.1(d)(ii)
estimates:
certain significant, 6.3(d)
use of, 6.3(c)
fair value disclosures, 6.1(d)(ii)
generally, 6.1(a), 6.1(c)
historical background, 6.1(b)
independent auditor involvement, 6.4
liquidity disclosures, 6.1(d)(ii)
nature of operations, 6.3(b)
newly issued but not yet effective accounting standards, 6.2(d)
non-GAAP measures, 6.2(c)
requirements, 6.2(a)
risks and uncertainties, 6.3(a)
smaller reporting companies, 6.1(d)(i)
Manufacturing inventory:
finished goods, 13.3(b)(iii)
generally, 13.3(b)
raw materials, 13.3(b)(i)
supplies, 13.3(b)(iv)
work in process, 13.3(b)(ii)
Market efficiency, 1.1(b)(ii)
Materiality:
not-for-profit organizations, 28.4(c)
prospective financial statements, 21.5(e)
Regulation S-X, 5.4(e)
Securities Act criterion:
assessment of materiality, 5.2(c)(i)
generally, 5.2(c)
intentional immaterial misstatements, 5.2(c)(iii)
misstatements, 5.2(c)(ii), 5.2(c)(iii)
MD&A, *see* Management Discussion and Analysis

Measurement. *See also* Valuation
  fair value, *see* Fair value measurement(s)
  impairment of value; assets to be held and used, 16.3(b)(ii)
Mining:
  commodities transactions, 34.7(d)
  exploration/development costs, 34.7(a)
  futures transactions, 34.7(d)
  GAAP, sources of, 34.6(b)
  impairment of long-lived assets, 34.7(g)
  inventories, 34.7(c)(i), 34.7(c)(ii)
  materials and supplies, 34.7(c)(ii)
  metal and mineral inventories, 34.7(c)(i)
  operations, 34.6(a)
  production costs, 34.7(b)
  reclamation/remediation, 34.7(e)
  royalty revenues, 34.8(b)
  sales of minerals, 34.8(a)
  shutdowns, 34.7(f)
  tolling revenues, 34.8(b)
Minority interests:
  exchange of ownership interests, 8.3(e)(i)
  generally, 8.3(e)
  simultaneous common control mergers, 8.3(e)(ii)
Mortgage banking activities:
  accounting guidance, 30.3(b)
  generally, 30.1(c)(ii), 30.3(a)
  mortgage loans:
    held for investment, 30.3(d)
    held for sale, 30.3(c)
  sales of mortgage loans/securities:
    accounting guidance, 30.2(p)(v)
    gain/loss on, 30.3(e)(i)
    generally, 30.3(e)
    loan servicing, 30.2(p)(iii)
    prepayment, financial assets subject to, 30.3(e)(ii)
    regulatory guidance, 30.2(p)(iv)
    securitizations, 30.2(p)(ii)
    underwriting standards, 30.2(p)(i)
    valuation, 30.2(p)(vi)
  servicing rights, mortgage:
    amortization of, 30.3(f)(ii)
    fair value of, 30.3(f)(iv)
    generally, 30.3(f)
    impairment of, 30.3(f)(iii)
    initial capitalization of, 30.3(f)(i)
    retained interests and, 30.3(f)(vi)
    sales of, 30.3(f)(v)
    tax treatment of, 30.3(g)(i)
  taxation of banks:
    generally, 30.3(g)
    mark to market, 30.3(g)(ii)
    mortgage servicing rights, 30.3(g)(i)

Natural resources:
  disclosures, financial statement, 34.11
  exploration and producing operations, 34.2
  financial statements:
    disclosures on, 34.11
    ore reserves, supplementary information on, 34.9
  full cost accounting method:
    amortization, exclusion of costs from, 34.4(b)(ii)
    basic rules, 34.4(b)(i)
    ceiling test, 34.4(b)(iii)
    conveyances, 34.4(b)(iv)
  generally, 34.1
  hard-rock mining, *see subhead:* mining
  income taxation, 34.10
  joint operations involving:
    alternate procedures, 34.3(c)
    generally, 34.3
    nonoperator accounting, 34.3(b)
    operator accounting, 34.3(a)
    standards, 34.3(d)
  mining:
    commodities transactions, 34.7(d)
    exploration/development costs, 34.7(a)
    futures transactions, 34.7(d)
    GAAP, sources of, 34.6(b)
    impairment of long-lived assets, 34.7(g)
    inventories, 34.7(c)(i), 34.7(c)(ii)
    materials and supplies, 34.7(c)(ii)
    metal and mineral inventories, 34.7(c)(i)
    operations, 34.6(a)
    production costs, 34.7(b)
    reclamation/remediation, 34.7(e)
    royalty revenues, 34.8(b)
    sales of minerals, 34.8(a)
    shutdowns, 34.7(f)
    tolling revenues, 34.8(b)
  natural gas imbalances:
    entitlements method, 34.5(b)
    example, gas balancing, 34.5(c)
    generally, 34.5
    sales method, 34.5(a)

ore reserves, supplementary information on, 34.9
successful efforts accounting method:
basic rules, 34.4(a)(i)
conveyances, 34.4(a)(v)
exploratory vs. development wells, 34.4(a)(ii)
impairment test, 34.4(a)(iv)
undetermined outcome of exploratory wells, 34.4(a)(iii)
Nonprofit organizations. *See also* Not-for-profit organizations
cost-volume-revenue analysis for, *see* Cost-volume-revenue (CVR) analysis for nonprofit organizations
generally, 29
Not-for-profit health care entities:
balance sheet, 35.5(b)(i)
business combinations involving, 35.3(o)(i)
contributions to, 35.3(g)(i)
derivatives accounting with, 35.3(i)(i)
generally, 35.1(b)
joint operating agreements involving, 35.3(n)(iii)
operating statement, 35.5(c)(ii)
"public" vs. "private," 35.2(a)(ii)
reporting entity considerations with, 35.3(n)(i), 35.3(n)(iii)
Not-for-profit organizations:
accounting principles with:
AICPA Audit Guides, 28.1(a)(ii)
decisions, required, 28.1(a)(i)
FASB projects, upcoming, 28.1(a)(iii)
generally, 28.1(a), 28.3(c)(i)
and affiliated organizations:
generally, 28.2(k)
pass-through gifts, 28.2(k)(ii)
reporting entity, 28.2(k)(i)
appropriations by, 28.2(e)
audits of:
compliance auditing, 28.4(f)
consolidation of financial statements, 28.4(e)
generally, 28.4(a)
government requirements, 28.1(b)
and internal control, 28.4(b)
investments, 28.4(g)
materiality, 28.4(c)
taxes, 28.4(d)
unique areas, 28.4(h)
basis, accounting, 28.2(b)
bona fide pledges by donors, 28 (App4)
cash flows, statement of:
generally, 28.2(m)
voluntary health and welfare organizations, 28.3(a)(iv)
colleges and universities:
encumbrance accounting, 28.3(b)(ii)
fund accounting, 28.3(b)(i)
conditional vs. restricted gifts/pledges, 28 (App5)
contracts vs. restricted grants, 28 (App1)
contributions to:
expendable support, 28.2(i)(i)
gifts in kind, 28.2(i)(ii)
intermediary, not-for-profit organization as, 28.2(i)(iv)
not currently expendable support, 28.2(i)(iii)
services, 28 (App 2), 28 (App3)
depreciation of assets by, 28.2(g)
fixed assets of:
generally, 28.2(f)
grantor, reversion to, 28.2(f)(i)
fund accounting:
and classes vs. funds, 28.2(c)(i)
generally, 28.2(c)
reclassifications in, 28.2(d)
governmental vs. nongovernmental accounting with, 28.2(n)
investments by:
gains/losses on investments, 28.2(h)(ii)
generally, 28.2(h)
income, investment, 28.2(h)(i)
mergers and acquisitions of, 28.2(l)
operating vs. nonoperating items, 28 (App6)
reporting requirements for, 28.2(a)
restricted grants vs. contracts, 28 (App1)
services contributed to:
need for services, 28 (App3)
specialized skills required for, 28 (App2)
tax positions taken by, 28.2(j)
voluntary health and welfare organizations:
balance sheet, 28.3(a)(ii)
cash flows, statement of, 28.3(a)(iv)
financial statements of, 28.3(a)(i)
functional expenses, statement of, 28.3(a)(v)
generally, 28.3(a)

Not-for-profit organizations: (*Continued*)
statement of support, revenue/expenses, and changes in net assets, 28.3(a)(iii)

Operating budgets (state/local government accounting), 33.4(k)(i)
Overhead:
inventory valuation, 13.5(a)(v), 13.5(a)(vi)
on self-constructed assets, overhead on, 16.2(b)

Partnerships. *See also* Joint ventures
accounting peculiarities with, 20.2(a)
advantages/disadvantages of, 20.1(b)
average capital ratio example, 20.2(c)
change in partners:
capital ratios, adjustment of, 20.3(f)
effect of, 20.3(a)
closing of operating accounts:
division of profits (example), 20.2(e)(i)
generally, 20.2(e)
statement of partners' capitals (example), 20.2(e)(ii)
defined, 20.1(a)
formation of, 20.1(e)
importance of, 20.1(d)
and income taxation, 20.2(f)
incorporation of, 20.4
initial balance sheet of, 20.1(f)
limited:
accounting issues with, 20.6(d)(iii)
defined, 20.6(a)
financial statement disclosure issues with, 20.6(d)(ii)
financial statement reporting issues with, 20.6(d)(i)
formation of, 20.6(c)
general partnerships vs., 20.6(b)
liquidation of:
balance sheet example, 20.5(d)
generally, 20.5(a)
by installments, 20.5(c)
by single cash distribution, 20.5(b)
new partner's investment to acquire interest:
at book value, 20.3(c)(i)
generally, 20.3(c)
goodwill method, 20.3(c)(iv)
at less than book value, 20.3(c)(iii)
at more than book value, 20.3(c)(ii)
new partner's purchase of interest:
at book value, 20.3(b)(i)
generally, 20.3(b)
at less than book value, 20.3(b)(iii)
at more than book value, 20.3(b)(ii)
nonpublic investment, 20.7
profits and losses, dividing of, 20.2(b)
realization of assets of, 20.5(a). *See also subhead:* liquidation of
tax considerations with, 20.1(c)
transactions between partner and firm:
bonuses, 20.2(d)(iii)
and debtor–creditor relationship, 20.2(d)(iv)
generally, 20.2(d)
invested capital, interest on, 20.2(d)(i)
and landlord–tenant relationship, 20.2(d)(v)
salaries, partners', 20.2(d)(ii)
statement presentation of, 20.2(d)(vi)
withdrawing partner, using firm funds to settle with:
discount given by retiring partner, 20.3(e)(ii)
generally, 20.3(e)
premium paid to retiring partner, 20.3(e)(i)
withdrawing partner, using outside funds to settle with:
at book value, sale, 20.3(d)(i)
generally, 20.3(d)
at less than book value, sale, 20.3(d)(iii)
at more than book value, sale, 20.3(d)(ii)
Payments, share-based, *see* Share-based payments
PCAOB, *see* Public Company Accounting Oversight Board
PCAOB Staff Audit Practice Alert No. 2 (*Matters Related to Auditing Fair Value Measurements of Financial Instruments and the Use of Specialists*):
auditing of fair value measurements, 24.6(d)(i)
and FASB ASC 820, 24.6(d)(ii)
generally, 24.6(d)
pricing service, use of, 24.6(d)(iv)
valuation specialist, using work of, 24.6(d)(iii)
Pension plans. *See also* Postemployment benefits; Postretirement benefits
actuarial present value of benefits:

assumptions, 27.5(e)(i)
changes in, 27.5(f)
disclosures for, 27.5(e)(ii)
generally, 27.2(c)(v), 27.5(e)
administration of, 27.1(c)
assets, plan:
expected return on, 27.2(d)(iii)
generally, 27.2(e)
recognition of, 27.2(f)
basic elements in accounting for:
actuarial assumptions, 27.2(c)(ii)
actuarial present value of benefits, 27.2(c)(v)
attribution, 27.2(c)(i)
consistency, 27.2(c)(iv)
generally, 27.2(c)
interest rates, 27.2(c)(iii)
measurement date, 27.2(c)(vi)
business combinations, 8.3(g)(ix)
defined benefit plans:
medical benefits, postretirement, 27.5(k)
nonqualified, 27.4(d)
defined contribution plans:
financial statements for, 27.5(j)(iii)
generally, 27.2(i), 27.5(j)
nonqualified, 27.4(c)
separate accounts, 27.5(j)(i)
types of, 27.5(j)(ii)
development of private pensions:
growth, 27.1(b)(ii)
historical background, 27.1(b)(i)
present status, 27.1(b)(iii)
disclosures with:
actuarial present value of benefits, 27.5(e)(ii)
annuity contracts, 27.2(h)(iii)
generally, 27.2(h)
miscellaneous disclosures, 27.5(h)
nonpublic entities, 27.2(h)(ii)
nonrecurring events, 27.3(i)
public entities, 27.2(h)(i)
statement of net assets, 27.5(c)(ii)
evolution of accounting standards for, 27.1(d)
financial statement accounting for:
content of statements, 27.5(b)
decisions related to, 27.5(i)
disclosures, *see subhead:* disclosures with
example, 27.5(g)
historical background, 27.5(a)
net assets available for benefits, *see subhead:* net assets available for benefits
objective of statements, 27.5(b)
funding of, 27.2(m)
generally, 27.1(a)
income taxation of, 27.2(m)
interim measurements with, 27.2(g)
liabilities, recognition of, 27.2(f)
long-term liabilities, 18.8(h)
merger of, 27.3(e)
multiemployer plans, 27.2(k)
multiple employer plans, 27.2(l)
net assets available for benefits:
changes in, 27.5(d)
contributions receivable, 27.5(c)(iv)
disclosures for investments, 27.5(c)(ii)
generally, 27.5(c)
good-faith valuations, 27.5(c)(i)
operating assets, 27.5(c)(iii)
net periodic pension cost:
and amortization of net gains/losses, 27.2(d)(iv)
and amortization of net obligation/asset, 27.2(d)(vi)
and amortization of net prior service cost, 27.2(d)(v)
and expected return on plan assets, 27.2(d)(iii)
generally, 27.2(d)
interest cost, 27.2(d)(ii)
service cost, 27.2(d)(i)
nonqualified plans:
assets of, 27.4(b)
defined benefit plans, 27.4(d)
defined contribution plans, 27.4(c)
qualified vs., 27.4(a)
nonrecurring events with:
business combinations, 27.3(g)
curtailment, 27.3(c)
disclosure requirements, 27.3(i)
disposal of business, 27.3(d)
example, 27.3(j)
generally, 27.3(a)
mergers, plan, 27.3(e)
sequence of measurement steps for, 27.3(h)
settlements, *see subhead:* settlements
spinoffs, plan, 27.3(e)
termination, plan, 27.3(e)

Pension plans (*Continued*)
termination benefits, 27.3(f)
non-U. S. pension plans, 27.2(j)
qualified vs. nonqualified plans, 27.4(a)
recognition of liabilities/assets, 27.2(f)
settlements:
generally, 27.3(b)
maximum gain/loss, 27.3(b)(ii)
participating annuities, use of, 27.3(b)(iii)
timing of, 27.3(b)(i)
SFAS No. 87 and:
applicability, 27.2(b)
scope, 27.2(a)
spinoffs of, 27.3(e)
taxation, income, 27.2(m)
termination of:
benefits, 27.3(f)
generally, 27.3(e)
Personal financial statements:
and applicable professional standards, 22.2(d)
assets on:
closely held business, 22.3(h)
estimated current value of, 22.3(a)
future interests, 22.3(l)
intangible assets, 22.3(k)
life insurance, 22.3(g)
limited partnership interests, 22.3(d)
marketable securities, 22.3(c)
options on other than marketable securities, 22.3(f)
personal property, 22.3(j)
precious metals, 22.3(e)
real estate, 22.3(i)
receivables, 22.3(b)
audits of, 22.10
basis of accounting for, 22.1(d)
changes in net worth, statement of:
defined, 22.6(a)
format, 22.6(c)
uses of, 22.6(b)
for client internal use only, 22.12
compilation of, 22.8
defined, 22.1(a)
disclosures on:
generally, 22.7
income tax provision, 22.5(d), 22.5(e)
and due diligence in accountant-client relationship, 22.2(a)
income taxes on:
computation of provision for, 22.5(b)
disclaimer statement, 22.5(d)
as liability, 22.4(d)
omission of disclosure, 22.5(e)
provision for, 22.5(a)
and tax basis, 22.5(c)
individual vs. family, 22.1(b)
liabilities on:
contingencies, 22.4(c)
estimated current amount, 22.4(a)
fixed commitments, 22.4(b)
income taxes, 22.4(d)
risks and uncertainties, 22.4(c)
listing of assets/liabilities on, 22.1(d)
operating rules for, 22.2(d)
purpose of, 22.1(a), 22.1(c)
reports and reporting:
generally, 22.11
prescribed forms, 22.11(d)
standard audit report, 22.11(g)
standard compilation report, 22.11(a)
standard review report, 22.11(f)
when accountant is not independent, 22.11(c)
when departing from GAAP, 22.11(e)
when substantially all disclosures omitted, 22.11(b)
review of, 22.9
and understanding of engagement by all parties, 22.2(b)
and value of written representations, 22.2(c)
Plant, *see* Property, plant and equipment (PP&E)
Plant closing costs, 8.3(c)(ii)
Postemployment benefits. *See also* Pension plans
disclosures, 27.7(b)(iv)
employers' accounting for:
generally, 27.7(a)
SFAS No. 112 and, *see subhead:* SFAS No. 112 and
generally, 27.1(a)
SFAS No. 112 and:
accrual accounting, differences in, 27.7(b)(ii)
and application of SFAS No. 43 vs. SFAS No. 5, 27.7(b)(i)
disclosures, 27.7(b)(iv)
example, 27.7(b)(v)
measurement issues, 27.7(b)(iii)

Postretirement benefits. *See also* Pension plans
accounting for, 27.6(a)
disclosures, 27.6(e)
evolution of accounting standards for, 27.1(d)
generally, 27.1(a)
nonrecurring events, 27.6(d)
SFAS No. 106 and:
actuarial assumptions, 27.6(c)
generally, 27.6(b)
SFAS No. 87 vs., 27.6(b)(i), 27.6(b)(ii)
PP&E, *see* Property, plant and equipment
Preferred stock, 19.2(c)
callable, 19.2(c)(v)
convertible, 19.2(c)(ix)
cumulative, 19.2(c)(vi)
fully participating, 19.2(c)(vii)
increasing-rate, 19.2(c)(x)
mandatory redeemable:
carrying amount of, 19.2(c)(iv)
classification requirements, 19.2(c)(ii)
dividends on, 19.2(c)(iii)
generally, 19.2(c)(i)
partially participating, 19.2(c)(viii)
ratios, 10.4(c)(v)
redeemable, 5.4(m)
Regulation S-X and, 5.4(m)
Professional societies, 1.11(b)
Property, plant and equipment (PP&E):
authoritative literature on, 16.1(c)
characteristics of, 16.1(b)
cost of:
debt, acquisition by issuing, 16.2(a)(ii)
determining, 16.2(a)
donated assets, 16.2(a)(v)
exchange, acquisition by, 16.2(a)(i)
interest capitalization, 16.2(c)
land, *see subhead:* cost of land
mixed acquisition for lump sum, 16.2(a)(iv)
research/development activities, assets held for, 16.2(e)
self-constructed assets, overhead on, 16.2(b)
stock, acquisition by issuing, 16.2(a)(iii)
cost of land:
carrying charges, 16.2(d)(iii)
generally, 16.2(d)
interest, 16.2(d)(ii)
purchase options, 16.2(d)(i)
defined, 16.1(a)
depreciation of, *see* Property, plant and equipment depreciation
disposals of:
casualties, 16.5(b)
generally, 16.5
retirements, 16.5(a)
sales, 16.5(a)
trade-ins, 16.5(a)
expenditures during ownership:
additions, 16.4(c)
asbestos removal/containment, 16.4(f)
capital vs. operating expenditures, 16.4(a)
environmental contamination costs, 16.4(g)
improvements, 16.4(c)
maintenance/repairs, *see subhead:* maintenance and repairs
rearrangement/reinstallation, 16.4(e)
rehabilitation, 16.4(d)
replacements, 16.4(c)
financial statement presentation:
construction in progress, 16.13(b)
fully depreciated/idle assets, 16.13(d)
general requirements, 16.13(a)
impairment of assets, *see subhead:* impairment of value
retirement, gain/loss on, 16.13(c)
segment information, 16.13(f)
impairment of value:
assets to be disposed of, 16.3(c), 16.13(e)(iii)
assets to be held and used, 16.3(b), 16.3(b)(i), 16.3(b)(ii), 16.13(e)(ii)
financial statement presentation, 16.13(e)(i)
pronouncements, authoritative, 16.3(a)
maintenance and repairs:
accounting alternatives, 16.4(b)(i)
effect of maintenance, 16.8(c)
extraordinary repairs, 16.4(b)(ii)
generally, 16.4(b)
retirement of:
disposals, 16.5(a)
initial recognition/measurement, 16.6(c)
subsequent recognition/measurement, 16.6(d)
service life of:
estimating, 16.8(d), 16.8(f)

Property, plant and equipment (PP&E): (*Continued*)
factors affecting, 16.8(b), 16.8(b)(i), 16.8(b)(ii)
functional factors and, 16.8(b)(ii)
of leasehold improvements, 16.8(e)
maintenance and, 16.8(c)
physical factors and, 16.8(b)(i)
physical life vs., 16.8(a)
revisions of estimated service lives, 16.8(f)
Property, plant and equipment depreciation:
base, depreciation:
assets to be disposed of, 16.9(d)
idle/auxiliary equipment, 16.9(c)
and net salvage value, 16.9(a)
property under construction, 16.9(b)
used assets, 16.9(e)
computation of, 16.7(b)
defined, 16.7(a)
generally, 16.7
methods of:
changing, 16.10(f)
decreasing-charge methods, 16.10(c)
generally, 16.10
interest methods, 16.10(d)(i), 16.10(d)(ii)
for partial periods, 16.10(e)
straight-line method, 16.10(a)
usage methods, 16.10(b)(i), 16.10(b)(ii)
rates of:
additions and, 16.11(c)
composite depreciation, 16.11(b)(ii)
group depreciation, 16.11(b)(i)
improvements and, 16.11(c)
replacements and, 16.11(c)
sources for, 16.11(a)
tools, 16.11(d)
for tax purposes:
additional first-year depreciation, 16.12(c)
current requirements, 16.12(a)
generally, 16.12
modified accelerated cost recovery system (MACRS), 16.12(b)
tools and related assets, 16.11(d)
Prospective financial statements:
and accountants' services:
compilation services, *see subhead:* compilation services
examination services, *see subhead:* examination services
internal use of statements, 21.4(c)
accountants' services related to:
assembly of statements, 21.5(b)(iii)
materiality criterion, 21.5(e)
objective of, 21.5(a)
partial presentations, 21.5(b)(i)
prohibited engagements, 21.5(d)
SEC rules, 21.5(f)
standard services, 21.5(b)
third-party use, 21.5(b)(ii)
agreed-upon procedures:
procedures, 21.8(b)
reports, 21.8(c)
scope of, 21.8(a)
compilation services:
assembly, 21.6(b)
deficiencies, presentation, 21.6(e)(ii)
independence, lack of, 21.6(e)(iii)
problem situations, 21.6(e)
procedures, 21.6(c)
reporting on compilations, 21.6(d)
scope, 21.6(a), 21.6(e)(i)
defined, 21.1(a)
development of:
assembly of statements, 21.3(d)
assumptions, 21.3(c)
general guidelines, 21.3(a)
key factors, identification of, 21.3(b)
length of prospective period, 21.3(c)(ii)
mathematical models, 21.3(c)(i)
disclosures in:
accounting principles, significant, 21.4(c)(iii)
assumptions, significant, 21.4(c)(ii)
authoritative guidance, 21.4(a)
date of presentation, 21.4(c)(iv)
description of presentation, 21.4(c)(i)
generally, 21.4(c)
examination services:
adverse report, 21.7(c)(ii)
assumptions, evaluation of, 21.7(a)(ii)
disclaimer, 21.7(c)(iii)
divided responsibility, 21.7(c)(iv)
independence of, 21.7(d)
modified examination reports, 21.7(c)
preparation, evaluation of, 21.7(a)(i)
presentation, evaluation of, 21.7(a)(iii)
qualified opinion, 21.7(c)(i)
scope, 21.7(a)
standard examination report, 21.7(b)

financial analyses vs., 21.1(b)(iv)
financial forecasts defined, 21.1(a)(i)
financial projections defined, 21.1(a)(ii)
internal use services:
formal reports, 21.9(d)(iii)
legends, 21.9(d)(ii)
plain paper, 21.9(d)(i)
procedures, 21.9(c)
reports, 21.9(d)
scope of, 21.9(a)
use of third parties vs., 21.9(b)
partial presentations vs., 21.1(b)(ii)
presentation of:
amounts presented, 21.4(b)(i)
authoritative guidance, 21.4(a)
form of statements, 21.4(b)
titles, 21.4(b)(ii)
presentations for wholly expired periods vs., 21.1(b)(i)
pro formas vs., 21.1(b)(iii)
use of:
generally, 21.2(a)
general use, 21.2(b)
internal use, 21.2(d)
limited use, 21.2(c)
Public colleges and universities, 33.6
Public Company Accounting Oversight Board (PCAOB):
advisory groups, 1.9(c)(i)
authority, 1.9(b)
background, 1.9(a)
board members, 1.9(c)(i)
inspections by:
generally, 1.9(f)
results, 1.9(f)(ii)
scope, 1.9(f)(i)
intangible assets, initial valuation of, 14.3(a)(ii)
investigations by, 1.9(g)
registration of firms with, 1.9(d)
Sarbanes-Oxley Act and, 1.9(a), 1.9(e)(i)
staff, 1.9(c)(i)
standards:
generally, 1.9(e)
process of setting, 1.9(e)(ii)
Sarbanes-Oxley mandated provisions, 1.9(e)(i)
structure, 1.9(c)
white-collar crime penalties, 1.9(h)
Publicly held companies, disclosure requirements for:
earnings per share, 4.8(c)(ii)
generally, 4.8(c)
interim reporting, 4.8(c)(iii)
segment disclosure, 4.8(c)(i)

Quasi reorganizations:
ASC Topic 740 on, 17.2(e)(iv)
retained earnings and, 19.7(l)
procedures, 19.7(l)(i)
readjustment, retained earnings after, 19.7(l)(ii)
tax loss carryforwards, 19.7(l)(iii)

Real estate. *See also* Land; Lease(s)
accounting policies and, 31.9(b)
bank-owned:
foreclosed assets, 30.2(q)(iii), 30.2(v)(vii)
former bank premises, 30.2(q)(ii)
investments, 30.2(q)(i)
taxation of, 30.2(v)(vii)
Codification and, 31.10(a)
defined, 15.9(a)
under development, 31.5(b)
disclosures, note, 31.9(c)
and FASB codification, 31.1(b)
financial statement presentation:
balance sheet, 31.9(a)(i)
statement of income, 31.9(a)(ii)
generally, 31.1(a)
investment trusts, 31.9(e)
mortgage loan borrowers, accounting by, 31.9(d)
note disclosures, 31.9(c)
on personal financial statements, 22.3(i)
Real estate capitalized costs:
abandonments, 31.3(k)
amenities, costs of, 31.3(j)
changes in use, 31.3(k)
construction costs, 31.3(d)
environmental contamination removal costs, 31.3(e)
foreclosed assets:
generally, 31.3(m)
income, held for production of, 31.3(m)(ii)
sale, held for, 31.3(m)(i)
general and administrative expenses, 31.3(i)
generally, 31.3(a)

Real estate capitalized costs: (*Continued*)
indirect project costs, 31.3(h)
insurance costs, 31.3(g)
interest costs:
amount capitalized, accounting for, 31.3(f)(iv)
generally, 31.3(f)
methods of capitalization, 31.3(f)(iii)
period, capitalization, 31.3(f)(ii)
qualifying assets, 31.3(f)(i)
land acquisition costs, 31.3(c)
land improvement and development costs, 31.3(d)
preacquisition costs, 31.3(b)
selling, costs associated with, 31.3(l)
taxes, 31.3(g)
Real estate investment trusts (REITs), 30.1(c)(ix)
Real estate transactions:
alternate accounting methods:
cost recovery method, 31.2(j)(iii)
coventure method, 31.2(j)(vii)
deposit method, 31.2(j)(i)
derecognition method, 31.2(j)(viii)
financing method, 31.2(j)(v)
generally, 31.2(j)
installment method, 31.2(j)(ii)
lease method, 31.2(j)(vi)
profit-sharing method, 31.2(j)(vii)
reduced profit method, 31.2(j)(iv)
analysis of, 31.2(a)
condominium sales:
accounting methods, 31.2(g)(ii)
future costs, estimated, 31.2(g)(iii)
generally, 31.2(g)
profit recognition, criteria for, 31.2(g)(i)
continued involvement of seller:
development and construction, 31.2(f)(ix)
future profits, participation in, 31.2(f)(i)
generally, 31.2(f)
general partner in limited partnership, 31.2(f)(iii)
guaranteed return on buyer's investment, 31.2(f)(v), 31.2(f)(vi), 31.2(f)(vii)
operations, initiation/support of, 31.2(f)(x)
partial sales, 31.2(f)(xi)
permanent financing, lack of, 31.2(f)(iv)
profit-sharing arrangement, 31.2(f)(iii)
repurchase, option/obligation to, 31.2(f)(ii)
sale–leaseback arrangements, 31.2(f)(vii)
services without adequate compensation, 31.2(f)(viii)
cost allocation methods:
area method, 31.4(a)(iii)
generally, 31.4(a)
specific identification method, 31.4(a)(i)
value method, 31.4(a)(ii)
down payment:
composition of, 31.2(d)(ii)
inadequate, 31.2(d)(iii)
size of, 31.2(d)(i)
receivable from buyer:
amortization of, 31.2(e)(ii)
collectability of, 31.2(e)(i)
future subordination, 31.2(e)(iii)
inadequate continuing investment, 31.2(e)(vi)
interest, imputation of, 31.2(e)(v)
release provisions, 31.2(e)(iv)
recognition of sale, 31.2(c)
retail land sales:
full accrual method, 31.2(h)(ii), 31.2(h)(iii)
generally, 31.2(h)
installment and deposit methods, 31.2(h)(v)
percentage-of-completion method, 31.2(h)(iv)
recording of sale, 31.2(h)(i)
sales generally, 31.2(b)
syndication fees, 31.2(i)
tenants in common (TIC):
accounting methods, 31.2(g)(ii)
future costs, estimated, 31.2(g)(iii)
generally, 31.2(g)
profit recognition, criteria for, 31.2(g)(i)
Real estate valuation:
under development, real estate, 31.5(b)
fair value measurements:
generally, 31.5(c)
hierarchy, fair value, 31.5(c)(i)
techniques, fair value, 31.5(c)(ii)
generally, 31.5
long-lived assets, impairment/disposal of:
disposed of, real estate to be, 31.5(a)(ii)
generally, 31.5(a)
held/used, real estate to be, 31.5(a)(i)
Real estate ventures:
accounting for:

current standards, 31.8(b)(ii)
historical background, 31.8(b)(i)
investor accounting issues, 31.8(c)
organization of, 31.8(a)
tax benefits from affordable housing investments, 31.8(d)
Receivables:
accounts receivables, 12.2(b)
credit card receivables, 12.2(d)
defined, 12.2(a)
notes receivables, 12.2(c)
Recognition, revenue, *see* Revenue recognition
Recordkeeping:
for estates:
final accounting, 38.2(b)(iii)
generally, 38.2(b)
going business, operation of, 38.2(b)(ii)
journals, 38.2(b)(i)
forensic:
acquisition notes, 42.15
analysis workpapers, 42.17
chain-of-custody documentation, 42.16
generally, 42.14
for inventory, 13.4(c)(i)
for trusts:
bond premium/discount, amortization of, 38.4(b)(iv)
depreciation, 38.4(b)(v)
expenses, payments of, 38.4(b)(vi)
generally, 38.4(b)
journals, 38.4(b)(i)
opening books of account, 38.4(b)(iii)
principal and income accounts, 38.4(b)(ii)
Regulated utilities:
alternative forms of regulation:
competition, regulated transition to, 36.4(g)(iv)
generally, 36.4(g)
non-fuel rate trackers/riders, 36.4(g)(vi)
price ceilings/caps, 36.4(g)(i)
rate moratoriums, 36.4(g)(ii)
revenue decoupling, 36.4(g)(v)
sharing formulas, 36.4(g)(iii)
ASC Topic 980, *see* Accounting Standards Codification (ASC) Topic 980 (*Regulated Operations*)
characteristics of, 36.1(b)
commissions, regulatory:
federal, 36.3(a)
rates, setting of, 36.4(a)
state, 36.3(b)
disclosures:
construction intermediaries, financing through, 36.10(d)(ii)
expanded footnote disclosures, 36.10(d)(vi)
jointly owned plants, 36.10(d)(iii)
nuclear decommissioning costs, 36.10(d)(iv)
purchase power contracts, 36.10(d)(i)
stranded costs, securitization of, 36.10(d)(v)
GAAP, rate regulation and:
APB Opinion No. 2, 36.5(c)(ii)
historical background, 36.5(c)(i)
generally, 36.1(a)
historical background:
Chicago, Milwaukee & St. Paul Railroad Co. v. Minnesota ex rel. Railroad & Warehouse Comm., 36.2(b)
generally, 36.2
Munn v. Illinois, 36.2(a)
Smyth v. Ames, 36.2(c)
income taxation of:
accounting for income taxes (ASC Topic 740), 36.10(a)(vi)
flow-through, 36.10(a)(ii)
generally, 36.10(a)
incentives, tax, 36.10(a)(iv)
Internal Revenue Code provisions, 36.10(a)(iii)
interperiod allocation, 36.10(a)(i)
investment tax credit, 36.10(a)(vii)
legislation, tax, 36.10(a)(v)
judicial precedents:
rate of return and, 36.4(e)
valuation, rate base, 36.4(d)(iv)
postretirement benefits other than pensions, 36.10(c)
rate base, 36.4(c)
rate base valuation:
fair value, 36.4(d)(ii)
generally, 36.4(d)
judicial precedents, 36.4(d)(iv)
and original cost, 36.4(d)(i)
and weighted cost, 36.4(d)(iii)
rate of return, 36.4(e)
rates:
formula for establishing, 36.4(b)

Regulated utilities: (*Continued*)
GAAP and regulation of, *see subhead:* GAAP, rate regulation and
moratoriums, 36.4(g)(ii)
and operating income, 36.4(f)
setting of, 36.4(a)
recent industry changes, 36.10(e)
reporting, regulatory vs. financial:
GAAP, *see subhead:* GAAP, rate regulation and
regulating agency, accounting authority of, 36.5(a)
SEC and FASB, 36.5(b)
revenue recognition; alternative programs, 36.10(b)
Regulation S-X:
accountants' reports, 5.4(b)
consolidated financial statements, 5.4(d)
disclosures:
compensating balances, 5.4(l)(i)
generally, 5.4(g)
income tax expense, 5.4(k)
short-term borrowings, 5.4(l)(ii)
sources of, 5.4(h)
by subsidiary, 5.4(i)
50-percent-or-less-owned equity method investees, 5.4(j)
financial statements:
consistency of chronological order in, 5.4(f)
consolidated, 5.4(d)
generally, 5.4(c)
fund transfers from subsidiary to parent company, 5.4(i)
generally, 5.4(a)
materiality tests, 5.4(e)
redeemable preferred stock, 5.4(m)
schedules, 5.4(n)
unconsolidated subsidiaries, 5.4(j)
REITs, *see* Real estate investment trusts
Rental operations. *See also* Lease(s)
costs of:
escalation, cost, 31.7(b)(i)
future periods, chargeable to, 31.7(c)(i)
period costs, 31.7(c)(ii)
and depreciation, 31.7(d)
expense, rental, 31.7(f)
generally, 31.7(a)
income from:
and cost escalation, 31.7(b)(i)
generally, 31.7(b)
percentage rents, 31.7(b)(ii)
initial:
sale, held for, 31.7(e)(ii)
in use, held, 31.7(e)(i)
Reporting. *See also* Disclosure(s); Financial accounting and reporting; Financial statements
by banks and savings institutions, 30.2(j)(ii)
in Chapter 11 bankruptcy:
balance sheet, 39.5(f)(i)
generally, 39.5(f)
statement of cash flows, 39.5(f)(iii)
statement of operations, 39.5(f)(ii)
and fair value for, 25.2(b)
goodwill; reporting unit:
disposal, 14.7(b)(vii)
generally, 14.7(b)(iv)
interim, 4.8(c)(iii)
international reporting:
foreign issuers in United States, 10.3(n)(ii)
IASB and, 10.3(n)(i)
by not-for-profit organizations, 28.2(a)
objectives of, 2.3(b)(i), 4.2(a)
prior-period adjustments to retained earnings:
reporting, 19.7(c)(ii)
segment; health care organizations, 35.5(f)
selection of entity for, 9.1(g)(i)
by state and local governments, *see* State and local government accounting
treasury stock transactions:
cost method, 19.5(c), 19.5(f)
par value method, 19.5(d), 19.5(f)
Retained earnings:
appropriations of:
generally, 19.7(n)
loss contingencies, 19.7(o)
defined, 19.7(a)
and dividends:
cash dividends, 19.7(g)
declaration dates, 19.7(f)
generally, 19.7(e)
liquidating dividends, 19.7(k)
property dividends, 19.7(i)
scrip or liability dividends, 19.7(j)
stock dividends, *see subhead:* stock dividends
events affecting, 19.7(b)

and prior-period adjustments, 19.7(c)
errors, correction of, 19.7(c)(i)
reporting, 19.7(c)(ii)
retroactive pronouncements, 19.7(d)
and quasi reorganization, 19.7(l)
procedures, 19.7(l)(i)
readjustment, retained earnings after, 19.7(l)(ii)
tax loss carryforwards, 19.7(l)(iii)
restrictions on, 19.7(m)
contractual, 19.7(m)(ii)
legal, 19.7(m)(i)
preferred stock, liquidating value of, 19.7(m)(iv)
voluntary, 19.7(m)(iii)
stock dividends, 19.7(h)
closely held corporations, 19.7(h)(iii)
large stock dividends, 19.7(h)(ii)
reasons for declaration, 19.7(h)(v)
record date, 19.7(h)(iv)
small stock dividends, 19.7(h)(i)
Revenue. *See also* Income
ancillary:
by-product sales, 12.6(f)
dividends, 12.6(a)
interest, 12.6(b)
joint product sales, 12.6(f)
loan guarantees, 12.6(h)
miscellaneous assets, profits on sales of, 12.6(c)
rents, 12.6(d)
royalties, 12.6(e)
scrap sales, 12.6(f)
shipping and handling fees, 12.6(g)
classification of, 12.1(b)
components of, 12.1(a)
defined, 12.1(a)
disclosures:
on balance sheet, 12.7(b)
on income statement, 12.7(a)
installment receivables, 12.7(b)(ii)
interest on receivables, 12.7(b)(iii)
single-payment accounts receivable, 12.7(b)(i)
earning of, 12.1(c)(ii)
measurement of, 12.1(c)(i)
realization of, 12.1(c)(iii)
recognition of, *see* Revenue recognition
Revenue adjustments and aftercosts:
allowances, 12.5(c)
generally, 12.5(a)
guarantees, 12.5(f)
incentives:
consideration, cash or equity, 12.5(d)(i)
consideration, not cash or equity, 12.5(d)(ii)
customers' accounting for, 12.5(d)(iii)
product defects, obligations related to, 12.5(g)
returns, 12.5(b)
uncollectible receivables:
aging-of-receivables method, 12.5(e)(iii)
percentage-of-receivables method, 12.5(e)(ii)
percentage-of-sales method, 12.5(e)(i)
warranties, 12.5(f)
Revenue recognition:
after delivery, 12.1(d)(iii)
alternatives to, 12.1(d)
asset received characteristics as criteria for:
collectability, 12.3(f)(iii)
generally, 12.3(f)
liquidity, 12.3(f)(i)
measurability, 12.3(f)(iv)
obligations/restrictions, absence of, 12.3(f)(ii)
characteristics of revenue recognized, 12.3(g)
construction, *see* Construction revenue recognition
at delivery, 12.1(d)(i)
before delivery, 12.1(d)(ii)
and entry vs. exit values, 12.3(b)
event or transaction, characteristics of, 12.3(e)
event/transaction characteristics as criteria for:
events, 12.3(e)(iii)
nonreversibility, 12.3(e)(i)
risks/rewards of ownership, transfer of, 12.3(e)(ii)
and FASB conceptual framework, 12.3(c)
FASB project on, 12.4(d)
general criteria for, 12.3(a)
generally, 12.1(c)(iii)
industry-specific issues with:
cable television companies, 12.4(b)(ii)
film and broadcasting industry, 12.4(b)(v)
franchising companies, 12.4(b)(iii)
generally, 12.4(b)

Revenue recognition: (*Continued*)
Internet companies, 12.4(b)(vii)
record and music industry, 12.4(b)(iv)
software companies, 12.4(b)(vi)
need for additional guidance in, 12.4(c)
outside United States, criteria used, 12.3(h)(vi)
SEC Staff's views on:
delivery and performance, 12.3(h)(ii)
generally, 12.3(h)
leased or licensed departments, sale of, 12.3(h)(iv)
outside United States, criteria used, 12.3(h)(vi)
persuasive evidence of arrangement, 12.3(h)(i)
SAB No. 114, 12.3(h)(v)
sales price, fixed/determinable, 12.3(h)(iii)
special problems with:
barter credits, 12.4(a)(vii)
extended warranty contracts, separately priced, 12.4(a)(viii)
future revenues, sales of, 12.4(a)(vi)
generally, 12.4(a)
multiple deliverables, sales with, 12.4(a)(ix)
product financing arrangements, 12.4(a)(iii)
product maintenance contracts, separately priced, 12.4(a)(viii)
right of return, 12.4(a)(iv)
same counterparty, purchases and sales with, 12.4(a)(x)
service transactions, 12.4(a)(v)
transfers of receivables, 12.4(a)(ii)
specific criteria for, 12.3(d)

Sales:
ancillary revenue from:
by-product sales, 12.6(f)
joint product sales, 12.6(f)
miscellaneous assets, profits on sales of, 12.6(c)
scrap sales, 12.6(f)
on income statement:
comparative trend analysis, 10.2(b)(iv)
components of sale trends, 10.2(b)(iii)
generally, 10.2(b)
trend analysis, 10.2(b)(i)
variability, 10.2(b)(ii)
of minerals, 34.8(a)
of property, plant and equipment (PP&E), 16.5(a)
real estate, *see* Real estate transactions
and revenue recognition:
fixed/determinable price, 12.3(h)(iii)
future revenues, sales of, 12.4(a)(vi)
multiple deliverables, sales with, 12.4(a)(ix)
same counterparty, purchases and sales with, 12.4(a)(x)
short, 30.2(r)(iii)
wash, 30.2(r)(ii)
Sarbanes-Oxley Act (2002):
and audit committees, 5.1(e)(ii)
generally, 5.1(e)
and independent auditors, 5.1(e)(iii)
intangible assets, management of, 14.2(h)(i)
and internal control:
effectiveness, 7.1(a)
generally, 7.1
and Public Company Accounting Oversight Board (PCAOB), 1.9(a), 1.9(e)(i)
and public company officers/directors, 5.1(e)(i)
Savings institutions, *see* Banks and savings institutions
SEC, *see* Securities and Exchange Commission
Securities, *see* Debt securities; Equity securities
Securities Act (1933). *See also* Securities and Exchange Commission (SEC)
auditors' responsibilities, 5.2(b)
covered transactions, 5.2(a)
exemptions from registration:
generally, 5.2(e)
miscellaneous exemptions, 5.2(e)(iii)
Regulation A, 5.2(e)(ii)
Regulation D, 5.2(e)(i)
"going private" transactions, 5.2(f)
initial filings, 5.2(g)
materiality criterion:
assessment of materiality, 5.2(c)(i)
generally, 5.2(c)
intentional immaterial misstatements, 5.2(c)(iii)
misstatements, 5.2(c)(ii), 5.2(c)(iii)
smaller reporting companies, 5.2(d)
Securities and Exchange Commission (SEC):

accountants' services on prospective financial statements:
  compilations of filings, 21.5(f)(i)
  generally, 21.5(f)
  independence rules, 21.5(f)(ii)
and accounting fraud, 5.1(g)
accounting profession and, 5.1(d)
annual report to stockholders:
  content of, 5.4(q)
  required disclosures, 5.4(q)
audit committees, 5.1(i)
banks and savings institutions:
  background, 30.2(j)(i)
  reporting requirements, 30.2(j)(ii)
and business combinations:
  disclosures in SEC filings, 8.3(o)
  recognition/measurement of assets and liabilities, 8.3(g)(xvii)
and consolidated financial statements:
  disclosures, miscellaneous, 9.1(g)(iii)
  intercompany items and transactions, 9.1(g)(ii)
  reporting entity, selection of, 9.1(g)(i)
contact with staff of, 5.1(j)
creation of, 5.1(a)
Division of Corporation Finance (DCF):
  EDGAR system, 5.1(c)(iv)
  extension of time to file, 5.1(c)(v)
  generally, 1.3(c)
  organization, 5.1(c)(ii)
  responsibilities, 5.1(c)(i)
  review procedures, 5.1(c)(iii)
Division of Enforcement, 1.3(e)
and Foreign Corrupt Practices Act:
  internal accounting control, 5.1(h)(ii)
  payments to foreign officials, 5.1(h)(i)
Form 8-K:
  acquisition/disposition of assets, 5.6(a)(i)
  certifying accountant, changes in, 5.6(a)(ii)
  Item 2.01, 5.6(a)(i)
  Item 4.01, 5.6(a)(ii)
  Item 4.02, 5.6(a)(iii)
  non-reliance on previous financial statements, 5.6(a)(iii)
  requirements of, 5.6(a)
Form 10-K:
  certifications, 5.4(p)(vi)
  generally, 5.4
  Part I of, 5.4(p)(i)
  Part II of, 5.4(p)(ii)
  Part III of, 5.4(p)(iii)
  Part IV of, 5.4(p)(iv)
  signatures, 5.4(p)(v)
  structure of, 5.4(p)
Form 10-Q:
  generally, 5.5
  Part I of, 5.5(a)(i)
  Part II of, 5.5(a)(ii)
  signatures, 5.5(a)(iii)
generally, 1.3
health care organizations:
  municipal securities market and, 35.6(a)
  in private sector, 35.2(a)(i)
historical background, 1.3(a)
investment companies, 30.4(a)(i), 30.4(f)
Office of the Chief Accountant (OCA), 1.3(d)
organization of, 5.1(b)
proxy statements:
  generally, 5.7(a)
  Regulation 14A and, 5.7(b)
  review requirements, 5.7(c)
public accountants practicing before, 5.1(f)
publications, 1.3(f)
regulated utilities, 36.5(b)
regulations, 1.3(f)
Regulation S-K, 5.4(o)
Regulation S-X, *see* Regulation S-X
and revenue recognition:
  delivery and performance, 12.3(h)(ii)
  generally, 12.3(h)
  leased or licensed departments, sale of, 12.3(h)(iv)
  outside United States, criteria used, 12.3(h)(vi)
  persuasive evidence of arrangement, 12.3(h)(i)
  SAB No. 114, 12.3(h)(v)
  sales price, fixed/determinable, 12.3(h)(iii)
Sarbanes-Oxley Act and, *see* Sarbanes-Oxley Act (2002)
and Securities Act, *see* Securities Act (1933)
and Securities Exchange Act, *see* Securities Exchange Act (1934)
and Special Committee on Cooperation with Stock Exchanges, 2.2(a)(iii)
structure, 1.3(b)
and valuation of intangible assets, 14.3(a)(ii)

Securities Exchange Act (1934). *See also* Securities and Exchange Commission (SEC)
disclosure requirements:
periodic reports, 5.3(b)(ii)
registration of securities, 5.3(b)(i)
scope of, 5.3(a)
Seidman Committee, 2.2(c)(ii)
Share-based payments:
employee stock ownership plans (ESOPs), 19.6(d)
dividends on, 19.6(d)(iii)
purchase of shares by, 19.6(d)(i)
redemption of, 19.6(d)(ii), 19.6(d)(iv)
release of shares, 19.6(d)(ii)
stock options, employee, 19.6(c)
disclosure requirements, 19.6(c)(ii)
share-based payments, 19.6(c)(i)
stock rights, 19.6(b)(v), 19.6(b)(vii)
use of, 19.6(a)
warrants:
exercise of, 19.6(b)(iv)
generally, 19.6(b)
issued for services, 19.6(b)(iii)
issued with debt, 19.6(b)(i)
lapsed, 19.6(b)(vii)
reacquisition of, 19.6(b)(viii)
sale of, 19.6(b)(ii)
Silver, on personal financial statements, 22.3(e)
Special Committee on Cooperation with Stock Exchanges. *See also* Financial accounting and reporting
"accepted principles of accounting," 2.2(a)(i)
generally, 2.2(a)
recommendations, 2.2(a)(ii)
and SEC, 2.2(a)(iii)
and Securities Exchange Act, 2.2(a)(iii)
State and local governments:
characteristics of, 33.2(d)
objectives of, 33.2(b)
organization of, 33.2(c)
structure of, 33.2(a)
State and local government accounting:
accounting principles, sources of, 33.3
audits of governmental units:
committees, audit, 33.7(b)(ii)
generally, 33.7
governmental rotation of auditors, 33.7(b)(i)
Single Audit Act Amendments (1996), 33.7(a)
basis of accounting:
expenditure transactions, 33.4(j)(iv)
generally, 33.4(c)(viii), 33.4(j)(i), 33.4(j)(ii)
nonexchange transactions, 33.4(j)(v)
revenue transactions, 33.4(j)(iii)
budgeting and budgetary control/reporting:
capital budgets, 33.4(k)(v)
comparisons, budgetary, 33.4(k)(vi)
execution of budget, 33.4(k)(iii)
generally, 33.4(c)(ix)
operating budgets, types of, 33.4(k)(i)
preparation of budget, 33.4(k)(ii)
proprietary fund budgeting, 33.4(k)(iv)
capabilities, accounting/reporting:
legal compliance, 33.4(e)(i)
reporting requirements, 33.4(e)(ii)
summary statement, 33.4(c)(i)
capital assets:
depreciation, calculating, 33.4(h)(i)
depreciation of, 33.4(c)(vi)
disposal/retirement of, 33.4(h)(iii)
generally, 33.4(c)(iv), 33.4(h)
impairment of, 33.4(c)(vi), 33.4(h)(iv)
subsidiary property records, 33.4(h)(ii)
valuation of, 33.4(c)(v)
classification, common:
generally, 33.4(c)(xi)
classification of accounts:
fund balance/equity, 33.4(l)(v)
generally, 33.4(c)(x)
government fund expenditures, 33.4(l)(ii)
government fund revenues, 33.4(l)(i)
miscellaneous transactions, 33.4(l)(iii)
proprietary fund revenues/expenses, 33.4(l)(iv)
depreciation of capital assets, 33.4(c)(vi)
expenditure accounts, 33.4(c)(x)
expense accounts, 33.4(c)(x)
financial reporting:
basic financial statements, 33.4(m)(ii)
Certificate of Achievement program, 33.4(m)(iv)
Comprehensive Annual Financial Report (CAFR), 33.4(m)(iii)
entity for, 33.4(m)(i)
popular reports, 33.4(m)(v)
financial reports:

interim/annual, 33.4(c)(xii)
users/uses of, 33.4(b)
fund accounting systems:
capability, 33.4(f)
summary statement, 33.4(c)(ii)
funds, types of:
fiduciary funds, 33.4(g)(iii)
generally, 33.4(c)(iii), 33.4(g)
governmental funds, 33.4(g)(i)
proprietary funds, 33.4(g)(ii)
generally, 33.1
and Governmental Accounting Standards Board (GASB), 33.3(b)
government-wide accounting systems:
capability, 33.4(f)
generally, 33.4(c)(ii)
long-term liabilities:
capabilities, 33.4(i)
generally, 33.4(c)(vii)
measurement focus of, 33.4(c)(viii), 33.4(j), 33.4(j)(i)
and National Council on Governmental Accounting (NCGA), 33.3(a)
private sector accounting vs., 33.4(a)
revenue accounts, 33.4(c)(x)
special-purpose governments, reporting by:
business-type activities, 33.5(b)
fiduciary-type activities, 33.5(c)
generally, 33.5
governmental activities, 33.5(a)
summary statement of principles, 33.4(c)
terminology, common, 33.4(c)(xi)
transfer accounts, 33.4(c)(x)
valuation of capital assets, 33.4(c)(v)
State boards of accountancy, 1.11(a)
Statement of cash flows:
financing activities, 4.6(c)
generally, 4.6, 4.10(b)
investing activities, 4.6(b)
operating activities, 4.6(a)
Statement of financial position, *see* Balance sheet
Statement of stockholders' equity, 4.5
Stock:
balance sheet presentation of, 19.2(g)
certificates representing shares of, 19.2(a)
common, 19.2(b)
disclosure of capital structure:
generally, 19.9
preferred stock, 19.9(a)
par vs. no par value, 19.2(d)
payments, share-based, *see* Share-based payments
preferred, *see* Preferred stock
recording issuance of, 19.2(e)
and stated capital, 19.2(f)
treasury, *see* Treasury stock
Stock-based compensation:
accounting for:
employee stock option plans (ESOPs), 23.2(d)
fair value, 23.2(a)
non-public company option, 23.2(b)
restricted stock options, 23.2(c)
Black-Scholes option pricing model:
dividends, expected, 23.3(a)(ii)
generally, 23.3(a)
option lives, expected, 23.3(a)(iii)
volatility, expected, 23.3(a)(i)
Codification, accounting standards, 23.6
disclosure:
example, 23.5(b)
notes to financial statements, 23.5(a)
earnings per share:
diluted, 23.4(f)(i)
generally, 23.4(f)
fair value, estimating:
changing methods, 23.3(b)(ii)
generally, 23.3
historical background:
backdating scandal, 23.1(a)
generally, 23.1
income taxation of, 23.4(e)
international standards, 23.7
lattice/binomial option pricing model:
computation of option price, 23.3(b)(i)
generally, 23.3(b)
liabilities, awards classified as, 23.4(b)
modification of awards, 23.4(d)
nonemployees, awards to, 23.4(a)
stock appreciation rights, 23.4(c)
supporting data, obtaining/retaining, 23.4(g)
Stockholders' equity. *See also* Stock
and combined financial statements, 19.8(b)
contributed equity, 4.3(c)(i)
generally, 4.3(c)
with investor/investee transactions, 19.8(c)
below book value, sale, 19.8(c)(iii)
book value, sale at, 19.8(c)(i)

Stockholders' equity. *See also* Stock (*Continued*)
excess of book value, sale in, 19.8(c)(ii)
no parent-subsidiary relationship, 19.8(c)(v)
SAB No. 51, 19.8(c)(iv)
and noncontrolling interests, 19.8(a)
and reporting comprehensive income, 19.8(d)
retained earnings, 4.3(c)(ii)
subclassifications of, 4.3(c)(iii)
Stock issuance:
authorized number of shares, 19.3(a)
for cash, 19.3(c)
cost of, 19.3(b)
at discount, 19.3(f)
at premium, 19.3(f)
for property or services, 19.3(d)
stock discount, 19.3(f)
on subscription basis, 19.3(e)
balance sheet presentation, 19.3(e)(ii)
defaulted subscriptions, 19.3(e)(iii)
defaulted subscriptions WORDING, 19.3(e)(iii)
recording, 19.3(e)(i)
Stock options, *see* Stock-based compensation
Stock splits:
with change in par value, 19.4(a)(i)
generally, 19.4(a)
with no change in par value, 19.4(a)(ii)
reverse splits, 19.4(a)(iii)
Subleases:
generally, 15.10(c)
lessor, original, 15.10(c)(iii)
non-relief of obligation, original lessee's, 15.10(c)(ii)
relief of obligation, original lessee's, 15.10(c)(i)
Subsidiaries:
ASC 740 and, 17.2(e)(v)
equity method, *see* Equity method
equity method with unconsolidated, 9.3(b)(i)
goodwill, impairment testing of, 14.7(b)(v)
property records; state/local government accounting, 33.4(h)(ii)
recognition of intangible assets upon acquisition of subsidiary, 14.2(d)
Regulation S-X and:
fund transfers from subsidiary to parent company, 5.4(i)
unconsolidated subsidiaries, 5.4(j)

Tax accounting, financial accounting and reporting vs., 2.1(b)
Tax services, by CPAs, 1.10(b)(iii)
Tenants in common (TIC):
accounting methods, 31.2(g)(ii)
future costs, estimated, 31.2(g)(iii)
generally, 31.2(g)
profit recognition, criteria for, 31.2(g)(i)
Translation:
about, 9.2
approximations in, 9.2(h)(iii)
assumptions concerning, 9.2(b)
consolidated financial statements, 9.1(c)
of current liabilities, 18.3(k)
disclosures concerning foreign operations, 9.2(i)
exchange rates, selection of, 9.2(h)(ii)
foreign currency transactions, 9.2(e)
foreign extensions of parent company, treatment of, 9.2(d)
foreign operations, 9.2(d), 9.2(i)
forward exchange contracts:
about, 9.2(f)
discounts or premiums, 9.2(f)(i)
gains or losses, 9.2(f)(ii)
historical summary of pronouncements, 9.4(b)
income, exclusion of gains/losses from:
about, 9.2(g)
deferral of gains and losses, 9.2(g)(ii)
treatment as translation adjustments, 9.2(g)(i)
income tax considerations with, 9.2(h)(i)
and intercompany profit eliminations, 9.2(h)(ii)
objectives of, 9.2(a)
parent company, foreign components/extensions of, 9.2(d)
tasks required for, 9.2(c)
adjustments, 9.2(c)(iv)
current rate, use of current rate, 9.2(c)(iii)
identification of functional currency, 9.2(c)(i)
reasurement into functional currency, 9.2(c)(ii)

Treasury bonds, treatment and reissue of, 18.6(g)
Treasury stock:
  agreements to purchase, 19.5(a)(ii)
  balance sheet presentation of, 19.5(b)
  cost method of transaction reporting, 19.5(c)
    disposition of, 19.5(c)(i)
    par value method vs., 19.5(f)
    retired, 19.5(c)(ii)
  donated, 19.5(e)
  generally, 19.5(a)
  market rate, purchase at higher price than, 19.5(h)
  par value method of transaction reporting, 19.5(d), 19.5(f)
  retained earnings, restrictions on, 19.5(a)(i)
  shareholders' equity presentation of, 19.5(g)
Trusts:
  accounting for, 38.4(a)
  accounting period for, 38.4(a)(i)
  beneficiaries, rights of, 38.3(i)
  bond discounts/premiums:
    amortization of, 38.4(b)(iv)
    generally, 38.3(k)(iv)
  funding of, 38.1(i)(xxvi)
  generally, 38.3(a)
  guardians, appointment of, 38.3(f)
  investment of funds, proper, 38.3(d)
  liabilities, treatment of, 38.4(a)(iv)
  multiple, 38.4(a)(iii)
  principal and income from:
    accounts and recordkeeping, 38.4(b)(ii)
    accrual of, 38.3(k)(ii)
    bond discounts/premiums, 38.3(k)(iv)
    charges to income, 38.3(j)(iv)
    depletion and, 38.3(k)(v)
    depreciation and, 38.3(k)(v)
    disbursements of income, 38.3(j)(iv)
    disbursements of principal, 38.3(j)(ii)
    distinguishing principal from income, 38.3(j)
    dividends, 38.3(k)(iii)
    generally, 38.3(j)
    receipts of income, 38.3(j)(iii)
    receipts of principal, 38.3(j)(i)
    recording, 38.4(a)(ii)
    unproductive property, sale of, 38.3(k)(i)
  private trusts, limitations on, 38.3(a)(i)
  record-keeping system for:
    bond premium/discount, amortization of, 38.4(b)(iv)
    depreciation, 38.4(b)(v)
    expenses, payments of, 38.4(b)(vi)
    generally, 38.4(b)
    journals, 38.4(b)(i)
    opening books of account, 38.4(b)(iii)
    principal and income accounts, 38.4(b)(ii)
  revocation of, 38.3(a)(ii)
  tax status of, 38.3(l)
  termination of, 38.3(m)
  types of, 38.3(a)
Trustee(s):
  acts of cotrustee, liability for, 38.3(e)
  appointment of:
    acceptance/disclaimer of appointment, 38.3(b)(iii)
    choice of, 38.3(b)(i)
    generally, 38.3(b)
    methods of appointment, 38.3(b)(ii)
  compensation of, 38.3(h)
  duties of, 38.3(c)(ii)
  personal liabilities of, 38.3(e)
  powers of, 38.3(c)(i)
  removal of, 38.3(b)(v)
  reports of, 38.4(c)
  resignation of, 38.3(b)(iv)
  testamentary, 38.3(g)

United States:
  accounting standards in, 1.2
  auditing standards, 1.8
Universities, public, 33.6
Utilities, regulated, *see* Regulated utilities

Valuation. *See also* Business valuation; Fair value measurement(s); Inventory valuation methods; Real estate valuation
  of closely held business, 22.3(h)
  by CPAs, 1.10(b)(iv)
  of estate assets, 38.1(i)(x)
  of intangible assets:
    acquired intangible assets, 14.3(a)
    and cost allocation, 14.3(a)(i)
    court opinions, 14.3(a)(iii)
    intangibles as distinct from goodwill, 14.3(a)(vi)
    SEC/PCAOB issues with, 14.3(a)(ii)
    by tech-transfer practitioners, 14.3(a)(iv)

Valuation (*Continued*)
Wall Street transactions, 14.3(a)(v)
mortgage loans and securities, sales of, 30.2(p)(vi)
of net assets available for benefits (pension plans), 27.5(c)(i)
of nonpublic companies, 25.1(a)
regulated utilities; rate base valuation:
fair value, 36.4(d)(ii)
generally, 36.4(d)
and original cost, 36.4(d)(i)
and weighted cost, 36.4(d)(iii)
and standards of value, 25.2
testing of valuation model, 24.6(c)(ii)
Value, standards of, 25.2

Wills:
execution of, 38.1(a)
powers not conferred by statute, 38.1(j)(ii)
powers vs. statutory powers distinction, 38.1(j)(iii)
probate procedures, 38.1(e)
provisions of, 38.1(b)
surviving spouse's right of election against, 38.1(i)(xxiii)